SOCIAL SECURITY LEGISLATION 2020/2021

VOLUME V:
UNIVERSAL CREDIT

SOCIAL SECURITY
LEGISLATION 2020/2021

General Editor
Nick Wikeley, M.A. (Cantab)

VOLUME V:
UNIVERSAL CREDIT

Commentary By

**John Mesher, B.A., B.C.L.
(Oxon), LL.M. (Yale)**
Retired Judge of the Upper Tribunal

Richard Poynter, B.C.L., M.A. (Oxon)
Judge of the Upper Tribunal

Nick Wikeley, M.A. (Cantab)
Judge of the Upper Tribunal
Emeritus Professor of Law, University of Southampton

Consultant Editor
Child Poverty Action Group

SWEET & MAXWELL  THOMSON REUTERS

Published in 2020 by
Thomson Reuters trading as Sweet & Maxwell
Registered in England & Wales, Company No 1679046.
Registered Office and address for service:
5 Canada Square, Canary Wharf,
London E14 5AQ

Typeset by Servis Filmsetting Ltd, Stockport, Cheshire
Printed and bound by CPI Group (UK) Ltd,
Croydon, CR0 4YY

For further information on our products and services,
visit www.sweetandmaxwell.co.uk

No natural forests were destroyed to make this product.
Only farmed timber was used and re-planted.

A CIP catalogue record for this book is
available from the British Library

ISBN (print): 978-0-414-07991-5
ISBN (e-book): 978-0-414-08120-8
ISBN (print and e-book): 978-0-414-08119-2

CHILD POVERTY ACTION GROUP

The Child Poverty Action Group (CPAG) is a charity, founded in 1965, which campaigns for the relief of poverty in the United Kingdom. It has a particular reputation in the field of welfare benefits law derived from its legal work, publications, training and parliamentary and policy work, and is widely recognised as the leading organisation for taking test cases on social security law.

CPAG is therefore ideally placed to act as Consultant Editor to this 5-volume work—Social Security Legislation 2020/21. CPAG is not responsible for the detail of what is contained in each volume, and the authors' views are not necessarily those of CPAG. The Consultant Editor's role is to act in an advisory capacity on the overall structure, focus and direction of the work.

For more information about CPAG, its rights and policy publications or training courses, its address is 30 Micawber Street, London, N1 7TB (telephone: 020 7837 7979—website: http://www.cpag.org.uk).

FOREWORD

The volumes which make up the Social Security Legislation, with their accompanying commentaries, remain an indispensable part of First-tier Tribunal decision making. In the face of ongoing complex reform as well as the continuing development of the jurisprudence that is applicable to the existing legislation, they provide an essential reference and a reliable source of information and guidance. We are immensely grateful to those whose commentaries, based on their learning and experience, significantly enhance the value of the Social Security Legislation series. I recommend these volumes to all those who have an interest in this area of the law.

Judge Mary Clarke,
Acting Chamber President, Social Entitlement Chamber
Social Security and Child Support,
Criminal Injuries Compensation,
Asylum Support

PREFACE

Universal Credit is Volume V of the series *Social Security Legislation 2020/21.* The companion volumes are Hooker, Mesher, Mitchell, Poynter, Ward and Wikeley, Volume I: *Non-Means Tested Benefits and Employment and Support Allowance*; Mesher, Poynter and Wikeley, Volume II: *Income Support, Jobseeker's Allowance, State Pension Credit and the Social Fund*; Rowland and Ward, Volume III: *Administration, Adjudication and the European Dimension*; and Wikeley, Mitchell and Hooker, Volume IV: *Tax credits and HMRC-administered Social Security Benefits*. Each of the volumes in the series provides a legislative text, clearly showing the form and date of amendments, and commentary up to date to April 10, 2020. The commentary sometimes includes references to later case law as well as to later administrative guidance and to expected legislative changes, particularly in relation to the coronavirus provisions.

The introduction of universal credit is the biggest change to the social security system since the abolition of supplementary benefit and its replacement with income support thirty years ago. Universal credit is intended to simplify the social security system and to ensure that claimants will always be better off in work. In the medium to long term, the Government intends to abolish six existing "legacy" benefits and tax credits: income support, income-based jobseeker's allowance, income-related employment and support allowance, housing benefit, child tax credit and working tax credit and replace them all with universal credit. In the short term, however, universal credit has been introduced on a phased basis, so the old and new systems are co-existing side by side. During this transitional period, universal credit is not a replacement benefit but an additional benefit. Universal credit was finally "rolled-out" to (nearly all) new claimants on December 12, 2018. Many existing claimants of legacy benefits have since been transferred across to universal credit by "natural migration" (e.g. following a change in circumstances), while the pilot for "managed migration", to be initiated by the Department, has been postponed in the wake of the Covid-19 pandemic.

Volume V is divided into six Parts. Part I provides a clear and comprehensive narrative overview and analysis of the scope and structure of universal credit. Part II comprises the relevant primary legislation, principally provisions in the Welfare Reform Act 2012, but also including sections from the Social Security Administration Act 1992 and the Social Security Act 1998. Part III for the most part consists of the main regulations, the Universal Credit Regulations 2013. Part IV contains the Universal Credit (Transitional Provisions) Regulations 2014 as well as relevant Commencement Orders, along with phasing provisions. Part V includes regulations governing both claims and payments and also decisions and appeals as they relate to universal credit. Part VI includes the key statutory provisions from immigration law which bear on universal credit entitlement (e.g. as regards the right to reside). The text includes both the key statutory material and commentary, including in particular discussion of the amendments to the legislation made from March 2020 onwards in the wake of the coronavirus crisis. There is also detailed analysis of the Court of Appeal's important decision on assessment periods and the attribution of earned income for certain categories of claimant (*Secretary of State for Work and Pensions v Johnson and others* [2020] EWCA Civ 778), as followed in *R. (on the application of Pantellerisco) v Secretary of State for Work and Pensions* [2020] EWHC 1944 (Admin). There is also a much-expanded treatment of the rules on capital.

The withdrawal agreement reached in late 2019 between the United Kingdom and the European Union provides for a period, variously referred to as the "transition period" or the "implementation period", which is due to end on December 31, 2020 unless extended. During that period EU law continues to apply within only relatively minor modifications. It is planned to address subsequent developments in the updating volume.

As always, revising and updating the legislative text and commentary has required considerable flexibility on the part of the publisher and a great deal of help from a number of sources, including CPAG as advisory editor to the series. We remain grateful for this assistance in our task of providing an authoritative reflection on the current state of the law. To maximise space for explanatory commentary in books which seem to grow in size year on year, we have provided lists of definitions only where the commentary to the provision is substantial, or where reference to definitions is essential for a proper understanding. Users of the book should always check whether particular words or phrases they are called on to apply have a particular meaning ascribed to them in legislation. Generally the first or second regulation in each set of regulations contains definitions of key terms (check the "Arrangements of Regulations" at the beginning of each set for an indication of the subject matter covered by each regulations). There are also definition or "interpretation" sections in primary legislation.

Users of the series, and its predecessor works, have over the years contributed to their effectiveness by providing valuable comments on our commentary, as well as pointing out where the text of some provision has been omitted in error, or become garbled, or not been brought fully up to date. In some cases, this has drawn attention to an error which might otherwise have gone unnoticed. In providing such feedback, users of the work have helped to shape the content and ensure the accuracy of our material, and for that we continue to be grateful. This is all the more important in the context of this new benefit. We therefore hope that users of the work will continue to provide such helpful input and feedback. Please write to the General Editor of the series, Professor Nick Wikeley, c/o School of Law, University of Southampton, Highfield, Southampton SO17 1BJ, email: njw@soton. ac.uk, and he will pass on any comments received to the appropriate commentator.

Our gratitude also goes to the acting President of the Social Entitlement Chamber of the First-tier Tribunal and her colleagues there for continuing the now long tradition of help and encouragement in our endeavours.

September 3, 2020.

John Mesher
Richard Poynter
Nick Wikeley

CONTENTS

Contents

PART III A
TRANSITIONAL PROVISIONS

PART III B
COMMENCEMENT ORDERS

Contents

Contents

PART III C
SAVINGS PROVISIONS

Contents

PART IV
UNIVERSAL CREDIT: CLAIMS & PAYMENTS AND DECISIONS
& APPEALS

Paras

PART V
IMMIGRATION STATUS AND THE RIGHT TO RESIDE

Paras

USING THIS BOOK: AN INTRODUCTION TO LEGISLATION AND CASE LAW

Introduction

This book is not a general introduction to, or general textbook on, the law relating to social security but it is nonetheless concerned with both of the principal sources of social security law—*legislation* (both primary and secondary) and *case law*. It sets out the text of the most important legislation, as currently in force, and then there is added commentary that refers to the relevant case law. Lawyers will be familiar with this style of publication, which inevitably follows the structure of the legislation.

This note is designed primarily to assist readers who are not lawyers to find their way around the legislation and to understand the references to case law, but information it contains about how to find social security case law is intended to be of assistance to lawyers too.

Primary legislation

Primary legislation of the United Kingdom Parliament consists of *Acts of Parliament* (also known as *Statutes*). They will have been introduced to Parliament as *Bills*. There are opportunities for Members of Parliament and peers to debate individual clauses and to vote on amendments before a Bill is passed and becomes an Act (at which point the clauses become sections). No tribunal or court has the power to disapply, or hold to be invalid, an Act of Parliament unless it is inconsistent with European Union law.

An Act is known by its "short title", which incorporates the year in which it was passed (e.g. the Social Security Contributions and Benefits Act 1992), and is given a chapter number (abbreviated as, for instance, "c.4" indicating that the Act was the fourth passed in that year). It is seldom necessary to refer to the chapter number but it appears in the running heads in this book.

Each *section* (abbreviated as "s." or, in the plural, "ss.") of an Act is numbered and may be divided into *subsections* (abbreviated as "subs." and represented by a number in brackets), which in turn may be divided into *paragraphs* (abbreviated as "para." and represented by a lower case letter in brackets) and *subparagraphs* (abbreviated as "subpara." and represented by a small roman numeral in brackets). Subparagraph (ii) of para.(a) of subs. (1) of s.72 will usually be referred to simply as "s.72(1)(a)(ii)". Upper case letters may be used where additional sections or subsections are inserted by amendment and additional lower case letters may be used where new paragraphs and subparagraphs are inserted. This accounts for the rather ungainly s.109B(2A)(aa) of the Social Security Adminstation Act 1992.

Sections of a large Act may be grouped into a numbered *Part*, which may even be divided into *Chapters*. It is not usual to refer to a Part or a Chapter unless referring to the whole Part or Chapter.

Where a section would otherwise become unwieldy because it is necessary to include a list or complicated technical provisions, the section may simply refer to a *Schedule* at the end of the Act. A Schedule (abbreviated as "Sch.") may be divided into paragraphs and subparagraphs and further divided into heads and subheads. Again, it is usual to refer simply to, say, "para.23(3)(b)(ii) of Sch.3". Whereas it is conventional to speak of a section *of* an Act, it is usual to speak of a Schedule *to* an Act.

Secondary legislation

Secondary legislation (also known as *subordinate legislation* or *delegated legislation*) is made by *statutory instrument* in the form of a set of *Regulations* or a set of *Rules* or an *Order*. The power to make such legislation is conferred on ministers and other persons or bodies by Acts of Parliament. To the extent that a statutory instrument is made beyond the powers (in Latin, ultra vires) conferred by primary legislation, it may be held by a tribunal or court to be invalid and ineffective. Secondary legislation must be laid before Parliament. However, most secondary legislation is not debated in Parliament and, even when it is, it cannot be amended although an entire statutory instrument may be rejected.

A set of Regulations or Rules or an Order has a name indicating its scope and the year it was made and also a number, as in the Social Security (Disability Living Allowance) Regulations 1991 (SI 1991/2890) (the 2890th statutory instrument issued in 1991). Because there are over a thousand statutory instruments each year, the number of a particular statutory instrument is important as a means of identification and it should usually be cited the first time reference is made to that statutory instrument.

Sets of Regulations or Rules are made up of individual *regulations* (abbreviated as "reg.") or *rules* (abbreviated as "r." or, in the plural, "rr."). An Order is made up of *articles* (abbreviated as "art."). Regulations, rules and articles may be divided into paragraphs, subparagraphs and heads. As in Acts, a set of Regulations or Rules or an Order may have one or more Schedules attached to it. The style of numbering used in statutory instruments is the same as in sections of, and Schedules to, Acts of Parliament. As in Acts, a large statutory instrument may have regulations or rules grouped into Parts and, occasionally, Chapters. Statutory instruments may be amended in the same sort of way as Acts.

Scottish legislation

Most of the social security legislation passed by the United Kingdom Parliament applies throughout Great Britain, *i.e.*, in England, Wales and Scotland, but a separate Scottish social security system is gradually being developed and the relevant legislation is included in the appropriate volumes in this series. Acts of the Scottish Parliament are similar to Acts of the United Kingdom Parliament and Scottish Statutory Instruments are also similar to their United Kingdom counterparts.

Northern Ireland legislation

Most of the legislation set out in this series applies only in Great Britain, social security not generally being an excepted or reserved matter in relation to Northern Ireland. However, Northern Irish legislation—both primary legislation, most relevantly in the form of *Orders in Council* (which, although statutory instruments, had the effect of primary legislation in Northern Ireland while there was direct rule from Westminster and still do when made under the Northern Ireland (Welfare Reform) Act 2015) and *Acts of the Northern Ireland Assembly,* and subordinate legislation, in the form of *statutory rules*—largely replicates legislation in Great Britain so that much of the commentary in this book will be applicable to equivalent provisions in Northern Ireland legislation. Although there has latterly been a greater reluctance in Northern Ireland to maintain parity with Great Britain, which led to some delay in enacting legislation equivalent to the Welfare Reform Act 2012, this has partially been resolved for the time being by the allocation of funds to allow the effects of some of the reforms to be mitigated in Northern Ireland while the broad legislative structure remains similar.

European Union legislation

Although the United Kingdom ceased to be a Member State of the European Union on January 31, 2020, the effect of the European Union (Withdrawal Act) 2018, as amended in 2020, is that most European Union law that was in force immediately before that date continues to be part of United Kingdom law during the implementation period ending on December 31, 2020.

European Union primary legislation is in the form of the *Treaties* agreed by the Member States. Relevant subordinate legislation is in the form of *Regulations,* adopted to give effect to the provisions of the Treaties, and *Directives,* addressed to Member States and requiring them to incorporate certain provisions into their domestic laws. Directives are relevant because, where a person brings proceedings against an organ of the State, as is invariably the case where social security is concerned, that person may rely on the Directive as having direct effect if the Member State has failed to comply with it. European Union Treaties, Regulations and Directives are divided into *Articles* (abbreviated as "Art.") United Kingdom legislation that is inconsistent with European Union legislation may be disapplied.

Finding legislation in this book

If you know the name of the piece of legislation for which you are looking, use the list of contents at the beginning of each volume of this series which lists the pieces of legislation contained in the volume. That will give you the paragraph reference to enable you to find the beginning of the piece of legislation. Then, it is easy to find the relevant section, regulation, rule, article or Schedule by using the running heads on the right hand pages. If you do not know the name of the piece of legislation, you will probably need to use the index at the end of the volume in order to find the relevant paragraph number but will then be taken straight to a particular provision.

The legislation is set out as amended, the amendments being indicated by numbered sets of square brackets. The numbers refer to the numbered entries under the heading "AMENDMENTS" at the end of the relevant section, regulation, rule, article or Schedule, which identify the amending statute or statutory instrument. Where an Act has been consolidated, there is a list of "DERIVATIONS" identifying the provisions of earlier legislation from which the section or Schedule has been derived.

Finding other legislation

Legislation in both its amended and its unamended form may now be found on *http://www.legislation.gov.uk*. Northern Ireland social security legislation may also be found at *https://www.communities-ni.gov.uk/services/ law-relating-social-security-northern-ireland-blue-volumes*. European Union legislation may be found at *http://eur-lex.europa.eu/collection/eu-law.html*.

Interpreting legislation

Legislation is written in English and generally means what it says. However, more than one interpretation is often possible. Most legislation itself contains definitions. Sometimes these are in the particular provision in which a word occurs but, where a word is used in more than one place, any definition will appear with others. In an Act, an interpretation section is usually to be found towards the end of the Act or of the relevant Part of the Act. In a statutory instrument, an interpretation provision usually appears near the beginning of the statutory instrument or the relevant Part of it. In the more important pieces of legislation in this series, there is included after every section, regulation, rule, article or Schedule a list of "DEFINITIONS", showing where definitions of words used in the provision are to be found.

However, not all words are statutorily defined and there is in any event more to interpreting legislation than merely defining its terms. Decision-makers and tribunals need to know how to apply the law in different types of situations. That is where case law comes in.

Case law and the commentary in this book

In deciding individual cases, courts and tribunals interpret the relevant law and incidentally establish legal principles. Decisions on questions of legal principle of the superior courts and appellate tribunals are said to be binding on decision-makers and the First-tier Tribunal, which means that decision-makers and the First-tier Tribunal must apply those principles. Thus the judicial decisions of the superior courts and appellate tribunals form part of the law. The commentary to the legislation in this series, under the heading "GENERAL NOTE" after a section, regulation, rule, article or Schedule, refers to this *case law*.

Much case law regarding social security benefits is still in the form of decisions of Social Security Commissioners and Child Support Commissioners. However, while there are still Commissioners in Northern Ireland, which has a largely separate judiciary and tribunal system, the functions of Commissioners in Great Britain were transferred to the Upper Tribunal and allocated to the Administrative Appeals Chamber of that tribunal on November 3, 2008. Consequently, social security case law is increasingly to be found in decisions of the Upper Tribunal.

The commentary in this series is not itself binding on any decision-maker or tribunal because it is merely the opinion of the author. It is what is actually said in the legislation or in the judicial decision that is important. The legislation is set out in this series, but it will generally be necessary to look elsewhere for the precise words used in judicial decisions. The way that decisions are cited in the commentary enables that to be done.

The reporting of decisions of the Upper Tribunal and Commissioners

About 50 of the most important decisions of the Administrative Appeals Chamber of the Upper Tribunal are selected to be "reported" each year in the Administrative Appeals Chamber Reports (AACR), using the same criteria as were formerly used for reporting Commissioners' decisions in Great Britain. The selection is made by an editorial board of judges and decisions are selected for reporting only if they are of general importance and command the assent of at least a majority of the relevant judges. The term "reported" simply means that they are published in printed form as well as on the Internet (see *Finding case law*, below) with headnotes (i.e. summaries) and indexes, but reported decisions also have a greater precedential status than ordinary decisions (see *Judicial precedent* below).

A handful of Northern Ireland Commissioners' decisions are also selected for reporting in the Administrative Appeals Chamber Reports each year, the selection being made by the Chief Social Security Commissioner in Northern Ireland.

Citing case law

As has been mentioned, much social security case law is still to be found in decisions of Social Security Commissioners and Child Support Commissioners, even though the Commissioners have now effectively been abolished in Great Britain.

Reported decisions of Commissioners were known merely by a number or, more accurately, a series of letters and numbers beginning with an "R". The type of benefit in issue was indicated by letters in brackets (e.g. "IS" was income support, "P" was retirement pension, and so on) and the year in which the decision was selected for reporting or, from 2000, the year in which it was published as a reported decision, was indicated by the last two digits, as in *R(IS) 2/08*. In Northern Ireland there was a similar system until 2009, save that the type of benefit was identified by letters in brackets after the number, as in *R 1/07 (DLA)*.

Unreported decisions of the Commissioners in Great Britain were known simply by their file numbers, which began with a "C", as in *CIS/2287/2008*. The letters following the "C" indicated the type of benefit in issue in the case. Scottish and, at one time, Welsh cases were indicated by a "S" or "W" immediately after the "C", as in *CSIS/467/2007*. The last four digits indicated the calendar year in which the case was registered, rather than the year it was decided. A similar system operated in Northern Ireland until 2009, save that the letters indicating the type of benefit appeared in brackets after the numbers and, from April 1999, the financial year rather than the calendar year was identified, as in *C 10/06-07 (IS)*.

Decisions of the Upper Tribunal, of courts and, since 2010, of the Northern Ireland Commissioners are generally known by the names of the parties (or just two of them in multi-party cases). In social security and some other types of cases, individuals are anonymised through the use of initials in the names of decisions of the Upper Tribunal and the Northern Ireland Commissioners. Anonymity is much rarer in the names of decisions of courts. In this series, the names of official bodies are also abbreviated in the names of decisions of the Upper Tribunal and the Northern Ireland Commissioners (*e.g.*, "SSWP" for the Secretary of State for Work and Pensions, "HMRC" for Her Majesty's Revenue and Customs, "CMEC" for the Child Maintenance and Enforcement Commission and "DSD" for the Department for Social Development in Northern Ireland). Since 2010, such decisions have also been given a "flag" in brackets to indicate the subject matter of the decision, which in social security cases indicates the principal benefit in issue in the case. Thus, the name of one jobseeker's allowance case is *SSWP v JB (JSA)*.

Any decision of the Upper Tribunal, of a court since 2001 or of a Northern Ireland Commissioner since 2010 that has been intended for publication has also given a *neutral citation number* which enables the decision to be more precisely identified. This indicates, in square brackets, the year the decision was made (although in relation to decisions of the courts it sometimes merely indicates the year the number was issued) and also indicates the court or tribunal that made the decision (e.g. "UKUT" for the Upper Tribunal, "NICom" for a Northern Ireland Commissioner, "EWCA Civ" for the Civil Division of the Court of Appeal in England and Wales, "NICA" for the Court of Appeal in Northern Ireland, "CSIH" for the Inner House of the Court of Session (in Scotland), "UKSC" for the Supreme Court and so on). A number is added so that the reference is unique and finally, in the case of the Upper Tribunal or the High Court in England and Wales, the relevant chamber of the Upper Tribunal or the relevant division or other part of the High Court is identified (e.g."(AAC)" for the Administrative Appeals Chamber, "(Admin)" for the Administrative Court and so on). Examples of decisions of the Upper Tribunal and a Northern Ireland Commissioner with their neutral citation numbers are *SSWP v JB (JSA)* [2010] UKUT 4 (AAC) and *AR v DSD (IB)* [2010] NICom 6.

If the case is reported in the Administrative Appeals Chamber Reports or another series of law reports, a reference to the report usually follows the neutral citation number. Conventionally, this includes either the year the case was decided (in round brackets) or the year in which it was reported (in square brackets), followed by the volume number (if any), the name of the series of reports (in abbreviated form, so see the Table of Abbreviations at the beginning of each volume of this series) and either the page number or the case number. However, before 2010, cases reported in the Administrative Appeals Chamber Reports or with Commissioners' decisions were numbered in the same way as reported Commissioners' decisions. *Abdirahman v Secretary of State for Work and Pensions* [2007] EWCA Civ 657; [2008] 1 W.L.R. 254 (also reported as *R(IS) 8/07)* is a Court of Appeal decision, decided in 2007 but reported in 2008 in volume 1 of the Weekly Law Reports at page 254 and also in the 2007 volume of reported Commissioners' decisions. *NT v SSWP* [2009] UKUT 37 (AAC), *R(DLA) 1/09* is an Upper Tribunal case decided in 2009 and reported in the Administrative Appeals Chamber Reports in the same year. *Martin v SSWP* [2009] EWCA Civ 1289; [2010] AACR 9 is a decision of the Court of Appeal that was decided in 2009 and was the ninth decision reported in the Administrative Appeals Chamber Reports in 2010.

It is usually necessary to include the neutral citation number or a reference to a series of reports only the first time a decision is cited in any document. After that, the name of the case is usually sufficient.

All decisions of the Upper Tribunal that are on their website have neutral citation numbers. If you wish to refer a tribunal or decision-maker to a decision of the Upper Tribunal that does not have a neutral citation number, contact the office of the Administrative Appeals Chamber (*adminappeals@*

justice.gov.uk) who will provide a number and add the decision to the website.

Decision-makers and claimants are entitled to assume that judges of both the First-tier Tribunal and the Upper Tribunal have immediate access to reported decisions of Commissioners or the Upper Tribunal and they need not provide copies, although it may sometimes be helpful to do so. However, where either a decision-maker or a claimant intends to rely on an unreported decision, it will be necessary to provide a copy of the decision to the judge and other members of the tribunal. A copy of the decision should also be provided to the other party before the hearing because otherwise it may be necessary for there to be an adjournment to enable that party to take advice on the significance of the decision.

Finding case law

The extensive references described above are used so as to enable people easily to find the full text of a decision. Most decisions of any significance since the late 1990s can be found on the Internet.

Decisions of the Upper Tribunal may be found at *https://www.gov.uk/ administrative-appeals-tribunal-decisions*. The link from that page to "decisions made in 2015 or earlier" leads also to decisions of the Commissioners in Great Britain. Decisions of Commissioners in Northern Ireland may be found on *https://iaccess.communities-ni.gov.uk/NIDOC*.

The Administrative Appeals Chamber Reports. They are also published by the Stationery Office in bound volumes which follow on from the bound volumes of Commissioners' decisions published from 1948.

Copies of decisions of the Administrative Appeals Chamber of the Upper Tribunal or of Commissioners that are otherwise unavailable may be obtained from the offices of the Upper Tribunal (Administrative Appeals Chamber) or, in Northern Ireland, from the Office of the Social Security and Child Support Commissioners.

Decisions of a wide variety of courts and tribunals in the United Kingdom may be found on the free website of the British and Irish Legal Information Institute, *http://www.bailii.org*. It includes all decisions of the Supreme Court and provides fairly comprehensive coverage of decisions given since about 1996 by the House of Lords and Privy Council and most of the higher courts in England and Wales, decisions given since 1998 by the Court of Session and decisions given since 2000 by the Court of Appeal and High Court in Northern Ireland. Some earlier decisions have been included, so it is always worth looking and, indeed, those decisions dating from 1873 or earlier and reported in the English Reports may be found through a link to *http://www.commonlii.org/uk/cases/EngR/*.

Decisions of the Court of Justice of the European Union are all to be found at *https://curia.europa.eu*.

Decisions of the European Court of Human Rights are available at *https://www.echr.coe.int*.

Most decisions of the courts in social security cases, including decisions of the Court of Justice of the European Union on cases referred by United Kingdom courts and tribunals, are reported in the Administrative Appeals Chamber Reports or with the reported decisions of Commissioners and may therefore be found on the same websites and in the same printed series of reported decisions. So, for example, *R(I) 1/00* contains Commissioner's decision *CSI/12/1998*, the decision of the Court of Session upholding the Commissioner's decision and the decision of the House of Lords in *Chief Adjudication Officer v Faulds*, reversing the decision of the Court of Session. The most important decisions of the courts can also be found in the various series of law reports familiar to lawyers (in particular, in the *Law Reports*, the *Weekly Law Reports*, the *All England Law Reports*, the *Public and Third Sector Law Reports*, the *Industrial Cases Reports* and the *Family Law Reports*) but these are not widely available outside academic or other law libraries, or subscription-based websites. See the Table of Cases at the beginning of each volume of this series for all the places where a decision mentioned in that volume is reported.

If you know the name or number of a decision and wish to know where in a volume of this series there is a reference to it, use the Table of Cases or the Table of Commissioners' Decisions 1948–2009 in the relevant volume to find the paragraph(s) where the decision is mentioned.

Judicial precedent

As already mentioned, decisions of the Upper Tribunal, the Commissioners and the higher courts in Great Britain become *case law* because they set binding precedents which must be followed by decision-makers and the First-tier Tribunal in Great Britain. This means that, where the Upper Tribunal, Commissioner or court has decided a point of legal principle, decision-makers and appeal tribunals must make their decisions in conformity with the decision of the Upper Tribunal, Commissioner or court, applying the same principle and accepting the interpretation of the law contained in the decision. So a decision of the Upper Tribunal, a Commissioner or a superior court explaining what a term in a particular regulation means, lays down the definition of that term in much the same way as if the term had been defined in the regulations themselves. The decision may also help in deciding what the same term means when it is used in a different set of regulations, provided that the term appears to have been used in a similar context.

Only decisions on points of law set precedents that are binding and, strictly speaking, only decisions on points of law that were necessary to the overall conclusion reached by the Upper Tribunal, Commissioner or court are binding. Other parts of a decision (which used to be known as obiter dicta) may be regarded as helpful guidance but need not be followed if a decision-maker or the First-tier Tribunal is persuaded that there is a better approach. It is particularly important to bear this in mind in relation to older decisions of Social Security Commissioners because, until 1987, most rights of appeal to a Commissioner were not confined to points of law.

Where there is a conflict between precedents, a decision-maker or the First-tier Tribunal is generally free to choose between decisions of equal status. For these purposes, most decisions of the Upper Tribunal and decisions of Commissioners are of equal status. However, a decision-maker or First-tier Tribunal should generally prefer a reported decision to an unreported one unless the unreported decision was the later decision and the Commissioner or Upper Tribunal expressly decided not to follow the earlier reported decision. This is simply because the fact that a decision has been reported shows that at least half of the relevant judges of the Upper

Tribunal or the Commissioners agreed with it at the time. A decision of a Tribunal of Commissioners (i.e. three Commissioners sitting together) or a decision of a three-judge panel of the Upper Tribunal must be preferred to a decision of a single Commissioner or a single judge of the Upper Tribunal.

A single judge of the Upper Tribunal will normally follow a decision of a single Commissioner or another judge of the Upper Tribunal, but is not bound to do so. A three-judge panel of the Upper Tribunal will generally follow a decision of another such panel or of a Tribunal of Commissioners, but similarly is not bound to do so, whereas a single judge of the Upper Tribunal will always follow such a decision.

Strictly speaking, the Northern Ireland Commissioners do not set binding precedent that must be followed in Great Britain but their decisions are relevant, due to the similarity of the legislation in Northern Ireland, and are usually regarded as highly persuasive with the result that, in practice, they are generally given as much weight as decisions of the Great Britain Commissioners. The same approach is taken in Northern Ireland to decisions of the Upper Tribunal on social security matters and to decisions of the Great Britain Commissioners.

Decisions of the superior courts in Great Britain and Northern Ireland on questions of legal principle are almost invariably followed by decision-makers, tribunals and the Upper Tribunal, even when they are not strictly binding because the relevant court was in a different part of the United Kingdom or exercised a parallel – but not superior – jurisdiction.

Decisions of the Court of Justice of the European Union come in two parts: the Opinion of the Advocate General and the decision of the Court. It is the decision of the Court which is binding. The Court is assisted by hearing the Opinion of the Advocate General before itself coming to a conclusion on the issue before it. The Court does not always follow its Advocate General. Where it does, the Opinion of the Advocate General often elaborates the arguments in greater detail than the single collegiate judgment of the Court. Decision-makers, tribunals and Commissioners must apply decisions of the Court of Justice of the European Union, where relevant to cases before them, in preference to other authorities binding on them.

The European Court of Human Rights in Strasbourg is quite separate from the Court of Justice of the European Union in Luxembourg and serves a different purpose: interpreting and applying the European Convention on Human Rights, which is incorporated into United Kingdom law by the Human Rights Act 1998. Since October 2, 2000, public authorities in the United Kingdom, including courts, Commissioners, tribunals and decision-makers have been required to act in accordance with the incorporated provisions of the Convention, unless statute prevents this. They must take into account the Strasbourg case law and are required to interpret domestic legislation, so far as it is possible to do so, to give effect to the incorporated Convention rights. Any court or tribunal may declare secondary legislation incompatible with those rights and, in certain circumstances, invalidate it. Only the higher courts can declare a provision of primary legislation to be incompatible with those rights, but no court, tribunal or Upper Tribunal can invalidate primary legislation. The work of the Strasbourg Court and the impact of the Human Rights Act 1998 on social security are discussed in the commentary in Part IV of this volume.

See the note to s.3(2) of the Tribunals, Courts and Enforcement Act 2007 in Part V of this volume for a more detailed and technical consideration of the rules of precedent.

Other sources of information and commentary on social security law

For a comprehensive overview of the social security system in Great Britain, CPAG's *Welfare Benefits and Tax Credits Handbook*, published annually each spring, is unrivalled as a practical introduction from the claimant's viewpoint.

From a different perspective, the Department for Work and Pensions publishes the 14-volume *Decision Makers' Guide* and the newer *Advice for Decision Making*, which covers personal independence payment, universal credit and the "new" versions of Jobseeker's Allowance and Employment and Support Allowance (search for the relevant guide by name at *https://www.gov.uk* under the topic "Welfare"). Similarly, Her Majesty's Revenue and Customs publish manuals relating to tax credits, child benefit and guardian's allowance, which they administer, see *https://www.gov.uk/government/collections/hmrc-manuals*. (Note that the *Child Benefit Technical Manual* also covers guardian's allowance.) These guides and manuals are extremely useful but their interpretation of the law is not binding on tribunals and the courts, being merely internal guidance for the use of decision-makers.

There are a number of other sources of valuable information or commentary on social security case law: see in particular publications such as the *Journal of Social Security Law*, CPAG's *Welfare Rights Bulletin*, *Legal Action* and the *Adviser*. As far as online resources go there is little to beat *Rightsnet* (*https://www.rightsnet.org.uk*). This site contains a wealth of resources for people working in the welfare benefits field but of special relevance in this context are Commissioners'/Upper Tribunal Decisions section of the "Toolkit" area and also the "Briefcase" area which contains summaries of the decisions (with links to the full decisions). Sweet and Maxwell's online subscription service *Westlaw* is another valuable source (*https://legalsolutions.thomsonreuters.co.uk/en/products-services/westlaw-uk.html*), as is LexisNexis *Lexis* (*https://www.lexisnexis.co.uk*).

Conclusion

The internet provides a vast resource but a search needs to be focused. Social security schemes are essentially statutory and so in Great Britain the legislation which is set out in this series forms the basic structure of social security law. However, the case law shows how the legislation should be interpreted and applied. The commentary in this series should point the way to the case law relevant to each provision and the Internet can then be used to find it where that is necessary.

EFFECTIVE DATES OF CHANGES TO UNIVERSAL CREDIT LEGISLATION

Once universal credit has been awarded, the general rule is that a super-seding decision based on a change of circumstances, takes effect from the first day of the assessment period in which that change occurred or is expected to occur (see the Decisions and Appeals Regulations 2013 reg.35 and Sch.1, Pt.III). This follows the rule for the "legacy" benefits (IS, HB, JSA(IB), and ESA(IR)) in which changes took effect from the first day of the benefit week in which they occurred or were expected to occur (see, e.g., the Social Security and Child Support (Decisions and Appeals) Regulations 1999 Schs 3A and 3C).

The administrative advantages of having a bright line rule about the effective dates for changes in circumstances are obvious: it avoids having to carry out more than one benefit calculation for each period by reference to which entitlement is administered.

However, the "legacy" benefits were paid on a weekly basis, so claim-ants could neither gain nor lose more than a week's benefit if a change in circumstances was taken into account early. By contrast, universal credit is administered by reference to monthly assessment periods. Having an adverse change that occurs towards the end of an assessment period taken into account up to a month early can have serious consequences for claim-ants (e.g., where a claimant ceases to be liable to pay rent and therefore to be eligible for the housing costs element).

It is therefore important to note that where the change in circumstances is a change in *legislation* the opposite rule often applies. In such cases, the amending Regulations may contain a provision in the following (or similar terms):

"(2) Where the amendments made by these Regulations apply in respect of an existing award of universal credit, they have effect for the purposes of that award—
(a) on [date] if there is an assessment period for that award that begins on that day; or
(b) if sub-paragraph (a) does not apply, on the first day of the next assessment period for the award beginning after that day.
(3) For the purposes of this regulation, "existing award of universal credit" means an award of universal credit that exists on [date]."

The effect is that the amended law apples to new claims for universal credit from the outset. However, where there is an existing award of universal credit, the amendment takes effect from the first day of the following assess-ment period.

In such cases, the Amendment sections of the commentary in this volume refer to "Assessment periods beginning on or after" the date on which the amending regulation comes into force (or similar), rather than just stating that date.

TABLE OF CASES

Table of Cases

TABLE OF COMMISSIONERS' DECISIONS

TABLE OF ABBREVIATIONS USED IN THIS SERIES

1975 Act	Social Security Act 1975
1977 Act	Marriage (Scotland) Act 1977
1979 Act	Pneumoconiosis (Workers' Compensation) Act 1979
1986 Act	Social Security Act 1986
1996 Act	Employment Rights Act 1996
1998 Act	Social Security Act 1998
2002 Act	Tax Credits Act 2002
2004 Act	Gender Recognition Act 2004
2006 Act	Armed Forces Act 2006
2008 Act	Child Maintenance and Other Payments Act 2008
2013 Act	Marriage (Same Sex Couples) Act 2013
2014 Act	Marriage and Civil Partnership (Scotland) Act 2014
A1P1	Art.1 of Protocol 1 to the European Convention on Human Rights
AA	Attendance Allowance
AA 1992	Attendance Allowance Act 1992
AAC	Administrative Appeals Chamber
AACR	Administrative Appeals Chamber Reports
A.C.	Law Reports, Appeal Cases
A.C.D.	Administrative Court Digest
Admin	Administrative Court
Admin L.R.	Administrative Law Reports
Administration Act	Social Security Administration Act 1992
Administration Regulations	Statutory Paternity Pay and Statutory Adoption Pay (Administration) Regulations 2002
AIP	assessed income period
All E.R.	All England Reports
All E.R. (E.C.)	All England Reports (European Cases)
AMA	Adjudicating Medical Authorities
AO	Adjudication Officer
AOG	*Adjudication Officers Guide*
art.	article
Art.	Article
ASD	Autistic Spectrum Disorder
ASPP	Additional Statutory Paternity Pay

Table of Abbreviations used in this Series

A.T.C.	Annotated Tax Cases
Attendance Allowance Regulations	Social Security (Attendance Allowance) Regulations 1991
AWT	All Work Test
BA	Benefits Agency
Benefits Act	Social Security Contributions and Benefits Act 1992
B.H.R.C.	Butterworths Human Rights Cases
B.L.G.R.	Butterworths Local Government Reports
Blue Books	*The Law Relating to Social Security*, Vols 1–11
B.P.I.R.	Bankruptcy and Personal Insolvency Reports
B.T.C.	British Tax Cases
BTEC	Business and Technology Education Council
B.V.C.	British Value Added Tax Reporter
B.W.C.C.	Butterworths Workmen's Compensation Cases
c.	chapter
C	Commissioner's decision
C&BA 1992	Social Security Contributions and Benefits Act 1992
CAA 2001	Capital Allowances Act 2001
CAB	Citizens Advice Bureau
CAO	Chief Adjudication Officer
CB	Child Benefit
CBA 1975	Child Benefit Act 1975
CBJSA	Contribution-Based Jobseeker's Allowance
C.C.L. Rep.	Community Care Law Reports
CCM	HMRC *New Tax Credits Claimant Compliance Manual*
C.E.C.	European Community Cases
CERA	cortical evoked response audiogram
CESA	Contribution-based Employment and Support Allowance
CFS	chronic fatigue syndrome
Ch.	Chancery Division Law Reports; Chapter
Citizenship Directive	Directive 2004/38/EC of the European Parliament and of the Council of April 29, 2004
CJEC	Court of Justice of the European Communities
CJEU	Court of Justice of the European Union
Claims and Payments Regulations	Social Security (Claims and Payments) Regulations 1987
Claims and Payments Regulations 1979	Social Security (Claims and Payments) Regulations 1979
Claims and Payments Regulations 2013	Universal Credit, Personal Independence Payment, Jobseeker's Allowance and Employment and Support Allowance (Claims and Payments) Regulations 2013
CM	Case Manager

CMA	Chief Medical Adviser
CMEC	Child Maintenance and Enforcement Commission
C.M.L.R.	Common Market Law Reports
C.O.D.	Crown Office Digest
COLL	*Collective Investment Schemes Sourcebook*
Community, The	European Community
Computation of Earnings Regulations	Social Security Benefit (Computation of Earnings) Regulations 1978
Computation of Earnings Regulations 1996	Social Security Benefit (Computation of Earnings) Regulations 1996
Consequential Provisions Act	Social Security (Consequential Provisions) Act 1992
Contributions and Benefits Act	Social Security Contributions and Benefits Act 1992
Contributions Regulations	Social Security (Contributions) Regulations 2001
COPD	chronic obstructive pulmonary disease
CP	Carer Premium; Chamber President
CPAG	Child Poverty Action Group
CPR	Civil Procedure Rules
Cr. App. R.	Criminal Appeal Reports
CRCA 2005	Commissioners for Revenue and Customs Act 2005
Credits Regulations 1974	Social Security (Credits) Regulations 1974
Credits Regulations 1975	Social Security (Credits) Regulations 1975
Crim. L.R.	Criminal Law Review
CRU	Compensation Recovery Unit
CSA 1995	Children (Scotland) Act 1995
CSIH	Inner House of the Court of Session (Scotland)
CSM	Child Support Maintenance
CS(NI)O 1995	Child Support (Northern Ireland) Order 1995
CSOH	Outer House of the Court of Session (Scotland)
CSPSSA 2000	Child Support, Pensions and Social Security Act 2000
CTA	Common Travel Area
CTA 2009	Corporation Tax Act 2009
CTA 2010	Corporation Tax Act 2010
CTB	Council Tax Benefit
CTC	Child Tax Credit
CTC Regulations	Child Tax Credit Regulations 2002
CTF	child trust fund
CTS	Carpal Tunnel Syndrome
DAC	Directive 2011/16/ EU (Directive on administrative co-operation in the field of taxation)
DAT	Disability Appeal Tribunal

dB	decibels
DCA	Department for Constitutional Affairs
DCP	Disabled Child Premium
Decisions and Appeals Regulations 1999	Social Security Contributions (Decisions and Appeals) Regulations 1999
Dependency Regulations	Social Security Benefit (Dependency) Regulations 1977
DfEE	Department for Education and Employment
DHSS	Department of Health and Social Security
Disability Living Allowance Regulations	Social Security (Disability Living Allowance) Regulations
DIY	do it yourself
DLA	Disability Living Allowance
DLA Regs 1991	Social Security (Disability Living Allowance) Regulations 1991
DLAAB	Disability Living Allowance Advisory Board
DLADWAA 1991	Disability Living Allowance and Disability Working Allowance Act 1991
DM	Decision Maker
DMA	Decision-making and Appeals
DMG	*Decision Makers' Guide*
DMP	Delegated Medical Practitioner
DP	Disability Premium
DPT	diffuse pleural thickening
DPTC	Disabled Person's Tax Credit
DRO	Debt Relief Order
DSD	Department for Social Development (Northern Ireland)
DSM IV; DSM-5	Diagnostic and Statistical Manual of Mental Disorders of the American Psychiatric Association
DSS	Department of Social Security
DTI	Department of Trade and Industry
DWA	Disability Working Allowance
DWP	Department for Work and Pensions
DWPMS	Department for Work and Pensions Medical Service
EAA	Extrinsic Allergic Alveolitis
EAT	Employment Appeal Tribunal
EC	European Community
ECHR	European Convention on Human Rights
ECJ	European Court of Justice
E.C.R.	European Court Reports
ECSC	European Coal and Steel Community
ECSMA	European Convention on Social and Medical Assistance
EEA	European Economic Area

EEC	European Economic Community
EESSI	Electronic Exchange of Social Security Information
E.G.	Estates Gazette
E.G.L.R.	Estates Gazette Law Reports
EHC plan	education, health and care plan
EHIC	European Health Insurance Card
EHRC	European Human Rights Commission
E.H.R.R.	European Human Rights Reports
EL	employers' liability
E.L.R	Education Law Reports
EMA	Education Maintenance Allowance
EMP	Examining Medical Practitioner
Employment and Support Allowance Regulations	Employment and Support Allowance Regulations 2008
EPS	extended period of sickness
Eq. L.R.	Equality Law Reports
ERA	evoked response audiometry
ERA scheme	Employment, Retention and Advancement scheme
ES	Employment Service
ESA	Employment and Support Allowance
ESA Regs 2013	Employment and Support Allowance Regulations 2013
ESA Regulations	Employment and Support Allowance Regulations 2008
ESA WCAt	Employment and Support Allowance Work Capability Assessment
ESC	employer supported childcare
ESE Scheme	Employment, Skills and Enterprise Scheme
ESE Regulations	Jobseeker's Allowance (Employment, Skills and Enterprise Scheme) Regulations 2011
ESES Regulations	Jobseeker's Allowance (Employment, Skills and Enterprise Scheme) Regulations 2011
ETA 1973	Employment and Training Act 1973
ETA(NI) 1950	Employment and Training Act (Northern Ireland) 1950
ETS	European Treaty Series
EU	European Union
Eu.L.R.	European Law Reports
EWCA Civ	Civil Division of the Court of Appeal (England and Wales)
EWHC Admin	Administrative Court, part of the High Court (England and Wales)
FA 1993	Finance Act 1993
FA 1996	Finance Act 1996
FA 2004	Finance Act 2004

Table of Abbreviations used in this Series

HP	Health Professional
HPP	Higher Pensioner Premium
HRA 1998	Human Rights Act 1998
H.R.L.R.	Human Rights Law Reports
HRP	Home Responsibilities Protection
HSE	Health and Safety Executive
IAC	Immigration and Asylum Chamber
IAP	Intensive Activity Period
IB	Incapacity Benefit
IB PCA	Incapacity Benefit Personal Capability Assessment
IB Regs	Social Security (Incapacity Benefit) Regulations 1994
IB Regulations	Social Security (Incapacity Benefit) Regulations 1994
IB/IS/SDA	Incapacity Benefits Regime
IBJSA	Income-Based Jobseeker's Allowance
IBS	Irritable Bowel Syndrome
ICA	Invalid Care Allowance
I.C.R.	Industrial Cases Reports
ICTA 1988	Income and Corporation Taxes Act 1988
IFW Regulations	Incapacity for Work (General) Regulations 1995
IH	Inner House of the Court of Session
I.I.	Industrial Injuries
IIAC	Industrial Injuries Advisory Council
IIDB	Industrial Injuries Disablement Benefit
ILO	International Labour Organization
Imm. A.R.	Immigration Appeal Reports
Incapacity for Work Regulations	Social Security (Incapacity for Work) (General) Regulations 1995
Income Support General Regulations	Income Support (General) Regulations 1987
IND	Immigration and Nationality Directorate of the Home Office
I.N.L.R.	Immigration and Nationality Law Reports
I.O.	Insurance Officer
IPPR	Institute of Public Policy Research
IRESA	Income-Related Employment and Support Allowance
I.R.L.R.	Industrial Relations Law Reports
IS	Income Support
IS Regs	Income Support Regulations
IS Regulations	Income Support (General) Regulations 1987
ISA	Individual Savings Account
ISBN	International Standard Book Number
ITA 2007	Income Tax Act 2007
ITEPA 2003	Income Tax, Earnings and Pensions Act 2003

I.T.L. Rep.	International Tax Law Reports
I.T.R.	Industrial Tribunals Reports
ITS	Independent Tribunal Service
ITTOIA 2005	Income Tax (Trading and Other Income) Act 2005
IVB	Invalidity Benefit
IW (General) Regs	Social Security (Incapacity for Work) (General) Regulations 1995
IW (Transitional) Regs	Incapacity for Work (Transitional) Regulations
Jobseeker's Allowance Regulations	Jobseeker's Allowance Regulations 1996
Jobseeker's Regulations 1996	Jobseeker's Allowance Regulations 1996
JSA	Jobseeker's Allowance
JSA 1995	Jobseekers Act 1995
JSA (NI) Regulations	Jobseeker's Allowance (Northern Ireland) Regulations 1996
JSA (Transitional) Regulations	Jobseeker's Allowance (Transitional) Regulations 1996
JSA Regs 1996	Jobseeker's Allowance Regulations 1996
JSA Regs 2013	Jobseeker's Allowance Regulations 2013
JS(NI)O 1995	Jobseekers (Northern Ireland) Order 1995
J.S.S.L.	Journal of Social Security Law
J.S.W.L.	Journal of Social Welfare Law
K.B.	Law Reports, King's Bench
L.& T.R.	Landlord and Tenant Reports
LCW	limited capability for work
LCWA	Limited Capability for Work Assessment
LCWRA	limited capability for work-related activity
LDEDC Act 2009	Local Democracy, Economic Development and Construction Act 2009
LEA	local education authority
LEL	Lower Earnings Limit
LET	low earnings threshold
L.G. Rev.	Local Government Review
L.G.L.R.	Local Government Reports
L.J.R.	Law Journal Reports
LRP	liable relative payment
L.S.G.	Law Society Gazette
Luxembourg Court	Court of Justice of the European Union (also referred to as CJEC and ECJ)
MA	Maternity Allowance
MAF	Medical Assessment Framework
Maternity Allowance Regulations	Social Security (Maternity Allowance) Regulations 1987
MDC	Mayoral development corporation
ME	myalgic encephalomyelitis

Medical Evidence Regulations	Social Security (Medical Evidence) Regulations 1976
MEN	Mandatory Employment Notification
Mesher and Wood	*Income Support, the Social Fund and Family Credit: the Legislation* (1996)
M.H.L.R.	Mental Health Law Reports
MHP	mental health problems
MIF	minimum income floor
MIG	minimum income guarantee
Migration Regulations	Employment and Support Allowance (Transitional Provisions, Housing Benefit and Council Tax Benefit (Existing Awards) (No.2) Regulations 2010
MP	Member of Parliament
MRSA	methicillin-resistant Staphylococcus aureus
MS	Medical Services
MWA Regulations	Jobseeker's Allowance (Mandatory Work Activity Scheme) Regulations 2011
MWAS Regulations	Jobseeker's Allowance (Mandatory Work Activity Scheme) Regulations 2011
NCB	National Coal Board
NDPD	Notes on the Diagnosis of Prescribed Diseases
NHS	National Health Service
NI	National Insurance
N.I..	Northern Ireland Law Reports
NICA	Northern Ireland Court of Appeal
NICom	Northern Ireland Commissioner
NICs	National Insurance Contributions
NINO	National Insurance Number
NIRS 2	National Insurance Recording System
N.L.J.	New Law Journal
NMC	Nursing and Midwifery Council
Northern Ireland Contributions and Benefits Act	Social Security Contributions and Benefits (Northern Ireland) Act 1992
N.P.C.	New Property Cases
NRCGT	non-resident capital gains tax
NTC Manual	Clerical procedures manual on tax credits
NUM	National Union of Mineworkers
NUS	National Union of Students
OCD	obsessive compulsive disorder
Ogus, Barendt and Wikeley	A. Ogus, E. Barendt and N. Wikeley, *The Law of Social Security* (1995)
Old Cases Act	Industrial Injuries and Diseases (Old Cases) Act 1975
OPB	One Parent Benefit
O.P.L.R.	Occupational Pensions Law Reports

OPSSAT	Office of the President of Social Security Appeal Tribunals
Overlapping Benefits Regulations	Social Security (Overlapping Benefits) Regulations 1975
P	retirement pension case
P. & C.R.	Property and Compensation Reports
para.	paragraph
Pay Regulations	Statutory Paternity Pay and Statutory Adoption Pay (General) Regulations 2002; Statutory Shared Parental Pay (General) Regulations 2014
PAYE	Pay As You Earn
PC	Privy Council
PCA	Personal Capability Assessment
PCC	Police and Crime Commissioner
PD	Practice Direction; prescribed disease
Pens. L.R.	Pensions Law Reports
Pensions Act	Pension Schemes Act 1993
PEP	Personal Equity Plan
Persons Abroad Regulations	Social Security Benefit (Persons Abroad) Regulations 1975
Persons Residing Together Regulations	Social Security Benefit (Persons Residing Together) Regulations 1977
PIE	Period of Interruption of Employment
PILON	pay in lieu of notice
Pilot Scheme Regulations	Universal Credit (Work-Related Requirements) In Work Pilot Scheme and Amendment Regulations 2015
PIP	Personal Independence Payment
P.I.Q.R.	Personal Injuries and Quantum Reports
Polygamous Marriages Regulations	Social Security and Family Allowances (Polygamous Marriages) Regulations 1975
PPF	Pension Protection Fund
Prescribed Diseases Regulations	Social Security (Industrial Injuries) (Prescribed Diseases) Regulations 1985
PSCS	Pension Service Computer System
Pt	Part
PTA	pure tone audiometry
P.T.S.R.	Public and Third Sector Law Reports
PTWR 2000	Part-time Workers (Prevention of Less Favourable Treatment) Regulations 2000
PVS	private and voluntary sectors
Q.B.	Queen's Bench Law Reports
QBD	Queen's Bench Division
QCS Board	Quality Contract Scheme Board
QEF	qualifying earnings factor
QYP	qualifying young person

r.	rule
R	Reported Decision
R.C.	Rules of the Court of Session
REA	Reduced Earnings Allowance
reg.	regulation
RIPA	Regulation of Investigatory Powers Act 2000
RMO	Responsible Medical Officer
rr.	rules
RR	reference rate
RSI	repetitive strain injury
RTI	Real Time Information
R.V.R.	Rating & Valuation Reporter
s.	section
S	Scottish Decision
SAP	Statutory Adoption Pay
SAPOE Regulations	Jobseeker's Allowance (Schemes for Assisting Persons to Obtain Employment) Regulations 2013
SAWS	Seasonal Agricultural Work Scheme
SAYE	Save As You Earn
SB	Supplementary Benefit
SBAT	Supplementary Benefit Appeal Tribunal
SBC	Supplementary Benefits Commission
S.C.	Session Cases
S.C. (H.L.)	Session Cases (House of Lords)
S.C. (P.C.)	Session Cases (Privy Council)
S.C.C.R.	Scottish Criminal Case Reports
S.C.L.R.	Scottish Civil Law Reports
Sch.	Schedule
SDA	Severe Disablement Allowance
SDP	Severe Disability Premium
SEC	Social Entitlement Chamber
SEN	special educational needs
SERPS	State Earnings Related Pension Scheme
ShPP	statutory shared parental pay
ShPP Regulations	Statutory Shared Parental Pay (General) Regulations 2014
SI	Statutory Instrument
SIP	Share Incentive Plan
S.J.	Solicitors Journal
S.J.L.B.	Solicitors Journal Law Brief
SLAN	statement like an award notice
S.L.T.	Scots Law Times
SMP	Statutory Maternity Pay

SMP (General) Regulations 1986	Statutory Maternity Pay (General) Regulations 1986
SPC	State Pension Credit
SPC Regulations	State Pension Credit Regulations 2002
SPCA 2002	State Pension Credit Act 2002
SPL Regulations	Shared Parental Leave Regulations 2014
SPP	Statutory Paternity Pay
ss.	sections
SS (No.2) A 1980	Social Security (No.2) Act 1980
SSA 1975	Social Security Act 1975
SSA 1977	Social Security Act 1977
SSA 1978	Social Security Act 1978
SSA 1979	Social Security Act 1979
SSA 1981	Social Security Act 1981
SSA 1986	Social Security Act 1986
SSA 1988	Social Security Act 1988
SSA 1989	Social Security Act 1989
SSA 1990	Social Security Act 1990
SSA 1998	Social Security Act 1998
SSAA 1992	Social Security Administration Act 1992
SSAC	Social Security Advisory Committee
SSAT	Social Security Appeal Tribunal
SSCBA 1992	Social Security Contributions and Benefits Act 1992
SSCB(NI)A 1992	Social Security Contributions and Benefits (Northern Ireland) Act 1992
SSCPA 1992	Social Security (Consequential Provisions) Act 1992
SSD	Secretary of State for Defence
SSHBA 1982	Social Security and Housing Benefits Act 1982
SSHD	Secretary of State for the Home Department
SSI	Scottish Statutory Instrument
SS(MP)A 1977	Social Security (Miscellaneous Provisions) Act 1977
SSP	Statutory Sick Pay
SSP (General) Regulations	Statutory Sick Pay (General) Regulations 1982
SSPA 1975	Social Security Pensions Act 1975
SSPP	statutory shared parental pay
SSWP	Secretary of State for Work and Pensions
State Pension Credit Regulations	State Pension Credit Regulations 2002
S.T.C.	Simon's Tax Cases
S.T.C. (S.C.D.)	Simon's Tax Cases: Special Commissioners' Decisions
S.T.I.	Simon's Tax Intelligence
STIB	Short-Term Incapacity Benefit
subpara.	subparagraph

subs.	subsection
T	Tribunal of Commissioners' Decision
T.C.	Tax Cases
TCA 1999	Tax Credits Act 1999
TCA 2002	Tax Credits Act 2002
TCC	Technology and Construction Court
TCEA 2007	Tribunals, Courts and Enforcement Act 2007
TCGA 1992	Taxation of Chargeable Gains Act 2002
TCTM	*Tax Credits Technical Manual*
TEC	Treaty Establishing the European Community
TENS	transcutaneous electrical nerve stimulation
TEU	Treaty on European Union
TFC	tax-free childcare
TFEU	Treaty on the Functioning of the European Union
TIOPA 2010	Taxation (International and Other Provisions) Act 2010
TMA 1970	Taxes Management Act 1970
T.R.	Taxation Reports
Transfer of Functions Act	Social Security Contributions (Transfer of Functions etc.) Act 1999
Tribunal Procedure Rules	Tribunal Procedure (First-tier Tribunal)(Social Entitlement Chamber) Rules 2008
UB	Unemployment Benefit
UC	Universal Credit
UC Regs 2013	Universal Credit Regulations 2013
UCITS	Undertakings for Collective Investments in Transferable Securities
UKAIT	UK Asylum and Immigration Tribunal
UKBA	UK Border Agency of the Home Office
UKCC	United Kingdom Central Council for Nursing, Midwifery and Health Visiting
UKFTT	United Kingdom First-tier Tribunal Tax Chamber
UKHL	United Kingdom House of Lords
U.K.H.R.R.	United Kingdom Human Rights Reports
UKSC	United Kingdom Supreme Court
UKUT	United Kingdom Upper Tribunal
UN	United Nations
Universal Credit Regulations	Universal Credit Regulations 2013
URL	uniform resource locator
USI Regs	Social Security (Unemployment, Sickness and Invalidity Benefit) Regulations 1983
USI Regulations	Social Security (Unemployment, Sickness and Invalidity Benefit) Regulations 1983
UT	Upper Tribunal

VAT	Value Added Tax
VCM	vinyl chloride monomer
Vol.	Volume
VWF	Vibration White Finger
W	Welsh Decision
WCA	Work Capability Assessment
WCAt	limited capability for work assessment
WFHRAt	Work-Focused Health-Related Assessment
WFI	work-focused interview
WFTC	Working Families Tax Credit
Wikeley, Annotations	N. Wikeley, "Annotations to Jobseekers Act 1995 (c.18)" in *Current Law Statutes Annotated* (1995)
Wikeley, Ogus and Barendt	Wikeley, Ogus and Barendt, *The Law of Social Security* (2002)
W.L.R.	Weekly Law Reports
WLUK	Westlaw UK
Workmen's Compensation Acts	Workmen's Compensation Acts 1925 to 1945
WP	Widow's Pension
WPS	War Pensions Scheme
WRA 2007	Welfare Reform Act 2007
WRA 2009	Welfare Reform Act 2009
WRA 2012	Welfare Reform Act 2012
W-RA Regulations	Employment and Support Allowance (Work-Related Activity) Regulations 2011
WRAAt	Work-Related Activity Assessment
WRPA 1999	Welfare Reform and Pensions Act 1999
WRP(NI)O 1999	Welfare Reform and Pensions (Northern Ireland) Order 1999
WRWA 2016	Welfare Reform and Work Act 2016
WSP (LCP) R (NI) 2016	Welfare Supplementary Payment (Loss of Carer Payments) Regulations (Northern Ireland) 2016
WSP (LDRP) R (NI) 2016	Welfare Supplementary Payment (Loss of Disability-Related Premiums) Regulations (Northern Ireland) 2016
WSPR (NI) 2016	Welfare Supplementary Payment Regulations (Northern Ireland) 2016
WTC	Working Tax Credit
WTC Regulations	Working Tax Credit (Entitlement and Maximum Rate) Regulations 2002

INTRODUCTION

Universal Credit—An Introduction

Despite the many criticisms that have been made of it, universal credit still appears to be destined to become the future of working-age social security in Great Britain. Its introduction is the biggest change to the social security system since the abolition of supplementary benefit and its replacement with income support ("IS") by the Social Security Act 1986.

The background: complexity and disincentives to work

Readers of Vols I to IV of this work will require no persuading that the social security system as a whole is complex. However, the changes since 1996—including the introduction of jobseeker's allowance ("JSA") in October 1996, the new tax credits in April 2003, and employment and support allowance ("ESA") in October 2008—destroyed the previous position of IS as a single benefit for all those poor enough to satisfy the means-test. Instead, the changes created a system for claimants of working age (i.e., those under pensionable age) that is more than usually Byzantine.

Before the introduction of universal credit, people of working age who needed to claim benefit because they were not working (or, though working, were not earning enough to meet their basic needs) had to choose from a complex array of benefits some of which complemented each other and others of which were mutually exclusive.

Those who were able to work, but could not find a job, generally had to claim JSA, entitlement to which was either "contribution-based", or "income-based" ("JSA(IB)") which was a euphemism for "means-tested". Those who could not work because they were prevented from doing so by illness or disability claimed ESA, which again could be contributory or "income-related" ("ESA(IR)"). Those who could not be expected to work for other reasons (e.g., because they were caring for a young child or for a disabled person) could claim IS, entitlement to which was based on a means-test and had no contributory component.

The three benefits listed above were administered by the Department for Work and Pensions ("DWP") and included elements to help meet a claimant's housing costs if (broadly speaking) the claimant was an owner-occupier. However, for claimants who rented their homes, help for housing costs was provided by a fourth benefit, housing benefit ("HB") which was administered by local authorities.

Moreover, ESA(IR) and—except in a limited class of transitional cases—JSA(IB) and IS were "adults only" benefits. For claimants whose families included children or "qualifying young persons" (people aged between 16 and 20 who are in education or training) state help for the cost of feeding, clothing and bringing up the child or qualifying young person was provided by HM Revenue & Customs ("HMRC") through two further benefits, child benefit and child tax credit ("CTC").

Finally, people working more than 16 hours a week were excluded from IS, JSA(IB) and ESA(IR). However, they could sometimes claim working tax credit ("WTC"), which was not open to anyone working fewer than 16 hours a week. HB had no hours rule (although, of course, the more hours a person worked, the more likely their claim might fail on income grounds).

The complexity of that system, in which a claimant with children living in rented property might have to claim four different benefits from three differ-ent agencies was further aggravated by the fact entitlement to tax credits was normally calculated with respect to, and paid over, an entire tax year whereas entitlement to IS, JSA(IB), ESA(IR) and HB was calculated weekly and usually paid fortnightly or, in the case of HB, four-weekly or monthly. It was often difficult to ensure that the two different calculation and payment systems meshed together properly, not least because the mechanisms for sharing information between the DWP, HMRC and local authorities were less than perfect. The whole system operated against the background that a mistake, whether by the claimant or the administering authority, could result in an overpayment, leaving the claimant in debt, often for thousands of pounds.

The old system had the further effect of providing financial disincentives to work at certain levels of income. Under the means-tests for IS, JSA(IB) and ESA(IR) only relatively small amounts of earnings were ignored. Claimants whose earnings exceeded those "disregards" had their benefits reduced penny for penny by the amount of the excess and therefore derived no further benefit from their earnings until they earned enough to lose enti-tlement to benefit altogether.

This is not the place for a detailed discussion of the poverty trap. An example should suffice to make the point.

During 2020/21, a single claimant, call her Jane, aged over 25 on the basic rate of JSA(IB) receives £74.35 per week. Jane's weekly earnings disregard is £5.00. Suppose she does one hour's work a week at the national minimum wage of £8.72 per hour. The first £5 of those earnings is disregarded but her JSA(IB) is reduced by £3.72 (the amount by which £8.72 exceeds £5) to £70.63. Jane's total weekly income is thus £79.35 (£8.72 in earnings plus JSA(IB) of £70.63).

Now, suppose Jane increases her working hours to nine per week. Her weekly earnings are now £78.46 (£8.72 × 9) but her earnings disregard is still £5. Therefore her weekly entitlement to JSA(IB) is reduced by £73.46 (£78.46 – £5.00) from £74.35 to £0.89, giving her a total weekly income of £79.35 (£78.46 in earnings plus £0.89 in JSA(IB)). In short, Jane's income remains exactly the same whether she works one hour per week or nine. It is only once she works ten hours a week, taking her earnings to £82.20 (£87.20 – £5.00) and losing entitlement to JSA(IB) altogether, that Jane begins to be better off. And at that stage, if she is in rented accommodation, she is likely to lose 65 pence in HB for each additional pound that she earns. She will also lose entitlement to "passported" advantages such as free prescriptions, which will provide a further disincentive to work.

Universal credit and the new system

Universal credit is designed to get rid of both the problems outlined above by simplifying the social security system and ensuring that claimants will always be better off in work.

The planned simplification of the system is to be achieved by abolishing six of the seven benefits referred to above (IS, JSA(IB), ESA(IR) HB, CTC and WTC) and replacing them with universal credit. As universal credit is administered and paid by the DWP, the effect will be to end the role of local authorities in social security administration and to restrict the role of HMRC to the administration of child benefit and guardian's allowance.

In the new system, child benefit continues unaffected and two new benefits, confusingly called "jobseeker's allowance" and "employment and support allowance"—and referred to as "new style" JSA and ESA to dis-tinguish them from the older, identically–named, "old style" benefits are paid without any means-test, but for limited periods, to those who meet the contribution conditions.

The new structure is undoubtedly simpler than the system it replaces.

The aim of simplification has, however, been frustrated by the decision to phase universal credit in over a period of years. That decision is entirely understandable, given the new benefit's reliance on information technology. It would be a recipe for disaster for universal credit to be introduced on a general basis before it had been established in pilot areas that it could be properly administered.

However, the effect of a phased introduction is that the two systems continue to co-exist, so that what has been achieved is not a simplification of the benefits system but a significant complication. During the transition, universal credit is not a *replacement* benefit but an *additional* benefit.

Moreover, it is inherent in the design of universal credit that it overlaps with each of the older benefits it is eventually intended to replace. That overlap means that, in addition to the complication of the old and new systems existing side-by-side (including having two different and mutually exclusive benefits both called JSA and two called ESA), it is also necessary to have legislation defining which set of rules applies to any particular claimant at any given time. That legislation is now to be found first, in the Universal Credit (Transitional Provisions) Regulations 2014 ("the 2014 Regulations") and, second, in a series of Commencement Orders that, even by the high standards set by past social security legislation, are bewilderingly complex.

If that were not enough, the procedures by which universal credit was introduced meant that, at least in relation to some issues, the benefit existed for a period in two forms with different substantive rules: see *Introduction of universal credit* below.

As a final complication, the need to devote departmental resources to the introduction of universal credit appears to have delayed the extension of the housing costs element of SPC to cover rent and other payments made by those who are not owner-occupiers. Further, even claimants who have become subject to the universal credit rules may still claim HB if they live in "exempt accommodation" (see the definition in Sch.1, para.1 to the Universal Credit Regulations, below). The effect is that local authorities will need to retain their benefits departments—and incur the associated costs and overheads that might otherwise have been saved—to deal with claims for HB from those who are above working age and in exempt accommodation.

All of that might not matter if the transition from the old system to the new had been relatively swift. However, that has not been the case. On July 9, 2020, the latest date for which statistics are available, and more than six years after the benefit was introduced—there were 5.6 million people on universal credit (a figure that reflects an increase of 2.6 million (87%) on the figure for March 2020 because of the Coronavirus pandemic). This compares with the original projection by the Office for Budget Responsibility in March 2013 that there would be 6.1 million people on universal credit in 2016-17. The benefit was finally "rolled-out" to all new claimants—or, at any rate, almost all: see *Introduction of universal credit* below—on December 12, 2018. It was then intended that the process of migrating claimants who are in receipt of IS, JSA(IB), ESA(IR) HB, CTC and WTC to the new benefit would begin a pilot phase in July 2019 and eventually end in March 2023. That deadline was met (just) by the Universal Credit (Managed Migration Pilot and Miscellaneous Amendments) Regulations 2019 (SI 2019/1152), regs 2 and 3 of which came into force on July 24, 2010. Those regulations establish a pilot scheme which will affect a maximum of 10,000 existing claimants, beginning with claimants in Harrogate. In answer to a Parliamentary question on January 27, 2020 (six months after the pilot began), it was announced that there were 80 claimants taking part of whom "around 13" had migrated to universal credit. At which rate, the pilot will take 384 years and 7½ months to complete. Or, rather it would have done had it not been suspended on March 30, 2020 because of the Coronavirus pandemic.

The slow pace of the transition also means that, for the vast majority of existing working age claimants, the benefits system continues to be as described in the opening paragraphs of this introduction: they will continue to deal with up to three different authorities and to be subject to disincentives to work from the poverty trap.

That having been said, the new scheme has some positive features.

First—and with the notable exception of the Commencement Orders—the legislation is better structured and easier to follow than social security lawyers have become accustomed to. The drafting still has some eccentricities. For example, the Regulations use the words "claimant" and "person" in an inconsistent and confusing way that assumes that they are precise synonyms for each other; and it is surprising to find what used to be the permitted work rule for those who have limited capability for work hidden away in a regulation (reg.41) that appears to be about when a work capability assessment may be carried out. However, overall, the Regulations and the 2014 Regulations are not unnecessarily opaque or complex, even though the rules for any benefit that replaces six other benefits are inevitably going to be detailed.

Second, although the universal credit scheme embodies political judgments about what claimants should be required to do in return for their benefit with which it is possible to disagree, progress has been made towards eliminating the poverty trap.

If we return to the example given above and suppose that, instead of claiming JSA, Jane had been eligible to claim universal credit, then her basic entitlement to universal credit (ignoring housing costs as we did implicitly in the JSA example) would be her "maximum amount" which would consist of the modified standard allowance (see the commentary to reg.36 of the Universal Credit Regulations) for a single person aged at least 25, namely £409.89 per month. That equates to £94.89 per week (£409.89 × 12 ÷ 52) and is therefore considerably higher than the equivalent personal allowance for JSA.

Jane then begins to work one hour a week at the minimum wage of £8.72 per hour. In an average month she would earn £37.79 (8.72 × 52 ÷ 12). From April 2016, Jane no is longer entitled to a work allowance (i.e., because she does not have responsibility for a child or qualifying young person and does not have limited capability for work). There would therefore be no equivalent of the £5 weekly disregard in the JSA calculation. However, under universal credit, from April 2017 only 63% of Jane's earnings will be deducted from the maximum amount, not the full amount of her (undisregarded) earnings as in JSA. In cash terms, the deduction is £23.81 (£37.79 × 63%) giving a monthly universal credit award of £386.08 (£409.89 – £23.81), equivalent to £89.09 per week (£386.08 × 12 ÷ 52). Jane's equivalent weekly income is therefore £97.81 (£89.09 in universal credit + £8.72 in earnings).

Jane is therefore £2.92 (£97.81 – £94.89) per week better off as a result of working 1 hour a week.

Jane's weekly income of £97.81 on universal credit compares favourably with the equivalent JSA figure of £78.35. Moreover, not many people work for just 1 hour a week and the more work Jane does, the more the universal credit rules begin to operate in her favour. If Jane works nine hours a week (at which level, it will be remembered, her combined weekly earnings and benefit under JSA would still have been £79.35), the equivalent weekly income from universal credit and earnings is £123.63.

However, Jane is considerably worse off under the new universal credit rules than she would have been under the rules that existed before April 2016 (see *The amounts to be deducted*, below).

Introduction of universal credit

Universal credit raises two transitional issues. The first is whether a person making a fresh claim for benefit is free to claim IS/HB/JSA/ESA or whether he or she must now claim universal credit. The second is in what circumstances existing recipients of IS/HB/JSA/ESA will be moved from those benefits to universal credit.

Fresh claims

The process of introducing universal credit was begun by the Universal Credit (Transitional Provisions) Regulations 2013 ("the 2013 Regulations"). The text of those Regulations (which have now been revoked) is set out on pp.305-354 of the 2013/14 edition of this volume. In summary, they provided that claimants may (and must) claim universal credit rather than IS/JSA/ESA if, at the time their claim was made or treated as made, they resided in one of the "relevant districts" and were either in the Pathfinder Group or had formerly been jointly entitled to universal credit as a member of a former couple. The relevant districts were postcode areas linked to particular Jobcentres and specified in the various Commencement Orders (see Pt IV below). The extension of universal credit proceeded by issuing further Commencement Orders that widened the geographical scope of the rules by adding further "relevant districts".

Membership of the Pathfinder Group was governed by regs 4-12 of the 2013 Regulations (pp.312-323 of the 2013/14 edition). The criteria for membership of the Pathfinder Group were so narrowly drawn that it, in summary, it only included single, adult, British citizens who would otherwise have had to claim JSA. The issues that were likely to give rise to disputes were narrower still because any claimant whose circumstances were likely to give rise to complications had been excluded from the Pathfinder Group and therefore had to continue to claim IS/JSA/ESA. Unsurprisingly in those circumstances, the initial experience of the Social Entitlement Chamber of the First-tier Tribunal was that universal credit appeals were overwhelmingly about backdating and the imposition of sanctions.

The 2013 Regulations were revoked by the 2014 Regulations with effect from June 16, 2014. Nothing equivalent to the former Pathfinder conditions appeared in the 2014 Regulations. Instead, a policy decision was taken that new "Gateway conditions" would be specified in Commencement Orders. This approach gave the government flexibility to vary those conditions for different areas, or to include no Gateway conditions at all.

That flexibility was used to establish two different models for the implementation of universal credit. From November 11, 2014, the No.20 Commencement Order (see Pt IV below) allowed (and required) claimants who lived in a small area of the SM5 postcode in the London Borough of Sutton to claim universal credit without having to satisfy the Gateway conditions. On the same day, the Universal Credit (Digital Service) Amendment Regulations 2014 (SI 2014/2887) came into force and made substantive changes to the Universal Credit Regulations, that only apply in what are described as "digital service" areas. At that time, the SM5 2 postcode area was the only such area. However, subsequent Commencement Orders have expanded the areas covered by the digital service and further statutory instruments (SI 2014/3225 and SI 2015/1647) have introduced additional amendments to the Universal Credit Regulations that only apply in such areas.

In keeping with its long-standing institutional reluctance to call anything by its correct statutory name, the DWP referred to digital service areas as "full service" areas and distinguished them from the areas in which the Gateway conditions still applied by referring to the latter as "live service" areas.

The distinction reflected the fact that, during this period, universal credit was administered using two separate and incompatible IT systems, depending on whether the claimant lived in a full/digital service area or a live service area.

Once the rules for universal credit were in force on at least a live service basis (i.e., for claimants who satisfied the Gateway Conditions) throughout Great Britain, the further roll-out of universal credit consisted of a process of "de-gatewayfication": instead of Commencement Orders extending universal credit to new geographical areas by prescribing additional relevant districts, they converted existing live service areas to full/digital service areas by revoking the Gateway conditions in those areas.

But even claims by people who lived in live service areas could raise issues that, if they had existed at the time of the original claim, would have meant that the Gateway conditions were not satisfied. This is because of what is known colloquially as the "lobster pot" principle. The editors of this volume profess no expertise in catching marine crstaceans, but it is understood that the analogy is to the fact that the route into a lobster pot is a narrow one, but that once inside there is more room and, more importantly, the lobster cannot get back out. The principle applies to universal credit because the Commencement Orders are structured so that the provisions of the Act that abolish JSA(IB) and ESA(IR) come into force in relation to a particular claimant when he or she makes a valid claim for, or is actually awarded universal credit. From that point on, the claimant cannot go back to the those benefits (i.e., because, in relation to him or her, they no longer exist) and must therefore continue to claim universal credit even if he or she no longer lives in a relevant district or has had a change of circumstances that is incompatible with the Gateway conditions. The other "legacy" benefits (IS, CTC, WTC and, in most cases, HB) cease to apply because regs 5-8 of the 2014 Regulations exclude those who are in receipt of universal credit from entitlement and prevent those who are not actually in receipt of universal credit but count as a universal credit claimant from making a new claim for them. In full/digital service areas, the relevant commencement orders prevented anyone living within the area from claiming a "legacy" benefit.

Existing claimants

At the time of going to press, the pilot scheme in Harrogate remains suspended, so that no "managed migration" of claimants from "legacy benefits" to universal credit is actually taking place.

However, in case that scheme resumes during the currency of this edition, it should be explained that the legal basis for the pilot can be found in Part 4 of the Universal Credit (Transitional Provisions) Regulations 2014 as substituted by reg.3(7) of the Universal Credit (Managed Migration Pilot and Miscellaneous Amendments) Regulations 2019 (SI 2019/1152). Migration is commenced by the Secretary of State issuing a "migration notice" under the substituted reg.44 to a person who is entitled to an award of an existing benefit. The notice must inform that person that all awards of any existing benefits to which they are entitled are to terminate and that they will need to make a claim for universal credit. It must also specify a day ("the deadline day") by which a claim for universal credit must be made. If no universal credit claim is made by the deadline day (which the Secretary of State can change to a later day: see reg.45) then all awards of any existing benefits to which the person is entitled terminate on the deadline day (except for awards of housing benefit, which terminate two weeks later: see reg.46). Under reg.46(3) and (4), a claimant who does not claim universal credit by the deadline day can retrieve the situation by claiming before "the final deadline", which is the day that would be the last day of the first assessment period in relation to an award commencing on the deadline day.

Unlike "natural migration", managed migration gives entitlement to transitional protection, so that claimants should not receive less in benefit immediately after the move to universal credit than they were receiving immediately before. Substituted regs 48-57 of the Transitional Provisions Regulations 2014 contain detailed rules on how the transitional protection operates.

The relevant law

The universal credit scheme is established by Part 1 of the Welfare Reform Act 2012 ("WRA 2012" or "the Act") and by the Schedules to the Act that are given effect by provisions in Part 1. The Act has subsequently been amended by the Welfare Reform and Work Act 2016 (WR & RA 2016). As is common in social security law, the Act sets out the structure of the scheme and confers extensive powers on the Secretary of State to make regulations prescribing matters of detail. The main regulations are the Universal Credit Regulations 2013 ("the Universal Credit Regulations" or "the Regulations"), but there are others including the 2014 Regulations and regulations dealing with claims and payments, and decisions and appeals, for universal credit, personal independence payment ("PIP"), new style JSA and new style ESA.

This volume contains all the statute law that directly affects entitlement to universal credit, including procedural issues. Provisions that relate indirectly to universal credit, i.e., by amending the rules for other benefits so that they refer to universal credit are taken into account in Vols I to IV.

The structure of universal credit

Any description of the structure of universal credit will involve at least an implicit decision about the level of detail that should be included. Almost any general proposition about social security law will be subject to qualifications and exceptions. Failing to note those qualifications and exceptions risks giving an unhelpfully approximate explanation of how the structure is meant to work. However, dealing with them in full risks obscuring the view of the wood by concentrating on the trees.

We have the advantage that the detailed rules about universal credit are dealt with in the annotations to the legislation in Parts II to V. The purpose of this introduction is to give the big picture. It therefore discusses details only where a particular rule is entirely new, or markedly different from the equivalent rules for existing benefits, or is likely to have important practical effects, or to give rise to disputes. There is never any substitute for looking at the actual words of the legislative text. Until they have checked both that text and the commentary to it, readers should assume that everything in this introduction is subject to unstated exceptions, particularly when such exceptions are implied by the use of words such as "normally" and "usually".

Universal credit is a non-contributory, means-tested, working age, social security benefit. That means that it is not "universal". With very limited exceptions, people who are not of working age are excluded from entitlement, as are (with no exceptions) those who do not satisfy the means-test. Moreover, as is the case with all non-contributory benefits, the rules contain residence and presence conditions (including a right to reside test) which exclude those who are felt not have a legitimate connection with Great Britain or who have been absent from the UK for an extended period.

In addition, the fact that universal credit is a social security benefit means that it is not "credit" in the sense in which that word is used in ordinary speech. Universal credit is a *payment*, made as a matter of legal right to those who meet the conditions of entitlement, not a *loan* to tide claimants over a period of reduced income. With the sole exception of the hardship payments made to those who have been sanctioned, universal credit that has been correctly paid does not have to be repaid.

Couples

One of the basic principles of universal credit is that it cannot usually be claimed by one member of a couple: WRA 2012 s.2(1) provides that a claim for universal credit may only be made a single person or by members of a couple jointly. It is implicit that any award of universal credit made on a joint claim will be a joint award to both members of the couple.

The basic conditions

Entitlement to universal credit depends upon satisfying both the "basic conditions" and the "financial conditions" set out in the Act (WRA 2012, s.3(1)). Where a joint claim is made, those conditions must usually be satisfied by both members of the couple (WRA 2012, s.3(2)).

The basic conditions are set out in s.4(1) of the Act. They are that the claimant:

- must be at least 18 years old;
- must not have reached the qualifying age for SPC (which is now pensionable age);
- is in Great Britain;
- is not receiving education; and
- has accepted a claimant commitment.

The last three of those conditions are further defined, or partially defined, in regulations. For example, a person who does not have a right to reside in the UK is treated as not being habitually resident here and hence as not being "in Great Britain": see reg.9 of the Universal Credit Regulations. All of those conditions are subject to exceptions which are specified in regulations. In addition, a person who meets the basic conditions cannot acquire entitlement to universal credit if he or she falls within the restrictions specified in s.6 of the Act and reg.19 of the Regulations.

It should be noted that it is not a condition of entitlement to universal credit that any claimant should be, or should not be, in remunerative work. The only way in which work affects universal credit is through the income that is earned from undertaking it.

The financial conditions

The financial conditions are set out in s.5 of the Act. They are that

- the claimant's capital (or, for couples, joint capital) is not greater than a prescribed amount (currently fixed at £16,000 by reg.18 of the Regulations); and that

- the claimant's income (or, for couples, joint income) is "such that, if the claimant were entitled to universal credit, the amount payable would not be less than any prescribed minimum" (currently fixed at one penny by reg.17 of the Regulations).

As is discussed above and below, entitlement to universal credit reduces as a claimant's income increases. The effect of the convoluted wording quoted in the second bullet point above is that if, as a result of that reduction, the amount of universal credit payable would be less than one penny (i.e., nil), the financial conditions are not satisfied. In other words, one cannot be entitled to universal credit at a nil rate.

As would be expected, the calculation of a claimant's income and capital are the subject of detailed provisions in the Regulations.

Assessment periods

Universal credit is a monthly benefit. Entitlement is normally assessed by reference to the claimant's circumstances during an "assessment period", which is defined by WRA 2012 s.7(2) and reg.21(1) of the Regulations as "a period of one month beginning with the first date of entitlement and each subsequent period of one month during which entitlement subsists". That entitlement is then normally paid monthly in arrears after the end of the assessment period to which the payment relates (see reg.47 of the Universal Credit, Personal Independence Payment, Jobseeker's Allowance and Employment and Support Allowance (Claims and Payments) Regulations 2013).

Calculation of entitlement to universal credit

Under s.8(1) of the Act, the amount of an award of universal credit is the balance of the "maximum amount" less "the amounts to be deducted".

The amount so calculated will normally be reduced by the "benefit cap" (see below) if the claimant's total entitlement to specified social security benefits would otherwise exceed the amount of the cap.

11

The maximum amount

The maximum amount is a monthly amount. It is conceptually equivalent to the weekly "applicable amount" used in the calculation of entitlement to IS, JSA(IB) and ESA(IR). It is the total of the standard allowance (equivalent to the personal allowances for IS/JSA/ESA) established by WRA 2012, s.9 and reg.36 of the Regulations, and any of the following amounts to which the claimant is (or the joint claimants are) entitled:

- the child element

  Under WRA 2012, s.10 and regs.24 & 36 of the Regulations, an amount is allowed for each child or qualifying young person for whom a claimant is responsible, up to (subject to exceptions and transitional savings) a maximum of two children or qualifying young persons. An additional amount is allowed for each child or qualifying young person who is entitled to disability living allowance ("DLA") or PIP. The amount is higher if entitlement is to the highest rate of the care component of DLA or the enhanced rate of the daily living component of PIP or if the child or qualifying young person is registered blind.

- the housing costs element

  The housing costs element is payable under WRA 2012, s.11 and regs 25 & 26 of, and Schs 1-5 to the Regulations. The rules are summarised below.

- the LCWRA element

  This is payable where the claimant has limited capability for work-related activity. It is equivalent to, but paid at a considerably higher rate than, the support component of ESA (see WRA 2012, s.12 and regs 27(1)(b) & 36 of the Regulations). The former LCW element (equivalent to the former work-related activity component of ESA) was abolished with effect from April 3, 2017 and is now only payable to claimants with transitional protection.

- the carer element

  This is equivalent to, and is paid at approximately the same rate as, the carer premium for IS/JSA/ESA (see WRA 2012, s.12 and regs 29 & 36 of the Regulations). To qualify, a claimant must satisfy the conditions of entitlement to carer's allowance other than having earnings below the prescribed limit and making a claim for that benefit (see regs 30(1) & (2) of the Regulations).

- the childcare costs element

  The childcare costs element is 85% of the charges incurred by a claimant for relevant childcare (defined in reg.35 of the Regulations) subject to a maximum of £646.35 pcm for one child or £1,108.04 pcm for two or more children (regs 34(1) and 36) and also to anti-abuse rules in reg.34(2). To qualify, a claimant must satisfy both the work condition (reg. 32) and the childcare costs condition (reg.33).

  The childcare costs element is not subject to the benefits cap (reg. 81(1)(b) and (2)).

The amounts of the standard allowance and the various elements are specified in a table that forms part of reg.36 of the Regulations.

The amounts to be deducted

Once the maximum amount has been ascertained, it is necessary to calculate the amounts to be deducted from it. By WRA 2012, s.8(3) & reg.22 of the Universal Credit Regulations, those amounts are:

- All the claimant's, or the claimants' combined, *unearned* income;

- Either (where the claimant does not have responsibility for a child or qualifying young person and does not have limited capability for work) 63% of his or her *earned* income; or

- (where the claimant has responsibility for a child or qualifying young person or has limited capability for work) 63% of the amount by which the claimant's, or the claimants' combined, *earned* income exceeds the work allowance.

The "work allowance" is what is described in IS/HB/JSA/ESA as an "earnings disregard". There are two rates, which are specified in a table that forms part of reg.22. The higher work allowance of £512.00 is applicable if the award of universal credit does not include the housing costs element: otherwise the lower work allowance of £292.00 applies.

Until April 2016, all claimants with earned income had work allowances, but, as indicated above, work allowances are now only available when the claimant (or at least one joint claimant) has responsibility for a child or qualifying young person or has limited capability for work. In addition, some of pre-April 2016 allowances were higher than is now the case. For some claimants who have responsibility for a child, the reduction in the work allowances were at least partially offset by the April 2016 increases in the maximum rates of the childcare costs elements (reg.36 of the Regulations) and the percentage of relevant childcare charges that is eligible to be met by universal credit (reg.34). However, the maximum increase in the child care costs element was £114.06 per month for one child and £192.54 for two or more children, By contrast, the higher work allowance for a single person with children was cut by £337 from £734 to £397 (now £512 in 2020/21).

In fairness, the cuts in the lower work allowance are considerably less than in the higher allowance (and it is likely that many claimants who have responsibility for a child or qualifying young person will have housing costs and so only be eligible for the lower allowance). So the combined effect of the cut in the work allowance and the increase in the childcare costs element will often be a modest increase in entitlement to universal credit.

However, that has been achieved at the cost of a swingeing reduction in work incentives for able-bodied, childless, claimants. Revisiting the example above, if Jane had been working nine hours a week at the minimum wage, she would still have been £10.41 per week worse off (more in real terms) on April 5, 2020 than she had been on April 5, 2015 (the calculations appear in the 2019/20 edition of this Introduction). As a result of the modification of the standard allowances for 2020/21, she would now be better off. However, unless the modification is continued in future years, Jane would be likely to revert to being worse off on April 6, 2021.

Calculation of income

Earned income

Employees

The treatment of the earned income of employees is another new feature of the universal credit scheme and one of the areas in which the benefit depends heavily upon the efficient operation of information technology. Most employers are now obliged to submit their PAYE returns to HMRC online and on a monthly basis under the "Real-Time Information" system. The idea is that that PAYE information should then be used to calculate the claimant's entitlement to universal credit for that month. If the system works, it has the advantage that claimants need not report fluctuations in their earnings (and therefore need not fear having to repay overpayments if they omit to do so). The possibility of treating earned income in this way was the main reason for establishing universal credit as a monthly, rather than weekly, benefit and for providing that payment should be in arrears after the end of the assessment period.

For those advantages to accrue the way in which earnings from employment are calculated are different from those for IS/HB/JSA/ESA. First, earnings are to be based on the actual amount received by the claimant during the assessment period (see reg.54(1)). Then, reg.55 defines "earned income" by reference to the income tax definition. Finally reg.61 provides that where the claimant's employer is a "Real Time Information employer", the information on which the Secretary of State bases his calculation of earned income is to be the information reported by that employer through the PAYE system and the claimant is normally treated as having received those earnings in the same assessment period as the Secretary of State received the information.

With effect from April 11, 2018 the new reg.54 introduces the rule that if a claimant's earned income (whether as an employee or as a self-employed person) is more than sufficient to wipe out entitlement to UC for an assessment period, the amount of the excess ("surplus earnings") is to be taken into account on any new claims within the following six months. There are complex provisions, with a potential to confuse claimants, for the erosion of surplus earnings within that six months by the making of claims that do not result in any entitlement.

The self-employed

The principle in reg.54(1) of the Universal Credit Regulations that earnings are to be taken as the actual amount received by the claimant during the assessment period also applies to self-employed earnings. Under reg.57(2), a person's self-employed earnings in respect of an assessment period are to be calculated by taking that person's "gross profits" (defined by reg.57(3) as "the actual receipts in [the assessment] period less any deductions for expenses allowed under regulation 58 or 59") and then deducting any payments of income tax and Class 2 and 4 national insurance contributions actually made to HMRC in that period and any "relievable pension contributions made" (as defined in s.188 of the Finance Act 2004, i.e., contributions to a registered pension scheme for which tax relief is available). Regs 58 & 59 establish an exhaustive list of the expenses that can be deducted. In particular, reg.59 provides for flat rate deductions for business mileage and the use of the claimant's home for business purposes.

Where a claimant would otherwise be subject to all work-related requirements—or is only exempt from all work-related requirements because their earnings exceed the earnings threshold (see below)—self-employed earnings are subject to a "minimum income floor" (see regs 62-64). The minimum income floor is usually an amount representing the person's "individual threshold" (see below) converted to a monthly figure and subjected to a notional deduction to reflect the tax and national insurance contributions payable on that level of self-employed earnings. Except during a start-up period (reg.63) self-employed claimants whose earnings in any assessment period are less than their minimum income floor are treated as having earnings equal to that floor.

The operation of the minimum income floor will be affected from April 2018 by the "surplus earnings" rule (see above). That, and the general calculations, will also be affected from the same date by the new provision (reg.57A and amendments to reg.57) for "unused losses" in past (but not pre-April 2018) assessment periods to be set against profits in the current assessment period.

Unearned income

Unearned income is deducted from the maximum amount without any disregard or taper. However, in contrast to the rules for IS/JSA/ESA and working-age HB, not all types of unearned income fall within the definition. Those that do are set out in reg.66 of the Universal Credit Regulations and include:

- retirement pension income;

- certain social security benefits (including "new style" JSA and ESA);

- spousal maintenance payments;

- student income (e.g., student loans and grants: see reg.68);

- payments under permanent health insurance policies and certain mortgage protection policies;

- income from (non-retirement) annuities and from trusts unless disregarded as compensation for personal injury (regs 75 & 76);

- income treated as the yield from capital under reg.72 (see below);

- miscellaneous income that is taxable under Part 5 of Income Tax (Trading and Other Income) Act 2005;

Unearned income is calculated as a monthly amount but—in contrast to earned income—does not necessarily represent the amount actually received by the claimant in the assessment period for which the award is made. Regulation 73 contains detailed rules for converting unearned income (other than student income) received in respect of periods other than a month into a monthly equivalent. Student income has its own detailed rules, which are set out in regs 69-71.

Treatment of capital

Capital is relevant to universal credit entitlement in two ways. First, there is a maximum capital limit of £16,000 for both single and joint claimants (see reg.18 of the Universal Credit Regulations). Claimants who have capital in excess of that limit do not satisfy the first financial condition (see WRA 2012 s.5) and are therefore not entitled to benefit. Second, claimants with capital of more than £6,000 but less than £16,000 are treated as receiving an amount of unearned income equal to an "assumed yield" on that income. Reg.72 of the Universal Credit Regulations provides that that assumed yield is to be £4.35 per assessment period for each £250 (or part thereof). Readers who are familiar with IS/HB/JSA/ESA will recognise the "tariff income" rule under a different name.

The calculation of capital is governed by regs.45-50. By reg.46(1) and (2), the whole of a claimant's capital (other than his or her personal possessions) is to be taken into account unless it is treated as income under regs 46(3) and (4) or disregarded under reg. 48 and Sch.10. The valuation rules closely follow those for IS/HB/JSA/ESA and reg.50 contains a notional capital rule which is similar, though not identical, to that for the older working age benefits.

The benefit cap

Awards of universal credit are subject to the "benefit cap" established by ss.96-97 of the Act and regs 78-83 of the Universal Credit Regulations. This means that, subject to limited exceptions, if an award of universal credit would lead to the claimant's total entitlement to social security benefits exceeding the level of the cap then the amount of universal credit that the claimant would otherwise be awarded for the assessment period is reduced by the amount of the excess.

The cap is fixed at four different levels. If the claimant is (or joint claimants are) resident in Greater London, the cap is £23,000 per annum–equivalent to £442.30 per week–for joint claimants or those responsible for a child or qualifying young person and £15,410 per annum—£296.35 per week—for other claimants. If the claimant is (or joint claimants are) not resident in Greater London, the equivalent levels are £20,000 per annum and £13,400 per annum (£384.62 per week and £257.69 per week). The higher levels in Greater London are intended to reflect the higher cost of accommodation in the capital. The childcare costs element of universal credit is not subject to the cap and the cap does not apply at all if the universal credit award contains the LCWRA element; if a claimant is receiving certain other benefits including new style ESA with the support component, industrial injuries disablement benefit and attendance allowance; or if any member of the household is receiving DLA or PIP.

Housing costs

Section 8(2)(c) of the Act provides that the maximum amount is to include "any amount included under s.11 (housing costs)". Section 11(1) says that an award of universal credit must include "an amount in respect of any liability of a claimant to make payments in respect of the accommodation they occupy as their home". By s.11(2), the accommodation must be in Great Britain and must be residential accommodation but need not be self-contained. The remainder of s.11 confers powers for the Secretary of

State to make regulations, which have been used to make regs 25 and 26 of, and Schs 1-5 to, the Universal Credit Regulations.

Regulation 25 establishes three conditions for eligibility, the "payment condition", the "liability condition" and the "occupation condition"(see reg.25(5)(b)).

The payment condition (reg.25(1)(a) and (2) is that payments must be rent payments (as defined in Sch.1, paras.2 and 3), owner-occupier payments (Sch.1, paras.4-6) or service charges payments (Sch.1, para.7). Until April 5, 2018, owner-occupiers were, in some circumstances, entitled to an amount of housing costs in respect of the interest on their mortgages or on loans taken out for repairs and improvements. However, from April 6, 2016 such housing costs have been replaced with loans under the Loans for Mortgage Interest Regulations 2017 (SI 2017/725): see below. As a result the only UC housing costs still payable to owner-occupiers are those in respect of service charges.

The inclusion of rent payments was a major change. Previously help with rent was given through HB which was administered by local authorities rather than the DWP. Many—but not all—of the rules about rental payments are similar to those for HB.

The liability condition (reg.25(1)(b) and (3)) is that the claimant (or either joint claimant) must either be liable to make the payments on a commercial basis, or treated as liable to make the payments (Pt 1 of Sch.2) and must not be treated as not liable to make the payments (Pt 2 of Sch.2).

The occupation condition (reg.25(1)(c) and (4)) is that the claimant must normally be treated as occupying the accommodation as his or her home (Pt 1 of Sch.3) and not be treated as not occupying it (Pt 2 of Sch.3)

The rules for the calculation of the housing costs element are set out in Schs 4 (for renters) and 5 (for the residual housing costs payable to owner occupiers).

Claimant responsibilities and the claimant commitment

The claimant commitment

Under s.4(1)(e) of the Act, it is a basic condition of entitlement to universal credit that the claimant "has accepted a claimant commitment". By s.14, a claimant commitment is "a record of a claimant's responsibilities in relation to an award of universal credit" and is to include a record of the requirements with which the claimant must comply, any prescribed information, and any other information the Secretary of State considers it appropriate to include. However, the claimant commitment does not itself impose requirements on the claimant and the condition that the clamant should accept it appears to have been included so that there is no doubt about what requirements have, in fact, been imposed. Any failure to comply with a requirement is dealt with by a sanction rather than by ending entitlement to benefit.

Claimant responsibilities

Work-related requirements

Section 13(1) of the Act empowers the Secretary of State "to impose work-related requirements with which claimants must comply". There are four different types of work-related requirement:

- the work-focused interview requirement (WRA 2012 s.15)

  As its name suggests, this is a "requirement that a claimant participate in one or more work-focused interviews as specified by the Secretary of State".

- the work preparation requirement (WRA 2012 s.16)

  This is a "requirement that a claimant take particular action specified by the Secretary of State for the purpose of making it more likely in the opinion of the Secretary of State that the claimant will obtain paid work (or more paid work or better-paid work)". Section 16(3) gives the following examples of actions that the Secretary of State may specify:

  o attending a skills assessment;
  o improving personal presentation;
  o participating in training;
  o participating in an employment programme;
  o undertaking work experience or a work placement;
  o developing a business plan;
  o any prescribed action.

  In addition any claimant with limited capability for work may also be required to participate in a work-focused health-related assessment.

- work search requirements (WRA 2012 s.17 and reg.95)

  There are two of these. The first is that a claimant must take all reasonable action for the purpose of obtaining paid work (or more paid work or better-paid work). The second is that he or she must also take any particular action specified by the Secretary of State for that purpose. Section 17(3) gives the following examples of actions that the Secretary of State may specify

  o carrying out work searches;
  o making applications;
  o creating and maintaining an online profile;
  o registering with an employment agency;
  o seeking references;
  o any prescribed action.

  Under reg.95, claimants are treated as not having complied with the first work search requirement unless they have spent at least the "expected number of hours each week minus any relevant deductions" taking action to obtain paid work unless the Secretary of State is satisfied that the claimant has taken all reasonable action for that purpose despite having spent fewer hours taking action.

  Reg.88 provides that the expected number of hours is 35 per week unless the claimant has caring responsibilities or is physically or mentally impaired and the Secretary of State agrees to a lesser number of hours. Reg.95(2) specifies that relevant deductions means the total of any time agreed by the Secretary of State for the claimant to carry out paid work, voluntary work, a work preparation requirement, or voluntary work preparation in that week or to deal with temporary childcare responsibilities, a domestic emergency, funeral arrangements or other temporary circumstances.

- work availability requirements (WRA 2012 s.18 and reg.96)

    This is a requirement that the claimant be available for work which is defined as "able and willing immediately to take up paid work (or more paid work or better-paid work)".

The work-related requirements which may be imposed on a claimant depend on which of the following groups the claimant falls into—

- Claimants subject to no work-related requirements (WRA 2012 s.19 and regs 89-90);

    These include claimants with limited capability for work and work-related activity, claimants with regular and substantial caring responsibilities for a severely disabled person, and claimants who are the responsible carer for a child under the age of 1, the claimant has reached the qualifying age for state pension credit; pregnant women within 11 weeks of the expected date of confinement and new mothers within 15 weeks of the birth, recent adopters, certain claimants in education and foster parents of children under 1.

    Claimants also fall within this group if they are in work and their earnings equal or exceed the threshold that applies to them. For most people that threshold will be the amount they would earn if they worked for their expected number of hours (usually 35 per week) at the minimum wage converted to a monthly figure. At current rates, that threshold is £1,245.18 (£8.21 x 35 x 52 ÷ 12) for those aged 25 or over. Lower thresholds apply to those aged less than 25, those who would otherwise be subject to the work-focused interview requirement only, or the work preparation requirement only, and apprentices. Couples have a joint threshold that applies to their combined weekly earnings.

- Claimants subject to the work-focused interview requirement only (WRA 2012 s.20 and reg.91);

    This group comprises the responsible carers of children who are aged 1 or more but are under 3 and certain foster parents and others caring for children.

- Claimants subject to the work-focused interview and work preparation requirements only (WRA 2012 s.21 and reg.91A);

    This group comprises claimants who have limited capability for work, but do not also have limited capability for work-related activity, or are responsible carers of children aged 3 or 4.

- Claimants subject to all work-related requirements (WRA 2012 s.22 and reg.92).

    This group comprises every claimant who is not in any of the other groups. The Secretary of State *must* impose the work search requirement and the work availability requirement on everyone in this group and *may* also impose the work-focused interview requirement and a work preparation requirement.

Reg.98 establishes special rules for the victims of domestic violence.

Connected requirements

Under s.23 of the Act, the Secretary of State may also impose a "connected requirement". There are three of these. First, claimants may be required to participate in an interview in connection with a work-related requirement. Second, they may be required to provide evidence to verify that they have complied with work-related requirements that have been imposed on them. Finally, they may be required to report specified changes in their circumstances which are relevant to work-related requirements.

Sanctions

It is not a condition of entitlement to universal credit that claimants should comply with requirements imposed by the Secretary of State under the provisions summarised above. Instead, compliance is enforced by the imposition of sanctions under which the amount of universal credit payable is reduced. Under regs 110-111 of the Universal Credit Regulations, the maximum reduction is the amount of the standard allowance applicable to the award of universal credit for the assessment period that is being considered or, where the sanction has only been imposed on one of two joint claimants, half the amount of that standard allowance.

There are four levels of sanction.

Higher-level sanctions are imposed under s.26 of the Act, which specifies that various actions or omissions by the claimant are to be "sanctionable failures". The definition of each of those failures is technical but, in broad terms, higher-level sanctions apply where, for no good reason, a claimant fails to undertake a work placement or apply for a vacancy when required to do so; fails to take up an offer of paid work; ceases work or loses pay voluntarily or through misconduct (whether before or after claiming universal credit). The sanction period is fixed by reg.102 of the Universal Credit Regulations. Again the rules are technical but for adults who commit a sanctionable failure during the currency of a claim, length of the sanction period depends upon whether there has been a previous sanctionable failure within the previous 365 days (including the date of the failure that led to the imposition of the current sanction). If not, then the sanction period is 91 days. If there was one previous sanctionable failure within the period, it is 182 days. The sanction period for a third or subsequent sanctionable failure within the 365 day period was originally 1095 days (3 years) but was reduced to 182 days with effect from November 27, 2019. Shorter periods apply if the claimant was under 18 when the sanctionable failure occurred or in the case of a failure that occurred before the claim for universal credit. Reg.102 is subject to reg.113 which specifies a number of circumstances in which a sanctionable failure does not result in a reduction of universal credit.

Medium-level sanctions, low-level sanctions and *lowest-level sanctions* are imposed under s.27 of the Act. That section provides that it is to be a sanctionable failure for a claimant to fail, for no good reason, to comply with a work-related requirement or a connected requirement unless that failure would also be a sanctionable failure under s.26, in which case the higher-level sanction applies. The level of sanction that such a failure attracts is prescribed in regs.103-105. The regulations themselves do not say so but it is important to remember that, by virtue of s.27, each of the failures discussed below is only sanctionable if it occurred for no good reason. Moreover, regs.103-105 are subject to reg.113 which specifies a number of circumstances in which a sanctionable failure does not result in a reduction of universal credit.

A failure to take all reasonable action to obtain paid work in breach of a work search requirement under s.17(1)(a) or a failure to comply with a work availability requirement attracts a medium-level sanction under reg.103. The sanction period is 28 days for the first such failure in any 365 day period and 91 days for a second or subsequent failure in that period.

Reg.104 provides that low-level sanctions apply to claimants who are subject to the work preparation requirement or to all work-related require-ments and who have failed to comply with a work-focused interview requirement, a work preparation requirement, or a connected requirement, or failed to take a particular action specified by the Secretary of State to obtain work in breach of a work search requirement. The sanction lasts until 7, 14 or 28 days (depending on the number of previous such failures in the preceding 65 days) after the claimant complies with the requirement, or has a change of circumstances so that he or she is not longer subject to any work-related requirements, or the requirement is withdrawn, or the award of universal credit ends. Again, the period for 16 and 17 year-olds is shorter.

Lowest-level sanctions are governed by reg.105. They apply to claimants who are subject to the work-focused interview requirement only (i.e., under WRA 2012, s.20) and who fail to comply with that requirement. The sanc-tion continues until the claimant complies with the requirement, or has a change of circumstances so that he or she is no longer subject to any work-related requirements, or the award of universal credit ends.

When deciding whether there has been a previous sanctionable failure within the 365 day period, failures occurring in the 14 days immediately preceding the failure in question are disregarded (reg.101(4)).

The total of all outstanding sanction periods in relation to a particular claimant, cannot exceed 1095 days (reg.101(3)).

Under reg.109, a sanction terminates (irrespective of the length of the unexpired sanction period) if, since the most recent sanction was imposed, the claimant has been in paid work for six months (not necessarily consecutively) and during each of those months his or her earnings were equal to or exceeded the applicable threshold (see above).

Regulations provide for the date on which the sanction period is to begin. Where a claimant is subject to more than one sanction, they run consecu-tively (reg.101(2)).

Where a 100% sanction has been imposed (but not where there has been a 40% reduction), the Secretary of State must make a hardship payment under WRA 2012, s.28 in the (very limited) circumstances prescribed by regs 115-118. Under reg.119, hardship payments are usually recoverable in accordance with s.71ZH of the Social Security Administration Act 1992. However, any hardship payment ceases to be recoverable if, since the last date on which the award of universal credit was subject to a sanction, the claimant (or the joint claimants) has (or have) been in paid work for six months (not necessarily consecutively) and during each of those months his or her earnings (or their joint earnings) were equal to or exceeded the applicable threshold (see above).

PART I

UNIVERSAL CREDIT: STATUTES

Social Security Administration Act 1992

(1992 C.5)

An Act to consolidate certain enactments relating to the administration of social   1.2
security and related matters with amendments to give effect to recommendations of
the Law Commission and the Scottish Law Commission.

[13th February 1992]

GENERAL NOTE

For the main provisions of this Act ("the SSAA 1992") and extensive commen-   1.3
tary, see Vol.III of this series. This Volume only includes certain of the amendments
made to SSAA 1992 by the WRA 2012, namely the insertion of new ss.71ZB to
71ZH inclusive.

Recovery of benefit payments

[¹ Recovery of overpayments of certain benefits

71ZB.—(1) The Secretary of State may recover any amount of the   1.4
following paid in excess of entitlement—
  (a) universal credit;
  (b) jobseeker's allowance;
  (c) employment and support allowance, *and*
  (d) *except in prescribed circumstances, housing credit (within the meaning of
      the State Pension Credit Act 2002).*
(2) An amount recoverable under this section is recoverable from—
  (a) the person to whom it was paid, or
  (b) such other person (in addition to or instead of the person to whom it
      was paid) as may be prescribed.
(3) An amount paid in pursuance of a determination is not recoverable
under this section unless the determination has been—
  (a) reversed or varied on an appeal, or
  (b) revised or superseded under section 9 or section 10 of the Social
      Security Act 1998,
except where regulations otherwise provide.

25

(4) Regulations may provide that amounts recoverable under this section are to be calculated or estimated in a prescribed manner.

(5) Where an amount of universal credit is paid for the sole reason that a payment by way of prescribed income is made after the date which is the prescribed date for payment of that income, that amount is for the purposes of this section paid in excess of entitlement.

(6) In the case of a benefit referred to in subsection (1) which is awarded to persons jointly, an amount paid to one of those persons may for the purposes of this section be regarded as paid to the other.

(7) An amount recoverable under this section may (without prejudice to any other means of recovery) be recovered—

    (a) by deduction from benefit (section 71ZC);

    (b) by deduction from earnings (section 71ZD);

    (c) through the courts etc (section 71ZE);

    (d) by adjustment of benefit (section 71ZF).]

AMENDMENT

1.5   1. Welfare Reform Act 2012 s.105(1) (April 29, 2013 for certain purposes, but at a date appointed for remaining purposes).

GENERAL NOTE

1.6   This new section marks a fundamental shift in the law relating to the recovery of overpayments of benefit. It deals (at present only) with the recovery of overpaid universal credit, JSA, ESA and the new housing credit element of state pension credit. However, it is not yet fully in force—see further below. Furthermore, so far as ESA and JSA are concerned, the present effect of the commencement provisions is that the new test applies only to overpayments of the new-style contributory versions of ESA and JSA, introduced as part of the universal credit regime.

The Secretary of State is given the power to recover any amount of Universal Credit, JSA and ESA, which has been paid in excess of entitlement (subs.(1)(a)–(c)). The same principle applies also to housing credit which has been paid in excess of entitlement, except in circumstances that will be prescribed in regulations (subs.(1)(d)). There is no requirement on the Secretary of State to establish either a misrepresentation or failure to disclose as a precondition for recovery. It follows that any payment of one of the relevant benefits in excess of the claimant's appropriate entitlement will be a recoverable overpayment, including those overpayments which arise purely as a result of official error. The underlying philosophy is that even the need for the Department to take responsibility for its own mistakes "does not give people the right to keep taxpayers' money that they are not entitled to" (Explanatory Memorandum to the Social Security (Overpayments and Recovery) Regulations 2013, para.7.2).

The overpaid benefit can be recovered from the person to whom it was paid or such other person as is prescribed (subs.(2); see further Security (Overpayments and Recovery) Regulations 2013 (SI 2013/384) reg.4). There must have been a relevant revision, supersession or appellate decision (subs.(3)). This requirement is broadly equivalent to the existing s.71(5A) of the SSAA 1992. However, note that reg.5 of the Security (Overpayments and Recovery) Regulations 2013 provides that "Section 71ZB(3) of the Act (recoverability of an overpayment dependent on reversal, variation, revision or supersession) does not apply where the circumstances of the overpayment do not provide a basis for the decision pursuant to which the payment was made to be revised under section 9 of the Social Security Act 1998 or superseded under section 10 of that Act."

Subsection (5) has the effect that where another income or benefit that would affect the award of universal credit is paid late, any amount of universal credit, which would not have been paid had the other income or benefit been paid on time, is treated as an overpayment and is recoverable from the universal credit recipient.

Where an award of benefit is made to persons jointly, an amount paid to one member of the couple may be treated as paid to the other and so recovered (subs. (6)).

The various methods of recovery are set out in subs.(7), namely deduction from   1.7
benefit (s.71ZC), by deduction from earnings (s.71ZD) (a new method akin to attachment of earnings), through the courts (s.71ZE) or by adjustment of subsequent benefit payments (s.71ZF).

Note that this section is not fully in force. Article 5(3)(a) of the Welfare Reform Act 2012 (Commencement No.8 and Savings and Transitional Provisions) Order 2013 (SI 2013/358) provided for the amending s.105(1) of the WRA 2012 to have effect in so far as it was not already in force "except in so far as it inserts section 71ZB(1)(d) of the 1992 Act and the word 'and' immediately preceding it" (the italicised text above). The Commencement No.8 Order was then modified by art.23(3) of the Welfare Reform Act 2012 (Commencement No.9 and Transitional and Transitory Provisions and Commencement No.8 and Savings and Transitional Provisions (Amendment)) Order 2013 (SI 2013/983), which provides that new s.71ZB(1)(b) and (c) "come into force on 29th April 2013 only in so far as they relate respectively to a new style JSA award and a new style ESA award".

Deduction from benefit

[¹ **71ZC.**—(1) An amount recoverable from a person under section 71ZB   1.8
may be recovered by deducting the amount from payments of prescribed benefit.

(2) Where an amount recoverable from a person under section 71ZB was paid to the person on behalf of another, subsection (1) authorises its recovery from the person by deduction—

(a) from prescribed benefits to which the person is entitled;

(b) from prescribed benefits paid to the person to discharge (in whole or in part) an obligation owed to that person by the person on whose behalf the recoverable amount was paid, or

(c) from prescribed benefits paid to the person to discharge (in whole or in part) an obligation owed to that person by any other person.

(3) Where an amount is recovered as mentioned in paragraph (b) of subsection (2), the obligation specified in that paragraph shall in prescribed circumstances be taken to be discharged by the amount of the deduction.

(4) Where an amount is recovered as mentioned in paragraph (c) of subsection (2), the obligation specified in that paragraph shall in all cases be taken to be so discharged.]

AMENDMENT

1. Welfare Reform Act 2012 s.105(1) (July 1, 2012 for the purpose only of prescribing under s.71ZC(1) the benefits from which deductions may be made in order to recover penalties, October 1, 2012 to the extent that it inserts s.71ZC(1) for the purpose only of enabling recovery of the penalties to take place by these methods; and April 29, 2013 for remaining purposes).

GENERAL NOTE

This section provides for the recovery of overpayments under the new s.71ZB   1.9
by deduction from benefit. Thus overpayments of universal credit, JSA, ESA and the housing credit can be recovered by making deductions from payments of prescribed benefits (subs.(1)). Where universal credit, JSA, ESA or the housing credit is paid to a third party (e.g. a landlord) on the claimant's behalf, overpay-

ments of those benefits may be recovered from prescribed benefits to which the third party is entitled; ongoing payments of prescribed benefits to the third party being made on the benefit claimant's behalf; or ongoing payments of prescribed benefits paid to the third party on other benefit claimants' behalf (e.g. if a landlord has other tenants who are in receipt of universal credit or housing credit) (subs.(2)). Furthermore, in circumstances to be prescribed by regulations, where deductions are made from payments of prescribed benefits to the third party on the claimant's behalf, then the claimant's obligations to the third party will be discharged, e.g. the landlord would not be able to put the claimant into arrears with their rent (subs.(3)). Similarly, in all cases where deductions are made from payments of prescribed benefits to the third party on behalf of other benefit claimants, the other claimants' obligations to the third party will likewise be discharged (and so the landlord would not be able to hold those other claimants as being in arrears with their rent) (subs.(4)). See further Social Security (Overpayments and Recovery) Regulations 2013 (SI 2013/384) P5 (regs 10–16) and especially reg.15.

Deduction from earnings

1.10   [¹ **71ZD**.—(1) Regulations may provide for amounts recoverable under section 71ZB to be recovered by deductions from earnings.

(2) In this section "earnings" has such meaning as may be prescribed.

(3) Regulations under subsection (1) may include provision—

(a) requiring the person from whom an amount is recoverable ("the beneficiary") to disclose details of their employer, and any change of employer, to the Secretary of State;

(b) requiring the employer, on being served with a notice by the Secretary of State, to make deductions from the earnings of the beneficiary and to pay corresponding amounts to the Secretary of State;

(c) as to the matters to be contained in such a notice and the period for which a notice is to have effect;

(d) as to how payment is to be made to the Secretary of State;

(e) as to a level of earnings below which earnings must not be reduced;

(f) allowing the employer, where the employer makes deductions, to deduct a prescribed sum from the beneficiary's earnings in respect of the employer's administrative costs;

(g) requiring the employer to keep records of deductions;

(h) requiring the employer to notify the Secretary of State if the beneficiary is not, or ceases to be, employed by the employer;

(i) creating a criminal offence for non-compliance with the regulations, punishable on summary conviction by a fine not exceeding level 3 on the standard scale;

(j) with respect to the priority as between a requirement to deduct from earnings under this section and—

(i) any other such requirement;

(ii) an order under any other enactment relating to England and Wales which requires deduction from the beneficiary's earnings;

(iii) any diligence against earnings.]

AMENDMENT

1. Welfare Reform Act 2012 s.105(1) (July 1, 2012).

DEFINITION

"earnings"—see subs.(2).

GENERAL NOTE

Under the previous arrangements, the Secretary of State typically recovered overpayment debts through deductions from ongoing benefit entitlement. However, once a claimant subject to an overpayment liability stopped receiving benefit, further recovery relied heavily on the debtor's compliance with repayment. The DWP estimates that about 350,000 people who are no longer in receipt of benefit owe some £500 million (DWP Impact Assessment, *Direct Earnings Attachment to Recover Overpaid Social Security Benefits*, September 2011, p.7). If a former claimant chose not to pay the money owed, then the Department's only option was to take court action, which was not always cost effective. In principle, however, the Department has always been able to apply to the magistrates' court for an attachment of earnings order as a means of recovering outstanding overpayments. Indeed, in the six months from April 2010, the Department obtained 824 orders under the Attachment of Earnings Act 1971, suggesting an annual case load of about 1,650 such cases (DWP Impact Assessment, p.9).

This new section for the first time empowers both the Department and local authorities to recover debt by attachment of earnings without the need for an application to court. The new Direct Earnings Attachments (DEA) are thus designed to act as an incentive to those liable for overpayments to make arrangements to repay their debts and, if they still refuse to repay, to provide the Department (or local authority) with a simpler alternative means to secure recovery. See further Social Security (Overpayments and Recovery) Regulations 2013 (SI 2013/384), especially Pt 6 (regs 17–30). These Regulations set out the circumstances in which a DEA can be issued, the type of earnings from which a deduction can be taken, the responsibilities of employers and the relevant rates of deduction where a DEA is in place.

The new DEA system may just be an interim measure. The DWP has also considered the possibility of recovering overpayments from former claimants who are now in employment through the PAYE system (DWP Impact Assessment, pp.6–7). However, this method could not be implemented for some years, presumably for operational or technical reasons as much as anything else. But note in this regard the increased powers for information sharing between the DWP and HMRC (see WRA 2012, s.127).

Court action etc.

[¹ **71ZE.**—(1) Where an amount is recoverable under section 71ZB from a person residing in England and Wales, the amount is, if [² the county court] so orders, recoverable—

(a) under section 85 of the County Courts Act 1984; or

(b) otherwise as if it were payable under an order of the court.

(2) Where an amount is recoverable under section 71ZB from a person residing in Scotland, the amount recoverable may be enforced as if it were payable under an extract registered decree arbitral bearing a warrant for execution issued by the sheriff court of any sheriffdom in Scotland.

(3) Any costs of the Secretary of State in recovering an amount of benefit under this section may be recovered by him as if they were amounts recoverable under section 71ZB.

(4) In any period after the coming into force of this section and before the coming into force of section 62 of the Tribunals, Courts and Enforcement Act 2007, subsection (1)(a) has effect as if it read "by execution issued from the county court".]

1.11

1.12

AMENDMENTS

1. Welfare Reform Act 2012 s.105(1) (October 1, 2012, for the purpose only of enabling recovery of the penalties to take place by these methods and April 29, 2013 for other purposes).
2. Crime and Courts Act 2013 s.17(5) and Sch.9(3) para.52(1)(b) (April 22, 2014).

GENERAL NOTE

1.13   This section provides for the recovery of overpayments under new s.71ZB through the courts. Thus overpayments are recoverable through the county courts for claimants residing in England and Wales (subs.(1)) and through the sheriff courts for those residing in Scotland (subs.(2)). The Secretary of State's normal practice is to try and recover court costs when there is a court judgment in his favour. However, under the previous law there was no mechanism for the Secretary of State to recover such associated costs in the same way as if they formed part of the overpayment debt (e.g. by deduction from benefit or by adjustment of subsequent payments of benefit). Accordingly, subs.(3) allows the Secretary of State to recover costs by the same method as the overpayment itself is recovered.

Adjustment of benefit

1.14   [¹ 71ZF. —Regulations may for the purpose of the recovery of amounts recoverable under section 71ZB make provision—
  (a) for treating any amount paid to a person under an award which it is subsequently determined was not payable—
    (i) as properly paid, or
    (ii) as paid on account of a payment which it is determined should be or should have been made,
and for reducing or withholding arrears payable by virtue of the subsequent determination;
  (b) for treating any amount paid to one person in respect of another as properly paid for any period for which it is not payable in cases where in consequence of a subsequent determination—
    (i) the other person is entitled to a payment for that period, or
    (ii) a third person is entitled in priority to the payee to a payment for that period in respect of the other person,
and by reducing or withholding any arrears payable for that period by virtue of the subsequent determination.]

AMENDMENTS

1. Welfare Reform Act 2012 s.105(1) (April 29, 2013).
2. Welfare Reform Act 2012 Sch.14(4) para.1 (April 29, 2013).

GENERAL NOTE

1.15   This section concerns the recovery of overpayments under new s.71ZB using the method of adjusting subsequent benefit payments. It provides that the Secretary of State may prescribe in regulations that in certain circumstances, amounts paid but subsequently determined as not payable, can be treated as properly paid and be set against future payments of benefit or against certain payments to third parties.

1.15.1   **[¹ 71ZG Recovery of payments on account**
(1) The Secretary of State may recover any amount paid under section 5(1)(r) (payments on account).

(2) An amount recoverable under this section is recoverable from—

(a) the person to whom it was paid, or

(b) such other person (in addition to or instead of the person to whom it was paid) as may be prescribed.

(3) Regulations may provide that amounts recoverable under this section are to be calculated or estimated in a prescribed manner.

(4) In the case of a payment on account of a benefit which is awarded to persons jointly, an amount paid to one of those persons may for the purposes of this section be regarded as paid to the other.

(5) Sections 71ZC, 71ZD and 71ZE apply in relation to amounts recoverable under this section as to amounts recoverable under section 71ZB.]

AMENDMENT

1. Welfare Reform Act 2012, s.105(1) (April 29, 2013 for certain purposes, but at a date appointed for remaining purposes).

[¹ 71ZH Recovery of hardship payments etc   1.15.2

(1) The Secretary of State may recover any amount paid by way of—

(a) a payment under section 28 of the Welfare Reform Act 2012 (universal credit hardship payments) which is recoverable under that section,

(b) [² . . .]

(c) a payment of a jobseeker's allowance under paragraph 8 or 8A of Schedule 1 to that Act (exemptions), where the allowance is payable at a prescribed rate under paragraph 9 of that Schedule and is recoverable under that paragraph,

(d) a payment of a jobseeker's allowance under paragraph 10 of that Schedule (claims yet to be determined etc) which is recoverable under that paragraph, or

(e) a payment which is recoverable under section 6B(5A)(d) or (7)(d), 7(2A)(d) or (4)(d), 8(3)(aa), (4)(d) or 9(2A)(d) or (4)(d) of the Social Security Fraud Act 2001.

(2) An amount recoverable under this section is recoverable from—

(a) the person to whom it was paid, or

(b) such other person (in addition to or instead of the person to whom it was paid) as may be prescribed.

(3) Regulations may provide that amounts recoverable under this section are to be calculated or estimated in a prescribed manner.

(4) Where universal credit or a jobseeker's allowance is claimed by persons jointly, an amount paid to one claimant may for the purposes of this section be regarded as paid to the other.

(5) Sections 71ZC to 71ZF apply in relation to amounts recoverable under this section as to amounts recoverable under section 71ZB.]

AMENDMENT

1. Welfare Reform Act 2012, s.105(1) (April 29, 2013 for certain purposes, but at a date appointed for remaining purposes).
2. Welfare Reform Act 2012 Sch.14(4) para.1 (April 29, 2013).

GENERAL NOTE

See further reg.119 of the Universal Credit Regulations.   1.15.3

Social Security Act 1998

(1998 c.14)

An Act to make provision as to the making of decisions and the determination of appeals under enactments relating to social security, child support, vaccine damage payments and war pensions; to make further provision with respect to social security; and for connected purposes.

[21st May 1998]

GENERAL NOTE

1.17   For the main provisions of this Act ("the SSA 1998"), see Vol.III of this series. This Volume only includes the core provisions in the SSA 1998 which are essential to understanding the structure of decision-making and appeals for universal credit. For detailed commentary on these and other provisions, see Vol.III.

CHAPTER II

SOCIAL SECURITY DECISIONS AND APPEALS

Decisions

Decisions by Secretary of State

1.18   **8.**—(1) Subject to the provisions of this Chapter, it shall be for the Secretary of State—

(a) to decide any claim for a relevant benefit;
(b) [⁶ ...] [¹ and]
(c) subject to subsection (5) below, to make any decision that falls to be made under or by virtue of a relevant enactment; [¹ ...]
(d) [¹ ...]

(2) Where at any time a claim for a relevant benefit is decided by the Secretary of State—

(a) the claim shall not be regarded as subsisting after that time; and
(b) accordingly, the claimant shall not (without making a further claim) be entitled to the benefit on the basis of circumstances not obtaining at that time.

(3) In this Chapter "relevant benefit" [² ...] means any of the following, namely—

(a) benefit under Parts II to V of the Contributions and Benefits Act;
[⁸(aa) universal credit;]
[⁹ (ab) state pension or a lump sum under Part 1 of the Pensions Act 2014;]
[¹⁰ (ac) bereavement support payment under section 30 of the Pensions Act 2014;]
(b) a jobseeker's allowance;
[⁵(ba) an employment and support allowance;]
[⁷(baa) personal independence payment;]
[³(bb) state pension credit;]
[¹¹(bc) a loan under section 18 of the Welfare Reform and Work Act 2016;
(c) income support;
(d) [⁴ . . .]
(e) [⁴ . . .]
(f) a social fund payment mentioned in section 138(1)(a) or (2) of the Contributions and Benefits Act;
(g) child benefit;
(h) such other benefit as may be prescribed.

(4) In this section "relevant enactment" means any enactment contained in this Chapter, the Contributions and Benefits Act, the Administration Act, the Social Security (Consequential Provisions) Act 1992 [³, the Jobseekers Act] [⁵, the State Pension Credit Act 2002 [⁸, Part 1 of the Welfare Reform Act 2007, Part 1 of the Welfare Reform Act 2012] [⁷ [⁹, Part 4 of that Act or Part 1 of the Pensions Act 2014]], [¹⁰ [¹¹, section 30 of that Act or sections 18 to 21 of the Welfare Reform and Work Act 2016]] other than one contained in—

(a) Part VII of the Contributions and Benefits Act so far as relating to housing benefit and council tax benefit; or
(b) Part VIII of the Administration Act (arrangements for housing benefit and council tax benefit and related subsidies).

[¹ (5) Subsection (1)(c) above does not include any decision which under section 8 of the Social Security Contributions (Transfer of Functions, etc) Act 1999 falls to be made by an officer of the Inland Revenue.]

AMENDMENTS

1. Social Security Contributions (Transfer of Functions, etc.) Act 1999 s.18 and Sch.7, para.22 (April 1, 1999). **1.19**

2. Welfare Reform and Pensions Act 1999 s.88 and Sch.13 (April 6, 2000).

3. State Pension Credit Act 2002 s.11 and Sch.1, para.6 (July 2, 2002 for the purpose of exercising any power to make regulations or orders and April 7, 2003 for other purposes).

4. Tax Credits Act 2002 s.60 and Sch.6 (April 8, 2003, subject to a saving in respect of outstanding questions concerning working families' tax credit and disabled person's tax credit—see Tax Credits Act 2002 (Commencement No.4, Transitional Provisions and Savings) Order 2003 (SI 2003/962), art.3(1)–(3)).

5. Welfare Reform Act 2007 s.28(1) and Sch.3, para.17(1)(and (3) (March 18, 2008 for regulation-making purposes and July 27, 2008 for other purposes).

6. Welfare Reform Act 2012 s.147 and Sch.14, Pt 8 (April 1, 2013).

7. Welfare Reform Act 2012 s.91 and Sch.9, paras 37 and 39 (February 25, 2013 for regulation-making purposes and April 8, 2013 for other purposes).

8. Welfare Reform Act 2012 s.31 and Sch.2, paras 43 and 45 (February 25, 2013 for regulation-making purposes and April 29, 2013 for other purposes).

9. Pensions Act 2014 Sch.12(1) para.33 (April 6, 2016).

10. Pensions Act 2014 Sch.16 paras 39(2) and (3) (April 6, 2017).

11. Welfare Reform and Work Act 2016 s.20(4) (July 27, 2018).

DEFINITIONS

"the Administration Act"—see SSA 1998 s.84.

"claim"—by virtue of SSA 1998 s.39(2), see SSAA 1992, s.191.

"claimant"—see SSA 1998 s.39(1), and by virtue of SSA 1998 s.39(2), see SSAA 1992 s.191.

"the Contributions and Benefits Act"—see SSA 1998 s.84.

"Inland Revenue"—by virtue of SSA 1998 s.39(2), see SSAA 1992 s.191 but note that the Inland Revenue has been merged into HMRC (Her Majesty's Revenue and Customs) by the Commissioners for Revenue and Customs Act 2005.

"the Jobseekers Act"—see SSA 1998 s.84.

"prescribed"–*ibid.*

"relevant benefit"—see subs.(3).

"relevant enactment"—see subs.(4).

Revision of decisions

1.21   **9.**—(1) [¹ ...] Any decision of the Secretary of State under section 8 above or section 10 below may be revised by the Secretary of State—

(a) either within the prescribed period or in prescribed cases or circumstances; and

(b) either on an application made for the purpose or on his own initiative;

and regulations may prescribe the procedure by which a decision of the Secretary of State may be so revised.

(2) In making a decision under subsection (1) above, the Secretary of State need not consider any issue that is not raised by the application or, as the case may be, did not cause him to act on his own initiative.

(3) Subject to subsections (4) and (5) and section 27 below, a revision under this section shall take effect as from the date on which the original decision took (or was to take) effect.

(4) Regulations may provide that, in prescribed cases or circumstances, a revision under this section shall take effect as from such other date as may be prescribed.

(5) Where a decision is revised under this section, for the purpose of any rule as to the time allowed for bringing an appeal, the decision shall be regarded as made on the date on which it is so revised.

(6) Except in prescribed circumstances, an appeal against a decision of the Secretary of State shall lapse if the decision is revised under this section before the appeal is determined.

AMENDMENT

1. Welfare Reform Act 2012 s.147 and Sch.14, Pt 8 (April 1, 2013).

DEFINITION

"prescribed"—see SSA 1998 s.84.

Decisions superseding earlier decisions

1.22   **10.**—(1) Subject to [¹ subsection (3)] [⁴ ...] below, the following, namely—

(a) any decision of the Secretary of State under section 8 above or this section, whether as originally made or as revised under section 9 above; [³ ...]

[³(aa) any decision under this Chapter of an appeal tribunal or a Commissioner; and]

(b) any decision under this Chapter [² of the First-tier Tribunal or any decision of the Upper Tribunal which relates to any such decision],

may be superseded by a decision made by the Secretary of State, either on an application made for the purpose or on his own initiative.

(2) In making a decision under subsection (1) above, the Secretary of State need not consider any issue that is not raised by the application or, as the case may be, did not cause him to act on his own initiative.

(3) Regulations may prescribe the cases and circumstances in which, and the procedure by which, a decision may be made under this section.

(4) [¹ ...]

(5) Subject to subsection (6) and section 27 below, a decision under this section shall take effect as from the date on which it is made or, where applicable, the date on which the application was made.

(6) Regulations may provide that, in prescribed cases or circumstances, a decision under this section shall take effect as from such other date as may be prescribed.

[³ (7) In this section—

"appeal tribunal" means an appeal tribunal constituted under Chapter 1 of this Part (the functions of which have been transferred to the First-tier Tribunal);

"Commissioner" means a person appointed as a Social Security Commissioner under Schedule 4 (the functions of whom have been transferred to the Upper Tribunal), and includes a tribunal of such persons.]

AMENDMENTS

1. Social Security Contributions (Transfer of Functions, etc.) Act 1999, s.18 and Sch.7, para.23 (April 1, 1999).
2. Transfer of Functions Order 2008 (SI 2008/2833) art.6 and Sch.3, paras 14 and 148 (November 3, 2008).
3. Welfare Reform Act 2012 s.103 and Sch.12, para.4 (check date, 2013).
4. Welfare Reform Act 2012 s.147 and Sch.14, Pt 8 (April 1, 2013).

DEFINITIONS

"appeal tribunal"—see subs.(7).
"Commissioner"—*ibid.*
"prescribed"—SSA 1998 s.84.

Appeals

Appeal to [² First-tier Tribunal]

12.—(1) This section applies to any decision of the Secretary of State   1.22.1
under section 8 or 10 above (whether as originally made or as revised under section 9 above) which—

(a) is made on a claim for, or on an award of, a relevant benefit, and does not fall within Schedule 2 to this Act; [¹ or]
(b) is made otherwise than on such a claim or award, and falls within Schedule 3 to this Act; [¹ ...]
(c) [¹ ...]

[¹ (2) In the case of a decision to which this section applies, the claimant and such other person as may be prescribed shall have a right to appeal to [² the First-tier Tribunal], but nothing in this subsection shall confer a right of appeal—

[³(a)] in relation to a prescribed decision, or a prescribed determination embodied in or necessary to a decision;

  (b) where regulations under subsection (3A) so provide.]]

(3) Regulations under subsection (2) above shall not prescribe any decision or determination that relates to the conditions of entitlement to a relevant benefit for which a claim has been validly made or for which no claim is required.

[³(3A) Regulations may provide that, in such cases or circumstances as may be prescribed, there is a right of appeal under subsection (2) in relation to a decision only if the Secretary of State has considered whether to revise the decision under section 9.

  (3B) The regulations may in particular provide that that condition is met only where—

  (a) the consideration by the Secretary of State was on an application;

  (b) the Secretary of State considered issues of a specified description, or

  (c) the consideration by the Secretary of State satisfied any other condition specified in the regulations.

  (3C) The references in subsections (3A) and (3B) to regulations and to the Secretary of State are subject to any enactment under or by virtue of which the functions under this Chapter are transferred to or otherwise made exercisable by a person other than the Secretary of State.]

[⁵(3D) In the case of a decision relating to child benefit or guardian's allowance, the making of any appeal under this section against the decision as originally made must follow the Commissioners for Her Majesty's Revenue and Customs first deciding, on an application made for revision of that decision under section 9, not to revise the decision.]

(4) Where the Secretary of State has determined that any amount is recoverable under or by virtue of section 71[⁴, 71ZB, 71ZG, 71ZH,] or 74 of the Administration Act, any person from whom he has determined that it is recoverable shall have the same right of appeal to [² the First-tier Tribunal] as a claimant.

(5) In any case where—

  (a) the Secretary of State has made a decision in relation to a claim under Part V of the Contributions and Benefits Act; and

  (b) the entitlement to benefit under that Part of that Act of any person other than the claimant is or may be, under Part VI of Schedule 7 to that Act, affected by that decision,

that other person shall have the same right of appeal to [² the First-tier Tribunal] as the claimant.

(6) A person with a right of appeal under this section shall be given such notice of a decision to which this section applies and of that right as may be prescribed.

(7) Regulations may—

[³(a)] make provision as to the manner in which, and the time within which, appeals are to be brought;

  [(b) provide that, where in accordance with regulations under subsection (3A) there is no right of appeal against a decision, any purported appeal may be treated as an application for revision under section 9].

(8) In deciding an appeal under this section, [² the First-tier Tribunal]—

(a) need not consider any issue that is not raised by the appeal; and

(b) shall not take into account any circumstances not obtaining at the time when the decision appealed against was made.

(9) The reference in subsection (1) above to a decision under section 10 above is a reference to a decision superseding any such decision as is mentioned in paragraph (a) or (b) of subsection (1) of that section.

AMENDMENTS

1. Social Security Contributions (Transfer of Functions, etc.) Act 1999 s.18 and Sch.7, para.25 (April 1, 1999).

2. Transfer of Functions Order 2008 (SI 2008/2833) art.6 and Sch.3, paras 143 and 149 (November 3, 2008).

3. Welfare Reform Act 2012 s.102(1)–(4) (February 25, 2013).

4. Welfare Reform Act 2012 s.105(6) (April 29, 2013).

5. Tax Credits, Child Benefit and Guardian's Allowance Reviews and Appeals Order 2014/886 art.4(1) (April 6, 2014).

DEFINITIONS

"the Administration Act"—see SSA 1998 s.84.

"claim"—by virtue of SSA 1998 s.39(2), see SSAA 1992 s.191.

"claimant"—see SSA 1998 s.39(1), and by virtue of SSA 1998 s.39(2), see SSAA 1992 s.191.

"the Contributions and Benefits Act"—see SSA 1998 s.84.

"prescribed"—*ibid.*

"relevant benefit"—see s.8(3).

Finality of decisions

17.—(1) Subject to the provisions of this Chapter [¹ and to any provision made by or under Chapter 2 of Part 1 of the Tribunals, Courts and Enforcement Act 2007], any decision made in accordance with the foregoing provisions of this Chapter shall be final; and subject to the provisions of any regulations under section 11 above, any decision made in accordance with those regulations shall be final.

(2) If and to the extent that regulations so provide, any finding of fact or other determination embodied in or necessary to such a decision, or on which such a decision is based, shall be conclusive for the purposes of—

(a) further such decisions;

(b) decisions made under the Child Support Act; and

(c) decisions made under the Vaccine Damage Payments Act.

1.23

AMENDMENT

1. Transfer of Functions Order 2008 (SI 2008/2833) art.6 and Sch.3, paras 143 and 155 (November 3, 2008).

DEFINITIONS

"the Child Support Act"—see SSA 1998 s.84.

"the Vaccine Damage Act"—*ibid.*

SCHEDULE 2

DECISIONS AGAINST WHICH NO APPEAL LIES

Jobseeker's allowance for persons under 18

1.24

1. In relation to a person who has reached the age of 16 but not the age of 18, a decision—
  (a) whether section 16 of the Jobseekers Act is to apply to him; or
  (b) whether to issue a certificate under section 17(4) of that Act.

Christmas bonus

2. A decision whether a person is entitled to payment under section 148 of the Contributions and Benefits Act.

Priority between persons entitled to [³ carer's allowance]

3. A decision as to the exercise of the discretion under section 70(7) of the Contributions and Benefits Act.

Priority between persons entitled to child benefit

4. A decision as to the exercise of the discretion under paragraph 5 of Schedule 10 to the Contributions and Benefits Act.

Persons treated as if present in Great Britain

5. A decision whether to certify, in accordance with regulations made under section 64(1), 71(6), 113(1) or 119 of the Contributions and Benefits Act, that it is consistent with the proper administration of that Act to treat a person as though he were present in Great Britain.

[¹ Work-focused interviews

5A. A decision terminating or reducing the amount of a person's benefit made in consequence of any decision made under regulations under section 2A [⁴ or 2AA] of the Administration Act (work-focused interviews).]

Alteration of rates of benefit

6. A decision as to the amount of benefit to which a person is entitled, where it appears to the Secretary of State that the amount is determined by—
  (a) the rate of benefit provided for by law; or
  (b) an alteration of a kind referred to in—
      (i)   section 159(1)(b) of the Administration Act (income support); [² ...]
      (ii) section 159A(1)(b) of that Act (jobseeker's allowance)[;²
      (iii) section 159B(1)(b) of that Act (state pension credit)]] [⁵;
      (iv) section 159C(1)(b) of that Act (employment and support allowance)] [⁷; or
      (v)   section 159D(1)(b) of that Act (universal credit)].

Increases in income support due to attainment of particular ages

7. A decision as to the amount of benefit to which a person is entitled, where it appears to the Secretary of State that the amount is determined by the recipient's entitlement to an increased amount of income support or income-based jobseeker's allowance in the circumstances referred to in section 160(2) or 160A(2) of the Administration Act.

[⁸ Increases in universal credit due to attainment of particular ages

7A. *A decision as to the amount of benefit to which a person is entitled, where it appears to the Secretary of State that the amount is determined by the recipient's entitlement to an increased amount of universal credit in the circumstances referred to in section 160C(2) of the Administration Act.]*

Reduction in accordance with reduced benefit decision

8. A decision to reduce the amount of a person's benefit in accordance with a reduced benefit decision (within the meaning of section 46 of the Child Support Act).

[⁶ Reduction on application of benefit cap

8A. A decision to apply the benefit cap in accordance with regulations under section 96 of the Welfare Reform Act 2012.]

Power to prescribe other decisions

9. Such other decisions as may be prescribed.

AMENDMENTS

1. Welfare Reform and Pensions Act 1999 s.81 and Sch.11, para.87 (November 11, 1999).
2. State Pension Credit Act 2002 s.11 and Sch.1, para.11 (July 2, 2002 for the purpose of exercising any power to make regulations or orders and October 6, 2003 for all other purposes).
3. Regulatory Reform (Carer's Allowance) Order 2002 (SI 2002/1457) art.2(1) and Sch., para.3(b) September 2002 for the purposes of exercising powers to make subordinate legislation and October 28, 2002 for all other purposes).
4. Employment Act 2002 s.53 and Sch.7, para.51 (July 5, 2003).
5. Welfare Reform Act 2007 Sch.3, para.17(1) and (8) (October 27, 2008).
6. Welfare Reform Act 2012 s.97(6) (April 15, 2013).
7. Welfare Reform Act 2012 s.31, Sch.2, paras 43, 50(1), (2) (April 29, 2013).
8. *Welfare Reform Act 2012 s.31, Sch.2, paras 43, 50(1), (3) (not yet in force).*

DEFINITIONS

"the Administration Act"—see SSA 1998, s.84.
"benefit"—see SSA 1998, s.39(1), and by virtue of SSA 1998 s.39(2), see SSAA 1992, s.191.
"the Child Support Act"—see SSA 1998, s.84.
"the Contributions and Benefits Act"—*ibid.*
"the Jobseekers Act"—*ibid.*
"prescribed"—*ibid.*

Section 12(1)

SCHEDULE 3

DECISIONS AGAINST WHICH AN APPEAL LIES

PART I

BENEFIT DECISIONS

Entitlement to benefit without a claim

1. In such cases or circumstances as may be prescribed, a decision whether a person is enti-   1.25
tled to a relevant benefit for which no claim is required.
2. If so, a decision as to the amount to which he is entitled.

Payability of benefit

3. A decision whether a relevant benefit (or a component of a relevant benefit) to which a person is entitled is not payable by reason of—
  (a) any provision of the Contributions and Benefits Act by which the person is disqualified for receiving benefit;
  (b) regulations made under section 72(8) of that Act (disability living allowance);
  (c) regulations made under section 113(2) of that Act (suspension of payment);
  (d) [⁸ . . .]
[⁵ (da) [⁸ . . .]]
  [¹ (e) [⁶ . . .] [² or
  (f) section [⁷ 6B,] 7, 8 or 9 of the Social Security Fraud Act 2001] [⁴; [¹⁰ . . .]
  (g) section 18 of the Welfare Reform Act 2007];
  [¹⁰ (h) regulations made under section 85(1) or 86(1) of the Welfare Reform Act 2012; or
  (i) section 87 of that Act].

[⁹ **3A.** A decision as to the amount of a relevant benefit that is payable to a person by virtue of regulations under section 6B, 7, 8 or 9 of the Social Security Fraud Act 2001.]

Payments to third parties

4. Except in such cases or circumstances as may be prescribed, a decision whether the whole or part of a benefit to which a person is entitled is, by virtue of regulations, to be paid to a person other than him.

Recovery of benefits

5. A decision whether payment is recoverable under section 71 or 71A of the Administration Act.

6. If so, a decision as to the amount of payment recoverable.

[¹¹**6A.** *A decision as to whether payment of housing credit (within the meaning of the State Pension Credit Act 2002) is recoverable under section 71ZB of the Administration Act.*]

¹⁰**6B.** A decision as to the amount of payment recoverable under section 71ZB, 71ZG or 71ZH of the Administration Act.]

State pension: prisoners and overseas residents

[¹²**6C.** A decision that a state pension under Part 1 of the Pensions Act 2014 is not payable by reason of regulations under section 19 of that Act (prisoners).

6D. A decision that a person is not entitled to increases in the rate of a state pension under Part 1 of the Pensions Act 2014 by reason of regulations under section 20 of that Act (overseas residents).]

Industrial injuries benefit

7. A decision whether an accident was an industrial accident for the purposes of industrial injuries benefit.

Jobseekers' agreements

8. A decision in relation to a jobseeker's agreement as proposed to be made under section 9 of the Jobseekers Act, or as proposed to be varied under section 10 of that Act.

[⁵*State Pension Credit*

8A. A decision whether to specify a period as an assessed income period under section 6 of the State Pension Credit Act 2002.

8B. If so, a decision as to the period to be so specified.

8C. A decision whether an assessed income period comes to an end by virtue of section 9(4) or (5) of that Act.

8D. If so, a decision as to when the assessed income period so ends.]

Power to prescribe other decisions

9. Such other decisions relating to a relevant benefit as may be prescribed.

PART II

CONTRIBUTIONS DECISIONS

10.–15. *[Omitted].*

Responsibilities at home

1.26

16. A decision whether a person was (within the meaning of regulations) precluded from regular employment by responsibilities at home.

Earnings and contributions credits

17. A decision whether a person is entitled to be credited with earnings or contributions in accordance with regulations made under section 22(5) of the Contributions and Benefits Act.

18.–29. *[Omitted].*

AMENDMENTS

1. Child Support, Pensions and Social Security Act 2000, s.66 and Sch.9, Pt V (October 15, 2001).
2. Social Security Fraud Act 2001, s.12(2) (April 1 2002).
3. State Pension Credit Act 2002, Sch.1, para.12 (July 2, 2002 for the purpose of exercising any power to make regulations or orders and October 6, 2003 for other purposes).
4. Welfare Reform Act 2007, Sch.3, para.17(1) and (9) (October 27, 2008).
5. Welfare Reform Act 2009, s.1(4) and Sch.3, para.4 (November 12, 2009).
6. Welfare Reform Act 2009, Sch.7 (March 22, 2010).
7. Welfare Reform Act 2009, Sch.4, para.10 (April 1, 2010).
8. Welfare Reform Act 2012, s.46(4) (October 22, 2012).
9. Welfare Reform Act 2012, s.31 and Sch.2, paras 43 and 51 (April 1, 2013).
10. Welfare Reform Act 2012, s.91 and Sch.9, paras 37 and 43 (April 8, 2013).
11. Welfare Reform Act 2012, s.105(7) (April 29, 2013).
12. Pensions Act 2014 Sch.12(1) para.37 (April 6, 2016).

DEFINITIONS

"the Administration Act"—see SSA 1998 s.84.
"benefit"—see SSA 1998 s.39(1), and by virtue of SSA 1998, s.39(2) see SSAA 1992 s.191.
"claim"—*ibid.*
"the Child Support Act"—see SSA 1998 s.84.
"the Contributions and Benefits Act"—*ibid.*
"industrial injuries benefit"—see SSA 1998 s.39(1), and by virtue of SSA 1998 s.39(2), see SSAA 1992 s.191.
"the Jobseekers Act"—see SSA 1998 s.84.
"prescribed"—*ibid.*
"relevant benefit"—see SSA 1998 s.8(3).

Immigration and Asylum Act 1999

(1999 C.33)

SECTION REPRODUCED

PART VI

SUPPORT FOR ASYLUM-SEEKERS

Exclusions

115.   Exclusion from benefits.   1.26.1

Exclusion from benefits

115.—(1) No person is entitled to [¹⁰ to universal credit under Part 1 of   1.26.2
the Welfare Reform Act 2012] income-based jobseeker's allowance under
the Jobseekers Act 1995 [⁴ or to state pension credit under the State Pension
Credit Act 2002] [⁶ or to income-related allowance under Part 1 of the

41

Welfare Reform Act 2007 (employment and support allowance)] [⁹ or to personal independence payment] or to—
  (a) attendance allowance,
  (b) severe disablement allowance,
  (c) [¹carer's allowance],
  (d) disability living allowance,
  (e) income support,
  (f) [². . .]
  (g) [². . .]
  (h) a social fund payment,
[⁷ (ha) health in pregnancy grant;]
  (i) child benefit,
  (j) housing benefit, [⁸ . . .]
  (k) [⁸ . . .]
under the Social Security Contributions and Benefits Act 1992 while he is a person to whom this section applies.

(2) [*Omitted*]

(3) This section applies to a person subject to immigration control unless he falls within such category or description, or satisfies such conditions, as may be prescribed.

(4) Regulations under subsection (3) may provide for a person to be treated for prescribed purposes only as not being a person to whom this section applies.

(5) In relation to [⁷ health in pregnancy grant or] [³ child benefit], "prescribed" means prescribed by regulations made by the Treasury.

(6) In relation to the matters mentioned in subsection (2) (except so far as it relates to [⁷ health in pregnancy grant or] [³ child benefit]), "prescribed" means prescribed by regulations made by the Department.

(7) Section 175(3) to (5) of the Social Security Contributions and Benefits Act 1992 (supplemental powers in relation to regulations) applies to regulations made by the Secretary of State or the Treasury under subsection (3) as it applies to regulations made under that Act.

(8) Sections 133(2), 171(2) and 172(4) of the Social Security Contributions and Benefits (Northern Ireland) Act 1992 apply to regulations made by the Department under subsection (3) as they apply to regulations made by the Department under that Act.

(9) "A person subject to immigration control" means a person who is not a national of an EEA State and who—
  (a) requires leave to enter or remain in the United Kingdom but does not have it;
  (b) has leave to enter or remain in the United Kingdom which is subject to a condition that he does not have recourse to public funds;
  (c) has leave to enter or remain in the United Kingdom given as a result of a maintenance undertaking; or
  (d) has leave to enter or remain in the United Kingdom only as a result of paragraph 17 of Schedule 4.

(10) "Maintenance undertaking", in relation to any person, means a written undertaking given by another person in pursuance of the immigration rules to be responsible for that person's maintenance and accommodation.

AMENDMENTS

1. Regulatory Reform (Carer's Allowance) Order 2002 (SI 2002/1457) art.2(1) and Sch. para.3(c) (April 1, 2003).
2. Tax Credits Act 2002 s.60 and Sch.6 (April 8, 2003).
3. Tax Credits Act 2002 s.51 and Sch.4 paras 20–21 (February 26, 2003).
4. State Pension Credit Act 2002 s.4(2) (October 6, 2003).
5. State Pension Credit Act (Northern Ireland) 2002 s.4(2) (October 6, 2003).
6. Welfare Reform Act 2007 Sch.3 para.19 (October 27, 2008).
7. Health and Social Care Act 2008 s.138 (January 1, 2009).
8. Welfare Reform Act 2012 s.147 and Sch.1 Pt 1 (April 1, 2013).
9. Welfare Reform Act 2012 s.91 and Sch.9 para.44 (April 8, 2013).
10. Welfare Reform Act 2012 s.31 and Sch.2 para.54 (April 29, 2013).

GENERAL NOTE

See the notes to the Social Security (Immigration and Asylum) Consequential   **1.26.3** Amendments Regulations 2000 (Part IV below).

Paragraph 17 of Sch.4 to the Act was repealed on April 1, 2003 by Sch.9 para.1 of the Nationality, Immigration and Asylum Act 2002 but the reference to the repealed provision in s.115(9)(d) has not itself been repealed. By virtue of s.17(2) of the Interpretation Act 1978, that reference should now be construed as a reference to s.3C(1) and (2)(b) of the Immigration Act 1971 which was inserted into that Act by the 2002 Act (but not as a reference to the former s.3D of that Act): see *EE v City of Cardiff (HB)* [2018] UKUT 418 (AAC).

Health in Pregnancy Grants were abolished for women who reached the 25th week of their pregnancy on or after January 1, 2011: see s.3(2) of the Savings Accounts and Health in Pregnancy Grant Act 2010. However, s.115(1)(ha) has not been repealed to reflect that circumstance.

Welfare Reform Act 2012

(2012 C.5)

ARRANGEMENT OF SECTIONS

PART 1

UNIVERSAL CREDIT

CHAPTER 1

ENTITLEMENT AND AWARDS

Introductory

Entitlement

CHAPTER 2

CLAIMANT RESPONSIBILITIES

CHAPTER 3

SUPPLEMENTARY AND GENERAL

Supplementary and consequential

Universal credit and other benefits

General

Regulations

PART 5

SOCIAL SECURITY: GENERAL

Benefit cap

PART 7

FINAL

SCHEDULES

An Act to make provision for universal credit and personal independence payment; to make other provision about social security and tax credits; to make provision about the functions of the registration service, child support maintenance and the use of jobcentres; to establish the Social Mobility and Child Poverty Commission and otherwise amend the Child Poverty Act 2010; and for connected purposes.

[8th March 2012]

PART 1

UNIVERSAL CREDIT

CHAPTER 1

ENTITLEMENT AND AWARDS

Introductory

1.31 **Universal credit**

1.—(1) A benefit known as universal credit is payable in accordance with this Part.

(2) Universal credit may, subject as follows, be awarded to—

(a) an individual who is not a member of a couple (a "single person"), or

(b) members of a couple jointly.

(3) An award of universal credit is, subject as follows, calculated by reference to—

(a) a standard allowance;

(b) an amount for responsibility for children or young persons;

(c) an amount for housing; and

(d) amounts for other particular needs or circumstances.

DEFINITIONS

"child"—see s.40.
"couple"—see ss.39 and 40.

GENERAL NOTE

1.32   Part 1 of the Welfare Reform Act 2012 ("WRA 2012") contains the provisions and confers regulation-making powers in relation to universal credit. Universal credit is to be the new means-tested, non-contributory benefit for people of working age. It replaces income support, income-based jobseeker's allowance (JSA), income-related employment and support allowance (ESA), housing benefit, working tax credit and child tax credit. Thus it will be paid to people both in and out of work. State pension credit will continue for people who are over the qualifying age for state pension credit (this is gradually rising in line with the staged increase in pensionable age for women until it reaches 65 in November 2018 and will increase to 66 by October 2020)—see s.4(4), which applies the definition of "the qualifying age" for state pension credit in s.1(6) of the State Pension Credit Act 2002 (see Vol.II in this series) for the purposes of universal credit. ESA and JSA will also continue but as contributory benefits only.

Note that "a person who is subject to immigration control" is not entitled to universal credit (Immigration and Asylum Act 1999, s.115, as amended by WRA 2012, Sch.2, para.54 with effect from April 29, 2013).

Initially universal credit was introduced only for people in the "pathfinder group" and only on an extremely limited geographical basis. See the Introduction and the General Note at the beginning of Part IV of this Volume for a summary of the process by which universal credit has been "rolled out" on a national basis up to August 8, 2016.

As usual, Part 1 creates the legislative framework and the detail is to be found in the Universal Credit Regulations 2013 (SI 2013/376)—on which see Pt III of this Volume.

Subsection (2)

This provides that in the case of a couple awards are to be made to the couple **1.33** jointly. Note the definition of "claimant" in s.40, which states that "claimant" in Pt 1 of the Act means "a single claimant or each of joint claimants".

Subsection (3)

Depending on the claimant's (or claimants') circumstances, an award of universal **1.34** credit will include a standard allowance (see s.9 and reg.36 of the Universal Credit Regulations), an amount for children and young persons for whom the claimant is responsible (see s.10 and regs 24 and 36 of the Universal Credit Regulations), housing costs (see s.11 and regs 25–26 of, and Schs 1–5 to, the Universal Credit Regulations) and an amount for "other particular needs or circumstances" (see s.12 and regs 23(2) and 27–35 of, and Schs 6-9 to, the Universal Credit Regulations). Note that although subs.(3)(b) refers to an amount for children and young persons, in the case of the latter, s.10 restricts this to "qualifying young persons". For who counts as a "qualifying young person" see s.40 and reg.5 of the Universal Credit Regulations.

Claims

2.—(1) A claim may be made for universal credit by— **1.35**

(a) a single person; or

(b) members of a couple jointly.

(2) Regulations may specify circumstances in which a member of a couple may make a claim as a single person.

DEFINITIONS

"claim"—see s.40.
"couple"—see ss.39 and 40.
"single person"—see s.40.

GENERAL NOTE

In the case of a couple, claims for universal credit are to be made jointly. This does **1.36** not apply in prescribed circumstances (subs.(2)). On subs.(2), see reg.3(3) of the Universal Credit Regulations and note reg.3(4)-(6).

For the rules for claims for universal credit see the Universal Credit, Personal Independence Payment, Jobseeker's Allowance and Employment and Support Allowance (Claims and Payments) Regulations 2013 (SI 2013/380) in Part V of this Volume. Generally a claim for universal credit has to be made online. Note reg.6 (claims not required for entitlement to universal credit in certain cases).

Entitlement

Entitlement

1.37   **3.**—(1) A single claimant is entitled to universal credit if the claimant meets—
  (a) the basic conditions; and
  (b) the financial conditions for a single claimant.
  (2) Joint claimants are jointly entitled to universal credit if—
  (a) each of them meets the basic conditions; and
  (b) they meet the financial conditions for joint claimants.

DEFINITIONS

  "claim"—see s.40.
  "claimant"—*ibid.*
  "joint claimants"—*ibid.*
  "single claimant"—*ibid.*

GENERAL NOTE

1.38   This sets out the general conditions of entitlement to universal credit. A single claimant has to meet all of the basic conditions (see s.4) and the financial conditions (i.e., the means-test) (see s.5). In the case of joint claimants, both of them have to meet all of the basic and the financial conditions. Note, however, s.4(2) which allows for regulations to provide for exceptions from any of these conditions, either in the case of a single claimant, or one or both joint claimants.

Basic conditions

1.39   **4.**—(1) For the purposes of section 3, a person meets the basic conditions who—
  (a) is at least 18 years old;
  (b) has not reached the qualifying age for state pension credit;
  (c) is in Great Britain;
  (d) is not receiving education; and
  (e) has accepted a claimant commitment.
  (2) Regulations may provide for exceptions to the requirement to meet any of the basic conditions (and, for joint claimants, may provide for an exception for one or both).
  (3) For the basic condition in subsection (1)(a) regulations may specify a different minimum age for prescribed cases.
  (4) For the basic condition in subsection (1)(b), the qualifying age for state pension credit is that referred to in section 1(6) of the State Pension Credit Act 2002.
  (5) For the basic condition in subsection (1)(c) regulations may—
  (a) specify circumstances in which a person is to be treated as being or not being in Great Britain;

(b) specify circumstances in which temporary absence from Great Britain is disregarded.

(c) modify the application of this Part in relation to a person not in Great Britain who is by virtue of paragraph (b) entitled to universal credit.

(6) For the basic condition in subsection (1)(d) regulations may—

(a) specify what "receiving education" means;

(b) specify circumstances in which a person is to be treated as receiving or not receiving education.

(7) For the basic condition in subsection (1)(e) regulations may specify circumstances in which a person is to be treated as having accepted or not accepted a claimant commitment.

DEFINITIONS

"claim"—see s.40.
"claimant"—*ibid.*
"joint claimants"—*ibid.*

GENERAL NOTE

Subsection (1) lists the basic conditions that have to be satisfied for entitlement to universal credit. Subsection (2) allows for regulations to provide for exceptions from any of these conditions, either in the case of a single claimant, or one or both joint claimants.   **1.40**

Subsection (1)(a)

The minimum age for entitlement to universal credit is generally 18. However, under subs.(3) regulations can provide for a lower age in certain cases. See reg.8 of the Universal Credit Regulations for the cases where the minimum age is 16.   **1.41**

Subsection (1)(b)

This subsection excludes the possibility that a person could be entitled to both state pension credit and universal credit by providing that no person who has reached "the qualifying age for state pension credit" will meet the basic conditions for universal credit. But note subs.(2) and see reg.3(2) of the Universal Credit Regulations. The effect of reg.3(2) is that a couple may still be entitled to universal credit even if one member is over the qualifying age for state pension credit, provided that the other member of the couple is under that age.   **1.42**

Subsection (4) applies the definition of "the qualifying age" for state pension credit in s.1(6) of the State Pension Credit Act 2002 (see Vol.II in this series) for the purposes of universal credit. The effect of that definition is that the qualifying age for state pension credit for both men and women is the pensionable age for women (this was 60 but since April 2010 has been gradually rising and will reach 65 in November 2018).

Subsection (1)(c)

It is a basic condition of entitlement to universal credit that the person is in Great Britain. Note subs.(5) under which regulations may treat a person as being or not being in Great Britain (see reg.9 of the Universal Credit Regulations for when a person is treated as not being in Great Britain, and reg.10 on Crown servants and armed forces) and may provide for the circumstances in which temporary absence from Great Britain is ignored (see reg.11).   **1.43**

Subsection (1)(d)

A person must not be "receiving education" to be eligible for universal credit. For the regulations made under subs.(6) see regs 12–14 of the Universal Credit Regulations.   **1.44**

49

Subsection (1)(e)

1.45   The concept of a claimant commitment as a condition of receiving benefit is an important part of the underlying policy behind the Government's welfare benefit reforms. See s.14 below and the notes to that section. Note that the condition is met merely by having accepted the most up-to-date version of the claimant commitment. A failure to comply with the claimant commitment does not entail any breach of subs.(1)(e), nor is that in itself any ground for a sanction, although sanctions may be imposed for failures to comply with work-related and connected requirements that are recorded in the claimant commitment and other legal consequences may follow from failures to carry out other obligations. Under subs.(7) regulations may specify the circumstances in which a person can be treated as having accepted or not accepted a claimant commitment—see reg.15 of the Universal Credit Regulations. In addition, subs.(2) allows regulations to provide exceptions to the requirement to meet any basic condition.

That power has been exercised in relation to the condition of having accepted a claimant commitment in reg.16, which may be of particular importance during the 2020 coronavirus outbreak, when "conditionality" was suspended for three months from March 30, 2020. Since there was no new legislation to lift the operation of s.4(1)(e) during that period, in contrast to the position on the work search and work availability requirements (see the notes to ss.17 and 18), allowing entitlement on new claims without s.4(1)(e) being met appears to be the key to not imposing those requirements. Regulation 16(b) (exceptional circumstances make it unreasonable to expect the claimant to accept a claimant commitment) could clearly be applied (see further in the notes to reg.16). For existing claimants, who had already accepted a commitment, the work search and work availability requirements were expressly lifted. For other requirements, there were to be no sanctions imposed for failing to comply and/or a flexibility in reviewing requirements over the telephone.

On July 1, 2020 it was announced in Parliament (Under-Secretary of State, Mims Davies, WQ 62431) that from that date the requirement for universal credit claimants (among others) to accept a claimant commitment was being reintroduced. The commitments of existing claimants would be reviewed and up-dated as capacity allowed. It appears that the reintroduction for new claimants is also being phased in.

Financial conditions

1.46   **5.**—(1) For the purposes of section 3, the financial conditions for a single claimant are that—

(a) the claimant's capital, or a prescribed part of it, is not greater than a prescribed amount, and

(b) the claimant's income is such that, if the claimant were entitled to universal credit, the amount payable would not be less than any prescribed minimum.

(2) For those purposes, the financial conditions for joint claimants are that—

(a) their combined capital, or a prescribed part of it, is not greater than a prescribed amount, and

(b) their combined income is such that, if they were entitled to universal credit, the amount payable would not be less than any prescribed minimum.

DEFINITIONS

"claim"—see s.40.
"claimant"—*ibid.*
"joint claimants"—*ibid.*
"prescribed"—*ibid.*
"single claimant"—*ibid.*

GENERAL NOTE

This section contains the means-test for universal credit. Both the capital and the   1.47
income condition have to be met. For joint claimants it is their combined capital and
their combined income that counts (subs.(2)).

Capital

The capital limit for universal credit for both a single claimant and joint claimants   1.48
is £16,000 (see reg.18(1) of the Universal Credit Regulations). Note that where a
claimant who is a member of a couple makes a claim as a single person (see reg.3(3)
of the Universal Credit Regulations for the circumstances in which this may occur)
the capital of the other member of the couple counts as the claimant's (reg.18(2)).

Thus the capital limit for universal credit is the same as for income support,
income-based JSA, income-related ESA and housing benefit. There is no capital
limit for working tax credit and child tax credit. See further the notes to s.134(1)
SSCBA 1992 in Vol. II of this series.

For the rules on calculating capital see regs 45–50 and 75–77 of, and Sch 10 to,
the Universal Credit Regulations.

Income

The effect of subs.(1)(b) in the case of a single claimant and subs.(2)(b) in the   1.49
case of joint claimants is that there will be no entitlement to universal credit if the
amount payable is less than the minimum amount. The minimum amount is 1p (see
reg.17 of the Universal Credit Regulations and note reg.6(1) on rounding). Thus it
is possible for a person to be entitled to universal credit of 1p.

Note that where a claimant who is a member of a couple makes a claim as a single
person (see reg.3(3) of the Universal Credit Regulations for the circumstances in
which this may occur) the combined income of the couple is taken into account
when calculating an award (reg.22(3)(a)).

Any income of a child is not taken into account.

See also the regulation-making powers as regards the calculation of capital and
income in para.4 of Sch.1.

Restrictions on entitlement

6.—(1) Entitlement to universal credit does not arise—   1.50
(a) in prescribed circumstances (even though the requirements in
section 3 are met);
(b) if the requirements in section 3 are met for a period shorter than a
prescribed period.
(c) for a prescribed period at the beginning of a period during which
those requirements are met.

(2) A period prescribed under subsection (1)(b) or (c) may not exceed
seven days.

(3) Regulations may provide for exceptions to subsection (1)(b) or (c).

DEFINITION

"prescribed"—see s.40.

GENERAL NOTE

This enables regulations to be made which provide that a person will not be enti-   1.51
tled to universal credit: (i) even though they meet the basic and financial conditions
(subs.(1)(a)); (ii) if they meet those conditions for seven days or less (subs.(1)(b)
and subs.(2)); or (iii) for a period of seven days or less at the beginning of a period
during which those conditions are met (subs.(1)(c) and subs.(2)).

The power conferred by subs.(1)(a) has been exercised to make reg.19 of the Universal Credit Regulations and that conferred by subs.(1)(c) to make reg.19A. No regulations have yet been made under subs.(1)(b).

Awards

Basis of awards

1.52   7.—(1) Universal credit is payable in respect of each complete assessment period within a period of entitlement.

(2) In this Part an "assessment period" is a period of a prescribed duration.

(3) Regulations may make provision—

(a) about when an assessment period is to start;

(b) for universal credit to be payable in respect of a period shorter than an assessment period;

(c) about the amount payable in respect of a period shorter than an assessment period.

(4) In subsection (1) "period of entitlement" means a period during which entitlement to universal credit subsists.

GENERAL NOTE

1.53   See the commentary to reg.21 of the Universal Credit Regulations.

Calculation of awards

1.54   8.—(1) The amount of an award of universal credit is to be the balance of—

(a) the maximum amount (see subsection (2)), less

(b) the amounts to be deducted (see subsection (3)).

(2) The maximum amount is the total of—

(a) any amount included under section 9 (standard allowance);

(b) any amount included under section 10 (responsibility for children and young persons);

(c) any amount included under section 11 (housing costs), and

(d) any amount included under section 12 (other particular needs or circumstances).

(3) The amounts to be deducted are—

(a) an amount in respect of earned income calculated in the prescribed manner (which may include multiplying some or all earned income by a prescribed percentage), and

(b) an amount in respect of unearned income calculated in the prescribed manner (which may include multiplying some or all unearned income by a prescribed percentage).

(4) In subsection (3)(a) and (b) the references to income are—

(a) in the case of a single claimant, to income of the claimant, and

(b) in the case of joint claimants, to combined income of the claimants.

DEFINITIONS

"claim"—see s.40.
"claimant"—*ibid.*
"joint claimants"—*ibid.*
"prescribed"—*ibid.*
"single claimant"—*ibid.*

See the commentary to reg.22 of the Universal Credit Regulations. 1.55

Elements of an award

Standard allowance

9.—(1) The calculation of an award of universal credit is to include an 1.56
amount by way of an allowance for—
(a) a single claimant, or
(b) joint claimants.
(2) Regulations are to specify the amount to be included under subsection (1).
(3) Regulations may provide for exceptions to subsection (1).

DEFINITIONS

"claim"—see s.40.
"claimant"—*ibid.*

GENERAL NOTE

See the commentary to regs 23 and 36 of the Universal Credit Regulations. 1.57

Responsibility for children and young persons

10.—(1) The calculation of an award of universal credit is to include an 1.58
amount for each child or qualifying young person for whom a claimant is
responsible.
[¹ (1A) But the amount mentioned in subsection (1) is to be available in
respect of a maximum of two persons who are either children or qualifying
young persons for whom a claimant is responsible.]
(2) Regulations may make provision for the inclusion of an additional
amount [¹ for each] child or qualifying young person [¹ for whom a claimant
is responsible who] is disabled.
(3) Regulations are to specify, or provide for the calculation of, amounts
to be included under subsection (1) or (2).
(4) Regulations may provide for exceptions to subsection (1) [¹ or (1A)].
(5) In this Part, "qualifying young person" means a person of a prescribed description.

AMENDMENT

1. Welfare Reform and Work Act 2016 s.14(1)-(4) (April 6, 2017).

DEFINITIONS

"child"—see s.40.
"disabled"—*ibid.*

GENERAL NOTE

See the commentary to regs 24 and 36 of the Universal Credit Regulations. 1.59

Housing costs

11.—(1) The calculation of an award of universal credit is to include an 1.60
amount in respect of any liability of a claimant to make payments in respect
of the accommodation they occupy as their home.

(2) For the purposes of subsection (1)—

(a) the accommodation must be in Great Britain;

(b) the accommodation must be residential accommodation;

(c) it is immaterial whether the accommodation consists of the whole or part of a building and whether or not it comprises separate and self-contained premises.

(3) Regulations may make provision as to—

(a) what is meant by payments in respect of accommodation for the purposes of this section [¹ ...];

(b) circumstances in which a claimant is to be treated as liable or not liable to make such payments;

(c) circumstances in which a claimant is to be treated as occupying or not occupying accommodation as their home (and, in particular, for temporary absences to be disregarded);

(d) circumstances in which land used for the purposes of any accommodation is to be treated as included in the accommodation.

(4) Regulations are to provide for the determination or calculation of any amount to be included under this section.

(5) Regulations may—

(a) provide for exceptions to subsection (1);

(b) provide for inclusion of an amount under this section in the calculation of an award of universal credit—

(i) to end at a prescribed time, or

(ii) not to start until a prescribed time.

AMENDMENT

1. Welfare Reform and Work Act 2016 s.20(9) (April 6, 2018).

DEFINITIONS

"claim"—see s.40.
"claimant"—*ibid.*
"prescribed"—*ibid.*

GENERAL NOTE

1.61   This provides for an award of universal credit to include an amount in respect of the claimant's (or claimants') liability to make payments in respect of the accommodation they occupy as their home. It will cover payments both by people who are renting their homes and by owner occupiers (as well as service charges).

Under subs.(2), the accommodation must be residential accommodation and must be in Great Britain. It can be the whole or part of a building and need not comprise separate and self-contained premises.

For the rules relating to housing costs see regs 25–26 of, and Schs 1–5 to, the Universal Credit Regulations.

Other particular needs or circumstances

1.62   **12.**—(1) The calculation of an award of universal credit is to include amounts in respect of such particular needs or circumstances of a claimant as may be prescribed.

(2) The needs or circumstances prescribed under subsection (1) may include—

(a) [¹ . . .]

(b) the fact that a claimant has limited capability for work and work-related activity;

(c) the fact that a claimant has regular and substantial caring responsibilities for a severely disabled person.

(3) Regulations are to specify, or provide for the determination or calculation of, any amount to be included under subsection (1).

(4) Regulations may—

(a) provide for inclusion of an amount under this section in the calculation of an award of universal credit—

(i) to end at a prescribed time, or

(ii) not to start until a prescribed time;

(b) provide for the manner in which a claimant's needs or circumstances are to be determined.

AMENDMENT

1. Welfare Reform and Work Act 2016 s.16 (April 3, 2017).

DEFINITIONS

"claim"—see s.40.
"claimant"—*ibid.*
"limited capability for work"—*ibid.*
"prescribed"—*ibid.*
"work"—*ibid.*

GENERAL NOTE

See the commentary to regs 27–36 of the Universal Credit Regulations.   **1.63**

CHAPTER 2

CLAIMANT RESPONSIBILITIES

Introductory

Work-related requirements: introductory

13.—(1) This Chapter provides for the Secretary of State to impose   **1.64**
work-related requirements with which claimants must comply for the purposes of this Part.

(2) In this Part "work-related requirement" means—

(a) a work-focused interview requirement (see section 15);

(b) a work preparation requirement (see section 16);

(c) a work search requirement (see section 17);

(d) a work availability requirement (see section 18).

(3) The work-related requirements which may be imposed on a claimant depend on which of the following groups the claimant falls into—

(a) no work-related requirements (see section 19);

(b) work-focused interview requirement only (see section 20);

(c) work-focused interview and work preparation requirements only (see section 21);

(d) all work-related requirements (see section 22).

1.65   The remaining sections of this Chapter of the WRA 2012 in the main set out what sort of work-related requirements can be imposed on which universal credit claimants, as well as the system for imposing sanctions (reductions in benefit) on claimants for failure to comply with those requirements. Although s.13(1) refers only to work-related requirements as defined in ss.15–18, s.23 allows the Secretary of State to require a claimant to participate in an interview for various related purposes and to provide information and evidence. A failure to comply with a requirement under s.23 can lead to a sanction under s.27(2)(b) in the same way as can a failure to comply with any work-related requirement under s.27(2)(a). Section 14 contains rules about the "claimant commitment", acceptance of which is a condition of entitlement under s.4(1)(e).

There is a handy summary of the sanctions framework in Chapter 47 of CPAG's *Welfare Benefits and Tax Credits Handbook* (2020/2021 edn.).

It was noted in paras 17 and 18 of *S v SSWP (UC)* [2017] UKUT 477 (AAC) that s.13(1) means that a work-related requirement can only come into being when it has been *imposed* by the Secretary of State (under the duty in s.22). See the discussion in the notes to s.14 for the important implications for the effect in law of the standard terms of claimant commitments.

Note that if a claimant is entitled to both universal credit and new style JSA, reg.5 of the JSA Regulations 2013 provides that no work-related requirements can be imposed under the new style JSA regime (ss.6B-6G of the new style Jobseekers Act 1995) and that the provisions for reduction of JSA on sanctions under ss.6J and 6K of that Act do not apply. See the annotations to reg.5 in Vol.II of this series for discussion of the consequences, and the notes to reg.111 of and Sch.11 to the Universal Credit Regulations. There is an equivalent provision in reg.42 of the ESA Regulations 2013 in relation to new style ESA.

Claimant commitment

1.66   **14.**—(1) A claimant commitment is a record of a claimant's responsibilities in relation to an award of universal credit.

(2) A claimant commitment is to be prepared by the Secretary of State and may be reviewed and updated as the Secretary of State thinks fit.

(3) A claimant commitment is to be in such form as the Secretary of State thinks fit.

(4) A claimant commitment is to include—

(a) a record of the requirements that the claimant must comply with under this Part (or such of them as the Secretary of State considers it appropriate to include),

(b) any prescribed information, and

(c) any other information the Secretary of State considers it appropriate to include.

(5) For the purposes of this Part a claimant accepts a claimant commitment if, and only if, the claimant accepts the most up-to-date version of it in such manner as may be prescribed.

"claimant"—see s.40.
"prescribed"—*ibid.*

1.67   Under s.4(1)(e) the final basic condition of entitlement is that the claimant has accepted a claimant commitment. Section 14 defines the nature of a claimant commitment and there are further provisions in regs 15 and 16 of the Universal Credit

Regulations. Where a claim has to be made jointly by both members of a couple, both are claimants and subject to this condition.

See the notes to s.4(1)(e) and reg.16 for the position during the 2020 coronavirus outbreak, as well as the notes on the work search and work availability require-ments. It appears that at least for the period from March 30, 2020 to June 30, 2020 the power to award entitlement without having met the basic condition of having accepted a claimant commitment was invoked. On July 1, 2020 it was announced in Parliament (Under-Secretary of State, Mims Davies, WQ 62431) that from that date the requirement for universal credit claimants (among others) to accept a claimant commitment was being reintroduced. The commitments of existing claimants would be reviewed and up-dated as capacity allowed. It appears that the reintroduction for new claimants is also being phased in. The answer stressed that claimant commitments agreed or reviewed from July 1, 2020 would have to be rea-sonable for the "new normal" and acknowledge the reality of a person's local jobs market and personal circumstances.

Note that the condition is met merely by having accepted the most up-to-date version of the claimant commitment, as discussed below. A failure to comply with the claimant commitment does not entail any breach of s.4(1)(e), nor is that in itself any ground for a sanction, although sanctions may be imposed for failures to comply with work-related and connected requirements that are recorded in the claimant commitment and other legal consequences may follow from failures to carry out other obligations.

It is an important element of the universal credit scheme, in contrast to the schemes that it has replaced, that the acceptance of the claimant commitment is a condition of entitlement for all categories of claimant, not merely those who would previously have been within the ambit of old style JSA. However, for those other categories the commitment can only be a much more generalised statement of responsibilities (see below), since the application of "conditionality" in the full sense to the claimant's personal circumstances will not be in issue.

Subsections (1) and (2) define a claimant commitment as a record prepared by the Secretary of State (in such form as he thinks fit: subs.(3)) of a claimant's respon-sibilities in relation to an award of universal credit. In particular, by subs.(4)(a), the record is to include the requirements that the particular claimant must comply with under the WRA 2012. These will in the main be work-related and connected requirements (see ss.15-25). However, in relation to those with limited capability for work or work-related activity the requirements will include those to provide information or evidence and to submit to a medical examination (s.37(5)-(7) and regs 43 and 44 of the Universal Credit Regulations). Work-related requirements can sometimes be to take specific action (e.g. to participate in a particular interview under s.15 or to take particular action to improve prospects of paid work under s.16 or to obtain paid work under s.17), although often the specification of such action by the Secretary of State will take place outside the claimant commitment (see the discussion in *JB v SSWP (UC)* [2018] UKUT 360 (AAC), detailed near the end of the notes to s.14). Nonetheless, the document will need to be detailed and closely related to the claimant's circumstances as they are from time to time. As such, it may be subject to frequent change, although there is a discretion in subs.(4) (a) to omit requirements if appropriate. The process of review and updating under subs.(2) appears to be completely informal, in stark contrast to the process for vari-ation of a jobseeker's agreement under s.10 of the old style Jobseekers Act 1995, so can accommodate that. Each updating will trigger a new requirement to accept the most up-to-date version. Subsection (4)(b) requires the record to contain any prescribed information. Regulations have not as yet prescribed any such informa-tion. Subsection (4)(c) requires the record to contain any other information (note, information, not a further requirement) that the Secretary of State considers appro-priate. For the claimant commitment to serve the basic purpose discussed below, that information must at least include information about the potential consequences under the Act of receiving a sanction for failure to carry out a requirement.

Since subs.(4) is, though, not an exhaustive statement of what a claimant commitment can contain, merely a statement of elements that it must contain, there is no reason why other responsibilities in relation to an award of universal credit cannot also be recorded, along with any appropriate accompanying information, although the perceived need to include subs.(4)(c) could be argued to cast doubt on that conclusion. For instance, the general obligations under regs 38 and 44 of the Claims and Payments Regulations 2013 to supply information and evidence in connection with an award and to notify changes of circumstances should probably be recorded, as it is in the example mentioned below.

Very limited exceptions from the application of the basic condition in s.4(1)(e) are set out in reg.16 of the Universal Credit Regulations. The WRA 2012 does not seek to define what is meant by acceptance of a claimant commitment beyond the provision in subs.(5) that it must be the most up-to-date version that has been accepted in such manner as prescribed in regulations. Regulation 15 of the Universal Credit Regulations provides for the time within which and the manner in which the claimant commitment must be accepted, but says nothing about what accepting the commitment entails in substance. In practice, the normal method specified under reg.15 is via a "To Do" action placed on the claimant's electronic journal, where a button must be clicked to indicate acceptance (Williams, Lack of commitment?, *Welfare Rights Bulletin 274* (February 2020) p.4).

1.68 Since the commitment is the record of the particular claimant's responsibilities as imposed by or under the legislation itself it does not seem that acceptance can mean much more than an acknowledgement of its receipt or possibly also that the claimant understands the implications of the requirements set out. There can be no question of a claimant having to express any agreement with the justice or reasonableness of the requirements, let alone of the policy behind universal credit. Nor does acceptance seem to involve any personal commitment to carrying out the stated requirements, despite the language used in the example mentioned below. A failure to comply with any requirement imposed by the Secretary of State is a matter for a potential sanction under ss.26 or 27, not for a conclusion that the basic condition of entitlement in s.4(1)(e) is no longer met. There is no direct sanction for a failure to comply with a requirement just because it is included in the claimant commitment, nor does such a failure show that the claimant commitment has ceased to be accepted in the sense suggested above.

However, this distinction may be of little significance in practice, since inclusion in the claimant commitment appears to be a sufficient means of notifying a claimant of the imposition of a requirement (see s.24(4) below) and a failure for no good reason to comply with any work-related requirement attracts a sanction under s.27(2) at the least. For instance, if the Secretary of State acting under s.17(2)(b) (work search requirement) specifies in the claimant commitment an impossibly large or internally inconsistent number of actions per week, then a failure to carry out the actions is at least prima facie a sanctionable failure and the question of whether what was specified was unreasonable would appear to be relevant only to "good reason" (though see the further discussion in the notes to ss.26 and 27). It is not like the actively seeking employment condition in old style JSA where, whatever was set out in a jobseeker's agreement, the fundamental test was whether claimants had in any week taken such steps as they could reasonably have been expected to have done to have the best prospects of securing employment.

Despite the incontrovertible nature of the legal framework, official sources continue to describe an essential feature of the claimant commitment as being that it and its conditionality requirements have been agreed by the claimant. See the DWP's statement of the aim of conditionality and sanctions set out in para.10 of the House of Commons Work and Pensions Committee's report of November 6, 2018 on *Benefit Sanctions* (HC 995 2017-19) and the Committee's own description of the claimant commitment as recording "the actions a [...] claimant has agreed to undertake as a condition of receiving their benefit". Even the Social Security Advisory Committee's March 19, 2019 call for evidence on the operation of the claimant commitment in universal credit for those subject to all work-related requirements talked of the commitment setting out what a claimant has agreed to do to prepare for work, or to increase their earnings if they are already working, and what will happen if a claimant fails to meet the agreed responsibilities. It might not matter much if such terminology is restricted to policy discussions. No doubt, for the sort of reasons mentioned below, it will always be better if the requirements set out in the claimant commitment have been worked out after a full and co-operative discussion with the work coach and the claimant agrees that the requirements are realistic and achievable. But there is evidence that the approach has infected the standard terms of claimant commitments, with consequent problems in ascertaining whether the legal requirements for the imposition of sanctions have been made out (see the discussion below of the standard terms and of the decision in *JB v SSWP (UC)* [2018] UKUT 360 (AAC)).

Chapter J1 of *Advice for Decision Making* says that the claimant commitment is generated as the result of a conversation with the claimant (para.J1010) and that claimants who fall into the all work-related requirements group or the work preparation group will need to have a discussion with an adviser before a claimant commitment can be drawn up and accepted. Claimant commitments for claimants not in either of those groups may be accepted as part of the normal claims process (para.J1011). The meaning of that last phrase is not entirely clear, but may refer to those groups of claimants on whom it is clear from the outset that no personalised requirements will be imposed. There is a recognition that claimants may well not feel able to accept on the spot at a first interview with an adviser (now called a work coach) the full range of requirements set out in the claimant commitment, so that if the claimant declines to accept the document then, a "cooling-off period" of a maximum of seven days must be allowed for reconsideration (para.J1010). The legislative basis for this is under reg.15(1) of the Universal Credit Regulations, which provides that s.4(1)(e) is to be treated as satisfied from the outset when the claimant commitment is accepted within such period after the making of the claim as the Secretary of State specifies. It must in law be open to a work coach, depending on the particular circumstances, to specify a longer period or to alter the period initially specified. See the notes to reg.15 for further discussion of the dates on which claimant commitments are deemed to be accepted.

Work requirements are supposed to be set through a one-to-one relationship between work coach and claimant, enabling the development of a good understanding of the claimant's circumstances, so that the work coach can best help the claimant find work (see the DWP's evidence to the Work and Pensions Committee in para.87 of the report above). However, the Committee received evidence that many claimant commitments were "generic" in nature, failing to take account of individual circumstances, and that "easements" (i.e. circumstances in which in accordance with regulations the requirement in question could be lifted) were insufficiently used. Taking the view that it was unrealistic for claimants to know the rules about when easements could apply or for them to pour out the details of their personal lives at each meeting, the Committee recommended that the DWP develop a standard set of questions that work coaches routinely ask claimants when developing their claimant commitments, as well as improve the information available to claimants on easements. The DWP's response (House of Commons Work and Pensions Committee, *Benefit Sanctions: Government Response* (HC 1949 2017-19, February 11, 2019, paras 55-65) was that current training, guidance and monitoring of work coaches involved standard key questions to identify things like caring responsibilities, health conditions and other complex circumstances that could impact ability to meet requirements. Additional easements were said to be more specific and sensitive, so should not be presented as if they would apply to the majority of claimants. Instead, a new information package on easements to be provided at the start of the claim was to become available in Spring 2019.

Thus, when it was announced (Parliamentary answer, Under-Secretary of State, Mims Davies, WQ 62431) that from July 1, 2020 the requirement for universal

credit claimants (among others) to accept a claimant commitment was being reintroduced, it was stressed that claimant commitments agreed or reviewed from that
date would have to be reasonable for the "new normal" and acknowledge the reality
of a person's local jobs market and personal circumstances. That must entail an
increased focus on "easements", but doubts have been expressed about the practi-
cality of that when the length of meetings is being restricted, at least initially, to 30
minutes.

The Social Security Advisory Committee's (SSAC's) September 2019 study on
The effectiveness of the claimant commitment in Universal Credit (Occasional Paper
No.21) contains much interesting information on policy and the practical operation
of the claimant commitment, without addressing the mismatch suggested above
with the legal framework. It puts forward, within the overarching principle that the
process of developing a commitment for a particular claimant should be reasonable
and based on evidence of what works to help people move into sustained employment, five principles for the effectiveness of a commitment for a claimant in the
intensive work search regime. It should be accessible, clear, tailored to the needs
of each claimant, accepted by both parties and the claimant should have the right
information. The SSAC identified many examples of good practice by work coaches,
but also examples of failure to meet those principles, especially on the tailoring to
individual needs and circumstances.

The notion of the claimant commitment is in many ways at the heart of what
"conditionality" is meant to achieve under universal credit. It looks on its face to be
an expression of what Charles Reich in his classic essay *The New Property* (1964) 73
Yale Law Journal 733 called "the New Feudalism". The universal credit claimant not
only has, as the price of securing entitlement to the benefit, to accept a defined status
that involves the giving up of some rights normally enjoyed by ordinary citizens, but
appears to have to undertake some kind of oath of fealty by accepting a commitment
to the feudal duties of that status. However, in reality the claimant commitment is
a much more prosaic, and more sensible, thing. In its interesting paper *Universal
Credit and Conditionality* (Social Security Advisory Committee Occasional Paper
No. 9, 2012) the SSAC reported research findings that many claimants of current
benefits subject to a sanctions regime did not understand what conduct could lead to
a sanction, how the sanctions system worked (some not even realising that they had
been sanctioned) and in particular what the consequences of a sanction would be on
current and future entitlement. Paragraph 3.12 of the paper states:

> "The lessons to be learned from the research ought to be relatively straight-
> forward to implement, although providing the appropriate training for a large
> number of Personal Advisers may present a considerable challenge:
>
> - claimants need to have the link between conditionality and the application
>   of sanctions fully explained at the start of any claim
> - clear and unambiguous communication about the sanctions regime
>   between advisers and claimants is vital at the start of any claim and must
>   form a key element in the Claimant Commitment
> - claimants need to know when they are in danger of receiving a sanction and
>   to be told when a sanction has been imposed, the amount and the duration
> - claimants need to know what actions they have to take to reverse a sanc-
>   tion—the process and consequences of re-compliance."

If one of the main aims of conditionality, of encouraging claimants to avoid
behaviour that would impede a possible return to or entry into work and thus reducing the incidence of the imposition of sanctions or of more severe sanctions, is to
be furthered, it therefore makes sense to build into the system a requirement to set
out each claimant's responsibilities and the consequences of not meeting them in
understandable terms. However, as the SSAC suggests, the nature of the personal
interaction between personal advisers, now known as work coaches, and claimants

may be much more important than a formal written document in getting over the realities of the situation and in encouraging claimants to take steps to avoid or reduce dependence on benefit.

A similar line of thought seems to be behind what was set out in paras 65 and **1.69** 66 of the joint judgment of Lords Neuberger and Toulson in *R (on the application of Reilly and Wilson) v Secretary of State for Work and Pensions* [2013] UKSC 68; [2014] 1 A.C. 453, in relation to the JSA regime, after noting the serious consequence of imposing a requirement to engage in unpaid work on a claimant on pain of discontinuance of benefits:

> "65. Fairness therefore requires that a claimant should have access to such information about the scheme as he or she may need in order to make informed and meaningful representations to the decision-maker before a decision is made. Such claimants are likely to vary considerably in their levels of education and ability to express themselves in an interview at a Jobcentre at a time when they may be under considerable stress. The principle does not depend on the categorisation of the Secretary of State's decision to introduce a particular scheme under statutory powers as a policy: it arises as a matter of fairness from the Secretary of State's proposal to invoke a statutory power in a way which will or may involve a requirement to perform work and which may have serious consequences on a claimant's ability to meet his or her living needs.
>
> 66. Properly informed claimants, with knowledge not merely of the schemes available, but also of the criteria for being placed on such schemes, should be able to explain what would, in their view, be the most reasonable and appropriate scheme for them, in a way which would be unlikely to be possible without such information. Some claimants may have access to information downloadable from a government website, if they knew what to look for, but many will not. For many of those dependent on benefits, voluntary agencies such as Citizens Advice Bureaus play an important role in informing and assisting them in relation to benefits to which they may be entitled, how they should apply, and what matters they should draw to the attention of their Jobcentre adviser."

These principles were discussed by the Court of Appeal in *SSWP v Reilly and Hewstone* and *SSWP v Jeffrey and Bevan* [2016] EWCA Civ 413; [2017] Q.B. 657; [2017] AACR 14 in relation to Mr Bevan's cross-appeal against the decision of the three-judge panel of the Upper Tribunal in *SSWP v TJ (JSA)* [2015] UKUT 56 (AAC). There was a detailed description and discussion of the decision in *TJ* in the 2015/16 edition of Vol.II, which need not be repeated here in the light of the Court of Appeal's decision. The Upper Tribunal had concluded, in the terms of its own summary in para.13(vi), that in the case of schemes which were mandatory both at the stages of referral onto them and once on them, no basis could be identified on which *meaningful* representations could be made prior to the decision to refer, in the sense of those representations being able to affect the decision to refer. In the 2015/16 edition of Vol.II there was some criticism of the Upper Tribunal's use of the word "mandatory" in this context.

The Court of Appeal first held that the Upper Tribunal had been right on the particular facts of Mr Bevan's case (where his complaint was that he could not afford the bus fare to attend the appointment given, so needed payment in advance rather than a refund) to find that it would have made no difference to what he would have said to the provider about the fares if he had known about what *The Work Programme Provider Guidance* issued by the DWP said about ability to use transportation.

So far as the Upper Tribunal's general guidance is concerned, the Court said this in para.172 about the submission that the Upper Tribunal had erred in saying that there was no scope for making representations in connection with a decision to refer a claimant to the Work Programme since referral was mandatory:

> "We do not believe that that is a fair reading of what the Tribunal said; and if it is properly understood there does not seem to be any dispute of principle between

the parties. The Tribunal was not laying down any absolute rule. The Secretary of State's policy, embodied in the guidance, is that referral to the Programme should be automatic (ignoring the specified exceptions) if the criteria are met. All that the Tribunal was doing was to point out that, that being so, any representations would have to address the question why he should depart from the policy; and that it was not easy to see what such representations might be. That seems to us an obvious common sense observation, particularly since referral to the Work Programme does not as such involve any specific obligation: see para.151 above. But it does not mean that there could never be such cases, and indeed para.224 is expressly addressed to that possibility. The Tribunal did not depart from anything that the Supreme Court said in [*Reilly and Wilson*]. It was simply considering its application in the particular circumstances of referral to the Work Programme."

The Court considered that in the real world application of the prior information duty was unlikely to be important at the point of initial referral to the Work Programme under the old style JSA legislation, as claimants were unlikely to object at that stage, before any specific requirements were imposed. Problems were likely to emerge when particular requirements were imposed on claimants that they considered unreasonable or inappropriate. The Upper Tribunal had appeared to say in para.249 of its decision that there was little or no scope for the operation of the duty at that stage. The Court of Appeal says this in paras 177 and 178:

"177. Mr de la Mare [counsel for Mr Bevan] submitted that that is wrong. If it is indeed what the Tribunal meant, we agree. So also does Ms Leventhal [counsel for the Secretary of State], who explicitly accepted in her written submissions that 'the requirements of fairness continue to apply after referral'. In principle, JSA claimants who are required, or who it is proposed should be required, under the Work Programme to participate in a particular activity should have sufficient information to enable them to make meaningful representations about the requirement – for example, that the activity in question is unsuitable for them or that there are practical obstacles to their participation. The fact that participation is mandatory if the requirement is made is beside the point: the whole purpose of the representations, and thus of the claimant having the relevant information to be able to make them, is so that the provider may be persuaded that the requirement should not be made, or should be withdrawn or modified.

178. However we should emphasise that the foregoing is concerned with the position in principle. It is quite another matter whether the Work Programme as operated in fact fails to give claimants such information. The Secretary of State's evidence before the Tribunal was that the relevant guidance in fact provides for them to be very fully informed. We have already referred to the Tribunal's findings about the information given at the referral interview. But it was also the evidence that at the initial interview with the provider post-referral, which is designed to find out how the claimant can be best supported, and in the subsequent interactions between claimant and provider claimants are supposed to be given both information and the opportunity to make representations. Whether in any particular case there has nevertheless been a failure to give information necessary to enable the claimant to make meaningful representations will have to be judged on the facts of the particular case. Tribunals will no doubt bear in mind the point made in [*Reilly and Wilson*] that it is important not to be prescriptive about how any necessary information is provided: see para.74 of the judgment of Lord Neuberger and Lord Toulson."

It is understood that Mr Bevan, who had been represented by CPAG, abandoned the possibility of applying for permission to appeal to the Supreme Court against the Court of Appeal's decision, having been unable to obtain legal aid. The Supreme Court refused Mr Hewstone's application for permission to appeal on the ground that it did not raise a point of law that deserved consideration at that point, as the outcome would not have affected the position of the parties to the case. That was because the claimants had succeeded on the point on art.6 of the ECHR and had only been seeking a declaration of incompatibility with the ECHR. The judges did indicate, though, that the issue whether the 2013 Act breached art.1 of Protocol 1 of the ECHR might deserve consideration in another case in which its resolution could affect the outcome.

A proposed remedial Order, under the powers in s.10(2) of the Human Rights Act 1998, was laid before Parliament in June 2018 for extensive consultation. The proposal is to add a new s.1A to the 2013 Act to require the appeals pending before March 26, 2013 and still undecided to be determined, usually by revision by the Secretary of State, in the claimants' favour. The Explanatory Memorandum estimates that around 3789 – 4303 claimants will be affected. A draft Jobseekers (Back to Work Schemes) Act 2013 (Remedial) Order 2019, following the form of the June 2018 proposed order, was laid before Parliament for affirmative resolution on September 5, 2019. In a report published on March 13, 2020, the Joint Committee on Human Rights recommended that both Houses of Parliament approve the draft Order.

In relation to the universal credit scheme, there might well be scope therefore for the application of the general principle of fairness at the stage of the application of a work-related or connected requirement and at the stage of specification of particular actions or activities. However, the process of discussion leading to the drawing up of a claimant commitment and its notification of the requirements imposed, as described above, certainly gives full opportunity for the provision of sufficient information to enable claimants to make meaningful representations about the content of the claimant commitment and to decide whether or not to accept initially and to make meaningful representations and decisions about taking particular specified actions further down the line. But the crucial questions in any appeals will most likely be, as suggested in para.178 of *Jeffrey and Bevan*, how the process was actually carried out in the particular case in question.

In *NM v SSWP (JSA)* [2016] UKUT 351 (AAC) Judge Wright held, as eventually conceded by the Secretary of State, that the inability to show that relevant DWP guidance had been considered before the claimant was given notice to participate in a Mandatory Work Activity scheme meant either that the claimant should not have been referred to the scheme (because the officer either would have followed the guidance or could have been persuaded to do so on representations from the claimant) or that he had good reason for not participating in the scheme. The appeal related to a sanction for failing to participate, through behaviour on the scheme. The guidance, in something called *Mandatory Work Activity Guidance* or *Operational Instructions–Procedural Guidance–Mandatory Work Activity–January 2012*, was relevant because at the time it instructed that claimants should not be considered for referral to Mandatory Work Activity if, among other circumstances, they were currently working (paid or voluntary). The claimant had been volunteering in a Sue Ryder shop, which he had to give up to attend the required scheme as a volunteer in a Salvation Army shop. The Secretary of State submitted that the guidance had since been changed to introduce an element of discretion about referral of claimants doing voluntary work. Judge Wright held that this would not excuse a failure by an officer of the Secretary of State to consider his own guidance or, on any appeal, a failure to provide the guidance to a First-tier Tribunal in accordance with the principles of natural justice.

Judge Wright has since emphasised some important elements of the application of the prior information duty, that should serve to rein in an over-enthusiastic use of the principle in some First-tier Tribunals, but only when properly placed in context. In *SSWP v SD (JSA)* [2020] UKUT 39 (AAC) he stressed, by reference both to the Supreme Court in *Reilly and Wilson* and the Court of Appeal in *Reilly and Hewstone* and *Jeffrey and Bevan*, that even if there has been a breach of the duty at the stage of initial referral to the Work Programme the notice of referral would only be invalidated if the breach was material. In the particular case, the claimant had never objected to his referral and his appeal against a sanction for failing to participate by non-attendance at a notified appointment was solely based on the ground that he had previously been told not to attend by his work coach. The tribunal, which had raised and sought evidence on the prior information point on its own initiative, failed to explain why it considered any breach of the duty material. In substituting a decision the judge rejected any unfairness in the referral to the Work Programme and rejected on the evidence the claimant's contention about the appointment.

In *SSWP v CN (JSA)* [2020] UKUT 26 (AAC), the claimant's sole ground of appeal against a sanction for failing to participate in the Work Programme by not attending an appointment was that she had never failed to keep an appointment (i.e. implicitly that she could not have received the notice of the appointment and/or had good cause under the regulations then in force). The tribunal allowed her appeal on the ground that the bundle did not contain a copy of the notice referring her to the Work Programme (i.e. the WP05) so that it was not satisfied that she had properly been notified of the requirement to participate. The tribunal appeared to think that that issue was one "raised by the appeal" within s.12(8)(a) of the SSA 1998, which it manifestly was not as the Secretary of State's submission in the bundle was that there was no dispute that the claimant was referred to the Work Programme. Nor did it give any explanation, if it had exercised its discretion under s.12(8)(a) to consider the issue, as to why it did so and how it was clearly apparent from the evidence so as to be capable of being dealt with under that discretion. Even if those hurdles had been overcome, the Secretary of State had not been given a fair opportunity to deal with the point. It is not necessary for the Secretary of State in all sanctions cases to provide evidence in the appeal bundle that *all* preconditions for the imposition of the sanction are satisfied. It depends what issues have been put in dispute in the appeal. Having therefore set the tribunal's decision aside, the judge substituted a decision finding on the evidence that the claimant had received the letter notifying her of the appointment in question.

The judge's statement that the Secretary of State need not in all sanctions cases provide evidence in the appeal bundle to support the satisfaction of all the preconditions to imposing a sanction must be read in the light of the approach in *SSWP v DC (JSA)* [2017] UKUT 464 (AAC), reported as [2018] AACR 16, and *PO'R v DFC (JSA)* [2018] NI Com 1. There it was said that the Secretary of State should in all cases involving a failure to participate in some scheme or interview where notice of certain details of the scheme etc. was required to be given, as well as notice of date, time and place, include in the appeal bundle a copy of the appointment letter, whether the claimant had raised any issue as to the terms of the letter or not. That was on the basis that unrepresented claimants could not be expected to identify technical issues about the validity of notices and it could not be predicted what particular issues might arise in the course of an appeal. If the letter was not included in the initial bundle, the decisions approved the action of tribunals in directing its production as a proper exercise of their inquisitorial jurisdiction. That exercise must rest on a use of the discretion in s.12(8)(a) to consider issues not raised by the appeal. The resolution of the approaches is no doubt that whenever a tribunal exercises that discretion it must do so consciously and explain why it has done so in any statement of reasons, and give the Secretary of State a fair opportunity to produce the document(s). It may be that an adequate explanation is to be found more readily when it is a notice of a specific appointment is in issue rather than an initial reference to a scheme.

A sample claimant commitment has been produced by the DWP in response to a freedom of information request (available at *https://www.gov.uk/government/publications/foi-query-universal-credit-claimant-commitment-example* (accessed January 27, 2014), or through a link in the universal credit part of the discussion forum on the Rightsnet website). The document puts things in terms of what the claimant says he or she will do. It is suggested above that that is not quite what the legislation requires, but there is obviously a tension with an attempt to use everyday and simple language. Nevertheless, the document is long and complicated. In the sample, there is no attempt to specify the precise length of the sanction that would be imposed for a failure for no good reason (the document says "without good reason") to comply with a requirement, but the maximum possible duration is included, plus the words "up to". It is arguable that this information is insufficiently precise.

No more recent sample claimant commitment has become publicly available. However, examples that have emerged in tribunal documents display the same fundamental defects and, it is submitted, a misunderstanding of the DWP's own legislation. The emphasis is on what claimants commit themselves to doing, in terms of finding and taking work and the actions and activities involved, rather than making any record of the requirements imposed on them under the legislation. Examples would be "I will be available to attend a job interview immediately [and to] start work immediately", "I will normally spend 35 hours per week looking and preparing for work" and "I will also attend and take part in appointments with my adviser when required". Thus, it appears that claimant commitments in themselves may fail to carry out the duty in s.14(3)(a) to record "the requirements that the claimant must comply with" under Part I of the WRA 2012. As noted in paras 17 and 28 of *S v SSWP (UC)* [2017] UKUT 477 (AAC) (see the introductory part of the note to s.26), s.13(1) means that a work-related requirement only comes into being when imposed by the Secretary of State and s.22(2) requires the Secretary of State to impose a work search requirement and a work availability requirement on claimants who are not exempted from those requirements (with a discretion to impose a work-focused interview requirement and/or a work preparation requirement on non-exempt claimants). Requirements must be *imposed*, with notification required by s.24(4), not merely undertaken by claimants.

In *JB v SSWP (UC)* [2018] UKUT 360 (AAC) the claimant was made subject to a sanction under s.27(2)(a) of the WRA 2012 for failing for no good reason to comply with a work-related requirement under s.15 (work-focused interview requirement). He had failed to attend an appointment with an adviser on January 12, 2017, saying later that he had thought that the appointment was for the next day and later still that he did not attend because of health issues.

The First-tier Tribunal found that the claimant had signed and agreed a claimant commitment on October 27, 2016 that included a requirement to attend and take part in appointments with advisers when required and had been notified at a previous appointment of the requirement to attend on January 12, 2017. In fact the provision before the tribunal was "I will attend and take part in appointments with my adviser when required". The tribunal rejected his argument that he had had good reason for failing to attend. However, the claimant commitment supplied in evidence by the SSWP was not signed or dated and contained a provision for action to be taken by September 20, 2016. It was therefore improbable that the document in the papers had been notified to the claimant on October 27, 2016 and the SSWP had not supplied any other evidence of what claimant commitment had been accepted and what requirements might have been notified in it. Accordingly, although the unrepresented claimant had not raised the issue of whether he had been properly notified of the requirement to attend the particular appointment, the tribunal went wrong in law by proceeding on the basis that a claimant commitment agreed by the claimant on October 27, 2016 imposed a work-related requirement to attend a work-focused interview. Nor had the SSWP put forward coherent evidence of what had been said at an earlier appointment. The written submission relied on an attendance on June 1, 2016, which did not work because the universal credit claim began on September 7, 2016. The appointment history showed a "work-focused review" on December 21, 2016, but there was no evidence of any notification then of a future appointment. There could be no reliance on any presumption of regularity because there was no evidence of a general practice or "script" of what claimants are told at appointments about the need to attend work-focused interviews. Although it was implicit in the claimant's position that he knew of the appointment on January 12, 2017, a sanction could only be imposed if there had been proper notification of the requirement in question and the SSWP had failed to show that. The case was remitted to a new tribunal for rehearing, as it was fair (the issue not having been raised until the Upper Tribunal judge gave permission to appeal), to allow the SSWP an opportunity to produce further evidence.

Judge Poole QC therefore did not need to decide whether the terms of the claimant commitment in the papers were capable of constituting a notification of a requirement to participate in work-focused interviews when notified of appointments. However, she did make interesting observations on that and other wider issues. The SSWP had submitted that the standard terms of claimant commitments were prepared so that claimants could understand them, but were clear and imperative, and that in the context of a system including sanctions claimants and advisers knew that when they were requested to attend interviews it was obligatory to turn up. Judge Poole did not in so many words either accept or reject that submission, but her observations indicate that it could only be accepted subject to heavy qualifications.

In her introductory discussion of the legal principles, the judge stressed that while the universal credit legislation gave the SSWP considerable flexibility, the flip side of that was that in sanctions cases the SSWP had to be able to evidence the imposition of the requirement in question. The more informal the means of communication to a claimant the more efficient its recording systems will have to be, so that copies can be produced in cases of appeal. Her opinions on the wider issues were set out as follows in para.29:

> "29.1 The UC legislation is deliberately drafted to leave a degree of flexibility for the SSWP, and permits multiple methods of communication to claimants (paragraphs 16 and 17 above). There is a flexibility in the manner and means of notification. Given this legislative intention, it would be inappropriate for the Upper Tribunal to set out particular requirements for wording of notifications, or the means by which this is done.
>
> 29.2 In cases where the issue arises, the key matter for tribunals to consider is whether fair notice has been given, having regard to all the communications between the SSWP and the claimant (paragraphs 18 – 20 above). What tribunals need to do is look at the evidence produced by the SSWP, in the context in which it arises, together with any evidence taken from the claimant, and ask the question: does the evidence show that the substance of the relevant requirement and consequences of non-compliance were notified to the claimant? The answer to this question will turn on the particular circumstances of a case.
>
> 29.3 There is a virtue in plain English, and in couching notifications about what a claimant has to do in terms that claimants can readily understand. The Upper Tribunal Judge who granted permission raised the issue of whether requirements should be spelled out expressly and not left to implication. In my view it is not necessary that there is reproduction of statutory wording or reference to particular section or regulation numbers, or indeed any prescribed form of wording. *What is important is the substance. In this case the question was whether it could fairly be said, on the totality of the evidence, that the claimant had been notified of an obligation to attend a work-focused interview and the consequences of non-compliance.* [emphasis added by editor]
>
> 29.4 Unless the only evidence bearing on the imposition of a requirement in a sanctions case is the claimant commitment, it is artificial to focus on the sufficiency of the precise terms of the claimant commitment. This is because requirements can be imposed in various ways, including by a combination of documents (paragraph 20 above). Indeed, in this case the SSWP does not maintain that the wording in the claimant commitment of itself imposed a work-related requirement to attend a work-focused interview on 12 January 2017. Where a claimant commitment is part of the evidence, general reference to 'appointments' in the claimant commitment seems to me to be a sensible shorthand way of conveying a need to attend meetings but leaving flexibility to impose requirements at a later stage under either Section 15 or Section 23 of the 2012 Act. I also consider the passages set out in paragraph 26 above about sanctions for not meeting require-

ments, giving detail of how payments are cut, and sanctions for not meeting requirements. So where the claimant commitment has been notified, then those requirements have to be considered in conjunction with other evidence before the tribunal bearing on communication to the claimant of requirements and consequences of non-compliance. This can include, for example, later appointment cards, texts about appointments, and verbal communications at interview. It seems to me that when considering the efficacy of verbal communication, although the SSWP's record keeping will be key, it is permissible to take into account a regular pattern of interviews. For example, a claimant may have been asked at interview to come back for the same sort of interview two weeks later. The claimant's experience from earlier interviews may be relevant to whether they have been informed of the substance of a requirement and consequences of non-compliance. Further, while intimation of date, time and place of appointment is a necessary component of intimation, that will be insufficient of itself unless linked in some way to notification to a claimant of a requirement to attend and consequences of non-compliance. The overall point is that tribunals have to consider not only the wording of the claimant commitment, but of all the evidence bearing on whether the substance of the relevant requirement and consequences of non-compliance were notified to the claimant.

29.5 [Deals with some of the consequences of the differences between the powers in s.15 and s.23 of the WRA 2012]."

That overall approach may not be too difficult to apply if the DWP takes on board at all levels the lessons of *JB* and routinely maintains and provides to tribunals clear and consistent records of the requirements imposed on claimants. However, if the familiar lazy assumptions exemplified in *JB* continue (or appear in older cases from before a hoped-for change of practice), a sharper focus may be necessary on how to resolve the tensions between some of the principles canvassed in para.29 in the circumstances of individual cases. For instance, at a broad level it might continue wrongly to be assumed that, if what is done (e.g. in the drafting of the standard form of terms in claimant commitments) is sensible in policy terms, the actual terms of the relevant legislation have been complied with. At a more grassroots level, there might well continue to be a failure to realise the need to provide tribunals with copies of all the evidence beyond the claimant commitment necessary to show the imposition of the requirement in question and the consequences of non-compliance. In either case, it might become necessary to address directly the effect of the standard form of terms in the claimant commitment. As well as the provision about appointments in issue in *JB*, drafted in terms of what the claimant said he would do rather than in terms of the imposition of a requirement, other standard provisions take the same form (see the examples given above from the sample claimant commitment). It is submitted that the principle expressed at the end of para.29.3 (and in earlier paragraphs) of *JB* that the test is whether the evidence shows that the claimant has been notified of an obligation becomes primary and that there is a fundamental difference between a commitment being undertaken by a claimant and a requirement being imposed by the SSWP.

In para.34 of *JB*, Judge Poole mentions two documents produced to the Upper Tribunal by the SSWP, of potential relevance in the rehearing. One was a computer printout recording the signing, acceptance and issue of a claimant commitment on September 13, 2016, together with something called a "claimant pack". The other was a standard form document headed "Your meeting plan" with spaces for entering dates, times and contacts of next meeting, with a warning on the back that missing meetings without rearranging in advance risks a sanction. According to the SSWP, the meeting plan document is issued with the "commitment pack", which the judge noted might or might not be the same thing as the "claimant pack". Such documents, in particular a complete copy of the claimant or commitment pack, might well be relevant in future cases, but only if properly put into evidence before tribunals. It is also understood that a leaflet "About Sanctions" is routinely uploaded to a claimant's electronic journal early in the course of an award.

Quite rigorous guidance has been issued to decision-makers in the universal credit context in Memo ADM 5/19. It in general emphasises the necessity for the SSWP to be able, in order to show that any failure to comply with a requirement is sanctionable, to evidence that the requirement has been imposed and that the claimant has been properly been informed of the substance of the requirement and the consequences of non-compliance. The Memo accepts that evidence other than the claimant commitment will be crucial and that copies of all relevant communications will need to be included in any appeal papers to found a notification by a combination of means. Paragraph 7 states that:

"it is expected that the SSWP will produce to a tribunal, as a minimum, copies of
1. the claimant commitment
2. any appointment letters ((for example, standard notification letters used for referring to employment programmes such as sbwa [sector based work academy], WHP [Work and Health Programme] etc)
3. records of telephone or electronic communications (for example, a copy of the relevant 'to-do' or journal notes)
4. internal electronic records (for example, a copy of the sanctions information screen)
5. any other relevant documents (for example a copy of the relevant ALP [Action List Prompt]) that shows the imposition of any work-related requirement and the consequences of non-compliance to the claimant."

Paragraph 14 says rather oddly that the ordinary meaning of "substance" is "to specify the intended purpose or subject matter". The meaning surely is not so restricted, but the Memo emphasises that where interviews are concerned the claimant must be told the purpose of the interview and the reason for it. There is now more comprehensive guidance in the section on Public Law Principles of Fairness in Ch.K1 of the ADM.

In para.29 of *S v SSWP (UC)* [2017] UKUT 477 (AAC), the judge accepted that if the Secretary of State failed to carry out the s.22(2) duty, the claimant should not bear the consequences of that (which must entail that the requirement(s) in question had not been imposed and there could be no sanction for failing to comply).

In *S*, it was said that the imposition of the work search requirement was not in issue, but the evidence to support that conclusion was not spelled out. The decision should not therefore be taken as any endorsement of a view that terms of a claimant commitment like that in *S* would be sufficient in themselves to impose work-related requirements on a claimant. Nor should the language used by Judge Jacobs in *SP v SSWP (UC)* [2018] UKUT 227 (AAC), where he talked of a claimant having to make a commitment, in that case about attendance at work-focused interviews, and about the standard term in the claimant commitment not becoming effective until made specific by a notification of the date, time and place of a particular interview by the Secretary of State. The issue in the case was whether the claimant had received the letter notifying him of the interview. Nothing in the decision undermines the principle that work-related requirements must be *imposed* and that on any sanction appeal the Secretary of State must provide evidence of such an imposition (compare the approach in *SSWP v DC (JSA)* [2017] UKUT 464 (AAC), reported as [2018] AACR 16, to the need for evidence of appointment letters to attend schemes under s.17A of the old style Jobseekers Act 1995 and in *MB v SSWP (PIP)* [2018] UKUT 213 (AAC) to the need for evidence of a requirement to attend and participate in a consultation under regulation 9 of the Social Security (Personal Independence Payment) Regulations 2013).

There is some difficulty in working out what remedies a claimant would have who disagrees with the imposition of a requirement included in the claimant commitment. If the claimant declines to accept the Secretary of State's form of the record, at the outset of the claim or as later reviewed and up-dated, then any initial disallowance of the claim or subsequent supersession of an awarding decision would be appealable. However, it is not clear whether such an appeal could succeed on the basis that a requirement in fact included in the claimant commitment should not have been imposed under the conditions in ss.19–24. If the requirement was one whose imposition was prohibited by the legislation and the claimant was prepared to accept everything else in the document, it is submitted that it could properly be concluded that the condition in s.4(1)(e) had been satisfied (compare the approach of Judge Rowland in *CJSA/1080/2002* and *GM v SSWP (JSA)* [2014] UKUT 57 (AAC) in holding that a claimant was to be accepted as satisfying a condition of attendance at a Jobcentre when he had in fact not attended after being informed that he was not entitled to JSA so that attendance was pointless: see further the notes to reg.23 of the JSA Regulations 1996 in Vol.II). If it was a matter of the Secretary of State's discretion under s.22(3), the result might be different. A claimant who accepts a claimant commitment under protest about some requirement may no doubt request the Secretary of State not to impose the challenged requirement and in consequence to review the claimant commitment. However, it appears that the claimant cannot appeal directly either against the imposition of the requirement or the content of the claimant commitment or against a refusal by the Secretary of State to remove a requirement and to review the claimant commitment. See the discussion in the note to s.24 below, which would apply equally to any of the kinds of decision mentioned. None of them are "outcome" decisions.

Work-related requirements

Work-focused interview requirement

15.—(1) In this Part a "work-focused interview requirement" is a requirement that a claimant participate in one or more work-focused interviews as specified by the Secretary of State.   1.70

(2) A work-focused interview is an interview for prescribed purposes relating to work or work preparation.

(3) The purposes which may be prescribed under subsection (2) include in particular that of making it more likely in the opinion of the Secretary of State that the claimant will obtain paid work (or more paid work or better-paid work).

(4) The Secretary of State may specify how, when and where a work-focused interview is to take place.

DEFINITION

"claimant"—see s.40.

GENERAL NOTE

This section defines what a "work-focused interview" is and makes the related requirement "participation" in the interview. This is for the purposes of ss.20–22, and in particular s.20, which applies the requirement to participate in such an interview to the great majority of claimants within the general work-seeking ambit, although on a discretionary basis. Note the circumstances specified in and under s.19 in which no work-related requirement may be imposed.   1.71

Under subss.(2) and (3) regulations must prescribe the purposes, relating to work or work preparation, for which an interview may be required. The prescription, in very wide terms, is in reg.93 of the Universal Credit Regulations. "Paid work" is not defined in the Act, but when that phrase is used in reg.93 the definition in reg.2 will apply (see the note to reg.93). The Secretary of State is allowed under subss.(1) and (4) to specify how, when and where the interview is to take place, so that there is no straightforward limit on the number or frequency of the interviews that may be specified, or on the persons who may conduct the interview. The interviews must of course properly be for one of the purposes prescribed in reg.93. The requirement to participate in an interview cannot be used for punitive purposes or simply as a means of control of a claimant. No doubt it is also to be implied that only rational requirements may be imposed, so that a specification of two interviews in different places at the same time or so that they could not practically be coordinated could be disregarded (see the approach of Judge Rowland in *GM v SSWP (JSA)* [2014] UKUT 57 (AAC): notes to s.14 above). Rationality would also require that what was specified should not be incompatible with other requirements, in particular the work search and work availability requirements where there is no discretion under s.22(2) about their imposition. Thus a claimant could not validly be required to attend so many interviews that it made it impossible to take work search actions for the hours specified under s.17, unless there was a corresponding reduction in the s.17 requirements. These are rather extreme examples, which it is hoped would not arise in practice. Because, as discussed in the notes to s.24, there is no right of appeal against an imposition of a work-related or connected requirement as such, the issues will normally arise in the course of challenges to or appeals against removal of entitlement for failing to accept a claimant commitment containing the requirement(s) in questions or against reductions in benefit following a sanction for non-compliance. The main focus in the latter case may be on whether the claimant had a good reason for not complying with the requirement, but sight should not be lost of whether there had been non-compliance with the requirement as properly interpreted (see below).

However, there may also often be questions whether a requirement has in fact been imposed. There appear to be two stages. The Secretary of State may indicate in general that a claimant will be required to participate in interviews (although see the notes to s.14 for serious doubts whether the current standard form of claimant commitment achieves that result). But the requirement under subs.(1) appears not to arise, in the sense of a requirement that the claimant can comply with or fail to comply with for sanctions purposes, until the Secretary of State has specified the particular interview or interviews under subs.(4) and probably (although subs.(1) is not entirely clear) that the claimant participate. See the notes to s.14 for extensive discussion of the decision in *JB v SSWP (UC)* [2018] UKUT 360 (AAC) on the evidence that the SSWP needs to produce to show that a requirement to participate in a s.15 interview has been imposed and the guidance given to decision-makers in Memo ADM 5/19. Paragraph 6 of *JB* states that it is a condition precedent of imposing any sanction under s.27(2)(a) that the claimant was subject to the work-related requirement in issue, thus confirming the approach in para.29 of *S v SSWP (UC)* [2017] UKUT 477 (AAC) that if a specific requirement has not been imposed by the SSWP, no sanction can follow.

SP v SSWP (UC) [2018] UKUT 227 (AAC) is consistent with such a two-stage approach, but see the discussion in the notes to s.14 for how the language used should not be taken as contrary to the argument made there about evidence of the imposition of a requirement.

Specification must necessarily imply communication to the claimant in time to attend the interview.

There is no requirement that the specification under subs.(4) of how, when and where an interview is to take place should be in writing or in other permanent form. However, good practice, plus the potential need for acceptable evidence of the existence and terms of the specification in the light of the principle that the claimant should in sanctions cases be given the benefit of any doubt that might reasonably arise (*DL v SSWP (JSA)* [2013] UKUT 295 (AAC)), must surely point to the need for written or computer records to be kept and to be available to the claimant for reference. Arguably, the "prior information duty" (see the notes to s.14 for detailed discussion) would require that information about the purpose of the particular interview be given in the specification. Arguably also, in accordance with the approach in *SSWP v DC (JSA)* [2017] UKUT 464 (AAC), reported as [2018] AACR 16, and *PO'R v DFC (JSA)* [2018] NI Com 1, a copy of the appointment letter should be included in the Secretary of State's submission on any appeal against a sanction for failing to comply with a requirement to participate in the interview. There it was said that the Secretary of State should in all cases involving a failure to participate in some scheme or interview where notice of certain details of the scheme etc was required to be given, as well as notice of date, time and place, include in the appeal bundle a copy of the appointment letter, whether the claimant had raised any issue as to the terms of the letter or not. That was on the basis that unrepresented claimants could not be expected to identify technical issues about the validity of notices and it could not be predicted what particular issues might arise in the course of an appeal. If the letter was not included in the initial bundle, the decisions approved the action of tribunals in directing its production as a proper exercise of their inquisitorial jurisdiction. That exercise must, if the claimant has not taken the point, rest on a use of the discretion in s.12(8)(a) of the SSA 1998 to consider issues not raised by the appeal. The resolution with the approach in *SSWP v SD (JSA)* [2020] UKUT 39 (AAC) and *SSWP v CN (JSA)* [2020] UKUT 26 (AAC) (see the notes to s.14) is no doubt that whenever a tribunal exercises that discretion it must do so consciously and explain why it has done so in any statement of reasons, and give the Secretary of State a fair opportunity to produce the document(s). It may be that an adequate explanation is to be found more readily when it is a notice of a specific appointment that is in issue rather than an initial reference to a scheme.

Note that the requirement, as now for both old style and new style JSA, is not attendance at an interview at the specified time and date, but participation in it. This would appear to mean that a claimant can be required to participate in an interview over the telephone, providing that that manner of conducting it has been specified under subs.(4). In an ambiguous (so far as JSA is concerned) Parliamentary answer on 24 November 2015 (UIN 17005), the Minister of State Priti Patel said:

"Under JSA, claimants are not sanctioned for failing to answer their telephone. In Universal Credit, claimants who have a prearranged telephone interview with their Work Coach, and who fail to participate without good reason, can be referred for a sanction decision."

There is no further provision about what participating in a work-focused interview entails. It must at least entail turning up at the place and time specified, although the decision of Judge Knowles in *SA v SSWP (JSA)* [2015] UKUT 454 (AAC) (see the notes to s.27 for full discussion) would indicate that tribunals should consider, in cases where the claimant arrives not very late, whether it is proportionate to the nature of all the circumstances to regard that as a failure to participate in an interview. There were all sorts of mitigating circumstances in *SA*, that may well not be present in other cases. See *SN v SSWP (JSA)* [2018] UKUT 279 (AAC), detailed in the notes to s.26(2)(a) and 27(2)(a), for discussion of what might amount to a failure to participate (in that case in a mandatory work activity scheme and involving conduct before the scheme started) and the expression in para.45 of some doubt about the result in *SA*.

The requirement to participate must also extend to making some meaningful contribution to the interview, but the limits will probably not be established until there have been some more sanctions appeals in JSA or universal credit that reach the Upper Tribunal. Behaviour that leads to the premature termination of the interview may well amount to a failure to participate (see the facts of *DM v SSWP (JSA)* [2015] UKUT 67 (AAC) in the notes to s.27(2)(b)). There may, though, in cases of uncooperative claimants or heavy-handed officials or a combination, be difficult questions about when an interview has ceased to exist, so that subsequent behaviour cannot be relevant to whether there has been a failure to participate (see *PH v SSWP (ESA)* [2016] UKUT 119 (AAC) on failing to submit to a medical examination).

It was recognised in *CS v SSWP (JSA)* [2019] UKUT 218 (AAC), detailed in the notes to s.26(2)(a), that it was legitimate for a scheme provider to require an attender to verify their identity before starting a scheme, so that a refusal to do so would usually amount to a failure to participate in the scheme. The same principle could apply to an interview, but the particular issues that arose in *CS*, to do with a scheme provider external to the DWP, are unlikely to arise if it is an interview with a work coach or other adviser that has been notified.

A failure for no good reason to comply with any work-related requirement is sanctionable under s.27(2)(a). That is the context in which what amounts to a failure to comply will be identified, as well as what might amount to a good reason for non-compliance. For instance, there appear to be no provisions prescribing the length of notice of an interview to be given or how far a claimant can be required to travel, but there could plainly be a good reason for failing to comply with unreasonable requirements, especially if the claimant had attempted in advance to draw any problem with attendance to the Secretary of State's attention. Claimants who are found not in fact to have been aware of an interview must have a good reason for failing to comply, whether or not the requirement is said to have been imposed in such circumstances (*SP v SSWP (UC)* [2018] UKUT 227 (AAC)).

Note that under s.23(1) the Secretary of State is empowered to require a claimant to attend an interview relating to the imposition of a work-related requirement on the claimant or assisting the claimant to comply with a requirement.

Work preparation requirement

1.72   **16.**—(1) In this Part a "work preparation requirement" is a requirement that a claimant take particular action specified by the Secretary of State for the purpose of making it more likely in the opinion of the Secretary of State that the claimant will obtain paid work (or more paid work or better-paid work).

(2) The Secretary of State may under subsection (1) specify the time to be devoted to any particular action.

(3) Action which may be specified under subsection (1) includes in particular—

(a) attending a skills assessment;
(b) improving personal presentation;
(c) participating in training;
(d) participating in an employment programme;
(e) undertaking work experience or a work placement;
(f) developing a business plan;
(g) any action prescribed for the purpose in subsection (1).

(4) In the case of a person with limited capability for work, the action which may be specified under subsection (1) includes taking part in a work-focused health-related assessment.

(5) In subsection (4) "work-focused health-related assessment" means an assessment by a health care professional approved by the Secretary of State which is carried out for the purpose of assessing—

(a) the extent to which the person's capability for work may be improved by taking steps in relation to their physical or mental condition, and
(b) such other matters relating to their physical or mental condition and the likelihood of their obtaining or remaining in work or being able to do so as may be prescribed.

(6) In subsection (5) "health care professional" means—

(a) a registered medical practitioner,
(b) a registered nurse,
(c) an occupational therapist or physiotherapist registered with a regulatory body established by an Order in Council under section 60 of the Health Act 1999, or
(d) a member of such other profession regulated by a body mentioned in section 25(3) of the National Health Service Reform and Health Care Professions Act 2002 as may be prescribed.

DEFINITIONS

"claimant"—see s.40.
"limited capability for work"—*ibid.*

GENERAL NOTE

This section defines "work preparation requirement" for the particular pur-   1.73
poses of ss.21 and 22. The requirement is to take particular action specified by the
Secretary of State for the purpose of making it more likely that the claimant will
obtain paid work or obtain more or better-paid such work. If a specific requirement
has not been imposed, then no sanction can follow (*S v SSWP (UC)* [2017] UKUT
477 (AAC) para.29). See the notes to s.14 for extensive discussion of the decision
in *JB v SSWP (UC)* [2018] UKUT 360 (AAC) on the evidence that the SSWP
needs to produce to show that a requirement (in that case to participate in a s.15
interview) has been imposed and the guidance given to decision-makers in Memo
ADM 5/19. Paragraph 6 of *JB* states that it is a condition precedent of imposing any
sanction under s.27(2)(a) that the claimant was subject to the work-related requirement in issue, thus confirming the approach in para.29 of *S*.

Subsection (3) gives a non-exhaustive list of actions that may be specified, including under para.(g) any action prescribed in regulations. No regulations have as yet
been made under para.(g). The list is in fairly broad terms, not further defined in
the legislation, even "employment programme". The sorts of activities required do
not themselves have to be paid, so long as they can legitimately be related to the
purpose of improving prospects of obtaining paid work or more or better paid work
(see below and the notes to s.26(2)(a)). So unpaid work experience or placements
(e.g. as an intern) or voluntary work can be made mandatory. See the notes to s.15
above for the need for the co-ordination with the practical application of other
work-related or connected requirements for the specification of any particular work
preparation requirement to be rational.

The Secretary of State has a discretion under ss.21 and 22(3) whether to impose
a work preparation requirement in any particular case. It appears that the requirement therefore cannot arise until the Secretary of State has specified the particular
action, so that general statements in a claimant commitment about normally spending 35 hours a week looking and preparing for work (even if they could be regarded
as *imposed* by the Secretary of State: see the notes to s.14) would not be enough in
themselves. Also note the circumstances specified in and under s.19 in which no
work-related requirement may be imposed.

The Secretary of State may under subs.(2) specify the time to be devoted to any
particular action, but in practice this is likely to be less controversial than the similar
power in s.17(2) in relation to a work search requirement. Subsections (4)–(6) allow
the application of a particular requirement to take part in a work-focused health-
related assessment to claimants with limited capability for work (only claimants
who also have limited capability for work-related activity being exempted from all
work-related requirements under s.19(2)(a)). Paragraph 15 of *JS v SSWP (ESA)*;
[2013] UKUT 635 (AAC) suggests that if a claimant is patently not going to be able
to obtain work at any stage or is already in a suitable apprenticeship or placement no
action could make it more likely that work or more work would be obtained, so that
no action could be legitimately specified.

There is no requirement that the specification under subs.(1) and (2) of the
particular action to be taken and the time to be devoted to it should be in writing
or in other permanent form. However, good practice, plus the potential need for
acceptable evidence of the existence and terms of the specification in the light of
the principle that the claimant should in sanctions cases be given the benefit of
any doubt that might reasonably arise (*DL v SSWP (JSA)* [2013] UKUT 295
(AAC)), must surely point to the need for written or computer records to be kept
and to be available to the claimant for reference. See *NM v SSWP (JSA)* [2016]
UKUT 351 (AAC), discussed in para.1.69 above, for circumstances in which

failure to consider relevant DWP guidance about the circumstances in which there should or should not be referral to a scheme, with sufficient information to the claimant to allow the making of meaningful representations, undermines the applicability of any sanction for failure to comply with a requirement. The principles of natural justice require that the terms of the relevant guidance be provided to a tribunal on any appeal.

Arguably, the "prior information duty" (see the notes to s.14 for detailed discussion) would require that information about the purpose of the particular course, programme, placement etc. be given in the specification. Arguably also, in accordance with the approach in *SSWP v DC (JSA)* [2017] UKUT 464 (AAC), reported as [2018] AACR 16, and *PO'R v DFC (JSA)* [2018] NI Com 1, a copy of the appointment letter should be included in the Secretary of State's submission on any appeal against a sanction for failing to comply with a requirement under s.16. There it was said that the Secretary of State should in all cases involving a failure to participate in some scheme or interview where notice of certain details of the scheme etc. was required to be given, as well as notice of date, time and place, include in the appeal bundle a copy of the appointment letter, whether the claimant had raised any issue as to the terms of the letter or not. That was on the basis that unrepresented claimants could not be expected to identify technical issues about the validity of notices and it could not be predicted what particular issues might arise in the course of an appeal. If the letter was not included in the initial bundle, the decisions approved the action of tribunals in directing its production as a proper exercise of their inquisitorial jurisdiction. That exercise must, if the claimant has not taken the point, rest on a use of the discretion in s.12(8)(a) of the SSA 1998 to consider issues not raised by the appeal. The resolution with the approach in *SSWP v SD (JSA)* [2020] UKUT 39 (AAC) and *SSWP v CN (JSA)* [2020] UKUT 26 (AAC) (see the notes to s.14) is no doubt that whenever a tribunal exercises that discretion it must do so consciously and explain why it has done so in any statement of reasons, and give the Secretary of State a fair opportunity to produce the document(s). It may be that an adequate explanation is to be found more readily when it is a notice of a specific appointment that is in issue rather than an initial reference to a scheme.

A failure for no good reason by a claimant subject to all work-related requirements to comply with a requirement under this heading to undertake a work placement of a prescribed description (i.e. the Mandatory Work Activity Scheme: reg.114 of the Universal Credit Regulations) is sanctionable under s.26(2)(a) (higher-level sanctions). The scheme has not operated after April 2016. Outside that limited category, failure for no good reason to comply with any work-related requirement is sanctionable under s.27(2)(a). That is the main context in which there will be exploration of what action can be said to make it more likely that the claimant will obtain paid work or more or better-paid work, since the addition of the Secretary of State's opinion in subs.(1) will not be allowed to take away the power of tribunals to reach their own conclusions on that matter. What amounts to a failure to comply will also be identified, as well as what might amount to a good reason for non-compliance. The issue may also arise in challenges to the removal of entitlement following a failure to accept a claimant commitment containing a disputed work preparation requirement (see the notes to s.14).

Note that under s.23(1) the Secretary of State is empowered to require a claimant to participate in an interview relating to the imposition of a work-related requirement on the claimant or assisting the claimant to comply with a requirement. Under s.23(3) he can require the provision of information and evidence for the purpose of verifying compliance and that the claimant confirm compliance in any manner.

Work search requirement

1.74   **17.**—(1) In this Part a "work search requirement" is a requirement that a claimant take—

   (a) all reasonable action, and

(b) any particular action specified by the Secretary of State,

for the purpose of obtaining paid work (or more paid work or better-paid work).

(2) The Secretary of State may under subsection (1)(b) specify the time to be devoted to any particular action.

(3) Action which may be specified under subsection (1)(b) includes in particular—

(a) carrying out work searches;

(b) making applications;

(c) creating and maintaining an online profile;

(d) registering with an employment agency;

(e) seeking references;

(f) any action prescribed for the purpose in subsection (1).

(4) Regulations may impose limitations on a work search requirement by reference to the work to which it relates; and the Secretary of State may in any particular case specify further such limitations on such a requirement.

(5) A limitation under subsection (4) may in particular be by reference to—

(a) work of a particular nature,

(b) work with a particular level of remuneration,

(c) work in particular locations, or

(d) work available for a certain number of hours per week or at particular times,

and may be indefinite or for a particular period.

DEFINITION

"claimant"—see s.40.

GENERAL NOTE

Temporary Coronavirus Provisions

Regulation 6(1)(a) and (b) of the Social Security (Coronavirus) (Further Measures)   **1.75**
Regulations 2020 (SI 2020/371) provides that for a period of three months beginning on March 30, 2020 the Secretary of State cannot impose a work search requirement on anyone who has an award of universal credit and any existing work search requirement ceases to have effect from that date. Although reg.6 refers to the provision being a consequence of the outbreak of coronavirus disease, it is not necessary that the claimant in question be affected in any way by that outbreak or the resulting economic disruption. It is not clear what is intended by the restriction to someone who has an award of universal credit. There would be no consistency in lifting the work search requirement for someone who happened to have an existing award on March 30, 2020, but not allowing an award to be made on a new claim because the claimant had not accepted a claimant commitment containing the requirement that the Secretary of State was bound to impose under s.22(2)(a), so that reg.6 of the Further Measures Regulations was never reached because the claimant never had an award. Such a result was plainly not intended (and was not applied in practice), so is to be avoided if possible, but para.11 of Memo ADM 04/20 gives no clue as to the mechanism for doing so. It is suggested that, provided that it had been accepted under reg.16(b) of the Universal Credit Regulations that the claimant could be entitled without having accepted a claimant commitment (see the notes to s.4(1)(e) and reg.16) and all the other basic conditions in s.4(1) were met, an award could be made to the claimant before consideration of what work-related requirements were to be imposed, so that then reg.6 could apply to modify the Secretary of State's s.22(2) duty to impose the work search and work availability requirements.

See the notes to s.18 for the effect of reg.6 on the work availability requirement.

The effect of reg.6 expires at the end of November 12, 2020 (reg.10(2)), subject to any amendment. The power to extend the three-month period was not exercised before it expired. When it was announced (Parliamentary answer, Under-Secretary of State, Mims Davies, WQ 62431) that from July 1, 2020 the requirement for universal credit claimants to accept a claimant commitment was being reintroduced, it was stressed that claimant commitments agreed or reviewed from that date (i.e. the work-related requirements included) would have to be reasonable for the "new normal" and acknowledge the reality of a person's local jobs market and personal circumstances.

1.75.1   This section defines "work search requirement" for the particular purpose of s.22, under which the requirement must be imposed on all claimants except those exempted by s.19, 20 or 21. See the notes to s.14 for discussion of whether the current standard terms of claimant commitments are sufficient in themselves to *impose* such a requirement. It is a requirement that a claimant take both all reasonable action (subs.(1)(a)) and any particular action specified by the Secretary of State (subs.(1)(b)) for the purpose of obtaining paid work or more or better-paid work. "Paid work" is not defined in the Act, nor is it defined in regulations for the specific purpose of ss.17 and 22. However, under the power in s.25, regs 94 and 95 of the Universal Credit Regulations deem the work search requirement not to have been complied with in certain circumstances and make references to "paid work". For those purposes, the definition in reg.2 will apply, i.e. work done for payment or in expectation of payment, excluding work for a charity or voluntary organisation, or as a volunteer, in return for expenses only. Regulation 87 adds nothing to the terms of s.17 itself. Thus it appears that both self-employment and employment can be considered both under the reg.2 definition and under the ordinary meaning of the phrase "paid work" and that voluntary work or unpaid internships or work placements are excluded. According to the then Minister of State Esther McVey (House of Commons written answers April 2, 2014 and September 1, 2014) guidance to Jobcentre Plus staff is that, in contrast to the position for JSA, universal credit claimants can be mandated to apply for vacancies for zero hours contracts. At the time it appeared not to matter whether there was an exclusivity clause in the contract or not, but such clauses were made unenforceable from May 26, 2015 by the new s.27A of the Employment Rights Act 1996. There will be a question in challenges to and appeals against sanctions decisions whether claimants have a good reason for not complying with a requirement to search for zero hours contracts.

Subsections (4) and (5) allow regulations to impose limitations on the kind of work search which can be required and also allow the Secretary of State to specify further limitations. Regulation 97 contains the prescribed limitations, in terms of hours of work for carers and those with a disability, of the maximum time for travel to and from work and of the type of work recently undertaken. See the notes to reg.97. There appears to be no limitation on the number of hours a week that work could involve while still falling for consideration, apart from in the cases of the particular categories of claimant identified in reg.97(2). Note also that reg.99 exempts claimants from the work search requirement in a variety of individual circumstances that would make the carrying out of any work search impracticable. See the notes to reg.99 for the details. The circumstances include several to do with care of children, the carrying out of various worthwhile activities, unfitness for work for short and (subject to conditions) more extended periods and, particularly important to the structure of universal credit, where earnings are at a defined level. Regulation 98 exempts recent victims of domestic violence for a fixed period.

What is "all reasonable action" under subs.(1)(a) for the purpose of obtaining paid work within any applicable limitations is obviously in general a matter of judgment. That includes a judgment about what counts as "action" and about the significance of any potential action that has not been taken. The actions mentioned in subs.(3) might be a starting point, but other things could plainly count, such as carrying out research into the job market or potential for self-employment. No doubt just sitting and thinking falls the other side of the line, but can often form an essential element of the hours devoted to some more active action. Subsection (3) does not include in its list accepting an offer of suitable work. However, it could certainly be argued that a claimant who failed to accept such an offer had failed to take all reasonable action for the purpose of obtaining paid work. A medium-level sanction could then follow under s.27(2)(a) if the failure was for no good reason unless the case fell within s.26(2)(c) (failing for no good reason to comply with a work availability requirement by taking up an offer of paid work). There is a certain artificiality to the s.26(2)(c) sanction (see the notes to that section) but no doubt in practice decision-makers will prefer to use that provision first in a case where an offer of work has not been taken up. If for any reason that provision does not apply, it can be argued that s.27(2)(a) and s.17(1)(a) should be considered in addition. It seems very unlikely that in practice the Secretary of State would ever be in a position to specify under sub.(1) that a claimant should accept a particular offer of paid work.

Regulation 95 of the Universal Credit Regulations deems a claimant not to have complied with the requirement unless quite stringent conditions about the weekly hours devoted to work search are satisfied. See the notes to reg.95 and remember that the sanctions in s.26(4)(a), in relation to having, before claiming universal credit, failed to take up an offer of paid work, and s.27(2)(a) can only be imposed when there was no good reason for the failure to comply. But note that the two alternative conditions in reg.95(1)(a) of spending at least the "expected hours" under reg.88 (starting point, 35) per week or of taking all reasonable action though for fewer than the expected hours are logically of equal status. A rigid approach that claimants are in general expected to devote 35 hours a week to work search is likely to lead into error. It is also arguable that if a claimant shows, say, that they have spent 35 hours on work search action in a week, they should only be regarded as not having taken all reasonable action in that week if that action does not give them the best prospects of obtaining work (reg.95(1)(b)). Paragraph 15 of *JS v SSWP (ESA)* [2013] UKUT 635 (AAC) suggests that if a claimant is patently not going to be able to obtain work at any stage or is already in a suitable apprenticeship or placement no action could make it more likely that work or more work would be obtained, so that no action could be legitimately specified.

The particular action that can be specified by Secretary of State under subs.(1)   **1.76**
(b) can, by subs.(3), include a number of actions, including those prescribed in regulations. No relevant regulation has yet been made. The list includes, at (c), creating and maintaining an online profile. That was relied on by the DWP to support requiring claimants to create a public profile and a public CV in Universal Jobmatch. There is helpful guidance on this in Memo ADM 15/16 of June 2016, which recognised that claimants could not be mandated to do that or create an email account from day one of their claim, merely encouraged, and that mandation was not to follow until the claimant had had an initial work search interview with a work coach. The requirement was not to be imposed unless the benefits of Universal Jobmatch had been explained, its use was reasonable in the claimant's individual circumstances (including health, learning problems, whether English was a second language, lack of appropriate literacy and numeracy skills), the claimant had access to the internet (including at a Jobcentre) and the cookies fact sheet had been issued. From May 14, 2018 Universal Jobmatch has been replaced by the Find a job service, run by Adzuna. Paragraphs K5171 – K5209 of the ADM apply effectively the same approach to Find a job. Paragraphs K5174 and K5175 explain the differences between Universal Jobmatch and the new service.

Particular vacancies could also be notified to a claimant within Universal Jobmatch and a requirement to apply notified through the claimant commitment. A failure for no good reason to comply with such a requirement leads to a higher-level sanction under s.26(2)(b). Memo ADM 15/16 suggests that if a claimant subject to such a sanction has also failed to take all reasonable action for the purposes of obtaining paid work by not applying for enough notified vacancies, there can also be a medium-level sanction under s.27(2)(a). However, it is arguable that an imposition of the medium-level sanction in those circumstances would contravene s.27(3) (no s.27 sanction if failure is also a s.26 sanctionable failure).

Where a claimant has been required to apply for a particular vacancy, reg.94 of the Universal Credit Regulations deems the work search requirement not to have been complied with where the claimant fails to participate in an interview offered in connection with the vacancy.

There is no requirement that the specification under subss.(1)(b), (2) and (3) of the particular actions to be taken and the time to be devoted to them should be in writing or in other permanent form. However, good practice, plus the potential need for acceptable evidence of the existence and terms of the specification in the light of the principle that the claimant should in sanctions cases be given the benefit of any doubt that might reasonably arise (*DL v SSWP (JSA)* [2013] UKUT 295 (AAC)), must surely point to the need for written or computer records to be kept and to be available to the claimant for reference. See the notes to ss.14 and 16 for the potential application of the "prior information duty" in requiring the claimant to be given an opportunity to make informed and meaningful representations about the actions proposed to be specified before they are imposed.

Note that under s.23(1) the Secretary of State is empowered to require a claimant to participate in an interview relating to the imposition of a work-related requirement on the claimant or assisting the claimant to comply with a requirement. Under s.23(3) he can require the provision of information and evidence for the purpose of verifying compliance and that the claimant confirm compliance in any manner. A failure for no good reason to comply with any of those connected requirements is also sanctionable under s.27(2)(b).

Work availability requirement

1.77   **18.**—(1) In this Part a "work availability requirement" is a requirement that a claimant be available for work.

(2) For the purposes of this section "available for work" means able and willing immediately to take up paid work (or more paid work or better-paid work).

(3) Regulations may impose limitations on a work availability requirement by reference to the work to which it relates; and the Secretary of State may in any particular case specify further such limitations on such a requirement.

(4) A limitation under subsection (3) may in particular be by reference to—

(a) work of a particular nature,
(b) work with a particular level of remuneration,
(c) work in particular locations, or
(d) work available for a certain number of hours per week or at particular times,

and may be indefinite or for a particular period.

(5) Regulations may for the purposes of subsection (2) define what is meant by a person being able and willing immediately to take up work.

DEFINITION

"claimant"—see s.40.

GENERAL NOTE

Temporary Coronavirus Provisions
1.78   Regulation 6(1)(c) of the Social Security (Coronavirus) (Further Measures) Regulations 2020 (SI 2020/371) provides that for a period of three months beginning on March 30, 2020 any work availability requirement imposed on anyone who has an award of universal credit is to operate as if "able and willing immediately to take up paid work" means able and willing to do so, or to attend an interview, once reg.6 ceases to apply. Although reg.6 refers to the provision being a consequence of the

outbreak of coronavirus disease, it is not necessary that the claimant in question be affected in any way by that outbreak or the resulting economic disruption. It is not clear what is intended by the restriction to someone who has an award of universal credit. There would be no consistency in suspending the work availability requirement for someone who happened to have an existing award on March 30, 2020, but not allowing an award to be made on a new claim because the claimant had not accepted a claimant commitment containing the requirement that the Secretary of State was bound to impose under s.22(2)(b), so that reg.6 of the Further Measures Regulations was never reached because the claimant never had an award. Such a result was plainly not intended (and was not applied in practice), so is to be avoided if possible, but para.11 of Memo ADM 04/20 gives no clue as to the mechanism for doing so. It is suggested that, provided that it had been accepted under reg.16(b) of the Universal Credit Regulations that the claimant could be entitled without having accepted a claimant commitment (see the notes to s.4(1)(e) and reg.16) and all the other basic conditions in s.4(1) were met, an award could be made to the claimant before consideration of what work-related requirements were to be imposed, so that then reg.6 could apply to modify the Secretary of State's s.22(2) duty to impose the work search and work availability requirements.

See the notes to s.17 for the effect of reg.6 on the work search requirement.

The effect of reg.6 expires at the end of November 12, 2020 (reg.10(2)), subject to any amendment. The power to extend the three-month period was not exercised before it expired. When it was announced (Parliamentary answer, Under-Secretary of State, Mims Davies, WQ 62431) that from July 1, 2020 the requirement for universal credit claimants to accept a claimant commitment was being reintroduced, it was stressed that claimant commitments agreed or reviewed from that date (i.e. the work-related requirements included) would have to be reasonable for the "new normal" and acknowledge the reality of a person's local jobs market and personal circumstances.

This section defines "work availability requirement" for the particular purpose of s.22, under which the requirement must be imposed on all claimants except those exempted by s.19, 20 or 21. See the notes to s.14 for discussion of whether the current standard terms of claimant commitments are sufficient in themselves to *impose* such a requirement. It requires in general that a claimant be able and willing immediately to take up paid work, or more or better-paid work. "Paid work" is not defined in the Act, nor is it defined in regulations for the specific purpose of ss.18 and 22. However, under the power in s.25, reg.96 of the Universal Credit Regulations deems the work availability requirement not to have been complied with in certain circumstances and to have been satisfied in other circumstances and makes references to "paid work". For those purposes, the definition in reg.2 will apply, i.e. work done for payment or in expectation of payment, excluding work for a charity or voluntary organisation, or as a volunteer, in return for expenses only. Regulation 87 adds nothing to the terms of s.18 itself. Thus it appears that willingness to take up both self-employment and employment can be considered. Under the ordinary meaning of the phrase "paid work" it would seem that voluntary work or unpaid internship or work placements are excluded (but see s.16 on work preparation).

For some suggestions as to a common sense approach to "immediately", in the specific context of reg.7 of the JSA Regulations 1996, see Simon Brown LJ in *Secretary of State for Social Security v David*, reported in *R(JSA) 3/01*, at paras 25 and 26:

1.78.1

"That 'immediately' means within a very short space of time indeed is clear not only from the word itself but also from regulation 5 which provides for exceptions to this requirement in the case of those with caring responsibilities or engaged in voluntary work (who need only be willing and able to take up employment on 48 hours' notice) and certain others engaged in providing a service (who get 24 hours' notice). No doubt the requirement for immediate availability allows the claimant time to wash, dress and have his breakfast, but strictly it would seem inconsistent with, say, a claimant's stay overnight with a friend or relative, or attendance at a weekend cricket match, or even an evening at the cinema (unless perhaps he had left a contact number and had not travelled far).

26. In these circumstances, claimants ought clearly to be wary of entering into an agreement which offers unrestricted availability throughout the entire week, day and night, weekdays and weekends."

Subsections (3) and (4) allow regulations to impose limitations on the kind of work for which a claimant can be required to be available and also allow the Secretary of State to specify further limitations. Regulation 97 contains the prescribed limitations, in terms of hours of work for carers and those with a disability, of the maximum time for travel to and from work and of the type of work recently undertaken. See the notes to reg.97. There appears to be no limitation on the number of hours a week that work could involve while still falling for consideration, apart from in the cases of the particular categories of claimant identified in reg.97(2).

Subsection (5) allows regulations to define what is meant in subs.(1) by being able and willing immediately to take up work. Regulation 99(1)(b) of the Universal Credit Regulations uses this power to provide that claimants in any of the circumstances set out in reg.99(3), (4), (4A) or (5) are regarded as being available for work if able and willing to take up paid work or attend an interview immediately after the relevant circumstance ceases to apply. See also the provisions of reg.99(2B) with (5A) and reg.99(2C) with (5B). Regulation 96(1) deems the work availability requirement not to be complied with if the claimant is not able and willing immediately to attend an interview in connection with finding paid work. Regulation 96(2) to (5) defines circumstances in which carers, those doing voluntary work and those in paid employment are to be treated as having complied with the requirement, where it is accepted that some longer notice than "immediately" is needed. Those provisions can only apply subject to any modifications to the availability requirement made by reg.99. Regulation 98 prevents the imposition of any work-related requirement on recent victims of domestic violence.

1.79 It is notable, by contrast with the position that will be familiar to many readers from old style JSA and, before it, unemployment benefit, that being available for work is not a condition of entitlement to universal credit, failure to satisfy which means that there can be no entitlement to benefit at all, although it is a condition of entitlement under s.4(1)(e) to accept a claimant commitment that should record the requirement. Instead, a failure to comply with the work availability requirement, if imposed on a claimant, is merely a potential basis for a sanction under ss.26 or 27. Under s.26(2)(c) a higher-level sanction can be imposed if a claimant fails for no good reason to comply by not taking up an offer of paid work. Section 27(2)(a) allows the imposition of a medium-level sanction for a failure for no good reason to comply with any work-related requirement.

Note that under s.23(1) the Secretary of State is empowered to require a claimant to participate in an interview relating to the imposition of a work-related requirement on the claimant or assisting the claimant to comply with a requirement. Under s.23(3) he can require the provision of information and evidence for the purpose of verifying compliance and that the claimant confirm compliance in any manner. A failure for no good reason to comply with any of those connected requirements is also sanctionable under s.27(2)(b).

Application of work-related requirements

Claimants subject to no work-related requirements

1.80 **19.**—(1) The Secretary of State may not impose any work-related requirement on a claimant falling within this section.

(2) A claimant falls within this section if—

(a) the claimant has limited capability for work and work-related activity,

(b) the claimant has regular and substantial caring responsibilities for a severely disabled person,

(c) the claimant is the responsible carer for a child under the age of 1, or

(d) the claimant is of a prescribed description.

(3) Regulations under subsection (2)(d) may in particular make provision by reference to one or more of the following—

(a) hours worked;

(b) earnings or income;

(c) the amount of universal credit payable.

(4) Regulations under subsection (3) may—

(a) in the case of a claimant who is a member of the couple, make provision by reference to the claimant alone or by reference to the members of the couple together;

(b) make provision for estimating or calculating any matter for the purpose of the regulations.

(5) Where a claimant falls within this section, any work-related requirement previously applying to the claimant ceases to have effect.

(6) In this Part "responsible carer", in relation to a child means—

(a) a single person who is responsible for the child, or

(b) a person who is a member of a couple where—

(i) the person or the other member of the couple is responsible for the child, and

(ii) the person has been nominated by the couple jointly as responsible for the child.

DEFINITIONS

"claimant"—see s.40.
"limited capability for work"—*ibid.*
"limited capability for work-related activity"—*ibid.*
"regular and substantial caring responsibilities"—*ibid.*
"severely disabled"—*ibid.*
"work-related requirement"—see ss.40 and 13(2).

GENERAL NOTE

The default position in s.22 is that a claimant is, unless falling within ss.19–21, **1.81** to be subject to all work-related requirements, i.e. the work search and work availability requirements, with the optional additions of a work-focused interview and/ or a work preparation requirement. Section 19 defines the circumstances in which no work-related requirement at all may be imposed. Under reg.98 of the Universal Credit Regulations, made under s.24(5) below, recent victims of domestic violence must be free of any work-related requirement for a period of 13 weeks, subject to an extension for a further 13 weeks in relation to the work search and work availability requirements for responsible carers of children (reg.98(1A)). Where a claim has to be made jointly by both members of a couple, both are claimants and it must be asked separately whether work-related requirements can be imposed on each. Note that a claimant who cannot, by virtue of s.19, have any work-related requirement imposed may nevertheless be required by the Secretary of State under s.23(1)(a) to participate in an interview relating to the possible imposition of any such requirement.

Subsection (2)

Three categories are specifically identified in subs.(2)(a)–(c). Others can, and **1.82** have been, prescribed in regulations (subss.(2)(d) and (3)–(4)):

(a) Claimants who have limited capability for work and for work-related activity cannot have any work-related requirement imposed. Once claimants who currently qualify for employment and support allowance (ESA) fall within the ambit of universal credit, limited capability will be tested in essentially the same way as for ESA. Note that claimants who do not fall within s.19(2)(a) are exempted from the application of the work search and work availability requirements if they have limited capability for work, but not limited capability for work-related activity (s.21(1)(a)). Under reg.99 of the Universal Credit Regulations claimants who are unfit for work (not further defined) and provide prescribed evidence cannot have the work search requirement imposed and have the work availability requirement modified, for limited periods. See the notes to reg.99 for the details of the various permutations of circumstances covered.

(b) Claimants who have regular and substantial caring responsibilities for a severely disabled person cannot have any work-related requirement imposed. Although s.40 allows the meaning of "regular and substantial caring responsibilities" and "severely disabled person" to be prescribed separately in regulations, reg.30 of the Universal Credit Regulations defines the two phrases in combination in terms of meeting the conditions of entitlement to carer's allowance, disregarding the earnings conditions. There seems no reason why that should not be valid. The test is therefore, in brief, that the person cared for is entitled to attendance allowance, at least the middle rate of the care component of disability living allowance, the standard or enhanced rate of the daily living component of personal independence payment or armed forces independence payment and that the carer devotes at least 35 hours per week to caring for such a person. But note that by virtue of reg.30(3) anyone who derives any earnings from the caring is excluded from the definition. See the extension in reg.89(1)(b) of the Universal Credit Regulations, under para.(d) below.

(c) Claimants who are the responsible carer for a child under the age of one cannot have any work-related requirement imposed. By subs.(6) a responsible carer is a person who is responsible for a child or, for couples, either partner nominated jointly provided one is responsible for the child. Regulation 4 of the Universal Credit Regulations, made under para.5 of Sch.1 to the WRA 2012, sets out how responsibility is to be determined. See the notes to reg.4.

(d) Regulations 89 and 90 of the Universal Credit Regulations set out the additional categories of claimant who cannot have any work-related requirement imposed. Regulation 90 covers the special rules needed by virtue of the special characteristic of universal credit as both an in-work and an out-of-work benefit. It thus exempts claimants whose earnings are of an amount at least equal to a threshold figure, calculated by reference to the national minimum wage and differing weekly hours for different groups of claimants. That in most cases produces a relatively high figure. For claimants with earnings below that threshold, see the effect of reg.99 on the work search and work availability requirements.

Regulation 89 covers more general categories. Regulation 89(1)(b) allows in some claimants who do not quite meet the conditions of subs.(2)(b). Regulation 89(1)(d) and (f) allow in some claimants who do not quite meet the conditions of subs.(2)(c). Regulation 89(1)(a) applies to claimants who have reached the qualifying age for state pension credit, i.e. state pension age. Regulation 89(1)(c) brings in women for shortish periods before and after confinement. Regulation 89(1)(e) brings in some claimants in education.

Claimants subject to work-focused interview requirement only

1.83   **20.**—(1) A claimant falls within this section if—

(a) the claimant is the responsible carer for a child who is aged [¹1], or

(b) the claimant is of a prescribed description.

(2) The Secretary of State may, subject to this Part, impose a work-focused interview requirement on a claimant falling within this section.

(3) The Secretary of State may not impose any other work-related requirement on a claimant falling within this section (and, where a claimant falls within this section, any other work-related requirement previously applying to the claimant ceases to have effect).

AMENDMENT

1. Welfare Reform and Work Act 2016 s.17(1)(a) (April 3, 2017).

DEFINITIONS

"claimant"—see s.40.
"responsible carer"—see ss.40 and 19(6).
"work-focused interview requirement"—see ss.40 and 15(1).
"work-related requirement"—see ss.40 and 13(2).

GENERAL NOTE

The default position in s.22 is that a claimant is, unless falling within ss.19–21, to be subject to all work-related requirements, i.e. the work search and work availability requirements, with the optional additions of a work-focused interview and/or a work preparation requirement. Section 20 defines the circumstances in which a claimant who does not fall within s.19 (no work-related requirements) can have a work-focused interview requirement, but not any other requirement, imposed. If the conditions of s.20(1) are met, there is a discretion whether actually to impose the work-focused interview requirement (subs.(2): "may"). Where a claim has to be made jointly by both members of a couple, both are claimants and it must be asked separately whether work-related requirements can be imposed on each. Note that under s.23 the Secretary of State may require a claimant to participate in an interview for purposes relating to the imposition of any work-related requirement, verifying compliance with any work-related requirement or assisting the claimant's compliance with any work-related requirement. He may also require the reporting of relevant changes of circumstances.

1.84

See s.24 for the process of imposing a requirement.

Section 19(1)(c) exempts responsible carers (defined in s.19(6)) of children under the age of one from all work-related requirements (and there are slight extensions in reg.89 of the Universal Credit Regulations). So no further protection is needed where a child is under the age of one. The scope of the protection given by s.20 to limit the permissible work-related requirements that can be imposed on a claimant has been narrowed considerably since April 2013. Initially, in combination with reg.91(1), subs.(1)(a) applied where the child in question was aged less than five. In April 2014, the crucial age was reduced to three, but with some further protection under s.21(1)(b) in combination with a new reg.91A for responsible carers of children aged three or four, who could not have any work-related requirements other than the work-focused interview or work preparation requirement imposed. The April 2017 amendments limit subs.(1)(a) to responsible carers of a child aged one (not under or over that age) and take away the power to prescribe any different age in regulations. As a result, reg.91(1), which had carried out the prescription previously required by subs.(1)(a), has been revoked. The further protection under s.21(1) has been limited to responsible carers of children aged two (subs.(1)(aa)) and reg.91A has been revoked.

Under s.20(1)(b), reg.91(2) continues to extend the effect of the provision to responsible foster carers of any child aged from one to 15 and to certain categories of foster parents and "friend and family carers". It seems anomalous that "ordinary" responsible carers should be treated less favourably then those groups, but no challenge under the Human Rights Act 1998 on the ground of discrimination could lead to any finding that the amendments were invalid, since they were all carried out by primary legislation.

The nature of the requirement and the purposes of the interview are defined in s.15 and reg.93 of the Universal Credit Regulations.

Claimants subject to work preparation requirement

1.85   **21.**—(1) A claimant falls within this section if the claimant does not fall within section 19 or 20 and—

(a) the claimant has limited capability for work,

[¹ (aa) the claimant is the responsible carer for a child who is aged 2,] or

(b) the claimant is of a prescribed description.

(2) The Secretary of State may, subject to this Part, impose a work preparation requirement on a claimant falling within this section.

(3) The Secretary of State may also, subject to this Part, impose a work-focused interview requirement on a claimant falling within this section.

(4) The Secretary of State may not impose any other work-related requirement on a claimant falling within this section (and, where a claimant falls within this section, any other work-related requirement previously applying to the claimant ceases to have effect).

(5) [¹ . . .]

AMENDMENT

1. Welfare Reform and Work Act 2016 s.17(1) (April 3, 2017).

DEFINITIONS

"claimant"—see s.40.
"limited capability for work"—see ss.40 and 37(1).
"prescribed"—see s.40.
"responsible carer"—see ss.40 and 19(6).
"work preparation requirement"—see ss.40 and 16(1).
"work-focused interview requirement"—see ss.40 and 15(1).
"work-related requirement"—see ss.40 and 13(2).

GENERAL NOTE

1.86   The default position in s.22 is that a claimant is, unless falling within ss.19–21, to be subject to all work-related requirements, i.e. the work search and work availability requirements, with the optional additions of a work-focused interview and/or a work preparation requirement. Section 21 defines the circumstances in which a claimant who does not fall within ss.19 or 20 (no work-related requirements or work-focused interview requirement only) can have a work preparation requirement and, under subs.(3), a work-focused interview requirement, but not any other requirement, imposed. Under s.23(1) the Secretary of State is empowered to require a claimant to attend an interview relating to the imposition of a work-related requirement, verifying compliance with any work-related requirement or assisting the claimant's compliance with any work-related requirement. He may also require the reporting of relevant changes of circumstances. Where a claim has to be made jointly by both members of a couple, both are claimants and it must be asked separately whether work-related requirements can be imposed on each.

See s.24 for the process of imposing a requirement. Note that there is a discretion ("may") to impose the requirement if the conditions are met.

Initially, the only claimants covered by s.21 were those with limited capability for work (but not limited capability for work-related activity, which would take the claimant into s.19(2)(a)) under subs.(1)(a), because no regulations had been made under subs.(1)(b). The duty in subs.(5) to make regulations did not arise in practice because any claimant who was the responsible carer for a child aged three or four fell within s.20(1)(b) by virtue of reg.91(1) of the Universal Credit Regulations as they stood at the time. In the period from April 6, 2014, when the crucial age under s.20(1)(a) was reduced to three, a prescription became necessary, which produced a new reg.91A. With effect from April 3, 2017 and the restriction of the effect of s.20(1)(a) to children aged one (and not under or over that age), the protection of s.21 has been limited to responsible carers of a child aged two (and not under or over that age). The former duty in subs.(5) to make regulations in certain circumstances has been removed and reg.91A has been revoked.

The nature of the work preparation requirement is defined in s.16.

Claimants subject to all work-related requirements

22.—(1) A claimant not falling within any of sections 19 to 21 falls within this section.   1.87

(2) The Secretary of State must, except in prescribed circumstances, impose on a claimant falling within this section—

(a) a work search requirement, and

(b) a work availability requirement.

(3) The Secretary of State may, subject to this Part, impose either or both of the following on a claimant falling within this section—

(a) a work-focused interview requirement;

(b) a work preparation requirement.

DEFINITIONS

"claimant"—see s.40.
"prescribed"—*ibid.*
"work availability requirement"—see ss.40 and 18(1).
"work preparation requirement"—see ss.40 and 16(1).
"work search requirement"—see ss.40 and 17(1).
"work-focused interview requirement"—see ss.40 and 15(1).

GENERAL NOTE

Temporary Coronavirus Provisions

Regulation 6(1)(a) and (b) of the Social Security (Coronavirus) (Further   1.88
Measures) Regulations 2020 (SI 2020/371) provides that for a period of three months beginning on March 30, 2020 the Secretary of State cannot impose a work search requirement on anyone who has an award of universal credit and any existing work search requirement ceases to have effect from that date. Regulation 6(1)(c) provides that for the same period any work availability requirement imposed on anyone who has an award of universal credit is to operate as if "able and willing immediately to take up paid work" means able and willing to do so, or to attend an interview, once reg.6 ceases to apply. Thus, circumstances have been prescribed in which the duty in s.22(2) does not apply.

Although reg.6 refers to the provisions being a consequence of the outbreak of coronavirus disease, it is not necessary that the claimant in question be affected in any way by that outbreak or the resulting economic disruption. It is not clear what is intended by the restriction to someone who has an award of universal credit. There would be no consistency in lifting the work search requirement and suspending the work availability requirement for someone who happened to have an existing award on March 30, 2020, but not allowing an award to be made on a new claim because the claimant had not accepted a claimant commitment containing those requirements that the Secretary of State was bound to impose under s.22(2), so that reg.6 of the Further Measures Regulations was never reached because the claimant never had an award. Such a result was plainly not intended (and was not applied in practice), so is to be avoided if possible, but para.11 of Memo ADM 04/20 gives no clue as to the mechanism for doing so. It is suggested that, provided that it had been accepted under reg.16(b) of the Universal Credit Regulations that the claimant could be entitled without having accepted a claimant commitment (see the notes to s.4(1)(e) and reg.16) and all the other basic conditions in s.4(1) were met, an award could be made to the claimant before consideration of what work-related requirements were to be imposed, so that then reg.6 could apply to modify the Secretary of State's s.22(2) duty to impose the work search and work availability requirements.

The effect of reg.6 expires at the end of November 12, 2020 (reg.10(2)), subject to any amendment. The power to extend the three-month period was not exercised before it expired. When it was announced (Parliamentary answer, Under-Secretary of State, Mims Davies, WQ 62431) that from July 1, 2020 the requirement for universal credit claimants to accept a claimant commitment was being reintroduced, it was stressed that claimant commitments agreed or reviewed from that date (i.e. the work-related requirements included) would have to be reasonable for the "new normal" and acknowledge the reality of a person's local jobs market and personal circumstances.

1.88.1   This section sets out the default position that a claimant of universal credit is, unless falling within ss.19–21, to be subject to all work-related requirements, i.e. the work search and work availability requirements, with the optional additions of a work-focused interview and/or a work preparation requirement. Under s.23(1) the Secretary of State is empowered to require a claimant to attend an interview relating to the imposition of a work-related requirement, to the verification of compliance or to assisting the claimant to comply with a requirement. By contrast with other provisions, where this section applies the work search and work availability requirements *must*, subject to the exceptions prescribed in regs 98 and 99 of the Universal Credit Regulations, be imposed (subs.(2)), but there is a discretion about the other requirements (subs.(3)). See the notes to ss.19–21 for the circumstances in which either no or only some work-related requirements may be imposed. The content of the requirements is set out in ss.15–18 and associated regulations. Where a claim has to be made jointly by both members of a couple, and both are claimants it must be asked separately whether work-related requirements can be imposed on each. See s.24 for the process of imposing a requirement.

See the notes to s.14 for discussion of *JB v SSWP (UC)* [2018] UKUT 360 (AAC) and the question whether the current standard terms of claimant commitments (e.g. in the form of provisions like "I will also attend and take part in appointments with my adviser when required", "I will be available to attend a job interview immediately [and to] start work immediately" or "I will normally spend 35 hours per week looking and preparing for work") are sufficient in themselves to carry out the duty in s.22(1) and the power in s.22(2) to impose the specified work-related requirements. The judge considered that that question would rarely arise in practice and that what was important was whether consideration of all the evidence produced by the SSWP of communications to the claimant showed that the substance of the requirement in issue and the consequences of non-compliance had been properly notified to the claimant. In para.29 of *S v SSWP (UC)* [2017] UKUT 477 (AAC), the judge accepted that, if the SSWP failed to carry out the s.22(1) duty, the claimant should not bear the consequences of that (which must entail that the requirement(s) in question had not been imposed and there could be no sanction for failing to comply). That approach has in effect been confirmed in para.6 of *JB*, where it was said to be a condition precedent of the imposition of a sanction under s.27(2)(a) that the claimant was subject to the work-related requirement in question. See also the notes to ss.13, 14 and 24.

Work-related requirements: supplementary

Connected requirements

23.—(1) The Secretary of State may require a claimant to participate in   **1.89**
an interview for any purpose relating to—

(a) the imposition of a work-related requirement on the claimant;

(b) verifying the claimant's compliance with a work-related requirement;

(c) assisting the claimant to comply with a work-related requirement.

(2) The Secretary of State may specify how, when and where such an interview is to take place.

(3) The Secretary of State may, for the purpose of verifying the claimant's compliance with a work-related requirement, require a claimant to—

(a) provide to the Secretary of State information and evidence specified by the Secretary of State in a manner so specified;

(b) confirm compliance in a manner so specified.

(4) The Secretary of State may require a claimant to report to the Secretary of State any specified changes in their circumstances which are relevant to—

(a) the imposition of work-related requirements on the claimant;

(b) the claimant's compliance with a work-related requirement.

DEFINITIONS

"claimant"—see s.40.
"work-related requirement"—see ss.40 and 13(2).

GENERAL NOTE

This section gives the Secretary of State power to require a claimant to do various   **1.90**
things related to the imposition of work-related requirements, verifying compliance and assisting claimants to comply: to participate in an interview (subss.(1) and (2)); for the purpose of verifying compliance, to provide specified information and evidence or to confirm compliance (subs.(3)); or to report specified changes in a claimant's circumstances relevant to the imposition of or compliance with requirements. Such requirements do not fall within the meaning of "work-related requirement", but there is a separate ground of sanction under s.27(2)(b) for failing for no good reason to comply with them, but only for claimants subject to all work-related requirements or to the work preparation requirement (see reg.104(1) of the Universal Credit Regulations in conjunction with regs 102, 103 and 105). The Secretary of State is allowed under subs.(2) to specify how, when and where any interview under subs.(1) is to take place, so that there is no straightforward limit on the number or frequency of the interviews that may be specified, or on the persons who may conduct the interview. The interviews must of course properly be for one of the purposes specified in subs.(1). The requirement to participate in an interview cannot be used for punitive purposes or simply as a means of control of a claimant. The requirement, as now for new style JSA, is not attendance at an interview at the specified time and date, but participation in it. This would appear to mean that a claimant can be required to participate in an interview over the telephone, providing that that manner of conducting it has been specified under subs.(2). In an ambiguous (so far as JSA is concerned) Parliamentary answer on 24 November 2015 (UIN 17005), the Minister of State Priti Patel said:

"Under JSA, claimants are not sanctioned for failing to answer their telephone. In Universal Credit, claimants who have a prearranged telephone interview with their Work Coach, and who fail to participate without good reason, can be referred for a sanction decision."

There is no further provision about what participating in a work-focused interview entails. It must at least entail turning up at the place and time specified, although the decision of Judge Knowles in *SA v SSWP (JSA)* [2015] UKUT 454 (AAC) (see the notes to s.27 for full discussion) would indicate that tribunals should consider, in cases where the claimant arrives not very late, whether it is proportionate to the nature of all the circumstances to regard that as a failure to participate in an interview. There were all sorts of mitigating circumstances in *SA*, that may well not be present in other cases. See *SN v SSWP (JSA)* [2018] UKUT 279 (AAC), detailed in the notes to ss.26(2)(a) and 27(2)(a), for discussion of what might amount to a failure to participate (in that case in a mandatory work activity scheme) and the expression in para.45 of some doubt about the result in *SA*.

The requirement to participate must also extend to making some meaningful contribution to the interview, but the limits will probably not be established until some more sanctions appeals in JSA or universal credit reach the Upper Tribunal. Behaviour that leads to the premature termination of the interview may well amount to a failure to participate (see the facts of *DM v SSWP (JSA)* [2015] UKUT 67 (AAC) in the notes to s.27(2)(b)). There may, though, in cases of uncooperative claimants or heavy-handed officials or a combination, be difficult questions about when an interview has ceased to exist, so that subsequent behaviour cannot be relevant to whether there has been a failure to participate (see *PH v SSWP (ESA)* [2016] UKUT 119 (AAC) on failing to submit to a medical examination).

The compulsory imposition of a sanction for failure for no good reason to report specified changes in circumstances, to provide specified information and evidence or to confirm compliance with a work-related requirement is a new departure.

It was recognised in *CS v SSWP (JSA)* [2019] UKUT 218 (AAC), detailed in the notes to s.26(2)(a), that it was legitimate for a scheme provider to require an attender to verify their identity before starting a scheme, so that a refusal to do so would usually amount to a failure to participate in the scheme. The same principle could apply to an interview, but the particular issues that arose in *CS*, to do with a scheme provider external to the DWP, are unlikely to arise if it is an interview with a work coach or other adviser that has been notified.

See s.24 for the process of imposing a requirement.

Imposition of requirements

1.91
24.—(1) Regulations may make provision—
  (a) where the Secretary of State may impose a requirement under this Part, as to when the requirement must or must not be imposed;
  (b) where the Secretary of State may specify any action to be taken in relation to a requirement under this Part, as to what action must or must not be specified;
  (c) where the Secretary of State may specify any other matter in relation to a requirement under this Part, as to what must or must not be specified in respect of that matter.

(2) Where the Secretary of State may impose a work-focused interview requirement, or specify a particular action under section 16(1) or 17(1) (b), the Secretary of State must have regard to such matters as may be prescribed.

(3) Where the Secretary of State may impose a requirement under this Part, or specify any action to be taken in relation to such a requirement, the Secretary of State may revoke or change what has been imposed or specified.

(4) Notification of a requirement imposed under this Part (or any change to or revocation of such a requirement) is, if not included in the claimant commitment, to be in such manner as the Secretary of State may determine.

(5) Regulations must make provision to secure that, in prescribed circumstances, where a claimant has recently been a victim of domestic violence—
   (a) a requirement imposed on that claimant under this Part ceases to have effect for a period of 13 weeks, and
   (b) the Secretary of State may not impose any other requirement under this Part on that claimant during that period.
(6) For the purposes of subsection (5)—
   (a) "domestic violence" has such meaning as may be prescribed;
   (b) "victim of domestic violence" means a person on or against whom domestic violence is inflicted or threatened (and regulations under subsection (5) may prescribe circumstances in which a person is to be treated as being or not being a victim of domestic violence);
   (c) a person has recently been a victim of domestic violence if a prescribed period has not expired since the violence was inflicted or threatened.

DEFINITIONS

"claimant"—see s.40.
"work-focused interview requirement"—see ss.40 and 15(1).

GENERAL NOTE

This section contains a variety of powers and duties in relation to the imposition by the Secretary of State of either a work-related requirement or a connected requirement under s.23. It makes the imposition of a requirement and the notification to the claimant a moderately formal process, which raises the question of whether the decision of the Secretary of State to impose a requirement is a decision that is appealable to a First-tier Tribunal under s.12(1) of the SSA 1998, either as a decision on a claim or award or one which falls to be made under the WRA 2012 as a "relevant enactment" (s.8(1)(a) and (c) of the SSA 1998). However, if it is a decision not made on a claim or award, it is not covered in Sch.3 to the SSA 1998 (or in Sch.2 to the Decisions and Appeals Regulations 2013 (see below and in Vol.III)), so could not be appealable under that heading. The discussion in the note to s.12(1) of the SSA 1998 in Vol.III would indicate that, since the imposition of a requirement is not an "outcome" decision determining entitlement or payability of universal credit or the amount payable, it is not appealable under s.12(1)(a) as a decision on a claim or award or as a decision on another basis.

1.92

Thus, it appears that a direct challenge to the imposition of any particular requirement, including any element specified by the Secretary of State, and/or its inclusion in a claimant commitment under s.14 of this Act, can only be made by way of judicial review in the High Court, with the possibility of a discretionary transfer to the Upper Tribunal. Otherwise, a challenge by way of appeal appears not be possible unless and until a reduction of benefit for a sanctionable failure is imposed on the claimant for a failure to comply with a requirement. It must therefore be arguable that in any such appeal the claimant can challenge whether the conditions for the imposition of the requirement in question were met, with the result that, if that challenge is successful, the sanction must be removed. That appears to have been the assumption of the Supreme Court in *R. (on the application of Reilly and Wilson) v Secretary of State for Work and Pensions* [2013] UKSC 68; [2014] 1 A.C. 453. In para.29 of their judgment, Lords Neuberger and Toulson mentioned without any adverse comment Foskett J's holding at first instance that a consequence of a breach of a regulation requiring a claimant to be given notice of a requirement to participate in a scheme was that no sanctions could lawfully be imposed on the claimants for failure to participate in the scheme. Paragraph 6 of *JB v SSWP (UC)* [2018] UKUT 360 (AAC) states that it is a condition precedent of imposing any sanction under s.27(2)(a) that the claimant was subject to the work-related requirement in issue, thus confirming the approach in para.29 of *S v SSWP (UC)* [2017] UKUT 477 (AAC) that if a specific requirement has not been imposed by the SSWP no sanction can follow.

Subsection (1)

1.93   Regulation 99 of the Universal Credit Regulations is made in part under para.(a), reg.98 on domestic violence falling more specifically under subss.(5) and (6). No regulations appear to have been made under paras (b) and (c).

Subsection (2)

1.94   No regulations appear to have been made under this provision.

Subsection (3)

1.95   The inclusion of this express power to revoke or change any requirement, or any specification of action, is an indication of the formality entailed in the imposition of a requirement. However, there appears to be no restriction on the circumstances in which the Secretary of State may carry out such a revocation or change, subject of course to the legislative conditions being met for whatever the new position is. A mere change of mind without any change in circumstances or mistake or error as to the existing circumstances will do.

Subsection (4)

There is serious doubt whether the standard terms currently used in universal credit claimant commitments are sufficient in themselves to impose any work-related requirements (see the notes to s.14 for extensive discussion of the effect of the decision in *JB v SSWP (UC)* [2018] UKUT 360 (AAC)). If they are not, the necessity for notification by some other means, as allowed by subs.(4), becomes more important. It is necessarily implied in subs.(4) in conjunction with ss.13(1) and 22 that claimants are not subject to a work-related requirement if the Secretary of State has not notified them of its imposition: see para.29 of *S v SSWP (UC)* [2017] UKUT 477 (AAC), *SP v SSWP (UC)* [2018] UKUT 227 (AAC) and now para.6 of *JB* (above)). Careful consideration will need to be given by tribunals to what evidence of imposition by the Secretary of State and notification to the claimant has been put before them.

It is plainly arguable that no work-related or connected requirement can be imposed unless the claimant has received sufficient information about the requirement to enable them to make meaningful representations about whether the requirement should be imposed or not (the "prior information duty"). That duty stems from principles stated by the Supreme Court in *Reilly and Wilson* (above) and elaborated by the Court of Appeal in *Secretary of State for Work and Pensions v Reilly and Hewstone* and *Secretary of State for Work and Pensions v Jeffrey and Bevan* [2016] EWCA Civ 413; [2017] Q.B. 657; [2017] AACR 14. See the discussion in the notes to s.14, especially for points about when any breach of the duty might be material and when issues about the duty arise on appeals. If the process for the production of claimant commitments as described in the notes to s.14 is followed, there should be ample opportunity for the giving of sufficient information, although what happened in practice in individual cases will be what matters.

1.96   This provision allows the Secretary of State to notify the claimant of the imposition of any requirement, if not included in a claimant commitment under s.14, in any manner. Thus, it may be done orally (or presumably even through the medium of mime), but it is a necessary implication that a requirement must be notified to the claimant. That in turn implies that, whatever the manner of notification, the content must be such as is reasonably capable of being understood by the particular claimant with the characteristics known to the officer of the Secretary of State (so perhaps the medium of mime will not do after all). Less flippantly, this principle may be important for claimants with sensory problems, e.g. hearing or vision difficulties. The expectation of course is that the requirements imposed under the Act will be included in the claimant commitment, one of whose aims is to ensure that claimants know and understand what is being required of them and the potential consequences of failing to comply. That expectation may not in practice have been fulfilled. However, it is clear in law that the validity of a requirement is not dependent on inclusion in the claimant commitment. There is no such express condition and under s.14(4)(a) the Secretary of State is only under a duty to record in the claimant commitment such of the requirements under the Act as he considers it appropriate to include. It may be that the fact that a requirement is not recorded in the claimant commitment could be put forward as part of an argument for there having been a good reason for failing to comply with the requirement.

Subsections (5) and (6)

The duty to make regulations providing that no work-related requirement or connected requirement under s.23 may be imposed for a period of 13 weeks on a claimant who has recently been a victim of domestic violence is partially carried out in reg.98 of the Universal Credit Regulations. Most of the meat is in the regulation, including the definition of "domestic violence", which has been amended since April 2013. See the note to reg.98 for the details. However, subs.(6)(b) does define "victim" to include not just those on whom domestic violence is inflicted but also those against whom it is threatened.   1.97

Regulation 98 appears to be defective in that it applies only to work-related requirements, which in accordance with the definition in s.13(2) do not include connected requirements under s.23. Thus the duty in subs.(5) in relation to any requirement under Part 1 of the Act has not been fulfilled in relation to connected requirements. That defect cannot affect the application of reg.98 to work-related requirements.

Compliance with requirements

25. Regulations may make provision as to circumstances in which a claimant is to be treated as having—   1.98

    (a) complied with or not complied with any requirement imposed under this Part or any aspect of such a requirement, or

    (b) taken or not taken any particular action specified by the Secretary of State in relation to such a requirement.

GENERAL NOTE

Under subs.(a) regulations may deem a claimant either to have or not to have complied with any work-related requirement or connected requirement under s.23 in particular circumstances. Regulations 94–97 of the Universal Credit Regulations make use of this power, mainly in treating claimants as not having complied. No regulations appear to have been made as yet under subs.(b).   1.99

Reduction of benefit

Higher-level sanctions

26.—(1) The amount of an award of universal credit is to be reduced in accordance with this section in the event of a failure by a claimant which is sanctionable under this section.   1.100

(2) It is a failure sanctionable under this section if a claimant falling within section 22—

    (a) fails for no good reason to comply with a requirement imposed by the Secretary of State under a work preparation requirement to undertake a work placement of a prescribed description;

    (b) fails for no good reason to comply with a requirement imposed by the Secretary of State under a work search requirement to apply for a particular vacancy for paid work;

(c) fails for no good reason to comply with a work availability requirement by not taking up an offer of paid work;

(d) by reason of misconduct, or voluntarily and for no good reason, ceases paid work or loses pay.

(3) It is a failure sanctionable under this section if by reason of misconduct, or voluntarily and for no good reason, a claimant falling within section 19 by virtue of subsection (3) of that section ceases paid work or loses pay so as to cease to fall within that section and to fall within section 22 instead.

(4) It is a failure sanctionable under this section if, at any time before making the claim by reference to which the award is made, the claimant—

(a) for no good reason failed to take up an offer of paid work, or

(b) by reason of misconduct, or voluntarily and for no good reason, ceased paid work or lost pay,

and at the time the award is made the claimant falls within section 22.

(5) For the purposes of subsections (2) to (4) regulations may provide—

(a) for circumstances in which ceasing to work or losing pay is to be treated as occurring or not occurring by reason of misconduct or voluntarily;

(b) for loss of pay below a prescribed level to be disregarded.

(6) Regulations are to provide for—

(a) the amount of a reduction under this section;

(b) the period for which such a reduction has effect, not exceeding three years in relation to any failure sanctionable under this section.

(7) Regulations under subsection (6)(b) may in particular provide for the period of a reduction to depend on either or both of the following—

(a) the number of failures by the claimant sanctionable under this section;

(b) the period between such failures.

(8) Regulations may provide—

(a) for cases in which no reduction is to be made under this section;

(b) for a reduction under this section made in relation to an award that is terminated to be applied to any new award made within a prescribed period of the termination;

(c) for the termination or suspension of a reduction under this section.

DEFINITIONS

"claimant"—see s.40.
"prescribed"—*ibid.*
"work availability requirement"—see ss.40 and 18(1).
"work preparation requirement"—see ss.40 and 16(1).
"work search requirement"—see ss.40 and 17(1).

GENERAL NOTE

1.101 Sections 26–28 set up a very similar structure of sanctions leading to reductions in the amount of universal credit to that already imposed in the new ss.19–20 of the old style Jobseekers Act 1995 substituted by the WRA 2012 and in operation from October 22, 2012 (see Vol.II of this series). The similarity is in the creation of higher-level sanctions, here under s.26, and of medium, low and lowest-level sanctions, here under s.27, and in the stringency of the periods and the amount of reductions to be imposed, in particular for higher-level sanctions. See the discussion in the notes to s.19 of the Jobseekers Act 1995 in Vol.II. There are even more similarities to the structure of sanctions in ss.6J and 6K of the new style Jobseekers Act 1995, also introduced by the WRA 2012 and only in operation in relation to claimants to whom the universal credit provisions have started to apply. In all three places the maximum length of a higher-level sanction was initially three years, a very considerable increase on the previous position. On May 9, 2019, following a report of November 6, 2018 by the House of Commons Work and Pensions Committee on *Benefit Sanctions* (HC 995 2017–19), the Secretary of State (Amber Rudd) made a written statement to Parliament (HCWS1545) including the following:

> "I have reviewed my Department's internal data, which shows that a six-month sanction already provides a significant incentive for claimants to engage with the labour market regime. I agree with the Work and Pensions Select Committee that a three-year sanction is unnecessarily long and I feel that the additional incentive provided by a three-year sanction can be outweighed by the unintended impacts to the claimant due to the additional duration. For these reasons, I have now decided to remove three year sanctions and reduce the maximum sanction length to six months by the end of the year."

That decision was implemented, subject to qualification, in relation to universal credit by the amendment to reg.102 of the Universal Credit Regulations with effect from November 27, 2019 (see below).

There are, however, some differences in the wording of otherwise similar provisions made by different parts of the WRA 2012, which will be noted below. The sanctions framework is limited to the operation of work-related and connected requirements, so that universal credit claimants who fall outside that ambit cannot be sanctioned (although other consequences might follow failure to comply with some requirements). That result is secured through the general restriction of the application of s.26 to claimants who are subject to all work-related requirements under s.22 (except under subs.(3)) and through the scope of s.27 being limited to failures to comply with work-related or connected requirements.

The test of being subject to all work-related requirements is applied at the date of the sanctionable failure (or award of universal credit for pre-claim failures) and it does not in general affect the continuing operation of the sanction if the claimant ceases to be so subject. The reduction rate drops from 100% of the standard allowance to nil if the claimant begins to have limited capability for work and work-related activity (Universal Credit Regulations, reg.111(3)). The reduction rate drops to 40% if the claimant comes within s.19 (no work-related requirements) because of certain caring responsibilities for children under one (reg.111(2)). The DWP rejected the Work and Pensions Committee's recommendation in its report on *Benefit Sanctions* (above) that sanctions be cancelled when a claimant ceased to be subject to the requirement that led to the sanction (House of Commons Work and Pensions Committee, *Benefit Sanctions: Government Response* (HC 1949 2017-19, February 11, 2019, paras 49-51). It was said that that would undermine the incentive effect of the sanctions and that the mitigations in reg.111 were adequate. Note also the termination of a reduction when the claimant has been in paid work at a weekly rate of 35 times the hourly national minimum wage for 26 weeks (reg.109).

Note the important provision in reg.5 of the JSA Regulations 2013 that, if a claimant is entitled to both universal credit and new style JSA, no work-related requirements can be imposed under the new style JSA regime (ss.6B-6G of the new style Jobseekers Act 1995) and that the provisions for reduction of JSA on sanctions under ss.6J and 6K of that Act do not apply. See the annotations to reg.5 in Vol.II for discussion of the consequences.

The central concept under these provisions is of a "sanctionable failure", which under s.26(1) (subject to reg.113 of the Universal Credit Regulations), and s.27(1), is to lead to a reduction in the amount of an award of universal credit. For higher-level sanctions under s.26, the reduction for most adult claimants initially was in brief of 100 per cent of the claimant's individual standard allowance for 91 days for a first higher-level failure, 182 days for a second such failure (or a new style ESA or JSA failure) within a year and 1095 days for a third or subsequent such failure within a year. However, the amendment with effect from November 27, 2019 has changed the period in the third category to 182 days. That is in fulfilment of Amber Rudd's undertaking noted above. Regulation 5(3) of the amending Regulations makes the transitional provision that, where an award of universal credit is subject to a 1095-day reduction under s.26 as at November 27, 2019, that reduction is to be terminated where the award had been reduced for at least 182 days.

It must, though, be noted that there has been no amendment to reg.101(3) of the Universal Credit Regulations, which imposes a 1095-day limit on the total outstanding reduction period that is allowed. Because by virtue of reg.101(2) reduction periods under universal credit (as for new style JSA, but not old style JSA) run consecutively, the result is still that a claimant subject to a series of higher-level sanctions, each individually limited to 182 days, may be subject to a continuous reduction of benefit for up to 1095 days. The precise words of Amber Rudd's pledge set out above may thus have been carried out, but the effect is not as comprehensive as may have been thought.

There is no discretion under either ss.26 or 27 as to whether or not to apply a reduction if the conditions are met and no discretion under the regulations as to the amount and period of the reduction as calculated under the complicated formulae there. Regulation 113 of the Universal Credit Regulations, made under ss.26(8)(a) and 27(9)(a), sets out circumstances in which no reduction is to be made for a sanctionable failure. There is also provision for hardship payments under s.28.

As a matter of principle, a claimant has to be able, in any appeal against a reduction in benefit on the imposition of a sanction, to challenge whether the conditions for the imposition of sanction were met. See the note to s.24.

It has recently been stated that the Secretary of State need not in all sanctions cases provide evidence in the appeal bundle to support the satisfaction of all the preconditions to imposing a sanction, but that principle must be properly understood in context. In *SSWP v CN (JSA)* [2020] UKUT 26 (AAC), the claimant's sole ground of appeal against a sanction for failing to participate in the Work Programme by not attending an appointment was that she had never failed to keep an appointment (i.e. implicitly that she could not have received the notice of the appointment and/or had good cause under the regulations then in force). The tribunal allowed her appeal on the ground that the bundle did not contain a copy of the notice referring her to the Work Programme (i.e. the WP05) so that it was not satisfied that she had properly been notified of the requirement to participate. The tribunal appeared to think that that issue was one "raised by the appeal" within s.12(8)(a) of the SSA 1998, which it manifestly was not as the Secretary of State's submission in the bundle was that there was no dispute that the claimant was referred to the Work Programme. Nor did it give any explanation, if it had exercised its discretion under s.12(8)(a) to consider the issue, as to why it did so and how it was clearly apparent from the evidence so as to be capable of being dealt with under that discretion. Even if those hurdles had been overcome, the Secretary of State had not been given a fair opportunity to deal with the point. What evidence it was necessary for the Secretary of State to provide in the appeal bundle depended what issues have been put in dispute in the appeal. Having therefore set the tribunal's decision aside, Judge Wright substituted a decision finding on the evidence that the claimant had received the letter notifying her of the appointment in question.

The same approach was applied in *SSWP v SD (JSA)* [2020] UKUT 39 (AAC). There, the tribunal had raised and sought evidence on its own initiative on the issue whether the "prior information duty" (on which see the notes to s.14) had bee satisfied at the stage of initial referral to the Work Programme, which the claimant had never challenged. As well as the s.12(8)(a) problem, the tribunal had failed to explain why, even if there was a breach of the duty at that stage, the beach was material. In substituting a decision the judge rejected any unfairness in the referral to the

Work Programme and rejected on the evidence the claimant's contention about the appointment.

That view of what evidence must be provided in the appeal bundle as to satisfaction of the preconditions to imposing a sanction must be read in the light of the approach in *SSWP v DC (JSA)* [2017] UKUT 464 (AAC), reported as [2018] AACR 16, and *PO'R v DFC (JSA)* [2018] NI Com 1. There it was said that the Secretary of State should in all cases involving a failure to participate in some scheme or interview where notice of certain details of the scheme etc was required to be given, as well as notice of date, time and place, include in the appeal bundle a copy of the appointment letter, whether the claimant had raised any issue as to the terms of the letter or not. That was on the basis that unrepresented claimants could not be expected to identify technical issues about the validity of notices and it could not be predicted what particular issues might arise in the course of an appeal. If the letter was not included in the initial bundle, the decisions approved the action of tribunals in directing its production as a proper exercise of their inquisitorial jurisdiction. That exercise must rest on a use of the discretion in s.12(8)(a) to consider issues not raised by the appeal. The resolution of the approaches is no doubt that whenever a tribunal exercises that discretion it must do so consciously and explain why it has done so in any statement of reasons, and give the Secretary of State a fair opportunity to produce the document(s). It may be that an adequate explanation is to be found more readily when it is a notice of a specific appointment is in issue rather than an initial reference to a scheme. See also para.6 of *JB v SSWP (UC)* [2018] UKUT 360 (AAC), detailed in the notes to s.14.

Another important concept is that of a "good reason" for the conduct or failure to comply with a requirement under the WRA 2012. Most of the definitions of sanctionable failures in ss.26 and 27 incorporate the condition that the failure was "for no good reason". Paragraph 8 of Sch.1 to the Act allows regulations to prescribe circumstances in which a claimant is to be treated as having or as not having a good reason for an act or omission and to prescribe matters that are or are not to be taken into account in determining whether a claimant has a good reason. No regulations have been made under this power. There is no equivalent to reg.72 of the JSA Regulations 1996 (but the problem dealt with there is covered for universal credit by the allowance of limitations on work search and work availability requirements). The House of Commons Work and Pensions Committee (in para.111 of its report on *Benefit Sanctions*, above) recommended that regulations be introduced containing a non-exhaustive list of circumstances that could constitute good reason. The DWP (paras 66-69 of *Benefit Sanctions: Government Response*, above) rejected that recommendation as undermining flexibility, while noting that a list of good reasons is available in the DMG and on GOV.uk (the link provided in the response is to chapter K2 of the ADM for universal credit).

Thus, the concept of "good reason" remains an open-ended one, no doubt requir-   **1.102** ing consideration of all relevant circumstances but also containing a large element of judgment according to the individual facts of particular cases. The amount and quality of information provided to the claimant in the claimant commitment or otherwise about responsibilities under the WRA 2012 and the consequences of a failure to comply will no doubt be relevant, especially in the light of the approach of the Supreme Court in paras 65 and 66 of *R (on the application of Reilly and Wilson) v Secretary of State for Work and Pensions* [2013] UKSC 68; [2014] 1 A.C. 453 and of the Court of Appeal in *SSWP v Reilly and Hewstone* and *SSWP v Jeffrey and Bevan* [2016] EWCA Civ 413; [2017] Q.B. 657; [2017] AACR 14 (see the notes to s.14 above). Probably, in addition, as in the previously familiar concept of "just cause", a balancing is required between the interests of the claimant and those of the community whose contributions and taxes finance the benefit in question. See the discussion under the heading of "Without a good reason" in the note to s.19 of the old style Jobseekers Act 1995 in Vol.II of this series.

In *SA v SSWP (JSA)* [2015] UKUT 454 (AAC), a decision on s.19A(2)(c) of the old style Jobseekers Act 1995 and failing to carry out a jobseeker's direction,

Judge Knowles accepted the Secretary of State's submission that in determining whether a good reason had been shown for the failure all the circumstances should be considered and that the question was whether those circumstances would have caused a reasonable person (with the characteristics of the claimant in question) to act as the claimant did. Expressing the approach in such terms tends to point away from the notion of a balance.

However, there is a potentially significant difference in wording. In ss.26 and 27 and in ss.6J and 6K of the new style Jobseekers Act 1995 the condition is that the claimant fails "for no good reason", not that the claimant acts or omits to act "without a good reason". It may eventually be established that these two phrases have the same meaning, but in the ordinary use of language the phrase "for no good reason" carries a suggestion that something has been done or not done capriciously or arbitrarily, without any real thought or application of reason. It could therefore be argued that it is easier for a claimant to show that they did not act for no good reason and on that basis that the balancing of interests mentioned above could not be applicable. It would be enough that the claimant acted or failed to act rationally in the light of his or her own interests. It can of course be objected that such an argument fails to give the proper weight to the identification of what is a good reason and that it would seem contrary to the overall policy of the legislation if it was much easier to escape a universal credit sanction than an old style JSA sanction. On the other hand, it can be asked why Parliament chose to use a different phrase for the purposes of universal credit sanctions than "without a good reason" when the latter phrase could have fitted happily into ss.26 and 27. It is to be hoped that the ambiguity will be resolved in early decisions of the Upper Tribunal.

One of the points raised when permission to appeal to the Upper Tribunal was given in *S v SSWP (UC)* [2017] UKUT 477 (AAC) was whether "for no good reason" has any different meaning from "without a good reason". In para.54 Judge Mitchell expresses the view that there is no material difference and that both phrases refer to the absence of a good reason. However, the point made in the previous paragraph about a possible difference in meaning may not yet have been conclusively rejected, as it is not clear that in the particular circumstances of *S* it would have mattered which was adopted.

The case actually decides only a relatively short point about the meaning of "for no good reason" in ss.26 and 27 of the WRA 2012. The First-tier Tribunal had said that the claimant's professed ignorance of the effect of work (including part-time work) on his universal credit entitlement could not amount to a good reason for failing to undertake all reasonable work search action because ignorance of the law was no defence. On the claimant's appeal to the Upper Tribunal the Secretary of State accepted that, by analogy with the well-established case law on good cause for a delay in claiming, ignorance of the law was capable of constituting a good reason. The judge agreed that the tribunal had erred in law, but concluded that the error was not material because the only proper conclusion on the evidence was that the claimant could reasonably have been expected to raise with his work coach or other DWP official any concerns or confusions over the financial implications on his universal credit award of taking any of the sorts of work he had agreed to search for. Thus, even on the correct approach the claimant did not have a good reason for what the tribunal had concluded was a failure under s.27(2)(a).

It may also be that the analogy with good cause (indeed in para.57 the judge said that "good reason" expressed the same concept as "good cause" but in more modern language) is misleading or at least incomplete. That is because when considering good cause for a delay in claiming there is no difficulty in adopting the general meaning approved in *R(SB) 6/83* of some fact that, having regard to all the circumstances (including a claimant's state of health and the information that he had or might have obtained), would probably have caused a reasonable person of the same age and experience to act or fail to act as the claimant had done. It was in that context that the principle that a reasonable ignorance or mistaken belief as to rights could constitute good cause was established. But the question there is what a reasonable person could be expected to do to secure an advantage to them in the form of the benefit claimed late. In the context of universal credit sanctions, the notion of reasonableness carries a distinctly different force. So where the work search requirement under s.17(1)(a) to take all reasonable action to obtain paid work is concerned, reasonableness must be based on what level of activity the community that funds universal credit is entitled to expect from a claimant as a condition of receipt of the benefit. Similar, although not necessarily identical, factors are present in relation to the other work-related requirements and the sanctions for voluntarily and for no good reason ceasing work or losing pay. Although all personal circumstances are relevant, the notion of a balance between those circumstances and the claimant's proper responsibilities is not captured by the traditional concept of "good cause". The better analogy would seem to be with "just cause" as used in unemployment benefit and in old style JSA before the 2012 amendments. The adoption of the "good cause" approach in relation to claimed ignorance of rights in S cannot be taken as excluding such an approach. The full meaning of "for no good reason" remains to be worked out.

Subsections (2)–(4) set out what can be a sanctionable failure for the purposes of s.26 and higher-level sanctions. All except subs.(3) are restricted to claimants who are at the time of the sanctionable failure or the imposition of the sanction subject to all work-related requirements under s.22. Thus, claimants excused from all work-related requirements under s.19 (e.g. those with limited capability for work and work-related activity or with specified caring responsibilities) or from some element of such requirements under s.20 or 21 cannot be subject to higher level sanctions. They can be subject to s.27 sanctions. Subsections (5)–(8) give regulation-making powers.

Subsection (2)

(a) It is a higher-level sanctionable failure for a claimant subject to all work-related requirements to fail for no good reason (on which see the note above) to comply with a work preparation requirement under s.16 to undertake a work placement of a description prescribed in regulations. Regulation 114(1) of the Universal Credit Regulations prescribes Mandatory Work Activity as a work placement for the purposes of this provision (although the scheme has ceased to operate after April 2016) and reg.114(2) in its substituted form gives sufficient details of the scheme to satisfy the requirement in subs.(2)(a) to give a description and not just a label (the problem identified by the Court of Appeal in relation to the then state of the JSA legislation in *R (on the application of Reilly and Wilson) v Secretary of State for Work and Pensions* [2013] EWCA Civ 66; [2013] 1 W.L.R. 2239), as approved by the Supreme Court ([2013] UKSC 68; [2014] 1 A.C.453). That was decided in relation to s.17A(1) of the old style Jobseekers Act 1995 and reg.2 of the Jobseeker's Allowance (Mandatory Work Activity Scheme) Regulations 2011 (where the description of the scheme is in substance the same as in reg.114) by Hickinbottom J in *R (Smith) v Secretary of State for Work and Pensions* [2014] EWHC 843 (Admin). That conclusion and the judge's reasoning was in essence endorsed by the Court of Appeal on the claimant's appeal ([2015] EWCA Civ 229).

Before undertaking a Mandatory Work Activity scheme could have become a work preparation requirement under s.16 it must have been specified for the claimant in question by the Secretary of State and meet the condition of improving the particular claimant's work prospects. See *DM v SSWP (JSA)* [2015] UKUT 67 (AAC) on the sanction for failing to carry out a jobseeker's direction under s.19A(2) (c) and (11) of the old style Jobseekers Act 1995. There Judge Rowley, having referred to official guidance in the DMG, held that to be valid a direction had to be personalised and appropriate to the individual claimant. There was insufficient evidence to show that the "Group Information Session" in which the claimant had been directed to participate and which apparently turned out to be about the sanctions regime would have assisted the particular claimant to find employment or

1.103

improve his prospects of doing so, so that a sanction should not have been applied. The requirement is to take the action specified by the Secretary of State, so that the detail of the specification will be important in determining what amounts to a failure to comply with the requirement. There will be familiar issues, e.g. whether turning up to a scheme and then declining to co-operate or doing so only grudgingly amounts to a failure to comply.

In *PL v DSD (JSA)* [2015] NI Com 72, the Chief Commissioner for Northern Ireland has approved and applied the *obiter* suggestion of Judge Ward in *PL v SSWP (JSA)* [2013] UKUT 227 (AAC) (on the pre-October 2012 form of the Great Britain legislation) that in deciding whether a claimant had good cause for failing to avail himself of a reasonable opportunity of a place on a training scheme or employment programme a tribunal erred in law, where the circumstances raised the issue, in failing to consider the appropriateness of the particular scheme or programme to the claimant in the light of his skills and experience and previous attendance on any placements. Judge Ward's suggestion had been that the test was whether the claimant had reasonably considered that what was provided would not help him. It seems likely that a similar general approach will be taken to issues of "good reason" under s.26(2)(a) and (b) and, in the particular context of para.(a), the appropriateness of the work placement. It may though still need to be sorted out how far the issue turns on the claimant's subjective view, within the bounds of reasonableness, in the light of the information provided at the time, as against a tribunal's view of the appropriateness of what was to be provided. The Chief Commissioner made no comment on the treatment of the claimant's refusal to complete and sign forms with information about criminal convictions and health, that the First-tier Tribunal had found were reasonably required by the training provider as part of its application process for the scheme, as a failure by the claimant to avail himself of a reasonable opportunity of a place on the training scheme.

In *NM v SSWP (JSA)* [2016] UKUT 351 (AAC) Judge Wright held, as eventually conceded by the Secretary of State, that the inability to show that relevant DWP guidance had been considered before the claimant was given notice to participate in a Mandatory Work Activity scheme meant either that the claimant should not have been referred to the scheme (because the officer either would have followed the guidance or could have been persuaded to do so on representations from the claimant) or that he had good reason for not participating in the scheme. The appeal related to a sanction for failing to participate, through behaviour on the scheme. The guidance, in something called *Mandatory Work Activity Guidance* or *Operational Instructions – Procedural Guidance – Mandatory Work Activity – January 2012*, was relevant because at the time it instructed that claimants should not be considered for referral to Mandatory Work Activity if, among other circumstances, they were currently working (paid or voluntary). The claimant had been volunteering in a Sue Ryder shop, which he had to give up to attend the required scheme as a volunteer in a Salvation Army shop. The Secretary of State submitted that the guidance had since been changed to introduce an element of discretion about referral of claimants doing voluntary work. Judge Wright held that this would not excuse a failure by an officer of the Secretary of State to consider his own guidance or, on any appeal, to provide the guidance to a First-tier Tribunal in accordance with the principles of natural justice. The claimant in *NM* might also have had a good argument that in the light of his existing voluntary work the condition of making it more likely that the claimant would obtain paid work was not met.

SN v SSWP (JSA) [2018] UKUT 279 (AAC) discusses, from para.42 onwards, what can amount to a failure to participate in a scheme (at a time when the consequent sanction was under reg.8 of the MWAS Regulations, rather than s.19(2)(e) of the old style Jobseekers Act 1995). It confirms that conduct of the claimant related to the ordinary requirements of the work activity in question leading to the termination of their placement can amount to a failure to participate. The same principle could apply to a work placement prescribed under s.16 if the requirement were in terms of participation. In particular, it is held in paras 59-62 that actions before the start of the scheme can be relevant. In *SN* the claimant was required to work for four weeks as a retail assistant in a charity shop. As found by Upper Tribunal Judge Wright in substituting a decision on the appeal, the claimant visited the shop about a week before the placement was due to start, to find out what would be entailed. During the visit he used offensive language to one member of staff and about the nature of the work involved, that was unreasonable in any work setting. He attended at the shop at the specified time for the start of the placement, but, as the representative of the programme provider was not to arrive for about 20 minutes, retired to a changing cubicle to sit down, took off his shoes and appeared to go to sleep. When the representative arrived, the deputy manager of the shop told him that the claimant would not be allowed to work there in view of his earlier offensive conduct. The judge concludes that the combination of the claimant's behaviour on the earlier visit and his attitude of antagonism and lack of interest on the first day of the placement meant that he had failed to meet the notified requirements for participation in the scheme. There was no good cause for the failure to participate. Some doubt is expressed in para.45 about the result in *SA v SSWP (JSA)* [2015] UKUT 454 (AAC), where the claimant arrived 10 minutes late for a one-hour course (see para.1.114 below).

In *CS v SSWP (JSA)* [2019] UKUT 218 (AAC) Judge Hemingway accepted that it was legitimate for a scheme provider to require an attender to verify their identity before starting the scheme, so that a refusal to do so would usually amount to a failure to participate in the scheme (and, it would seem, to a failure to comply with a work preparation requirement to undertake a work placement under s.16 or to participate in an interview in relation to a requirement to apply for a particular vacancy under s.17). However, in the particular case the claimant had declined to verify various items of information about him appearing on a computer screen, largely because of misguided views about the effect of the Data Protection Act 1998, but also because of concerns about the security of social security information held by scheme providers. The judge held that the tribunal had erred in law by failing to make findings of fact about whether the claimant had been offered the opportunity to verify his identity by other means, e.g. by producing a passport or driving licence or other document in addition to the appointment letter that he had already produced. In the absence of such findings the tribunal had not been entitled to conclude that the claimant had refused to confirm his identity rather than merely refused to confirm it by the method initially put forward by the scheme provider. It might in other cases be relevant to enquire what the appointment letter or other documents do or do not say about confirming identity.

For a further example on its own facts (and no more than that) of a potential good reason for not undertaking a placement, see *GR v SSWP (JSA)* [2013] UKUT 645 (AAC), where it was held that a claimant with a genuine fear that prevented him going to the town where a course was to take place had good cause (under reg.7 of the Jobseeker's Allowance (Employment, Skills and Enterprise Scheme) Regulations 2011) for failing to participate in the scheme.

(b) It is a higher-level sanctionable failure for a claimant subject to all work-related requirements to fail for no good reason (on which see the note above) to comply with a work search requirement under s.17 to apply for a particular vacancy for paid work. It would seem that for there to have been a requirement to apply for a particular vacancy the taking of that action must have been specified by the Secretary of State under s.17(1)(b). See the note to s.17 for discussion of the meaning of "paid work", the notification of vacancies through Universal Jobmatch and requirements to apply for vacancies in the claimant commitment. It appears in the nature of the word "vacancy" that it is for employment as an employed earner, or possibly some form of self-employment that is closely analogous to such employment, e.g. through an agency.

In *MT v SSWP (JSA)* [2016] UKUT 72 (AAC) doubts were expressed whether registration with an employment agency could fall within the equivalent provision for old style JSA (s.19(2)(c) of the old style Jobseekers Act 1995), at least without evidence of some specific vacancy. It is not entirely clear whether a vacancy has actually to exist at the time that the Secretary of State specifies that the claimant is to apply for it or whether it is enough that a vacancy is about to arise at that point (compare the terms of s.19(2)(c)). It may be that it is enough that the requirement is conditional on the post becoming open for applications before the next meeting with the work coach, but the "failure" cannot take place until applications are possible. And the claimant must have been given sufficient information about the vacancy in order to have been able to make meaningful representations at the time about whether the requirement should be imposed (see notes to s.14 for discussion of the "prior information duty"). Some doubt was expressed in *CJSA/4179/1997* whether the offer of a "trial" as a part-time car washer properly fell within s.19(2)(c). It was suggested that if it did not, the case should have been considered under s.19(2)(d) (neglect to avail oneself of a reasonable opportunity of employment), to which there is no direct equivalent in the universal credit legislation (see the notes to para.(c) below). But if applying for or accepting the offer of the trial had been specified by the Secretary of State as a work search action under s.17, failure to comply for no good reason would be a sanctionable failure under s.27(2)(a) of the WRA 2012.

There is no express provision that the vacancy is for work that is suitable for the claimant in question. However, plainly the question of suitability would be relevant to the issue of whether a claimant had no good reason for failing to apply for the vacancy, even in the absence of the decisions in *PL v DSD (JSA)* and *PL v SSWP (JSA)* discussed in the note to para.(a) above. Regulation 113(1)(a) of the Universal Credit Regulations prevents any reduction in benefit being made when the vacancy was because of a strike arising from a trade dispute. According to the then Minister of State Esther McVey (House of Commons written answers April 2, 2014 and September 1, 2014) the instruction to Jobcentre Plus staff not to mandate claimants to apply for zero hours contracts applies only to JSA, not universal credit. However, again, and even though exclusivity clauses have been made unenforceable from May 26, 2015 by the new s.27A of the Employment Rights Act 1996, the suitability of such a contract for the particular claimant will certainly be relevant to the issue of no good reason.

1.104   Failure to apply for a vacancy no doubt encompasses an outright refusal to apply and also behaviour that is "tantamount to inviting a refusal by the employer to engage [the claimant]" (*R(U) 28/55*, para.7). In that case the claimant had presented himself for an interview for a job as a parcel porter in what the employer had described as a dirty and unshaven state, as a result of which he was not engaged. The Commissioner accepted that on the employer's evidence the claimant had neglected to avail himself of a reasonable opportunity of suitable employment. There is no reason why that general approach should not also apply in the present context.

It has long been accepted that a refusal or failure to complete an unobjectionable application form can amount to a failure to apply (see *R(U) 32/52* and *CJSA/2692/1999*). As Commissioner Howell noted in para.5 of *CJSA/4665/2001* there will be cases:

> "where the way a claimant completes or spoils a job application will be unsatisfactory and unfit to put in front of any employer so as to prevent it counting as a genuine application at all, so that he or she will have 'failed to apply': it is all a question of fact."

In *CJSA/4665/2001* itself, though, the Employment Service had refused to pass on otherwise properly completed application forms because the claimant had included criticisms of the Service and of government training initiatives. The Commissioner held that in the absence of any evidence that employers had been or would have been put off from considering the claimant by his comments or of any evidence of an intention to spoil his chances it had not been shown that he had failed to apply for the vacancies. A similar approach has been taken by Commissioner Rowland in a case in which the claimant disputed the necessity of including a photograph with the application form (*CJSA/2082/2002* and *CJSA/5415/2002*). As the employment officer did not have clear information from the employer contrary to the claimant's contention and had not tested the matter by submitting a form without a photograph, the sanction should not have been applied.

See the notes to para.(a) above for further discussion of good reason. Apart from the suitability and location of the work, personal, domestic and financial circumstances might be relevant. No doubt, as in the past, conscientious or religious objections would need particularly careful consideration. For instance, in *R(U) 2/77* (on neglect to avail) the claimant's sincerely held objection on what he described as moral grounds to joining a trade union were held to make to make an opportunity of employment unsuitable and unreasonable (and see *R(U) 5/71* for a case where a more intellectual conviction against joining a teachers' registration scheme did not have that effect). For a further example on its own facts (and no more than that) of a potential good reason for not applying for a vacancy, see *GR v SSWP (JSA)* [2013] UKUT 645 (AAC), where it was held that a claimant with a genuine fear that prevented him going to the town where a course was to take place had good cause (under reg.7 of the Jobseeker's Allowance (Employment, Skills and Enterprise Scheme) Regulations 2011) for failing to participate in the scheme.

In *KB v SSWP (UC)* [2019] UKUT 408 (AAC) the claimant failed to apply for a vacancy (as a barista) as she had agreed with her work coach to do. She said that she had later concluded that there was no point in applying, as she was temperamentally unsuited to the employer's requirements (she did not have "a passion for coffee" and was an introvert). The judge suggests that, in the absence of any further consultation with the work coach about the matter, there could not be a good reason for the failure. Although there was a misguided emphasis by the Secretary of State and the First-tier Tribunal on what the claimant agreed to do in her claimant commitment, there was no dispute that the Secretary of State had, through the work coach, "required" her to take the specified action of applying for the vacancy by, after discussion, saving the details to her Universal Jobmatch account.

Regulation 94 of the Universal Credit Regulations deems a claimant not to have complied with a requirement to apply for a particular vacancy for paid work where the claimant fails to participate in an interview offered in connection with the vacancy. Participation must at least entail turning up at the place and time for the interview, although the decision of Judge Knowles in *SA v SSWP (JSA)* [2015] UKUT 454 (AAC) (see the notes to s.27 for full discussion) would indicate that tribunals should consider, in cases where the claimant arrives not very late, whether it is proportionate to the nature of all the circumstances to regard that as a failure to participate in an interview. There were all sorts of mitigating circumstances in *SA*, that may well not be present in other cases. Participation must also extend to making some meaningful contribution to the interview, but the limits will probably not be established until there have been some more sanctions appeals to the Upper Tribunal. Behaviour that leads to the premature termination of the interview may well amount to a failure to participate (see the facts of *DM v SSWP (JSA)* [2015] UKUT 67 (AAC) in the notes to s.27(2)(b)). There may, though, in cases of uncooperative claimants or heavy-handed officials or a combination, be difficult questions about when an interview has ceased to exist, so that subsequent behaviour cannot be relevant to whether there has been a failure to participate (see *PH v SSWP (ESA)* [2016] UKUT 119 (AAC) on failing to submit to a medical examination).

See *SN v SSWP (JSA)* [2018] UKUT 279 (AAC) and *CS v SSWP (JSA)* [2019] UKUT 218 (AAC), detailed in the notes to para.(a) above, for further helpful discussion of what might amount to a failure to participate (in those cases in a mandatory work activity scheme and a work programme scheme) and the expression in para.45 of *SN* of some doubt about the result in *SA*.

Where non-compliance with the requirement to apply for a vacancy is constituted by failure to participate in an interview, good reason must extend to good reason for that failure to participate. There appear to be no provisions prescribing the length of notice of an interview to be given or how far a claimant can be required to travel, but there could plainly be a good reason for failing to comply with unreasonable requirements, especially if the claimant had attempted in advance to draw any problem with attendance to the attention of the Secretary of State or the potential employer. See reg.113(1)(a) of the Universal Credit Regulations excluding reductions in benefit on consideration of vacancies due to strikes arising from trade disputes.

(c) It is a higher-level sanctionable failure for a claimant subject to all work-related requirements to fail for no good reason (on which see the note above) to comply with a work availability requirement under s.18 by not taking up an offer of paid work. See the note to s.17 for discussion of the meaning of "paid work". Since the requirement under s.18 is in the very general terms of being able and willing immediately to take up paid work, the relevance of not taking up an offer can only be in revealing an absence of such ability or willingness. Therefore, both any limitations under reg.97 of the Universal Credit Regulations on the kinds of paid work that a claimant must be able and willing to take up immediately and the provisions of reg.96(2)–(5) on when a claimant is deemed to have complied with the requirement despite not being able to satisfy the "immediately" condition must be taken into account in determining whether a claimant has failed to comply with the requirement. See the discussion in the note to s.19(2)(c) of the old style Jobseekers Act 1995 in Vol.II of this series for what might amount to refusing or failing without a good reason to accept a situation, if offered, in any employment, but note that there may be differences between failing to accept a situation in employment and failing to accept an offer of paid work. Presumably a claimant escapes a sanction under this head by showing either a good reason for not accepting the particular offer, if that offer is compatible with the availability requirements currently imposed by the Secretary of State, or a good reason why those requirements should have been different in some way. See the notes to para.(a) above for discussion of the relevance of the suitability of the work in question for the particular claimant and *GR v SSWP (JSA)* [2013] UKUT 645 (AAC) and *KB v SSWP (UC)* [2019] UKUT 408 (AAC) mentioned there and at the end of the note to subs.(2)(b). See also reg.113(1)(a) of the Universal Credit Regulations excluding reductions in benefit on consideration of vacancies due to strikes arising from trade disputes.

(d) It is a higher-level sanctionable failure for a claimant subject to all work-related requirements to cease paid work or lose pay by reason of misconduct or voluntarily and for no good reason (on which see the note above). Since by definition the claimant must, if already subject to s.22, have an award of universal credit, this sanction can only apply to those claimants who are entitled to the benefit while in work. See the note to s.17 for discussion of the meaning of "paid work". See the note to subs.(4) below for discussion of the meanings of "misconduct" and "voluntarily and for no good reason", as well as of the implications of fixed and severe sanctions for losing pay apparently no matter what the amount of loss, subject to the exception from reductions in benefit in reg.113(1)(g) of the Universal Credit Regulations (earnings have not fallen below the level set in reg.99(6)). See the further exceptions in reg.113(1)(b) (trial periods in work where the claimant attempts hours additional to a limitation under ss.17(4) or 18(3)); (c) (voluntarily ceasing paid work or losing pay because of a strike); (d) (voluntarily ceasing paid work or losing pay as a member of the regular or reserve forces); and (f) (volunteering for redundancy or lay-off or short-time).

Subsection (3)

1.105
This provision applies to claimants with an award of universal credit who are subject to no work-related requirements under s.19(2)(d) because reg.90 of the Universal Credit Regulations, made under the specific powers in s.19(3), applies s.19 where the claimant's earnings equal or exceed the individual threshold, called by the DWP the conditionality earnings threshold. If the claimant ceases the paid work from which those earnings are derived or loses pay so that the earnings are then below the individual threshold, either by reason of misconduct or voluntarily and for

no good reason (on which see the note above), and does not fall within either s.20 or 21, a higher-level sanction is to be imposed. See the note to subs.(4) below for discussion of the meanings of "misconduct" and "voluntarily and for no good reason". The exception in reg.113(1)(g) of the Universal Credit Regulations (earnings have not fallen below the level set in reg.99(6)) cannot by definition apply if this provision applies. If reg.99(6) (weekly earnings exceed amount of old style JSA personal allowance by £5 or £10, called by the DWP the administrative earnings threshold) applies to the new level of earnings, no work search requirement can be imposed and the claimant therefore does not fall within s.22 (subject to all work-related requirements). In that case, subs.(3) cannot apply under its own terms and no exception is needed. If, as part of the ongoing process of working out an acceptable approach to in-work conditionality by subjecting claimants to pilot schemes under the Universal Credit (Work-Related Requirements) In Work Pilot Scheme and Amendment Regulations 2015 (in Part III below and see the notes to reg.99(6) and (6A) of the Universal Credit Regulations for discussion), entitlement is to be determined on the basis that reg.99(6) does not exist, then the terms of the exception in reg.113(1)(g) cannot apply either. A very slight decrease in earnings could, in a marginal case, have the effect identified in subs.(3), yet (no regulations having been made under subs.(5)(b)) the full force of the higher-level sanction must be imposed. It may be that in such circumstances it will be correspondingly easier for a claimant to show that a voluntary loss of pay was not "for no good reason". These issues will have to be worked out during the operation of the in-work conditionality pilot schemes mentioned above, which apparently expose claimants subject to them to very severe sanctions rules, although the DWP has stated that sanctions will be applied for failures to comply with in-work requirements under a pilot scheme "in the last resort" (see the notes to reg.99(6) and (6A)). See also the further exceptions in reg.113(1)(c) (voluntarily ceasing paid work or losing pay because of a strike); (d) (voluntarily ceasing paid work or losing pay as a member of the regular or reserve forces); and (f) (volunteering for redundancy or applying for a redundancy payment after lay-off or short-time).

Subsection (4)

Where a claimant has an award of universal credit and is subject to all work-related **1.106** requirements under s.22 it is a higher-level sanctionable failure if before making the claim relevant to the award the claimant for no good reason failed to take up an offer of paid work (para.(a)) or by reason of misconduct or voluntarily and for no good reason ceased paid work or lost pay (para.(b)). A practical limit to how far back before the date of claim such action or inaction can be to lead to a reduction of benefit is set by regs 102(4) and 113(1)(e) of the Universal Credit Regulations. If the gap between the action or inaction and the date of claim is longer than or equal to the period of the reduction that would otherwise be imposed, there is to be no reduction. Thus a lot depends on whether it is a first, second or subsequent "offence" within a year. These two grounds of sanction are the most similar to the familiar JSA grounds now in s.19(2)(a), (b) and (c) of the old style Jobseekers Act 1995.

Under para.(a), see the discussion in the note to subs.(2)(c), but note that this sanction applies to any offer of paid work. Therefore, all questions of whether the work is suitable for the claimant and whether or not it was reasonable for the claimant not to take it up will have to be considered under the "no good reason" condition. See the introductory part of the note to this section for the meaning of that phrase as compared with "without a good reason".

Under para.(b), it would appear that misconduct and voluntarily ceasing work will have the same general meaning as misconduct and leaving employment voluntarily for the purposes of old style JSA and, before it, unemployment benefit. See the extensive discussion in the notes to s.19(2)(a) and (b) of the old style Jobseekers Act 1995 in Vol.II of this series, which will not even be summarised here. The scope of the sanction has to be wider to take account of the nature of universal credit. Ceasing paid work certainly has a significantly wider meaning than losing employment as an employed earner if it encompasses self-employment in addition, as suggested in the note to s.17. The notion of ceasing paid work seems in itself wider than that of losing employment and to avoid difficulties over whether suspension from work without dismissal and particular ways of bringing a contract of employment to an end are covered. But remember that under reg.113(1)(f) of the Universal Credit Regulations a reduction cannot be applied on the ground of voluntarily ceasing work where the claimant has volunteered for redundancy or has claimed a redundancy payment after being subject to lay-off or short-time working, although the action remains a sanctionable failure. See also the exceptions for voluntarily ceasing paid work or losing pay because of a strike arising from a trade dispute or as a member of the regular or reserve forces (reg.113(1)(c) and (d)).

1.107   The other particularly significant widening of the scope of the sanction as compared with those in old style JSA is in the application of this and the similar sanctions under previous subsections to losing pay as well as to ceasing paid work. This is necessary, both in relation to circumstances before the date of claim and later, because it is possible for a claimant to be entitled to universal credit while still in paid work. If the earnings from the work are below the amount of the claimant's work allowance (if and as applicable according to circumstances) they are disregarded in the calculation of any award (see reg.22(1)(b) of the Universal Credit Regulations). If they exceed that amount, 63 per cent of the excess is taken into account as income to be set against the maximum amount of universal credit. If a claimant does not have a work allowance, 63 per cent of earnings are taken into account. There are also the rules, under s.19(2)(d) and (3), in reg.90 of the Universal Credit Regulations making a claimant subject to no work-related conditions if earnings are at least equal to an individual threshold (in the standard case the National Minimum Wage for 35 hours per week, with lesser hours used in defined circumstances), the conditionality earnings threshold. The sanction regime under subs.(4) can only apply when at the time of the award in question the claimant is subject to all work-related requirements under s.22 and so cannot be receiving earnings at or above that individual threshold. Subsection (3) above deals with the situation where during the course of an award of universal credit a claimant moves from having earnings at least equal to the individual threshold to a situation where the earnings are lower than that threshold. For loss of pay, short of the ceasing of work, prior to the date of claim to trigger the application of the sanction under subs.(3) it must be within a fairly narrow limit. To bring the claimant within the scope of s.22 the loss of pay must leave earnings below the individual threshold.

Subsection (5)

1.108   Regulations may deem ceasing work or losing pay not to be by reason of misconduct or voluntarily in certain circumstances and may provide that loss of pay below a prescribed level is to be disregarded. No such regulations have been made. Regulation 113 of the Universal Credit Regulations is made under the powers in subs.(8)(a) and only affects whether a reduction in benefit is to be imposed, not whether there is or is not a sanctionable failure.

Subsections (6) and (7)

1.109   See regs 101 and 106—111 of the Universal Credit Regulations for the amount and period of the reduction in benefit under a higher-level sanction. The three-year limit is imposed in subs.(6)(b) and cannot be extended in regulations.

Subsection (8)

1.110   Under para.(a), see reg.113 of the Universal Credit Regulations. Under para.(b), see reg.107. Under para.(c), see regs 108 and 109.

Other sanctions

1.111   27.—(1) The amount of an award of universal credit is to be reduced in accordance with this section in the event of a failure by a claimant which is sanctionable under this section.

(2) It is a failure sanctionable under this section if a claimant—

(a) fails for no good reason to comply with a work-related requirement;

(b) fails for no good reason to comply with a requirement under section 23.

(3) But a failure by a claimant is not sanctionable under this section if it is also a failure sanctionable under section 26.

(4) Regulations are to provide for—

(a) the amount of a reduction under this section, and

(b) the period for which such a reduction has effect.

(5) Regulations under subsection (4)(b) may provide that a reduction under this section in relation to any failure is to have effect for—

(a) a period continuing until the claimant meets a compliance condition specified by the Secretary of State,

(b) a fixed period not exceeding 26 weeks which is—

    (i) specified in the regulations, or

    (ii) determined in any case by the Secretary of State, or

(c) a combination of both.

(6) In subsection (5)(a) "compliance condition" means—

(a) a condition that the failure ceases, or

(b) a condition relating to future compliance with a work-related requirement or a requirement under section 23.

(7) A compliance condition specified under subsection (5)(a) may be—

(a) revoked or varied by the Secretary of State;

(b) notified to the claimant in such manner as the Secretary of State may determine.

(8) A period fixed under subsection (5)(b) may in particular depend on either or both the following—

(a) the number of failures by the claimant sanctionable under this section;

(b) the period between such failures.

(9) Regulations may provide—

(a) for cases in which no reduction is to be made under this section;

(b) for a reduction under this section made in relation to an award that is terminated to be applied to any new award made within a prescribed period of the termination;

(c) for the termination or suspension of a reduction under this section.

DEFINITIONS

"claimant"—see s.40.

"work-related requirement"—see ss.40 and 13(2).

GENERAL NOTE

See the introductory part of the note to s.26 for the general nature of the universal credit sanctions regime under ss.26 and 27 and for discussion of the meaning of "for no good reason". Section 27(1) and (2) requires there to be a reduction, of the amount and period set out in regulations, wherever the claimant has failed for no good reason to comply with any work-related requirement or a connected requirement under s.23. There is no general discretion whether or not to apply the prescribed deduction, but that is subject first to the rule in subs.(3) that if a failure is sanctionable under s.26 (and therefore subject to the higher-level regime) it is not to be sanctionable under s.27 and to the rules in reg.113 of the Universal Credit Regulations about when a reduction is not to be applied although there is a sanctionable failure (none of which currently apply to s.27). While the power and duty under subs.(4) for regulations to provide for the amount and period of the reduction

1.112

105

to be imposed is in fact more open-ended than that in s.26(6), because it does not have the three-year limit, subss.(5)–(7) introduce the specific power (that does not of course have to be used) for regulations to provide for the period of the reduction for a particular sanctionable failure to continue until the claimant meets a "compliance condition" (subs.(6)) or for a fixed period not exceeding 26 weeks specified in regulations or determined by the Secretary of State or a combination of both. The 26-week limit in subs.(5)(b) appears not to have any decisive effect because a longer period could always be prescribed under subs.(4)(b), unless "may" is to be construed as meaning "may only".

In practice, the powers have been used in the Universal Credit Regulations to set up a structure of medium-level (reg.103), low-level (reg.104) and lowest-level (reg.105) sanctions. See the notes to those regulations for the details.

The medium-level sanction applies only to failures to comply with a work search requirement under s.17(1)(a) to take all reasonable action to obtain paid work etc. or to comply with a work availability requirement under s.18(1). A failure to comply with a work search requirement under s.17(1)(b) to apply for a particular vacancy attracts a higher-level sanction under s.26(2)(b) if the claimant is subject to all work-related requirements. The reduction period under reg.103 is 28 days for a first "offence" and 91 days for a second "offence" or subsequent offence within a year of the previous failure (7 and 14 days for under-18s).

1.113   The low-level sanction under reg.104 applies where the claimant is subject either to all work-related requirements under s.22 or to the work preparation requirement under s.21 and fails to comply with a work-focused interview requirement under s.15(1), a work preparation requirement under s.16(1), a work search requirement under s.17(1)(b) to take any action specified by the Secretary of State or a connected requirement in s.23(1), (3) or (4). Note that this is the sanction that applies to a failure for no good reason to report specified changes in circumstances (s.23(4)) or to provide specified information and evidence (s.23(3)) as well as to failure to participate in an interview. The reduction period under reg.104 lasts until the claimant complies with the requirement in question, comes within s.19 (no work-related requirements), a work preparation requirement to take particular action is no longer imposed or the award terminates, plus seven days for a first "offence", 14 days for a second "offence" within a year of the previous failure and 28 days for a third or subsequent "offence" within a year (plus seven days in all those circumstances for under-18s).

The lowest-level sanction under reg.105 applies where a claimant is subject to s.20 and fails to comply with a work-focused interview requirement. The reduction period under reg.105 lasts until the claimant complies with the requirement, comes within s.19 (no work-related requirements), a work preparation requirement to take particular action is no longer imposed or the award terminates.

For the purposes of regs 104 and 105, "compliance condition" is defined in subs.(6) to mean either a condition that the failure to comply ceases or a condition relating to future compliance. A compliance condition may be revoked or varied by the Secretary of State, apparently at will, and may be (not must be) notified to the claimant in such manner as the Secretary of State might determine (subs.(7)). But under regs 104 and 105 a compliance condition has to be "specified" by the Secretary of State. On the one hand, it is difficult to envisage it being decided that the Secretary of State can specify such a condition to himself, rather than to the claimant. On the other hand, it is difficult to envisage it being decided that a claimant who has in fact complied with a requirement has not met a compliance condition merely because the Secretary of State failed to give proper notice of the condition. It appears that during the 2020 coronavirus outbreak any contact by the claimant with the DWP is being treated as compliance with any condition, thus bringing that part of the reduction period to an end.

The test of being subject to the work-related requirement in question is applied at the date of the sanctionable failure and it does not in general affect the continuing operation of the sanction if the claimant ceases to be so subject. The reduction rate drops from 100% of the standard allowance to nil if the claimant begins to have limited capability for work and work-related activity (Universal Credit Regulations, reg.111(3)). The reduction rate drops to 40% if the claimant comes within s.19 (no work-related requirements) because of certain caring responsibilities for children under one (reg.111(2)). The DWP rejected the House of Commons Work and Pensions Committee's recommendation in its report of November 6, 2018 on *Benefit Sanctions* (HC 995 2017-19) that sanctions be cancelled when a claimant ceased to be subject to the requirement that led to the sanction (House of Commons Work and Pensions Committee, *Benefit Sanctions: Government Response* (HC 1949 2017-19, February 11, 2019, paras 49 - 51). It was said that that would undermine the incentive effect of the sanctions and that the mitigations in reg.111 were adequate. Note also the termination of a reduction when the claimant has been in paid work at a weekly rate of 35 times the hourly national minimum wage for 26 weeks (reg.109).

Regulation 113 of the Universal Credit Regulations, made in part under subs.(9) **1.114** (a), prescribes circumstances in which no reduction is to be made for a sanctionable failure under s.27, but none of the circumstances covered seem relevant to s.27.

Under para.(b) of subs.(9), see reg.107. Under para.(c), see regs 108 and 109.

Many of the requirements that can give rise to sanctions under s.27 involve undertaking or participating in interviews, courses, assessments, programmes etc that that have a specified start time. In *SA v SSWP (JSA)* [2015] UKUT 454 (AAC) the claimant, who had hearing difficulties and wore a hearing aid in one ear, was directed by an employment officer to attend and complete a CV writing course with Learn Direct two days later from 11.15 a.m. to 12.15 p.m. He was given a letter to confirm the time and date. The claimant arrived at 11.25 a.m. and was told that he was too late and so had been deemed to have missed his appointment. He immediately went to the Jobcentre Plus office to rebook an appointment for the course and explained that he had misheard the time for the appointment as 11.50, the time that he normally signed on. A fixed four-week sanction for failing, without a good reason, to carry out a reasonable jobseeker's direction was imposed. On appeal the claimant said that at the meeting with the employment officer he had not been wearing his hearing aid and that he had not thought to check the time of the appointment on the letter as he genuinely thought that it was the same as his two previous appointments. The First-tier Tribunal regarded it as clear that the direction had been reasonable and that the claimant had failed to comply with it, so that the sole question was whether he had had a good reason for the failure. On that question, the tribunal concluded that, although the error was genuine, that did not in itself give him a good reason and that he had failed to take reasonable steps to confirm the time of the appointment and dismissed his appeal. In setting aside the tribunal's decision and substituting her own decision reversing the imposition of the sanction (as had been suggested by the Secretary of State), Judge Knowles held that the tribunal had erred in law by failing to consider the question of whether the claimant had failed to comply with the direction. In the substituted decision, she concluded that, the claimant not having refused to carry out the direction and taking into account that his error was genuine and that he took immediate steps to rebook, it was disproportionate to treat his late arrival in isolation as amounting to a failure to comply with the direction. That can only be regarded as a determination on the particular facts that does not constitute any sort of precedent to be applied as a matter of law in other cases. The outcome may have reflected an understandable desire in a deserving case to get around the absence of any scope for varying the fixed period of four weeks for a sanction under s.19A of the old style Jobseekers Act 1995 for a "first offence". However, there could have been nothing unreasonable about a conclusion that arriving 10 minutes after the beginning of a course that only lasted for an hour amounted to a failure to comply with a direction to attend and complete the course, no matter how genuine the error that led to the late arrival.

SN v SSWP (JSA) [2018] UKUT 279 (AAC) discusses, from para.42 onwards, what can amount to a failure to participate in a scheme (at a time when the consequent sanction was under reg.8 of the MWAS Regulations, rather than s.19(2)(e) of the old style Jobseekers Act 1995). It confirms that conduct of the claimant related to the ordinary requirements of the work activity in question leading to the termination of their placement can amount to a failure to participate. In particular, it is held in paras 59-62 that actions before the start of the scheme can be relevant. In *SN* the claimant was required to work for four weeks as a retail assistant in a charity shop. As found by Upper Tribunal Judge Wright in substituting a decision on the appeal, the claimant visited the shop about a week before the placement was due to start, to find out what would be entailed. During the visit he used offensive language to one member of staff and about the nature of the work involved, that were unreasonable in any work setting. He attended at the shop at the specified time for the start of the placement, but, as the representative of the programme provider was not to arrive for about 20 minutes, retired to a changing cubicle to sit down, took off his shoes and appeared to go to sleep. When the representative arrived, the deputy manager of the shop told him that the claimant would not be allowed to work there in view of his earlier offensive conduct. The judge concludes that the combination of the claimant's behaviour on the earlier visit and his attitude of antagonism and lack of interest on the first day of the placement meant that he had failed to meet the notified requirements for participation in the scheme. There was no good cause for the failure to participate. Some doubt is expressed in para.45 about the result in *SA*.

In *CS v SSWP (JSA)* [2019] UKUT 218 (AAC) Judge Hemingway accepted that it was legitimate for a scheme provider to require an attender to verify their identity before starting the scheme, so that a refusal to do so would usually amount to a failure to participate in the scheme. However, in the particular case the claimant had declined to verify various items of information about him appearing on a computer screen, largely because of misguided views about the effect of the Data Protection Act 1998, but also because of concerns about the security of social security information held by scheme providers. The judge held that the tribunal had erred in law by failing to make findings of fact about whether the claimant had been offered the opportunity to verify his identity by other means, e.g. by producing a passport or driving licence or other document in addition to the appointment letter that he had already produced. In the absence of such findings the tribunal had not been entitled to conclude that the claimant had refused to confirm his identity rather than merely refused to confirm it by the method initially put forward by the scheme provider. It might in other cases be relevant to enquire what the appointment letter or other documents do or do not say about confirming identity.

Claimants who are found not in fact to have been aware of an interview must have a good reason for failing to comply, whether or not the requirement is said to have been imposed in such circumstances (*SP v SSWP (UC)* [2018] UKUT 227 (AAC)).

Hardship payments

1.115   **28.**—(1) Regulations may make provision for the making of additional payments by way of universal credit to a claimant ("hardship payments") where—

(a) the amount of the claimant's award is reduced under section 26 or 27, and

(b) the claimant is or will be in hardship.

(2) Regulations under this section may in particular make provision as to—

(a) circumstances in which a claimant is to be treated as being or not being in hardship;

(b) matters to be taken into account in determining whether a claimant is or will be in hardship;

(c) requirements or conditions to be met by a claimant in order to receive hardship payments;

(d) the amount or rate of hardship payments;
(e) the period for which hardship payments may be made;
(f) whether hardship payments are recoverable.

DEFINITION

"claimant"—see s.40.

GENERAL NOTE

The provision of hardship payments is an important part of the sanctions regime   1.116
for universal credit. The payments are to be made by way of universal credit.
However, it will be seen that s.28, first, does not require the making of provision
for hardship payments in regulations and, second, gives almost complete freedom
in how any regulations define the conditions for and amounts of payments. The
provisions made are in regs 115–119 of the Universal Credit Regulations, which
contain stringent conditions and a restricted definition of "hardship", which nevertheless retains a number of subjective elements. Payments are generally recoverable, subject to exceptions. See the notes to those regulations for the details and
the relevant parts of Ch.53 of CPAG's *Welfare benefits and tax credits handbook
2019/2020* for helpful explanations and examples. There seems to be no reason
why a decision of the Secretary of State to make or not to make hardship payments
on an application under reg.116(1)(c) should not be appealable to a First-tier
Tribunal.

Administration

Delegation and contracting out

29.—(1) The functions of the Secretary of State under sections 13 to 25   1.117
may be exercised by, or by the employees of, such persons as the Secretary
of State may authorise for the purpose (an "authorised person").

(2) An authorisation given by virtue of this section may authorise the
exercise of a function—
(a) wholly or to a limited extent;
(b) generally or in particular cases or areas;
(c) unconditionally or subject to conditions.

(3) An authorisation under this section—
(a) may specify its duration;
(b) may be varied or revoked at any time by the Secretary of State;
(c) does not prevent the Secretary of State or another person from exercising the function to which the authorisation related.

(4) Anything done or omitted to be done by or in relation to an authorised person (or an employee of that person) in, or in connection with, the
exercise or purported exercise of the function concerned is to be treated for
all purposes as done or omitted to be done by or in relation to the Secretary
of State or (as the case may be) an officer of the Secretary of State.

(5) Subsection (4) does not apply—
(a) for the purposes of so much of any contract made between the
authorised person and the Secretary of State as relates to the exercise
of the function, or
(b) for the purposes of any criminal proceedings brought in respect of
anything done or omitted to be done by the authorised person (or an
employee of that person).

(6) Where—
(a) the authorisation of an authorised person is revoked, and

(b) at the time of the revocation so much of any contract made between the authorised person and the Secretary of State as relates to the exercise of the function is subsisting, the authorised person is entitled to treat the contract as repudiated by the Secretary of State (and not as frustrated by reason of that revocation).

DEFINITION

"person"—see Interpretation Act 1978, Sch.1.

GENERAL NOTE

1.118   This section allows the Secretary of State to authorise other persons (which word in accordance with the Interpretation Act 1978 includes corporate and unincorporated associations, such as companies) and their employees to carry out any of his functions under ss.13–25. Any such authorisation will not in practice cover the making of regulations, but may well (depending on the extent of the authorisations given) extend to specifying various matters under those sections. The involvement of private sector organisations, operating for profit, in running various schemes within the scope of the benefit system is something that claimants sometimes object to. Such a generalised objection, even if on principled grounds, is unlikely to amount in itself to a good reason for failing to engage with a scheme in question (although see the discussion in the note to s.26 on whether "for no good reason" has a restricted meaning). An objection based on previous experience with the organisation concerned or the nature of the course may raise more difficult issues. See also the discussion in *R(JSA) 7/03* plus *CSJSA/495/2007* and *CSJSA/505/2007*.

In *DH v SSWP (JSA)* [2016] UKUT 355 (AAC), an old style JSA case under the Jobseeker's Allowance (Schemes for Assisting Persons to Obtain Employment) Regulations 2013, it was held that the First-tier Tribunal erred in law in apparently dismissing the claimant's objections to attending a Work Programme run by a particular provider (on the grounds that staff of the company concerned had lied in a police statement and in court about whether travel expenses had been refunded to him and had bullied him) as, even if true, irrelevant to whether he had a good reason for failing to comply with requirements to attend. The tribunal had said that the claimant's remedies were to contact the police and to use appropriate complaints procedures, not to refuse to attend interviews or courses. The judge asked the rhetorical question in para.20 what could amount to good reason if such matters did not. The circumstances are to be distinguished from those in *R(JSA) 7/03*, not mentioned in *DH*, where the claimant's objection was a generalised one to the involvement of private companies in the provision of such schemes.

CHAPTER 3

SUPPLEMENTARY AND GENERAL

Supplementary and consequential

Supplementary regulation-making powers

1.119   **30.** Schedule 1 contains supplementary regulation-making powers.

Supplementary and consequential amendments

1.120   **31.** Schedule 2 contains supplementary and consequential amendments.

Power to make supplementary and consequential provision etc.

1.121   **32.**—(1) The appropriate authority may by regulations make such consequential, supplementary, incidental or transitional provision in relation to any provision of this Part as the authority considers appropriate.

(2) The appropriate authority is the Secretary of State, subject to subsection (3).

(3) The appropriate authority is the Welsh Ministers for—

(a) provision which would be within the legislative competence of the National Assembly for Wales were it contained in an Act of the Assembly;

(b) provision which could be made by the Welsh Ministers under any other power conferred on them.

(4) Regulations under this section may amend, repeal or revoke any primary or secondary legislation (whenever passed or made).

Universal credit and other benefits

Abolition of benefits

33.—(1) The following benefits are abolished— 1.122

(a) income-based jobseeker's allowance under the Jobseekers Act 1995;

(b) income-related employment and support allowance under Part 1 of the Welfare Reform Act 2007;

(c) income support under section 124 of the Social Security Contributions and Benefits Act 1992;

(d) housing benefit under section 130 of that Act;

(e) council tax benefit under section 131 of that Act;

(f) child tax credit and working tax credit under the Tax Credits Act 2002.

(2) In subsection (1)—

(a) "income-based jobseeker's allowance" has the same meaning as in the Jobseekers Act 1995;

(b) "income-related employment and support allowance" means an employment and support allowance entitlement to which is based on section 1(2)(b) of the Welfare Reform Act 2007.

(3) Schedule 3 contains consequential amendments.

DEFINITIONS

"income-related employment and support allowance"—see subs(2)(b).
"income-based jobseeker's allowance"—see subs.(2)(a).

GENERAL NOTE

Subsection (1)

The purpose of this provision is simple enough. Sub-section (1) provides for 1.123
the abolition of income-based JSA, income-related ESA, income support, housing benefit, council tax benefit, child tax credit and working tax credit. The implementation of this section is much less straightforward. Council tax benefit was abolished in favour of localised schemes from April 2013. As a general rule abolition of the other benefits will only happen when all claimants have been transferred to universal credit. The exception to this rule is that when a claimant in the Pathfinder Group claims JSA, ESA or universal credit, this action of itself triggers the abolition at that point (and for that individual) of income-based JSA and income-related ESA (see Commencement Order No.9, art.4).

This sub-section is modelled on the drafting of s.1(3) of the Tax Credits Act (TCA) 2002, which provided for the abolition of e.g. the personal allowances for children in the income support and income-based JSA schemes. Section 1(3) of the TCA 2002 has never been fully implemented. The fate of subs.(1) here remains to be seen.

1.124   This introduces Sch.3, which makes consequential amendments relating to the abolition of these benefits. Those changes remove references in other legislation to contributory ESA or JSA, as these will be unnecessary once ESA and JSA are contributory benefits only, and update references to other legislation which has been amended.

Universal credit and state pension credit

1.125   **34.** Schedule 4 provides for a housing element of state pension credit in consequence of the abolition of housing benefit by section 33.

GENERAL NOTE

1.126   This section provides for a new housing credit element of state pension credit to replace housing benefit for claimants above the qualifying age for state pension credit. In its original form under the SPCA 2002, state pension credit was made up of two elements: the guarantee credit (performing the same function as income support used to) and the savings credit (providing a small top-up for those claimants with modest savings). Schedule 4 amends the SPCA 2002 to create a new third credit to cover housing costs. This will provide support for people who have reached the qualifying age for state pension credit (or for couples where both members have reached the qualifying age) once housing benefit is no longer available following the introduction of universal credit.

Universal credit and working-age benefits

1.127   **35.** Schedule 5 makes further provision relating to universal credit, jobseeker's allowance and employment and support allowance.

GENERAL NOTE

1.128   This section (and Sch.5) deals with the inter-relationship between universal credit, JSA and ESA. After the introduction of universal credit, ESA and JSA will continue to be available but only as contributory benefits.

Migration to universal credit

1.129   **36.** Schedule 6 contains provision about the replacement of benefits by universal credit.

GENERAL NOTE

1.130   This section gives effect to Sch.6, which makes provision relating to the replacement of the benefits that will be abolished under s.33, as well as any other prescribed benefits, and the consequential migration (or transfer) of claimants to universal credit.

General

Capability for work or work-related activity

1.131   **37.**—(1) For the purposes of this Part a claimant has limited capability for work if—

(a) the claimant's capability for work is limited by their physical or mental condition, and

(b) the limitation is such that it is not reasonable to require the claimant to work.

(2) For the purposes of this Part a claimant has limited capability for work-related activity if—

(a) the claimant's capability for work-related activity is limited by their physical or mental condition, and

(b) the limitation is such that it is not reasonable to require the claimant to undertake work-related activity.

(3) The question whether a claimant has limited capability for work or work-related activity for the purposes of this Part is to be determined in accordance with regulations.

(4) Regulations under this section must, subject as follows, provide for determination of that question on the basis of an assessment (or repeated assessments) of the claimant.

(5) Regulations under this section may for the purposes of an assessment—

(a) require a claimant to provide information or evidence (and may require it to be provided in a prescribed manner or form);

(b) require a claimant to attend and submit to a medical examination at a place, date and time determined under the regulations.

(6) Regulations under this section may make provision for a claimant to be treated as having or not having limited capability for work or work-related activity.

(7) Regulations under subsection (6) may provide for a claimant who fails to comply with a requirement imposed under subsection (5) without a good reason to be treated as not having limited capability for work or work-related activity.

(8) Regulations under subsection (6) may provide for a claimant to be treated as having limited capability for work until—

(a) it has been determined whether or not that is the case, or

(b) the claimant is under any other provision of regulations under subsection (6) treated as not having it.

(9) Regulations under this section may provide for determination of the question of whether a claimant has limited capability for work or work-related activity even where the claimant is for the time being treated under regulations under subsection (6) as having limited capability for work or work-related activity.

DEFINITIONS

"claim"—see s.40.
"claimant"—*ibid.*
"limited capability for work"—*ibid.*
"prescribed"—*ibid.*
"work search requirement"—*ibid.*

GENERAL NOTE

If a person has limited capability for work or limited capability for work and work-related activity, this is relevant to universal credit in three ways. Firstly, it affects the amount of the award of universal credit (see ss.1(3)(d) and 12(2)(a) and (b) and regs 27–28 and 36 of the Universal Credit Regulations). Secondly, it determines the work-related requirements that can be imposed. Under s.19(1) and (2)(a) no work-related requirements can be imposed on a claimant who has limited capability for work and work-related activity and under s.21(1)(a) a claimant who has limited capability for work (and who does not fall within s.19 or 20) is only subject to the work preparation requirement. Thirdly, it enables the application of the appropriate work allowance (see s. 8(3)(a) and reg. 22 of the Universal Credit Regulations).

This section contains provisions that are broadly equivalent to those in ss.1(4), 2(5), 8 and 9 of the Welfare Reform Act 2007. Thus the question of whether a person has limited capability for work or limited capability for work and work-related activity, will be determined in the same way as for ESA.

In relation to subs.(7), note also the regulation-making power in para.8 of Sch.1.

1.132

Information

1.133   **38.** Information supplied under Chapter 2 of this Part or section 37 is to be taken for all purposes to be information relating to social security.

Couples

1.134   **39.**—[¹ ² (1) In this Part "couple" means—
(a) two people who are married to, or civil partners of, each other and are members of the same household; or
(b) two people who are not married to, or civil partners of, each other but are living together [³ as if they were a married couple or civil partners].]
(2) [¹ ² ...]
(3) For the purposes of this section regulations may prescribe—
(a) circumstances in which the fact that two persons are [¹ ² married] or are civil partners is to be disregarded;
(b) circumstances in which [¹ ² two people are to be treated as living together [³ as if they were a married couple or civil partners]]];
(c) circumstances in which people are to be treated as being or not being members of the same household.

AMENDMENTS

1.   Marriage (Same Sex Couples) Act 2013 (Consequential and Contrary Provisions and Scotland) Order 2014 (SI 2014/560) art.2 and Sch.1, para.36 (March 13, 2014). This amendment extended to England and Wales only.

2.   Marriage and Civil Partnership (Scotland) Act 2014 and Civil Partnership Act 2004 (Consequential Provisions and Modifications) Order 2014 (SI 2014/3229) art.29 and Sch.5, para.20 (December 16, 2014). This amendment extended to Scotland only. However, as it was in the same terms as the amendment made in England and Wales by SI 2014/560 (see above), the effect is that the law is now the same throughout Great Britain.

3.   Civil Partnership (Opposite-sex Couples) Regulations 2019 (SI 2019/1458) reg.41(a) and Sch.3 Pt.1 para.35 (December 2, 2019).

GENERAL NOTE

1.135   See the commentary to reg.3 of the Universal Credit Regulations.

Interpretation of Part 1

1.136   **40.** In this Part—
"assessment period" has the meaning given by section 7(2);
"child" means a person under the age of 16;
"claim" means claim for universal credit;
"claimant" means a single claimant or each of joint claimants;
"couple" has the meaning given by section 39;
"disabled" has such meaning as may be prescribed;
"joint claimants" means members of a couple who jointly make a claim or in relation to whom an award of universal credit is made;
"limited capability for work" and "limited capability for work-related activity" are to be construed in accordance with section 37(1) and (2);
"prescribed" means specified or provided for in regulations;
"primary legislation" means an Act, Act of the Scottish Parliament or Act or Measure of the National Assembly for Wales;

"qualifying young person" has the meaning given in section 10(5);

"regular and substantial caring responsibilities" has such meaning as may be prescribed;

"responsible carer", in relation to a child, has the meaning given in section 19(6);

"secondary legislation" means an instrument made under primary legislation";

"severely disabled" has such meaning as may be prescribed;

"single claimant" means a single person who makes a claim for universal credit or in relation to whom an award of universal credit is made as a single person;

"single person" is to be construed in accordance with section 1(2)(a);

"work" has such meaning as may be prescribed;

"work availability requirement" has the meaning given by section 18(1);

"work preparation requirement" has the meaning given by section 16(1);

"work search requirement" has the meaning given by section 17(1);

" work-focused interview requirement" has the meaning given by section 15(1);

"work-related activity", in relation to a person, means activity which makes it more likely that the person will obtain or remain in work or be able to do so;

"work-related requirement" has the meaning given by section 13(2).

Regulations

Pilot schemes

41.—(1) Any power to make—   1.137

(a) regulations under this Part,

(b) regulations under the Social Security Administration Act 1992 relating to universal credit, or

(c) regulations under the Social Security Act 1998 relating to universal credit, may be exercised so as to make provision for piloting purposes.

(2) In subsection (1), "piloting purposes", in relation to any provision, means the purposes of testing—

(a) the extent to which the provision is likely to make universal credit simpler to understand or to administer,

(b) the extent to which the provision is likely to promote—

(i) people remaining in work, or

(ii) people obtaining or being able to obtain work (or more work or better-paid work), or

(c) the extent to which, and how, the provision is likely to affect the conduct of claimants or other people in any other way.

(3) Regulations made by virtue of this section are in the remainder of this section referred to as a "pilot scheme".

(4) A pilot scheme may be limited in its application to—

(a) one or more areas;

(b) one or more classes of person;

(c) persons selected—

(i) by reference to prescribed criteria, or

(ii) on a sampling basis.

(5) A pilot scheme may not have effect for a period exceeding three years, but—

    (a) the Secretary of State may by order made by statutory instrument provide that the pilot scheme is to continue to have effect after the time when it would otherwise expire for a period not exceeding twelve months (and may make more than one such order);

    (b) a pilot scheme may be replaced by a further pilot scheme making the same or similar provision.

(6) A pilot scheme may include consequential or transitional provision in relation to its expiry.

GENERAL NOTE

1.138   This section was brought into force for all purposes on September 15, 2014 by art.6 of the Welfare Reform Act 2012 (Commencement No. 19 and Transitional and Transitory Provisions and Commencement No. 9 and Transitional and Transitory Provisions (Amendment)) Order 2014 (SI 2014/2321).

This important provision is similar to that in s.29 of the Jobseekers Act 1995. It contains the power to pilot changes in regulations across particular geographical areas and/or specified categories of claimants for up to three years, although this period can be extended, or the pilot scheme can be replaced by a different pilot scheme making the same or similar provision (subs.(5)). The power can only be exercised in relation to the types of regulation listed in subs.(1) and with a view to assessing whether the proposed changes are likely to make universal credit simpler to understand or administer, to encourage people to find or remain in work (or more or better-paid work) or "to affect the conduct of claimants or other people in any other way" (subs.(2)). Regulations made under this section are subject to the affirmative resolution procedure (s.43(4)). On past experience in relation to JSA, it seems likely that this power will be exercised on a fairly regular basis.

Regulations: general

1.139   **42.**—(1) Regulations under this Part are to be made by the Secretary of State, unless otherwise provided.

(2) A power to make regulations under this Part may be exercised—

    (a) so as to make different provision for different cases or purposes;

    (b) in relation to all or only some of the cases or purposes for which it may be exercised.

(3) Such a power includes—

    (a) power to make incidental, supplementary, consequential or transitional provision or savings;

    (b) power to provide for a person to exercise a discretion in dealing with any matter.

(4) Each power conferred by this Part is without prejudice to the others.

(5) Where regulations under this Part provide for an amount, the amount may be zero.

(6) Where regulations under this Part provide for an amount for the purposes of an award (or a reduction from an award), the amount may be different in relation to different descriptions of person, and in particular may depend on—

    (a) whether the person is a single person or a member of couple.

    (b) the age of the person.

(7) Regulations under section 11(4) or 12(3) which provide for the determination or calculation of an amount may make different provision for different areas.

DEFINITIONS

"couple"—see ss.39 and 40.
"single person"—see s.40.
"work"—*ibid.*

Regulations: procedure

43.—(1) Regulations under this Part are to be made by statutory instru-   1.140
ment.

(2) A statutory instrument containing regulations made by the Secretary
of State under this Part is subject to the negative resolution procedure,
subject as follows.

(3) A statutory instrument containing the first regulations made by the
Secretary of State under any of the following, alone or with other regulations, is subject to the affirmative resolution procedure—

(a) section 4(7) (acceptance of claimant commitment);
(b) section 5(1)(a) and (2)(a) (capital limits);
(c) section 8(3) (income to be deducted in award calculation);
(d) section 9(2) and (3) (standard allowance);
(e) section 10(3) and (4) (children and young persons element);
(f) section 11 (housing costs element);
(g) section 12 (other needs and circumstances element);
(h) section 18(3) and (5) (work availability requirement);
(i) section 19(2)(d) (claimants subject to no work-related requirements);
(j) sections 26 and 27 (sanctions);
(k) section 28 (hardship payments);
(l) paragraph 4 of Schedule 1 (calculation of capital and income);
(m) paragraph 1(1) of Schedule 6 (migration), where making provision
under paragraphs 4, 5 and 6 of that Schedule.

(4) A statutory instrument containing regulations made by the Secretary
of State by virtue of section 41 (pilot schemes), alone or with other regulations, is subject to the affirmative resolution procedure.

(5) A statutory instrument containing regulations made by the Secretary
of State under this Part is subject to the affirmative resolution procedure
if—

(a) it also contains regulations under another enactment, and
(b) an instrument containing those regulations would apart from this
section be subject to the affirmative resolution procedure.

(6) For the purposes of subsections (2) to (5)—

(a) a statutory instrument subject to the "negative resolution procedure"
is subject to annulment in pursuance of a resolution of either House
of Parliament;
(b) a statutory instrument subject to the "affirmative resolution procedure" may not be made unless a draft of the instrument has
been laid before, and approved by resolution of, each House of
Parliament.

(7) A statutory instrument containing regulations made by the Welsh
Ministers under section 32 may not be made unless a draft of the instru-
ment has been laid before, and approved by resolution of, the National
Assembly for Wales.

"child"—see s.40.
"claim"—*ibid.*
"claimant"—*ibid.*
"work"—*ibid.*
"work availability requirement"—*ibid.*

PART 5

SOCIAL SECURITY: GENERAL

Benefit cap

Benefit cap

1.141   **96.**—(1) Regulations may provide for a benefit cap to be applied to the welfare benefits to which a single person or couple is entitled.

(2) For the purposes of this section, applying a benefit cap to welfare benefits means securing that, where a single person's or couple's total entitlement to welfare benefits in respect of the reference period exceeds the relevant amount, their entitlement to welfare benefits in respect of any period of the same duration as the reference period is reduced by an amount up to or equalling the excess.

(3) In subsection (2) the "reference period" means a period of a pre-scribed duration.

(4) Regulations under this section may in particular—

(a) make provision as to the manner in which total entitlement to welfare benefits for any period, or the amount of any reduction, is to be determined;

(b) make provision as to the welfare benefit or benefits from which a reduction is to be made;

(c) provide for exceptions to the application of the benefit cap;

(d) make provision as to the intervals at which the benefit cap is to be applied;

(e) make provision as to the relationship between application of the benefit cap and any other reduction in respect of a welfare benefit;

(f) provide that where in consequence of a change in the relevant amount, entitlement to a welfare benefit increases or decreases, that increase or decrease has effect without any further decision of the Secretary of State;

(g) make supplementary and consequential provision.

[^{1} (5) Regulations under this section may make provision for determining the "relevant amount" for the reference period applicable in the case of a single person or couple by reference to the annual limit applicable in the case of that single person or couple.

(5A) For the purposes of this section the "annual limit" is—

(a) £23,000 or £15,410, for persons resident in Greater London;

(b) £20,000 or £13,400, for other persons.

(5B) Regulations under subsection (5) may—

(a) specify which annual limit applies in the case of—

(i) different prescribed descriptions of single person;

(ii) different prescribed descriptions of couple;

   (b) define "resident" for the purposes of this section;

   (c) provide for the rounding up or down of an amount produced by dividing the amount of the annual limit by the number of periods of a duration equal to the reference period in a year.]

(6) [¹ ...]

(7) [¹ ...]

(8) [¹ ...]

(9) Regulations under this section may not provide for any reduction to be made from a welfare benefit—

   (a) provision for which is within the legislative competence of the Scottish Parliament;

   (b) provision for which is within the legislative competence of the National Assembly for Wales;

   (c) provision for which is made by the Welsh Ministers, the First Minister for Wales or the Counsel General to the Welsh Assembly Government.

(10) In this section—

"couple" means two persons of a prescribed description;

"prescribed" means prescribed in regulations;

"regulations" means regulations made by the Secretary of State;

"single person" means a person who is not a member of a couple;

"welfare benefit" [¹ means—

   (a) bereavement allowance (see section 39B of the Social Security Contributions and Benefits Act 1992),

   (b) child benefit (see section 141 of the Social Security Contributions and Benefits Act 1992),

   (c) child tax credit (see section 1(1)(a) of the Tax Credits Act 2002),

   (d) employment and support allowance (see section 1 of the Welfare Reform Act 2007), including income-related employment and support allowance (as defined in section 1(7) of the Welfare Reform Act 2007),

   (e) housing benefit (see section 130 of the Social Security Contributions and Benefits Act 1992),

   (f) incapacity benefit (see section 30A of the Social Security Contributions and Benefits Act 1992),

   (g) income support (see section 124 of the Social Security Contributions and Benefits Act 1992),

   (h) jobseeker's allowance (see section 1 of the Jobseekers Act 1995), including income-based jobseeker's allowance (as defined in section 1(4) of the Jobseekers Act 1995),

   (i) maternity allowance under section 35 or 35B of the Social Security Contributions and Benefits Act 1992,

   (j) severe disablement allowance (see section 68 of the Social Security Contributions and Benefits Act 1992),

   (k) universal credit,

   (l) widow's pension (see section 38 of the Social Security Contributions and Benefits Act 1992),

   (m) widowed mother's allowance (see section 37 of the Social Security Contributions and Benefits Act 1992), or

   (n) widowed parent's allowance (see section 39A of the Social Security Contributions and Benefits Act 1992).

(11) [¹ ...]

AMENDMENT

1. Welfare Reform and Work Act 2016 s.8(1)-(5) (assessment periods beginning on or after November 7, 2016: see SI 2016/910).

GENERAL NOTE

1.142   See the commentary to regs 78–83 of the Universal Credit Regulations.

[¹ Benefit cap: review

1.143   **96A.**—(1) The Secretary of State must at least once in each Parliament review the sums specified in section 96(5A) to determine whether it is appropriate to increase or decrease any one or more of those sums.

(2) The Secretary of State may, at any other time the Secretary of State considers appropriate, review the sums specified in section 96(5A) to determine whether it is appropriate to increase or decrease any one or more of those sums.

(3) In carrying out a review, the Secretary of State must take into account—

(a) the national economic situation, and

(b) any other matters that the Secretary of State considers relevant.

(4) After carrying out a review, the Secretary of State may, if the Secretary of State considers it appropriate, by regulations amend section 96(5A) so as to increase or decrease any one or more of the sums specified in section 96(5A).

(5) Regulations under subsection (4) may provide for amendments of section 96(5A) to come into force—

(a) on different days for different areas;

(b) on different days for different cases or purposes.

(6) Regulations under subsection (4) may make such transitional or transitory provision or savings as the Secretary of State considers necessary or expedient in connection with the coming into force of any amendment made by regulations under subsection (4).

(7) Regulations under subsection (6) may in particular—

(a) provide for section 96(5A) to have effect as if the amendments made by regulations under subsection (4) had not been made, in relation to such persons or descriptions of persons as are specified in the regulations or generally, until a time or times specified in a notice issued by the Secretary of State;

(b) provide for the Secretary of State to issue notices under paragraph (a) specifying different times for different persons or descriptions of person;

(c) make provision about the issuing of notices under paragraph (a), including provision for the Secretary of State to issue notices to authorities administering housing benefit that have effect in relation to persons specified, or persons of a description specified, in the notices.

(8) Section 176 of the Social Security Administration Act 1992 (consultation with representative organisations) does not apply in relation to regulations under subsection (4).

(9) If an early parliamentary general election is to take place in accordance with section 2 of the Fixed-term Parliaments Act 2011, the duty in subsection (1) is to be disregarded.]

AMENDMENT

1. Welfare Reform and Work Act 2016 (c.7) s.9(1) (November 7, 2016).

Benefit cap: supplementary

97.—(1) Regulations under section 96 [³ or 96A] may make different   1.144
provision for different purposes or cases.

(2) Regulations under section 96 [³ or 96A] must be made by statutory
instrument.

(3) [² ...]

(4) A statutory instrument containing [² ...] regulations under section
96 is subject to annulment in pursuance of a resolution of either House of
Parliament.

[³ (4A) A statutory instrument containing regulations under section 96A
may not be made unless a draft of the instrument has been laid before, and
approved by a resolution of, each House of Parliament.]

(5) [¹ ...]

(6) In Schedule 2 to the Social Security Act 1998 (decisions against
which no appeal lies) after paragraph 8 there is inserted—

"Reduction on application of benefit cap

8A A decision to apply the benefit cap in accordance with regulations
under section 96 of the Welfare Reform Act 2012."

AMENDMENTS

1. Welfare Reform and Work Act 2016 s.9(6) (March 16, 2016).
2. Welfare Reform and Work Act 2016 s.8(6) (assessment periods beginning on or
after November 7, 2016: see SI 2016/910).
3. Welfare Reform and Work Act 2016 s.9(2)-(5) (November 7, 2016).

GENERAL NOTE

See the commentary to regs 78–83 of the Universal Credit Regulations.   1.145

PART 7

FINAL

Repeals

147. *[Omitted]*   1.146

Financial provision

148. There shall be paid out of money provided by Parliament—   1.147
(a) sums paid by the Secretary of State by way of universal credit or
personal independence payment;
(b) any other expenditure incurred in consequence of this Act by a
Minister of the Crown or the Commissioners for Her Majesty's
Revenue and Customs;
(c) any increase attributable to this Act in the sums payable under any
other Act out of money so provided.

Extent

149.—(1) This Act extends to England and Wales and Scotland only,   1.148
subject as follows.

(2) The following provisions extend to England and Wales, Scotland and Northern Ireland—

(a) section 32 (power to make consequential and supplementary provision: universal credit);

(b) section 33 (abolition of benefits);

(c)–(f) *[Omitted]*

(g) this Part, excluding Schedule 14 (repeals).

(3) *[Omitted]*

(4) Any amendment or repeal made by this Act has the same extent as the enactment to which it relates.

Commencement

1.149   **150.**—(1) The following provisions of this Act come into force on the day on which it is passed—

(a)–(e)   *[Omitted]*

(f) this Part, excluding Schedule 14 (repeals).

(2) *[Omitted]*

(3) The remaining provisions of this Act come into force on such day as the Secretary of State may by order made by statutory instrument appoint.

(4) An order under subsection (3) may—

(a) appoint different days for different purposes;

(b) appoint different days for different areas in relation to—

(i) any provision of Part 1 (universal credit) or of Part 1 of Schedule 14;

(ii)–(iii) *[Omitted]*

(iv) section 102 (consideration of revision before appeal);

(c) make such transitory or transitional provision, or savings, as the Secretary of State considers necessary or expedient.

Short title

1.150   **151.** This Act may be cited as the Welfare Reform Act 2012.

SCHEDULES

Section 30

SCHEDULE 1

UNIVERSAL CREDIT: SUPPLEMENTARY REGULATION-MAKING POWERS

Entitlement of joint claimants

1.151   1. Regulations may provide for circumstances in which joint claimants may be entitled to universal credit without each of them meeting all the basic conditions referred to in section 4.

Linking periods

2. Regulations may provide for periods of entitlement to universal credit which are separated by no more than a prescribed number of days to be treated as a single period.

Couples

3.—(1) Regulations may provide—

(a) for a claim made by members of a couple jointly to be treated as a claim made by one member of the couple as a single person (or as claims made by both members as single persons);

(b) for claims made by members of a couple as single persons to be treated as a claim made jointly by the couple.

(2) Regulations may provide—

(a) where an award is made to joint claimants who cease to be entitled to universal credit as such by ceasing to be a couple, for the making of an award (without a claim) to either or each one of them—

(i) as a single person, or

(ii) jointly with another person;

(b) where an award is made to a single claimant who ceases to be entitled to universal credit as such by becoming a member of a couple, for the making of an award (without a claim) to the members of the couple jointly;

(c) for the procedure to be followed, and information or evidence to be supplied, in relation to the making of an award under this paragraph.

Calculation of capital and income

4.—(1) Regulations may for any purpose of this Part provide for the calculation or estimation of—

(a) a person's capital,

(b) a person's earned and unearned income, and

(c) a person's earned and unearned income in respect of an assessment period.

(2) Regulations under sub-paragraph (1)(c) may include provision for the calculation to be made by reference to an average over a period, which need not include the assessment period concerned.

(3) Regulations under sub-paragraph (1) may—

(a) specify circumstances in which a person is to be treated as having or not having capital or earned or unearned income;

(b) specify circumstances in which income is to be treated as capital or capital as earned income or unearned income;

(c) specify circumstances in which unearned income is to be treated as earned, or earned income as unearned;

(d) provide that a person's capital is to be treated as yielding income at a prescribed rate;

(e) provide that the capital or income of one member of a couple is to be treated as that of the other member.

(4) Regulations under sub-paragraph (3)(a) may in particular provide that persons of a prescribed description are to be treated as having a prescribed minimum level of earned income.

(5) In the case of joint claimants the income and capital of the joint claimants includes (subject to sub-paragraph (6)) the separate income and capital of each of them.

(6) Regulations may specify circumstances in which capital and income of either of joint claimants is to be disregarded in calculating their joint capital and income.

Responsibility for children etc

5.—(1) Regulations may for any purpose of this Part specify circumstances in which a person is or is not responsible for a child or qualifying young person.

1.152

(2) Regulations may for any purpose of this Part make provision about nominations of the responsible carer for a child (see section 19(6)(b)(ii)).

Vouchers

6.—(1) This paragraph applies in relation to an award of universal credit where the calculation of the amount of the award includes, by virtue of any provision of this Part, an amount in respect of particular costs which a claimant may incur.

(2) Regulations may provide for liability to pay all or part of the award to be discharged by means of provision of a voucher.

(3) But the amount paid by means of a voucher may not in any case exceed the total of the amounts referred to in sub-paragraph (1) which are included in the calculation of the amount of the award.

(4) For these purposes a voucher is a means other than cash by which a claimant may to any extent meet costs referred to in sub-paragraph (1) of a particular description.

(5) A voucher may for these purposes—

    (a) be limited as regards the person or persons who will accept it;

    (b) be valid only for a limited time.

Work-related requirements

    7.—Regulations may provide that a claimant who—

    (a) has a right to reside in the United Kingdom under the EU Treaties, and

    (b) would otherwise fall within section 19, 20 or 21,is to be treated as not falling within that section.

Good reason

1.153   8.—Regulations may for any purpose of this Part provide for—

    (a) circumstances in which a person is to be treated as having or not having a good reason for an act or omission;

    (b) matters which are or are not to be taken into account in determining whether a person has a good reason for an act or omission.

DEFINITIONS

    "assessment period"—see s.40 and s.7(2).

    "child"—see s.40.

    "claim"—*ibid.*

    "claimant"—*ibid.*

    "couple"—see ss.39 and 40.

    "joint claimants"—see s.40.

    "prescribed"—*ibid.*

    "single claimant"—*ibid.*

    "single person"—*ibid.*

Section 31

SCHEDULE 2

UNIVERSAL CREDIT: AMENDMENTS

[Omitted]

SCHEDULE 3

ABOLITION OF BENEFITS: CONSEQUENTIAL AMENDMENTS

Social Security Contributions and Benefits Act 1992 (c.4)

1.154   1. The Social Security Contributions and Benefits Act 1992 is amended as follows.

    2. In section 22 (earnings factors), in subsections (2)(a) and (5), for "a contributory" there is substituted "an".

    3. In section 150 (interpretation of Part 10), in subsection (2), in the definition of "qualifying employment and support allowance", for "a contributory allowance" there is substituted "an employment and support allowance".

Social Security Administration Act 1992 (c.5)

1.155   4. The Social Security Administration Act 1992 is amended as follows.

    5. In section 7 (relationship between benefits), in subsection (3), for "subsections (1) and (2)" there is substituted "subsection (1)".

    6. In section 73 (overlapping benefits), in subsections (1) and (4)(c), for "a contributory" there is substituted "an".

    7. In section 159B (effect of alterations affecting state pension credit), for "a contributory", wherever occurring, there is substituted "an".

    8. In section 159D (as inserted by Schedule 2 to this Act) (effect of alterations affecting universal credit), for "a contributory", wherever occurring, there is substituted "an".

Immigration and Asylum Act 1999 (c.33)

9. In the Immigration and Asylum Act 1999, in section 115 (exclusion from benefits of persons subject to immigration control)—   **1.156**
   (a) in subsection (1), after paragraph (ha) there is inserted "or";
   (b) in subsection (2)(b) for "(a) to (j)" substitute "(a) to (i)".

Child Support, Pensions and Social Security Act 2000 (c.19)

10. The Child Support, Pensions and Social Security Act 2000 is amended as follows.   **1.157**
11. (1) Section 69 (discretionary financial assistance with housing) is amended as follows.
(2) In subsection (1)—
   (a) for "relevant authorities" there is substituted "local authorities";
   (b) in paragraph (a), the words from "housing benefit" to "both," are repealed.
(3) In subsection (2)—
   (a) in paragraph (b), for "relevant authority" there is substituted "local authority";
   (b) in paragraph (e), for "relevant authorities" there is substituted "local authorities";
   (c) in paragraphs (f), (g) and (h), for "relevant authority" there is substituted "local authority".
(4) In subsection (5), for "relevant authorities" there is substituted "local authorities".
(5) In subsection (7), for the definition of "relevant authority" there is substituted—
""local authority" has the meaning given by section 191 of the Social Security Administration Act 1992."
12. (1) Section 70 (grants towards cost of discretionary housing payments) is amended as follows.
(2) In subsection (1), after "payments" there is inserted "("grants")".
(3) For subsection (2) there is substituted—
"(2) The amount of a grant under this section shall be determined in accordance with an order made by the Secretary of State with the consent of the Treasury."
(4) In subsection (8)—
   (a) for the definition of "relevant authority" there is substituted—
""local authority" has the same meaning as in section 69;";
   (b) the definition of "subsidy" is repealed.
13. After section 70 there is inserted—

"70A. Payment of grant
   (1) A grant under section 70 shall be made by the Secretary of State in such instalments, at   **1.158**
such times, in such manner and subject to such conditions as to claims, records, certificates, audit or otherwise as may be provided by order of the Secretary of State with the consent of the Treasury.
   (2) The order may provide that if a local authority has not complied with the conditions specified in it within such period as may be specified in it, the Secretary of State may estimate the amount of grant under section 70 payable to the authority and employ for that purpose such criteria as he considers relevant.
   (3) Where a grant under section 70 has been paid to a local authority and it appears to the Secretary of State that—
   (a) the grant has been overpaid, or
   (b) there has been a breach of any condition specified in an order under this section, he may recover from the authority the whole or such part of the payment as he may determine.
   (4) Without prejudice to the other methods of recovery, a sum recoverable under this section may be recovered by withholding or reducing subsidy.
   (5) An order under this section may be made before, during or after the end of the period to which it relates.
   (6) In this section "local authority" has the same meaning as in section 69.
   (7) Section 70(5) to (7) applies to orders under this section."

Capital Allowances Act 2001 (c.2)

14. In Schedule A1 to the Capital Allowances Act 2001 (first-year tax credits), in paragraph   **1.159**
17(1)(b) after "sick pay," there is inserted "or".

Social Security Fraud Act 2001 (c.11)

1.160   15. The Social Security Fraud Act 2001 is amended as follows.

16. In section 6B (loss of benefit for conviction etc), in subsection (5), for "to (10)" there is substituted "and (8)".

17. In section 7 (loss of benefit for repeated conviction etc), in subsection (2), for "to (5)" there is substituted "and (4A)".

18. In section 11 (regulations), in subsection (3)(c), for the words from "section" to the end there is substituted "section 6B(5A) or (8), 7(2A) or (4A) or 9(2A) or (4A)".

Commissioners for Revenue and Customs Act 2005 (c.11)

1.161   19. The Commissioners for Revenue and Customs Act 2005 is amended as follows.

20. In section 5 (initial functions), in subsection (1), after paragraph (a) there is inserted "and".

21. In section 44 (payment into Consolidated Fund), in subsection (3), after paragraph (b) there is inserted "and".

Welfare Reform Act 2007 (c. 5)

1.162   22. The Welfare Reform Act 2007 is amended as follows.

23. In section 1 (employment and support allowance), in subsection (3)(d), at the end there is inserted "and".

24. In section 2 (amount of contributory allowance), in subsection (1), for "In the case of a contributory allowance, the amount payable" there is substituted "The amount payable by way of an employment and support allowance".

25.(1) Section 27 (financial provisions) is amended as follows.

(2) In subsection (1), for the words from "so much of" to the end there is substituted "any sums payable by way of employment and support allowance".

(3) In subsection (3), for "contributory" there is substituted "employment and support".

26. In each of the following provisions, for "a contributory allowance" there is substituted "an employment and support allowance"

(a) section 1A(1), (3), (4), (5) and (6) (as inserted by section 51 of this Act);

(b) section 1B(1) (as inserted by section 52 of this Act);

(c) section 3(2)(d);

(d) section 18(4);

(e) section 20(2), (3)(a), (b) and (c), (4), (5)(a), (b) and (c), (6), (7)(a), (b) and (c);

(f) in Schedule 1, paragraphs 1(5)(d) and 3(2)(a);

(g) in Schedule 2, paragraphs 6 and 7(2)(d).

Corporation Tax Act 2009 (c. 4)

1.163   27. The Corporation Tax Act 2009 is amended as follows.

28. In section 1059 (relief relating to SME R&D: total amount of company's PAYE and NICs liabilities), in subsection (5) after "sick pay" there is inserted "or".

29. In section 1108 (relief relating to vaccine research etc: total amount of company's PAYE and NICs liabilities), in subsection (5) after "sick pay" there is inserted "or".

GENERAL NOTE

1.164   The amendments contained in this Schedule to other primary legislation fall into two main categories.

First, and for the most part, the amendments are consequential upon the abolition of income support, housing benefit, council tax benefit, child tax credit, working tax credit and the income-based forms of ESA and JSA. So, for example, references in other Acts to "a contributory employment and support allowance" are changed to "an employment and support allowance". This is because, after the full implementation of universal credit, the only form of ESA which will be available will be a contributory allowance.

The second category of amendments concerns those made to the Child Support, Pensions and Social Security Act 2000. These amend the provisions relating to discretionary housing payments and are consequential on the abolition of council tax benefit and housing benefit.

SCHEDULE 4

HOUSING CREDIT ELEMENT OF STATE PENSION CREDIT

PART 1

AMENDMENTS TO STATE PENSION CREDIT ACT 2002

State Pension Credit Act 2002 (c. 16)

1. The State Pension Credit Act 2002 is amended as follows.　　　　　　　　　　　**1.165**

2. In section 1 (entitlement), in subsection (2)(c), at the end there is inserted "or (iii) the conditions in section 3A(1) and (2) (housing credit)."

3. In that section, in subsection (3)—
   (a) after paragraph (b)　　there is inserted "or
   (c) to a housing credit, calculated in accordance with section 3A, if he satisfies the conditions in subsections (1) and (2) of that section,";
   (b) for the words from "(or to both)" to the end there is substituted "(or to more than one of them, if he satisfies the relevant conditions)".

4. After section 3 there is inserted—

"3A. Housing credit
   (1) The first of the conditions mentioned in section 1(2)(c)(iii) is that the claimant is liable　**1.166**
to make payments in respect of the accommodation he occupies as his home.

   (2) The second of the conditions mentioned in section 1(2)(c)(iii) is that the claimant's capital and income are such that the amount of the housing credit payable (if he were entitled to it) would not be less than a prescribed amount.

   (3) Where the claimant is entitled to a housing credit, the amount of the housing credit shall be an amount calculated in or determined under regulations (which may be zero).

   (4) For the purposes of subsection (1)—
   (a) the accommodation must be in Great Britain;
   (b) the accommodation must be residential accommodation;
   (c) it is immaterial whether the accommodation consists of the whole or part of a building and whether or not it comprises separate and self-contained premises.

   (5) Regulations may make provision as to—
   (a) the meaning of "payments in respect of accommodation" for the purposes of this section (and, in particular, as to the extent to which such payments include mortgage payments);
   (b) circumstances in which a claimant is to be treated as liable or not liable to make such payments;
   (c) circumstances in which a claimant is to be treated as occupying or not occupying accommodation as his home (and, in particular, for temporary absences to be disregarded);
   (d) circumstances in which land used for the purposes of any accommodation is to be treated as included in the accommodation.

   (6) Regulations under this section may make different provision for different areas."

5. In section 7 (fixing of retirement provision for assessed income period), at the end there is inserted—

   "(10) Regulations may prescribe circumstances in which subsection (3) does not apply for the purposes of determining the amount of a housing credit to which the claimant is entitled."

6. In section 12 (polygamous marriages), in subsection (2)(b), after "savings credit" there is inserted "or housing credit".

7. In section 17 (interpretation), in subsection (1), after the definition of "guarantee credit" there is inserted—""housing credit" shall be construed in accordance with sections 1 and 3A;".

8. In Schedule 2 (consequential amendments etc), paragraph 9(5)(a) is repealed.

PART 2

AMENDMENTS TO OTHER ACTS

Social Security Administration Act 1992 (c.5)

1.167   9. The Social Security Administration Act 1992 is amended as follows.

10. In section 5 (regulations about claims and payments) in subsection (6), before "subsection" there is inserted "or housing credit (within the meaning of the State Pension Credit Act 2002)".

11. [¹ ...].

12. (1)Section 122F (supply by rent officers of information) is amended as follows.

(2) In subsection (3)(a) at the end of the words in brackets there is inserted "or housing credit".

(3) In subsection (4) at the end there is inserted "or housing credit".

(4) After that subsection there is inserted—

"(5) In this section "housing credit" has the same meaning as in the State Pension Credit Act 2002".

Housing Act 1996 (c.52)

1.168   13.(1) Section 122 of the Housing Act 1996 (rent officers) is amended as follows.

(2) In the heading, at the end there is inserted "and housing credit".

(3) In subsection (1), at the end there is inserted "or housing credit (within the meaning of the State Pension Credit Act 2002)".

Child Support, Pensions and Social Security Act 2000 (c.19)

1.169   14. In section 69 of the Child Support, Pensions and Social Security Act 2000 (discretionary financial assistance with housing), in subsection (1)(a), after "universal credit" there is inserted "or housing credit (within the meaning of the State Pension Credit Act 2002)".

AMENDMENT

1. Welfare Reform and Work Act 2016 s.20(11)(f)(ii) (April 6, 2018).

GENERAL NOTE

1.170   Schedule 4 (which at the time of writing is not yet in force) amends the State Pension Credit Act 2002 to create a new type of credit within state pension credit to cover housing costs. This will provide support for people who qualify for state pension credit once housing benefit is no longer available. The key provision is para.4, which inserts a new s.3A into the SPCA 2002. This provision sets out the conditions of entitlement to the housing credit (subss.(1) and (2)); it also provides the power to set out the manner in which the housing credit is to be calculated or determined in regulations (subs.(3)). The policy intention is that claimants will be entitled to broadly the same amount of support under the housing credit as they would previously have been entitled to by way of housing benefit. Subsection (5) of new s.3A simply adds detail to the power in subs.(3) by listing a number of specific matters in respect of which regulations may be made. Subsection (6) provides that regulations may make different provision for different areas. The underlying aim is to ensure that persons in different but abutting areas may be treated in a different manner depending on the circumstances obtaining in that area (e.g. to reflect different local taxation applied by different local authorities).

The other provision of note is para.5, which inserts a new s.7(10) into the SPCA 2002. Section 7 provides for assessed income periods in state pension credit, during which a person's retirement provision as assessed at the start of the period is taken to be the same throughout the period. The power exists in s.6(2)(b) to prescribe circumstances in which an assessed income period may not be set. The new s.7(10) provides that regulations may prescribe circumstances in which a person's retirement provision is not taken to be the same throughout the assessed income period for the purposes of determining the amount of housing credit to which a person is entitled. This power is inserted in order to replicate the current position in respect of housing benefit, which does not operate a system based on assessed income periods.

SCHEDULE 5

UNIVERSAL CREDIT AND OTHER WORKING-AGE BENEFITS

General

1.(1) In this Schedule "relevant benefit" means—
  (a) jobseeker's allowance, or
  (b) employment and support allowance.
(2) In this Schedule "work-related requirement" means—
  (a) a work-related requirement within the meaning of this Part,
  (b) a work-related requirement within the meaning of the Jobseekers Act 1995, or
  (c) a work-related requirement within the meaning of Part 1 of the Welfare Reform Act 2007.
(3) In this Schedule "sanction" means a reduction of benefit under—
  (a) section 26 or 27,
  (b) section 6J or 6K of the Jobseekers Act 1995, or
  (c) section 11J of the Welfare Reform Act 2007.

1.171

Dual entitlement

2. (1) Regulations may make provision as to the amount payable by way of a relevant benefit where a person is entitled to that benefit and universal credit.
(2) Regulations under sub-paragraph (1) may in particular provide for no amount to be payable by way of a relevant benefit.
(3) Regulations may, where a person is entitled to a relevant benefit and universal credit—
  (a) make provision as to the application of work-related requirements;
  (b) make provision as to the application of sanctions.
(4) Provision under sub-paragraph (3)(a) includes in particular—
  (a) provision securing that compliance with a work-related requirement for a relevant benefit is to be treated as compliance with a work-related requirement for universal credit;
  (b) provision disapplying any requirement on the Secretary of State to impose, or a person to comply with, a work-related requirement for a relevant benefit or universal credit.
(5) Provision under sub-paragraph (3)(b) includes in particular—
  (a) provision for the order in which sanctions are to be applied to awards of relevant benefit and universal credit;
  (b) provision to secure that the application of a sanction to an award of a relevant benefit does not result in an increase of the amount of an award of universal credit.

1.172

Movement between working-age benefits

3. Regulations may provide—
  (a) in a case where a person ceases to be entitled to universal credit and becomes entitled to a relevant benefit, for a sanction relating to the award of universal credit to be applied to the award of the relevant benefit;
  (b) in a case where a person ceases to be entitled to a relevant benefit and becomes entitled to universal credit, for a sanction relating to the award of the relevant benefit to be applied to the award of universal credit;
  (c) in a case where a person ceases to be entitled to one relevant benefit and becomes entitled to the other, for a sanction relating to the award of the former to apply to the award of the latter.

1.173

Hardship payments

4. Regulations under section 28 (hardship payments) may be made in relation to a person whose award of universal credit is reduced by virtue of regulations under paragraph 2(3)(b) or 3(b) as in relation to a person whose award is reduced under section 26 or 27.

1.174

1.175   5. In section 4 of the Jobseekers Act 1995 (amount payable by way of a jobseeker's allowance), in subsection (1)(b)—
(a) after "making" there is inserted—
"(i) deductions in respect of earnings calculated in the prescribed manner (which may
include multiplying some or all earnings by a prescribed percentage), and
(b) "earnings," (before "pension payments") is repealed.
6. (1) Section 2 of the Welfare Reform Act 2007 (amount of contributory allowance) is
amended as follows.
(2) In subsection (1)(c), after "making" there is inserted—
"(i) deductions in respect of earnings calculated in the prescribed manner (which may
include multiplying some or all earnings by a prescribed percentage), and
(3) At the end there is inserted—
"(6) In subsection (1)(c)(i) the reference to earnings is to be construed in accordance with
sections 3, 4 and 112 of the Social Security Contributions and Benefits Act 1992."

DEFINITIONS

"relevant benefit"—para.1(1)
"sanction"—para.1(3)
"work-related requirement"—para.1(2)

GENERAL NOTE

1.176   Schedule 5 makes provision to allow the Secretary of State to prescribe details of
the relationship between universal credit on the one hand and ESA and JSA on the
other. At the time of writing only paras 1-3 inclusive are in force; paras 4-6 are yet
to be brought into force.

Paragraph 2
1.177   In certain circumstances claimants may meet the conditions of entitlement to
both universal credit and JSA or ESA (as contributory benefits only). Paragraph 2
enables the Secretary of State to make provision as to the amount of contributory
benefit payable where a person is entitled to both a contributory benefit and universal credit. According to the Department, Memorandum from the Department for
Work and Pensions, *Welfare Reform Bill, as brought from the House of Commons on 16
June 2011*, House of Lords Select Committee on Delegated Powers and Regulatory
Reform (at para.166):

"It is intended that the power will in particular be used to:
a) specify whether, in cases where the claimant might be entitled to both universal
credit and either ESA or JSA, the claimant will be paid to only universal credit, or
only the contributory benefit, or to both.
b) make provision in relation to cases where a claimant might be able to
choose which benefit to claim, in the event of them being potentially entitled
to both.
c) provide for exceptions, if appropriate, from the general rule.
d) prescribe how work-related requirements are to apply in such cases.
e) set out, if sanctions are applicable, which benefit is to be reduced first (in a case
where a claimant is receiving both), what limitations any reductions are subject
to, and to provide, if appropriate, that the application of a sanction to one benefit
does not increase payment of the other."

Paragraph 3
1.178   Paragraph 3(a) and (b) allows for regulations to provide that where a person is
entitled to universal credit and has their award reduced by a sanction, and then
becomes entitled to JSA or ESA, the sanction can be applied to the new JSA or ESA
award. This is obviously designed to ensure that claimants cannot avoid a sanction
simply because they move between universal credit and JSA or ESA. Paragraph
3(c) makes similar provision for regulations to provide that sanctions imposed on

claimants entitled to JSA or ESA can be applied to a subsequent award of the other benefit.

Paragraph 4

This allows for regulations made under s.28 (hardship payments) to apply to a person whose universal credit award is reduced by virtue of either para.2(3)(b) or 3(b) above. Section 28 only allows for universal credit hardship payments to be made to claimants who have their universal credit award reduced under ss.26 or 27, and so para.4 allows for claimants whose awards are reduced under other provisions to also be eligible for universal credit hardship payments.

1.179

Paragraph 5

This amendment to s.4 of the Jobseekers Act 1995 creates a power which allows the Secretary of State to deduct earnings which have been calculated in a prescribed manner, which may include multiplying some or all of the earnings by a prescribed percentage. The intention is to make provision for the amount of benefit payable to be tapered as earnings increase and to allow for some earnings to be disregarded before the taper is applied.

1.180

Paragraph 6

This amends s.2 of the Welfare Reform Act 2007, and has similar effect on provision for the calculation of earnings in ESA as does para.(5) in relation to JSA.

1.181

SCHEDULE 6

MIGRATION TO UNIVERSAL CREDIT

General

1.(1) Regulations may make provision for the purposes of, or in connection with, replacing existing benefits with universal credit.

1.182

(2) In this Schedule "existing benefit" means—

    (a) a benefit abolished under section 33(1);

    (b) any other prescribed benefit.

(3) In this Schedule "appointed day" means the day appointed for the coming into force of section 1.

Claims before the appointed day

2. (1) The provision referred to in paragraph 1(1) includes—

1.183

    (a) provision for a claim for universal credit to be made before the appointed day for a period beginning on or after that day;

    (b) provision for a claim for universal credit made before the appointed day to be treated to any extent as a claim for an existing benefit;

    (c) provision for a claim for an existing benefit made before the appointed day to be treated to any extent as a claim for universal credit.

(2) The provision referred to in paragraph 1(1) includes provision, where a claim for universal credit is made (or is treated as made) before the appointed day, for an award on the claim to be made in respect of a period before the appointed day (including provision as to the conditions of entitlement for, and amount of, such an award).

Claims after the appointed day

3. (1) The provision referred to in paragraph 1(1) includes—

1.184

    (a) provision permanently or temporarily excluding the making of a claim for universal credit after the appointed day by—

        (i) a person to whom an existing benefit is awarded, or

        (ii) a person who would be entitled to an existing benefit on making a claim for it;

    (b) provision temporarily excluding the making of a claim for universal credit after the appointed day by any other person;

    (c) provision excluding entitlement to universal credit temporarily or for a particular period;

    (d) provision for a claim for universal credit made after the appointed day to be treated to any extent as a claim for an existing benefit;

(e) provision for a claim for an existing benefit made after the appointed day to be treated to any extent as a claim for universal credit.

(2) The provision referred to in paragraph 1(1) includes provision, where a claim for universal credit is made (or is treated as made) after the appointed day, for an award on the claim to be made in respect of a period before the appointed day (including provision as to the conditions of entitlement for, and amount of, such an award).

Awards

1.185

4.(1) The provision referred to in paragraph 1(1) includes—
  (a) provision for terminating an award of an existing benefit;
  (b) provision for making an award of universal credit, with or without application, to a person whose award of existing benefit is terminated.

(2) The provision referred to in sub-paragraph (1)(b) includes—
  (a) provision imposing requirements as to the procedure to be followed, information to be supplied or assessments to be undergone in relation to an award by virtue of that sub-paragraph or an application for such an award;
  (b) provision as to the consequences of failure to comply with any such requirement;
  (c) provision as to the terms on which, and conditions subject to which, such an award is made, including—
    (i) provision temporarily or permanently disapplying, or otherwise modifying, conditions of entitlement to universal credit in relation to the award;
    (ii) provision temporarily or permanently disapplying, or otherwise modifying, any requirement under this Part for a person to be assessed in respect of capability for work or work-related activity;
  (d) provision as to the amount of such an award;
  (e) provision that fulfilment of any condition relevant to entitlement to an award of an existing benefit, or relevant to the amount of such an award, is to be treated as fulfilment of an equivalent condition in relation to universal credit.

(3) Provision under sub-paragraph (2)(d) may secure that where an award of universal credit is made by virtue of sub-paragraph (1)(b)—
  (a) the amount of the award is not less than the amount to which the person would have been entitled under the terminated award, or is not less than that amount by more than a prescribed amount;
  (b) if the person to whom it is made ceases to be entitled to universal credit for not more than a prescribed period, the gap in entitlement is disregarded in calculating the amount of any new award of universal credit.

Work-related requirements and sanctions

1.186

5.(1) The provision referred to in paragraph 1(1) includes—
  (a) provision relating to the application of work-related requirements for relevant benefits;
  (b) provision relating to the application of sanctions.

(2) The provision referred to in sub-paragraph (1)(a) includes—
  (a) provision that a claimant commitment for a relevant benefit is to be treated as a claimant commitment for universal credit;
  (b) provision that a work-related requirement for a relevant benefit is treated as a work-related requirement for universal credit;
  (c) provision for anything done which is relevant to compliance with a work-related requirement for a relevant benefit to be treated as done for the purposes of compliance with a work-related requirement for universal credit;
  (d) provision temporarily disapplying any provision of this Part in relation to work-related requirements for universal credit.

(3) The provision referred to in sub-paragraph (1)(b) includes—
  (a) provision for a sanction relevant to an award of a relevant benefit to be applied to an award of universal credit;
  (b) provision for anything done which is relevant to the application of a sanction for a relevant benefit to be treated as done for the purposes of the application of a sanction for universal credit;
  (c) provision temporarily disapplying any provision of this Part in relation to the application of sanctions.

(4) In this paragraph—
"relevant benefit" means—
  (a) jobseeker's allowance,

   (b) employment and support allowance, and
   (c) income support;
"work-related requirement" means—
   (a) for universal credit, a work-related requirement within the meaning of this Part;
   (b) for jobseeker's allowance, a requirement imposed—
        (i) by virtue of regulations under section 8 or 17A of the Jobseekers Act 1995,
        (ii) by a jobseeker's direction (within the meaning of section 19A of that Act),
        (iii) by virtue of regulations under section 2A, 2AA or 2D of the Social Security Administration Act 1992, or
        (iv) by a direction under section 2F of that Act;
   (c) for employment and support allowance, a requirement imposed—
        (i) by virtue of regulations under section 8, 9, 11, 12 or 13 of the Welfare Reform Act 2007,
        (ii) by a direction under section 15 of that Act,
        (iii) by virtue of regulations under section 2A, 2AA or 2D of the Social Security Administration Act 1992, or
        (iv) by a direction under section 2F of that Act;
   (d) for income support, a requirement imposed—
        (i) by virtue of regulations under section 2A, 2AA or 2D of the Social Security Administration Act 1992, or
        (ii) by a direction under section 2F of that Act;
"sanction" means a reduction of benefit under—
   (a) section 26 or 27 above,
   (b) section 19, 19A or 19B of the Jobseekers Act 1995,
   (c) section 11, 12 or 13 of the Welfare Reform Act 2007, or
   (d) section 2A, 2AA or 2D of the Social Security Administration Act 1992.

Tax credits

6. In relation to the replacement of working tax credit and child tax credit with universal credit, the provision referred to in paragraph 1(1) includes—   **1.187**
   (a) provision modifying the application of the Tax Credits Act 2002 (or of any provision made under it);
   (b) provision for the purposes of recovery of overpayments of working tax credit or child tax credit (including in particular provision for treating overpayments of working tax credit or child tax credit as if they were overpayments of universal credit).

Supplementary

7. Regulations under paragraph 1(1) may secure the result that any gap in entitlement to an existing benefit (or what would, but for the provisions of this Part, be a gap in entitlement to an existing benefit) is to be disregarded for the purposes of provision under such regulations.   **1.188**

DEFINITIONS

   "appointed day"—see para.1(3).
   "existing benefit"—see para.1(2).
   "relevant benefit"—see para.5(4).
   "sanction"—*ibid.*
   "work-related requirement"—*ibid.*

GENERAL NOTE

Schedule 6 (which at the time of writing is partly in force and partly not yet in force) contains regulation-making powers to make provision in connection with replacing the existing means-tested benefits system with universal credit, and more particularly with the "migration" of claimants from one benefit to the other. Regulations made under this Schedule were subject to the affirmative resolution procedure where the power in para.1(1) was used in a way described in paras.4, 5 or 6 for the first time.   **1.189**

Paragraph 1

1.190   The principal such regulations are the Transitional Provisions Regulations 2014.

Paragraph 2

1.191   Regulations may specify when a claim can be treated as a claim for an existing benefit and when a claim can be treated as a claim for universal credit. For example, regulations may provide that a claim for an existing benefit made before the day that universal credit comes into effect, but for a period beginning after universal credit is introduced, (i.e. people making advance claims), can be treated as a claim for universal credit.

Paragraph 3

1.192   Regulations may provide that after the appointed day (i.e. the day universal credit is introduced), existing benefits cannot be claimed (see Transitional Provisions Regulations 2014 regs 5 and 6). Regulations can also provide for a claim to universal credit to be treated as a claim for existing benefit. This might be used where e.g. a claimant's benefit is backdated to a period before universal credit was introduced. Regulations may also provide that these cases may be awarded universal credit on terms, which match wholly or partly, the existing benefit.

Paragraph 4

1.193   Regulations will be able to make provision for the "migration" of existing claimants onto universal credit. Such migration may be voluntary or mandatory. Regulations can prescribe the timing, conditions, kind and amount of any such entitlement to universal credit which was previously an award for an existing benefit. As regards para.4(1), see further the Transitional Provisions Regulations 2014.

Paragraph 5

1.194   This makes provision for the continuity of both work-related requirements and sanctions; see further especially regs 30–34 of the Transitional Provisions Regulations 2014 as regards sanctions.

Paragraph 6

1.195   This provides that the Secretary of State may, through regulations, modify any provision of the Tax Credits Act 2002 (or regulations) as necessary for the purposes of transferring people from working tax credit and child tax credit to universal credit. This power may be used to align certain tax credit rules more closely with universal credit to facilitate the transition process (para.(a)). Paragraph 6 also makes it clear that for overpayments of tax credits could, through the transitional regulations, be treated as overpayments of universal credit (para.(b)).See further regs 11-12A of the Transitional Provisions Regulations 2014.

Welfare Reform and Work Act 2016

(2016 C.7)

SECTIONS REPRODUCED

Welfare benefits

Loans for mortgage interest etc

Final

An Act to make provision about reports on progress towards full employment and the apprenticeships target; to make provision about reports on the effect of certain support for troubled families; to make provision about life chances; to make provision about the benefit cap; to make provision about social security and tax credits; to make provision for loans for mortgage interest and other liabilities; and to make provision about social housing rents.
[March 16, 2016]

GENERAL NOTE

Sections 8-21 of, and Schedule 1 to, this Act are of potential relevance to entitle-   1.196.1
ment to social security benefits and tax credits. They have been reproduced below to the extent that they are in force, do not make amendments that have been reproduced in the text of other legislation in this work, and have not been reproduced in other volumes.

Sections 1-7 concern social policy, section 22 governs an aspect of social security administration that cannot give rise to an appeal and sections 23-33 make provision about social housing rents. They are therefore beyond the scope of this work,

Welfare benefits

Benefit cap

8.—(1)-(7) *[Omitted]*   1.197

(8) Regulations made by the Secretary of State may make such transitional or transitory provision or savings as the Secretary of State considers necessary or expedient in connection with the coming into force of subsections (1) to (6).

(9) Regulations under subsection (8) may in particular—

(a) provide for section 96 to have effect as if the amendments made by subsections (2) to (5) and (7) had not been made, in relation to such persons or descriptions of persons as are specified in the regulations or generally, until a time or times specified in a notice issued by the Secretary of State;

(b) provide for the Secretary of State to issue notices under paragraph (a) specifying different times for different persons or descriptions of person;

(c) make provision about the issuing of notices under paragraph (a), including provision for the Secretary of State to issue notices to authorities administering housing benefit that have effect in relation to persons specified, or persons of a description specified, in the notices.

(10) Section 176 of the Social Security Administration Act 1992 (consultation with representative organisations) does not apply in relation to regulations under subsection (8).

(11) Regulations under subsection (8) must be made by statutory instrument.

(12) A statutory instrument containing regulations under subsection (8) is subject to annulment in pursuance of a resolution of either House of Parliament.

GENERAL NOTE

1.198   Section 8 was brought into force on March 16, 2016 for the purpose of making regulations (s.36(3)(a)), and on November 7, 2016 for all purposes (SI 2016/910, reg.2(1)). It extends to England, Wales and Scotland (s.35(3)). Subss.(1)-(6) amend WRA 2012 ss.96 and 97 (above) and subs.(7) revokes Pensions Act 2014 Sch.12 para.52. The regulation-making powers conferred by subs.(8)-(12) have been exercised to make the Benefit Cap (Housing Benefit and Universal Credit) (Amendment) Regulations 2016 (SI 2016/909).

Changes to child element of universal credit

1.199   14.—(1)-(5) *[Omitted]*

(6) The Secretary of State may by regulations make such transitional or transitory provision or savings as the Secretary of State considers necessary or expedient in connection with the coming into force of this section.

(7) Regulations under subsection (6) must be made by statutory instrument.

(8) A statutory instrument containing regulations under subsection (6) is subject to annulment in pursuance of a resolution of either House of Parliament.

GENERAL NOTE

1.200   Subss.(1)-(5), which amend Welfare Reform Act 2012 s.10 and Universal Credit Regulations, reg.24 came into force on April 6, 2017 (see SI 2017/111 reg.4). The other sub-sections came into force on February 8, 2017 (see SI 2017/111 reg.2(a)). The section as a whole extends to England and Wales and Scotland (s.35(3)(c)).

The regulation-making powers in subss.(6)-(8) have been used to make the Social Security (Restrictions on Amounts for Children and Qualifying Young Persons) Amendment Regulations 2017 (SI 2017/376) which amend Universal Credit Regulations, regs 2 and 24 and introduce new regs 24A and 24B and a new Sch.12 into those Regulations: see the commentary to regs 24-24B below.

Loans for mortgage interest etc

Loans for mortgage interest etc

1.201   18.—(1) The Secretary of State may by regulations provide for loans to be made in respect of a person's liability to make owner-occupier payments in respect of accommodation occupied by the person as the person's home.

(2) The regulations may make provision about eligibility to receive a loan under the regulations.

(3) Regulations under subsection (2) may in particular require that a person—

(a) is entitled to receive income support, income-based jobseeker's allowance, income-related employment and support allowance, state pension credit or universal credit;

(b) has received such a benefit for a period prescribed by the regulations.

(4) The regulations may make provision about the liabilities in respect of which a loan under the regulations may be made.

(5) Regulations under subsection (4) may in particular provide that a loan under the regulations may only be made if, and to the extent that, a person's liability to make owner-occupier payments was incurred for purposes prescribed by the regulations.

(6) Regulations under subsection (4) may in particular make provision about—

(a) determining or calculating the amount of a person's liabilities;

(b) the maximum amount of a person's liabilities in respect of which a loan under the regulations may be made.

(7) The regulations may—

(a) make provision about determining or calculating the amount that may be paid by way of loan under the regulations;

(b) require that a loan under the regulations be secured by a mortgage of or charge over a legal or beneficial interest in land or, in Scotland, by a heritable security.

(8) The regulations may define "owner-occupier payment".

(9) Regulations under this section may make different provision for different purposes.

(10) Regulations under this section must be made by statutory instrument.

(11) A statutory instrument containing regulations under this section is subject to annulment in pursuance of a resolution of either House of Parliament.

GENERAL NOTE

This section (and ss.19 & 21 below) came into force on April 3, 2017 (SI 2017/111 reg.3(d)-(f)). Section 20, which repeals and amends primary legislation governing mortgage interest support for IS, income-based JSA, SPC, income-related ESA and universal credit, came into force on July 27, 2018 (sub-ss (2)-(7) and (10): see SI 2017/802) and April 6, 2018 (sub-ss (1), (8)-(9) and (11): see SI 2018/438). All four sections extend to England and Wales and Scotland (s.35(3)(g)).   1.202

Taken together, ss.18, 19 and 21 confer powers on the Secretary of State to make regulations which replace the housing costs element for owner-occupiers under Universal Credit Regulations, reg.25(2) and Sch.5 (and the equivalent payments under IS Regulations, Sch.3; Jobseeker's Allowance Regulations 1996, Sch.2; SPC Regulations, Sch.2; and ESA Regulations, Sch.6) with repayable loans.

However, by the final date for the inclusion of legislation in this edition (and also at the time of going to press) no regulations had been made and so the legislation listed in the previous paragraph remains in force. It is understood that the Department intends to begin replacing owner-occupier payments with loans from April 2018. The existence of the powers to make transitional provision in s.21 suggest that the new rules may be piloted and then "rolled out" rather than introduced for all claimants and in all areas at the same time.

Section 18: further provision

19.—(1) This section makes further provision about regulations under section 18.   1.203

(2) The regulations may make provision about—

(a) circumstances in which a person is to be treated as liable or not liable to make owner-occupier payments;

(b) circumstances in which a person is to be treated as occupying or not occupying particular accommodation as a home.

(3) The regulations may include—

(a) provision about applying for a loan;

(b) provision requiring a person to satisfy requirements prescribed by the regulations before a loan may be made under the regulations, including requirements about receiving financial advice;

(c) provision about entering into an agreement (which may contain such terms and conditions as the Secretary of State thinks fit, subject to what may be provided in the regulations);

(d) provision about the time when, and manner in which, a loan must be repaid;

(e) provision about other terms upon which a loan is made;

(f) provision about the payment of interest, including provision prescribing or providing for the determination of the rate of interest;

(g) provision enabling administrative costs to be charged;

(h) provision about adding administrative costs to the amount of a loan;

(i) provision about accepting substituted security.

(4) The regulations may make provision—

(a) requiring that, in circumstances prescribed by the regulations, money lent in respect of a person's liability to make owner-occupier payments—

(i) is paid directly to the qualifying lender;

(ii) is applied by the qualifying lender towards discharging the person's liability to make owner-occupier payments;

(b) for the costs of administering the making of payments to qualifying lenders to be defrayed, in whole or in part, at the expense of the qualifying lenders, whether by requiring them to pay fees prescribed by the regulations, by deducting and retaining such part as may be prescribed by the regulations of the amounts that would otherwise be paid to them or otherwise;

(c) for requiring a qualifying lender, in a case where by virtue of paragraph (b) the amount paid to the lender is less than it would otherwise have been, to credit against the liability in relation to which the amount is paid the amount of the difference (in addition to the payment actually made);

(d) for enabling a body which, or person who, would otherwise be a qualifying lender to elect not to be regarded as a qualifying lender for the purposes of this section (other than this paragraph);

(e) for the recovery from any body or person—

(i) of any sums paid to that body or person by way of payment under the regulations that ought not to have been so paid;

(ii) of any fees or other sums due from that body or person by virtue of paragraph (b);

(f) for cases where the same person is liable to make owner-occupier payments under more than one agreement to make such payments.

(5) The regulations may provide for the Secretary of State to make arrangements with another person for the exercise of functions under the regulations.

(6) The regulations may include—

(a) provision requiring information and documents to be provided;

(b) provision authorising the disclosure of information.

(7) The bodies and persons who are "qualifying lenders" for the purposes of this section are—

(a) a deposit taker;

(b) an insurer;

(c) a county council, a county borough council, a district council, a London Borough Council, the Common Council of the City of London or the Council of the Isles of Scilly;

(d) a council constituted under section 2 of the Local Government etc. (Scotland) Act 1994;

(e) a new town corporation;

(f) other bodies or persons prescribed by regulations under section 18.

(8) In this section—

"deposit taker" means—

(a) a person who has permission under Part 4A of the Financial Services and Markets Act 2000 to accept deposits, or

(b) an EEA firm of the kind mentioned in paragraph 5(b) of Schedule 3 to that Act which has permission under paragraph 15 of that Schedule (as a result of qualifying for authorisation under paragraph 12 of that Schedule) to accept deposits;

"insurer" means—

(a) a person who has permission under Part 4A of the Financial Services and Markets Act 2000 to effect and carry out contracts of insurance, or

(b) an EEA firm of the kind mentioned in paragraph 5(d) of Schedule 3 to that Act which has permission under paragraph 15 of that Schedule (as a result of qualifying for authorisation under paragraph 12 of that Schedule) to effect and carry out contracts of insurance.

(9) The definitions of "deposit taker" and 'insurer' in this section must be read with—

(a) section 22 of the Financial Services and Markets Act 2000;

(b) any relevant order under that section;

(c) Schedule 2 to that Act.

GENERAL NOTE

See the General note to s.18 above. 1.204

Consequential amendments

20. *[Not reproduced]* 1.205

GENERAL NOTE

The amendments made by s.20 have been reproduced at the appropriate places in the text of this, and the other volumes. 1.206

Transitional provision

21.—(1) Regulations made by the Secretary of State may make such transitional or transitory provision or savings as the Secretary of State considers necessary or expedient in connection with the coming into force of sections 18 to 20. 1.207

(2) The regulations may include provision for temporarily excluding the making of a loan under regulations under section 18 after the coming into force of sections 18 to 20.

(3) Regulations under subsection (2) may in particular—

(a) provide for a temporary exclusion to continue until a time or times specified in a notice issued by the Secretary of State;

(b) enable the Secretary of State to issue notices under paragraph (a) specifying different times for different persons or descriptions of person.

(4) The regulations may include provision for enabling assistance with payments in respect of accommodation occupied as a home to be given by means of a qualifying benefit after the coming into force of sections 18 to 20 (including where the making of loans is temporarily excluded).

(5) Regulations under subsection (4) may in particular—

(a) provide for legislation that has been repealed or revoked to be treated as having effect;

(b) provide for assistance by means of a qualifying benefit to continue until a time or times specified in a notice issued by the Secretary of State;

(c) enable the Secretary of State to issue notices under paragraph (b) specifying different times for different persons or descriptions of person.

(6) In this section "qualifying benefit" means income support, income-based jobseeker's allowance, income-related employment and support allowance, state pension credit or universal credit.

(7) Regulations under this section may make different provision for different areas, cases or purposes.

(8) Regulations under this section must be made by statutory instrument.

(9) A statutory instrument containing regulations under this section is subject to annulment in pursuance of a resolution of either House of Parliament.

GENERAL NOTE

1.208   See the General note to s.18 above.

Final

Power to make consequential provision

1.209   **34.**—(1) The Secretary of State may by regulations make such amendments and revocations of subordinate legislation (whenever made) as appear to the Secretary of State to be necessary or expedient in consequence of any provision of this Act.

(2) In this section "subordinate legislation" has the same meaning as in the Interpretation Act 1978.

(3) Regulations under this section must be made by statutory instrument.

(4) A statutory instrument containing regulations under this section is subject to annulment in pursuance of a resolution of either House of Parliament.

PART II

UNIVERSAL CREDIT: REGULATIONS

The Universal Credit Regulations 2013

(SI 2013/376)

Made on February 25, 2013 by the Secretary of State for Work and Pensions in exercise of the powers conferred by sections 2(2), 4(2), (3), (5), (6) and (7), 5, 6(1)(a) and (3), 7(2) and (3), 8(3), 9(2) and (3), 10(2) to (5), 11(3) to (5), 12(1), (3) and (4), 14(5), 15(2), 17(3) and (4), 18(3) and (5), 19(2)(d), (3) and (4), 20(1), 22(2), 24(1), (5) and (6), 25, 26(2)(a), (6) and (8), 27(4), (5), (9), 28, 32(1), 37(3) to (7), 39(3)(a), 40, 96 and 97 of, and paragraphs 1, 4, 5 and 7 of Schedule 1 and paragraphs 2 and 3 of Schedule 5 to, the Welfare Reform Act 2012; a draft having been laid before Parliament in accordance with section 43(3) of the Welfare Reform Act 2012 and approved by a resolution of each House of Parliament; and without the instrument having been referred to the Social Security Advisory Committee because it contains only regulations made by virtue of or consequential on Part 1 and sections 96 and 97 of, and Schedules 1 and 5 to, the Welfare Reform Act 2012 and is made before the end of the period of 6 months beginning with the coming into force of those provisions.

2.1

[In force April 2013 but see Pt IV]

ARRANGEMENT OF REGULATIONS

PART 1

INTRODUCTION

2.2

PART 2

ENTITLEMENT

PART 3

AWARDS

PART 4

ELEMENTS OF AN AWARD

PART 5

CAPABILITY FOR WORK OR WORK-RELATED ACTIVITY

PART 6

CALCULATION OF CAPITAL AND INCOME

CHAPTER 1

CAPITAL

CHAPTER 2

EARNED INCOME

CHAPTER 3

UNEARNED INCOME

CHAPTER 4

MISCELLANEOUS

PART 7

THE BENEFIT CAP

PART 8

CLAIMANT RESPONSIBILITIES

CHAPTER 1

WORK-RELATED REQUIREMENTS

CHAPTER 2

SANCTIONS

CHAPTER 3

HARDSHIP

SCHEDULES

PART 1

INTRODUCTION

Citation and commencement

2.4   **1.**—These Regulations may be cited as the Universal Credit Regulations 2013 and come into force on 29th April 2013.

GENERAL NOTE

2.5   Although the Regulations come into force on April 29, 2013, they do not apply to all claimants. See further the Universal Credit (Transitional Provisions) Regulations 2014 and the commencement orders in Pt IV of this Volume.

Interpretation

2.6   **2.**—In these Regulations—
"the Act" means the Welfare Reform Act 2012;
[⁸ . . .]
[² "adopter" has the meaning in regulation 89(3)(a);]
"attendance allowance" means—
(a) an attendance allowance under section 64 of the Contributions and Benefits Act;
(b) an increase of disablement pension under section 104 or 105 of that Act (increases where constant attendance needed and for exceptionally severe disablement);
(c) [³ . . .]
(d) a payment by virtue of article 14, 15, 16, 43 or 44 of the Personal Injuries (Civilians) Scheme 1983 or any analogous payment;
(e) any payment based on the need for attendance which is paid as an addition to a war disablement pension;
[¹(f) armed forces independence payment under the Armed Forces and Reserve Forces (Compensation Scheme) Order 2011;]
"bereavement allowance" means an allowance under section 39B of the Contributions and Benefits Act;
[⁶ "blind" means certified as severely sight impaired or blind by a consultant ophthalmologist;]
"care leaver" has the meaning in regulation 8;
"carer's allowance" means a carer's allowance under section 70 of the Contributions and Benefits Act;
"carer element" has the meaning in regulation 29;
"childcare costs element" has the meaning in regulation 31;
"child element" has the meaning in regulation 24;
"close relative", in relation to a person, means—
(a) a parent, parent-in-law, son, son-in-law, daughter, daughter-in-law, step-parent, step-son, step-daughter, brother or sister; and
(b) if any of the above is a member of a couple, the other member of the couple;
"confinement" has the meaning in regulation 8;
"Contributions and Benefits Act" means the Social Security Contributions and Benefits Act 1992;
"course of advanced education" has the meaning in regulation 12;

"disability living allowance" means an allowance under section 71 of the Contributions and Benefits Act;

"earned income" has the meaning in Chapter 2 of Part 6;

"EEA Regulations" means the [14 Immigration (European Economic Area) Regulations 2016];

"employment and support allowance" means an allowance under Part 1 of the Welfare Reform Act 2007 as amended by Schedule 3 and Part 1 of Schedule 14 to the Welfare Reform Act 2012 (removing references to an income-related allowance);

[4 "enactment" includes an enactment comprised in, or an instrument made under, an Act of the Scottish Parliament or the National Assembly of Wales;]

"ESA Regulations" means the Employment and Support Allowance Regulations 2013;

"expected number of hours per week" has the meaning in regulation 88;

"foster parent" means—

(a) in relation to England, a person with whom a child is placed under the Fostering Services Regulations 2011;

(b) in relation to Wales, a person with whom a child is placed under the Fostering Services (Wales) Regulations 2003;

(c) in relation to Scotland, a foster carer or kinship carer with whom a child is placed under the Looked After Children (Scotland) Regulations 2009;

"grant" has the meaning in regulation 68;

"health care professional" means (except in regulation 98)—

(a) a registered medical practitioner;

(b) a registered nurse; or

(c) an occupational therapist or physiotherapist registered with a regulatory body established by Order in Council under section 60 of the Health Act 1999;

"housing costs element" has the meaning in regulation 25;

"individual threshold" has the meaning in regulation 90(2);

"industrial injuries benefit" means a benefit under Part 5 of the Contributions and Benefits Act;

"ITEPA" means the Income Tax (Earnings and Pensions) Act 2003;

"jobseeker's allowance" means an allowance under the Jobseekers Act 1995 as amended by Part 1 of Schedule 14 to the Act (removing references to an income-based allowance);

"local authority" means—

(a) in relation to England, a county council, a district council, a parish council, a London borough council, the Common Council of the City of London or the Council of the Isles of Scilly;

(b) in relation to Wales, a county council, a county borough council or a community council;

(c) in relation to Scotland, a council constituted under section 2 of the Local Government etc. (Scotland) Act 1994;

[12 "LCWRA element" has the meaning in regulation 27;]

"looked after by a local authority" in relation to a child or young person means a child or young person who is looked after by a local authority within the meaning of section 22 of the Children Act 1989 [10 , section 17(6) of the Children (Scotland) Act 1995 or section 74 of the Social Services and Well-being (Wales) Act 2014];

"maternity allowance" means a maternity allowance under section 35 [5 or 35B] of the Contributions and Benefits Act;

"Medical Evidence Regulations" means the Social Security (Medical Evidence) Regulations 1976;

[9 "monthly earnings" has the meaning in regulation 90(6);]

"national insurance contribution" means a contribution under Part 1 of the Contributions and Benefits Act;

[11 "National Minimum Wage Regulations" means the National Minimum Wage Regulations 2015;]

"[8 ...] statutory paternity pay" means [8 ...] statutory paternity pay under Part 12ZA of the Contributions and Benefits Act;

"paid work" means work done for payment or in expectation of payment and does not include being engaged by a charitable or voluntary organisation, or as a volunteer, in circumstances in which the payment received by or due to be paid to the person is in respect of expenses;

"partner" means (except in regulation 77) the other member of a couple;

"personal independence payment" means an allowance under Part 4 of the Welfare Reform Act 2012;

"prisoner" means—

(a) a person who is detained in custody pending trial or sentence upon conviction or under a sentence imposed by a court; or

(b) is on temporary release in accordance with the provisions of the Prison Act 1952 or the Prisons (Scotland) Act 1989,

other than a person who is detained in hospital under the provisions of the Mental Health Act 1983 or, in Scotland, under the provisions of the Mental Health (Care and Treatment) (Scotland) Act 2003 or the Criminal Procedure (Scotland) Act 1995;

"qualifying young person" has the meaning in regulation 5;

"redundancy" has the meaning in section 139(1) of the Employment Rights Act 1996;

[6 ...]

"regular and substantial caring responsibilities for a severely disabled person" has the meaning in regulation 30;

"relevant childcare" has the meaning in regulation 35;

"responsible for a child or qualifying young person" has the meaning in regulation 4;

"statutory adoption pay" means a payment under Part 12ZB of the Contributions Benefits Act;

"statutory maternity pay" means a payment under Part 12 of the Contributions and Benefits Act;

[15 "statutory parental bereavement pay" means statutory parental bereavement pay payable in accordance with Part 12ZD of the Contributions and Benefits Act;]

[7 "statutory shared parental pay" means statutory shared parental pay payable in accordance with Part 12ZC of the Contributions and Benefits Act;]

"statutory sick pay" means a payment under Part 11 of the Contributions and Benefits Act;

[13 "step-parent", in relation to a child or qualifying young person ("A"), means a person who is not A's parent but—

(a) is a member of a couple, the other member of which is a parent of A, where both are responsible for A; or

(b) was previously a member of a couple, the other member of which was a parent of A, where immediately prior to ceasing to be a member of that couple the person was, and has since continued to be, responsible for A.]

"student loan" has the meaning in regulation 68;

"terminally ill" means suffering from a progressive disease where death in consequence of that disease can reasonably be expected within 6 months;

"total outstanding reduction period" has the meaning in regulation 101(5);

"trade dispute" has the meaning in section 244 of the Trade Union and Labour Relations (Consolidation) Act 1992;

"unearned income" has the meaning in Chapter 3 of Part 6;

"war disablement pension" means any retired pay, pension or allowance payable in respect of disablement under an instrument specified in section 639(2) of ITEPA;

[1 . . .]

"widowed mother's allowance" means an allowance under section 37 of the Contributions and Benefits Act;

"widowed parent's allowance" means an allowance under section 39A of the Contributions and Benefits Act;

"widow's pension" means a pension under section 39 of the Contributions and Benefits Act.

AMENDMENTS

1. Armed Forces and Reserve Forces Compensation Scheme (Consequential Provisions: Subordinate Legislation) Order 2013 (SI 2013/591) art.7 and Sch., para.54 (April 8, 2013).

2. Universal Credit (Miscellaneous Amendments) Regulations 2013 (SI 2013/803) reg.2(1) and (2) (April 29, 2013).

3. Social Security (Miscellaneous Amendments) (No.2) Regulations 2013 (SI 2013/1508) reg.3(1) and (2) (October 29, 2013).

4. Universal Credit and Miscellaneous Amendments Regulations 2014 (SI 2014/597) reg.2(1) and (2) (April 28, 2014).

5. Social Security (Maternity Allowance) (Miscellaneous Amendments) Regulations 2014 (SI 2014/884) reg.6(1) (May 18, 2014).

6. Universal Credit and Miscellaneous Amendments (No.2) Regulations 2014 (SI 2014/2888) reg.3(1)(a) (Assessment periods beginning on or after November 26, 2014).

7. Shared Parental Leave and Statutory Shared Parental Pay (Consequential Amendments to Subordinate Legislation) Order 2014 (SI 2014/3255) art.28(1) and (2)(c) (December 31, 2014).

8. Shared Parental Leave and Statutory Shared Parental Pay (Consequential Amendments to Subordinate Legislation) Order 2014 (SI 2014/3255) art.28(1) and (2)(a) and (b) (April 5, 2015). The amendments are subject to the transitional provision in art.35 (see below).

9. Universal Credit and Miscellaneous Amendments Regulations 2015 (SI 2015/1754) reg.2 (Assessment periods beginning on or after November 4, 2015).

10. Universal Credit (Care Leavers and Looked After Children) Amendment Regulations 2016 (SI 2016/543) reg.2(1) and (2) (May 26, 2016).

11. Social Security (Jobseeker's Allowance, Employment and Support Allowance and Universal Credit) (Amendment) Regulations 2016 (SI 2016/678) reg.5(1) and (2) (July 25, 2016).

12. Employment and Support Allowance and Universal Credit (Miscellaneous Amendments and Transitional and Savings Provisions) Regulations 2017 (SI 2017/204) reg. 4(1) and (2) (April 3, 2017).

13. Social Security (Restrictions on Amounts for Children and Qualifying Young Persons) Amendment Regulations 2017 (SI 2017/376) reg.2(1) and (2) (April 6, 2017).

14. Social Security (Income-related Benefits) (Updating and Amendment) (EU Exit) Regulations 2019 (SI 2019/872) reg.8(1) and (2) (May 7, 2019).

15. Parental Bereavement Leave and Pay (Consequential Amendments to Subordinate Legislation) Regulations 2020 (SI 2020/354) reg.28(1) and (2) (April 6, 2020).

MODIFICATION

The definition of "prisoner" in para.(3) is modified with effect from April 8, 2020 by reg.2(1) and (2)(e) of the Social Security (Coronavirus) (Prisoners) Regulations 2020 (SI 2020/409). The modification provides that the Universal Credit Regulations "are to be read as if the definition of "prisoner" did not include a person on temporary release in accordance with the provisions of the Prison Act 1952". By reg.6 of SI 2020/409, the modification will expire at the end of November 12, 2020.

DEFINITIONS

"child"—see WRA 2012 s.40.
"couple"—see WRA 2012 ss.39 and 40.
"disabled"—see WRA 2012 s.40.
"qualifying young person"—see WRA 2012 ss.40 and 10(5).
"work"—see WRA 2012 s.40.

GENERAL NOTE

2.7 Most of these definitions are either self-explanatory, or references to definitions in other regulations, or discussed in the commentary to the regulations where the defined terms are used. A number are similar to terms defined for the purposes of IS, JSA and ESA: see further the commentary to reg.2(1) of the ESA Regulations 2008 in Vol.I of this series and to reg.2(1) of the IS Regulations and reg.1(2) of the JSA Regulations 1996 in Vol.II.

The Benefit Unit

Couples

2.8 **3.**—(1) This regulation makes provision in relation to couples, including cases where both members of a couple may be entitled to universal credit jointly without each of them meeting all the basic conditions referred to in section 4 of the Act (see paragraph (2)) and cases where a person whose partner does not meet all the basic conditions [1 or is otherwise excluded from entitlement to universal credit] may make a claim as a single person (see paragraph (3)).

(2) A couple may be entitled to universal credit as joint claimants where—
- (a) one member does not meet the basic condition in section 4(1)
  - (b) (under the qualifying age for state pension credit) if the other member does meet that condition; or
- (b) one member does not meet the basic condition in section 4(1)(d) (not receiving education) and is not excepted from that condition if the other member does meet that condition or is excepted from it.

(3) A person who is a member of a couple may make a claim as a single person if the other member of the couple—
- (a) does not meet the basic condition in section 4(1)(a) (at least 18 years old) and is not a person in respect of whom the minimum age specified in regulation 8 applies;

(b) does not meet the basic condition in section 4(1)(c) (in Great Britain);

(c) is a prisoner; [¹ . . .]

(d) is a person other than a prisoner in respect of whom entitlement does not arise by virtue of regulation 19 (restrictions on entitlement) [; or

(e) is a person to whom section 115 of the Immigration and Asylum Act 1999 (exclusion from benefits) applies,]

and regulations 18 (capital limit), 36 (amount of elements) and 22 (deduction of income and work allowance) provide for the calculation of the award in such cases.

(4) Where two people are parties to a polygamous marriage, the fact that they are husband and wife is to be disregarded if—

(a) one of them is a party to an earlier marriage that still subsists; and

(b) the other party to that earlier marriage is living in the same household,

and, accordingly, the person who is not a party to the earlier marriage may make a claim for universal credit as a single person.

(5) In paragraph (4) "polygamous marriage" means a marriage during which a party to it is married to more than one person and which took place under the laws of a country which permits polygamy.

(6) Where the claimant is a member of a couple, and the other member is temporarily absent from the claimant's household, they cease to be treated as a couple if that absence is expected to exceed, or does exceed, 6 months.

DEFINITIONS

"claim"—see WRA 2012 s.40.
"claimant"—*ibid.*
"prisoner"—see reg.2 as modified by SI 2020/409.
"single person"—see WRA 2012 ss.40 and 1(2)(a).
"couple"—see WRA 2012 ss.39 and 40.

AMENDMENT

1. Universal Credit (Consequential, Supplementary, Incidental and Miscellaneous Provisions) Regulations 2013 (SI 2013/630) reg.8(1) and (2) (April 29, 2013).

GENERAL NOTE

This regulation is the first of four under the sub-heading, "The Benefit Unit". That phrase is used extensively in departmental guidance (e.g., Chapter E2 of ADM) but is not defined anywhere in WRA 2012 or these Regulations. The Department intends the phrase to mean all the people in a given household who may, or must, be included in a claim for universal credit. That is consistent with these Regulations because identifying those people is also the subject-matter of regs 3–5 inclusive, which appear under the sub-heading.

It is not generally possible for a person who is a member of a couple to claim, or be awarded, universal credit as a single person. By s.2(1) WRA 2012, members of a couple must claim jointly and by s.1(2) any award of benefit is made jointly to both members of the couple. Further, under s.3(2)(a), the basic conditions of entitlement must be met by both members of the couple and, by ss.3(2)(b) and 5(2), whether or not they satisfy the financial conditions is assessed by reference to their combined income and capital.

It is therefore important for claimants to know whether or not they are members of a couple. The word is defined by s.39(1) and (2) WRA 2012 in terms which follow the standard definition for income-related benefits (e.g., in s.137 SSCBA 1992). It covers:

2.9

- two people who are married to each other (whether they are of different sexes or the same sex), or are civil partners of each other, and are members of the same household; and

- two people who are not married to, or civil partners of, each other but are living together as a married couple

see further the commentary to reg.2(1) of the IS Regulations in Vol.II. Note also the commentary to para.(6) below as regards temporary absence.

Paragraph (2)

2.10   Under s.4(2) WRA 2012, the Secretary of State has a general power to make regulations which provide for exceptions to the requirement to meet any of the basic conditions for universal credit. In the case of joint claimants, that power can be used to make an exception for one or both of them. Similarly, WRA 2012 Sch.1, para.1 empowers the Secretary of State to make regulations providing for circumstances in which joint claimants may be entitled to universal credit without each of them meeting all the basic conditions referred to in s.4. Those powers have been exercised to make para.(2) (among other regulations).

Under s.4(1)(b) it is a basic condition for universal credit that a person should not have reached the qualifying age for SPC (as defined in s.4(4) and s.1(6) SPCA 2002). However, under para.2(a) a couple may be jointly entitled to universal credit if one member is over that age, as long as the other member is under it. In those circumstances, the couple may be better off if the older member claims SPC. That will depend on a number of circumstances, the most important of which are likely to be whether either member has housing costs or is responsible for a child or qualifying young person. The universal credit rules include a 63% taper for earned income and, in some cases, a "work allowance" (see reg.22) which may well be more generous than the equivalent rules for SPC. However, for universal credit, owner occupiers who have earned income get a higher work allowance but do not get any amount for housing costs as part of universal credit (see para.4 of Sch.5), whereas, under SPC housing costs are paid. A couple where one member is over SPC age, and the other is not, should therefore seek advice about which benefit to claim.

Under s.4(1)(d), it is a basic condition for universal credit that a person should not be "receiving education". For the definition of that phrase, see regs 12 and 13. Note also that by s.4(2) and reg.14 some people are exempt from the condition imposed by s.4(1)(b). The effect of para.(2)(b) is that a couple may be jointly entitled to universal credit even though one member is receiving education (and does not fall within reg.14) as long as the other member is not receiving education (or does fall within reg.14).

Note that couples who fall within para.(2) must still claim universal credit jointly. The exceptions are from the requirement that both should meet the basic conditions, not the requirement for a joint claim.

Paragraph (3)

2.11   By contrast, a member of a couple who falls within para.(3) may claim universal credit as a single person.

The paragraph is made under s.3(2) WRA 2012 which empowers the Secretary of State to make regulations that "specify circumstances in which a member of a couple may make a claim as a single person". There is no express power to make regulations which disapply the requirement in s.1(2) that universal credit must be awarded jointly where the claimants are members of a couple. However, it is implicit that a member of a couple who may lawfully *claim* universal credit as a single person may also lawfully be *awarded* benefit in that capacity.

Under para.(3) a member of a couple may claim universal credit as a single person if the other member:

- is aged less than 18 (and is not a person who is entitled to claim universal credit from the age of 16 under reg.8): para.(3)(a);

- is not in Great Britain for the purposes of s.4(1)(c) WRA 2012 (see reg.9): para.(3)(b);

- is a prisoner (as defined in reg.2 as modified by SI 2020/409): para.(3)(c).

(Note that, under reg.19(2), certain prisoners retain entitlement to the housing costs element of universal credit during the first six months of their sentence. However, para.(3)(c) applies whenever the other member of the couple is a prisoner. There is no additional requirement, as there is under para.(3)(d)—which also covers people who fall within reg.19—that the other member of the couple should be excluded from entitlement by that regulation. The implication is that the member of the couple who is not in prison can immediately make a claim as a single person.)

- is a member of a religious order or serving a sentence of imprisonment detained in hospital and excluded from entitlement to universal credit by reg.19: para.(3)(d); or

- is a person subject to immigration control who is excluded from entitlement to benefit under s.115 Immigration and Asylum Act 1999 (see in particular s.115(3) and (9) and the commentary to the 1999 Act in Vol.II): para.(3)(e)

There are special rules for calculating entitlement under claims made by virtue of para.(3). Under reg.36(3) the claimant's maximum amount is calculated using the standard allowance for a single claimant. However, under reg.22(3) the couple's combined income is taken into account when calculating the income to be deducted from that amount. and, under reg.18(2), the claimant's capital is treated as including the capital of the other member of the couple.

Note that the restricted standard allowance under reg.36(3) only applies to a member of a couple who claims as a single person under para.(3). It does *not* affect claims by those who are able to make a joint claim by virtue of para.(2).

Under reg.9(1) of the Claims and Payments Regulations 2013, if a person who is a member of a couple but is entitled to claim as a single person under para.(3), instead makes a joint claim, that claim is treated as made by that person as a single person.

Paragraphs (4) and (5)

Paragraphs (4) and (5) apply to those in a polygamous marriage. "Polygamous marriage" is defined by para.(5) as "a marriage during which a party to it is married to more than one person and which took place under the laws of a country which permits polygamy". That definition could clearer. A possible interpretation is that once a party to the marriage has been married to more than one person, the marriage is to be treated as polygamous for as long as it lasts (i.e., because it is a marriage "during which" there were, at least for a period, more than two members). However, it is suggested that in the context of the regulation of the whole, that interpretation is not correct. The use of the present tense ("is married") and the provisions made by para.(4)—which can only apply if the marriage has more than two members—indicate that the head (a) of the definition is to be read as meaning that a marriage is polygamous *during any period in which* a party to it is married to more than one person. In other words, the definition preserves the distinction, which applies elsewhere in social security law, between a marriage that is actually polygamous and one that is only potentially polygamous, so that where neither party is actually married to more than one person, the marriage is not polygamous for universal credit purposes.

For the definition to apply, the party who is married to more than one person must be legally married to them under the law of England and Wales or the law of Scotland (as the case may be). This can raise complex issues of the private international law: see further the commentary to the Social Security and Family Allowances Regulations 1975 (SI 1975/561) in Vol.I and s.4 of Ch.17 of Dicey, Morris & Collins *The Conflict of Laws* 15th edn (Sweet & Maxwell, London, 2012).

2.12

The effect of para.(4) is that where a marriage is actually polygamous, and at least three members of that marriage live in the same household, the parties to the earlier or earliest marriage are treated as a couple and all other members of the marriage may make a claim for universal credit as a single person. Where such member of the marriage actually makes a joint claim with another member, that claim is treated as a claim made by that member as a single person (reg.9(2) and (3) of the Claims and Payments Regulations 2013).

Paragraph (6)

2.13   At first sight, the drafting of para.6 is puzzling. It seems to draw a distinction between the member of the couple who is "the claimant" who, it is implied, is the head of "the claimant's household" and that person's partner who is "the other member", when, as noted above, the structure of universal credit is that if a claim is to be made by a member of a couple, *both* parties must normally be *joint* claimants. However, WRA 2012, s.40, defines "claimant" as including "each of joint claimants". Therefore, the effect of para.(6) is that when either member of the couple is temporarily absent from the household, they cease to be treated as a couple if the absence is expected to last, or actually lasts, for more than six months.

Relationship formation and breakdown

2.14   TCA 2002 s.3, which requires couples to make a joint claim for tax credits, contains an express provision (s.3(4)), that entitlement to tax credits ceases if the claim was made by a couple and the members of that couple split up ("could no longer make a joint claim") or if, in the case of a single claim, the claimant becomes a member of a couple ("could no longer make a single claim"). By contrast, WRA 2012 does not include any such provision relating to universal credit. Various provisions in these Regulations and of the Claims and Payments Regulations 2013 *assume* that a joint award comes to an end when a couple separate and that an award to a single claimant ends if the claimant becomes a member of a couple. However, it is not permissible to interpret primary legislation on the basis of assumptions made in the secondary legislation made under it. It is more persuasive that the same assumption is made by WRA 2012, Sch.1, para.3(2), but even that paragraph empowers the Secretary of State to make regulations about what happens *if* an award of universal credit comes to an end because of a relationship change, rather than saying that is automatically the case.

One can argue that it is inherent in the concept of a joint award to a couple, that it should come to an end if that couple no longer exists. But if that is the case, why was it felt necessary to make express provision for the situation in TCA 2002? And, when one thinks about it further, it becomes less and less clear why—in the absence of any provision equivalent to s.3(4) TCA 2002—ceasing to be a couple, or becoming one, should not be treated like any other change of circumstances, like a change of address, or a change in the amount of income or capital, rather than as a change which brings the award of benefit to an end irrespective of the circumstances of the claimants after that change. The rules in reg.9(6)-(8) and (10) of the Claims and Payments Regulations (which dispense with the need for a fresh claim where people who have been awarded universal credit become, or cease to be, members of a couple) and reg.21(3)-(3B) (under which new awards of universal credit in such cases adopt the assessment periods of the old awards) mean that, in practice, that will often be the effect of relationship formation and breakdown, even though, formally, the regulations assume that a previous entitlement to universal credit comes to an end in such circumstances.

When a person is responsible for a child or qualifying young person

2.15   **4.**—(1) Whether a person is responsible for a child or qualifying young person for the purposes of Pt 1 of the Act and these Regulations is determined as follows.

(2) A person is responsible for a child or qualifying young person who normally lives with them.

(3) But a person is not responsible for a qualifying young person if the two of them are living as a couple.

(4) Where a child or qualifying young person normally lives with two or more persons who are not a couple, only one of them is to be treated as responsible and that is the person who has the main responsibility.

(5) The persons mentioned in paragraph (4) may jointly nominate which of them has the main responsibility but the Secretary of State may determine that question—

(a) in default of agreement; or

(b) if a nomination or change of nomination does not, in the opinion of the Secretary of State, reflect the arrangements between those persons.

(6) [¹ Subject to regulation 4A,] a child or qualifying young person is to be treated as not being the responsibility of any person during any period when the child or qualifying young person is—

(a) looked after by a local authority; or

(b) a prisoner,

[¹ . . .]

(7) Where a child or qualifying young person is temporarily absent from a person's household the person ceases to be responsible for the child or qualifying young person if—

(a) the absence is expected to exceed, or does exceed, 6 months; or

(b) the absence is from Great Britain and is expected to exceed, or does exceed, one month unless it is in circumstances where an absence of a person for longer than one month would be disregarded for the purposes of regulation 11(2) or (3) (medical treatment or convalescence or death of close relative etc.).

DEFINITIONS

"the Act"—see reg.2.
"child"—see WRA 2012 s.40.
"couple"—see WRA 2012 ss.39 and 40.
"looked after by a local authority"—see reg.2.
"qualifying young person"—see WRA 2012 s.40 and 10(5) and regs 2 and 5.

AMENDMENT

1. Social Security (Miscellaneous Amendments) (No.2) Regulations 2013 (SI 2013/1508) reg.3(1) and (3) (July 29, 2013).

GENERAL NOTE

Whether or not a claimant is responsible for a child or qualifying young person is relevant to their maximum amount under Pt 4, to the level of any work allowance under reg.22 and to the imposition of work-related requirements under Pt 8.   2.16

Paragraphs (1)–(5)

The general rule is that a person is responsible for a child or qualifying young person who normally lives with them (para.(2)) unless (in the case of a qualifying young person) the two of them are living together as a couple (para.(3)).   2.17

Where a child or qualifying young person normally lives with two people who are a couple, both members of the couple are responsible for him or her (because that is the effect of para.(2) and no other rule applies).

However, where he or she lives with two or more persons who are not a couple, only one of them is to be treated as responsible and that is the person who has the

157

main responsibility for him or her (para.(4)). In those circumstances, the people with whom the child or qualifying young person lives may agree which of them has the main responsibility. However, the Secretary of State may overrule that agreement, if in his opinion, it does not reflect the arrangements those people have made (i.e., for the care of the child or qualifying young person) (para.(5)(b)). The Secretary of State may also decide who has main responsibility if the people with whom the child or qualifying young person lives do not agree who has the main responsibility (para.(5)(a)).

The application of para.(4) was considered by the Upper Tribunal (Judge Wikeley) in *MC v SSWP (UC)* [2018] UKUT 44 (AAC). In that case, the claimant was the father of a daughter who—to put the matter neutrally—stayed overnight and took her meals at her godparent's home for 12 days a fortnight. She did so to facilitate her attendance at a college near the godparent's house. However, the daughter spent every other weekend with the claimant and he contributed the cost of her keep and was responsible for all other aspects of her upbringing. Judge Wikeley rejected Departmental guidance to the effect that "a child or qualifying young person normally lives with a person where they spend more time with that person than anyone else" in favour of a "more holistic approach" in which the proportion of time spent living with an adult was a factor to be taken into consideration but was not necessarily determinative. Paras (2) and (4) established a two-stage test for first identifying who the child or young person normally lives with, and then ascribing main responsibility if more than one adult is involved. On the facts of *MC*, Judge Wikeley, decided that the daughter was "normally living" with both her father and her godparent but that her father had main responsibility for her. As far as the "normally lives with" limb of the two-stage test is concerned, it should be applied with a focus on the *quality* rather than *quantification* of the normality. As regards main responsibility, Judge Wikeley took the view that the guidance at paragraph F1065 of *Advice for decision makers* is "a good starting point". That guidance is in the following terms:

> "If the DM [decision maker] is required to determine who has main responsibility they should note that main responsibility is not defined in regulations and should be given the meaning of the person who is normally answerable for, or called to account for the child or young person. In determining who has the main responsibility for a child or young person consideration should be given to:
> 1. Who the child normally lives with
> 2. Who makes day to day decisions about the child's welfare including, for example, arranging and taking them to visits to the doctor or dentist or enrolling and taking the child to and from school?
> 3. Who provides the child with clothing, shoes, toiletries and other items needed for daily use?
> 4. Who is the main contact for the child's school, doctor and dentist?
> 5. Who cares for the child when the child is ill?
> This list should not be considered exhaustive."

Judge Wikeley also endorsed the approach recommended by Judge Jacobs in *PG v HMRC and NG (TC)* [2016] UKUT 216 (AAC); [2016] AACR 45. That decision relates to child tax credit. However, the statutory test is similar.

Paragraph (6)

2.18   Children or qualifying young persons who are being looked after by a local authority or are prisoners (as defined in reg.2) are treated as not being the responsibility of any person. The effect is that the child or qualifying young person is disregarded for the purposes of reg.22, Pt 4 and Pt 8 even if he or she normally lives with the claimant or claimants.

However, para.(6) is subject to reg.4A, so that the child or qualifying young person is not treated as not being the responsibility of any person during any period in which he or she is being looked after by a local authority and either:

- his or her absence is "in the nature of a planned short term break, or is one of a series of such breaks, for the purpose of providing respite for the person who normally cares for" him or her; or

- (though being formally looked after by a local authority) the child or qualifying young person is placed with, or continues to live with, their parent or a person who has parental responsibility for them. For the definition of parental responsibility, see reg.4A(2).

Paragraph (7)

Paragraph 7 deals with the temporary absence of a child or qualifying young **2.19** person from a claimant's (or the claimants') household. In those circumstances, the person who was previously responsible for the child or qualifying young person ceases to be so as soon as the absence is expected to exceed six months or if, unexpectedly, it actually exceeds six months (para.7(a)). That period is reduced to one month if the child or qualifying young person is also absent from Great Britain unless that absence would be disregarded under reg.11(1) by virtue of reg.11(2) or (3).

[¹ Responsibility for children looked after by a local authority

4A.—(1) There is excluded from regulation 4(6)(a)— **2.20**
   (a) any period which is in the nature of a planned short term break, or is one of a series of such breaks, for the purpose of providing respite for the person who normally cares for the child or qualifying young person;
   (b) any period during which the child or qualifying young person is placed with, or continues to live with, their parent or a person who has parental responsibility for them.
   (2) For the purposes of this regulation, a person has parental responsibility if they are not a foster parent and—
   (a) in England and Wales, they have parental responsibility within the meaning of section 3 of the Children Act 1989; or
   (b) in Scotland, they have any or all of the legal responsibilities or rights described in sections 1 or 2 of the Children (Scotland) Act 1995.]

Amendment

1. Social Security (Miscellaneous Amendments) (No.2) Regulations 2013 (SI 2013/1508) reg.3(1) and (4) (July 29, 2013).

Definitions

   "child"—see WRA 2012 s.40.
   "qualifying young person"—see WRA 2012 ss.40 and 10(5) and regs 2 and 5.
   "looked after by a local authority"—see reg.2.
   "local authority"—*ibid.*

General Note

See the general note to reg.4(6) above. **2.20.1**

Meaning of "qualifying young person"

5.—(1) A person who has reached the age of 16 but not the age of 20 is **2.21** a qualifying young person for the purposes of Part 1 of the Act and these Regulations—
   (a) up to, but not including, the 1st September following their 16th birthday; and

(b) up to, but not including, the 1st September following their 19th birthday, if they are enrolled on, or accepted for, approved training or a course of education—

    (i) which is not a course of advanced education,

    (ii) which is provided at a school or college or provided elsewhere but approved by the Secretary of State, and

    (iii) where the average time spent during term time in receiving tuition, engaging in practical work or supervised study or taking examinations exceeds 12 hours per week.

(2) Where the young person is aged 19, they must have started the education or training or been enrolled on or accepted for it before reaching that age.

(3) The education or training referred to in paragraph (1) does not include education or training provided by means of a contract of employment.

(4) "Approved training" means training in pursuance of arrangements made under section 2(1) of the Employment and Training Act 1973 or section 2(3) of the Enterprise and New Towns (Scotland) Act 1990 which is approved by the Secretary of State for the purposes of this regulation.

(5) A person who is receiving universal credit, an employment and support allowance or a jobseeker's allowance is not a qualifying young person.

MODIFICATION

With effect from June 16, 2014, reg. 5 is modified by reg. 28 of the Universal Credit (Transitional Provisions) Regulations 2014 (SI 2014/1230) (see Pt IV of this book). The modification applies where a person who would otherwise be a "qualifying young person" within the meaning of reg. 5 is entitled to an "existing benefit" (namely income-based JSA, income-related ESA, income support, housing benefit, child tax credit or working tax credit: see reg.2(1) of SI 2014/1230). The modifications are (i) that such a person is not a qualifying young person for the purposes of the Universal Credit Regulations, and (ii) that reg. 5(5) applies as if, after "a person who is receiving" there were inserted "an existing benefit (within the meaning of the Universal Credit (Transitional Provisions) Regulations 2014),".

DEFINITIONS

"employment and support allowance"—see reg.2.
"jobseeker's allowance"—*ibid.*

GENERAL NOTE

2.22   Under s.8(2)(b) and s.10(1) WRA 2012 the calculation of an award of universal credit includes an amount for a qualifying young person for whom the claimant is responsible. Regulation 5 defines who is a qualifying young person. The definition is similar to that which applies for the purposes of child benefit (see by way of comparison regs 3, 7 and 8 of the Child Benefit (General) Regulations 2006 in Vol.IV of this series) but not quite. In particular, the concept of "terminal date" has gone.

Under reg.5, a person who is aged 16 or over but under 20 counts as a qualifying young person:

    (i) up to (but not including) the 1st September following their 16th birthday if they are aged 16; or

    (ii) up to (but not including) the 1st September following their 19th birthday if they are aged 16–19 and has been accepted for (or has enrolled on) approved training (defined in para.(4)) or non-advanced education at a school or college (or elsewhere as approved by the Secretary of State; note that in the case of education provided other than at a school or college there is no requirement that the qualifying young person must have been receiving such education before they became 16, as there is for child benefit (see reg.3(3) of the 2006 Regulations in Vol.IV of this series and *JH v HMRC (CHB)* [2015] UKUT 479 (AAC)). In the case of a course of education at least 12 hours on average a week must be spent on tuition, practical work, supervised study or examinations. Meal breaks and unsupervised study are not included. *R(F) 1/93* held that "supervised study" (in reg.5 of the Child Benefit Regulations 1976) "would normally be understood to import the presence or close proximity of a teacher or tutor". If the person is aged 19, they must have started (or been accepted for or enrolled on) the education or training before reaching 19. The education or training must not be provided as part of a contract of employment.

But note that if a person is receiving universal credit, new style ESA or new style JSA in their own right, they cannot be a qualifying young person (para.(5)). Note also the modification to para.(5) in reg. 28 of SI 2014/1230 referred to above, which has the effect that if the person is receiving income-based JSA, income-related ESA, income support, housing benefit, child tax credit or working tax credit they are not a qualifying young person.

See also reg.12(1) which provides that if a person is a qualifying young person they are regarded as receiving education and so will not meet the basic condition in s.4(1)(d) WRA 2012 (unless they come within one of the exceptions to this requirement in reg.14).

Rounding

6.—(1) Where the calculation of an amount for the purposes of these Regulations results in a fraction of a penny, that fraction is to be disregarded if it is less than half a penny and otherwise it is to be treated as a penny.

[¹ (1A) Where the calculation of an amount for the purposes of the following [³ provisions] results in a fraction of a pound, that fraction is to be disregarded—

[² (za) regulation 82(1)(a) (exceptions – earnings);]

(a) regulation 90 (claimants subject to no work-related requirements – the earnings thresholds); and

(b) regulation 99(6) (circumstances in which requirements must not be imposed) [³[⁴ . . .] and

(c) [⁴ . . .].]

(2) This regulation does not apply to the calculation in regulation 111 (daily rate for a reduction under section 26 or 27 of the Act).

2.23

AMENDMENTS

1. Universal Credit and Miscellaneous Amendments Regulations 2015 (SI 2015/1754), reg.4 (November 4, 2015, or in the case of existing awards, the first assessment period beginning on or after November 4, 2015).

2. Universal Credit (Benefit Cap Earnings Exception) Amendment Regulations 2017 (SI 2017/138) reg.2(2) (April 1, 2017).

3. Universal Credit (Housing Costs Element for claimants aged 18 to 21) (Amendment) Regulations 2017 (SI 2017/252) reg.2(2) (April 1, 2017).

4. Universal Credit and Jobseeker's Allowance (Miscellaneous Amendments) Regulations 2018 (SI 2018/1129) reg.3(2) (December 31, 2018).

DEFINITION

"the Act"—see reg.2.

PART 2

ENTITLEMENT

Introduction

2.24   7. This Part contains provisions about—
 (a) the requirement to meet the basic conditions in section 4 of the Act, including exceptions from that requirement;
 (b) the maximum amount of capital and the minimum amount of universal credit for the financial conditions in section 5 of the Act; and
 (c) cases where no entitlement to universal credit arises even if the basic conditions and the financial conditions are met.

DEFINITION

   "the Act"—see reg.2.

Minimum age

Cases where the minimum age is 16

2.25   8.—(1) For the basic condition in section 4(1)(a) of the Act (at least 18 years old), the minimum age is 16 years old where a person—
 (a) has limited capability for work;
 (b) is awaiting an assessment under Part 5 to determine whether the person has limited capability for work and has a statement given by a registered medical practitioner in accordance with the Medical Evidence Regulations which provides that the person is not fit for work;
 (c) has regular and substantial caring responsibilities for a severely disabled person;
 (d) is responsible for a child;
 (e) is a member of a couple the other member of which is responsible for a child or a qualifying young person (but only where the other member meets the basic conditions in section 4 of the Act);
 (f) is pregnant, and it is 11 weeks or less before her expected week of confinement, or was pregnant and it is 15 weeks or less since the date of her confinement; or
 (g) is without parental support (see paragraph (3)).
   (2) Sub-paragraphs (c), (f) and (g) of paragraph (1) do not include any person who is a care leaver.
   (3) For the purposes of paragraph (1)(g) a young person is without parental support where that person is not being looked after by a local authority and—
 (a) has no parent;
 (b) cannot live with their parents because—
   (i) the person is estranged from them, or
   (ii) there is a serious risk to the person's physical or mental health,

or that the person would suffer significant harm if the person lived with them; or

(c) is living away from their parents, and neither parent is able to support the person financially because that parent—

    (i) has a physical or mental impairment,

    (ii) is detained in custody pending trial or sentence upon conviction or under a sentence imposed by a court, or

    (iii) is prohibited from entering or re-entering Great Britain.

(4) In this regulation—

"parent" includes any person acting in the place of a parent;

"care leaver" means—

(a) in relation to England [¹ ...], an eligible child for the purposes of paragraph 19B of Schedule 2 to the Children Act 1989 or a relevant child for the purposes of section 23A of that Act;

[¹ (b) in relation to Scotland, a person under the age of 18 who—

    (i) is looked after by a local authority; or

    (ii) has ceased to be looked after by a local authority but is a person to whom a local authority in Scotland is obliged to provide advice and assistance in terms of section 29(1) of the Children (Scotland) Act 1995 or a person who is being provided with continuing care under section 26A of that Act,

and who, since reaching the age of 14 has been looked after by a local authority for a period of, or periods totalling, 3 months or more (excluding any period where the person has been placed with a member of their family);

(c) in relation to Wales, a category 1 young person or category 2 young person within the meaning of section 104(2) of the Social Services and Well-being (Wales) Act 2014.]

"confinement" means—

(a) labour resulting in the birth of a living child; or

(b) labour after 24 weeks of pregnancy resulting in the birth of a child whether alive or dead,

and where a woman's labour begun on one day results in the birth of a child on another day she is to be taken to be confined on the date of the birth.

AMENDMENT

1. Universal Credit (Care Leavers and Looked After Children) Amendment Regulations 2016 (SI 2016/543) reg.2(3) (May 26, 2016).

DEFINITIONS

"the Act"—see reg.2.

"child"—see WRA 2012, s.40.

"limited capability for work"—see WRA 2012, ss.40 and 37(1).

"local authority"—see reg.2.

"looked after by a local authority"—*ibid.*

"Medical Evidence Regulations"— *ibid.*

"qualifying young person"—see regs 2 and 5.

"regular and substantial caring responsibilities"—see WRA 2012, s.40 and reg.30.

"responsible for a child or qualifying young person"—see reg.4.

GENERAL NOTE

2.26   One of the basic conditions for entitlement to universal credit is that the claimant must be at least 18 years old (s.4(1)(a) WRA 2012). Regulation 8 provides for the exceptions to that rule.

Under para.(1) a person aged 16 or 17 (who satisfies the other basic conditions) can qualify for universal credit if they:

    (a) have limited capability for work; or

    (b) are waiting for a work capability assessment and have submitted a medical certificate stating that they are not fit for work; or

    (c) have "regular and substantial caring responsibilities for a severely disabled person" (see reg.30), but not if they are a "care leaver" (defined in para. (4)); or

    (d) are responsible for a child (see reg.4 for when a person is responsible for a child); or

    (e) are a member of a couple and the other member satisfies the basic conditions and is responsible for a child or a qualifying young person (see reg.5 for who counts as a qualifying young person); or

    (f) are pregnant and it is 11 weeks or less before their expected week of confinement (defined in para.(4)), or was pregnant and it is 15 weeks or less since the date of confinement, but not if they are a care leaver; or

    (g) are "without parental support" (defined in para.(3)), but not if they are a care leaver.

In relation to the definition of "care leaver", for who is an "eligible child" for the purposes of para.19B of Sch.2 to the Children Act 1989 or a "relevant child" for the purposes of s.23A of that Act, or a "category 1 young person" or "category 2 young person" within the meaning of s.104(2) of the Social Services and Well-being (Wales) Act 2014, see the Children (Leaving Care) Act 2000 and the notes to that Act in Vol.II of this series.

2.27   A care leaver who is aged 16 or 17 is not entitled to a housing costs element for rent payments (see Sch.4, para.4) But note that a person aged 18-21, who was a care leaver before they became 18, is exempt from the "shared accommodation rate" for renters (see para.29(2) of Sch.4).

On para.(1)(g), a young person is "without parental support" if they are not being looked after by a local authority and come within one of the categories listed in para. (3). These categories are similar to those in reg.13(2)(c), (d) and (e) of the Income Support Regulations (see the notes to those provisions in Vol.II of this series). Note the definition of "parent" in para.(4). On para.(3)(b)(ii), para.E1055 of ADM gives examples of "serious risk" as: (i) having a brother or sister who is a drug addict, which poses a risk to the young person who is exposed to the drugs at the parental home; (ii) having a history of mental illness which is made worse by the parent's attitude; or (iii) suffering from chronic bronchitis, which is made worse by the damp conditions of the parent's home.

Note that under reg.3(3)(a) a person who is a member of a couple (and is either 18 or over or falls within para.(1)) but whose partner is under 18 and does not fall within para.(1) can claim universal credit as a single person.

A person is not normally eligible for universal credit if they are receiving education (see s.4(1)(d) WRA 2012). However, see reg.14 for the exceptions.

In Great Britain

Persons treated as not being in Great Britain

2.28   **9.**—(1) For the purposes of determining whether a person meets the basic condition to be in Great Britain, except where a person falls within paragraph (4), a person is to be treated as not being in Great Britain if the person is not habitually resident in the United Kingdom, the Channel Islands, the Isle of Man or the Republic of Ireland.

(2) A person must not be treated as habitually resident in the United Kingdom, the Channel Islands, the Isle of Man or the Republic of Ireland unless the person has a right to reside in one of those places.

(3) For the purposes of paragraph (2), a right to reside does not include a right which exists by virtue of, or in accordance with—

(a) regulation 13 of the EEA Regulations or Article 6 of Council DirectiveNo.2004/38/EC; [² . . .]

[² (aa) regulation 14 of the EEA Regulations(3), but only in cases where the right exists under that regulation because the person is–

   (i) a qualified person for the purposes of regulation 6(1) of those Regulations as a jobseeker; or

   (ii) a family member (within the meaning of regulation 7 of those Regulations) of such a jobseeker; [³ . . .]]]

(b) [³ regulation 16] of the EEA Regulations, but only in cases where the right exists under that regulation because [³ the person] satisfies the criteria in [³ regulation 16(5)] of those Regulations or article 20 of the Treaty on the Functioning of the European Union (in a case where the right to reside arises because a British citizen would otherwise be deprived of the genuine enjoyment of their rights as a European citizen [³ ; or].

[³ (c) a person having been granted limited leave to enter, or remain in, the United Kingdom under the Immigration Act 1971 by virtue of—

   (i) Appendix EU to the immigration rules made under section 3(2) of that Act; or

   (ii) being a person with a Zambrano right to reside as defined in Annex 1 of Appendix EU to the immigration rules made under section 3(2) of that Act.]

(4) A person falls within this paragraph if the person is—

(a) a qualified person for the purposes of regulation 6 of the EEA Regulations as a worker or a self-employed person;

(b) a family member of a person referred to in sub-paragraph (a) within the meaning of regulation 7(1)(a), (b) or (c) of the EEA Regulations;

(c) a person who has a right to reside permanently in the United Kingdom by virtue of regulation 15(1)(c), (d) or (e) of the EEA Regulations;

(d) a refugee within the definition in Article 1 of the Convention relating to the Status of Refugees done at Geneva on 28th July 1951, as extended by Article 1(2) of the Protocol relating to the Status of Refugees done at New York on 31st January 1967;

[¹(e) a person who has been granted, or who is deemed to have been granted, leave outside the rules made under section 3(2) of the Immigration Act 1971 where that leave is—

   (i) discretionary leave to enter or remain in the United Kingdom,

   (ii) leave to remain under the Destitution Domestic Violence concession, or

   (iii) leave deemed to have been granted by virtue of regulation 3 of the Displaced Persons (Temporary Protection) Regulations 2005;]

(f) a person who has humanitarian protection granted under those rules; or

(g) a person who is not a person subject to immigration control within the meaning of section 115(9) of the Immigration and Asylum Act 1999 and who is in the United Kingdom as a result of their deportation, expulsion or other removal by compulsion of law from another country to the United Kingdom.

AMENDMENT

1. Social Security (Miscellaneous Amendments) (No.2) Regulations 2013 (SI 2013/1508) reg.3(1) and (5) (October 29, 2013).

2. Universal Credit (EEA Jobseekers) Amendment Regulations 2015 (SI 2015/546) reg.2 (June 10, 2015).

3. Social Security (Income-related Benefits) (Updating and Amendment) (EU Exit) Regulations 2019 (SI 2019/872) reg.8(1) and (3) (May 7, 2019).

DEFINITION

"EEA Regulations"—see reg.2.

GENERAL NOTE

2.29   Under s.4(1)(c) WRA 2012, it is a basic condition of entitlement to universal credit that the claimant is "in Great Britain" and s.4(5)(a) empowers the Secretary of State to make regulations specifying "circumstances in which a person is to be treated as being, or not being, in Great Britain". Regulation 9 is made under that power. The general rule (para.(1)) is that to be "in Great Britain" a person must be habitually resident in the United Kingdom, the Channel Islands, the Isle of Man or the Republic of Ireland. Apart from people who fall within para.(4), everyone who is not so habitually resident is treated as not being in Great Britain.

The habitual residence test in para.(1) is supplemented by para.(2) which establishes an ancillary right to reside test: no-one may treated as habitually resident in the United Kingdom, the Channel Islands, the Isle of Man or the Republic of Ireland for universal credit purposes unless the person has a right to reside in one of those places, other than a right to reside specified in para.(3).

Paragraph (3)(c) was added with effect from May 7, 2019 as a consequence of the EU Settlement Scheme in Appendix EU to the Immigration Rules. EU nationals who wish to continue to live in the UK after the end of the "implementation period"— see under the heading, *The United Kingdom's withdrawal from the European Union*, in the General Note to the Immigration (European Economic Area) Regulations 2016 (below)—must apply under the Scheme. Applicants who can satisfy the Home Office that they meet the criteria in paras EU11 or EU12 of the Appendix, and that they should not be refused on grounds of suitability (paras EU15 and EU16), will be given indefinite leave to remain (also known in this context as "settled status"). Those who have been granted settled status have a right to reside in the UK that counts for the purposes of all income-related benefits: para.(3)(c) does not affect them.

Applicants who do not qualify for settled status will be given limited leave to remain for five years (also known as "pre-settled status") if they meet the criteria in para.EU14. Those with pre-settled status may apply for settled status as soon as they meet the criteria in paras EU11 or EU12. In the meantime, however, although their right of residence counts for immigration purposes, it does not count for the purposes of the right to reside test. That is the effect of para.(3)(c)(i).

In *R (Fratila and Tanase) v Secretary of State for the Home Department* [2020] EWHC 998 (Admin), the High Court (Swift J) upheld the validity of regulation 9(3)(c)(i) in the face of a submission that it discriminated unlawfully on the grounds of nationality contrary to art.18 TFEU. The reasoning underlying that decision applies equally to the equivalent regulations for the benefits and tax credits that universal credit is replacing.

Note that, until the end of the implementation period, EU nationals with pre-settled status may have other rights of residence under Directive 2004/38/EC and the Immigration (European Economic Area) Regulations 2016 that count for the purposes of the right to reside test even though pre-settled status does not.

For the exclusion of those with a "Zambrano right to reside" by para.(3)(c)(ii), see under the heading, *Carers of British Citizens*, in the General Note to reg.16 of the Immigration (European Economic Area) Regulations 2016.

For a detailed analysis of the habitual residence and right to reside tests, see the commentary to the Immigration (European Economic Area) Regulations 2016 (below), to reg.21AA of the IS Regulations in Vol.II, and to the provisions of EU law in Pt III of Vol.III.

Crown servants and members of Her Majesty's forces posted overseas

10.—(1) The following persons do not have to meet the basic condition   2.30
to be in Great Britain—
- (a) a Crown servant or member of Her Majesty's forces posted overseas;
- (b) in the case of joint claimants, the partner of a person mentioned in sub-paragraph (a) while they are accompanying the person on that posting.

(2) A person mentioned in paragraph (1)(a) is posted overseas if the person is performing overseas the duties of a Crown servant or member of Her Majesty's forces and was, immediately before their posting or the first of consecutive postings, habitually resident in the United Kingdom.

(3) In this regulation—

"Crown servant" means a person holding an office or employment under the Crown; and

"Her Majesty's forces" has the meaning in the Armed Forces Act 2006.

DEFINITIONS

"joint claimants"—see WRA 2012 s.40.
"partner"—see reg.2.

GENERAL NOTE

Under s.4(1)(c) WRA 2012, it is a basic condition of entitlement to univer-   2.31
sal credit that the claimant is "in Great Britain". However s.4(2) empowers the Secretary of State to make regulations that "provide for exceptions to the requirement to meet any of the basic conditions". Regulation 10 is made under that power.

Crown Servants and members of Her Majesty's forces who are posted overseas (as defined in para.(2)) do not have to meet the basic condition to be in Great Britain.

Neither does the partner of such a Crown Servant or member of Her Majesty's forces, if a joint claim for universal credit is made. However, as it seems probable that a Crown Servant or member of Her Majesty's forces who has been posted overseas will be in full-time work, many such joint claims seem likely to fail on the basis that the financial conditions are not met.

By para.(3), the phrase "Her Majesty's forces" has the meaning in the Armed Forces Act 2006. However, that phrase is not defined in that Act except to the extent that ""Her Majesty's forces" . . . do not include any Commonwealth force" (see s.374). "Commonwealth force" is defined by the same section as meaning "a force of a Commonwealth country".

Temporary absence from Great Britain

2.32   **11.**—(1) A person's temporary absence from Great Britain is disregarded in determining whether they meet the basic condition to be in Great Britain if—

    (a) the person is entitled to universal credit immediately before the beginning of the period of temporary absence; and

    (b) either—

        (i) the absence is not expected to exceed, and does not exceed, one month, or

        (ii) paragraph (3) or (4) applies.

(2) The period of one month in paragraph (1)(b) may be extended by up to a further month if the temporary absence is in connection with the death of—

    (a) the person's partner or a child or qualifying young person for whom the person was responsible; or

    (b) a close relative of the person, or of their partner or of a child or qualifying young person for whom the person or their partner was responsible,

and the Secretary of State considers that it would be unreasonable to expect the person to return to Great Britain within the first month.

(3) This paragraph applies where the absence is not expected to exceed, and does not exceed, 6 months and is solely in connection with—

    (a) the person undergoing—

        (i) treatment for an illness or physical or mental impairment by, or under the supervision of, a qualified practitioner, or

        (ii) medically approved convalescence or care as a result of treatment for an illness or physical or mental impairment, where the person had that illness or impairment before leaving Great Britain; or

    (b) the person accompanying their partner or a child or qualifying young person for whom they are responsible for treatment or convalescence or care as mentioned in sub-paragraph (a).

(4) This paragraph applies where the absence is not expected to exceed, and does not exceed, 6 months and the person is—

    (a) a mariner; or

    (b) a continental shelf worker who is in a designated area or a prescribed area.

(5) In this regulation—

"continental shelf worker" means a person who is employed, whether under a contract of service or not, in a designated area or a prescribed area in connection with any activity mentioned in section 11(2) of the Petroleum Act 1998;

"designated area" means any area which may from time to time be designated by Order in Council under the Continental Shelf Act 1964 as an area within which the rights of the United Kingdom with respect to the seabed and subsoil and their natural resources may be exercised;

"mariner" means a person who is employed under a contract of service either as a master or member of the crew of any ship or vessel, or in any other capacity on board any ship or vessel where—

    (a) the employment in that other capacity is for the purposes of that ship or vessel or its crew or any passengers or cargo or mails carried by the ship or vessel; and

(b) the contract is entered into in the United Kingdom with a view to its performance (in whole or in part) while the ship or vessel is on its voyage;

"medically approved" means certified by a registered medical practitioner;

"prescribed area" means any area over which Norway or any member State (other than the United Kingdom) exercises sovereign rights for the purpose of exploring the seabed and subsoil and exploiting their natural resources, being an area outside the territorial seas of Norway or such member State, or any other area which is from time to time specified under section 10(8) of the Petroleum Act 1998;

"qualified practitioner" means a person qualified to provide medical treatment, physiotherapy or a form of treatment which is similar to, or related to, either of those forms of treatment.

DEFINITIONS

"child"—see WRA 2012 s.40.
"close relative"—see reg.2.
"partner"—*ibid.*
"prescribed"—see WRA 2012 s.40.
"responsible for a child or qualifying young person"—see regs 2, 4 and 4A.
"qualifying young person"—see WRA 2012 s.40 and 10(5) and regs 2 and 5.

GENERAL NOTE

Under s.4(1)(c) WRA 2012, it is a basic condition of entitlement to universal credit that the claimant is "in Great Britain". However s.4(5)(b) and (c) empowers the Secretary of State to make regulations that specify circumstances in which temporary absence from Great Britain is disregarded (subs.(5)(b)) and modify the application of WRA 2012 in relation to a person who is not in Great Britain but who is entitled to universal credit by virtue of subs.(5)(b) (subs.(5)(c)). Regulation 11 is made under the former power.   **2.33**

Paragraphs (1) and (2)
The general rule is that a person who is entitled to universal credit retains that entitlement during a temporary absence—for whatever reason—that is not expected to exceed one month and does not in fact exceed that period (para.(1)(b)(i)). By para.(1)(a), there must be an existing entitlement to universal credit for the rule to apply. It is not possible to claim universal credit for the first time while temporarily absent abroad.

The one-month period in para.(1)(b)(i) can be extended by up to a further month in the circumstances set out in para.(2)(a) and (b) if the Secretary of State considers it would be unreasonable to expect the person to return home during the first month.

Paragraphs (3) and (4)
The one-month period in para.(1)(b)(i) is also extended to six months if either para.(3) or para.(4) applies. Those paragraphs are not subject to the condition that the Secretary of State should consider that it would be unreasonable to expect the person to return home sooner.   **2.34**

Paragraph (3) permits an extended temporary absence for medical treatment, physiotherapy, or a treatment that is similar to either of those forms of treatment, or medically approved convalescence in the circumstances set out in para.(3)(a) and (b). Note the definitions of "medically approved" and "qualified practitioner" in para.(5). The phrase, "registered medical practitioner" is further defined by para.1 of Sch.1 Interpretation Act 1978 as meaning "a fully registered person within the meaning of the Medical Act 1983 who holds a licence to practise under that Act."

Paragraph (4) permits an extended temporary absence for a "mariner" and a "continental shelf worker" who is in a "designated area" or a "prescribed area". All four of those terms are defined in para.(5). The definition of "mariner" is self-explanatory. The definition of "continental shelf worker" is more technical but, to summarise, it means a person working on an oil or gas rig in a specified area. Readers are referred to the Continental Shelf Act 1964, the Petroleum Act 1998 and the Orders in Council made under those Acts for further details of the areas concerned.

2.35   Note that paras (2) and (3) are also relevant to the question whether a person remains responsible for a child or qualifying young person during the temporary absence of that child or qualifying young person: see the commentary to reg.4(7) above.

Receiving education

Meaning of "receiving education"

2.36   **12.**—[¹ (1) This regulation applies for the basic condition in section 4(1)(d) of the Act (not receiving education).

(1A) A qualifying young person is to be treated as receiving education, unless the person is participating in a [² relevant training scheme]

(1B) In paragraph (1A) [² "relevant training scheme" means—

(a) a traineeship, or

(b) a course or scheme which—

(i) comprises education or training designed to assist a claimant to gain the skills needed to obtain paid work (or more paid work or better-paid work);

(ii) is attended by a claimant falling within section 22 of the Act as a work preparation requirement or as voluntary work preparation, and

(iii) the claimant has been referred to by the Secretary of State;]

"traineeship" means a course which—

(a) is funded (in whole or in part) by, or under arrangements made by, the—

(i) Secretary of State under section 14 of the Education Act 2002, or

(ii) Chief Executive of [² Education and Skills Funding];

(b) lasts no more than 6 months;

(c) includes training to help prepare the participant for work and a work experience placement; and

(d) is open to persons who on the first day of the course have reached the age of 16 but not 25;]

(2) [¹ Except in circumstances where paragraph (1A) applies] "receiving education" means—

(a) undertaking a full-time course of advanced education; or

(b) undertaking any other full-time course of study or training at an educational establishment for which a student loan or grant is provided for the person's maintenance.

(3) In paragraph (2)(a) "course of advanced education" means—

(a) a course of study leading to—

(i) a postgraduate degree or comparable qualification,

(ii) a first degree or comparable qualification,

(iii) a diploma of higher education,

(iv) a higher national diploma; or

(b) any other course of study which is of a standard above advanced GNVQ or equivalent, including a course which is of a standard above a general certificate of education (advanced level), or above a Scottish national qualification (higher or advanced higher).

(4) A claimant who is not a qualifying young person and is not undertaking a course described in paragraph (2) is nevertheless to be treated as receiving education if the claimant is undertaking a course of study or training that is not compatible with any work-related requirement imposed on the claimant by the Secretary of State.

AMENDMENTS

1. Social Security (Traineeships and Qualifying Young Persons) Amendment Regulations 2015 (SI 2015/336) reg.4 (March 27, 2015).
2. Social Security (Qualifying Young Persons Participating in Relevant Training Schemes) (Amendment) Regulations 2017 (SI 2017/987) reg.4 (November 6, 2017).

DEFINITIONS

"claimant"—see WRA 2012 s.40.
"qualifying young person"—see WRA 2012 ss.40 and 10(5) and regs 2 and 5.

GENERAL NOTE

It is a condition of entitlement to universal credit that the person is not receiving   2.37
education (s.4(1)(d) WRA 2012) (but see reg.14 for the exceptions to this rule).

Note that a couple may be entitled to universal credit as joint claimants even where one member of the couple is receiving education (and does not come within reg.14), provided that the other member is not receiving education, or comes within reg.14 (see reg.3(2)(b)).

Regulation 12 defines who counts as receiving education. Firstly, a qualifying young person (see reg.5 for who is a qualifying young person) is deemed to be receiving education, unless they are participating in a relevant training scheme (para.(1A)). "Relevant training scheme" is defined in para.(1B) as either a traineeship (further defined in para.(1B)) or certain courses or schemes as defined therein. Where someone is participating in a relevant training scheme as so defined they will not count as receiving education for the purposes of s.4(1)(d).

If para.(1A) does not apply, receiving education means being on a full-time course of advanced education (defined in para.(3)) or on another full-time course of study or training at an educational establishment for which a student loan or grant is provided for the person's maintenance (para.(2)). But in addition a claimant will also be treated as receiving education if they are on a course of study or training that is not compatible with the work-related requirements imposed on them (para.(4)).

The definition of "course of advanced education" in reg.12(3) is the same as the definition in reg.61(1) of the Income Support Regulations (see Vol.II in this series). "Full-time" is not defined.

See reg.13 for when a person is regarded as being on a course.

Meaning of "undertaking a course"

13.—(1) For the purposes of these Regulations a person is to be regarded   2.38
as undertaking a course of education [1, study] or training—
 (a) throughout the period beginning on the date on which the person starts undertaking the course and ending on the last day of the course or on such earlier date (if any) as the person finally abandons it or is dismissed from it; or
 (b) where a person is undertaking a part of a modular course, for the

period beginning on the day on which that part of the course starts and ending—

    (i) on the last day on which the person is registered as undertaking that part, or

    (ii) on such earlier date (if any) as the person finally abandons the course or is dismissed from it.

(2) The period referred to in paragraph (1)(b) includes—

    (a) where a person has failed examinations or has failed to complete successfully a module relating to a period when the person was undertaking a part of the course, any period in respect of which the person undertakes the course for the purpose of retaking those examinations or completing that module; and

    (b) any period of vacation within the period specified in paragraph (1)(b) or immediately following that period except where the person has registered to attend or undertake the final module in the course and the vacation immediately follows the last day on which the person is to attend or undertake the course.

(3) In this regulation "modular course" means a course which consists of two or more modules, the successful completion of a specified number of which is required before a person is considered by the educational establishment to have completed the course.

(4) A person is not to be regarded as undertaking a course for any part of the period mentioned in paragraph (1) during which the following conditions are met—

    (a) the person has, with the consent of the relevant educational establishment, ceased to attend or undertake the course because they are ill or caring for another person;

    (b) the person has recovered from that illness or ceased caring for that person within the past year, but not yet resumed the course; and

    (c) the person is not eligible for a grant or student loan.

AMENDMENT

1. Universal Credit (Consequential, Supplementary, Incidental and Miscellaneous Provisions) Regulations 2013 (SI 2013/630) reg.38(3) (April 29, 2013).

DEFINITIONS

"grant"—see regs 2 and 68(7).
"student loan"—*ibid.*

GENERAL NOTE

2.39   Paragraphs (1) to (3) of reg.13 reproduce the rules in reg.61(2) to (4) of the Income Support Regulations. See the notes to reg.61 in Vol.II of this series.

Paragraph (4) is similar to the provision in reg.1(3D) and (3E) of the JSA Regulations 1996 (see Vol.II in this series). The person must have recovered from the illness or their caring responsibilities must have ended within the past year for para.(4) to apply (see para.(4)(b)). See further *RVS v SSWP (ESA)* [2019] UKUT 102 (AAC), a decision on a similar provision in reg.17 of the ESA Regulations 2008; however, note that the ESA Regulations 2008 do not have a provision equivalent to para. (4).

Exceptions to the requirement not to be receiving education

2.40   **14.** A person does not have to meet the basic condition in s.4(1)(d) of the Act (not receiving education) if—

    (a) the person—

      (i) is undertaking a full-time course of study or training which is not a course of advanced education,

      (ii) is under the age of 21, or is 21 and reached that age whilst undertaking the course, and

      (iii) is without parental support (as defined in regulation 8(3));

(b) the person is entitled to attendance allowance, disability living allowance or personal independence payment and has limited capability for work;

(c) the person is responsible for a child or a qualifying young person;

(d) the person is a single person and a foster parent with whom a child is placed;

(e) the person is a member of a couple, both of whom are receiving education, and the other member is—

      (i) responsible for a child or qualifying young person, or

      (ii) a foster parent with whom a child is placed; or

(f) the person—

      (i) has reached the qualifying age for state pension credit, and

      (ii) is a member of a couple the other member of which has not reached that age.

DEFINITIONS

"the Act"—see reg.2.
"attendance allowance"—*ibid.*
"child"—see WRA 2012 s.40.
"couple"—see WRA 2012 ss.39 and 40.
"course of advanced education"—see reg.12(3).
"disability living allowance"—see reg.2.
"foster parent"—*ibid.*
"personal independence payment"—*ibid.*
"qualifying young person"—see WRA 2012 ss.40 and 10(5) and regs 2 and 5.
"qualifying age for state pension credit"—see WRA 2012 s.4(4), SPCA 2002 s.1(6).

GENERAL NOTE

This regulation sets out the exceptions to the rule in s.4(1)(d) WRA 2012 that a person must not be receiving education. Note that most student funding will count as income—see regs 68–71. If a person who comes within reg.14 has student income in relation to the course that they are undertaking which is taken into account in the calculation of their universal credit award, they will not have any work requirements (see reg.89(1)(e)(ii)). **2.41**

The following are exempt from the condition in s.4(1)(d):

● a person who is on a course which is not a course of advanced education (see reg.12(3) for what counts as a course of advanced education) and who is under 21 (or is 21 and reached that age while on the course) and who is "without parental support" (see reg.8(3) for who counts as without parental support) (para.(a)). Such a person will have no work requirements (see reg.89(1)(e)(i));

● a person who has limited capability for work (see reg.39(1)) and who is entitled to disability living allowance, personal independence payment, attendance allowance or armed forces independence payment (see the definition of "attendance allowance" in reg.2 which includes armed forces independence payment) (para.(b));

● a person who is responsible for a child or qualifying young person (para.(c));

- a single person who is a foster parent with whom a child is placed (para.(d));

- a member of a couple, both of whom are receiving education, whose partner is responsible for a child or qualifying young person or is a foster parent with whom a child is placed (para.(e)); or

- a member of a couple who has reached the qualifying age for state pension credit but whose partner is below that age (para.(f)).

Note that a person who falls within reg.13(4) is not regarded as undertaking a course and so is not treated as receiving education (see reg.12(2)).

Note also that a couple may be entitled to universal credit as joint claimants even where one member of the couple is receiving education (and does not come within this regulation), provided that the other member is not receiving education, or comes within this regulation (see reg.3(2)(b)).

Accepting a claimant commitment

Claimant commitment—date and method of acceptance

2.42   **15.**—(1) For the basic condition in section 4(1)(e) of the Act, a person who has accepted a claimant commitment within such period after making a claim as the Secretary of State specifies is to be treated as having accepted that claimant commitment on the first day of the period in respect of which the claim is made.

(2) In a case where an award may be made without a claim, a person who accepts a claimant commitment within such period as the Secretary of State specifies is to be treated as having accepted a claimant commitment on the day that would be the first day of the first assessment period in relation to the award in accordance with regulation 21(3) [¹or (3A)].

(3) The Secretary of State may extend the period within which a person is required to accept a claimant commitment or an updated claimant commitment where the person requests that the Secretary of State review—

   (a) any action proposed as a work search requirement or a work availability requirement; or

   (b) whether any limitation should apply to those requirements,

and the Secretary of State considers that the request is reasonable.

(4) A person must accept a claimant commitment by one of the following methods, as specified by the Secretary of State—

   (a) electronically;

   (b) by telephone; or

   (c) in writing.

AMENDMENT

1. Income Support (Digital Service) Amendment Regulations 2014 (SI 2014/2887) reg.3(1)(a) (November 26, 2014).

DEFINITIONS

"claimant commitment"—see WRA 2012 s.14(1)
"work availability requirement"—see WRA 2012 ss.40 and 18(1)
"work search requirement"—see WRA 2012 ss.40 and 17(1)

GENERAL NOTE

2.43   By virtue of s.4(1)(e) of the WRA 2012 it is one of the basic conditions for making an award of universal credit that a claimant, including each of joint claimants, has accepted a claimant commitment, the meaning of which is then set out in s.14. See that provision and its annotations for the nature of a claimant commitment (i.e. a record of the claimant's responsibilities under the WRA 2012) and what is entailed in accepting such a record. There are exceptions from the basic condition in reg. 16 below. Regulation 15 deals with the time within which and the method by which a claimant commitment must be accepted. The relevant regulation-making powers are in s.14(5) of the WRA 2012, which requires the most up-to-date version of a claimant commitment to be accepted "in such manner as may be prescribed", and in s.4(7), which allows regulations to specify circumstances in which a person is to be treated as having or as not having accepted a claimant commitment.

Note that, before there can be a question of acceptance, a claimant commitment must have been prepared on behalf of the Secretary of State and offered for acceptance. A claimant should not be found to have failed to satisfy the basic condition in s.4(1)(e) merely by failing to attend a commitments interview with a work coach.

Paragraph (1)

On a new claim, if the claimant commitment is accepted within the time specified   2.44
by the Secretary of State (as extended under para.(3) if applicable), and by a method prescribed in para.(4), the basic condition is deemed to be satisfied from the first day of the period claimed for. Otherwise, the condition would only be met from the date on which the acceptance by a prescribed method actually took place. Paragraph (1) must therefore be made under s.4(7) of the WRA 2012. Under s.14(2) of the WRA 2012, the Secretary of State may review and up-date a claimant commitment as he thinks fit and under s.14(5) a claimant has to accept the most-up-date version. Such circumstances do not seem to fall within either paras (1) or (2), although para. (3) refers to a period within which a claimant is required to accept an up-dated claimant commitment and its possible extension. There is doubt whether an acceptance under such circumstances strictly takes effect only from its actual date or from the date of the preparation of the up-dated version, but no-one is likely to complain if the Secretary of State gives retrospective effect to an acceptance of an up-dated version within a specified time, as consistency would suggest is fair.

Paragraph (2)

Where no claim is required to be made (see reg.6 of the Claims and Payments   2.45
Regulations 2013), effectively the same rule is applied as in para.(1) with effect from the first day of the award.

Paragraph (3)

This paragraph allows the Secretary of State, in defined circumstances, to extend   2.46
the period within which a person is required (which is only in the sense of required in order to take advantage of giving a retrospective effect to the acceptance) to accept a claimant commitment or an up-dated version. It is arguable that no such authorisation is needed to allow the Secretary of State to extend any period as first specified under paras (1) or (2), so that the form of the restrictions in sub-paras (a) and (b) may not matter too much. Those provisions purport to apply when a claimant has requested that the Secretary of State review any action proposed as a work search or work availability requirement (see ss.17(1)(b) and 18 of the WRA 2012) or whether any limitation should apply to those requirements (see reg.97 below). The main difficulty with them, apart from the fact that s.18 contains no power for the Secretary of State to specify particular action in relation to a work availability requirement, is that the legislation contains no formal process of review of the "proposals" mentioned. The reference must presumably be to the power under s.24(3) of the WRA 2012 for the Secretary of State to revoke or change any requirement imposed under the Act or any specification of action to be taken and to a request to exercise that power in relation to action specified under ss.17 or 18. Those difficulties perhaps reinforce the argument for the Secretary of State being able to extend the period for acceptance of the claimant whenever it appears reasonable to do so, although that would involve giving no effective force to para.(3). See the notes to s.14 of the WRA 2012 for the administrative guidance on "cooling-off periods".

Paragraph (4)

2.47   This paragraph, as allowed by s.14(5) of the WRA 2012, requires that any acceptance of a claimant commitment that can count for the purposes of s.4(1)(e) be done electronically, by telephone or in writing, with the Secretary of State able to specify which in any particular case. "Electronically" will no doubt cover a range of methods, but in practice the method specified is via a "To Do" action placed on the claimant's electronic journal where a button must be clicked to indicate acceptance. It seems bizarre that acceptance orally or otherwise face-to-face is not allowed, although the telephone is covered. Both methods are capable of being recorded in some permanent form. But the standard method is in keeping with the imperative towards on-line administration, even though claimants who think that everything was agreed in the meeting with their work coach may easily get confused. In so far as no account is taken of the circumstances of claimants with disabilities and the problem cannot be taken care of under reg.16 this provision must be vulnerable to a challenge under the Human Rights Act 1998 for discrimination contrary to art.14 of the European Convention on Human Rights.

Claimant commitment—exceptions

2.48   **16.** A person does not have to meet the basic condition to have accepted a claimant commitment if the Secretary of State considers that—

(a) the person cannot accept a claimant commitment because they lack the capacity to do so; or

(b) there are exceptional circumstances in which it would be unreasonable to expect the person to accept a claimant commitment.

DEFINITION

"claimant commitment"—see WRA 2012 s.14(1)

GENERAL NOTE

2.49   As authorised by s.4(2), the basic condition in s.4(1)(e) of the WRA 2012 does not have to be met where the claimant either lacks the capacity to accept a claimant commitment (para.(a)) or there are exceptional circumstances in which it would be unreasonable to expect the claimant to accept a claimant commitment (para.(b)). Both provisions, but especially para.(b), contain elements of judgment. If "accepting" a claimant commitment has the restricted meaning suggested in the notes to s.14 of the WRA 2012, that will affect when it might be unreasonable to expect a claimant to do so. If a claimant would be unable or experience undue difficulty in accepting a claimant commitment by one of the methods required by reg.15(4), that would suggest that it would be unreasonable to expect the claimant to take those steps to accept the claimant commitment. See Williams, Lack of commitment?, *Welfare Rights Bulletin 274* (February 2020) p.4 for some suggestions of arguments that might possibly be made relying on reg.16(b), e.g. where a claimant genuinely believed that there was no need to do more to accept a commitment after agreement at an interview with the work coach or where the claimant commitment contained unlawful conditions (but note the corrections on some technical matters in the online version of this article).

The rule in reg.16(b) may have been of particular importance during the 2020 coronavirus outbreak, when "conditionality" was suspended for three months from March 30, 2020. Since there was no new legislation to lift the operation of s.4(1)(e) during that period, in contrast to the position on the work search and work availability requirements (see the notes to ss 17 and 18), allowing entitlement on new claims without s.4(1)(e) being met appears to be the key to not imposing those requirements. The terms of reg.16(b) on exceptional circumstances and unreasonableness would plainly be met. So an award of universal credit could then be made without needing to consider what work-related requirements might be imposed and need to be included in the claimant commitment. That would then allow the condition in reg.6(1) of the Social Security (Coronavirus) (Further Measures) Regulations 2020 (SI 2020/371) that a new claimant has an award of universal credit to be met, so that sub-paras (a) and (c) could be applied to lift the work search requirement and suspend the work availability requirement. Although para.11 of Memo ADM 04/20, purporting to explain the effect of reg.6, gives no clue that those provisions are linked (presumably because the Further Measures Regulations did not need to amend reg.16 at all), it is submitted that such a mechanism must have been envisaged. For existing claimants as at March 30, 2020, who had already accepted a commitment, the work search and work availability requirements were expressly lifted by reg.6(1)(b). For other requirements, there were to be no sanctions for failing to comply and/or a flexibility in reviewing requirements over the telephone.

The effect of reg.6 of the Further Measures Regulations expired at the end of June 30, 2020, the power to extend the period of application not having been exercised. On July 1, 2020 it was announced in Parliament (Under-Secretary of State, Mims Davies, WQ 62431) that from that date the requirement for universal credit claimants (among others) to accept a claimant commitment was being reintroduced. The commitments of existing claimants would be reviewed and up-dated as capacity allowed. It appears that the reintroduction for new claimants is also being phased in.

It is unclear whether, in a case in which a claimant is entitled to both universal credit and new style JSA (so that in accordance with reg.5 of the JSA Regulations 2013 no work-related or connected requirements can be imposed in relation to JSA), the claimant would still be required to accept a claimant commitment to retain entitlement to JSA. Even if the claimant is so required, the effect of reg.5 would be that it was the universal credit claimant commitment that was the controlling document.

Financial conditions

Minimum amount

17. For the purposes of section 5(1)(b) and (2)(b) of the Act (financial conditions: amount payable not less than any prescribed minimum) the minimum is one penny.

2.50

DEFINITION

"the Act"—see reg.2.

Capital limit

18.—(1) For the purposes of section 5(1)(a) and (2)(a) of the Act (financial conditions: capital limit)—

(a) the prescribed amount for a single claimant is £16,000; and

(b) the prescribed amount for joint claimants is £16,000.

(2) In a case where the claimant is a member of a couple, but makes a claim as a single person, the claimant's capital is to be treated as including the capital of the other member of the couple.

2.51

DEFINITIONS

"claimant"—see WRA 2012 s.40.
"couple"—see WRA 2012 ss.39 and 40.
"joint claimants"—see WRA 2012 s. 40.
"prescribed"—*ibid.*
"single claimant"—*ibid.*
"single person"—see WRA 2012 ss.40 and 1(2)(a).

GENERAL NOTE

2.52   This provides that the capital limit for universal credit for both a single claimant and joint claimants is £16,000. Thus the capital limit for universal credit is the same as for income support, income-based JSA, income-related ESA and housing benefit (there is no capital limit for working tax credit and child tax credit). See further the notes to s.134(1) SSCBA 1992 in Vol.II of this series.

Under para.(2), where a claimant who is a member of a couple makes a claim as a single person (see reg.3(3) for the circumstances in which this may occur) the capital of the other member of the couple counts as the claimant's.

For the rules on calculating capital, including important disregards, see regs 45–50 and 75–77 and Sch.10.

With effect from July 24, 2019, reg.51 of the Transitional Provisions Regulations 2014, as inserted by reg.3 of the Universal Credit (Managed Migration Pilot and Miscellaneous Amendments) Regulations 2019 (SI 2019/1152), supplies a transitional capital disregard to claimants who (i) were previously entitled to a tax credit and had capital exceeding £16,000; (ii) are given a migration notice that existing benefits are to terminate; and (iii) claim universal credit within the deadline. The disregard is of any capital exceeding £16,000. The disregard can apply only for 12 assessment periods and ceases (without the possibility of revival) following any assessment period in which the amount of capital the claimant has falls below £16,000. See regs 56 and 57 of the Transitional Provisions Regulations for further provisions on termination of the protection. Paragraph 7 of Sch.2 to the Transitional Provisions Regulations, inserted by the same Regulations, contains a disregard as capital of any amount paid as a lump sum by way of a "transitional SDP amount" under that Schedule.

Restrictions on entitlement

Restrictions on entitlement—prisoners etc.

2.53   **19.**—(1) Entitlement to universal credit does not arise where a person is—

(a) a member of a religious order who is fully maintained by their order;

(b) a prisoner; or

(c) serving a sentence of imprisonment detained in hospital.

(2) Paragraph (1)(b) does not apply during the first 6 months when the person is a prisoner where—

(a) the person was entitled to universal credit immediately before becoming a prisoner, and the calculation of their award included an amount for the housing costs element; and

(b) the person has not been sentenced to a term in custody that is expected to extend beyond that 6 months.

(3) In the case of a prisoner to whom paragraph (2) applies, an award of universal credit is not to include any element other than the housing costs element.

(4) In paragraph (1)(c) a person serving a sentence of imprisonment detained in hospital is a person who is—

(a) being detained—

(i) under section 45A or 47 of the Mental Health Act 1983 (power of higher courts to direct hospital admission; removal to hospital of persons serving sentence of imprisonment etc), and

(ii) before the day which the Secretary of State certifies to be that person's release date within the meaning of section 50(3) of that Act (in any case where there is such a release date); or

   (b) being detained under—
      (i) section 59A of the Criminal Procedure (Scotland) Act 1995 (hospital direction), or
      (ii) section 136 of the Mental Health (Care and Treatment) (Scotland) Act 2003 (transfer of prisoners for treatment of mental disorder).

DEFINITIONS

"housing costs element"—see regs 2 and 25.
"prisoner"—see reg.2 as modified by SI 2020/409.

GENERAL NOTE

WRA 2012, s.6(1)(a) provides that "entitlement to universal credit does not arise . . . in prescribed circumstances even though the requirements of section 3 [i.e., the requirements to satisfy the basic conditions and the financial conditions] are met". Regulation 19 is made under that power. Its effect is that, where a person's circumstances fall within para.(1), entitlement to universal credit "does not arise" even though that person otherwise meets all the conditions of entitlement. Those circumstances as that the claimant is a fully maintained member of a religious order, a prisoner (subject to para.(2)), or serving a sentence of imprisonment in a hospital (as defined in para.(4)).   **2.54**

The wording "entitlement . . . does not arise" in both s.6 and reg.19 creates problems. It would have been more natural to say that a person whose circumstances fall within para.(1) "is not entitled to Universal Credit" even if he or she satisfies s.3.

One possibility is that the wording may have been chosen to forestall any suggestion that the rules in reg.19 amount to conditions of disentitlement or disqualification (in which case, subject to the principles enunciated by the House of Lords in *Kerr v Department of Social Development*, [2004] UKHL 23 (also reported as *R 1/04 (SF)*), the burden would be on the Secretary of State to show that affected claimants were not entitled to universal credit, rather than for the claimants to prove that they were). However, this seems unlikely. Whether or not a person is a fully maintained member of a religious order, a prisoner, or serving a sentence of imprisonment in a hospital are not questions that would normally raise difficult issues of proof. And if this was the intention, it is not entirely clear that s.6 and reg.19 achieve it.

Whatever the reason for the wording, the problem it creates is that (to use prisoners as an example) although departmental policy is that prisoners should generally have no entitlement to universal credit other than under reg.19(2) (see ADM E3030 and E3040), that is not what s.6 and reg.19 say. They only say that entitlement does not arise where a person is a prisoner. But that does not cover the position in which entitlement has already arisen but the claimant subsequently becomes a prisoner. If s.6 and reg.19 contained a clear statement that a person who is a prisoner "is not entitled" to universal credit (except where reg.19(2) applies), then imprisonment would be a relevant change of circumstances and a ground for superseding the decision awarding universal credit. As it is, the effect of reg.19 appears to be limited to cases in which a new claim is made by a person who is already a prisoner because it is only in such cases that there is any issue about whether entitlement has "arisen". This view is reinforced by s.6(1)(b) and (c) and (2) which provide that entitlement to universal credit does not arise if the basic conditions or the financial conditions are met for a period shorter than a prescribed period or for up to seven days at the beginning of a period during which those conditions are met. In those provisions the "entitlement . . . does not arise" wording is being applied to circumstances where there is no existing entitlement, as is apt.   **2.55**

Paragraphs (2) and (3)
The above analysis, creates some difficulties in the interpretation of para.(2). This says that para.(1)(b) "does not apply" during the first six months when the   **2.56**

person is a prisoner where that person was entitled to universal credit immediately before becoming a prisoner, and certain other circumstances exist. If what is said above is correct, then para.(1)(b) does not apply at all in such a case, irrespective of the other circumstances. (That is not an objection to the analysis. The "entitlement . . . does not arise" wording is in primary legislation and the way in which the Secretary of State has interpreted that wording when making secondary legislation is not a guide to what it actually means).

The policy which para.(2) seeks to implement is that where someone with an existing award of universal credit that includes the housing costs element is sentenced to a term in custody that is not expected to extend beyond that 6 months, entitlement to universal credit is retained but the award may not include any element other than the housing costs element.

See also the commentary under the headings *Members of religious orders* and *Person serving a sentence of imprisonment in hospital* in the General Note to reg.21 of the IS Regulations in Vol.II.

[¹ **Waiting Days**

2.57   **19A.** [⁴ . . .]]

AMENDMENTS

1. Universal Credit (Waiting Days) (Amendment) Regulations 2015 (SI 2015/1362) reg.2(1)(a) (August 3, 2015).
2. Universal Credit and Miscellaneous Amendments Regulations 2015 (SI 2015/1754) reg.2(3) (Assessment periods beginning on or after November 4, 2015).
3. Universal Credit and Miscellaneous Amendments Regulations 2015 (SI 2015/1754) reg.5 (Assessment periods beginning on or after November 4, 2015).
4. Universal Credit (Miscellaneous Amendments, Saving and Transitional Provision) Regulations 2018 (SI 2018/65) reg.3(3) (February 14, 2018).

DEFINITIONS

"terminally ill"—*ibid.*
"weekly earnings"—*ibid.*
"work-related requirements"—see WRA 2012 s.13.

GENERAL NOTE

2.58   WRA 2012 s.6(1)(c) provides that "entitlement to universal credit does not arise . . . for a prescribed period at the beginning of a period during which" the claimant satisfies the basic and financial conditions for universal credit (i.e., as required by WRA 2012 s.3). By s.6(2), the period for which there is no entitlement may not exceed seven days.

2.59   Regulation 19A was made under the power conferred by s.6(1)(c) and provided that with effect from August 3, 2015, entitlement to universal credit was normally deferred for seven "waiting days". The regulation was revoked with effect from February 4, 2018. See the commentary on p.161 of the 2017/18 edition of this Volume for details of how the regulation operated when it was in force.

PART 3

AWARDS

Introduction

2.60   **20.** This Part contains provisions for the purposes of sections 7 and 8 of the Act about assessment periods and about the calculation of the amount of an award of universal credit.

DEFINITIONS

"the Act"—see reg.2.
"assessment period"—see WRA 2012 ss.40 and 7(2).

GENERAL NOTE

Part 3 is made under powers conferred by ss.7 to 12 WRA 2012 and is concerned   2.61
with the calculation of an award of universal credit. There are two underlying principles. The first is that an award is made by reference to an "assessment period" (s.7
and reg.21). The second is that the amount of the award is calculated by ascertaining the claimant's (or claimants') "maximum amount" and then deducting "the
amounts to be deducted", namely all unearned income and some earned income
(s.8 and reg.22).

[¹ Awards

20A. [² . . .]]   2.62

AMENDMENTS

1. Universal Credit (Waiting Days) (Amendment) Regulations 2015 (SI
2015/1362) reg.2(1)(b) (August 3, 2015).
2. Universal Credit (Miscellaneous Amendments, Saving and Transitional
Provision) Regulations 2018 (SI 2018/65) reg.3(4) (February 14, 2018).

GENERAL NOTE

When it was in force between August 3, 2015 and February 14, 2018, reg.20A   2.63
clarified that where entitlement to another benefit is conditional on a person
"having an award of universal credit" a person does not have such an award on
any day when they are not entitled to universal credit (e.g., on waiting days).
The intention was to prevent the reasoning of the Upper Tribunal in *SSWP v
SJ (IS)* [2015] UKUT 0127 (AAC) (see the commentary to reg.7(3) and (4) of
the Social Fund Maternity and Funeral Expenses (General) Regulations 2005
in Vol.II) from being extended to universal credit. Following the abolition of
waiting days by the revocation of reg.19A with effect from February 14, 2018,
reg.20A would no longer have served any purpose and it has therefore been
revoked too.

Assessment periods

21.—(1) An assessment period is [⁴ . . .] a period of one month beginning   2.64
with the first date of entitlement and each subsequent period of one month
during which entitlement subsists.
[²(1A) [³ . . .]]
(2) Each assessment period begins on the same day of each month except
as follows—
  (a) if the first date of entitlement falls on the 31st day of a month, each
      assessment period begins on the last day of the month; and
  (b) if the first date of entitlement falls on the 29th or 30th day of a
      month, each assessment period begins on the 29th or 30th day of the
      month (as above) except in February when it begins on the 27th day
      or, in a leap year, the 28th day.
[⁴ (2A) But paragraphs (1) and (2) are subject to regulation 21A (assessment period cycle to remain the same following change in the first date of
entitlement).]
[¹ (3) Where a new award is made to a single person without a claim by

virtue of regulation 9(6)(a) or (10) of the Claims and Payments Regulations (old award has ended when the claimant ceased to be a member of a couple) each assessment period for the new award begins on the same day of each month as the assessment period for the old award.

(3A) Where a new award is made to members of a couple jointly without claim by virtue of regulation 9(6)(b) or (7) of the Claims and Payments Regulations (two previous awards have ended when the claimants formed a couple) each assessment period for the new award begins on the same day of each month as the assessment period for whichever of the old awards ended earlier.

(3B) Where a claim is treated as made by virtue of regulation 9(8) of the Claims and Payments Regulations (old award ended when a claimant formed a couple with a person not entitled to universal credit), each assessment period in relation to the new award begins on the same day of each month as the assessment period for the old award.

(3C) Where a claim is made by a single person or members of a couple jointly and the claimant (or either joint claimant) meets the following conditions—

(a) the claimant was previously entitled to an award of universal credit the last day of which fell within the 6 months preceding the date on which the claim is made; and

(b) during that 6 months—

(i) the claimant has continued to meet the basic conditions in section 4 of the Act (disregarding the requirement to have accepted a claimant commitment and any temporary period of absence from Great Britain that would be disregarded during a period of entitlement to universal credit); and

(ii) the claimant was not excluded from entitlement by regulation 19 (restrictions on entitlement – prisoners etc.),

each assessment period for the new award begins on the same day of each month as the assessment period for the old award or, if there was an old award in respect of each joint claimant, the assessment period that ends earlier in relation to the date on which the claim is made.

(3D) For the purposes of this regulation it does not matter if, at the beginning of the first assessment period of the new award, the following persons do not meet the basic conditions in section 4(1)(a) and (c) of the Act (at least 18 years old and in Great Britain) or if they are excluded from entitlement under regulation 19 (restrictions on entitlement – prisoners etc.) provided they meet those conditions (and are not so excluded) at the end of that assessment period—

(a) in a case to which paragraph (3B) applies, the member of the couple who was not entitled to universal credit; or

(b) in a case to which paragraph (3C) applies, the member of the couple who does not meet the conditions mentioned in that paragraph.

(3E) In this regulation "the Claims and Payments Regulations" means the Universal Credit, Personal Independence Payment, Jobseeker's Allowance and Employment and Support Allowance (Claims and Payments) Regulations 2013.]

(5) [¹ ...]

(6) [¹ ...]

AMENDMENTS

1. Universal Credit (Digital Service) Amendment Regulations 2014 (SI 2014/2887) reg.3(1) (November 26, 2014). The amendment is subject to the saving provision in reg.5 of SI 2014/2887 (see Pt IV).
2. Universal Credit (Waiting Days) (Amendment) Regulations 2015 (SI 2015/1362) reg.2(1)(c) (August 3, 2015).
3. Universal Credit (Miscellaneous Amendments, Saving and Transitional Provision) Regulations 2018 (SI 2018/65) reg.3(5) (February 14, 2018).
4. Universal Credit (Miscellaneous Amendments, Saving and Transitional Provision) Regulations 2018 (SI 2018/65) reg.3(5) (April 11, 2018).

DEFINITIONS

"assessment period"—see WRA 2012 ss.40 and 7(2).
"claim"—see WRA 2012 s.40.
"couple"—see WRA 2012 ss.39 and 40.
"jobseeker's allowance"—see reg.2.
"personal independence payment"—*ibid.*

GENERAL NOTE

The effect of the saving provision in reg.5 of SI 2014/2887 is that the text of the regulation reproduced above only applies in "Full Service" (or "Digital Service") areas (see *Universal Credit—An Introduction*, above). For claims that are subject to the "Live Service" rules, see the text of, and commentary, to reg.21 on pp.134-136 of the 2013-2014 edition (and, for the provisions governing repeat claims now contained in reg.21(3C), reg.6 of the Claims and Payments Regulations 2013 on pp.432-433). Note, however that the insertion of the new para.(1A) with effect from August 3, 2015 applies in both Full Service and Live Service cases.   **2.65**

WRA 2012, s.7(1) provides that universal credit "is payable in respect of each complete assessment period within a period of entitlement". "Assessment period" is defined by s.7(2) as a "period of prescribed duration" and "period of entitlement" is defined by s.7(4) as a "period during which entitlement to universal credit subsists". Section 7(3) empowers the Secretary of State to make regulations about when an assessment period is to start, for universal credit to be payable in respect of a period shorter than an assessment period and for the amount payable in respect of a period shorter than an assessment period. Regulation 21 is made under the powers conferred by s.7(2) and (3).

Paragraph (1) provides that an assessment period is a period of one month beginning with the first date of entitlement and each subsequent period of one month during which entitlement subsists.   **2.66**

Paragraph (1A) clarifies that where the waiting days rule applies (see the General Note to reg.19A), the first day of entitlement (and therefore the first day of the assessment period) is the day after the expiry of the seven waiting days.   **2.67**

Paragraph (2) makes provision to avoid the administrative problems that would otherwise occur in shorter months. The general rule is that each assessment period begins on the same day of each month. But that is not always possible when the first assessment period began on the 29th, 30th or 31st of a month because not all months have more than 28 days. Therefore: **2.68**

- if the first date of entitlement falls on the 31st day of a month, each subsequent assessment period begins on the last day of the month (para.(2)(a)); or

- if the first date of entitlement falls on the 29th or 30th day of a month, each subsequent assessment period begins on the 29th or 30th day of the month except in February when it begins on the 27th day or, in a leap year, the 28th day.

2.69 *Paragraphs (3)-(3B):* Reg.9(6)-(8) and (10) of the Claims and Payments Regulations 2013 (see the definition in para.(3E)) specify circumstances in which it is possible to become entitled to universal credit without making a claim for it. All of those circumstances involve there having been a previous award of universal credit. Paras (3)-(3B) govern the day on which the first assessment period begins under the new award:

- *Paragraph (3)* applies where an award is made to a single person who had previously been awarded universal credit as one of two joint claimants, but who has ceased to be a member of a couple, either through relationship breakdown (reg.9(6)(a) of the Claims and Payments Regulations 2013) or through death (reg.9(10)). In such circumstances, each assessment period for the new award begins on the same period of each month as the assessment period for the old award.

- *Paragraph (3A)* applies either (1) where a joint award of universal credit ends because one former joint claimant has formed a new couple with a third person who is already entitled to universal credit (reg.9(6)(b)) or (2) where two single claimants who are already entitled to universal credit form a couple. In those cases, the dates on which the assessment periods began under the previous awards will not necessarily be the same, so para.(3A) provides that the assessment periods for the new award will begin on the same day of each month as the assessment period for whichever of the two old awards ended earlier.

- *Paragraph (3B)* applies if a joint award of universal credit ends because one former joint claimant has formed a new couple with a third person who was not previously entitled to universal credit (reg.9(8)), and provides that each assessment period for the new award begins on the same period of each month as the assessment period for the old award. This rule applies even if—at the beginning of the first assessment period under the new award—one member of the new couple was under 18, or was not in Great Britain, or was excluded from entitlement under reg.19,as long as they were 18 or over, in Great Brittan, and not excluded from entitlement at the end of that assessment period (para.(3D)).

2.70 *Paragraph (3C)* is not—or, at any rate, not necessarily—concerned with relationship formation or breakdown, but rather with repeat claims. It applies if a new claim for universal credit is made and the claimant (or either or both joint claimants) was (or were) entitled to universal credit within the previous six months and, during the period between the old award and the new claim, the claimant (or both claimants):

- were at least 18 years old, below state pension credit age, in Great Britain (other than for periods of temporary absence that would have been disregarded under reg.11 if there had been an award of universal credit at the time) and were not receiving education; and

- were not excluded from entitlement to universal credit by reg.19 as a member of a religious order, as a prisoner, or as a person serving a sentence of imprisonment detained in hospital.

If the new claim is made by a couple, and—at the beginning of the first assessment period under the new award—one member was under 18, or was not in Great Britain, or was excluded from entitlement under reg.19, the conditions in the two bullet points above are treated as having been met provided was 18 or over, in Great Britain and not excluded from entitlement at the end of that assessment period (para.(3D)).

Where para.(3C) applies, each assessment period for the new award begins on the same day of the month as each assessment period of the old award or, if there were two old assessment periods (*i.e.,* because two people who were previously single claimants have formed a couple between the end of the old award and the new claim), on the same day of the month as whichever assessment period of the old award ended earlier.

Under reg.26(5) of the Claims and Payments Regulations 2013, a claim must be made before the end of the assessment period in respect of which it is made in order to benefit from para.(3C).

This will normally be more favourable to claimants that the rules for initial claims. The claims process for repeat claimants is intended to be simpler. In addition, the fact that the first assessment period of the new award will normally begin before the date of the new claim (*i.e.*, unless that date happens to coincide with the start of an assessment period) means that the claimant(s) will be entitled to universal credit before that date (although any income earned during the assessment period from a previous employment will be brought into account). However, where any claimant is not in work at the date of the new claim and has ceased being in paid work since the old award ended, the amount of universal credit paid for the first assessment period is reduced (technically, "apportioned") unless the new claim is made within seven days of the date on which work ceased: see reg.22A, below.

[¹Assessment period cycle to remain the same following change in the first date of entitlement

21A.—(1) This regulation applies where—   2.71
(a) the first date of entitlement has been determined;
(b) it is subsequently determined that the first date of entitlement falls on a different date (the "start date"); and
(c) applying regulation 21(1) and (2) following that subsequent determination (and thereby changing the beginning of each assessment period) would, in the opinion of the Secretary of State, cause unnecessary disruption to the administration of the claim.

(2) Where this regulation applies—
(a) the first assessment period is to be a period of a length determined by the Secretary of State beginning with the start date;
(b) the amount payable in respect of that first assessment period is to be calculated as follows—

$$N \times \left(\frac{A \times 12}{365} \right)$$

where—
N is the number of days in the period; and
A is the amount calculated in relation to that period as if it were an assessment period of one month; and
(c) regulation 21(1) and (2) apply to the second and subsequent assessment periods as if the day after the end of the first assessment period were the first date of entitlement.]

AMENDMENT

1. Universal Credit (Miscellaneous Amendments, Saving and Transitional Provision) Regulations 2018 (SI 2018/65) reg.3(6) (April 11, 2018).

Deduction of income and work allowance

22.—(1) The amounts to be deducted from the maximum amount in   2.72
accordance with section 8(3) of the Act to determine the amount of an
award of universal credit are—

   (a) all of the claimant's unearned income (or in the case of joint claimants all of their combined unearned income) in respect of the assessment period; and

[¹ (b) the following amount of the claimant's earned income (or, in the case of joint claimants, their combined earned income) in respect of the assessment period—

     (i) in a case where no work allowance is specified in the table below (that is where a single claimant does not have, or neither of joint claimants has, responsibility for a child or qualifying young person or limited capability for work), [² 63%] of that earned income; or

     (ii) in any other case, [² 63%] of the amount by which that earned income exceeds the work allowance specified in the table.]

(2) The amount of the work allowance is—

   (a) if the award contains no amount for the housing costs element, the applicable amount of the higher work allowance specified in the table below; and

   (b) if the award does contain an amount for the housing costs element, the applicable amount of the lower work allowance specified in that table.

[¹ (3) In the case of an award where the claimant is a member of a couple, but makes a claim as a single person, the amount to be deducted from the maximum amount in accordance with section 8(3) of the Act is the same as the amount that would be deducted in accordance with paragraph (1) if the couple were joint claimants.]

[¹ Higher work allowance	
Single claimant—	
responsible for one or more children or qualifying young persons and/or has limited capability for work	[⁴£512]
Joint claimants	
responsible for one or more children or qualifying young persons and/or where one or both have limited capability for work	[⁴£512]
Lower work allowance	
Single claimant—	
responsible for one or more children or qualifying young persons and/or has limited capability for work	[⁴£292]
Joint claimants—	
responsible for one or more children or qualifying young persons and/or where one or both have limited capability for work]	[⁴£292]

AMENDMENTS

   1. Universal Credit (Work Allowance) Amendment Regulations 2015 (SI 2015/1649) reg.2 (Assessment periods beginning on or after April 11, 2016).

   2. Universal Credit (Reduction of the Earnings Taper Rate) Amendment Regulations 2017 (SI 2017/348) reg.2(1) and (2) (Assessment periods beginning on or after April 10, 2017).

   3. Universal Credit (Miscellaneous Amendments, Saving and Transitional Provision) Regulations 2018 (SI 2018/65) reg.3(7) (April 9, 2018).

   4. Social Security Benefits Up-rating Order 2020 (SI 2020/234) art.31(1) (Assessment periods beginning on or after April 6, 2019).

DEFINITIONS

"the Act"—see reg.2.
"assessment period"—see WRA 2012, ss.40 and 7(2).
"child"—see WRA 2012, s.40.
"claimant"—*ibid.*
"couple"—see WRA 2012, ss.39 and 40.
"earned income"—see reg.2.
"housing costs element"—see regs 2 and 25.
"joint claimants"—see WRA 2012, s.40.
"limited capability for work"—see WRA 2012, ss.40 and 37(1).
"qualifying young person"—see WRA 2012, ss.40 and 10(5) and regs 2 and 5.
"responsible for a child or qualifying young person"—see regs 2, 4 and 4A.
"single claimant"—see WRA 2012, s.40.
"unearned income"—see reg.2.
"work"—see WRA 2012, s.40.

GENERAL NOTE

Under s.8(1) WRA 2012, the amount of an award of universal credit is the balance of the maximum amount less the amounts to be deducted which, by s.8(3), are to be two prescribed amounts, one in respect of earned income and the other in respect of unearned income. Regulation 22 is made under s.8(3) and specifies how those prescribed amounts are to be determined.   2.73

Paragraph (1) contains the three general principles. First, the claimant's (or the claimants' combined) *unearned* income (i.e., as calculated in accordance with regs 65-74) is deducted in full (para.(1)(a)). Second, where no claimant has either responsibility for a child or qualifying young person or limited capability for work, 63% of *earned* income (i.e., as calculated in accordance with regs 51-64) is deducted. Third, where any claimant has responsibility for a child or qualifying young person or limited capability for work, the deduction is 63% of the amount by which the claimant's (or the claimant's combined) earned income exceeds the "work allowance" specified in the table to the regulation (para.(1)(b)(ii)).   2.74

Paragraph (3) modifies those principles where a member of a couple is claiming as a single claimant under reg.3(3): the couple's combined income is take into account when calculation earned and unearned income, even though the circumstances of the other member of the couple will be excluded when calculating his or her maximum amount (see reg.36(3)).   2.75

Paragraph (1)(b) is—or, at any rate, was until April 11, 2016 see below—the main mechanism by which the policy that, under universal credit, claimants will always be better off in work is achieved. The "work allowance" is what would previously have been described as an earnings disregard: an amount deducted from a claimant's earnings before any means-test is carried out. But, even at the lowest rate, it is a more generous disregard than applied for the purposes of IS, income-based JSA and income-related ESA. Even where there is no responsibility for a child or qualifying young person—and therefore no work allowance—the 63% "taper" means that the claimant keeps 35 pence in every additional pound he or she earns, whereas under IS, income-based JSA and income-related ESA, benefit was reduced pound for pound so that, once a claimant's earnings exceeded the earnings disregard (and ignoring any potential entitlement to WTC), there was no financial incentive to work unless he or she could earn enough to come off income-related benefits altogether.
Before April 11, 2016, the work allowances specified in most cases were higher than those that now appear above. In addition, work allowances were also specified for claimants who were not responsible for a child or qualifying young person, For a more detailed discussion of the effects of the reduction and removal of work allowances in those cases, see *Universal Credit—An Introduction* above.

Paragraph (2)

2.76   The amount of the work allowance to be deducted from earned income in cases where a claimant has responsibility for a child or qualifying young person is specified in para.(2) and the table at the end of the regulation. The higher work allowance is applicable when the award of universal credit does not contain the housing costs element and the lower work allowance when it does. Very few universal credit claimants will not have to pay anything towards housing costs. The most likely recipients of the higher work allowance are, those living as non-dependants in another person's household, owner-occupiers whose earnings exclude them from entitlement to housing costs under Sch.5, para.4 and those renters treated as not liable to make payments under Sch.2, paras 5 to 10.

[1 **Apportionment where re-claim delayed after loss of employment**

2.77   **22A.**—(1) This regulation applies where—
- (a) a new award is made in a case to which regulation 21(3C) (new claim within 6 months of a previous award) applies; and
- (b) the claimant (or either joint claimant) is not in paid work and has ceased being in paid work since the previous award ended, other than in the 7 days ending with the date on which the claim is made.

(2) In calculating the amount of the award for the first assessment period in accordance with section 8 of the Act—
- (a) the amount of each element that is to be included in the maximum amount; and
- (b) the amount of earned and unearned income that is to be deducted from the maximum amount,

are each to be reduced to an amount produced by the following formula—

$$N \times \left(\frac{A \times 12}{365} \right)$$

Where—

N is the number of days in the period beginning with the date on which the claim is made and ending with the last day of the assessment period; and

A is the amount of the element that would otherwise be payable for that assessment period or, as the case may be, the amount of earned and unearned income that would otherwise be deducted for that assessment period.

(3) The period of 7 days in paragraph (1)(b) may be extended if the Secretary of State considers there is good reason for the delay in making the claim.

AMENDMENT

1. Universal Credit (Digital Service) Amendment Regulations 2014 (SI 2014/2887) reg.3(1)(d) (November 26, 2014). The amendment is subject to the saving provision in reg.5 of SI 2014/2887 (see Pt.IV).

DEFINITIONS

    "assessment period"—see WRA 2012 ss.40 and 7(2) and reg.21.
    "claim"—see WRA 2012 s.40.
    "claimant"—*ibid*.
    "earned income"—see reg.2 and regs 51-64.
    "joint claimants"—see WRA 2012 s.40.
    "maximum amount"—see WRA 2012 s.8(2).
    "unearned income"—see reg.2 and regs 65-74.

GENERAL NOTE

2.78   The effect of the saving provision in reg.5 of SI 2014/2887 is that the new reg.22A only applies in "Full Service" (or "Digital Service") areas (see *Universal Credit—An*

Introduction, above). It does not affect claims that are subject to the "Live Service" rules (as to which see the commentary to reg.6 of the Claims and Payments Regulations 2013 (below) and pp.432-3 of the 2013/14 edition).

Until November 25, 2014, it was unnecessary in some circumstances to re-claim universal credit if there had been a gap in entitlement of no more than six months. However, in Full Service cases only, and from November 26, 2014, a claim is now necessary but such repeat claims are subject to more favourable rules (see reg.21(3C) above). In particular, the assessment period from the old award of universal credit is adopted, with the effect that the claimant will normally become entitled to universal credit before the date of his or her claim.

However, in cases where the new claim is made more than seven days after any claimant ceased paid work, reg.22A removes the benefit of that more favourable rule. The monthly amounts of each element included in the maximum amount for the assessment period and of the earned and unearned income received in the assessment period are apportioned by multiplying by 12 and dividing by 365 to give a daily rate and then multiplying by the number of days between the date of claim and the end of the assessment period. Note that the apportioned result is likely to less favourable to the claimant than simply starting a new assessment period on the date of claim would have been. Under the apportionment, income earned during the assessment period in the claimant's former employment is taken into account, albeit at a reduced rate. If the assessment period had started at the date of claim, that income would have been received before it started and would not be taken into account.

According to the explanatory memorandum to SI 2014/2887 reg.22A was introduced ". . . to encourage claimants to re-claim universal credit as quickly as possible. Evidence has shown that where claimants enter a conditionality regime within two weeks of losing a job it significantly decreases their time between periods of employment".

Under para.(3), the seven day time limit for re-claiming may be extended if the Secretary of State (and, on appeal, the First-tier Tribunal or Upper Tribunal) considers there is good reason for the delay in making the claim.

Note finally that, where reg.21(3C) applies, the waiting days rule does not: see reg.19A(3)(a)(ii).

PART 4

ELEMENTS OF AN AWARD

Introduction

23.—(1) This Part contains provisions about the amounts ("the elements") under—   2.79

    (a) section 9 (the standard allowance);

    (b) section 10 (responsibility for children and young persons);

    (c) section 11 (housing costs); and

    (d) section 12 (particular needs and circumstances),

of the Act that make up the maximum amount of an award of universal credit, as provided in section 8(2) of the Act.

(2) The elements to be included in an award under section 12 of the Act in respect of particular needs or circumstances are—

    (a) [¹ . . .] the LCWRA element

    (b) the carer element (see regulations 29 and 30); and

    (c) the childcare costs element (see regulations 31 to 35).

AMENDMENT

1. Employment and Support Allowance and Universal Credit (Miscellaneous Amendments and Transitional and Savings Provisions) Regulations 2017 (SI 2017/204) reg. 4(1) and (3) (April 3, 2017).

DEFINITION

"the Act"—see reg.2.

GENERAL NOTE

2.80   The maximum amount for the purposes of s.8 WRA is the total of:

- the standard allowance: WRA 2012, s.9 and reg.36;

- an amount for each child or young person for whom a claimant is responsible ("the child element") WRA 2012, s.10 and reg.24;

- any amount included in respect of any liability of the claimant to make payments in respect of the accommodation they occupy as their home ("the housing costs element"): WRA 2012, s.11 and regs 25 and 26; or

- any amount included in respect of "other particular needs and circumstances": WRA 2012, s.12 and regs.27 to 35.

The amounts to be included in respect of other particular needs and circumstances are the LCWRA element (regs 27 and 28), the carer element (see regs 29 and 30) and the childcare costs element (regs 31–35). The former LCW element was abolished with effect from April 3, 2017 by the Employment and Support Allowance and Universal Credit (Miscellaneous Amendments and Transitional and Savings Provisions) Regulations 2017 (SI 2017/204) subject to the transitional and savings provisions in Sch.2, Pt.2 to those Regulations (see below).

Responsibility for children or young persons

The child element

2.81   **24.**—(1) The amount to be included in an award of universal credit for each child or qualifying young person for whom a claimant is responsible [² and in respect of whom an amount may be included under section 10] ("the child element") is given in the table in regulation 36.

(2) An additional amount as shown in that table is to be included in respect of each child or qualifying young person who is disabled and that amount is—

   (a) the lower rate, where the child or qualifying young person is entitled to disability living allowance or personal independence payment (unless sub-paragraph (b) applies); or

   (b) the higher rate where the child or qualifying young person is—

      (i) entitled to the care component of disability living allowance at the highest rate or the daily living component of personal independence payment at the enhanced rate, or

      (ii) [¹ . . .] blind.

AMENDMENTS

1. Universal Credit and Miscellaneous Amendments (No.2) Regulations 2014 (SI 2014/2888) reg.3(1)(b) (Assessment periods beginning on or after November 26, 2014).

2. Welfare Reform and Work Act 2016 (c.7) s.14(5)(a) (April 6, 2017).

DEFINITIONS

"blind"—see reg.2.
"child"—see WRA 2012, s.40.
"child element"—see reg.2.

"disability living allowance"—*ibid.*
"disabled"—see WRA 2012, s.40.
"personal independence payment"—see reg.2.
"responsible for a child or qualifying young person"—see regs 2, 4 and 4A.
"qualifying young person"—see WRA 2012, s.40 and 10(5) and regs 2 and 5.

GENERAL NOTE

The child element includes two amounts, which are specified in reg.36. The first,   **2.82**
which is included for each child or qualifying young person for whom a claimant
is responsible, is £235.83 per assessment period subject to a maximum of two children: see regs 24A and 24B and Sch.12.

Before April 6, 2017 the rate of the child element was higher for the first child
or qualifying young person for whom the claimant was responsible. Under reg.43
of the Transitional Provisions Regulations 2014, the higher rate continues to apply
where the claimant is responsible for a child or qualifying young person born before
April 6, 2017. The transitionally protected higher rate was £277.08 from 2017/18–
2019/20 and is £281.20 in 2020/21: see art.31(2) of, and Sch.13 to, SI 2020/234.

An additional amount is included for each child or qualifying young person who
is entitled to disability living allowance or personal independence payment or is
registered as blind. The higher amount of £409.29 per assessment period is included
where the child or qualifying young person is blind or entitled to the highest rate of
the care component of disability living allowance or the enhanced rate of personal
independence payment; the lower amount of £128.25 is included in any other case.

[¹ Availability of the child element where maximum exceeded

24A.—(1) Where a claimant is responsible for more than two children or   **2.83**
qualifying young persons, the amount mentioned in section 10(1) of the Act
is to be available in respect of—
[² (za) any child or qualifying young person in relation to whom an exception applies in the circumstances set out in—
   (i) paragraph 3 (adoptions) or paragraph 4 (non-parental caring
     arrangements) of Schedule 12; or
   (ii) paragraph 6 of Schedule 12 by virtue of an exception under
     paragraph 3 of that Schedule having applied in relation to a
     previous award;]
 (a) the first and second children or qualifying young persons in the
    claimant's household; and
 (b) the third and any subsequent child or qualifying young person in the
    claimant's household if—
   (i) the child or qualifying young person is transitionally protected;
    or
   (ii) an exception applies in relation to that child or qualifying young
     person [² in the circumstances set out in paragraph 2 (multiple
     births), paragraph 5 (non-consensual conception) or, except
     where sub-paragraph (za)(ii) applies, paragraph 6 (continuation
     of existing exception in a subsequent award) of Schedule 12].

(2) A reference in paragraph (1) to a child or qualifying young person
being the first, second, third or subsequent child or qualifying young person
in the claimant's household is a reference to the position of that child or
qualifying young person in the order determined in accordance with regulation 24B.

(3) A child or qualifying young person is transitionally protected [³ if the
child or qualifying young person was born before 6th April 2017.]

(4) [² ...]]

AMENDMENT

1. Social Security (Restrictions on Amounts for Children and Qualifying Young Persons) Amendment Regulations 2017 (SI 2017/376) reg.2(1) and (3) (April 6, 2017).

2. Universal Credit and Jobseeker's Allowance (Miscellaneous Amendments) Regulations 2018 (SI 2018/1129) reg.3(1) and (3) (November 28, 2018).

3. Universal Credit (Restriction on Amounts for Children and Qualifying Young Persons) (Transitional Provisions) Amendment Regulations 2019 (SI 2019/27) reg.3 (February 1, 2019).

GENERAL NOTE

2.84   From April 6, 2017 until October 31, 2018, the rules described in this Note applied to existing universal credit claimants only (including those who claimed after April 6, 2017 and subsequently became responsible for two or more children or qualifying young persons). During that interim period, a person who was responsible for two or more children or qualifying young persons could not make a new claim for universal credit—and therefore needed to claim IS/JSA/ESA and CTC (and, where relevant, HB) instead—unless the claim was made within six months of a previous award terminating under reg.21(3C) or was made by a single person within one month of an award of universal credit terminating because that person ceased to be a member of a couple. See generally, reg.39 of the Transitional Provisions Regulations 2014.

From April 6, 2017 s.10(1A) of the WRA 2012 (as inserted by WR&WA 2016, s.14(1)-(4)) provides that the child element of universal credit established by s.10(1) "is to be available in respect of a maximum of two persons who are either children or qualifying young persons for whom a claimant is responsible." However, s.10(4) provides that "[r]egulations may provide for exceptions to subsection (1) or (1A). Regulations 24A and 24B are made under that power. Reg.24A and Sch.12 create exceptions to the "two-child limit".

In the interests of brevity, the rest of this note will refer to "child" and "children" as if those words included qualifying young persons.

2.85   *Paragraph (1)* provides that where a claimant is responsible for two or more children, the child element is to be available in respect of:

- any child to whom the exceptions (see below) for adoptions or non-parental caring arrangements in paras 3 and 4 of Sched 12 (including any extension of an adoption exception under para. 6 of Sch.12) apply: see subpara.(za).

  Children into whom these exceptions apply are excluded when determining the order of children under reg.24B: see reg.24B(2A);

- the first and second children (as determined in accordance with reg.24B): see subpara.(a) and para.(2); and

- any additional child:

  – who was born before 6 April 2017 and is therefore transitionally protected: see subpara.(b)(i) and para.(3); or

  – to whom the exceptions for multiple births or non-consensual conception in paras 2 and 5 of Sch.12: see subpara (b)(ii); or

  – who have the benefit of any continuing exception under para.6 of Sch.12 except for a continuing exception for adoption (which is already covered by subpara.(za)(ii)): see, again, subpara.(b)(ii).

2.86   Children to whom these exceptions apply are not excluded when determining the order of children under reg.24B. The exceptions therefore only apply to third and subsequent children because if a first or second child fell within the exception s/he would be eligible for a child element in any event under sub-para.(a).

Exceptions

These are set out in Sch.12. They apply in certain cases where there has been: 2.87

- a multiple birth (para.2);

- an adoption (para.3);

- a "non-parental caring arrangement" (para.4);

- non-consensual conception (para.5); or

- a previous exception where the claimant is a step-parent of the child.

Multiple births

The childcare element is available for the third or subsequent child in a household 2.88
where that child was one of two or more children born as the result of the same pregnancy, the claimant is the child's (non-adoptive) parent and is responsible for at least two of the children born as a result of that pregnancy and the child is not the first in order (*i.e.*, under reg.24B) of the children born as a result of that pregnancy (see Sch.12, para.2).

In plain English what this means is that the childcare element is included for all children born as a result of a multiple birth as long as the household did not already include two or more older children.

Adoption

The childcare element is available for an adoptive child (irrespective of how many 2.89
other children the household already includes) except where, the claimant (or their partner) was the child's step parent immediately before the adoption or is the child's (non-adoptive) parent (see Sch.12, para.3). There are also exceptions in certain cases where the child has been adopted in or from another country.

Non-parental caring arrangements

The childcare element is available for the third or subsequent child in a household 2.90
where the child's parent is herself (or himself) a child (not, in this case, a qualifying young person) and the claimant (or either joint claimant) is responsible for the child's parent: see para.4(1)(b).

There is a further exception where the claimant (or either joint claimant) is a "friend or family carer" as defined in para.4(2): see para.4(1)(a). That definition covers people who are responsible for a child but who are not (and whose partner, if any, is not) a parent or step parent of the child and have care of the child under a variety of different statutes, or who are entitled to guardian's allowance for the child or who have undertaken the care of the child in circumstances where it is likely that the child would otherwise be looked after by a local authority.

Non-consensual conception

This exception applies where the claimant is the child's parent and the Secretary 2.91
of State (or, on appeal, a Tribunal) accepts that the child "is likely to have been conceived as a result of sexual intercourse to which the claimant did not agree by choice or did not have the freedom and capacity to agree by choice": see para.5(1) (a) and (b). It is also a condition that the claimant "is not living at the same address as the other party to the intercourse". The use of the present tense ("is not living") suggests that the exception can apply if the claimant lived with the other party at the time of the non-consensual conception but no longer does so. That is implicitly confirmed by para.5(5)(b) (see below).

There is a partial definition of the circumstances in which the claimant is to be treated as not having the freedom or capacity to agree by choice to sexual intercourse in para.5(2). They include (but are not limited to) circumstances in which (at the time of conception) the two parties were "personally connected", the other party was "repeatedly or continuously engaging in behaviour towards [the claimant] that was controlling or coercive" and that behaviour had a "serious effect" on the claimant.

Under para.5(5), the claimant and other party are "personally connected" if, at or around the time of the conception, the were in an intimate personal relationship with each other, or were living together as members of the same family having previously been in an intimate personal relationship with each other.

Under para.5(6), behaviour is to be regarded as having a "serious effect" on the claimant if it caused her to fear, on at least two occasions, that violence would be used against her or caused her serious alarm or distress which had a substantial adverse effect on her day-to-day activities.

The Secretary of State may accept the claimant's unsupported word that she is not living at the same address as the other party (para.5(4)). However, under para.5(3), he may only determine that the child is likely to have been conceived as a result of sexual intercourse to which the claimant did not agree by choice or did not have the freedom and capacity to agree by choice in two sets of circumstances.

The first set of circumstances apply if:

- there has been a conviction for rape or controlling or coercive behaviour in an intimate family relationship, or an analogous offence under the law of a country outside Great Britain; or

- an award of compensation has been made has been made under the Criminal Injuries Compensation Scheme in respect of a "relevant criminal injury" (as defined in para.5(7)); and

where the offence was committed, or the criminal injury caused, by the other party and resulted in the conception or diminished the claimant's freedom or capacity to agree by choice to the sexual intercourse that resulted in the conception (see para5(3)(b)).

The second set of circumstances apply if the claimant provides evidence from an "approved person" which demonstrates that the claimant has had contact with that, or another, approved person and her circumstances "are consistent with those of a person to whom" paras 5(1)(a) and (1)(b)(i) apply. "Approved person" is defined by para.5(7) as "a person of a description specified on a list approved by the Secretary of State … and acting in their capacity as such". That list can be found in Form NCC1, *Support for a child conceived without your consent (England, Scotland and Wales)*, which those claiming to have conceived a child non-consensually must complete. The list reads:

- a healthcare professional in a Sexual Assault Referral Centre, or

- other healthcare professionals, such as a doctor, midwife, nurse or health visitor

- a registered social worker

- a specialist support worker from an approved organisation as listed on http://www.gov.uk/government/publications/support-for-a-child-conceived-without-your-consent

At the time of going to press, that website lists:

- members of The Survivors Trust;

- members of Rape Crisis England and Wales;

- Refuge;

• certain member organisations of Women's Aid Federation Northern Ireland and Women's Aid Federation of England.

Note that there is no restriction on when the claimant must have had contact with the approved person.

Under reg. 42 of the Transitional Provisions Regulations 2013, the Secretary of State may treat the requirement for evidence from an approved person as satisfied where the claimant has previously provided such evidence to HMRC for the purposes of the corresponding exception in relation to CTC.

Continuation of an existing exception for step-parents

Para.5 of Sch.12 applies where the claimant is the step-parent of a child ("A"); has previously had the benefit of an exception in a joint award of universal credit with one of A's parents; in that award the claimant was also responsible for one or more children born as a result of the same pregnancy as A; A is not the first in order (*i.e.*, under reg.24B) of the children born as a result of that pregnancy; and that award ended because the step-parent and parent ceased to be a couple, or in any other circumstances in which the assessment periods for a later award begin and end on the same day of each month as an earlier award under reg.21.

2.92

In those circumstances, if the step-parent continues to be responsible for A, under the new award, the childcare element continues to be available for A, even if they are the third or subsequent child in a household.

Finally, under reg.41 of the Transitional Provisions Regulations 2014, a similar exception applies where, within 6 months before the step-parent became entitled to universal credit, they had an award of CTC, IS or old style JSA in which an exception corresponding with one of those set out above applied in respect of A.

[¹ Order of children and qualifying young persons

24B.—(1) Subject to to [² paragraphs (2) and (2A)], the order of children or qualifying young persons in a claimant's household is to be determined by reference to [² the date of birth of each child or qualifying young person for whom the claimant is responsible, taking the earliest date first.]

2.93

(2) In a case where—

(a) the date in relation to two or more children or qualifying young persons for whom the claimant is responsible (as determined under paragraph (1)) is the same date; [² . . .]

(b) [² . . .]

the order of those children or qualifying young persons (as between themselves only) in the claimant's household is the order determined by the Secretary of State that ensures that the amount mentioned in section 10(1) of the Act is available in respect of the greatest number of children or qualifying young persons.

[² (2A) Any child or qualifying young person to whom regulation 24A(1) (za) applies is to be disregarded when determining the order of children and qualifying young persons under this regulation.]

(3) In this regulation and Schedule 12, "claimant" means a single claimant or either of joint claimants.]

AMENDMENTS

1. Social Security (Restrictions on Amounts for Children and Qualifying Young Persons) Amendment Regulations 2017 (SI 2017/376) reg.2(1) and (3) (April 6, 2017).

2. Universal Credit and Jobseeker's Allowance (Miscellaneous Amendments) Regulations 2018 (SI 2018/1129) reg.3(1) and (4) (November 28, 2018).

GENERAL NOTE

2.94   This regulation establishes the rules for determining the order of children and qualifying young persons ("children" as in the General Note to reg.24A) in a household for the purposes of the "two-child limit" in s.10(1A) WRA 2012 (see the General Note to reg.24A above) by allocating a date to each child for whom the claimant is responsible. The child with the earliest date is first in the order and so on.

The general rule in *para. (1)* is that where the claimant (or either joint claimant) is the child's parent or step-parent (other than by adoption) the date is the child's date of birth. Otherwise, the date is the date on which the claimant became responsible for the child or, if two joint claimants became responsible on different dates, the earlier of those dates.

2.95   *Paragraph (2)* establishes a qualification and an exception to that general rule. The qualification applies where the para.(1) rule determines the same date for two or more children. The exception applies where a claimant gives birth to a child less than 10 months after becoming responsible for another child as a result of a "non-parental caring arrangement" (see Sch.12, para.4). In either case, the Secretary of State must determine the order of those children so as to maximise the number of children for whom the child element is available.

Paragraph (2A) provides that children and young persons who fall within reg.24A(1)(za)—*i.e.,* those to whom the exceptions for adoptions or non-parental caring arrangements in paras 3 and 4 of Sched 12 (including any extension of an adoption exception under para.6 of Sch.12) apply.

Housing costs

The housing costs element

2.96   **25.**—(1) Paragraphs (2) to (4) specify for the purposes of section 11 of the Act (award of universal credit to include an amount in respect of any liability of a claimant to make payments in respect of the accommodation they occupy as their home)—

(a) what is meant by payments in respect of accommodation (see paragraph (2));

(b) the circumstances in which a claimant is to be treated as liable or not liable to make such payments (see paragraph (3));

(c) the circumstances in which a claimant is to be treated as occupying or not occupying accommodation and in which land used for the purposes of any accommodation is to be treated as included in the accommodation (see paragraph (4)).

(2) The payments in respect of accommodation must be—

(a) payments within the meaning of paragraph 2 of Schedule 1 ("rent payments");

(b) [¹ . . .];

(c) payments within the meaning of paragraph 7 of that Schedule ("service charge payments").

(3) The circumstances of the liability to make the payments must be such that—

(a) the claimant (or either joint claimant)—

(i) has a liability to make the payments which is on a commercial basis, or

(ii) is treated under Part 1 of Schedule 2 as having a liability to make the payments; and

(b) none of the provisions in Part 2 of that Schedule applies to treat the claimant (or either joint claimant) as not being liable to make the payments.

(4) The circumstances in which the accommodation is occupied must be such that—

(a) the claimant is treated under Part 1 of Schedule 3 as occupying the accommodation as their home (including any land used for the purposes of the accommodation which is treated under that Part as included in the accommodation); and

(b) none of the provisions in Part 2 of that Schedule applies to treat the claimant as not occupying that accommodation.

(5) References in these Regulations—

(a) to the housing costs element are to the amount to be included in a claimant's award under section 11 of the Act;

(b) to a claimant who meets the payment condition, the liability condition or the occupation condition are, respectively, to any claimant in whose case the requirements of paragraph (2), (3) or (4) are met (and any reference to a claimant who meets all of the conditions specified in this regulation is to be read accordingly).

AMENDMENT

1. Loans for Mortgage Interest Regulations 2017 (SI 2017/725) reg.18 and Sch.5 para.5(a) (April 6, 2018).

DEFINITIONS

"the Act"—see reg.2.
"claimant"—see WRA 2012, s.40.

GENERAL NOTE

Since universal credit replaces benefits which can include an amount for house 2.97 purchase costs (income support, income-based JSA and income-related ESA) and housing benefit, the housing costs element of universal credit covers payments both by people who are renting their homes and by owner-occupiers (as well as service charges).

Section 11 WRA 2012 allows for universal credit to include "an amount in respect of any liability of a claimant to make payments in respect of the accommodation they occupy as their home". It also provides that the accommodation must be residential accommodation and must be in Great Britain, and that the accommodation can be the whole or part of a building and need not comprise separate and self-contained premises. All the other detailed rules relating to the housing costs element are in this regulation and reg.26 and in Schs 1–5 to these Regulations (made under the powers in s.11).

Paragraphs (2) to (4) contain the three basic conditions for the payment of a housing costs element: the payment condition (para.(2)), the liability condition (para.(3)) and the occupation condition (para.(4)).

Under para.(2) and Sch.1 the payments in respect of the accommodation must be "rent payments", "owner-occupier payments" or "service charges" (referred to hereafter as "eligible payments"). See the notes to Sch.1 for further discussion.

Under para.(3) and Sch.2 the claimant (or either joint claimant) must be liable to make the eligible payments on a commercial basis, or be treated as liable to make them, and must not be treated as not liable to make them. See the notes to Sch.2.

Under para.(4) and Sch.3 the claimant (or each claimant in the case of joint claimants: s.40 WRA 2012) must be treated as occupying the accommodation as their home, and not be treated as not occupying it. See the notes to Sch.3.

Note:

- Paragraph 4 of Sch.4 which excludes any 16 or 17 year old who is a care leaver (defined in reg.8(4)) from entitlement to a housing costs element.

- If the claimant (and/or other member of the couple, in the case of couples) who is an owner-occupier has *any* earned income during an assessment period (i.e. month), no housing costs element will be payable (Sch.5, para.4, although in the case of a shared ownership tenancy (see reg.26(6)), rent payments and service charges can still be met).

- The lower work allowance applies if an award includes a housing costs element (reg.22(2)(b)). This will only affect people in rented accommodation because owner-occupiers cannot get a housing costs element if they have any earned income (see above).

- People who live in "specified accommodation" (see Sch.1, paras 3(h) and 3A, together with the definition of "exempt accommodation" in para.1 of Sch.1) do not receive help with housing costs through universal credit but for the time being at least this will continue to be provided by way of housing benefit.

- There are no deductions for non-dependants (referred to as a housing cost contribution) in the case of owner-occupiers.

Amount of the housing costs element—renters and owner-occupiers

2.98   **26.**—(1) This regulation provides for the amount to be included in an award in respect of an assessment period in which the claimant meets all the conditions specified in regulation 25.

(2) Schedule 4 has effect in relation to any claimant where—

(a) the claimant meets all of those conditions; and

(b) the payments for which the claimant is liable are rent payments (whether or not service charge payments are also payable).

(3) Schedule 5 has effect in relation to any claimant where—

(a) the claimant meets all of those conditions; and

(b) the payments for which the claimant is liable are—

    (i) [¹ . . .]

    (ii) service charge payments [¹ . . .].

(4) Where both paragraphs (2) and (3) apply in relation to a claimant who occupies accommodation under a shared ownership tenancy—

(a) an amount is to be calculated under each of Schedules 4 and 5; and

(b) the amount of the claimant's housing cost element is the aggregate of those amounts.

(5) But where, in a case to which paragraph (4) applies, there is a liability for service charge payments, the amount in respect of those payments is to be calculated under Schedule 4.

(6) "Shared ownership tenancy" means—

(a) in England and Wales, a lease granted on payment of a premium calculated by reference to a percentage of the value of accommodation or the cost of providing it;

(b) in Scotland, an agreement by virtue of which the tenant of accommodation of which the tenant and landlord are joint owners is the tenant in respect of the landlord's interest in the accommodation or by virtue of which the tenant has the right to purchase the accommodation or the whole or part of the landlord's interest in it.

AMENDMENT

1. Loans for Mortgage Interest Regulations 2017 (SI 2017/725) reg.18 and Sch.5, para.5(b) and (c) (April 6, 2018).

DEFINITION

"claimant"—see WRA 2012 s.40.

GENERAL NOTE

This provides that the amount of the housing costs element for renters (whether   **2.99** or not service charges are also payable) is to be calculated in accordance with Sch.4 (para.(2)). The amount for owner-occupiers (whether or not service charges are also payable) is calculated in accordance with Sch.5 (para.(3)(a) and (b)(i)). Schedule 5 also applies if only service charges are payable (para.(3)(b)(ii)). If the claimant occupies the accommodation under a shared ownership tenancy (defined in para.(6)), the amount of the claimant's (or claimants') housing costs element is the aggregate of the amount calculated under Schs 4 and 5 (para.(4)); in the case of shared ownership any amount for service charges is calculated under Sch.4 (para.(5)).

Note reg.39(4) of the Decisions and Appeals Regulations 2013 which provides that if the Secretary of State considers that he does not have all the relevant information or evidence to decide what housing costs element to award, the decision will be made on the basis of the housing costs element that can immediately be awarded.

Particular needs or circumstances—capability for work

Award to include [¹ LCWRA element]

27.—[¹ (1) An award of universal credit is to include an amount in   **2.100** respect of the fact that a claimant has limited capability for work and work-related activity ("the LCWRA element").]

(2) The [¹ amount of that element is] given in the table in regulation 36.

(3) Whether a claimant has limited capability for [¹ . . .] work and work-related activity is determined in accordance with Part 5.

[¹ (4) In the case of joint claimants, where each of them has limited capability for work and work-related activity, the award is only to include one LCWRA element.]

AMENDMENT

1. Employment and Support Allowance and Universal Credit (Miscellaneous Amendments and Transitional and Savings Provisions) Regulations 2017 (SI 2017/204) reg.4(1) and (4) (April 3, 2017).

DEFINITIONS

"claimant"—see WRA 2012 s.40.
"limited capability for work"—see WRA 2012 ss.40 and 37(1).
"limited capability for work-related activity"—see WRA 2012 ss.40 and 37(2).
"work-related activity"— see WRA 2012 s.40.

GENERAL NOTE

Section 12(2)(a) and (b) WRA 2012 allows for an award of universal credit to   **2.101** include an additional element if the claimant (or each claimant in the case of joint claimants: s.40 WRA 2012) has limited capability for work and work-related activity ("LCWRA"). Paras (1) and (2) establish that element at a rate (in 2020/21) of £341.92. See reg.29(4) where the claimant also qualifies for the carer element (note if it is the other member of the couple that qualifies for the carer element reg.29(4) will not apply).

If both joint claimants have LCWRA, only one additional element will be included (para.(4)).

See reg.36 for the amount of the LCWRA element and reg.28 for when it will be included.

The former LCW element was abolished with effect from April 3, 2017 by the Employment and Support Allowance and Universal Credit (Miscellaneous Amendments and Transitional and Savings Provisions) Regulations 2017 (SI 2017/204) subject to the transitional and savings provisions in Sch.2, Pt.2 to those Regulations (see below). In 2020/21, the transitional rate of the LCW element is £128.25: see art.31(2) of, and Sch.13 to, SI 2020/234. See pp.166-167 of the 2016/17 edition of this volume for the rules that apply if Sch.2. Pt.2 applies and both joint claimants are entitled to the LCW or LCWRA elements or one is entitled to the LCW element and the other is entitled to the LCWRA element.

LCW and LCWRA are assessed in accordance with Part 5 of these Regulations. Under reg.39(1) a claimant will have LCW if it has been decided on the basis of an assessment under these Regulations or Part 4 of the ESA Regulations 2013 that they have LCW, or if they are treated as having LCW because any of the circumstances in Sch.8 apply (see reg.39(6)). Similarly, under reg.40(1), a claimant will have LCWRA if it has been decided on the basis of an assessment under these Regulations that they have LCW and LCWRA or under Part 5 of the ESA Regulations 2013 that they have LCWRA, or if they are treated as having LCW and LCWRA because any of the circumstances in Sch.9 apply (see reg.40(5)).

See reg.41 as to when an assessment may be carried out.

Note regs 19 to 27 of the Universal Credit (Transitional Provisions) Regulations 2014 (see Pt IV of this Volume) which concern the transition from old style ESA, income support on the ground of incapacity for work or disability and other incapacity benefits to universal credit.

In relation to the effect of a determination of LCW (or not), see reg.40(1) and (2) of the Decisions and Appeals Regulations 2013 which is the equivalent of reg.10 of the Social Security and Child Support (Decisions and Appeals) Regulations 1999. See the notes to reg.10 in Vol.III of this series.

Period for which the [² . . .] LCWRA element is not to be included

2.102

28.—(1) An award of universal credit is not to include the [² . . .] LCWRA element until the beginning of the assessment period that follows the assessment period in which the relevant period ends.

(2) The relevant period is the period of three months beginning with—

(a) if regulation 41(2) applies (claimant with [¹ monthly] earnings equal to or above the relevant threshold) the date on which the award of universal credit commences or, if later, the date on which the claimant applies for the [² . . .] LCWRA element to be included in the award; or

(b) in any other case, the first day on which the claimant provides evidence of their having limited capability for work in accordance with the Medical Evidence Regulations.

(3) But where, in the circumstances referred to in paragraph (4), there has been a previous award of universal credit—

(a) if the previous award included the [² . . .] LCWRA element, paragraph (1) does not apply; and

(b) if the relevant period in relation to that award has begun but not ended, the relevant period ends on the date it would have ended in relation to the previous award.

(4) The circumstances are where—

(a) immediately before the award commences, the previous award has ceased because the claimant ceased to be a member of a couple or became a member of a couple; or

(b) within the six months before the award commences, the previous award has ceased because the financial condition in section 5(1)(b) (or, if it was a joint claim, section 5(2)(b)) of the Act was not met.

(5) Paragraph (1) also does not apply if—

(a) the claimant is terminally ill; or

(b) the claimant—

    (i) is entitled to an employment and support allowance that includes the support component [2 . . .], or

    (ii) was so entitled on the day before the award of universal credit commenced and has ceased to be so entitled by virtue of section 1A of the Welfare Reform Act 2007 (duration of contributory allowance).

(6) [2 . . .]

(7) Where, by virtue of this regulation, the condition in section 5(1)(b) or 5(2)(b) of the Act is not met, the amount of the claimant's income (or, in the case of joint claimants, their combined income) is to be treated during the relevant period as such that the amount payable is the prescribed minimum (see regulation 17).

AMENDMENTS

1. Universal Credit and Miscellaneous Amendments Regulations 2015 (SI 2015/1754), reg.2(3) (November 4, 2015, or in the case of existing awards, the first assessment period beginning on or after November 4, 2015).

2. Employment and Support Allowance and Universal Credit (Miscellaneous Amendments and Transitional and Savings Provisions) Regulations 2017 (SI 2017/204) reg.4(1) and (5) (April 3, 2017).

DEFINITIONS

    "the Act"—see reg.2.
    "assessment period"—see WRA 2012 ss.40 and 7(2) and reg.21.
    "claim"—see WRA 2012 s.40.
    "claimant"—*ibid.*
    "couple"—see WRA 2012 ss.39 and 40.
    "employment and support allowance"—see reg.2.
    "joint claimants"—see WRA 2012 s.40.
    "LCW element"—see regs.2 and 27.
    "LCWRA element"—*ibid.*
    "limited capability for work"—see WRA 2012 ss.40 and 37(1).
    "limited capability for work-related activity"—see WRA 2012 ss.40 and 37(2).
    "Medical Evidence Regulations"—see reg.2.
    "monthly earnings"—see regs 2 and 90(6).
    "work-related activity"—see WRA 2012 s.40.

GENERAL NOTE

The LCWRA element will not normally be included until the beginning of the assessment period following the assessment period in which the "relevant period" ends (para.(1)), but see the exceptions below.

2.103

The "relevant period" is a three months waiting period, starting on the first day on which the claimant submits a medical certificate, or if reg.41(2) applies because the claimant has monthly earnings equal to or above the "relevant threshold" (16 × the national minimum national wage, which is £7.83 per hour from April 1, 2018, converted to a monthly amount by multiplying by 52 and dividing by 12), the date on which the claimant's universal credit award starts, or the date the claimant applies for the LCWRA element to be included, if later (para.(2)).

A claimant does not have to serve the three months waiting period if they:

- were previously entitled to universal credit including the LCWRA element, or the three months waiting period for the LCWRA element in relation to the previous award had started but not ended, and the previous award ended immediately before the current award started because the claimant had stopped being or become a couple, or ended in the six months before the current award started because the income condition was not met (and note para.(7)). If the three month waiting period in the previous award had not been completed, the claimant will have to serve the remainder of it (paras.(3) and (4));

- are terminally ill (para.(5)(a)); or

- are entitled to ESA that includes the support component, or was so entitled on the day before the universal credit award started but the ESA ended because of the 52 week limit on entitlement to contributory ESA (para.(5)(b)).

Particular needs or circumstances–carers

Award to include the carer element

2.104
29.—(1) An award of universal credit is to include an amount ("the carer element") specified in the table in regulation 36 where a claimant has regular and substantial caring responsibilities for a severely disabled person, but subject to paragraphs (2) to (4).

(2) In the case of joint claimants, an award is to include the carer element for both joint claimants if they both qualify for it, but only if they are not caring for the same severely disabled person.

(3) Where two or more persons have regular and substantial caring responsibilities for the same severely disabled person, an award of universal credit may only include the carer element in respect of one them and that is the one they jointly elect or, in default of election, the one the Secretary of State determines.

[¹ (4) Where an amount would, apart from this paragraph, be included in an award in relation to a claimant by virtue of paragraphs (1) to (3), and the claimant has limited capability for work and work-related activity (and, in the case of joint claimants, the LCWRA element has not been included in respect of the other claimant), only the LCWRA element may be included in respect of the claimant.]

AMENDMENT

1. Employment and Support Allowance and Universal Credit (Miscellaneous Amendments and Transitional and Savings Provisions) Regulations 2017 (SI 2017/204) reg.4(1) and (6) (April 3, 2017).

DEFINITIONS

"carer element"—see reg.2.
"claimant"—see WRA 2012 s.40.

"disabled"—*ibid.*
"joint claimants"—see WRA 2012 s.40.
"LCW element"—see regs 2 and 27.
"LCWRA element"—*ibid.*
"limited capability for work"—see WRA 2012 ss.40 and 37(1).
"limited capability for work-related activity"—see WRA 2012 ss.40 and 37(2).
"regular and substantial caring responsibilities for a severely disabled person"—
    see regs 2 and 30.
"severely disabled"—*ibid.*
"work"—*ibid.*
"work-related activity"—*ibid.*

GENERAL NOTE

The carer element (£162.92 per assessment period: see reg.36) is included in the maximum amount if a claimant has "regular and substantial caring responsibilities for a severely disabled person" (as defined in reg.30): para.(1). Where there is a joint claim, and both parties have regular and substantial caring responsibilities for a severely disabled person, the amount is included twice, as long as they are caring for different severely disabled people: para.(2). However, if awards would also include the LCWRA element (see regs 27 and 28) as well as the carer element, then only the LCWRA element is included, unless (in the case of a joint claim), the LCWRA element has been included in respect of the other member of the couple (see reg.27(4)). This reflects the fact that, at £162.92 per assessment period, the carer element is not as high as the LCWRA element at £341.92.   2.105

Paragraph (3) governs the situation where two or more people have regular and substantial caring responsibilities for the same person. Only one of those carers can have the carer element included in an award of universal credit. They can agree between them which it is to be but, if they do not do so, the Secretary of State will decide. Under reg.50(2) and Sch.3, para.4 of the Decisions and Appeals Regulations 2013, there is no right of appeal against the Secretary of State's decision on that point.

Meaning of "regular and substantial caring responsibilities for a severely disabled person"

30.—(1) For the purposes of Part 1 of the Act and these Regulations, a person has regular and substantial caring responsibilities for a severely disabled person if they satisfy the conditions for entitlement to a carer's allowance or would do so but for the fact that their earnings have exceeded the limit prescribed for the purposes of that allowance.   2.106

(2) Paragraph (1) applies whether or not the person has made a claim for a carer's allowance.

(3) But a person does not have regular and substantial caring responsibilities for a severely disabled person if the person derives earned income from those caring responsibilities.

DEFINITIONS

"carer's allowance"—see reg.2.
"disabled"—see WRA 2012 s.40.
"prescribed"—see WRA 2012 s.40.
"severely disabled"—see WRA 2012 s.40.

GENERAL NOTE

A claimant has regular and substantial caring responsibilities for a severely disabled person if he or she satisfies the conditions of entitlement to carer's allowance (see Vol.I) as long as he or she does not have earned income from those responsibilities. It is not necessary for the claimant to have claimed carer's allow-   2.107

ance (para.(2)): it is enough that they would meet the conditions of entitlement if they did.

Particular needs or circumstances—childcare costs

Award to include childcare costs element

2.108 **31.** An award of universal credit is to include an amount in respect of childcare costs ("the childcare costs element") in respect of an assessment period in which the claimant meets both—

(a) the work condition (see regulation 32); and

(b) the childcare costs condition (see regulation 33).

DEFINITION

"childcare costs element"—see reg.2.

GENERAL NOTE

2.109 The childcare costs element is included in the maximum amount if a claimant satisfies both the work condition (reg.32) and the childcare costs condition (reg.33). By reg.34, the amount of the element is 85 per cent cases of the charges incurred by the claimant for "relevant childcare" up to a maximum of £646.35 per assessment period for a single child or £1,108.04 for two or more children (reg.36). The childcare costs element is not reduced under the benefit cap: see reg.81(1) and (2).

The work condition

2.110 **32.**—(1) The work condition is met in respect of an assessment period if—

(a) the claimant is in paid work or has an offer of paid work that is due to start before the end of the next assessment period; and

(b) if the claimant is a member of a couple (whether claiming jointly or as a single person), the other member is either in paid work or is unable to provide childcare because that person—

(i) has limited capability for work,

(ii) has regular and substantial caring responsibilities for a severely disabled person, or

(iii) is temporarily absent from the claimant's household.

(2) For the purposes of meeting the work condition in relation to an assessment period a claimant is to be treated as being in paid work if—

(a) the claimant has ceased paid work—

(i) in that assessment period,

(ii) in the previous assessment period, or

(iii) if the assessment period in question is the first or second assessment period in relation to an award, in that assessment period or in the month immediately preceding the commencement of the award; or

(b) the claimant is receiving statutory sick pay, statutory maternity pay, [2 ...] statutory paternity pay, [2 ...] statutory adoption pay [1 , statutory shared parental pay] [3 , statutory parental bereavement pay] or a maternity allowance.

AMENDMENTS

1. Shared Parental Leave and Statutory Shared Parental Pay (Consequential Amendments to Subordinate Legislation) Order 2014 (SI 2014/3255) art.28(1) and (3)(c) (December 31, 2014).

2. Shared Parental Leave and Statutory Shared Parental Pay (Consequential Amendments to Subordinate Legislation) Order 2014 (SI 2014/3255) art.28(1) and (3)(a) and (b) (April 5, 2015). The amendments are subject to the transitional provision in art.35 (see below).

3. Parental Bereavement Leave and Pay (Consequential Amendments to Subordinate Legislation) Regulations 2020 (SI 2020/354) reg.28(1) and (3) (April 6, 2020).

DEFINITIONS

"assessment period"—see WRA 2012, ss.40 and 7(2).
"claimant"—see WRA 2012, s.40.
"maternity allowance"—see reg.2.
"paid work"—ibid.
"single person"—see WRA 2012, ss.40 and 1(2)(a).
"statutory adoption pay"—see reg.2.
"statutory maternity pay"—*ibid.*
"statutory paternity pay"—*ibid.*
"statutory shared parental pay"—*ibid.*
"statutory sick pay"—*ibid.*
"work"—see WRA 2012, s.40.

GENERAL NOTE

A claimant satisfies the work condition if she or he is in paid work or has an offer of paid work that is due to start before the end of the next assessment period: para. (1)(a). For joint claims (or in cases where by a member of a couple claims as a single person under reg.3(3)) there is an additional condition that the other member is either in paid work or is unable to provide childcare for one of the reasons set out in heads (i)–(iii). Claimants are treated as if they were still in paid work if they have stopped work within the periods set out in para.(2)(a) or if they are receiving statutory sick pay, statutory maternity pay, statutory paternity pay, statutory shared parental pay, statutory adoption pay (see Vol.IV) or a maternity allowance (see Vol.I).   **2.111**

The childcare costs condition

33.—(1) The childcare costs condition is met in respect of an assessment period if—   **2.112**

[¹ (za) the claimant has paid charges for relevant childcare that are attributable to that assessment period (see regulation 34A) and those charges have been reported to the Secretary of State [² before the end of the assessment period that follows the assessment period in which they were paid];]

  (a) [¹ the charges are in respect of]—
    (i) a child, or
    (ii) a qualifying young person who has not reached the 1st September following their 16th birthday,
for whom the claimant is responsible; and
  (b) the charges are for childcare arrangements—
    (i) that are to enable the claimant to take up paid work or to continue in paid work, or
    (ii) where the claimant is treated as being in paid work by virtue of regulation 32(2), that are to enable the claimant to maintain childcare arrangements that were in place when the claimant ceased paid work or began to receive those benefits.

[¹ (2) The late reporting of charges for relevant childcare may be accepted in the same circumstances as late notification of a change of circumstances may be accepted under regulation 36 of the Universal Credit, Personal Independence Payment, Jobseeker's Allowance and Employment and Support Allowance (Decisions and Appeals) Regulations 2013 and, in such cases, subject to regulation 34A below, all or part of any such charges may be taken into account in any assessment period to which they relate.]

[² (3) For the purposes of paragraph (2), "the relevant notification period" in regulation 36 of the Universal Credit, Personal Independence Payment, Jobseeker's Allowance and Employment and Support Allowance (Decisions and Appeals) Regulations 2013 means a period of time ending on the last day of the assessment period that follows the assessment period in which the charges for relevant childcare were paid.]

AMENDMENT

1. Universal Credit (Digital Service) Amendment Regulations 2014 (SI 2014/2887) reg.2(1) and (2) (November 26, 2014). The amendment is subject to the saving provision in reg.5 of SI 2014/2887 (see Pt.IV).
2. Universal Credit (Childcare Costs and Minimum Income Floor) (Amendment) Regulations 2019 (SI 2019/1249) reg.2 (October 3, 2019).

DEFINITIONS

"assessment period"—see WRA 2012, ss.40 and 7(2).
"claimant"—see WRA 2012, s.40.
"paid work"—see reg.2.
"relevant childcare"—see reg.35.
"responsible for a child or qualifying young person"—see regs 2, 4 and 4A.

GENERAL NOTE

2.113   The effect of the saving provision in reg.5 of SI 2014/2887 is that the amendments to reg.33 with effect from November 26, 2014 only apply in "Full Service" (or "Digital Service") cases (see *Universal Credit—An Introduction* above). For the text of the unamended regulation (which continues to apply in "Live Service" cases) see p.149 of the 2013/14 edition.

A claimant satisfies the childcare costs condition in the circumstances set out in para.(1)(za), (a) and (b). Those paragraphs are cumulative. All three must apply before the childcare costs condition is satisfied.

Paragraph (1)(za) applies if a claimant pays charges for relevant childcare (as defined in reg.35) that are attributable to the assessment period under consideration and, subject to para.(2), have been reported to the Secretary of State before the end of that period. Reg.34A governs the assessment period to which charges are attributable.

2.114   *Paragraph (1)(a)* applies if the charges are in respect of a child or a qualifying young person for whom she the claimant is responsible. A qualifying young person ceases to count for these purposes on September 1st following his or her 16th birthday.

2.115   *Paragraph (1)(b)* applies if the charges are for childcare arrangements to enable the claimant to work or to maintain childcare arrangements that were in place before a period when she or he is not in paid work but is treated by reg.32(2) as if she or he were.

Under para.(2) the Secretary of State may accept childcare charges that are reported after the end of the assessment period after the end of the assessment period to which they are attributable, in the same circumstances as any late notification of a change of circumstances may be accepted under reg.36 of the Decisions and Appeals Regulations 2013 (see Pt.IV below).

Amount of childcare costs element

34.—(1) The amount of the childcare costs element for an assessment   2.116
period is the lesser of—

[¹ (a) [² 85%] of the charges paid for relevant childcare that are attributable to that assessment period; or]

(b) the maximum amount specified in the table in regulation 36.

(2) In determining the amount of charges paid for relevant childcare,
there is to be left out of account any amount—

(a) that the Secretary of State considers excessive having regard to the
extent to which the claimant (or, if the claimant is a member of a
couple, the other member) is engaged in paid work; or

(b) that is met or reimbursed by an employer or some other person or is
covered by other relevant support.

(3) "Other relevant support" means payments out of funds provided by
the Secretary of State or by Scottish or Welsh Ministers in connection with
the claimant's participation in work-related activity or training.

AMENDMENT

1. Universal Credit (Digital Service) Amendment Regulations 2014 (SI
2014/2887) reg.2(1) and (3) (November 26, 2014). The amendment is subject to
the saving provision in reg.5 of SI 2014/2887 (see Pt.IV).

2. Universal Credit and Miscellaneous Amendments Regulations 2015 (SI
2015/1754) reg.6 (Assessment periods beginning on or after April 11, 2016).

DEFINITIONS

"childcare costs element"—see reg.2.
"claimant"—see WRA 2012, s.40.
"couple"—see WRA 2012, ss.39 and 40.
"relevant childcare"—see reg.2 and reg.35.
"work"—see WRA 2012, s.40.

GENERAL NOTE

Paragraph (1): See the note to reg.31.   2.117
The effect of the saving provision in reg.5 of SI 2014/2887 is that the amendment
to para.(1) with effect from November 26, 2014 (but not the increase in the rate at
which childcare costs are met from 70% to 85% with effect from April 11, 2016)
only applies in "Full Service" (or "Digital Service") cases (see *Universal Credit—An
Introduction* above). For the text of para.(1) as it continues to apply in "Live Service"
cases (except for the change from 70% to 85%), see p.150 of the 2013/14 edition.

Paragraphs (2) and (3): Charges for relevant childcare are not taken into account   2.118
to the extent that the Secretary of State considers them excessive; if they are reimbursed by the claimant's employer or some other person; or if they are covered by
"other relevant support" (as defined in para.(3)) paid to claimants participating in
work-related activity or training.

[¹ Charges attributable to an assessment period

34A.—(1) Charges paid for relevant childcare are attributable to an   2.119
assessment period where—

(a) those charges are paid in that assessment period for relevant childcare in respect of that assessment period; or

(b) those charges are paid in that assessment period for relevant childcare in respect of a previous assessment period; or

(c) those charges were paid in either of the two previous assessment periods for relevant childcare in respect of that assessment period.

(2)   For the purposes of paragraph (1)(c), where a claimant pays charges for relevant childcare in advance, the amount which they have paid in respect of any assessment period is to be calculated as follows:

Step 1

Take the total amount of the advance payment (leaving out of account any amount referred to in regulation 34(2)).

Step 2

Apply the formula—

$$\left(\frac{PA}{D}\right) \times AP$$

Where—

PA is the amount resulting from step 1;

D is the total number of days covered by the payment referred to in step 1, and

AP is the number of days covered by the payment which also fall within the assessment period in question.

(3)   In this regulation, a reference to an assessment period in which charges are paid, or in respect of which charges are paid, includes any month preceding the commencement of the award that begins on the same day as each assessment period in relation to a claimant's current award.

AMENDMENT

1. Universal Credit (Digital Service) Amendment Regulations 2014 (SI 2014/2887) reg.2(1) and (4) (November 26, 2014). The amendment is subject to the saving provision in reg.5 of SI 2014/2887 (see Pt IV).

DEFINITIONS

"assessment period"—see WRA 2012 ss.40 and 7(2) and reg.21.
"claimant"—see WRA 2012 s.40.
"relevant childcare"—see reg.2 and reg.35.

GENERAL NOTE

2.120   The effect of the saving provision in reg.5 of SI 2014/2887 is that reg.34A only applies in "Full Service" (or "Digital Service") cases (see *Universal Credit—An Introduction* above).

Reg.34A governs when childcare charges are attributable to an assessment period for the purposes of reg.33(1)(za).

Para.(1) provides that charges are attributable either:

● to the assessment period in which they are paid if they are for relevant childcare in that period or (in arrears) for relevant childcare in a previous assessment period (sub-paras (a) and (b)) including, in the latter case, periods before the start of the award of universal credit (para.(3)); or

● to the assessment period in which the relevant childcare is provided if they were paid in advance in one of the two previous assessment periods (sub-para.(1)(c)). In practice, this means that childcare charges can be paid at least two months, and sometimes up to three months, in advance. Again, the previous periods can be before the start of the award of universal credit (para.(3)).

Para.(2) sets out the formula for deciding the amount of childcare charges paid in advance under para.(1)(c) that is to be attributed to an assessment period. The full amount of the advance payment (other than sums that are to be left out of account under reg.34(2) because they are excessive or are met or reimbursed by another person) is divided it by the number of days to which it relates, to produce a daily rate, and then multiplied by the number of days in the assessment period.

Meaning of "relevant childcare"

35.—(1) "Relevant childcare" means any of the care described in paragraphs (2) to (5) other than care excluded by paragraph (7) or (8).   2.121

(2) Care provided in England for a child—

(a) by a person registered under Part 3 of the Childcare Act 2006; or

[¹(b) by or under the direction of the proprietor of a school as part of the school's activities—

    (i) out of school hours, where a child has reached compulsory school age, or

    (ii) at any time, where a child has not yet reached compulsory school age; or]

[¹(c) by a domiciliary care provider registered with the Care Quality Commission in accordance with the requirements of the Health and Social Care Act 2008.]

(3) Care provided in Scotland for a child—

(a) by a person in circumstances in which the care service provided by the person consists of child minding or of day care of children within the meaning of [¹ schedule 12 to the Public Services Reform (Scotland) Act 2010 and is registered under Part 5 of that Act; or]

(b) by a childcare agency where the care service consists of or includes supplying, or introducing to persons who use the service, childcarers within the meaning of [¹ paragraph 5 of schedule 12 to the Public Services Reform (Scotland) Act 2010; or]

(c) by a local authority in circumstances in which the care service provided by the local authority consists of child minding or of day care of children within the meaning of [¹ schedule 12 to the Public Services Reform (Scotland) Act 2010 and is registered under Part 5 of that Act].

(4) Care provided in Wales for a child—

(a) by a person registered under Part 2 of the Children and Families (Wales) Measure 2010;

(b) in circumstances in which, but for articles 11, 12 or 14 of the Child Minding and Day Care Exceptions (Wales) Order 2010, the care would be day care for the purposes of Part 2 of the Children and Families (Wales) Measure 2010;

(c) by a childcare provider approved in accordance with a scheme made by the National Assembly for Wales under section 12(5) of the Tax Credits Act 2002;

[¹(d) out of school hours, by a school on school premises or by a local authority;]

[¹ (e) by a person who is employed, or engaged under a contract for services, to provide care and support by the provider of a domiciliary support service within the meaning of Part 1 of the Regulation and Inspection of Social Care (Wales) Act 2016; or]

(f) by a foster parent in relation to the child (other than one whom the foster parent is fostering) in circumstances in which the care would be child minding or day care for the purposes of Part 2 of the Children and Families (Wales) Measure 2010 but for the fact that the child is over the age of the children to whom that Measure applies.

(5) Care provided anywhere outside Great Britain by a childcare provider approved by an organisation accredited by the Secretary of State.

[¹ (5A) In paragraph (2)(b), "school" means a school that Her Majesty's Chief Inspector of Education, Children's Services and Skills is, or may be, required to inspect.]

(6) In paragraphs (2)(b) and (4)(d)—

(a) "proprietor", in relation to a school, means—
    (i) the governing body incorporated under section 19 of the Education Act 2002, or
    (ii) if there is no such governing body, the person or body of persons responsible for the management of the school; and

(b) "school premises" means premises that may be inspected as part of an inspection of the school.

(7) The following are not relevant childcare—

(a) care provided for a child by a close relative of the child, wholly or mainly in the child's home; and

(b) care provided by a person who is a foster parent of the child.

(8) Care is not within paragraph (2)(a) if it is provided in breach of a requirement to register under Part 3 of the Childcare Act 2006.

(9) In this regulation "child" includes a qualifying young person mentioned in regulation 33(1)(a)(ii).

AMENDMENT

1. Social Security (Miscellaneous Amendments) (No.2) Regulations 2013 (SI 2013/1508) reg.3(1) and (6) (July 29, 2013).
2. Social Security and Child Support (Regulation and Inspection of Social Care (Wales) Act 2016) (Consequential Provision) Regulations 2018 (SI 2018/228) reg.14 (April 2, 2018).

DEFINITIONS

"child"—see WRA 2012 s.40 and para.(9).
"foster parent"—see reg.2.
"local authority"—ibid.
"qualifying young person"—see WRA 2012 s.40 and 10(5) and regs 2 and 5.

GENERAL NOTE

2.122   Under reg.33(1)(a), charges only count for the purposes of the childcare costs condition if they are paid for "relevant childcare". Regulation 35 defines that phrase. By para.(1) care is "relevant childcare" if it falls within paras (2) to (5) unless it is excluded by paras (7) or (8).

2.123   *Paragraphs (2)–(5)*: The details differ as between England, Scotland and Wales but the rule may be summarised as being that to qualify as relevant childcare, the care must be provided by a person authorised or approved by an organ of the state to do so. In England and Wales, it can also be provided by the "proprietor" of a "school" on "school premises". The words and phrase in quotation marks are defined in paras (5A) and (6).

2.124   *Paragraphs (7) and (8)*: Care is not relevant childcare if it is provided by an unregistered childminder (para.(8)), by a foster parent (para.(7)(b) or by a close relative of the child (or qualifying young person: see para.(9)) wholly or mainly in the child's own home (para.(7)(a)).

General

Table showing amounts of elements

36.—(1) The amounts of the standard allowance, the child element, the [³ LCWRA element] and the carer element (which are all fixed amounts) and the maximum amounts of the childcare costs element are given in the following table.

2.125

(2) The amount of the housing costs element is dealt with in regulation 26.

(3) In the case of an award where the claimant is a member of a couple, but claims as a single person, the amounts are those shown in the table for a single claimant.

Element	Amount for each assessment period
Standard allowance—	
single claimant aged under 25	[⁵ £256.05] (*£342.72)
single claimant aged 25 or over	[⁵ £323.22] (*£409.89)
joint claimants both aged under 25	[⁵ £401.92] (*£488.59)
joint claimants where either is aged 25 or over	[⁵ £507.37] (*£594.04)
Child element—	
[⁵ ...]	[⁵ ...]
[⁵ each] child or qualifying young person	[⁵ £235.83]
Additional amount for disabled child or qualifying young person—	
lower rate	[⁵ £128.25]
higher rate	[⁵ £409.29]
[³ LCWRA element]—	
[³ ...]	[³ ...]
limited capability for work and work-related activity	[⁵ £341.92]
Carer element	[⁵ £162.92]
Childcare costs element—	
maximum amount for one child	[⁵ £646.35]
maximum amount for two or more children	[⁵ £1,108.04]

AMENDMENTS

1. Welfare Benefits Up-rating Order 2015 (SI 2015/30) art.13 and Sch. 5 (Assessment periods beginning on or after April 6, 2015).
2. Universal Credit and Miscellaneous Amendments Regulations 2015 (SI 2015/1754) reg.6 (Assessment periods beginning on or after April 11, 2016).
3. Employment and Support Allowance and Universal Credit (Miscellaneous Amendments and Transitional and Savings Provisions) Regulations 2017 (SI 2017/204) reg.4(1) and (7) (April 3, 2017).

4. Welfare Reform and Work Act 2016 s.14(5)(b) (April 6, 2017).

5. Social Security Benefits Up-rating Order 2020 (SI 2020/234) art.31(2) and Sch.13 (Assessment periods beginning on or after April 6, 2019).

MODIFICATION

The amounts of the standard allowances prescribed by art.31(2) of, and Sch.13 to, SI 2020/234 are modified to the higher amounts shown in round brackets and marked with asterisks in the table above by reg.3(1) of the Social Security (Coronavirus) (Further Measures) Regulations 2020 (SI 2020/371). By reg.3(2), the modification takes effect in the first assessment period that *ends* on or after April 6, 2020 and continues to have effect only for the 2020/21 tax year.

DEFINITIONS

"assessment period"—see WRA 2012, ss.40 and 7(2).
"carer element"—see reg.2.
"child element"—*ibid.*
"childcare costs element"—see reg.2.
"claimant"—see WRA 2012, s.40.
"disabled"—*ibid.*
"housing costs element"—see regs 2 and 25.
"joint claimants"—see WRA 2012, s.40.
"LCWRA element"—see regs 2 and 27.
"limited capability for work"—see WRA 2012, ss.40 and 37(1).
"limited capability for work-related activity"—see WRA 2012, ss.40 and 37(2).
"qualifying young person"—see WRA 2012, s.40 and 10(5) and regs 2 and 5.
"single claimant"—see WRA 2012, s.40.

GENERAL NOTE

2.126   The amount of each element in the universal credit calculation is prescribed by the table (other than the housing costs element, the amount of which is prescribed by reg.26(2)). Para.(3) provides that where a member of a couple claims as a single person (i.e., under reg.3(3)), it is the amounts for a single person that apply.

For the rules about entitlement to each of the elements, see the notes to the earlier regulations in Pt.4.

The amounts in the table have been up-rated three times since the first edition of this volume. The current amounts are as set out above and, with two exceptions, apply from April 6, 2020 (but see the note on p.xxv about when legislative changes to the rules for universal credit take effect in an individual case).

The two exceptions referred to above are the two amounts for the childcare costs element. The original 2013/14 rates of £532.29 and £912.50 were continued through 2014/2015 and 2015/2016 but were increased from the first assessment period beginning on or after April 11, 2016, and have not been up-rated further.

The other current amounts would normally also have been up-rated in April 2016. However, on March 16, 2016, s.11 and Sch.1 of the Welfare Reform and Work Act 2016 came into force. As a result the following amounts were frozen at their 2015/16 levels for four tax years and were not up-rated again until April 6, 2020:

- all the rates of the standard allowance (para.1(j) of Sch.1 to the 2016 Act);

- the lower rate of the additional amount for a disabled child or qualifying young person (para.1(k)); and

- the LCW element (para.1(l)).

The amounts for the child element, the higher rate of the additional amount for a disabled child or qualifying young person, the LCWRA element, the carer element, the childcare costs element, and the housing costs element were not subject to the four-year freeze. However, they were not up-rated for 2016/17 as the Secretary of State decided that those amounts has maintained their value in relation to prices as measured by the Consumer Prices Index over the 12 month period ending September 2015 (which had showed negative inflation of 0.1%): see para.4.2 of the Explanatory Memorandum to SI 2016/230.

Before April 6, 2017 the rate of the child element was higher for the first child or qualifying young person for whom the claimant was responsible. Under reg.43 of the Transitional Provisions Regulations 2014, the higher rate continues to apply where the claimant is responsible for a child or qualifying young person born before April 6, 2017. In 2018/2019, the transitionally protected higher rate is £277.08.

Run-on after a death

37. In calculating the maximum amount of an award where any of the following persons has died—

(a) in the case of a joint award, one member of the couple;

(b) a child or qualifying young person for whom a claimant was responsible; [¹ . . .]

(c) in the case of a claimant who had regular and substantial caring responsibilities for a severely disabled person, that person [¹ ; or

(d) a person who was a non-dependant within the meaning of paragraph 9(2) of Schedule 4,]

the award is to continue to be calculated as if the person had not died for the assessment period in which the death occurs and the following two assessment periods.

2.127

AMENDMENT

1. Universal Credit and Miscellaneous Amendments Regulations 2014 (SI 2014/597) reg.2(1) and (3) (April 28, 2014).

DEFINITIONS

"assessment period"—see WRA 2012, ss.40 and 7(2).
"claimant"—see WRA 2012, s.40.
"couple"—see WRA 2012, ss.39 and 40.
"regular and substantial caring responsibilities for a severely disabled person"—see regs 2 and 30.
"responsible for a child or qualifying young person"—see regs 2, 4 and 4A.
"severely disabled"—see WRA 2012, s.40.

GENERAL NOTE

Where a joint claimant, a child or qualifying young person for whom a claimant is responsible, a severely disabled person for whom a claimant had regular and substantial caring responsibilities or, from April 28, 2014, a non-dependant dies, the award of universal credit runs-on (i.e., it continues as if that person had not died) for the assessment period in which the death occurred and the following two assessment periods.

2.128

PART 5

CAPABILITY FOR WORK OR WORK-RELATED ACTIVITY

Introduction

2.129   **38.** The question whether a claimant has limited capability for work, or for work and work-related activity, is to be determined for the purposes of the Act and these Regulations in accordance with this Part.

DEFINITIONS

"the Act"—see reg.2.
"work-related activity"—see WRA 2012, s.40.

GENERAL NOTE

2.130   The question of whether a person has limited capability for work ("LCW") or limited capability for work and work-related activity ("LCWRA") is relevant for three reasons. Firstly, if a person has LCW or LCWRA, it affects the work require-ments that can or cannot be imposed on him/her (see ss.19(2)(a) and 21(1)(a) WRA 2012). Secondly, it will entitle him/her to an additional element as part of their universal credit (see regs 27–28), although note reg.29(4) where the claimant is also eligible for the carer element. Thirdly, it determines which level of the lower or higher work allowance (if applicable) applies (see reg. 22).
    Note also that the minimum age for claiming universal credit is 16 (not 18) if a person has LCW or is waiting for a work capability assessment and has submitted a medical certificate stating that they are not fit for work (see reg.8(1)(a) and (b)). In addition, if a claimant's universal credit award includes the LCWRA element, or the claimant (or either or both joint claimants) is receiving new style ESA that includes the support component, the benefit cap does not apply (see reg.83(1)(a)).

Limited capability for work

2.131   **39.**—(1) A claimant has limited capability for work if—
    (a) it has been determined that the claimant has limited capability for work on the basis of an assessment under this Part or under Part 4 of the ESA Regulations; or
    (b) the claimant is to be treated as having limited capability for work (see paragraph (6)).
    (2) An assessment under this Part is an assessment as to the extent to which a claimant who has some specific disease or bodily or mental disa-blement is capable of performing the activities prescribed in Schedule 6 or is incapable by reason of such disease or bodily or mental disablement of performing those activities.
    (3) A claimant has limited capability for work on the basis of an assess-ment under this Part if, by adding the points listed in column (3) of Schedule 6 against each descriptor listed in column (2) of that Schedule that applies in the claimant's case, the claimant obtains a total score of at least—
    (a) 15 points whether singly or by a combination of descriptors specified in Part 1 of that Schedule;
    (b) 15 points whether singly or by a combination of descriptors specified in Part 2 of that Schedule; or

(c) 15 points by a combination of descriptors specified in Parts 1 and 2 of that Schedule.

(4) In assessing the extent of a claimant's capability to perform any activity listed in Schedule 6, it is a condition that the claimant's incapability to perform the activity arises—

(a) in respect of any descriptor listed in Part 1 of Schedule 6, from a specific bodily disease or disablement;

(b) in respect of any descriptor listed in Part 2 of Schedule 6, from a specific mental illness or disablement; or

(c) in respect of any descriptor or descriptors listed in—

(i) Part 1 of Schedule 6, as a direct result of treatment provided by a registered medical practitioner for a specific physical disease or disablement, or

(ii) Part 2 of Schedule 6, as a direct result of treatment provided by a registered medical practitioner for a specific mental illness or disablement.

(5) Where more than one descriptor specified for an activity applies to a claimant, only the descriptor with the highest score in respect of each activity which applies is to be counted.

(6) [¹ Subject to paragraph (7),] A claimant is to be treated as having limited capability for work if any of the circumstances set out in Schedule 8 applies.

[¹ (7) Where the circumstances set out in paragraph 4 or 5 of Schedule 8 apply, a claimant may only be treated as having limited capability for work if the claimant does not have limited capability for work as determined in accordance with an assessment under this Part.]

AMENDMENT

1. Universal Credit and Miscellaneous Amendments Regulations 2014 (SI 2014/597) reg. 2(4) (April 28, 2014).

DEFINITIONS

"the Act"—see reg.2.
"claimant"—see WRA 2012 s.40.
"ESA Regulations"—see reg.2.
"limited capability for work"—see WRA 2012 ss.40 and 37(1).

GENERAL NOTE

A claimant will have LCW if it has been decided on the basis of an assessment under these Regulations or Part 4 of the ESA Regulations 2013 that they have LCW, or if they are treated as having LCW because any of the circumstances in Sch.8 apply (paras (1) and (6)). The effect of para.(7) is that a claimant can only be treated as having LCW under para.4 of Sch.8 (substantial risk to their health or that of someone else) or para.5 of Sch.8 (life threatening disease) once a work capability assessment has been carried out and they have been assessed as not having LCW.

2.132

Note that if a claimant has reached the qualifying age for state pension credit (the qualifying age for state pension credit for both men and women is the pensionable age for women (s.4(4) WRA 2012 and s.1(6) State Pension Credit Act 2012)—since April 2010 this has been increasing from 60 and will reach 65 in November 2018) and is entitled to disability living allowance or personal independence payment, they are treated as having LCW (para.6 of Sch.8).

See Sch.6 for the activities and descriptors for assessing LCW. They are the same as the activities and descriptors in Sch.2 to the ESA Regulations 2008 for assessing LCW. See the notes to Sch.2 in Vol.I of this series. They are also the same as the activities and descriptors in Sch.2 to the ESA Regulations 2013.

Limited capability for work and work-related activity

2.133

40.—(1) A claimant has limited capability for work and work-related activity if—

(a) it has been determined that—
  (i) the claimant has limited capability for work and work-related activity on the basis of an assessment under this Part, or
  (ii) the claimant has limited capability for work related activity on the basis of an assessment under Part 5 of ESA Regulations; or
(b) the claimant is to be treated as having limited capability for work and work-related activity (see paragraph (5)).

(2) A claimant has limited capability for work and work-related activity on the basis of an assessment under this Part if, by reason of the claimant's physical or mental condition—

(a) at least one of the descriptors set out in Schedule 7 applies to the claimant;
(b) the claimant's capability for work and work-related activity is limited; and
(c) the limitation is such that it is not reasonable to require that claimant to undertake such activity.

(3) In assessing the extent of a claimant's capability to perform any activity listed in Schedule 7, it is a condition that the claimant's incapability to perform the activity arises—

(a) in respect of descriptors 1 to 8, 15(a), 15(b), 16(a) and 16(b)—
  (i) from a specific bodily disease or disablement; or
  (ii) as a direct result of treatment provided by a registered medical practitioner for a specific physical disease or disablement; or
(b) in respect of descriptors 9 to 14, 15(c), 15(d), 16(c) and 16(d)—
  (i) from a specific mental illness or disablement; or
  (ii) as a direct result of treatment provided by a registered medical practitioner for a specific mental illness or disablement.

(4) A descriptor applies to a claimant if that descriptor applies to the claimant for the majority of the time or, as the case may be, on the majority of the occasions on which the claimant undertakes or attempts to undertake the activity described by that descriptor.

(5) [¹ Subject to paragraph (6),] A claimant is to be treated as having limited capability for work and work-related activity if any of the circumstances set out in Schedule 9 applies.

[¹ (6) Where the circumstances set out in paragraph 4 of Schedule 9 apply, a claimant may only be treated as having limited capability for work and work-related activity if the claimant does not have limited capability for work and work-related activity as determined in accordance with an assessment under this Part.]

AMENDMENT

1. Universal Credit and Miscellaneous Amendments Regulations 2014 (SI 2014/597) reg.2(5) (April 28, 2014).

DEFINITIONS

"the Act"—see reg.2.
"claimant"—see WRA 2012 s.40.
"ESA Regulations"—see reg.2.
"limited capability for work"—see WRA 2012 ss.40 and 37(1).
"limited capability for work-related activity"—see WRA 2012 ss.40 and 37(2).

GENERAL NOTE

A claimant will have LCW and LCWRA if it has been decided on the basis of an   2.134
assessment under these Regulations that they have LCW and LCWRA or under
Part 5 of the ESA Regulations 2013 that they have LCWRA, or if they are treated
as having LCW and LCWRA because any of the circumstances in Sch.9 apply (see
paras (1) and (5)). The effect of para.(6) is that a claimant can only be treated as
having LCW and LCWRA under para.4 of Sch.9 (substantial risk to their health or
that of someone else) once a work capability assessment has been carried out and
they have been assessed as not having LCW and LCWRA.

Note that if a claimant has reached the qualifying age for state pension credit (the
qualifying age for state pension credit for both men and women is the pensionable
age for women (s.4(4) WRA 2012 and s.1(6) State Pension Credit Act 2012)—since
April 2010 this has been increasing from 60 and will reach 65 in November 2018)
and is entitled to the highest rate of the care component of disability living allowance, the enhanced rate of the daily living component of personal independence
payment, attendance allowance or armed forces independence payment (see the
definition of "attendance allowance" in reg.2 which includes armed forces independence payment) they are treated as having LCW and LCWRA (para.5 of Sch.9).

See Sch.7 for the activities and descriptors for assessing LCW and LCWRA. They
are the same as the activities and descriptors in Sch.3 to the ESA Regulations 2008
for assessing LCWRA. See the notes to Sch.3 in Vol.1 of this series. They are also
the same as the activities and descriptors in Sch.3 to the ESA Regulations 2013.

Work Capability Assessment

When an assessment may be carried out

41.—(1) The Secretary of State may carry out an assessment under this   2.135
Part where—
  (a) it falls to be determined for the first time whether a claimant has
      limited capability for work or for work and work-related activity; or
  (b) there has been a previous determination and the Secretary of State
      wishes to determine whether there has been a relevant change of
      circumstances in relation to the claimant's physical or mental condi-
      tion or whether that determination was made in ignorance of, or was
      based on a mistake as to, some material fact,
but subject to paragraphs (2) to (4).

  (2) If the claimant has [¹ monthly] earnings that are equal to or exceed
the relevant threshold, the Secretary of State may not carry out an assessment under this Part unless—
  (a) the claimant is entitled to attendance allowance, disability living
      allowance or personal independence payment; or
  (b) the assessment is for the purposes of reviewing a previous determi-
      nation that a claimant has limited capability for work or for work and
      work-related activity that was made on the basis of an assessment
      under this Part or under Part 4 or 5 of the ESA Regulations,

and, in a case where no assessment may be carried out by virtue of this paragraph, the claimant is to be treated as not having limited capability for work unless they are treated as having limited capability for work or for work and work-related activity by virtue of regulation 39(6) or 40(5).

(3) The relevant threshold for the purposes of paragraph (2) is the amount that a person would be paid at the hourly rate set out in [[2] regulation 4 of the National Minimum Wage Regulations] for 16 hours a week [[1], converted to a monthly amount by multiplying by 52 and dividing by 12].

(4) If it has previously been determined on the basis of an assessment under this Part or under Part 4 or 5 of the ESA Regulations that the claimant does not have limited capability for work, no further assessment is to be carried out unless there is evidence to suggest that—

(a) the determination was made in ignorance of, or was based on a mistake as to, some material fact; or

(b) there has been a relevant change of circumstances in relation to the claimant's physical or mental condition.

AMENDMENTS

1. Universal Credit and Miscellaneous Amendments Regulations 2015 (SI 2015/1754), reg.2(4) (November 4, 2015, or in the case of existing awards, the first assessment period beginning on or after November 4, 2015).

2. Social Security (Jobseeker's Allowance, Employment and Support Allowance and Universal Credit) (Amendment) Regulations 2016 (SI 2016/678), reg.5(3) (July 25, 2016).

DEFINITIONS

"attendance allowance"—see reg.2.
"claimant"—see WRA 2012 s.40.
"disability living allowance"—see reg.2.
"ESA Regulations"—*ibid.*
"limited capability for work"—see WRA 2012 ss.40 and 37(1).
"limited capability for work-related activity"—see WRA 2012 ss.40 and 37(2).
"monthly earnings"–see regs 2 and 90(6).
"National Minimum Wage Regulations" – see reg. 2.
"personal independence payment"—*ibid.*
"work-related activity"—see WRA 2012 s.40.

GENERAL NOTE

2.136   *Paragraph (1)*
This provides when a work capability assessment can be carried out but it is subject to paras (2)–(4).

2.137   *Paragraphs (2) and (3)*
The effect of these two paragraphs is that a claimant who has monthly earnings that are equal to or above the "relevant threshold" (16 × the national minimum national wage, which is £7.83 per hour from April 1, 2018, converted to a monthly amount by multiplying by 52 and dividing by 12) is treated as not having LCW (unless they are deemed to have LCW under reg.39(6) and Sch.8 or LCW and LCWRA under reg.40(5) and Sch.9) and no assessment may be carried out. But this rule does not apply if the claimant:

- is entitled to disability living allowance, personal independence payment, attendance allowance or armed forces independence payment (see the definition of "attendance allowance" in reg.2 which includes armed forces independence payment); or

- has already been assessed as having LCW or LCW and LCWRA under these Regulations or Pt 4 or 5 of the ESA Regulations 2013 and the purpose of the assessment is to review that determination.

Paragraphs (2) and (3) thus contain what could be viewed as a rump of a "permitted work rule" (somewhat oddly placed in a regulation that is also concerned with when an assessment may be carried out). But the effect of para.(2)(b) is that a claimant will only be treated as not having LCW under para.(2) if their weekly earnings are equal to or above the relevant threshold (see para.(3)) *and* they have not yet been assessed under the work capability assessment. If the claimant has already been assessed as having LCW or LCW and LCWRA, para.(2) will not apply, although the work capability assessment may well be re-applied in these circumstances. Until it is determined that the claimant does not have LCW or LCW and LCWRA, the claimant's universal credit award will continue to include the LCW or LCWRA element (as appropriate) (confirmed in para.G1035 ADM).

Note reg.40(1) and (2) of the Decisions and Appeals Regulations 2013 which provides that a determination that a person has, or does not have, LCW, or is to be treated as having, or not having, LCW, that has been made for the purposes of new style ESA or universal credit is conclusive for the purpose of any further decision relating to that benefit.

Paragraph (4) 2.138

If it has been decided that the claimant does not have LCW either under these Regulations or the ESA Regulations 2013, no further assessment will be carried out for the purposes of universal credit unless the evidence suggests that the decision was made in ignorance of or mistake as to a material fact or that there has been a relevant change in the claimant's physical or mental condition (para.(4)). Note that this provision applies without time limit.

Assessment—supplementary

42.—(1) The following provisions apply to an assessment under this Part. 2.139

(2) The claimant is to be assessed as if the claimant were fitted with or wearing any prosthesis with which the claimant is normally fitted or normally wears or, as the case may be, wearing or using any aid or appliance which is normally, or could reasonably be expected to be, worn or used.

(3) If a descriptor applies in the case of the claimant as a direct result of treatment provided by a registered medical practitioner for a specific disease, illness or disablement, it is to be treated as applying by reason of the disease, illness or disablement.

DEFINITION

"claimant"—see WRA 2012 s.40.

Information requirement

43.—(1) The information required to determine whether a claimant has 2.140 limited capability for work or for work and work-related activity is—
  (a) any information relating to the descriptors specified in Schedule 6 or 7 requested by the Secretary of State in the form of a questionnaire; and
  (b) any additional information that may be requested by the Secretary of State.

(2) But where the Secretary of State is satisfied that there is enough information to make the determination without the information mentioned in paragraph (1)(a), that information is not required.

(3) Where a claimant fails without a good reason to comply with a request under paragraph (1), the claimant is to be treated as not having limited capability for work or, as the case may be, for work and work- related activity.

(4) But paragraph (3) does not apply unless the claimant was sent a further request to provide the information at least 3 weeks after the date of the first request and at least 1 week has passed since the further request was sent.

DEFINITIONS

"claimant"—see WRA 2012 s.40.
"limited capability for work"—see WRA 2012 ss.40 and 37(1).
"limited capability for work-related activity"—see WRA 2012 ss.40 and 37(2).
"work-related activity"—see WRA 2012 s.40.

GENERAL NOTE

2.141   On paras (3) and (4), see regs 22 and 37 of the ESA Regulations 2008 and the notes to those regulations in Vol.I of this series.

Medical examinations

2.142   **44.**—(1) Where it falls to be determined whether a claimant has limited capability for work or for work and work-related activity, the claimant may be called by or on behalf of a health care professional approved by the Secretary of State to attend a medical examination.

(2) Where a claimant who is called by or on behalf of such a health care professional to attend a medical examination fails without a good reason to attend or submit to the examination, the claimant is to be treated as not having limited capability for work or, as the case may be, for work and work-related activity.

(3) But paragraph (2) does not apply unless—
  (a) notice of the date, time and place of the examination was given to the claimant at least 7 days in advance; or
  (b) notice was given less than 7 days in advance and the claimant agreed to accept it.

DEFINITIONS

"claimant"—see WRA 2012 s.40.
"health care professional"—see reg.2.
"limited capability for work"—see WRA 2012 ss.40 and 37(1).
"limited capability for work-related activity"—see WRA 2012 ss.40 and 37(2).
"work-related activity"—see WRA 2012 s.40.

GENERAL NOTE

2.143   See regs 23 and 38 of the ESA Regulations 2008 and the notes to those regulations in Vol.I of this series. But note that unlike regs 23 and 38, the notice under reg.44 does not have to be in writing (see para.(3)).

PART 6

CALCULATION OF CAPITAL AND INCOME

CHAPTER 1

CAPITAL

Introduction

45. This Chapter provides for the calculation of a person's capital for the purpose of section 5 of the Act (financial conditions) and section 8 of the Act (calculation of awards).   **2.144**

DEFINITION

"the Act"—see reg. 2.

GENERAL NOTE

A claimant's resources are either capital or income. There is nothing in between. On the distinction between capital and income, see the notes to reg. 23 of the Income Support Regulations in Vol. II of this series. Those general principles are not explored here, because the approach to income other than earnings to be taken into account in universal credit is different from that in income support, earnings have their own special definitions and deemings and, as noted below, there is a simpler approach to capital. There will be reference back to the general principles at the appropriate places.   **2.145**

Compared with income support, income-based JSA, income-related ESA and housing benefit, the rules for the treatment of capital under universal credit are refreshingly concise. For example, there are only 19 paragraphs in Sch. 10 (capital to be disregarded), whereas Sch. 10 to the Income Support Regulations has over 70 (although a few have been omitted over the years).

The capital limit for universal credit for both a single claimant and joint claimants is £16,000 (see reg. 18(1)). Note that where a claimant who is a member of a couple makes a claim as a single person (see reg. 3(3) for the circumstances in which this may occur) the capital of the other member of the couple counts as the claimant's (reg. 18(2)).

With effect from July 24, 2019, reg. 51 of the Transitional Provisions Regulations 2014, as inserted by reg. 3 of the Universal Credit (Managed Migration Pilot and Miscellaneous Amendments) Regulations 2019 (SI 2019/1152), supplies a transitional capital disregard to claimants who (i) were previously entitled to a tax credit and had capital exceeding £16,000; (ii) are given a migration notice that existing benefits are to terminate; and (iii) claim universal credit within the deadline. The disregard is of any capital exceeding £16,000. The disregard can apply only for 12 assessment periods and ceases (without the possibility of revival) following any assessment period in which the amount of capital the claimant has falls below £16,000. See regs 56 and 57 of the Transitional Provisions Regulations for further provisions on termination of the protection. Paragraph 7 of Sch. 2 to the Transitional Provisions Regulations, inserted by the same Regulations, contains a disregard as capital of any amount paid as a lump sum by way of a "transitional SDP amount" under that Schedule.

What is included in capital?

46.—(1) The whole of a person's capital is to be taken into account unless—   **2.146**

(a) it is to be treated as income (see paragraphs (3) and (4)); or

(b) it is to be disregarded (see regulation 48).

(2) A person's personal possessions are not to be treated as capital.

(3) Subject to paragraph (4), any sums that are paid regularly and by reference to a period, for example payments under an annuity, are to be treated as income even if they would, apart from this provision, be regarded as capital or as having a capital element.

(4) Where capital is payable by instalments, each payment of an instalment is to be treated as income if the amount outstanding, combined with any other capital of the person (and, if the person is a member of a couple, the other member), exceeds £16,000, but otherwise such payments are to be treated as capital.

GENERAL NOTE

2.147   The whole of a claimant's capital, both actual and notional (see reg.50), counts towards the £16,000 limit, except if it is treated as income under paras (3) and (4), or is ignored under Sch.10 or regs 75 and 76 (para.(1)). There is also the important provision in para.(2) that personal possessions, however acquired, are not to be treated as capital and so cannot count towards the capital limits (see the detailed notes below). In the case of joint claimants, it is their combined capital that counts towards the £16,000 limit (s.5(2)(a) WRA 2012). A child's capital is not taken into account.

Note reg.49 which maintains the rule that applies for income support, old style JSA, old style ESA and housing benefit that it is only if a debt is secured on a capital asset that it can be deducted.

There is a great deal of case law, both in the context of other social security benefits and more generally, that will be equally applicable in the context of universal credit. See also the notes to reg.23 of the Income Support Regulations on the distinction between income and capital.

Distinguishing between actual and notional capital

2.147.1   *AB v SSWP and Canterbury CC (IS and HB)* [2014] UKUT 212 (AAC) emphasises the importance of decision-makers and tribunals making a clear distinction in their findings of fact as to whether the claimant has actual or notional capital. If it is found that the claimant has actual capital over £16,000, there will usually be no entitlement to income support. If the claimant shows that they possess capital of less than £16,000, because some of it has been spent or otherwise disposed of, it is usually necessary to consider whether they should be treated as possessing notional capital (see reg.50(1) and the notes to that regulation). In this case the claimant's wife had received an inheritance. On the DWP's discovery of this, supersession of the claimant's income support and housing benefit was sought. The burden therefore shifted to the claimant to show that his wife no longer possessed that capital. See *R(SB) 38/85* where Commissioner Hallett held at para.18:

> "The claimant says that he expended this sum of £18,700 in repaying loans. It is for him to prove that this is so. Failing a satisfactory account of the way in which the money has been disposed of, it will be open to the tribunal, and a natural conclusion, to find that the claimant still has, in some form or other, that resource and consequently to conclude that his actual resources are above the prescribed limit."

The tribunal's statement of reasons in *AB* concluded that the claimant "should be deemed to still have, through his partner, capital in excess of £16,000". Judge Wikeley held that the ambiguity inherent in the use of the word "deemed" (or "treated") meant that it was not sufficiently clear whether the tribunal had found that the claimant, through his wife, still had the capital from the inheritance in some form or whether he had deprived himself of it for the purpose of obtaining benefit such as to be fixed with notional capital. In addition, the tribunal had failed to adequately explain why it did not accept the claimant's wife's explanation. In relation to this issue Judge Wikeley emphasises the importance of having a sound evidential basis for an adverse credibility finding against a claimant.

Actual capital

There is a good deal of law on actual capital.

2.147.2

The first condition is of course that the capital resource is the claimant's or their partner's. This is not as simple as it sounds.

In *CIS/634/1992* the claimant was made bankrupt on November 29, 1990. However, his trustee in bankruptcy was not appointed until April 1991. Between November 29 and December 28, 1990, when he claimed income support the claimant divested himself of most of his capital. Under the Insolvency Act 1986 (subject to certain exceptions) a bankrupt's property does not vest in his trustee in bankruptcy on the making of a bankruptcy order, but only when the trustee is appointed. The appointment does not have retrospective effect. It is held that since he had failed to give a satisfactory account of how he had disposed of his capital he was to be treated as still possessing it (*R(SB) 38/85* referred to in the notes to reg.50). Thus the claimant was not entitled to income support prior to the appointment of the trustee in bankruptcy because until then he possessed actual capital over the income support limit.

KS v SSWP (JSA) [2009] UKUT 122 (AAC), reported as [2010] AACR 3, however, disagrees with *CIS/634/1992*. Judge Mark points out that a person cannot realise or use any part of his capital after a bankruptcy order has been made and that, subject to any order of the court, it will vest in his trustee in due course. Whether the capital remained the claimant's with a nil value or whether it ceased to be his capital at all (on which Judge Mark did not reach any firm conclusion), the result was that the claimant had no capital, or no capital of any value, after the bankruptcy order had been made.

In *SH v SSWP* [2008] UKUT 21 (AAC) Judge Turnbull also does not reach a final conclusion as to whether money in a bank account or other property that is subject to a restraint order under s.77 of the Criminal Justice Act 1988 (now the Proceeds of Crime Act 2002) or a freezing order ceases to be the claimant's capital. He was inclined to think that such assets remained the claimant's capital. However, their market value would be nil since the claimant was prohibited by court order from disposing of them. *CS v Chelmsford BC (HB)* [2014] UKUT 518 (AAC) takes the same view as *SH* but again without reaching a final conclusion on the point. In *CS*, which concerned assets subject to a restraint order under the Proceeds of Crime Act 2002, Judge Markus points out that not only is a restraint order under the Proceeds of Crime Act 2002 not expressed to deprive people of their interest in the property but also the terminology of the Act consistently presupposes that they retain their interest in property that is subject to a restraint order. Its market value, however, would be nil.

See also *CIS/1189/2003*, which concerned a claimant who was the sole residuary beneficiary under her mother's will. The estate had remained unadministered for several years so that her mother's property had not actually vested in the claimant. However, the property counted as the claimant's actual capital for the purposes of income support since, subject only to the formalities needed to perfect her title, she had for all practical purposes an entitlement in respect of the property that was equivalent to full beneficial ownership.

R(IS) 9/04 confirms that assets being administered on a patient's behalf either at the Court of Protection or by their receiver remain the patient's assets which have to be valued at their current market value (see reg.49) (following *CIS/7127/1995*). Such assets are held under a "bare trust" with the entire beneficial ownership remaining with the patient. The fact that the Court had discretionary powers of control over the management of the patient's property for their benefit did not mean that the patient's beneficial ownership had ceased.

However, capital that a claimant is under a "certain and immediate liability" to repay at the moment of its receipt by, or attribution to, the claimant, will not count as their capital (*CIS/2287/2008*). In *CIS/2287/2008* the Commissioner decides that the principle in *Chief Adjudication Officer v Leeves*, reported as *R(IS) 5/99*, does apply to capital as well as income. However, it only applies at the moment of receipt or attribution and is relevant only to the issue of whether money or an asset should be classified as the claimant's capital. *Leeves* does not apply if the liability to repay arises after something has become capital in the claimant's hands. That issue continues to be governed by the principle in *R(SB) 2/83* that, in calculating capital, liabilities are not to be deducted, except those expressly provided for in the legislation. *SSWP v GF (ESA)* [2017] UKUT 333 (AAC), discussed later in this note under the heading *Deduction of liabilities*, is a recent application of the principle of *R(SB) 2/83*. See also *JH v SSWP* [2009] UKUT 1 (AAC) which explains that *Leeves* only operates where, outside trust relationships, there is a certain obligation of immediate repayment or return of the asset to the transferor. It does not bite where the claimant is under some liability to a third party.

Beneficial ownership

2.147.3   The mere fact that an asset or a bank or building society account is in the claimant's sole name does not mean that it belongs to the claimant. It is the "beneficial ownership" which matters. It is only such an interest that has a market value. The claimant may hold the asset under a trust which means that they cannot simply treat the asset as theirs, but must treat it as if it belonged to the beneficiary or beneficiaries under the trust. It is they who are "beneficially entitled." A trustee may also be a beneficiary, in which case the rule in reg.47 may come into play, or may have no beneficial interest at all (see further below under *Claimant holding as trustee*).

The basic principle was confirmed, as might have been thought unnecessary, by Judge Poynter in *SSWP v LB of Tower Hamlets and CT* (IS & HB) [2018] UKUT 25 (AAC) (see the notes under *Claimant holding as a trustee* for the details). However, it appeared that local authorities had routinely been submitting in housing benefit cases, wrongly taking a single sentence from the same judge's earlier decision in *CH/715/2006* out of context, that only legal interests were relevant.

These issues often arise in the context of attributing the beneficial ownership of former matrimonial assets. One example is *R(IS) 2/93*. The claimant had a building society account in her sole name, which she had had since before her marriage. Her husband deposited the bulk of the money in it, including his salary. On their separation, the AO and the SSAT treated the entire amount in the account as part of the claimant's capital. The Commissioner holds that she was not solely beneficially entitled to the money so that the equivalent of reg.47 had to operate. There is helpful guidance on the limited circumstances in which the "presumption of advancement" (i.e. that when a husband puts an asset into his wife's name he intends to make an outright gift of it) will operate in modern circumstances. (Note that the presumption of advancement was due to be abolished by s.199 of the Equality Act 2010 but this section has not yet been brought into force.) And see *CIS/982/2002* on the valuation of a share in a frozen joint bank account. Note also *R(IS) 10/99* below. In *CIS/553/1991*, where a house was in the husband's sole name, it was held that its valuation should take into account the wife's statutory right of occupation under the Matrimonial Homes Act 1967. See also *R(IS) 1/97*, where the claimant, who separated from his wife, agreed that she could live in the former matrimonial home, which was in his sole name, for her lifetime, which the Commissioner considered created a constructive trust.

In most cases of spouses or civil partners, in whoever's name the asset is, there will be some degree of joint ownership. But if an asset is in the sole name of one, the other should not be treated as having a half share as a beneficial tenant in common under reg.47 until it has been established that they do own at least part of it. On this, see *R(IS) 1/03*, which holds that a person's right to seek a lump sum payment or property transfer order under the Matrimonial Causes Act 1973 is not a capital asset. Moreover, *CIS/984/2002* should also be noted in this context. This holds that money held by the claimant's solicitor pending quantification of the statutory charge to the Legal Services Commission under s.10(7) of the Access to Justice Act 1999 was not part of the claimant's capital. Until that quantification had been carried out, it was not possible to identify any particular amount as the claimant's capital. Another way of looking at it was to treat the statutory charge as an incumbrance for the purpose of the equivalent of reg.49(1)(b) (see *CIS/368/1993*). Nor was any part of the money available to the claimant on application for the purposes of reg.51(2) of the Income Support Regulations. See also *CIS/7097/1995*, discussed in the notes to reg.47.

In *LC v Bournemouth Borough Council (HB)* [2016] UKUT 175 (AAC), the proceeds of sale of a former matrimonial home were being held in a solicitors' client account until the claimant's partner and his ex-wife agreed how the sum was to be split or the issue was resolved by a court order after a Financial Dispute Resolution hearing. In the judge's view the value of the capital prior to agreement or an order of the court would be minimal. The local authority had jumped the gun by treating the claimant as having capital in excess of £16,000 from the date the proceeds were placed in the client account.

Claimant holding as trustee

It would take many whole books to explore all the circumstances in which a trust relationship arises such that a person who holds the legal ownership of assets is subject to trust duties towards other people and so is a trustee and either has no beneficial interest in the assets or only a partial interest. The notes that follow concentrate on the social security case law, but only the barest outline of the general law can be given. In novel or complex cases there may need to be reference to specialist trust books. Sometimes the social security cases refer helpfully to the more general authorities. See, for recent examples, *SSWP v LB of Tower Hamlets and CT (IS & HB)* [2018] UKUT 25 (AAC) on resulting trusts and *VMcC v SSWP (IS)* [2018] UKUT 63 (AAC) on the *Quistclose* principle, both discussed further below.

The following notes first deal briefly with express trusts, where the existence and terms of the trust are stated or accepted, then with circumstances in which trusts arise by some form of implication, i.e implied, resulting or constructive trusts.

A trust can be created by declaration when assets are acquired (e.g. the familiar transfer of a house to a couple as beneficial joint tenants or tenants in common) or over assets already owned. In relation to assets other than land, no particular formality is required, although there must be certainty as to the assets covered by the trust and the beneficiaries as well as on the intention to create a trust. There may therefore be difficult questions in particular cases over whether there is sufficient persuasive evidence of the existence of a trust (as exemplified in several cases discussed below). It is in general for a claimant who has been shown to be the legal owner of an asset to show that they are not a beneficial owner (*MB v Royal Borough of Kensington and Chelsea (HB)* [2011] UKUT 321 (AAC) and *CT*, above).

In relation to trusts of land, *SB v SSWP (IS)* [2012] UKUT 252 (AAC) is a useful reminder that s.53(1)(b) of the Law of Property Act 1925 only requires a trust relating to land to be evidenced in writing. Absence of writing makes the trust unenforceable but not void. The tribunal had found that there was no trust of the property in question because there was no trust deed. That error of law had led the tribunal to fail to investigate and make findings on whether there had been a declaration of trust, whether the scope of the trust was certain, the subject matter of the trust, the objects/persons intended to benefit from any such trust and (in the absence of any documentation) whether the surrounding circumstances were consistent with the existence of a trust. It follows from the principle that the trust is merely unenforceable that the existence of later evidence in writing satisfies s.53(1) from the date of the original declaration. It is also said that the statute cannot be used as an instrument of fraud, so that a person who has taken the property knowing of the trust cannot be heard to deny the trust, despite there being no evidence in

2.147.4

writing. Note also that s.53(1) does not apply to implied, resulting or constructive trusts.

In *R(IS) 1/90*, the claimant established a building society account in his own name which was to be used solely to finance his son's medical education. He executed no documents about the account. It was argued that there was sufficient evidence of a declaration of trust over the account, but the Commissioner held that the claimant had not unequivocally renounced his beneficial interest in the sum in the account. Although he had earmarked the money for the son's education, the situation was like an uncompleted gift and there was insufficient evidence of a declaration of trust.

For the position under Scots law see *R(IS) 10/99*. The claimant agreed that he would pay his former wife (from whom he was separated) £22,250, representing a share of his pension. When he claimed income support, the claimant had £15,500 in his bank account that he said he was holding for his wife. The Commissioner decides that the £15,500 was not subject to a trust. That was because there had been no delivery of the subject of the trust, nor any satisfactory equivalent to delivery, "so as to achieve irrevocable divestiture of the truster [the equivalent of the settlor in English law] and investiture of the trustee in the trust estate", as required by Scots law (see *Clark Taylor & Co Ltd v Quality Site Development (Edinburgh) Ltd* 1981 S.C. 11). There was no separate bank account and there had been no clear indication to the claimant's wife that the money was held on trust for her. In addition, as the truster would have been the sole trustee, the Requirements of Writing (Scotland) Act 1995 required the trust to be proved in writing. That had not been done. Nor was there an "incumbrance" within the meaning of the equivalent of reg.49(1)(b) preventing the claimant disposing of the money. The consequence was that the £15,500 counted as the claimant's capital. No doubt the result would have been the same if the principles of trust law in England and Wales had been applied. Mere mental earmarking of an asset for a particular purpose is not enough to show the existence of a trust.

For a further case which considered whether a trust had been validly constituted for the purposes of Scots law, see *CSIS/639/2006*.

One particular instance of a resulting trust is where a person gives or loans some amount to another to be used for a particular purpose. In *R(SB) 53/83* the claimant's son had paid him £2,850 to be used for a holiday in India. The claimant died without taking the holiday or declaring the existence of the money to the DHSS. The Commissioner, applying the principle of *Barclays Bank Ltd v Quistclose Investments Ltd* [1970] A.C. 567, held that there was a trust to return the money to the son if the primary purpose of the loan was not carried out. Since the Commissioner held that there had been no overpayment while the claimant was alive, this must mean that the claimant held the money on trust to use it for the specified purpose or to return it. It was not part of the claimant's resources. This is an important decision, which overtakes some of the reasoning of *R(SB) 14/81* (see the notes to reg.49). The actual decision in *R(SB) 53/83* was reversed (by consent) by the Court of Appeal, because the Commissioner had differed from the appeal tribunal on a point of pure fact. *R(SB) 1/85* holds that this does not affect its authority on the issue of principle. In *R(SB) 1/85*, the claimant's mother-in-law had some years previously provided the money for the purchase of the lease of a holiday chalet for the use of the claimant's mentally handicapped son, Keith. The lease was in the claimant's name and its current value was probably about £5,000. The AO's initial statement of the facts was that the mother-in-law had bought the chalet in the claimant's name. The Commissioner held that this would give rise to a presumption of a resulting trust in her favour, so that the claimant would have no beneficial interest in the chalet—nothing he could sell. The presumption could be rebutted if in fact the mother-in-law had made an outright gift to the claimant, or to Keith. In the second case the claimant again would have no beneficial interest. In the first, he would be caught, for even if he had said that he intended to use the chalet purely for Keith, there was not the necessary written evidence of the trust (Law of Property Act 1925 s.53). Another possibility was that the mother-in-law had made a gift to the claimant subject to an express (but unwritten) trust in favour of Keith, when again the claimant clearly would not be the beneficial owner, as that would be a fraud. This is a very instructive decision, which will give valuable guidance in sorting out many family-type arrangements.

The dangers and difficulties of *Quistclose* were pointed out in *CSB/1137/1985*, particularly where family transactions are concerned. There, the claimant had received loans of £1,000 and £500, to fund a trip to India, from friends originally from the same village, who both later provided letters to say that, as the trip had not been taken, they had asked for, and received, their money back. Commissioner Rice held that the tribunal had gone wrong in law in concluding, following *R(SB) 53/83*, that the claimant did not have any beneficial interest in the funds, because the relationship between the lenders and the claimant indicated that nothing as sophisticated as the imposition of a trust had been intended. Rather, it had not been shown that there was any restriction on the claimant's use of the money.

Judge Wikeley in *VMcC v SSWP (IS)* [2018] UKUT 63 (AAC) has recently helpfully summarised the test required for the imposition of a *Quistclose* trust as set out in recent authority (in particular *Twinsectra Ltd v Yardley* [2002] 2 A.C. 164 and *Bellis v Challenor* [2015] EWCA Civ 59) and also discussed the distinction between *R(SB) 53/83* and *CSB/1137/1985*. The summary in para.42 is this:

> "The funds must be transferred on terms, typically for a stated purpose, which do not leave them at the free disposal of the transferee;
> There must be an intention to create what is, viewed objectively, a trust;
> A person creates a trust by their words or conduct, not their innermost thoughts;
> If such a trust is created, then the beneficial interest in the property remains in the transferor unless and until the purposes for which it has been transferred have been fulfilled;
> If such a trust is not created, then the ordinary consequence is that the money becomes the property of the transferee, who is free to apply it as they choose."

In addition, *Twinsectra* established that if there is a lack of clarity in identifying the stated purpose such that the funds cannot be applied the transferor's beneficial interest continues. Judge Wikeley acknowledged that there appeared to be a very thin line between the circumstances in *R(SB) 53/83* and *CSB/1137/1985*, but suggested in para.48 that, as well as the purpose being more specific, it might have been significant that the funds in *R(SB) 53/83* had been transferred, while the transaction in *CSB/1137/1985* was described in terms of a loan. With respect, it is hard to see why the transaction being a loan should point towards the claimant in *CSB/1137/1985* being subject to no trust obligations. It might be thought that the distinction, fine though it may be, was more in there not having been the necessary words or conduct, rather than innermost thoughts.

Cases in which *Quistclose* has been applied include the following. In *R(SB) 12/86*, £2,000 was lent to the claimant on condition that she did not touch the capital amount, but only took the interest, and repaid the £2,000 on demand. The £2,000 was not part of her capital, never having been at her disposal. The Commissioner in *CSB/975/1985* was prepared to apply the principle to a loan on mortgage from a Building Society for property renovation. But it would have to be found that the loan was made for no other purpose and was to be recoverable by the Building Society if for any reason the renovations could not be carried out. The furthest extension so far of the *Quistclose* principle is in *CFC/21/1989*. The claimant's father paid her each month an amount to meet her mortgage obligation to a building society. The Commissioner accepts that the money was impressed with a trust that it should be used only for that purpose and did not form part of her capital. The extension is that the purpose was to meet expenditure on an item that could be covered by income support.

The facts in *VMcC* were very unusual. The claimant, who was a member of the Traveller community, had two accounts with TSB and Nationwide opened in her own name when she was a child (probably when she was about seven) for members of her family to put money in for her future education. When she became pregnant at the age of 19 she was disowned by her family and claimed income support in April 2015, disclosing two bank accounts, but not the TSB and Nationwide accounts. She said she only became aware of those accounts at a compliance interview in July 2015 and in August produced evidence that both accounts had been closed. She said that all the amounts in the accounts (some £13,000) had been returned to the family members by her mother, save for £2,000 that she was allowed to keep for her baby. The decision-maker treated all the amounts as the claimant's, generating a tariff income, and that was upheld on appeal. The tribunal found that as the claimant had opened the accounts she would have known of them and concluded that she could have used the money as she pleased. If her mother or the family had wanted to set aside money for her education they could have opened a trustee account. Judge Wikeley set the tribunal's decision aside because there was not evidence to support the finding that the claimant had opened the TSB and Nationwide accounts and gave some guidance to a new tribunal on rehearing. In para.44 he cited what had been said in the commentary in Vol.II of this series, that there may well be evidential difficulties in establishing the components of a *Quistclose* trust in the context of family arrangements, not least because there is often no contemporary documentation, but stressed that the absence of a paper trail is not necessarily determinative. In principle a *Quistclose* trust can be created informally and by word of mouth, although very careful fact-finding is necessary. After comparing the outcomes of *R(SB) 53/83* and *CSB/1137/1995* (see above), he mentioned in para.47 two particular factors to be considered in family-type cases:

> "The first is that in practice it is unusual for informal family arrangements to be contemporaneously evidenced in writing (whether within the Traveller community or elsewhere). The second is that if the Appellant's account about being cast out by the community is accepted, that in itself may explain the failure of witnesses to attend an oral hearing to support her."

The question was not what was objectively reasonable (or what a High Street solicitor would have advised) but whether the claimant's account could be accepted in the light of what was customary in the particular community (para.61). It should also be noted that the Secretary of State accepted that an account may contain funds subject to a trust mixed with funds that are not so subject (para.51).

Cases in which *Quistclose* has not been applied include the following, many of which illustrate the thinness of the line between an outright gift or loan and one subject to an implied trust. *R(IS) 5/98* reached a similar outcome without any mention of *Quistclose*. The claimant had transferred her flat to her daughter partly on the condition that her daughter looked after her. It was held that the gift failed when this condition was not fulfilled and the daughter held the flat on trust for her mother. An appeal against this decision was dismissed by the Court of Appeal (*Ellis v Chief Adjudication Officer*, reported as part of *R(IS) 5/98*). The claimant had argued that the condition was void for uncertainty but this was rejected by the Court (and in accordance with the principles summarised in *VMcC* that would have led to the beneficial interest remaining with the mother from the outset).

In *YH v SSWP (IS)* [2015] UKUT 85 (AAC) the claimant raised a loan on his property and gave the money to his sons to establish a business. The sons used the money to set up the business and made the repayments on the loan. The *Quistclose* principle did not apply because there was no evidence to suggest that the lender had advanced the money on the condition that it was only to be used to establish the sons' business. A borrower does not create a trust in favour of the lender simply by having their own clear intention as to the application of the money. There was no separation between legal and beneficial interest so far as the sons were concerned, so that there was a question of whether the claimant had notional capital on the deprivation under the equivalent of reg.50(1).

A further example occurred in *CIS/5185/1995*, which held that *Quistclose* did not apply to a student grant which the claimant became liable to repay to the education authority when he left his course early. The grant could not be disregarded under the *Quistclose* principle because the education authority retained no beneficial interest in the grant. The authority merely reserved the right to demand repayment of a sum calculated according to the unexpired balance of the relevant term when the person ceased to be a student. In *Chief Adjudication Officer v Leeves*, reported as *R(IS) 5/99*, it was conceded on behalf of the claimant that there was no constructive trust in these circumstances, since no proprietary right had been retained by the education authority, nor had any fiduciary obligation been created.

In *MW v SSWP (JSA)* [2016] UKUT 469 (AAC), reported as [2017] AACR 15, a Scottish case, it was held that circumstances which would in England and Wales have given rise to a *Quistclose* trust did not do so as a matter of Scots law, because Scots law did not recognise a trust where the sole beneficiary was a trustee. The claimant had been lent money by his mother in order to buy his house. If it was not used for that purpose it was to be returned. Judge Gamble held that nevertheless the claimant was subject to a personal obligation to his mother to use the money only for the specified purpose, which in Scots law had a similar effect to a *Quistclose* trust, so that for the period in question the money lent did not form part of his capital. It is perhaps unclear to a non-Scots lawyer just why a trust could not be recognised (would not the mother also be a beneficiary?), but that appears not to matter as the essence of the decision is in the effect of the personal obligation identified by the judge.

So far as resulting trusts in general are concerned, the most authoritative statement is that of Lord Browne-Wilkinson, speaking for the majority of the House of Lords, in *Westdeutsche Landesbank Girozentrale v Islington LBC* [1996] A.C. 669 at 708:

> "Under existing law a resulting trust arises in two sets of circumstances: (A) where A makes a voluntary payment to B or pays (wholly or in part) for the purchase of property which is vested either in B alone or in the joint names of A and B, there is a presumption that A did not intend to make a gift to B: the money or property is held on trust for A (if he is the sole provider of the money) or in the case of a joint purchase by A and B in shares proportionate to their contributions. It is important to stress that this is only a presumption, which presumption is easily rebutted either by the counter-presumption of advancement or by direct evidence of A's intention to make an outright transfer .... (B) [*Quistclose* cases]."

That statement was cited in para.48 of *SSWP v LB of Tower Hamlets and CT (IS & HB)* [2018] UKUT 25 (AAC), where it was also noted that in *R(SB) 49/83* Commissioner Hallett stated that "the principle that purchase of land in the name of another gives rise to a resulting trust for the true purchaser has been settled for centuries". The principle rests on giving effect to the common intention of the parties.

In *R(SB) 49/83* the claimant had bought a house, but said that this was on behalf of his son, who had not been able to obtain a loan in his own name but was paying off the loan. The Commissioner held that if this could be established, the claimant would hold the house on a resulting trust for his son. However, he stressed that the credibility of the claimant's evidence, in the light of any further documents that came forward, needed to be carefully tested. For instance why did the house have to be transferred into the claimant's name, rather than him guaranteeing a loan to his son?

In *CT* the claimant bought a house in her sole name with a buy-to-let mortgage, intending that the mortgage interest would be met by the rental income. The purchase price and expenses came to £377,728.09. The mortgage loan was for £310,215. The claimant only had £250 capital to contribute, so agreed with a friend, Mr G, for him to contribute the remaining £67,263.09. They could reach no agreement at the time about what interest that gave him in the property. On claims for income support and housing benefit the claimant was initially treated as having capital of the value of the house less the amount of the incumbrance of the mortgage and 10% for expenses of sale. A tribunal held that she held the property on a resulting trust for Mr G. That decision was upheld by the Upper Tribunal on the basis that the claimant's beneficial interest was only 0.04% of the value (£250 as against £67,362.09). That result would follow from the plain application of the general resulting trust principles, in that the payments of mortgage had no effect on the beneficial interests, as while the house was let they came out of the rent (to which the two would have been entitled in proportion to their beneficial interests). That was not affected by a period in which the claimant was forced to live in the house while her own home was uninhabitable and she paid the mortgage interest. That was equivalent to her paying an occupation rent.

The main submission made by the Secretary of State on the appeal to the Upper Tribunal was that the tribunal's approach was incompatible with that of the Supreme Court in *Jones v Kernott* [2011] UKSC 53; [2012] 1 A.C. 776, under which what was fair in the light of the whole course of dealings between the parties was determinative. Judge Poynter provides a helpful analysis of the effect of the decisions in *Stack v Dowden* [2007] UKHL 17; [2007] 2 A.C. 432 and *Jones v Kernott* in "family home" type cases. The principles applicable in such cases were summarised as follows in para.51 of the joint judgment of Lady Hale and Lord Walker in *Jones v Kernott* (the words in square brackets in sub-para.(1) were added by Judge Poynter when citing this passage in *CT*):

> "*Conclusion*
> 51. In summary, therefore, the following are the principles applicable in a case such as this, where a family home is bought in the joint names of a cohabiting couple who are both responsible for any mortgage, but without any express declaration of their beneficial interests.
> (1) The starting point is that equity follows the law and they are joint tenants both in law and in equity. [As this decision will be read by people who are not legally qualified, I should explain that the phrase "joint tenants" in this context has a technical legal meaning and is not a generic reference to any co-owner. To summarise, the distinction being drawn by the Supreme Court is between "joint enants", who always own a property equally, and "tenants in common" who may own a property in equal shares but do not necessarily do so.]
> (2) That presumption can be displaced by showing (a) that the parties had a different common intention at the time when they acquired the home, or (b) that they later formed the common intention that their respective shares would change.
> (3) Their common intention is to be deduced objectively from their conduct:
>
>> "the relevant intention of each party is the intention which was reasonably understood by the other party to be manifested by that party's words and conduct notwithstanding that he did not consciously formulate that intention in his own mind or even acted with some different intention which he did not communicate to the other party" (Lord Diplock in *Gissing v Gissing* [1971] A.C. 886, 906).
>
> Examples of the sort of evidence which might be relevant to drawing such inferences are given in *Stack v Dowden*, at para 69.
> (4) In those cases where it is clear either (a) that the parties did not intend joint tenancy at the outset, or (b) had changed their original intention, but it is not possible to ascertain by direct evidence or by inference what their actual intention was as to the shares in which they would own the property, "the answer is that each is entitled to that share which the court considers fair having regard to the whole course of dealing between them in relation to the property": Chadwick LJ in *Oxley v Hiscock* [2005] Fam 211, para.69. In our judgment, "the whole course of dealing ... in relation to the property" should be given a broad meaning, enabling a similar range of factors to be taken into account as may be relevant to ascertaining the parties' actual intentions.
> (5) Each case will turn on its own facts. Financial contributions are relevant but there are many other factors which may enable the court to decide what shares were either intended (as in case (3)) or fair (as in case (4))."

Judge Poynter took the view that, while the "family home" category has been expanded to some extent beyond the confines of cohabiting couples, it could not apply in *CT*, where the purchase of the house was intended as an investment, with no intention of the claimant and Mr G living together there or anywhere else. Therefore the traditional resulting trust approach was correct.

However, the important, but somewhat inconclusive, Privy Council case of *Marr v Collie* [2017] UKPC 17, [2018] A.C. 631 shows that things are not as simple as that, while not throwing doubt on the actual result in *CT*.

Mr Marr, a banker, and Mr Collie, a building contractor, were in a personal relationship in the Bahamas from 1991 to 2008. During that time a number of properties were acquired, not for them to live in, that were conveyed into their joint names. Mr Marr provided the purchase price and paid the mortgage instalments. According to Mr Marr, Mr Collie repeatedly assured him that he would make an equal contribution to the costs, but never did. According to Mr Collie, he was to carry out renovations and works on the properties, some of which he did. There were also purchases of a truck and a boat that were registered in joint names. After the relationship broke down Mr Marr brought proceedings claiming that he was entitled to full beneficial ownership of those properties and the truck and boat. At first instance, the judge, relying on *Laskar v Laskar* [2008] EWCA Civ 347, [2008] 1 W.L.R. 2695, held that the *Stack v Dowden* presumption that a conveyance into joint names indicated a legal and beneficial joint tenancy unless the contrary was proved applied only in the "domestic consumer context". So, as the properties were intended primarily as investments, that presumption did not apply even though there was a personal relationship between the parties and there was a presumption that there was a resulting trust in favour of Mr Marr unless Mr Collie could demonstrate that a gift to him had been intended, which the judge concluded he had failed to do. On appeal, the Court of Appeal of the Bahamas found that there was cogent evidence of Mr Marr having intended that the beneficial interest in the properties be shared equally, so that the presumption of a resulting trust was rebutted. However, that was in large part in reliance on a 2005 email from Mr Marr that he had not been given the opportunity to comment on. For that reason and because the Court of Appeal's conclusions on the common intention of the parties failed to address a number of factual findings by the first instance judge, the Privy Council allowed Mr Marr's appeal, but was unable to substitute a decision in view of the absence of a proper examination of the parties' intentions. Thus the discussion of the general principles noted below was not anchored in a concrete application to specific findings of fact.

Lord Kerr, giving the judgment of a Board that included both Lady Hale and Lord Neuburger, opined in para.40 that by stating in para.58 of *Stack v Dowden* that the starting point, at least in the domestic consumer context, was that conveyance into joint names indicates both legal and beneficial joint tenancy, unless and until the contrary is proved, Lady Hale did not intend that the principle be confined to the purely domestic setting. Nor was *Laskar*, a case of the purchase of the claimant's council house, for letting out, effectively funded by the claimant's daughter, to be regarded as an authority to the contrary. Thus where a property was bought in the joint names of a cohabiting couple, even if that was as an investment, the "resulting trust solution" did not provide the inevitable answer on beneficial ownership (para.49). However, "save perhaps where there is no evidence from which the parties' intentions can be identified", the answer was not to be provided by the triumph of one presumption over another (Lady Hale's starting point as against the resulting trust solution). Rather, the context of the parties' common intention, or lack of it, was crucial (para.54) and apparently (it is not entirely clear) it was accepted that that common intention could alter after the initial acquisition of the property (para.55).

Applying those principles to the facts of *CT*, it would seem that there was a lack of any common intention both at the time of acquisition of the property and subsequently about what beneficial interest the claimant and Mr G should have.

Accordingly, either the case was one where the resulting trust solution should apply for that reason (most probable) or it was one where the lack of common intention in the context of an investment property was sufficient to displace the starting point of the beneficial interests following the legal ownership.

The main lesson to be taken from *Marr v Collie* is perhaps that great care needs to be taken in making findings of fact about the parties' intentions, common or otherwise, both at the time of acquisition of the property in question and subsequently. In addition it is noteworthy that the Privy Council apparently accepted that the same approach applied to the acquisition of chattels, in the form of the truck and boat, as to the acquisition of real property. What in particular is left unclear, even though the notion of a clash of presumptions was rejected, is on which party does the burden fall of showing that the common intention works in their favour. Or is the common intention to be identified on an objective analysis of the evidence, including the evaluation of credibility, without resort to propositions about burden of proof?

The same principle can apply to cases where a claimant has an account into which someone else's money is put either solely or mixed with the claimant's own money. In *R(IS) 9/08* payments of a boarding-out allowance which the foster parent had saved up over the years were not held on trust for the children in her care. However, *MC v SSWP (IS)* [2015] UKUT 600 (AAC) reaches the opposite conclusion where the claimant had saved up her daughters' disability living allowance in an account in the claimant's name. A tribunal accepted that in relation to an earlier period the claimant was holding the money on trust for her daughters. However, when she used a substantial part of the money to meet rent arrears, the tribunal considered that this suggested that what was previously held on trust had been subsequently "converted" into the claimant's capital by her actions. Judge Wikeley holds, however, that this was wrong in law. First, as the claimant had been made an appointee by DWP to act on behalf of her daughters in benefit matters, she was acting as a de facto trustee. Second, this was an obvious example of an informal trust over money, created without any legal formalities. Third, paying off rent arrears helped to keep a roof over the daughters' heads and was a perfectly reasonable use of their savings, consistent with the purposes of the trust. See also *DL v Southampton CC (CTB)* [2010] UKUT 453 (AAC) for a case where the tribunal failed to make adequate findings of fact about the circumstances in which the claimant's daughter had transferred funds into the claimant's savings account, so as to be able to decide whether there was a resulting trust or not.

JK v SSWP (JSA) [2010] UKUT 437 (AAC), reported as [2011] AACR 26, holds that by asking whether there was a trust the tribunal had posed the wrong question in relation to Scots law. It should have considered whether the presumption of ownership had been rebutted under Scots law. The claimant had contended that some of the money in his and his wife's joint account belonged to his mother-in-law. Applying the principle in *Cairns v Davidson* 1913 S.C. 1053, the tribunal should have considered, by way of such written or oral evidence available to it that it accepted, whether the presumption in favour of all the money in the joint account belonging to the claimant and his wife had been rebutted, so as to establish whether or not some of it belonged to his mother-in law.

It will sometimes be the case that the claimant's explanation as to why they are holding capital for someone else may involve some unlawful purpose, e.g. in order to conceal assets from the HMRC. In *MC v SSWP* [2010] UKUT 29 (AAC) the claimant had purchased a house for £26,000 in her own name. The money had come from her bank account. She asserted that £14,000 of the £26,000 had been paid into her account by her husband by way of a gift for their son and that the remaining £12,000 was her son's money which had been paid into her bank account because he had no bank account of his own. The tribunal found that the only explanation for her son providing the £12,000 was to "deny monies obtained illicitly to the revenue or that the sums were obtained from some illegal sources" and that as a consequence her son was estopped from denying that the capital belonged to the claimant. Judge Turnbull points out, however, that this was wrong in law. As the

House of Lords held in *Tinsley v Milligan* [1994] 1 A.C. 340, the principle that prevents a person putting forward evidence of his own wrongdoing in order to establish a resulting trust in his favour only applies where the person needs to put forward that evidence in order to rebut the presumption of advancement or of resulting trust. It does not apply where the person does not need to assert the illegality and only needs to show that he paid or contributed to the purchase price. In this case the claimant's son would be able to rely on the presumption of resulting trust without asserting any illegality. The question therefore was, in so far as it was accepted that the money was provided by her son, whether there was a resulting trust in his favour or whether he had intended to make a gift to the claimant.

DF v SSWP (ESA) [2015] UKUT 611 (AAC) concerns the question of whether the claimant could argue that he was not the beneficial owner of the funds in an Individual Savings Account (ISA) that was in his name. One of the conditions for an ISA account is that money invested in the account is in the beneficial ownership of the account holder (see reg.4(6) of the Individual Savings Account Regulations 1998 (SI 1998/1870) (ISA Regulations 1998)). The claimant maintained that the money in his ISA account really belonged to his daughter. His daughter confirmed this, stating that the ISA was designed to keep her money away from an unreliable partner. The Secretary of State argued that a person in whose name an ISA is held has to be regarded as the beneficial owner of the money in the account, relying on the decision in *CIS/2836/2006*. While that decision concerned the Personal Equity Plan Regulations 1989 (SI 1989/469), the ISA Regulations 1998 were said to be identical.

Judge Mitchell, however, concludes that *CIS/2836/2006* is restricted to "presumption of advancement" cases, i.e. cases in which the money is given by someone standing in loco parentis to a child, or by a husband to a wife, where there is a presumption that a gift was intended (note that the presumption of advancement was due to be abolished by s.199 of the Equality Act 2010 but this section has not yet been brought into force). To the extent that *CIS/2836/2006* could be read as going further, in his view it was not consistent with the decision in *Tinsley v Milligan* (above). He also holds that *CIS/2836/2006* did not decide that ISA-type legislation operates to extinguish beneficial interests of third parties in ISA deposits. Neither the ISA Regulations 1998 nor the enabling power under which they were made (Income and Corporation Taxes Act 1988 s.333(2)) had the effect of altering existing rights in relation to property. The legislation was only concerned with creating a special account with special tax advantages.

Judge Mitchell then goes on to reject the Secretary of State's argument that the law of illegality meant that, as a matter of public policy, the claimant could not rely on a beneficial interest that he had previously denied. This was inconsistent with the Supreme Court's decision in *Hounga v Allen* [2014] UKSC 47; [2014] 1 W.L.R. 2889 and the Court of Appeal's decision in *R. (Best) v Secretary of State for Justice (Rev 1)* [2015] EWCA Civ 17. In his view it was better for a First-tier Tribunal in an ISA case to ignore the role that may or may not be played by the law of illegality and simply focus on whether it accepted that the beneficial interest in the funds lay elsewhere. He does, however, point out the risks that a claimant runs in arguing that a third party has a beneficial interest in the sums deposited in an ISA, namely conceding that any ISA tax reliefs were improperly awarded and the possibility of criminal proceedings for a tax offence under s.106A of the Taxes Management Act 1970 (see para.17 of the decision).

An illustration of a constructive trust, which does not operate on the basis of a common intention but on it being unconscionable for the person with the legal interest to deny the beneficial interest of another, is *R(SB) 23/85*. The claimant's wife in a home-made and legally ineffective deed of gift purported to give an uninhabitable property to her son. He, as intended, carried out the works to make it habitable. The Commissioner holds that, although a court will not normally "complete" such an "uncompleted gift" in favour of someone who has not given valuable consideration, one of the situations in which a transfer of the property will be ordered is where the intended recipient is induced to believe that he has or will have an interest in the property and acts on that belief to his detriment. Thus in the meantime the claimant's wife held the property merely as a "bare trustee" and could not lawfully transfer it to anyone but the son. There is discussion of what kind of action might give rise to the right to complete the gift in *R(SB) 7/87*, where there was evidence of the claimant's intention to give a flat to her two sons, but all that one son had done in reliance was to redecorate the flat prior to its sale. See also *CIS/807/1991* on proprietary estoppel.

Note also the doctrine of secret trusts, under which a person who receives property under an intestacy when the deceased refrained from making a will in reliance on that person's promise to carry out their expressed intentions, holds the property on trust to carry out those intentions (*CSB/989/1985*). The doctrine also applies to property left by will where on the face of the will the property has been left to A but this is on the understanding that A is merely a trustee of it in favour of B.

For an example of where there may have been a secret trust, see *GK v SSWP (JSA)* [2012] UKUT 115 (AAC). In that case the claimant had inherited money from her aunt which she understood from conversations with her aunt was to be shared between her five children and herself. She used the money to purchase some land, which, although in her sole name, she regarded as belonging to all six of them. Judge Mark held that the tribunal had erred in not considering whether there was a secret trust.

CIS/213/2004 and *CIS/214/2004* concerned the applicability of French law. A property in France had been purchased in the name of the claimant but the purchase price and renovation costs had been met by Ms V. Ms V was not the claimant's partner but they had a son and the purpose of putting the property in the claimant's name was so that their son and not Ms V's other children would inherit it (under French law all five of Ms V's children would otherwise have been entitled to an interest in the property). On the same day that the property was purchased the claimant executed a holograph will bequeathing a "usufruct" (the French equivalent of a life interest) in the property to Ms V. Applying the Recognition of Trusts Act 1987, which implements the Hague Convention of 1986 on the law applicable to trusts and their recognition, the Commissioner concludes that French law was the applicable law. But since French law does not recognise the concept of a trust, it followed that there was no resulting or constructive trust in favour of Ms V (although in the Commissioner's view if English law had been applicable the facts would have given rise to such a trust). The Commissioner directed the Secretary of State to obtain a further opinion as to the remedies available under French law to Ms V if the claimant decided to treat the property as his own, but after receiving this concluded that there was no reason under French law or otherwise why the value of the property should not be included in the claimant's capital. The claimant appealed against this decision to the Court of Appeal but the appeal was dismissed (*Martin v Secretary of State for Work and Pensions* [2009] EWCA Civ 1289; [2010] AACR 9).

It will be an error of law if a tribunal fails to consider the question of the applicable law in relation to property abroad (*MB v Royal Borough of Kensington & Chelsea (HB)* [2011] UKUT 321 (AAC)). The claimant in *MB* was an Irish national, who had, while domiciled and resident in Ireland, bought a property in Ireland with the assistance of a mortgage from an Irish bank. In those circumstances it was difficult to see how the applicable law could be other than Irish law, but the tribunal had not referred to this issue at all, nor had it sought any evidence as to the nature and content of Irish law and the Irish law of trusts (foreign law is a question of fact (see *R(G) 2/00*, at para.20)).

Choses in action

2.147.5   There is also a remarkable range of interests in property which do have a present market value and so are actual capital resources. These are usually things in action (or choses in action), rights to sue for something. Debts, even where they are not due to be paid for some time, are things in action which can be sold. A good example is *R(SB) 31/83* where the claimant in selling a house allowed the purchaser a mort-gage of £4,000, to be redeemed in six months. The debt conferred a right to sue and had to be valued at what could be obtained on the open market. In *CJSA/204/2002* the claimant had lent her son £8,500 for the deposit on a flat. The Commissioner holds that the legal debt owed by the son to the claimant had to be valued in order to decide whether the claimant had actual capital in excess of £8,000 (which was then the prescribed limit). The terms of the loan, including the rate of any interest and whether there was any security for the loan, as well as the terms of repayment, were clearly relevant to this valuation. Once the value of the loan had been determined, the question of deprivation of capital then had to be considered. To the extent that the value of the loan was less than £8,500, to that extent the claimant had deprived herself of capital. However, on the facts the Commissioner found that the claimant had not deprived herself of the capital for the purpose of securing entitlement to, or increasing the amount of, jobseeker's allowance (see further the note to reg.50(1)). See also *JC v SSWP* [2009] UKUT 22 (AAC) which points out that the value of the loan will depend on whether it is likely to be recoverable. If the claimant had lent the money with no expectation of getting it back, he had in effect reduced the value of the chose in action to nil. The issue of deprivation of capital then arose. *R 2/09(IS)*, a Northern Ireland decision, gives further guidance on the approach to choses in action and their value.

In *GS v DSD (IS)* [2012] NI Com 284 (another Northern Ireland decision) the claimant agreed in June 2004 to buy a house (not yet built) from Mr McK in return for the transfer of ownership of the claimant's present house, plus £33,000. The £33,000 was paid by cheque in August 2006. However, the building work was delayed due to the illness of Mr McK's brother and the house was only eventually built during 2009. But by March 2010 (the date of the decision under appeal) the agreement still had not been fulfilled due to difficulties with Mr McK's title to the land. Mr McK accepted that the £33,000 deposit would be returned if these dif-ficulties could not be resolved. Commissioner Stockman points out that a chose in action can only arise upon breach of contract, or possibly frustration of contract; the mere existence of the contract did not give rise to the right to sue for return of the deposit. The difficulty was determining whether there had been a breach of contract and in identifying when that occurred. In the circumstances of this case, where there was no date for the completion of the contract and the delay in completing the building work had been waived by the claimant because of the personal friendship between Mr McK and himself, the claimant would not have had a strong case for breach of contract for unreasonable delay. This would have a resultant effect on the value of the chose in action, for which there was unlikely to be a ready market. The Commissioner decides that the value of the chose in action was nil from August 2006 and £3,000 from November 2008 up to March 2010.

An action for breach of fiduciary duty against an attorney appointed under the Enduring Powers of Attorney Act 1985 who had used the claimant's capital to repay her own debts also constitutes actual capital; so too would a claim against the attor-ney for misapplication of capital on the ground that she had made gifts outside the circumstances sanctioned by s.3(5) of the 1985 Act (this allows an attorney to make gifts (to herself or others) "provided that the value of each such gift is not unreason-able having regard to all the circumstances and in particular the size of the donor's estate") (*R(IS) 17/98*).

Bank or building society accounts

A more direct way of holding capital is in a bank or building society account. In *CSB/296/1985* the claimant's solicitor received £12,000 damages on behalf of the claimant and placed the money on deposit, presumably in the solicitor's client account. The Commissioner held that the £12,000 was an actual resource of the claimant, on the basis that there was no difference in principle between monies being held by a solicitor on behalf of a client and monies held by a bank or building society on behalf of a customer. This decision was upheld by the Court of Appeal in

2.147.6

Thomas v Chief Adjudication Officer, reported as *R(SB) 17/87*. Russell LJ says "the possession of this money by the solicitors as the agent for the claimant was, in every sense of the term, possession by the claimant."

However, note *CIS/984/2002* which holds that money held by the claimant's solicitor pending quantification of the statutory charge to the Legal Services Commission under s.10(7) of the Access to Justice Act 1999 was not part of the claimant's capital. Until that quantification had been carried out, it was not possible to identify any particular amount as the claimant's capital. Another way of looking at it was to treat the statutory charge as an incumbrance for the purpose of the equivalent of reg.49(1) (b) (see *CIS/368/1993*).

See also *LC v Bournemouth Borough Council (HB)* [2016] UKUT 175 (AAC), where the proceeds of sale of a former matrimonial home were being held in a solicitors' client account until the claimant's partner and his ex-wife could agree how the sum was to be split or the issue was resolved by a court order after a Financial Dispute Resolution hearing. In Judge White's view the value of the capital prior to agreement or an order of the court would be minimal.

The approach taken in *Thomas* seems to involve valuing the amount of money directly, not as a technical chose in action. However, the importance of the legal relationship between a bank and a customer being one of debtor and creditor was revealed in *CSB/598/1987*. A large cheque was paid into the claimant's wife's bank account on October 9, 1987. The amount was credited to her account on that date, but the cheque was not cleared until October 15. The bank's paying-in slips reserved the bank's right to "postpone payment of cheques drawn against uncleared effects which may have been credited to the account." The effect was that the bank did not accept the relationship of debtor and creditor on the mere paying in of a cheque. Thus the amount did not become part of the claimant's actual resources until October 15. A person who deliberately refrains from paying in a cheque may be fixed with notional capital under reg.50(1).

CIS/255/2005 concerned the effect on capital of the issue of a cheque. The Commissioner holds that the claimant's capital was reduced from the date that the cheque was issued (this would not apply if the cheque was postdated). After that time she could not honestly withdraw money from her bank account so as to leave insufficient funds to meet the cheque.

In *R(IS) 15/96* the Commissioner confirms that money in a building society or bank (or solicitor's client) account is an actual resource in the form of a chose in action. It is not, as the SSAT had decided, held in trust. If the money is in an account from which it can be withdrawn at any time, its value is the credit balance (less any penalties for early withdrawal, etc.). But if the money cannot be withdrawn for a specified term the value will be less (although the notional capital rules may come into play in respect of the difference in value: *CIS/494/1990*; see also *R(15) 8/04*.

Interests in trusts

2.147.7   The nature of interests in capital under trusts gives rise to several problems. It is clear that a person may have an absolute vested interest under a trust, although payment is deferred, e.g. until the age of 21. This was the case in *R(SB) 26/86*, where the resource was held to be the person's share of the fund. However, an interest may be contingent on reaching a particular age. This appears to have been one of the assumptions on which the Court of Appeal decided the unsatisfactory case of *Peters v Chief Adjudication Officer*, reported as *R(SB) 3/89*. It was conceded that sums were held on trust to be paid over to each of three sisters on attaining the age of 18, with the power to advance up to 50 per cent of the capital before then. In the end, the Court of Appeal accepted the valuation of half of the full value for each sister under 18. The precise finding may depend on the supplementary benefit rule on discretionary trusts, which was not translated into the income support or universal credit legislation. But some statements about the general market value of such interests are made. May LJ says "in an appropriate market a discretionary entitlement of up to 50 per cent now and at least 50 per cent in, say, six months in a given case, or three to four years in another, could well be said to have a value greater than 50 per cent of the capital value of the trust." This clearly supports the view that a contingent interest has a market value and so is actual capital. See also *CTC 4713/2002* which concerned a similar trust in favour of the claimant's son to that in *Peters* (although in this case the trustees had power to advance the whole of the fund). The Commissioner notes that in *Peters* the Court of Appeal had accepted the valuation agreed by the parties without argument. He acknowledged that each case must turn on its facts and that valuation of different interests would differ depending on such factors as the nature of the underlying investments (there was evidence in this case that due to lack of investor confidence the market value of the fund was much diminished); in addition in this case, unlike *Peters*, the whole of the fund could be advanced. However, he concluded that the Court of Appeal's approach in *Peters* led to a valuation of the claimant's son's equitable interest as being more or less equal to the whole net value of the trust fund (less 10 per cent for the expenses of sale).

A life interest in a trust fund or the right to receive income under a liferent in Scots law is a present asset which can be sold and has a market value (*R(SB) 2/84, R(SB) 43/84, R(SB) 15/86* and *R(SB) 13/87*). The practical effect is reversed for income support by para.13 of Sch.10 to the Income Support Regulations, but no such disregard is included in Sch.10 to the present Regulations.

All interests which can be sold or borrowed against will need to be considered. However, in the case of an interest under a discretionary trust, the DWP will normally only take payments of capital (or income) into account when they are actually made.

In *R(IS) 9/04* it was argued that funds held by the Court of Protection were analogous to those held by a discretionary trustee. Since neither the claimant nor her receiver could insist on the Court releasing any part of the funds it was contended that the market value of the claimant's actual interest was so small as to be negligible. However, the Commissioner followed *CIS/7127/1995* in holding that the entire beneficial interest in the funds administered by the Court remained with the claimant to whom alone they belonged. The fact the Court had discretionary powers of control over the management of a patient's property for his or her benefit did not mean that the patient's beneficial ownership had ceased. The funds therefore had to be valued at their current market value, less any appropriate allowance for sale expenses, in the normal way (see reg.49).

Realisation of assets

R (SB) 18/83 stresses that there are more ways of realising assets than sale. In particular, assets can be charged to secure a loan which can be used to meet requirements. In that case the asset was a minority shareholding in a family company. The Commissioner says that only a person prepared to lend money without security would do so in such circumstances. The articles of association of the company provided that if a shareholder wanted to sell shares they were to be offered to the existing shareholders at the fair value fixed by the auditors. The Commissioner holds that the regulations do not require assets to be valued at a figure higher than anything the person would realise on them, i.e. the auditor's fair value. This is in line with the purpose of the capital cut-off that a claimant can draw on resources until they fall below the limit.

This approach to valuation can usefully deal with unrealisable assets. See the notes to reg.49. However, it is no part of the definition of capital that it should be immediately realisable, although its market value may be affected by such factors. It remains possible for claimants to be fixed with large amounts of actual capital that are not immediately available to them by everyday means, but may have a value in some specialised market.

2.147.8

Deduction of liabilities

2.147.9   The general rule is that the whole of a capital resource is to be taken into account. Liabilities are not to be deducted from the value (*R(SB) 2/83*). In general, the "remedy" if the capital limits are in issue, is for the claimant to discharge the liability, the amount of which cannot, by virtue of reg.50(2) constitute notional capital under the deprivation rule.

SSWP v GF (ESA) [2017] UKUT 333 (AAC) is an illustration of the application of the principle. For one part of the period in issue the claimant's brother-in-law had paid a costs order of some £48,000 made against the claimant in the expectation at least that he would be repaid once the 120-day notice period for withdrawal of funds in the claimant's building society bond with a balance of £75,000 had expired. On the evidence available the judge rightly concluded that there was no implied, resulting or constructive trust and that the claimant's debt did not change the beneficial ownership of the funds in the bond. However, there could in other similar cases be evidence of discussions or arrangements before the brother-in-law made his payment that could lead to a conclusion either that the debt had been secured on the claimant's rights in the bond or that the claimant had made a declaration of trust. In *GF* itself no such argument could have helped the claimant because even if he had not been the beneficial owner of £48,000 of the balance in the bond, the value of the remainder (even subject to the 120-day notice provision) would no doubt have exceeded £16,000.

Otherwise, it is only if a debt is secured on the capital asset that it can be deducted, at the stage specifically required by reg.49 (*R(IS) 21/93*). See the notes to reg.49 and note *JRL v SSWP (JSA)* [2011] UKUT 63 (AAC), reported as [2011] AACR 30. There, the claimant had three accounts with the same bank, of which one was in credit, one was overdrawn, and one had a nil balance. The three-judge panel pointed out that this meant that the claimant was both a creditor and a debtor of the same body. Under the bank's terms and conditions, the bank had a contractual right to debit at any time any of a customer's accounts which were in credit with sums sufficient to clear the customer's indebtedness to the bank. This created what was effectively a charge on the customer's credit balance(s). The market value of the account that was in credit was therefore its net value after deduction of the amount of the claimant's overdraft on his other account.

Personal possessions

Note that personal possessions are not treated as capital (para.(2)). There is no equivalent to the rule for income support, old style JSA, old style ESA and housing benefit that personal possessions are taken into account if they have been acquired with the intention of reducing capital in order to secure, or increase, entitlement to benefit (see, e.g., para.10 of Sch.10 to the Income Support Regulations in Vol.II of this series). However, in such circumstances claimants may be found to have notional capital under reg.50(1) and (2), by reason of having deprived themselves of capital through the mechanism of acquisition of personal possessions. For reg.50(1) to operate, the deprivation must have been for the purpose of securing entitlement to or increasing the amount of universal credit (rather than any other benefit), which may significantly limit its effect in relation to acquisitions some way in the past. In addition, reg.50(2), in a provision not replicated in relation to any other benefits (except state pension credit), prevents claimants being treated as having deprived themselves of capital if they have purchased goods or services and the expenditure was reasonable in the circumstances (see further in the notes to that provision).

R(H) 7/08 was a case about whether a moveable but static caravan, attached to mains services on a non-residential site, was a "personal possession" for the purposes of the disregard in the housing benefit legislation. A tribunal had decided that it was not, so that its value counted as capital. The Commissioner held that it erred in law in doing so. After a discursive discussion of the legislative background and the scant authority, he said this in para.53:

"My conclusion is that 'personal possessions' mean any physical assets other than land and assets used for business purposes. . . . [This] avoids uncertainty of scope and difficulties of application. It is consistent with the legislative history of the disregard and the more humane approach to resource-related benefits that has increasingly been shown over the period of the welfare state. It recognises the increased emphasis that has been given over recent decades to ways of assisting claimants off welfare by not requiring particular categories of possessions to be disposed of for what may be a relatively short period on benefit."

That approach would seem to require that the actual value of items acquired mainly, or even solely, as investments be disregarded, but there will sometimes be very difficult lines to be drawn in particular circumstances even if that basis were accepted. At what point might coins, say, or gold bars cease to be regarded as personal possessions and be regarded as a way of holding capital in the same way as everyday cash?

Might it still be argued that, as Commissioner Jacobs was not directly concerned in *R(H) 7/08* with any line between personal possessions and investments, the decision does not exclude a conclusion that the adjective "personal" is an indication that something has to be used at least partly for personal or domestic or household purposes, not solely for investment? Prior to its amendment in October 2014 by s.3(1) of the Inheritance and Trustees' Powers Act 2014, the definition of "personal chattels" in s.55(1)(x) of the Administration of Estates Act 1925 (for the purposes of identifying how an estate is to be distributed on intestacy), as well as setting out a long list of specific items, included "articles of household or personal use or ornament". The courts, bearing in mind the test in terms of the use made of the article at the time of death, took quite a generous approach to when that use had a personal element. In one case, *Re Reynolds' Will Trusts* [1966] 1 W.L.R. 19, the aptly named Stamp J, having held the intestate's valuable stamp collection, built up since childhood as his main hobby, to be part of his personal chattels, suggested that if he had gone into a shop and bought a similar collection that he then installed in his flat it could hardly be said that that was an article of personal use. Regulation 46(2) makes no express reference to the use made of any possession, but it may be arguable that the word "personal" entails the exclusion of items with no element of personal enjoyment or cherishing (such as collections of jewellery, art work, stamps etc locked away in a safe or bank vault and never inspected). However, such an approach would again involve the drawing of difficult lines after careful investigation that it may be thought that the legislation was intended to avoid. It would have been helpful if matters had been made plainer on the face of the legislation.

No doubt, whatever the general answer, the more evidence there is that an item was acquired by a person for investment, the stronger the argument would be for its cost having been a deprivation of capital under reg.50(1), subject to the working out of the scope of the exception in reg.50(2)(b) for purchasing goods and services where the expenditure was reasonable.

Capital treated as income

Under paras (3) and (4), certain payments that might otherwise be capital are treated as income (and therefore do not count as capital).

Paragraph (4) deals with capital payable by instalments. If the amount outstanding plus the claimant's (including, in the case of couples, the other member of the couple's) other capital is more than £16,000, each instalment when paid is treated as income. Otherwise the payment counts as capital. See the notes to reg.41(1) of the Income Support Regulations in Vol.II of this series.

Paragraph (3) applies to sums (other than capital payable by instalments) that are paid regularly and by reference to a period, such as payments under an annuity, that may otherwise be capital or have a capital element. They are treated as income. This is wider than the existing rule in, e.g., reg.41(2) of the Income Support Regulations (which only applies to payments under an annuity) and would seem to be an attempt to draw more of a line between capital and income. See the notes to reg.23

of the Income Support Regulations in Vol.II of this series on the distinction between capital and income.

Capital that is treated as income under paras (3) or (4) is included in a person's unearned income (see reg.66(1)(l)).

Note the "assumed yield from capital" rule in reg.72(1) (the equivalent to the "tariff income rule" for income support, old style JSA, old style ESA and housing benefit). Actual income from capital (unless the capital is disregarded or the income is taken into account under reg.66(1)(i) or (j)) is treated as capital from the day it is due to be paid (reg.72(3)).

Jointly held capital

2.148   **47.** Where a person and one or more other persons have a beneficial interest in a capital asset, those persons are to be treated, in the absence of evidence to the contrary, as if they were each entitled to an equal share of the whole of that beneficial interest.

GENERAL NOTE

2.149   This provision is much the same in structure as the income support and income-based JSA equivalents (reg.52 of the Income Support Regulations and reg.115 of the JSA Regulations 1996), with the addition of the apparently significant words "in the absence of evidence to the contrary". However, close analysis suggests that those words are meaningless and ineffective and that reg.47, like its equivalents, achieves only limited results of substance.

That conclusion follows from the decision of the Court of Appeal in *Hourigan v Secretary of State for Work and Pensions* [2002] EWCA Civ 1890, reported as *R(IS) 4/03*. There the claimant bought her council house with a contribution of five-sixths of the purchase price from her son. The legal estate was transferred to her in her sole name, but it was accepted that in those circumstances she held the legal estate on trust for herself and her son as tenants in common in the proportions of their contributions to the purchase price. The Secretary of State argued that reg.52 of the Income Support Regulations applied because the claimant and her son were beneficially entitled to the capital asset of the equitable interest in the house and that as a result she had to be treated as having a half share in the equitable interest, although her actual share was one-sixth. It was argued that it was that deemed half share that had to be valued as capital, in which case the claimant was not entitled to income support because the capital limit was breached. Brooke LJ held that it would be a misuse of language to say that the claimant and her son were both beneficially entitled to a capital asset in the form of the house because the beneficial interest of each as a tenant in common was a separately disposable asset. To interpret reg.52 in the way contended for by the Secretary of State would require very much clearer words. Not only was it unfair to the claimant to treat her as possessing more capital than she could actually realise, but the Secretary of State's argument could also work unfairly in favour of claimants (e.g. if it had been a claimant who had a five-sixths share who was deemed to have only a half-share). Thus it was only the claimant's actual one-sixth share as tenant in common that fell to be valued as capital.

Brooke LJ accepted that the language of reg.52 could apply to circumstances in which the claimant and one or more persons were jointly entitled to the equitable interest in the same capital asset. In that situation the effect of reg.52 was to treat the joint tenancy as severed and to deem the claimant to have an equal share (with the other joint tenants), with there being a tenancy in common as between the claimant and the other joint tenant(s).

That appears correct, but the limit of the effect of reg.47 (just as for reg.52 of the Income Support Regulations) would appear to be in deeming that there has been a severance of the joint tenancy of the beneficial interest (as can be carried out by a joint tenant at any time or by selling or otherwise alienating or attempting to alienate the interest as a joint tenant). The limit is because there is no need for any regulation to deem that the claimant's share on severance is proportionate to the number of former joint tenants (i.e. a half share if there were previously two, a third share if there were previously three etc). That consequence follows from the nature of a joint tenancy, where there is only one interest (the so-called unity of interest), so that the interest of each tenant must be the same in extent, nature and duration. *Goodman v Gallant* [1985] EWCA Civ 15, [1986] Fam. 106 establishes that the sole exception could be where the terms of the trust establishing the joint tenancy expressly provided that on any severance the shares were not to be equal (which would be a vanishingly rare circumstance). There is no room at the stage of severance (or deemed severance) for going back to, say, the amount of contribution to the purchase price, to justify anything other than an equal share. (But do not forget that tenancies in common created in other ways can, and often do, have unequal shares). Thus, if the claimant in *Hourigan* had expressly had the council house conveyed to her to hold in trust for herself and her son as joint tenants, there could have been no escape, regardless of any regulations, from the consequence on a severance (actual or deemed) of the joint tenancy in the beneficial interest that her share as tenant in common was one-half. It could make no difference that the son had contributed five-sixths of the purchase price. It is a common elementary student error to think otherwise, one into which it appears that Auld LJ fell in *Hourigan*.

The upshot is that, once it is determined that reg.47 is restricted to joint tenancies, the reference to the absence of evidence to the contrary becomes redundant. The purported relevance of the phrase "in the absence of evidence to the contrary" to the deeming in reg.47 can only be to the shares in which the beneficial interest is to be held under the tenancy in common (the phrase "in equal shares" having long been accepted as indicating a tenancy in common). Evidence to the contrary cannot prevent the deeming of a tenancy in common because in all circumstances where there was still actually a joint tenancy there would be evidence to the contrary, i.e. whatever the evidence was that produced that actual result, and the regulation could then never apply at all. However, no evidence to the contrary can influence the shares under the deemed tenancy in common, because the equal shares follow from the nature of a joint tenancy as noted above.

In cases, like the above, involving real property, there will usually be no difficulty in identifying the property subject to a joint tenancy. It may not be so easy when the joint interest is in some other asset or in a bank or building society account. That is shown by *CIS/7097/1995*. There, the claimant's husband went to live permanently in a nursing home. To help finance the cost of that accommodation, £7,000 of the husband's National Savings certificates were cashed in and the proceeds paid into the couple's joint bank account, so that the nursing home could be paid regularly by direct debit. There was evidence that the intention had not been that the sum should form part of the joint money in the account. The £7,000 had been declared as the husband's own money in an application to the local authority for financial assistance with the fees and a separate tally was kept of the use of that money. The AO treated the claimant's capital as including half of the balance in the joint account, including the proceeds of the husband's National Savings certificates, which took her over the limit, so that she was not entitled to income support. The Commissioner reversed that decision. There was clear evidence that the normal presumption of joint beneficial ownership between a husband and wife operating a joint bank account did not apply in relation to the £7,000. It was obviously intended that the proceeds of the husband's National Savings certificates were to remain his sole property and had been paid into the joint account merely for convenience. They did not form part of the claimant's capital. The Commissioner also analysed the nature of joint beneficial ownership and ownership in equal shares in a way consistent with what is said above.

A similar approach was taken in the Scottish case of *JK v SSWP (JSA)* [2010] UKUT 437 (AAC), reported as [2011] AACR 26. The claimant contended that some of the money in his and his wife's joint bank account belonged to his mother-in-law. It was held that the First-tier Tribunal, instead of asking whether there was a trust in favour of the mother-in-law, should have considered, by reference to such oral or written evidence available to it that it accepted, whether under Scots law (see *Cairns v Davidson* 1913 S.C. 1053) the presumption in favour of all the money in the joint account belonging to the claimant and his wife had been rebutted, so as to establish whether or not some of it belonged to the mother-in-law.

Valuation under regulation 47

2.149.1   It is the deemed equal share that has to be valued, not the proportionate share of the overall value (see the Court of Appeal's decision in *Chief Adjudication Officer v Palfrey*, reported as part of *R(IS) 26/95*, which had upheld the Tribunal of Commissioners' decisions in *CIS/391/1992* and *CIS/417/1992* (reported as part of *R(IS) 26/95*). The Tribunal of Commissioners gave detailed guidance as to the basis of a proper valuation of such a share (*CIS 391/1992*, paras 53 and 54), which is still relevant as a foundation for later decisions. In both *CIS/391/1992* and *CIS/417/1992* ownership was shared with relatives who were unable or unwilling to sell the property or buy the claimant's interest. The Commissioners recognised, as did the Court of Appeal, that the market value in such cases may well be nil, although as discussed below all will depend on the circumstances of particular cases.

In *Palfrey* the Tribunal of Commissioners state that the SSAT should have exercised its inquisitorial jurisdiction to call for the documents under which the property was acquired in order to sort out the beneficial ownership, but that may not be necessary where there is no dispute about the actual conveyancing history (*CIS/127/1993*).

The current guidance to decision makers in Ch.H1 of the ADM (in particular paras H1638 – H1642) suggests that they should obtain an expert opinion on the market value of a deemed share in land/premises. It gives quite rigorous and detailed guidance, in the main firmly based on the case law discussed below fleshing out what is entailed by the principle laid down in *Palfrey*, on the criteria for a valuation to be acceptable. For instance, the guidance states that where the other owners will not buy the share or agree to a sale of the asset as a whole, the expert should not simply assume that a court would order a sale but must consider the particular circumstances and take into account legal costs, length of time to obtain possession, etc. The guidance also says that the expert would need to explain whether on the facts of the case there was any market for the deemed share, explain what assumptions, if any, have been made, whether and, if so what, comparables have been considered and indicate how the value of the deemed share had been calculated. The expert should also indicate their experience and/or knowledge of the market for shared interests in real property. Slightly oddly, it is said in para.H1641 that in working out the reg.49(1) value of the premises, only 10 per cent for expenses of sale should be deducted and not anything for encumbrances, because they will already have been taken into account in the expert's valuation. That may work out if the expert has had full information about the nature and amount of the encumbrances, but that may need to be checked before the process as set out in reg.49(1) is short-circuited.

If that guidance was carefully followed, there would little problem in the production of acceptable evidence on behalf of the Secretary of State, although of course there would always be room for differences of opinion as a matter of judgment. However, experience over the years shows continuing difficulties in the production of valuations that properly adopt the principles of *Palfrey*. There have also been some differences of expression in the cases that have created some uncertainties, although it is submitted below that the basic principles have not been subverted.

R(IS) 3/96 contains a useful discussion as to whether the District Valuer's opinion supplied in that case met the requirements of *CIS/391/1992*. *R(JSA) 1/02* was concerned with valuing the claimant's interest in his former matrimonial home. His wife, from whom he was separated and who was in ill-health, continued to live there with their daughter, who had learning difficulties. The valuation obtained by the Jobcentre on a standard form (A64A/LA1) gave the open market value as £30,000 and the claimant's deemed undivided share as £9,200. No reasons were given for that conclusion. The property was leasehold but there was no evidence as to the remaining term of the lease, or as to the condition of the property. There was also no evidence as to the age of the daughter and no consideration as to whether a court would order a sale (which seemed very unlikely, given the purpose for which the property had been acquired and the purpose for which it was being used). The Commissioner, referring to *CIS/191/1994*, holds that there was no evidence that the claimant's capital exceeded the then prescribed limit of £8,000. He stated that everything depended on the facts and the evidence before the tribunal. In this case the valuation evidence was so unsatisfactory as to be worthless. He set out the following guidance on valuation:

"13. Proper valuation evidence should include details of the valuer's expertise, the basis on which he or she holds him or herself out as able to give expert evidence in relation to the property in question. Where it is the sale of a share in a property which is in issue, the evidence should deal with the valuer's experience in relation to such shares, and their sale. The property, and any leasehold interest, should be described in sufficient detail, including details of the length of any lease, of any special terms in it, and of the location, size and condition of the property, to show that the factors relevant to its value have been taken into account, and the reasons for the conclusion as to the value should be given. A similar approach should be applied to a share of a property, and an explanation should be given of the factors identified as relevant to the valuation, and how they affect it. The expert should also give evidence of any comparables identified, or of other reasons why it is concluded that the share could be sold at any particular price. If there is no evidence of actual sales of such interests, an acceptable explanation of the absence of such evidence should be given.

14. I appreciate that, in cases of this kind, this will on occasions be a counsel of perfection which cannot be realised. Where a valuer does not have relevant information, and proceeds upon assumptions, the report should state what is missing, and should also state the assumptions upon which it is based. This will normally give the claimant the opportunity to correct any mistaken assumptions or other errors of fact in the report."

See also *JC-W v Wirral Metropolitan BC (HB)* [2011] UKUT 501 (AAC), paras 13–18, for Judge Mark's critical comments in relation to the District Valuer's valuation in that case, and *MN v LB Hillingdon (HB)* [2014] UKUT 427 (AAC) and *PE v SSWP (SPC)* [2014] UKUT 387 (AAC) noted below.

It will not always be the case that a deemed equal share in a property will be of minimal value, even if the other co-owners are unwilling to sell. As *Wilkinson v Chief Adjudication Officer*, CA, March 24, 2000, reported as *R(IS) 1/01*, illustrates, the purposes for which the joint ownership was established will need to be scrutinised in order to assess whether a court would order a sale. In *Wilkinson* the claimant's mother had died, leaving her home to the claimant and her brother jointly "to do with as they wish". It was accepted that the mother had expressed the hope that the claimant's brother would live in the house with his son when his divorce proceedings in Australia were resolved (although there was nothing in the will to that effect). The claimant contended that the capital value of her half-share in the property was of a nominal value only, because her brother was unwilling to leave the property and unwilling to sell his share in it. She maintained that a court would not order a sale under s.30 of the Law of Property Act 1925 (repealed with effect from January 1, 1998 and replaced by ss.14 and 15 of the Trusts of Land and Appointment of Trustees Act 1996). But the Court of Appeal, by a majority (Mummery and Potter LJJ), disagreed. This was not a case like *Palfrey* where property had been acquired by joint owners for a collateral purpose (e.g. for them to live in as long as they wished) and that purpose would be defeated by ordering a sale. On the contrary, this was a case where an order for sale would enable the claimant's mother's wishes, as expressed in her will, to be carried out. Her brother's unwillingness to sell or pay the claimant for the value of her share was in fact having the effect of defeating that testamentary purpose. Potter LJ said that the proper starting point for valuation of the claimant's half-share was half the market value of the house with vacant possession, with a discount for any factors materially affecting her ability to market the house on that basis. The tribunal's conclusion that in the circumstances the value of her half-share was half of the market value of the house less 10% for expenses of sale and a charge to the testatrix's former husband was upheld. Evans LJ, however, took the opposite view. He considered that the claimant's share should be valued on the basis that a sale would not be ordered because this would defeat the mother's wish that her son and grandson be allowed to live in the property. As this case illustrates, much will depend on the circumstances in a particular case (and the view that is taken of those circumstances).

On very similar facts (a mother leaving a property to the claimant and his two sisters in equal shares, with no restriction or superadded purpose expressed in the will) the approach in *Wilkinson* was applied to the same effect in *JM v Eastleigh Borough Council (HB)* [2016] UKUT 464 (AAC).

Those cases were ones where there was no obstacle to the sale of the property with vacant possession, even though there might have been some normal delay in the process during which the disregard in para.6 of Sch.10 could come into play. The approach of starting with the market value of the property as a whole and then dividing by the number of joint owners, but not ignoring other factors, does not undermine the fundamental principle that under reg.47 it is the claimant's deemed severed share (i.e. as a deemed tenant in common) that must be valued. The following decisions illustrate some of problems of valuation in the more complicated cases where there is real doubt whether a court would order a sale if other joint owners were unwilling to agree.

In *CIS/3197/2003* the claimant owned a house with her daughter, who had a two-thirds share. (As we now know as a result of *Hourigan*, such circumstances do not fall within reg.47, but the approach to valuation is still relevant). The claimant went into a nursing home, leaving the house in the occupation of her daughter and the daughter's disabled child. The daughter would not agree to a sale of the house nor was she willing to buy out the claimant's share. It seemed unlikely that a court would order a sale. In view of the Secretary of State's failure to provide proper evidence of the value of the claimant's share the Commissioner found that the value of the claimant's interest was nil. However, he added that tribunals should not approach the matter in this way. If the evidence was incomplete, they should adjourn with directions as to the ways in which the evidence should be supplemented and should not decide the case on the burden of proof. Clearly where there has been no attempt to obtain any valuation evidence this should apply. However, if such attempts have been made and the evidence remains inadequate, it is suggested that the burden of proof may need to come into play (and indeed this was the approach taken in both *R(IS) 3/96* and, in effect, *R(JSA) 1/02*). For example, in *R(IS) 3/96* it was held that grounds for revising the claimant's award had not been shown in the light of the deficiencies in the District Valuer's report and in *R(JSA) 1/02* the Commissioner substituted his own decision on the existing evidence despite such deficiencies.

Despite the above case law, examples have continued to crop up of a claimant's share in a property being wrongly valued simply as a proportion of the whole, rather than the claimant's actual or deemed share being properly valued, taking into account all the relevant circumstances. See, for instance, *R(IS) 5/07* and *AM v SSWP (SPC)* [2010] UKUT 134 (AAC).

Examples of inadequate valuation evidence from the District Valuer, where a tribunal erred in law by relying on it, also continue to arise, such as *MN v London Borough of Hillingdon (HB)* [2014] UKUT 427 (AAC). The claimant there had been living in the jointly-owned matrimonial home with his wife, who had serious mental health problems, and their severely disabled son. However, it became necessary for the claimant and his son to leave, due to deterioration in his wife's health. Judge Ovey, after noting that the District Valuer appeared to have arrived at her valuation by halving the total value of the property and deducting just under 1 per cent, despite having been given details of the circumstances of the case, stated:

"32. . . . As a matter of common sense, it seems unlikely in the extreme that a purchaser would pay just under half the vacant possession value of a property for a half interest which would not enable him to occupy the property without first obtaining some form of court order against a defendant suffering from paranoid schizophrenia who was in occupation of a former matrimonial home, bought for the purpose of being a home, and who might be entitled to a property adjustment order. . . ."

See also *PE v SSWP (SPC)* [2014] UKUT 387 (AAC) which concerned the value of the claimant's interest in his former home, which remained occupied by his wife, son and step-son (the step-son had mental health problems). The District Valuer's valuation was based on an assumption that there had been a hypothetical application under the Trusts of Land and Appointment of Trustees Act 1996. The Secretary of State argued that in the circumstances of the case the District Valuer's assumption was unrealistic. Although no divorce proceedings were in place at the time, any application under the 1996 Act would be likely to generate such proceedings by the other party who was likely to obtain a more favourable outcome under the Matrimonial Causes Act 1973. Judge Jacobs accepted that the evidence relied on by the tribunal as to valuation was therefore flawed and decided, with the consent of the Secretary of State, that there were no grounds to supersede the decision awarding state pension credit.

There is a difficult balance between what might be a counsel of perfection (as in *R(JSA) 1/02*) and a realistic approach to what assumptions are acceptable in the inevitably imprecise exercise of valuing hypothetical interests. *Reigate and Banstead BC v GB (HB)* [2018] UKUT 225 (AAC) shows that tribunals should not go overboard in picking holes in a District Valuer's report. On the assumption (quite possibly inaccurate) that the claimant and his daughter were beneficial joint tenants and that there had not already been a severance, the tribunal went wrong in the reasons it relied on to find that the District Valuer had not properly valued the claimant's deemed equal share as a tenant in common and had not taken into account the possible need for an application to the court, as the property was occupied by the daughter and her son. In particular, the District Valuer did not need to provide evidence of a local market for an interest of the kind the claimant was deemed to have. There is undoubtedly a market for actual interests of the kind deemed to exist by reg.47 (see the many cases discussed above), often in specialist auctions, although that is no doubt not well-known to claimants. But there remains a question how much detail a District Valuer needs to give of the existence of such a market and of the prices fetched for comparable interests to validly underpin the valuation.

Capital disregarded

48.—(1) Any capital specified in Schedule 10 is to be disregarded from the calculation of a person's capital (see also regulations 75 to 77).   2.150

(2) Where a period of 6 months is specified in that Schedule, that period may be extended by the Secretary of State where it is reasonable to do so in the circumstances of the case.

GENERAL NOTE

The number of disregards in Sch.10 is considerably reduced from those that   2.151
apply for income support, old style JSA, old style ESA and housing benefit but they cover many of the same items, such as premises, business assets, rights in pension schemes, earmarked assets, etc. But note that some of the disregards that are in Schedules for the purposes of those benefits are to be found elsewhere in these Regulations, e.g., in regs 46(2), 49(3), 75 and 76. See also reg.77 in relation to companies in which the person is like a sole trader or partner. And note that with effect from May 21, 2020 there is a disregard as capital (for 12 months from the date of

receipt) for the self-employed of any payment in respect of a furloughed employee under the Coronavirus Job Retention Scheme or "by way of a grant or loan to meet the expenses or losses of the trade, profession or vocation in relation to the outbreak of coronavirus disease" (Universal Credit (Coronavirus) (Self-employed Claimants and Reclaims) (Amendment) Regulations 2020 (SI 2020/522) reg.2(2)) (see discussion in the note to para.7 of Sch.10).

Note the general extension on the grounds of reasonableness that can be applied to the six months' period in any of the provisions in Sch.10 (para.(2)).

With effect from July 24, 2019, reg.51 of the Transitional Provisions Regulations 2014, as inserted by reg.3 of the Universal Credit (Managed Migration Pilot and Miscellaneous Amendments) Regulations 2019 (SI 2019/1152), supplies a transitional capital disregard to claimants who (i) were previously entitled to a tax credit and had capital exceeding £16,000; (ii) are given a migration notice that existing benefits are to terminate; and (iii) claim universal credit within the deadline. The disregard is of any capital exceeding £16,000. The disregard can apply only for 12 assessment periods and ceases (without the possibility of revival) following any assessment period in which the amount of capital the claimant has falls below £16,000. See regs 56 and 57 of the Transitional Provisions Regulations for further provisions on termination of the protection. Paragraph 7 of Sch.2 to the Transitional Provisions Regulations, inserted by the same Regulations, contains a disregard as capital of any amount paid as a lump sum by way of a "transitional SDP amount" under that Schedule.

Valuation of capital

2.152   **49.**—(1) Capital is to be calculated at its current market value or surrender value less—

(a) where there would be expenses attributable to sale, 10 per cent; and

(b) the amount of any encumbrances secured on it.

(2) The market value of a capital asset possessed by a person in a country outside the United Kingdom is—

(a) if there is no prohibition in that country against the transfer of an amount equal to the value of that asset to the United Kingdom, the market value in that country; or

(b) if there is such a prohibition, the amount it would raise if sold in the United Kingdom to a willing buyer.

(3) Where capital is held in currency other than sterling, it is to be calculated after the deduction of any banking charge or commission payable in converting that capital into sterling.

GENERAL NOTE

2.153   The rules for the valuation of capital are the same as for income support, old style ESA and JSA and housing benefit. Paragraph (1) is the equivalent of reg.49 of the Income Support Regulations. Paragraph (2) on assets outside the UK is the equivalent of reg.50. Paragraph (3) on capital held in foreign currency previously took the form of a disregard (para.21 of Sch.10 to the Income Support Regulations).

The general rule under para.(1) is that the market value of the asset is to be taken. The surrender value will be taken if appropriate (the disregard in para.9 of Sch.10 of the value of life insurance policies must refer to whichever value has been chosen). The value at this stage does not take account of any encumbrances (always spelt with an "i" in the former legislation) secured on the assets, since those come in under sub-para.(b) (*R(IS) 21/93*). There is no definitive requirement that there be a local market (*Reigate and Banstead BC v GB (HB)* [2018] UKUT 225 (AAC)), but the way in which markets work in practice in whatever asset is in question must be taken into account.

In *R(SB) 57/83* and *R(SB) 6/84* the test taken is the price that would be commanded between a willing buyer and a willing seller at a particular date. In *R(SB)*

6/84 it is stressed that in the case of a house it is vital to know the nature and extent of the interest being valued. Also, since what is required is a current market value, the Commissioner holds that an estate agent's figure for a quick sale was closer to the proper approach than the District Valuer's figure for a sale within three months. All the circumstances must be taken into account in making the valuation. Arguments have been raised that during the 2020 coronavirus outbreak, in the period when estate agents' offices were closed and most viewings impossible, there was no market in existence for domestic properties. In *CIS/553/1991* it is held that in valuing a former matrimonial home the wife's statutory right of occupation under the Matrimonial Homes Act 1967 has to be taken into account. See further the decisions discussed under *Valuation under reg. 47* in the notes to reg.47.

Reigate and Banstead BC v GB (above, and in detail in the notes to reg.47) is a helpful example of valuation of an interest as a tenant in common, in that case a deemed such interest, and of an acceptable District Valuer's report.

RM v Sefton Council (HB) [2016] UKUT 357 (AAC), reported as [2017] AACR 5, provides a good practical example of the valuation of a property with sitting shorthold tenants.

Similarly, if chattels are being valued, it is what they could be sold for that counts, not simply what was paid for them (*CIS/494/1990, CIS/2208/2003*). See also *JJ v SSWP (IS)* [2012] UKUT 253 (AAC) which points out that where a sale of a chattel is by auction there are buyer's premiums added as well as seller's commission and that this could result in the seller being treated as having much more capital than he would realise on a sale. In the judge's view this was not the object of the regulations and the valuation had to be based on the standard test of what the claimant could expect to realise on a transaction between a willing seller and a willing buyer. Despite the disregard in universal credit of the value of personal possessions (reg.46(2)) and of business assets (paras 7 and 8 of Sch.10), it may occasionally be necessary to take the value of chattels, e.g. if a claimant retains former business assets beyond the limits of para.8 of Sch.10 or if investment assets are found to fall outside the meaning of "personal possessions" (see the notes to re.46(2)).

Sometimes a detailed valuation is not necessary, such as where the value of an asset is on any basis clearly over the prescribed limit of £16,000) (*CIS/40/1989*). That, however, has the undesirable result that no baseline has been established for assessing the effects of future disposals of the assets.

Shares

It is accepted that the test of the willing buyer and the willing seller is the starting point for the valuation of shares (*R(SB) 57/83, R(SB) 12/89* and *R(IS) 2/90*). The latter case emphasises that in the income support context, as would also be the case for universal credit, the value must be determined on the basis of a very quick sale, so that the hypothetical willing seller would be at a corresponding disadvantage. In the case of private companies there is often a provision in the articles of association that a shareholder wishing to sell must first offer the shares to other shareholders at a "fair value" fixed by the auditors (this was the case in *R(SB) 18/83* and *R(IS) 2/90*). Then the value of the shares ought not to be higher than the fair value, but for benefit purposes may well be less. The possible complications are set out in *CSB/488/1982* (quoted with approval in *R(SB) 12/89* and *R(IS) 2/90*). In *R(IS) 8/92* it is suggested that the market value is what a purchaser would pay for the shares subject to the same restriction. Whether the shareholding gives a minority, equal or controlling interest is particularly significant. All the circumstances of the share structure of the company must be considered. For instance, in *R(SB) 12/89* shares could only be sold with the consent of the directors, which it was indicated would not be forthcoming. It seems to be agreed that valuation according to Revenue methods is not appropriate (*R(SB) 18/83* and *R(IS) 2/90*), although it is suggested in *R(SB) 12/89* that the Revenue Shares Valuation Division might be able to assist tribunals. It is not known if this is so. What is absolutely clear is that the total value of the company's shareholding cannot simply be divided in proportion to the claimant's holding (*R(SB) 18/83*).

2.153.1

However, in para.14 of *P v SSWP and P (CSM)* [2018] UKUT 60 (AAC) it was said, in a passage not necessary to the decision, that the tribunal in that child support case:

"was correct in basing the value of the shares on the book value of the company's net assets, without making any discount to reflect the difficulty in selling part of the shareholding in a private company. In *Ebrahimi v Westbourne Galleries Limited* [1973] A.C. 360 it was held that in some circumstances a limited company could co-exist with a 'quasi-partnership' between those involved in the company, for example, if the shareholders were bound by personal relationships involving mutual confidence, if the shareholders were in practice involved in the conduct of the business, and if the transfer of the shares was restricted. In *re Bird Precision Bellows Ltd.* [1986] Ch. 658 Oliver LJ held [674A] that in a 'quasi-partnership' case it was appropriate that: 'the shares of the company should be valued as a whole and that the petitioners should then simply be paid the proportionate part of that value which was represented by their shareholding, without there being made a discount for the fact that this was a minority shareholding'."

It is not though clear how far that approach should be translated to means-tested benefits and how far it turns on the particular context of the child support variation provisions with their stress on a parent's control in practice over a company (see para.15 of *P*). But the application of reg.77 (company analogous to a partnership or one-person business) would have to be considered in such circumstances. If that provision applies, reg.77(2) expressly requires that the actual value of the claimant's shareholding be disregarded and the claimant be treated as owning the capital of the company, or the appropriate proportion of it (see the notes to reg.77 for further discussion).

In the case of shares in companies quoted on the London Stock Exchange the Revenue method of valuation should be used (*R(IS) 18/95*). This involves looking at all the transactions relating to the relevant share during the previous day, taking the lowest figure and adding to this a quarter of the difference between the lowest and the highest figure. The Commissioner considered that decision-makers could use the valuation quoted in newspapers (which is the mean between the best bid and best offer price at the close of business the previous day) to obtain approximate valuations. However, where a completely accurate valuation was essential, the Revenue method would need to be adopted. See also *DW v SSWP (JSA)* [2012] UKUT 478 (AAC).

Valuation affected by difficulties in realisation

2.153.2   The proper approach to valuation can usefully deal with unrealisable assets. Sometimes their market value will be nil (e.g. a potential interest under a discretionary trust: *R(SB) 25/83*; assets that are subject to a restraint or freezing order: *SH v SSWP* [2008] UKUT 21 (AAC); *CS v Chelmsford BC (HB)* [2014] UKUT 518 (AAC)); sometimes it will be very heavily discounted. However, if the asset will be realisable after a time, it may have a current value. The claimant may be able to sell an option to purchase the asset in the future (see *R(IS) 8/92*) or borrow, using the asset as security. But the valuation must reflect the fact that the asset is not immediately realisable. In *R(IS) 4/96* the claimant had on his divorce transferred his interest in the former matrimonial home to his wife in return for a charge on the property which could only be enforced if she died, remarried or cohabited for more than six months. The claimant's former wife was 46 and in good health. A discount had to be applied to the present day value of the charge to reflect the fact that it might not be realisable for as long as 40 years or more; consequently it was unlikely to be worth more than £3,000. See also *CIS/982/2002* in which the Commissioner sets out a number of detailed questions that had to be considered when valuing the claimant's share (if any) in a joint bank account that had been frozen following the claimant's separation from her husband. And note *LC v Bournemouth Borough Council (HB)* [2016] UKUT 175 (AAC), discussed in the notes to reg.46.

In *JC-W v Wirral MBC (HB)* [2011] UKUT 501 (AAC) Judge Mark concluded that nobody would be willing to purchase (for more than a nominal amount) the claimant's beneficial interest pending divorce in two heavily mortgaged properties, one of which was only partly built, in respect of which the claimant's parents-in-law claimed an interest in the proceeds of sale, and which the claimant's husband was unwilling to sell.

As the Tribunal of Commissioners in *R(SB) 45/83* point out, the market value (in that case of an interest in an entire trust fund) must reflect the outlay the purchaser would expect to incur in obtaining transfer of the assets and the profit they would expect as an inducement to purchase. If there might be some legal difficulty in obtaining the underlying asset (as there might have been in *R(SB) 21/83* and in *R(IS) 13/95*, where shares were held in the names of the claimant's children) this must be taken into account.

See also *MB v Wychavon DC (HB)* [2013] UKUT 67 (AAC) which concerned the valuation of the claimant's beneficial interest under a declaration of trust made by his mother in relation to a property held in the mother's name. The claimant had contributed 10 per cent towards the purchase price. In the absence of a family member willing to purchase the claimant's share, Judge Mark finds that the market value of the claimant's interest was substantially less than the amount of his contribution to the purchase price (he decided it was less than half that amount). However, it was possible that there would be no market at all for the claimant's share, in which case its value would be nil.

Where the property is jointly owned, see the decisions discussed under *Valuation under reg. 47* in the notes to reg.47.

Deductions from market value

The general rule is that the whole of a capital resource is to be taken into account.   **2.153.3** Liabilities are not to be deducted from the value (*R(SB) 2/83* and *SSWP v GF (ESA)* [2017] UKUT 333 (AAC)). The "remedy" in such a case is for the claimant to discharge the liability, which does not give rise to notional capital under the deprivation rule (see reg.50(2)(a)). It is only where a debt is secured on the capital asset that it is deducted under reg.49(1)(b).

In this connection, note *JRL v SSWP (JSA)* [2011] UKUT 63 (AAC), reported as [2011] AACR 30. The claimant had three accounts with the same bank, of which one was in credit, one was overdrawn and one had a nil balance. The Three-Judge Panel pointed out that this meant that the claimant was both a creditor and a debtor of the same body. Under the bank's terms and conditions, the bank had a contractual right to debit at any time any of a customer's accounts which were in credit with sums sufficient to clear the customer's indebtedness to the bank. This created what was effectively a charge on the customer's credit balance(s). The market value of the account that was in credit was therefore its net value after deduction of the amount of the claimant's overdraft on his other account.

The first deduction to be made is a standard 10 per cent if there would be any expenses attributable to sale, as there almost always will be. The second is the amount of any encumbrance secured on the asset. There is particularly full and helpful guidance on the nature of incumbrances on real property and the evidence which should be examined in *R(IS) 21/93*, and see below. In *R(IS) 10/99* the Commissioner points out that the word "encumbrance" is unknown to the law of Scotland, but goes on to interpret the equivalent of sub-para.(b) as meaning that there must be something attached to the capital in question that prevents the claimant from disposing of it.

The standard case of a debt being secured on a capital asset is a house that is mortgaged. The amount of capital outstanding will be deducted from the market value of the house. In *R(SB) 14/81* the claimant had been lent £5,000 for work on his bungalow, which was mortgaged to secure the debt. He had £3,430 left. Although he was obliged to make monthly repayments this liability could not be deducted from the £3,430, for the debt was not secured on the money. However, the principle of *R(SB) 53/83* (see the notes to reg.46) would make the money not part of the claimant's resources. In *JH v SSWP* [2009] UKUT 1 (AAC) the site owner's commission payable on the sale of a beach hut was not "an incumbrance secured on" the hut but a personal contractual obligation on the seller which could not be enforced against the asset itself.

In *R(SB) 18/83* the Commissioner says that personal property such as shares (or money) can be charged by a contract for valuable consideration (e.g. a loan) without any writing or the handing over of any title documents. But this is not the case in Scots law (*R(SB) 5/88*). In *R(IS) 18/95* the claimant's brokers had a lien on his shares for the cost of acquisition and their commission which fell to be offset against the value of the shares. *CIS/368/1993* concerned money held under a solicitor's undertaking. £40,000 of the proceeds of sale of the claimant's house was retained by his solicitors in pursuance of an undertaking to his bank given because of a previous charge on the property. The Commissioner decides that the undertaking was an incumbrance within the equivalent of sub-para.(b). It was the equivalent of a pledge or lien and was secured on the proceeds of sale. Thus the £40,000 did not count as part of the claimant's resources. See also *CIS/984/2002* which concerned money held by the claimant's solicitor pending quantification of the statutory charge to the Legal Services Commission under s.10(7) of the Access to Justice Act 1999. The Commissioner holds that this was not part of the claimant's capital until the charge had been quantified, as until then it was not possible to identify any particular amount as the claimant's capital. He added that another way of looking at it was to treat the statutory charge as an incumbrance for the purpose of the equivalent of sub-para.(b).

In *R(IS) 5/98* the claimant transferred her flat to her daughter on the understanding that the daughter would care for her in the flat and pay off the mortgage. The daughter complied with the second condition, but evicted her mother from the flat. The Commissioner decides that the gift of the flat to the daughter had been subject to the condition that she looked after her mother. As that condition had not been fulfilled, the gift failed and the daughter held the property on trust for the claimant. In valuing the claimant's interest, the mortgage was to be deducted because the daughter was to be treated as subrogated to the rights of the mortgagee. In addition, the costs of the litigation to recover the property from the daughter also fell to be deducted. The claimant appealed against this decision to the Court of Appeal but her appeal was dismissed (*Ellis v Chief Adjudication Officer*, reported as part of *R(IS) 5/98*).

Notional capital

2.154

50.—(1) A person is to be treated as possessing capital of which the person has deprived themselves for the purpose of securing entitlement to universal credit or to an increased amount of universal credit.

(2) A person is not to be treated as depriving themselves of capital if the person disposes of it for the purposes of—

(a) reducing or paying a debt owed by the person; or

(b) purchasing goods or services if the expenditure was reasonable in the circumstances of the person's case.

(3) Where a person is treated as possessing capital in accordance with this regulation, then for each subsequent assessment period (or, in a case where the award has terminated, each subsequent month) the amount of capital the person is treated as possessing ("the notional capital") reduces—

(a) in a case where the notional capital exceeds £16,000, by the amount which the Secretary of State considers would be the amount of an award of universal credit that would be made to the person (assuming they met the conditions in section 4 and 5 of the Act) if it were not for the notional capital; or

(b) in a case where the notional capital exceeds £6,000 but not £16,000 (including where the notional capital has reduced to an amount equal to or less than £16,000 in accordance with sub-paragraph (a)) by the amount of unearned income that the notional capital is treated as yielding under regulation 72.

DEFINITION

"unearned income"—see reg.2.

GENERAL NOTE

Paragraph (1)

Under universal credit the only circumstance in which someone will be treated as having notional capital is where they have deprived themselves of it for the purpose of securing, or increasing, entitlement to universal credit (although note also reg.77(2) in relation to companies in which the person is like a sole trader or partner).

There is a considerable amount of case law on the "deprivation rule"—see the extensive notes to reg.51(1) of the Income Support Regulations in Vol.II of this series. But note that some of the case law will need to be read in the light of para. (2). The very important exceptions there for reducing or paying a debt or purchasing reasonable goods and services take a lot of formerly contentious areas out of consideration for universal credit.

In particular, the principle laid down in *R(SB) 38/85* will no doubt be relevant, that once it is shown that a person did possess, or received, a capital asset, the burden shifts to that person to show that it has ceased to be part of their actual capital. If the person fails to show that, the proper conclusion is then that the asset remains part of their actual capital, rather than to invoke any notional capital rule (see *R(SB) 40/85*). Tribunals should therefore in such circumstances avoid vague formulations such as 'the claimant is treated as having capital of £x' and make it clear whether the conclusion is that the person has actual or notional capital of that amount (see *AB v SSWP and Canterbury CC (IS and HB)* [2014] UKUT 212 (AAC)). One consequence of the difference is that, if a person is found to have actual capital as a consequence of not having shown that some asset or assets have been disposed of, there is no statutory diminishing capital rule to be applied. Normally where a claimant is not entitled to benefit because the amount of capital exceeds the £16,000 limit (or the amount of assumed tariff income from capital over £6,000 precludes entitlement) the 'remedy' is to dip into the capital to meet living and/or other reasonable expenses or pay off some debt and to claim again when the amount of capital has reduced to the level that allows entitlement. However, a claimant may be in difficulty in making such an argument while maintaining that the assets in question had been disposed of.

It should also be remembered that another result of *R(SB) 38/85* and *R(SB) 40/85* is that there is a deprivation of capital whenever a person ceases by their own act to possess some asset, even though some other asset is received in return. Otherwise it would be possible to convert capital that counts towards the limits into a form in which it is disregarded without falling foul of the notional capital rule. However, para.(2) of the present regulation sets out important limitations on the effect of that principle, which are not present in the income support or old style ESA or JSA legislation (see below).

There is no equivalent in reg.50 (or in reg.75) to reg.51(1)(a) of the Income Support Regulations (reg.115(1)(a) of the ESA Regulations 2008 and reg.113(1)(a) of the JSA Regulations 1996) excluding the operation of the deprivation rule where the capital disposed of is derived from a payment made in consequence of a personal injury and is placed on trust. If the sum was initially paid without restriction and that action, or the purchase of an annuity, was not taken, then after the expiry of the 12 months allowed for a reg.75 disregard by reg.75(6) there would be no applicable disregard. Therefore, depending on the amounts involved and the other

2.155

circumstances, it could appear on the face of it that such a transfer of the capital either before or after the expiry of the 12 months was for the purpose of securing entitlement to universal credit or increasing its amount. The person would then have to be treated (as there is no discretion) as still possessing the amount disposed of. However, it is suggested that the policy behind reg.75 is so clear that where funds deriving from a personal injury are held in the ways specified in paras.(2) – (5) of reg.75 there should be no effect on universal credit entitlement, that the notional capital rule should not be applied in these circumstances.

There is a great deal of case law on when there has been a deprivation for the purpose of securing entitlement to or increasing the amount of benefit, including the issue of how much knowledge of the capital limits is necessary for it to be concluded that the deprivation had that purpose. See the notes to reg.51(1) of the Income Support Regulations in Vol.II of this series for extensive discussion. No doubt, the principle that it is enough that that purpose is a significant operative purpose and need not be the sole or main purpose will be maintained here. There is no equivalent in reg.50 to the rule in reg.60(2) below (notional earned income) treating the prohibited purpose as having existed where entitlement or higher entitlement to universal credit did result and was a foreseeable and intended consequence of the deprivation.

The operation of para.(1) is restricted to circumstances where the person's purpose is related to entitlement to universal credit. That is in contrast to the terms of reg.113(1) of the JSA Regulations 1996 (which covers purposes related to both old style JSA and income support) and of reg.115(1) of the ESA Regulations 2008 (which covers purposes related to all of old style ESA and JSA and income support), but not to the terms of reg.51(1) of the Income Support Regulations (which is restricted to income support). *R(IS) 14/93* was concerned with a similar problem on the transfer to income support from the corresponding supplementary benefit provisions in 1988. That was whether claimants who deprived themselves of capital under the supplementary benefit regime, before income support existed, could be said to have done so for the purpose of securing entitlement to income support so as to be caught by reg.51(1) once the income support legislation had come into force. The decisions on the point do not now need to be examined in detail. *R(IS) 14/93* holds that the words "income support" in reg.51(1) cannot be taken to refer to means-tested benefits that previously went under the name of supplementary benefit. Thus, if a deprivation of capital occurs while a person is receiving, or contemplating a claim for, income support or old style JSA or ESA, it may be arguable, depending on the exact circumstances, that if there is later a claim for universal credit the purpose of the deprivation was not to secure entitlement to universal credit. It may also be slightly more onerous to establish the person's knowledge of the capital rules in universal credit, as a new and not yet familiar benefit, especially if previous entitlement had been to tax credits, where the amount of capital did not affect entitlement.

Paragraph (2)

2.156   Paragraph (2)(a) provides that someone will not be treated as having deprived themselves of capital if they have used it to repay or reduce a debt. This provision avoids a lot of difficult issues under the notional capital rules for other benefits about the exact circumstances in which paying off debts in whole or part might indicate that securing entitlement to or increasing the amount of benefit was not a significant operative purpose of the deprivation. It appears to have a very wide application. There is no requirement that the debt is legally enforceable, or even that it is due to be repaid, or any restriction as to the type of debt involved. It should therefore apply to the repayment of loans from family or friends (subject to possible issues about when there is sufficient evidence to establish the existence of the debt on the balance of probabilities) and to the repayment of overdrafts or credit card balances as well as mortgages, personal loans etc. Although para.(2)(a) expressly refers to debts owed by the person who carries out the deprivation, it is submitted that where the person is a member of a couple (whose capital would be aggregated under reg.18(2) or s.5(2) of the WRA 2012) payment of a debt owed by the other member of the couple would be covered.

Under para.(2)(b) the deprivation rule is not to apply if the deprivation takes the form of purchase of goods or services and the expenditure was reasonable in the circumstances of the person concerned. It is not at all clear what might be covered by the word "goods". Regulation 46(2) provides that personal possessions are not to be treated as capital. In the notes to that provision the approach in *R(H) 7/08* is mentioned, that personal possessions mean any physical assets other than land and assets used for business purposes, with no distinctions to be drawn, say to exclude assets acquired for investment. However, a question is raised there whether the use of the adjective "personal" could be taken to exclude items used solely as investments. It could be argued here that "goods" should not have any narrower meaning than whatever is the correct meaning of personal possessions in reg.46(2). Indeed, it would seem that in the absence of the adjective "personal" the meaning should include things used for business purposes. On the other hand, it could be argued that the word "goods" suggests items used in the course of daily living, even though they might be regarded as capital purchases, so that it would not cover items acquired for investment. The practical importance of such uncertainties may be lessened by the condition of reasonableness. That test must depend on reasonableness as at the date of the potential deprivation, rather than as assessed later with the benefit of hindsight. Although the relevant circumstances will include the person's financial situation and prospects at the time, including the likelihood of having to claim a means-tested benefit and how much the person actually knew about the capital limits for such benefits, it is submitted that the assessment of benefit must balance the principle that in general people are free to spend their own money on whatever they like against what is reasonable in relation to the community of taxpayers who fund universal credit.

Note that if neither of the two situations in para.(2) apply, it remains necessary to consider whether the person did deprive themselves of the capital for the purpose of securing, or increasing, entitlement to universal credit. That will be the case, for instance, where a claimant buys some interest in property, e.g. in the home.

Paragraph (3)
This paragraph contains the diminishing notional capital rule for universal credit. 2.157
If the notional capital is more than £16,000, it is reduced in each subsequent assessment period, or each subsequent month if the universal credit award has ceased, by the amount of universal credit that the person would have received but for the notional capital. In the case of a person who has notional capital of between £6,000 and £16,000, the notional capital reduces by the amount of income deemed to be generated by that amount of capital under the "assumed yield from capital" rule in reg.72(1).

This diminishing notional capital rule is different from that in income support (reg.51A of the Income Support Regulations), old style ESA (reg.116 of the ESA Regulations 2008) or old style JSA (reg.114 of the JSA Regulations 2006). Those provisions apply whenever taking the notional capital into account has either taken the claimant out of entitlement or resulted in a reduction in the amount of benefit received. Then the amount of notional capital is reduced week by week by the amount of benefit in question that would otherwise have been paid for that week. Thus the rule can apply regardless of the initial amount of the notional capital. What matters is whether the combination of actual capital (if any) and notional capital takes the claimant over a relevant limit.

By contrast, para.(3) on its face applies only where the amount of notional capital alone exceeds either £16,000 or £6,000. If a claimant has actual capital of £15,000 and is then fixed with £2,000 of notional capital, so that there can no longer be entitlement to universal credit, the terms of para.(3) are not met and there apparently can be no reduction in the £2,000 of notional capital. If the claimant had no actual capital and was fixed with £17,000 of notional capital para.(3) could apply. That difference in treatment within universal credit and between different means-tested benefits seems inequitable. However, it may be that there is unjustified double counting in the other benefits in favour of claimants who have actual capital. In the example quoted of £15,000 actual capital and £2,000 notional capital, the claimant would need to dip into actual capital to meet essential living expenses in the absence of the previous benefit payments, and that expenditure on goods and services would no doubt be accepted as reasonable under para.(2)(b). So once the actual capital had reduced below £14,000, there could be entitlement again. The difference is that a universal credit claimant cannot take advantage of a reduction in the amount of notional capital in addition to that reduction in actual capital, whereas it appears that income support, old style ESA and old style JSA claimants can. There are similar problems where it is a combination of actual and notional capital that takes the claimant over the £6,000 limit for an assumed yield under reg.72(1). It may be that the problems and inequities are so great that the references to notional capital exceeding £6,000 or £16,000 must be interpreted as references to the amount of notional capital taking the claimant over one or other of those limits, whether on its own or in combination with actual capital.

Presumably a person's notional capital will be calculated in the same way as if it were actual capital, that is, by applying any relevant disregard, although neither reg.50 nor reg.48 specifically states this. This is assumed in para.H1885 ADM.

CHAPTER 2

EARNED INCOME

Introduction

2.158   **51.** This Chapter provides for the calculation or estimation of a person's earned income for the purposes of section 8 of the Act (calculation of awards).

DEFINITIONS

"the Act"—see reg.2.
"earned income"—see reg.52.

GENERAL NOTE

2.159   In the case of joint claimants their income is aggregated (see s.8(4)(b) of the WRA 2012). If a member of a couple is claiming as a single person (see reg.3(3) for the circumstances in which this can happen) the income of the other member of the couple is taken into account when calculating the universal credit award (see reg.22(3)).

Any income of a child is ignored.

In calculating universal credit, 63 per cent of the claimant's, or the claimants' combined earned income, or, where a work allowance is applicable, 63 per cent of the excess over the amount of the allowance is taken into account (see s.8(3) WRA 2012 and reg.22).

Regulations 52–64 deal with the calculation of earned income and regs 65–74 with unearned income. Regulations 75–77 contain a number of additional rules in relation to treatment of a person's capital and income.

Meaning of "earned income"

2.160   **52.** "Earned income" means—
  (a) the remuneration or profits derived from—
      (i) employment under a contract of service or in an office, including elective office,
      (ii) a trade, profession or vocation, or
      (iii) any other paid work; or

(b) any income treated as earned income in accordance with this Chapter.

DEFINITION

"paid work"—see reg.2.

GENERAL NOTE

Paragraph (a) spells out what counts as earned income. It comprises earnings as 2.161
an employee, as an office-holder, including a holder of elective office, such as a local
councillor, self-employed earnings, and remuneration or profits from any other paid
work (for the definition of "paid work" see reg.2).

What might fall within sub-para.(iii) as paid work that does not already fall within
sub-para.(i) (contract of employment or office) or (ii) (self-employment) remains
obscure. There are no other regulations saying how remuneration or profit derived
from other paid work should be calculated or taken into account. Regulations 55 on
employed earnings and 58 and 59 on self-employed earnings contain rules about
the calculation of such earnings that involve disregards of certain kinds of receipts
and deductions from gross receipts. It plainly cannot be the case that such elements
come back into consideration under sub-para.(iii). The exclusion of their amount in
the calculation process does not alter their status as remuneration or profit derived
from employment or self-employment and so cannot count as derived from "other"
paid work. Possibly the category is meant to cover casual and informal work that
lacks the organisation to qualify as a trade, vocation or profession (see *Hakki v
Secretary of State for Work and Pensions* [2014] EWCA Civ 530 on a "professional"
poker player held not to be a self-employed earner on that ground). The reasoning in
Hakki has been somewhat uncritically endorsed in the further child support case of
French v SSWP and another [2018] EWCA Civ 474; [2018] AACR 25. However, in
gambling type cases the activities might not be regarded as work and it would seem
that there is no expectation of payment, as opposed to gain.

It appears that para.(a) establishes an overarching condition that payments that
would fall to be calculated as employed earnings or self-employed earnings be remuneration or profit derived from the sources specified. That would cover the provisions in reg.55 for adopting income tax principles as a matter of calculation and in
regs 57–59 on self-employed earnings.

On para.(b), see regs 55(4) and (4A), 62 (minimum income floor) and 77(3)
(person standing in a position analogous to that of a sole owner or partner in relation to a company carrying on a trade). Note also reg.60 on notional earned income.

Meaning of other terms relating to earned income

53.—(1) In this Chapter—
"car" has the meaning in section 268A of the Capital Allowances Act 2.162
2001;
"employed earnings" has the meaning in regulation 55;
"gainful self-employment" has the meaning in regulation 64;
"HMRC" means Her Majesty's Revenue and Customs;
"motor cycle" has the meaning in section 268A of the Capital Allowances
Act 2001;
"PAYE Regulations" means the Income Tax (Pay As You Earn)
Regulations 2003;
"relievable pension contributions" has the meaning in section 188 of the
Finance Act 2004;
"self-employed earnings" has the meaning in regulation 57; and
"start-up period" has the meaning in regulation 63.

(2) References in this Chapter to a person participating as a service user
are to—
(a) a person who is being consulted by or on behalf of—

(i) a body which has a statutory duty to provide services in the field of health, social care or social housing; or

(ii) a body which conducts research or undertakes monitoring for the purpose of planning or improving such services,

in their capacity as a user, potential user, carer of a user or person otherwise affected by the provision of those services; or

[¹ (ab) a person who is being consulted by or on behalf of—

(i) the Secretary of State in relation to any of the Secretary of State's functions in the field of social security or child support or under section 2 of the Employment and Training Act 1973; or

(ii) a body which conducts research or undertakes monitoring for the purpose of planning or improving such functions,

in their capacity as a person affected or potentially affected by the exercise of those functions or the carer of such a person;]

(b) the carer of a person consulted under [¹ sub-paragraphs (a) or (ab)].

AMENDMENT

1. Social Security (Miscellaneous Amendments) Regulations 2015 (SI 2015/67) reg.2(1)(g) and (2) (February 23, 2015).

DEFINITION

"Her Majesty's Revenue and Customs"—see Interpretation Act 1978 Sch.1.

Calculation of earned income—general principles

2.163   **54.**—(1) The calculation of a person's earned income in respect of an assessment period is, unless otherwise provided in this Chapter, to be based on the actual amounts received in that period.

(2) Where the Secretary of State—

(a) makes a determination as to whether the financial conditions in section 5 of the Act are met before the expiry of the first assessment period in relation to a claim for universal credit; or

(b) makes a determination as to the amount of a person's earned income in relation to an assessment period where a person has failed to report information in relation to that earned income,

that determination may be based on an estimate of the amounts received or expected to be received in that assessment period.

DEFINITIONS

"the Act"—see reg.2.
"assessment period"—see WRA 2012 ss.40 and 7(2) and reg.21.
"claim"—see WRA 2012 s.40.
"earned income"—see reg.52.

GENERAL NOTE

2.164   Under para.(1), the normal rule is that a person's earned income (as defined in reg.52 and so covering both employed earnings and self-employed earnings as well as remuneration or profit derived from other paid work, whatever that is) is to be based on the actual amount received during an assessment period.

In *PT v SSWP (UC)* [2015] UKUT 696 (AAC) the claimant claimed universal credit on January 6, 2015 and received his final wages from his previous job on January 16, 2015. These were taken into account in calculating his entitlement to universal credit in the first assessment period. The claimant contended that they should not have been taken into account as his job had ended. Judge Jacobs raises the question of how there can be an assessment period before a decision has been made that the claimant is entitled to universal credit. He accepts the Secretary of State's explanation that the answer lies in s.5(1)(b) of the WRA 2012. The assessment period is fixed by reference to the first date of entitlement (reg.21(1)). Until the decision is made on entitlement, s.5(1)(b) provides for income to be calculated on the assumption that an award will be made. The earnings were received during the first assessment period and so fell to be taken into account under para.(1). It did not matter that the employment had ceased to exist by the time the wages were paid. Nor can it matter that the wages were earned in respect of weeks prior to the first assessment period. It is the time of receipt that is crucial.

However, para.(2) allows an estimate to be made (i) where the calculation is made before the expiry of the first assessment period or (ii) where there has been a failure to report information about earned income in an assessment period.

A judicial review challenge to the inflexibility of the structure of assessment periods and the attribution of earned income actually received in each period (or information received from HMRC under the real time information provisions of reg.61), which, as operated by the DWP, could easily lead to two regular monthly payments being counted in one assessment period and none in another, was first heard in November 2018. However, the Divisional Court (*R. (Johnson) v Secretary of State for Work and Pensions* [2019] EWHC 23 (Admin), Singh LJ and Lewis J) decided that it did not need to address the issues of irrationality, breach of art.14 (discrimination) of the ECHR and breach of the Equality Act 2010 that had been raised originally. That was because it concluded that the DWP had been interpreting regs 54 and 61 wrongly and that the correct interpretation removed the claimants' problems. That conclusion has now been overturned by the Court of Appeal on the Secretary of State's appeal in *Secretary of State for Work and Pensions v Johnson* [2020] EWCA Civ 778. The regulations were to be interpreted in the way put forward by the DWP, but the court rejected the Secretary of State's appeal because the claimants' case succeeded on the ground that there was irrationality in the failure, when the regulations were drafted and subsequently, to make an express adjustment to avoid the adverse consequences for those in the claimants' circumstances of applying the basic reg.54 rule of using the date of receipt of earned income to decide in which assessment period it counted. There was then no need to consider the alternative ground of discrimination.

The court did not in either of the judgments suggest that any part of reg.54 or 61 was invalid or say what the consequences of its conclusions on irrationality were on the entitlement decisions challenged by the four claimants. However, as discussed below, the declaration contained in the order dated June 30, 2020, presumably accepted on behalf of the Secretary of State as consistent with the judgments, appears to go further. On June 25, 2020, the Under-Secretary of State, Will Quince, confirmed in Parliament that the DWP did not intend to appeal against the judgment (HC Hansard, Vol.677, col.1456).

The four claimants were all single claimants of youngish children, so qualifying for the work allowance, and in monthly paid employment. All of their employers were Real Time Information (RTI) employers. Ms Johnson was paid on the last working day of each month, unless (according to Rose LJ) that was a non-banking day, in which case she was paid earlier. Ms Barrett was paid on the 28th of each month, unless that was a non-banking day, in which case she was paid on the last working day before the 28th. Ms Woods was paid on the last working day of each month (presumably with a similar dispensation if that was a non-banking day). Ms Stewart was paid on the 28th of each month (again presumably with a similar dispensation) Ms Johnson's assessment period ran from the last day of each month to the penultimate day of the following month. Ms Barrett's and Ms Stewart's assessment periods ran from the 28th of each month to the 27th of the following month. Ms Woods' assessment period ran from the 30th of each month to the 29th of the following month. The problems arose when the attribution of payments to a particular assessment period was affected by what Rose LJ called "the non-banking day salary shift".

To take the facts of Ms Johnson's case as an example, she was paid her salary for November 2017 on November 30, 2017 and her salary for December 2017 on December 29, 2017, since December 30 and 31, 2017 were a Saturday and Sunday. (Note that it is accordingly not entirely clear whether that represented payment on the contractual pay-day, Saturday and Sunday not being working days, rather than being a precise example of non-banking day salary shift, but that term might have been intended not to exclude situations where there was in fact no shift from the contractual pay-day). It appears that her employer reported the payments through the RTI system to HMRC on the dates of payment and the information transmitted to the DWP on the same date. A decision-maker took the view that, since the information about both payments was received within the assessment period running from November 30, 2017 to December 30, 2017, reg.61 required them both to be taken into account in that assessment period. The result was that 63% of the excess of the amount of the two payments (after the deductions required by reg.55(5)) over her work allowance of £192 was deducted from the maximum amount of universal credit for that period. It was the decision to that effect on January 6, 2018 that Ms Johnson challenged in her judicial review application. It was accepted that, on that basis, her earnings in the assessment period running from December 31, 2017 to January 30, 2018 would be nil (payment of the January 2018 salary being due on Wednesday January 31, 2018). There would then be no deduction at all for earnings from the maximum amount of universal credit for that assessment period, resulting in a much higher amount of universal credit than in a one-payment assessment period, but Ms Johnson would have been "deprived" of the ability to use £192 worth of work allowance against each separate payment of salary (see further below for discussion of the amount of net losses involved). Ms Woods' challenge was in essence the same, to a decision on January 3, 2018 taking both November and December salary payments into account in the assessment period running from November 30, 2017 to December 29, 2017.

Ms Barrett and Ms Stewart were more definite examples of non-banking day salary shift. If their pay-day of the 28th of the month was a Saturday or Sunday or a bank holiday, they would be paid at least a day earlier, the payment apparently to be taken into account in the assessment period ending on the 27th of that month (see below for why the employers' RTI returns should in accordance with HMRC guidance/instructions nevertheless have designated payment as made on the 28th).

The Divisional Court concluded that in both reg.54(1) and 61, but with the emphasis on the former, the use of the formula that the amount of earned income "in respect of" an assessment period is to be "based on" the actual amounts received in that period, or the HMRC information received by the Secretary of State in that period, meant that there was "intended to be some other factor, not the mere mechanical addition of monies received in a particular period, which the calculation has to address" (para.51). That other factor was said to be the period in respect of which the earned income was earned, so that there might need to be an adjustment where it was clear that the amounts received in an assessment period did not, in fact, reflect the amounts received in respect of the period of time included within that assessment period. There was a direction that claimants' earned income was to be calculated in accordance with that principle. It is not now necessary to go into more detail on the Divisional Court's reasoning or into the criticisms made of it in the 2019/20 edition of this volume (at 2.164), because its conclusion has been shortly rejected by the Court of Appeal as a matter of construction.

Rose LJ, giving the lead judgment, held that the terms "to be based on" and "in respect of" did not have to be given the meaning given by the Divisional Court to have some substantial content. Looking at the use of different phrases throughout the legislation, "in respect of" meant no more than "in" or "for". The formula of "to be based on" made sense in support of the DWP's approach because of the need to take account of provisions like reg.55(3) on the disregard of certain categories of receipts, which entailed not using the full amount of actual receipts. The Divisional Court's approach also left open many questions about other circumstances in which an adjustment might be made, that reg.54 was intended to avoid, in particular because the universal credit system was designed to be automated, so that decisions could be made by computer without the need for a manual intervention. Another important factor was that "earned income" as defined in reg.52 covered a very wide range of payments, including many where the pattern of payment might well be genuinely irregular. The general principle in reg.54 had to apply to all such payments and in general it made sense for the amount actually received in the assessment period to be not only the starting point but also the finishing point. It was then not possible to give the phrase "is to be based on" in reg.61(2)(a) any different meaning from that in reg.54.

The Secretary of State's challenge to the Divisional Court's reasoning was thus found to be soundly based, but her appeal was nonetheless dismissed because the claimants' arguments on irrationality were accepted. Despite the challenge to specific decisions, Rose LJ described the irrationality arguments, on the basis of her acceptance of the general good sense of the reg.54 rule, as directed at "the initial and ongoing failure of the SSWP to include in the Regulations a further express adjustment to avoid the consequence of the combination of the non-banking day salary shift and the application of regulation 54 for claimants in the position of the Respondents" (para.47).

Counsel for the Secretary of State had accepted that the result of reg.54 for the claimants was arbitrary and that there was no policy reason why they should be faced with the difficulties involved, but submitted that no solution to their difficulties had been found that was not outweighed by other factors. Rose LJ agreed with the Divisional Court that the way that reg.54, as construed in the way she accepted, applied to the claimants was "odd in the extreme". She accepted that there was a wide and frequent oscillation in the amounts of universal credit payable and the total income available to the claimants assessment period to assessment period, leading to budgeting difficulties, the expense of taking out loans or going into overdraft, the effect on entitlement to other advantages (e.g. council tax reduction) and associated stress and anxiety. She also accepted that, through the loss of the benefit of the work allowance in assessment periods when no earned income was received, the claimants suffered an overall loss of income compared with a claimant whose assessment period was dated in a way that required each regular payment of monthly salary to be taken into account in its own assessment period. (Despite that acceptance, it appears in fact very difficult to work out whether any individual claimant would be worse or better off by sometimes having two monthly salaries counted in one assessment period and sometimes none: the calculations are too complicated to explore here). There could also possibly be an effect on other aspects of the universal credit scheme, such as the earnings exemption from the benefit cap, but that did not affect any of the claimants involved.

Rose LJ rejected the Secretary of State's submission that the oscillation was a reflection of a central feature of the scheme in responding immediately to changes in claimants' circumstances as they move in and out of work. Rather, there was no change here in the claimants' circumstances or irregularity in the pattern of their receipt of monthly payments. The oscillation was a response only to whether the regular monthly pay date coincided with the end date of the assessment period. There was no practical way for the claimants to alter the dates of their assessment periods once they were set at the date of claim (having received no warning of the potential consequences) or to alter their contractual pay-day, but there was evidence that the consequences cut across the overall policy of the scheme by creating perverse employment incentives for the claimants to change or turn down employment on the basis of payment patterns.

The Secretary of State had put forward three reasons for not resolving the problems of non-banking day salary shift either initially or once the scheme was in operation, linked it seems by the argument that to do so would undermine the coherence of the universal credit scheme as a whole. The first was that the suggested irrationality was based on the misconception of aligning an assessment period with a calendar month or that the problem arose from the irregularity of payment set against the intended regular and fixed pattern of assessment periods. Rose LJ rejected that characterisation of the origin of the difficulty. The second reason was the need for "bright lines" in the rules for the attribution of receipts of earned income, that would inevitably lead to some hard cases falling just on the wrong side. Rose LJ accepted the need for bright lines in many circumstances, but noted that the regulations contained several exceptions to such lines where the policy imperative overrode the need for simplicity and that, as the claimants submitted, flexibility was allowed when it was in the Secretary of State's interests. Careful and detailed drafting had been adopted to address specific issues. It could not be impossible to draft an exception to cover the particular problem highlighted in *Johnson*, which involved significant and predictable, but arbitrary, effects, and it was not a valid argument against doing so that there might be other groups of claimants for whom such a solution could not be found. The third reason was the need for a rule that would allow the calculation of the amount of a universal credit award to take place in an automated way without the need for manual intervention. Such automation was said to have many advantages for claimants and the cost of rebuilding the calculator in the computer system was said to be substantial. Rose LJ could not accept that the computer programme could not be altered to recognise cases where the end of a claimant's assessment period coincided with the salary pay date, so that action might be needed to prevent two payments counting in one assessment period when there was a non-banking day salary shift.

Rose LJ also took into account the potential size of the cohort affected, suggesting (without adjudicating between the competing figures put forward by the parties) that many tens of thousand were likely to be involved. That was because 75% of working people are paid monthly, the most common pay-day being the last working day of the month followed by the 28th, and many claims are made towards the end of the month when jobs come to an end. She also considered it significant that there was no practical way for the claimants to get themselves out of the situation, that the problem was arbitrary in nature and without prior warning to the claimant (increasing stress) and in particular involved inconsistency with the policy of incentivising work. Thus there were serious personal consequences for those affected and results that ran counter to some fundamental features of the universal credit scheme.

Although the threshold for establishing irrationality was very high, here the refusal to put in place a solution to the very specific problem was an outcome that no reasonable Secretary of State would have adopted. There was to be a direction (to be agreed by counsel) focusing on that specific problem, that would leave it to the Secretary of State to consider the best way to solve the problem (para.110). Underhill LJ agreed, saying that there was nothing to justify a conclusion that no solution could be devised without causing unacceptable cost or problems elsewhere in the system, but also that the case turned on its own particular circumstances. He added, at para.116, that the case turned on its own very particular circumstances and had no impact on the lawfulness of the universal credit system more generally.

The court's discussion of the construction of reg.54 was rather limited and it is arguable that a proper basis had not been established for regarding the need for automated calculation (not mentioned anywhere in the legislation) as a significant factor in identifying the purpose that the provision was intended to achieve. However, since the closer textual analysis, especially in the relationship with reg.61(2)(b), set out in para.2.164 of the 2019/20 edition of this volume, supports the same construction, that may not matter. It appears unlikely that any of the claimants in *Johnson* will seek to appeal to the Supreme Court, so the issue appears settled unless it is raised again in some other case that reaches the Court of Appeal at least.

It is also arguable that the Court of Appeal here, perhaps because of the way that the court below had approached the issues, gave insufficient attention in general to reg.61 and the various specific provisions within it, since all the employers concerned were RTI employers. Those specific provisions could possibly have qualified the general principle in reg.54 and it was accepted that reg.61(2) applied. Rose LJ said two interesting things, possibly inconsistent, about reg.61. In para.44 she rejected the submission for the claimants that they could rely on reg.61(3), on the ground that there was nothing inaccurate or untimely in the information the employers were providing to HMRC and the DWP, so that there was nothing incorrect in a way specified in reg.61(3). In para.86 she referred to HMRC guidance/instructions that employers should report payment on the contracted pay date in the RTI feed even if payment was made earlier. She cited guidance dealing with Easter 2019 and information on behalf of the claimants that such general guidance had been in place since at least 2018. The guidance may, therefore, not have been in place at the time of the particular decisions challenged by the four claimants, but surely should have played a much more prominent part in the discussion of the ongoing rationality. If an employer in a non-banking day salary shift case where payment is made early enters the date of actual payment in the relevant field (43) of the Full Payment Submission instead of the contractual date, surely it is arguable that the information received from HMRC is incorrect in a material respect within s.61(3)(b)(ii), so that the general rule in reg.61(2) need not apply. Regulation 54 would then apply, but with the power to treat a payment of employed earnings received in one assessment period as received in a later period (reg.61(5)(a)). As Rose LJ notes, the following of the HMRC guidance would have obviated the problems for claimants paid on the last day of the month (and, it would seem, for most of those paid on a fixed day of the month, such as the 28th), but not for those paid on the last working day of the month (like Ms Johnson and Ms Woods). That would be because the "early" date of actual payment would still be the contractual or usual pay date. The following of the HMRC guidance/instruction by employers and the use of reg.61(3)(b)(ii) when it was not followed would greatly decrease the size of the cohort subject to extremely odd outcomes. See the notes to reg.61 for further details of the HMRC guidance/ instructions.

It is not at all clear how the Court of Appeal's decision on irrationality leaves the four claimants concerned in practical terms or affects other monthly-paid claimants whose usual pay day is close to the end of their assessment period. The nature of the irrationality accepted and para.110 of Rose LJ's judgment seems to envisage that the terms of the applicable provisions would only be changed through amendment once the Secretary of State, as directed, had come up with a solution to the specific problem. That would have raised difficult questions about whether the Secretary of State would have been required to make any such amendment retrospective, so as to affect the amount of universal credit that should have been awarded (under the terms of the amendment) in the decisions specifically challenged by the four claimants in *Johnson* and in the cases of other claimants. However, the declaration made in the order of June 30, 2020 is as follows:

> "It is declared that the earned income calculation method in Chapter 2 of Part 6 of the Universal Credit Regulations 2013 is irrational and unlawful as employees paid monthly salary, whose universal credit claim began on or around their normal pay date, are treated as having variable earned income in different assessment periods when pay dates for two (consecutive) months fall in the same assessment period in the way described in the judgment."

Thus, rather than a focus on the process of legislating a solution to the specific problem in *Johnson*, the declaration appears to bite on the substance of the legislation and to declare the outcome of the application of regs 54 and 61 for claimants affected by that problem to be "irrational and unlawful". That would in principle be so from the date that those provisions first came into effect. While such a declaration does not directly invalidate any part of those provisions, the inevitable effect must be that the four *Johnson* claimants cannot now, in relation to the decisions challenged, have an irrational and unlawful outcome applied. But what outcome is to be applied? Must the answer await the Secretary of State's coming up with a drafting solution, which is then to be applied retrospectively through the force of the declaration? Or can the four claimants now demand payment of whatever universal credit they would have been entitled to if only one monthly payment, instead of two, had been reported in the particular assessment period in issue? The same questions apply to other claimants in the same situation who either have appeals or mandatory reconsideration applications already lodged or are awaiting decisions that had been deferred under the Secretary of State's powers in s.25 of the SSA 1998 and reg.53 of the Decisions and Appeals Regulations 2013. For claimants who now wish to challenge past decisions there are the hurdles of being in time for a valid challenge and of decisions made before *Johnson* not having arisen for "official error" because the error was only revealed by the Court of Appeal's decision. They may, though, wish to try the discrimination argument on which the court expressed no opinion to argue for invalidity of the regulations in so far as they have the outcome found irrational by the Court of Appeal.

But note again the suggestion made above that the problems for those paid on the last day of the month or on a fixed day of the month could be obviated by employers properly following HMRC instructions, where payment is made earlier because the contractual or usual pay day is a non-banking day, to report payment as made on the contractual or usual day. Then, if an employer fails to follow that instruction and reports the actual payment date, which circumstance is drawn to the DWP's attention, it is suggested that payment can be treated as made in another assessment period because the information received from HMRC is incorrect in a material respect (reg.61(3)(b)(ii), (4) and (5)(a)).

Very similar problems can arise for claimants who are paid four-weekly, bi-weekly or weekly, regardless of whether the normal pay day is a non-banking day or not. For instance, the pattern of four-weekly payment, being out of sync with the pattern of monthly assessment periods, will inevitably sometimes lead to two payments being counted in one assessment period and sometimes none. The Secretary of State appears to have taken the view, based in particular on Underhill LJ's statements in *Johnson* and Rose LJ's acceptance at para.47 that in the great majority of circumstances the use of actual receipts was sensible and right, that the decision meant that the effect of the regulations could not be found irrational for any pay patterns other than monthly and that to do so would reintroduce the uncertainty for which the Court of Appeal had criticised the Divisional Court's approach. That seems to have been the central submission to the Administrative Court in *R. (Pantellerisco) v Secretary of State for Work and Pensions* [2020] EWHC 1944 (Admin), a case of four-weekly earnings, decided shortly after *Johnson* with the parties given the opportunity of comment on that decision and the direction given. Garnham J rightly rejected that submission. The only reasonable inference that could be drawn from the Court of Appeal's necessary restriction of its reasoning to the facts and evidence before it and from its observations that its conclusions did not undermine the whole structure of universal credit, or even the general structure of earnings calculation, is that there was no intention to exclude the possible application of a similar logic to other specific categories of case.

The context of *Pantellerisco* was the earnings exemption from the benefit cap under reg.82(1) (see further in the notes to reg.82) where a claimant's earnings in an assessment period equal or exceed the amount of the national minimum wage per hour times 16, converted to a monthly figure. The claimant was employed for 16 hours a week at the national minimum wage and was paid four-weekly. Because in 11 assessment periods out of 12 only one four-weekly payment was received and the monthly conversion then came out below the crucial level she had the benefit cap applied to her in those 11 assessment periods. If she had been paid at the same rate on a monthly basis, she would not have had the benefit cap applied at all and would have received perhaps £400 per month more. The judge carefully went through the same factors as identified in *Johnson* and came to the same conclusion that, the outcome of the balance being obvious and irresistible, no reasonable Secretary of

State could have struck the balance in the way done in the regulations. Indeed, he continued in para.87:

"[I]t can fairly be said that the logic applies with even greater force. First, four-weekly payments are genuinely and consistently regular; they do not incorporate the inevitable, if occasional, irregularity that comes with monthly payments as described by the Court of Appeal. Second, in monthly payment cases the difficulty arises in a few months each year; with lunar monthly cases such as the First Claimant's it arises in 11 months out of 12. In those circumstances, it seems to me that the case for the Regulations making an exception for such claimants is even stronger than it was in *Johnson*. The one substantial ground on which a Secretary of State might reasonably decline to make such an exception is if the availability of data by RTI threatened the integrity of the automated processing of claims. And such evidence as there is points in the opposite direction on that issue."

Accordingly, and in line with what was done in *Johnson*, it was declared that:

"the calculation required by regulation 82(1)(a) read together with regulation 54 of the Universal Credit Regulations 2013 is irrational and unlawful in so far as employees who are paid on a four weekly basis (as opposed to a calendar monthly basis) are treated as having earned income of only 28 days' earnings in 11 out of 12 assessment periods a year."

It is suggested that that formulation entails the same unanswered questions as that in *Johnson* (above).

An assessment period is normally a period of one month beginning with the first day of entitlement to universal credit and each subsequent month while entitlement continues (see reg.21(1)). See regs 57-59 below (with the addition of the new reg.54A on surplus earnings and reg.57A on unused losses, plus reg.62 on the minimum income floor) for the provisions on the calculation of self-employed earnings, including some inroads into the focus on actual receipts and expenditure in a particular assessment period. See regs.54A-56 and 61 for the provisions on the calculation of employed earnings involving slightly fewer inroads. The notes to reg.55 discuss the question of identifying the amount to be regarded as received. See the discussion of *SSWP v RW (rule 17) (UC)* [2017] UKUT 347 (AAC) and of *Johnson* in the notes to reg.61 below for circumstances in which the rules in that provision for taking account of real time information reported by an employer to HMRC and received by the Secretary of State in a particular assessment period must give way to the ordinary rule in reg.54 depending on date of receipt by the claimant.

Also see the notes to reg.61 for discussion of whether any alterations of existing awards resulting from increases or reductions in the amount of earned income are appealable.

[¹Surplus earnings

2.165

54A.—(1) This regulation applies in relation to a claim for universal credit where—
  (a) the claimant, or either of joint claimants, had an award of universal credit (the "old award") that terminated within the 6 months ending on the first day in respect of which the claim is made;
  (b) the claimant has not, or neither of joint claimants has, been entitled to universal credit since the old award terminated; and
  (c) the total earned income in the month that would have been the final assessment period for the old award, had it not terminated, exceeded the relevant threshold.

(2) Where this regulation applies in relation to a claim, any surplus earnings determined in accordance with paragraph (3) are to be treated as earned income for the purposes of determining whether there is entitlement to a new award and, if there is entitlement, calculating the amount of the award.

(3) Surplus earnings are—

(a) if the claim in question is the first since the termination of the old award, the amount of the excess referred to in paragraph (1)(c) ("the original surplus");

(b) if the claim in question is the second since the termination of the old award, the amount, if any, by which—

    (i) the original surplus, plus

    (ii) the total earned income in the month that would have been the first assessment period in relation to the first claim,

exceeded the relevant threshold ("the adjusted surplus");

(c) if the claim in question is the third since the termination of the old award, the amount, if any, by which—

    (i) the adjusted surplus from the second claim, plus

    (ii) the total earned income in the month that would have been the first assessment period in relation to the second claim,

exceeded the relevant threshold;

(d) if the claim in question is the fourth or fifth since the termination of the old award, an amount calculated in the same manner as for the third claim (that is by taking the adjusted surplus from the previous claim).

(4) For the purposes of paragraph (3)—

(a) if the claim in question is the first joint claim by members of a couple, each of whom had an old award (because each was previously entitled to universal credit as a single person or as a member of a different couple), the amounts of any surplus earnings from the old award or from a previous claim that would have been treated as earned income if they had each claimed as a single person are to be aggregated; and

(b) if the claim in question is—

    (i) a single claim where the claimant had an old award, or made a subsequent claim, as a joint claimant, or

    (ii) a joint claim where either claimant had an old award, or made a subsequent claim, as a member of a different couple,

the original surplus, or any adjusted surplus, in relation to the old award is to be apportioned in the manner determined by the Secretary of State.

(5) No amount of surplus earnings is to be taken into account in respect of a claimant who has, or had at the time the old award terminated, recently been a victim of domestic violence (within the meaning given by regulation 98).

(6) In this regulation—

"total earned income" is the earned income of the claimant or, if the claimant is a member of a couple, the couple's combined earned income, but does not include any amount a claimant would be treated as having by virtue of regulation 62 (the minimum income floor);

"the nil UC threshold" is the amount of total earned income above which there would be no entitlement to universal credit, expressed by the following formula—

$$\frac{(M - U)}{[^{3}63]} \times 100 + WA$$

where—

M is the maximum amount of an award of universal credit;

U is unearned income;

WA is the work allowance; and

"the relevant threshold" is the nil UC threshold plus £300 [²£2,500].]

AMENDMENTS

1. Universal Credit (Surpluses and Self-employed Losses) (Digital Service) Amendment Regulations 2015 (SI 2015/345) reg.2(2), as amended by Universal Credit (Miscellaneous Amendments, Saving and Transitional Provision) Regulations 2018 (SI 2018/65) reg.7(3) (April 11, 2018).

2. Universal Credit (Surpluses and Self-employed Losses) (Digital Service) Amendment Regulations 2015 (SI 2015/345) reg.5, as inserted by Universal Credit (Miscellaneous Amendments, Saving and Transitional Provision) Regulations 2018 (SI 2018/65) reg.7(6) (modification effective from April 11, 2018 to March 31, 2019 as extended by the Secretary of State to March 31, 2021).

3. Universal Credit (Reduction of the Earnings Taper Rate) Amendment Regulations 2017 (SI 2017/348) reg.2(3) (April 11, 2018).

DEFINITIONS

"assessment period"—see WRA 2012 ss.40 and 7(2) and reg.21.

"claim"—see WRA 2012 s.40.

"claimant"—*ibid.*

"couple"—see WRA 2012 ss.40 and 39.

"earned income"—see reg.52.

"joint claimants"—see WRA 2012 s.40.

"maximum amount of an award of universal credit"—see WRA s.8(2).

"unearned income"—see regs 2 and 65 - 74.

"victim of domestic violence"—see WRA 2012 s.24(6)(b).

"work allowance"—see reg.22.

GENERAL NOTE

The general purpose of reg.54A is described as follows in the Explanatory **2.166** Memorandum attached to SI 2018/65:

"7.7   This instrument makes a number of changes to the Universal Credit (Surpluses and Self-employed Losses) (Digital Service) Amendment Regulations 2015 which make provision to smooth the peaks and troughs of losses and earnings so that a fairer assessment as to Universal Credit entitlement is made over a period of time, longer than one month. This has, however, proved difficult to operate and simplification is required.

7.8   The current provision provides that the carrying forward of surplus earnings will apply to both employed and self-employed claimants. Where there is an increase in earnings that means Universal Credit is lost, the amount of that increase over the "relevant threshold" (which includes a de minimis of £300, but see below) will be taken into account and applied to future Universal Credit awards, for a maximum of 6 assessment periods. This ensures that those with fluctuating earning patterns are not unduly penalised or unfairly rewarded by receiving less or more Universal Credit than they would if they earned the same amount but were paid monthly. It also reduces the risk of claimants manipulating payment patterns to receive bigger payments of Universal Credit.

7.9   This instrument will also change the way that surplus earnings are applied when people reclaim Universal Credit within 6 months. Instead of taking account of earnings over the whole period of Universal Credit, only the earnings in the month where people make a claim will be counted. Where couples separate there will be more scope for flexibility in the way the surplus is apportioned. These changes will also increase the de minimis from £300 to £2500 for one year (which may be extended by the Secretary of State). This will assist the smooth implementation by the reducing the numbers affected in the early stages."

It seems odd to refer to sums like £2,500 or £300 as "de minimis" and that term is not used in the regulation itself. It could more accurately be described as an effective disregard of those amounts in determining whether the claimant has surplus earnings in any months. The initial use of the sum of £2,500 has restricted the effect of the regulation in the first three years from April 2018 (see the extensions noted below, with the possibility of further extensions) to fairly extreme upward variations in earned income and exclude the more routine fluctuations that might be covered by the unmodified form. Potential problems may therefore be to some extent masked during this period, although on the other hand there may also be the opportunity for further amendment before the provision begins to bite more routinely. The modification of the definition of "relevant threshold" in para.(6) and the identification of the "temporary de minimis period" for which it has effect is to be found in reg.5 of the Universal Credit (Surpluses and Self-employed Losses) (Digital Service) Amendment Regulations 2015 (SI 2015/345), as set out at the end of this Part of Vol.V. That provision first applied the modification to £2,500 for one year down to March 31, 2019, but on February 5, 2019 it was announced that the Secretary of State had made a determination to extend the period to March 31, 2020, as allowed by reg.5(2). There was a further extension of a year announced on March 5, 2020. The extensions are collected in the DWP's Guidance on regulations under the Welfare Reform Act 2012 on gov.uk.

The Social Security Advisory Committee (SSAC) expressed a number of serious misgivings about the proposals as amended by SI 2018/65 (set out in the letter of January 19, 2018 from the Chairman to the Secretary of State in their Report of January 2018 and response by the Secretary of State). They will be mentioned at appropriate points below.

Regulation 54A appears to be validly made in terms of the powers in para.4(1) and (3)(a) of Sch.1 to the WRA 2012 in the light of the decision of the Court of Appeal in *Owen v Chief Adjudication Officer*, April 29, 1999, dismissing an argument that shifting income from the period in which it was received to a different period was neither "calculation" nor "estimation" (see the notes to reg.35(2) of the Income Support Regulations in Vol.II of this series). But see the note to para.(2) below for an argument on irrationality. The provision applies only in digital service (full service) cases (see the saving provision in reg.4(1) of SI 2015/345).

See the notes to reg.61 for discussion of whether any alterations of existing awards resulting from increases or reductions in the amount of earned income to be taken into account are appealable.

Regulation 54A entails the attribution of surplus earnings to assessment periods subsequent to the period in which the amount over the threshold was received. Since, by definition that receipt will have precluded entitlement in that period on income grounds, there is no need to enquire about the immediate effect on the claimant's capital. However, in relation to subsequent assessment periods for which a claim is made or treated as made, there is a question whether any funds actually still possessed by the claimant constitute capital if surplus earnings are to be treated under reg.54A as existing in that period (for instance through the receipt of a grant from the Coronavirus Self-Employed Income Support Scheme (SEISS)). On general principle (see *R(IS) 3/93* and *R(IS) 9/08*) income, and in particular earnings, does not metamorphose into capital until after the end of the period to which it is attributed under the relevant legislation. Although matters are not so clear in universal credit as in income support and similar benefits, that principle would seem to hold because of the irrationality of treating the same amount as both income and capital at the same time.

The principle could arguably extend to assessment periods in which surplus earnings are treated as possessed, so that any actual funds retained from the initial receipt are treated as earnings and not capital to the extent of the amount of surplus earnings taken into account in the period in question. Another way of looking at the situation might be to invoke the further principle in *R(SB) 2/83* that income does not metamorphose into capital until relevant liabilities, including tax liabilities, have been deducted. It could be argued that the operation of the surplus earnings rule on later claims is a relevant liability that should therefore lead to a corresponding reduction in the amount of capital to be taken into account. In income support and similar benefits the metamorphosis principle cannot apply to self-employed earnings, because of the method of calculating such earnings *(CIS/2467/2003)*. However, since for universal credit both self-employed and employed earnings are calculated by reference to receipts and expenditure in particular assessment periods, the metamorphosis principle can be applied just as much to one as the other. One difference, though, is that in so far as the self-employed have capital in the form of sums deriving from payments that have caused surplus earnings, the disregards of business assets in paras 7 and 8 of Sch.10 can apply. And note that with effect from May 21, 2020 there is a disregard as capital (for 12 months from the date of receipt) for the self-employed of any payment in respect of a furloughed employee under the Coronavirus Job Retention Scheme or "by way of a grant or loan to meet the expenses or losses of the trade, profession or vocation in relation to the outbreak of coronavirus disease" (Universal Credit (Coronavirus) (Self-employed Claimants and Reclaims) (Amendment) Regulations 2020 (SI 2020/522) reg.2(2)).

Paragraph (1) sets out the basic conditions for the application of the regulation, which are subject to the exclusion in para.(5) of claimants who have recently been the victims of domestic violence. Paragraph (2) sets out the rule as to treating surplus earnings in one assessment period as earned income in certain later assessment periods. Paragraph (3) says what surplus earnings are and how they may be reduced or extinguished. Paragraph (4) deals with circumstances where surplus earnings were received when a couple had a joint claim, but later claim as single or as part of a different couple. Paragraph (6) supplies important definitions.

Paragraph (1)

The issue of surplus earnings arises on a claim for universal credit when the claimant or either of joint claimants had previously had an award of universal credit ("the old award") that had terminated within the six months before the first day of the period claimed for (sub-para.(a)). It does not matter by what method the award terminated, by virtue of a decision of the Secretary of State on revision or supersession or by the claimant withdrawing the claim. But the six months establishes the outer limit of how far back surplus earnings can be relevant on a new claim. The claimant or either joint claimant must not have been entitled to universal credit since that termination (remembering that there can be entitlement while nothing is payable) (sub-para.(b)). Then the final condition is that in the month that would have been the final assessment period for the old award if it had not terminated, total earned income in that month exceeded the "relevant threshold" (sub-para.(c)). It is that excess that is the starting point for calculating surplus earnings under para.(3). The relevant threshold is defined by way of a complicated formula in para.(6). The starting point is basically the amount of earned income that, after taking account of any unearned income (which counts in full), the appropriate work allowance, if any, and the 63% taper applied to earned income, would lead to there being no entitlement to universal credit. That is the "nil UC threshold". In the simple case of a single claimant of 25 and over with no work allowance and no unearned income, that threshold would be £650.60 (the amount of which the standard allowance as specially increased for the year from April 2020 of £409.89 is 63%). Then the amount of £2,500 (currently, to revert to £300 after March 31, 2021 unless the substitution is further extended) is added to make the "relevant threshold".

Paragraph (1) thus applies to any form of earned income (defined in reg.52):

2.167

employed earnings; self-employed earnings; and remuneration from any other paid work (whatever that means), as well as notional earned income. The latter category will cover amounts treated as possessed under regs 60 and 77(3), but any amount the claimant is treated as possessing under reg.62 (minimum income floor) is expressly excluded from the definition of "total earned income" in para.(6). The existence of surplus earnings need not have been the reason for the termination of the old award. That could have been, for instance, failing to accept a new claimant commitment or the withdrawal of the claim by the claimant. All that is necessary under sub-para.(c) is that in what would have been the final assessment period of the old award there were surplus earnings. Thus, claimants cannot avoid the operation of reg.54A by, once they know that the earned income received or to be received in a current assessment period will exceed the relevant threshold, quickly withdrawing their claim for that assessment period. That assessment period would seem still to be caught by sub-para.(c). The use of the words "final ... had it not terminated" is not problem-free. They cannot mean that the termination is to be ignored completely, because then the award might have continued into the future and it cannot be said what might have been the final assessment period. To make any sense, the words must be taken as referring to the month following the last actual assessment period under the old award, that would have been an assessment period if entitlement had not ceased after the last day of the last actual assessment period. However, that does seem to mean that if a claimant can predict in advance that a particularly large one-off receipt of earnings is to arrive at a particular time it might be worth withdrawing the universal credit claim for the assessment period immediately preceding the period in which the receipt is expected. That period would not then be caught by sub-para.(c) and a new claim for universal credit after the end of that period would not attract any surplus earnings, so that entitlement would be assessed on actual earned income receipts in the new assessment period. However, it would require very careful calculation whether the loss of two months' universal credit would outweigh the benefit of future freedom from the surplus earnings rule.

Paragraph (2)

2.168   Paragraph (2) provides that, where the conditions in para.(1) are met, surplus earnings as worked out under para.(3) are to be treated as earned income in determining entitlement under the new claim and calculating the amount of any award. Paragraph (3) deals with the consequences on the erosion of the amount of surplus earnings where the taking into account of the surplus earnings results in there not being entitlement on the first claim after the termination of the old claim and so on for further unsuccessful claims (see below for the details).

This process marks the clearest difference from the original 2015 form of the amending regulations, which spread the surplus earnings and thus their erosion over the six months following the assessment period in which the surplus earnings were received, regardless of whether a claim for universal credit was made in those months or not. The rule that the amount of surplus earnings will only be eroded, before the expiry of the six-month limit, for any month in which a claim is made, was one of the main causes of disquiet in the SSAC.

However, para.(3) says nothing about the consequences if the taking into account of surplus earnings on that first or a subsequent claim results in an award of universal credit, but of a lower amount than would have been calculated if they were not taken into account. That works in relation to the first assessment period under the new claim and award, but there is nothing in reg.54A to prevent the same amount of surplus earnings being taken into account for future assessment periods within the same period of entitlement under the award. Paragraph (2) is expressly in terms of an award and the amount of the award, not a particular assessment period. Paragraph (3) only provides for the erosion of the surplus earnings on a new or subsequent *claim*. Once a claim has been successful and an award has been made there can be no further claim during the period of entitlement and no scope for the mechanism of para.(3) to apply. Nor could even the six-month limit apply to stop that continuing effect, because under para.(1)(a) that applies by reference to the first day of the period for which the new claim is made, not each successive assessment period. The result on the face of it is that in such circumstances the claimant is fixed for ever (or at least within the same continuing period of entitlement) with the remaining amount of surplus earnings taken into account in the first assessment period under the new award. Indeed, that seemed to be the assumption in some of the examples given in Memo ADM 11/18 (although several of the original examples contained misleading or incomplete calculations). The examples now given in para.H3311 of the ADM and in Appendix 2 to chap.H3 include claimants who start off with a level of entitlement based on regular earnings and end up after the para.(3) process with a lower level of entitlement when an award is eventually made and the advice says that "surplus earnings have been eroded and no longer apply". But there is no explanation of how in the terms of reg.54A the surplus earnings that have been taken into account in the first assessment period under the new award cease to be taken into account in subsequent assessment periods.

It may well have been thought that para.(1)(b) (claimant has not been entitled to universal credit since the old award terminated) has the effect of preventing the attribution of surplus earnings beyond the first assessment period of some entitlement to universal credit. However, that does not work, because para.(1) contains the conditions for application of the surplus earnings rule in relation to a *claim*, not to an award. In the circumstances described above (and worked through in the example in the notes to para.(3) below), once some entitlement has been awarded for one assessment period there can be no new claim for the following assessment period. The award made for the first assessment period of entitlement continues into the next and subsequent assessment periods on the basis of the claim made for the first assessment period of entitlement. In relation to that claim, the condition in para. (1)(b) was satisfied because *at the date of that claim* the claimant will not have been entitled to universal credit since the old award terminated. It might in some circumstances be possible, in order to produce an equitable result, to interpret the word "claim" as extending to an award and a continuing award. However, that does not seem possible in the context of reg.54A, which so carefully distinguishes between claims and awards throughout.

That result is so obviously unfair, both in fixing claimants with deemed earnings that total more than the surplus earnings involved and in treating different claimants differently by the pure chance of the amount of surplus earnings, large or small, that is left at the end of the last para.(3) calculation that allows an award to be made (see the end of the example worked through in the note to para.(3) below), that it cannot be allowed to stand. However, it is difficult, if not impossible, to identify a technical means of interpretation by which the result can be avoided. Is the unfairness so intractable that the amending provisions can be regarded as irrational and ultra vires on that ground?

This problem would not have arisen on the original 2015 form of the amending regulations, where the erosion of surplus earnings would simply have followed month by month until eroded completely or six months was reached.

Paragraph (3)

Once an old award has terminated when there is an excess of total earned income over the relevant threshold, as identified in para.(1)(c), that "original surplus" (see para.(3)(a)) sits there waiting potentially to come into play once a new claim is made. But the amount of the original surplus remains the same if no claim is made until the six months in para.(1)(a) expires. The only way in the terms of reg.54A that the amount of the original surplus can reduce is by the making of new claims. That may involve a claimant in making multiple new claims that will be bound not to lead to entitlement in order to reduce the amount of surplus earnings to a level that will allow satisfaction of the financial condition in s.5(1)(b) or 5(2)(b) of the WRA 2012.

2.169

Regulation 3 of the Universal Credit (Coronavirus) (Self-employed Claimants and Reclaims) (Amendment) Regulations 2020 (SI 2020/522) introduces with effect from May 21, 2020 a new reg.32A of the Claims and Payments Regulations 2013 allowing the Secretary of State, subject to any appropriate conditions, to treat a claimant as making a new universal credit claim on the first day of each of five subsequent potential assessment periods after non-entitlement because income is too high. That provision is quite general (as expressed in the guidance in Memo ADM 10/20), but the primary intention expressed in para.7.10 of the Explanatory Memorandum to the Regulations is to use the power where it is earnings received by a furloughed employee supported through the Coronavirus Job Retention Scheme or a grant from the Self-Employed Income Support Scheme (SEISS) that prevents the claimant from satisfying the financial conditions in s.5 of the WRA 2012. That is said to be to make it easier to bring claimants back into universal credit entitlement if actual earnings reduce in those subsequent periods and the surplus earnings are exhausted. There can be circumstances in which a claimant is, depending on the pattern of actual earnings and household circumstances, better off by not making a new universal credit claim for a particular period. It is not clear how the administrative arrangements for deemed claims in cases affected by coronavirus schemes might be able to take that into account or whether claimants might be able to assert that they should not be treated as making a claim. The problem of surplus earnings in this context is most likely to arise for actual (or deemed under reg.77) self-employed claimants.

One of the most serious misgivings of the SSAC was whether claimants would sufficiently understand the need to make multiple unsuccessful claims so as to take the most beneficial action, especially as there are some circumstances (e.g. where a claimant's earnings do not immediately return to the regular level after a peak assessment period, but continue at a higher than regular, but not as high as the peak, level) when it will be more beneficial not to make new claims. As it was put in the chairman's letter of January 19, 2018:

"One of our main concerns about these proposals is the assumption that claimants will have a detailed understanding of this complex policy, when in reality it seems likely most will not. Many may be disadvantaged simply due to that lack of detailed understanding of the complex rules underpinning this policy.

For example, the only way that claimants can successfully erode surplus earnings that have taken them off Universal Credit is to make repeated monthly claims. But these are destined to fail until the surplus is eroded and entitlement resumes. Requiring claims to be made where it is known that they will be unsuccessful is, at best, counterintuitive and risks damaging the credibility of both this policy and Universal Credit more widely.

...

There is also an assumption that it will be obvious to claimants making a repeat claim whether or not their circumstances have changed in a way that is likely to affect their Universal Credit entitlement. This may be the case where the only change is an increase or decrease in the claimant's earnings. But some changes of circumstances have less predictable outcomes, and multiple changes within a single assessment period are likely to create uncertainty. This might arise, for example, in situations where both members of a couple are in some form of paid work, one member's earnings can go up whilst the other member's goes down, or there may be changes in the household composition."

The Secretary of State's response to that concern was this:

"The re-claim process in Universal Credit is a simplified one, intentionally designed as a simple and swift process for claimants. For claimants whose only change is the level of earnings, the average time to complete a re-claim could be just eight minutes. The need for affected claimants to re-claim each month does not differ significantly from the current situation. Currently, where the level of earnings causes the UC entitlement to reduce to NIL and the claim to close, claimants need to re-claim if there is a change to their circumstances or level of earnings.

This is also the case with surplus earnings, the claimant has the same need to re-claim as there are no re-awards in Full Service. Notification from DWP on claim closure would advise the claimant of the need to re-claim if their circumstances change.

In addition, the Department will ensure that messaging and guidance, both for those claimants impacted by surplus earnings and for work coaches helping claimants, reinforces this message so that the claimant's responsibilities are clear and they are kept well-informed."

That response, apart from the objectionable nature of much of the terminology (e.g. "claim closure" etc), might be thought almost wilfully to ignore the difference between realising the need to make a claim when the circumstances suggest that entitlement is a real possibility and realising a need when the circumstances point against such a possibility. There was also no answer to the point that had been raised by the SSAC, about circumstances in which claiming would not be beneficial. Overall it is very hard to have any confidence in the ability of the information given at the time of the termination of the old award or in assistance to be given by work coaches to guide claimants through the labyrinth when the experienced experts drafting the DWP's advice to decision-makers could not get even simple examples of the operation of the rules right. And will claimants whose earnings have returned to what they regard as normal appreciate that there has been a change of circumstances?

The technical operation of para.(3) is this. On the first claim (within six months) since the termination of the old award the amount of the original surplus (paras (1) (c) and (3)(a)) is simply added into the calculation for the first assessment period under the claim along with the actual earned and unearned income in that period. If that, after applying the 63% taper to the earned income, leaves the claimant's income below the appropriate maximum amount of universal credit there is entitlement at that reduced level for that assessment period, with the uncertain consequences for future assessment periods under the award as discussed in the note to para.(2) above. If that leaves the claimant's income above the maximum amount there is no entitlement for the month that would have been an assessment period if there had been entitlement. On the next (second) claim, which cannot be made for any period starting earlier than the month for which no entitlement has been determined, surplus earnings will have to be considered under para.(3)(b). For that purpose one has to consider how far in the calculation on the first claim the original surplus plus any actual earned income in that month exceeded the relevant threshold. If there is no excess (i.e. the sum exactly equalled the relevant amount in the previous month), there are no longer any surplus earnings to be carried forward to the second claim. If there is an excess, that is the "adjusted surplus" to be taken into account in determining the second claim. The process then continues under sub-paras (c) and (d), but on these claims taking forward the adjusted surplus from the previous period rather than the original surplus, until there is no longer a surplus to be carried forward or entitlement arises or the six months expires.

That is all fairly impenetrable as an abstract explanation. Trying to work through an example may help the explanation (with caution in view of the criticisms above of the initial official guidance).

Imagine a single universal credit claimant with no children who is also a contributor to an annual book of social security legislation and has no other source of income. The claimant is paid an annual fee of £10,000 on September 10, 2019, in the middle of the assessment period running from September 1 to September 30, and no income tax or national insurance contribution is paid in that period. Entitlement will therefore terminate after the end of the previous assessment period as 63% of the self-employed earnings exceeds the maximum amount of universal credit at that date (£317.82 standard allowance with no work allowance).

On the immediate claim for the period from October 1, 2019, in which there will be no actual earned income, surplus earnings from the previous month must be considered under para.(3)(a). The nil UC threshold is £504.82 (the amount of which £317.82 is 63%) and the relevant threshold is £3,004.48 (£504.82 + £2,500). The claimant's earned income of £10,000 exceeds that relevant threshold, so the excess (£6,995.52) is surplus earnings (the original surplus) to be taken into account on this first new claim. The result is that there is no entitlement, as 63% of that amount (£4,407.18) exceeds the maximum amount of universal credit.

On the second new claim for the period from November 1, 2019, surplus earnings from the previous month must be considered under sub-para.(b). There is no actual earned income. The original surplus is £6,995.52 and the relevant threshold is £3,004.48, so that the excess is £3,991.04. That again is clearly enough to prevent entitlement after the 63% taper. But £3,991.04 then becomes the adjusted surplus to be carried forward to the next claim.

On the third new claim for the period from December 1, 2019, surplus earnings must be considered under sub-para.(c). The adjusted surplus of £3,991.04 from the previous month still exceeds the relevant threshold of £3,004.48, so that the excess of £986.56 is to be taken into account as surplus earnings. The amount after the 63% taper (£621.53) exceeds the maximum amount of universal credit, so there is no entitlement. But £986.56 becomes the adjusted surplus to be carried forward to the next claim.

On the fourth new claim for the period from January 1, 2020, surplus earnings must be considered under sub-para.(d). The adjusted surplus of £986.56 from the previous month does not exceed the relevant threshold of £3,004.48, so that no surplus earnings can be taken into account and the claimant becomes entitled to universal credit of the maximum amount.

If the fee had been £9,000 the claimant would have become entitled to the maximum amount on the third new claim. If the fee had been £9,500, the claimant would have become entitled to universal credit, but only of a small amount, on the third claim, because the excess of the adjusted surplus from the second claim (£3,491.04) over the relevant threshold would have been £496.56, 63% of which is £312.83, less than the maximum amount of £317.82. So the award would have been only £5.01 for the assessment period beginning on December 1, 2019. There would then be no surplus earnings to carry forward to a new claim, but no new claim would be possible as the claimant already had an award. Common sense and fairness dictate that the claimant in those circumstances should not be treated as having earned income of £496.56 for January 2020 and subsequent months, but as discussed in the notes to para.(2) the plain words of para.(2) seem to require that result.

Remember always that surplus earnings cannot be applied on any *claim* more than six months after the termination of the old award (para.(1)(a)).

Paragraph (4)

2.170   Since the effect of a significant increase in the amount of earned income can under reg.54A affect claims up to six months in the future, claimants may well move in to and out of partnerships with others in that period. Paragraph (4) deals with those circumstances.

Sub-paragraph (a) covers new claims following the termination that are the first joint claim by a couple, both of whom have surplus earnings from an old award or claim when they were either single or members of a different couple that would have been taken into account if they had each claimed as a single person. In those circumstances the surplus earnings that would have counted if they had claimed as single persons are aggregated. That is straightforward if the previous awards or claims were as single persons. If they were as joint claimants, then that seems to bring in the rule in sub-para.(b) about apportionment.

Sub-paragraph (b) covers two alternatives. One is where the relevant claim is as a single person and the claimant had an old award or made a subsequent claim as a joint claimant. The other is where one or other member of a couple (or both) making a joint claim has an old award or made a subsequent claim as a member of a different couple. In both those cases the surplus, original or adjusted, is to be apportioned in the manner determined by the Secretary of State. There is thus a completely open-ended discretion, that of course must be exercised by reference to all the relevant circumstances and the aims of the legislation, as to the share of the surplus to be attributed to the claimant in question, a discretion that on any appeal is to be exercised by the tribunal on its own judgment of the circumstances. However, the guidance in para.H3313 of the ADM is that the proportion between the joint claimants is to be 50% unless there are any exceptional circumstances. Such guidance is inconsistent with the terms of para.(4)(b), under which to adopt any starting point (in effect a default position) that could be differed from only in exceptional circumstances would be placing an unlawful fetter on the discretion given.

The letter of January 19, 2018 from the chairman of the SSAC to the Secretary of State contained the following under the heading "Equality impact":

"The Committee noted that an equality impact had shown that there were no adverse effects on anyone with a protected characteristic. However it is clear that having, by default, a simple 50/50 apportionment of surplus earnings in the event that a couple separate would adversely affect any non-working partner, or the partner earning a lower amount relative to the current situation of allocating the surplus in proportion to the earnings of each individual of a couple. Some of the non-working partners, or partners on lower wages, are likely to have a protected characteristic (for example gender or those with a mental health condition), therefore we were surprised by the Department's assertion. Although, as was made clear to us, the legislation would give discretion for a different apportionment to be applied, the default position would be 50/50 and it would fall to individual claimants to make a request for it to be changed. Some individuals adversely affected might lack the understanding to request a revision of that decision; others may be put under some pressure from their former partner to accept the Department's decision."

The Secretary of State's response was as follows:

"The Department has changed the apportionment rules to provide greater clarity to claimants in understanding how a surplus is recovered. The apportionment rules would only come into force in the event a couple separating at the same time a surplus is outstanding also re-claimed within 6 months of the original surplus being created.

It is reasonable that a couple and their household would equally benefit from household income such as a one off bonus. As such, the surplus should be equally apportioned unless there are grounds that this is unreasonable.

Additionally, the regulations allow for a decision maker acting on behalf of the Secretary of State to consider the reasonableness of an individual's circumstances when looking at a decision on apportionment, allowing discretion to ensure claimants are adequately protected.

[Reference to the recent domestic violence exception to remove any financial disincentive from leaving an abusive relationship]."

Apart from it being laughable to suggest that greater clarity had been provided for claimants, either that response demonstrates a complete misunderstanding of the effect of para.(4)(b) or a change was made in its terms before SI 2018/65 was made. As it is, the guidance in the ADM appears to reflect the view set out in that response rather than the requirements of the legislation.

Paragraph (5)   2.171

This exclusion of the effect of reg.54A for recent victims of domestic violence can operate if the claimant has that status either at the time the old award terminated or at the time of the new claim being considered. Paragraph (5) refers on to reg.98, which contains the very wide definition of "domestic violence", what counts as recent and some conditions about having reported the domestic violence and notified the Secretary of State. Section 24(6)(b) of the WRA 2012 says when a person is to be regarded as a "victim" of domestic violence.

Employed earnings

2.172   **55.**—(1) This regulation applies for the purposes of calculating earned income from employment under a contract of service or in an office, including elective office ("employed earnings").

(2) Employed earnings comprise any amounts that are general earnings, as defined in section 7(3) of ITEPA, but excluding—

   (a) amounts that are treated as earnings under Chapters 2 to 11 of Part 3 of ITEPA (the benefits code); and

   (b) amounts that are exempt from income tax under Part 4 of ITEPA.

(3) In the calculation of employed earnings the following are to be disregarded—

   (a) expenses that are allowed to be deducted under Chapter 2 of Part 5 of ITEPA; and

   (b) expenses arising from participation as a service user (see regulation 53(2)).

(4) The following benefits are to be treated as employed earnings—

   (a) statutory sick pay;

   (b) statutory maternity pay;

   (c) [³ ...] statutory paternity pay;

   (d) [³ ...]

   (e) statutory adoption pay [² ; and]

[² (f) statutory shared parental pay.]

[¹ (4A) A repayment of income tax or national insurance contributions received by a person from HMRC in respect of a tax year in which the person was in paid work is to be treated as employed earnings unless it is taken into account as self-employed earnings under regulation 57(4).]

(5) In calculating the amount of a person's employed earnings in respect of an assessment period, there are to be deducted from the amount of general earnings or benefits specified in paragraphs (2) to (4)—

   (a) any relievable pension contributions made by the person in that period;

   (b) any amounts paid by the person in that period in respect of the employment by way of income tax or primary Class 1 contributions under section 6(1) of the Contributions and Benefits Act; and

   (c) any sums withheld as donations to an approved scheme under Part 12 of ITEPA (payroll giving) by a person required to make deductions or repayments of income tax under the PAYE Regulations.

AMENDMENTS

1. Universal Credit and Miscellaneous Amendments (No.2) Regulations 2014 (SI 2014/2888) reg.4(2) (November 26, 2014, or in the case of existing awards, the first assessment period beginning on or after November 26, 2014).

2. Shared Parental Leave and Statutory Shared Parental Pay (Consequential Amendments to Subordinate Legislation) Order 2014 (SI 2014/3255) art.28(4)(c) and (d) (December 31, 2014).

3. Shared Parental Leave and Statutory Shared Parental Pay (Consequential Amendments to Subordinate Legislation) Order 2014 (SI 2014/3255) art.28(4)(a) and (b) (April 5, 2015). The amendments are subject to the transitional provision in art.35 (see Pt IV of this book).

"Contributions and Benefits Act"—see reg.2.
"earned income"—see reg.52.
"ITEPA"—see reg.2.
"relievable pension contributions" —see reg.53(1).
"PAYE Regulations" —*ibid.*
"statutory adoption pay"—see reg.2.
"statutory maternity pay"—*ibid.*
"statutory shared parental pay"—*ibid.*
"statutory sick pay"—*ibid.*

GENERAL NOTE

This regulation applies to employed earnings (i.e., under a contract of service or   **2.173**
as an office holder) (para.(1)). By reason of the overarching definition of "earned
income" in reg.52, payments must be derived from such employment. See regs
57-59 for the calculation of self-employed earnings.

Unlike income support, old style JSA, old style ESA and housing benefit, what
counts as employed earnings for the purposes of universal credit is defined in
terms of the income tax rules (paras (2) and (3)(a)). However, not all amounts that
HMRC treats as earnings count for universal credit purposes (see para.(2)(a)).
Under para.(2))(a) benefits in kind, for example living accommodation provided by
reason of the employment, are excluded.

The meaning of "general earnings" in s.7(3) of ITEPA (the Income Tax (Earnings
and Pensions) Act 2003), which the beginning of para.(2) makes the starting point
for calculating earned income, is earnings within Chap.1 of Part 3 of ITEPA or
any amount treated as earnings, excluding exempt earnings. Section 62 of ITEPA,
which constitutes Chap.1 of Part 3, provides in subs.(2) that earnings means:

"(a)   any salary, wages or fee;
(b)   any gratuity or other profit or incidental benefit of any kind obtained by
the employee if it is money or money's worth; and
(c)   anything else that constitutes an emolument of the employment."

That meaning is thus very broad, but is immediately narrowed for universal credit
purposes by para.(2)(a) of reg.55 in the exclusion of amounts treated as earnings in
Chaps 2–11 of Part 3 of ITEPA. Those items covers matters like expenses, vouch-
ers, provision of living accommodation, cars, vans and related benefits and loans.
The exclusion by para.(2)(b) of amounts exempt from income tax under Part 4
of ITEPA would have followed in any event under the terms of s.7(3) of ITEPA.
Those exemptions include mileage or transport allowances, travel and subsistence
allowances, benefits for training and learning, recreational benefits etc and some
payments on the termination of employment (see the separate section below).

As a matter of general principle, any payment, whether of an income or capital
nature, can be a profit or emolument within s.62(2) of ITEPA, providing that it is a
reward for past services or an incentive to enter into employment and provide future
services. See *AH v HMRC (TC)* [2019] UKUT 5 (AAC), where Judge Wikeley discusses the relevant income tax case law, and *Minter v Kingston upon Hull CC* and *Potter
v Secretary of State for Work and Pensions* [2011] EWCA Civ 1155; [2012] AACR 21,
where Thomas LJ in para.29 emphasised the width of the phrase "any remuneration
or profit derived from employment" in reg.35(1) of the Income Support Regulations,
such that the essential issue was whether any payment was made in consideration of
the employee's services, so as to be derived from the employment, whether it was on
general principle to be regarded as capital or income.

There have been amendments to s.7 of ITEPA with effect from April 6, 2018, by
virtue of the Finance (No.2) Act 2017, that in particular affect what sorts of payments on termination of employment fall within the meaning of "general earnings".
See the separate section below.

It is difficult to say how the principle adopted in *R(TC) 2/03* (a case on the meaning of "earnings" in reg.19(1) of the Family Credit Regulations) might apply to the identification of the "amount" that is to be taken into account under reg.55, and regarded as "received" under reg.54. In *R(TC) 2/03* the claimant's partner's employer made deductions from his current salary in order to recover an earlier overpayment of salary. His payslips showed the "gross for tax" figure as £76 less than his usual salary. The Commissioner held that his gross salary for the relevant months was the reduced figure, most probably on the basis that there had been a consensual variation of the contract of employment, so that the lower figure was the remuneration or profit derived from employment in the relevant months. In *MH v SSWP and Rotherham MBC (HB)* [2017] UKUT 401 (AAC) Judge Wikeley adopted and applied the analysis in *R(TC) 2/03*. The claimant received a redundancy payment of nearly £15,000 in March 2016, which was used to pay off debts and make home improvements. In May 2016 he was offered his old job back on condition that he repaid the employer the amount of the redundancy payment by monthly deductions from salary within the 2016/17 tax year. The claimant accepted those terms. On his monthly payslips his basic salary was stated as £2,719.04 before overtime with deductions including income tax and national insurance and the sum of £1,222,22 described as "BS loan". On his claim for housing benefit the local authority (and the First-tier Tribunal) decided that under the equivalent of regs 35 and 36 of the Income Support Regulations the gross earnings had to be taken into account and there was nothing to allow the deduction or disregard of the £1,222.22 repayment. The judge held that the proper analysis was that the claimant's contract of employment had been varied by agreement so that he was only entitled to receive a salary reduced by the amount of the repayment and that that amount was his gross earnings. In fact, the case appears stronger than that of *R(TC) 2/03* because the initial terms on which the claimant was re-engaged incorporated the repayments of the redundancy payment.

It is not clear in *MH* what amount was regarded as subject to PAYE income tax. If it was the reduced figure, as in *R(TC) 2/03*, then that would appear to be the amount to taken into account under reg.55 and regarded as received under reg.54. The receipt would presumably also be reflected in the real time information provided by HMRC to the DWP under reg.61. If the employer had regarded the higher figure as subject to PAYE income tax then it seems arguable that the amount to be treated as remuneration or profit derived from the employment (reg.52) and received under reg.54 is the lower figure. If the real time information reflected the higher figure, then it would have to be argued that reg.61(2) did not apply because the information was incorrect or failed to reflect the definition in reg.55 in some material respect (reg.61(3)(b)(ii)).

Under para.(3)(a) expenses that are deductible under ITEPA, Pt 5, Ch.2, are disregarded in calculating employed earnings—this includes, for example, expenses that are "wholly, exclusively and necessarily" incurred in the course of the claimant's employment (see s.336(1) of ITEPA). In addition, expenses from participation as a service user (defined in reg.53(2)) are ignored (para.(3)(b)), although payments for attendance at meetings, etc., will count as earnings.

Note that employed earnings are to be treated as also including statutory sick pay, statutory maternity pay, statutory paternity pay, statutory adoption pay and statutory shared parental pay (para.(4)).

Paragraph (4A), inserted with effect from November 26, 2014, treats a repayment of income tax or NI contributions in respect of a tax year in which the person was in paid work as employed earnings, unless it is taken into account as self-employed earnings. According to DWP (see Memo ADM 24/14), this will include repayments of income tax that relate to other sources, such as unearned income, as long as the claimant was in paid work in the tax year to which the repayment relates. Memo ADM 24/14 gives as an example a case in which a claimant receives a cheque for £200 from HMRC, which relates to an overpayment of £600 income tax in the tax year 2011/12 in which the claimant was in paid work and an underpayment of £400 in the following year. The amount that counts as employed earnings is £200, which is the repayment that the claimant received.

In calculating a person's employed earnings in an assessment period the following are deducted: any income tax and Class 1 contributions paid in that assessment period, together with any contributions to a registered pension scheme and any charity payments under a payroll giving scheme made in that period (para.(5)). Since the definition of "relievable pension contributions" in reg.53(1) is by reference only to s.188 of the Finance Act 2004 it is arguable that the annual and lifetime limits imposed in other sections of that Act are not incorporated for universal credit purposes.

Information on a person's employed earnings and deductions made will normally be taken from what is recorded on PAYE records. See further the note to reg.61.

Earnings on cessation of employment

There are no special provisions for the treatment of final earnings under universal credit. A claimant's final earnings will be taken into account in the assessment period in which they are paid under the general rule in reg.54(1), subject to the operation of reg.61 on real time information. See in particular *PT v SSWP (UC)* [2015] UKUT 696 (AAC), discussed in the notes to reg.54 and *SSWO v RW (rule 17) (UC)* [2017] UKUT 347 (AAC), discussed in the notes to reg.61. In *Secretary of State for Work and Pensions v Johnson* [2020] EWCA Civ 778 the Court of Appeal rejected the approach of the Divisional Court below to the interpretation of regs 54 and 61 and its reliance on the phrase "in respect of" in those provisions to introduce other factors than date of receipt into the identification of the assessment period to which a payment is attributed. In para.41 Rose LJ says that the phrase usually means nothing different from "for" or "in". That seems to have put paid to any argument that, say, final payments of earnings should be attributed to the relevant period of employment rather than to the assessment period in which the payment is received.

Termination payments (e.g., contractual payments in lieu of notice and holiday pay) are "general earnings" under ss.7(3)(a) and 62 of ITEPA (see HMRC, *Employment Income Manual*, para.12850) and so will be taken into account for the purposes of universal credit. The dividing line in principle between payments that are general earnings and payments that fall within s.401 of ITEPA as made in connection with the termination of employment, and so not within s.62, is this. If the payment (including a part of a payment) is in satisfaction of a right to remuneration under the contract of employment it falls within s.62. If it is compensation for a breach of the contract of employment it falls within s.401. So, employment tribunal awards for unfair dismissal, damages for breach of contract and redundancy payments (statutory and contractual) will not count as they are only taxable under s.401 of ITEPA and so do not come within s.7(3) (see *Employment Income Manual*, paras 12960, 12970, 12978, 13005 and 13750). For other employment tribunal awards which do count as earnings see para.02550 of the *Employment Income Manual*.

There have been amendments to s.7 of ITEPA and new ss.402A–402E added by the Finance (No.2) Act 2017, that apply to certain payments made on or after April 6, 2018 on the termination of employment that would otherwise fall within s.401. To be a "relevant" termination award the payment must not be a redundancy payment (statutory or contractual). Then so much of the payment as counts as post-employment notice pay (PENP) is taxable as general earnings. PENP is in essence the amount of basic pay to which the employee would have been entitled after the date of termination of the contract if full statutory notice had been given, less the amount of any contractual payment in lieu of notice that was made. That appears to mean that if an employer makes some sort of global payment on termination, without it being broken down into particular elements, the PENP is to be taken into account as employed earnings for universal credit purposes.

The policy and legislative background to the amendments has been comprehensively described in House of Commons Library Briefing Paper No.8084 (May 8, 2018), *Taxation of termination payments*. That paper reproduces as an appendix a helpful statement of the legal background produced in 2013 by the amusingly named Office of Tax Simplification. There was on the existing law a distinction

2.174

between a payment in lieu of notice on termination of the contract on less than the contractual notice that was provided for in the contract of employment (within s.62) and a payment made where there was no such provision or where the employer chose to terminate the contract without making a contractual payment in lieu of notice but made a payment for breach of the contract of employment instead (not within s.62). That distinction was considered not only to be very difficult to draw in particular cases but also to be unjustified.

The use of the ITEPA classification in reg.55 appears to avoid the problems of distinguishing between compensation payments which are capital in the recipient's hands and those which are income, discussed in the notes to regs 23 and 35(1) of the Income Support Regulations in Vol.II of this series. If a payment falls within the meaning of "employed earnings" in reg.55 it is to be taken into account as such regardless of whether it might otherwise have been categorised as capital (see *AH v HMRC (TC)* [2019] UKUT 5 (AAC), where Judge Wikeley discusses the relevant income tax case law on s.62(2) of ITEPA). Arguably the words are clear enough to be an exercise of the power in para.4(3)(b) of Sch.1 to the WRA 2012 to treat capital as earned income (see the notes to reg.57(2) below).

Dividends

2.175 The overriding principle set out in reg.52(a) that earned income from employment under a contract of service or in an office must be remuneration or profit derived from that employment or office suggests that payments of dividends on shares cannot be earned income. They are derived from the ownership of the shares. However, sometimes payments that are described as dividends are not properly to be treated as such. The formal company law and accounting processes for declaring a dividend may not have been gone through or the whole transaction may be a sham. There may be other situations in which, although the payments are properly to be regarded as dividends they are derived from employment or an office, so are taxable as general earnings. See the discussion in *H v SSWP and C (CSM)* [2015] UKUT 621 (AAC), citing extensively from the decision in *CCS 2533/2014* (not currently on the AAC website), which itself relied on the decision (described as instructive) of the Court of Appeal in the tax case of *HMRC v PA Holdings Ltd* [2011] EWCA Civ 1414. The overall approach adopted by the Court of Appeal is to look at the substance, or reality, not the form. There, contractual bonuses were structured so as to be paid out as dividends from a company separate from the employing personal service company and were held to be taxable as general earnings. Such highly artificial arrangements are perhaps unlikely to be encountered in universal credit. In more routine cases, there may be little reason to dispute a division between the taking of earnings as an employee or director and taking of dividends as a shareholder.

Dividends are chargeable to income tax under Part 4 of the Income Tax (Trading and Other Income) Act 2005 (ITTOIA), so cannot as such fall within the definition of general earnings in s.7(3) of ITEPA. However, if in substance the payments constitute remuneration derived from employment or an office they do fall within that definition. As a matter of principle, a decision-maker or tribunal would not be bound by HMRC having accepted payments as in substance of dividends taxable only under ITTOIA, but would have to come to an independent judgment on all the evidence available about whether payments were general earnings. However, how HMRC treated the payments would of course be a relevant factor to be considered., with the weight to be given to that treatment depending on how far it was based on a mere acceptance of statements on a tax return or on any further consideration of the particular circumstances.

See reg.77 for deemed capital and self-employed earnings where the claimant is like a sole trader or partner in relation to a company carrying on a trade.

Employee involved in trade dispute

2.176 **56.** A person who has had employed earnings and has withdrawn their labour in furtherance of a trade dispute is, unless their contract of service has been terminated, to be assumed to have employed earnings at the same level as they would have had were it not for the trade dispute.

DEFINITIONS

"employed earnings"—see regs 53(1) and 55.
"trade dispute"—see reg.2.

GENERAL NOTE

Anyone who is involved in a trade dispute but still employed is treated as having the same level of earnings as they would have had but for the trade dispute. "Trade dispute" has the same meaning as in s.244 of the Trade Union and Labour Relations (Consolidation) Act 1992 (reg.2). For the terms of the s.244 definition see the notes to reg.113 (below). 　　　　　　　　　　　　　　　　　　　　　　　　2.177

Self-employed earnings

57.—(1) This regulation applies for the purpose of calculating earned income that is not employed earnings and is derived from carrying on a trade, profession or vocation ("self-employed earnings").　　2.178

[²(2) A person's self-employed earnings in respect of an assessment period are to be calculated as follows.

Step 1

Calculate the amount of the person's profit or loss in respect of each trade, profession or vocation carried on by the person by—

(a) taking the actual receipts in that assessment period; and

(b) deducting any amounts allowed as expenses under regulation 58 or 59.

Where a trade, profession or vocation is carried on in a partnership, take the amount of the profit or loss attributable to the person's share in the partnership.

Step 2

If the person has carried on more than one trade, profession or vocation in the assessment period, add together the amounts resulting from step 1 in respect of each trade, profession or vocation.

Step 3

Deduct from the amount resulting from step 1 or (if applicable) step 2 any payment made by the person to HMRC in the assessment period [³by way of national insurance contributions or income tax in respect of any trade, profession or vocation carried on by the person.]

If the amount resulting from steps 1 to 3 is nil or a negative amount, the amount of the person's self-employed earnings in respect of the assessment period is nil (and ignore the following steps).

Step 4

If the amount resulting from step 3 is greater than nil, deduct from that amount any relievable pension contributions made by the person in the assessment period (unless a deduction has been made in respect of those contributions in calculating the person's employed earnings).

If the amount resulting from this step is nil or a negative amount, the person's self-employed earnings in respect of the assessment period are nil (and ignore the following step).

Step 5

If the amount resulting from step 4 is greater than nil, deduct from that amount any unused losses (see regulation 57A), taking the oldest first.

If the amount resulting from this step is greater than nil, that is the amount of the person's self-employed earnings for the assessment period.

If the amount resulting from this step is nil or a negative amount, the amount of the person's self-employed earnings in respect of the assessment period is nil.]

(3) [²...]

(4) The receipts referred to in [³paragraph (2)] include receipts in kind and any refund or repayment of income tax, value added tax or national insurance contributions relating to the trade, profession or vocation.

[¹(5) Where the purchase of an asset has been deducted as an expense in any assessment period and, in a subsequent assessment period, the asset is sold or ceases to be used for the purposes of a trade, profession or vocation carried on by the person, the proceeds of sale (or, as the case may be, the amount that would be received for the asset if it were sold at its current market value) are to be treated as a receipt in that subsequent assessment period].

AMENDMENTS

1. Universal Credit and Miscellaneous Amendments (No.2) Regulations 2014 (SI 2014/2888) reg.4(3) (November 26, 2014, or in the case of existing awards, the first assessment period beginning on or after November 26, 2014).

2. Universal Credit (Surpluses and Self-employed Losses) (Digital Service) Amendment Regulations 2015 (SI 2015/345) reg.3(2) (April 11, 2018).

3. Universal Credit (Surpluses and Self-employed Losses) (Digital Service) Amendment Regulations 2015 (SI 2015/345) reg.3(3) (April 11, 2018).

4. Universal Credit (Miscellaneous Amendments, Saving and Transitional Provision) Regulations 2018 (SI 2018/65) reg.7(4)(a), (April 11, 2018, text to be inserted by SI 2015/345 amended with effect from February 14, 2018).

DEFINITIONS

"assessment period"—see WRA 2012, ss.40 and 7(2) and reg.21.
"Contributions and Benefits Act"—see reg.2.
"earned income"–see reg.52.
"employed earnings"—see regs 53(1) and 55.
"HMRC"—see reg.53(1).
"relievable pension contributions"—see reg.53(1).

GENERAL NOTE

2.179   This regulation, now from April 2018 supplemented by reg.57A on unused losses, applies for the purpose of calculating self-employed earnings. As with employed earnings, it is the actual amount received during the assessment period that is taken into account. Thus those who are self-employed will need to report their earnings every month.

Self-employed earnings are earnings that are not employed earnings and are derived from carrying on a trade, profession or vocation (para.(1)). On the tests for deciding whether a person is an employed earner or in self-employment, see, for example, *CJSA/4721/2001*. Guidance on what amounts to a trade can also be taken from the cases on what is a business for the purposes of the disregard of the assets of a business (Sch.10 para.7), such as *R(FC) 2/92* and *RM v Sefton Council*

(HB) [2016] UKUT 357 (AAC), reported as [2017] AACR 5, on the question of when the ownership of a tenanted house is a business. Whether particular earnings are self-employed earnings for the purposes of universal credit is not determined by how they have been treated for other purposes, e.g. contribution purposes (see *CIS/14409/1996* and para.H4017 ADM).

Thus the first question is whether the person is engaged in self-employment. The issue will have to be determined according to the facts. Paragraph H4013 ADM quotes as examples someone who sells their two classic cars after losing their job because they can no longer afford their upkeep (who is not engaged in a trade) and someone who buys 10,000 toilet rolls from a wholesaler with the intention of selling them for a profit (who is so engaged). If it is decided that the person is engaged in self-employment, the question of whether they are in "gainful self-employment" will also need to be considered for the purpose of applying the minimum income floor rule (see the note to reg.62). If the person is not in gainful self-employment, no minimum income floor will apply and the person's actual self-employed earnings will be taken into account for the purposes of calculating their universal credit award.

This is not the place for any extensive discussion of how to distinguish between employed earners (i.e. those employed under a contract of service (employees) or office-holders) and self-employed earners. In most cases there will be no difficulty in identifying a claimant who falls within reg.57 as opposed to reg.55. There is a still helpful, although now dated, summary of the traditional factors in pp.98–103 of Wikeley, Ogus & Barendt, *The Law of Social Security* (5th edn). See also *CJSA/4721/2001*. There is perhaps a recent tendency to give particular significance to who takes the financial risk of operations as between the person doing the work and the employer/customer. Someone who sets up a limited company of which they are the sole or main employee and who controls the company through being the sole or majority shareholder is an employee, but reg.77 supplies a special regime in which they are treated as self-employed and the income of the company is to be calculated under reg.57.

There may be circumstances that fall outside both categories, in which case the category of "other paid work" in reg.52(a)(iii) would have to be considered. See the decision of the Court of Appeal in the child support case *Hakki v Secretary of State for Work and Pensions* [2014] EWCA Civ 530 in which a "professional" poker player was held not to be a self-employed earner on the ground that his activities lacked the necessary degree of organisation to amount to a trade, profession or vocation. The reasoning has been somewhat uncritically endorsed in the further child support case of *French v SSWP and another* [2018] EWCA Civ 474; [2018] AACR 25.

There are no specific rules excluding certain payments from being self-employed earnings (contrast, for example, reg.37(2) of the Income Support Regulations in Vol.II of this series).

The April 2018 re-casting of paras (2) and (3) into para.(2) does not change the basic substance of the method of calculation of self-employed earnings, apart from new rules on the treatment of losses including the incorporation of the operation of reg.57A on unused losses, but now expressly specifies a series of steps. The whole provision is directed to the calculation for a particular assessment period. The amendment operates only in relation to digital service (full service) cases by a detailed prescription of categories of claimant (see reg.4(1) of the Universal Credit (Surpluses and Self-employed Losses) (Digital Service) Amendment Regulations 2015 (SI 2015/345), as amended). See previous editions for the previous form of reg.57(2) and (3), which has been subject to slight amendment in its application in live service cases (now extinct).

Step 1

Now the starting point in full service cases in step 1 is the actual receipts in the particular assessment period, regardless of when the work to earn those receipts was done, with the deduction of any allowable expenses under reg.58 or 59 (which

2.179.1

apply to amounts paid in a particular assessment period, by necessary implication the same assessment period as for the actual receipts). Thus, it is not necessary that a claimant be engaged in self-employment in the assessment period in question, merely that there are actual receipts or allowable expenses incurred in that period that are derived from self-employment.

It is important that step 1 requires the calculation not just of a profit but also of a loss for each self-employment. Where the trade etc is carried on by a partnership, the claimant's share, which will depend on the terms of the partnership agreement, is taken. Note that drawings from a partnership or from a trade carried on as a self-employed person are not earnings from self-employment (*AR v Bradford Metropolitan DC* [2008] UKUT 30 (AAC), reported as *R(H) 6/09*), nor can they be regarded as unearned income. They are irrelevant to the method of calculation under reg.57 and, even if they did not fall outside the categories of unearned income in reg.66, to regard them as unearned income would entail an unfair double counting. Under para.(4) receipts include receipts in kind and any refund or repayment of income tax, VAT or national insurance contributions for the self-employed. See the notes on para.(5) below for sale of stock and other assets. This method of calculating self-employed earnings is based on HMRC's "cash basis and simplified expenses accounting system" (the cash basis model, or "cash in/cash out"). According to para.H4141 of ADM, self-employed claimants will be asked to report monthly between seven days before and 14 days after the end date of each assessment period details of actual income receipts and actual expenditure on allowable expenses during the assessment period that has just come to an end. The work of compiling the necessary information and getting through to report it will be quite burdensome. If there is a failure to report on time, an estimate can be made under reg.54(2)(b).

It must be the case that, as accepted in para.H4190 of ADM, capital receipts do not form part of actual receipts for the purposes of reg.57. Examples would be loans, grants, capital introduced into the business by the claimant or others or the proceeds of the sale of capital assets (where such a sale is not part of the business itself). The basic reasoning in *R(FC) 1/97* (and see the other cases mentioned in the notes to reg.37(1) of the Income Support Regulations in Vol.II of this series) would seem to apply, although there are some differences between the family credit legislation considered there and the provisions in these Regulations. However, it is plain that the object of reg.57 is to calculate the amount of earned *income* as defined in reg.52, as was important in *R(FC) 1/97*, in addition to the principle that the power to treat capital as earned income (in the terms of para.4(3)(b) of Sch.1 to the WRA 2012) can only be exercised by the use of express words in the regulation.

Coronavirus payments

2.179.2   It appeared that that principle might be tested in 2020 in relation to grants under the Coronavirus Self-Employed Income Support Scheme (SEISS), but amending regulations have short-circuited the problem. These grants, for those who meet the conditions, were described in the March 26, 2020 HMRC guidance as taxable grants of 80% of taxable profits (as calculated by reference to an average over the previous three tax years, or fewer if that is all the evidence available) up to £2,500 per month. Two of the conditions for the grant are that the person's business has been adversely affected due to the coronavirus outbreak and that they intend to continue to trade in the tax year 2020/21. The amount of the grant does not, as confirmed in the Treasury Direction authorising the expenditure on the scheme (Coronavirus Act 2020 Functions of Her Majesty's Revenue and Customs (Self-Employment Income Support Scheme) Direction, signed on April 30, 2020), vary according to the degree of loss of current trading profits. Everyone who qualifies and applies gets the 80% subject to the upper limit. The initial payment in late May or June 2020 is to cover three months' worth of the annual figure. One further payment for the following three months has been made available to be claimed from August 17, 2020.

There is extensive discussion in the notes to reg.37 of the Income Support Regulations (which have not been amended) in Vol.II of this series of whether the grants are on general principle income or capital receipts. That discussion is not relevant to universal credit because, with effect from May 21, 2020, before any SEISS grants were to be made, reg.2(1)(a) of the Universal Credit (Coronavirus) (Self-employed Claimants and Reclaims) (Amendment) Regulations 2020 (SI 2020/522) requires SEISS grants to be treated as a receipt at step 1 of reg.57 in the assessment period in which they are received. That would seem adequate if it was necessary for the regulation to treat capital as earned income of that category. See the notes to reg.54A and to Sch.10 for the resulting operation of the surplus earnings rule, the possible attribution as capital and the disregards of capital in subsequent assessment periods.

Payments from the Small Business Grant Fund or the Retail, Hospitality and Leisure Fund are undifferentiated, in the sense that their purpose is not expressed any more specifically than that of general support for the businesses covered. The conditions for payment are rather different from those for SEISS and the March 2020 Department for Business, Energy & Industrial Strategy guidance says nothing about taxability. The grants can be made to business ratepayers who get certain forms of rate relief (one grant per property) and are to be paid at two rates: £10,000 if the rateable value of the property is up to £15,000 and £25,000 if the rateable value is over £15,000 up to £51,000. There is no condition that there has been any loss of trading income. It therefore seems probable that the nature of the grant is sufficiently far from that of compensation for loss of what would have been revenue receipts to be properly a capital receipt, akin to an injection of capital into the business, and thus not to be included as a receipt at step 1. Loans under the Business Interruption Loan Scheme or the Bounce Back Loan Scheme appear even more likely to be capital receipts, although the terms of particular agreements may need to be considered. That appears to be the assumption of the drafters of the Self-employed Claimants and Reclaims Regulations because reg.2(2) merely provides for a disregard as capital of grants or loans to claimants carrying on a trade etc. "to meet the expenses or losses of the trade, profession or vocation in relation to the outbreak of coronavirus disease" and the Regulations say nothing about treatment under step 1. See the notes to Sch.10 for whether the disregard succeeds in covering the grants and loans just mentioned or SEISS payments.

Self-employed claimants who have employees and a PAYE scheme may also receive payments under the Coronavirus Job Retention Scheme (CJRS) if they have one or more employees who have been "furloughed" under that scheme. Claimants trading through companies as if they are sole owners or partners who are deemed by reg.77 to be self-employed, so that the income of the company is to be treated as self-employed earnings calculated under reg.57, may also be treated as having the CJRS payments as a consequence of furloughing themselves. Paragraph 2.1 of the Schedule to the Coronavirus Act 2020 Functions of Her Majesty's Revenue and Customs (Coronavirus Job Retention Scheme) Direction signed on May 20, 2020 (modifying the scheme in the direction signed on April 15, 2010) describes the purpose of the scheme as to provide for payments to be made to employers "incurring costs of employment in respect of furloughed employees arising from the health, social and economic emergency in the United Kingdom resulting from coronavirus and coronavirus disease" and para.2.2 says that it is integral that payments are only made in reimbursement of qualifying expenditure incurred or to be incurred by the employer. Any payment must be returned if the employer becomes unwilling or unable to use it for the specified purpose (para.2.4(b)). Those strict conditions showing the purpose of replacing (up to the initial limits of 80% of qualifying expenditure and £2,500 per month, more limited assistance being available from August to the end of October 2020) what would otherwise have been revenue expenditure indicates that CJRS payments should be regarded as income receipts.

That again is the assumption of the drafters of the Self-employed Claimants and Reclaims Regulations. Paragraph 7.7 of the Explanatory Memorandum to the Regulations says that CJRS payments will "not be taken into account in the self-employed claimants UC as earnings (and the claimant will not be able to treat the wages covered by CJRS as expenses in the calculation of their earnings)". However, the actual terms of the Regulations appear to achieve the very opposite of that primary aim. They contain nothing to say that the payments are not to be treated as actual receipts under para.(a) of step 1, but para.2(1)(b) provides that no deduction is to be made at para.(b) of step 1 for "expenses comprising the salary or wages paid to an employee in so far as those expenses are covered by a payment under the [CJRS]". That seems to have the effect that the CJRS payment counts towards the person's profit in the assessment period of receipt, but in so far as the payment is used for its proper purpose that expenditure cannot be deducted. Regulation 2(2)(a) provides that a CJRS payment is to be disregarded as capital for 12 months, but that cannot affect the inevitable conclusion, accepted in the Explanatory Memorandum, that the payment to the self-employed person is an income receipt. Perhaps decision-makers will apply the policy rather than the words of the Regulations. The word "covered" presumably allows the no-deduction rule to be imposed in the particular assessment period to which a CJRS payment relates, even if the payment was not actually received in that period.

If the analysis above is correct, the intention stated in para.7.8 of the Explanatory Memorandum has been implemented, that where "self-employed UC claimants who are trading through a limited company which "employs" them [and are] supported as a furloughed employee under CJRS ... payments will be treated as earnings and applied to the UC award". See the notes to reg.77 for further explanation. What remains mysterious is how the Regulations achieve any differential treatment between such claimants and ordinary self-employed claimants.

Step 2

Step 2 applies only where the person carries on more than one trade, profession or vocation in the assessment period in question and requires the adding together of the respective results under step 1. Thus a loss in one trade etc goes to offset a profit in another.

Step 3

Step 3 requires the deduction from the figure produced by step 1 (and 2, if applied) of any payment actually made in the assessment period in question to HMRC by way of self-employed national insurance contributions or income tax. Many self-employed people do not pay national insurance contributions and income tax regularly, but they can arrange with HMRC to make such payments monthly. It will obviously be to their advantage for universal credit purposes (to minimise fluctuations in the amounts of earned income to be taken into account) to do so. The process of calculation may stop at the end of step 3. If the resulting figure is nil or a negative amount, then the self-employed earnings for the assessment period are nil. If there is a negative amount there will then be an "unused loss" as defined in reg.57A(1) that can be taken into account in subsequent assessment periods if the process then gets to step 5.

Step 4

Step 4 applies if step 3 results in a positive amount. Then the amount of any relievable pension contributions made in the assessment period in question is deducted, unless already deducted in calculating employed earnings (under reg.55(5)—presumably if not all of the amount was needed to reduce employed earnings to nil, the remainder can be deducted under step 4). See the notes to reg.55 for discussion of "relievable pension contributions". If the resulting figure is nil or a negative amount, then the self-employed earnings for the assessment period are nil. If there is a negative amount at this stage there is not an "unused loss" under reg.57A(1).

Step 5

Step 5 applies if step 4 results in a positive amount. Then at that final stage any unused losses from past assessment periods that have not been extinguished under reg.57A are to be deducted. If the resulting figure is positive, that is the amount of self-employed earnings for the assessment period in question. If the resulting figure is nil or a negative amount, the self-employed earnings are nil. The oldest unused losses are to be looked at first. Although it would have been better if the process had been spelled out, for the structure of regs 57 and 57A to be workable it must be assumed that once deducting a particular unused loss produces a nil result or a negative figure, no more recent unused losses are to be deducted. See the notes to reg.57A for how that affects the amount of unused losses available in subsequent assessment periods.

Note in particular the effect of the saving provision in reg.4(4) of the Universal Credit (Surpluses and Self-employed Losses) (Digital Service) Amendment Regulations 2015, as amended, which provides that there is to be no unused loss under reg.57A from any assessment period that began before April 11, 2018.

Under para.(5), where the purchase of an asset has been deducted as an expense in any assessment period, and in a subsequent assessment period the asset is sold, or ceases to be used for the purpose of the claimant's self-employment, the proceeds of sale, or the amount that would have been received if the asset had been sold at its current market value, will be treated as a receipt in that subsequent period. Paragraph H4181 of the ADM advises decision makers that the full amount of the proceeds of sale (or deemed proceeds of sale) is to be taken into account, even if only a proportion of the purchase price was deducted as a expense in the assessment period in which the asset was purchased because the claimant's self-employed earnings in that assessment period were less than the price of the asset. This provision would seem to embody a somewhat rigid approach which does not take into account the realities of self-employment which usually needs to be viewed over a much longer period than an assessment period (i.e., a month). To quote an example given in the ADM, if a claimant pays £400 for display material in an assessment period in which their earnings are only £100, so that only £100 of the expense is taken into account as this reduces their earnings to nil, it does not seem fair that the whole of the sale price (or deemed sale price) should count as a receipt in a subsequent assessment period, rather than the equivalent of the expenses reduction they were allowed. But now the unused loss in the assessment period in which the display material was purchased can be taken into account under step 5 and reg.57A in subsequent assessment periods, so that the unfairness is diminished. The guidance accepts that if an asset was only to be used partially for business purposes, only that proportion of the proceeds of sale is to be taken into account as a receipt.

This method of calculation, even on the assumption that claimants will be able to supply accurate information month by month, might be expected in many cases to produce considerable fluctuations between assessment periods depending on the chance of when receipts come in and when expenses are incurred. In the case of fluctuations downwards, reg.62 on the minimum income floor may come into play. If a self-employed person is in gainful self-employment as defined in reg.64, would apart from the operation of reg.62 or 90 be subject to all work-related requirements and their actual earned income in an assessment period is below the minimum income floor (usually the hourly national minimum wage times 35), their earned income is deemed to be equal to that threshold. However, the test for gainful self-employment is quite strict. The person must be carrying on a trade, profession or vocation as their main employment and derive self-employed earnings from that. In addition, the trade, profession or vocation must be "organised, developed, regular and carried on in the expectation of profit". Those last conditions, and also the exclusion of the 12-month start-up period under reg.63, will exclude many claimants with fluctuating or more casual operations. See the notes to reg.64 for further discussion. If reg.62 does not apply, the actual level of self-employed earnings as calculated under the present regulation must be taken. Even if reg.62 does apply to some assessment periods, it supplies no mechanism for evening out fluctuations to a higher level for other assessment periods. If earned income exceeds the minimum income floor in any assessment period, the actual level must be taken.

The April 2018 provisions on taking account of losses will give some mitigation in evening out fluctuations in the level of self-employed earnings, but may also lead to an increased application of the minimum income floor. In addition, the new provisions on surplus earnings in reg.54A will add to the unpredictability of outcomes when, as is likely to be the case for any self-employed person, there are continual fluctuations month by month in actual receipts and in expenditure. There are still likely to be differences in total annual income between those universal credit claimants whose earnings are of a regular monthly amount and those (many of whom will be self-employed) who earn the same amount over the year but subject to fluctuations. See the House of Commons Work and Pensions Committee's May 2018 report *Universal Credit: supporting self-employment* (HC 997).

See also reg.77 for the special rules that apply to those whose control of a company is such that they are like a sole trader or a partner. In those circumstances, amongst other things, the company's income or the person's share of it is to be treated as the person's income and calculated under reg.57 as if it were self-employed earnings. It is, though, far from clear how that notional conversion is to take place. Under reg.57, in the case of actual self-employed earnings, the calculation is based on actual receipts in any assessment period less permitted deductions for expenses under regs 58 and 59. Presumably therefore, "the income of the company" does not mean the net income of the company as might be calculated for corporation tax purposes or under ordinary accounting principles. Presumably it means the actual receipts of the company in the assessment period in question less the deductions for expenses under regs 58 and 59, looking at expenditure on behalf of the company rather than by the person in question. It is difficult to say whether in practice information will be available as to such receipts and expenditure in a current assessment period of a month. A further problem is how to calculate the deductions from gross profits under step 3 of para. (2) for national insurance contributions and income tax paid to HMRC in the assessment period and relievable pension contributions made in that period, when the person's actual tax and national insurance status will not have been as a self-employed earner. But some difficulties may be avoided by the provision in reg.77(3)(c) that if the person's activities in the course of the company's trade are their main employment reg.62 (minimum income floor) is to be applied.

See the notes to reg.61 for discussion of whether any alterations of existing awards resulting from increases or reductions in the amount of earned income, including self-employed earnings, are appealable.

[¹Unused losses

2.180   **57A.**—(1) For the purposes of regulation 57(2), a person has an unused loss if—

    (a) in calculating the person's self-employed earnings for any of the previous [²...] assessment periods, the amount resulting from steps 1 to 3 in regulation 57(2) was a negative amount (a "loss"); and

    (b) the loss has not been extinguished in a subsequent assessment period.

(2) For the purposes of paragraph (1)(b) a loss is extinguished if no amount of that loss remains after it has been deducted at step 5 in regulation 57(2).

(3) Where a person was entitled to a previous award of universal credit and the last day of entitlement in respect of that award fell within the 6 months preceding the first day of entitlement in respect of the new award, the Secretary of State may, for the purposes of this regulation (provided the person provides such information as the Secretary of State requires), [²treat—

    (a) the assessment periods under the previous award; and

(b) any months between that award and the current award in respect of which a claim has been made,

as assessment periods under the current award.]]

AMENDMENTS

1. Universal Credit (Surpluses and Self-employed Losses) (Digital Service) Amendment Regulations 2015 (SI 2015/345) reg.3(4) (April 11, 2018).

2. Universal Credit (Miscellaneous Amendments, Saving and Transitional Provision) Regulations 2018 (SI 2018/65) reg.7(4)(b) (text to be inserted by SI 2015/345 amended with effect from February 14, 2018) (April 11, 2018).

DEFINITIONS

"assessment period"—see WRA 2012 ss.40 and 7(2) and reg.21.
"self-employed earnings"—see regs 53(1) and 57.

GENERAL NOTE

Although reg.57A came into force on April 11, 2018, the saving provision in reg.4(4) of the Universal Credit (Surpluses and Self-employed Losses) (Digital Service) Amendment Regulations 2015 (SI 2015/345), as amended, secures that no unused loss is to be produced from any assessment period that began before that date. It will therefore take some months at least for practical consequences to build up. In addition, reg.4(1) restricts the effect of this new regulation to digital service (full service) awards, by a detailed prescription of categories of claimant.

2.181

An "unused loss" arises in any previous assessment period under reg.57A(1) when the result after step 3 of the calculation of self-employed earnings in reg.57(2) produces a negative figure. That requires calculating profit or loss (i.e. actual receipts in the assessment period less allowable expenses incurred in the same period) for each trade, profession or vocation, combining the figures if more than one trade etc is carried on, and deducting income tax and national insurance payments made to HMRC in that period. Note that the reg.57A test is applied without taking any account of the deduction of the amount of relievable pension contributions under step 4 in reg.57(2). The loss in the form of the negative amount is then "unused" in the sense that the amount of self-employed earnings taken into account in the assessment period in question can never be less than nil.

On the face of it, when such an unused loss is to be taken into account in a subsequent assessment period under reg.57(2), where it comes in at step 5, there is no time limit on how far in the past the relevant assessment period was (subject to the saving that only assessment periods beginning on or after April 11, 2018 can count). The limit to 11 previous assessment periods that existed in previous forms of the amending regulation was removed in the final form. However, the DWP's view is that the rule only operates for assessment periods within the same continuous period of entitlement to universal credit as under the current award, subject to the linking rule in para.(3) of reg.57A, so that a break in entitlement prevents the taking into account of unused losses in pre-break assessment periods. That view must be based on the definition of assessment period in reg.21(1) as "a period of one month beginning with the first date of entitlement and each subsequent period of one month *during which entitlement subsists*" (emphasis added), as well as on the perceived need for para.(3). There may be some doubt about the validity of the emphasised part of reg.21(1) under the powers given in s.7(2) of the WRA 2012 and elsewhere. But leaving that aside and assuming that a month only amounts to an "assessment period" when within a period of universal credit entitlement, that seems to supply no reason why what were undoubtedly assessment periods during the pre-break period of entitlement are not "previous assessment periods" under para.(1)(a). It is suggested that some specific words would have been needed in reg.57A to produce the result that only assessment periods in the current period of entitlement could count and that the existence of para.(3) is insufficient to produce a necessary implication that the plain words of para.(1)(a) do not mean what they say. Thus it is arguable that a break in entitlement does not break the ability to go back to previous assessment periods for unused losses.

If that argument does not work, then para.(3) allows the Secretary of State, where the break in entitlement is of less than six months, to treat the assessment periods in the pre-break period of entitlement and the months in the break as assessment periods under the current award. If that is done, the unused losses in the pre-break period of entitlement and in the deemed assessment periods during the break can then be taken into account if necessary under reg.57(2). There is a discretion ("may") as to whether the deeming should be done, subject to the condition that the claimant provides any required information (presumably mainly as to receipts and expenses in months in the break which were not actually assessment periods). It is not clear what sort of factors might indicate that the basic rule should not be applied. On any appeal a tribunal can make its own judgment as to the exercise of the discretion.

Unused losses are only to be taken into account in step 5 in reg.57(2) if they have not been extinguished (reg.57A(1)(b)). Paragraph (2) links that matter to such use in step 5, but in slightly peculiar terms. It is clear enough that, if the process suggested in the notes to reg.57(2) is followed and only the unused losses, starting with the oldest, that are needed to reduce the final figure to nil or a negative amount are deducted under step 5, the losses that have not needed to be deducted at all are not extinguished. The peculiarity is in relation to the final or sole loss used. Say, for instance, that the figure remaining at the end of step 4 is £300 and the oldest or sole unextinguished unused loss is £500. That produces a negative amount of £200 in step 5 and the amount of self-employed earnings to be taken into account is nil. But to what extent is the unused loss of £500 extinguished by that operation? One would expect it to have been extinguished to the extent of £300. However, para. (2) seems to assume that a loss is either extinguished in its entirety or not extinguished in its entirety and states that a loss is extinguished if "no amount of that loss remains" after it has been deducted in step 5. That test is not clear. In one sense the whole of the £500 unused loss in the example was deducted, producing a negative figure and an amount of self-employed earnings of nil. What does it mean to ask if no amount of the loss "remains"? It seems that, to make any sense, it must mean that in the example £200 remained, because that amount was not needed to reduce the final figure to nil. That then is hard to reconcile with the apparent effect of the plain words of para.(2) that the whole of the £500 unused loss remains unextinguished, because it cannot be said that no amount of that loss remains. That is not the approach taken in the examples given in para.H4503 of the ADM, which are consistent with the carrying forward in the example above of only £200 of unused loss. That would involve interpreting "loss" in para.(2) as meaning something like the whole or part of the original unused loss as identified in para.(1), in so far as not already used up in step 5 of a reg.57 calculation.

Remember of course that if the result of bringing in unused losses results in a low or nil amount of self-employed earnings, the minimum income floor under reg.62 may well come into play.

Permitted expenses

2.182

58.—(1) The deductions allowed in the calculation of self-employed earnings are amounts paid in the assessment period in respect of—

(a) expenses that have been wholly and exclusively incurred for purposes of the trade, profession or vocation; or

(b) in the case of expenses that have been incurred for more than one purpose, an identifiable part or proportion that has been wholly and exclusively incurred for the purposes of the trade, profession or vocation, excluding any expenses that were incurred unreasonably.

(2) Payments deducted under paragraph (1) may include value added tax.

(3) No deduction may be made for payments in respect of—

(a) expenditure on non-depreciating assets (including property, shares or other assets held for investment purposes);

(b) [² . . .]

(c) repayment of capital [¹ . . .] in relation to a loan taken out for the purposes of the trade, profession or vocation;

(d) expenses for business entertainment.

[¹(3A) A deduction for a payment of interest in relation to a loan taken out for the purposes of the trade, profession or vocation may not exceed £41.]

(4) This regulation is subject to regulation 59.

AMENDMENTS

1. Social Security (Miscellaneous Amendments) (No.2) Regulations 2013 (SI 2013/1508) reg.3(7) (July 29, 2013).

2. Universal Credit (Surpluses and Self-employed Losses) (Digital Service) Amendment Regulations 2015 (SI 2015/345) reg.3(5) (April 11, 2018).

DEFINITIONS

"assessment period"—see WRA 2012, ss.40 and 7(2) and reg.21.
"self-employed earnings"—see reg 53(1) and 57.

GENERAL NOTE

This regulation, and reg.59, provide for the deductions that can be made from self-employed earnings. Only these deductions can be made in addition to those under steps 3 and 4 of reg.57(2) for national insurance contributions and income tax paid to HMRC and relievable pension contributions.

2.183

The amount of the deduction will normally be the actual amount of the permitted expenses paid in the assessment period, but note para.(4). The effect of para.(4) is that the alternative deductions under reg.59 in respect of the expenses referred to in paras (2)–(4) of that regulation may be made instead. However, note that in the case of a car, the actual costs involved in acquiring or using it are not allowable and the only deduction that can be made is a flat rate deduction for mileage under reg.59(2). Regulation 53(1) gives "car' the same meaning as in s.268A(1) of the Capital Allowances Act 2001. That provision excludes motorcycles, vehicles of a construction primarily suited for the conveyance of goods or some other burden and vehicles of a type not commonly used as a private vehicle and unsuitable for such use. The ADM (paras H4231 and H4234) accepts that black cabs or hackney carriages are not cars, because they are specially adapted for business use, in contrast to minicabs or taxis of that kind.

To be deductible, the expenses must have been paid in the assessment period, be reasonable and have been "wholly and exclusively" incurred for the purposes of the self-employment (para.(1)), but note para.(1)(b). See para.H4214 ADM for examples of allowable expenses. Permitted expenses include value added tax (para.(2)).

Paragraph (1)(b) specifically provides for the apportionment of expenses that have been incurred for more than one purpose (e.g., for business and private purposes). In such a case, a deduction will be made for the proportion of the expenses that can be identified as wholly and exclusively incurred for the purposes of the self-employment. See *R(FC) 1/91* and *R(IS) 13/91* which hold that any apportionment already agreed by HMRC should normally be accepted. But note the alternative flat-rate deductions for expenses if someone uses their home for business purposes in reg.59(3). See also reg.59(4) which provides for flat-rate deductions from expenses if business premises are also used for personal use.

No deduction can be made for the payments listed in para.(3). The limitation of sub-para.(a) to non-depreciating assets confirms that reasonable capital expenditure on depreciating assets or stock-in-trade is to be deducted. Sub-paragraph (b) formerly excluded the deduction of losses from previous assessment periods, but has now been overtaken by the new form of reg.57(2) and reg.57A.

Repayments of capital on a loan taken out for the purposes of the self-employment are not deductible (para.(3)(c)) but deductions can be made for interest paid on such a loan up to a limit of £41 per assessment period (para.(3A)). Paragraph (3A) was introduced to bring universal credit into line with the tax rules which now allow a deduction of up to £500 annually for interest payments made on loans taken out for the purposes of a business. This will include interest on credit cards and overdraft charges if the original expense related to the business. According to para.H4217 ADM only £41 can be deducted in any assessment period, regardless of the number of relevant loans a person has and for what purposes. It might just be arguable that the terms of para.(3A) are sufficient to rebut the normal presumption under s.6(c) of the Interpretation Act 1978 that the singular includes the plural, especially if the person carries on more than one trade etc.

Flat rate deductions for mileage and use of home and adjustment for personal use of business premises

2.184

59.—(1) This regulation provides for alternatives to the deductions that would otherwise be allowed under regulation 58.

(2) Instead of a deduction in respect of the actual expenses incurred in relation to the acquisition or use of a motor vehicle, the following deductions are allowed according to the mileage covered on journeys undertaken in the assessment period for the purposes of the trade, profession or vocation—

(a) in a car, van or other motor vehicle (apart from a motorcycle), 45 pence per mile for the first 833 miles and 25 pence per mile thereafter; and

(b) on a motorcycle, 24 pence per mile,

and, if the motor vehicle is a car [¹ . . .], the only deduction allowed for the acquisition or use of that vehicle is a deduction under this paragraph.

(3) Where a person carrying on a trade, profession or vocation incurs expenses in relation to the use of accommodation occupied as their home, instead of a deduction in respect of the actual expenses, a deduction is allowed according to the number of hours spent in the assessment period on income generating activities related to the trade, profession or vocation as follows—

(a) at least 25 hours but no more than 50 hours, £10;

(b) more than 50 hours but no more than 100 hours, £18;

(c) more than 100 hours, £26.

(4) Where premises which are used by a person mainly for the purposes of a trade, profession or vocation are also occupied by that person for their personal use, whether alone or with other persons, the deduction allowed for expenses in relation to those premises is the amount that would be allowed under regulation 58(1) if the premises were used wholly and exclusively for purposes of the trade, profession or vocation, but reduced by the following amount according to the number of persons occupying the premises for their personal use—

(a) £350 for one person;

(b) £500 for two persons;

(c) £650 for three or more persons.

AMENDMENT

1. Social Security (Miscellaneous Amendments) (No.2) Regulations 2013 (SI 2013/1508) reg.3(8) (July 29, 2013).

DEFINITIONS

"the Act"—see reg.2.
"assessment period"—see WRA 2012 ss.40 and 7(2) and reg.21.
"car"—see reg.53(1).
"motor cycle"—*ibid.*

GENERAL NOTE

This regulation provides for alternative deductions to those that would otherwise   2.185
be permitted under reg.58 to be chosen (para.(1)). However, note that in the case of a
car, there is no choice: only a flat rate deduction for mileage is allowed and no deduction can be made for the actual cost of buying or using the car (para.(2)). This does
not apply to other motor vehicles. See the notes to reg.58 for the meaning of "car".

Under para.(2), a deduction for mileage on journeys undertaken for the purposes
of the business in the assessment period:

- on a motorcycle, of 24 pence per mile; or

- in a car, van or other motor vehicle (other than a motorcycle), of 45 pence per
  mile for the first 833 miles and 25 pence per mile after that,

can be made instead of the actual cost of buying or using the motor vehicle (in the
case of a car this is the only permitted deduction).

If someone uses their own home for the purposes of their self-employment, a flat-
rate deduction of:

- £10 for at least 25 hours but no more than 50 hours;

- £18 for more than 50 hours but no more than 100 hours; or

- £26 for more than 100 hours,

of "income generating activities" related to the self-employment in an assessment
period can be made instead of the actual expenses incurred in the use of the home
(para.(3)). The guidance in paras H4241–H4242 ADM suggests that "income generating activities" include providing services to customers, general administration
of the business (e.g. filing and record-keeping) and action to secure business (e.g.
sales and marketing) but do not include being on call (e.g. a taxi driver waiting for
customers to ring), the use of the home for storage or time spent on completing tax
returns (presumably on this basis DWP would also discount any time spent collating
evidence of actual receipts and expenses for the purposes of the person's universal
credit claim).

For the alternative provision for apportionment of expenses, see reg.58(1)(b).

Paragraph (4) provides that if the person lives in premises that are mainly used
for business purposes, the expenses that would be allowed if the premises were used
wholly and exclusively for the purposes of the person's self-employment are to be
reduced by a set amount depending on the number of people living in the premises.
The reduction is £350 for one person, £500 for two and £650 for three or more
people in each assessment period. It is not entirely clear but the reduction under this
paragraph appears to be a set rule, rather than an alternative to an apportionment
under reg.58(1)(b).

Notional earned income

60.—(1) A person who has deprived themselves of earned income, or   2.186
whose employer has arranged for them to be so deprived, for the purpose of

securing entitlement to universal credit or to an increased amount of universal credit is to be treated as possessing that earned income.

(2) Such a purpose is to be treated as existing if, in fact, entitlement or higher entitlement to universal credit did result and, in the opinion of the Secretary of State, this was a foreseeable and intended consequence of the deprivation.

(3) If a person provides services for another person and—

(a) the other person makes no payment for those services or pays less than would be paid for comparable services in the same location; and

(b) the means of the other person were sufficient to pay for, or pay more for, those services,

the person who provides the services is to be treated as having received the remuneration that would be reasonable for the provision of those services.

(4) Paragraph (3) does not apply where—

(a) the person is engaged to provide the services by a charitable or voluntary organisation and the Secretary of State is satisfied that it is reasonable to provide the services free of charge or at less than the rate that would be paid for comparable services in the same location;

(b) the services are provided by a person who is participating as a service user (see regulation 53(2)); or

(c) the services are provided under or in connection with a person's participation in an employment or training programme approved by the Secretary of State.

DEFINITIONS

"earned income"—see reg.52.
"a person who is participating as a service user"—see reg.53(2).

GENERAL NOTE

2.187   This regulation treats a person as having employed or self-employed earnings in two situations. For the rules relating to notional unearned income, see reg.74.

Paragraphs (1)–(2)

2.188   This contains the deprivation of earnings rule for universal credit. It applies if someone has deprived themselves of earned income, for the purpose of securing entitlement to, or increasing the amount of, universal credit. It also applies if the person's employer has "arranged for" the deprivation. Presumably this will only apply if the person's purpose was to secure, or increase, entitlement to universal credit by way of the arrangement and the employer's purpose is not relevant.

See the extensive notes to regs 42(1) and 51(1) of the Income Support Regulations in Vol.II of this series on the deprivation rule.

The operation of para.(1) is restricted to circumstances where the person's purpose is related to entitlement to universal credit. That is in contrast to the terms of reg.105(1) of the JSA Regulations 1996 (which covers purposes relating to both old style JSA and income support) and of reg.106(1) of the ESA Regulations 2008 and reg.42(1) of the Income Support Regulations (which both cover purposes relating to all of old style ESA and JSA and income support). *R(IS) 14/93* was concerned with a similar problem on the transfer to income support from the corresponding supplementary benefit provisions in 1988 in relation to the notional capital. That was whether claimants who deprived themselves of capital under the supplementary benefit regime, before income support existed, could be said to have done so for the purpose of securing entitlement to income support so as to be caught by reg.51(1) of the Income Support Regulations once the income support legislation had come into force. The Commissioner holds that the words "income support" in reg.51(1) cannot be taken to refer to means-tested benefits that previously went under the name of supplementary benefit. Thus, if a deprivation of earned income occurs while a person is receiving, or contemplating a claim for, income support or old style JSA or ESA, it may be arguable, depending on the exact circumstances, that if there is later a claim for universal credit the purpose of the deprivation was not to secure entitlement to universal credit. But there might in such circumstances be a continuing deprivation for that purpose if there was not an earlier permanent deprivation.

Note, however, para.(2). The effect of para.(2) is that the person will be deemed to have the necessary purpose if they did obtain universal credit, or more universal credit, and in the opinion of the Secretary of State, this was "a foreseeable and intended consequence" of the deprivation. To some extent para.(2) represents a codification of the case law on the "purpose" part of the traditional deprivation rule. However, it seems likely that much will continue to depend on the view taken by the Secretary of State (and on appeal a tribunal) of the person's intention. It is far from clear what difference there is meant to be between *an* "intended consequence" in para.(2) and "purpose" (interpreted as meaning significant operative purpose) in para.(1). If there is no difference there would be no point in including the deeming in para.(2). It may have been thought that the conditions in para.(2) are easier to determine one way or the other, but it is submitted that a consequence is not intended as well as foreseeable just because a person realises that it will result from the deprivation.

Paragraphs (3)–(4)

This is similar but not identical to the notional earnings rule for income support, old style JSA, old style ESA and housing benefit. For example, the exception in para.(4)(a) only applies if the person is engaged to provide the services by a charitable or voluntary organisation and does not also include the situation where the person is simply a volunteer (on the meaning of "volunteer" see *R(IS) 12/92*).

See the notes to reg.42(6) and (6A) of the Income Support Regulations in Vol.II of this series.

2.189

[¹Information for calculating earned income - real time information etc

61.—(1) Unless paragraph (2) applies, a person must provide such information for the purposes of calculating their earned income at such times as the Secretary of State may require.

(2) Where a person is, or has been, engaged in an employment in respect of which their employer is a Real Time Information employer—

(a) the amount of the person's employed earnings from that employment for each assessment period is to be based on the information which is reported to HMRC under the PAYE Regulations and is received by the Secretary of State from HMRC in that assessment period; and

(b) for an assessment period in which no information is received from HMRC, the amount of employed earnings in relation to that employment is to be taken to be nil.

(3) The Secretary of State may determine that paragraph (2) does not apply—

(a) in respect of a particular employment, where the Secretary of State considers that the information from the employer is unlikely to be sufficiently accurate or timely; or

(b) in respect of a particular assessment period where—

(i) no information is received from HMRC and the Secretary of

2.190

State considers that this is likely to be because of a failure to report information (which includes the failure of a computer system operated by HMRC, the employer or any other person); or

(ii) the Secretary of State considers that the information received from HMRC is incorrect, or fails to reflect the definition of employed earnings in regulation 55, in some material respect.

(4) Where the Secretary of State determines that paragraph (2) does not apply, the Secretary of State must make a decision as to the amount of the person's employed earnings for the assessment period in accordance with regulation 55 (employed earnings) using such information or evidence as the Secretary of State thinks fit.

(5) When the Secretary of State makes a decision in accordance with paragraph (4) the Secretary of State may—

(a) treat a payment of employed earnings received by the person in one assessment period as received in a later assessment period (for example where the Secretary of State has received the information in that later period or would, if paragraph (2) applied, have expected to receive information about that payment from HMRC in that later period); or

(b) where a payment of employed earnings has been taken into account in that decision, disregard information about the same payment which is received from HMRC.

(6) Paragraph (5) also applies where the Secretary of State makes a decision under regulation 41(3) of the Universal Credit, Personal Independence Payment, Jobseeker's Allowance and Employment and Support Allowance (Decisions and Appeals) Regulations 2013 in a case where the person disputes the information provided by HMRC.

(7) In this regulation "Real Time Information Employer" has the meaning in regulation 2A(1) of the PAYE Regulations.]

Amendment

1. Universal Credit and Miscellaneous Amendments (No.2) Regulations 2014 (SI 2014/2888) reg.4(4) (November 26, 2014, or in the case of existing awards, the first assessment period beginning on or after November 26, 2014).

Definitions

"assessment period"—see WRA 2012, ss.40 and 7(2) and reg.21.
"earned income"–see reg.52.
"employed earnings"—see regs 53(1) and 55.
"HMRC"—see reg.53(1).
"PAYE Regulations"—*ibid.*

General Note

2.191   This regulation is concerned with the collection of information in relation to employed earnings. One of the new features of universal credit is that normally PAYE information is to be used to calculate a person's employed earnings (and thus their entitlement to universal credit) and that direct reporting of employed earnings by a claimant (or "self-reporting") is only to be the fall-back position. It is mainly for this reason that universal credit is assessed on a monthly basis and paid in arrears after the end of the assessment period.

This regulation was re-cast on November 26, 2014 as DWP's "on-going process of monitoring and evaluation identified some circumstances where it is not appropriate for Universal Credit purposes simply to take the RTI [Real Time Information] at face value or where the Secretary of State should clarify contingency arrangements" (see the Explanatory Memorandum which accompanied SI 2014/2888). The re-casting involves a distinct change in emphasis, as well as clarifying a number of points.

Paragraph (1) contains a general rule that a claimant must provide the information that the Secretary of State requires for the purposes of calculating their earned income (note that earned income includes not only employed earnings, but also earnings as an office-holder, self-employed earnings, remuneration from any other paid work and income treated as earned income: see reg.52).

However, that is subject to para.(2) and it is para.(2) that will apply in most cases of employed earnings. Under para.(2), if the claimant's employer is a "Real Time Information employer" (defined in para. (7)), the calculation of the claimant's employed earnings is to be based on the information that is reported to HMRC through the PAYE system and received by the Secretary of State from HMRC in that assessment period (sub-para.(a)). If no information is received from HMRC for an assessment period, the claimant's earnings from that employment are to be taken as nil (sub-para.(b)). It should especially be noted that the language of sub-para.(b) is different from that of sub-para.(a) ("is to be taken" as opposed to "is to be based on").

The instructions to employers on reporting are to record amounts on the normal payment date. HMRC's October 2019 (Issue 80) *Employer Bulletin* contains a clarification of the rules about the date on which pay should be reported in a Real Time Information Full Payment Submission as having been made when the normal payment date falls on a non-banking day. Whether the payment is made before or after the normal payment date it should be reported as having been made on the normal date. The Bulletin also contains guidance relating to early payments around Christmas 2019, applying the same rule. What was described as a temporary "easement" for Christmas 2018 has been made permanent. The same should apply when a payment is not made on the normal payment date for any other reason. Those instructions have been repeated with general application in section 1.8 of HMRC *Guidance 2020 to 2021: Employer further guide to PAYE and National Insurance contributions* (CWG2, as updated on May 14, 2020 and available on the internet). What perhaps started as mere guidance has been firmed up into what are now very precise instructions.

Initially, it was considered that para.(2) established a rigid rule that could only be displaced under the conditions in para.(3). That certainly was the assumption in *SSWP v RW (rule 17) (UC)* [2017] UKUT 347 (AAC), discussed below in relation to para.(3). However, the decision of the Divisional Court in *R. (Johnson and others) v Secretary of State for Work and Pensions* [2019] EWHC 23 (Admin) cast doubt on that assumption by rejecting the Secretary of State's interpretation of regs 54 and 61. That doubt was been removed by the Court of Appeal's decision on appeal (*Secretary of State for Work and Pensions v Johnson* [2020] EWCA Civ 778) and there is now no need to repeat the criticisms of the Divisional Court's approach to the interpretation of reg.61 made in the 2019/20 edition of this volume (at 2.191). However, the Secretary of State's appeal was not allowed, because the court found that it had been irrational for her not to have included some provision in the legislation to avoid the problems arising for the four monthly-paid claimants from the extremely odd results of applying the accepted interpretation to them. See the notes to reg.54 for a full discussion of the Court of Appeal's decision and the unanswered questions arising about its effect.

One weakness of the Court of Appeal's decision, probably stemming from the flawed concentration of the Divisional Court below on reg.54, rather than reg.61, was similarly to give limited attention to reg.61 in a case where all four claimants had Real Time Information (RTI) employers. In particular, Rose LJ, at para.44, appears to have been too hasty in rejecting the claimants' argument that they could rely on reg.61(3) (no doubt relying on sub-para.(b)(ii): information received from HMRC incorrect in a material respect). In the cases of Ms Barrett and Ms Stewart (whose usual pay days were the 28th of the month), when the 28th was a non-banking day (Saturday, Sunday or bank holiday) and they were paid on last working day before the 28th their employers reported the date of actual payment on their Full Payment Submission. The judge says that there was nothing inaccurate or untimely in the information provided by the employers to HMRC and the DWP. But, as she noted at para.86, HMRC guidance/instructions (or what was called an "easement" in relation to Easter 2019) had been from at least 2018 to report payment on the usual pay day. There is therefore some doubt whether those instructions were in effect at the date of the decisions challenged in *Johnson* and, if so, how strong the instructions/guidance was. However, the court was considering a continuing failure to make legislative provision for the specific problem of monthly-paid claimants with assessment periods ending near the end of the month and it was clear from the limited evidence it had that HMRC were from 2018 or 2019 telling employers that that was how they were to report payment dates. Rose LJ then did not connect up that evidence with her conclusion in para.44. Surely, doing no more than applying the everyday meaning of "incorrect", it must be arguable that where the employer has failed to follow HMRC instructions the information passed on to the DWP as incorrect in a material respect under sub-para.(b)(ii). That would, as explained in more detail below, allow the Secretary of State or a tribunal on appeal to treat earnings actually received on one date as received on the usual pay day, if that results in it counting in a later assessment period (para.(5)). A practical problem is whether the DWP is able to identify that information is incorrect in the sense above from what is sent to it from HMRC or whether claimants would need to alert the DWP to the occurrence of a shift.

Note that the argument above would appear not to be of assistance to claimants who, like Ms Johnson and Ms Woods, are usually paid on the last working day of the month. That is because if the "non-banking day salary shift" occurs it would merely identify what is the last working day of the month and the date of actual payment would be correctly reported by the employer as the usual pay day. It could possibly help some claimants like those in *R. (Pantellerisco) v Secretary of State for Work and Pensions* [2020] EWHC 1944 (Admin) (see the notes to reg.54 for the details) who are paid four-weekly, but only in very occasional circumstances (say where payment on a Thursday instead of a bank holiday Friday would take a payment into a different assessment period). The argument would not impinge on the systemic disadvantage and irrationality identified in *Pantellerisco*.

Since October 6, 2013 most employers have been Real Time Information employers (see reg.2A(1)(d) of the Income Tax (Pay As You Earn) Regulations 2003 (SI 2003/2682) ("the PAYE Regulations"). Under reg.67B of the PAYE Regulations a Real Time Information employer is required to deliver specified information to HMRC before or at the time of making payments to an employee. During the period October 6, 2013 to April 5, 2014 this requirement was relaxed for Real Time Information employers with less than 49 employees in that they only had to provide the information by the last day of the tax month, i.e. by the 5th of the following calendar month. In December 2013 HMRC announced a further relaxation of this rule that applied only until April 2016 but only to existing employers with nine or fewer employees. They were required to provide the information on or before the last pay day of the month.

Paragraph (3) allows the Secretary of State to decide that para.(2) does not apply

- in relation to a particular employment, where the information from the employer is "unlikely to be sufficiently accurate or timely"; or

- in respect of a particular assessment period where

(i) no information is received from HMRC and this is likely to be due to a failure to report (including the failure of a computer system); or

(ii) the information received from HMRC is incorrect, or the payment does not fall within the meaning of employed earnings in reg.55, in some material respect.

If the Secretary of State decides that para.(2) does not apply, they have to decide the amount of the claimant's employed earnings for the assessment period, using such information or evidence as they think fit (para.(4)). Presumably the claimant will be asked to provide the necessary information (see para.(1)). Note also the Secretary of State's power under reg. 54(2)(b) to estimate a claimant's employed earnings where the claimant has failed to report.

There would seem to be a relatively thin line between the circumstances in which para.(2)(b) (no information received from HMRC) will apply and those in which para.(3)(b)(i) (no information received from HMRC which is likely to be due to a failure to report) applies. Unless the claimant does not have employed earnings in a particular assessment period, it seems likely that in most instances the lack of information will be due to some failure to report (bearing in mind that failure to report includes the failure of a computer system: see para.(3)(b)(i)).

In *SSWP v RW (rule 17) (UC)* [2017] UKUT 347 (AAC), the Secretary of State's submission to the Upper Tribunal supported the application of para.(3)(b)(i) in a way that appears wrong. HMRC's real time earnings feed showed notification on two dates in February 2016 (February 1, 2016 and February 29, 2016) of the claimant having received earnings. Her assessment period ran from the first of each calendar month to the last day of that month. Both receipts were taken into account in relation to February 2016, resulting in a much reduced universal credit entitlement. The claimant's case on mandatory reconsideration and appeal was that her January 2016 earnings were received on Sunday January 31, 2016, but not reported by her employer until the next day (as apparently confirmed in HMRC documents). She had no control over when the earnings information was reported. The First-tier Tribunal, in allowing the claimant's appeal, rejected the Secretary of State's argument at that stage that para.(3) did not justify any departure from the basic rule in para.(2)(a) that, where the employer is a RTI employer, the amount of a claimant's earnings for any assessment period is to be based on the information which is both reported to HMRC *and* received by the Secretary of State from HMRC in that assessment period. The tribunal relied on two alternative reasons: that under para.(3)(b)(i) no information had been received from HMRC in respect of the January assessment period and that under para.(3)(b)(ii) the information received in respect of the February 2016 assessment period failed to reflect the definition of employed earnings in reg.55 in some material respect. The Secretary of State appealed to the Upper Tribunal, but on receipt of detailed directions from Judge Wright, applied to withdraw the appeal, saying after further directions that it had been concluded that the case could be brought within para.(3)(b)(i) on the basis that reporting a payment by an employer after the date on which it was actually made can be considered a failure by the employer (and drawing attention to the provisions of paras (4) and (5)). In the light of that explanation Judge Wright consented to the withdrawal of the appeal. He directed that his decision recording that withdrawal, although it determined none of the issues involved, go onto the AAC website as the Secretary of State's reasoning might be relevant in other cases.

However, the reliance on para.(3)(b)(i) in relation to the January 2016 assessment, even if justified, appears to be a red herring. Paragraph (3)(b) applies in respect of a particular assessment period. If no information was received from HMRC because of a failure by the employer that could only have affected entitlement in the January 2016 assessment period and not entitlement in the February 2016 assessment period. It appears that the tribunal altered the amount of entitlement for the February 2016 assessment period and it not clear what, if any, adjustment was made in relation to the January 2016 assessment period. Further, it appears a more natural reading of para.(3)(b)(i) that it applies only where no information has been received from HMRC by the date on which a decision is made about a particular assessment period, not where information has been received by that date but involves some late recording of receipts. Thus the reason for the Secretary of State's support of the tribunal's decision in relation to the February 2016 assessment period appears flawed.

The alternative basis adopted by the tribunal under para.(3)(b)(ii) also appears flawed in so far as it relied on the information received from HMRC having failed to reflect the definition of employed earnings in reg.55. Regulation 55 is concerned with the nature of the categories of payments that count or do not count as such earnings and with allowable deductions, not with any rules as to the assessment period to which any payment is to be attributed. It is reg.54(1) that supplies the general principle that, unless otherwise provided in Chap.2 of the Regulations, the calculation of earned income in respect of any assessment period is to be based on the actual amounts received in that period. The information received from HMRC in *RW* did not fail to reflect any element of the definition in reg.55. It failed to reflect the fact that the claimant received a payment (which plainly fell within reg.55) on January 31, 2016, which is a different thing. The tribunal in its statement of reasons referred to reg.55(5) as indicating that the purpose of reg.55 was to find the employed earnings in an assessment period. It is true that reg.55(5), on deductions for national insurance, income tax and pension contributions, refers to those being for the purpose of calculating the amount of employed earnings in respect of an assessment period, but that merely sets the context and does not make the definition in reg.55 include any requirement that amounts be notified in the same assessment period as they were received in.

However, the tribunal's decision may be supported on a rather simpler and more straightforward basis. Why could it not have been concluded that the circumstances fell within para.(3)(b)(ii) because the information received from HMRC was incorrect in a material respect? The word "incorrect" is one that can legitimately be given a relatively broad interpretation. The information notified by HMRC on Monday February 1, 2016 was incorrect in the sense that, whether the delay in reporting over the preceding weekend was the employer's or HMRC's, the dating of the notification on the first available working day created a materially misleading impression. The way would then be open, as the effect of satisfaction of para.(3) is that para. (2) does not apply, to apply the ordinary rules in regs 54 and 55 to both assessment periods in accordance with reg.61(4) and (5).

Such a conclusion would now be strengthened by the evidence noted above of HMRC's instructions that earnings are to be reported as paid on the usual pay day even if actually paid earlier or later, e.g. because the usual day is a non-banking day or falls in a Christmas and New Year period. If the employer fails to follow that instruction the information received from HMRC is strongly arguable to be incorrect in a material respect (see the discussion of *Johnson* and *Pantellerisco* above).

Paragraph (4) requires the Secretary of State, and therefore any tribunal on appeal, in any case in which para.(2) does not apply, to decide the amount of earnings in accordance with reg.54, with a very general discretion to use such information or evidence as is thought fit in doing so.

Under para.(5), if the Secretary of State makes a decision under para.(4), they can treat a payment of employed earnings received in one assessment period as received in a later assessment period, or, where the decision under para.(4) took account of a payment of employed earnings, disregard information about the same payment received from HMRC.

Paragraph (6) provides that the flexibility in para.(5) also applies where the Secretary of State makes a decision under reg.41(3) of the Decisions and Appeals Regulations 2013 where the claimant has disputed the information provided by HMRC. Under subs.(1)(b)(vi) of s.159D (effect of alterations affecting universal credit) of SSAA 1992 (Vol.III of this series), inserted by s.31 of, and para.23 of Sch.2 to, WRA 2012, and reg.41 of the Decisions and Appeals Regulations

2013 (Pt. V of this volume), an alteration (i.e., an increase or decrease) in the amount of a claimant's employed earnings as a result of information provided to the Secretary of State by HMRC takes effect without any further decision by the Secretary of State. However, if the claimant disputes the figure used in accordance with reg.55 to calculate their employed earnings in any assessment period, they can ask the Secretary of State to give a decision in relation to that assessment period (which must be given within 14 days of the request, or as soon as practicable thereafter).

The point of that provision might appear to be to give the claimant a right of appeal, but there are obstacles to such a conclusion in the unnecessary obscurities in the chain of legislation involved. Paragraph 6(b)(v) of Sch.2 to the SSA 1998 (Pt. I of this volume) provides that no appeal lies against a decision as to the amount of benefit to which a person is entitled where the amount is determined by an alteration of a kind referred to in s.159D(1)(b) of the SSAA. Thus, even though the alteration is given effect through a Secretary of State's decision, rather than without such a decision as in the general application of s.159D, at first sight there can be no appeal against the decision. It would appear that para.6(b)(v) applies as much to a decision removing entitlement entirely as well as to one reducing the amount of entitlement. The claimant would then be restricted to applying for revision on the "any time" ground in reg.10(a) of the Decisions and Appeals Regulations 2013 (with consequently no right of appeal if unsuccessful) or to an application for judicial review.

However, that effect would arguably be inconsistent with art.6 of the ECHR (fair trial) under the Human Rights Act 1998, on the basis that revision or judicial review would not be adequate alternatives to a right to appeal. There would then be an obligation under s.3 to interpret legislation in a way compatible with ECHR rights. It is possible to interpret the phrase "an alteration of a kind referred to" in s.159D(1)(b) of the SSAA 1992 as used in para.6(b) of Sch.2 to the SSA 1998 as only applying to an alteration that is not merely referred to in s.159D(1)(b) but is not subject to any exception or condition that requires a decision to be given by the Secretary of State. Subsection (1) of s.159D makes its effect subject to such exceptions and conditions as may be prescribed. Regulation 41(3) of the Decisions and Appeals Regulations 2013 may legitimately be regarded as such an exception or condition. Thus, if the process under reg.41(3) leads to the giving of a decision by the Secretary of State, para.6(b) can be interpreted as not standing in the way of there being a right of appeal in the normal way.

That interpretation of para.6(b) of Sch.2 to the SSA 1998 could also lessen, but not completely remove, the adverse consequences of the wider effect of s.159D(1) (b) of the SSAA 1992. Section 159D(1)(b) on alterations to existing awards of universal credit applies to a much wider range of circumstances than the equivalent provisions for other benefits. In addition to alterations in the statutory rates of universal credit or of new style ESA or JSA or other benefit income, head (iii) applies to an alteration in any amount to be deducted in respect of earned income under s.8(3)(a) of the WRA 2012. "Earned income", in accordance with reg.52, covers not just employed earnings, but also remuneration or profit derived from a trade, profit or vocation (i.e. self-employed earnings) or from any other paid work. Thus the prohibition in para.6(b)(v) of Sch.2 would appear to have applied to the circumstances covered by reg.41 even if those circumstances had not been prescribed for the purposes of s.159D(1)(b)(vi). Further, and more seriously, the prohibition on its face extends to any decision on an existing award turning on an alteration for any reason in the amount of any kind of earned income (all of which fall to be deducted from the maximum amount of universal credit under s.8(3)(a)). There is some doubt whether reg.41(3) of the Decisions and Appeals Regulations, establishing the exception from or condition relating to s.159D(1)(b) applies only in relation to cases where there is a dispute under reg.61(6) about the information provided by HMRC and not to other disputes about the amount of employed earnings. Does reg.41(3) only operate as a qualification to reg.41(1) on s.159D(b)(vi) cases or does it have a stand-alone operation on its own terms, which could then apply to any dispute about the amount of employed earnings? The obligation under s.3 of the Human Rights Act 1998 to interpret legislation so as to be compatible with ECHR rights would probably lead to the second alternative being adopted, protecting the right of appeal in those cases. However, can the terms of reg.41(3), with the express reference to reg.55 of the Universal Credit Regulations and employed earnings, possibly be interpreted as also applying to the other forms of earned income that count under s.8(3)(a) of the WRA 2012, i.e. self-employed earnings, other paid work and, it appears, notional earned income (see reg.52)? That would arguably entail the addition or substitution of too many words changing the substance of the provision to be considered part of any legitimate process of interpretation. If reg.41(3) is thus restricted to employed earnings, there is nothing to prevent the operation of s.159D(1)(b)(iii) and para.6(b) in requiring alterations in amounts of self-employed earnings, other paid work and notional earned incomes to take effect without any Secretary of State decision and therefore without anything to appeal against. If that outcome would be considered to entail an inconsistency with art.6 (fair trial) of the ECHR, then the argument at the level of the First-tier or Upper Tribunal would probably have to be that the terms of the secondary legislation cannot be allowed to stand in the way of the provision of a fair trial in any individual case, without seeking to say how the defect in the legislation should be remedied generally.

See also para.22 of Sch.1 to the Decisions and Appeals Regulations 2013 which provides that a supersession decision made where a claimant's employed earnings have reduced and they have provided the information for the purpose of calculating those earnings at the times required by the Secretary of State takes effect from the first day of the assessment period in which that change occurred.

Gainful self-employment

[¹Minimum income floor

2.192
62.—(1) This regulation applies to a claimant who—
  (a) is in gainful self-employment (see regulation 64); and
  (b) would, apart from this regulation [⁴or regulation 90], fall within section 22 of the Act (claimants subject to all work-related requirements).

(2) Where this regulation applies to a single claimant, for any assessment period in respect of which the claimant's earned income is less than their individual threshold, the claimant is to be treated as having earned income equal to that threshold.

(3) Where this regulation applies to a claimant who is a member of a couple, for any assessment period in respect of which—
  (a) the claimant's earned income is less than their individual threshold; and
  (b) the couple's combined earned income is less than the couple threshold,

the claimant is to be treated as having earned income equal to their individual threshold minus any amount by which that amount of earned income combined with their partner's earned income would exceed the couple threshold.

(4) In this regulation, references to the claimant's individual threshold and to the couple threshold are to the amounts set out in regulation 90(2) and 90(3) respectively, converted to net [² ...] amounts by—

(a) [² . . .]

(b) deducting such amount for income tax and national insurance contributions as the Secretary of State considers appropriate.

[³(4A) Where this regulation applies in respect of an assessment period in which surplus earnings are treated as an amount of earned income under regulation 54A (surplus earnings), that amount is to be added to the claimant's earned income before this regulation is applied and, in the case of joint claimants, it is to be added to the earned income of either member of the couple so as to produce the lowest possible amount of combined earned income after this regulation is applied.]

(5) An assessment period referred to in this regulation does not include an assessment period which falls wholly within a start-up period or begins or ends in a start-up period.]

AMENDMENTS

1. Universal Credit and Miscellaneous Amendments (No.2) Regulations 2014 (SI 2014/2888) reg.4(5) (November 26, 2014, or in the case of existing awards, the first assessment period beginning on or after November 26, 2014).

2. Universal Credit and Miscellaneous Amendments Regulations 2015 (SI 2015/1754) reg.2(5) (November 4, 2015, or in the case of existing awards, the first assessment period beginning on or after November 4, 2015).

3. Universal Credit (Surpluses and Self-employed Losses) (Digital Service) Amendment Regulations 2015 (SI 2015/345) reg.2(3) (April 11, 2018).

4. Universal Credit (Childcare Costs and Minimum Income Floor) (Amendment) Regulations 2019 (SI 2019/1249) reg.3 (October 3, 2019).

DEFINITIONS

"assessment period"—see WRA 2012, ss.40 and 7(2) and reg.21.
"claimant"—see WRA 2012, s.40.
"couple"—see WRA 2012, ss.39 and 40.
"earned income"–see reg.52.
"gainful self-employment"—see regs 53(1) and 64.
"individual threshold"–see regs 2 and 90(2).
"joint claimants"—see WRA 2012 s.40.
"national insurance contribution"—see reg.2.
"start-up period"—see regs 53(1) and 63.
"work-related requirement"—see WRA 2012, ss.40 and 13(2).

GENERAL NOTE

Temporary coronavirus provisions

With effect from March 13, 2020 to March 29, 2020, reg.4 of the Employment and Support Allowance and Universal Credit (Coronavirus Disease) Regulations 2020 (SI 2020/289) allowed the Secretary of State to determine that reg.62 did not apply to a claimant in the assessment period in which they ceased to be treated as having limited capability for work by virtue of reg.3 and in further periods as considered appropriate. Thus, for those few weeks the possibility of lifting the normal application of reg.62 was limited to situations where a claimant was previously treated as having limited capability for work because of being infected or contaminated with coronavirus disease (COVID-19), being in isolation to prevent such infection or contamination or looking after a child or qualifying young person who was so affected or in isolation. During such a period itself reg.62 could not apply because the claimant would, by virtue of reg.3 be exempted from the work search and work availability requirements. Then reg.4 gave the discretion to continue the

2.193

non-application of reg.62 for the assessment period in which the reg.3 deeming ceased, and for following assessment periods. Regulations 10(3) of the Further Measures Regulations (below) brought the operation of regs 3 and 4 in universal credit to an end on March 30, 2020.

With effect from March 30, 2020 to November 12, 2020 (subject to any amendment), reg.2 of the Social Security (Coronavirus) (Further Measures) Regulations 2020 (SI 2020/371) gives the Secretary of State a very broad discretion, "where it appears expedient as a consequence of the outbreak of coronavirus disease", to alter the normal application of many aspects of reg.62, both more and less restrictively. These are noted at the appropriate places in the notes below. There appear to be difficult questions whether a First-tier Tribunal may exercise that discretion in any appeal against an outcome decision on entitlement to or the amount of universal credit resulting from an application of the regulation on a normal basis.

Note, however, that reg.6 of the Further Measures Regulations prevents the Secretary of State, for three months beginning with March 30, 2020, from imposing a work search requirement on anyone with an award of universal credit and brings any such already imposed requirement to an end. Thus for that period no-one can be subject to all work-related requirements under universal credit and no-one can have the MIF imposed. That is regardless of whether the claimant is or is not affected or by the coronavirus outbreak or its consequences.

2.193.1   This regulation, authorised by para.4(1), (3)(a) and (4) of Sch.1 to the WRA 2012, provides for the "minimum income floor" which applies to certain self-employed claimants and deems them to be receiving that level of income although their actual earnings from self-employment, plus employed earnings, if any, are lower. It is an anti-abuse provision which was presumably introduced partly because of the difficulties of checking the hours of work and takings of the self-employed and partly to provide an incentive against sitting back in unproductive self-employment while relying on universal credit to make up income. The operation of the rule has been considerably affected from April 2018 by the operation of the provisions in reg.54A for spreading surplus earnings and in regs 57(2) and 57A on unused losses in self-employment.

A judicial review challenge to the general operation of reg.62, based on alleged differences in treatment of the self-employed and employed earners was rejected by the Administrative Court (Laing J) in *R. (on the application of Parkin) v Secretary of State for Work and Pensions* [2019] EWHC 2356 (Admin).

Ms Parkin had worked in the theatre as a self-employed person for some years before she claimed universal credit in 2017. Her profits in the 2017/18 tax year were £2,306 and in 2018/19 £2,842.24. She also had some earnings as an employee. A minimum income floor (MIF) of £861.11 per month was applied to her on the basis that she was in gainful self-employment within the meaning of reg.64. Her appeal against that on the ground that she was not in gainful self-employment was refused by a First-tier Tribunal in May 2019. Over the 20 months of her universal credit award down to June 2019 she received £5,318.65 less in universal credit for herself and the one child included in the award than if she had been employed with equivalent earnings and £610.86 less than if she had not been employed at all.

The first ground of Ms Parkin's judicial review challenge to the effect of reg.62 was that there was a breach of art.14 of the ECHR. Laing J accepted that art.8 (respect for family life) and probably art.1 of Protocol 1 (protection of property) was engaged and that there was a difference in treatment between self-employed and employed earners. However, she held that the self-employed and employed earners were not in relevantly analogous circumstances and that, even if that was wrong, the difference in treatment was not manifestly without reasonable foundation and so was justified. The essence of her reasoning appears in paras 103, 107 and 108 of the judgment:

> "103. It is clear that one of the intentions of the statutory scheme is to make work pay, and to encourage claimants to do more productive activities in order

to encourage them, over time, to reduce their reliance on benefits. The practical effects of the legal distinctions between the two groups mean that a work requirement imposed on an employee has an immediate, predictable and measurable effect. There is no directly effective practical equivalent in the case of a self-employed claimant. If Parliament and the executive wanted to achieve the aims I have described in the case of self-employed claimants, a different mechanism had to be designed in order to influence their behaviour. I therefore consider that employed and self-employed claimants are not in relevantly analogous situations for the purposes of this scheme. I also consider, for that reason, that I can, and should, conclude at this stage of the analysis that this part of the claim fails.

107. The question then is whether the MIF, in particular, because it applies to [gainfully self-employed] claimants and not to employed or unemployed claimants, is [manifestly without reasonable foundation]. As I have said in paragraph 103, above, a work requirement and an [individual threshold] amount to a practical and objective tool for influencing the behaviour of employed claimants. Their combined effects are visible and can be measured. The differences between claimants which flow from their decisions to be employed or self-employed mean that a work requirement and an [individual threshold] cannot produce the same effects for self-employed claimants. The imposition of a work requirement on a self-employed claimant would not necessarily make his business more profitable, which is what is at issue.

108. The MIF, however, is such a mechanism. Its effect coheres with the aims I have described, because it encourages self-employed claimants who are in [gainful self-employment] and who wish to claim UC, but whose enterprises consistently generate low profits, to think carefully about whether they should continue to be in [gainful self-employment]. The MIF encourages such thought because its effect is to treat a self-employed claimant as generating profits equivalent to what he would earn from employment at the [national minimum wage], whether or not he in fact generates such profits. It encourages a rational claimant in that position to ask whether continuing in [gainful self-employment] is in his own best interests, and whether he should take up employment instead, or change the balance of his activities between self-employment and employment so that, while continuing to be self-employed, self-employment is no longer his main employment, with the result that he would cease to be in [gainful self-employment] for the purposes of the scheme, and be subject to work requirements instead."

The same reasoning supported the rejection of the argument that the MIF regulations were irrational at common law. There had also been compliance with s.149 of the Equality Act 2010 by reference to the impact of the universal credit scheme as a whole.

It may be arguable that the judge's suggestions about how a claimant could alter the balance between employment and self-employment, so that self-employment would no longer be the main employment and therefore fall outside the meaning of gainful self-employment (see further in the notes to reg.64) and the reach of the MIF, are not entirely realistic. However, that would probably not be enough to undermine the reasoning completely. Note that self-employment falls outside the meaning of gainful self-employment if there is not an expectation of profit.

A new form of reg.62 was introduced on November 26, 2014 in order to make "clearer provision about the calculation of the MIF [minimum income floor] when a self-employed person is a member of a couple (or when both members of a couple are self-employed)" (see the Explanatory Memorandum which accompanies SI 2014/2888). It is a distinct improvement on the previous form of reg.62. However, some confusion still remains, partly because the phrase "individual threshold" as used in reg.62 does not have quite the same meaning as that phrase in reg.90, even though reg.62(4) cross-refers to reg.90. This is because under para.(4)(b) of this regulation "appropriate" deductions for income tax and NI contributions may be made when calculating a claimant's individual threshold, which is not the case under reg.90 (see below).

There was a further amendment, said to implement the original policy intention, with effect from October 3, 2019. In the condition in para.(1)(b) for the application of the MIF that the claimant would be subject to all work-related requirements, not only is the effect of reg.62 itself to be ignored but also the effect of reg.90 on earnings thresholds. See the notes below on *Would be subject to all work-related requirements*.

Regulation 62 will only apply if in any assessment period a claimant

- is in "gainful self-employment" (as defined in reg.64) (para.(1)(a)); *and*

- is not in a "start-up period" (see reg.63) (para. (5)); *and*

- would, apart from this regulation, fall within s. 22 WRA 2012 (claimant subject to all work-related requirements) (para.(1)(b)); *and*

- in the case of a single claimant, their self-employed earnings, together with any other earned income (as defined in reg.52), are below their individual threshold (para.(2)); *or*

  in the case of a couple, their self-employed earnings, together with any other earned income, are below their individual threshold, and the couple's combined earned income is below the couple threshold (para.(3)).

If all four of those conditions are met (subject to the temporary coronavirus provisions) then claimants are deemed to have earned income equal to the threshold even though their actual earned income is lower.

Gainful self-employment

2.193.2   For what might or might not count as gainful self-employment and for the effect of reg.2(1)(b) and (c) of the Coronavirus Further Measures Regulations, see the notes to reg.64. The conditions in reg.64 go a good way beyond the simple issue of whether the activity is carried on in the expectation of gain and must be carefully considered. In particular, the trade, profession or vocation must be the claimant's main employment and must be organised, developed and regular.

Not in start-up period

2.193.3   See the notes to reg.63 for what is a start-up period and how long it can last. In brief, it can start to run where the claimant started the trade, profession or vocation that is now the main employment in the 12 months before the beginning of the first assessment period in which it is determined that the claimant is in gainful self-employment and is taking active steps to increase the earnings from that self-employment to the level of the individual threshold. Then the period lasts for 12 months starting with that assessment period unless the claimant ceases to be in gainful self-employment or ceases to take the active steps to increase earnings. Note that with effect from March 30, 2020, the Secretary of State has a discretion (intended for use where expedient as a consequence of the coronavirus outbreak) to extend a start-up period as appropriate (reg.2(1)(d) of the Coronavirus Further Measures Regulations). See the notes to reg.63.

Would be subject to all work-related requirements

2.193.4   The requirement that the claimant would, apart from the operation of the MIF or reg.90, fall within s.22 of the WRA 2012 and thus not be exempted from the imposition of any work-related requirement adds an important limitation, that must not be overlooked in a focus on the level of earned income in the particular assessment period (see further below). The final condition is that the claimant or claimants' earned income is below the reg.62 individual or couple threshold as appropriate. Remember, as noted at the very beginning of this note, that reg.6 of the Further

Measures Regulations prevents the Secretary of State, for three months beginning with March 30, 2020, from imposing a work search requirement on anyone with an award of universal credit and brings any such already imposed requirement to an end (as well as suspending the work availability requirement). Thus, for that period no-one can be subject to all work-related requirements under universal credit and no-one can have the MIF imposed. That is regardless of whether the claimant is or is not affected or by the coronavirus outbreak or its consequences.

The following notes deal with the situation free of those temporary provisions.

It must, because of the third condition (in para.(1)(b)), be asked in all cases whether some provision in or under ss.19—22 exempts the claimant from one or more work-related requirements. In particular, prior to October 3, 2019 the operation of reg.90 needed to be considered. As discussed below, this provision exempts claimants from all work-related requirements if their monthly earnings before any deduction for income tax, national insurance contributions or relievable pension contributions (reg.90(6)(a)) at least equal their individual threshold under reg.90(2), called the conditionality earnings threshold. In the great majority of cases anyone with earnings at that level would not fall within the scope of reg.62, but it should be noted that reg.90(6)(b) requires, in cases where earned income fluctuates or is likely to fluctuate, a monthly averaging over any identifiable cycle or otherwise over three months or such other period as may enable the average to be determined more accurately. That can apply to earnings from employment or other paid work as well as to earnings from self-employment. However, it is in the nature of self-employment in particular that earned income (i.e. actual receipts less allowable expenses in each assessment period) will fluctuate month by month, even in businesses that are well established and large scale. Thus if in a particular assessment period the amount of a claimant's earned income fell below the reg.62 individual threshold it could not immediately be assumed that the MIF would apply. The monthly average could at least equal the reg.90 individual threshold (the conditionality earnings threshold) so that the claimant remained exempted from all work-related requirements.

The position changed with the October 2019 amendment so that if a claimant is only exempted from work-related requirements through the operation of reg.90 that does not prevent the application of the MIF. The change was said by the DWP to restore the original policy intention and was explained in the Explanatory Memorandum as follows:

"7.9 [The amendment is] to make clear that a reference to a claimant in the All Work Related Requirements conditionality group includes those who are exempt from the requirement to look for work only because their earnings exceed the Conditionality Earnings Threshold.

7.10 The Conditionality Earnings Threshold is only relevant to employed claimants and, as such, has no role in the application of the Minimum Income Floor. For example, a claimant could meet the Conditionality Earnings Threshold as a result of average earnings over a period of time if they are an employed earner. However, self-employed universal credit claimants are expected to plan for fluctuations in income in the same way as all other self-employed people must do and which is part of running a sustainable business. Gainfully self-employed claimants are expected to earn at or above the set assumed level in each assessment period and, where earnings fall short of this, the Minimum Income Floor is applied."

If the Explanatory Memorandum intended to suggest that reg.90 only applies to employed earners, that is incorrect. "Earned income" is plainly defined in reg.52 to cover both earnings derived from a contract of service or office and earnings derived from self-employment. So the suggestion must have been more that the mechanism of reg.90 was inadequate in itself to apply the appropriate pressure to self-employed claimants either to abandon unproductive self-employment or to make it more productive. That may be debateable, but what is clear is that the amendment has from October 2019 onwards rendered redundant the discussion above of whether the averaging provision in reg.90(6) might prevent the application of the MIF in an assessment period in which earnings fell below the MIF.

The reference in para.(1)(b) to "apart from this regulation" is necessary because of reg.90(5), which exempts any claimant who is treated by reg.62 as having earned income from all work-related requirements (by putting them within s.19 of the WRA 2012). If it were not for that qualification there would be an endless loop by which application of the MIF led to the conditions for its application not being met. The effect of reg.90(5) should not, though, be forgotten while the MIF is in operation. While the Coronavirus Further Measures Regulations are in force, if those special temporary provisions result in the MIF not being applied, so that the claimant could no longer benefit from the deeming in reg.90(5) and would then fall within s.22 of the WRA 2012 (all work-related requirements), the Secretary of State is given the discretion to exempt the claimant from a work search or work availability requirement (reg.2(1)(e)).

Actual earned income below individual or couple's threshold

2.193.5

Note that with effect from March 30, 2020, the Secretary of State has a discretion (intended for use where expedient as a consequence of the coronavirus outbreak) to treat the individual or couple's threshold as zero or as a lesser amount than under reg.90(2) (reg.2(1)(a) of the Coronavirus Further Measures Regulations). That makes it easier for claimants to escape application of the MIF while reg.2 is in effect, if that has not occurred at some earlier stage in the process.

Although "earned income" is defined in reg.52(a) merely in terms of the remuneration or profits derived from employment, self-employment or other paid work, it would seem that paras (2) and (3) must be taken as referring to the amount of earned income to be taken into account for universal credit purposes, thus requiring the deduction of income tax, national insurance contributions and relievable pension contributions (employed earnings: reg.55(5) (plus payroll giving); self-employed earnings: reg.57(2)). But note that under para.(4)(b) there is no power to deduct relievable pension contributions or payroll giving from the individual or couple threshold. Claimants who made large pension contributions might therefore have particular need of the possibility that the MIF does not apply because they are exempted from all work-related requirement under reg.90. Although the MIF cannot apply unless the self-employment is the claimant's main employment, employed earnings may come into the calculation, especially in the case of joint claimants.

The new (April 2018) para.(4A) confirms that where surplus earnings calculated under reg.54A are to be applied in any assessment period they are to be taken into account as part of claimants' earned income for reg.62 purposes. If the surplus earnings are sufficient on their own to wipe out entitlement to universal credit that consequence does not matter. If the surplus earnings on their own do not have that effect, then they may, depending on their level, help lift earned income up to the individual or couple threshold, so that MIF does not apply and actual earnings plus surplus earnings are taken against the maximum amount of universal credit. Income deemed to exist by reg.62 does not count in the calculation of surplus earnings under reg.54A (reg.54A(5)). The new (April 2018) provision on unused losses for the self-employed (reg.57A) may work in the opposite direction. Unused losses (unused in the sense that a claimant's self-employed earnings to be counted against the maximum amount in the assessment period in which received cannot be less than nil) from any past assessment period can now operate to reduce the amount of self-employed earnings as calculated under reg.57(2). That could have the effect of taking the amount of earned income in the current assessment period below the individual or couple threshold and triggering the application of the MIF when it would not be triggered on the current earnings. The fairness entailed in the operation of reg.57A on its own would be impaired by that. Fluctuations in earnings, and in particular the new taking into account of fluctuations in terms of past losses by the self-employed, are likely to have unpredictable, and sometimes harsh effects, on the application of the MIF.

Some claimants might think of forming limited companies of which they are the sole or main employee and director in order to pursue the business that would otherwise have been the trade, profession or vocation followed as a self-employed person, aiming not to be self-employed at all and so free of the MIF rules. That does not work because of the effect of reg.77(3)(b) and (c). Where a person stands in a position analogous to that of a sole trader or partner in relation to a company carrying on a trade or property business the company's income or the claimant's share of it is to be treated as the claimant's income and calculated under reg.57 as if it were self-employed earnings and, if the claimant's activities in the course of the trade are their main employment, reg.62 is to apply. See the notes to regs 57 and 77 for some complications and the limited exceptions in reg.77(5).

For a claimant's individual threshold for the purposes of reg.62, the starting point is reg.90(2). This provides that a claimant's individual threshold is the hourly rate of the national minimum wage for a claimant of that age multiplied by, in the case of a claimant who would otherwise be subject to all work-related requirements under s.22 of the WRA 2012, the expected number of hours per week (usually 35, see reg.88). In the case of a claimant who would otherwise fall within ss.20 or 21, the multiplier is 16. That can be relevant when one of joint claimants is subject to all work-related requirements, but their partner is not (see below for couples). This amount is then multiplied by 52 and divided by 12 (to make it monthly), from which is deducted "such amount for income tax and national insurance contributions as the Secretary of State considers appropriate" (para.(4)). Presumably this will normally be the amount for income tax and NI contributions that would be payable if the claimant's actual earned income was at this level but para.(4)(b) does not actually say that.

If the claimant's earned income is less than this figure (the minimum income floor) they will be treated as having earned income equal to this figure (para.(2)). If it equals or exceeds this figure reg.62 does not apply and the claimant's actual earnings will be taken into account in the normal way.

Example 1

Michael is single, aged 25 and a self-employed plumber. He declares earnings of £580 (£700 less permitted expenses of £120) for the current assessment period. He also has employed earnings of £200 a month as he works in a hardware store on Saturday mornings. His minimum income floor is £1,202.66 a month (35 hours a week x £8.72 x 52 ÷ 12, less £119.87 for notional tax and NI contributions). As his self-employed earnings and employed earnings added together amount to £780, this is less than his minimum income floor and so he is treated as having earnings of £1,202.66 and his universal credit is assessed on that basis.

2.194

In the case of a couple, the position is more complicated. Under para.(3), in addition to the condition that the claimant's earned income is less than their individual threshold (as calculated under para.(4)), the couple's combined earned income must also be less than the couple threshold (as calculated under para.(4)) for reg.62 to apply. The starting point for calculating the couple threshold under para.(4) is reg.90(3). This provides that in the case of joint claimants their individual thresholds are added together (see reg.90(3)(b) for how the threshold is calculated in the case of a person who is a member of a couple but claims as a single person by virtue of reg.3(3)). This amount is then multiplied by 52 and divided by 12 (to make it monthly), from which is deducted "such amount for income tax and national insurance contributions as the Secretary of State considers appropriate" (para.(4)(b)).

If these two conditions are met, the claimant will be treated as having earned income equal to their individual threshold, less any amount by which that deemed earned income combined with their partner's earned income exceeds the couple threshold (para.(3)).

Example 2

2.195   Rafiq and Maggie are a couple (both over 25) and they have one child, Charlie, who is aged 2. Rafiq has a photography business and Maggie works in a pub in the evenings. Maggie's earnings are £700 and Rafiq's are £500 in the current assessment period.

Maggie has been accepted as the "responsible carer" for Charlie and so falls within s.21(1)(aa) of the WRA 2012. Her individual threshold is therefore £604.59 (16 hours a week x £8.72 x 52 ÷ 12 = £604.59), with no tax or NI contribution deductions at this level of earnings).

Rafiq's individual threshold is £1,202.66 a month (35 hours a week x £8.72 x 52 ÷ 12, less £119.87 for tax and NI contributions).

Rafiq and Maggie's actual combined earnings are £1,200 (£500 + £700).

This is below the sum of their joint earnings thresholds of £1,807.25 (£1,202.66 for Rafiq + £604.59 for Maggie).

However, adding Rafiq's minimum income floor to Maggie's actual earnings gives £1,902.66 (£1,202.66 + £700). That is £95.41 above their joint earnings thresholds of £1,807.25, so Rafiq is treated as having earnings of £1,107.25 (£1,202.66 less £95.41). Their universal credit is assessed on the basis of earned income of £1,807.25 (Rafiq's deemed earnings of £1,107.25 plus Maggie's actual earnings of £700).

Note that if reg.62 does apply in an assessment period, a claimant will not be subject to work-related requirements in that assessment period (see reg.90(1) and (5)).

Note also that income a claimant is deemed to have by virtue of reg.62 does not count as earned income for the purpose of the benefit cap (see reg.82(4)).

See the notes to reg.61 for discussion of whether any alterations of existing awards resulting from increases or reductions in the amount of earned income apart from employed earnings, which could include such changes resulting from the application of the MIF, are appealable.

Start-up period

2.196   **63.**—(1) A "start-up period" is a period of 12 months and applies from the beginning of the assessment period in which the Secretary of State determines that a claimant is in gainful self-employment where—

> (a) the claimant has begun to carry on the trade, profession or vocation which is their main employment in the 12 months preceding the beginning of that assessment period; and
>
> (b) the claimant is taking active steps to increase their earnings from that employment to the level of the claimant's individual threshold (see regulation 90).

(2) But no start-up period may apply in relation to a claimant where a start-up period has previously applied in relation to that claimant, whether in relation to the current award or any previous award of universal credit, unless that previous start-up period—

> (a) began more than 5 years before the beginning of assessment period referred to in paragraph (1); and
>
> (b) applied in relation to a different trade, profession or vocation which the claimant has ceased to carry on.

(3) The Secretary of State may terminate a start-up period at any time if the person is no longer in gainful self-employment or is no longer taking the steps referred to in paragraph (1)(b).

DEFINITIONS

"assessment period"—see WRA 2012 ss.40 and 7(2) and reg.21.
"claimant"—see WRA 2012 s.40.
"gainful self-employment"—see regs 53(1) and 64.
"individual threshold"—see regs 2 and 90(2).

GENERAL NOTE

Temporary coronavirus provisions

See the notes to reg.62 for the temporary provisions allowing an alteration or sus-   **2.197**
pension of the minimum income floor (MIF). In particular, reg.2(1)(d) of the Social
Security (Coronavirus) (Further Measures) Regulations 2020 (SI 2020/371 (in effect
from March 30, 2020 to November 12, 2020, unless extended or curtailed by amendment) allows the Secretary of State to extend a start-up period as long as appropriate.

If the claimant is in a "start-up period", the minimum income floor does not apply   **2.197.1**
even if they are in gainful self-employment (as defined in reg.64) (see reg.62(5)).
A start-up period is a period of 12 months starting from the beginning of the assessment period in which the Secretary of State decides that the claimant is in gainful
self-employment, provided that the claimant (i) started the trade, profession or vocation which is now the main employment in the 12 months before the beginning of
that assessment period and (ii) is taking active steps to increase their earnings from
that self-employment to the level of their individual threshold under reg.90, i.e., the
level at which they will no longer have to meet work-related requirements (para.(1)).
Note that with effect from July 24, 2019, reg.59 of the Universal Credit
(Transitional Provisions) Regulations 2014 (SI 2014/1230), as inserted by reg.3 of
the Universal Credit (Managed Migration Pilot and Miscellaneous Amendments)
Regulations 2019 (SI 2019/1152), gives a special meaning to "start-up period"
where a claimant in receipt of a legacy benefit has received a notice that existing
benefits are to terminate ("a notified person") and claims universal credit before the
deadline. Regulation 63 is then to be applied as if para.(1)(a) were omitted. Thus
the condition that the claimant began to carry on the self-employment that is their
main employment in the 12 months before the Secretary of State determines that
the claimant is in gainful self-employment does not apply. The start-up period can
still only apply for 12 months from the beginning of the assessment period in which
the Secretary of State makes that determination.
Although it is often said that the start-up period only protects the first 12 months
of self-employment from the operation of the MIF, in fact the combination of the
conditions in para.(1) can extend to 24 months. The forward 12 months only starts
to run with the assessment period in which the Secretary of State recognises that
the claimant is in gainful self-employment as defined in reg.64. Before that date the
claimant needs no protection from the MIF because regulation 62 will not apply
(reg.62(1)(a)), although of course any profits from the self-employment will count
as earned income. The encouragement not to continue in some disorganised or
irregular way, so avoiding the MIF, for an extended time is in the rule that there is
to be no start-up period where the trade, profession or vocation that has become
gainful self-employment was started more than 12 months before the assessment
period in which that was recognised by the Secretary of State.
If the claimant is no longer in gainful self-employment, or is not taking active
steps to increase their earnings as required by para.(1)(b), the Secretary of State can
end the start-up period (para.(3)). If the Secretary of State chooses to terminate the
start-up period in such circumstances, a consequence is that if the claimant later
becomes gainfully self-employed again or starts taking the required active steps,
application of the MIF can no longer be suspended except on the conditions in
para.(2)(a) and (b) (see below). Any challenge to that choice would appear to have
to be by way of judicial review or possibly by way of appeal against the entitlement

decision in the new circumstances. If the Secretary of State chooses not to terminate the start-up period in such circumstances, it appears to follow that the 12-month period continues to run even though the MIF can no longer be applied. The same would appear to follow if the MIF ceased to apply because the claimant ceased to be subject to all work-related requirements.

A claimant can only have one start-up period in relation to the same trade, profession or vocation. In addition, a claimant who has had a previous start-up period can only have a further start-up period in relation to a different trade, profession or vocation if the previous start-up period began more than five years before the start of the assessment period in which the new one begins (para.(2)).

Meaning of "gainful self-employment"

2.198

64. A claimant is in gainful self-employment for the purposes of regulations 62 and 63 where the Secretary of State has determined that—

    (a) the claimant is carrying on a trade, profession or vocation as their main employment;

    (b) their earnings from that trade, profession or vocation are self-employed earnings; and

    (c) the trade, profession or vocation is organised, developed, regular and carried on in expectation of profit.

DEFINITIONS

"claimant"—see WRA 2012, s.40.
"self-employed earnings"—see regs 53(1) and 57.

GENERAL NOTE

Temporary coronavirus provisions

2.199

See the notes to reg.62 for the temporary provisions allowing an alteration or suspension of the MIF and the period for which the MIF cannot be imposed on anyone because of the prohibition on imposing the work search requirement on anyone. In particular, reg.2(1)(b) and (c) of the Social Security (Coronavirus) (Further Measures) Regulations 2020 (in effect from March 30, 2020 to November 12, 2020, unless extended or curtailed by amendment) allow the Secretary of State, as expedient, to delay making a determination that a claimant is in gainful self-employment and, if such a determination has been made, treat the claimant as not in gainful self-employment.

2.199.1

This defines when a claimant is in "gainful self-employment". This is important because it determines whether the "minimum income floor" (see reg.62) applies to the claimant's earned income. Although the regulation does not expressly say that a claimant is *only* in gainful self-employment when its conditions are met, it appears to be a necessary implication that a claimant is not in gainful self-employment when the conditions are not met.

Claimants are in gainful self-employment if they are carrying on a trade, profession or vocation as their main employment, the earnings from which are self-employed earnings, and the trade, profession or vocation is "organised, developed, regular and carried on in expectation of profit". The mere hope of profit is not enough. There must be a realistic expectation not just of bringing money in, but of profit. If any of these conditions are not met, the claimant will not be in gainful self-employment. It appears that if the claimant's earnings are from "other paid work" (reg.52(a)(iii)) reg.64 cannot apply, but it is not at all clear what sort of work can fall into that category.

In order to decide whether claimants are in gainful self-employment, they will be asked to attend a Gateway interview soon after making a claim for universal credit or after declaring that they are in self-employment.

There is lengthy guidance on the gainful self-employment test at paras H4020–4058 ADM.

Carrying on a trade etc.

The guidance gives little attention to the question of whether and when a claim-   **2.199.2**
ant is carrying on a trade etc under para.(b), treating that as mainly subsumed in the
issue of regularity under para.(c). However, it appears that there is a prior condition
that the claimant is both carrying on a trade etc and doing so as their main employment. There may be difficult questions whether a claimant is currently carrying on
a trade etc, for instance where there are seasonal periods of non-activity or some
circumstances intervene to interrupt activity and in which the future of the trade
cannot be predicted. In *KD v SSWP (UC)* [2020] UKUT 18 (AAC), a case where
there was apparently just a slackening off in gardening work in the winter rather
than a period of complete inactivity, the judge did not think that authorities on the
rules for other benefits were of any help in deciding how the minimum income floor
(MIF) rules were to apply. But there may be some guidance in the cases on whether
a person is engaged in remunerative work under reg.5 of the Income Support
Regulations (and equivalents) or has ceased to be employed as a self-employed
earner for the purposes of para.3 of Sch.8 (disregard of earnings). See the notes to
those provisions in Vol.II of this series for full discussion.

In *R(JSA) 1/09* Judge Rowland took the view that there is a distinction between
whether a person is employed as a self-employed earner, which he took to mean
trading, and whether the person, if so employed, is engaged in remunerative work or
part-time work as a self-employed earner (in particular for the purposes of the condition of entitlement of not being engaged in remunerative work). That distinction
has sometimes been summarised as the difference between being in work and being
at work (see para.18 of *R(JSA) 1/07*, in the context of employed earners). He also
took the view that a person ceased to be so employed on no longer being employed
in the former sense. Although some of the reasoning in that case has been doubted
in subsequent decisions, it is submitted that the basic distinction remains. The
notion of carrying on a trade etc in reg.64 appears to be equivalent to the question
of whether a person is employed, in the above sense of trading, rather than to being
engaged in self-employment.

Paragraph 27020 of the DMG (repeated in substance in para.H4055 of ADM)
suggests nine factors potentially relevant to whether a person is no longer trading,
rather than there merely being an interruption in the person's activities in a continuing employment. The substance of that approach (although then directed to whether
the claimant was in gainful employment within the definition of self-employment)
was approved in *CIS/166/1994*, although in some other cases reservations have been
expressed. The nine factors overlap somewhat and it is recognised that not all will
be relevant in a particular case, but represent a sensible approach. In summary, they
are whether the person has reasonable prospects of work in the near future; whether
the business is a going concern and regarded as such by others; whether the person
is genuinely available for and seeking alternative work; whether the person hopes or
intends to resume work when conditions improve; whether the person is undertaking any activities in connection with the self-employment; whether there is any work
in the pipeline; whether the person is regarded as self-employed by HMRC; whether
the person is making it known that the business can take on work; and whether the
interruption is part of the normal pattern of the business.

It has though been made clear in some recent decisions that neither an intention to resume self-employment in the future nor the existence of a past seasonal
pattern of activity and non-activity in itself requires a conclusion for income support
and equivalent purposes that the person is still trading and is still employed in self-
employment. The old style JSA claimant in *Saunderson v Secretary of State for Work
and Pensions* [2012] CSIH 102; [2013] AACR 16 had worked as a self-employed golf
caddie in St Andrews in the spring and summer months for several years. The claim
was after the end of the summer season, when his authorisation to act as a caddie

had been withdrawn and there was no commitment that he would be able to work in the next or subsequent years. The question was whether entitlement was excluded by reason of the claimant being treated as engaged in remunerative work in periods in which he carried out no activities. The Inner House of the Court of Session held that such a deeming could only operate when the claimant was "in work" in the ordinary meaning of the word. That seems to involve essentially the same factors as the question of whether the person is carrying on trade. The court remitted the question to a new tribunal for decision but said this in para.20 (the language being coloured by arguments that the self-employed had to be treated differently from employees):

> "Plainly there may be many self-employed trading or professional activities in which it is not difficult to say that the professional or trading activity continues notwithstanding an idle period. An example might be the arable farmer who, having ploughed and sowed the winter wheat in the autumn, has relatively little to do until the arrival of the spring. In some respects, one might draw an analogy with a schoolteacher whom one would readily say was in work albeit that his teaching duties are punctuated by school holidays in which he has little by way of professional activity to perform. But conversely, there will be seasonally pursued activities which, while treated in their exercise for contractual or fiscal reasons as a 'self-employed' activity, are in their substance little different from employment. Typically (but not exclusively), such *quasi* employed activities might be those in which the individual has no significant commercial capital invested and the temporal limit on his exercise of that technically self-employed activity is dictated by seasonal factors affecting demand for the person's services."

A Northern Ireland Commissioner followed *Saunderson* in *TC v DSD (JSA)* [2013] NI Com 65. He held that the claimant had ceased self-employment as an eel-fisherman when he made his claim in September 2011 although he hoped to resume fishing in May 2012. For the months of January to April statutory rules prohibited fishing and it was not economically worthwhile to fish from October to December. In the particular year the gearbox of his engine broke in early August and he could not afford a repair or source a replacement in time to resume fishing that season. Some further discussion of the weighing-up of the factors considered relevant would have been helpful. In particular, the steps that the claimant was taking and intended to take in the months before May 2012, to get his boat in a condition to resume fishing, and possibly to recruit helpers, could have been said to point to his continuing to be in work. But the uncertainty of the outcome of such steps as at the date of decision perhaps outweighed that factor in the context of the length of the break and the test not requiring a permanent cessation of employment. What was clear was that the mere fact that the claimant had fished during the restricted season for several years did not automatically lead to a conclusion that the self-employment had not ceased in August 2011.

There may be specific testing of the meaning of carrying on a trade in 2020 in the context of the disruption to business caused by the coronavirus outbreak. As detailed in the notes to reg.62, the prohibition on the imposition of a work search requirement and the suspension of the work availability requirement for the three months from March 30, 2020 prevents any application of the MIF. But once that period ends, the general discretion in reg.2 of the Further Measures Regulations (above) on treating claimants as not in gainful self-employment becomes relevant. There may be many cases in which it can be argued that the use of that discretion is unnecessary and that the claimant is no longer "carrying on" a trade etc. during continued inactivity. The length of any period of enforced inactivity and the realistic prospects of being able to resume profitable trading with the necessary adaptations for hygiene and personal protection measures, even with the assistance of the various governmental grant and loan schemes, might be particularly relevant. In addition, the application of the capital disregard of assets used or previously used for the purposes of a trade etc that a person is or was carrying on (paras 7 and 8 of Sch.10) would need to be considered.

Main employment

The ADM guidance suggests that the question of whether the self-employment is the claimant's main employment will depend on a number of factors, such as the hours spent undertaking it each week, whether this is a significant proportion of the claimant's expected hours per week, how many hours (if any) the claimant spends on employed activity, the amount of income received, whether the claimant receives a greater proportion of their income from self-employed or employed activity, and whether self-employment is the claimant's main aim. The ordinary use of language would suggest that if the self-employed activity in question, however slight or unprofitable beyond a de minimis level, is all that the claimant does by way of employment, then that has to be their main employment. However, that is not the view taken in para.H4023 of the ADM, where it is said that in such circumstances, if the activity is for only a few hours a week or is on a low-paid basis, it should not be regarded as the main employment. There are various elaborate examples given where either of those factors on their own are said to have that effect, so as to avoid the need to examine the criteria laid down in para.(c).

Organised, developed, regular and expectation of profit

In order to decide whether the self-employment is "organised, developed, regular and carried on in expectation of profit", the guidance suggests that factors such as whether the work is undertaken for financial gain, the number of hours worked each week, whether there is a business plan, the steps being taken to increase the income from the work, whether the business is being actively marketed or advertised, how much work is in the pipeline and whether HMRC regard the activity as self-employment may be relevant. None of those factors seem related specifically to regularity, which will have to be determined in accordance with the overall pattern of activity. Difficult questions may arise where the nature of the trade etc carried on creates seasonal fluctuations or even seasonal periods of non-activity.

JF v HMRC (TC) [2017] UKUT 334 (AAC) concerned the definition of "self-employed" in reg.2(1) of the Working Tax Credit (Entitlement and Maximum Rate) Regulations 2002 as in force with effect from April 6, 2015 (see Vol.IV of this series), which includes a condition that the trade, profession or vocation be "organised and regular". Judge Wikeley gave guidance that, in assessing organisation and regularity for the purposes of WTC, HMRC should "get real" and adjust expectations about the documentary support to be expected for the modest enterprises often involved. Nor should the facts that a claimant did not have an accountant or a business plan necessarily mean that the condition was not met. However, by contrast with the position in WTC, self-employed universal credit claimants will no doubt often be arguing that their business is not organised, developed and regular, so as to avoid the operation of the minimum income floor under reg.62, rather than the other way round, to qualify for WTC.

In *KD v SSWP (UC)* [2020] UKUT 18 (AAC), the gardener's case mentioned above, the judge did not wish, having not had argument on both sides, to express a definitive conclusion on whether regular meant having a constant frequency or merely according to a standard pattern over some period, so that the trade would continue to be regular through a predictable shortage of work. However, he considered that it would be going too far to say that almost constant frequency was required and was not prepared to overturn the tribunal's conclusion that the claimant was in gainful self-employment although the level of his work and income fell off in the winter months. Again, there may be a testing of the matter in the context of the 2020 coronavirus outbreak, especially once the person starts to undertake some activities, such as preparation in adapting premises or procedures for being able to start earning money again. Could such activity be said to be "regular" in that special context?

Clearly if the claimant's business is an established one that has been operating for some time and is still receiving income, it may be relatively straightforward to decide that the claimant is in gainful self-employment. If, however, the business is receiving little or no income, it may be that the self-employment is no longer "organised", "regular" or "carried on in expectation of profit". All the circumstances will need to be considered, including future prospects and whether this is part of the normal pattern of the claimant's work. A claimant may still be in gainful employment while unable to work through illness but in that situation should consider submitting medical certificates with a view to no longer being subject to all work-related requirements and thus the minimum income floor not applying. And at some point it would be said that the claimant had ceased to carry on the business.

If the claimant is not in gainful self-employment, the minimum income floor will not apply and the claimant's actual self-employed earnings will be taken into account.

CHAPTER 3

UNEARNED INCOME

Introduction

2.200   **65.** This Chapter provides for the calculation of a person's unearned income for the purposes of section 8 of the Act (calculation of awards).

DEFINITION

"the Act"—see reg.2.

What is included in unearned income?

2.201   **66.**—(1) A person's unearned income is any of their income, including income the person is treated as having by virtue of regulation 74 (notional unearned income), falling within the following descriptions—
   (a) retirement pension income (see regulation 67) [² to which the person is entitled, subject to any adjustment to the amount payable in accordance with regulations under section 73 of the Social Security Administration Act 1992 (overlapping benefits)];
   (b) any of the following benefits to which the person is entitled, subject to any adjustment to the amount payable in accordance with regulations under section 73 of the Social Security Administration Act 1992 (overlapping benefits)—
       (i) jobseeker's allowance,
      (ii) employment and support allowance,
     (iii) carer's allowance,
      (iv) [¹ ...],
       (v) widowed mother's allowance,
      (vi) widowed parent's allowance,
     (vii) widow's pension,
    (viii) maternity allowance, or
      (ix) industrial injuries benefit, excluding any increase in that benefit under section 104 or 105 of the Contributions and Benefits Act (increases where constant attendance needed and for exceptionally severe disablement);
   (c) any benefit, allowance, or other payment which is paid under the law of a country outside the United Kingdom and is analogous to a benefit mentioned in sub-paragraph (b);
   (d) payments made towards the maintenance of the person by their

spouse, civil partner, former spouse or former civil partner under a court order or an agreement for maintenance;

[²(da) foreign state retirement pension;]

  (e) student income (see regulation 68);

  (f) a payment made under section 2 of the Employment and Training Act 1973 or section 2 of the Enterprise and New Towns (Scotland) Act 1990 which is a substitute for universal credit or is for a person's living expenses;

  (g) a payment made by one of the Sports Councils named in section 23(2) of the National Lottery etc. Act 1993 out of sums allocated to it for distribution where the payment is for the person's living expenses;

  (h) a payment received under an insurance policy to insure against—

    (i) the risk of losing income due to illness, accident or redundancy, or

    (ii) the risk of being unable to maintain payments on a loan, but only to the extent that the payment is in respect of owner-occupier payments within the meaning of paragraph 4 of Schedule 1 in respect of which an amount is included in an award for the housing costs element;

  (i) income from an annuity (other than retirement pension income), unless disregarded under regulation 75 (compensation for personal injury);

  (j) income from a trust, unless disregarded under regulation 75 (compensation for personal injury) or 76 (special schemes for compensation);

  (k) income that is treated as the yield from a person's capital by virtue of regulation 72;

  (l) capital that is treated as income by virtue of regulation 46(3) or (4);

[²(la) PPF periodic payments;]

  (m) income that does not fall within sub-paragraphs [²(a) to (la)] and is taxable under Part 5 of the Income Tax (Trading and Other Income) Act 2005(miscellaneous income).

[²(2) In this regulation—

  (a) in paragraph (1)(da) "foreign state retirement pension" means any pension which is paid under the law of a country outside the United Kingdom and is in the nature of social security;

  (b) in paragraph (1)(f) and (g) a person's "living expenses" are the cost of—

    (i) food;

    (ii) ordinary clothing or footwear;

    (iii) household fuel, rent or other housing costs (including council tax),

for the person, their partner and any child or qualifying young person for whom the person is responsible;

  (c) in paragraph (1)(la) "PPF periodic payments" has the meaning given in section 17(1) of the State Pension Credit Act 2002.]

AMENDMENTS

1. Pensions Act 2014 (Consequential, Supplementary and Incidental Amendments) Order 2017 (SI 2017/422) art.43(3) (April 6, 2017, subject to arts 2 and 3).

2. Universal Credit (Miscellaneous Amendments, Saving and Transitional Provision) Regulations 2018 (SI 2018/65) reg.3(9) (April 11, 2018).

DEFINITIONS

"bereavement allowance"—see reg.2.
"carer's allowance" —*ibid.*
"child" —see WRA 2012 s.40
"employment and support allowance" —see reg.2.
"industrial injuries benefit" —*ibid.*
"jobseeker's allowance" —*ibid.*
"maternity allowance" —*ibid.*
"partner"—*ibid.*
"qualifying young person" —see WRA 2012 ss.40 and 10(5) and regs 2 and 5.
"retirement pension income"—see reg.67.
"widowed mother's allowance" —see reg.2.
"widowed parent's allowance" —*ibid.*
"widow's pension"—*ibid.*

MODIFICATION

With effect from June 16, 2014, reg.66 is modified by reg.25 of the Universal Credit (Transitional Provisions) Regulations 2014 (SI 2014/1230) (see Pt IV of this Volume). The modification applies where an award of universal credit is made to a claimant who is entitled to incapacity benefit or severe disablement allowance, in which case reg.66 applies as if incapacity benefit or, as the case may be, severe disablement allowance were added to the list of benefits in reg.66(1)(b).

2.202   GENERAL NOTE

Paragraph (1)
Universal credit adopts the general approach taken in state pension credit of specifying what is to be included as unearned income. If a type of income is not listed as included, it is ignored and does not affect the claimant's (or claimants') award. Accordingly, there is no need for any general provisions disregarding specified kinds of unearned income (but see regs 75 and 76, expressly mentioned in para. (1)(i) and (j)). However, note that rather than, as for state pension credit, providing in regulations that all social security benefits count as unearned income except those specified as excluded, reg.66 lists the benefits that do count. That leaves occasional difficulty in deciding whether certain payments count as within the wide meaning given to "retirement pension income".

In calculating universal credit, all of the claimant's, or the claimants' combined, unearned income that counts is taken into account in full (see s.8(3) of the WRA 2012 and reg.22). There are also some circumstances in which income not listed in reg.66 will affect the application of particular provisions, e.g. the amount of charges allowed in the childcare costs element under reg.34 is reduced to the extent that they are met or reimbursed by some other person or by other relevant support (i.e. in connection with participation in work-related activity or training).

Unearned income also includes notional unearned income (see reg.74).

On para.(1)(a) (retirement pension income), see the note to reg.67, in particular on the meanings of occupational pensions, and on para.(1)(e) (student income), see the note to reg.68. In so far as retirement pension income consists of elements of the state retirement pension (all of which are covered in reg.67), the April 2018 amendment confirms that the amount to be taken into account is the figure after any adjustment under the Overlapping Benefits Regulations. The new para.(1)(da) includes a foreign state retirement pension (defined in para.(2)(a)) and the new para.(1)(la) includes PPF periodic payments (defined in para.(2)(c)—the PPF is the Pension Protection Fund).

Not all benefit income is taken into account—see para.(1)(b) for the benefits that do count in addition to those within the meaning of retirement pension income (note that this will also include incapacity benefit or severe disablement allowance if the claimant is entitled to either of these benefits: see the modification made to para. (1)(b) by reg.25 of SI 2014/1230 referred to above). Thus, for example, child benefit is ignored, as is disability living allowance, attendance allowance and personal independence payment. War disablement pension and war widows', widowers' or surviving civil partners' pensions are also ignored (for income support, old style JSA, old style ESA and housing benefit there is only a £10 disregard). Bereavement allowance, which has been abolished prospectively for deaths on or after April 6, 2017 has been taken out of the list of benefits in para.(1)(b), but remains in the list in relation to awards of the allowance made before April 6, 2017 or to awards made in relation to deaths before that date (see arts 2 and 3 of the amending Order, SI 2017/422). The monthly payments of the new bereavement support payment have not been put into the list, so will not count as income for universal credit purposes, whether paid on time or in arrears. In so far as any payment of arrears is to be treated as capital it is disregarded as such under para.18(1)(c) of Sch.10. The initial one-off lump sum payment appears to have the character of capital and is disregarded as such under the new para.20 of Sch.10.

The definitions of JSA and ESA (listed in heads (i) and (ii)) in reg.2(1) are in terms restricting the meaning to new style JSA and new style ESA. Thus when a claimant previously entitled to a legacy benefit is entitled to the two-week run-on of housing benefit, extended to income support, IBJSA and IRESA from July 22, 2020, none of those receipts count as unearned income under reg.66(1). None of those benefits is listed in sub-para.(b).

By virtue of reg.10 of the Universal Credit (Transitional Provisions) Regulations 2014 (see the notes to that provision in Pt.IIIA), any payment of an "existing benefit" (IRJSA, IBESA, income support or housing benefit, but excluding for these purposes joint claim JSA and any tax credits) made to a claimant who is not entitled to it in respect of a period that falls within a universal credit assessment period is to fall within reg.66(1)(b) as unearned income. The overpayment involved is not then recoverable in the ordinary way. It will in effect be recovered through the deduction in the calculation of universal credit.

In a case brought on the application of Moore, and supported by CPAG, the inclusion of maternity allowance in the list of social security benefits that count as unearned income (para.(1)(b)(viii)) is being challenged. The claimant did not qualify for statutory maternity pay (SMP), which counts as earned income, because she had not worked for her current employer for long enough when she started her maternity leave. If she had received SMP she would have benefited from the work allowance once her daughter was born and from the 63% taper in the amount taken into account whether the work allowance applied or not. It is being argued that the difference in treatment is discriminatory contrary to art.14 of the EHRC, is unreasonable at common law and that there had been a failure to exercise the public sector equality duty under s.149 of the Equality Act 2010 in relation to the contrast with the tax credit position. A "rolled up" hearing took place on June 24 and 25, 2020.

Under para.(1)(d) payments "towards the maintenance of a person" from their spouse, or former spouse, or civil partner, or former civil partner, under a court order or maintenance agreement count. Thus maintenance payments that are not made pursuant to an agreement (e.g., ad hoc voluntary payments) will be ignored. There is also no provision for treating such payments as unearned income if they are made directly to a third party. Maintenance for a child is ignored.

The list in reg.66 does not include charitable or voluntary payments and so these will be ignored. On the meaning of charitable and voluntary payments, see the notes to para.15 of Sch.9 to the Income Support Regulations in Vol.II of this series.

Payments from employment and training programmes under s.2 of the Employment and Training Act 1973 or s.2 of the Enterprise and New Towns

(Scotland) Act 1990 are only taken into account in so far as they are a substitute for universal credit (e.g., a training allowance) or for a person's living expenses (para. (1)(f)). See para.(2)(b) for what counts as "living expenses".

Under para.(1)(h) payments under an insurance policy count but only if the policy was to insure against the contingencies in heads (i) and (ii). Under head (ii) payments under a mortgage (or other loan) protection policy will only be taken into account if the payment is to pay interest on a mortgage or loan secured on the person's home or to meet "alternative finance payments" (see the notes to paras 4–6 of Sch.1) *and* if the person's universal credit award includes a housing costs element under para.4 of Sch.1. Thus insurance policy payments to meet, e.g., capital repayments or policy premiums, will be ignored.

Income from an annuity (other than retirement pension income) counts unless it was purchased with personal injury compensation (reg.75) as does income from a trust (unless it is disregarded under regs 75 or 76) (para.(1)(i) and (j)).

On para.(1)(k), "assumed yield from capital" (the equivalent to the "tariff income rule" for income support, old style JSA, old style ESA and housing benefit), see the note to reg.72. That applies where the claimant has capital (thus excluding any disregarded capital) in excess of £6,000, when an income of £4.35 per month for each £250 of excess is assumed. If any such income is assumed, reg.72(3) provides that any actual income derived from that capital ("for example rental, interest or dividends") is to be treated as part of the person's capital from the day it is due to be paid. That produces some strange consequences where a claimant is in receipt of rent or some payment for occupation of premises, where not trading in lettings as a self-employed person (see the notes to reg.57). The plain assumption in reg.72(3) is that such income is to be treated as derived from capital in the sense of the value of whatever interest the claimant has in the premises. But neither actual income derived from capital nor rental payments, nor contributions towards household expenses is included in the list of what counts as unearned income. There can only be the assumed income where the value of capital is over £6,000, with the consequence of adding the actual income to the amount of capital, which will go towards keeping it over the £6,000. Regulation 72 can never apply where the income is from letting out some part of the claimant's home, because the capital value of the home is disregarded, so that no yield can be assumed from it.

Paragraph (1)(l) includes as income capital that is treated as income under reg.46(3) or (4)—see the note to reg.46.

Paragraph (1)(m) covers income that does not fall within paras (1)(a)–(la) but which is taxable under Pt 5 of the Income Tax (Trading and Other Income) Act 2005. The types of income that are taxable under Pt 5 include royalty payments, income from films and sound recordings, and income from estates in administration.

Note that dividends are not included as unearned income, but see the notes to regs 55 (employed earnings) and 77(4) for when they might properly be regarded in substance as remuneration derived from employment or an office.

Unearned income is calculated monthly in accordance with reg.73, except in the case of student income which is calculated in accordance with reg.71.

What neither reg.66 nor any other provision on unearned income does is to provide any general rule at to how to decide to which assessment periods particular receipts are to be attributed. Regulation 68 does provide a rule for student income, but otherwise the Regulations are silent, as is Chapter H5 of the ADM. There is no equivalent of reg.31 of the Income Support Regulations (Vol.II of this series) with a general rule that income other than earnings is to be treated as paid on the date it is due to be paid. Nor is there any equivalent of the final part of reg.29(2), that the period to which income other than earnings is attributed begins with the date on which the payment is treated as made under reg.31.

In most cases, where a regular amount of income is received monthly or more frequently, there will be no practical problem. However, a couple of examples can be taken to indicate the problem. First, suppose that a claimant receives income from a trust (para.(1)(j)) or instalments of capital that are treated as income (para. (1)(l)) on a quarterly basis in arrears, that the most recent receipt was on April 1 and that the first assessment period in the universal credit claim begins on May 1. Second, suppose that either before or during an existing universal credit award the claimant receives a lump sum payment (less than £5,000) of arrears of a social security benefit falling within para.(1)(a) or (b) that relates to a period before the beginning of entitlement to universal credit. Although such a payment would not be disregarded as capital under para.18 of Sch.10 or reg.10A of the Universal Credit (Transitional Provisions) Regulations 2014, it is arguable that benefit that would have been income if paid on the due date retains its character as income even though paid as a lump sum as arrears (see the notes to para.18 of Sch.10).

On the first example, reg.73(2)(c) tells us that the monthly equivalent is to be calculated by multiplying by four and dividing by 12. But that leaves open the question whether the monthly equivalent of the payment received on April 1 is to be treated as income in the assessment periods beginning on May 1 and June 1 or whether, since that payment was received before entitlement to universal credit started, nothing should be taken into account until the assessment period beginning on July 1. On the one hand, the claimant "had" the three months' worth of income available on April 1 to be used for living expenses and could be said to have had it available until the end of June. If it was to be taken into account in the assessment periods beginning on May 1 and June 1, the only question would then be the calculation of the monthly amount under reg.73. But if the test is of the period in respect of which the payment was made, that was the three months prior to April 1, so that the payment on that date could not affect the universal credit assessment, except to the extent that any amount retained out of the payment would count as capital. On that basis, a subsequent payment made on July 1 would be in respect of the prior three months, including the assessment periods beginning on May 1 and June 1. But there seems to be no mechanism for retrospectively attributing two months' income to those assessment periods. And could it be assumed on May 31 and June 30, before the July 1 payment was made, that a payment in respect of those assessment periods would be made?

On the second example, on the assumption that a lump sum payment of benefit arrears is income, if the test is whether a claimant "has" income in an assessment period, that test would certainly be met in the assessment period in which the payment is received. Arguably, that would also be the case for all the subsequent assessment periods impacted by the number of weeks' benefit by which the arrears were calculated. But, is the right test whether the claimant "has" income? In income support and similar benefits it is established that a payment of arrears of benefit that would have been income if paid on time is income and is to be taken into account in the weeks in which it would have been taken into account if paid on the due dates (*R(SB)* 4/89, relying on the principle in *McCorquodale v Chief Adjudication Officer*, reported as *R(SB)* 1/88). But that was on the basis of express provisions about the date on which benefit income was to be treated as paid equivalent to regs 29(2) and 31 of the Income Support Regulations.

In the absence of such express provisions in the universal credit scheme, can any firm inferences be drawn from the structure of the legislation and individual provisions? Paragraph 4(3)(a) of Sch.1 to the WRA 2012 authorises the making of regulations specifying circumstances in which a person is to be treated as "having or not having" unearned income, which perhaps points towards a test of having such income, as do the terms of the deeming of having such income in regs 68 (student income) and 74(1) (notional income). But that in itself does not tell us in what assessment period any amount of unearned income is to be taken into account. Similarly, s.8(3)(b), providing for the deduction of an amount "in respect of unearned income calculated in the prescribed manner" in calculating entitlement and the authorisation in para.4(1)(c) of Sch.1 of regulations providing for the calculation or estimation of unearned income in respect of an assessment period do not take the issue further forward. They do not tell us how any amount is to be attached to any assessment period. Regulation 22(1)(a) provides that the amount to be deducted from the maximum amount of universal credit in any assessment period includes all of the claimant's unearned income "in respect of the assessment period". That could point towards using "in respect of" as the test of attribution, or could merely reflect the terms of s.8(3)(b). Finally and the most specifically, reg.73(2A) seems to operate on the assumption that it is the period in respect of which the payment was made that matters, not the period for which the payment is available to be used as income. It applies when the period in respect of which income is paid begins or ends during an assessment period and then supplies a method of calculation of the amount to reflect the number of days in respect of which the unearned income was paid that fall within the assessment period in question. Thus, it is submitted that the balance of the inferences is in favour of the "in respect of" test. However, for the reasons sketched in above in the discussion of the examples it is very difficult to see how there can be a practical operation of that test within the overall structure of the scheme. What the proper approach is remains obscure.

It is very unfortunate that there should have to be such speculation about matters that would have been expected to be settled clearly by straightforward regulations.

Meaning of "retirement pension income"

2.203   **67.**—(1) Subject to paragraph (2), in regulation 66(1)(a) "retirement pension income" has the same meaning as in section 16 of the State Pension Credit Act 2002 as extended by regulation 16 of the State Pension Credit Regulations 2002.

(2) Retirement pension income includes any increase in a Category A or Category B retirement pension mentioned in section 16(1)(a) of the State Pension Credit Act 2002 which is payable under Part 4 of the Contributions and Benefits Act in respect of a person's partner.

DEFINITIONS

"Contributions and Benefits Act"—see reg.2.
"partner"—*ibid.*

GENERAL NOTE

2.204   "Retirement pension income" has the same meaning for the purposes of universal credit as it does for state pension credit. See the notes to s.16 of the State Pension Credit Act 2002 and reg.16 of the State Pension Credit Regulations 2002 in Vol.II of this series. The definition covers most kinds of UK state retirement pension provision and occupational or personal pension payments. Presumably para.(2) is felt to be necessary because s.16(1)(a) of the 2002 Act does not refer to such increases (although in the case of a couple it is their combined income that counts (s.8(4)(b) of the WRA 2012)).

In relation to occupational and personal pension schemes it is necessary to follow a longer chain of references, through s.17(1) of the 2002 Act to s.1 of the Pension Schemes Act 1993. Personal pension schemes are relatively easily identified, but there are sometimes difficulties in differentiating occupational pension schemes, income from which does count in universal credit, and other sorts of schemes income from which does not. The definition in s.1 of the 1993 Act has been amended over the years. The reference for purposes of the Universal Credit Regulations is presumably to the current form, rather than the form in force at the time when the 2002 Regulations were laid. In summary, s.1(1) gives the meaning as "a pension scheme" established for the purpose of providing benefits to, or in respect of, people with service in employment, or to, or in respect of, other people by an employer, employee or some representative body. That on its face seems rather circular, but s.1(5) provides that "pension scheme" means a scheme or other arrangement comprised in one or more instruments or arrangements, having or capable of having effect so as to provide benefits to or in respect of people (a) on retirement;

(b) on having reached a particular age; or (c) on termination of employment. That can cover schemes that include death in service benefits to partners, children or dependants of employees and benefits on early retirement or termination of employment for medical reasons. It can then be difficult to work out whether employers' schemes for benefits payable on disablement or death come within that definition. For instance, although various Armed Forces Pension Schemes are clearly within the definition, what about the various pre-2005 War Pensions Schemes and similar and the Armed Forces Compensation Scheme? It is submitted that the latter are not occupational pension schemes. A possible test (no more than that) might be that if a scheme does not provide any benefits on retirement, reaching a particular age or termination of employment independent of incapacity, disablement or death of the employee, it is not an occupational pension scheme.

There is not the space here to mention most of the further categories listed in s.16 of the 2002 Act as extended by reg.16 of the 2002 Regulations. Income from retirement annuity contracts and from annuities bought with the proceeds of personal pension schemes are covered, as are regular payments under an equity release scheme. Payments from a former employer, i.e. not from an occupational scheme as such, on early retirement for ill-health or disability are also covered.

Note the category of notional unearned income in reg.74(3) and (4), where a person has failed to apply for retirement pension income that is available or has deferred taking an annuity or income drawdown that is available from a scheme.

Person treated as having student income

68.—(1) A person who is undertaking a course [¹of education, study or training] (see regulation 13) and has a student loan[², a postgraduate master's degree loan] or a grant in respect of that course, is to be treated as having student income in respect of—

    (a) an assessment period in which the course begins;

    (b) in the case of a course which lasts for two or more years, an assessment period in which the second or subsequent year begins;

    (c) any other assessment period in which, or in any part of which, the person is undertaking the course, excluding—

        (i) an assessment period in which the long vacation begins or which falls within the long vacation, or

        (ii) an assessment period in which the course ends.

(2) Where a person has a student loan [² or a postgraduate master's degree loan], their student income for any assessment period referred to in paragraph (1) is to be based on the amount of that loan.

(3) Where paragraph (2) applies, any grant in relation to the period to which the loan applies is to be disregarded except for—

    (a) any specific amount included in the grant to cover payments which are rent payments in respect of which an amount is included in an award of universal credit for the housing costs element;

    (b) any amount intended for the maintenance of another person in respect of whom an amount is included in the award.

(4) Where paragraph (2) does not apply, the person's student income for any assessment period in which they are treated as having that income is to be based on the amount of their grant.

(5) A person is to be treated as having a student loan [² or a postgraduate master's degree loan] where the person could acquire [² a student loan or a postgraduate master's degree loan] by taking reasonable steps to do so.

(6) Student income does not include any payment referred to in regulation 66(1)(f) (training allowances).

(7) In this regulation and regulations 69 to 71—

2.205

"grant" means any kind of educational grant or award, excluding a student loan or a payment made under a scheme to enable persons under the age of 21 to complete courses of education or training that are not advanced education;

"the long vacation" is a period of no less than one month which, in the opinion of the Secretary of State, is the longest vacation during a course which is intended to last for two or more years;

[² "postgraduate master's degree loan" means a loan which a student is eligible to receive under the Education (Postgraduate Master's Degree Loans) Regulations 2016;]

"student loan" means a loan towards a student's maintenance pursuant to any regulations made under section 22 of the Teaching and Higher Education Act 1998, section 73 of the Education (Scotland) Act 1980 or Article 3 of the Education (Student Support) (Northern Ireland) Order 1998 and includes, in Scotland, a young student's bursary paid under regulation 4(1)(c) of the Students' Allowances (Scotland) Regulation 2007.

AMENDMENTS

1. Universal Credit (Consequential, Supplementary, Incidental and Miscellaneous Provisions) Regulations 2013 (SI 2013/630) reg. 38(5) (April 29, 2013).

2. Social Security (Treatment of Postgraduate Master's Degree Loans and Special Support Loans) (Amendment) Regulations 2016 (SI 2016/743) reg. 6(2) (August 4, 2016).

DEFINITIONS

"assessment period"—see WRA 2012, ss.40 and 7(2) and reg.21.
"housing costs element"—see regs 2 and 25.

GENERAL NOTE

2.206 See the notes to reg.13 for when a person is regarded as undertaking a course of education, study or training. If someone who is exempt from the requirement not to be receiving education under reg.14 has student income that is taken into account in calculating their universal credit award, they will not have any work requirements (see reg.89(1)(e)(ii) and reg.89(1)(da) for couples where only one partner is a student). If the person leaves their course, student income is taken into account up to the end of the assessment period before the one in which they leave the course. That is because the person is no longer undertaking the course and so para.(1) of this regulation does not apply (the change of circumstance will take effect from the first day of the assessment period in which it occurs—para.20 of Sch.1 to the Decisions and Appeals Regulations 2013). As any student income that is left over at the end of a course or when a person finally abandons or is dismissed from it does not fall within any other paragraph in reg.66(1), it will be ignored.

Paragraph (1)

2.207 This provides for the assessment periods (i.e. months) in which student income will be taken into account. These are any assessment periods during which, or during part of which, the person is undertaking the course of education, study or training, including the assessment period in which the course begins, or any subsequent year of the course begins. But student income will be ignored in the assessment period in which the course ends, in the assessment period in which the long vacation (defined in para.(7)) starts and in any assessment periods that fall wholly within the long vacation.

Paragraphs (2)–(7)

These paragraphs define what counts as student income. It does not include training allowances and payment for living expenses taken into account under reg.66(1)(f) (para.(6)). 2.208

If a person has a student loan or a postgraduate master's degree loan (both defined in para.(7)), or is treated as having a student loan or a postgraduate master's degree loan under para.(5), the amount of that loan counts as income and any grant (defined in para.(7)) paid for the same period as the loan is ignored. But any specific amount included in the grant for rent payments which are being met by universal credit, or any amount intended for the maintenance of another person included in the person's universal credit award, will count as income (paras (2) and (3)).

If the person does not have, and is not treated under para.(5) as having, a student loan or a postgraduate master's degree loan, grant income is taken into account (para.4)).

Note the exclusion from the definition of "grant" of payments made to enable people under 21 to complete courses of non-advanced education or training. This means that payments from the 16–19 Bursary Fund and educational maintenance allowances (in so far as they still exist) do not count as student income (they are fully disregarded for the purposes of income support, old style JSA, old style ESA and housing benefit). Paragraph H6008 ADM also states that grant income does not include any payment derived from Access Funds (although the basis for this is not clear).

"Student loan" for the purposes of regs 68–71 only includes a loan towards the student's maintenance (see para.(7)). In Scotland it also includes a young student's bursary. Any loan for tuition fees will be ignored.

See regs 69–71 for the calculation of student income. There is a disregard for student income of £110 per assessment period (reg.71).

Calculation of student income—student loans [¹ and postgraduate master's degree loans]

69.—(1) Where, in accordance with regulation 68(2), a person's student income is to be based on the amount of a student loan for a year, the amount to be taken into account is the maximum student loan (including any increases for additional weeks) that the person would be able to acquire in respect of that year by taking reasonable steps to do so. 2.209

[¹ (1A) Where, in accordance with regulation 68(2), a person's student income is to be based on the amount of a postgraduate master's degree loan for a year, the amount to be taken into account is 30 per cent. of the maximum postgraduate master's degree loan that the person would be able to acquire by taking reasonable steps to do so.]

(2) For the purposes of calculating the maximum student loan in paragraph (1) [¹ or the maximum postgraduate master's degree loan in paragraph (1A)] it is to be assumed no reduction has been made on account of—

    (a) the person's means or the means of their partner, parent or any other person; or

    (b) any grant made to the person.

AMENDMENT

1. Social Security (Treatment of Postgraduate Master's Degree Loans and Special Support Loans) (Amendment) Regulations 2016 (SI 2016/743) reg. 6(3) (August 4, 2016).

"partner"—see reg.2.
"postgraduate master's degree loan--see reg.68(7).
"student loan"—see regs 2 and 68(7).

GENERAL NOTE

2.210   The amount of a student loan that is taken into account is the maximum amount
(including any increases for additional weeks) that the person could obtain for that
year if they took reasonable steps to do so (para.(1)). In the case of a postgraduate master's degree loan, it is 30 per cent. of the maximum postgraduate master's
degree loan that the person could obtain for that year if they took reasonable steps to
do so (para.(1A)). No reduction is made for any assessed contribution from a parent
or partner (or any other person) or for any grant which may have reduced the loan.

In *CH/4429/2006* the claimant's partner had a religious objection to taking out
a loan and it was argued that that made it unreasonable for him to do so. The
Commissioner rejected that argument on the basis that "reasonable" only qualified
the steps that could be taken to acquire a student loan. It is understood that that
decision is under challenge in an appeal currently before the Upper Tribunal.

See reg.71 for how the amount of student income to be taken into account in an
assessment period is calculated (note the disregard of £110).

Calculation of student income—grants

2.211   **70.** Where, in accordance with regulation 68(4), a person's student
income is to be based on the amount of a grant, the amount to be taken into
account is the whole of the grant excluding any payment—
  (a) intended to meet tuition fees or examination fees;
  (b) in respect of the person's disability;
  (c) intended to meet additional expenditure connected with term
       time residential study away from the person's educational establish-
       ment;
  (d) intended to meet the cost of the person maintaining a home at a
       place other than that at which they reside during their course, except
       where an award of universal credit includes an amount for the
       housing costs element in respect of those costs;
  (e) intended for the maintenance of another person, but only if an award
       of universal credit does not include any amount in respect of that
       person;
  (f) intended to meet the cost of books and equipment;
  (g) intended to meet travel expenses incurred as a result of the person's
       attendance on the course; or
  (h) intended to meet childcare costs.

DEFINITION

"grant"—see regs 2 and 68(7).

GENERAL NOTE

2.212   If a grant counts as student income (on which see reg.68 and the note to that
regulation), the whole of the grant is taken into account, subject to the disregards
in paras (a)–(h). The disregards in paras (d) and (e) do not apply if the person's
universal credit award includes an amount in respect of housing costs (para.(d)) or
for the maintenance of another person (para.(e)) (see also reg.68(3)).

See reg.71 for how the amount of student income to be taken into account in an
assessment period is calculated (note the disregard of £110).

Calculation of student income—amount for an assessment period

71. The amount of a person's student income in relation to each assess-   2.213
ment period in which the person is to be treated as having student income
in accordance with regulation 68(1) is calculated as follows.

Step 1

Determine whichever of the following amounts is applicable—
  (a) [¹ in so far as regulation 68(2) applies to a person with a student
      loan,] the amount of the loan (and, if applicable, the amount of any
      grant) in relation to the year of the course in which the assessment
      period falls; [¹ . . .]
  [¹ (aa) in so far as regulation 68(2) applies to a person with a postgraduate
      master's degree loan, 30 per cent. of the amount of the loan in relation
      to the year of the course in which the assessment period falls; or]
  (b) if regulation 68(4) applies (person with a grant but no student loan
      [¹ or postgraduate master's degree loan]) the amount of the grant in
      relation to the year of the course in which the assessment period falls.
But if the period of the course is less than a year determine the amount of
the grant or loan in relation to the course.

Step 2

Determine in relation to—
  (a) the year of the course in which the assessment period falls; or
  (b) if the period of the course is less than a year, the period of the course,
the number of assessment periods for which the person is to be treated as
having student income under regulation 68(1).

Step 3

Divide the amount produced by step 1 by the number of assessment
periods produced by step 2.

Step 4

Deduct £110.

AMENDMENT

1. Social Security (Treatment of Postgraduate Master's Degree Loans and Special
Support Loans) (Amendment) Regulations 2016 (SI 2016/743) reg. 6(4) (August
4, 2016).

DEFINITIONS

   "grant"—see regs 2 and 68(7).
   "postgraduate master's degree loan" – see reg.68(7).
   "student loan" – see regs 2 and 68(7).

GENERAL NOTE

   The amount of a person's student income that is to be taken into account in each   2.214
assessment period (i.e. month) is worked out as follows:
Step 1:
  (a) if the person has, or is treated as having, a student loan, calculate the annual
      amount of the loan, plus, if applicable, the annual amount of any grant that
      is to be taken into account (see regs 68 and 70), for that year of the course;
      or

(b) if the person has, or is treated as having, a postgraduate master's degree loan, calculate 30 per cent. of the loan for that year of the course; or

(c) if the person has a grant but does not have, and is not treated as having, a student loan, or a postgraduate master's degree loan, calculate the amount of the grant for that year of the course; or

(d) if the course lasts for less than a year, calculate the amount of the loan and/ or grant for the course.

Step 2: calculate the number of assessment periods for which the person is to be treated as having student income in that year of the course, or if the course lasts for less than a year, during the course, in accordance with reg.68(1). Note that this will include assessment periods during which the person was under-taking the course and which count under reg.68(1), even if the person had not made a claim for universal credit at that time. See H6140-6144 ADM (example 2).

Step 3: divide the amount in Step 1 by the number of assessments periods in Step 2.

Step 4: deduct £110, as £110 of student income is ignored in each assessment period.

General

Assumed yield from capital

2.215   **72.**—(1) A person's capital is to be treated as yielding a monthly income of £4.35 for each £250 in excess of £6,000 and £4.35 for any excess which is not a complete £250.

(2) Paragraph (1) does not apply where the capital is disregarded or the actual income from that capital is taken into account under regulation 66(1)(i) (income from an annuity) or (j) (income from a trust).

(3) Where a person's capital is treated as yielding income, any actual income derived from that capital, for example rental, interest or dividends, is to be treated as part of the person's capital from the day it is due to be paid to the person.

GENERAL NOTE

2.216   This contains the universal credit equivalent of the tariff income rule that applies for income support, old style JSA, old style ESA and housing benefit. Under universal credit it is referred to as "assumed yield from capital".

If a person has capital above £6,000 but below £16,000, it is treated as producing £4.35 per month for each complete £250 above £6,000 and £4.35 per month for any odd amount left over (para.(1)). But this does not apply if the capital is disregarded (see Sch.10 and regs 75 and 76), or if the actual income is taken into account under reg.66(1)(i) (income from an annuity) or (j) (income from a trust) (para.(2)). And remember the deductions that must be made under reg.49 in reaching the value of capital.

If the assumed yield from capital rule does apply, actual income from the capital counts as part of the person's capital from the day it is due to be paid (para. (3)). This rule could produce some tricky conundrums if the amount of the claimant's capital is very close to the £6,000 boundary or to a boundary between different amounts of assumed yield. Say that a claimant with an assessment period from the first to last day of the calendar month and with no other capital owns a heavily mortgaged second property whose capital value for universal credit purposes is £5,900 and which is rented out for £500 a month, payable on the 21st. Prima facie, when the rent is received it does not count as actual unearned income as it is not listed in reg.66(1), nor is it to be added to the claimant's capital because the capital is not treated under para.(1) as yielding an income. If the claimant retained the amount of the rent into the next assessment period, their capital would increase to £6,400, but if the £500 had immediately been spent on mortgage interest, that would not happen. However, if the capital value of the property was £6,100, what would happen? Would the £500 be treated as capital because at the date it was due to be paid income was being assumed and, if so, would the assumed income for that assessment period be based on £6,100 or £6,600? Or should the calculation not be made until the end of the assessment period? If by that date the claimant had used the £500 for the mortgage interest and so no longer had that capital, should the assumed yield be based on £6,100? Readers can no doubt think up more complicated scenarios.

Unearned income calculated monthly

73.—(1) A person's unearned income is to be calculated as a monthly amount.

(2) Where the period in respect of which a payment of income is made is not a month, an amount is to be calculated as the monthly equivalent, so for example—

  (a) weekly payments are multiplied by 52 and divided by 12;

  (b) four weekly payments are multiplied by 13 and divided 12;

  (c) three monthly payments are multiplied by 4 and divided by 12; and

  (d) annual payments are divided by 12.

[[1](2A) Where the period in respect of which unearned income is paid begins or ends during an assessment period the amount of unearned income for that assessment period is to be calculated as follows—

$$N \times \left(\frac{M \times 12}{365} \right)$$

where N is the number of days in respect of which unearned income is paid that fall within the assessment period and M is the monthly amount referred to in paragraph (1) or, as the case may be, the monthly equivalent referred to in paragraph (2).]

(3) Where the amount of a person's unearned income fluctuates, the monthly equivalent is to be calculated—

  (a) where there is an identifiable cycle, over the duration of one such cycle; or

  (b) where there is no identifiable cycle, over three months or such other period as may, in the particular case, enable the monthly equivalent of the person's income to be determined more accurately.

(4) This regulation does not apply to student income.

2.217

AMENDMENT

1. Universal Credit (Digital Service) Amendment Regulations 2014 (SI 2014/2887) reg.4 (November 26, 2014). The amendment is subject to the saving provision in reg.5 of SI 2014/2887 (see Pt IV of this Volume).

DEFINITIONS

"assessment period"–see WRA 2012 ss.40 and 7(2) and reg.21.

"student income"—see reg.68.

Paragraphs (1) and (2)

2.218   Unearned income is calculated as a monthly amount (paras (1) and (2)). But unlike earned income the amount taken into account in an assessment period (i.e. month) is not necessarily the amount actually received in that month. If the amount of the unearned income varies, the monthly equivalent is calculated in accordance with para.(3)).

See the notes to reg.66 for discussion of how payments of unearned income are to be attributed to particular assessment periods in the absence of specific provisions providing a general rule.

Paragraph (2A)

2.219   This paragraph provides an exception to the general rule that unearned income is calculated as a monthly amount. For assessment periods (i.e. months) during which unearned income starts and/or finishes, only an amount based on the actual days in respect of which the income is paid will be taken into account. That is likely mainly to affect benefit payments and pensions.

Note that the amendment which inserted para.(2A) is subject to a saving provision–see reg. 5 of the Universal Credit (Digital Service) Amendment Regulations 2014 in Part IV. The effect is that para.(2A) only applies to awards in relation to claims from people living in areas where the "digital service" (also referred to by DWP as the "full service") is in operation or from such persons who subsequently form a new couple or who separate after being part of a couple.

Paragraph (3)

2.220   This provides that if there is an identifiable cycle, the amount of unearned income received during that cycle is converted into a monthly amount (para.(3)(a)). If there is no cycle, the amount taken into account is averaged over three months, or over another period if this produces a more accurate monthly equivalent (para.(3)(b)). See the notes to reg.5(2)–(3A) of the Income Support Regulations in Vol.II of this series for discussion of when there is a recognisable cycle, making the necessary allowances for the present regulation applying only to unearned income. There is no equivalent here to paras (3)–(3A) of reg.5. "Identifiable" cannot mean anything different from "recognisable".

Paragraph (4)

2.221   This regulation does not apply to the calculation of student income. See reg.71 for the amount of a person's student income that is to be taken into account in each assessment period.

Notional unearned income

2.222   **74.**—(1) If unearned income would be available to a person upon the making of an application for it, the person is to be treated as having that unearned income.

(2) Paragraph (1) does not apply to the benefits listed in regulation 66(1)(b).

(3) A person who has reached the qualifying age for state pension credit is to be treated as possessing the amount of any retirement pension income for which no application has been made and to which the person might expect to be entitled if a claim were made.

(4) The circumstances in which a person is to be treated as possessing retirement pension income for the purposes of universal credit are the same as the circumstances set out in regulation 18 of the State Pension Credit Regulations 2002 in which a person is treated as receiving retirement pension income for the purposes of state pension credit.

DEFINITION

"retirement pension income"—see reg.67.

GENERAL NOTE

Paragraphs (1) and (2)

A person is treated as having unearned income if "it would be available to [them]   2.223
upon the making of an application for it". But that does not apply to the benefits
listed in reg.66(1)(b).

A person should only be treated as having unearned income under para.(1) if it
is clear that it would be paid if an application for it was made. Thus, for example,
para.(1) would not apply to payments from a trust that are within the discretion of
the trustees.

Paragraphs (3) and (4)

A person who has reached the qualifying age for state pension credit will be   2.224
treated as having retirement pension income (defined in reg.67) in the same circumstances as they would be so treated for the purposes of state pension credit under
reg.18 of the State Pension Credit Regulations 2002. See the notes to reg.18 and to
reg.42(2ZA)–(2C) of the Income Support Regulations in Vol.II of this series. Very
much in general, the following are covered. A person who defers taking their state
pension is treated as having the amount applicable if the pension had been taken
at the qualifying age. A person who defers taking benefits from an occupational
pension scheme beyond the scheme's retirement age, where the scheme allows that,
is treated as having the amount of pension that would have been received if benefits
had started at the normal age. A person in a defined contribution occupational
pension scheme who does not buy an annuity or take advantage of income drawdown after state pensionable age is treated as having the amount of the annuity that
could have been bought with the fund. The qualifying age for state pension credit
was 60 but since April 2010 it has gradually risen in line with the staged increase
in pensionable age for women and reached 65 in November 2018; thereafter state
pension age for both men and women started to rise from 65 in December 2018,
to reach 66 by October 2020. Although it is a condition of entitlement to universal
credit that a person is below the qualifying age for state pension credit (see s.4(1)
(b) of the WRA 2012), a couple may still be entitled if one member of the couple is
under that age (see reg.3(2)) and the other is not.

If a person below the qualifying age for state pension credit chooses not to apply
for retirement pension income, he or she will not be caught by this rule.

For the rules relating to notional earned income, see reg.60.

CHAPTER 4

MISCELLANEOUS

Compensation for personal injury

75.—(1) This regulation applies where a sum has been awarded to a   2.225
person, or has been agreed by or behalf of a person, in consequence of a
personal injury to that person.

(2) If, in accordance with an order of the court or an agreement, the person
receives all or part of that sum by way of regular payments, those payments
are to be disregarded in the calculation of the person's unearned income.

(3) If the sum has been used to purchase an annuity, payments under the
annuity are to be disregarded in the calculation of the person's unearned
income.

(4) If the sum is held in trust, any capital of the trust derived from that sum is to be disregarded in the calculation of the person's capital and any income from the trust is to be disregarded in the calculation of the person's unearned income.

(5) If the sum is administered by the court on behalf of the person or can only be disposed of by direction of the court, it is to be disregarded in the calculation of the person's capital and any regular payments from that amount are to be disregarded in the calculation of the person's unearned income.

(6) If the sum is not held in trust or has not been used to purchase an annuity or otherwise disposed of, but has been paid to the person within the past 12 months, that sum is to be disregarded in the calculation of the person's capital.

GENERAL NOTE

2.226   This regulation provides for an extensive disregard of compensation for personal injury, both as capital and income.

Firstly, the compensation is ignored for 12 months from the date it is paid to the person (para.(6)). Thus if it is spent during that 12 months or reduces to £6,000 or less, it will not have any effect on universal credit. Secondly, if the compensation is held in trust (on which see *Q v SSWP (JSA)* [2020] UKUT 49 (AAC): any form of trust will do, including where funds are held in a joint bank account with another person), it will be disregarded as capital indefinitely and any income from the trust will be disregarded in the calculation of the person's unearned income (para.(4) and reg.66(1)(j)). Similarly, if the compensation payment is administered by a court, or can only be disposed of by direction of a court, its capital value is ignored and any regular payments from it are ignored in the calculation of the person's unearned income (para.(5)). Thirdly, if the compensation is used to purchase an annuity, payments under the annuity are disregarded as unearned income (para.(3) and reg.66(1)(i)). Fourthly, if, in accordance with a court order or agreement, the person receives all or part of the compensation by way of regular payments, these are ignored as unearned income (see para.(2)).

Although paras (3)–(5) refer to "the sum" awarded or agreed, in contrast to para. (2), which refers to all or part of that sum, it is submitted that in the overall context, "the sum" in paras (3)–(5) must be interpreted to include part of that sum and amounts derived from the original award or agreement.

There appears to be no problem with the relationship with reg.50(1) on notional capital (deprivation for the purpose of securing entitlement to or increasing the amount of universal credit) if the court order or agreement directly requires the making of regular payments (para.(2)) or the holding of the compensation payment on trust (para.(4)) or control by a court (para.(5)). However, an apparent problem could arise in cases in which the payment has initially been paid to the person concerned and later some or all of the amount is placed into a trust or is used to purchase an annuity. If that action had not been taken, the disregard under para. (6) could not have lasted for longer than 12 months. Therefore, depending on the amounts involved and other circumstances, it could appear on the face of it that the transfer of the capital was for the purpose of securing entitlement to universal credit or increasing its amount after the running out of that 12 months, so that the person would be treated as still possessing the amount disposed of. There is no equivalent in reg.50 to reg.51(1)(a) of the Income Support Regulations (reg.113(1)(a) of the JSA Regulations 1996 and reg.115(1)(a) of the ESA Regulations 2008) excluding its operation where the capital disposed of is derived from a payment made in consequence of a personal injury and is placed on trust. However, as suggested in the notes to reg.50(1) above, the intention of reg.75 is so clearly that the holding of funds in the ways set out in paras (3)–(5) should not affect entitlement to universal credit that it is submitted that the notional capital rule cannot be applied in those circumstances. The only penalty for continuing to hold funds as capital with no restrictions after the expiry of 12 months from the date of initial payment should be the loss of the para.(6) disregard for so long as the funds remain held in that way.

See the notes to para.12 of Sch.10 to the Income Support Regulations in Vol.II of this series, as to what constitutes personal injury.

Special schemes for compensation etc.

76.—(1) This regulation applies where a person receives a payment from a scheme established or approved by the Secretary of State or from a trust established with funds provided by the Secretary of State for the purpose of—

  (a) providing compensation [[1]or support] in respect of—

      (i) a person having been diagnosed with variant Creutzfeldt-Jacob disease or infected from contaminated blood products,

     (ii) the bombings in London on 7th July 2005,

    (iii) persons who have been interned or suffered forced labour, injury, property loss or loss of a child during the Second World War; [[1]...]

    [[1](iv) the terrorist attacks in London on 22nd March 2017 or 3rd June 2017,

     (v) the bombing in Manchester on 22nd May 2017; or]

  (b) supporting persons with a disability to live independently in their accommodation.

(2) Any such payment, if it is capital, is to be disregarded in the calculation of the person's capital and, if it is income, is to be disregarded in the calculation of the person's income.

(3) In relation to a claim for universal credit made by the partner, parent, son or daughter of a diagnosed or infected person referred to in paragraph (1)(a)(i) a payment received from the scheme or trust, or from the diagnosed or infected person or from their estate is to be disregarded if it would be disregarded in relation to an award of state pension credit by virtue of paragraph 13 or 15 of Schedule 5 to the State Pension Credit Regulations 2002.

2.227

AMENDMENT

1. Social Security (Emergency Funds) (Amendment) Regulations 2017 (SI 2017/689) reg.9 (June 19, 2017).

DEFINITIONS

  "claim"—see WRA 2012 s.40.
  "partner"—see reg.2.

GENERAL NOTE

This regulation disregards payments from various compensation and support schemes and schemes to support people with a disability to live independently set up or approved by the Government. Any payment from these schemes or trusts is ignored as capital if it is capital, and as income if it is income (para.(2) and reg.66(1) (j)). Payments of capital under para.(3) that are made to a parent of a person diagnosed with variant Creutzfeldt-Jacob disease are disregarded for two years; in the case of a payment to a parent of a person infected from contaminated blood products they are ignored until two years after the date of the person's death.

2.228

Company analogous to a partnership or one person business

77.—(1) Where a person stands in a position analogous to that of a sole owner or partner in relation to a company which is carrying on a trade or a

2.229

property business, the person is to be treated, for the purposes of this Part, as the sole owner or partner.

(2) Where paragraph (1) applies, the person is to be treated, subject to paragraph (3)(a), as possessing an amount of capital equal to the value, or the person's share of the value, of the capital of the company and the value of the person's holding in the company is to be disregarded.

(3) Where paragraph (1) applies in relation to a company which is carrying on a trade—

(a) any assets of the company that are used wholly and exclusively for the purposes of the trade are to be disregarded from the person's capital while they are engaged in activities in the course of that trade;

(b) the income of the company or the person's share of that income is to be treated as the person's income and calculated in the manner set out in regulation 57 as if it were self-employed earnings; and

(c) where the person's activities in the course of the trade are their main employment, the person is to be treated as if they were in gainful self-employment and, accordingly, regulation 62 (minimum income floor) applies [¹ . . .].

(4) Any self-employed earnings which the person is treated as having by virtue of paragraph (3)(b) are in addition to any employed earnings the person receives as a director or employee of the company.

(5) This regulation does not apply where the person derives income from the company that is employed earnings by virtue of Chapter 8 (workers under arrangements made by intermediaries)[², Chapter 9 (managed service companies) or Chapter 10 (workers' services provided through intermediaries) of Part 2 of ITEPA and that income is derived from activities that are the person's main employment].

(6) In paragraph (1) "property business" has the meaning in section 204 of the Corporation Tax Act 2009.

AMENDMENTS

1. Universal Credit and Miscellaneous Amendments (No.2) Regulations 2014 (SI 2014/2888) reg.4(6) (November 26, 2014, or in the case of existing awards, the first assessment period beginning on or after November 26, 2014).

2. Universal Credit and Jobseeker's Allowance (Miscellaneous Amendments) Regulations 2018 (SI 2018/1129) reg.3(5) (November 5, 2018).

DEFINITIONS

"employed earnings"—see regs 53(1) and 55.
"ITEPA"—see reg.2.
"self-employed earnings"—see regs 53(1) and 57.

GENERAL NOTE

2.230   If a person's control of a company, which is carrying on a trade or a property business (defined in para.(6)), is such that they are like a sole trader or a partner, the value of the person's shareholding is disregarded and they are treated as having a proportionate share of the capital of the company (para.(2)) and a proportionate share of the company's income as if that was self-employed earnings (para.(3)(b)). However, the general rule in para.(3)(a) is that so long as the person is engaged in activities in the course of the company's trade the company's assets are disregarded as capital. Those rules are similar to those in reg.51(4) and (5) of the Income Support Regulations (see the notes in Vol.II of this series), reg.115(6) and (7) of the ESA Regulations 2008 and reg.113(4) and (5) of the JSA Regulations 1996, but by no means identical. Some unpacking and identification of potential problems is necessary.

First, note that under para.(5) the regulation as a whole does not apply where the person concerned receives employed earnings from the company that are chargeable to income tax under Chapter 8 (workers under arrangements made by intermediaries), 9 (managed service companies) or, from November 5, 2018, 10 (workers' services provided through intermediaries) of Part 2 of the Income Tax (Earnings and Pensions) Act 2003 (ITEPA). The November 2018 amendment also introduced the important condition for the application of the exception in para.(5) that the activities producing those earnings are the person's main employment. There is no such exclusion in the income support and old style ESA and JSA rules. Chapter 8 of Part 2 of ITEPA is concerned with what are known as IR35 or "off-payroll" arrangements, under which a person provides services to a client who would be an employer except that the arrangements are made by a third party to whom the client makes the payments in return for the services. Then, subject to conditions, the payments to the third party are treated as employed earnings of the person concerned and chargeable to income tax. Chapter 9 applies to similar effect where the intermediary is a managed service company, i.e. one under the control of the service provider(s). Chapter 10 has, from April 6, 2017, applied special rules to cases where the client is a public authority.

Paragraph (1)

The addition of the reference to a property business in para.(1) is unique. The definition in s.204 of the Corporation Tax Act 2009, as referred to in para.(6), is unhelpful in itself, merely saying that the term includes both UK and overseas property businesses. One has to go on to ss.205-207 to find provisions: (a) that a property business consists of every business which the company carries on for generating income from land in the UK or outside, as the case may be, and every transaction entered into for that purpose otherwise than in the course of the business; and (b) that generating income from land means exploiting it as a source of rents or other income. It is not clear why it was felt necessary to add the reference to a property business. Presumably, it would have been regarded as a trade under the Income Support Regulations, the ESA Regulations 2008 and the JSA Regulations 1996 in the general meaning of the word, it being irrelevant that the profits of a company from trade are chargeable to tax under a different Part of the Corporation Tax Act 2009 from the profits of a property business. But the reference causes problems of interpretation mentioned below.

2.231

Paragraph (2)

The approach adopted in *R(IS) 13/93* to the income support rule must also apply to para.(2) in that the value of the company's capital (by reference to which the amount of the person's notional capital is assumed) means the net total value after liabilities have been taken into account. The fact that the company owns some particularly valuable asset or assets does not on its own mean that the claimant's notional capital must be over the limit. The net worth must be identified, no doubt by looking at accounts and using standard accounting practices. Where the person's position is not analogous to that of a sole owner, but to a partner, the identification of the proportionate share may raise difficult issues of judgment. In *R(IS) 13/93* the Commissioner seemed prepared to adopt the proportionate shareholding as the criterion. There should then be no difficulty in the disregarding under para.(2) of the actual value of the person's shareholding in the company.

2.232

Paragraph (3)

There are further departures from the income support and old style ESA and JSA position in para.(3), in deeming the person's proportionate share of the company's income to be self-employed earnings (sub-para.(b)) and in applying the minimum income floor where the person's activities in the trade are their main employment (sub-para.(c)). There is a preliminary problem in that para.(3) only applies where para.(1) applies in relation to a company that is carrying on a trade. There is no

2.233

mention of a company carrying on a property business. Can it really have been intended that the consequences in sub-paras.(b) and (c) and, more importantly, the disregard of the capital value of the company's assets under sub-para.(a) are not to be applied where a company is carrying on a property business? There seems no element of policy or logic behind such a difference of treatment. Accordingly, especially if it is accepted, as suggested above, that outside the particular context of the tax regime under the Corporation Tax Act 2009, a property business would be regarded as a trade, it may be that in context the reference in para.(3) to carrying on a trade is to all trades including property businesses. The discussion below proceeds on that basis. However, some authoritative elucidation of the relationship between paras (1) and (3) in relation to property businesses would be welcome. On when a trade is being carried on see the notes to reg.64 (gainful self-employment).

Under para.(3)(b) the income of the company or a proportionate share is to be treated as income of the person concerned and calculated under reg.57 as if it were self-employed earnings. That appears to be so even if the person concerned undertakes no activities in the course of the business. It is far from clear how the notional conversion is to take place. Under reg.57, in the case of actual self-employed earnings, the calculation is based on actual receipts in any assessment period less permitted deductions for expenses under regs 58 and 59. Presumably, therefore "the income of the company" does not mean the net income of the company as might be calculated for corporation tax purposes or under ordinary accounting principles. Presumably it means the actual receipts of the company in the assessment period in question less the deductions for expenses under regs 58 and 59, looking at expenditure on behalf of the company rather than by the person in question. It is difficult to say whether in practice information will be available as to such receipts and expenditure in a current assessment period of a month. Even if that is so, there might well be large fluctuations month by month. A further problem is how to calculate the deductions from gross profits under steps 3 and 4 of reg.57(2) for national insurance contributions and income tax paid to HMRC in the assessment period and relievable pension contributions made in that period, when the person's actual tax and national insurance status will not have been as a self-employed earner. See para.(4) for the effect of the person having employed earnings.

See the notes to reg.57 for payments made under the Coronavirus Job Retention Scheme (CJRS) to claimants caught by reg.77 who had furloughed themselves as employees in law and the effect of the Universal Credit (Coronavirus) (Self-employed Claimants and Reclaims) (Amendment) Regulations 2020 (SI 2020/522), in force from May 21, 2020. As explained in those notes, such payments must be treated as income receipts of the company, that then are to be taken into account as an actual receipt at step 1 of reg.57(2), by virtue of reg.77(3)(b). There is nothing in the Self-employed Claimants Regulations to prevent that effect and no specific reference to reg.77. But reg.2(1)(b) provides that no deduction is to be made under step 1 of reg.57(2) for salary or wages paid to an employee in so far as that payment is covered by a payment under the CJRS. Thus the income of the company with which the self-employed person is fixed by the operation of reg.77 includes the CJRS payment, with a deduction for the furloughed employee's salary only in so far as the company paid the employee more than the initial 80% (or the later lower amounts covered by the CJRS) of qualifying salary. In order for the CJRS payment to have been properly received a corresponding payment out must have been made by the employer, that the scheme then reimbursed. That appears to be fair when reg.77(4) is considered. If the deemed self-employed person also has employed earnings from the company (as the person must have done to get the CJRS payment) those earnings are to be taken into account as earned income as well as the deemed self-employed earnings. Normally, although those employed earnings would count, the expense of the salary paid to the deemed self-employed person would be deducted at step 1 of reg.57(2).

In the light of the difficulties with para.(3)(b), the effect of para.(3)(c) may be particularly important. Where the person's activities in the course of the company's trade are their main employment they are deemed to be in gainful self-employment, so that reg.62 on the minimum income floor applies. For any assessment period in which reg.62 applies (see the notes to that provision) and the claimant's earned income is less than their individual threshold, the earned income is deemed to be equal to that amount. The weekly amount is effectively the hourly national minimum wage multiplied by the expected number of hours under reg.88. That level of income exempts the claimant from all work-related requirements (reg.90(1) and (5) and s.19 of the WRA 2012), but the deemed amount would be taken into account in calculating the amount of benefit payable.

The other element of para.(3) is the disregard of assets of the company that would otherwise be deemed to be part of the claimant's capital by reason of the person's deemed status as sole owner or partner in the business (sub-para.(a)). There are two conditions. The person must be engaged in activities in the course of the company's trade. In reg.51(4) and (5) of the Income Support Regulations, reg.115(6) and (7) of the ESA Regulations 2008 and reg.113(4) and (5) of the JSA Regulations 1996 the condition is that the person undertakes activities in the course of the business of the company. On that form of words the Commissioner in *R(IS) 13/93* was satisfied that the claimant's wife, who took telephone messages and received mail for the company, as well as being a director, was taking part in the company's business. He also said that although the activities were low key, he was far from certain that they were de minimis. It is not entirely clear that he was intending to lay down a rule that any activity beyond something that was de minimis (i.e. so trivial as to be equivalent to nothing) would do, rather than merely describing the circumstances of the particular case, but a principle that anything of substance would do appears right. Does a test in the terms of being engaged in activities in the course of the company's trade require a different approach? In *Chief Adjudication Officer v Knight*, reported as part of *R(IS) 14/98*, the Court of Appeal was concerned with the disregard of the assets of a business in which a person was engaged as a self-employed earner. The claimant was described as a sleeping partner in a farming business with her son and his wife. The court held that that the risking of her assets in the business and her right to a share of profits did not constitute a sufficient positive involvement to conclude that she was engaged in the business. But it was recognised that each case would have to be decided individually. That does not suggest any plain difference in approach, and it is submitted that the word "engaged" does not in its ordinary meaning require anything more extensive than "undertaking activities".

It should be noted that para.(3)(a) applies only while the person is actually engaged in activities. No doubt short breaks, such as for weekends or longer holidays, are to be ignored. But there is no provision in it, as there is in para.6 of Sch.10 to the Income Support Regulations and in para.8 of Sch.10 to the present Regulations (business assets) for an extension where the person has ceased to carry on a trade, business or vocation within the previous six months (extendable) in certain circumstances such as incapacity being thought not to be permanent. It may be arguable that the disregard in para.8 of Sch.10 can apply to the notional capital to be possessed under para.(2) if its conditions would have applied if the person had actually previously been carrying on the business as a self-employed person.

The second condition for the disregard under para.(3)(a) is that the assets are used wholly and exclusively for the purposes of the company's trade. That is not a condition in reg.51(5) of the Income Support Regulations, reg.115(7) of the ESA Regulations 2008 or reg.113(5) of the JSA Regulations 1996, under which the whole of the person's deemed capital under the equivalent of para.(2) is disregarded. Does the phrase "wholly and exclusively" exclude the disregarding of the value of assets that have a dual use? An obvious example would be a vehicle used for both business and personal purposes. In relation to the deduction of expenses in the calculation of the net profits of self-employed earners under reg.38(3)(a) of the Income Support Regulations (reg.98(3)(a) of the ESA Regulations 2008 and reg.101(4)(a) of the JSA Regulations 1996), where it is a condition that the expenses were wholly and exclusively defrayed for the purposes of the employment, it has been held that apportionment can extend not only to items where specific different uses can be identified (e.g. telephone calls or petrol costs) but also to items where there can be an apportionment on a time basis (e.g. vehicle insurance): *R(FC) 1/91, CFC/26/1989* and *R(IS) 13/91*. However, there are still some expenses that are not capable of apportionment, such as the cost of clothing or lunches. Where the use of an asset is in issue, there will be less room for apportionment. To take the example of a vehicle to be used equally for business and for personal purposes, for example, although the expenditure on vehicle tax, insurance and maintenance costs could be apportioned just as much as fuel costs, when looked at as a single asset to be valued it is hard to see how it could be said to be wholly and exclusively used for the purposes of the company's trade if it was used for any non-trivial non-trade purpose. Nonetheless, there might possibly be some things, like money in a bank account or a stock of stationery that could be regarded as made up of some assets used wholly and exclusively for the purposes of the company's trade and some not so used. Nor is it necessarily fatal to a conclusion that the asset is used wholly and exclusively for the purposes of the company's trade that a person derives some private advantage from it (e.g. a particularly comfortable office chair or one adapted to a person's disability or physiology).

The second condition seems unfairly restrictive compared to the position in income support and old style ESA and JSA and also compared to the treatment under universal credit of those actually in self-employment. There, para.7 of Sch.10 requires the disregard of assets used "wholly or mainly" for the purposes of the trade, business or vocation being carried on. In view of the express condition in para.(3)(a), it appears that a person could not rely on the wider disregard in para.7 of Sch.10 in relation to their deemed notional capital, on the same basis as suggested above in relation to para.8 of Sch.10. Indeed, that may cast doubt on the validity of the argument about para.8.

Paragraph (4)

2.234   If someone treated as having self-employed earnings under para.(3)(b) also has employed earnings from the company, either as an employee or in the office of director, the two sources of income are both to be taken into account. Dividends are not normally employed earnings, being derived from the ownership of the shares on which they are paid. But sometimes the label of dividend cannot properly be applied to the payments made or dividends properly so called can constitute remuneration derived from a contract of employment or in an office. Dividends cannot constitute unearned income because they do not appear in the exhaustive list in reg.66(1). They are not remuneration or profit derived from employment under a contract of employment or in an office (reg.52(a)(i)). Nor are they general earnings as defined in s.7(3) of ITEPA, being chargeable to income tax under Chapters 3–5 of Part 4 of the Income Tax (Trading and Other Income) 2005 (ITTOIA). It is different if the labelling as dividends is a sham or, taking the broader approach of recent authority, the payments are in substance or reality earnings. See the further discussion in the notes to reg.55 under the heading *Dividends*.

PART 7

THE BENEFIT CAP

GENERAL NOTE

Introduction

2.235   Regulations 78–83 are made under ss.96–97 of the WRA 2012. They establish a "benefit cap" under which affected claimants can receive no more in social security benefits than £23,000 pa or £15,410 pa in Greater London and £20,000 pa or £13,400 pa elsewhere. In both cases, the higher of those limits applies to joint claimants or those responsible for a child or qualifying young person and the lower to single claimants who are not responsible a child or a qualifying young person. The £23,000 limit is equivalent to £1,916.67 per assessment period or approximately £442.35 per week. The equivalents for £20,000 are £1,666.67 and £384.62; for £15,410 they are £1,284.17 and £296.35; and for £13,400 they are £1,116.67 and £257.69. The higher rates apply irrespective of how many people are in the benefit unit: families consisting of a couple with six children are capped at the same rate as a single parent with one.

How the benefit cap works

Under reg.79, the benefit cap applies where the total amount of the "welfare bene-   **2.236**
fits" (as defined in WRA 2012 s.96(10)) exceed whichever "relevant amount" applies: see reg.80A. The amount of universal credit that the claimant would otherwise be awarded for the assessment period is reduced by the amount of the excess: reg.81.

Calculation of entitlement to welfare benefits

Regulation 80 deals with how the amount of the claimant's (or claimants') entitle-   **2.237**
ment to "welfare benefits" is calculated. The rule is that the total entitlement to all specified benefits during the assessment period is taken into account except where that entitlement is not payable because of the overlapping benefit rules: reg.80(1). Under reg.66, many of the benefits listed in WRA 2012 s.96(10) are taken into account as unearned income when calculating entitlement to universal credit. Regulation 80(4) provides that they are to be taken into account for benefit cap purposes at the same rate as they are taken into account under reg.66. Universal credit itself is (obviously) taken into account at the rate to which the claimant(s) would be entitled if the benefit cap did not apply: reg.80(2). Regulation 80(3) provides (presumably for the avoidance of doubt) that where a claimant is disqualified from receiving (new-style) ESA by virtue of reg.93 ESA Regulations 2013, that benefit is not taken into account. Finally, reg.80(5) provides that where a "welfare benefit" is awarded in respect of a period other than a month (which will always be the case, except for universal credit itself) the monthly equivalent is to be calculated in the same way as for other unearned income under reg.73.

Exceptions

There are a number of exceptions, where the benefit cap does not apply, or the   **2.238**
reduction is less than the full amount of the excess. The benefit cap does not apply in any assessment period:

- where the award of universal credit includes the LCWRA element, or the carer element, or a claimant (including one or more joint claimants) is receiving "new-style" ESA at a rate that includes the support component: reg.83(1)(a) and (j);

- during which a claimant or a qualifying young person for whom they are responsible is receiving carer's allowance or a claimant is receiving industrial injuries benefit, attendance allowance, disability living allowance or personal independence payment, or guardian's allowance: reg.83(1)(b), (c), (f), (g), (i) and (k) and note that—for obvious reasons—those benefits are not "welfare benefits" as defined in WRA 2012 s.96(10);

- a child or qualifying young person for whom a claimant is responsible is receiving disability living allowance or personal independence payment: reg.83(1)(f) and (g); and

- a claimant is receiving a war pension (as defined in reg.83(2))or certain payments under the Armed Forces and Reserve Forces Compensation Scheme: reg.83(1)(d) and (c).

Where a claimant (or a child or qualifying young person) is entitled to attendance allowance, disability living allowance, personal independence payment—or a war pension or a relevant payment under the Armed Forces Compensation Scheme— but is not receiving it because he or she is in a hospital or a care home, the benefit cap does not apply by virtue of reg.83(1)(h).

Under reg.82(1), the benefit cap does not apply if the claimant's earned income (or the claimants' combined earned income) in the assessment exceeds "the amount of earnings that a person would be paid at the hourly rate set out in regulation 4 of the National Minimum Wage Regulations for 16 hours per week, converted to a monthly amount by multiplying by 52 and dividing by 12" or during the nine month "grace period" as defined in reg.82(2). The rules on the "minimum income floor" in reg.62 (which, in this instance, would be advantageous for the claimant(s)) do not apply to the calculation of earned income in this context.

Finally, where the award of universal credit includes the childcare costs element, the amount of that element is deducted from the amount of the reduction under reg.81. If that amount exceeds the excess of the total entitlement to welfare benefits over the relevant amount, then no reduction is made: reg.81(1) and (2).

Legal challenges

2.239   On March 18, 2015, in *R (SG and others (previously JS and others) v Secretary of State for Work and Pensions* [2015] UKSC 16, the Supreme Court (Lords Reed, Carnwath and Hughes, Lady Hale and Lord Kerr dissenting) rejected a legal challenge to the benefit cap on the grounds that it unlawfully discriminated against women in breach of art.14 of, read with art.1 of the First Protocol to, ECHR; and infringed art.3(1) of the United Nations Convention on the Rights of the Child.

On November 26, 2015, in *Hurley v Secretary of State for Work And Pensions* [2015] EWHC 3382 (Admin), Collins J held that the failure to exempt individual family carers caring for adult family members from the benefit cap constituted unlawful discrimination contrary to contrary to Art.14 of—taken together with Art.1 of the First Protocol to, or Art.8 of—the ECHR. The government responded to the judgment by removing carer's allowance from the list of "welfare benefits" in WRA 2012 s.96(10) (see WR&WA 2016 s.8(4)) and by adding exceptions to reg.83 where the claimant (or a qualifying young person for whom they are responsible) is entitled to carer's allowance; or where the carer element is included in the ward of universal credit; or where the claimant is entitled to guardian's allowance.

On June 22, 2017 in *R (DA and Others) v Secretary of State for Work and Pensions* [2017] EWHC 1446 (Admin), Collins J ruled that the application of the benefit cap (under the equivalent provisions of the Housing Benefit Regulations 2006) to lone parents of children under two infringed their Convention Rights under arts 8 and 14 ECHR taken together. In particular, the applicants were unable to work for 16 hours a week (i.e., so as to take advantage of the earnings exception: see reg.82) because of their caring responsibilities and the cost of childcare. However, on March 15, 2018, the Court of Appeal (Leveson P and Sir Patrick Elias, McCombe LJ dissenting) allowed the Secretary of State's appeal against Collins J's decision ([2018] EWCA Civ 504), and on May 15, 2019, the Supreme Court (Lords Reed, Wilson, Carnwath, Hughes and Hodge, Lady Hale and Lord Kerr dissenting) dismissed a further appeal together with another appeal backed by CPAG: see further, *R (DA and others and DS and others) v Secretary of State for Work and Pensions* [2019] UKSC 21.

On July 20, 2020, the High Court (Garnham J) allowed a challenge to the benefit cap as it affects UC claimants who are paid four-weekly: see *R (Pantellerisco) v Secretary of State for Work and Pensions* [2020] EWHC 1944 (Admin). As there are 13 four-week periods in each year and only 12 assessment periods, the Regulations treated the claimant as earning 1/13 of her annual salary in 11 of those assessment periods and 2/13 in one of them. By regulation 82(1)(a) the benefits cap does not apply to assessment periods in which the claimant's earned income is equal to or exceeds the amount of earnings that a person would be paid for 16 hours work at the national minimum wage, converted to a monthly amount by multiplying by 52 and dividing by 12. As the claimant actually did work 16 hours a week at the national minimum wage, she would have been exempt from the benefit cap for the whole year if she had been treated as earning 1/12 of her annual salary in each assessment period. However, in 11 out of 12 assessment periods, the universal credit earned income calculation treated her as if she had only worked for 28 days with the result that she was not exempt from the cap. In the claimant's case, that left her approximately £463 worse off in each of the 11 assessment periods in respect of which her benefit was capped. The judge described this issue as the "lunar month problem". It is similar to the "non-banking day salary shift" problem: see the discussion of *Secretary of State for Work and Pensions v Johnson and others* [2020] EWCA Civ 778 in the General Note to reg.54. Following the Court of Appeal's reasoning in *Johnson*, the judge allowed the application for judicial review and made a declaration to the effect that "the earned income calculation is irrational and unlawful in respect of employees paid on a four-weekly basis". It is understood that the Secretary of State is seeking permission to appeal to the Court of Appeal.

Introduction

78.—(1) This Part makes provision for a benefit cap under section 96 of the Act which, if applicable, reduces the amount of an award of universal credit.   2.240

(2) In this Part "couple" means—

(a) joint claimants; or

(b) a single claimant who is a member of a couple within the meaning of section 39 of the Act and the other member of that couple,

and references to a couple include each member of that couple individually.

DEFINITION

"the Act"—see reg.2.

Circumstances where the benefit cap applies

79.—(1) Unless regulation 82 or 83 applies, the benefit cap applies where the welfare benefits to which a single person or couple is entitled during the reference period exceed the relevant amount [¹ determined under regulation 80A (relevant amount)].   2.241

(2) The reference period for the purposes of the benefit cap is the assessment period for an award of universal credit.

(3) [¹. . .]

(4) [¹. . .]

AMENDMENT

1. Benefit Cap (Housing Benefit and Universal Credit) (Amendment) Regulations 2016 (SI 2016/909) reg.3(1) and (2) (assessment periods beginning on or after November 7, 2016).

DEFINITIONS

"assessment period"—see WRA 2012 ss.40 and 7(2).
"bereavement allowance"—see reg.2.
"carer's allowance"—*ibid.*
"child"—see WRA 2012 s.40.
"claimant"—*ibid.*
"Contributions and Benefits Act"—see reg.2.
"couple"—see reg.78(2).
"employment and support allowance"—see reg.2.
"jobseeker's allowance"—*ibid.*
"joint claimants"—see WRA 2012 s.40.
"maternity allowance"—see reg.2.
"qualifying young person"—see WRA 2012 s.40 and 10(5) and regs 2 and 5.
"responsible for a child or qualifying young person"—see regs 2, 4 and 4A.

"single claimant"—see WRA 2012 s.40.
"single person"—see WRA 2012 ss.40 and 1(2)(a).
"welfare benefit"—see WRA 2012 s.96(10).
"widowed mother's allowance"—see reg.2.
"widowed parent's allowance"—*ibid.*
"widow's pension"—*ibid.*

GENERAL NOTE

2.242   Although "couple" is defined by reg.78(2) as including a member of a couple who is permitted to claim as a single person under reg.3(3), the higher "relevant amount" in reg.79(3)(a) is only available to "joint claimants" and those responsible for a child or a qualifying young person. A member of a couple claiming as a single person who is not responsible for a child or a qualifying young person, will therefore be capped at the lower rate.

The welfare benefits to which reg.79 applies are defined by WRA 2012 s.96(10) as bereavement allowance, child benefit, child tax credit, ESA, housing benefit, incapacity benefit, IS, JSA, maternity allowance, severe disablement allowance, universal credit, widow's pension, widowed mother's allowance and widowed parent's allowance.

Manner of determining total entitlement to welfare benefits

2.243   **80.**—(1) Subject to the following provisions of this regulation, the amount of a welfare benefit to be used when determining total entitlement to welfare benefits is the amount to which the single person or couple is entitled during the reference period subject to any adjustment to the amount payable in accordance with regulations under section 73 of the Social Security Administration Act 1992 (overlapping benefits).

(2) Where the welfare benefit is universal credit, the amount to be used is the amount to which the claimant is entitled before any reduction under regulation 81 or under section 26 or 27 of the Act.

[¹ (2A) Where the welfare benefit is housing benefit under section 130 of the Contributions and Benefits Act, the amount to be used is nil.]

(3) Where a person is disqualified for receiving an employment and support allowance by virtue of section 18 of the Welfare Reform Act 2007, it is disregarded as a welfare benefit.

(4) Where an amount of a welfare benefit is taken into account in assessing a single person's or a couple's unearned income for the purposes of an award of universal credit the amount to be used is the amount taken into account as unearned income in accordance with regulation 66.

(5) Where a welfare benefit is awarded in respect of a period that is not a month, the amount is to be calculated as the monthly equivalent as set out in regulation 73 (unearned income calculated monthly).

AMENDMENT

1. Benefit Cap (Housing Benefit and Universal Credit) (Amendment) Regulations 2016 (SI 2016/909) reg.3(1) and (3) (assessment periods beginning on or after November 7, 2016).

DEFINITIONS

"couple"—see reg.78(2).
"earned income"—see reg.2.
"single person"—see WRA 2012 ss.40 and 1(2)(a).
"unearned income"—see reg.2.

[¹ Relevant amount

80A.—(1) The relevant amount is determined by dividing the applicable   2.244
annual limit by 12.

(2) The applicable annual limit is—

(a) £15,410 for a single claimant resident in Greater London who is not responsible for a child or qualifying young person;

(b) £23,000 for—
   (i) joint claimants where either joint claimant is resident in Greater London;
   (ii) a single claimant resident in Greater London who is responsible for a child or qualifying young person;

(c) £13,400 for a single claimant not resident in Greater London who is not responsible for a child or qualifying young person;

(d) £20,000 for—
   (i) joint claimants not resident in Greater London;
   (ii) a single claimant not resident in Greater London who is responsible for a child or qualifying young person.

(3) For the purposes of section 96 of the Act (benefit cap) and this regulation a claimant is resident in Greater London if—

(a) where the housing costs element is included in the claimant's award of universal credit—
   (i) accommodation in respect of which the claimant meets the occupation condition is in Greater London; or
   (ii) the claimant is in receipt of housing benefit in respect of a dwelling (which has the meaning given in section 137 of the Contributions and Benefits Act) in Greater London;

(b) where the housing costs element is not included in the claimant's award of universal credit—
   (i) accommodation that the claimant normally occupies as their home is in Greater London; or
   (ii) where there is no accommodation that the claimant normally occupies as their home, the Jobcentre Plus office to which the Secretary of State has allocated their claim is in Greater London.]

AMENDMENT

1. Benefit Cap (Housing Benefit and Universal Credit) (Amendment) Regulations 2016 (SI 2016/909) reg.3(1) and (4) (assessment periods beginning on or after November 7, 2016).

Reduction of universal credit

81.—(1) Where the benefit cap applies in relation to an assessment   2.245
period for an award of universal credit, the amount of the award for that
period is to be reduced by—

(a) the excess; minus

(b) any amount included in the award for the childcare costs element in relation to that assessment period.

(2) But no reduction is to be applied where the amount of the childcare costs element is greater than the excess.

(3) The excess is the total amount of welfare benefits that the single person or the couple are entitled to in the reference period, minus the relevant amount [¹ determined under regulation 80A].

AMENDMENT

1. Benefit Cap (Housing Benefit and Universal Credit) (Amendment) Regulations 2016 (SI 2016/909) reg.3(1) and (5) (assessment periods beginning on or after November 7, 2016).

DEFINITIONS

"childcare costs element"—see reg.2.
"assessment period"—see WRA 2012 ss.40 and 7(2).

Exceptions—earnings

2.246   **82.**—(1) The benefit cap does not apply to an award of universal credit in relation to an assessment period where—

(a) the claimant's earned income or, if the claimant is a member of a couple, the couple's combined earned income, is equal to or exceeds [¹ the amount of earnings that a person would be paid at the hourly rate set out in regulation 4 of the National Minimum Wage Regulations for 16 hours per week, converted to a monthly amount by multiplying by 52 and dividing by 12]; or

(b) the assessment period falls within a grace period or is an assessment period in which a grace period begins or ends.

(2) A grace period is a period of 9 consecutive months that begins on the most recent of the following days in respect of which the condition in paragraph (3) is met—

(a) a day falling within the current period of entitlement to universal credit which is the first day of an assessment period in which the claimant's earned income (or, if the claimant is a member of a couple, the couple's combined earned income is [¹ less than—

    (i) where the assessment period began before 1st April 2017, £430; or

    (ii) in any other case, the amount calculated in accordance with paragraph (1)(a)];

(b) a day falling before the current period of entitlement to universal credit which is the day after a day on which the claimant has ceased paid work.

(3) The condition is that, in each of the 12 months immediately preceding that day, the claimant's earned income or, if the claimant was a member of a couple, the couple's combined earned income was equal to or [¹ exceeded—

(a) in any month beginning before 1st April 2017, £430; and

(b) in any other case, the amount calculated in accordance with paragraph (1)(a)].

(4) "Earned income" for the purposes of this regulation does not include income a person is treated as having by virtue of regulation 62 (minimum income floor).

AMENDMENT

1. Universal Credit (Benefit Cap Earnings Exception) Amendment Regulations 2017 (SI 2017/138) reg.2(1) and (3) (Assessment periods beginning on or after April 1, 2017).

DEFINITIONS

"assessment period"—see WRA 2012 ss.40 and 7(2).
"claimant"—see WRA 2012 s.40.

"couple"—see reg.78(2).
"earned income"—see reg.2 and para.(4).

GENERAL NOTE

See the discussion of *R (Pantellerisco) v Secretary of State for Work and Pensions* [2020] EWHC 1944 (Admin) in the General Note to Part 7 (above).

Exceptions—entitlement or receipt of certain benefits

83.—(1) The benefit cap does not apply in relation to any assessment period where—   2.247

(a) the LCWRA element is included in the award of universal credit or the claimant is receiving an employment and support allowance that includes the support component;

(b) a claimant is receiving industrial injuries benefit;

(c) a claimant is receiving attendance allowance;

(d) a claimant is receiving a war pension;

(e) a claimant is receiving a payment under article 15(1)(c) or article 29(1)(a) of the Armed Forces and Reserve Forces (Compensation Scheme) Order 2011;

(f) a claimant, or a child or qualifying young person for whom a claimant is responsible, is receiving disability living allowance;

(g) a claimant, or a qualifying young person for whom a claimant is responsible, is receiving personal independence payment;

(h) a claimant, or a child or qualifying young person for whom a claimant is responsible, is entitled to a payment listed in [¹ sub-paragraphs (b) to (g)] but—

   (i) is not receiving it by virtue of regulation 6 (hospitalisation) or regulation 7 (persons in care homes) of the Social Security (Attendance Allowance) Regulations 1991,

   (ii) it is being withheld by virtue of article 53 of the Naval, Military and Air Forces etc (Disablement and Death) Service Pensions Order 2006 (maintenance in hospital or an institution),

   (iii) is not receiving it by virtue of regulation 8 (hospitalisation) or regulation 9 (persons in care homes) of the Social Security (Disability Living Allowance) Regulations 1991, or

   (iv) in the case of personal independence payment, is not receiving it by virtue of regulations under section 85 (care home residents) or 86 (hospital in-patients) of the Act.

[¹ (i) a claimant, or a qualifying young person for whom a claimant is responsible, is entitled to carer's allowance;

(j) the carer element is included in the award of universal credit;

(k) a claimant is entitled to guardian's allowance under section 77 of the Contributions and Benefits Act.]

(2) For the purposes of this regulation, "war pension" means—

(a) any pension or allowance payable under any of the instruments listed in section 639(2) of ITEPA—

   (i) to a widow, widower or a surviving civil partner, or

   (ii) in respect of disablement;

(b) a pension payable to a person as a widow, widower or surviving civil partner under any power of Her Majesty otherwise than under an enactment to make provision about pensions for or in respect of persons who have been disabled or have died in consequence of service as members of the armed forces of the Crown;

(c) a payment which is made under any of—

    (i) the Order in Council of 19th December 1881,

    (ii) the Royal Warrant of 27th October 1884, or

    (iii) the Order by His Majesty of 14th January 1922,

to a widow, widower or surviving civil partner of a person whose death was attributable to service in a capacity analogous to service as a member of the armed forces of the Crown and whose service in such capacity terminated before 31st March 1973;

(d) a pension paid by the government of a country outside the United Kingdom which is analogous to any of the pensions, allowances or payments mentioned in paragraphs (a) to (c).

AMENDMENT

1. Benefit Cap (Housing Benefit and Universal Credit) (Amendment) Regulations 2016 (SI 2016/909) reg.3(1) and (6) (assessment periods beginning on or after November 7, 2016).

DEFINITIONS

    "the Act"—see reg.2.

    "attendance allowance"—see reg.2.

    "child"—see WRA 2012, s.40.

    "claimant"—*ibid.*

    "disability living allowance"—see reg.2.

    "employment and support allowance"—*ibid.*

    "industrial injuries benefit"—*ibid.*

    "ITEPA"—*ibid.*

    "partner"—see reg.2.

    "personal independence payment"—see reg.2.

    "responsible for a child or qualifying young person"—see regs 2, 4 and 4A.

    "qualifying young person"—see WRA 2012, s.40 and 10(5) and regs 2 and 5.

AMENDMENT

1. Universal Credit (Consequential, Supplementary, Incidental and Miscellaneous Provisions) Regulations 2013 (SI 2013/630) reg.38(1) and (6) (April 29, 2013).

PART 8

CLAIMANT RESPONSIBILITIES

CHAPTER 1

WORK-RELATED REQUIREMENTS

Introductory

Introduction

2.248   **84.** This Chapter contains provisions about the work-related requirements under sections 15 to 25 of the Act, including the persons to whom they are to be applied, the limitations on those requirements and other related matters.

DEFINITION

"work-related requirement"—see WRA 2012 ss.40 and 13(2)

Meaning of terms relating to carers

85. In this Chapter—   2.249
"relevant carer" means—

(a) a parent of a child who is not the responsible carer, but has caring responsibilities for the child; or
(b) a person who has caring responsibilities for a person who has a physical or mental impairment; and

"responsible foster parent" in relation to a child means a person who is the only foster parent in relation to that child or, in the case of a couple both members of which are foster parents in relation to that child, the member who is nominated by them in accordance with regulation 86.

DEFINITIONS

"child"—see WRA 2012 s.40
"couple"—see WRA 2012 ss.40 and 39
"foster parent"—see reg.2
"responsible carer"—see WRA 2012 ss.40 and 19(6)

GENERAL NOTE

The definitions of "relevant carer" and "responsible foster parent" are relevant for   2.250
the purposes of regs 86, 88, 89(1)(f), 91(2), 96(3) and 97(2). A child is a person under the age of 16. Responsibility for a child is to be determined in accordance with the rules in regs 4 and 4A, under which the basic test is whether the child normally lives with the person in question. The definition of "relevant carer" allows the inclusion into that category of people who do not count as responsible under the reg.4 rules but nevertheless have caring responsibilities (not further defined) for the child in question or have caring responsibilities for a person of any age who has a physical or mental impairment (not further defined). If a child has only one foster parent, that person is the "responsible foster parent". If both members of a couple are foster parents of the child, there must be a nomination of one of them under reg.86.

Nomination of responsible carer and responsible foster parent

86.—(1) This regulation makes provision for the nomination of the   2.251
responsible carer or the responsible foster parent in relation to a child.

(2) Only one of joint claimants may be nominated as a responsible carer or a responsible foster parent.

(3) The nomination applies to all the children, where there is more than one, for whom either of the joint claimants is responsible.

(4) Joint claimants may change which member is nominated—

(a) once in a 12 month period, starting from the date of the previous nomination; or
(b) on any occasion where the Secretary of State considers that there has been a change of circumstances which is relevant to the nomination.

DEFINITIONS

"child"—see WRA 2012 s.40
"joint claimant"—*ibid.*
"responsible carer"—see WRA 2012 ss.40 and 19(6)
"responsible foster parent"—see reg.85

GENERAL NOTE

2.252   This regulation provides, for the purposes of s.19(6) of the WRA 2012 and reg.85, for the nomination by a couple of which one of them is to be the "responsible carer" or "responsible foster parent". Under s.19(6) the nomination has to be made jointly. Presumably that is implied where the nomination is of the responsible foster parent under reg.85. Where more than one child is involved, the same nomination must cover all of them. The nomination can be changed once within 12 months from the date of the previous nomination or when there has been a relevant change of circumstances

References to paid work

2.253   **87.** References in this Chapter to obtaining paid work include obtaining more paid work or [¹better-paid work].

AMENDMENT

1. Social Security (Qualifying Young Persons Participating in Relevant Training Schemes) (Amendment) Regulations 2017 (SI 2017/987) reg.4(5) (November 6, 2017, in full service areas only).

DEFINITION

"paid work"—see reg.2

GENERAL NOTE

2.254   References to obtaining paid work, which appears to include self-employment as well as employment, includes obtaining more or better-paid work. This provision does not appear to add anything to the conditions of most of the provisions to which obtaining paid work is relevant. The amendment adding the hyphen between "better" and "paid" applies only for digital service (full service) cases.

Expected hours

2.255   **88.**—(1) The "expected number of hours per week" in relation to a claimant for the purposes of determining their individual threshold in regulation 90 or for the purposes of regulation 95 or 97 is 35 unless some lesser number of hours applies under paragraph (2).
(2) The lesser number of hours is—
(a) where—
  (i) the claimant is a relevant carer, a responsible carer [¹(subject to the following sub-paragraphs)] or a responsible foster parent, and
  (ii) the Secretary of State is satisfied that the claimant has reasonable prospects of obtaining paid work,
  the number of hours that the Secretary of State considers is compatible with those caring responsibilities;
[¹(aa) where the claimant is a responsible carer of a child who has not yet reached compulsory school age, the number of hours that the Secretary of State considers is compatible with those caring responsibilities;]

(b) where the claimant is a responsible carer for a child [¹who has reached compulsory school age but who is] under the age of 13, the number of hours that the Secretary of State considers is compatible with the child's normal school hours (including the normal time it takes the child to travel to and from school); or

(c) where the claimant has a physical or mental impairment, the number of hours that the Secretary of State considers is reasonable in light of the impairment.

AMENDMENT

1. Employment and Support Allowance and Universal Credit (Miscellaneous and Transitional and Savings Provisions) Regulations 2017 (SI 2017/204) reg.6 (April 3, 2017).

DEFINITIONS

"child"—see WRA 2012 s.40.
"claimant"—*ibid.*
"relevant carer"—see reg.85.
"responsible carer"—see WRA 2012 ss.40 and 19(6).
"responsible foster parent"—see reg.85.

GENERAL NOTE

Regulation 90 calculates the amount of earnings that will take a claimant out of being subject to all work-related requirements under s.22 of the WRA 2012 by reference to the "expected number of hours per week" and the national minimum wage. Regulation 95 uses the same number as one of the tests for the time that a claimant has to spend in action aimed at obtaining paid work to avoid being deemed not to have complied with the work search requirement under s.17 of the WRA 2012. Regulation 97(2) allows certain claimants to limit the work for which they must be available and for which they must search to work for the expected number of hours per week. Regulation 88 defines the expected number of hours for all these purposes.

2.256

The number under para.(1) is 35, unless some lesser number is applicable under para.(2). Can the number be reduced to zero? Why not? Zero is a number and it is less than 35. There are four alternative categories in para.(2).

Sub-paragraph (a) applies where the claimant is a relevant carer, a responsible carer (for a child (under 16) or anyone else, unless already covered by one of sub-paras. (aa)-(c)) or a responsible foster parent (see s.19(6) of the WRA 2012 and reg.85 above), and so has some substantial caring responsibility. Then, if the claimant nonetheless has reasonable prospects of obtaining paid work (including obtaining more or better-paid work), the expected hours are what is compatible with those caring responsibilities.

Sub-paragraph (aa) applies where the claimant is the responsible carer (as defined in s.19(6) of the WRA 2012 simply in terms of responsibility for the child, on which see reg.4) of a child under compulsory school age, where the number of hours is to be reduced to what is compatible with those caring responsibilities, without any condition of having reasonable prospects of obtaining paid work. Compulsory school age is reached at the beginning of the school terms following 1 January, 1 April or 1 September, according to which date first follows the child's fifth birthday.

Sub-paragraph (b) applies where the claimant is a responsible carer (as defined in s.19(6) of the WRA 2012) for a child under the age of 13, when the expected hours are those compatible with the child's normal school and travel hours. How should this apply in home-schooling cases?

Sub-paragraph (c) applies where the claimant has a physical or mental impairment (not further defined), when the expected hours are those reasonable in the light of the impairment. This is an important rule in the structure of the application of work-related requirements in a benefit not restricted to jobseekers, and one where the argument that the expected hours under reg.88 can be zero is particularly relevant.

Note that the application of the deeming of non-compliance with the work search requirement under reg.95(1) if the expected hours of action are not taken is subject to deductions of hours under reg.95(2), including for temporary circumstances. Also note regs 96–99 on circumstances in which the work availability and work search requirements cannot be imposed or are moderated, particularly reg.96(4) (voluntary work), reg.96(5) (existing employment), reg.97(2) (physical or mental impairment) and reg.99(4) and (5)(c) (unfitness for work for short periods).

Work-related groups

Claimants subject to no work-related requirements

2.257   **89.**—(1) A claimant falls within section 19 of the Act (claimants subject to no work-related requirements) if—

(a) the claimant has reached the qualifying age for state pension credit;

(b) the claimant has caring responsibilities for one or more severely disabled persons for at least 35 hours a week but does not meet the conditions for entitlement to a carer's allowance and the Secretary of State is satisfied that it would be unreasonable to require the claimant to comply with a work search requirement and a work availability requirement, including if such a requirement were limited in accordance with section 17(4) or 18(3) of the Act;

(c) the claimant is pregnant and it is 11 weeks or less before her expected week of confinement, or was pregnant and it is 15 weeks or less since the date of her confinement;

(d) the claimant is an adopter and it is 12 months or less since—

(i) the date that the child was placed with the claimant, or

(ii) if the claimant requested that the 12 months should run from a date within 14 days before the child was expected to be placed, that date;

[²(da) the claimant is a member of a couple entitled to universal credit by virtue of regulation 3(2)(b) and has student income in relation to the course they are undertaking which is taken into account in the calculation of the award;]

(e) the claimant does not have to meet the condition in section 4(1)(d) of the Act (not receiving education) by virtue of regulation 14 and—

(i) is a person referred to in paragraph (a) of that regulation (under 21, in non-advanced education and without parental support), or

(ii) has student income in relation to the course they are undertaking which is taken into account in the calculation of the award; or

(f) the claimant is the responsible foster parent of a child under the age of 1.

(2) In paragraph (1)(b) "severely disabled" has the meaning in section 70 of the Contributions and Benefits Act.

(3) In paragraph (1)(d)—

(a) "adopter" means a person who has been matched with a child for adoption and who is, or is intended to be, the responsible carer for the child, but excluding a person who is a foster parent or close relative of the child; and

(b) a person is matched with a child for adoption when it is decided by an adoption agency that the person would be a suitable adoptive parent for the child.

[¹(4) For the purposes of paragraph (1)(e)(ii), a claimant is not to be treated as having student income where—

(a) that income is a postgraduate master's degree loan; and

(b) the course in respect of which the loan is paid is not a full-time course.

(5) In paragraph (4), "postgraduate master's degree loan" has the meaning given in regulation 68(7).]

AMENDMENTS

1. Social Security (Treatment of Postgraduate Master's Degree Loans and Special Support Loans) (Amendment) Regulations 2016 (SI 2016/743) reg.6(5) (August 4, 2016).

2. Universal Credit (Miscellaneous Amendments, Saving and Transitional Provision) Regulations 2018 (SI 2018/65) reg.3(10) (April 11, 2018).

DEFINITIONS

"child"—see WRA 2012 s.40.
"claimant"—*ibid.*
"close relative"—see reg.2.
"Contributions and Benefits Act"—*ibid.*
"postgraduate master's degree loan"—see para.(5) and reg.68(7).
"responsible carer"—see WRA 2012 ss.40 and 19(6).
"responsible foster parent"—see reg.85.

GENERAL NOTE

Temporary Coronavirus Provisions

Regulation 6(1)(a) and (b) of the Social Security (Coronavirus) (Further Measures) Regulations 2020 (SI 2020/371) provide that for a period of three months beginning on March 30, 2020 the Secretary of State cannot impose a work search requirement on anyone who has an award of universal credit and any existing work search requirement ceases to have effect from that date. Although reg.6 refers to the provision being a consequence of the outbreak of coronavirus disease, it is not necessary that the claimant in question be affected in any way by that outbreak or the resulting economic disruption. It is not clear what is intended by the restriction to someone who has an award of universal credit. There would be no consistency in lifting the work search requirement for someone who happened to have an existing award on March 30, 2020, but not allowing an award to be made on a new claim because the claimant had not accepted a claimant commitment containing the requirements that the Secretary of State was bound to impose under s.22(2)(a), so that reg.6 of the Further Measures Regulations was never reached because the claimant never had an award. Such a result was plainly not intended (and was not applied in practice), so is to be avoided if possible, but para.11 of Memo ADM 04/20 gives no clue as to the mechanism for doing so. It is suggested that, provided that it had been accepted under reg.16(b) of the Universal Credit Regulations that the claimant could be entitled without having accepted a claimant commitment (see the notes to s.4(1)(e) and reg.16) and all the other basic conditions in s.4(1) were met, an award could be made to the claimant before consideration of what work-related requirements were to be imposed, so that then reg.6 could apply to modify the Secretary of State's s.22(2) duty to impose the work search and work availability requirements.

Regulation 6(1)(c) of the Further Measures Regulations provides that for the same period any work availability requirement imposed on anyone who has an award of universal credit is to operate as if "able and willing immediately to take up paid work" means able and willing to do so, or to attend an interview once reg.6 ceases to apply.

The effect of reg.6 expires at the end of November 12, 2020 (reg.10(2)), subject

2.258

to any amendment. The power to extend the three-month period was not exercised before it expired. When it was announced (Parliamentary answer, Under-Secretary of State, Mims Davies, WQ 62431) that from July 1, 2020 the requirement for universal credit claimants to accept a claimant commitment was being reintroduced, it was stressed that claimant commitments agreed or reviewed from that date (i.e. the work-related requirements included) would have to be reasonable for the "new normal" and acknowledge the reality of a person's local jobs market and personal circumstances.

2.258.1   Section 19(2) of the WRA 2012 sets out in paras (a), (b) and (c) three categories of claimants who can be subject to no work-related requirements: (a) those who have limited capability for work and work-related activity; (b) those who meet the definition of having regular and substantial caring responsibilities for a severely disabled person (i.e. satisfy the conditions, apart from level of earnings and claiming, for carer's allowance, but gain no earned income from the caring: reg.30); and (c) those who are the responsible carer for a child under the age of one. Paragraph (d) of s.19(2) includes claimants of a description prescribed in regulations. Regulation 89(1) sets out categories prescribed for this purpose, as noted below. Regulation 90 prescribes another category, dependent on earnings. See also reg.98 on recent victims of domestic violence.

The categories prescribed for the purpose of s.19(2)(d) are as follows:

(a) Claimants who have reached the qualifying age for state pension credit. The qualifying age for men is the same as for a woman born on the same day and for women depends on the date of birth in accordance with a complicated formula. See p.776 of and Appendix 11 to CPAG's *Welfare benefits and tax credits handbook* (2019/2020 edition) for the details. For anyone born before April 6, 1950 the age is 60. For those born on or after that date there is a sliding scale that rose to 65 in November 2018, and is scheduled to reach 66 by October 2020 and 67 by some date from 2026.

(b) Claimants who do not meet the conditions of entitlement for carer's allowance, but have caring responsibilities for at least 35 hours per week for a severely disabled person (defined in the same way as for carer's allowance: para.(2)), where it would be unreasonable to expect the claimant to comply with a work search and a work availability requirement, even with limitations. Some claimants who fall within this category will already be covered by s.19(2)(b) and it is not easy to work out who could benefit from the extension. Perhaps the main category would be those who are paid for the caring, who are expressly excluded from the scope of s.19(2)(b) by the definition in reg.30 above.

(c) Claimants who are pregnant in the period from 11 weeks before the expected date of confinement and 15 weeks after the date of confinement.

(d) Claimants who are "adopters" (i.e. who have been matched with a particular child for adoption under the complicated conditions in para.(3)) within 12 months or so of placement. It does not matter how old the child is, so long as below the age of 16. Any person who is actually the responsible carer of a child under the age of one is already covered by s.19(2)(c). It appears that para.(d) can continue to apply after the child has actually been adopted, for the 12 months following placement. See para.(f) for foster parents.

(da) Claimants who are part of a joint claim couple where one claimant fails to meet the basic condition in s.4(1)(d) of the WRA 2012 not to be receiving education, but the other meets that condition or is excepted from it, but only where student income for the course being attended has been taken into account in the calculation of the award of universal credit. Regulation 3(2)(b) allows such a couple to be entitled to universal credit. See regs 68-71 for student income and how it is taken into account. The aim of this addition in April 2018 was to provide uniformity for couples with the treatment of single claimants in education under sub-para.(e).

(e) Claimants who, by virtue of reg.14(1)(a), do not have to meet the basic condition in s.4(1)(d) of the WRA 2012 of not receiving education or who have student income (see regs 68-71) that is taken into account in the award of universal credit.

(f) Claimants who are the responsible foster parent (there can only be one under reg.85) of a child under the age of one. It appears that such a person cannot get within s.19(2)(c) because reg.4(6)(a) prevents their being treated as responsible for the child while the child is "looked after" by a local authority under s.22 of the Children Act 1989 or s.17(6) of the Children (Scotland) Act 1995.

Claimants subject to no work-related requirements—the earnings thresholds

90.—(1) A claimant falls within section 19 of the Act (claimants subject to no work-related requirements) if the claimant's [²monthly] earnings are equal to or exceed the claimant's individual threshold.

2.259

(2) A claimant's individual threshold is the amount that a person of the same age as the claimant would be paid at the hourly rate applicable under [³regulation 4 or regulation 4A(1)(a) to (c)] of the National Minimum Wage Regulations for—

(a) 16 hours per week, in the case of a claimant who would otherwise fall within section 20 (claimants subject to work-focused interview requirement only) or section 21 (claimants subject to work-preparation requirement) of the Act; or

(b) the expected number of hours per week in the case of a claimant who would otherwise fall within section 22 of the Act (claimants subject to all work-related requirements)[²,

converted to a monthly amount by multiplying by 52 and dividing by 12].

(3) A claimant who is a member of a couple falls within section 19 of the Act if the couple's combined [²monthly] earnings are equal to or exceed whichever of the following amounts is applicable—

(a) in the case of joint claimants, the sum of their individual thresholds; or

(b) in the case of a claimant who claims universal credit as a single person by virtue of regulation 3(3), the sum of—

(i) the claimant's individual threshold, and

(ii) the amount a person would be paid for 35 hours per week at the hourly rate specified in [³regulation 4] of the National Minimum Wage Regulations[²,

converted to a monthly amount by multiplying by 52 and dividing by 12].

(4) A claimant falls within section 19 of the Act if the claimant is employed under a contract of apprenticeship and has [²monthly] earnings that are equal to or exceed the amount they would be paid for—

(a) 30 hours a week; or

(b) if less, the expected number of hours per week for that claimant,

at the rate specified in [³ regulation 4A(1)(d)] of the National Minimum Wage Regulations[², converted to a monthly amount by multiplying by 52 and dividing by 12].

[¹(5) A claimant falls within section 19 of the Act if they are treated as having earned income in accordance with regulation 62 (minimum income floor).]

(6) [² A person's monthly earnings are]—

(a) [² the person's] earned income calculated or estimated in relation to the current assessment period before any deduction for income tax, national insurance contributions or relievable pension contributions; or

(b) in a case where the person's earned income fluctuates (or is likely to fluctuate) the amount of that income[², calculated or estimated before

any deduction for income tax, national insurance contributions or relievable pension contributions, taken as a monthly average]—
  (i) where there is an identifiable cycle, over the duration of one such cycle, or
  (ii) where there is no identifiable cycle, over three months or such other period as may, in the particular case, enable the [²monthly] average to be determined more accurately,
[²and the Secretary of State may, in order to enable monthly earnings to be determined more accurately, disregard earned income received in respect of an employment which has ceased.]
  (7) [³...]

AMENDMENTS

1. Universal Credit and Miscellaneous Amendments (No.2) Regulations 2014 (SI 2014/2888) reg.4(7) (November 16, 2014).
2. Universal Credit and Miscellaneous Amendments Regulations 2015 (SI 2015/1754) reg.2(6) (November 4, 2015).
3. Social Security (Jobseeker's Allowance, Employment and Support Allowance and Universal Credit) (Amendment) Regulations 2016 (SI 2016/678) reg.5(4) (July 25, 2016).

DEFINITIONS

"the Act"—see reg.2.
"assessment period"—see WRA 2012 ss.40 and 7(2), and reg.21.
"claimant"—see WRA 2012 s.40(1).
"couple"—see WRA 2012 ss.40 and 39.
"earned income"—see regs 2 and 52.
"joint claimants"—see WRA 2012 s.40.
"National Minimum Wage Regulations"—see reg.2.
"single person"—see WRA 2012 ss.40 and 1(2)(a).

GENERAL NOTE

2.260
Regulation 90 prescribes additional circumstances, beyond those prescribed by reg.89, in which a claimant falls within s.19(2)(d) of the WRA 2012 and therefore can be subject to no work-related requirements. The basic test under para.(1) is that the claimant's monthly earnings are at least equal to their "individual threshold", known administratively as the conditionality earnings threshold. This provision is necessary because universal credit, in contrast to the terms of pre-existing benefits, can be payable while a claimant is in work. The policy is that if a claimant is already earning above a minimum level there is no need to require them to do anything to seek further paid work. Entitlement then depends on the income calculation under s.8 of the WRA 2012. See further the notes to reg.99.
Paragraph (3) applies the para.(1) test to couples. For joint claimants their individual thresholds are added together, as are their monthly earnings. The threshold is calculated under para.(2) by multiplying the hourly rate of national minimum wage by, in the case of a claimant who would otherwise be subject to all work-related requirements under s.22 of the WRA 2012, the expected number of hours per week (see reg.88, starting point 35). In the case of a claimant who would otherwise fall within s.20 or 21, the multiplier is 16.
Under para.(6) monthly earnings are earned income as calculated under Chapter 2 of Part 6 of the Universal Credit Regulations (i.e. regs 51–64) in each monthly assessment period but without deductions for income tax, national insurance contributions or pension contributions, subject to an averaging provision in sub-para. (b) where earned income fluctuates or is likely to fluctuate. The ordinary calculation in regs 51–64 involves the use of "real time" information. In the case of both

employment and self-employment the calculation of earned income in respect of any assessment period (i.e. month) is to be based on amounts received in that assessment period (regs 54, 55, 57 and 57A), as now confirmed as a matter of construction by the Court of Appeal in *Secretary of State for Work and Pensions v Johnson* [2020] EWCA Civ 778 and the Administrative Court in *R. (Pantellerisco) v Secretary of State for Work and Pensions* [2020] EWHC 1944 (Admin), discussed in detail in the notes to regs 54 and 61. Those decisions found that the outcome, especially the fluctuations in the amounts of earnings taken into account in different assessment periods when the general pattern of earnings was regular, was irrational and unlawful for claimants in the very particular categories involved. It is yet to be seen what method of calculation might be accepted as rational, but for most claimants the general rule in regs 54 and 61 is to be applied. In those cases, it may be proper for the amount of universal credit to fluctuate month by month or for the claimant to fall in and out of entitlement on the means test. However, if entitlement continues there are plainly arguments against a claimant drifting in and out of exemption from all work-related requirements on the basis of the amount of earned income. That is presumably the thinking behind para. (6)(b). The reference to fluctuation of earned income must be to fluctuation over more than one assessment period, because fluctuation within each assessment period does not affect the total for that month. Under sub-para.(i) it is not clear whether the identifiable cycle refers merely to the pattern of receipts or to the pattern of the employment or self-employment or other paid work that produces the income. It would appear that there cannot be an identifiable cycle until it has started and come to an end, which is by definition the start of the next cycle, at least once. Given the difficulties that the notion of a recognisable cycle has given in other contexts it may be that most cases will be dealt with by sub-para.(ii), which requires the taking of an average over the previous three months or such other period as in the particular case enables the weekly average to be determined more accurately. That gives a very wide discretion.

Note also the important power at the end of para.(6) to disregard earned income from an employment that has ceased.

In relation to self-employment some of the problems mentioned above will be avoided by the application of the reg.62 minimum income floor (para.(5)). Providing that a person meets the quite stringent conditions in reg.64 for being in gainful self-employment and is not in a 12-month start-up period (reg.63), earned income below the individual threshold is deemed to be at that level. In those circumstances the claimant is exempted from all work-related requirements by para.(5). If as result of the application of the Secretary of State's discretion in reg.2(1) of the Social Security (Coronavirus) (Further Measures) Regulations 2020 (SI 2020/371, in effect from March 30, 2020) a claimant is not treated as having earned income under the MIF when they normally would be, so that para.(5) does not apply, reg.2(1)(e) allows the Secretary of State to exempt the claimant from any work search or work availability requirement.

Prior to October 3, 2019, in the converse situation where a person was exempted from all work-related requirements through the operation of reg.90 apart from para.(5), the provisions of reg.62 on the MIF could not apply (reg.62(1)(b) in its original form). See the notes to reg.62 for how that, and in particular the averaging process under reg.90(6), could then affect the MIF. According to the Explanatory Memorandum to the Universal Credit (Childcare Costs and Minimum Income Floor) (Amendment) Regulations 2019 (SI 2019/1249), that did not reflect the policy intention. Regulation 3 of those Regulations inserts into reg.62(1)(b), with effect from October 3, 2019, the rule that for the MIF to apply the claimant must be subject to all work-related requirements not only apart from the effect of reg.62, but also apart from the effect of reg.90. It remains the case that, if a claimant in exempted from any work-related requirement under any provision apart from reg.62 or 90, the MIF cannot apply.

Claimants subject to work-focused interview requirement only

2.261   **91.**—(1) [¹ . . .].

(2) A claimant falls within section 20 of the Act if—

(a) the claimant is the responsible foster parent in relation to a child aged at least 1;

(b) the claimant is the responsible foster parent in relation to a qualifying young person, and the Secretary of State is satisfied that the qualifying young person has care needs which would make it unreasonable to require the claimant to comply with a work search requirement or a work availability requirement, including if such a requirement were limited in accordance with section 17(4) or 18(3) of the Act;

(c) the claimant is a foster parent, but not the responsible foster parent, in relation to a child or qualifying young person, and the Secretary of State is satisfied that the child or qualifying young person has care needs which would make it unreasonable to require the claimant to comply with a work search requirement or a work availability requirement, including if such a requirement were limited in accordance with section 17(4) or 18(3) of the Act;

(d) the claimant has fallen within paragraph (a), (b) or (c) within the past 8 weeks and has no child or qualifying young person currently placed with them, but expects to resume being a foster parent; or

(e) the claimant has become a friend or family carer in relation to a child within the past 12 months and is also the responsible carer in relation to that child.

(3) In paragraph (2)(e) "friend or family carer" means a person who is responsible for a child, but is not the child's parent or step-parent, and has undertaken the care of the child in the following circumstances—

(a) the child has no parent or has parents who are unable to care for the child; or

(b) it is likely that the child would otherwise be looked after by a local authority because of concerns in relation to the child's welfare.

AMENDMENT

1. Welfare Reform and Work Act 2016 s.17(2)(a) (April 3, 2017).

DEFINITIONS

"the Act"—see reg.2.
"child"—see WRA 2012 s.40.
"claimant"—*ibid.*
"foster parent"—see reg.2.
"qualifying young person"—see regs 2 and 5.
"responsible carer"—see WRA 2012 ss.40 and 19(6).
"responsible foster parent"—see reg.85.
"work availability requirement"—see WRA 2012 ss.40 and 18(1).
"work search requirement"—see WRA 2012 ss.40 and 17(1).

GENERAL NOTE

Paragraph (1)

2.262   Paragraph (1) had formerly prescribed the relevant maximum age of a child for the purposes of s.20(1)(a) of the WRA 2012 to enable a responsible carer to be exempted from all work-related requirements except the work-focused interview requirement (initially five and then, from April 2014, three). From April 3, 2017 the operation of s.20(1)(a) has by its terms been restricted to responsible carers of a child aged one (responsible carers of a child under one being exempted from all work-related requirements under s.19(1)(c)). There is no longer any power to prescribe an age in regulations.

Paragraph (2)

This provision prescribes the categories of claimant who are subject only to the work-focused interview requirement under s.20(1)(b) and any connected requirements under s.23. They cover mainly foster parents.   **2.263**

Under sub-para.(a) responsible foster parents of children of any age from one to 15 are covered. Responsible foster parents of children under one are exempted from all work-related requirements under reg.89(1)(f).

That is extended to young persons in education up to the age of 19 if it would be unreasonable to subject the claimant to other work-related requirements (sub-para. (b)).

Sub-paragraph (c) extends the scope of sub-paras (a) and (b) to foster parents who do not meet the condition of being "responsible" if the child or qualifying young person has care needs that make it unreasonable to subject the claimant to other work-related requirements.

Sub-paragraph (d) allows the effect of sub-paras (a)–(c) to continue for eight weeks after the claimant ceases to have any child or qualifying young person placed with them, if a new placement is expected.

Sub-paragraph (e) applies to claimants who are responsible carers of a child of any age up to 15 if they fall within the meaning of "friend or family carer" in para.(3).

[¹Claimants subject to work preparation requirement

91A. [² . . .].]   **2.264**

AMENDMENTS

1. Income Support (Work-Related Activity) Miscellaneous Amendments Regulations 2014 (SI 2014/1097) reg.16(3) (April 28, 2014).
2. Welfare Reform and Work Act 2016 s.17(2)(b) (April 3, 2017).

GENERAL NOTE

See the notes to s.21 of the WRA 2012. The operation of that section in so far as it exempts responsible carers of a child from all work-related requirements except the work-focused interview and work preparation requirement has from April 3, 2017 been directly controlled by the terms of s.21 (the child must be aged two and no less or more). There is thus no need for a prescription of conditions including an age in regulations and the former duty in s.21(5) so to do has also been removed.   **2.265**

Claimants subject to all work-related requirements—EEA jobseekers

92.[¹ . . .]   **2.266**

AMENDMENT

1. Universal Credit (EEA Jobseekers) Amendment Regulations 2015 (SI 2015/546) reg.3 (June 10, 2015).

GENERAL NOTE

For the discriminatory effect of this provision on the entitlement of certain EEA claimants with a right to reside before its revocation in June 2015 see the notes to the 2013/14 edition. Now see reg.9 above, as also amended in June 2015.   **2.267**

The work-related requirements

Purposes of a work-focused interview

2.268   **93.** The purposes of a work-focused interview are any or all of the following—
   (a) assessing the claimant's prospects for remaining in or obtaining paid
        work;
   (b) assisting or encouraging the claimant to remain in or obtain paid
        work;
   (c) identifying activities that the claimant may undertake that will make
        remaining in or obtaining paid work more likely;
   (d) identifying training, educational or rehabilitation opportunities for
        the claimant which may make it more likely that the claimant will
        remain in or obtain paid work or be able to do so;
   (e) identifying current or future work opportunities for the claimant that
        are relevant to the claimant's needs and abilities;
   (f) ascertaining whether a claimant is in gainful self-employment or
        meets the conditions in regulation 63 (start-up period).

DEFINITIONS

   "claimant"—see WRA 2012 s.40.
   "obtaining paid work"—see reg.87.
   "paid work"—see reg.2.

GENERAL NOTE

2.269   This provision prescribes the purposes of a work-focused interview under the definition in s.15(2) of the WRA 2012. The purposes could probably not be set out more
widely, especially given that obtaining paid work includes obtaining more or better
paid work and that s.15 covers work preparation as well as work. Arguably, even if
there is no realistic prospect of a claimant obtaining any kind of paid work, the purpose
of assessing those prospects or lack of prospects in an interview could still be fulfilled.

Work search requirement—interviews

2.270   **94.** A claimant is to be treated as not having complied with a work search
requirement to apply for a particular vacancy for paid work where the
claimant fails to participate in an interview offered to the claimant in connection with the vacancy.

DEFINITIONS

   "claimant"—see WRA 2012, s.40.
   "paid work"—see reg.2.
   "work search requirement"—see WRA 2012 ss.40 and 17(1).

GENERAL NOTE

2.271   This provision, made under s.25(a) of the WRA 2012, applies when the Secretary
of State has required under s.17(1)(b) that the claimant take the particular action
of applying for a specified vacancy for paid work. If the claimant fails to participate
in an interview offered in connection with the vacancy the work search requirement
is deemed not to have been complied with. See the notes to s.17, and the notes to
ss.15 and 27 for "participation" in an interview.

Work search requirement—all reasonable action

2.272   **95.**—(1) A claimant is to be treated as not having complied with a work search requirement to take all reasonable action for the purpose of obtaining paid work in any week unless—

(a) either—
    (i) the time which the claimant spends taking action for the purpose of obtaining paid work is at least the claimant's expected number of hours per week minus any relevant deductions, or
    (ii) the Secretary of State is satisfied that the claimant has taken all reasonable action for the purpose of obtaining paid work despite the number of hours that the claimant spends taking such action being lower than the expected number of hours per week; and

(b) that action gives the claimant the best prospects of obtaining work.

(2) In this regulation "relevant deductions" means the total of any time agreed by the Secretary of State—

(a) for the claimant to carry out paid work, voluntary work, a work preparation requirement, or voluntary work preparation in that week; or

(b) for the claimant to deal with temporary childcare responsibilities, a domestic emergency, funeral arrangements or other temporary circumstances.

(3) For the purpose of paragraph (2)(a) the time agreed by the Secretary of State for the claimant to carry out voluntary work must not exceed 50% of the claimant's expected number of hours per week.

(4) "Voluntary work preparation" means particular action taken by a claimant and agreed by the Secretary of State for the purpose of making it more likely that the claimant will obtain paid work, but which is not specified by the Secretary of State as a work preparation requirement under section 16 of the Act.

DEFINITIONS

"claimant"—see WRA 2012 s.40.
"expected number of hours"—see regs 2 and 88.
"obtaining paid work"—see reg.87.
"paid work"—see reg.2.
"work preparation requirement"—see WRA 2012 ss.40 and 16(1).
"work search requirement"—see WRA 2012 ss.40 and 17(1).

GENERAL NOTE

Temporary Coronavirus Provisions
    Regulation 6(1)(a) and (b) of the Social Security (Coronavirus) (Further   2.273
Measures) Regulations 2020 (SI 2020/371) provide that for a period of three months beginning on March 30, 2020 the Secretary of State cannot impose a work search requirement on anyone who has an award of universal credit and any existing work search requirement ceases to have effect from that date. Although reg.6 refers to the provision being a consequence of the outbreak of coronavirus disease, it is not necessary that the claimant in question be affected in any way by that outbreak or the resulting economic disruption. It is not clear what is intended by the restriction to someone who has an award of universal credit. There would be no consistency in lifting the work search requirement for someone who happened to have an existing award on March 30, 2020, but not allowing an award to be made on a new claim because the claimant had not accepted a claimant commitment containing the requirement that the Secretary of State was bound to impose under s.22(2)(a), so that reg.6 of the Further Measures Regulations was never reached because the claimant never had an award. Such a result was plainly not intended (and was not applied in practice), so is to be avoided if possible, but para.11 of Memo ADM 04/20 gives no clue as to the mechanism for doing so. It is suggested that, provided that it had

been accepted under reg.16(b) of the Universal Credit Regulations that the claimant could be entitled without having accepted a claimant commitment (see the notes to s.4(1)(e) and reg.16) and all the other basic conditions in s.4(1) were met, an award could be made to the claimant before consideration of what work-related requirements were to be imposed, so that then reg.6 could apply to modify the Secretary of State's s.22(2) duty to impose the work search and work availability requirements.

The effect of reg.6 expires at the end of November 12, 2020 (reg.10(2)), subject to any amendment. The power to extend the three-month period was not exercised before it expired. When it was announced (Parliamentary answer, Under-Secretary of State, Mims Davies, WQ 62431) that from July 1, 2020 the requirement for universal credit claimants to accept a claimant commitment was being reintroduced, it was stressed that claimant commitments agreed or reviewed from that date (i.e. the work-related requirements included) would have to be reasonable for the "new normal" and acknowledge the reality of a person's local jobs market and personal circumstances.

2.273.1   This regulation, made under s.25(a) of the WRA 2012, deems certain claimants not to have complied with a work search requirement under s.17(1)(a) of the WRA 2012 to take all reasonable action for the purpose of obtaining paid work (including more or better paid work). Although in form meeting the conditions in reg.95 merely lifts the deeming of non-compliance if its conditions are met, there would seem to be little point in making such detailed provision if claimants were not to be positively treated as having complied if the conditions are met. See the notes to s.17 and see reg.97 for limitations on the kind of work that needs to be searched for. A failure for no good reason to comply with the requirement under s.17(1)(a) can lead to a medium-level sanction under s.27(2)(a) of the WRA 2012 and reg.103(1)(a).

To avoid the deeming a claimant must get within *both* sub-paras.(a) *and* (b) of para.(1).

There are two alternative routes to getting within sub-para.(a). Although the route in head (i), relating to spending the "expected hours" (starting point under reg.88, 35), has been described as the "primary" rule in previous editions, it is now submitted that that is misleading. Although head (ii), with the route of having taken all reasonable action in the week in question, applies only if the claimant spent less than the expected hours, logically the two routes are of equal status. One of the routes had to appear before the other in sub-para.(a) and the two routes could with the same effect have been put in the opposite order. The effect of reading the two provisions together is that there is no rigid rule that claimants be held to spending the expected hours in work search week after week, even though that may be the easiest point to start the enquiry. The ultimate test is what is reasonable. The sentence in the middle of para.32 of *S v SSWP (UC)* [2017] UKUT 477 (AAC) (see the notes to s.14 of the WRA 2012 for the details) saying that if "a claimant spends less than 35 hours, or the quality of the work search is disputed, he will need to rely on section 27(2) [i.e. the "for no good reason" rule] if he seeks to avoid a sanction" is not to be taken to indicate the contrary. That sentence is immediately followed by an acknowledgement of the effect of head (ii).

The para.(1)(a)(i) route requires that the claimant must spend at least the "expected number of hours per week" (reg.88), less deductions for work, voluntary work or work-related activities or various emergency, urgent or other temporary difficulties (para.(2), subject to the further rules in paras (3) and (4)), in taking action for the purpose of obtaining paid work. Note that the starting point of expected hours under reg.88 may be reduced from 35 (arguably to nil, if appropriate) to take account of responsibility for certain categories of young children, of certain other regular caring responsibilities and physical or mental impairments. The time to count as a deduction under para.(2) must be agreed by the Secretary of State. The words might suggest that the agreement must come in advance of the activity that might qualify. However, it would seem unrealistic for claimants to predict, say, the future occurrence of domestic emergencies so as to seek the Secretary of State's agreement in advance. Thus, it would seem, and would be in line with the normal pattern of claimants making a declaration that they have been seeking work in the assessment period that is ending, that a subsequent agreement will do (although no doubt it would be sensible for claimants to raise potential issues in advance where possible). It must be the case that, while the Secretary of State appears to have an open-ended discretion whether or not to agree to any particular hours being deducted under para.(2), on appeal against any sanction for failure to comply with the work search requirement under s.17(1)(a) of the WRA 2012 a tribunal is allowed to substitute its own judgment about what should have been agreed. Even if it were to be held that whatever had or had not been agreed by the Secretary of State has to control whether there had been a sanctionable failure, the reasonableness or otherwise of the Secretary of State's view would be relevant to whether a failure to comply was "for no good reason". The deductions for hours spent in paid work and voluntary work are important, as is that for work preparation requirements in securing a rational co-ordination among the various work-related requirements. Would para.(2)(b) allow the Secretary of State to allow short "holidays" from work search responsibilities, under the heading of temporary circumstances or temporary child care responsibilities (cf. reg.19(1)(p) and (2) of the JSA Regulations 1996)? Or would such an allowance fall more naturally under reg.99(5)(b) (work search requirement not to be imposed where it would be unreasonable to do so because of temporary child care responsibilities or temporary circumstances)?

If the claimant does not meet the expected hours condition, which for the majority of claimants will be 35 hours per week, sub-para.(a) can nevertheless be satisfied through head (ii) if the claimant has taken all reasonable action in the week in question for the purpose of obtaining paid work. This is an important provision which, if properly applied, would go a good way to meeting the commonly expressed criticism that in the real world it is impossible for many claimants to fill 35 hours week after week with meaningful work search action.

In *RR v SSWP (UC)* [2017] UKUT 459 (AAC), the First-tier Tribunal, in upholding two medium-level sanctions on the basis that the claimant had not taken work-search action for the 35 expected hours in two weeks, failed to consider whether there should be deductions from 35 hours under reg.95(2)(b) when there was evidence of circumstances (having to deal with the fall-out from divorce or other family proceedings) that could have amounted to a domestic emergency or other temporary circumstances. The tribunal appeared to think that the 35 hours were immutable, which was plainly an error of law. Alternatively, the claimant could have been taken to satisfy the condition in s.17(1)(a) through reg.95(1)(a)(ii), which applies even though the expected hours, less deductions, are not met. The decision-maker and the tribunal put some emphasis on the claimant having agreed in her claimant commitment to prepare and look for work for 35 hours a week. Judge Wikeley pointed out that the claimant commitment was only in terms of "normally" spending 35 hours a week, but in fact the number of hours specified in a claimant commitment cannot be directly relevant unless they establish a lesser number of hours under reg.88(2) or an agreement to a deduction of hours under reg.95(2). The test is in terms of the expected hours less deductions, which the claimant commitment merely records, or "all reasonable action" under reg.95(1)(a)(ii). It is worth noting that the claimant commitment in *RR* (following what appears to be a standard form) specified 35 hours normally for a combination of work preparation (s.16(1) of the WRA 2012) *and* work search, so did incorporate an unquantified deduction under reg.95(2)(a).

The judge, in re-making the decision in the claimant's favour, did not expressly consider the condition that a deduction under para.(2) be agreed by the Secretary of State. He must either have regarded that condition as one on which a First-tier Tribunal was entitled to substitute its own agreement or have regarded the Secretary of State's support of the appeal in the Upper Tribunal and of the substitution of a decision as necessarily involving agreement to a deduction. He also suggested that an alternative way of looking at the case could have been to consider whether reg.99(5)(b) applied (domestic emergency or temporary circumstances), so that no work search requirement could be imposed for the weeks in question. See the notes to reg.99.

Under (b), the action under (a) must give the claimant the best prospects of obtaining work. Taken at face value that condition imposes an almost impossibly high standard, because there will nearly always be something extra that the claimant could do to improve prospects of obtaining work. The condition must therefore be interpreted in a way that leaves some work for condition (a) to do and with some degree of common sense, taking account of all the circumstances, especially any factors that have led to a reduction in the expected hours below 35 or a deduction under para.(1)(a)(i) and (2), as well as matters such as the state of the local labour market, what the claimant has done in previous weeks and how successful or otherwise those actions were (compare reg.18(3) of the JSA Regulations 1996).The work search requirement in s.17(1)(a) of the WRA 2012 is only to take all reasonable action.The reference here in secondary legislation to the best prospects of obtaining work cannot be allowed to make the test as set out in the primary legislation stricter than that.There will of course be considerable difficulty in checking on the precise number of hours spent in taking relevant action, depending on what might count as action (see the notes to s.17), and in what might be required from claimants in the way of record keeping. It may be that it will be much easier to define non-compliance with the requirement in s.17(1)(b) to take particular action specified by the Secretary of State, although such a failure will only attract a low-level sanction under s.27(2)(a) and reg.104(1)(b)(iii).

In the Upper Tribunal's substituted decision in *RR* (above) there was no express consideration of the overriding condition in sub-para.(b). That must be regarded as having been satisfied in the absence of it having been raised on behalf of the Secretary of State in the support of the appeal to the Upper Tribunal.

In *S v SSWP (UC)* [2017] UKUT 477 (AAC) (see the notes to s.14 of the WRA 2012 for the details), the basis on which the First-tier Tribunal seemed to have accepted that the claimant had failed to take all reasonable action for the purpose of obtaining paid work in the various weeks in question was that he had failed to apply for vacancies outside the healthcare sector that the DWP said were suitable. The claimant's evidence was somewhat inconsistent and unconvincing, but he appears to have said that, although he did not apply for any vacancies, he had spent 35 hours in each week checking jobs websites and local newspapers. If that had been accepted, it could have been argued (see the beginning of this note) that, subject to the operation of para.(2)(b), the claimant not only escaped the deeming of non-compliance in para.(1) but fell to be treated as having complied with the s.17(1)(a) requirement. That point was not addressed in the Upper Tribunal's substituted decision dismissing the claimant's appeal (on the issue of "no good reason"). There was certainly evidence on which it could have been concluded that the action taken by the claimant, even if taking up 35 hours each week, had not given him the best prospects of obtaining work. It would have been better if it had been spelled out just where the inadequacy of the claimant's job search fitted into the legislative structure. Did the claimant fail the expected hours test in para.(2)(a)(i) without being rescued by para. (2)(a)(ii) or did he get within para.(2)(a)(i), but fail the para.(2)(b) test?

Work availability requirement—able and willing immediately to take up paid work

2.274   **96.**—(1) Subject to paragraph (2) a claimant is to be treated as not having complied with a work availability requirement if the claimant is not able and willing immediately to attend an interview offered to the claimant in connection with obtaining paid work.

(2) But a claimant is to be treated as having complied with a work availability requirement despite not being able immediately to take up paid work, if paragraph (3), (4) or (5) applies.

(3) This paragraph applies where—

(a) a claimant is a responsible carer or a relevant carer;

(b) the Secretary of State is satisfied that, as a consequence the claimant needs a longer period of up to 1 month to take up paid work, or up to 48 hours to attend an interview in connection with obtaining work, taking into account alternative care arrangements; and

(c) the claimant is able and willing to take up paid work, or attend an interview, on being given notice for that period.

(4) This paragraph applies where—

(a) a claimant is carrying out voluntary work;

(b) the Secretary of State is satisfied that, as a consequence, the claimant needs a longer period of up to 1 week to take up paid work, or up to 48 hours to attend an interview in connection with obtaining work; and

(c) the claimant is able and willing to take up paid work, or attend an interview, on being given notice for that period.

(5) This paragraph applies where a claimant—

(a) is employed under a contract of service;

(b) is required by section 86 of the Employment Rights Act 1996, or by the contract of service, to give notice to terminate the contract;

(c) is able and willing to take up paid work once the notice period has expired; and

(d) is able and willing to attend an interview on being given 48 hours notice.

DEFINITIONS

"claimant"—see WRA 2012 s.40.
"obtaining paid work"—see reg.87.
"paid work"—see reg.2.
"relevant carer"—see reg.85.
"responsible carer"—see WRA 2012 ss.40 and 19(6).
"work availability requirement"—see WRA 2012 ss.40 and 18(1).

GENERAL NOTE

Temporary Coronavirus Provisions

Regulation 6(1)(c) of the Social Security (Coronavirus) (Further Measures) Regulations 2020 (SI 2020/371) provides that for a period of three months beginning on March 30, 2020 any work availability requirement imposed on anyone who has an award of universal credit is to operate as if "able and willing immediately to take up paid work" means able and willing to do so, or to attend an interview, once reg.6 ceases to apply. Although reg.6 refers to the provision being a consequence of the outbreak of coronavirus disease, it is not necessary that the claimant in question be affected in any way by that outbreak or the resulting economic disruption. It is not clear what is intended by the restriction to someone who has an award of universal credit. There would be no consistency in suspending the work availability requirement for someone who happened to have an existing award on March 30, 2020, but not allowing an award to be made on a new claim because the claimant had not accepted a claimant commitment containing the requirement that the Secretary of State was bound to impose under s.22(2)(b), so that reg.6 of the Further Measures Regulations was never reached because the claimant never had an award. Such a result was plainly not intended (and was not applied in practice), so is to be avoided if possible, but para.11 of Memo ADM 04/20 gives no clue as to the mechanism for doing so. It is suggested that, provided that it had been accepted under reg.16(b) of the Universal Credit Regulations that the claimant could be entitled without having accepted a claimant commitment (see the notes to s.4(1)(e) and reg.16) and all the other basic conditions in s.4(1) were met, an award could be made to the claimant before consideration of what work-related requirements were to be imposed, so that then reg.6 could apply to modify the Secretary of State's s.22(2) duty to impose the work search and work availability requirements.

2.275

361

The effect of reg.6 expires at the end of November 12, 2020 (reg.10(2)), subject to any amendment. The power to extend the three-month period was not exercised before it expired. When it was announced (Parliamentary answer, Under-Secretary of State, Mims Davies, WQ 62431) that from July 1, 2020 the requirement for universal credit claimants to accept a claimant commitment was being reintroduced, it was stressed that claimant commitments agreed or reviewed from that date (i.e. the work-related requirements included) would have to be reasonable for the "new normal" and acknowledge the reality of a person's local jobs market and personal circumstances.

2.275.1   This regulation is made under s.25 of the WRA 2012 and relates to the work availability requirement under s.18(1) and (2) of being able and willing immediately to take up paid work or more or better paid work. See reg.97 for limitations on the kind of work for which a claimant must be available and reg.99, and in particular para. (5), for other situations in which the ordinary test of being able and willing immediately to take up work or attend an interview is modified.

Paragraph (1)

2.276   Paragraph (1) simply confirms that the requirement of being able and willing immediately to take up paid work extends to being able and willing immediately to attend an interview in connection with obtaining paid work, subject to the exemptions in paras (3)-(5), through the operation of para.(2).

Paragraphs (2) to (5)

2.277   A claimant who falls within paras (3), (4) or (5) is to be treated as complying with the work availability requirement, including as extended by para.(1). Paragraph (3) applies to those with child-care or other caring responsibilities who would need to take up to one month to take up paid work or up to 48 hours to attend an interview and are able and willing to do so if given that length of notice. Can para.(3)(b) allow claimants with caring responsibilities (noting that such claimants do not need to have sole or main responsibility) to have a holiday without needing to arrange some means of taking up work offers or interviews immediately? Or would such an allowance fall more naturally under reg.99(5A) or (5B) with (5)(b) (no need to be available immediately where work search requirement not to be imposed because it would be unreasonable to do so because of temporary child care responsibilities or temporary circumstances)? Paragraph (4) applies to claimants doing voluntary work (not further defined), subject to the same conditions. Paragraph (5) applies to claimants in employment who are required to give notice to terminate their contract of employment and who are able and willing to take up paid work once that notice has expired and to attend an interview on 48 hours' notice.

Work search requirement and work availability requirement—limitations

2.278   **97.**—(1) Paragraphs (2) to (5) set out the limitations on a work search requirement and a work availability requirement.

(2) In the case of a claimant who is a relevant carer or a responsible carer or who has a physical or mental impairment, a work search and work availability requirement must be limited to the number of hours that is determined to be the claimant's expected number of hours per week in accordance with regulation 88.

(3) A work search and work availability requirement must be limited to work that is in a location which would normally take the claimant—

    (a) a maximum of 90 minutes to travel from home to the location; and

    (b) a maximum of 90 minutes to travel from the location to home.

(4) Where a claimant has previously carried out work of a particular nature, or at a particular level of remuneration, a work search requirement

and a work availability requirement must be limited to work of a similar nature, or level of remuneration, for such period as the Secretary of State considers appropriate, but only if the Secretary of State is satisfied that the claimant will have reasonable prospects of obtaining paid work in spite of such limitation.

(5) The limitation in paragraph (4) is to apply for no more than 3 months beginning with—

(a) the date of claim; or

(b) if later, the date on which the claimant ceases paid work after falling within section 19 of the Act by virtue of regulation 90 (claimants subject to no work-related requirements- the earnings thresholds).

(6) Where a claimant has a physical or mental impairment that has a substantial adverse effect on the claimant's ability to carry out work of a particular nature, or in particular locations, a work search or work availability requirement must not relate to work of such a nature or in such locations.

DEFINITIONS

"claimant"—see WRA 2012 s.40.
"expected number of hours per week"—see regs 2 and 88.
"relevant carer"—see reg.85.
"responsible carer"—see WRA 2012 ss.40 and 19(6).
"work availability requirement"—see WRA 2012 ss.40 and 18(1).
"work search requirement"—see WRA 2012 ss.40 and 17(1).

GENERAL NOTE

This regulation is made under ss.17(4) and (5) (work search requirement) and 18(3) and (4) (work availability requirement) of the WRA 2012. It sets out limitations on the kind of work that a claimant can be required to search for or be able and willing immediately to take up. See reg.99 for other situations in which the ordinary tests for those requirements are modified.

2.279

Paragraph (2)

This paragraph establishes an important limitation on the kind of work that can be considered, but only for the particular categories of claimant identified: those with child care responsibilities and the disabled (anyone with a physical or mental impairment). Those categories of claimant can only be required to search for or be able and willing to take up work for no more than the number of hours per week compatible with those circumstances, as worked out under reg.88 (which could, it is suggested in the notes to reg.88, be zero). So, as far as the work search requirement is concerned, this limitation appears to apply as much to the sort of work in relation to which the Secretary of State may specify particular action under s.17(1)(b) of the WRA 2012 as to the requirement under s.17(1)(a) to take all reasonable action for the purpose of obtaining paid work or more or better paid work. Although the drafting of para. (2) appears to limit the hours for which either requirement is applicable, it can only, in view of the terms of the regulation-making powers in ss.17(4) and 18(3), relate to the hours of work to which the relevant requirement can be attached. See para.(6) for permissible limitations relating to the location and nature of employment.

Note that under s.19(1) and (2)(a) no work-related requirements can be imposed on a claimant who has limited capability for work and work-related activity, nor can any be imposed on a claimant with regular and substantial caring responsibilities for a severely disabled person (s.19(2)(b)) or who is the responsible carer for a child under the age of one (s.19(2)(c)). Note the other categories prescribed in reg.89. Other groups of claimants with caring responsibilities are free of the work search and work availability requirements under ss.20 and 21 of the WRA 2012. Claimants with limited capability for work fall into that category by reason of s.21(1)(a).

2.280

Paragraph (3)

2.281   A work search or availability requirement cannot relate to work in a location where the claimant's normal travel time either from home to work or from work to home would exceed 90 minutes, subject to the further limitation in para.(6) for some disabled claimants. Travel times below that limit could be relevant in relation to a sanction for non-compliance with a requirement, on the question of whether the claimant had no good reason for the failure to comply. On that question all circumstances could be considered, including the effect of any physical or mental impairment not serious enough to count under para.(6), whereas under this provision time is the conclusive factor unless the location is completely excluded under para.(6).

Paragraphs (4) and (5)

2.282   A claimant who has previously carried out work of a particular nature or at a particular level of remuneration is to have the kind of work to be considered limited to similar conditions for so long as considered appropriate up to three months from the date of claim or ceasing to fall within s.19 of the WRA 2012 by virtue of the level of earnings (para.(5)). But the rule only applies if and so long as the claimant will have reasonable prospects of work subject to that limitation.

Paragraph (6)

2.283   A claimant who has a physical or mental impairment which has a substantial adverse effect on their ability to carry out work of a particular nature or in particular locations (a significant additional condition over and above that of impairment on its own) is to have the kind of work to be considered under the work search and work availability requirements limited to avoid such work.

Victims of domestic violence

2.284   **98.**—(1) Where a claimant has recently been a victim of domestic violence, and the circumstances set out in paragraph (3) apply—
    (a) a work-related requirement imposed on that claimant ceases to have effect for a period of 13 consecutive weeks starting on the date of the notification referred to in paragraph (3)(a); and
    (b) the Secretary of State must not impose any other work-related requirement on that claimant during that period.
[²(1A) Where a claimant referred to in paragraph (1) is a person who falls within section 22 of the Act (claimants subject to all work-related requirements) and is the responsible carer of a child, the Secretary of State must not impose a work search requirement or a work availability requirement on that claimant for a further period of 13 consecutive weeks beginning on the day after the period in paragraph (1)(a) expires.]
(2) A person has recently been a victim of domestic violence if a period of 6 months has not expired since the violence was inflicted or threatened.
(3) The circumstances are that—
    (a) the claimant notifies the Secretary of State, in such manner as the Secretary of State specifies, that domestic violence has been inflicted on or threatened against the claimant by the claimant's partner or former partner or by a family member during the period of 6 months ending on the date of the notification;
    (b) this regulation has not applied to the claimant for a period of 12 months before the date of the notification;
    (c) on the date of the notification the claimant is not living at the same address as the person who inflicted or threatened the domestic violence; and
    (d) as soon as possible, and no later than 1 month, after the date of the

notification the claimant provides evidence from a person acting in an official capacity which demonstrates that—

(i) the claimant's circumstances are consistent with those of a person who has had domestic violence inflicted or threatened against them during the period of 6 months ending on the date of the notification, and

(ii) the claimant has made contact with the person acting in an official capacity in relation to such an incident, which occurred during that period.

(4) In this regulation—

[¹"coercive behaviour" means an act of assault, humiliation or intimidation or other abuse that is used to harm, punish or frighten the victim;

"controlling behaviour" means an act designed to make a person subordinate or dependent by isolating them from sources of support, exploiting their resources and capacities for personal gain, depriving them of the means needed for independence, resistance or escape or regulating their everyday behaviour;

"domestic violence" means any incident, or pattern of incidents, of controlling behaviour, coercive behaviour, violence or abuse, including but not limited to—

(a)   psychological abuse;

(b)   physical abuse;

(c)   sexual abuse;

(d)   emotional abuse;

(e)   financial abuse,

regardless of the gender or sexuality of the victim;]

"family member", in relation to a claimant, means the claimant's grandparent, grandchild, parent, step-parent, parent-in-law, son, step-son, son-in-law, daughter, step-daughter, daughter-in-law, brother, step-brother, brother-in-law, sister, step-sister, sister-in law and, if any of those persons is member of a couple, the other member of the couple;

"health care professional" means a person who is a member of a profession regulated by a body mentioned in section 25(3) of the National Health Service Reform and Health Care Professions Act 2002;

"person acting in an official capacity" means a health care professional, a police officer, a registered social worker, the claimant's employer, a representative of the claimant's trade union, or any public, voluntary or charitable body which has had direct contact with the claimant in connection with domestic violence;

"registered social worker" means a person registered as a social worker in a register maintained by—

[⁴(a) Social Work England;]

[³(b) Social Care Wales;]

(c)   The Scottish Social Services Council; or

(d)   The Northern Ireland Social Care Council.

AMENDMENTS

1. Social Security (Miscellaneous Amendments) (No.2) Regulations 2013 (SI 2013/1508) reg.3(1) (October 29, 2013).

2. Universal Credit and Miscellaneous Amendments (No.2) Regulations 2014 (SI 2014/2888) reg.8(2) (November 26, 2014).

3. Social Security (Social Care Wales) (Amendment) Regulations 2017 (SI 2017/291) reg.2 (April 1, 2017).

4. Children and Social Work Act 2017 (Consequential Amendments) (Social Workers) Regulations 2019 (SI 2019/1094) reg.2(c) and Sch.3 para.30 (July 9, 2019).

DEFINITIONS

"claimant"—see WRA 2012 s.40.
"partner"—see reg.2.
"victim of domestic violence"—see WRA 2012 s.24(6)(b).
"work-related requirement"—see WRA 2012 ss.40 and 13(2).

GENERAL NOTE

2.285 This regulation, made as required by s.24(5) and (6) of the WRA 2012, exempts recent victims of domestic violence from the imposition of any work-related requirements for a period of 13 weeks from the date of notification to the Secretary of State under para.(3)(a) and lifts the effect of any existing imposition for the same period. The regulation appears to be defective to the extent that it makes no provision for exemption from the imposition of a connected requirement under s.23 of the WRA 2012, which is not a "work-related requirement" as defined in s.13(2). Thus the duty in s.24(5) to exempt recent victims of domestic violence from any requirement under Part 1 of the Act has not been fully carried out, but that would not seem to affect the validity of what has been provided in reg.98.

Paragraph (1A), in effect from November 26, 2014, requires the extension of the normal 13-week suspension under para.(1) for a further 13 weeks where the claimant is the responsible carer (see ss.19(6) and 40 of the WRA 2012 and reg.4) of a child.

For these purposes, para.(4) now provides a comprehensive definition of "domestic violence", instead of the former reference to a particular page of a difficult to find Department of Health document. It uses the terms of the government's official approach to the meaning of domestic violence across departments, which had not previously been used as a statutory definition. Note that the new criminal offence of controlling or coercive behaviour in intimate or familial relationships under s.76 of the Serious Crime Act 2015, while using the terms of controlling and coercive behaviour (the meaning of which is discussed in Home Office Statutory Guidance of December 2015) contains conditions that are different from those in reg.98. While the definition here expressly includes coercive behaviour and controlling behaviour (both given their own definition in para.(4)), any other incident of abuse of any kind can come within the ambit of domestic violence. Thus, although the specific definition of "coercive behaviour" requires the act or abuse to be used to harm, punish or frighten the victim and the specific definition of "controlling behaviour" is restricted to acts designed to make the victim subordinate or dependant by particular means (as taken to extremes by the vile Rob Titchener in *The Archers*), abuse of similar kinds where that specific form of intention or purpose is not present or is difficult to prove can nonetheless be domestic violence. The width of that makes the specific conditions in para.(3) for the application of reg.98 particularly important.

Section 24(6)(b) of the WRA 2012 defines a victim of domestic violence as a person on or against whom domestic violence (as defined above) is inflicted or threatened. Under s.24(6)(c) and para.(2) a person is to be treated as having recently been a victim of domestic violence if no more than six months has expired since the infliction or threat.

Paragraph (3)

2.286 This paragraph lays down four quite restrictive conditions that must all be satisfied for reg.98 to apply. Under sub-para.(a) the claimant must have notified the Secretary of State of the infliction or threatening of domestic violence by a partner, former partner or family member (as defined in para.(4)) within the previous six months. Under sub-para.(b), reg.98 must not have applied within the 12 months before the notification. Under sub-para.(c), the claimant must not on the date of the notification have been living at the same address as the person named as the assailant. Under sub-para.(d), the claimant must also provide, as soon as possible and no more than one month after the notification, evidence from a person acting in an official capacity (defined quite widely in para.(4)) both that the claimant's circumstances are consistent with having had domestic violence inflicted or threatened in the six months before notification and that the claimant had made contact (apparently not necessarily within the six months) with the person in relation to an incident of infliction or threat of domestic violence that occurred during the six months before notification.

Circumstances in which requirements must not be imposed

99.—(1) Where paragraph (3), (4)[², (4A)] [¹ . . .] or (6) applies—   2.287
  (a) the Secretary of State must not impose a work search requirement on a claimant; and
  (b) "able and willing immediately to take up work" under a work availability requirement means able and willing to take up paid work, or attend an interview, immediately once the circumstances set out in paragraph (3), (4)[², (4A)] [¹ . . .] or (6) no longer apply.

(2) A work search requirement previously applying to the claimant ceases to have effect from the date on which the circumstances set out in paragraph (3), (4)[², (4A)] [¹ . . .] or (6) begin to apply.

[¹(2A) Where paragraph (5) applies—
  (a) the Secretary of State must not impose a work search requirement on a claimant; and
  (b) a work search requirement previously applying to the claimant ceases to have effect from the date on which the circumstances set out in paragraph (5) begin to apply.

(2B) Where paragraph (5A) applies "able and willing to take up work" under a work availability requirement means able and willing to take up paid work, or to attend an interview, immediately once the circumstances set out in paragraph (5A) no longer apply.

(2C) Where paragraph (5B) applies, "able and willing to take up work" under a work availability requirement means—
  (a) able and willing to take up paid work immediately once the circumstances set out in paragraph (5B) no longer apply; and
  (b) able and willing to attend an interview before those circumstances no longer apply.]

(3) This paragraph applies where—
  (a) the claimant is attending a court or tribunal as a party to any proceedings or as a witness;
  (b) the claimant is a prisoner;
  (c) regulation 11(3) (temporary absence from Great Britain for treatment or convalescence) applies to the claimant;
  (d) any of the following persons has died within the past 6 months—
      (i) where the claimant was a member of a couple, the other membe
      (ii) a child or qualifying young person for whom the claimant or, where the claimant is a member of a couple, the other member, was responsible, or
      (iii) a child, where the claimant was the child's parent;
  (e) the claimant is, and has been for no more than 6 months, receiving and participating in a structured recovery-orientated course of alcohol or drug dependency treatment;

(f) the claimant is, and has been for no more than 3 months, a person for whom arrangements have been made by a protection provider under section 82 of the Serious Organised Crime and Police Act 2005; or

(g) the claimant is engaged in an activity of a kind approved by the Secretary of State as being in the nature of a public duty.

(4) [⁵Subject to paragraph (4ZA), this paragraph] applies where the claimant—

(a) is unfit for work—

    (i) for a period of no more than 14 consecutive days after the date that the evidence referred to in sub-paragraph (b) is provided, and

    (ii) for no more than 2 such periods in any period of 12 months; and

(b) provides to the Secretary of State the following evidence—

    (i) for the first 7 days when they are unfit for work, a declaration made by the claimant in such manner and form as the Secretary of State approves that the claimant is unfit for work, and

    (ii) for any further days when they are unfit for work, if requested by the Secretary of State, a statement given by a doctor in accordance with the rules set out in Part 1 of Schedule 1 to the Medical Evidence Regulations which provides that the person is not fit for work.

[⁵(4ZA) Where paragraph (4ZB) applies, paragraph (4) will only apply to a claimant if the Secretary of State makes a decision to carry out an assessment under regulation 41(1)(b).

(4ZB) This paragraph applies where—

(a) (i) it has previously been determined on the basis of an assessment under Part 5 of these Regulations or under Part 4 or 5 of the ESA Regulations that the claimant does not have limited capability for work; or

    (ii) the claimant has previously been treated as not having limited capability for work or, as the case may be, for work and work-related activity under regulation 43(3) or 44(2); and

(b) the condition specified in the evidence provided by the claimant in accordance with paragraph (4)(b) is in the opinion of the Secretary of State the same, or substantially the same, as the condition specified in the evidence provided by the claimant before the date—

    (i) of the determination that the claimant does not have limited capability for work; or

    (ii) that the claimant was treated as not having limited capability for work or, as the case may be, for work and work-related activity.]

[²(4A) This paragraph applies for one or more periods of one month, as provided for in paragraphs (4B) and (4C), where the claimant is the responsible carer of a child and an event referred to in sub-paragraph (a) or (b) has taken place in the last 24 months and has resulted in significant disruption to the claimant's normal childcare responsibilities—

(a) any of the following persons has died—

    (i) a person who was previously the responsible carer of that child;

    (ii) a parent of that child;

    (iii) a brother or sister of that child; or

    (iv) any other person who, at the time of their death, normally lived in the same accommodation as that child and was not a person who was liable to make payments on a commercial basis in respect that accommodation; or

(b) the child has been the victim of, or witness to, an incident of violence or abuse and the claimant is not the perpetrator of that violence or abuse.

(4B) Paragraph (4A) is not to apply for more than one period of one month in each of the 4 consecutive periods of 6 months following the event (and, if regulation 98 or paragraph (3)(d) of this regulation applies in respect of the same event, that month is to run concurrently with any period for which that regulation or paragraph applies).

(4C) Each period of one month begins on the date specified by the Secretary of State after the claimant has notified the Secretary of State of the circumstances in paragraph (4A) provided that the Secretary of State is satisfied that the circumstances apply.]

(5) This paragraph applies where the Secretary of State is satisfied that it would be unreasonable to require the claimant to comply with a work search requirement [¹ . . .], including if such a requirement were limited in accordance with section 17(4) [¹ . . .] of the Act, because [⁵ . . .]

(a) [⁵the claimant] is carrying out a work preparation requirement or voluntary work preparation (as defined in regulation 95(4));

(b) [⁵the claimant] has temporary child care responsibilities or is dealing with a domestic emergency, funeral arrangements or other temporary circumstances; [⁵ . . .]

(c) [⁵the claimant] has been unfit for work for longer than the period of 14 days specified in paragraph (4)(a) or for more than 2 such periods in any period of 12 months and, where requested by the Secretary of State, provides the evidence mentioned in paragraph (4)(b)(ii). [⁵; or

(d) paragraph (4) would apply to the claimant but for paragraph (4ZA).]

[¹(5A) This paragraph applies where the Secretary of State is satisfied that it would be unreasonable to require the claimant to comply with a work availability requirement to be able and willing to—

(a) take up paid work; and

(b) attend an interview,

(including if such a requirement were limited in accordance with section 18(3) of the Act) because the claimant falls within [⁵sub-paragraph (a), (b), (c) or (d)] of paragraph (5).

(5B) This paragraph applies where the Secretary of State is satisfied that it would be—

(a) unreasonable to require the claimant to comply with a work availability requirement to be able and willing to take up paid work because the claimant falls within [⁵sub-paragraph (a), (b), (c) or (d)] of paragraph (5); and

(b) reasonable to require the claimant to comply with a work availability requirement to attend an interview,

including if such a requirement were limited in accordance with section 18(3) of the Act.]

[³[⁴(6) This paragraph applies where the claimant has monthly earnings or, if the claimant is a member of a couple, the couple has combined monthly earnings (excluding in either case any that are not employed earnings) that are equal to, or more than, the following amount multiplied by 52 and divided by 12—

(a) in the case of a single claimant, £5 plus the applicable amount of the personal allowance in a jobseeker's allowance for a single person aged 25 or over (as set out in Part 1 of Schedule 1 to the Jobseeker's Allowance Regulations 1996); or

(b) in the case of a claimant who is a member of a couple, £10 plus the applicable amount of the personal allowance in a jobseeker's allowance for a couple where both members are aged 18 or over (as set out in that Part).]

(6A) In paragraph (6) "employed earnings" has the meaning in regulation 55.]

(7) In this regulation "tribunal" means any tribunal listed in Schedule 1 to the Tribunals and Inquiries Act 1992.

AMENDMENTS

1. Universal Credit and Miscellaneous Amendments Regulations 2014 (SI 2014/597) reg.2(7) (April 28, 2014).

2. Universal Credit and Miscellaneous Amendments) (No. 2) Regulations 2014 (SI 2014/2888) reg.8(3) (November 26, 2014).

3. Universal Credit (Work-Related Requirements) In Work Pilot Scheme and Amendment Regulations 2015 (SI 2015/89) reg.3 (February 19, 2015).

4. Universal Credit and Miscellaneous Amendments Regulations 2015 (SI 2015/1754) reg.2(7) (November 4, 2015).

5. Universal Credit (Miscellaneous Amendments, Saving and Transitional Provision) Regulations 2018 (SI 2018/65) reg.3(11) (April 11, 2018).

DEFINITIONS

"child"—see WRA 2012 s.40.
"claimant"—*ibid.*
"couple"—see WRA 2012, ss.40 and 39.
"ESA Regulations"—see reg.2.
"Medical Evidence Regulations"—*ibid.*
"paid work"—*ibid.*
"prisoner"—*ibid.*
"qualifying young person"—see WRA 2012 ss.40 and 10(5).
"responsible carer"—see WRA 2012 ss.40 and 19(6).
"voluntary work preparation"—see reg.95(4).
"work availability requirement"—see WRA 2012 ss.40 and 18(1).
"work preparation requirement"—see WRA 2012 ss.40 and 16(1).
"work search requirement"—see WRA 2012 ss.40 and 17(1).

GENERAL NOTE

Temporary Coronavirus Provisions

2.288 Regulation 6(1)(a) and (b) of the Social Security (Coronavirus) (Further Measures) Regulations 2020 (SI 2020/371) provides that for a period of three months beginning on March 30, 2020 the Secretary of State cannot impose a work search requirement on anyone who has an award of universal credit and any existing work search requirement ceases to have effect from that date. Although reg.6 refers to the provision being a consequence of the outbreak of coronavirus disease, it is not necessary that the claimant in question be affected in any way by that outbreak or the resulting economic disruption. It is not clear what is intended by the restriction to someone who has an award of universal credit. There would be no consistency in lifting the work search requirement for someone who happened to have an existing award on March 30, 2020, but not allowing an award to be made on a new claim because the claimant had not accepted a claimant commitment containing the requirement that the Secretary of State was bound to impose under s.22(2)(a), so that reg.6 of the Further Measures Regulations was never reached because the claimant never had an award. Such a result was plainly not intended (and was not applied in practice), so is to be avoided if possible, but para.11 of Memo ADM 04/20 gives no clue as to the mechanism for doing so. It is suggested that, provided that it had been accepted under reg.16(b) of the Universal Credit Regulations that the claimant could be entitled without having accepted a claimant commitment (see the notes to s.4(1)(e) and reg.16) and all the other basic conditions in s.4(1) were met, an award could be made to the claimant before consideration of what work-related requirements were to be imposed, so that then reg.6 could apply to modify the Secretary of State's s.22(2) duty to impose the work search and work availability requirements.

Regulation 6(1)(c) of the Further Measures Regulations provides that for the same period any work availability requirement imposed on anyone who has an award of universal credit is to operate as if "able and willing immediately to take up paid work" means able and willing to do so, or to attend an interview once reg.6 ceases to apply.

Note in addition that the definition of "prisoner" in reg.2(3) is modified for the period from April 8, 2020 to November 12, 2020 by reg.2 of the Social Security (Coronavirus) (Prisoners) Regulations 2020 (SI 2020/409) to exclude any prisoner on temporary release. The modification is relevant to reg.19(3)(b).

The effect of reg.6 expires at the end of November 12, 2020 (reg.10(2)), subject to any amendment. The power to extend the three-month period was not exercised before it expired. When it was announced (Parliamentary answer, Under-Secretary of State, Mims Davies, WQ 62431) that from July 1, 2020 the requirement for universal credit claimants to accept a claimant commitment was being reintroduced, it was stressed that claimant commitments agreed or reviewed from that date (i.e. the work-related requirements included) would have to be reasonable for the "new normal" and acknowledge the reality of a person's local jobs market and personal circumstances.

This regulation is made under ss.22(2) and 24(1)(a) of the WRA 2012 in respect **2.288.1** of the work search and availability requirements and under s.18(5) in respect of the work availability requirement. Its structure was revised in 2014 to make its operation somewhat clearer, although at the cost of a more complicated interaction of various paragraphs. Some requirements were tightened and some relaxed, also.

The central rule is under paras (1) and (2) and operates where any of paras (3), (4), (4A) (incorporating (4B) and (4C)) or (6) applies. Under para.(1)(a) no work search requirement can be imposed in those circumstances (and any already imposed requirement lapses: para.(2)) and under para.(1)(b) the work availability requirement is adjusted to require only that the claimant be willing and able to take up paid work or attend an interview immediately once the circumstances in question cease to apply. Paragraphs (3), (4), (4A) and (6) cover fairly specifically defined circumstances, dealt with separately below.

Paragraph (2A) operates where para.(5) applies, to the same effect as under paras (1)(a) and (2) on the work search requirement in relation to the circumstances in para.(5). Paragraph (5) also covers fairly specifically defined circumstances, but with the additional condition that it be unreasonable to require compliance with the work search requirement, and is dealt with separately below.

Paragraph (2B) operates where para.(5A) applies, to the same effect as under para.(1)(b) in relation to the circumstances in para.(5A). Paragraph (5A) involves a judgment that it would be unreasonable to require the claimant to be able and willing to take up paid work <u>and</u> attend an interview (see further below).

Paragraph (2C) operates where para.(5B) applies, but only so as to lift the requirement to be willing and able to take up an offer of paid work, not to lift the requirement to be willing and able to attend an interview. The judgment required under para.(5B) is thus that it would be unreasonable to require the claimant to be able and willing to take up paid work, but reasonable to require willingness and ability to attend an interview (see further below).

Paragraph (3)

2.289   Paragraph (3) lists a number of categories of claimant where the circumstances mean that the claimant could not be expected to look for or take up work or attend an interview, generally of a temporary nature:

(a)   Attending a court or tribunal (defined in para.(7)) as a party to proceedings or as a witness, apparently so long as the hearing continues for a party and so long as attendance is required for a witness.

(b)   A prisoner, under the reg.2 definition covering those detained in custody pending trial or sentence on conviction or under sentence or on temporary release, but excluding anyone detained in hospital under mental health legislation. Under the temporary coronavirus modification mentioned above, prisoners on temporary release are excluded from this provision for the period from April 8, 2020 to November 12, 2020 (see the notes to reg.15(2) of the JSA Regulations 1996 in Vol.II of this series for further details).

(c)   Temporary absence from Great Britain in connection with medical treatment for illness etc or convalescence, or accompanying a partner or child or qualifying young person undergoing such treatment or convalescence, under the conditions in reg.11(3). See the notes to that provision.

(d)   The claimant's then partner, a child or qualifying young person for whom the claimant or partner was responsible or a child of the claimant has died within the previous six months. See para.(4A)(a) for circumstances in which the operation of paras (1) and (2) can be triggered by the death within the previous 24 months of various people connected with a child.

(e)   Attending a structured recovery-oriented course of alcohol or drug dependency treatment, for no more than six months.

(f)   Having protection arrangements made under s.82 of the Serious Organised Crime and Police Act 2005 (protection of persons involved in investigations or proceedings whose safety is considered to be at risk), for no more than three months. Arrangements for protection are made by protection providers (e.g. Chief Constables and any of the Commissioners for HMRC).

(g)   Any other activity of a kind approved by the Secretary of State as being in the nature of a public duty, apparently for as long as the activity and approval lasts. It is therefore unclear whether on any appeal against a sanction where the application of this paragraph is in issue a First-tier Tribunal is required to accept non-approval of an activity by the Secretary of State or can substitute its own judgment.

Paragraphs (4)-(4ZB)

2.290   A claimant who is unfit for work (not further defined) and provides a self-certificate for the first seven days and, if requested, a statement from a doctor under the Medical Evidence Regulations (see Vol.I of this series) for any further days falls within the basic rules in para.(1) on both the work search and the work availability requirement. But the benefit of para.(4) is limited to a period of no more than 14 days after the evidence is provided and to no more than two such periods in any 12 months. There is a possible extension of those restrictions under para.(5)(c) in relation to the work search requirement or under para.(5A) or (5B) in relation to the work availability requirement.

There appears on the original form of para.(4) no reason why a claimant should not take the benefit of its provisions from the first day of entitlement to universal credit. But from April 2018 an additional limitation on the operation of para.(4) has been created by the new paras (4ZA) and (4ZB), designed to deal with the common circumstances where a claimant's entitlement to new style ESA has been terminated by reason of a determination following an assessment that they do not have limited capability for work or such a determination has been made under the universal credit provisions, so that the claimant no longer has an automatic exemption from the work search and work availability requirements under s.21(1)(a), or the claimant has previously been deemed not to have limited capability for work or work-related activity for failing to comply with an information requirement or failing to attend or submit to a medical examination (regs 43(3) and 44(2)). Such a universal credit determination would result in a decision removing the limited capability for work or limited capability for work and work-related activity element which would be appealable, but there is no provision for deeming capability and qualification for the appropriate element while the appeal is pending. If the claimant has appealed against the new style ESA decision after the mandatory reconsideration process, the circumstances in which limited capability for work will be deemed for those purposes has been severely restricted. If that deeming does operate, it appears not to translate into universal credit. The effect under regs 39(1)(a) and 40(1)(a)(ii) only follows a new style ESA determination that a claimant does have limited capability for work or for work-related activity.

In the circumstances described above, as prescribed in para.(4ZB)(a), a claimant can only take unrestricted advantage of para.(4) if the condition specified in the medical evidence provided under para.(4)(b) is not the same or substantially the same as the condition specified in the evidence provided by the claimant before the determination of not having limited capability for work (para.(4ZB)(b)). Paragraph (4ZA), which applies the conditions in para.(4ZB), then restricts a claimant who cannot satisfy that test from taking advantage of para.(4) except where the Secretary of State decides to carry out an assessment under reg.41(1)(b) (see the discussion below for the limited circumstances covered). Thus, the claimant is not in general permitted for these purposes to undermine the judgment on capability for work embodied in the adverse new style ESA or universal credit determination. However, paras (5)(d) and (5A) and (5B) allow the application of para.(4) where it would be unreasonable to require a claimant who would otherwise be caught by para.(4ZA) to comply with a work search or availability requirement.

The Explanatory Memorandum for SI 2018/65 describes the effect of these amendments as follows in paras 7.14 and 7.15:

"7.14 This instrument amends regulation 99 of the Universal Credit Regulations (and makes equivalent amendments to regulation 16 of the Jobseeker's Allowance Regulations 2013) to prevent work search and work availability requirements being automatically switched off for illness in certain circumstances. The amendments apply to claimants who have undergone a work capability assessment and been found not to have limited capability for work, and to claimants who have failed to attend a medical examination or comply with a request for information and are treated as not having limited capability for work. In other words, claimants who are, or are treated as being, fit for work. Where such claimants produce evidence that they are unfit for work and the condition mentioned in the evidence is the same, or substantially the same, as the condition for which they were assessed in the work capability assessment, work search and work availability requirements will only be switched off if they have been referred for another assessment as to their capability for work.

7.15 If such a claimant has not been referred for another assessment, regulations will continue to allow for work search and work availability requirements to be switched off if it would be unreasonable for a claimant to comply with such requirements."

That seems accurate so far as universal credit is concerned, but not for new style JSA (see the notes to reg.16 of the JSA Regulations 2013 in Vol.II of this series).

A number of points need brief mention. Note first that paras (4ZA) and (4ZB) only apply where the previous assessment and determination of no limited capability for work or deeming was for the purposes of new style ESA or universal credit. It does not apply if it was for the purposes of old style ESA. Then on its face it applies whenever in the past the adverse determination was made. It may need to be decided whether in order to operate in a rational and fair way the provisions should be limited to the most recent determination of no limited capability for work under new style ESA or universal credit. Third, the comparison to be made in para.(4ZB)(b) is between the condition(s) specified in the evidence provided by the claimant before the previous adverse determination or deeming and the condition(s) specified in the evidence put forward by the claimant in support of the application of para.(4). The evidence provided by the claimant before the adverse determination will presumably cover primarily a GP's medical certificate, but also any questionnaire completed by the claimant and any other evidence, from medical professionals or otherwise, put forward (and, it would seem, the claimant's oral evidence to any tribunal and any further evidence put forward there). It will not cover the opinions of any approved health care professional who has carried out a medical examination, even though it is usually on the basis of those opinions that adverse determinations are made, because that evidence was not provided by the claimant. The evidence to be provided under para.(4)(b) is a self-certificate for the first week and then a GP's medical certificate. Difficulties can be anticipated in making a comparison between what may be a fairly informal and short specification in a self-certificate and the previous evidence. And is it enough to trigger para.(4ZB)(b) that, say, the sole condition specified in the new self-certificate or GP's certificate is substantially the same as one, but only one, out of several that were specified before the adverse determination? The reference to "the condition specified" seems to require that a mere worsening in the condition(s) previously specified, even a substantial worsening, does not result in a condition that is not the same. But what if, say, a condition affecting one part of the body starts to affect another part? Is that the same condition?

The rule in para.(4ZA) allowing the lifting of the work search and work availability requirements on the ordinary para.(4) basis, despite the previous determination or deeming, only where the Secretary of State makes a decision to carry out an assessment under reg.41(1)(b) has much more limited scope than first appears. An assessment is not the medical examination (if any) under reg.44, but the assessment by a decision-maker on behalf of the Secretary of State of the extent to which a claimant is or is not capable of carrying out the activities prescribed in Sch.6 (i.e. the points-scoring exercise) (reg.39(2)). There may well be doubt about the exact point when the Secretary of State makes a decision to carry out an assessment, but no doubt it can be accepted that one has been made if the Secretary of State starts the evidence-gathering process by sending a questionnaire to the claimant and/or referring the case to the organisation running medical examinations by health care professionals. However, the Secretary of State's powers to carry out an assessment are circumscribed. Paragraph (4ZA) operates only where the power under reg.41(1)(a) is used, which is limited to cases where the Secretary of State wishes to determine whether since a previous limited capability for work determination there has been a relevant change of circumstances in relation to the claimant's physical or mental condition or whether the previous determination was made in ignorance of or was based on a mistake as to some material fact. Those are terms that relate primarily to the exercise of powers of supersession or revision. It might be thought that if the Secretary of State is merely considering what determination to make under paras (4)–(4ZB) as the result of a claimant's producing medical evidence under para. (4)(b) she does not need to determine any of the things mentioned. However, the further restriction in reg.41(4), to which reg.41(1) is expressly subject, prohibits the carrying out of a further assessment where there has been a previous new style ESA or universal credit determination adverse to the claimant unless there is evidence to suggest ignorance or mistake of material fact or a relevant change of circumstances. Thus, a mere assertion by the claimant that the previous determination was wrong will probably not do, but otherwise the regulations appear to leave a great deal of discretion to the Secretary of State as to when to carry out an assessment following a previous adverse determination.

Remember the provision in paras (2A) and (5)(d), in effect disapplying the effect of paras (4ZA) and (4ZB) when it is unreasonable to require the claimant to comply with any work search requirement and that in paras (2B) and (2C) and (5A) - (5C) modifying the work availability requirement on similar conditions. See the notes to para.(5)(c) below for the suggestion that it allows, where reasonable, the lifting of the requirements from those unfit for work for longer periods than allowed under para.(4) regardless of the existence of any previous determination or deeming.

Paragraphs (4A) to (4C)

Paragraph (4A) supplies a number of further circumstances, all related to chil-   2.291
dren, in which paras (1) and (2) operate to lift the work search requirement and modify the work availability requirement. The claimant must be the responsible carer of a child (as defined in s.19(6) of the WRA 2012 and see regs 4 and 4A for how responsibility is determined) and reg.26 on nomination by joint claimants. Then one of the events specified in sub-paras (a) and (b) must have occurred in the 24 months prior to the week in question and have resulted in significant disruption to the claimant's normal childcare responsibilities. Although it is not entirely clear, it seems to be necessary that the event is continuing to result in significant disruption in the week in question, not just at or shortly after the time of the event. "Normal childcare responsibilities" should be given its ordinary everyday meaning.

Sub-paragraph (a) applies when one of the persons listed (i.e. a parent or responsible carer or brother or sister of the child or someone else who lived in the same accommodation other than a commercial lodger) has died. Sub-paragraph (b) applies where the child has been the victim of or has witnessed an incident of violence or abuse not perpetrated by the claimant.

Paragraphs (4B) and (4C) limit each application of para.(4A) to a period of one month and to no more than one such application in each of the four periods of six months following the incident in question. Note the possibility of the application of para.(5)(b) without those limits in some circumstances that could have fallen within para.(4A).

Note also that under s.19(2)(c) of the WRA 2012 no work-related requirements may be imposed on the responsible carer of a child under the age of one, that under s.20(1)(a) only the work-focused interview requirement may be imposed on a claimant who is the responsible carer of a child aged one and that under s.21(1)(b) only the work-focused interview and work preparation requirements may be imposed on a claimant who is the responsible carer of a child aged two.

Paragraph (5)

The direct operation of para.(5) has since April 28, 2014 been limited to the work   2.292
search requirement. See paras (5A) and (5B) for the effect on the work availability requirement where one of the conditions in para.(5)(a)–(d) is satisfied.

In four sorts of circumstances the imposition of a work search requirement, even as limited under reg.97, is prohibited where it would be unreasonable for the claimant to comply.

Sub-paragraph (a) applies if the claimant is carrying out a work preparation requirement (s.16(1) of the WRA 2012) or voluntary work preparation (reg.95(4)). It appears that voluntary work preparation could include the doing of voluntary work if agreed by the Secretary of State (see the definition in reg.95(4)).

Sub-paragraph (b) applies if the claimant has temporary child care responsibilities (for any child) or is dealing with a domestic emergency, funeral arrangements (for a claimant who is already covered by para.(3)(d)) or with other temporary circumstances. In *RR v SSWP (UC)* [2017] UKUT 459 (AAC) (see the notes to reg.95), Judge Wikeley suggested that another way of looking at the case, rather than exploring deductions from 35 as the expected number of hours under reg.95(2), was to consider whether a work search requirement could not be imposed for the weeks in question on the basis that the claimant was dealing with a domestic emergency or other temporary circumstances (reg.99(5)(b)). His suggestion that reg.99(2A) and (5) apply only when the circumstances are such that it is unreasonable to require the claimant to comply with any work search requirement at all, rather than merely to undertake more than reduced hours of work search action under reg.95, appears right. The evidence in *RR* probably did not support such a conclusion.

Sub-paragraph (c) applies where the claimant is unfit for work and produces a GP's medical certificate if required and the restrictions in para.(4) have been exceeded. This is an important extension to the provision in para.(4) but subject to the overriding condition that it is unreasonable to require the claimant to undertake any work search activities. It must surely be the case, especially in view of the insertion of sub-para.(d) in April 2018, that sub-para.(c) applies regardless of the existence of any previous determination or deeming that the claimant does not have limited capability for work or work-related activity. It is enough, subject to the reasonableness and evidence conditions, that the claimant has been unfit for work for more than 14 days or has exceeded the two periods limit.

Sub-paragraph (d) mitigates the rigour of the paras (4ZA) and (4ZB) rules by in effect disapplying them when it would be unreasonable to require the claimant to comply with any work search requirement.

Would para.(5)(b) allow the Secretary of State to allow short "holidays" from work search responsibilities (and a modification of work availability requirements under para.(5A) or (5B)), under the heading of temporary circumstances or temporary child care responsibilities if satisfied that it would be reasonable to do so (cf. reg.19(1)(p) and (2) of the JSA Regulations 1996)? It is a feature of the universal credit scheme that it will apply to claimants in substantial work, who will have statutory holiday entitlements, as will family members of claimants not themselves in work. If so allowed, there would then be no need to consider the possible application of reg.95(2)(b) or 96(3)(b).

Paragraphs (5A) and (5B)

2.293   Where it would be unreasonable, because of the satisfaction of any of the conditions in para.(5)(a)–(d), for the claimant to be required to be able and willing immediately either to take up paid work or attend an interview, the work availability requirement is adjusted to require the claimant to be willing and able to do so immediately the condition ceases to be satisfied (paras (5A) and (1)(b)). Paragraph (5B) produces the equivalent effect where it would be unreasonable to require the claimant to be willing and able immediately to take up paid work, but reasonable to require willingness and ability to attend an interview.

Paragraphs (6) and (6A)

2.294   Where a claimant or joint claimants are not already free of all work-related requirements by reason of having earnings of at least the individual earnings threshold or the combined thresholds, the "conditionality earnings threshold" (reg.90), the work search requirement is not to be imposed if the monthly earnings, converted to a weekly equivalent, exceed the applicable amount of the personal allowance for a single person aged 25 or over in the JSA Regulations 1996 by £5 or more (£10 over the couple's personal allowance for a couple). That level, called by the DWP the administrative earnings threshold, was increased in April 2020 from £338 to £343 per month for a single person (£549 for a couple). In addition, the work availability requirement is adjusted to require only willingness and ability to take up paid work or attend an interview immediately after the earnings fall below the specified level. The DWP calls this level of conditionality the light touch approach. Where earnings are below the administrative earnings threshold, the normal rules on work-related requirements, as set by the regulations apart from para.(6), apply.

Prior to February 19, 2015, the test was in terms of the earnings being at a level where the Secretary of State was satisfied that the work search and availability requirements should not be imposed at the time in question. According to para.7.4 of the Explanatory Memorandum to the Universal Credit (Work-Related Requirements) In Work Pilot Scheme and Amendment Regulations 2015, para.(6) was initially put in that form because it had not been worked out what form of intervention in support of the principle of conditionality was likely to be most effective in cases where claimants were in work. The test was therefore made discretionary, with the intention of usually applying the level of earnings that would take a claimant or claimants out of entitlement to old style income-based JSA and with the prospect that para.(6) would later be revoked completely (apparently because it would then be known how the work search and availability requirements could be operated in an appropriate way).

The Pilot Scheme Regulations (see later in this Volume) represent an interim position. The February 2015 form of para.(6) now applies a hard-edged limit, adjusted from November 2015 to take account of the general change to the calculation of earnings for UC purposes on a monthly basis. The Pilot Scheme Regulations allow the Secretary of State to select on a random basis certain "qualifying claimants" who would otherwise benefit from para.(6), i.e. who would otherwise be subject to light touch conditionality, to be treated on the basis that para.(6) does not exist. The other conditions under reg.7 of those Regulations for being a "qualifying claimant" are falling within s.22 of the WRA 2012 (subject to all work-related requirements), not falling within reg.98 (victims of domestic violence) and not falling within reg.99(3) (except sub-para.(a) or (g)) or (5)(c). The effect of the Regulations was to expire after three years from February 19, 2015, but that period has been extended, as allowed by s.41(5) of the WRA 2012, for a further three years so far (Universal Credit (Work-Related Requirements) In Work Pilot Scheme (Extension) Order 2018 (SI 2018/168), as supplemented by the 2019 and 2020 Universal Credit (Work-Related Requirements) In Work Pilot Scheme (Extension) Orders (SIs 2019/249 and 2020/152) and may well, in view of the slow development of policy described below, be extended further.

This is a very important provision, allowing experiments ("test and learn") to take place on how to apply the principle of conditionality to those in more than merely subsidiary work, a question apparently not worked out when the scheme to which in-work conditionality was central was legislated for or in the several years since. The claimants selected for the experiments will bear the brunt of any unfairness or rough justice or impracticability revealed in the experiments. Although the large trial described below has finished, so that the terms of para. (6) will apply unaffected in most cases, smaller-scale research and testing will continue.

See the House of Commons Work and Pensions Committee's report on *In-work progression in Universal Credit* (Tenth Report of Session 2010-16, May 2016, HC 549) for a critical but supportive description of the pilot scheme. The government's response to the report was published as HC 585 on July 21, 2016, in which it was anticipated that the necessary 15,000 participants would have been identified by early autumn 2016, to be randomly allocated into groups receiving either frequent, moderate or minimal support. This was known as the randomised controlled trial (RCT). The DWP's evidence to the Committee was that sanctions would be applied for failures to meet in-work requirements without good reason "as a last resort" (para.47 of HC 549), a phrase repeated in para.27 of HC 585. It is not clear how this can operate in practice, as a decision-maker has no discretion not to impose a sanction or to modify its effects if the statutory conditions for imposition are met. Presumably, the intention is that work coaches or other officers will only refer cases to a decision-maker for a sanction as a last resort. On March 23, 2017 the DWP published *In-Work Progression Trial Progress Update: April 2015 to October 2016*. This revealed that 15,455 people had been on the trial and that during the update period 319 sanctions had been imposed, mainly at the low level for failing to participate in meetings or telephone calls.

The Social Security Advisory Committee published an interesting paper, *In-work progression and Universal Credit* (Occasional Paper No.19) in November 2017. The paper welcomed the DWP's adoption of a cautious test and learn approach and the current RCT, but recommended that the DWP should test a wider range of interventions and quickly develop a wider understanding of the variety of circumstances of working claimants who will fall within the ambit of universal credit. It also recommended tackling operational complexities that can be an obstacle to in-work progression and clarifying policy in a number of areas, such as where claimants are working part-time in order to study, re-train or pursue other interests. The government's response in the policy paper *DWP response to SSAC report on In-work progression and Universal Credit: government response* (March 6, 2018) was to welcome the report, but to stress that the DWP considered itself as still at a relatively early stage in understanding what works and that developments would be informed by a "multi-faceted suite of tests and trials" over the following four years. Clarification of policy and the appropriate guidance to and training of work coaches would emerge from that process.

The Work and Pensions Committee returned to the topic in its report of November 6, 2018 on *Benefit Sanctions* (HC 995 2017-19). The DWP's September 2018 report on the completion of the RCT had found a positive impact on behaviours and increased earnings 52 weeks on (an effect subsequently confirmed at 78 weeks: DWP Ad hoc Report 75, October 2019) for those in the more supported groups. However, the important thing was the tailoring of the support to individual needs rather than frequency. Experience of being sanctioned had no apparent effect on outcomes. The Committee recommended that conditionality and sanctions should not be applied to in-work claimants until universal credit had been fully rolled out and then only on the basis of robust evidence of effectiveness. The DWP (House of Commons Work and Pensions Committee, *Benefit Sanctions: Government Response* (HC 1949 2017-19, February 11, 2019), partially accepted that recommendation, but only to the extent of agreeing that the development of policy should be evidence-based and committing to a cautious approach, involving further research and testing of a range of interventions and a better understanding of structural barriers to progression for in-work claimants.

CHAPTER 2

SANCTIONS

Introduction

2.295   **100.**—(1) This Chapter contains provisions about the reduction in the amount of an award of universal credit in the event of a failure by a claimant which is sanctionable under section 26 or 27 of the Act ("a sanctionable failure").

[[1](1A) In this Chapter references to a "current sanctionable failure" are to a sanctionable failure in relation to which the Secretary of State has not yet determined whether the amount of an award of universal credit is to be reduced under section 26 or 27 of the Act.]

(2) How the period of the reduction for each sanctionable failure is to be determined is dealt with in regulations 101 to 105.

(3) When the reduction begins or ceases to have effect is dealt with in regulations 106 to 109.

(4) How the amount of a reduction is calculated for an assessment period in which the reduction has effect is set out in regulations 110 and 111.

(5) Regulations 112 to 114 provide for some miscellaneous matters (movement of sanctions from a jobseeker's allowance or an employment and support allowance, cases in which no reduction is made for a sanctionable failure and prescription of work placement scheme for the purposes of section 26(2)(a) of the Act).

AMENDMENT

1. Social Security (Jobseeker's Allowance, Employment and Support Allowance and Universal Credit) (Amendment) Regulations 2016 (SI 2016/678) reg.5(5) (July 25, 2016).

Definitions

Definitions

"the Act"—see reg.2.
"assessment period"—see WRA 2012 ss.40 and 7(2) and reg.21.
"claimant"—see WRA 2012 s.40.
"employment and support allowance"—see reg.2.
"jobseeker's allowance"—*ibid.*

Reduction periods

General principles for calculating reduction periods

101.—(1) The number of days for which a reduction in the amount of an award is to have effect ("the reduction period") is to be determined in relation to each sanctionable failure in accordance with regulations 102 to 105, but subject to paragraphs (3) and (4).

(2) Reduction periods are to run consecutively.

(3) If the reduction period calculated in relation to a sanctionable failure in accordance with regulations 102 to 105 would result in the total outstanding reduction period exceeding 1095 days, the reduction period in relation to that failure is to be adjusted so that the total outstanding reduction period does not exceed 1095 days.

(4) [¹...]

(5) In paragraph (3) "the total outstanding reduction period" is the total number of days for which no reduction in an award under section 26 or 27 of the Act has yet been applied.

2.296

Amendment

1. Social Security (Jobseeker's Allowance, Employment and Support Allowance and Universal Credit) (Amendment) Regulations 2016 (SI 2016/678) reg.5(6) (July 25, 2016).

Definitions

"the Act"—see reg.2.
"sanctionable failure"—see reg.100(1).

General Note

Under reg.100 and this provision the way in which a sanction bites is through a reduction in the amount of an award of universal credit for a period determined under regs 101–105 (the "reduction period": para.(1)) for each sanctionable failure. A sanctionable failure is a failure which is sanctionable under s.26 or 27 of the WRA 2012. This regulation contains some general rules on sanctions.

Under para.(2) reduction periods for separate reduction periods run consecutively. That is subject to the general overall three-year limit in paras (3) and (5). The drafting is fairly impenetrable, but the upshot seems to be that if adding a new reduction period to the end of an existing period or, more likely, chain of reduction periods would take the total days in the periods over 1095 days the new reduction period is to be adjusted to make the total 1095 days exactly. Now that the rule previously in para.(4), about previous sanctionable failures in the 13 days before another sanctionable failure not counting, has been incorporated into the specific provisions in regs 102 – 104 and tidied up, there can be no question of that rule qualifying the effect of para.(3) to allow a total outstanding reduction period to exceed 1095 days, as had been suggested in the 2013/14 edition of this Volume.

Note also the circumstances prescribed in reg.109 (earnings over the individual threshold for 26 weeks) in which a reduction is to be terminated and the circumstances prescribed in reg.113 where there is to be no reduction despite the existence

2.297

of a sanctionable failure. Under reg.111(3) the amount of the reduction is nil in an assessment period at the end of which the claimant is subject to no work-related requirements because of having limited capability for work and work-related activity under s.19 of the WRA 2012.

On May 9, 2019, following a report of November 6, 2018 by the House of Commons Work and Pensions Committee on *Benefit Sanctions* (HC 995 2017-19), the Secretary of State (Amber Rudd) made a written statement to Parliament (HCWS1545) including the following:

> "I have reviewed my Department's internal data, which shows that a six-month sanction already provides a significant incentive for claimants to engage with the labour market regime. I agree with the Work and Pensions Select Committee that a three-year sanction is unnecessarily long and I feel that the additional incentive provided by a three-year sanction can be outweighed by the unintended impacts to the claimant due to the additional duration. For these reasons, I have now decided to remove three year sanctions and reduce the maximum sanction length to six months by the end of the year."

That decision was implemented (perhaps not fully in spirit) in the November 2019 amendment to reg.102. Note in particular that there was no amendment to reg.101(3), so that in combination with the rule in para.(2) on reduction periods running consecutively it is still possible for a claimant subject to multiple reduction periods to have a total outstanding reduction period of 1095 days.

Higher-level sanction

2.298   **102.**—(1) This regulation specifies the reduction period for a sanctionable failure under section 26 of the Act ("higher level sanction").

[¹(2) Where the sanctionable failure is not a pre-claim failure, the reduction in the circumstances described in the first column of the following table is the period set out in—

(a) the second column, where the claimant is aged 18 or over on the date of the sanctionable failure;

(b) the third column, where the claimant is aged 16 or 17 on the date of the sanctionable failure.

Circumstances in which reduction period applies	Reduction period where claimant aged 18 or over	Reduction period where claimant aged 16 or 17
Where there has been no previous sanctionable failure by the claimant giving rise to a higher-level sanction	91 days	14 days
Where there have been one or more previous sanctionable failures by the claimant giving rise to a higher-level sanction and the date of the most recent previous sanctionable failure is not within 365 days beginning with the date of the current sanctionable failure	91 days	14 days
Where there have been one or more previous sanctionable failures by the claimant giving rise to a higher-level sanction and the date of the most recent previous sanctionable		

Circumstances in which reduction period applies	Reduction period where claimant aged 18 or over	Reduction period where claimant aged 16 or 17
failure is within 365 days, but not within 14 days, beginning with the date of the current sanctionable failure and the reduction period applicable to the most recent previous sanctionable failure is—		
(a) 14 days	–	28 days
(b) 28 days	–	28 days
(c) 91 days	182 days	–
(d) 182 days	[²182 days]	–
[²...]		
Where there have been one or more previous sanctionable failures by the claimant giving rise to a higher-level sanction and the date of the most recent previous sanctionable failure is within 14 days beginning with the date of the current sanctionable failure and the reduction period applicable to the most recent previous sanctionable failure is—		
(a) 14 days	–	14 days
(b) 28 days	–	28 days
(c) 91 days	91 days	–
(d) 182 days	182 days	–
[²...]		–.]

(3) But where the other sanctionable failure referred to in paragraph (2) was a pre-claim failure it is disregarded in determining the reduction period in accordance with that paragraph.

(4) Where the sanctionable failure for which a reduction period is to be determined is a pre-claim failure, the period is the lesser of—

(a) the period that would be applicable to the claimant under paragraph (2) if it were not a pre-claim failure; or

(b) where the sanctionable failure relates to paid work that was due to last for a limited period, the period beginning with the day after the date of the sanctionable failure and ending with the date on which the limited period would have ended,

minus the number of days beginning with the day after the date of the sanctionable failure and ending on the day before the date of claim.

[¹(5) In this regulation—

"higher-level sanction" means a sanction under section 26 of the Act;

"pre-claim failure" means a failure sanctionable under section 26(4) of the Act.]

AMENDMENTS

1. Social Security (Jobseeker's Allowance, Employment and Support Allowance and Universal Credit) (Amendment) Regulations 2016 (SI 2016/678) reg.5(7) (July 25, 2016).

2. Jobseeker's Allowance and Universal Credit (Higher-Level Sanctions) (Amendment) Regulations 2019 (SI 2019/1357) reg.3 (November 27, 2019).

DEFINITIONS

"the Act"—see reg.2.
"claimant"—see WRA 2012 s.40.
"current sanctionable failure"—see reg.100(1A).
"reduction period"—see reg.101(1).
"sanctionable failure"—see reg.100(1).

GENERAL NOTE

2.299   Higher-level sanctions are applicable to failures under s.26 of the WRA 2012. Such failures fall outside the scope of regs 103–105 and no failures under s.27 can come within the present regulation. Note the effect of reg.113 in specifying circumstances in which no reduction is to be applied although there has been a sanctionable failure. There is a distinction between "pre-claim failures", i.e. a failure under s.26(4) (before the relevant claim failing for no good reason to take up an offer of paid work or ceasing paid work or losing pay by reason of misconduct or voluntarily and for no good reason), and other failures.

The form of para.(2), specifying the length of sanctions reduction periods for non-pre-claim failures, was re-cast with effect from July 25, 2016 to spell out more precisely much the same effect as previously. It is unhelpful that the individual entries in the table are not numbered. Boxes have been added by the publishers to aid clarity. The rules for 16 and 17-year-olds are no longer separated out from those for claimants aged at least 18, but now appear in column 3 of the table. None of the rules set out below may take the overall length of a total outstanding reduction period (reduction periods run consecutively) over 1095 days (reg.101(2) and (3)).

The general rule for adults in the first entry in column 2 is that the reduction period is 91 days if there have been no other higher-level UC sanctionable failures (or equivalent new style ESA or JSA failures if the claimant moved to universal credit with some days of an ESA or JSA reduction period outstanding: reg.112 and Sch.11 para.3) within the previous 365 days (counting the day of the current sanctionable failure). Contrary to what was said in the note to reg.113 in the 2013/14 edition of this Volume, it appears that if no reduction of benefit was imposed in relation to a previous sanctionable failure, by reason of reg.113, that failure has not "given rise to" a higher-level sanction so as to count for the purposes of the table. However, if a reduction has been terminated under reg.109, the failure would appear to count because it has given rise to a sanction, even though the period of the reduction has not lasted as long as originally set. It might be argued, for the purposes of the later parts of the table, that the relevant period of reduction was no longer applicable, but the definition of "reduction period" in reg.101(1) is in terms of the initial fixing of the period, with no reference to the effect of reg.109. However, para.(3) secures that pre-claim sanctionable failures (only failures under s.26(4) of the WRA 2012: para.(5)) do not count in this process.

Matters become more complicated when there has been a previous relevant failure within the 365 days. But the amendment with effect from November 27, 2019 has led to a considerable simplification through the removal of the category requiring a reduction period of 1095 days. To start at the end of the table, if the sole or most recent previous sanctionable failure was within the 13 days immediately preceding the date of the current failure, the period of reduction for the current failure is of equal length (either 91 or 182 days) to that for the previous failure. But note that the result of reg.101(2) and (3) is that the new period is to be added on to the end of the previous period, subject to the overall 1095-day limit. If the most recent previous sanctionable failure falls outside that 13-day period but within the 364 days immediately preceding the date of the current failure, the period of reduction for the current failure is 182 days. But note again the effect of reg.101(2) and (3).

The November 2019 amendment is in strict fulfilment of the decision announced by the then Secretary of State, Amber Rudd (written statement to Parliament, HCWS1545, May 9, 2019), set out in the notes to reg.101, to remove three-year sanctions for third or subsequent failures and to reduce the maximum sanction length to six months by the end of the year. However, as explained above and in the notes to reg.101, in universal credit and new style JSA, by contrast with the position for old style JSA (see reg.70(2) of the JSA Regulations 1996), the effect of the rules that reduction periods run consecutively, which has not been amended, is that if there have been multiple sanctionable failures within a year a claimant may have a total outstanding reduction period of up to 1095 days imposed. Thus, the precise terms of the decision have been carried out, but it may be said that the spirit of the reasoning behind it has not been adopted for universal credit and new style JSA.

Regulation 5(3) of the amending regulation made the transitional provision that, where an award of universal credit was subject to a 1095-day reduction under s.26 (or such a reduction was treated as falling under s.26) as at November 27, 2019, that reduction was to be terminated where the award had been reduced for at least 182 days. That appears to apply whether the 182 days expired before, on or after November 27, 2019, provided that the award was subject to the 1095-day reduction on that date. It then appears that, once the 1095-day reduction had been terminated the reduction period "applicable" to the previous sanctionable failure became 182 days, so that the case would fall within the new form of para.(d) of the third part of the table.

There is a similar structure for 16 and 17-year-olds, with only two levels of reduction period, at 14 and 28 days.

For pre-claim sanctionable failures, under para.(4) the number of days between the date of the failure and the date of the relevant claim is deducted from the number of days in the reduction period calculated as under para.(2). That is subject to the further rule that if the sanctionable failure relates to paid work that was due to last only for a limited period, the period down to the date when the work was due to end is substituted for the para.(2) period in the calculation. Presumably that is to give an incentive to people to take such work. See also reg.113(1)(e).

Medium-level sanction

103.—(1) This regulation specifies the reduction period for a sanctionable failure under section 27 of the Act (other sanctions) where it is a failure by the claimant to comply with— 2.300

(a) a work search requirement under section 17(1)(a) (to take all reasonable action to obtain paid work etc.); or

(b) a work availability requirement under section 18(1).

[¹(2) The reduction in the circumstances described in the first column of the following table is the period set out in—

(a) the second column, where the claimant is aged 18 or over on the date of the sanctionable failure;

(b) the third column, where the claimant is aged 16 or 17 on the date of the sanctionable failure.

Circumstances in which reduction period applies	Reduction period where claimant aged 18 or over	Reduction period where claimant aged 16 or 17
Where there has been no previous sanctionable failure by the claimant that falls within paragraph (1)	28 days	7 days

Circumstances in which reduction period applies	Reduction period where claimant aged 18 or over	Reduction period where claimant aged 16 or 17
Where there have been one or more previous sanctionable failures by the claimant that fall within paragraph (1) and the date of the most recent previous sanctionable failure is not within 365 days beginning with the date of the current sanctionable failure	28 days	7 days
Where there have been one or more previous sanctionable failures by the claimant that fall within paragraph (1) and the date of the most recent previous sanctionable failure is within 365 days, but not within 14 days, beginning with the date of the current sanctionable failure and the reduction period applicable to the most recent previous sanctionable failure is—		
(a) 7 days	–	14 days
(b) 14 days	–	14 days
(c) 28 days	91 days	–
(d) 91 days	91 days	–
Where there have been one or more previous sanctionable failures by the claimant that fall within paragraph (1) and the date of the most recent previous sanctionable failure is within 14 days beginning with the date of the current sanctionable failure and the reduction period applicable to the most recent previous sanctionable failure is—		
(a) 7 days	–	7 days
(b) 14 days	–	14 days
(c) 28 days	28 days	–
(d) 91 days	91 days	–.]

AMENDMENT

1. Social Security (Jobseeker's Allowance, Employment and Support Allowance and Universal Credit) (Amendment) Regulations 2016 (SI 2016/678) reg.5(8) (July 25, 2016).

DEFINITIONS

"the Act"—see reg.2.
"claimant"—see WRA 2012 s.40.
"current sanctionable failure"—see reg.100(1A).
"reduction period"—see reg.101(1).
"sanctionable failure"—see reg.100(1).

GENERAL NOTE

This regulation applies to failures for no good reason to comply with two par-   **2.301**
ticular work-related requirements to which the claimant in question is subject: the
requirement under s.17(1)(a) of the WRA 2012 to take all reasonable action to
obtain paid work (but note, not the requirement under s.17(1)(b) to take particular action specified by the Secretary of State, where only some failures to comply
fall under s.26 and the higher-level sanctions regime) and the work availability
requirement in s.18(1). Note that none of the circumstances specified in reg.113
(no reduction to be applied though sanctionable failure) are relevant to medium-
level sanctions under s.27.

The form of para.(2), specifying the length of the sanction reduction period, has
been re-cast with effect from July 25, 2016 to spell out more precisely much the
same effect as previously. It is unhelpful that the individual entries in the table are
not numbered. Boxes have been added by the publishers to aid clarity. The rules
for 16 and 17-year-olds are no longer separated out from those for claimants aged
at least 18, but now appear in column 3 of the table. None of the rules set out
below may take the overall length of a total outstanding reduction period (reduction
periods run consecutively) over 1095 days (reg.101(2) and (3)).

The general rule for adults in the first entry in column 2 is that the reduction
period is 28 days if there have been no other medium-level UC sanctionable failures (or equivalent new style ESA or JSA failures if the claimant moved to universal
credit with some days of an ESA or JSA reduction period outstanding: reg.112 and
Sch.11 para.3) within the previous 365 days (counting the day of the current sanctionable failure). Arguably, the effect of there having been no reduction of benefit
in relation to a previous sanctionable failure, by reason of reg.113, is not quite the
same as under reg.102, because here there is no reference to the previous failure
having "given rise to" a medium-level sanction. If reg.113 applies there is still a
sanctionable failure, although no reduction of benefit is to be applied. However,
for the purposes of the later parts of the table, a reduction period applicable to
the previous sanctionable failure must be identified. If reg.113 has been applied to
that failure there can be no reduction period applicable. Consequently it must be
arguable that for the purposes of the table as a whole previous sanctionable failures
to which reg.113 has been applied do not count. See the notes to reg.102 for the
opposite effect where a reduction period has been terminated under reg.109.

The reduction period under para.(1) as from July 25, 2016 is 28 days if there have
been no other medium-level sanctionable failures (or equivalent new style ESA or
JSA sanctionable failures) at all or only outside the past period of 365 days including
the date of the current sanctionable failure. If the most recent relevant sanctionable
failure was in the past period of 14 days including the date of the current sanctionable failure, the length of the reduction period is equal to that for the most recent
failure. Where the most recent relevant failure was further in the past but still within
the 365 days, the length of the reduction period is 91 days. That is in substance the
same result as under the previous form of reg.20 and reg.101(4).

There is a similar structure for 16 and 17-year-olds, with only two levels of reduction period, at seven and 14 days.

Low-level sanction

104.—(1) This regulation specifies the reduction period for a sanction-   **2.302**
able failure under section 27 of the Act (other sanctions) where—
   (a) the claimant falls within section 21 (claimants subject to work
      preparation requirement) or 22 (claimants subject to all work-related
      requirements) of the Act on the date of that failure; and
   (b) it is a failure to comply with—
      (i) a work-focused interview requirement under section 15(1),
      (ii) a work preparation requirement under section 16(1),

    (iii) a work search requirement under section 17(1)(b) (to take any particular action specified by the Secretary of State to obtain work etc.), or

    (iv) a requirement under section 23(1), (3) or (4) (connected requirements: interviews and verification of compliance).

(2) Where the claimant is aged 18 or over on the date of the sanctionable failure, the reduction period is the total of—

    (a) the number of days beginning with the date of the sanctionable failure and ending with—

       (i) the day before the date on which the claimant meets a compliance condition specified by the Secretary of State,

       (ii) the day before the date on which the claimant falls within section 19 of the Act (claimant subject to no work-related requirements),

      (iii) the day before the date on which the claimant is no longer required to take a particular action specified as a work preparation requirement by the Secretary of State under section 16, or

      (iv) the date on which the award terminates (other than by reason of the claimant ceasing to be, or becoming, a member of a couple),

    whichever is soonest; and

[1(b) in the circumstances described in the first column of the following table, the number of days in the second column.

Circumstances applicable to claimant's case	Number of days
Where there has been no previous sanctionable failure by the claimant that falls within paragraph (1)	7 days
Where there have been one or more previous sanctionable failures by the claimant that fall within paragraph (1) and the date of the most recent previous sanctionable failure is not within 365 days beginning with the date of the current sanctionable failure	7 days
Where there have been one or more previous sanctionable failures by the claimant that fall within paragraph (1) and the date of the most recent previous sanctionable failure is within 365 days, but not within 14 days, beginning with the date of the current sanctionable failure and the reduction period applicable to the most recent previous sanctionable failure is— (a) 7 days (b) 14 days (c) 28 days	 14 days 28 days 28 days
Where there have been one or more previous sanctionable failures by the claimant that fall within paragraph (1) and the date of the most recent previous sanctionable failure is within 14 days beginning with the date of the current sanctionable failure and the reduction period applicable to the most recent previous sanctionable failure is— (a) 7 days (b) 14 days (c) 28 days	 7 days 14 days 28 days]

(3) Where the claimant is aged 16 or 17 years on the date of the sanction-able failure, the reduction period is—

(a) the number of days beginning with the date of the sanctionable failure and ending with—

    (i) the day before the date on which the claimant meets a compliance condition specified by the Secretary of State,

    (ii) the day before the date on which the claimant falls within section 19 of the Act (claimant subject to no work-related requirements),

    (iii) the day before the date on which the claimant is no longer required to take a particular action specified as a work preparation requirement by the Secretary of State under section 16, or

    (iv) date on which the award terminates (other than by reason of the claimant ceasing to be, or becoming, a member of a couple),

whichever is soonest; and

[[1](b) if there was another sanctionable failure of a kind mentioned in paragraph (1) within 365 days, but not within 14 days, beginning with the date of the current sanctionable failure, 7 days.]

AMENDMENT

1. Social Security (Jobseeker's Allowance, Employment and Support Allowance and Universal Credit) (Amendment) Regulations 2016 (SI 2016/678) reg.5(9) (July 25, 2016).

DEFINITIONS

"the Act"—see reg.2.
"claimant"—see WRA 2012 s.40.
"compliance condition"—see WRA 2012 s.27(6).
"current sanctionable failure"—see reg.100(1A).
"reduction period"—see reg.101(1).
"sanctionable failure"—see reg.100(1).

GENERAL NOTE

This regulation applies only to claimants who are subject to all work-related   **2.303** requirements under s.22 of the WRA 2012 or to the work preparation requirement under s.21 at the time of the sanctionable failure. Then a low-level sanction is attracted by a failure for no good reason to comply with a work-focused interview requirement under s.15(1), a work preparation requirement under s.16(1), a work search requirement under s.17(1)(b) to take particular action specified by the Secretary of State (see reg.103—medium-level sanction—for failures to comply with the requirement to take all reasonable action to obtain paid work under s.17(1)(a)) or one of the extensive connected requirements under s.23.

The calculation of the reduction period under para.(2) is more complicated than that for higher and medium-level sanctions. It is made up of a period of flexible length depending on the ongoing circumstances under sub-para.(a) plus a fixed period of days under sub-para.(b) to be added to the sub-para.(a) period. Note that none of the circumstances specified in reg.113 (no reduction to be applied though sanctionable failure) are relevant to low-level sanctions under s.27.

The basic rule in sub-para.(a) is that the period runs until any compliance condition specified by the Secretary of State is met. See the notes to s.27(5) of the WRA 2012 for the authorisation for this provision. A compliance condition is either that the failure to comply ceases to exist (e.g. the claimant attends a work-focused interview) or a condition as to future compliance. The condition must in accordance with s.27(5)(a) and sub-para.(a)(i) be specified by the Secretary of State. Although s.27(7) allows the Secretary of State to notify a claimant of a compliance condition in such manner as he determines, the approach of the Supreme Court in *R (on the application of Reilly and Wilson) v Secretary of State for Work and Pensions* [2013] UKSC 68; [2014] 1 A.C. 453 and of the Court of Appeal in *SSWP v Reilly and Hewstone* and *SSWP v Jeffrey and Bevan* [2016] EWCA Civ 413; [2017] 3 Q.B. 657; [2017] AACR 14 to the "prior information duty" and the requirements of fairness might possibly be relevant to the substance of what must be specified (and see the further discussion in the notes to s.27(5)). The sub-para.(a) period will also end if the claimant becomes subject to no work-related requirements for any reason under s.19 of the WRA 2012, is no longer required to take a specific action as a work preparation requirement or the award of universal credit terminates.

It is understood that during the 2020 coronavirus outbreak any contact by the claimant with the DWP is being treated as meeting a compliance condition.

Under sub-para.(b) the additional number of days is seven if there have been no other low-level sanctionable failures (or equivalent new style ESA or JSA failures if the claimant moved to universal credit with some days of an ESA or JSA reduction period outstanding: reg.112 and Sch.11 para.3) in the previous 365 days (counting the day of the current sanctionable failure). Arguably, the effect of there having been no reduction of benefit in relation to a previous sanctionable failure, by reason of reg.113, is not quite the same as under reg.102, because here there is no reference to the previous failure having "given rise to" a low-level sanction. If reg.113 applies there is still a sanctionable failure, although no reduction of benefit is to be applied. However, for the purposes of the later parts of the table, a reduction period applicable to the previous sanctionable failure must be identified. If reg.113 has been applied to that failure there can be no reduction period applicable. Consequently it must be arguable that for the purposes of the table as a whole previous sanctionable failures to which reg.113 has been applied do not count. See the notes to reg.102 for the opposite effect where a reduction period has been terminated under reg.109.

The second general rule, where there has been at least one previous low-level sanctionable failure in the 365 day period, is that the para.(b) reduction period is 14 days, where the reduction period for the most recent sanctionable failure was seven days and 28 days in all other cases (subject to the possible application of reg.101(3)). The exception to that general rule is where the most recent sanctionable failure occurred within 14 days before the current sanctionable failure, including the day of that failure. In that case, the reduction period is to be of the same length as that applicable to the previous sanctionable failure.

Under para.(3) for claimants aged under 18, the same rules as in para.(2)(a) apply, plus an additional seven days if there has been one or more low-level sanctionable failures in the previous 365 days (excluding the most recent 14 days).

Lowest-level sanction

2.304   **105.**—(1) This regulation specifies the reduction period for a sanctionable failure under section 27 of the Act (other sanctions) where it is a failure by a claimant who falls within section 20 of the Act (claimants subject to work-focused interview requirement only) to comply with a requirement under that section.

(2) The reduction period is the number of days beginning with the date of the sanctionable failure and ending with—

    (a) the day before the date on which the claimant meets a compliance condition specified by the Secretary of State;

    (b) the day before the date on which the claimant falls within section 19 of the Act (claimant subject to no work-related requirements); or

(c) the day on which the award terminates (other than by reason of the claimant ceasing to be, or becoming, a member of a couple),

whichever is soonest.

Definitions

"the Act"—see reg.2.
"claimant"—see WRA 2012 s.40.
"compliance condition"—see WRA 2012 s.27(6).
"reduction period"—see reg.101(1).
"sanctionable failure"—see reg.100(1).

General Note

This regulation applies only to claimants who are subject only to the work-focused interview requirement under s.20 of the WRA 2012. The reduction period for a sanctionable failure to comply with that requirement runs until the claimant meets a compliance condition specified by the Secretary of State (see notes to reg.104), becomes subject to no work-related requirements for any reason under s.19 or the award of universal credit terminates.

2.305

When reduction to have effect

Start of the reduction

106. A reduction period determined in relation to a sanctionable failure takes effect from—

2.306

(a) the first day of the assessment period in which the Secretary of State determines that the amount of the award is to be reduced under section 26 or 27 of the Act (but see also regulation 107(2));

(b) if the amount of the award of universal credit for the assessment period referred to in paragraph (a) is not reduced in that period, the first day of the next assessment period; or

(c) if the amount of the award for the assessment period referred to in paragraph (a) or (b) is already subject to a reduction because of a previous sanctionable failure, the first day in respect of which the amount of the award is no longer subject to that reduction.

Definitions

"the Act"—see reg.2.
"assessment period"—see WRA 2012 ss.40 and 7(2) and reg.21.
"claimant"—see WRA 2012 s.40.
"reduction period"—see reg.101(1).
"sanctionable failure"—see reg.100(1).

General Note

These rules for the start of the reduction period follow fairly logically from the structure of the sanctions regime. Where no other reduction period is running the reduction period starts either in the assessment period (month) in which the decision to make the reduction is made or in the following assessment period (paras. (a) and (b)). If there is already a reduction applied in that assessment period, then,

2.307

unless affected by the overall limit in reg.101(3) and (5), the new period starts on the expiry of the existing one.

Reduction period to continue where award terminates

2.308
107.—(1) If an award of universal credit terminates while there is an outstanding reduction period, the period continues to run as if a daily reduction were being applied and if the claimant becomes entitled to a new award (whether as single or joint claimant) before that period expires, that award is subject to a reduction for the remainder of the total outstanding reduction period.

(2) If an award of universal credit terminates before the Secretary of State determines that the amount of the award is to be reduced under section 26 or 27 of the Act in relation to a sanctionable failure and that determination is made after the claimant becomes entitled to a new award the reduction period in relation to that failure is to have effect for the purposes of paragraph (1) as if that determination had been made on the day before the previous award terminated.

DEFINITIONS

"the Act"—see reg.2.
"claimant"—see WRA 2012 s.40.
"joint claimants"—*ibid.*
"reduction period"—see reg.101(1).
"sanctionable failure"—see reg.100(1).
"single claimant"—see WRA 2012 s.40.

GENERAL NOTE

2.309
If an award of universal credit terminates while there is an outstanding reduction period, subsequent days count as if an actual reduction of benefit were being applied, so that on any further claim for universal credit the claimant is subject to the reduction only for the remainder of the period (para.(1)). If an award of universal credit terminates before the Secretary of State has made a decision about a reduction for a sanctionable failure, but a new award is in place by the time the decision is made (so that under reg.106 the reduction period would otherwise take effect in the current assessment period), the reduction period starts as if the decision had been made on the day before the previous award terminated.

Note that if on or after the termination of entitlement to universal credit the claimant is entitled to new style JSA, the reduction of benefit under the universal credit sanction for its unexpired period transfers to the award of JSA (JSA Regulations 2013 reg.30)

Suspension of a reduction where fraud penalty applies

2.310
108.—(1) A reduction in the amount of an award under section 26 or 27 of the Act is to be suspended for any period during which the provisions of section 6B, 7 or 9 of the Social Security Fraud Act 2001 apply to the award.

(2) The reduction ceases to have effect on the day on which that period begins and begins again on the day after that period ends.

DEFINITION

"the Act"—see reg.2.

When a reduction is to be terminated

109.—(1) A reduction in the amount of an award under section 26 or 27   2.311
of the Act is to be terminated where—
  (a) since the date of the most recent sanctionable failure which gave rise
      to a reduction, the claimant has been in paid work for a period of, or
      for periods amounting in total to, at least [¹six months]; and
  (b) the claimant's [¹monthly] earnings during that period or those
      periods were equal to or exceeded—
        (i) the claimant's individual threshold, [²...]
    [²(ia) where the claimant has no individual threshold, the amount that
           a person would be paid at the hourly rate specified in regulation
           4 or regulation 4A(1)(a) to (c) of the National Minimum Wage
           Regulations for 16 hours per week, converted to a monthly
           amount by multiplying by 52 and dividing by 12, or]
       (ii) if paragraph (4) of regulation 90 applies (threshold for an
            apprentice) the amount applicable under that paragraph.
  (2) The termination of the reduction has effect—
  (a) where the date on which paragraph (1) is satisfied falls within a
      period of entitlement to universal credit, from the beginning of the
      assessment period in which that date falls; or
  (b) where that date falls outside a period of entitlement to universal
      credit, from the beginning of the first assessment period in relation
      to any subsequent award.
  (3) A claimant who is treated as having earned income in accordance
with regulation 62 (minimum income floor) in respect of an assessment
period is to be taken to have [¹ monthly] earnings equal to their individual
threshold in respect of [¹ . . .] that assessment period.

AMENDMENTS

  1. Universal Credit and Miscellaneous Amendments Regulations 2015 (SI
2015/1754) reg.2(8) (November 4, 2015).
  2. Social Security (Jobseeker's Allowance, Employment and Support Allowance
and Universal Credit) (Amendment) Regulations 2016 (SI 2016/678) reg.5(10)
(July 25, 2016).

DEFINITIONS

  "the Act"—see reg.2.
  "assessment period"—see WRA 2012, ss.40 and 7(2) and reg.21.
  "claimant"—see WRA 2012, s.40.
  "individual threshold"—see regs 2 and 90(2).
  "sanctionable failure"—see reg.100(1).
  "National Minimum Wage Regulations"—see reg.2.

GENERAL NOTE

  Any reduction for any level of sanction or sanctions terminates where since the   2.312
date of the most recent sanctionable failure the claimant has been in paid work with
earnings at least equal to the appropriate individual threshold for at least six months,
not necessarily consecutive. It does not matter what the total outstanding reduction
period is. The claimant could have had a reduction period of 1095 days imposed, yet
after six months' work at minimum wage level (which will have reduced the outstanding period accordingly) the basis for the entire reduction disappears, just as much as
if the outstanding period was much shorter. Paragraph (2) confirms that the termina-

tion takes effect immediately if the condition in para.(1) is met while the claimant is entitled to universal credit. If the claimant is not then entitled to universal credit the termination takes effect from the beginning of the first assessment period under any new award. Note that this regulation does not take away the status of any sanctionable failure(s) on which the terminated reduction period was based. Thus for the purpose of asking in the future whether there have been other sanctionable failures within 364 days of a new sanctionable failure all such sanctionable failures must be counted.

See also reg.119(3) below, under which any hardship payments made under the conditions in reg.116 cease to be recoverable where the claimant has had earnings of the same level as specified in reg.109 for six months after the last day on which a reduction was applied.

There was a technical difficulty in the operation of reg.109(1)(b) in that under the definition of "individual threshold" in reg.90(2) only claimants who would otherwise (if it were not for the effect of reg.90(1) and s.19 of the WRA 2012) be subject to some work-related requirement could have an individual threshold and so take advantage of the provision in para.(1). That gap has been filled by the new para.(1)(b)(ia), specifying an amount of earnings in terms of the national minimum wage hourly rate and 16 hours per week for claimants without an individual threshold as such.

Amount of reduction

Amount of reduction for each assessment period

2.313
110. Where it has been determined that an award of universal credit is to be reduced under section 26 or 27 of the Act, the amount of the reduction for each assessment period in respect of which a reduction has effect is to be calculated as follows.

Step 1

Take the number of days—
  (a) in the assessment period; or
  (b) if lower, the total outstanding reduction period,
and deduct any days in that assessment period for which the reduction is suspended in accordance with regulation 108.

Step 2

Multiply the number of days produced by step 1 by the daily reduction rate (see regulation 111).

Step 3

If necessary, adjust the amount produced by step 2 so that it does not exceed—
  (a) the amount of the standard allowance applicable to the award; or
  (b) in the case of a joint claim where a determination under section 26 or 27 of the Act applies only in relation to one claimant, half the amount of that standard allowance.

Step 4

Deduct the amount produced by steps 2 and 3 from the amount of the award for the assessment period after any deduction has been made in accordance with Part 7 (the benefit cap).

DEFINITIONS

"the Act"—see reg.2.
"assessment period"—see WRA 2012 ss.40 and 7(2) and reg.21.
"claimant"—see WRA 2012, s.40.
"standard allowance"—see WRA 2012, s.9.

GENERAL NOTE

This apparently complex calculation will work out easily enough in practice. Its   2.314
main point is to translate the daily rate of reduction under reg.111 into the appropriate amount for an assessment period, depending on the number of days in the
period affected by a reduction. There is a rule of substance concealed in step 3, in
that the reduction can never exceed the amount of the claimant's standard allowance, or half of a couple's standard allowance.

However, see the notes to reg.111 below for discussion of the capricious results
that can follow from the way in which the daily reduction rate is calculated under
reg.111 and from the principle that in accordance with ss.26 and 27 of the WRA
2012 the reduction is to be applied to the overall award of universal credit, however
that is made up.

See those notes and the notes to reg.5 of the JSA Regulations 2013 in Vol.II of
this series and to paras 1 and 2 of Sch.11 to the present Regulations for further
discussion of the anomalous results where a universal credit recipient is also entitled another social security benefit (in particular new style ESA or JSA) and for the
non-use of regulation-making powers that could have avoided them.

Daily reduction rate

111.—(1) The daily reduction rate for the purposes of regulation 110 is,   2.315
unless paragraph (2), or (3) applies, an amount equal to the amount of the
standard allowance that is applicable to the award multiplied by 12 and
divided by 365.

(2) The daily reduction rate is 40 per cent of the rate set out in paragraph
(1) if, at the end of the assessment period—

(a) the claimant is aged 16 or 17;

(b) the claimant falls within section 19 of the Act (claimant subject to no
work-related requirements) by virtue of—

　(i) subsection (2)(c) of that section (responsible carer for a child
under the age of 1), or

　(ii) regulation 89(1)(c),(d) or (f) (adopter, claimant within 11
weeks before or 15 weeks after confinement or responsible
foster parent of a child under the age of 1); or

(c) the claimant falls within section 20 (claimant subject to work-
focused interview only).

(3) The daily reduction rate is nil if, at the end of the assessment period,
the claimant falls within section 19 of the Act by virtue of having limited
capability for work and work-related activity.

(4) The amount of the rate in [¹paragraphs (1) and (2)] is to be rounded
down to the nearest 10 pence.

(5) In the case of joint claimants—

(a) each joint claimant is considered individually for the purpose of
determining the rate applicable under paragraphs (1) to (3); and

(b) half of any applicable rate is applied to each joint claimant accordingly.

AMENDMENT

1. Universal Credit (Consequential, Supplementary, Incidental and Miscellaneous Provisions) Regulations 2013 (SI 2013/630) reg.38(7) (April 29, 2013).

DEFINITIONS

    "the Act"—see reg.2.
    "assessment period"—see WRA 2012 ss.40 and 7(2) and reg.21.
    "claimant"—see WRA 2012, s.40.
    "joint claimants"—*ibid.*
    "limited capability for work and work-related activity"—see WRA 2012, ss.40 and 37(1) and (2).
    "single claimant"—see WRA 2012, s.40.
    "standard allowance"—see WRA 2012, s.9.

GENERAL NOTE

2.316   The basic rule under para.(1) is that the reduction for the purposes of the calculation in reg.110 is by the whole amount equal to that of the claimant's standard allowance under s.9 of the WRA 2012. There is on the face of it no reduction to the elements that can make up the maximum amount of universal credit for responsibility for children and young persons (s.10), housing costs (s.11) or particular needs and circumstances (s.12). In the case of joint claimants, under para.(5) each claimant is considered separately for the purposes of calculating the reduction and treated as having half of the standard allowance applicable to them as joint claimants.

    Under para.(2) the reduction is by 40 per cent of the standard allowance, rather than 100 per cent, for claimants under 18, claimants subject to no work-related requirements under s.19 of the WRA 2012 by virtue of s.19(2)(c) (responsible carer of a child under one) or reg.89(1)(c), (d) or (f) and claimants subject to the work-focused interview requirement only under s.20.

    Despite the apparent simplicity of these rules, there are a number of complicating elements that create a degree of uncertainty. First, the effect of the rounding down under para.(4) to the nearest 10p in producing the daily rate of reduction from the amount of the standard allowance, which is expressed in reg.36 as a monthly amount, i.e. for each assessment period, is fairly clear. When the daily rate is multiplied by the number of days affected by the sanction in each assessment period in step 2 of reg.110 the result will often be less than the exactly proportionate share of the actual standard allowance. If a claimant's universal credit award was made up only of the standard allowance, then even a 100% reduction could leave some small amount still payable.

    Second, the specification of the reduction rate in terms of the amount of the standard allowance, rather than the amount of the claimant's award of universal credit, creates problems in certain circumstances. In particular, this is so where the claimant has income to be deducted from the "maximum amount" (the appropriate standard allowance plus any additional elements for children, childcare costs, housing costs etc). Take a simple example of a single universal credit claimant of 25 doing no work who is also entitled to new style JSA of £74.35 per week through satisfaction of the contribution-based conditions. The standard allowance as specially and temporarily increased from April 2020 is £409.89 per month, which is also the maximum amount. That would appear to produce a universal credit award of £87.71 per month. If the claimant were then made subject to a 100% sanction for a 30-day assessment period, multiplying the daily reduction rate of £13.40 by 30 would produce a figure of £402. But the concept of a reduction cannot allow the amount of universal credit otherwise payable to go below zero, so that the reduction could be by no more than £87.71 per month. It must not then be forgotten that reg.5 of the JSA Regulations 2013 prevents any reduction being applied to the claimant's new style JSA entitlement when there is also entitlement to universal credit, even though there may have been a sanctionable failure under the new style JSA legislation. Regulation 42 of the ESA Regulations 2013 does the same in relation to new style ESA.

However, things would become much more complicated if the claimant had a housing costs and/or a children element included in the universal credit maximum amount, so that the amount payable was higher. The basic calculation of the amount of the reduction under reg.110 by reference to the standard allowance would stay the same. But, since ss.26 and 27 of the WRA 2012 and reg.110 provide simply for the reduction of the amount of an award of universal credit by the amount calculated under reg.110, there appears to be nothing to prevent the reduction in this second case biting into potentially the whole of universal credit award, subject only to the limit under step 3 of reg.110 of the amount of the standard allowance. These results appear arbitrary and unrelated to the merits of cases, but equally appear to follow inexorably from the structure of the universal credit legislation. In the example used, the claimant will still have the £74.35 per week of new style JSA intact (or some other source of income in other cases), which can be used to meet essential expenses.

Those simple examples do no more than scratch the surface of other complexities that may arise. They make the existence of the provision for hardship payments, now restricted to 100% reduction cases, in regs 115–119 even more important, although the conditions for payment are extremely restrictive.

Under para.(3) a nil reduction is to be applied, apparently for a whole assessment period, if at the end of that period the claimant is subject to no work-related requirements under s.19 by virtue of having limited capability for work and work-related activity (see s.19(2)(a)). The effect of applying a daily reduction, but making the rate nil, appears to be that any assessment periods falling within para.(3) count as part of the period of reduction under the sanction in question.

See reg.113 for circumstances in which no reduction is to be applied despite the existence of a sanctionable failure that would otherwise trigger a reduction and reg.109 for the termination of all outstanding reductions if a claimant has earnings equal to the individual threshold (see reg.90(2)) for 26 weeks.

Miscellaneous

Application of ESA or JSA sanctions to universal credit

112. Schedule 11 has effect in relation to persons who are, or have been, entitled to an employment and support allowance or a jobseeker's allowance and who are, or become, entitled to universal credit.   2.317

DEFINITIONS

"employment and support allowance"—see reg.2.
"jobseeker's allowance"—*ibid.*

GENERAL NOTE

The general effect of Sch.11 is that if a claimant moves from new style ESA or JSA   2.318
to universal credit with some days of an ESA or JSA reduction period outstanding, the reduction for those days translates to the universal credit awards. The failures giving rise to those reductions count as previous sanctionable failures at the equivalent level for the purpose of calculating the length of the reduction period for higher, medium and low-level sanctions under regs 102–104.

Failures for which no reduction is applied

2.319   **113.**—(1) No reduction is to be made under section 26 or 27 of the Act for a sanctionable failure where—

(a) the sanctionable failure is listed in section 26(2)(b) or (c) (failure to apply for a particular vacancy for paid work, or failure to take up an offer of paid work) and the vacancy is because of a strike arising from a trade dispute;

(b) the sanctionable failure is listed in section 26(2)(d) (claimant ceases paid work or loses pay), and the following circumstances apply—

   (i) the claimant's work search and work availability requirements are subject to limitations imposed under section 17(4) and 18(3) in respect of work available for a certain number of hours,

  (ii) the claimant takes up paid work, or is in paid work and takes up more paid work that is for a greater number of hours, and

 (iii) the claimant voluntarily ceases that paid work, or more paid work, or loses pay,

within a trial period;

(c) the sanctionable failure is that the claimant voluntarily ceases paid work, or loses pay, because of a strike arising from a trade dispute;

(d) the sanctionable failure is that the claimant voluntarily ceases paid work as a member of the regular or reserve forces, or loses pay in that capacity;

(e) the sanctionable failure is listed in section 26(4) (failure to take up an offer of paid work, or to cease paid work or lose pay before making a claim), and the period of the reduction that would otherwise apply under regulation 102(4) is the same as, or shorter than, the number of days beginning with the day after the date of the sanctionable failure and ending with the date of claim;

(f) the sanctionable failure is that the claimant voluntarily ceases paid work in one of the following circumstances—

   (i) the claimant has been dismissed because of redundancy after volunteering or agreeing to be dismissed,

  (ii) the claimant has ceased work on an agreed date without being dismissed in pursuance of an agreement relating to voluntary redundancy, or

 (iii) the claimant has been laid-off or kept on short-time to the extent specified in section 148 of the Employment Rights Act 1996, and has complied with the requirements of that section; or

(g) the sanctionable failure is that the claimant by reason of misconduct, or voluntarily and for no good reason, ceases paid work or loses pay, but the claimant's [¹ monthly] earnings (or, if the claimant is a member of a couple, their joint [¹ monthly] earnings) have not fallen below [¹the amount specified in] regulation 99(6) (circumstances in which requirements must not be imposed).

(2) In this regulation "regular or reserve forces" has the same meaning as in section 374 of the Armed Forces Act 2006.

AMENDMENT

1. Universal Credit and Miscellaneous Amendments Regulations 2015 (SI 2015/1754) reg.2(9) (November 4, 2015).

DEFINITIONS

"the Act"—see reg.2.
"claimant"—see WRA 2012 s.40.
"couple"—see WRA 2012 ss.40 and 39.
"paid work"—see reg.2.
"redundancy"—*ibid.*
"sanctionable failure"—see reg.100(1).
"trade dispute"—see reg.2.
"work availability requirement"—see WRA 2012 ss.40 and 18(1).
"work search requirement"—see WRA 2012 ss.40 and 17(1).

GENERAL NOTE

This is an important provision in prescribing, under ss.26(8)(a) and 27(9)(a) of   **2.320**
the WRA 2012, cases of sanctionable failure for which no reduction of benefit can
be imposed. However, none of the circumstances specified are relevant to medium,
low or lowest-level sanctions arising under s.27. Note that if a case comes within this
regulation that does not affect the status of the sanctionable failure in question. It
can still count if in relation to a future sanctionable failure it has to be asked whether
there have been any sanctionable failures at the equivalent level in the previous 365
days. See the notes to regs 103 and 104 for further discussion. It will be different if, as
under reg.102, the question to be asked is whether there has been a previous sanctionable failure giving rise to a sanction. If reg.113 has applied, the failure would appear
not have given rise to a sanction. There remains scope for argument that in some of
the circumstances listed there is a good reason for the particular claimant's failure to
comply with the requirement in question, so that there is not in fact a sanctionable
failure.

The cases are as follows:

(a) Where the sanctionable failure is failing for no good reason to apply for a particular vacancy for paid work or to take up an offer of paid work (WRA 2012,
s.26(2)(b) or (c)), no reduction is to be imposed if the vacancy arose because
of a strike arising from a trade dispute. "Trade dispute" is defined in reg.2 by
adopting the rather long definition in s.244 of the Trade Union and Labour
Relations (Consolidation) Act 1992:

"(1) In this Part a "trade dispute" means a dispute between workers and
their employer which relates wholly or mainly to one or more of the following—

(a) terms and conditions of employment, or the physical conditions in
which any workers are required to work;

(b) engagement or non-engagement, or termination or suspension of
employment or the duties of employment, of one or more workers;

(c) allocation of work or the duties of employment between workers or
groups of workers;

(d) matters of discipline;

(e) a worker's membership or non-membership of a trade union;

(f) facilities for officials of trade unions; and

(g) machinery for negotiation or consultation, and other procedures,
relating to any of the above matters, including the recognition by
employers or employers' associations of the right of a trade union to
represent workers in such negotiation or consultation or in the carrying out of such procedures.

(2) A dispute between a Minister of the Crown and any workers shall, notwithstanding that he is not the employer of those workers, be treated as a
dispute between those workers and their employer if the dispute relates to
matters which—

(a) have been referred for consideration by a joint body on which, by virtue
of provision made by or under any enactment, he is represented, or

397

(b) cannot be settled without him exercising a power conferred on him by or under an enactment.

(3) There is a trade dispute even though it relates to matters occurring outside the United Kingdom, so long as the person or persons whose actions in the United Kingdom are said to be in contemplation or further-ance of a trade dispute relating to matters occurring outside the United Kingdom are likely to be affected in respect of one or more of the matters specified in subsection (1) by the outcome of the dispute.

(4) An act, threat or demand done or made by one person or organisation against another which, if resisted, would have led to a trade dispute with that other, shall be treated as being done or made in contemplation of a trade dispute with that other, notwithstanding that because that other submits to the act or threat or accedes to the demand no dispute arises.

(5) In this section—

"employment" includes any relationship whereby one person personally does work or performs services for another; and

"worker", in relation to a dispute with an employer, means—

(a) a worker employed by that employer; or

(b) a person who has ceased to be so employed if his employment was terminated in connection with the dispute or if the termination of his employment was one of the circumstances giving rise to the dispute."

That is a fairly comprehensive definition, although as compared with s.35(1) of the Jobseekers Act 1995 it does not cover disputes between employees and employees. "Strike" is not defined. It is possible that vacancies could arise because of industrial action short of a strike. There seems no good reason why claimants who on principle are not prepared to apply for such vacancies or accept offers should not also be protected. Perhaps it is arguable that in any event they have a good reason for failing to comply with the requirement in question, so that there is no sanctionable failure.

(b) This provision protects claimants who take up work for a trial period, but only current universal credit claimants who are required only to search for and be available for work subject to limitations as to hours of work under reg.97, made under ss.17(4) and 18(3) of the WRA 2012. Then if such a claimant takes up work, or more work, for more than the hours of limitation for a trial period, but then voluntarily gives up that work or extra work or loses pay within the trial period, there is to be no reduction. As above, it would be arguable there was good reason for such action, so no sanctionable failure.

(c) This provision provides the same protection as under sub-para.(a) for volun-tarily ceasing paid work or losing pay because of a strike arising from a trade dispute.

(d) Members of the armed forces, both regular and reserve forces, who voluntarily cease paid work as such or lose pay, cannot suffer a reduction on that ground, whatever the circumstances.

(e) Where there is a pre-claim sanctionable failure and the reduction period nor-mally applicable would expire on or before the date of the relevant universal credit claim, there is to be no reduction. It may be that the same result is achieved by reg.102(4).

(f) This provides protection in the same circumstances as prescribed in reg.71 of the JSA Regulations 1996 for old style JSA purposes (see the notes to reg.71 in Vol II), except that there the claimant is deemed not to have left employment voluntarily and so not subject to any sanction. Here the claimant is merely protected from having a reduction of benefit imposed, subject to any argument that there was a good reason under general principles for voluntarily ceasing work, so no sanctionable failure.

(g) Under reg.99(6) it may be determined that a claimant's or joint claimants' earnings are at a level where a work search or work availability requirement is not to be imposed, although the earnings are below the individual threshold or combined individual thresholds that has to be reached to make the claimant(s) subject to no work-related requirements under s.19 of the WRA 2012 and reg.90. If that decision is made after a claimant by reason of misconduct or voluntarily and for no good reasons ceases paid work or loses pay, no reduction of benefit is to be imposed.

Sanctionable failures under section 26—work placements

[¹**114.**—(1) A placement on the Mandatory Work Activity Scheme is a prescribed placement for the purpose of section 26(2)(a) of the Act (sanctionable failure not to comply with a work placement).

2.321

(2) In paragraph (1) "the Mandatory Work Activity Scheme" means a scheme provided pursuant to arrangements made by the Secretary of State and known by that name that is designed to provide work or work-related activity for up to 30 hours per week over a period of 4 consecutive weeks with a view to assisting claimants to improve their prospects of obtaining employment.]

AMENDMENT

1. Universal Credit (Consequential, Supplementary, Incidental and Miscellaneous Provisions) Regulations 2013 (SI 2013/630) reg.38(8) (April 29, 2013).

DEFINITIONS

"the Act"—see reg.2.
"claimant"—see WRA 2012 s.40.
"paid work"—see reg.2.
"work-related activity"—see WRA 2012 s.40.

GENERAL NOTE

See the notes to s.26(2)(a) of the WRA 2012 for the validity of this provision in giving sufficient detail of the nature of the Mandatory Work Activity Scheme to constitute a description of the scheme, as required by s.26(2)(a), not just a label, and for the circumstances in which failure to comply with a requirement to undertake a placement could give rise to a sanction. Note that the scheme need not be designed to provide work that is paid and that prospects of employment (not further defined) can in their ordinary meaning include prospects of self-employment. The scheme has ceased to operate after April 2016.

2.322

Chapter 3

HARDSHIP

Introduction

115. This Chapter contains provisions under section 28 of the Act for the making of hardship payments where the amount of an award is reduced under section 26 or 27 of the Act.

2.323

DEFINITION

"the Act"—see reg.2.

Conditions for hardship payments

2.324

116.—(1) The Secretary of State must make a hardship payment to a single claimant or to joint claimants only where—

(a) the claimant in respect of whose sanctionable failure the award has been reduced under section 26 or 27 of the Act is aged 18 or over;

(b) the single claimant or each joint claimant has met any compliance condition specified by the Secretary of State under regulation 104(2) (a)(i);

(c) the single claimant or either joint claimant completes and submits an application—

(i) approved for the purpose by the Secretary of State, or in such other form as the Secretary of State accepts as sufficient, and

(ii) in such manner as the Secretary of State determines;

(d) the single claimant or either joint claimant furnishes such information or evidence as the Secretary of State may require, in such manner as the Secretary of State determines:

(e) the single claimant or each joint claimant accepts that any hardship payments that are paid are recoverable;

(f) the Secretary of State is satisfied that the single claimant or each joint claimant has complied with all the work-related requirements that they were required to comply with in the 7 days proceeding the day on which the claimant or joint claimants submitted an application in accordance with sub-paragraph (c); [¹ . . .]

(g) the Secretary of State is satisfied that the single claimant or each joint claimant is in hardship; [¹and

(h) the daily reduction rate in regulation 111(1) applies for the purposes of the reduction in respect of the claimant under section 26 or 27 of the Act.]

(2) For the purposes of paragraph (1)(g) a single claimant or joint claimants must be considered as being in hardship only where—

(a) they cannot meet their immediate and most basic and essential needs, specified in paragraph (3), or the immediate and most basic and essential needs of a child or qualifying young person for whom the single claimant or either of joint claimants is responsible, only because the amount of their award has been reduced—

(i) under section 26 or 27 of the Act, by the daily reduction rate set out in [¹regulation 111(1)], or

(ii) by the daily reduction rate prescribed in regulations made under section 6B(5A), 7(2A) or 9(2A) of the Social Security Fraud Act 2001 which is equivalent to the rate referred to in paragraph (i);

(b) they have made every effort to access alternative sources of support to meet, or partially meet, such needs; and

(c) they have made every effort to cease to incur any expenditure which does not relate to such needs.

(3) The needs referred to in paragraph (2) are—

(a) accommodation;

(b) heating;

(c) food;

(d) hygiene.

AMENDMENT

1. Universal Credit and Miscellaneous Amendments Regulations 2014 (SI 2014/597) reg.2(12) (April 28, 2014).

DEFINITIONS

"the Act"—see reg.2.
"claimant"—see WRA 2012 s.40.
"joint claimants"—*ibid.*
"sanctionable failure"—see reg.100(1).
"single claimant"—see WRA 2012 s.40.
"work-related requirement"—see WRA 2012 ss.40 and 13(2).

GENERAL NOTE

This regulation is made under s.28 of the WRA 2012 and sets out the very strin-   **2.325**
gent conditions for the making of hardship payments to claimants to whom a sanction has been applied under s.26 or 27, that limitation being imposed by reg.115
and s.28(1)(a). The amount and period of any payment is dealt with in regs 117
and 118. Paragraph (1) of reg.116 lays down seven conditions, all of which must
be satisfied. Paragraphs (2) and (3) provide a further exhaustive definition of when
claimants can be considered to be in hardship for the purpose of condition (g) in
para.(1). No payment can be made under reg.117 for any period prior to the date
on which all the conditions in para.(1) are met.

The opening words of para.(1), by providing that the Secretary of State *must*
make a hardship payment only where all its conditions are met, appear to open the
door to the Secretary of State making payments on a discretionary basis where the
conditions are not met. However, that is not the case, because s.28 only allows additional payments of universal credit to be made in hardship cases when regulations
so provide. It must remain open to the Secretary of State to make payments, not of
universal credit, on an extra-statutory basis, but no doubt the circumstances would
have to be truly exceptional to persuade them to do so.

Paragraph (1)
The seven conditions are as follows: **2.326**
(a) The claimant to whom the sanction has been applied must be aged at least 18.
     Under-18s can be sanctioned, but will not have the amount of benefit reduced
     to nil, as for most over-18s (see reg.111(1) and (2)).
(b) Under reg.104(2)(a) reduction periods for low-level sanctions last unless and
     until the claimant satisfies a compliance condition specified by the Secretary
     of State, i.e. the failure to comply with the work-related requirement in ques-
     tion has come to an end or a condition about future compliance is met (WRA
     2012, s.27(6)), plus a fixed period on top. If such a compliance condition has
     been specified, a hardship payment can only be made after it has been met. The
     result is that in these cases a hardship payment can only be made during the
     final fixed period.
(c) The claimant or one of joint claimants must make an application for a hardship
     payment. The Secretary of State may accept an application in any sufficient
     form, but it is not clear what could also be required by the additional condition
     of the submission of the application being in such manner as determined by the
     Secretary of State. Condition (f) below can make the timing of an application
     important, but there seems nothing to stop multiple applications being made
     day by day.
(d) The claimant must have supplied any information or evidence required by the
     Secretary of State.
(e) The claimant or both joint claimants must accept that any hardship payments
     are recoverable. Since the recoverability is imposed by reg.119 and s.71ZH

401

of the Administration Act, independent of any advance agreement by the claimant, it is not clear quite what level or manner of acceptance will satisfy this condition. The claimant in a sense has no option but to submit to what the law requires, no matter how vehemently dislike of the result is expressed.

(f)   The claimant or both joint claimants must have complied with all work-related requirements imposed in the seven days preceding, presumably immediately preceding, the day of submission of the application under condition (c).

(g)   The most fundamental condition is that the claimant or both joint claimants are in hardship, presumably as at the date of making the payment or possibly as at the date of the application in question. Because of the use of the present tense, it is arguable that it is not a necessary condition that the claimant or claimants are expected to be in hardship for the duration of the period covered by the payment. Paragraphs (2) and (3) define when a claimant can be accepted as in hardship.

(h)   The effect of this provision, operative from April 2014, is to prevent any entitlement to a hardship payment arising for a claimant whose reduction in benefit under the sanction is only by 40% under reg.111(2), rather than by 100% under reg.111(1).

Paragraphs (2) and (3)

2.327   The use of the word "only" means that claimants can only be accepted as in hardship if they meet all three of the following conditions:

(a)   The claimant or both joint claimants must be unable to meet their most immediate and basic and essential needs, or those of children or young person for whom they are responsible, only by reason of the reduction in benefit due to a sanction or of a reduction for a benefit offence under the Social Security Fraud Act 2001. The only needs to be considered are accommodation, heating, food and hygiene (para.(3)) and then this condition limits consideration to immediate, basic and essential needs of those kinds. That plainly involves a large element of judgment, but the highly restrictive intention is made clear. There is no specific category of need relating to children no matter how young, e.g. for bedding, clothing or education.

(b)   The claimant or both joint claimants must have made every effort to access alternative sources of support to at least go towards meeting needs within condition (a). Some limitations must necessarily be implied either in terms of what efforts can be required or in terms of what alternative sources of support can be considered. The alternative source must at least be lawful. But presumably claimants are not to be required to beg on the streets. Are they to be required to go to back street or payday lenders? How far are they required to explore sources from which there is no practical possibility of support?

(c)   The claimant or both joint claimants must have made every effort to cease to incur expenditure not related to condition (a) needs. Given the restrictive scope of those needs, the range of expenditure to be considered is wide. But again some notions of reasonableness and practicability must necessarily be implied, especially if avoiding immediate expenditure in the short term might lead to disproportionate financial penalties or burdens in the longer term.

The period of hardship payments

2.328   [¹117.—(1) A hardship payment is to be made in respect of a period which—

(a)   begins with the date on which all the conditions in regulation 116(1) are met; and

(b)   unless paragraph (2) applies, ends with the day before the normal payment date for the assessment period in which those conditions are met.

(2) If the period calculated in accordance with paragraph (1) would be 7 days or less, it does not end on the date referred to in paragraph (1)(b) but instead ends on the normal payment date for the following assessment period or, if earlier, the last day on which the award is to be reduced under section 26 or 27 of the Act or under section 6B(5A), 7(2A) or 9(3A) of the Social Security Fraud Act 2001.

(3) In this regulation "the normal payment date" for an assessment period is the date on which the Secretary of State would normally expect to make a regular payment of universal credit in respect of an assessment period in a case where payments of universal credit are made monthly in arrears.]

AMENDMENT

1. Universal Credit (Consequential, Supplementary, Incidental and Miscellaneous Provisions) Regulations 2013 (SI 2013/630) reg.38(9) (April 29, 2013).

DEFINITIONS

"assessment period"—see WRA 2012 ss.40 and 7(2) and reg.21.
"joint claimants"—see WRA 2012 s.40.
"single claimant"—*ibid.*

GENERAL NOTE

The substituted form of reg.117 (in operation from the outset of the universal credit scheme) represents a simplification and clarification of the original form. Each hardship payment is made for a limited period. Once each period expires a new application must be made. Under para.(1)(a) the period of a payment starts when all the conditions in reg.116(1) are met. For that to be so the claimant must, amongst other things, have completed and submitted an application either on the approved form or in some other manner accepted by the Secretary of State (reg.116(1)(c)). The period ends under the general rule in para.(1)(b) on the day before the normal payment day for the assessment period in which the application was made, following which a new application has to be made for the next period. Under para.(2), if the application of para.(1)(b) would result in a period of hardship payment of less than eight days the period extends to the day before the normal payment day for the next assessment period.

The amount of hardship payments

118. The amount of a hardship payment for each day in respect of which such a payment is to be made is to be determined in accordance with the formula—

$$60\% \text{ of} \left(\frac{(A \times 12)}{365} \right)$$

where A is equal to the amount of the reduction in the single claimant's or joint claimants' award calculated under regulation 110 for the assessment period preceding the assessment period in which an application is submitted under regulation 116(1)(c).

DEFINITIONS

"assessment period"—see WRA 2012, ss.40 and 7(2), and reg.21.
"joint claimants"—see WRA 2012, s.40.
"single claimant"—*ibid.*

2.329

2.330

2.331   The amount of any hardship payment payable per day is effectively 60 per cent of the reduction in the amount of benefit in the assessment period before that in which the application is made. See reg.111 for the daily reduction rate for different categories of claimant.

Recoverability of hardship payments

2.332   **119.**—(1) Subject to paragraphs (2) and (3), hardship payments are recoverable in accordance with section 71ZH of the Social Security Administration Act 1992.

[¹(2) Paragraph (1) does not apply in relation to any assessment period in which—

(a) the single claimant, or each joint claimant, falls within section 19 of the Act by virtue of regulation 90 (claimants subject to no work-related requirements – the earnings threshold);

(b) where regulation 90 applies to one of the joint claimants only, the joint claimants' combined monthly earnings are equal to or exceed the amount of the individual threshold; or

(c) where regulation 90 does not apply to the single claimant or to either of the joint claimants, that claimant or the joint claimants' combined monthly earnings are equal to or exceed the amount that a person of the same age as the claimant, or the youngest of the joint claimants, would be paid at the hourly rate specified in regulation 4 or regulation 4A(1)(a) to (c) of the National Minimum Wage Regulations for 16 hours per week, converted to a monthly amount by multiplying by 52 and dividing by 12,

(3) Paragraph (1) ceases to apply where, since the last day on which the claimant's or the joint claimants' award was subject to a reduction under section 26 or 27 of the Act—

(a) the single claimant, or each joint claimant, has fallen within section 19 of the Act by virtue of regulation 90 (claimants subject to no work-related requirements – the earnings threshold);

(b) where regulation 90 applied to one of the joint claimants only, the joint claimants' have had combined monthly earnings that are equal to or exceed the amount of the individual threshold; or

(c) where regulation 90 did not apply to the single claimant or to either of the joint claimants, that claimant or the joint claimants' have had combined monthly earnings that are equal to or exceed the amount that a person of the same age as the claimant, or the youngest of the joint claimants, would be paid at the hourly rate specified in regulation 4 or regulation 4A(1)(a) to (c) of the National Minimum Wage Regulations for 16 hours per week, converted to a monthly amount by multiplying by 52 and dividing by 12,

for a period of, or more than one period where the total of those periods amounts to, at least 6 months.]

1. Social Security (Jobseeker's Allowance, Employment and Support Allowance and Universal Credit) (Amendment) Regulations 2016 (SI 2016/678) reg.5(11) (July 25, 2016).

DEFINITIONS

"the Act"—see reg.2.
"claimant"—see WRA 2012 s.40.
"individual threshold"—see regs 2 and 90(2).
"joint claimants"—see WRA 2012 s.40.
"National Minimum Wage Regulations"—see reg.2
"single claimant"—see WRA 2012 s.40.

GENERAL NOTE

The basic rule is that any hardship payment is recoverable from the person to   2.333
whom it was paid (Administration Act, s.71ZH(2)(a)), by the means provided in
ss.71ZC to 71ZF. A payment made to one of joint claimants is treated as also paid to
the other (s.71ZH(4)). The amount is not recoverable during any assessment period
in which the claimant or both joint claimants are subject to no work-related requirements by reason of having earnings of at least the individual threshold(s) under
reg.90 (para.(2)(a) and (b)). The same applies under the new provision in para.(2)
(c) to claimants who do not have an individual threshold as defined in reg.90(2)
because they would not otherwise have been subject to any work-related requirement who meet the test of earnings at the rate of 16 times the national minimum
wage hourly rate. It appears from the contrast with the terms of para.(3) that once
the reason for freedom from any work-related requirements ceases, the payment
becomes recoverable again. Under para.(3) recoverability ceases if since the end of
the sanction period the claimant or both joint claimants have had earnings of at least
the para.(2) level for a period or periods amounting to six months.

The maximum rate of recovery from payments of universal credit is 40% of the
standard allowance (Social Security (Overpayments and Recovery) Regulations
2013 (Vol.III of this series) reg.11(2)(a) and (3)(b)). The report of November 6,
2018 by the House of Commons Work and Pensions Committee on *Benefit Sanctions*
(HC 995 2017-19), para.132, recommended that the rate should be no higher than
what was affordable by the claimant, with a default rate of 5% of the standard
allowance. The DWP (House of Commons Work and Pensions Committee, *Benefit
Sanctions: Government Response* (HC 1949 2017-19, February 11, 2019, paras
90-93) rejected the 5% suggestion as unacceptably diluting the effect of sanctions.
It stated that it had announced in November 2018 that to assist those in debt it had
reduced the normal maximum rate of deduction to 30% of the standard allowance.
Where other higher priority deductions are in place there is a corresponding adjustment to the rate of recovery of hardship payments.

Regulation 25(2)

SCHEDULE 1

MEANING OF PAYMENTS IN RESPECT OF ACCOMMODATION

General

Interpretation
1. In this Schedule—   2.334
    "approved premises" means premises approved by the Secretary of State under section 13
        of the Offender Management Act 2007 (which contains provision for the approval etc. of
        premises providing accommodation for persons granted bail in criminal proceedings or for
        or in connection with the supervision or rehabilitation of persons convicted of offences);
    "care home"—
    (a) in England [4 ...], means a care home within the meaning of section 3 of the Care
        Standards Act 2000;

[(aa) in Wales, means a place at which a care home service within the meaning of Part 1 of the Regulation and Inspection of Social Care (Wales) Act 2016 is provided wholly or mainly to persons aged 18 or over;]

    (b) in Scotland, means a care home service within the meaning of paragraph 2 of Schedule 12 to the Public Services Reform (Scotland) Act 2010; and

    (c) in [⁴ any of the above cases], includes an independent hospital;

[¹ "exempt accommodation" has the meaning given in paragraph 4(10) of Schedule 3 to the Housing Benefit and Council Tax Benefit (Consequential Provisions) Regulations 2006;]

"housing association" has the meaning given by section 1(1) of the Housing Associations Act 1985;

"independent hospital"—

    (a) in England, means a hospital as defined by section 275 of the National Health Service Act 2006 that is not a health service hospital as defined by that section;

    (b) in Wales, has the meaning assigned to it by section 2 of the Care Standards Act 2000;

    (c) in Scotland, means an independent health care service as defined in section 10F(1)(a) and (b) of the National Health Service (Scotland) Act 1978;

"registered charity" means a charity entered in the register of charities maintained under Part 4 of the Charities Act 2011 or a body entered on the register of charities maintained under the Charities and Trustee Investment (Scotland) Act 2005;

"shared ownership tenancy" has the meaning given in regulation 26(6);

"tent" means a moveable structure that is designed or adapted (solely or mainly) for the purpose of sleeping in a place for any period and that is not a caravan, a mobile home or a houseboat;

[¹ . . .]

"voluntary organisation" means a body (other than a public or local authority) whose activities are carried on otherwise than for profit.

Rent payments

Rent payments

2.335   **2.** "Rent payments" are such of the following as are not excluded by paragraph 3—

    (a) payments of rent;

    (b) payments for a licence or other permission to occupy accommodation;

    (c) mooring charges payable for a houseboat;

    (d) in relation to accommodation which is a caravan or mobile home, payments in respect of the site on which the accommodation stands;

    (e) contributions by residents towards maintaining almshouses (and essential services in them) provided by a housing association which is—

        (i) a registered charity, or

        (ii) an exempt charity within Schedule 3 to the Charities Act 2011.

Payments excluded from being rent payments

2.336   **3.** The following are excluded from being "rent payments"—

    (a) payments of ground rent;

    (b) payments in respect of a tent or the site on which a tent stands;

    (c) payments in respect of approved premises;

    (d) payments in respect of a care home;

    (e) [¹ . . .]

    (f) payments which are owner-occupier payments [² within the meaning of Schedule 1 of the Loans for Mortgage Regulations 2017];

    (g) payments which are service charge payments within the meaning of paragraph 7.

[¹ (h) payments in respect of accommodation specified in paragraph 3A] [³ ;

    (i) payments in respect of accommodation specified in paragraph 3B.]

[¹ Specified accommodation

2.337   **3A.**—(1) The accommodation referred to in paragraph 3(h) is accommodation to which one or more of the following sub-paragraphs applies.

    (2) This sub-paragraph applies to accommodation which is exempt accommodation.

    (3) This sub-paragraph applies to accommodation—

    (a) which is provided by a relevant body;

    (b) into which the claimant has been admitted in order to meet a need for care, support or supervision; and

    (c) where the claimant receives care, support or supervision.

(4) This sub-paragraph applies to accommodation which—
(a) is provided by a local authority or a relevant body to the claimant because the claimant has left the home as a result of domestic violence; and
(b) consists of a building, or part of a building, which is used wholly or mainly for the non-permanent accommodation of persons who have left their homes as a result of domestic violence.

(5) This sub-paragraph applies to accommodation—
(a) which would be a hostel within the meaning of paragraph 29(10) (renters excepted form shared accommodation) of Schedule 4 (housing costs element for renters) but for it being owned or managed by a local authority; and
(b) where the claimant receives care, support or supervision.

(6) In this paragraph—
"domestic violence" has the meaning given in regulation 98 (victims of domestic violence);
"relevant body" means a—
(a) council for a county in England for each part of which there is a district council;
(b) housing association;
(c) registered charity; or
(d) voluntary organisation].

[¹ Temporary Accommodation

3B.—(1) The accommodation referred to in paragraph (3)(i) is accommodation which falls within Case 1 or Case 2.   **2.338**

(2) Case 1 is where—
(a) rent payments are payable to a local authority;
(b) the local authority makes the accommodation available to the renter—
(i) to discharge any of the local authority's functions under Part II of the Housing (Scotland) Act 1987, Part VII of the Housing Act 1996 or Part 2 of the Housing (Wales) Act 2014, or
(ii) to prevent the person being or becoming homeless within the meaning of Part II of the Housing (Scotland) Act 1987, Part VII of the Housing Act 1996 or Part 2 of the Housing (Wales) Act 2014; and
(c) the accommodation is not exempt accommodation.

(3) Case 2 is where—
(a) rent payments are payable to a provider of social housing other than a local authority;
(b) that provider makes the accommodation available to the renter in pursuance of arrangements made with it by a local authority—
(i) to discharge any of the local authority's functions under Part II of the Housing (Scotland) Act 1987, Part VII of the Housing Act 1996 or Part 2 of the Housing (Wales) Act 2014, or
(ii) to prevent the person being or becoming homeless within the meaning of Part II of the Housing (Scotland) Act 1987, Part VII of the Housing Act 1996 or Part 2 of the Housing (Wales) Act 2014; and
(c) the accommodation is not exempt accommodation.

(4) Sub-paragraph (1) applies irrespective of whether the renter is also liable to make service charge payments.

(5) In sub-paragraph (3), "provider of social housing" has the meaning given in paragraph 2 of Schedule 4.]

Owner-occupier payments

Owner-occupier payments
4.—[² . . .]   **2.339**

Meaning of "loan interest payments"
5. [² . . .]   **2.340**

Meaning of "alternative finance payments"
6.—[² . . .]   **2.341**

Service charge payments

Service charge payments
7.—(1) "Service charge payments" are payments which—   **2.342**
(a) fall within sub-paragraph (2);

(b) are not excluded by sub-paragraph (3); and

(c) in any case to which paragraph 8 applies, meet all of the conditions set out in that paragraph.

(2) The payments falling within this sub-paragraph are payments of amounts which are, in whole or in part—

(a) payments of, or towards, the costs of or charges for providing services or facilities for the use or benefit of persons occupying accommodation; or

(b) fairly attributable to the costs of or charges for providing such services or facilities connected with accommodation as are available for the use or benefit of persons occupying accommodation.

(3) Payments are excluded by this sub-paragraph where—

(a) [² a qualifying loan within the meaning of regulation 2 of the Loans for Mortgage Interest Regulations 2017] was taken out for the purposes of making the payments; or

(b) the services or facilities to which the payments relate are provided for the use or benefit of any person occupying—

(i) a tent,

(ii) approved premises,

(iii) a care home, or

(iv) exempt accommodation.

(4) It is irrelevant for the purposes of sub-paragraph (2)—

(a) whether or not the payments are separately identified as relating to the costs or charges referred to in sub-paragraph (2);

(b) whether they are made in addition to or as part of any other payment (including a payment that would otherwise be regarded as a rent payment within the meaning of paragraph 2);

(c) whether they are made under the same or a different agreement as that under which the accommodation is occupied.

Additional conditions: social rented sector renters and owner-occupiers

2.343   **8.**—(1) This paragraph applies for the purposes of calculating the amount of housing costs element to be included in a claimant's award of universal credit but only as regards calculations made under—

(a) Part 5 of Schedule 4 (social rented sector [³ ...]); or

(b) Schedule 5 (housing costs element for owner-occupiers).

(2) The following are the conditions referred to in paragraph 7(1)(c).

(3) The first condition is that making the payments is a condition on which the right to occupy the accommodation depends.

(4) The second condition is that the payments fall within one or more of the following categories:

Category A—Payments to maintain the general standard of the accommodation

Payments within this category are for—

(a) the external cleaning of windows, but only in relation to upper floors of a multi-storey building;

(b) other internal or external maintenance or repair of the accommodation, but only where the payments are separately identifiable as relating to such maintenance or repair and payable by—

(i) a claimant who occupies accommodation under a shared ownership tenancy, or

(ii) a claimant in whose case any amount of housing costs element to be included in their award in respect of those payments would fall to be calculated under Schedule 5.

Category B—Payments for the general upkeep of areas of communal use

Payments within this category are for ongoing maintenance or cleaning of, and the supply of water, fuel or any other commodity relating to the common use of, internal or external areas, including areas for reasonable facilities (such as laundry rooms or children's play areas).

Category C—Payments in respect of basic communal services

Payments within this category are for provision, ongoing maintenance, cleaning or repair in connection with basic services generally available to all persons living in the accommodation (such as refuse collection, communal lifts, secure building access or wireless or television aerials to receive a service free of charge).

Category D—Accommodation-specific charges

Payments within this category are specific to the particular accommodation occupied by a claimant but are limited to payments for the use of essential items contained in it (such as furniture or domestic appliances).

(5) The third condition is that the costs and charges to which the payments relate are of a reasonable amount and relate to services or facilities of such description as it is reasonable to provide.

(6) The fourth condition is that the payments are none of the following—

(a) payments to the extent that they relate to the costs of or charges for providing services or facilities in respect of which payments out of public funds might otherwise be made (irrespective of whether the claimant has any entitlement to payments so made);

(b) payments in connection with the use of an asset which result in the transfer of the asset or any interest in it;

(c) payments to the extent that they relate to the costs of or charges for providing food, medical services or personal services (including personal care) of any description.

(7) Payments that are not service charge payments within the meaning of paragraph 7 by reason only that they fail to meet any of the conditions set out in sub-paragraphs (3) to (6) are nevertheless to be treated as if they were such service charge payments for the purposes of paragraphs 3(g) and 4(2).

AMENDMENTS

1. Housing Benefit and Universal Credit (Supported Accommodation) (Amendment) Regulations 2014 (SI 2014/771) reg.2(2) (November 3, 2014).

2. Loans for Mortgage Interest Regulations 2017 (SI 2017/725) reg.18 and Sch.5, para.5(e) (April 6, 2018).

3. Universal Credit (Miscellaneous Amendments, Saving and Transitional Provision) Regulations 2018 (SI 2018/65) reg.3(12) (April 11, 2018).

4. Social Security and Child Support (Regulation and Inspection of Social Care (Wales) Act 2016) (Consequential Provision) Regulations 2018 (SI 2018/228) reg.14(1) and (2) (April 2, 2018).

DEFINITION

"claimant"—see WRA 2012 s.40.

GENERAL NOTE

In order to be eligible for a housing costs element, the claimant (or claimants) must meet the three basic conditions in reg.25(2) to (4): the payment condition, the liability condition, and the occupation condition. This Schedule is concerned with the payment condition.

Under reg.25(2) there are three types of payments that can be met: rent payments, owner-occupier payments and service charge payments.

2.344

Paragraphs 2, 3 and 3A

Paragraph 2 lists the payments that are eligible as rent payments and para.3 the payments that are not eligible. Note that the amount of the housing costs element may be restricted under Sch.4 if the rent is higher than allowed (private tenants and temporary accommodation) or the accommodation is larger than allowed (social rented sector).

The payments listed in para.2 include most of the payments that can be met by housing benefit but not all, e.g. payments by way of mesne profits (or, in Scotland, violent profits) are not included.

Under para.3 payments in respect of ground rent and in respect of a tent and the site on which it stands are excluded (para.3(a) and (b)). These qualify as "other housing costs" for income support, old style JSA and old style ESA but there seems to be no provision for such payments under universal credit.

2.345

Payments by Crown tenants no longer seem to be excluded (as they are for housing benefit).

Paragraph 3(h), together with para.3A, inserted with effect from November 3, 2014, excludes payments in respect of "specified accommodation". There are four categories of "specified accommodation", the first of which, exempt accommodation, was previously excluded under para. 3(e) (now omitted).

The four categories are: (i) "exempt accommodation" (as defined in para.1–this is accommodation which is a "resettlement place" or accommodation provided by a non-metropolitan county council, a housing association, a registered charity or a voluntary organisation, where care, support or supervision is provided to the claimant by that body or a person acting on its behalf); (ii) accommodation provided by a "relevant body" (as defined in para. 3A(6)) into which the claimant has been admitted because of a need for care, support or supervision, which they receive; (iii) temporary accommodation provided by a local authority or a relevant body for people who have left home because of domestic violence, e.g., a women's refuge (note the definition of "domestic violence" in reg. 98(4), which is quite wide); and (iv) hostels owned or managed by a local authority where the claimant receives care, support or supervision. Note that in the case of categories (ii) and (iv) the care, support or supervision does not have to be provided by the relevant body or on its behalf, or by the local authority or on its behalf, as it does in the case of exempt accommodation.

Claimants living in specified accommodation are eligible for housing benefit. Corresponding amendments have been made to the Housing Benefit Regulations 2006 (SI 2006/213), the effect of which is to exclude housing benefit paid to claimants living in specified accommodation from the HB benefit cap for housing benefit purposes (see regs 75C(2)(a) and 75H of those Regulations–the exemption previously only applied to claimants living in exempt accommodation). Housing benefit is not included in the list of welfare benefits in reg. 79(4) to which the universal credit benefit cap applies.

Paragraphs 4–6

2.346   The owner-occupier payments that can be met are "loan interest payments" and "alternative finance payments". They do not include service charge payments that come within para.7.

Note the £200,000 limit on loans in step 3 of para.10(2) of Sch.5 (except for loans for adaptations for disablement needs: see para.10(3) of Sch.5) and on the purchase price of the accommodation in the case of alternative finance payments in step 2 of para.11(2) of Sch.5. Note also that any increase, or decrease, in the amount of a loan, or in the amount owing under the alternative financial arrangements, during the currency of an award is only taken into account from the anniversary date (see paras 10(4) and 11(4) respectively of Sch.5).

"Loan interest payments" are defined in para.5 as "payments of interest on a loan which is secured on the accommodation in respect of which the claimant meets the occupation condition".

Thus payments of interest will be eligible (as calculated under Sch.5), provided only that the loan is secured on the accommodation that the claimant (or claimants: s.40 WRA 2012) is occupying, or is treated as occupying, as their home. Note that there is no requirement as to the purpose for which the loan (or loans) was taken out. Compare the income support, old style JSA and old style ESA provisions under which the loan has to be taken out to acquire an interest in the home or for the purpose of repairs or improvements (but does not have to be secured on the home, although it normally will be). Thus this could include a loan taken out, for example, to pay service charges (payments on loans secured on a claimant's home which were taken out to meet service charges are not eligible as service charge payments (see para.7(1)(b) and (3)(a)), or for repairs. But it could also include a loan taken out for any other purpose, for example, to buy a car, as long as the loan is secured on the claimant's home. This does seem surprising but is acknowledged in the examples given in para.F4082 ADM. Furthermore, a remortgage to roll up arrears of interest would also be covered. Thus a claimant may receive a housing costs element in respect of interest payments on loans that include arrears of interest (provided that they are secured on the home), which is a significant change from the position under the income support, old style JSA and old style ESA housing costs rules.

"**Alternative finance payments**" are defined in para.6. This will cover home financing schemes designed to be compliant with Shari'a principles. Such schemes are not eligible for income support (or old style JSA or old style ESA) housing costs (see the notes to para.15 of Sch.3 to the Income Support Regulations in Vol.II of this series).

Note that there is normally a qualifying period (i.e. waiting period) for owner-occupier payments (and for service charge payments if these are also payable). In the case of a new award of universal credit on or after April 1, 2016 the waiting period is nine consecutive assessments periods (i.e. months) (see Pt 3 of Sch.5). Before April 1, 2016 the waiting period was only three consecutive months. The amendment which increased the waiting period to nine months is subject to a saving provision (see reg. 8 of the Social Security (Housing Costs Amendments) Regulations 2015 in Pt.IV of this Volume and see the note to paras 5-7 of Sch.5).

Note also that if the claimant (or other member of the couple, in the case of couples) has *any* earned income during an assessment period (i.e. month) no housing costs element will be payable (Sch.5, para.4), although in the case of a shared ownership tenancy (defined in reg.26(6)) rent payments and service charges can still be met (Sch.5, para.4(3)). In addition, any break in entitlement to a housing costs element under Sch.5 (e.g. because of earnings), or if the owner-occupier ceases to qualify for a housing costs element under Sch. 5 during a waiting period, means that a whole new waiting period has to be served (see Sch.5, para.5).

Unlike income support, old style JSA and old style ESA, there is no rule that a housing costs element cannot be paid if the loan was taken out while the claimant (or either joint claimant) was in receipt of universal credit.

Paragraphs 7 and 8

Service charge payments are eligible payments if they fall within para.7(2) and are not excluded under para.7(3). They do not have to be separately identified, nor does it matter if they are paid in addition to, or as part of, any other payment (including a rent payment within the meaning of para.2), or if they are paid under the same or a different agreement than that under which the accommodation is occupied (para.7(4)).   2.347

Note the additional conditions in para.8 that have to be met in the case of service charge payments by social sector renters (other those in temporary accommodation) and owner-occupiers. This does not apply to private renters.

According to para.F2074 ADM, where service charges are for the provision of an eligible service, the relevant proportion of staffing costs of a person (e.g. a concierge, groundskeeper or caretaker) employed to provide the eligible service can be included, as can the relevant proportion of the costs of managing and administering eligible services, if the claimant is liable for these costs.

Regulation 25(3)

SCHEDULE 2

CLAIMANT TREATED AS LIABLE OR NOT LIABLE TO MAKE PAYMENTS

PART I

TREATED AS LIABLE TO MAKE PAYMENTS

Certain other persons liable to make payments

1.—(1) A claimant is to be treated as liable to make payments where the person who is liable to make the payments is—   2.348

(a) any child or qualifying young person for whom the claimant (or if the claimant is a member of a couple, either member) is responsible; or

(b) in the case of a claimant who is a member of a couple claiming as a single person, the other member of the couple.

(2) Sub-paragraph (1)(b) does not apply to a person who is claiming as a single person by virtue of regulation 3(4).

Failure to pay by the person who is liable

2.349

2.—(1) A claimant is to be treated as liable to make payments where all of the conditions specified in sub-paragraph (2) are met.

(2) These are the conditions—

(a) the person who is liable to make the payments is not doing so;

(b) the claimant has to make the payments in order to continue occupation of the accommodation;

(c) the claimant's circumstances are such that it would be unreasonable to expect them to make other arrangements;

(d) it is otherwise reasonable in all the circumstances to treat the claimant as liable to make the payments.

(3) In determining what is reasonable for the purposes of sub-paragraph (2)(d) in the case of owner-occupier payments, regard may be had to the fact that continuing to make the payments may benefit the person with the liability to make the payments.

Payments waived in return for repair work

2.350

3. A claimant is to be treated as liable to make payments where—

(a) the liability to make payments is waived by the person ("P") to whom the liability is owed; and

(b) the waiver of that liability is by way of reasonable compensation for reasonable repair or re-decoration works carried out by the claimant to the accommodation which P would otherwise have carried out or been required to carry out.

Rent free periods

2.351

4.—(1) Where the arrangements under which the claimant occupies the accommodation provide for rent free periods, the claimant is to be treated as liable to make rent payments and service charge payments in respect of accommodation for the whole of any rent free period.

(2) In paragraph (1), "rent free period" has the meaning given in paragraph 7(4) of Schedule 4.

PART 2

TREATED AS NOT LIABLE TO MAKE PAYMENTS

Liability to make rent and other payments to close relative

2.352

5.—(1) A claimant is to be treated as not liable to make rent payments where the liability to make them is owed to a person who lives in the accommodation and who is—

(a) if the claimant is a member of a couple, the other member; or

(b) a child or qualifying young person for whom—

    (i) the claimant is responsible, or

    (ii) if the claimant is a member of a couple, the other member is responsible; or

(c) a close relative of—

    (i) the claimant, or

    (ii) if the claimant is a member of a couple, the other member, or

    (iii) any child or qualifying young person who falls within paragraph (b).

(2) A claimant who is treated under sub-paragraph (1) as not liable to make rent payments to any person is also to be treated as not liable to make service charge payments where the liability to make the service charge payments is to the same person.

Liability to make rent and other payments to company

2.353

6.—(1) A claimant is to be treated as not liable to make rent payments where the liability to make them is owed to a company and the owners or directors of the company include—

(a) the claimant;

(b) if the claimant is a member of a couple, the other member;

(c) a qualifying young person for whom a person who falls within paragraph (a) or (b) is responsible; or

(d) a close relative of any of the above who lives in the accommodation with the claimant.

(2) A claimant who is treated under sub-paragraph (1) as not liable to make rent payments

to the company is also to be treated as not liable to make service charge payments where the liability to make the service charge payments is to—

    (a) the same company; or

    (b) another company of which the owners or directors include any of the persons listed in sub-paragraph (1)(a) to (d).

(3) In this paragraph, "owner", in relation to a company ("C"), means a person ("A") who has a material interest in C.

(4) For the purposes of sub-paragraph (3), A has a material interest in C if A—

    (a) holds at least 10% of the shares in C; or

    (b) is able to exercise a significant influence over the management of C by virtue of A's shareholding in C; or

    (c) holds at least 10% of the shares in a parent undertaking ("P") of C; or

    (d) is able to exercise a significant influence over the management of P by virtue of A's shareholding in P; or

    (e) is entitled to exercise, or control the exercise of, voting power in C which, if it consists of voting rights, constitutes at least 10% of the voting rights in C; or

    (f) is able to exercise a significant influence over the management of C by virtue of A's entitlement to exercise, or control the exercise of, voting rights in C; or

    (g) is entitled to exercise, or control the exercise of, voting power in P which, if it consists of voting rights, constitutes at least 10% of the voting rights in P; or

    (h) is able to exercise a significant influence over the management of P by virtue of A's entitlement to exercise, or control the exercise of, voting rights in P.

(5) For the purposes of sub-paragraph (4), references to "A" are to—

    (a) the person; or

    (b) any of the person's associates; or

    (c) the person and any of the person's associates taken together.

(6) For the purposes of sub-paragraph (5), "associate", in relation to a person ("A") holding shares in an undertaking ("X") or entitled to exercise or control the exercise of voting power in relation to another undertaking ("Y"), means—

    (a) the spouse or civil partner of A;

    (b) a child or step-child of A (if under 18);

    (c) the trustee of any settlement under which A has a life interest in possession (in Scotland a life interest);

    (d) an undertaking of which A is a director;

    (e) a person who is an employee or partner of A;

    (f) if A has with any other person an agreement or arrangement with respect to the acquisition, holding or disposal of shares or other interests in X or Y, that other person;

    (g) if A has with any other person an agreement or arrangement under which they undertake to act together in exercising their voting power in relation to X or Y, that other person.

(7) In sub-paragraph (6)(c), "settlement" means any disposition or arrangement under which property is held on trust (or subject to comparable obligations).

(8) For the purposes of this paragraph—

"parent undertaking" has the same meaning as in the Financial Services and Markets Act 2000 (see section 420 of that Act);

"shares" means—

    (a) in relation to an undertaking with shares, allotted shares (within the meaning of Part 17 of the Companies Act 2006);

    (b) in relation to an undertaking with capital but no share capital, rights to share in the capital of the body;

    (c) in relation to an undertaking without capital, interests—

        (i) conferring any right to share in the profits, or liability to contribute to the losses, of the body, or

        (ii) giving rise to an obligation to contribute to the debts or expenses of the undertaking in the event of a winding up;

"voting power", in relation to an undertaking which does not have general meetings at which matters are decided by the exercise of voting rights, means the rights under the constitution of the undertaking to direct the overall policy of the undertaking or alter the terms of its constitution.

Liability to make rent and other payments to a trust

    7.—(1) A claimant is to be treated as not liable to make rent payments where the liability to make them is owed to a trustee of a trust and the trustees or beneficiaries of the trust include—

    (a) the claimant;

    2.354

(b) if the claimant is a member of a couple, the other member;

(c) a child or qualifying young person for whom a person who falls within paragraph (a) or (b) is responsible; or

(d) a close relative of any of the above who lives in the accommodation with the claimant.

(2) A claimant who is treated under sub-paragraph (1) as not liable to make rent payments to the trustee of a trust is also to be treated as not liable to make service charge payments where the liability to make the service charge payments is to—

(a) a trustee of the same trust; or

(b) a trustee of another trust of which the trustees or beneficiaries include any of the persons listed in sub-paragraph (1)(a) to (d).

Liability to make owner-occupier and other payments to member of same household

2.355   **8.**—(1) A claimant is to be treated as not liable to make owner-occupier payments where the liability to make the payments is owed to a person who lives in the claimant's household.

(2) A claimant who is treated under sub-paragraph (1) as not liable to make owner-occupier payments to any person is also to be treated as not liable to make service charge payments where the liability to make the service charge payments is to the same person.

(3) A claimant is to be treated as not liable to make service charge payments where—

(a) there is no liability to make rent payments or owner-occupier payments; but

(b) the liability to make service charge payments is to a person who lives in the claimant's household.

Arrears of payments

2.356   **9.**—(1) A claimant is to be treated as not liable to make payments in respect of any amount which—

(a) represents an increase in the sum that would be otherwise payable; and

(b) is the result of—

(i) outstanding arrears of any payment or charge in respect of the accommodation,

(ii) outstanding arrears of any payment or charge in respect of other accommodation, previously occupied by the claimant, or

(iii) any other unpaid liability to make a payment or charge.

(2) Sub-paragraph (1) does not apply if the claimant is treated as not liable to make the payments under any of the preceding provisions of this Part of this Schedule.

Contrived liability

2.357   **10.**—(1) A claimant is to be treated as not liable to make payments where the Secretary of State is satisfied that the liability to make the payments was contrived in order to secure the inclusion of the housing costs element in an award of universal credit or to increase the amount of that element.

(2) Sub-paragraph (1) does not apply if the claimant is treated as not liable to make the payments under any of the preceding provisions of this Part of this Schedule.

DEFINITIONS

"child"—see WRA 2012 s.40.

"claimant"—*ibid.*

"close relative"—see reg.2.

"couple"—see WRA 2012 ss.39 and 40.

"partner"—see reg.2.

"qualifying young person"—see WRA 2012 ss.40 and 10(5) and regs 2 and 5.

"rent free period"—see Sch.4, para.7(4).

"single person"—see WRA 2012 ss.40 and 1(2)(a).

GENERAL NOTE

2.358   In order to be eligible for a housing costs element, the claimant (or claimants) must meet the three basic conditions in reg.25(2) to (4): the payment condition, the liability condition, and the occupation condition. This Schedule is concerned with the liability condition.

Under reg.25(3) the claimant (or either joint claimant) must be liable to make rent payments, owner-occupier payments or service charge payments on a commercial basis, or be treated as liable to make them, and must not be treated as not liable to make them. "Liable" is not defined but presumably requires a legal (as opposed to a moral) liability (see *R v Rugby BC HBRB ex parte Harrison* [1994] 28 HLR 36 and the discussion on the meaning of "liability" in the notes to reg.8 of the Housing Benefit Regulations in *CPAG's Housing Benefit and Council Tax Reduction Legislation*; it is also the view taken in para.F2081 ADM).

For the meaning of "on a commercial basis", see the notes to *"Board and lodging accommodation"* in reg.2 of the Income Support Regulations in Vol.II of this series and the notes to reg.9(1)(a) of the Housing Benefit Regulations in *CPAG's Housing Benefit and Council Tax Reduction Legislation*.

Paragraphs 1–4

Under para.1 a claimant is treated as liable to make payments if the person who is liable is (i) a child or qualifying young person for whom the claimant (or the other member of the couple in the case of a couple) is responsible (sub-para.(1)(a)); or (ii) the other member of the couple, if the claimant is a member of a couple but claiming as a single person (see reg.3(3) for the circumstances in which this can apply) (sub-para.(1)(b)); note that sub-para.(1)(b) does not apply in the case of polygamous marriages (sub-para.(2)).

2.359

A claimant is also treated as liable to make payments if the payments have been waived by the person to whom they were due (e.g. a landlord) as reasonable compensation for the claimant carrying out reasonable repair or redecoration works which the person would otherwise have had to carry out (para.3), or, in the case of rent and service charge payments, during rent free periods (para.4).

Paragraph 2 applies where the person who is liable to make the payments is not doing so. The claimant will be treated as liable if the claimant has to make the payments in order to continue to occupy the accommodation, it would be unreasonable to expect the claimant to make other arrangements and it is reasonable to treat the claimant as liable. These conditions are similar to those in, e.g., reg.8(1)(c) of the Housing Benefit Regulations and para.2(1)(b) of Sch.3 to the Income Support Regulations (see the notes to para.2 of Sch.3 in Vol.II of this series), except for the added condition that it would be unreasonable to expect the claimant to make other arrangements.

Note para.2(3) which provides that in the case of owner-occupier payments, in deciding whether it would be reasonable to treat the claimant as liable, account may be taken of the fact that the payments continuing to be made may benefit the person who is liable to make the payments. Paragraph F2090 ADM gives the following example of where this might apply. A couple split up and C, the member in whose name the mortgage is, moves out and refuses to pay the mortgage. The other member, P, remains in the property. A decision-maker decides not to include a housing costs element in P's universal credit award as C could still pay the mortgage.

Paragraphs 5–10

These paragraphs deal with when the claimant will be treated as not liable to make payments in respect of their home. Note that some of the exclusions only apply to some types of eligible payments. The situations in which this rule applies to rent payments are reduced compared with housing benefit (see reg.9 of the Housing Benefit Regulations). Note that the "on a commercial basis" requirement applies to any liability to make payments in respect of accommodation under universal credit (see reg.25(3)(a)(i)).

2.360

Paragraphs 5–7

A claimant is treated as not liable to make rent payments and service charges payments if the liability is to the following:

2.361

- Someone who also lives in the accommodation, and who is (i) the other member of the couple if the claimant is a member of a couple; (ii) a child or qualifying young person for whom the claimant or other member of the couple is responsible (see reg.4); or (iii) a close relative (defined in reg.2) of the claimant, the other member of the couple or the child or qualifying person (para.5).

"Lives in the accommodation" probably means the same as "resides in the dwelling" in reg.9(1)(b) of the Housing Benefit Regulations (see the notes to reg.9(1)(b) in *CPAG's Housing Benefit and Council Tax Reduction Legislation*).

- A company, and the owners or directors of the company include (i) the claimant; (ii) the other member of the couple if the claimant is a member of a couple; (iii) a qualifying young person for whom the claimant or other member of the couple is responsible; or (iv) a close relative of the claimant, other member of the couple or qualifying young person (in the case of a close relative, they must live in the accommodation with the claimant) (para.6(1) and (2)).

Note that the claimant will also be treated as not liable to pay the service charges if the liability for them is to another company whose owners or directors include any of the people listed in para.6(1) (para.6(2)(b)).

An owner of a company for the purposes of para.6 is a person who has a "material interest" in it (para.6(3)). See para.6(4)–(8) for the detail.

- A trustee of a trust, and the trustees or beneficiaries of the trust include (i) the claimant; (ii) the other member of the couple if the claimant is a member of a couple; (iii) a child or qualifying young person for whom the claimant or other member of the couple is responsible; or (iv) a close relative of the claimant, other member of the couple or child or qualifying young person (in the case of a close relative, they must live in the accommodation with the claimant) (para.7(1) and (2)).

Note that the claimant will also be treated as not liable to pay the service charges if the liability for them is to a trustee of another trust whose trustees or beneficiaries include any of the people listed in para.7(1) (para.7(2) (b)).

See the notes to reg.9(1)(e) and (f) of the Housing Benefit Regulations in *CPAG's Housing Benefit and Council Tax Reduction Legislation*.

Paragraph 8

2.362   Paragraph 8(1) and (2) are concerned with owner-occupier payments and service charges payments. They treat a claimant as not liable to make owner-occupier payments and service charges payments if the liability is to a person who is lives in the claimant's household. Clearly this is different from "lives in the accommodation" under paras 5 to 8. On the meaning of "household", see the notes to "*couple*" (under the heading "*Spouses and civil partners*") in reg.2 of the Income Support Regulations in Vol.II of this series.

Under para.8(3) a claimant is treated as not liable to make service charges payments if they are not liable for rent payments or owner-occupier payments and the liability for the service charges is to someone who is a member of the claimant's household.

Paragraph 9

2.363   This paragraph only applies if paras 5–8 do not apply (sub-para.(2)). It applies to all types of eligible payments.

It treats a claimant as not liable to pay any increase in the amount that they would otherwise be liable to pay, if that increase is the result of outstanding arrears of any payment or charge in respect of their current or previous accommodation. This also applies in respect of "any other unpaid liability to make a payment or charge" (see sub-para.(1)(b)(iii)) but only if that results in an increase in the amount the claimant is liable to pay.

What does "an increase in the sum that would otherwise be payable" mean? According to para.F2136 ADM, in relation to owner-occupier payments, because any loan secured on the claimant's home is eligible for inclusion in the calculation of the housing costs element (see para.5 of Sch.1) (subject to the £200,000 limit on loans in step 3 of para.10(2) of Sch.5), any increase in the loan (or loans) does not "represent an increase in the sum that would otherwise be payable" and so is not caught by para.9. This will include the situation when the loan is a remortgage to roll up arrears of interest. Thus a claimant may receive a housing costs element in respect of interest payments on loans that include arrears of interest (provided that they are secured on the home), which is a significant change from the position under the income support, old style JSA and old style ESA housing costs rules. Presumably this is because the arrears of interest are not "outstanding" if the remortgage has rolled up the arrears of interest.

An example of a payment that would come within para.9 is where a tenant has agreed to pay off arrears of rent by paying an increased amount of rent each month. They will be treated under para.9 as not liable to pay the extra amount above the rent that was originally agreed.

Paragraph 10

This paragraph only applies if paras 5–8 do not apply (sub-para.(2)). It applies to all types of eligible payments. **2.364**

It contains a similar rule to the contrived tenancy provision in housing benefit (see reg.9(1)(l) of the Housing Benefit Regulations). See the notes to reg.9(1)(l) in *CPAG's Housing Benefit and Council Tax Reduction Legislation*. But note that reg.9(1)(l) refers to the liability being "created to take advantage of the housing benefit scheme", whereas the test under para.10 is that the liability "was contrived in order to secure the inclusion of the housing costs element". There may be a distinction between "created" and "contrived".

Regulation 25(4)

SCHEDULE 3

CLAIMANT TREATED AS OCCUPYING OR NOT OCCUPYING ACCOMMODATION

PART I

TREATED AS OCCUPYING ACCOMMODATION

The occupation condition: the general rule

1.—(1) The general rule is that a claimant is to be treated as occupying as their home the accommodation which the claimant normally occupies as their home. **2.365**

(2) Subject to the following provisions of this Part, no claimant is to be treated as occupying accommodation which comprises more than one dwelling.

(3) Where none of those provisions applies and the claimant occupies more than one dwelling, regard is to be had to all the circumstances in determining which dwelling the claimant normally occupies as their home, including (among other things) any persons with whom the claimant occupies each dwelling.

(4) "Dwelling"—
  (a) in England and Wales, means a dwelling within the meaning of Part 1 of the Local Government Finance Act 1992;
  (b) in Scotland, means a dwelling within the meaning of Part 2 of that Act.

Croft land included in accommodation

2.—(1) Where accommodation which a claimant normally occupies as their home is situated on or pertains to a croft, croft land used for the purposes of the accommodation is to be treated as included in the accommodation. **2.366**

(2) "Croft" means a croft within the meaning of section 3(1) of the Crofters (Scotland) Act 1993.

Claimant living in other accommodation during essential repairs

2.367   **3.**—(1) Where a claimant—

(a) is required to move into accommodation ("the other accommodation") on account of essential repairs being carried out to the accommodation the claimant normally occupies as their home;

(b) intends to return to the accommodation which is under repair; and

(c) meets the payment condition and the liability condition in respect of either the other accommodation or the accommodation which they normally occupy as their home (but not both),

the claimant is to be treated as normally occupying as their home the accommodation in respect of which those conditions are met.

(2) A claimant is subject to the general rule in paragraph 1 where—

(a) sub-paragraph (1)(a) and (b) apply to the claimant; but

(b) the claimant meets the payment condition and the liability condition in respect of both the other accommodation and the accommodation which they normally occupy as their home.

Claimant housed in two dwellings by provider of social housing

2.368   **4.**—(1) In sub-paragraph (2), "relevant claimant" means a claimant who meets all of the following conditions—

(a) the first condition is that the claimant has been housed in two dwellings ("accommodation A" and "accommodation B") by a provider of social housing on account of the number of children and qualifying young persons living with the claimant;

(b) the second condition is that the claimant normally occupies both accommodation A and accommodation B with children or qualifying young persons for whom the claimant is responsible;

(c) the third condition is that the claimant meets the payment condition and the liability condition in respect of both accommodation A and accommodation B (and for these purposes it is irrelevant whether the claimant's liability is to the same or a different person).

(2) In the case of a relevant claimant, both accommodation A and accommodation B are to be treated as the single accommodation which the relevant claimant normally occupies as their home.

(3) In sub-paragraph (1), "provider of social housing" has the meaning given in paragraph 2 of Schedule 4.

Moving home: adaptations to new home for disabled person

2.369   **5.**—(1) Sub-paragraph (2) applies where—

(a) the claimant has moved into accommodation ("the new accommodation") and, immediately before the move, met the payment condition and liability condition in respect of the new accommodation; and

(b) there was a delay in moving in that was necessary to enable the new accommodation to be adapted to meet the disablement needs of a person specified in sub-paragraph (3).

(2) The claimant is to be treated as occupying both the new accommodation and the accommodation from which the move was made ("the old accommodation") if—

(a) immediately before the move, the claimant was entitled to the inclusion of the housing costs element in an award of universal credit in respect of the old accommodation; and

(b) the delay in moving into the new accommodation was reasonable.

(3) A person is specified in this sub-paragraph if the person is—

(a) a claimant or any child or qualifying young person for whom a claimant is responsible; and

(b) in receipt of—

(i) the care component of disability living allowance at the middle or highest rate,

(ii) attendance allowance, or

(iii) the daily living component of personal independence payment.

(4) No claimant may be treated as occupying both the old accommodation and the new accommodation under this paragraph for more than one month.

Claimant living in other accommodation because of reasonable fear of violence

2.370   **6.**—(1) This paragraph applies where—

(a) a claimant is occupying accommodation ("the other accommodation") other than the accommodation which they normally occupy as their home ("the home accommodation"); and

(b) it is unreasonable to expect the claimant to return to the home accommodation on account of the claimant's reasonable fear of violence in the home, or by a former partner, against the claimant or any child or qualifying young person for whom the claimant is responsible; but

(c) the claimant intends to return to the home accommodation.

(2) The claimant is to be treated as normally occupying both the home accommodation and the other accommodation as their home if—

(a) the claimant meets the payment condition and the liability condition in respect of both the home accommodation and other accommodation; and

(b) it is reasonable to include an amount in the housing costs element for the payments in respect of both the home accommodation and the other accommodation.

(3) Where the claimant meets the payment condition and the liability condition in respect of one accommodation only, the claimant is to be treated as normally occupying that accommodation as their home but only if it is reasonable to include an amount in the housing costs element for the payments in respect of that accommodation.

(4) No claimant may be treated as occupying both the home accommodation and the other accommodation under sub-paragraph (2) for more than 12 months.

Moving in delayed by adaptations to accommodation to meet disablement needs

7.—(1) The claimant is to be treated as having occupied accommodation before they moved into it where—　　2.371

(a) the claimant has since moved in and, immediately before the move, met the payment condition and the liability condition in respect of the accommodation;

(b) there was a delay in moving in that was necessary to enable the accommodation to be adapted to meet the disablement needs of a relevant person; and

(c) it was reasonable to delay moving in.

(2) "Relevant person" means a person specified in paragraph 5(3).

(3) No claimant may be treated as occupying accommodation under this paragraph for more than one month.

Moving into accommodation following stay in hospital or care home

8.—(1) The claimant is to be treated as having occupied accommodation before they moved into it where—　　2.372

(a) the claimant has since moved in and, immediately before the move, met the payment condition and the liability condition in respect of that accommodation; and

(b) the liability to make the payments arose while the claimant was a patient or accommodated in a care home (or, in the case of a joint claim, while both joint claimants were patients or were accommodated in a care home).

(2) No claimant may be treated as occupying the accommodation under this paragraph for more than one month.

(3) In this paragraph—

"care home" has the meaning given in paragraph 1 of Schedule 1;

"patient" means a person who is undergoing medical or other treatment as an in-patient in any hospital or similar institution.

PART 2

TREATED AS NOT OCCUPYING ACCOMMODATION

Periods of temporary absence exceeding 6 months

9.—(1) Subject to sub-paragraphs (2) and (3), a claimant is to be treated as no longer occupying accommodation from which they are temporarily absent where the absence exceeds, or is expected to exceed, 6 months.　　2.373

(2) Sub-paragraph (1) does not apply to a claimant who falls within paragraph 3.

(3) Where a claimant who falls within paragraph 6 is temporarily absent from the accommodation which they normally occupy as their home, the claimant is to be treated as no longer occupying that accommodation where the absence exceeds, or is expected to exceed, 12 months.

DEFINITIONS

"attendance allowance"—see reg.2.

"care home"—see Sch.1, para.1.

"child"—see WRA 2012 s.40.

"claimant"—*ibid.*
"disability living allowance"—see reg.2.
"partner"—*ibid.*
"personal independence payment"—*ibid.*
"provider of social housing"—see Sch.4, para.2.
"qualifying young person"—see WRA 2012 ss.40 and 10(5) and regs 2 and 5.

GENERAL NOTE

2.374   In order to be eligible for a housing costs element, the claimant (or claimants) must meet the three basic conditions in reg.25(2) to (4): the payment condition, the liability condition, and the occupation condition. This Schedule is concerned with the occupation condition.

Under reg.25(4) the claimant (or each claimant in the case of joint claimants: s.40 WRA 2012) must be treated as occupying the accommodation as his/her home and not be treated as not occupying it. Croft land is included (see para.2).

Paragraph 1

2.375   This contains the general rule that the claimant must be normally occupying the accommodation as their home (sub-para(1)). On the meaning of "normally occupying", see the notes to "dwelling occupied as the home" in reg.2 of the Income Support Regulations in Vol.II of this series.

In addition, the claimant cannot usually be treated as occupying accommodation which comprises more than one dwelling (sub-para.(2)). However, there are exceptions to these rules (see below). Where these exceptions do not apply, and the claimant (or claimants: s.40 WRA 2012) occupies more than one dwelling, to decide which is the dwelling normally occupied as the home, all the circumstances, including the people who live with the claimant (or claimants) in each dwelling, are to be taken into account (sub-para.(3)).

On the question of whether in certain circumstances two physically separate buildings can constitute one "dwelling", see the notes to reg.2 of the Income Support Regulations in Vol.II of this series. Where a claimant is housed in two dwellings by a "provider of social housing" (defined in Sch.4, para.2), see para.4 below.

Paragraph 3

2.376   If the claimant has to move into temporary accommodation because essential repairs (see *R(SB) 10/81*) are being carried out to their normal home, intends to return to that home, and satisfies the payment and liability conditions for either the temporary accommodation or their normal home (but not both), they are treated as occupying as their home the accommodation in respect of which the payment and liability conditions are met (sub-para.(1)). If the claimant satisfies the payment and liability conditions for both the temporary accommodation and their normal home, they are treated as occupying the accommodation that they normally occupy as their home (sub-para.(2)). This may not necessarily be the accommodation that was their normal home.

There is no time limit in para.3 itself as to how long it can apply.

Paragraph 4

2.377   This allows a housing costs element to be paid for two dwellings in the following circumstances. If the claimant (or claimants: s.40 WRA 2012) has been housed in two dwellings by a "provider of social housing" (defined in para.2 of Sch.4) due to the number of children and qualifying young persons living with them, the claimant normally occupies both dwellings with children or qualifying young persons (see reg.5) for whom they are responsible (see reg.4) and the claimant meets the payment and liability conditions in respect of both dwellings, the claimant will be treated as normally occupying both dwellings as their home.

This paragraph can apply without time limit.

See para.17 of Sch.4 as to how the housing costs element is calculated under para.4. A single calculation is made for both dwellings together. This will be carried out under Pt 5 of Sch.4 if the rent is paid to a social sector landlord for both dwellings and neither is temporary accommodation (see para.21 of Sch.4 for the meaning of "temporary accommodation"). Otherwise, the calculation is made under Pt 4 of Sch.4, including applying the four bedroom limit. Note that under para.25(3)–(4) of Sch.4, if the cap rent for the two dwellings is different (e.g. because they are in different areas), the cap rent that is lower at the time the housing costs element is first calculated is the cap rent that applies. The calculation of the renter's housing costs element will continue to be based on that cap rent for as long as the renter is housed in those two homes.

Paragraphs 5 and 7

Under para.5 a claimant (or claimants) can be treated as occupying two homes for up to one month if the claimant: **2.378**

- (i)   has moved into their new home;
- (ii) met the payment and liability conditions for that home immediately before they moved in,
- (iii) was entitled to a housing costs element in respect of their old home immediately before the move; and
- (iv) the delay in moving in was reasonable and was necessary to enable the new home to be adapted to the disablement needs (not defined) of the claimant (or claimants: s.40 WRA 2012) or any child or qualifying young person for whom the claimant (or claimants) is responsible. The person with the disablement needs must be in receipt of the middle or highest rate of the care component of disability living allowance, the daily living component of personal independence payment (either rate), attendance allowance or armed forces independence payment (note that the definition of "attendance allowance" in reg.2 includes armed forces independence payment).

If the above circumstances apply but the claimant was not receiving a housing costs element in respect of their old home immediately before they moved in, para.7 will apply to treat the claimant as occupying their home for up to one month before they move in.

On the meaning of "moving in" see *R(H) 9/05* and on "adapting the accommodation to meet disablement needs" see the notes to para.3(7)(c)(i) of Sch.3 to the Income Support Regulations in Vol.II of this series.

See para.18 of Sch.4 as to how the housing costs element is calculated under para.5. Note that any housing cost contributions for non-dependants are only deducted from the housing costs element for the old home.

Paragraph 6

If the claimant is living in accommodation other than the accommodation they normally occupy as their home because of a reasonable fear of violence in the home, or from a former partner against them or any child or qualifying young person (see reg.5) for whom they are responsible (see reg.4), and they intend to return to the accommodation they normally occupy as their home, they can be treated as occupying both for up to 12 months. This applies if they meet the payment and liability conditions in respect of both the accommodation they normally occupy as their home and the other accommodation, provided that it is reasonable to pay a housing costs element for both. If the claimant only satisfies the payment and liability conditions in respect of one accommodation, they will be treated as occupying that accommodation as their home but only if it is reasonable to pay a housing costs element for that accommodation.   **2.379**

If a claimant in these circumstances is living in a refuge, it is unlikely that they will meet the payment condition for that accommodation (see para.3(h), together with para.3A, of Sch.1, under which payments in respect of "specified accommodation" do not count as rent payments. "Specified accommodation" includes temporary accommodation provided by a local authority or a "relevant body" (defined in para.3A(6)) for people who have left home because of domestic violence (defined in reg.98(4)) (para.3A(4))). However, if they are living in "specified accommodation", they can claim housing benefit for that accommodation.

Note para.9(3) which provides that such a claimant can no longer be treated as temporarily absent from the accommodation which they normally occupy as their home if the absence lasts, or is expected to last, more than 12 months.

See para.19 of Sch.4 as to how the housing costs element is calculated under para.6 where the claimant is entitled to a housing costs element for both homes. This will be calculated for each home under Pt 4 of Sch.4 or under Pt 5 of Sch.4, as the case may be. Note that any housing cost contributions for non-dependants are only deducted from the housing costs element for the home that the claimant is normally occupying.

Paragraph 8

2.380   Under this paragraph a claimant can be treated as occupying their home for up to one month before they move in if they met the payment and liability conditions immediately before moving in and they became liable to make the payments while they were a patient (defined in sub-para.(3)) or in a care home (defined in para.1 of Sch.1), or in the case of joint claimants, while both of them were patients or in a care home.

Paragraph 9

2.381   Unless the absence is due to essential repairs (see para.3) or a fear of violence (see para.6), if a claimant is temporarily absent from the accommodation, they will be treated as no longer occupying it if the absence has lasted, or is expected to last, more than six months.

This is a considerably simplified provision compared with the rules for temporary absence that apply for the purposes of housing benefit and income support, old style JSA and old style ESA housing costs.

If at any time during the six months it becomes clear that the absence is likely to exceed six months, the claimant will be treated as no longer occupying the accommodation from that point (this could apply from the start if the absence was expected to last more than six months from the beginning). However, if the claimant returns to the accommodation for a period, even a very short period (24 hours?), the six months should restart (see *R v Penrith DC Housing Benefit Review Board ex p. Burt* (1990) 22 H.L.R. 292). See further the notes to para.3(8) to (12) of Sch.3 to the Income Support Regulations in Vol. II of this series.

Note that if a person was entitled to universal credit which included a housing costs element immediately before becoming a prisoner (defined in reg.2 as modified by SI 2020/409), and they have not been sentenced to a term in custody which is expected to last more than six months, they will be entitled to universal credit consisting of a housing costs element only during their first six months' absence as a prisoner (see reg.19(2) and (3)).

Regulation 26(2)

Schedule 4

Housing Costs Element for Renters

Part I

General

Introduction

2.382   **1.**—(1) This Schedule contains provisions about claimants to whom regulation 26(2) applies.
(2) Claimants who fall within sub-paragraph (1) are referred to in this Schedule as "renters" (and references to "joint renters" are to joint claimants to whom regulation 26(2) applies).

(3) Part 2 of this Schedule sets out [¹² [¹⁶ an exception]] to section 11(1) of the Act for certain renters in whose case an award of universal credit is not to include an amount of housing costs element calculated under this Schedule.

(4) The following Parts of this Schedule provide for the calculation of the amount of housing costs element to be included under regulation 26(2) in a renter's award of universal credit—

    (a) Part 3 contains general provisions that apply to all calculations, whether under Part 4 or Part 5;

    (b) Part 4 applies in relation to renters who occupy accommodation in the private rented sector [¹⁴ ...]; and

    (c) Part 5 applies in relation to renters who occupy accommodation in the social rented sector [¹⁴ ...].

Interpretation

2. In this Schedule—   **2.383**

[⁸ "exempt accommodation" has the meaning given in paragraph 4(10) of Schedule 3 to the Housing Benefit and Council Tax Benefit (Consequential Provisions) Regulations 2006;]

"extended benefit unit" has the meaning given in paragraph 9;

"Housing Act functions" means functions under section 122 of the Housing Act 1996 (functions of rent officers in connection with universal credit, housing benefit and rent allowance subsidy and housing credit);

"housing cost contribution" has the meaning given in paragraph 13;

"joint renter" has the meaning given in paragraph 1(2);

"listed persons", in relation to a renter, means—

    (a) the renter;

    (b) where the renter is a member of a couple, the other member of the couple; and

    (c) any child or qualifying young person for whom the renter (or either joint renter) is responsible;

[¹ "member of the armed forces" means a member of the regular forces or the reserve forces within the meaning of section 374 of the Armed Forces Act 2006;]

"non-dependant" has the meaning given in paragraph 9(2);

"provider of social housing" means—

    (a) a local authority;

    (b) a non-profit registered provider of social housing;

    (c) in relation to accommodation which is social housing, a profit-making registered provider of social housing;

    (d) a registered social landlord;

"registered social landlord" means—

    (a) a body which is registered in the register maintained by the Welsh Ministers under Chapter 1 of Part 1 of the Housing Act 1996;

    (b) a body which is registered in the register maintained by the Scottish Housing Regulator under section 20(1) of the Housing (Scotland) Act 2010;

"relevant payments" has the meaning given in paragraph 3;

"the Rent Officers Order 2013" means the Rent Officers (Universal Credit Functions) Order 2013;

"renter" means a single renter within the meaning of paragraph 1(2) or each of joint renters;

"renter who requires overnight care" is to be understood in accordance with paragraph 12(3) to (5);

"shared accommodation" has the meaning given in paragraph 27;

"social housing" has the meaning given in sections 68 to 77 of the Housing and Regeneration Act 2008.

"Relevant payments" for purposes of this Schedule

3.—(1) "Relevant payments" means one or more payments of any of the following descrip-   **2.384**
tions—

    (a) rent payments;

    (b) service charge payments.

(2) "Rent payments", in relation to any calculation under Part 4 or 5 of this Schedule, has the meaning given in paragraph 2 of Schedule 1.

(3) "Service charge payments"—

    (a) for the purposes of calculations under Part 4 of this Schedule, has the meaning given in paragraph 7 of Schedule 1;

    (b) for the purposes of calculations under Part 5 of this Schedule, is to be understood in accordance with paragraphs 7 and 8 of Schedule 1.

PART 2

[^{12} [^{16} EXCEPTION]] TO INCLUSION OF HOUSING COSTS ELEMENT

No housing costs element for 16 or 17 year old care leavers

2.385
4. Section 11(1) of the Act (housing costs) does not apply to any renter who is 16 or 17 years old and is a care leaver.

[^{12} No housing costs element for certain renters aged at least 18 but under 22

2.386
4A. [^{16} ...]]

Persons to whom paragraph 4A does not apply – general

2.387
4B. [^{16} ...]]

Persons to whom paragraph 4A does not apply – periods of work

2.388
4C. [^{16} ...]]]

PART 3

GENERAL PROVISIONS ABOUT CALCULATION OF AMOUNT OF
HOUSING COSTS ELEMENT FOR RENTERS

Application of Part 3

2.389
5. This Part contains provisions of general application in calculating the amount of a renter's housing costs element under Part 4 or 5 of this Schedule.

Payments taken into account

Relevant payments to be taken into account

2.390
6.—(1) Where a renter meets the payment condition, liability condition and occupation condition in respect of one or more descriptions of relevant payment, each such description is to be taken into account for the purposes of the calculation under Part 4 or 5 of this Schedule.

(2) No account is to be taken of any amount of a relevant payment to the extent that all of the conditions referred to in sub-paragraph (1) are not met in respect of that amount.

(3) Any particular payment for which a renter is liable is not to be brought into account more than once, whether in relation to the same or a different renter (but this does not prevent different payments of the same description being brought into account in respect of an assessment period).

Relevant payments calculated monthly

2.391
7.—(1) Where any relevant payment is to be taken into account under paragraph 6, the amount of that payment is to be calculated as a monthly amount.

(2) Where the period in respect of which a renter is liable to make a relevant payment is not a month, an amount is to be calculated as the monthly equivalent, so for example—

    (a) weekly payments are multiplied by 52 and divided by 12;

[^{7} (aa) two-weekly payments are multiplied by 26 and divided by 12;]

    (b) four-weekly payments are multiplied by 13 and divided by 12;

    (c) three-monthly payments are multiplied by 4 and divided by 12; and

    (d) annual payments are divided by 12.

(3) Where a renter is liable for relevant payments under arrangements that provide for one or more rent free periods, [^{7} subject to sub-paragraph (3A),] the monthly equivalent is to be calculated over 12 months by reference to the total number of relevant payments which the renter is liable to make in that 12 month period.

[^{7} (3A) Where sub-paragraph (3) applies and the relevant payments in question are—

    (a) weekly payments, the total number of weekly payments which the renter is liable to make in any 12 month period shall be calculated by reference to the formula—

$$52 - RFP;$$

    (b) two-weekly payments, the total number of two-weekly payments which the renter is liable to make in any 12 month period shall be calculated by reference to the formula—

$$26 - RFP;$$

    (c) four-weekly payments, the total number of four-weekly payments which the renter is liable to make in any 12 month period shall be calculated by reference to the formula—

13 – *RFP*;

where "RFP" is the number of rent free periods in the 12 month period in question.].

(4) "Rent free period" means any period in respect of which the renter has no liability to make one or more of the relevant payments which are to be taken into account under paragraph 6.

Room allocation

Size criteria applicable to the extended benefit unit of all renters

8.—(1) In calculating the amount of the renter's housing costs element under Part 4 or 5 of this Schedule, a determination is to be made in accordance with the provisions referred to in sub-paragraph (2) as to the category of accommodation which it is reasonable for the renter to occupy, having regard to the number of persons who are members of the renter's extended benefit unit (see paragraph 9).

(2) The provisions referred to in this sub-paragraph are the following provisions of this Schedule—

    (a) in respect of a calculation under Part 4, paragraphs 9 to 12 and 26 to 29;

    (b) in respect of a calculation under Part 5, paragraphs 9 to 12.

2.392

Extended benefit unit of a renter for purposes of this Schedule

9.—(1) For the purposes of this Schedule, the members of a renter's extended benefit unit are—

    (a) the renter (or joint renters);

    (b) any child or qualifying young person for whom the renter or either joint renter is responsible; and

    (c) any person who is a non-dependant.

(2) A person is a non-dependant if the person [6 normally] lives in the accommodation with the renter (or joint renters) and is none of the following—

    (a) a person within sub-paragraph (1)(a) or (b);

    (b) where the renter is a member of a couple claiming as a single person, the other member of the couple;

    (c) a foster child;

    (d) a person who is liable to make payments on a commercial basis in respect of the person's occupation of the accommodation (whether to the renter, joint renters or another person);

    (e) a person to whom the liability to make relevant payments is owed or a member of their household;

    (f) a person who has already been treated as a non-dependant in relation to a claim for universal credit by another person liable to make relevant payments in respect of the accommodation occupied by the renter.

[6 (g) a child or qualifying young person for whom no-one in the renter's extended benefit unit is responsible.]

(3) "Foster child" means a child in relation to whom the renter (or either joint renter) is a foster parent.

2.393

Number of bedrooms to which a renter is entitled

10.—(1) A renter is entitled to one bedroom for each of the following categories of persons in their extended benefit unit—

    (a) the renter (or joint renters);

    (b) a qualifying young person for whom the renter or either joint renter is responsible;

    (c) a non-dependant who is not a child;

    (d) two children who are under 10 years old;

    (e) two children of the same sex;

    (f) any other child.

(2) A member of the extended benefit unit to whom two or more of the descriptions in sub-paragraph (1) apply is to be allotted to whichever description results in the renter being entitled to the fewest bedrooms.

(3) In determining the number of bedrooms to which a renter is entitled, the following must also be taken into account—

    (a) the provisions of paragraph 11 as to treatment of periods of temporary absence of members of the renter's extended benefit unit;

    (b) any entitlement to an additional bedroom in accordance with paragraph 12;

    (c) for the purpose of any calculation under Part 4 of this Schedule, the additional requirements in paragraphs 26 to 29.

2.394

Temporary absence of member of renter's extended benefit unit

2.395   **11.**—(1) A member of the renter's extended benefit unit who is temporarily absent from the accommodation occupied by the renter is to be included in a determination of the number of bedrooms to which the renter is entitled ("relevant determination") in the circumstances specified in sub-paragraphs (2) to (4).

(2) In the case of a child or qualifying young person, the circumstances specified in this sub-paragraph are that the relevant determination relates to any time—

     (a) during the first 6 months of the absence of a child or qualifying young person for whom the renter is treated as not being responsible in accordance with regulation 4(6) (a) (child or qualifying young person looked after by local authority) where, immediately before the local authority started looking after them, the child or qualifying young person was included in the renter's extended benefit unit and the renter's award included the housing costs element;

     (b) during the first 6 months of the absence of a child or qualifying young person for whom the renter is treated as not being responsible in accordance with regulation 4(6) (b) (child or qualifying young person is a prisoner) where—

         (i) immediately before becoming a prisoner, the child or qualifying young person was included in the renter's extended benefit unit and the renter's award included the housing costs element, and

         (ii) the child or qualifying young person has not been sentenced to a term in custody that is expected to extend beyond that 6 months; or

     (c) before the renter or joint renter ceases to be responsible for a temporarily absent child or qualifying young person in accordance with regulation 4(7) (absence exceeding specified duration).

(3) In the case of a renter, the circumstances specified in this sub-paragraph are that the relevant determination relates to any time when—

     (a) the temporary absence from Great Britain of the renter is disregarded in accordance with regulation 11(1) or (2); or

     (b) the renter is a prisoner to whom regulation 19(2) (existing award includes housing costs when person becomes a prisoner) applies.

(4) In the case of a non-dependant, the circumstances specified in this sub-paragraph are that—

     (a) the relevant determination relates to any time during a period specified in sub-paragraph (5); and

     (b) immediately before the start of that period, the non-dependant was included in the renter's extended benefit unit and [², in the circumstances specified in sub-paragraph (5)(a) to (c),] the renter's award included the housing costs element.

(5) The specified periods are—

     (a) the first month of the non-dependant's temporary absence from Great Britain and, if the circumstances of the non-dependant are such as would be disregarded for the purposes of regulation 11(2) (death of a close relative), a further one month;

     (b) the first 6 months of the non-dependant's temporary absence from Great Britain in the circumstances described in regulation 11(3)(a) (absence solely in connection with treatment for illness or physical or mental impairment);

     (c) the first 6 months that the non-dependant is a prisoner where the non-dependant has not been sentenced to a term in custody that is expected to extend beyond that 6 months.

[³ (d) any period during which a non-dependant who is the son, daughter, step-son or step-daughter of a renter or joint renters is a member of the armed forces away on operations.]

(6) Any non-dependant who is temporarily absent from the accommodation occupied by the renter in circumstances other than those specified in sub-paragraphs (4) and (5) is not to be treated as being a member of the renter's extended benefit unit if that absence exceeds, or is expected to exceed, 6 months.

[⁶ **Additional room**

2.396   **12.**—[¹¹ (A1) A renter is entitled to an additional bedroom if one or more of the following persons satisfies the overnight care condition (see sub-paragraph (3))—

     (a) the renter;

     (b) a person in the renter's extended benefit unit;

     (c) a child in respect of whom the renter satisfies the foster parent condition (see sub-paragraphs (4) and (5)).]

(1) A renter is entitled to an additional bedroom if they satisfy any of the following conditions—

(a) [¹¹ . . .]

(b) the foster parent condition [¹¹ . . .]; or

(c) the disabled child condition (see sub-paragraph (6)) [¹¹;

(d) the disabled person condition (see sub-paragraph (6A))].

[¹¹ (2) Sub-paragraphs (A1) and (1) apply subject to sub-paragraphs (8) and (9).]

(3) [¹¹ A person satisfies] the overnight care condition if—

(a) they are in receipt of—

(i) the care component of disability living allowance at the middle or highest rate;

(ii) attendance allowance; or

(iii) the daily living component of personal independence payment;

(b) one or more persons who do not live in the renter's accommodation are engaged to provide overnight [¹¹ care for the person] and stay overnight in the accommodation on a regular basis; and

(c) overnight care is provided under arrangements entered into for that purpose.

(4) A renter satisfies the foster parent condition if the renter is—

(a) a foster parent; or

(b) an adopter with whom a child has been placed for adoption.

(5) For the purposes of sub-paragraph (4) "foster parent" includes a person who would be a foster parent, but for the fact that they do not currently have any child placed with them, provided that any period since the date when their last placement ended (or, if they have not yet had a child placed with them, since the date when they were approved to be a foster parent) does not exceed 12 months.

(6) A renter satisfies the disabled child condition if they or another member of their extended benefit unit are responsible for a child who would (but for the provisions of this paragraph) be expected to share a bedroom and that child is—

(a) in receipt of the care component of disability living allowance at the middle or highest rate; and

(b) by virtue of their disability, not reasonably able to share a room with another child.

[¹¹ (6A) A renter satisfies the disabled person condition if they would (but for the provisions of this paragraph) be expected to share a bedroom with a joint renter and—

(a) the renter is in receipt of—

(i) the care component of disability living allowance at the middle or highest rate;

(ii) attendance allowance at the higher rate;

(iii) the daily living component of personal independence payment; and

(b) the renter is, by virtue of their disability, not reasonably able to share a bedroom with the joint renter.]

(7) [¹¹ . . .]

(8) Where a renter, or one or both of joint renters, satisfy the disabled child condition in relation to one or more children, they are entitled to as many additional bedrooms as are necessary to ensure that each such child has their own bedroom.

[¹¹ (9) The renter is, or joint renters are, entitled to one additional bedroom for each of the following that apply—

(a) one or more persons satisfy the overnight care condition;

(b) the renter, or one or both of joint renters, satisfies the foster parent condition;

(c) the renter, or one or both of joint renters, satisfies the disabled child condition; or

(d) the renter, or one or both of joint renters, satisfies the disabled person condition.]]

Housing cost contributions

Housing cost contributions

13.—(1) In calculating the amount of the housing costs element under Part 4 or 5 of this Schedule, a deduction is to be made in respect of each non-dependant who is a member of the renter's extended benefit unit.   2.397

(2) Paragraph (1) is subject to paragraphs 15 and 16.

(3) Any amount to be deducted under sub-paragraph (1) is referred to in this Schedule as a "housing cost contribution".

Amount of housing cost contributions

14.—(1) The amount of each housing cost contribution to be deducted under paragraph 13 is [¹⁷ £75.15].   2.398

(2) Deductions are not to be made until the amount has been determined which results from all other steps in the calculation required in relation to the renter under Parts 4 and 5 of this Schedule.

(3) Where the sum of all the housing cost contributions to be deducted in the renter's case exceeds the amount referred to in sub-paragraph (2)—

    (a) the amount determined under this Schedule is to be reduced to nil; but

    (b) no further reduction in respect of housing cost contributions is to be made from the renter's award.

Exempt renters

2.399   **15.**—(1) No deduction is to be made under paragraph 13 in the case of—

    (a) any renter who is a single person to whom sub-paragraph (2) applies; or

    (b) any joint renter where at least one joint renter is a person to whom sub-paragraph (2) applies.

(2) This sub-paragraph applies to—

    (a) a person who is [⁹ . . .] blind;

    (b) a person in receipt of the care component of disability living allowance at the middle or highest rate;

    (c) a person in receipt of attendance allowance;

    (d) a person in receipt of the daily living component of personal independence payment;

    (e) a person who is entitled to a payment within paragraph (b), (c) or (d) but is not receiving it under, as the case may be—

        (i) regulation 8 of the Social Security (Disability Living Allowance) Regulations 1991,

        (ii) regulation 6 of the Social Security (Attendance Allowance) Regulations 1991,

        (iii) regulation 21 of the Social Security (General Benefit) Regulations 1982, or

        (iv) regulations under section 86 of the Act (payment of personal independence payment while a person is a hospital in-patient).

No deduction for housing cost contributions in respect of certain non-dependants

2.400   **16.**—(1) No deduction is to be made under paragraph 13 in respect of any non-dependant who is a member of the renter's extended benefit unit to whom sub-paragraph (2) applies.

(2) This sub-paragraph applies to—

    (a) a person who is under 21 years old;

    (b) a person in receipt of state pension credit;

    (c) a person in receipt of the care component of disability living allowance at the middle or highest rate;

    (d) a person in receipt of attendance allowance;

    (e) a person in receipt of the daily living component of personal independence payment;

    (f) a person who is entitled to a payment within paragraph (c), (d) or (e) but is not receiving it under, as the case may be—

        (i) regulation 8 of the Social Security (Disability Living Allowance) Regulations 1991,

        (ii) regulation 6 of the Social Security (Attendance Allowance) Regulations 1991,

        (iii) regulation 21 of the Social Security (General Benefit) Regulations 1982, or

        (iv) regulations under section 86 of the Act (payment of personal independence payment while a person is a hospital in-patient);

    (g) a person in receipt of carer's allowance;

    (h) a person who is a prisoner;

    (i) a person who is responsible for a child under 5 years old.

    [⁴ (j) a person who is a member of the armed forces away on operations who—

        (i) is the son, daughter, step-son or step-daughter of a renter or joint renters, and

        (ii) resided with the renter or joint renters immediately before leaving to go on operations and intends to return to reside with the renter or joint renters at the end of the operations.]

Calculations involving more than one accommodation

Single calculation for renter treated as occupying single accommodation

2.401   **17.**—(1) This paragraph applies to any renter where, under paragraph 4 of Schedule 3 (claimant housed in two dwellings by provider of social housing), two dwellings ("accommodation A" and "accommodation B") occupied by a renter are treated as the single accommodation in respect of which the renter meets the occupation condition.

(2) The amount of the renter's housing costs element is to be determined by a single calculation in respect of accommodation A and accommodation B as if they were one, taking account of—

(a) all relevant payments in respect of accommodation A and all relevant payments in respect of accommodation B; and

(b) the total number of bedrooms in accommodation A and accommodation B taken together.

[¹⁴ (3) The single calculation is to be made under Part 5 of this Schedule in any case where the renter's liability to make rent payments in respect of accommodation A and accommodation B is to a provider of social housing.]

(4) In any other case, the single calculation is to be made under Part 4 of this Schedule.

Calculation where move to new accommodation delayed for adaptations for disabled person

18.—(1) Sub-paragraph (2) applies to any renter where, under paragraph 5 of Schedule 3 (moving home: adaptations to new home for disabled person), the renter meets the occupation condition in respect of both the new accommodation and the old accommodation.

2.402

(2) The amount of the renter's housing costs element under this Schedule is to be calculated as follows.

Step 1

Calculate an amount in accordance with Part 4 or Part 5 of this Schedule (as the case may be) in respect of both—

(a) the new accommodation; and

(b) the old accommodation.

Step 2

Add together the amounts determined in step 1.

Step 3

If a deduction was made for housing cost contributions in respect of both the new accommodation and the old accommodation, take the amount of the housing costs contributions deducted in respect of the new accommodation and add that to the amount resulting from step 2.

(3) In this paragraph, references to "the new accommodation" and "the old accommodation" are to be understood in accordance with paragraph 5 of Schedule 3.

Calculation where renter moves out because of reasonable fear of violence

19.—(1) Sub-paragraph (2) applies to any renter where, under paragraph 6(2) of Schedule 3 (claimant living in other accommodation because of reasonable fear of violence), the renter meets the occupation condition in respect of both the home accommodation and the other accommodation.

2.403

(2) The amount of the renter's housing costs element under this Schedule is to be calculated as follows:

Step 1

Calculate an amount in accordance with Part 4 or Part 5 of this Schedule (as the case may be) in respect of—

(a) the home accommodation; and

(b) the other accommodation.

Step 2

Add together the amounts determined in step 1.

Step 3

If a deduction was made for housing cost contributions in respect of both the home accommodation and the other accommodation—

(c) determine which accommodation the renter normally occupies as their home; and

(d) take the amount of the housing costs contributions deducted in respect of the accommodation not so occupied and add that to the amount resulting from step 2.

(3) In this paragraph, references to "the home accommodation" and "the other accommodation" are to be understood in accordance with paragraph 6 of Schedule 3.

PART 4

PRIVATE RENTED SECTOR [¹⁴ ...]

Application of Part 4

2.404   **20.**—[¹⁴ (1) This Part applies to renters who are liable to make rent payments to a person other than a provider of social housing.]

     (2) Sub-paragraph (1) applies irrespective of whether renters are also liable to make service charge payments.

Meaning of "temporary accommodation"

2.405   **21.** [¹⁴ ...]

The calculation of the housing costs element under this Part

The amount of housing costs element under this Part

2.406   **22.** The amount of the renter's housing costs element under this Part is to be calculated as follows:

Step 1

     Determine—
         (a) the amount of the renter's core rent; and
         (b) the amount of the renter's cap rent,
and identify which is the lower amount (if both amounts are the same, that is the identified amount).

Step 2

     Deduct the sum of the housing cost contributions (if any) under paragraph 13 from the amount identified in step 1.
     The result is the amount of the renter's housing costs element calculated under this Part.

Core rent

2.407   **23.** Except where paragraph 24 applies, the renter's core rent is to be determined as follows:

Step 1

     Determine the amount of each relevant payment to be taken into account under paragraph 6.

Step 2

     Determine the period in respect of which each relevant payment is payable and, in accordance with paragraph 7, determine the amount of the payment in respect of a month.

Step 3

     If there is more than one relevant payment, add together the amounts determined in step 2 in relation to all relevant payments.
     The result is the renter's core rent.

Core rent for joint tenants

2.408   **24.**—(1) This paragraph applies where, in respect of the accommodation occupied by the renter, one or more persons other than the renter are liable to make relevant payments which are of the same description as those for which the renter is liable and which are to be taken into account under paragraph 6.

     (2) The following steps are to be taken in order to determine the renter's core rent.

Step 1

     Determine the total of all relevant payments referred to in sub-paragraph (1) for which the renter and others are liable in respect of the accommodation taken as a whole.

Step 2

     Determine the period in respect of which each relevant payment is payable and, in accordance with paragraph 7, determine the amount of the payment in respect of a month.

Step 3

Add together all of the amounts determined in step 2 in relation to all relevant payments.

Step 4

Find the allocated amount in accordance with whichever of sub-paragraphs (3) to (5) applies in the renter's case.

The result is the renter's core rent.

(3) Where the only persons liable to make relevant payments are listed persons, the allocated amount is the amount resulting from step 3 in sub-paragraph (2).

(4) Where the persons liable for the relevant payments are one or more listed persons and one or more other persons, the allocated amount is to be found by the applying the formula—

$$\left(\frac{A}{B} \right) \times C$$

where—

"A" is the amount resulting from step 3 in sub-paragraph (2),

"B" is the total number of all persons (including listed persons) liable to make the relevant payments, and

"C" is the number of listed persons [5 liable to make relevant payments].

(5) If the Secretary of State is satisfied that it would be unreasonable to allocate the amount resulting from step 3 in sub-paragraph (2) in accordance with sub-paragraph (4), that amount is to be allocated in such manner as the Secretary of State considers appropriate in all the circumstances, having regard (among other things) to the number of persons liable and the proportion of the relevant payments for which each of them is liable.

Cap rent

25.—(1) The renter's cap rent is to be determined as follows.   **2.409**

Step 1

Determine the category of accommodation to which the renter is entitled under paragraphs 8 to 12 and 26 to 29.

Step 2

Having regard to the determination at step 1, determine the maximum allowable amount for the renter under sub-paragraph (2) or (4) (as the case may be).

The result is the renter's cap rent.

(2) The maximum allowable amount to be used in relation to the renter is the local housing allowance which applies at the relevant time to—
  (a) the broad rental market area in which the renter's accommodation is situated; and
  (b) the category of accommodation determined at step 1 as that to which the renter is entitled.

(3) But the maximum allowable amount in relation to the renter is to be determined under sub-paragraph (4) in any case where—
  (a) paragraph 4 of Schedule 3 (claimant housed in two dwellings by provider of social housing) applies to the renter; and
  (b) the maximum allowable amount determined under sub-paragraph (2) for the renter in relation to accommodation A and the amount so determined in relation to accommodation B are different (references to accommodation A and accommodation B are to be understood in accordance with paragraph 4 of Schedule 3); and
  (c) a single calculation is to be made in relation to the renter under paragraph 17 (renter treated as occupying single accommodation).

(4) In any such case, the maximum allowable amount to be used in making the single calculation required by paragraph 17—
  (a) is to be determined by reference to the accommodation for which the amount referred to in sub-paragraph (3)(b) is lower when the calculation is first made; and
  (b) is to continue to be determined by reference to that accommodation for so long as paragraph 4 of Schedule 3 applies to the renter in respect of the same accommodation A and the same accommodation B; and
  (c) is to be re-determined in accordance with paragraphs (a) and (b) on each occasion when the renter is re-housed in any other accommodation, provided that paragraph 4 of Schedule 3 continues to apply to the renter.

(5) In this paragraph—

"broad rental market area" means the broad rental market area determined under article 3 of the Rent Officers Order 2013;

"local housing allowance", in relation to a broad rental market area, means the amount determined by a rent officer for that area under article 4 of the Rent Officers Order 2013;

"relevant time" means the time at which the amount of the renter's housing costs element is calculated under paragraph 22.

Further provisions about size criteria for cases to which this Part applies

Four bedroom limit

2.410   **26.** In calculating the amount of a renter's housing costs element under paragraph 22, no renter is entitled to more than 4 bedrooms.

Specified renters entitled to shared accommodation only

2.411   **27.**—(1) In calculating the amount of a renter's housing costs element under paragraph 22, any specified renter (within the meaning of paragraph 28) is entitled to shared accommodation only.

(2) "Shared accommodation" means the category of accommodation specified in paragraph 1(a) of Schedule 1 to the Rent Officers Order 2013.

Meaning of "specified renters"

2.412   **28.**—(1) For the purposes of paragraph 27, "specified renter" means a renter in respect of whom all of the following conditions are met.

(2) The first condition is that the renter is a single person (or a member of a couple claiming as a single person) who—

    (a) is under 35 years old; and

    (b) is not an excepted person under paragraph 29.

(3) The second condition is that the renter is not responsible for any children or qualifying young persons.

(4) The third condition is that no person is a non-dependant in relation to the renter.

Renters excepted from shared accommodation

2.413   **29.**—(1) "Excepted person" means any renter ("E") who falls within any of sub-paragraphs (2) to [15 (9A)].

[10 (2) E is at least 18 but under 22 years old and was a care leaver (within the meaning of regulation 8) before reaching the age of 18.]

(3) [10 . . .]

(4) E is at least 25 but under 35 years old and—

    (a) has, for a total of at least 3 months (whether or not continuously), lived in one or more hostels for homeless people; and

    (b) whilst E was living in such a hostel, was offered and has accepted services which the Secretary of State considers are intended to assist E to be rehabilitated or resettled within the community.

(5) E is under 35 years old and is in receipt of—

    (a) the care component of disability living allowance at the middle or highest rate;

    (b) attendance allowance; or

    (c) the daily living component of personal independence payment.

(6) In relation to England and Wales, E is under 35 years old and is the subject of active multi-agency management pursuant to arrangements established by a responsible authority under section 325(2) of the Criminal Justice Act 2003 (arrangements for assessing etc. risks posed by certain offenders).

(7) In relation to Scotland, E is under 35 years old and is the subject of active multi-agency risk management pursuant to arrangements established by the responsible authorities under section 10(1) of the 2005 Act (arrangements for assessing and managing risks posed by certain offenders).

(8) In relation to Scotland, E is under 35 years old and—

    (a) section 10(1) of the 2005 Act does not apply to E by reason only of the fact that section 10(1)(b) or (d) has not been brought fully into force; and

    (b) E is considered by the Secretary of State to be a person who may cause serious harm to the public at large.

(9) In relation to Scotland, E is under 35 years old and—

    (a) section 10(1) of the 2005 Act does not apply to E by reason only of the fact that section 10(1)(e) has not been brought fully into force; and

(b) by reason of an offence of which E has been convicted, E is considered by the Secretary of State to be a person who may cause serious harm to the public at large.
[¹⁵ (9A) E is under 35 years old and satisfies the foster parent condition (within the meaning of paragraph 12(4)).]

(10) In this paragraph—

"the 2005 Act" means the Management of Offenders etc. (Scotland) Act 2005;

"care home", "registered charity" and "voluntary organisation" have the meaning given in Schedule 1;

"hostel" means a building—

(a) in which there is provided, for persons generally or for a class of persons, domestic accommodation, otherwise than in separate and self-contained premises, and either board or facilities for the preparation of food adequate to the needs of those persons, or both; and

(b) which—

   (i) is managed or owned by a provider of social housing other than a local authority, or

   (ii) is operated other than on a commercial basis and in respect of which funds are provided wholly or in part by a government department or agency or a local authority, or

   (iii) is managed by a voluntary organisation or a registered charity and provides care, support or supervision with a view to assisting those persons to be rehabilitated or resettled within the community; and

(c) which is not a care home;

"hostel for homeless people" means a hostel the main purpose of which is to provide accommodation together with care, support or supervision for homeless people with a view to assisting such persons to be rehabilitated or resettled within the community.

PART 5

SOCIAL RENTED SECTOR [¹⁴ ...]

Application of Part 5

30.—[¹⁴ (1)This Part applies to renters who are liable to make rent payments to a provider of social housing.]   **2.414**

(2) Sub-paragraph (1) applies irrespective of whether renters are also liable to make service charge payments.

[¹³ Amount taken into account as the relevant payment]

Deduction from relevant payments of amounts relating to use of particular accommodation

31. In determining the amount of any relevant payment to be taken into account under paragraph 6, a deduction is to be made for any amount which the Secretary of State is satisfied—   **2.415**

(a) is included in the relevant payment; but

(b) relates to the supply to the accommodation of a commodity (such as water or fuel) for use by any member of the renter's extended benefit unit.

Power to apply to rent officer if relevant payments excessive

32.—(1) Sub-paragraph (2) applies where it appears to the Secretary of State that the amount of any relevant payment for which the renter is liable in respect of accommodation occupied by the renter is greater than it is reasonable to meet by way of the housing costs element under this Part.   **2.416**

(2) The Secretary of State may apply to a rent officer for a determination to be made as to the amount of the relevant payment by the officer in exercise of the officer's Housing Act functions.

(3) Sub-paragraph (4) applies in any case where a rent officer determines that a landlord might, at the time of the application under sub-paragraph (2), reasonably have expected to obtain a lower amount of the description of relevant payment referred to the rent officer.

(4) The lower amount determined by the rent officer is to be used in making the calculation under this Part, instead of the amount of the relevant payment for which the renter is liable, unless the Secretary of State is satisfied that it is not appropriate to use that lower amount.

[¹³ Reduction under tenant incentive scheme   **2.417**

32A.—(1) Where a reduction in the rent or service charge payments for which a renter would otherwise have been liable is applied by a provider of social housing under an approved tenant incentive scheme, the amount of any relevant payment to be taken into account under paragraph 6 is to be determined as if no such reduction had been applied.

(2) In paragraph (1) "approved tenant incentive scheme" means a scheme which is—

    (a) operated by a provider of social housing and designed to avoid rent arrears by allowing reductions in rent or service charges or other advantages in return for meeting specified conditions; and

    (b) approved by the Secretary of State.]

The calculation of the housing costs element under this Part

The amount of housing costs element

2.418   **33.** The amount of the renter's housing costs element under this Part is to be calculated by reference to the formula—

$$S - HCC$$

where—

"S" is the amount resulting from whichever of paragraph 34 or 35 applies in the renter's case, and

"HCC" is the sum of the housing cost contributions (if any) under paragraph 13.

Determining the amount from which HCC deductions are to be made

2.419   **34.** Except where paragraph 35 applies, amount S referred to in paragraph 33 is to be found as follows:

Step 1

Determine which relevant payments are to be taken into account under paragraph 6 and determine the amount of each of them (applying paragraphs 31 and 32(3) and (4) as necessary).

Step 2

Determine the period in respect of which each relevant payment is payable and, in accordance with paragraph 7, determine the amount of the payment in respect of a month.

Step 3

If there is more than one relevant payment, add together the amounts determined in step 2 in relation to all relevant payments.

Step 4

Determine under paragraph 36(1) whether an under-occupation deduction is to be made and, if one is to be made, determine the amount of the deduction under paragraph 36(2) and deduct it from the amount resulting from step 2 or 3 (as the case may be).

The result is amount S from which the sum of the housing costs contributions are to be deducted under paragraph 33.

Determining the amount from which HCC deductions are to be made: joint tenants

2.420   **35.**—(1) This paragraph applies where, in respect of the accommodation occupied by the renter, one or more persons other than the renter is liable to make relevant payments which are of the same description as those for which the renter is liable and which are to be taken into account under paragraph 6.

(2) Amount S referred to in paragraph 33 is to be found as follows:

Step 1

Determine the total of all relevant payments referred to in sub-paragraph (1) for which the renter and others are liable in respect of the accommodation taken as a whole (applying paragraphs 31 and 32(3) and (4) as necessary).

Step 2

Determine the period in respect of which each relevant payment is payable and, in accordance with paragraph 7, determine the amount of the payment in respect of a month.

Step 3

Add together all of the amounts determined in step 2 in relation to all relevant payments.

Step 4

Find amount S in accordance with whichever of sub-paragraphs (3) to (5) applies in the renter's case.

The result is amount S from which the sum of the housing costs contributions are to be deducted under paragraph 33.

(3) Where the only persons liable to make relevant payments are listed persons, amount S is the amount resulting from step 3 in sub-paragraph (2) less the amount of the under-occupation deduction (if any) required by paragraph 36.

(4) Where the persons liable for the relevant payments are one or more listed persons and one or more other persons, amount S is to be found by the applying the formula—

$$\left(\frac{A}{B}\right) \times C$$

where—

"A" is the amount resulting from step 3 in sub-paragraph (2),

"B" is the total number of all persons (including listed persons) liable to make the relevant payments, and

"C" is the number of listed persons [5 liable to make relevant payments].

(5) If the Secretary of State is satisfied that it would be unreasonable to determine amount S in accordance with sub-paragraph (4), amount S is to be determined in such manner as the Secretary of State considers appropriate in all the circumstances, having regard (among other things) to the number of persons liable and the proportion of the relevant payments for which each of them is liable.

Under-occupancy deduction

36.—(1) A deduction for under-occupancy is to be made under this paragraph where the number of bedrooms in the accommodation exceeds the number of bedrooms to which the renter is entitled under paragraphs 8 to 12.

2.421

(2) Where a deduction is to be made, the amount of the deduction is to be determined by the formula—

$$A \times B$$

where—

"A"—

  (a) in relation to any deduction under paragraph 34, is the amount resulting from step 2 or 3 in that paragraph (as the case may be), or

  (b) in relation to any deduction under paragraph 35(3), is the amount resulting from step 3 in paragraph 35(2);

"B" is the relevant percentage.

(3) The relevant percentage is 14% in the case of one excess bedroom.

(4) The relevant percentage is 25% in the case of two or more excess bedrooms.

(5) No deduction for under-occupation is to be made in calculating the amount of the renter's housing costs element under this Part in any case to which regulation 26(4) to (6) (shared ownership) applies.

AMENDMENTS

1. Universal Credit (Miscellaneous Amendments) Regulations 2013 (SI 2013/803), reg.2(3)(a) (April 29, 2013).

2. Universal Credit (Miscellaneous Amendments) Regulations 2013 (SI 2013/803), reg.2(3)(b)(i) (April 29, 2013).

3. Universal Credit (Miscellaneous Amendments) Regulations 2013 (SI 2013/803), reg.2(3)(b)(ii) (April 29, 2013).

4. Universal Credit (Miscellaneous Amendments) Regulations 2013 (SI 2013/803), reg.2(3)(e) (April 29, 2013).

5. Social Security (Miscellaneous Amendments) (No.2) Regulations 2013 (SI 2013/1508), reg.3(10) (July 29, 2013).

6. Housing Benefit and Universal Credit (Size Criteria) (Miscellaneous Amendments) Regulations 2013 (SI 2013/2828), reg.4 (December 4, 2013).

7. Universal Credit and Miscellaneous Amendments Regulations 2014 (SI 2014/597) reg.2(13) (April 28, 2014).

8. Housing Benefit and Universal Credit (Supported Accommodation) (Amendment) Regulations 2014 (SI 2014/771) reg.2(3) (November 3, 2014).

9. Universal Credit and Miscellaneous Amendments (No.2) Regulations 2014 (SI 2014/2888) reg.3(1)(c) (November 26, 2014, or in the case of existing awards, the first assessment period beginning on or after November 26, 2014).

10. Universal Credit (Care Leavers and Looked After Children) Amendment Regulations 2016 (SI 2016/543) reg.3 (May 26, 2016).

11. Housing Benefit and Universal Credit (Size Criteria) (Miscellaneous Amendments) Regulations 2017 (SI 2017/213) reg.6 (Assessment periods beginning on or after April 1, 2017).

12. Universal Credit (Housing Costs Element for claimants aged 18 to 21) (Amendment) Regulations 2017 (SI 2017/652) reg.2(1) and (3) (April 1, 2017).

13. Universal Credit (Tenant Incentive Scheme) Amendment Regulations 2017 (SI 2017/427) reg.2 (April 30, 2017).

14. Universal Credit (Miscellaneous Amendments, Saving and Transitional Provision) Regulations 2018 (SI 2018/65) reg.3(13) (April 11, 2018).

15. Universal Credit and Jobseeker's Allowance (Miscellaneous Amendments) Regulations 2018 (SI 2018/1129) reg.3(1) and (6)(d) (November 28, 2018).

16. Universal Credit and Jobseeker's Allowance (Miscellaneous Amendments) Regulations 2018 (SI 2018/1129) reg.3(1) and (6)(a)-(c) (December 31, 2018).

17. Social Security Benefits Up-rating Order 2020 (SI 2020/234) art.31(3) (Assessment periods beginning on or after April 6, 2019).

DEFINITIONS

"the Act"—see reg.2.
"assessment period"—see WRA 2012 ss.40 and 7(2) and reg.21.
"attendance allowance"—see reg.2.
"blind"—*ibid.*
"care leaver"—see regs 2 and 8.
"carer's allowance"—see reg.2.
"child"—see WRA 2012 s.40.
"claim"—*ibid.*
"claimant"—see WRA 2012 s.40.
"couple"—see WRA 2012 ss.39 and 40.
"disability living allowance"—see reg.2.
"disabled"—see WRA 2012 s.40.
"foster parent"—see reg.2.
"joint claimants"—see WRA 2012 s.40.
"local authority"—see reg.2.
"personal independence payment"—*ibid.*
"prisoner"—see reg.2 as modified by SI 2020/409.
"qualifying young person"—see WRA 2012 ss.40 and 10(5) and regs 2 and 5.
"registered as blind"—see reg.2.
"single person"—see WRA 2012 ss.40 and 1(2)(a).

GENERAL NOTE

2.422   *Paragraphs 1–7*
This Schedule concerns the calculation of the housing costs element for "renters" (see para.1(2)). For the definition of "renter" see para.2. References to "joint renters" are to joint claimants who are renters (para.1(2)).

For a renter (or joint renters) to be entitled to a housing costs element under this Schedule, they must meet the payment, liability and occupation conditions in respect of one or more "relevant payments" (para.6(1) and (2)).

"Relevant payments" for the purpose of Sch.4 mean rent payments (for the meaning of rent payments see para.2 of Sch.1 and note the exclusions in para.3) and service charges (on which see para. 7 of Sch.1 in relation to service charge payments calculated under Pt.4 of this Schedule and paras 7 and 8 of Sch.1 in relation to service charge payments calculated under Pt.5 of this Schedule (para.3)). Relevant payments are calculated as a monthly amount (see para.7). Where a renter has the benefit of rent and/or service charge free periods (see the definition of "rent free period" in para.7(4)), the conversion to a monthly figure is based on a standard 52 week year (see para. 7(3) and the formula in para.7(3A)).

Para 4 establishes an exception: no housing costs element is to be included in the universal credit award of any 16 or 17 year old renter who is a care leaver as defined in reg.8(4)). The former exclusion of certain 18-21 year olds from entitlement to hosuing costs (as to which see pp.359-360 and 388-389 of the 2018-19 edition of this volume) was revoked with effect from December 31, 2018 by SI 2018/1129.

Part 3 of this Schedule contains general provisions, which apply to all calculations under the Schedule. The rules in Pt 4 apply to renters in the private sector or who occupy temporary accommodation. Part 5 applies to renters in the social rented sector.

A housing costs element for renters is normally paid to the claimant as part of their universal credit award. However, it can be paid to another person (e.g. the claimant's landlord) if this appears to the Secretary of State to be necessary to protect the interest of the claimant, their partner, a child or qualifying young person for whom the claimant or their partner is responsible or a severely disabled person in respect of whom the claimant receives a carer element (see reg.58(1) of the Claims and Payments Regulations 2013).

Note also reg.39(4) of the Decisions and Appeals Regulations 2013 which provides that if the Secretary of State considers that he does not have all the relevant information or evidence to decide what housing costs element to award, the decision will be made on the basis of the housing costs element that can immediately be awarded.

Paragraphs 8–12 and 26–29

In order to calculate the amount of a renter's housing costs element, it is first **2.423** necessary to decide the number of "bedrooms"—a word that is not defined—that they are allowed under "the size criteria" (para.8). This depends on who counts as a member of the renter's "extended benefit unit".

The extended benefit unit comprises the renter, or joint renters, any child or qualifying young person (see reg.5) for whom the renter or either joint renter is responsible (see reg.4), and any non-dependant (para.9(1)).

A non-dependant is a person who normally lives in the renter's (or joint renters') accommodation and who is not excluded under para.9(2). There is no definition of "normally lives in the accommodation" but see the notes to reg.3(1) of the Income Support Regulations in Vol.II of this series on the general meaning of "residing with".

See paras 10–12 for the number of bedrooms allowed. Para.12 has been amended with effect from April 1, 2017 by SI 2017/213 to reflect the judgment of the Supreme Court in *R (Carmichael and Rourke) (formerly known as MA and Others) v Secretary of State for Work and Pensions* [2016] UKSC 58 that the previous law discriminated unlawfully against adult couples who cannot share a bedroom because of the disabilities of at least one member of the couple and renters who need an extra room to accommodate an overnight carer for a disabled child.

The effect of the *Carmichael* decision was that, as they related to those groups, the restrictions in paras 10-12 had been unlawful since they came into force (and that the equivalent restrictions in the housing benefit schemes had been unlawful since April 1, 2013, when they came into force). As the legislation was only amended to remove the discrimination with effect from April 1, 2017, the question arose what the First-tier Tribunal and Upper Tribunal should do in appeals relating to the intervening period. In *Secretary of State for Work and Pensions v Carmichael and Sefton Council* [2018] EWCA Civ 548, the Court of Appeal decided by a majority—and contrary to the previously orthodox view of the law—that courts and tribunals have no power to disapply either primary or secondary legislation that infringes Convention Rights. The Supreme Court has granted permission to appeal to claimants in two other cases, *DL and RR v Secretary of State for Work and Pensions*: see further [2018] UKUT 335 (AAC) and the discussion at para.4.21 of Vol.III.

Note that in the case of renters in the private sector or who occupy temporary accommodation (see para.21 for the meaning of "temporary accommodation") the maximum number of bedrooms allowed is four (see para.26). There is no limit for renters in the social rented sector. In addition, in the case of private sector renters and those in temporary accommodation, the housing costs element for single claimants (including a member of a couple who is claiming as a single person: see reg.3(3)) aged under 35, with no children or qualifying young persons for whom they are responsible and no non-dependants, is restricted to the local housing allowance rate for one bedroom shared accommodation, unless they are exempt from this restriction (see paras 27–29).

Under para.10, a renter is allowed one bedroom for each of the categories of people in they extended benefit unit listed in sub-para.(1). If a person falls into more than one category, they are treated as in the category that results in the renter being allowed the lowest number of bedrooms (see sub-para.(2)). Paragraph F3112 ADM gives the following example of when sub-para.(2) might apply. A couple have four children, two boys aged 15 and 6 and two girls aged 12 and 8. The two boys could be allocated one room and the two girls one room under sub-para.(1)(e). Alternatively, having allocated the two girls one room under sub-para.(1)(e), the boys could be allocated one room each under sub-para.(1)(f). But as the first alternative results in a fewer number of bedrooms, that will be the number of bedrooms (two) that is allocated.

Note that joint renters (i.e. joint claimants: see para.1(2)) are allowed one bedroom but a non-dependant couple will be allocated one bedroom each (although a housing cost contribution (see paras 13–16) may be made in respect of each of them).

Under para.12, a renter is allowed additional bedrooms for each of the following conditions that they meet: (i) the overnight care condition (for the test for this see sub-para.(3)); (ii) the foster parent condition (see sub-paras (4) and (5) for the test); or (iii) the disabled child condition (see sub-para.(6) for the test). If the renter satisfies two or more of the conditions, the number of additional bedrooms allowed will be the total for both or all conditions (sub-para.(9)).

If both joint renters (i.e. joint claimants: see para.1(2)) satisfy the overnight care condition, they will only be allowed one additional bedroom (sub-para.(7)). (Note that the overnight care condition does not apply in the case of a disabled child who needs overnight care, but see the Court of Appeal's judgment in *Rutherford* below.) Similarly, only one additional bedroom will be allowed if both joint renters meet the foster parent condition (sub-para.(7)). However, if one or both of them satisfies both these conditions, one additional bedroom will be allowed in respect of each condition.

Example

2.424   Amy and Nick are foster parents to two children. Nick also meets the overnight care condition. They are allowed two additional bedrooms. One for satisfying the overnight care condition and one for satisfying the foster parent condition.

If the disabled child condition is met, one additional bedroom will be allowed for each disabled child (see sub-para.(8)).

Note that the disabled child condition applies if it is the renter (or joint renters) *or* a member of the renter's extended benefit unit (i.e. including a non-dependant) who is responsible for the disabled child. The requirement under sub-para.(6)(b) that the child is "not reasonably able to share a room with another child" will be a matter of judgment, depending on the circumstances.

See para.11 for the circumstances in which a renter, a child or qualifying young person or a non-dependant will continue to count for the purpose of deciding the number of bedrooms allowed, despite being temporarily absent. Note also the temporary absence rule for a claimant (or claimants) in para.9 of Sch.3.

See also reg.37 (run-on after a death). Under this provision if a joint claimant, a child or qualifying young person (see reg.5) for whom a claimant was responsible (see reg.4), a severely disabled person for whom a claimant had regular and substantial caring responsibilities (see reg.30) or a non-dependant who was a member of the claimant's extended benefit unit (para.9(1)(c) and (2)) dies the claimant's universal credit award continues to be calculated as if the person had not died for the assessment period in which the death occurred and the following two assessment periods. Thus if such a death affects the number of bedrooms a renter is allowed, it will not do so for that run-on period.

Paragraphs 13–16

After the calculation of the renter's (or joint renters') housing costs element has been carried out under Pt 4 or 5 of this Schedule, a deduction (referred to as a "housing cost contribution") is made for non-dependants, unless they, or the renter, or joint renters, are exempt. The deduction has been £73.89 since April 8, 2019 for each non-dependant who is a member of the renter's extended benefit unit. **2.425**

Paragraphs 17–19

See the notes to paras 4, 5 and 6 of Sch.3. **2.426**

Paragraphs 20–25

The housing costs element for private sector renters and those in temporary accommodation (as defined in para.21) is calculated by taking the lower of the renter's core rent and their cap rent and deducting from that amount any housing cost contributions (para.22). **2.427**

Core rent

If the renter is solely liable to make the relevant payments, their core rent is the total of the monthly equivalents of the rent payments (as defined in para.2 of Sch.1) and service charges (see para.7 of Sch.1) that they are liable (or treated as liable) to pay (para.23). **2.428**

If the renter is jointly liable with another person or persons to make the relevant payments, their core rent is worked out by taking the total of the monthly equivalents of the rent payments and service charges for which they and the other person(s) are liable for the whole accommodation and applying the following rules.

If the only people who are jointly liable are "listed persons" (as defined in para.2) (i.e. the renter, their partner and any child or qualifying young person for whom either of them is responsible), the renter's core rent is that total amount (para.24(3)). If the liability is with one or more people who are not listed persons, the total amount is divided by the number of people who are liable and multiplied by the number of listed persons who are liable to make the relevant payments (para.24(4)). This is the renter's core rent. If, however, the Secretary of State (and on appeal a tribunal) is satisfied that it would be unreasonable to apportion the liability in this way, it is to be apportioned in a way that is appropriate in the circumstances (para.24(5)). Paragraph F3197 ADM gives the following example of where such an adjustment might be appropriate. Two brothers are joint tenants of a three bedroom property. One brother has his daughter living with him and pays two thirds of the rent. The decision maker considers that this is reasonable and that the appropriate core rent for that brother is two thirds (not half) of the rent payable.

Cap rent

2.429   A renter's cap rent depends on the category of dwelling, i.e. how many bedrooms they are allowed under the size criteria, subject to the four bedroom limit (see paras 8–12 and 26–29). Their cap rent is the local housing allowance that applies at the time their housing costs element is calculated for that category of dwelling in the area in which they live (para.25(1) and (2)). For how the cap rent is calculated if para.4 of Sch.3 (claimant housed in two dwellings by provider of social housing) applies, see the note to para.4 of Sch.3.

Paragraphs 30–36

2.430   The housing costs element for social sector renters (other than those in temporary accommodation, as defined in para.21) is calculated as follows. First, a deduction is made from any relevant payments (as defined in para.6) of any amount that is for the supply of a commodity (e.g. water or fuel) to the accommodation for use by the renter or any member of their extended benefit unit (para.31). Secondly, if, on the application of the Secretary of State, a rent officer has determined that a landlord might reasonably expect to get a lower amount than the amount of the relevant payment the renter pays, that lower figure will be used in the calculation of the renter's housing costs element, unless the Secretary of State (or on appeal a tribunal) considers that it is not appropriate to use that lower amount (para.32). An example might be where the rent is higher because it includes payment for modifications made to enable a disabled person to live in the property (see para.F3253 ADM) but the wording of para.32(4) is quite wide and is not restricted to this type of situation. Note, however, that (like housing benefit) there is no right of appeal against "so much of a decision as adopts a decision of a rent officer . . ." (para.6 of Sch.3 to the Decisions and Appeals Regulations 2013).

Thirdly, if the number of bedrooms in the accommodation is more than the number the renter is allowed under paras 8–12, an "under-occupation deduction" will be made. The reduction is 14 per cent in the case of one excess bedroom and 25 per cent in the case of two or more excess bedrooms (see para.36).

If a renter is solely liable to make the relevant payments, this deduction will be made from the monthly equivalent of the total of the rent payments and service charges that they are liable (or treated as liable) to pay, as reduced in accordance with paras 31 and 32(3) and (4), if applicable (para.34, step 4).

If the renter is jointly liable with another person or persons to make the relevant payments, an under-occupancy deduction will only be made if the only people who are jointly liable are "listed persons" (as defined in para.2) (i.e. the renter, their partner and any child or qualifying young person for whom either of them is responsible) (para.35(3)). If the joint liability is with one or more people who are not listed persons, no under-occupancy deduction will be made (there is no reference to such a deduction in para.35(4)).

Note also that no under-occupancy deduction is made in the case of a shared ownership tenancy (see para.36(5)).

Under para.35(3)-(5) the rules for working out the amount of the renter's housing costs element if they are jointly liable with another person or persons to make the relevant payments are the same that apply for the purpose of working out a renter's core rent under Part 4 of this Schedule (see above).

Finally, a deduction will be made for any housing cost contribution (para.33).

Regulation 26(3)

SCHEDULE 5

HOUSING COSTS ELEMENT FOR OWNER-OCCUPIERS

PART I

GENERAL

Introduction

1.—(1) This Schedule contains provisions about claimants to whom regulation 26(3)   **2.431**
applies.

(2) Claimants who fall within sub-paragraph (1) are referred to in this Schedule as "owner-occupiers" (and references to "joint owner-occupiers" are to joint claimants to whom regulation 26(3) applies).

(3) Part 2 of this Schedule sets out an exception to section 11(1) of the Act for certain owner-occupiers in whose case an award of universal credit is not to include an amount of housing costs element calculated under this Schedule.

(4) Part 3 of this Schedule provides for a qualifying period that is to elapse before an amount of housing costs element calculated under this Schedule may be included in an owner-occupier's award of universal credit.

(5) Part 4 provides for the calculation of the amount of housing costs element to be included under this Schedule in an owner-occupier's award of universal credit.

Interpretation

2. In this Schedule—   **2.432**

[¹[⁷ . . .]]

[⁷. . .]

"joint owner-occupier" has the meaning given in paragraph 1;

[⁷ ...]

"owner-occupier" means a single owner-occupier within the meaning of paragraph 1(2) or each of joint owner-occupiers;

"qualifying period" has the meaning given in paragraph 5;

[¹ "relevant date" means, in relation to an owner-occupier, the date on which an amount of housing costs element calculated under this Schedule is first included in the owner-occupier's award;]

"relevant payments" has the meaning given in paragraph 3;

[⁷. . .]

"Relevant payments" for purposes of this Schedule

3.—[⁷ (1) "Relevant payments" means one or more payments which are service charge payments.]   **2.433**

(2) [⁷ ...]

(3) "Service charge payments" is to be understood in accordance with paragraphs 7 and 8 of that Schedule.

PART 2

EXCEPTION TO INCLUSION OF HOUSING COSTS ELEMENT

No housing costs element where owner-occupier has any earned income

4.—(1) Section 11(1) of the Act (housing costs) does not apply to any owner-occupier in   **2.434**
relation to an assessment period where—

  (a) the owner-occupier has any earned income; or

  (b) if the owner-occupier is a member of a couple, either member of the couple has any earned income.

(2) Sub-paragraph (1) applies irrespective of the nature of the work engaged in, its duration or the amount of the earned income.

(3) Nothing in this paragraph prevents an amount calculated under Schedule 4 from

441

being included in the award of any claimant who falls within regulation 26(4) to (6) (shared ownership).

PART 3

NO HOUSING COSTS ELEMENT FOR QUALIFYING PERIOD

No housing costs element under this Schedule for qualifying period

2.435

5.—(1) An owner-occupier's award of universal credit is not to include any amount of housing costs element calculated under this Schedule until the beginning of the assessment period that follows the assessment period in which the qualifying period ends.

(2) "Qualifying period" means a period of—

(a) in the case of a new award, [⁶ 9] consecutive assessment periods in relation to which—

(i) the owner-occupier has been receiving universal credit, and

(ii) would otherwise qualify for the inclusion of an amount calculated under this Schedule in their award;

(b) in any case where an amount calculated under this Schedule has for any reason ceased to be included in the award, [⁶ 9] consecutive assessment periods in relation to which the owner-occupier would otherwise qualify for the inclusion of an amount calculated under this Schedule in their award.

(3) Where, before the end of a qualifying period, an owner-occupier for any reason ceases to qualify for the inclusion of an amount calculated under this Schedule—

(a) that qualifying period stops running; and

(b) a new qualifying period starts only when the owner-occupier again meets the requirements of sub-paragraph (2)(a) or (b).

Application of paragraph 5: receipt of JSA and ESA

2.436

6.—(1) This paragraph applies to any owner-occupier who immediately before the commencement of an award of universal credit is entitled to—

(a) a jobseeker's allowance; or

(b) an employment and support allowance.

(2) In determining when the qualifying period in paragraph 5 ends in relation to the owner-occupier, any period that comprises only days on which the owner-occupier was receiving a benefit referred to in sub-paragraph (1) may be treated as if it were the whole or part of one or more assessment periods, as determined by the number of days on which any such benefit was received.

Application of paragraph 5: joint owner-occupiers ceasing to be a couple

2.437

7.—(1) This paragraph applies where—

(a) an award of universal credit to joint owner-occupiers is terminated because they cease to be a couple;

(b) a further award is made to one of them (or to each of them); and

(c) in relation to the further award (or in relation to each further award), the occupation condition is met in respect of the same accommodation as that occupied by the joint owner-occupiers as their home.

(2) In determining when the qualifying period in paragraph 5 ends in relation to the further award (or each further award), the whole or part of any assessment period which would have counted in relation to the award that is terminated is to be carried forward and taken into account in relation to the further award (or each further award).

(3) But where, immediately before the joint owner-occupiers' award was terminated, an amount of housing costs element calculated under this Schedule was already included in the award, no qualifying period under paragraph 5 applies to the owner-occupier in relation to the commencement of the further award (or each further award).

(4) For the purposes of sub-paragraph (1)(b), it is irrelevant whether the further award—

(a) is made on a claim; or

(b) by virtue of regulation 9(6) of the Universal Credit, Personal Independence Payment, Jobseeker's Allowance and Employment and Support Allowance (Claims and Payments) Regulations 2013 is made without a claim.

PART 4

CALCULATION OF AMOUNT OF HOUSING COSTS ELEMENT FOR OWNER-OCCUPIERS

Payments to be taken into account

8.—(1) Where an owner-occupier meets the payment condition, liability condition and   **2.438**
occupation condition in respect of one or more relevant payments and the qualifying period
has ended, each of the relevant payments is to be taken into account for the purposes of the
calculation under this Part.

(2) No account is to be taken of any amount of a relevant payment to the extent that the
conditions referred to in sub-paragraph (1) are not met in respect of that amount.

(3) Any particular payment for which an owner-occupier is liable is not to be brought into
account more than once, whether in relation to the same or a different owner-occupier (but
this does not prevent different payments of the same description being brought into account
in respect of an assessment period).

The amount of housing costs element

9. The amount of the owner-occupier's housing costs element under this Schedule is [⁷ the   **2.439**
amount resulting from paragraph 13] in respect of all relevant payments which are to be taken
into account under paragraph 8.

Amount in respect of interest on loans

10. [⁷. . .]   **2.440**

Amount in respect of alternative finance arrangements

11.—[⁷. . .]   **2.441**

Standard rate to be applied under paragraphs 10 and 11

12.—[⁷. . .]   **2.442**

Amount in respect of service charge payments

13.—(1) This paragraph provides for the calculation of the amount to be included in the   **2.443**
owner-occupier's housing costs element under this Schedule in respect of relevant payments
which are service charge payments.

(2) The amount in respect of the service charge payments is to be calculated as follows.

Step 1

Determine the amount of each service charge payment.

Step 2

Determine the period in respect of which each service charge payment is payable and
determine the amount of the payment in respect of a month (see sub-paragraphs (3) and (4)).

Step 3

If there is more than one service charge payment, add together the amounts determined in
step 2.

The result is the amount to be included under this Schedule in respect of service charge
payments.

(3) Where the period in respect of which an owner-occupier is liable to make a service
charge payment is not a month, an amount is to be calculated as the monthly equivalent, so
for example—

   (a) weekly payments are multiplied by 52 and divided by 12;

[⁵ (aa) two-weekly payments are multiplied by 26 and divided by 12;]

   (b) four-weekly payments are multiplied by 13 and divided by 12;

   (c) three-monthly payments are multiplied by 4 and divided by 12; and

   (d) annual payments are divided by 12.

(4) Where an owner-occupier is liable for service charge payments under arrangements that
provide for one or more service charge free periods, [⁵ subject to sub-paragraph (4A),] the
monthly equivalent is to be calculated over 12 months by reference to the total number of
service charge payments which the owner-occupier is liable to make in that 12 month period.

[⁵ (4A) Where sub-paragraph (4) applies and the service charge payments in question are—

(a) weekly payments, the total number of weekly service charge payments which the owner-occupier is liable to make in any 12 month period shall be calculated by reference to the formula—

$$52 - SCFP;$$

(b) two-weekly payments, the total number of two-weekly service charge payments which the owner-occupier is liable to make in any 12 month period shall be calculated by reference to the formula—

$$26 - SCFP;$$

(c) four weekly payments, the total number of four-weekly service charge payments which the owner-occupier is liable to make in any 12 month period shall be calculated by reference to the formula—

$$13 - SCFP;$$

where "SCFP" is the number of service charge free periods in the 12 month period in question.]

(5) "Service charge free period" means any period in respect of which the owner-occupier has no liability to make one or more of the service charge payments which are to be taken into account under paragraph 8.

AMENDMENTS

1. Universal Credit and Miscellaneous Amendments Regulations 2014 (SI 2014/597) reg.2(14)(a) (April 28, 2014).
2. Universal Credit and Miscellaneous Amendments Regulations 2014 (SI 2014/597) reg.2(14)(b) (April 28, 2014).
3. Universal Credit and Miscellaneous Amendments Regulations 2014 (SI 2014/597) reg.2(14)(c) (April 28, 2014).
4. Universal Credit and Miscellaneous Amendments Regulations 2014 (SI 2014/597) reg.2(14)(d) (April 28, 2014).
5. Universal Credit and Miscellaneous Amendments Regulations 2014 (SI 2014/597) reg.2(14)(e) (April 28, 2014).
6. Social Security (Housing Costs Amendments) Regulations 2015 (SI 2015/1647) reg.5(2) (April 1, 2016). The amendment is subject to the saving provision in reg.8 of SI 2015/1647 (see Pt IV).
7. Loans for Mortgage Interest Regulations 2017 (SI 2017/725) reg.18 and Sch.5 para.5(f) (April 6, 2018).

DEFINITIONS

"the Act"—see reg.2.
"assessment period"—see WRA 2012, ss.40 and 7(2) and reg.21.
"claim"—see WRA 2012, s.40.
"claimant"—*ibid.*
"couple"—see WRA 2012, ss.39 and 40.
"earned income"—see reg.2.
"employment and support allowance"—*ibid.*
"jobseeker's allowance"—*ibid.*
"personal independence payment"—*ibid.*

GENERAL NOTE

2.444   *Paragraphs 1–4*
This Schedule concerns the calculation of the housing costs element for "owner-occupiers" (see para.1(2)). For the definition of "owner-occupier" see para.2. References to "joint owner-occupiers" are to joint claimants who are owner-occupiers (para.1(2)).

For an owner-occupier (or joint owner-occupier) to be entitled to a housing costs element under this Schedule, they must meet the payment, liability and occupation conditions in respect of one or more "relevant payments" (as defined in para.3) and the qualifying period (see paras 5–7) must have ended.

"Relevant payments" for the purposes of Sch.5 are owner-occupier payments (for the meaning of owner-occupier payments see para.4 of Sch.1) and service charges (on which see paras 7 and 8 of Sch.1). If the claimant (or claimants) is only liable for service charges payments, these will be calculated under this Schedule (see reg.26(3)). But if the claimant has a shared ownership tenancy, any service charges are calculated in accordance with Sch.4 (reg.26(5)).

Note the significant exclusion in para.4 from entitlement to a housing costs element under Sch.5. If an owner-occupier, or if they are a member of a couple, either member of the couple, has *any* earned income in an assessment period (i.e. month), they will not be entitled to a housing costs element in that assessment period. However, in the case of a shared ownership tenancy, rent payments and service charges can still be met (para.4(3)).

Paragraphs 5–7

There is a waiting period (referred to as "a qualifying period") for owner-occupier and service charges payments. In the case of a new award of universal credit, a housing costs element cannot be included until there have been nine consecutive assessment periods (i.e. months) during which the owner-occupier has been receiving universal credit *and* would otherwise have qualified for a housing costs element under Sch.5 (para.5(2)(a)). A housing costs element is included from the start of the next assessment period. If, once awarded, there is a break in entitlement to a housing costs element under Sch.5 (e.g. because of earnings), the owner-occupier has to serve a further nine consecutive months during which they would otherwise qualify for a housing costs element before they can be awarded a housing costs element under Sch.5 again (para.5(2)(b)). This applies even if the owner-occupier continues to be entitled to universal credit during the break in entitlement to a housing costs element under Sch.5. If during a waiting period an owner-occupier ceases to qualify for a housing costs element under Sch.5, that waiting period ends and a new waiting period will have to be served (para.5(3)).

2.445

Note that before April 1, 2016 the waiting period under para.5(2)(a) and (b) was only three consecutive assessment periods. The amendment which increased the waiting period to nine months is subject to a saving provision (see reg.8 of the Social Security (Housing Costs Amendments) Regulations 2015 in Pt IV of this Volume). The effect of the saving provision in relation to universal credit is that for those claimants who are entitled, or treated as entitled, to one or more relevant benefits (i.e., income support, old style JSA, old style ESA or universal credit) for a continuous period which includes March 31, 2016, the form of reg.5(2)(a) and (b) and of reg. 29 of the Universal Credit (Transitional) Regulations 2014 that were in force before the April 1, 2016 amendments continues to have effect. So for claimants who are in a waiting period on March 31, 2016 the waiting period for a housing costs element remains three consecutive assessment periods.

Paragraphs 6 and 7 contain exceptions to the rule in para.5.

If immediately before the owner-occupier's award of universal credit began, s/he was entitled to new style JSA or new style ESA, the days that s/he was only receiving one of these benefits can count towards the waiting period (para.6).

Under para.7, if a universal credit award made to joint owner-occupiers comes to an end because they have ceased to be a couple, and a further award is made to one of them who continues to occupy the same accommodation as they did when they were a couple, the further award will include a housing costs element under Sch.5 without a waiting period if a housing costs element was included in the joint award. If a housing costs element was not yet included in the joint award, any assessment period, or part of an assessment period, which counted towards the waiting period under the joint award counts towards the waiting period for the new award. If both members of the former couple remain in the same accommodation and both claim and are awarded universal credit again, this provision will apply to both of them.

The waiting period may also be extinguished or reduced under reg.29 of the Transitional Provisions Regulations 2014, which applies where in the one month before the claim for universal credit was made, or treated as made, the owner occupier, or his/her partner or former partner, was entitled to income support, old style JSA or old style ESA that included help with housing costs or did not yet do so only because a waiting period was being served.

Paras 8, 9 and 13

2.446   There is an upper limit of £200,000 for eligible loans (see para.10(2), step 3) and for the purchase price (defined in para.11(3)) of the accommodation and para.6(2) of Sch.1 in the case of alternative finance arrangements (see para.11(2), step 2). See para.2 and para.6(2) of Sch.1 for the definition of "alternative finance arrangements".

However, if a loan (or part of a loan) was taken out to make necessary adaptations to the accommodation to meet the disablement needs of the claimant (or claimants: s.40 WRA 2012) or any child or qualifying young person for whom the claimant (or either joint claimant) is responsible, that loan (or part of the loan) is disregarded in applying the £200,000 limit (para.10(3)). The person with disablement needs must be in receipt of the middle or highest rate of the care component of disability living allowance, the daily living component of personal independence payment (either rate), attendance allowance or armed forces independence payment (see the definition of "attendance allowance" in reg.2 which includes armed forces independence payment).

To calculate the housing costs element for loan interest payments, the amount of the capital outstanding on the eligible loan or loans (subject to the £200,000 limit) is multiplied by the standard rate (currently (in July 2016) 3.12 per cent) (para.10(2), steps 3 and 4). If the £200,000 limit applies, the housing costs element will also include loan interest payments on any loan (or part of a loan) for adaptations for disablement needs on top of loan interest payments on the £200,000 (para.10(3)).

In the case of alternative finance arrangements, the housing costs element is the "purchase price" of the accommodation (subject to the £200,000 limit) multiplied by the standard rate (para.11(2)). The "purchase price" of the accommodation is the price paid by a party to the alternative finance arrangements, other than the owner-occupier, to acquire an interest in the accommodation, minus (i) the amount of any initial payment made by the owner-occupier in acquiring that interest; and (ii) any subsequent payment by the owner-occupier made before the relevant date which reduces the amount owed by the owner-occupier under the alternative finance arrangements (para.11(3)). The relevant date is the date on which an amount for the housing costs element is first included in the owner-occupier's award (see para.2). Under para.11(4) variations in the amount owing under such alternative finance arrangements are taken into account on an annual basis, in the same way as for standard mortgages (on which see para.10(4)).

The amount for service charges that can be included in an owner-occupier's housing costs element is the monthly equivalent of the actual service charge payment or payments (see para.13). Where the owner-occupier has the benefit of service charge free periods (defined in para.13(5)), the conversion to a monthly figure is based on a standard 52 week year (see para. 13(4) and the formula in para.13(4A)).

Note:

- No "housing cost contribution" for a non-dependant is made in the case of amounts awarded under Sch.5 (this is to be contrasted with the position under income support, old style JSA and old style ESA).
- Any increase, or decrease, in the amount of a loan, or in the amount owing under alternative finance arrangements, during the currency of an award is

only taken into account from the anniversary date (see paras 10(4) and 11(4) respectively). But if a *new* (i.e. additional) loan is taken out that is secured on the home (or *additional* alternative finance arrangements are made), arguably that is a change of circumstances (rather than a variation in the amount owing) and so should take effect in accordance with Part III of Sch.1 to the Decisions and Appeals Regulations 2013).

- A housing costs element that is awarded in respect of payments of interest on a loan will be paid direct to the lender (see reg.59 of, and Sch.5 to, the Claims and Payments Regulations 2013).

- Under reg.39(4) of the Decisions and Appeals Regulations 2013, if the Secretary of State considers that he does not have all the relevant information or evidence to decide what housing costs element to award, the decision will be made on the basis of the housing costs element that can immediately be awarded.

Regulation 39(2) and(3)

SCHEDULE 6

ASSESSMENT OF WHETHER A CLAIMANT HAS LIMITED CAPABILITY FOR WORK

PART I

PHYSICAL DISABILITIES   **2.447**

(1)	(2)	(3)
Activity	Descriptors	Points
1. Mobilising unaided by another person with or without a walking stick, manual wheelchair or other aid if such aid is normally or could reasonably be worn or used.	1 (a) Cannot, unaided by another person, either: (i) mobilise more than 50 metres on level ground without stopping in order to avoid significant discomfort or exhaustion; or (ii) repeatedly mobilise 50 metres within a reasonable timescale because of significant discomfort or exhaustion.	15
	(b) Cannot, unaided by another person, mount or descend two steps even with the support of a handrail.	9
	(c) Cannot, unaided by another person, either: (i) mobilise more than 100 metres on level ground without stopping in order to avoid significant discomfort or exhaustion; or (ii) repeatedly mobilise 100 metres within a reasonable timescale because of significant discomfort or exhaustion.	9
	(d) Cannot, unaided by another person, either: (i) mobilise more than 200 metres on level ground without stopping in order to avoid significant discomfort or exhaustion; or (ii) repeatedly mobilise 200 metres within a reasonable timescale because of significant discomfort or exhaustion.	6
	(e) None of the above applies.	0

(1)	(2)	(3)
Activity	Descriptors	Points
2. Standing and sitting.	2 (a) Cannot move between one seated position and another seated position which are located next to one another without receiving physical assistance from another person.	15
	(b) Cannot, for the majority of the time, remain at a work station: (i) standing unassisted by another person (even if free to move around); (ii) sitting (even in an adjustable chair); or (iii) a combination of paragraphs (i) and (ii), for more than 30 minutes, before needing to move away in order to avoid significant discomfort or exhaustion.	9
	(c) Cannot, for the majority of the time, remain at a work station: (i) standing unassisted by another person (even if free to move around); (ii) sitting (even in an adjustable chair); or (iii) a combination of paragraphs (i) and (ii), for more than an hour before needing to move away in order to avoid significant discomfort or exhaustion.	6
	(d) None of the above applies.	0
3. Reaching.	3 (a) Cannot raise either arm as if to put something in the top pocket of a coat or jacket.	15
	(b) Cannot raise either arm to top of head as if to put on a hat.	9
	(c) Cannot raise either arm above head height as if to reach for something.	6
	(d) None of the above applies.	0
4. Picking up and moving or transferring by the use of the upper body and arms.	4 (a) Cannot pick up and move a 0.5 litre carton full of liquid.	15
	(b) Cannot pick up and move a one litre carton full of liquid.	9
	(c) Cannot transfer a light but bulky object such as an empty cardboard box.	6
	(d) None of the above applies.	0
5. Manual dexterity.	5 (a) Cannot press a button (such as a telephone keypad) with either hand or cannot turn the pages of a book with either hand.	15
	(b) Cannot pick up a £1 coin or equivalent with either hand.	15
	(c) Cannot use a pen or pencil to make a meaningful mark with either hand.	9
	(d) Cannot single-handedly use a suitable keyboard or mouse.	9
	(e) None of the above applies.	0

(1)	(2)		(3)
Activity	Descriptors		Points
6. Making self understood through speaking, writing, typing, or other means which are normally or could reasonably be used, unaided by another person.	6	(a) Cannot convey a simple message, such as the presence of a hazard.	15
		(b) Has significant difficulty conveying a simple message to strangers.	15
		(c) Has some difficulty conveying a simple message to strangers.	6
		(d) None of the above applies.	0
7. Understanding communication by: (i) verbal means (such as hearing or lip reading) alone; (ii) non-verbal means (such as reading 16 point print or Braille) alone; or (iii) a combination of sub-paragraphs (i) and (ii), using any aid that is normally or could reasonably be used, unaided by another person.	7	(a) Cannot understand a simple message, such as the location of a fire escape, due to sensory impairment.	15
		(b) Has significant difficulty understanding a simple message from a stranger due to sensory impairment.	
		(c) Has some difficulty understanding a simple message from a stranger due to sensory impairment.	15 6
		(d) None of the above applies.	0
8. Navigation and maintaining safety using a guide dog or other aid if either or both are normally used or could reasonably be used.	8	(a) Unable to navigate around familiar surroundings, without being accompanied by another person, due to sensory impairment.	15
		(b) Cannot safely complete a potentially hazardous task such as crossing the road, without being accompanied by another person, due to sensory impairment.	15
		(c) Unable to navigate around unfamiliar surroundings, without being accompanied by another person, due to sensory impairment.	9
		(d) None of the above applies.	0
9. Absence or loss of control whilst conscious leading to extensive evacuation of the bowel and/or bladder, other than enuresis (bed-wetting), despite the wearing or use of any aids or adaptations which are normally or could reasonably be worn or used.	9	(a) At least once a month experiences: (i) loss of control leading to extensive evacuation of the bowel and/or voiding of the bladder; or (ii) substantial leakage of the contents of a collecting device, sufficient to require cleaning and a change in clothing.	15
		(b) The majority of the time is at risk of loss of control leading to extensive evacuation of the bowel and/or voiding of the bladder, sufficient to require cleaning and a change in clothing, if not able to reach a toilet quickly.	6
		(c) Neither of the above applies.	0

(1)	(2)	(3)
Activity	Descriptors	Points
10. Consciousness during waking moments.	10 (a) At least once a week, has an involuntary episode of lost or altered consciousness resulting in significantly disrupted awareness or concentration.	15
	(b) At least once a month, has an involuntary episode of lost or altered consciousness resulting in significantly disrupted awareness or concentration.	6
	(c) Neither of the above applies.	0
11. Learning tasks.	11 (a) Cannot learn how to complete a simple task, such as setting an alarm clock.	15
	(b) Cannot learn anything beyond a simple task, such as setting an alarm clock.	9
	(c) Cannot learn anything beyond a moderately complex task, such as the steps involved in operating a washing machine to clean clothes.	6
	(d) None of the above applies.	0
12. Awareness of everyday hazards (such as boiling water or sharp objects).	12 (a) Reduced awareness of everyday hazards leads to a significant risk of: (i) injury to self or others; or (ii) damage to property or possessions, such that the claimant requires supervision for the majority of the time to maintain safety.	15
	(b) Reduced awareness of everyday hazards leads to a significant risk of: (i) injury to self or others; or (ii) damage to property or possessions, such that the claimant frequently requires supervision to maintain safety.	9
	(c) Reduced awareness of everyday hazards leads to a significant risk of: (i) injury to self or others; or (ii) damage to property or possessions, such that the claimant occasionally requires supervision to maintain safety.	6
	(d) None of the above applies.	0
13. Initiating and completing personal action (which means planning, organisation, problem solving, prioritising or switching tasks).	13 (a) Cannot, due to impaired mental function, reliably initiate or complete at least two sequential personal actions.	15
	(b) Cannot, due to impaired mental function, reliably initiate or complete at least two sequential personal actions for the majority of the time.	9
	(c) Frequently cannot, due to impaired mental function, reliably initiate or complete at least two sequential personal actions.	6
	(d) None of the above applies.	0
14. Coping with change.	14 (a) Cannot cope with any change to the extent that day to day life cannot be managed.	15

(1)	(2)	(3)
Activity	Descriptors	Points
	(b) Cannot cope with minor planned change (such as a pre-arranged change to the routine time scheduled for a lunch break), to the extent that, overall, day to day life is made significantly more difficult.	9
	(c) Cannot cope with minor unplanned change (such as the timing of an appointment on the day it is due to occur), to the extent that, overall, day to day life is made significantly more difficult.	6
	(d) None of the above applies.	0
15. Getting about.	15 (a) Cannot get to any place outside the claimant's home with which the claimant is familiar.	15
	(b) Is unable to get to a specified place with which the claimant is familiar, without being accompanied by another person.	9
	(c) Is unable to get to a specified place with which the claimant is unfamiliar without being accompanied by another person.	6
	(d) None of the above applies.	0
16. Coping with social engagement due to cognitive impairment or mental disorder.	16 (a) Engagement in social contact is always precluded due to difficulty relating to others or significant distress experienced by the claimant.	15
	(b) Engagement in social contact with someone unfamiliar to the claimant is always precluded due to difficulty relating to others or significant distress experienced by the claimant.	9
	(c) Engagement in social contact with someone unfamiliar to the claimant is not possible for the majority of the time due to difficulty relating to others or significant distress experienced by the claimant.	6
	(d) None of the above applies.	0
17. Appropriateness of behaviour with other people, due to cognitive impairment or mental disorder.	17 (a) Has, on a daily basis, uncontrollable episodes of aggressive or disinhibited behaviour that would be unreasonable in any workplace.	15
	(b) Frequently has uncontrollable episodes of aggressive or disinhibited behaviour that would be unreasonable in any workplace.	15
	(c) Occasionally has uncontrollable episodes of aggressive or disinhibited behaviour that would be unreasonable in any workplace.	9
	(d) None of the above applies.	0

PART II

2.448   MENTAL, COGNITIVE AND INTELLECTUAL FUNCTION ASSESSMENT

DEFINITIONS

"claimant"—see WRA 2012 s.40.
"limited capability for work"—see WRA 2012 ss.40 and 37(1).

GENERAL NOTE

2.449   The activities and descriptors for assessing whether a claimant has LCW are the same as the activities and descriptors in Sch.2 to the ESA Regulations 2008. See the notes to Sch.2 to the 2008 Regulations in Vol.I of this series. They are also the same as the activities and descriptors in Sch.2 to the ESA Regulations 2013.

Regulation 40(2) and (3)

2.450   SCHEDULE 7

ASSESSMENT OF WHETHER A CLAIMANT HAS LIMITED CAPABILITY FOR
WORK AND WORK-RELATED ACTIVITY

Activity	Descriptors
1. Mobilising unaided by another person with or without a walking stick, manual wheelchair or other aid if such aid is normally or could reasonably be worn or used.	1 Cannot either: (a) mobilise more than 50 metres on level ground without stopping in order to avoid significant discomfort or exhaustion; or (b) repeatedly mobilise 50 metres within a reasonable timescale because of significant discomfort or exhaustion.
2. Transferring from one seated position to another.	2. Cannot move between one seated position and another seated position located next to one another without receiving physical assistance from another person.
3. Reaching.	3 Cannot raise either arm as if to put something in the top pocket of a coat or jacket.
4. Picking up and moving or transferring by the use of the upper body and arms (excluding standing, sitting, bending or kneeling and all other activities specified in this Schedule).	4 Cannot pick up and move a 0.5 litre carton full of liquid.
5. Manual dexterity.	5 Cannot press a button (such as a telephone keypad) with either hand or cannot turn the pages of a book with either hand.
6. Making self understood through speaking, writing, typing, or other means which are normally, or could reasonably be, used unaided by another person.	6 Cannot convey a simple message, such as the presence of a hazard.

Activity	Descriptors
7. Understanding communication by: (i)　verbal means (such as hearing or lip reading) alone; (ii)　non-verbal means (such as reading 16 point print or Braille) alone; or (iii)　a combination of sub-paragraphs (i) and (ii), using any aid that is normally, or could reasonably, be used unaided by another person.	7　Cannot understand a simple message, such as the location of a fire escape, due to sensory impairment.
8. Absence or loss of control whilst conscious leading to extensive evacuation of the bowel and/or voiding of the bladder, other than enuresis (bed-wetting), despite the wearing or use of any aids or adaptations which are normally or could reasonably be worn or used.	8　At least once a week experiences: (a)　loss of control leading to extensive evacuation of the bowel and/or voiding of the bladder; or (b)　substantial leakage of the contents of a collecting device sufficient to require the individual to clean themselves and change clothing.
9. Learning tasks.	9　Cannot learn how to complete a simple task, such as setting an alarm clock, due to cognitive impairment or mental disorder.
10. Awareness of hazard.	10　Reduced awareness of everyday hazards, due to cognitive impairment or mental disorder, leads to a significant risk of: (a)　injury to self or others; or (b)　damage to property or possessions, such that the claimant requires supervision for the majority of the time to maintain safety.
11. Initiating and completing personal action (which means planning, organisation, problem solving, prioritising or switching tasks).	11　Cannot, due to impaired mental function, reliably initiate or complete at least two sequential personal actions.
12. Coping with change.	12　Cannot cope with any change, due to cognitive impairment or mental disorder, to the extent that day to day life cannot be managed.
13. Coping with social engagement, due to cognitive impairment or mental disorder.	13　Engagement in social contact is always precluded due to difficulty relating to others or significant distress experienced by the claimant.
14. Appropriateness of behaviour with other people, due to cognitive impairment or mental disorder.	14　Has, on a daily basis, uncontrollable episodes of aggressive or disinhibited behaviour that would be unreasonable in any workplace.
15. Conveying food or drink to the mouth.	15　(a)　Cannot convey food or drink to the claimant's own mouth without receiving physical assistance from someone else; (b)　Cannot convey food or drink to the claimant's own mouth without repeatedly stopping or experiencing breathlessness or severe discomfort;

Activity	Descriptors
	(c) Cannot convey food or drink to the claimant's own mouth without receiving regular prompting given by someone else in the claimant's presence; or (d) Owing to a severe disorder of mood or behaviour, fails to convey food or drink to the claimant's own mouth without receiving: (i) physical assistance from someone else; or (ii) regular prompting given by someone else in the claimant's presence.
16. Chewing or swallowing food or drink.	16 (a) Cannot chew or swallow food or drink; (b) Cannot chew or swallow food or drink without repeatedly stopping or experiencing breathlessness or severe discomfort; (c) Cannot chew or swallow food or drink without repeatedly receiving regular prompting given by someone else in the claimant's presence; or (d) Owing to a severe disorder of mood or behaviour, fails to: (i) chew or swallow food or drink; or (ii) chew or swallow food or drink without regular prompting given by someone else in the claimant's presence.

DEFINITIONS

"claimant"—see WRA 2012 s.40.
"limited capability for work"—see WRA 2012 ss.40 and 37(1).
"limited capability for work-related activity"—see WRA 2012 ss.40 and 37(2).

GENERAL NOTE

2.451   The activities and descriptors for assessing whether a claimant has LCW and LCWRA are the same as the activities and descriptors in Sch.3 to the ESA Regulations 2008 for assessing whether a claimant has LCWRA. See the notes to Sch.3 to the 2008 Regulations in Vol.I of this series. They are also the same as the activities and descriptors in Sch.3 to the ESA Regulations 2013.

Regulation 39(6)

SCHEDULE 8

CIRCUMSTANCES IN WHICH A CLAIMANT IS TO BE TREATED AS HAVING
LIMITED CAPABILITY FOR WORK

Receiving certain treatments
2.452   1. The claimant is receiving—
  (a) regular weekly treatment by way of haemodialysis for chronic renal failure;
  (b) treatment by way of plasmapheresis; or
  (c) regular weekly treatment by way of total parenteral nutrition for gross impairment of enteric function,
or is recovering from any of those forms of treatment in circumstances in which the Secretary of State is satisfied that the claimant should be treated as having limited capability for work.

In hospital
2.453   2.—(1) The claimant is—
  (a) undergoing medical or other treatment as [¹ a patient] in a hospital or similar institution; or
  (b) recovering from such treatment in circumstances in which the Secretary of

State is satisfied that the claimant should be treated as having limited capability for work.

(2) The circumstances in which a claimant is to be regarded as undergoing treatment falling within sub-paragraph (1)(a) include where the claimant is attending a residential programme of rehabilitation for the treatment of drug or alcohol dependency.

(3) For the purposes of this paragraph, a claimant is to be regarded as undergoing treatment as a patient in a hospital or similar institution only if that claimant has been advised by a health care professional to stay [² for a period of 24 hours or longer] following medical or other treatment.

Prevented from working by law

3.—(1) The claimant—   **2.454**
   (a) is excluded or abstains from work pursuant to a request or notice in writing lawfully made or given under an enactment; or
   (b) is otherwise prevented from working pursuant to an enactment,
by reason of it being known or reasonably suspected that the claimant is infected or contaminated by, or has been in contact with a case of, a relevant infection or contamination.

(2) In sub-paragraph (1) "relevant infection or contamination" means—
   (a) in England and Wales—
      (i) any incidence or spread of infection or contamination, within the meaning of section 45A(3) of the Public Health (Control of Disease) Act 1984 in respect of which regulations are made under Part 2A of that Act (public health protection) for the purpose of preventing, protecting against, controlling or providing a public health response to, such incidence or spread, or
      (ii) tuberculosis or any infectious disease to which regulation 9 of the Public Health (Aircraft) Regulations 1979 (powers in respect of persons leaving aircraft) applies or to which regulation 10 of the Public Health (Ships) Regulations 1979 (powers in respect of certain persons on ships) applies; and
   (b) in Scotland any—
      (i) infectious disease within the meaning of section 1(5) of the Public Health etc (Scotland) Act 2008, or exposure to an organism causing that disease; or
      (ii) contamination within the meaning of section 1(5) of that Act, or exposure to a contaminant,
      to which sections 56 to 58 of that Act (compensation) apply.

Risk to self or others

4.—(1) The claimant is suffering from a specific illness, disease or disablement by reason of   **2.455**
which there would be a substantial risk to the physical or mental health of any person were the claimant found not to have limited capability for work.

(2) This paragraph does not apply where the risk could be reduced by a significant amount by—
   (a) reasonable adjustments being made in the claimant's workplace; or
   (b) the claimant taking medication to manage their condition where such medication has been prescribed for the claimant by a registered medical practitioner treating the claimant.

Life threatening disease

5. The claimant is suffering from a life threatening disease in relation to which—   **2.456**
   (a) there is medical evidence that the disease is uncontrollable, or uncontrolled, by a recognised therapeutic procedure; and
   (b) in the case of a disease that is uncontrolled, there is a reasonable cause for it not to be controlled by a recognised therapeutic procedure.

Disabled and over the age for state pension credit

6. The claimant has reached the qualifying age for state pension credit and is entitled to disability living allowance or personal independence payment.   **2.457**

AMENDMENTS

1. Universal Credit (Consequential, Supplementary, Incidental and Miscellaneous Provisions) Regulations 2013 (SI 2013/630), reg.38(10) (April 29, 2013).

2. Social Security (Miscellaneous Amendments) (No.2) Regulations 2013 (SI 2013/1508), reg.3(11) (July 29, 2013).

Definitions

> "claimant"—see WRA 2012 s.40.
> "disability living allowance"—see reg.2.
> "health care professional"–*ibid.*
> "limited capability for work"—see WRA 2012 ss.40 and 37(1).

General Note

2.458   Paragraph 1 is similar, though not identical, to reg.26 of the ESA Regulations 2008; para. 2 is similar, though not identical, to reg.25 of those Regulations; and para. 3 is the same as reg.20(1)(c) and (2) of the 2008 Regulations. See the notes to regs 20, 25 and 26 of the 2008 Regulations in Vol.I of this series.

Note that Sch.8 does not contain provisions for treating a claimant who is (i) terminally ill; (ii) a pregnant woman whose health, or whose unborn child's health, is at serious risk of damage: or (iii) receiving treatment for cancer as having limited capability for work. Such a claimant will be treated as having LCW and LCWRA under paras 1 to 3 respectively of Sch.9 (see below).

There is no equivalent of para.6 in the ESA Regulations 2008.

Paragraphs 4 and 5 together contain very similar provisions to those in reg. 29 of the 2008 Regulations (see the notes to reg.29 in Vol.1 of this series). Note the amendment to reg. 39 made on April 28, 2014, the effect of which is that a claimant can only be treated as having LCW under paras 4 or 5 if they have been assessed as not having LCW. Regulation 29 of the 2008 Regulations already contains such a provision.

Regulation 40(5)

Schedule 9

Circumstances in which a Claimant is to be Treated as having Limited Capability for Work and Work-Related Activity

Terminal illness
2.459   1. The claimant is terminally ill.

Pregnancy
2.460   2. The claimant is a pregnant woman and there is a serious risk of damage to her health or to the health of her unborn child if she does not refrain from work and work-related activity.

Receiving treatment for cancer
2.461   3. The claimant is—
>   (a) receiving treatment for cancer by way of chemotherapy or radiotherapy;
>   (b) likely to receive such treatment within 6 months after the date of the determination of capability for work and work-related activity; or
>   (c) recovering from such treatment,

and the Secretary of State is satisfied that the claimant should be treated as having limited capability for work and work-related activity.

Risk to self or others
2.462   4. The claimant is suffering from a specific illness, disease or disablement by reason of which there would be a substantial risk to the physical or mental health of any person were the claimant found not to have limited capability for work and work-related activity.

Disabled and over the age for state pension credit
2.463   5. The claimant has reached the qualifying age for state pension credit and is entitled to attendance allowance, the care component of disability living allowance at the highest rate or the daily living component of personal independence payment at the enhanced rate.

Definitions

> "attendance allowance"—see reg.2.
> "child"—see WRA 2012, s.40.

"claimant"—*ibid.*
"limited capability for work"—see WRA 2012, ss.40 and 37(1).
"limited capability for work-related activity"—see WRA 2012, ss.40 and 37(2).
"personal independence payment"—see reg.2.

GENERAL NOTE

For the equivalent of (i) para.1, see regs 20(1)(a) and 35(1)(a) of the ESA   **2.464**
Regulations 2008; (ii) para.2, see regs 20(1)(d) and 35(1)(c) of those Regulations;
and (iii) para.3, see regs 20(1)(b) and 35(1)(b) of the 2008 Regulations. See the
notes to regs 20 and 35 of the 2008 Regulations in Vol.I of this series.

There is no equivalent of para.5 in the ESA Regulations 2008.

Paragraph 4 contains very similar provisions to those in regs 29(2)(b) and 35(2)
of the 2008 Regulations (see the notes to regs 29 and 35 in Vol.1 of this series).
Note the amendment to reg. 40 made on April 28, 2014, the effect of which is that a
claimant can only be treated as having LCW and LCWRA under para.4 if they have
been assessed as not having LCW and LCWRA. Regulations 29 and 35 of the 2008
Regulations already contain such a provision.

Regulation 48

SCHEDULE 10

CAPITAL TO BE DISREGARDED

Premises
   1.—(1) Premises occupied by a person as their home.   **2.465**
   (2) For the purposes of this paragraph and paragraphs 2 to 5, only one set of premises may
be treated as a person's home.
   2. Premises occupied by a close relative of a person as their home where that close
relative has limited capability for work or has reached the qualifying age for state pension
credit.
   3. Premises occupied by a person's former partner as their home where the person and their
former partner are not estranged, but living apart by force of circumstances, for example where
the person is in residential care.
   4.—(1) Premises that a person intends to occupy as their home where—
   (a) the person has acquired the premises within the past 6 months but not yet taken up
       occupation;
   (b) the person is taking steps to obtain possession and has commenced those steps within
       the past 6 months; or
   (c) the person is carrying out essential repairs or alterations required to render the prem-
       ises fit for occupation and these have been commenced within the past 6 months.
   (2) A person is to be taken to have commenced steps to obtain possession of premises
on the date that legal advice is first sought or proceedings are commenced, whichever is
earlier.
   5. Premises that a person has ceased to occupy as their home following an estrangement
from their former partner where—
   (a) the person has ceased to occupy the premises within the past 6 months; or
   (b) the person's former partner is a lone parent and occupies the premises as their home.
   6. Premises that a person is taking reasonable steps to dispose of where those steps have
been commenced within the past 6 months.

Business assets
   7. Assets which are used wholly or mainly for the purposes of a trade, profession or vocation   **2.466**
which the person is carrying on.
   8. Assets which were used wholly or mainly for a trade, profession or vocation that the
person has ceased to carry on within the past 6 months if—
   (a) the person is taking reasonable steps to dispose of those assets; or
   (b) the person ceased to be engaged in carrying on the trade, profession or vocation
       because of incapacity and can reasonably expect to be reengaged on recovery.

Rights in pensions schemes etc.

9. The value of any policy of life insurance.

2.467　　10.—(1) The value of any right to receive a pension under an occupational or personal pension scheme or any other pension scheme registered under section 153 of the Finance Act 2004.

(2) "Occupational pension scheme" and "personal pension scheme" have the meaning in section 1 of the Pension Schemes Act 1993.

11.—(1) The value of a funeral plan contract.

(2) "Funeral plan contract" means a contract under which the person makes payments to a person to secure the provision of a funeral and where the sole purpose of the plan is the provision of a funeral.

Amounts earmarked for special purposes

2.468　　12. An amount deposited with a housing association as a condition of the person occupying premises as their home.

13. An amount received within the past 6 months which is to be used for the purchase of premises that the person intends to occupy as their home where that amount—

    (a)　is attributable to the proceeds of the sale of premises formerly occupied by the person as their home;

    (b)　has been deposited with a housing association as mentioned in paragraph 12; or

    (c)　is a grant made to the person for the sole purpose of the purchase of a home.

14. An amount received under an insurance policy within the past 6 months in connection with the loss or damage to the premises occupied by the person as their home or to their personal possessions.

15. An amount received within the past 6 months that is to be used for making essential repairs or alterations to premises occupied or intended to be occupied as the person's home where that amount has been acquired by the person (whether by grant or loan or otherwise) on condition that it is used for that purpose.

Other payments

2.469　　16. A payment made within the past 12 months under Part 8 of the Contributions and Benefits Act (the social fund).

17.—(1) A payment made within the past 12 months by or on behalf of a local authority—

    (a)　under section 17, 23B, 23C or 24A of the Children Act 1989, section 12 of the Social Work (Scotland) Act 1968 [², or section 29 or 30 of the Children (Scotland) Act 1995 or section 37, 38, 109, 110, 114 or 115 of the Social Services and Well-being (Wales) Act 2014]; or

    (b)　under any other enactment in order to meet a person's welfare needs related to old age or disability, other than living expenses.

(2) In sub-paragraph (1) "living expenses" has the meaning in regulation 66(2).

18.—(1) A payment received within the past 12 months by way of arrears of, or compensation for late payment of—

    (a)　universal credit;

    (b)　a benefit abolished by section 33 of the Act; or

    (c)　a social security benefit which is not included as unearned income under regulation 66(1)(a) or (b).

(2) "Social security benefit" means a benefit under any enactment relating to social security in any part of the United Kingdom [⁵and includes armed forces independence payment under the Armed Forces and Reserve Forces (Compensation Scheme) Order 2011].

19. A payment to a person by virtue of being a holder of the Victoria Cross or George Cross.

[¹20. A payment made within the past 12 months of bereavement support payment in respect of the rate set out in regulation 3(2) or (5) of the Bereavement Support Payment Regulations 2017 (rate of bereavement support payment).]

[³21. Any early years assistance given within the past 12 months in accordance with section 32 of the Social Security (Scotland) Act 2018.]

[⁴22. Any funeral expense assistance given in accordance with section 34 of the Social Security (Scotland) Act 2018.]

Amendments

1. Pensions Act 2014 (Consequential, Supplementary and Incidental Amendments) Order 2017 (SI 2017/422) art.43(4) (April 6, 2017).

2. Social Services and Well-being (Wales) Act 2014 and the Regulation and Inspection of Social Care (Wales) Act 2016 (Consequential Amendments) Order 2017 (SI 2017/901) art.15 (November 2, 2017).

3. Social Security (Scotland) Act 2018 (Best Start Grants) (Consequential Modifications and Saving) Order 2018 (SI 2018/1138) art.11 (December 10, 2018).

4. Social Security (Scotland) Act 2018 (Funeral Expense Assistance and Early Years Assistance) (Consequential Modifications and Savings) Order 2019 (SI 2019/1060) art.19(2) (September 16, 2019).

5. Social Security (Capital Disregards) (Amendment) Regulations 2019 (SI 2019/1314) reg.8(2) (October 31, 2019).

DEFINITIONS

"close relative"—see reg.2.
"grant"—see regs 2 and 68(7).
"partner"—see reg.2.

GENERAL NOTE

The list of capital that is ignored for the purposes of universal credit is greatly   2.470
reduced compared with that which applies for the purposes of income support, old
style JSA, old style ESA and housing benefit. Many of the provisions in Sch.10 are
similar to those that apply for those benefits but not all. Paragraph 11—the disregard of the value of a funeral plan—is new.

The opportunity has been taken to group the disregards in a more coherent and
easy to follow structure. The notes below follow that structure and note the equivalences with and differences from the provisions in Sch.10 to the Income Support
Regulations (see Vol.II of this series for detailed discussion). The disregards can
apply to notional capital. By virtue of reg.48(2), where any period of six months is
specified in Sch.10 it can be extended by the Secretary of State (and on any appeal
by a tribunal) if it is reasonable to do so in the circumstances. Any specified period
of 12 months is not extendable.

Note that, in addition to the categories specified in Sch.10, there are specific
disregards of capital in reg.75(4), (5) and (6) (sums derived from compensation for personal injury to claimant), reg.76 (special compensation schemes) and
reg.77(3)(a) (assets of company where claimant treated as sole owner or partner).
Further, reg.51 of the Universal Credit (Transitional Provisions) Regulations
2014, as inserted by reg.3 of the Universal Credit (Managed Migration Pilot and
Miscellaneous Amendments) Regulations 2019 (SI 2019/1152) with effect from
July 24, 2019, supplies a transitional capital disregard to claimants who (i) were
previously entitled to a tax credit and had capital exceeding £16,000; (ii) are given
a migration notice that existing benefits are to terminate; and (iii) claim universal
credit within the deadline. The disregard is of any capital exceeding £16,000. The
disregard can apply only for 12 assessment periods and ceases (without the possibility of revival) following any assessment period in which the amount of capital the
claimant has falls below £16,000. See regs 56 and 57 of the Transitional Provisions
Regulations for further provisions on termination of the protection. There is no
capital limit for tax credits. Paragraph 7 of Sch.2 to the Transitional Provisions
Regulations, inserted by the same Regulations, contains a disregard as capital of
any amount paid as a lump sum by way of a "transitional SDP amount" under that
Schedule.

Finally, note that with effect from May 21, 2020, reg.2(2) of the Universal Credit
(Coronavirus) (Self-employed Claimants and Reclaims) (Amendment) Regulations
2020 (SI 2020/522) introduces a disregard as capital for 12 months of any payment
made to a self-employed claimant under the Coronavirus Job Retention Scheme or
by way of a grant or loan to meet the expenses or losses of the trade, profession or
vocation in relation to the outbreak of coronavirus disease. See further discussion
in the note to para.7.

The disregards can apply to capital that a claimant is treated as possessing under
reg.48 (notional capital), providing that the terms of the particular paragraph of

Sch.10 are satisfied (see discussion in the note to para.6). Although the references in Sch.10 are to a person, not to a claimant, that is merely in accord with 48(2) applying the Sch.10 disregards to the calculation of "a person's capital". Thus when a paragraph in Sch.10 refers to the circumstances of a person it means the person whose capital would otherwise count in the claimant's case, i.e. the claimant or either of joint claimants.

The categories of disregards under Sch.10 are as follows:

Para.1	Premises occupied as a person's home;
Para.2	Premises occupied as home by close relative with LCW or over pension age;
Para.3	Premises occupied as home by former partner living apart by force of circumstances;
Para.4	Various premises that person intends to occupy as home;
Para.5	Premises ceased to be occupied as home following estrangement;
Para.6	Premises where taking reasonable steps to dispose;
Para.7	Assets used for purposes of trade etc. being carried on;
Para.8	Assets previously used for purposes of trade etc no longer carried on;
Para.9	Life insurance policies;
Para.10	Pension rights;
Para.11	Funeral plan contracts;
Para.12	Housing association deposits;
Para.13	Amounts to be used to purchase new home;
Para.14	Insurance payments for home or personal possessions;
Para.15	Amounts received to be used for essential repairs or alterations;
Para.16	Social fund payments in past 12 months;
Para.17	Welfare payments in past 12 months;
Para.18	Arrears or compensation for late payment of certain benefits in past 12 months;
Para.19	Victoria Cross and George Cross payments;
Para.20	Lump sum bereavement support payments in past 12 months;
Para.21	Scottish early years assistance in past 12 months;
Para.22	Scottish funeral expense assistance.

Premises

2.471

Paragraph 1 (premises occupied as the home) is equivalent to para.1 of the income support Sch.10 except that it is in terms of premises rather than a dwelling. Only one set of premises (whatever the precise meaning of that might be: see the notes to reg.2(1) of the Income Support Regulations for cases on when separate properties could constitute one dwelling) can be treated as the home. That rule is expressly extended to paras 2–5, as is not done in the income support Sch.10. Presumably the premises need not be residential accommodation providing that they are lived in as a home. Presumably also the reference to one set of premises allows account to be taken of the provisions in Sch.3 allowing claimants to be treated as occupying more than one accommodation in limited circumstances. It would be consistent then to disregard the value of any interest the claimant has in either accommodation or both.

Paragraph 2 (premises occupied by a close relative as their home) is the equivalent of para.4(a) of the income support Sch.10, except that it is restricted to close relatives of the claimant instead of any relative or a partner. The alternative test (to that of having attained state pension credit qualifying age) of the relative having limited capability for work may possibly be more restrictive than that of being incapacitated. Regulations 38–44 only apply to determining whether a *claimant* has limited capability for work, or for work and work-related activity. Thus it is arguable either that the words "limited capability for work" merely have their ordinary meaning or that it is not necessary that the relative be in receipt of any benefit or credit based on a determination as to limited capability for work.

Paragraph 3 (premises occupied by a former partner as their home) is the equivalent of para.4(b) of the income support Sch.10, but with slightly different conditions. The application of para.4(b) is excluded where there has been a divorce from the former partner or a dissolution of a civil partnership as well as where the claimant and the former partner are estranged. The application of para.3 is not automatically excluded by divorce or the dissolution of a civil partnership, but is where there is estrangement, which may or may not follow such procedures, especially after some lapse of time. More important is the positive condition, not present in para.4(b) of the income support Sch.10, that the two are living apart by force of circumstances. That will prevent the application of the disregard for many non-estranged former partners. But it will apply to claimants who are in a residential home and so no longer share a household with their former partner for that reason. See also the potential disregard in para.5 where the claimant has ceased within the previous 6 months (or longer where the former partner is a lone parent) to occupy premises following an estrangement from their former partner.

Estrangement is a slippery concept that has generated case law in other benefits from which it is difficult to take clear guidance, not least because it is hard to see just what policy objective is served by preventing the application of the disregard when the claimant is estranged from the former partner. In the absence of any definition in the legislation, estrangement must be given its ordinary meaning in context. Some difference in expression among decisions, none of which purport to give definitions, is therefore to be expected and too much attention should not be given to such differences that may simply stem from the circumstances of the particular case in which the question was addressed (*CIS/4096/2005* and *AC v SSWP (IS)* [2015] UKUT 49 (AAC)). The discussion below attempts to concentrate on principles on which there is general agreement without citing all the decisions mentioned in past editions.

First, it is well established that estrangement is not the same as separation (*CIS/4843/2002*, *R(IS) 5/07*) and that separation does not necessarily imply estrangement (*R(IS) 5/05*). Nor does divorce or dissolution of a civil partnership necessarily imply estrangement, but no doubt normally the initial circumstances would indicate estrangement as discussed below and there would have to be some real intention to resume living together to found a different conclusion. By definition, to be a former partner the person must at least no longer be a member of the same household as the claimant. It must be remembered that, as pointed out in *R(IS) 5/05*, a person may temporarily be living away from a claimant and yet still be a member of the household. That is so on the general meaning of the term and as the basis of the special rule in reg.3(6), which purports to limit that effect of a temporary absence to six months (the form of reg.3(6) appears to be somewhat circular, because it refers to temporary absence from the claimant's household when a temporary absence would mean that the household was still shared, so "household" may have to have meant little more than accommodation). Examples might be where a spouse or partner is in a care or nursing home or hospital or caring for a sick relative or friend in another place for a time that is realistically hoped to be temporary. In such circumstances, the two remain a couple as defined in s.39 of the WRA 2012 and partners, so that the two must claim universal credit as joint claimants. But the value of the premises where the person is staying (if the other partner happened to have an interest in them) could not be disregarded under para.1 (because only one set of premises occupied as the home is covered) or para.2 (because a partner is not a close relative) or para.3 (because the person is not a *former* partner). If the separation has been permanent or open-ended from the outset (so as not to be merely temporary) or becomes non-temporary after a change of circumstances (including the time that it has continued), the person will be a former partner.

If there is separation such as to make the person a former partner, "estrangement" must entail something further in order to give some force to the condition of not being estranged. *R(IS) 5/05* agrees with *R(SB) 2/87* that estrangement has a "connotation of emotional disharmony". That has been accepted in subsequent decisions, but the important matter is the context in which such disharmony is to be assessed. There can be friendly relations between the claimant and former partner although they are estranged for the purposes of the disregard (*R(IS) 5/05*, para.12, *CPC/683/2007*, *CH/377/2007* and *Bristol CC v SJP (HB)* [2019] UKUT 360 (AAC), paras 34–37, where there is a helpful summary of the earlier decisions). The way that Commissioner Rowland put it in *R(IS) 5/05* was that the question was whether the parties had ceased to consider themselves a couple, as has been accepted and applied in later cases. That needs some unpacking because "couple" has a particular meaning within the legislation that by definition cannot be met where the person is a former partner. So the word must be used in a more general everyday sense.

In para.13 of *CPC/683/2007*, Commissioner Jacobs said this:

"It seems to me that the proper analysis of the relationship between the claimant and his wife is this. They remain married and have no plans to divorce. He would like to resume living with her, but she is opposed to the idea. The reality is that they will never resume living as husband and wife; the claimant accepts that. However, they are not hostile to each other on a personal level and he feels a continuing responsibility towards her. This leads him to help her when she cannot manage on account of her ill-health. In other words, there is no emotional disharmony between the claimant and his wife as adults, but there is emotional disharmony between them as partners. That is a key distinction, because the language used in the legislation is attempting to identify those cases in which the relationship between the parties is such that it is appropriate for their finances to be treated separately for the purposes of benefit entitlement. Once the facts of the case are set out, they seem to me to allow of only one interpretation, which is that the couple are estranged."

The distinction between disharmony as partners and disharmony as adults is a useful one. It is no doubt going too far to say, as the same judge did in *CH/117/2005*, that two people are not estranged if they retain all the indicia of partners apart from physical presence in the same household, at least if that were to be taken out of context to represent a test that separation equals estrangement unless that condition is met. That would not be compatible with a proper consideration of the circumstances of particular cases and an application of the ordinary meaning of estrangement. But it perhaps illustrates one end of the continuum, where although the person is a former partner, because the separation is non-temporary, they and the claimant would be members of the same household if it were not for the circumstances enforcing the separation. At the other end of the continuum are cases where a relationship has broken down such that there is no current prospect of a resumption of living together. Then, no matter how amicable and co-operative the parties might be about, say children, finances and other practical matters, there is estrangement. There is an emotional disharmony between them as partners.

In *CIS/4096/2005*, Commissioner Jupp, in a different context, indicated that estrangement does not require mutuality of feeling. Disharmony can arise from one person's attitude to another even though the other party may not wish the situation to be as it is. The form of para.3 does not ask whether one party is estranged from the other, as for other benefits, but whether the person and the former partner are not estranged. So the question is whether a state of estrangements exists between them. If the realistic position is that the attitude of one party prevents any resumption of a relationship as partners, the fact that the other party did not wish the situation to be as it was or hoped that the estrangement might not be permanent (*CH/377/2007*) does not on its own point against a conclusion that the other party is estranged from the first.

If estrangement is approached in the way suggested above there will be little work for the additional condition of living apart by force of circumstances to do. For the parties not to be estranged something very like that will have to be the case. Note that some people may be in residential care and yet estranged. And someone may be in residential care on a temporary basis, such that the parties remain a couple and the person is not a *former* partner.

Paragraph 4(1)(a) (premises acquired within past 6 months and intends to occupy as the home) is the equivalent of para.2 of the income support Sch.10, with a very slightly wider application. Paragraph 2 requires any extension to the period of 26 weeks from acquisition to be reasonable in the circumstances to enable the claimant to obtain possession and commence occupation. Under para.4(1)(a), provided as always that there is an intention to occupy the premises as the home, the extension to the period of six months under reg.48(2) can be made whenever it is reasonable in the circumstances.

Paragraph 4(1)(b) (commenced steps to obtain possession of premises within the past 6 months) is the equivalent of para.27 of the income support Sch.10. The provisions in sub-para.(2) about when a person is to be deemed to have commenced steps to obtain possession make the conditions the same as under para.27, except that any extension to the period of 6 months under reg.48(2) can be made whenever it is reasonable in the circumstances instead of being linked to enabling obtaining possession and commencing occupation.

Paragraph 4(1)(c) (essential repairs or alterations, commenced within the past 6 months, to render premises fit for occupation) is the equivalent of para.28 of the income support Sch.10, but with a narrower scope. The income support disregard starts from the date on which steps were first taken to effect the repairs, which can cover getting a grant or loan for the cost of the works, applying for permissions or consulting an architect or contractors. In para.4(1)(c) the person must be carrying out the essential repairs or alterations. It is not clear where in the preparatory process that might start. Nor is it entirely clear that alterations essential for occupation by the particular person (e.g. adaptations for someone who is disabled) are covered. The alterations might need to be required to render the premises fit for occupation by anyone. However, note that if the claimant has already taken up occupation as the home para.1 will apply and that if the premises were acquired within the previous six months (extendable) there is the more general disregard in para.4(1)(a). Regulation 48(2) allows the six months from commencement to be extended as reasonable.

Paragraph 5 (claimant ceased to occupy premises as home following estrangement from former partner) is the equivalent of para.25 of the income support Sch.10, except that it does not automatically apply on divorce or the dissolution of a civil partnership, only on estrangement. See the notes to para.3 for discussion of estrangement. The 6 months under sub-para.(b) can be extended where reasonable in the circumstances under reg.48(2).

Paragraph 6 (commenced taking reasonable steps to dispose of premises within past 6 months) is the equivalent of para.26 of the income support Sch.10. The 6 months can be extended where reasonable in the circumstances under reg.48(2). In both provisions the disregard applies to any premises, not just premises occupied as the home. Thus it should cover land without any building on it (*R(IS) 4/97*).

Steps to dispose of premises can include many preparatory steps before actually putting them on the market. Things that have been accepted include obtaining a solicitor's quotation for sale charges and obtaining an estate agent's valuation (*JT v Leicester CC (CTB)* [2012] UKUT 445 (AAC)), making a genuine approach to another tenant in common to agree a sale (*JH v SSWP* [2009] UKUT 1 (AAC)), bringing ancillary relief proceedings within a divorce suit (*R(IS) 5/05*) or even the bringing of divorce proceedings (*CIS/195/2007*). That last decision suggests that if, once steps have first been taken, there is some temporary suspension of activity (e.g. because of family pressures, threats of violence or efforts at reconciliation), that does not necessarily mean that steps are no longer being taken, but it would all depend on the circumstances. What are "reasonable" steps is a question of fact with a margin of judgment involved, but according to *R(IS) 4/97* the test is an objective one. So if a property is put up for sale at a totally unrealistic price, the disregard would not apply. If the asking price was later lowered to something realistic, it could start to apply and it would be that date at which reasonable steps commenced and at which the primary six months started to run.

In some cases, where reasonable steps stop being taken (as opposed to there being a mere temporary suspension or diminution of activity) and are later resumed it will be right to regard the commencement of reasonable steps as taking place at the beginning, not at the date of the resumption. But that is not necessarily always the case (see *SP v SSWP* [2009] UKUT 255 (AAC)). If premises are genuinely taken off the market and later, in different circumstances, are put on the market again, it is arguable that the disregard can start to be applied afresh, with a new six months starting to run. A gap in the receipt of benefit would not automatically have that effect, but could be one of the relevant circumstances to be taken into account.

It was decided in *CIS/30/1993* that the income support disregard could not apply to premises that the claimant had already disposed of, but was treated as still possessing the value of under the notional capital rule. That was because the income support disregard only applied if the claimant was taking reasonable steps to dispose of the premises, which was impossible as only the new owner could take such steps. That reasoning would apply equally to para.6 as the person who has to be taking the reasonable steps must be the person whose capital would be relevant to the universal credit claim were it not for the effect of reg.48(2) in applying the Sch.10 disregards.

Business assets

2.472   *Paragraph 7* (assets of business being carried on) is the equivalent of the first part of para.6(1) of the income support Sch.10. Income support para.6 uses the terms of assets of a business owned in whole or in part by the claimant for the purposes of which he is engaged as a self-employed earner. In view of the meaning of self-employed earner, the use here of the terms "used wholly or mainly for the purposes of a trade, profession or vocation" comes to the same thing. Paragraph 7 applies while the claimant is carrying on that trade, profession or vocation. See the notes to reg.64 for when a person is carrying on a trade etc, from which it is clear that a person may be trading in that sense ("in work") while not currently engaged in activities ("at work"). In this respect, it is arguable that the scope of para.7 is broader than that of the income support para.6(1). For those purposes, it has been held that to be "engaged in" a business a claimant must be performing some business activities in some practical sense as an earner (see the discussion of *Chief Adjudication Officer v Knight*, reported as part of *R(IS) 14/98*, in the notes to para.6(1) of the income support Sch.10 in Vol.II of this series). That appears to make the test whether the self-employed person is "at work". But the concept of "carrying on" a trade etc. in para.7 is significantly different. See the notes to para.8 below for the apparent resulting mismatch between the two provisions.

Note that with effect from May 21, 2020, reg.2(2) of the Universal Credit (Coronavirus) (Self-employed Claimants and Reclaims) (Amendment) Regulations 2020 (SI 2020/522) introduces a 12-month disregard as capital of any payment made to a self-employed claimant under the Coronavirus Job Retention Scheme (CJRS) or by way of a grant or loan to meet the expenses or losses of the trade, profession or vocation in relation to the outbreak of coronavirus disease. For the CJRS disregard to apply, the claimant must have one or more employees who were furloughed (see further in the notes to reg.57) or be a person deemed to be self-employed under reg.77 (company analogous to partnership or one-person business) who has furloughed themselves or other employees. The second disregard would appear to be intended to cover grants under the Self-Employed Income Support Scheme (SEISS), the Small Business Grant Fund or the Retail, Hospitality and Leisure Grant Fund (or similar funds) and loans under the Business Interruption Loan Scheme or the Bounce Back Loan Scheme or similar. The wording is problematic, because it is not clear that the conditions and method of calculation of all those schemes show that the payments are "to meet" expenses or losses (see the discussion in the notes to reg.57), rather than being undifferentiated in nature. Paragraph 7.12 of the Explanatory Memorandum to the Regulations mentions several of the above schemes, but oddly not the SEISS, as being covered. There is no guidance on the issue in para.4 of Memo ADM 10/20. It would appear, however, that, whether or not any payment was to be treated as an income receipt (see again the notes to reg.57), the capital represented by funds retained in the business after the assessment period of receipt would have been disregarded anyway under the principles discussed below while the claimant was continuing to carry on the trade etc (or under para.8 if the claimant had ceased to do so). The funds would be used for the purposes of the business.

The income support disregard applies to the assets of a business partly or wholly owned by a claimant. Here, para.7 applies to assets wholly or mainly "used" for the purposes of the trade etc. The income support disregard therefore appears to apply to any asset used to any extent beyond the de minimis in the business. For instance, the value of a vehicle used for 10% of the time for self-employment and for 90% of the time for personal purposes would seem to be disregarded under that rule. It is accordingly arguable that the universal credit position would be different, so that the value of the vehicle would not be disregarded under para.7 unless the business use amounted to more than 50%. But, if that test is met, the whole value of the asset is disregarded. There is no scope for any apportionment. By contrast, it seems that the use of the word "used" involves no more restrictive condition than under the income support disregard. There, business assets are distinguished from personal assets by asking whether they are "part of the fund employed and risked in the business" (*R(SB)* 4/85). The question whether assets are used for the purposes of a trade etc is substantially the same.

In answering those questions, the income tax and accounting position are factors to be taken into account, but are not conclusive (*CFC/10/1989*). The Commissioner in *R(SB)* 4/85 noted that, while people in a business partnership owe a duty to the other partner(s) to keep business assets severed from and not mixed with their own assets, the same does not apply to sole traders. They can mix their own and business assets together and can freely transfer items from business to personal assets and vice versa. Although so far as money is concerned it is much more straightforward if a self-employed person maintains a business account separate from any personal accounts and keeps receipts and expenditure to the appropriate account, many of those in small-scale self-employment will not maintain any separate bank or building society account. The account may even be a joint account with a person not involved in the business. That in itself is not fatal to the identification of some sums in the mixed account as employed and risked in the business. It becomes a matter of whether there is sufficient evidence (and no doubt it falls to the claimant to come forward with the evidence if there is no separate business account) to be able to identify such an asset. Thus, for instance, if claimants can show that they have a sum of money in a mixed account that is set aside to meet income tax due for payment in the future on their self-employed earnings, that would seem to fall within the scope of this disregard. By contrast, in *CIS/2467/2003* money put by an author into a Maxi ISA, designed for personal savings by medium or long term investment, was found not to have been employed in the business, but to be in the personal sphere as the proceeds of the business. The Commissioner stated that claimants who wished to benefit from the para.6 disregard in relation to money that was not in a separate business account would have to show a clear demarcation between the assets of the business and personal assets. However, it is submitted that that should be taken more as an explanation of why, on the circumstances of the particular case, the claimant had failed to show that he could benefit from the disregard than as a rule of thumb to be applied in place of the principle laid down in *R(SB)* 4/85. Everything depends on the assessment of the evidence in individual cases.

In the particular context of universal credit, the above principles may help to resolve a conundrum stemming from the method of calculating earnings, at least for the self-employed if not for employees. The rule for the self-employed in reg.57 is that income receipts are taken into account in the assessment period in which they are received. The principle that an amount cannot be income and capital at the same time (see *R(IS)* 3/93 and *R(IS)* 9/08) would then probably entail that the receipt and funds derived from it could not be capital during that assessment period. But any proceeds left over in future assessment periods would be capital, it appears regardless of whether surplus earnings would be attributed to those periods under reg.54A as result of the amount of the particular receipt. But the proceeds would still be assets used for the purposes of the trade etc, so would be disregarded as capital under para.7. There is no such escape route for employees. But see the notes to reg.54A (at 2.166) for the argument that the amount of any retained earnings to be taken into account as surplus earnings in any assessment period does not count as capital because the application of reg.54A represents a liability that has to be deducted before the metamorphosis from earnings to capital takes place. That argument can work for the self-employed and employees. See also the special disregard for the self-employed of some coronavirus payments or loans with effect from May 21, 2020 in reg.2(2) of the Self-employed Claimants and Regulations as noted above.

R(FC) 2/92 holds that the ownership by an individual of a tenanted house is not in itself a business, although there may come a point, depending on the circumstances, at which the amount of administration and/or activity involved even in the letting out of a single property could amount to self-employment. See also *RM v Sefton Council (HB)* [2016] UKUT 357 (AAC), reported as [2017] AACR 5, where there was an exceptionally comprehensive survey of the existing authorities. It concluded that, apart from the mere carrying out of the duties of a landlord of one dwelling being insufficient, there are no hard and fast rules, merely factors that point one way or the other.

Paragraph 8 (assets of business that ceased to carry on within the past 6 months) is the equivalent of the second part of para.6(1) and para.6(2) of the income support Sch.10. The disregard is arguably narrower in scope than the income support disregard because it applies only when the claimant has ceased to carry on the trade etc, which may, for the reasons given in the notes to para.7, entail a more definite cessation of trading as a whole, rather than a ceasing to be engaged in activities. Sub-para. (a), where the carrying on of trade ceased for any reason, is limited to circumstances where the claimant is taking reasonable steps to dispose of the assets. Presumably, that allows the value of only some assets, to which that applies, to be disregarded, leaving the value of the rest to count against the capital limits. Under sub-para.(b) the claimant must have ceased to be engaged in carrying on the trade etc because of incapacity (not further defined) and have a reasonable expectation of re-engaging on recovery. That is odd language, because if there has merely been a cessation of engagement in practical activities in the business, with the reasonable expectation of re-engagement once the incapacity is over, the conclusion in most cases would be that the claimant had not ceased to carry on the trade etc., so that the para.7 disregard would still apply. There would only be an easy fit with para.7 if that provision did not apply once a claimant had ceased to be engaged in activities. But on any basis a claimant should not be deprived of a disregard in the circumstances covered by para.8(b). Note that, by contrast with the income support position, incapacity has to be the reason for the cessation of engagement, not merely a reason for a continuation of a cessation started for another reason or a reason for not beginning to play a part in a business for the first time. The period of 6 months since ceasing to be engaged can be extended where reasonable in the circumstances under reg.48(2).

Note that where reg.77 applies (person in a position analogous to that of a sole trader or partner in relation to a company carrying on a trade treated as sole owner or partner and as possessing capital equal to the value of the company's capital, or a share), the value of that deemed capital is disregarded by reg.77(3)(a) while the person is engaged in activities in the course of that trade.

Rights in pensions schemes etc.

2.473 Note first that many provisions in the income support Sch.10 disregarding the capital value of the right to receive various forms of income are not replicated in the present Schedule (e.g. paras 11 (annuities, but see reg.46(3)), 12 (trust funds derived from personal injury compensation, but see reg.75(4)), 13 (life interests and liferents), 16 (capital payable by instalments, but see reg.46(4)), 24 (rent)).

Paragraph 9 (life insurance policies) is the equivalent of para.15 of the income support Sch.10. The latter refers to the surrender value. Paragraph 9 does not, but in the light of reg.49(1), the disregard must apply to whichever of the market value or surrender value has been applied to the policy.

Paragraph 10 (occupational or personal pension schemes) is the equivalent of para.23 of the income support Sch.10. As noted in Vol.II of this series, the right to receive a pension from the schemes mentioned is not capable of being bought or sold and so would have no capital value anyway. There is no equivalent in the present Schedule to para.23A of the income support Sch.10 disregarding the value of any funds held under a personal pension scheme. It is no doubt considered that such funds do not form part of the capital of the member of the scheme, whose interests are only in the rights under the scheme rather than in the fund itself.

Paragraph 11 (funeral plan contracts) has no equivalent in the income support Sch.10.

Amounts earmarked for special purposes

Paragraph 12 (housing association deposits as a condition of occupying the home) is the equivalent of para.9(a) of the income support Sch.10. The latter defines housing association.

2.474

Paragraph 13(a) (amounts received within the past 6 months attributable to proceeds of sale of previous home to be used for the purchase of premises to be occupied as the home) is the equivalent of para.3 of the income support Sch.10. Under the latter, the sum must be directly attributable to the proceeds of sale, rather than merely attributable. The emphasis of the 6-month condition is different. Under income support para.3 the intention must be to occupy new premises within 26 weeks of the sale of the previous home. Under para.13(a) there is simply a limit (extendable under reg.48(2)) of 6 months from the receipt of the proceeds of sale and no condition that the intention be to occupy the new home within any particular period. See *R(IS) 7/01* on the effect of the test of "is to be used". It was held there that there must not only be an intention to use the proceeds to buy a new home (which can include buying land to build a house on), but also "reasonable certainty" that it will be so used. A mere hope that the proceeds will be used at some future date for another home is not sufficient. It is understood that the correctness of *R(IS) 7/01* is under challenge in an appeal currently before the Upper Tribunal. A claimant who has a sum attributable to the proceeds of sale of home A and is currently living in home B may claim the advantage of the disregard provided that there is the requisite intention and reasonable certainty of use in relation to home C (*CIS/4269/2003*). However, the change in the condition for universal credit as compared to income support, of having received the sum within the previous six months (extendable) rather than intending to occupy the new home within 26 weeks (extendable) makes such a scenario more difficult to get within the terms of the disregard. The disregard cannot apply if the claimant has already bought a new home prior to the sale of the former home and at the time of the purchase it was not intended that the former home would be sold (*WT v DSD (IS)* [2011] NI Com 203).

Paragraph 13(b) (amounts received within the past 6 months to be used for the purchase of premises to be occupied as the home that have been deposited with a housing association) is the equivalent of para.9(b) of the income support Sch.10. See the notes to para.13(a) for "is to be used". The six months can be extended where reasonable in the circumstances under reg.48(2).

Paragraph 13(c) (grant received in the past 6 months for sole purpose of purchase of a home) appears to be the equivalent of para.37(a) of the income support Sch.10, but without any limitation as to the source of the grant. The definition of "grant" in reg.68(7) (see reg.2) does not seem applicable in the context of para.13(c). See the notes to para.13(a) for "is to be used". The six months can be extended where reasonable in the circumstances under reg.48(2).

Paragraph 14 (amount received within the past 6 months under an insurance policy in connection with loss of or damage to the home or personal possessions) is the equivalent of para.8(a) of the income support Sch.10, but without the condition that the sum be intended for repair and replacement. The 6 months can be extended where reasonable in the circumstances under reg.48(2).

Paragraph 15 (amount received within the past 6 months to be used for essential repairs or alterations to premises occupied or to be occupied as the home, where condition that it be used for that purpose) is the equivalent of para.8(b) of the income support Sch.10. See the notes to para.13(a) on the effect of the test of "is to be used". The 6 months can be extended where reasonable in the circumstances under reg.48(2).

Other payments

2.475   *Paragraph 16* (social fund payments made within the past 12 months) is the equivalent of para.18 of the income support Sch.10. The 12 months is not extendable.

Paragraph 17 (local authority welfare payments made within the past 12 months) appears to be the equivalent of paras 17(1) and (2), 18A and 67 of the income support Sch.10. Under sub-para.(b) there is no restriction to any particular legislative provision as the source of the power to make the payment, but an exception for payments for living expenses. However, it must be asked whether payments constitute capital rather than income in the first place. If income, amounts will metamorphose into capital only after the end of the period to which they are attributable as income under the principle of *R(IS) 3/93* and *R(IS) 9/08*. See the notes to reg.66 for the question of how payments of unearned income should be attributed to assessment periods. The 12 months is not extendable.

Paragraph 18 (arrears or compensation for late payment received within the past 12 months of universal credit and certain social security benefits) is the equivalent of para.7 of the income support Sch.10, although the specification of the other benefits covered is through a different method. The 12 months is not extendable. There is no provision, as there is for income support and other legacy benefits, for a longer disregard for large payments of arrears or compensation where the late payment was the result of official error or an error of law (but see reg.10A of the Transitional Provisions Regulations, mentioned below). The benefits abolished by s.33 of the WRA 2012 are income-based JSA, income-related ESA, income support, housing benefit, council tax benefit (already abolished), child tax credit and working tax credit. Benefits falling outside reg.66(1)(a) and (b) and therefore covered by the disregard will include child benefit, attendance allowance, any care or mobility component of disability living allowance, any daily living component or mobility component of personal independence payment and the monthly payments of the new bereavement support payment. Thus payments of arrears (or compensation for late payment) of the benefits listed in reg.66(1)(a) or (b), including retirement pension income and new style ESA and JSA, do not attract the capital disregard.

In principle, payments of benefits that would have had the character of income if paid on their due date should retain that character when paid in arrears as a lump sum (*R(SB) 4/89* and *CH/1561/2005*, and see *Minter v Kingston upon Hull CC* and *Potter v Secretary of State for Work and Pensions* [2011] EWCA Civ 1155, reported as [2012] AACR 21 on lump sum payments of compensation in settlement of equal pay claims, discussed in the notes to reg.23 of the Income Support Regulations in Vol.II of this series). In *R(SB) 4/89*, the Commissioner, relying on the principle in *McCorquodale v Chief Adjudication Officer*, reported as *R(SB) 1/88*, held that the income should be taken into account in the periods for which it would have been taken into account if paid on the due dates. In view of the absence of a clear rule in regs.66 and 73 on the assessment period in which payments of unearned income are to be taken into account (see the notes to reg.66), it is arguable that the same principle would apply to universal credit. But there is also a principle that if any amount of income is left over after the end of the period to which it is properly to be attributed that amount metamorphoses into capital (*R(SB) 2/83* and *R(IS) 3/93*). Looking at the date on which the payment of arrears or compensation is made, by definition all the periods to which the income would have been attributed if paid on the due dates would have passed, so that the lump sum would constitute capital from that point on. The disregard would therefore bite at that point, if applicable. If, however, the lump sum should be taken into account as unearned income for a forward period starting with the assessment period in which it is paid, it would not constitute capital in the assessment periods in which it was so attributed, except to the extent that there were amounts left over from that attributed to each succeeding assessment period.

See the new reg.10A of the Universal Credit (Transitional Provisions) Regulations 2014 (Pt.IVA of this volume), inserted with effect from September 11, 2018 by reg.8 of the Social Security (Treatment of Arrears of Benefit) Regulations 2018 (SI 2018/932). This allows a longer period of disregard as capital in cases where a payment of arrears of benefit, or of compensation for arrears due to the non-payment of benefit, amounts to £5,000 or more and the period of entitlement to which the payment relates began before legacy benefits are totally abolished (introductory part of reg.10A(1) and para.(1)(d)). All cases of arrears or compensation for non-payment of benefit are covered. Apparently any benefit can be involved, as there is no special definition of that word. There is no restriction to cases of official error or error of law. There are then two alternatives. The first (para.(1)(a)(i)) is that the payment is received during a current award of universal credit, in which case the disregard applies for 12 months from the date of receipt if the payment would have been disregarded if the claimant had been entitled to a legacy benefit or SPC. The second (para.(1)(ii)) is that the payment was received during an award of a legacy benefit or SPC and no more than a month elapsed between the ending of that award and the start of entitlement to universal credit. In that case the disregard applies for the same period if the payment was disregarded under the rules of the earlier award.

Paragraph 19 (Victoria Cross and George Cross) is the equivalent of para.46 of the income support Sch.10.

Paragraph 20 (lump sum bereavement support payment received within the previous 12 months) is the equivalent of the new para.72 of the income support Sch.10. The 12 months is not extendable. Payments of arrears of the monthly payments are disregarded as capital for 12 months from the date of receipt under para.18. In so far as they retain their character as income they fall outside the specification of what is unearned income in reg.66 (see reg.66(1)(b) as amended).

Paragraph 21 disregards as capital any Scottish early years assistance, but only where given within the 12 months before the date in question. The restriction of this disregard to receipts within the previous 12 months does not apply to other means-tested benefits (see, for instance, para.75 of Sch.10 to the Income Support Regulations). Early years assistance is not listed in reg.66 of the Universal Credit Regulations 2013, so cannot count as unearned income, although since it takes the form of lump sum payments it probably could not have constituted income in any event.

Paragraph 22 disregards as capital any Scottish funeral expense assistance, with no limit as to the past period in which it was received. The benefit is implemented by the Funeral Expense Assistance (Scotland) Regulations 2019 (SSI 2019/292) (see Pt VII of Vol.II of this series). Funeral expense assistance is not listed in reg.66, so cannot count as unearned income, although since it takes the form of lump sum payments would probably not have constituted income in any event.

Omissions

A number of categories disregarded for the purposes of income support and old style ESA and JSA are thus not included in the universal credit Sch.10 or regs 75–77. Some cover very specific circumstances, but all are apparently deserving. They include payments of expenses of attending various schemes relating to job-seeking, the value of the right to receive the outstanding amount of capital payable by instalments, payments under a council tax reduction scheme and educational maintenance allowances.

2.476

SCHEDULE 11

APPLICATION OF ESA OR JSA SANCTIONS TO UNIVERSAL CREDIT

Moving an ESA sanction to UC

2.477   1. (1) This paragraph applies where—
   (a) a person is, or has ceased to be, entitled to an employment and support allowance;
   (b) there is a reduction relating to the award of the employment and support allowance under section 11J of the Welfare Reform Act 2007; and
   (c) the person becomes entitled to universal credit.

(2) Any reduction relating to the award of the employment and support allowance is to be applied to the award of universal credit.

(3) The period for which the reduction is to have effect is the number of days which apply to the person under regulations 52 and 53 of the ESA Regulations minus—
   (a) any days which have already resulted in a reduction to the amount of the employment and support allowance; and
   (b) if the award of the employment and support allowance has terminated, any days falling after the date of that termination and before the date on which the award of universal credits starts, and that period is to be added to the total outstanding reduction period.

(4) The amount of the reduction in the award of universal credit for any assessment period in which the reduction is applied is the amount calculated in accordance with regulation 110.

Moving a JSA sanction to UC

2.478   2. (1) This paragraph applies where—
   (a) a person is, or has ceased to be, entitled to a jobseeker's allowance;
   (b) there is a reduction relating to the person's award of a jobseeker's allowance under section 6J or 6K of the Jobseekers Act 1995; and
   (c) the person becomes entitled to universal credit.

(2) Any reduction relating to the award of the jobseeker's allowance is to be applied to the award of universal credit.

(3) The period for which the reduction is to have effect is the number of days which apply to the person under regulations 19 to 21 of the Jobseeker's Allowance Regulations 2013 minus—
   (a) any days which have already resulted in a reduction to the amount of the jobseeker's allowance; and
   (b) if the award of the jobseeker's allowance has terminated, any days falling after the date of that termination and before the date on which the award of universal credits starts, and that period is to be added to the total outstanding reduction period.

(4) The amount of the reduction in the award of universal credit for any assessment period in which the reduction is applied is the amount calculated in accordance with regulation 110.

Effect of ESA or JSA sanction on escalation of UC sanction

2.479   3. Where—
   (a) a reduction in relation to an award of an employment and support allowance or an award of a jobseeker's allowance is applied to an award of universal credit by virtue of paragraph 1 or 2;
   (b) there is a subsequent sanctionable failure under section 26 or 27 of the Act; and
   (c) the failure giving rise to the reduction in relation to the award of an employment and support allowance or the award of a jobseeker's allowance ("the previous failure") and the reduction period determined for that failure correspond with a failure specified under section 26 or 27 of the Act to which the same reduction period would apply under Chapter 2 of Part 8 of these Regulations,

for the purposes of determining the reduction period for that subsequent failure, the previous failure is to be treated as if it were the corresponding failure under section 26 or 27 of the Act.

GENERAL NOTE

Paragraphs. 1 and 2

2.480   Paragraphs 1 and 2 constitute an important element of the relationship between new style ESA and JSA and universal credit. They provide that where a claimant is entitled to new style ESA or JSA and is subject to a sanction under s.11J of the WRA

2007 or s.6J or 6K of the WRA 2012 and then becomes entitled to universal credit, and also where the claimant ceases to be entitled to new style ESA or JSA, the ESA or JSA reduction is to be applied to the universal credit award. That works in practice if entitlement to ESA or JSA has ceased, but if that entitlement continues, it is the case that the unreduced (see reg.42 of the ESA Regulations 2013 and reg.5 of the JSA Regulations 2013 disapplying the sanctions regime for those benefits in the circumstances of dual entitlement) amount of ESA or JSA counts as income in the calculation of the amount of any universal credit award and so cuts into the amount available for reduction under the universal credit sanction. That sanction cannot as such reduce the amount of new style ESA or JSA payable. It is in the nature of a reduction in the amount of an award of benefit that the reduction cannot exceed the amount of that particular award. That has the anomalous results discussed in the notes to reg.5 of the JSA Regulations 2013 in Vol.II of this series.

The WRA 2012 contains a regulation-making power that could have been used to avoid these anomalous results. This is in para.2 of Sch.5, which applies when a claimant is entitled to both universal credit and a "relevant benefit", i.e. new style ESA or JSA. Paragraph 2(2) allows regulations in particular to provide in such circumstances for no amount to be payable by way of the relevant benefit. A Departmental memorandum to the House of Lords Select Committee on Delegated Powers and Regulatory Reform (see para.1.177) indicated that among the intended uses of the powers in para.2 was to specify in cases of dual entitlement whether the claimant would be paid only universal credit or only the relevant benefit or both. It was also intended to set out, if sanctions were applicable, which benefit was to be reduced first and to provide, if appropriate, that the application of a sanction to one benefit did not increase the amount of another. However, no regulations have been made to carry out those intentions. The only use of para.2 appears to have been in making reg.42 of the ESA Regulations 2013 and reg.5 of the JSA Regulations 2013, under the power in para.2(3), para.2(2) not being mentioned in the list of statutory powers invoked in the preamble to the Regulations. If regulations had provided that when there was dual entitlement no amount of new style ESA or JSA was to be payable, then there would have been no income from the benefit concerned to be taken into account in the calculation of the amount of universal credit payable and any reduction of benefit under a sanction would bite on the whole amount of the universal credit in the ordinary way. The non-application of the work-related and connected requirements for new style JSA and the sanctions regime under new style ESA and JSA would then have been part of a coherent structure. But that is not the actual state of the legislation.

It might be asked whether the provisions for reduction periods under the universal credit provisions to be applied to a new style ESA or JSA award and vice versa supply a way out of the anomalies. The answer is no. Regulation 61 of the ESA Regulations 2013 and reg.30 of the JSA Regulations 2013 only apply where a claimant ceases to be entitled to universal credit and is or becomes entitled to new style ESA or JSA. In those circumstances any universal credit sanction reduction period is applied to the ESA or JSA award. Regulations 61 and 30 do not apply during any period of dual entitlement. By contrast, when the opposite direction is considered, reg.43 of the ESA Regulations 2013 and reg.6 of the JSA Regulations 2013 apply only where the claimant is entitled to new style ESA or JSA subject to a sanction reduction period, becomes entitled to universal credit and *remains* entitled to new style ESA or JSA. But the result is that the reduction ceases to be applicable to the ESA or JSA award. That appears merely to reinforce the position under reg.42 of the ESA Regulations 2013 and reg.5 of the JSA Regulations 2013. The unreduced amount of ESA or JSA counts as income in the calculation of the amount of the universal credit award and only the "topping up" element of universal credit can be subject to reduction.

Paragraph 3

Under para.3, where a new style ESA or JSA sanction has been applied to universal credit under para.1 or 2, it can count as a "previous sanctionable failure" **2.481** for the purposes of calculating the length of the reduction period for a subsequent universal credit sanction under s.26 or 27 of the WRA 2012 (see regs 102–104). Where there have been previous universal credit (and these equivalent) sanctionable failures within the previous 365 days including the date of the current sanctionable failure (but not within the previous 14 days), that affects the length of the reduction period. Note that it is not every previous new style ESA or JSA sanction that has that effect under para.3. It is only such a sanction that has been applied to universal credit. The position is thus not the same as under regs 19–21 of the JSA Regulations 2013 where there is express reference to previous universal credit sanctions as well as new style JSA sanctions (and new style ESA sanctions in the case of reg.21) as capable of being previous sanctionable failures. Regulation 19 of the ESA Regulations 2013 refers to previous new style JSA sanctionable failures and universal credit sanctionable failures at the appropriate level as well as to previous new style ESA low-level sanctionable failures. It also appears that an old style ESA or JSA sanctionable failure occurring within the 365 days cannot count as a previous sanctionable failure.

[¹ Regulation 24A(4)]

SCHEDULE 12

Availability of the Child Element where Maximum Exceeded – Exceptions

Introduction
2.482   1. This Schedule provides for cases where, for the purposes of regulation 24A, an exception applies in relation to a child or qualifying young person for whom a claimant is responsible ("A").

Multiple births
2.483   2. An exception applies where—
    (a) the claimant is a parent (other than an adoptive parent) of A;
    (b) A was one of two or more children born as a result of the same pregnancy;
    (c) the claimant is responsible for at least two of the children or qualifying young persons born as a result of that pregnancy; and
    (d) A is not the first in the order of those children or qualifying young persons as determined under regulation 24B.

Adoptions
2.484   3. An exception applies where A has been placed for adoption with, or adopted by, the claimant in accordance with the Adoption and Children Act 2002 or the Adoption and Children (Scotland) Act 2007, but not where—
    (a) the claimant (or, if the claimant is a member of a couple, the other member)—
        (i) was a step-parent of A immediately prior to the adoption; or
        (ii) has been a parent of A (other than by adoption) at any time;
    (b) the adoption order made in respect of A was made as a Convention adoption order (as defined, in England and Wales, in section 144 of the Adoption and Children Act 2002 and in Scotland, in section 119(1) of the Adoption and Children Scotland Act 2007); or
    (c) prior to that adoption, A had been adopted by the claimant (or, if the claimant is a member of a couple, the other member) under the law of any country or territory outside the British Islands.

Non-parental caring arrangements
2.485   4.—(1) An exception applies where the claimant—
    (a) is a friend or family carer in relation to A; or
    (b) is responsible for a child who is a parent of A.
(2) In this paragraph, "friend or family carer" means a person who is responsible for A, but is not (or, if that person is a member of a couple, neither member is) A's parent or step-parent and—
    (a) is named in a child arrangements order under section 8 of the Children Act 1989, that is in force with respect to A, as a person with whom A is to live;
    (b) is a special guardian of A appointed under section 14A of that Act;
    (c) is entitled to a guardian's allowance under section 77 of the Contributions and Benefits Act in respect of A;

(d) in whose favour a kinship care order, as defined in section 72(1) of the Children and Young People (Scotland) Act 2014, subsists in relation to A;

(e) is a guardian of A appointed under section 5 of the Children Act 1989 or section 7 of the Children (Scotland) Act 1995;

(f) in whom one or more of the parental responsibilities or parental rights respectively described in section 1 and 2 of the Children (Scotland) Act 1995 are vested by a permanence order made in respect of A under section 80 of the Adoption and Children (Scotland) Act 2007;

(g) fell within any of paragraphs (a) to (f) immediately prior to A's 16th birthday and has since continued to be responsible for A; or

(h) has undertaken the care of A in circumstances in which it is likely that A would otherwise be looked after by a local authority.

Non-consensual conception

5.—(1) An exception applies where—   **2.486**

(a) the claimant ("C") is A's parent; and

(b) the Secretary of State determines that—

    (i) A is likely to have been conceived as a result of sexual intercourse to which C did not agree by choice, or did not have the freedom and capacity to agree by choice; and

    (ii) C is not living at the same address as the other party to that intercourse ("B").

(2) The circumstances in which C is to be treated as not having the freedom or capacity to agree by choice to the sexual intercourse are to include (but are not limited to) circumstances in which, at or around the time A was conceived—

(a) B was personally connected to C;

(b) B was repeatedly or continuously engaging in behaviour towards C that was controlling or coercive; and

(c) that behaviour had a serious effect on C.

(3) The Secretary of State may make the determination in sub-paragraph (1)(b)(i) only if—

(a) C provides evidence from an approved person which demonstrates that—

    (i) C had contact with that approved person or another approved person; and

    (ii) C's circumstances are consistent with those of a person to whom sub-paragraphs (1)(a) and (1)(b)(i) apply; or

(b) there has been—

    (i) a conviction for—

        (aa) an offence of rape under section 1 of the Sexual Offences Act 2003 or section 1 of the Sexual Offences (Scotland) Act 2009;

        (bb) an offence of controlling or coercive behaviour in an intimate or family relationship under section 76 of the Serious Crime Act 2015; or

        (cc) an offence under the law of a country outside Great Britain that the Secretary of State considers to be analogous to the offence mentioned in sub-paragraph (aa) or (bb) above; or

    (ii) an award under the Criminal Injuries Compensation Scheme in respect of a relevant criminal injury sustained by C,

where it appears likely to the Secretary of State that the offence was committed, or the criminal injury was caused, by B and resulted in the conception of A or diminished C's freedom or capacity to agree by choice to the sexual intercourse which resulted in that conception.

(4) The Secretary of State may make the determination in sub-paragraph (1)(b)(ii) where the only available evidence is confirmation by C that that sub-paragraph applies.

(5) For the purposes of sub-paragraph (2)(a), B was personally connected to C if, at or around the time A was conceived—

(a) they were in an intimate personal relationship with each other; or

(b) they were living together and—

    (i) were members of the same family; or

    (ii) had previously been in an intimate personal relationship with each other.

(6) For the purposes of sub-paragraph (2)(c), B's behaviour had a serious effect on C if—

(a) it caused C to fear, on at least two occasions, that violence would be used against C; or

(b) it caused C serious alarm or distress which had a substantial adverse effect on C's day-to-day activities.

(7) In sub-paragraph (3)—

"approved person" means a person of a description specified on a list approved by the Secretary of State for the purposes of sub-paragraph (3)(a) and acting in their capacity as such;

"Criminal Injuries Compensation Scheme" means the Criminal Injuries Compensation

Scheme under the Criminal Injuries Compensation Act 1995; and
"relevant criminal injury" means—

  (a) a sexual offence (including a pregnancy sustained as a direct result of being the victim of a sexual offence);

  (b) physical abuse of an adult, including domestic abuse; or

  (c) mental injury,

as described in the tariff of injuries in the Criminal Injuries Compensation Scheme.

(8) For the purposes of sub-paragraph (5)(b)(i), B and C were members of the same family if, at or around the time A was conceived—

  (a) they were, or had been, married to each other;

  (b) they were, or had been, civil partners of each other;

  (c) they were relatives (within the meaning given by section 63(1) of the Family Law Act 1996);

  (d) they had agreed to marry each other, whether or not the agreement had been terminated;

  (e) they had entered into a civil partnership agreement (within the meaning given by section 73 of the Civil Partnership Act 2004), whether or not the agreement had been terminated;

  (f) they were both parents of the same child; or

  (g) they had, or had had, parental responsibility (within the meaning given in regulation 4A(2)) for the same child.

Continuation of existing exception in a subsequent award

2.487   6. An exception applies where—

  (a) the claimant ("C") is A's step-parent;

  (b) none of the exceptions under paragraphs 2 to 5 above apply;

  (c) C has previously been entitled to an award of universal credit as a member of a couple jointly with a parent of A, in which an exception under paragraph 2, 3 or 5 above applied in relation to A;

  (d) since that award terminated, each award of universal credit to which C has been entitled has been made—

    (i) as a consequence of a previous award having ended when C ceased to be a member of a couple or became a member of a couple; or

    (ii) in any other circumstances in which the assessment periods for that award begin on the same day of each month as the assessment periods for a previous award under regulation 21 (assessment periods); and

  (e) where, in the award mentioned in sub-paragraph (c), an exception under paragraph 2 above applied in relation to A—

    (i) C is responsible for one or more other children or qualifying young persons born as a result of the same pregnancy as A; and

    (ii) A is not the first in the order of those children or qualifying young persons as determined under regulation 24B (order of children and qualifying young persons).

AMENDMENT

1. Social Security (Restrictions on Amounts for Children and Qualifying Young Persons) Amendment Regulations 2017 (SI 2017/376) reg.2(1) and (4) (April 6, 2017).

GENERAL NOTE

2.488   See the commentary to regs 24-24B.

The Rent Officers (Universal Credit Functions) Order 2013

(SI 2013/382) (AS AMENDED)

The Secretary of State for Work and Pensions makes the following Order in exercise of the powers conferred by section 122 of the Housing Act 1996.

[In force April 29, 2013]

Citation and commencement

1.—This Order may be cited as the Rent Officers (Universal Credit   2.489
Functions) Order 2013 and comes into force on 29th April 2013.

Interpretation

2.—In this Order—   2.490
"Welfare Reform Act" means the Welfare Reform Act 2012;
"the Universal Credit Regulations" means the Universal Credit
    Regulations 2013;
"accommodation" means any residential accommodation whether or not
    consisting of the whole or part of a building and whether or not com-
    prising separate and self-contained premises;
[² "assessment period" has the same meaning as in section 40 of the
    Welfare Reform Act.]
[¹ ...]
"assured tenancy"—
(a) in England and Wales, has the same meaning as in Part 1 of the
    Housing Act 1988, except that it includes—
    (i) a tenancy which would be an assured tenancy but for paragraph
        2, 8 or 10 of Schedule 1 (tenancies which cannot be assured
        tenancies) to that Act; and
    (ii) a licence which would be an assured tenancy (within the
        extended meaning given in this definition) were it a tenancy; and
(b) in Scotland, has the same meaning as in Part 2 of the Housing
    (Scotland) Act 1988, except that it includes—
    (i) a tenancy which would be an assured tenancy but for paragraph
        7 or 9 of Schedule 4 (tenancies which cannot be assured tenan-
        cies) to that Act; and
    (ii) any other form of occupancy which would be an assured
        tenancy (within the extended meaning given in this definition)
        were it a tenancy;
"broad rental market area" has the meaning given in article 3;
"housing payment" means a relevant payment within the meaning of

paragraph 3 of Schedule 4 (housing costs element for renters) to the Universal Credit Regulations;

"local authority" means—

(a) in relation to England, the council of a district or London borough, the Common Council of the City of London or the Council of the Isles of Scilly;

(b) in relation to Wales, the council of a county or county borough; and

(c) in relation to Scotland, a council constituted under section 2 (constitution of councils) of the Local Government etc. (Scotland) Act 1994;

"provider of social housing" has the meaning given in paragraph 2 of Schedule 4 to the Universal Credit Regulations;

"relevant time" means the time the request for the determination is made or, if earlier, the date the tenancy ends;

"service charge payments" has the meaning given in paragraph 7 of Schedule 1 (meaning of payments in respect of accommodation) to the Universal Credit Regulations;

"tenancy" includes—

(a) in England and Wales, a licence to occupy premises; and

(b) in Scotland, any other right of occupancy,

and references to rent, a tenant, a landlord or any other expression appropriate to a tenancy are to be construed accordingly;

"tenant" includes, where the tenant is a member of a couple within the meaning of section 39 of the Welfare Reform Act, the other member of the couple;

"working day" means any day other than—

(a) a Saturday or a Sunday;

(b) Christmas Day or Good Friday; or

(c) a day which is a bank holiday under the Banking and Financial Dealings Act 1971 in any part of Great Britain.

AMENDMENTS

1. Rent Officers (Housing Benefit and Universal Credit Functions) (Amendment) Order 2013 (SI 2013/1544), art.4(2) (September 1, 2013).

2. Rent Officers (Housing Benefit and Universal Credit Functions) (Local Housing Allowance Amendments) Order 2014 (SI 2014/3126) art.4(2) (January 8, 2015).

Broad rental market area determinations

2.491   **3.**—(1) Broad rental market area determinations taking effect on 29th April 2013 are determined in accordance with paragraph (7) and all other broad rental market area determinations are determined in accordance with paragraphs (2) to (6).

(2) A rent officer must, at such times as the rent officer considers appropriate and if the Secretary of State agrees—

(a) determine one or more broad rental market areas; and

(b) in respect of that broad rental market area, or those broad rental market areas, give to the Secretary of State a notice which identifies the local authority areas and the postcodes contained within the broad rental market area (or each of them).

[² (2A) The power in paragraph (2) is not limited by paragraph 2(2) of Schedule 1.]

(3) A broad rental market area is an area within which a person could reasonably be expected to live having regard to facilities and services for the purposes of health, education, recreation, personal banking and shopping, taking account of the distance of travel, by public and private transport, to and from those facilities and services.

(4) A broad rental market area must contain—

(a) residential premises of a variety of types, including such premises held on a variety of tenures; and

(b) sufficient privately rented residential premises to ensure that, in the rent officer's opinion, the local housing allowance for the categories of accommodation in the area for which the rent officer is required to determine a local housing allowance is representative of the rents that a landlord might reasonably be expected to obtain in that area.

(5) Every part of Great Britain must fall within a broad rental market area and a broad rental market area must not overlap with another broad rental market area.

(6) Any broad rental market area determination made in accordance with paragraph (2) is to take effect—

(a) on the day the determination is made for the purpose of enabling a rent officer to determine a local housing allowance for that area; and

[³ (b) for all other purposes—

(i) on the next relevant Monday following the day on which the determination is made; or

(ii) where the next relevant Monday is within 11 months beginning with the day on which the determination is made, on the next relevant Monday after that.]

(7) For broad rental market area determinations that take effect on 29th April 2013, a rent officer must use the broad rental market area determinations determined in accordance with article 4B of, and Schedule 3B to, the Rent Officers (Housing Benefit Functions) Order 1997 or the Rent Officers (Housing Benefit Functions) (Scotland) Order 1997 that apply on 29th April 2013.

[³ (8) "Relevant Monday" has the same meaning as in article 4(4).]

Amendments

1. Rent Officers (Housing Benefit and Universal Credit Functions) (Local Housing Allowance Amendments) Order 2013 (SI 2013/2978), art.4(2) (January 13, 2014).

2. Rent Officers (Housing Benefit and Universal Credit Functions) (Local Housing Allowance Amendments) Order 2016 (SI 2016/1179) art.4(1) and (2) (January 23, 2017).

3. Rent Officers (Housing Benefit and Universal Credit Functions) (Amendment) Order 2017 (SI 2017/1323) art.4(1) and (2) (January 26, 2018).

4. Rent Officers (Housing Benefit and Universal Credit Functions) (Amendment) Order 2020 (SI 2020/27) art.4(1) and (2) (January 30, 2020).

Local housing allowance determinations

4.—(1)[⁵ ...]   2.492

[⁵ (1)] [¹ In 2014 and in each subsequent year, on the date specified in paragraph [⁵ (2)],] a rent officer must—

(a) for each broad rental market area determine, in accordance with Schedule 1, a local housing allowance for each of the categories of accommodation set out in paragraph 1 of Schedule 1; and

(b) notify the Secretary of State of the local housing allowance determination made in accordance with sub-paragraph (a) for each broad rental market area.

[¹[³ [⁵ (2)] The date specified for the purposes of paragraph [⁵ (1)] is the last working day of January [⁶ and also the 31st March 2020].]]

[⁴ [⁵ (3) Any local housing allowance determination made in accordance with paragraph (1) is to take effect—

(a) in the case of a person with an existing UC entitlement—
  (i) on the relevant Monday where that is the first day of an assessment period for the person in question; or
  (ii) where the relevant Monday is not the first day of an assessment period for that person, on the first day of the next assessment period following that; or

(b) in any other case, on the relevant Monday.]]

[⁶ (3A) The determinations made in accordance with paragraph (1) on the 31st March 2020 shall take effect (under paragraph (3)) in place of the determinations made in accordance with paragraph (1) on the 31st January 2020.]

[⁵ (4) For the purposes of this article—

"a person with an existing UC entitlement" means a person who is entitled to universal credit on the relevant Monday;

"relevant Monday" means the first Monday in the first tax year that commences following the day on which the determination is made;

"tax year" means a period beginning with 6th April in one year and ending with 5th April in the next.]

AMENDMENTS

1. Rent Officers (Housing Benefit and Universal Credit Functions) (Amendment) Order 2013 (SI 2013/1544), art.4(3) (September 1, 2013).

2. Rent Officers (Housing Benefit and Universal Credit Functions) (Local Housing Allowance Amendments) Order 2013 (SI 2013/2978), art.4(2) (January 13, 2014).

3. Rent Officers (Housing Benefit and Universal Credit Functions) (Local Housing Allowance Amendments) Order 2014 (SI 2014/3126) art.4(3) (January 8, 2015).

4. Rent Officers (Housing Benefit and Universal Credit Functions) (Local Housing Allowance Amendments) Order 2014 (SI 2014/3126) art.4(4) (January 8, 2015).

5. Rent Officers (Housing Benefit and Universal Credit Functions) (Local Housing Allowance Amendments) Order 2015 (SI 2015/1753) art.4(2) (November 2, 2015).

6. Social Security (Coronavirus) (Further Measures) Regulations 2020 (SI 2020/371) reg.4(3)(a) (March 30, 2020).

DEFINITIONS

"accommodation"—see art.2.
"assessment period"—*ibid.*
"broad rental market area"—see arts 2 and 3.

Housing payment determination

2.493   **5.**—Where a rent officer receives a request from the Secretary of State for a determination in respect of housing payments for accommodation let by a provider of social housing, the rent officer must—

(a) determine in accordance with Schedule 2 whether each of the housing payments specified by the Secretary of State in that request is reasonable for that accommodation; and

(b) where the rent officer determines that a housing payment is not reasonable, determine in accordance with Schedule 2 the amount that is reasonable for the accommodation and notify the Secretary of State of that amount.

DEFINITIONS

"accommodation"—see art.2.
"assessment period"—*ibid.*
"housing payment"—see art.2 and Universal Credit Regs, Sch.4, para.3.

Redeterminations

6.—(1) Where a rent officer has made a determination under article 3, 4 or 5 ("the determination") and paragraph (2) applies, a rent officer must make a further determination ("a redetermination") and notify the Secretary of State of the redetermination.

(2) This paragraph applies where—

(a) the determination was made under article 3 or 4 and the rent officer considers that there is an error in relation to that determination; or

(b) the determination was made under article 5 and—

    (i) the Secretary of State requests that the rent officer makes a redetermination;

    (ii) the Secretary of State informs the rent officer that the information supplied when requesting the determination was incorrect or incomplete; or

    (iii) the rent officer considers that there is an error in relation to the determination.

(3) Where a rent officer makes a redetermination the rent officer must do so in accordance with the provisions of this Order that applied to the determination and use the same information that was used for the determination except that, where the information used was incorrect or incomplete, the rent officer must use the correct or complete information.

(4) Where a rent officer makes a redetermination by virtue of paragraph (2)(b)(i), the rent officer must have regard to the advice of at least one other rent officer in relation to that redetermination.

2.494

Information

7.—Where a rent officer considers that the information supplied by the Secretary of State or a landlord under regulation 40 (information to be provided to rent officers) of the Universal Credit, Personal Independence Payment, Jobseeker's Allowance and Employment and Support Allowance (Claims and Payments) Regulations 2013 is incomplete or incorrect, the rent officer must—

(a) notify the Secretary of State or the landlord of that fact; and

(b) request that the Secretary of State or the landlord supplies the further information or to confirm whether, in their opinion, the information already supplied is correct and, if they agree that it is not, to supply the correct information.

2.495

Means of giving notice

2.496   **8.**—Any notice given by a rent officer under this Order may be given in writing or by electronic means unless the Secretary of State requests that notice is given in writing only.

Article 4

SCHEDULE 1

LOCAL HOUSING ALLOWANCE DETERMINATIONS

Categories of accommodation

2.497   **1.** The categories of accommodation for which a rent officer is required to determine a local housing allowance in accordance with article 4 are—
    (a) accommodation where the tenant has the exclusive use of only one bedroom and where the tenancy provides for the tenant to share the use of one or more of—
        (i) a kitchen;
        (ii) a bathroom;
        (iii) a toilet; or
        (iv) a room suitable for living in;
    (b) accommodation where the tenant has the exclusive use of only one bedroom and exclusive use of a kitchen, a bathroom, a toilet and a room suitable for living in;
    (c) accommodation where the tenant has the use of only two bedrooms;
    (d) accommodation where the tenant has the use of only three bedrooms;
    (e) accommodation where the tenant has the use of only four bedrooms.

[1 Local housing allowance for category of accommodation in paragraph 1

2.498   **2.**—(1) Subject to paragraph 5 (anomalous local housing allowances) the rent officer must determine a local housing allowance for each category of accommodation in paragraph 1 as follows.
    [8 [9 (2) The local housing allowance for any category of accommodation is the lower of—
    (a) the rent at the 30th percentile determined in accordance with paragraph 3; and
    (b) for a category of accommodation listed in column 1 of the following table, the amount listed in column 2 of that table (maximum local housing allowance)—

1. Category of accommodation as specified in paragraph 1	2. Maximum local housing allowance for that category of accommodation
paragraph 1(a) (one bedroom, shared accommodation)	£ 1,283.96
Paragraph 1(b) (one bedroom, exclusive use)	£ 1,283.96
Paragraph 1(c) (two bedrooms)	£ 1,589.99
Paragraph 1(d) (three bedrooms)	£ 1,920.00
Paragraph 1(e) (four bedrooms)	£2,579.98]]

(4) Where the local housing allowance would otherwise not be a whole number of pence, it must be rounded to the nearest whole penny by disregarding any amount less than half a penny and treating any amount of half a penny or more as a whole penny.]

Rent at the 30th percentile

2.499   **3.**—(1) The rent officer must determine the rent at the 30th percentile in accordance with the following sub-paragraphs.
    (2) The rent officer must compile a list of rents.
    [1 (3) The rent officer must compile a list of rents in ascending order of the monthly rents which, in the rent officer's opinion, are payable—
    (a) for accommodation let under an assured tenancy for each category of accommodation specified in paragraph 1; and

(b) in the 12 month period ending on the 30th day of the September preceding the date of the determination.]

(4) The list must include any rents which are of the same amount.

(5) The criteria for including an assured tenancy on the list of rents in relation to each category of accommodation specified in paragraph 1 are that—

(a) the accommodation let under the assured tenancy is in the broad rental market area for which the local housing allowance for that category of accommodation is being determined;

(b) the accommodation is in a reasonable state of repair; and

(c) the assured tenancy permits the tenant to use exclusively or share the use of, as the case may be, the same number and type of rooms as the category of accommodation in relation to which the list of rents is being compiled.

[¹ (6) Sub-paragraph (7) applies where the rent officer is not satisfied that the list of rents in respect of any category of accommodation would contain sufficient rents, payable in the 12 month period ending on the 30th day of the September preceding the date of the determination for accommodation in the broad rental market area, to enable a local housing allowance to be determined which is representative of the rents that a landlord might reasonably be expected to obtain in that area.]

(7) In a case where this sub-paragraph applies, the rent officer may add to the list rents for accommodation in the same category in other areas in which a comparable market exists.

(8) Where rent is payable other than monthly the rent officer must use the figure which would be payable if the rent were to be payable monthly by calculating the rent for a year and dividing the total by 12.

(9) When compiling the list of rents for each category of accommodation, the rent officer must—

(a) assume that no-one had sought or is seeking the tenancy who would have been entitled to housing benefit under Part 7 of the Social Security Contributions and Benefits Act 1992(12) or universal credit under Part 1 of the Welfare Reform Act; and

(b) exclude the amount of any rent which, in the rent officer's opinion, is fairly attributable to the provision of services performed or facilities (including the use of furniture) provided for, or rights made available to, the tenant and which would not be classed as service charge payments.

(10) The rent at the 30th percentile in the list of rents ("R") is determined as follows—

(a) where the number of rents on the list is a multiple of 10, the formula is—

$$R = \frac{\text{the amount of the rent at P} + \text{the amount of the rent at P1}}{2}$$

where—

(i) P is the position on the list found by multiplying the number of rents on the list by 3 and dividing by 10; and

(ii) P1 is the following position on the list;

(b) where the number of rents on the list is not a multiple of 10, the formula is—

$$R = \text{the amount of the rent at P2}$$

where P2 is the position on the list found by multiplying the number of rents on the list by 3 and dividing by 10 and rounding the result upwards to the nearest whole number.

[¹ Maximum local housing allowance

4. [² [⁴ . . .]]]   2.500

Anomalous local housing allowances

5. Where—   2.501

(a) the rent officer has determined the local housing allowance for each of the categories of accommodation in paragraph 1 in accordance with the preceding paragraphs of this Schedule; and

(b) the local housing allowance for a category of accommodation in paragraph 1(b) to (e) is lower than the local housing allowance for any of the categories of accommodation which precede it,

that local housing allowance is to be the same as the highest local housing allowance which precedes it.

[⁵ 5A. [⁸ ...] [⁷ [⁸...]]]

6. [¹ [³ [⁴ . . .]]]

AMENDMENTS

1. Rent Officers (Housing Benefit and Universal Credit Functions) (Local Housing Allowance Amendments) Order 2013 (SI 2013/2978), art.4(3) (January 13, 2014).

2. Rent Officers (Housing Benefit and Universal Credit Functions) (Local Housing Allowance Amendments) Order 2014 (SI 2014/3126) art.4(5) (January 8, 2015).

3. Rent Officers (Housing Benefit and Universal Credit Functions) (Local Housing Allowance Amendments) Order 2014 (SI 2014/3126) art.4(6) and Sch.3 (January 8, 2015).

4. Rent Officers (Housing Benefit and Universal Credit Functions) (Local Housing Allowance Amendments) Order 2015 (SI 2015/1753) art.4(3) (November 2, 2015).

5. Rent Officers (Housing Benefit and Universal Credit Functions) (Local Housing Allowance Amendments) Order 2016 (SI 2016/1179) art.4(1) and (3) (January 23, 2017).

6. Rent Officers (Housing Benefit and Universal Credit Functions) (Amendment) Order 2017 (SI 2017/1323) art.4 (January 26, 2018).

7. Rent Officers (Housing Benefit and Universal Credit Functions) (Amendment) Order 2018 (SI 2018/1332) art.4 (January 25, 2019).

8. Rent Officers (Housing Benefit and Universal Credit Functions) (Amendment) Order 2020 (SI 2020/27) art.4(1) and (3) (January 30, 2020).

9. Social Security (Coronavirus) (Further Measures) Regulations 2020 (SI 2020/371) reg.4(3)(b) (March 30, 2020).

GENERAL NOTE

From January 30, 2020 to March 29, 2020, para.2(2) of Sch.1 read as follows:
"(2)   The local housing allowance for any category of accommodation is the lowest of—

(a) the rent at the 30th percentile determined in accordance with paragraph 3;

(b) the local housing allowance last determined for that category of accommodation (or, where the allowance is redetermined under article 6 (redeterminations), the allowance as so redetermined), increased by 1.7%; and

(c) for a category of accommodation listed in column 1 of the following table, the amount listed in column 2 of that table (maximum local housing allowance)—

1. Category of accommodation as in paragraph 1	2. Maximum local housing allowance for that accommodation
paragraph 1(a) (one bedroom, shared accommodation)	£1,218.57
paragraph 1(b) (one bedroom, exclusive use)	£1,218.57
paragraph 1(c) (two bedrooms)	£1,413.54
paragraph 1(d) (three bedrooms)	£1,657.25
paragraph 1(e) (four bedrooms)	£1,949.71".

Article 5

SCHEDULE 2

HOUSING PAYMENT DETERMINATION

1. The rent officer must determine whether, in the rent officer's opinion, each of the housing 2.502
payments payable for the tenancy of the accommodation at the relevant time is reasonable.

2. If the rent officer determines under paragraph 1 that a housing payment is not reasonable,
the rent officer must also determine the amount of the housing payment which is reasonable.

3. When making a determination under this Schedule, the rent officer must—
  (a) have regard to the level of similar payments under tenancies for accommodation
       which—
         (i)   is let by the same type of landlord;
         (ii) is in the same local authority area [¹ (but see paragraph 4)];
         (iii) has the same number of bedrooms; and
         (iv) is in the same reasonable state of repair,
       as the accommodation in respect of which the determination is being made;
  (b) exclude—
         (i)   the cost of any care, support or supervision provided to the tenant by the land-
               lord or by someone on the landlord's behalf;
         (ii) any payments for services performed or facilities (including the use of furniture)
               provided for, or rights made available to, the tenant which are not service charge
               payments; and
  (c) where the accommodation is let at an Affordable Rent, assume that the rent is reason-
       able.

4. Where the rent officer is not satisfied that the local authority area contains sufficient
accommodation to allow a determination of the housing payments which a landlord might
reasonably have been expected to charge, the rent officer may have regard to the level of
housing payments in one adjoining local authority area [¹ or one local authority area adjoining
an adjoining local authority area or, if the rent officer considers it necessary, more than one
such area].

5. For the purposes of this Schedule—
  (a) a housing payment is reasonable where it is not higher than the payment which the
       landlord might reasonably have been expected to obtain for the tenancy at the relevant
       time;
  (b) accommodation is let by the same type of landlord where—
         (i)   in a case where the landlord of the accommodation in respect of which the
               determination is being made is a local authority, the landlord of the other
               accommodation is also a local authority; and
         (ii) in a case where the landlord of the accommodation in respect of which the
               determination is being made is a provider of social housing other than a local
               authority, the landlord of the other accommodation is also a provider of social
               housing other than a local authority;
  (c) accommodation is let at an Affordable Rent where—
         (i)   the rent is regulated under a standard by the Regulator of Social Housing under
               section 194 of the Housing and Regeneration Act 2008(13) ("the 2008 Act")
               which requires the initial rent to be set at no more than 80% of the local market
               rent (including service charges); or
         (ii) the accommodation is let by a local authority and, under arrangements between
               the local authority and the Homes and Communities Agency (as established by
               section 1 of the 2008 Act), the Greater London Authority or the Secretary of
               State, the rent payable is set on the same basis as would be the case if the rent
               were regulated under a standard set by the Regulator of Social Housing under
               section 194 of the 2008 Act which requires the initial rent to be set at no more
               than 80% of the local market rent (including service charges).

AMENDMENT

1. Rent Officers (Housing Benefit and Universal Credit Functions) (Local
Housing Allowance Amendments) Order 2016 (SI 2016/1179) art.4(1) and (4)
(January 23, 2017).

DEFINITIONS

"accommodation"—see art.2.
"housing payment"—see art.2 and Universal Credit Regs, Sch.4, para.3.
"local authority"—see art.2.
"provider of social housing"—see art.2 and Universal Credit Regs, Sch.4, para.4.
"relevant time"—see art.2.
"service charge payments"—see art.2 and Universal Credit Regs, Sch.1 para.7.
"tenancy"—see art.2.
"tenant"—*ibid.*

The Universal Credit (Work-Related Requirements) In Work Pilot Scheme and Amendment Regulations 2015

(SI 2015/89)

Made on January 29, 2015 by the Secretary of State under sections 18(5), 22(2), 41(1)(a), (2)(b) and (4) and 42(2) and (3) of the Welfare Reform Act 2012, Part 3 being made with a view to ascertaining the extent to which the provision made by that Part is likely to promote people already in paid work remaining in work, or obtaining or being able to obtain, more work or better paid work, a draft having been laid before, and approved by resolution of, each House of Parliament in accordance with section 43(4) and (6)(b) of the Act, and the Social Security Advisory Committee having agreed in accordance with section 173(1) of the Social Security Administration Act 1992 that proposals in respect of these Regulations should not be referred to it.

2.503   *[In force February 19, 2015]*

REGULATIONS REPRODUCED

PART 1

INTRODUCTORY

1. Citation, commencement and duration
2. Interpretation

PART 2

AMENDMENT OF THE UNIVERSAL CREDIT REGULATIONS

3. New provision of suspension of mandatory work search and work availability requirements on account of earnings

PART 3

THE IN WORK PILOT SCHEME

GENERAL NOTE

See the annotation to reg.99(6) and (6A), the provisions affected by the amend-ment in reg.3 of the present Regulations, for the context in which the pilot schemes will operate. 2.504

PART 1

INTRODUCTORY

Citation and commencement

1. These Regulations may be cited as the Universal Credit (Work-Related Requirements) In Work Pilot Scheme and Amendment Regulations 2015, and come into force at the end of the period of 21 days beginning with the day on which they are made. 2.505

Interpretation

2. In these Regulations— 2.506
"the Act" means the Welfare Reform Act 2012;
[¹"monthly earnings" has the meaning in regulation 90(6) of the Universal Credit Regulations;]
"qualifying claimant" has the meaning in regulation 7;
"the Universal Credit Regulations" means the Universal Credit Regulations 2013; and
[¹ . . .].

AMENDMENT

1. Universal Credit and Miscellaneous Amendments Regulations 2015 (SI 2015/1754) reg.3(2) (November 4, 2015).

PART 2

AMENDMENT OF THE UNIVERSAL CREDIT REGULATIONS

New provision for suspension of mandatory work search and work availability requirements on account of earnings

2.507   **3.** – *The amendments effected by this regulation have been taken into account in the text of the Universal Credit Regulations 2013 elsewhere in this volume.*

PART 3

THE IN WORK PILOT SCHEME

Provision made for piloting purposes

2.508   **4.**—(1) The following provision is made in accordance with section 41 of the Act to test the extent to which the imposition of work-related requirements on persons already in paid work is likely to promote their remaining in work, or obtaining or being able to obtain, more work or better-paid work.

(2) Regulation 99 of the Universal Credit Regulations (which provides for the suspension of work search requirements and work availability requirements where the claimant's [¹ monthly] earnings from employment or, if the claimant is a member of a couple, their combined [¹ monthly] earnings from employment, reach a specified amount) is to apply as if paragraph (6) were omitted.

(3) The provision made by paragraph (2) is to apply only in relation to qualifying claimants who have been selected by the Secretary of State in accordance with regulation 5 and notified of that selection in accordance with regulation 6.

(4) The provision made by paragraph (2) ceases to apply to a person who has been selected in accordance with regulation 5 where—

(a) that person ceases to be a qualifying claimant (but see paragraph (5)); or

(b) the Secretary of State has determined that that provision should cease to apply because—

(i) the person has moved to live in a different geographical area; or

(ii) the Secretary of State has determined that the testing of particular work-related requirements that have been imposed on that person has concluded.

(5) Where a person has been selected in accordance with regulation 5 and, by reason only of an increase or decrease in their [¹ monthly] earnings (or, if they are a member of a couple, the [¹ monthly] earnings of the other member) the person is no longer a qualifying claimant, paragraph (2) applies again if the person becomes a qualifying claimant again unless, in the intervening period—

(a) paragraph (2) has ceased to apply for another reason; or

(b) the person has ceased to be entitled to universal credit for a continuous period of 6 months or more.

AMENDMENT

1. Universal Credit and Miscellaneous Amendments Regulations 2015 (SI 2015/1754) reg.3(3) (November 4, 2015).

DEFINITIONS

"the Act"—see reg.2.
"claimant"—see WRA 2012 s.40.
"monthly earnings"—see reg.2 and the Universal Credit Regulations 2013 reg.90(6).
"qualifying claimant"—see regs 2 and 7.
"the Universal Credit Regulations"—see reg.2
"work"—see WRA 2012 s.40.
"work availability requirement"—see WRA 2012 ss.40 and 18(2).
"work search requirement"—see WRA 2012 ss.40 and 17(1).
"work-related requirement"—see WRA 2012 ss.40 and 13(2).

Selection of participants

5.—(1) A selection for the purpose of regulation 4 is to be made by the Secretary of State on a random sampling basis from persons who, at the time of the selection, are qualifying claimants.

(2) The Secretary of State may make a selection in accordance with paragraph (1) on more than one occasion and, on each occasion, the Secretary of State may limit that selection to qualifying claimants living in a particular geographical area determined by the Secretary of State or to persons who have become qualifying claimants within a period determined by the Secretary of State.

2.509

DEFINITION

"qualifying claimant"—see regs 2 and 7.

Notification of participants

6.—(1) The Secretary of State must notify a claimant in writing when—
(a) the claimant is selected in accordance with regulation 5; and
(b) the provision made by regulation 4(3) ceases to apply to the claimant by virtue of regulation 4(4), unless it is because the claimant is no longer a qualifying claimant by reason only of a change in earnings.

(2) Where, for the purposes of this regulation, the Secretary of State sends a notice by post to the claimant's last known address, it is to be treated as having been given or sent on the day on which it was posted.

(3) Schedule 2 to the Universal Credit, Personal Independence Payments, Jobseeker's Allowance and Employment and Support Allowance (Claims and Payments) Regulations 2013 applies to the delivery of an electronic communication sent by the Secretary of State for the purposes of this regulation in the same manner as it applies to the delivery of electronic communications for the purposes of those Regulations.

2.510

DEFINITIONS

"claimant"—see WRA 2012 s.40.
"qualifying claimant"—see regs 2 and 7.

Meaning of "qualifying claimant"

2.511   **7.**—(1) A qualifying claimant is a person who—

    (a) falls within section 22 of the Act (claimants subject to all work-related requirements);

    (b) has [¹ monthly] earnings of such an amount (or, if the person is a member of a couple, the couple has combined [¹ monthly] earnings of such an amount) that, apart from regulation 4(2), regulation 99(6) of the Universal Credit Regulations would apply;

    (c) is not a person on whom the Secretary of State must not impose work-related requirements by virtue of regulation 98 of the Universal Credit Regulations (victims of domestic violence); and

    (d) is not a person to whom any of the following paragraphs of regulation 99 of the Universal Credit Regulations (circumstances in which requirements must not be imposed) applies—

        (i) paragraph (3) (which provides for suspension of work search and work availability requirements for various reasons, including imprisonment and treatment for alcohol or drug dependency), except sub-paragraph (a) (claimant attending court as a witness etc.) and sub-paragraph (g) (claimant engaged in a public duty); or

        (ii) paragraph (5)(c) (claimant unfit for work for longer than 14 days).

AMENDMENT

1. Universal Credit and Miscellaneous Amendments Regulations 2015 (SI 2015/1754) reg.3(3) (November 4, 2015).

DEFINITIONS

    "the Act"—see reg.2.
    "couple"—see WRA ss.40 and 39.
    "monthly earnings"—see reg.2 and the Universal Credit Regulations 2013 reg.90(6).
    "the Universal Credit Regulations"—see reg.2
    "work availability requirement"—see WRA 2012 ss.40 and 18(2).
    "work search requirement"—see WRA 2012 ss.40 and 17(1).

Expiry of the pilot scheme

2.512   **8.** This Part ceases to have effect at the end of the period of three years starting with the day on which these Regulations come into force, unless it continues in effect by order of the Secretary of State under section 41(5)(a) of the Act.

GENERAL NOTE

2.513   Part 3 of the Regulations (i.e. regs 4-8) continues in effect for the period of 12 months beginning with February 19, 2018 by virtue of the Universal Credit (Work-Related Requirements) In Work Pilot Scheme (Extension) Order 2018 (SI 2018/168), for the further period of 12 months beginning with February 19, 2019 by virtue of the Universal Credit (Work-Related Requirements) In Work Pilot Scheme (Extension) Order 2019 (SI 2019/249) and for a further 12 months beginning on February 19, 2020 by virtue of the Universal Credit (Work-Related Requirements) In Work Pilot Scheme (Extension) Order 2020 (SI 2020/152).

The Universal Credit (Surpluses and Self-employed Losses) (Digital Service) Amendment Regulations 2015

(SI 2015/345)

Made on February 23, 2015 by the Secretary of State in exercise of the powers conferred by s. 42(2) and (3) of, and para. 4(1), (3)(a) and (4) of Sch. 1 to, the Welfare Reform Act 2012, having been referred to the Social Security Advisory Committee in accordance with s. 172(1) of the Social Security Administration Act 1992.

[In force April 11, 2018]

Citation and commencement

1. These Regulations may be cited as the Universal Credit (Surpluses 　2.514
and Self-employed Losses) (Digital Service) Amendment Regulations 2015
and come into force on [¹11th April 2018].

AMENDMENT

1. Universal Credit (Miscellaneous Amendments, Saving and Transitional Provision) Regulations 2018 (SI 2018/65) reg.7(2) (February 14, 2018).

Carry forward of surplus earnings

2. *[Amendments incorporated into SI 2013/376]* 　　　　　　　　　2.515

Self-employed earnings – treatment of losses

3. *[Amendments incorporated into SI 2013/376]* 　　　　　　　　　2.516

[¹Saving

4.—(1) The amendments made by these Regulations do not apply to an 　2.517
award of universal credit unless it is—
   (a) an award to which a person has become entitled by reference to residence in a digital service area (whether or not the person is still living in that area);
   (b) an award to which a person who is living in a digital service area is entitled (whether or not the person was living in that area at the time that person became entitled);
   (c) an award, not falling within sub-paragraph (a) or (b), to which a person who has lived in a digital service area at any time after it became a digital service area is entitled but only if that award has been administered on the digital service computer system;
   (d) an award not falling within sub-paragraphs (a) to (c)--
      (i) which is made to members of a couple jointly as a consequence of a previous award having ended when the couple formed, or
      (ii) which is made to a single claimant as a consequence of a previous award having ended when the claimant ceased to be a member of a couple,

where that previous award was administered on the digital service computer system.

(2) Where the date on which these Regulations first apply to an existing award of universal credit by virtue of paragraph (1)(b) is not the first day of an assessment period, they are not to have effect in relation to that award until the first day of the next assessment period.

(3) In this regulation—

"a digital service area" means–

(a) postcode districts SM5 2, SM6 7 and SM6 8; and

(b) an area in respect of which no restrictions have been imposed in order for the universal credit provisions to come into force on a claim for universal credit (apart from with respect to residence and the date on which, or period in respect of which, universal credit is claimed) by an order under section 150 of the Welfare Reform Act 2012 or an area (apart from that referred to in (a)) in respect of which such restrictions have been, but are no longer, imposed;

"the digital service computer system" is the computer system operated by the Secretary of State in digital service areas;

"universal credit provisions" means the provisions listed in Schedule 2 to the Welfare Reform Act 2012 (Commencement No. 9 and Transitional and Transitory Provisions and Commencement No. 8 and Savings and Transitional Provisions (Amendment)) Order 2013.

(4) In regulation 54A of the Universal Credit Regulations 2013 (as inserted [² ...]), "the old award" does not include an award the last day of which fell before [²11th April 2018] and, in regulation 57A (as inserted by regulation 3(4)), "unused loss" does not include the loss from an assessment period that [²began] before that date.]

AMENDMENTS

1. Universal Credit and Miscellaneous Amendments Regulations 2015 (SI 2015/1754) reg.21 (November 3, 2015).

2. Universal Credit (Miscellaneous Amendments, Saving and Transitional Provision) Regulations 2018 (SI 2018/65) reg.7(5) (February 14, 2018).

[¹Transitional provision – temporary de minimis period

2.518   5.—(1) For the purposes of applying regulation 54A (surplus earnings) of the Universal Credit Regulations 2013 in relation to a claim for universal credit made in respect of a period that begins before the end of the temporary de minimis period, the meaning of "relevant threshold" in paragraph (6) of that regulation is modified by substituting "£2,500" for "£300".

(2) For the purposes of paragraph (1), the "temporary de minimis period" is the period beginning with the coming into force of regulation 54A and ending on 31st March 2019, but may be extended by the Secretary of State if the Secretary of State considers it necessary to do so to safeguard the efficient administration of universal credit.]

AMENDMENT

1. Universal Credit (Miscellaneous Amendments, Saving and Transitional Provision) Regulations 2018 (SI 2018/65) reg.7(6) (February 14, 2018).

GENERAL NOTE

See the notes to reg.54A of the Universal Credit Regulations 2013 for the effect of this important modification to the initial operation of the surplus earnings rules. On February 5, 2019 it was announced that the Secretary of State had made a determination under the power in para.(2) to extend the "temporary de minimis period" to March 31, 2020. There was a further extension of a year to March 31, 2021 announced on March 5, 2020 (see the DWP's Guidance on regulations under the WRA 2012 on gov.uk).

2.519

The Loans for Mortgage Interest Regulations 2017

(SI 2017/725)

Made on July 5, 2017 by the Secretary of State, in exercise of the powers conferred by sections 4(5), 35(1), 36(2) and (4) of the Jobseekers Act 1995, sections 2(3)(b) and sections 17(1) and 19(1) of the State Pension Credit Act 2002, sections 123(1)(a), 135(1), 137(1) and (2)(d) and 175(1), (3) and (4) of the Social Security Contributions and Benefits Act 1992, sections 4(2)(a), 24(1) and 25(2), (3) and (5)(a) of the Welfare Reform Act 2007, sections 11(3) and (4) and 42(1), (2) and (3)(a) of, and paragraph 1(1) of Schedule 6 to, the Welfare Reform Act 2012 and sections 18, 19 and 21 of the Welfare Reform and Work Act 2016.

This instrument contains only regulations made under, by virtue of, or consequential upon, sections 18, 19 and 21 of the Welfare Reform and Work Act 2016 and is made before the end of the period of 6 months beginning with the coming into force of those sections. Therefore, in accordance with section 173(5) of the Social Security Administration Act 1992, these Regulations are not required to be referred to the Social Security Advisory Committee.

[In force, see reg. 1 (2)]

Arrangement of Regulations

GENERAL NOTE

2.521   In the past, owner-occupiers who are entitled to IS, IBJSA, IRESA, SPC and universal credit could receive benefit to cover some of their housing costs. Such housing costs were paid as part of the applicable amount (IS, IBJSA and IRESA): see reg.17(1)(e) of, and Sch.3 to, the IS Regulations; reg.83(f) of, and Sch.2 to, the JSA Regulations 1996; reg. 67(1)(c) of, and Sch.6 to, the ESA Regulations; or of the guarantee credit (SPC): see reg.6(6)(c) of, and Sch.2 to, the SPC Regulations; or as the housing costs element of universal credit: see s.11 of the WRA 2012 and regs 25 and 26 of, and Schs 1-3 and 5 to, the UC Regs 2013.

    However, from April 6, 2018, these Regulations, which are made under ss.18, 19 and 21 WRWA 2016, provide for housing costs in respect of mortgage interest and interest on home improvement loans, to be replaced by repayable, interest-bearing, loans secured on the claimants' homes by way of a legal charge.

    The bulk of the Regulations have been in force since July 27, 2017. It was therefore possible for the Secretary of State to make an offer of a loan for mortgage interest before April 6, 2018. However, no amount was payable before that date: see reg.8(1)(a). The new rules commenced for practical purposes on April 6, 2018, when regs 18-21 and Sch.5, which repeal the Schedules referred to in the first paragraph of this Note as they relate to mortgage interest payments and interest on home improvement loans, came into force.

    Also, on July 27, 2017, ss 20(2)-(7) and (10) of WRWA 2016 were brought into force by reg.2 of the Welfare Reform and Work Act 2016 (Commencement No. 5) Regulations 2017 (SI 2017/802). Among other things, these amend s.8 SSA 1998 to empower the Secretary of State to make decisions about loans under s.18 WRWA 2016. The consequence is that an appeal lies to the First-tier Tribunal against such a decision under s.12 SSA 1998 and thence to the Upper Tribunal under s.11 TCEA 2007.

    The remaining parts of s.20 WRWA 2016, which amend the substantive statute law relating to entitlement to housing costs as part of a means-tested benefit were brought into force on April 6, 2018.

It must be stressed that the changes brought about by these Regulations relate exclusively to owner-occupiers. Renters will continue to be entitled to either the housing costs element of universal credit under section 11 of the WRA 2012 and regs 25 and 26 of, and Schs 1-4 to, the UC Regs 2013, or to the Housing Benefit Regulations, or the Housing Benefit (Persons who have attained the qualifying age for state pension credit) Regulations 2006.

Citation and commencement

1.—(1) These Regulations may be cited as the Loans for Mortgage Interest Regulations 2017.

(2) These Regulations come into force—

(a) for the purposes of regulations 18 to 21, on 6th April 2018;

(b) for all other purposes, on 27th July 2017.

2.522

Interpretation

2.—(1) In these Regulations—

"the Act" means the Welfare Reform and Work Act 2016;

[¹ "alternative finance arrangements" has the meaning given in paragraph 5(4) of Schedule 1 to these Regulations;]

"alternative finance payments" has the meaning given in paragraph 5(3) of Schedule 1 to these Regulations;

"applicable amount" means—

(a) in the case of employment and support allowance, the claimant's weekly applicable amount under regulations 67 to 70 of the ESA Regulations;

(b) in the case of income support, the claimant's weekly applicable amount under regulations 17 to 21AA of the IS Regulations;

(c) in the case of jobseeker's allowance, the claimant's weekly applicable amount under regulations 83 to 86C of the JSA Regulations;

(d) in the case of an SPC claimant, the claimant's weekly appropriate minimum guarantee under section 2 of the State Pension Credit Act 2002;

(e) in the case of a UC claimant, the maximum amount of a claimant's award of universal credit under regulation 23(1) of the UC Regulations;

"assessment period" has the meaning given in regulation 21 of the UC Regulations;

"benefit unit" means a single claimant and his or her partner (if any) or joint claimants;

"benefit week" has the meaning given—

(a) in the case of employment and support allowance, in regulation 2 of the ESA Regulations;

(b) the case of income support, in paragraph 4 of Schedule 7 to the Claims and Payment Regulations;

(c) in the case of jobseeker's allowance, in regulation 1 of the JSA Regulations;

(d) in the case of state pension credit, in regulation 1 of the SPC Regulations;

"charge by way of legal mortgage" has the meaning given in section 132(1) of the Land Registration Act 2002;

2.523

"child" means a person under the age of 16;

"claimant" means a single claimant or each of joint claimants;

"Claims and Payment Regulations" means the Social Security (Claims and Payments) Regulations 1987;

"close relative" means a parent, parent-in-law, son, son-in-law, daughter, daughter-in-law, step-parent, step-son, step-daughter, brother, sister, or, if any of the preceding persons is one member of a couple, the other member of that couple;

"couple" means—

(a) two people who are married to, or civil partners of, each other and are members of the same household;

(b) two people who are not married to, or civil partners of, each other but are living together as a married couple or civil partners;

"disabled person" has the meaning given—

(a) in the case of employment and support allowance, in paragraph 1(3) of Schedule 6 to the ESA Regulations,

(b) in the case of income support, in paragraph 1(3) of Schedule 3 to the IS Regulations;

(c) in the case of jobseeker's allowance, in paragraph 1(3) of Schedule 2 to the JSA Regulations;

(d) in the case of state pension credit, in paragraph 1(2)(a) of Schedule 2 to the SPC Regulations;

(e) in the case of universal credit, in paragraph 14(3) of Schedule 3 to these Regulations;

"dwelling"—

(a) in England and Wales, means a dwelling within the meaning of Part 1 of the Local Government Finance Act 1992;

(b) in Scotland, means a dwelling within the meaning of Part 2 of that Act;

"earned income" has the meaning given in Chapter 2 of Part 6 of the UC Regulations;

"ESA Regulations" means the Employment and Support Allowance Regulations 2008;

"existing claimant" means a claimant who is entitled to a qualifying benefit, including an amount for owner-occupier payments, on 5th April 2018;

"financial year" has the meaning given in section 25(2) of the Budget Responsibility and National Audit Act 2011;

"income" means any income which is, or which is treated as, an individual's, including payments which are treated as earnings, and which is not disregarded, under—

(a) in the case of employment and support allowance, Part 10 of the ESA Regulations;

(b) in the case of income support, Part 5 of the IS Regulations;

(c) in the case of jobseeker's allowance, Part 8 of the JSA Regulations;

(d) in the case of state pension credit, Part 3 of the SPC Regulations;

"IS Regulations" means the Income Support (General) Regulations 1987;

[¹ "joint claimants"—

(a) in the case of jobseeker's allowance means—

    (i) members of a joint-claim couple who have jointly made a claim for, and are entitled to, income-based jobseeker's allowance; or

    (ii) members of a joint-claim couple who have made a claim for, but are not entitled to, such a benefit by reason only that they have income—

        (aa) equal to or exceeding the applicable amount, but

        (bb) less than the sum of that applicable amount and the amount of a loan payment applicable to the joint-claim couple;

(b) in the case of universal credit means members of a couple who have jointly made a claim for, and are entitled to, universal credit;]

"joint-claim couple" has the meaning in section 1(4) of the Jobseekers Act 1995;

"JSA Regulations" means the Jobseeker's Allowance Regulations 1996;

"legacy benefit" means income-related employment and support allowance, income support or income-based jobseeker's allowance;

"legacy benefit claimant" means a claimant who is entitled to [¹, or is treated as entitled to,] a legacy benefit;

"legal estate" means any of the legal estates set out in section 1(1) of the Law of Property Act 1925;

"legal owner" means the owner, whether alone or with others, of a legal estate or, in Scotland, a heritable or registered interest, in the relevant accommodation;

"loan agreement" means an agreement entered into by a single claimant and his or her partner (if any), or each joint claimant, and the Secretary of State, which sets out the terms and conditions upon which the loan payments are made to the claimant;

"loan payments" means one or more payments, calculated under regulation 10, in respect of a claimant's liability to make owner-occupier payments in respect of the relevant accommodation;

"loan payments offer date" means the day on which the Secretary of State sends the loan agreement to a claimant;

"Modified Rules" means the Social Security (Housing Costs Special Arrangements) (Amendment and Modification) Regulations 2008;

"new claimant partner" has the meaning given in regulation 7 of the Transitional Provisions Regulations;

"non-dependant" has the meaning given—

(a) in the case of employment and support allowance, in regulation 71 of the ESA Regulations;

(b) in the case of income support, in regulation 3 of the IS Regulations;

(c) in the case of jobseeker's allowance, in regulation 2 of the JSA Regulations;

(d) in the case of state pension credit, in paragraph 1(4) of Schedule 2 to the SPC Regulations;

"owner-occupier payments" has the meaning given in regulation 3(2)(a);

"partner" means—

(a) where a claimant is a member of a couple, the other member of that couple;

(b) where a claimant is married polygamously to two or more members of the claimant's household, all such members;

"person who lacks capacity"—

(a) in England and Wales, has the meaning given in section 2 of the Mental Capacity Act 2005;

(b) in Scotland, means a person who is incapable under section 1(6) of the Adults with Incapacity (Scotland) Act 2000;

"polygamous marriage" means a marriage during which a party to it is married to more than one person and which took place under the laws of a country which permits polygamy;

"qualifying benefit" means income-related employment and support allowance, income support, income-based jobseeker's allowance, state pension credit or universal credit;

"qualifying lender" has the meaning given in section 19(7) of the Act;

"qualifying loan" means—

(a) in the case of a legacy benefit or state pension credit, a loan which qualifies under paragraph 2(2) or (4) of Schedule 1 to these Regulations;

(b) in the case of universal credit, a loan which qualifies under paragraph 5(2) of Schedule 1 to these Regulations;

"qualifying period" means a period of—

(a) nine consecutive assessment periods in which a claimant has been entitled to universal credit;

(b) 39 consecutive weeks in which a claimant—

   (i) has been entitled to a legacy benefit; or

   (ii) is treated as having been entitled to such a benefit under—

      (aa) paragraph 14 of Schedule 3 to the IS Regulations;

      (bb) paragraph 13 of Schedule 2 to the JSA Regulations; or

      (cc) paragraph 15 of Schedule 6 to the ESA Regulations;

"qualifying young person" has the meaning given—

(a) in the case of a legacy benefit, in section 142 of the Social Security Contributions and Benefits Act 1992;

(b) in the case of state pension credit, in regulation 4A of the SPC Regulations;

(c) in the case of universal credit, in regulation 5 of the UC Regulations;

"relevant accommodation" means the accommodation which the claimant occupies, or is treated as occupying, as the claimant's home under Schedule 3;

"relevant date", apart from in regulation 21, means the first day with respect to which a claimant's liability to make owner-occupier payments is met by a loan payment;

[¹ "single claimant" means—

(a) an individual who has made a claim for, and is entitled to, a qualifying benefit;

(b) an individual who has made a claim for, but is not entitled to, a legacy benefit or state pension credit by reason only that the individual has, or, if the individual is a member of a couple, they have, income—

   (i) equal to or exceeding the applicable amount, but

   (ii) less than the sum of that applicable amount and the amount of a loan payment applicable to the individual;]

"single person" means an individual who is not a member of a couple;

"SPC claimant" means a claimant who is entitled to [¹, or is treated as entitled to,] state pension credit;

"SPC Regulations" means the State Pension Credit Regulations 2002;

"standard security" has the meaning in Part 2 of the Conveyancing and Feudal Reform (Scotland) Act 1970;

"transitional end day" has the meaning given in regulations 19(1) [¹, 19A(1) and (5)] and 20(2);

"Transitional Provisions Regulations" means the Universal Credit (Transitional Provisions) Regulations 2014;

"UC claimant" means a claimant who is entitled to universal credit;

"UC Regulations" means the Universal Credit Regulations 2013; and

"unearned income" has the meaning given in Chapter 3 of Part 6 of the UC Regulations.

(2) For the purposes of these Regulations, a reference to—

(a) entitlement to a qualifying benefit is to be read as a reference to entitlement as determined under the ESA Regulations, IS Regulations, JSA Regulations, SPC Regulations and UC Regulations;

[[1](aa) a person being treated as entitled to a qualifying benefit is to be read as a reference to a person who satisfies sub-paragraph (a)(ii) of the definition of "joint claimants" or sub-paragraph (b) of the definition of "single claimant", except in the definition of "qualifying period", regulation 21(5)(b) and paragraph 3 of Schedule 1;]

(b) the claimant's family or to being a member of the claimant's family means a reference to the claimant's partner and any child or qualifying young person who is the responsibility of the claimant or the claimant's partner, where that child or qualifying young person is a member of the claimant's household;

(c) a person being responsible for a child or qualifying young person is to be read as a reference to a person being treated as responsible for a child or qualifying young person in the circumstances specified in—

    (i) in the case of employment and support allowance, regulation 156(10) of the ESA Regulations;

    (ii) in the case of income support, regulation 15 of the IS Regulations;

    (iii) in the case of jobseeker's allowance, regulation 77 of the JSA Regulations;

    (iv) in the case of state pension credit and universal credit, regulation 4 of the UC Regulations;

(d) a person being a member of a household is to be read as a reference to a person being treated as a member of the household in the circumstances specified in—

    (i) in the case of employment and support allowance, in regulation 156 of the ESA Regulations;

    (ii) in the case of income support, in regulation 16 of the IS Regulations;

    (iii) in the case of jobseeker's allowance, in regulation 78 of the JSA Regulations;

    (iv) in the case of state pension credit and universal credit, in regulation 5 of the SPC Regulations;

(e) a person being engaged in remunerative work is to be read as a reference to a person being treated as engaged in remunerative work—

    (i) in the case of employment and support allowance, in regulations 41 to 43 of the ESA Regulations;

    (ii) in the case of income support, in regulations 5 and 6 of the IS Regulations;

    (iii) in the case of jobseeker's allowance, in regulations 51 to 53 of the JSA Regulations;

    (iv) in the case of state pension credit, in paragraph 2 of Schedule 2 to the SPC Regulations.

AMENDMENT

1. Loans for Mortgage Interest and Social Fund Maternity Grant (Amendment) Regulations 2018 (SI 2018/307), reg.2(1) and (2) (April 6, 2018).

GENERAL NOTE

2.524   Most of the definitions listed above are self-explanatory. Where they are not, they are discussed in the commentary to the regulations in which the defined terms are used.

The offer of loan payments

2.525   **3.**—(1) The Secretary of State may make an offer of loan payments to a claimant in respect of any owner-occupier payments the claimant is, or is to be treated as, being liable to make in respect of the accommodation which the claimant is, or is to be treated as, occupying as the claimant's home, unless paragraph (4) applies.

(2) For the purposes of paragraph (1)—

(a) owner-occupier payments are—

    (i) in the case of a legacy benefit claimant or SPC claimant, payments within the meaning of Part 1 of Schedule 1;

    (ii) in the case of a UC claimant, payments within the meaning of Part 2 of Schedule 1;

(b) the circumstances in which a claimant is, or is to be treated as, being liable to make owner-occupier payments are—

    (i) in the case of a legacy benefit claimant or SPC claimant, the circumstances specified in Part 1 of Schedule 2;

    (ii) in the case of a UC claimant, the circumstances specified in Part 2 of Schedule 2;

(c) the circumstances in which a claimant is, or is to be treated as, occupying accommodation as the claimant's home are—

    (i) in the case of a legacy benefit claimant or SPC claimant, the circumstances specified in Part 2 of Schedule 3;

    (ii) in the case of a UC claimant, the circumstances specified in Part 3 of Schedule 3.

(3) Where the liability for owner-occupier payments is shared with a person not in the benefit unit, the claimant shall be, or shall be treated as, liable to make owner-occupier payments by reference to the appropriate proportion of the payments for which the claimant is responsible.

(4) A UC claimant shall not be eligible for the offer of loan payments if—

(a) where the claimant is a single person, the claimant has any earned income; or

(b) where the claimant is a member of a couple, either member of the couple has any earned income.

DEFINITIONS

"benefit unit"—reg.2(1).
"claimant"—*ibid.*
"couple"—*ibid.*
"earned income"—*ibid.*
"legacy benefit claimant"—*ibid.*
"loan payments"—*ibid.*
"owner-occupier payments"—regs 2(1) and 3(2)(a).

"single person"—reg.2(1).
"SPC claimant"—*ibid.*
"UC claimant"—*ibid.*

GENERAL NOTE

Paragraphs (1) and (2): Unless para.(4) applies, para.(1) empowers the Secretary of State to make "an offer of loan payments" in the following circumstances:

- first, the person to whom the offer is made must be a "claimant", defined in reg.2(1) as meaning "a single claimant or each of joint claimants";

- second, the offer can only be made in respect of "any owner-occupier payments".

   For "legacy benefit claimants" (i.e., those who are entitled to, or treated as entitled to, IRESA, IS or IBJSA: see reg.2(1)) and "SPC claimants" these are as defined in Sch.1, Pt.1. For "UC claimants", the definition is in Sch.1, Pt.2: see para.(2)(1)(a).

- third, the claimant must be liable, or treated as liable, to make those payments.

   The circumstances in which legacy benefit claimants and SPC claimants are, or are treated as, liable to make owner-occupier payments are set out in Sch.2, Pt.1. For UC claimants, those circumstances are set out in Sch.2, Pt.2: see para.(2)(1)(b). Where liability is shared, see also para.(2).

- fourth, the owner-occupier payments that the claimant is, or is treated as, liable to make must be in respect of accommodation which they are, or is treated as, occupying as his or her home.

   The circumstances in which legacy benefit claimants and SPC claimants are, or are treated as, occupying accommodation as their home, are set out in Sch.3, Pt.1. For UC claimants, those circumstances are set out in Sch.3, Pt.2: see para.(2)(1)(c).

The Secretary of State's offer will take the form of a draft loan agreement (as defined in reg.2(1)). The requirements for the offer to be accepted are set out in regs 4 and 5.

Paragraph (3) applies where the claimant is jointly liable for owner-occupier payments with someone who is not in the "benefit unit", which is defined by reg.2(1) as meaning "a single claimant and his or her partner (if any) or joint claimants". In those circumstances, the claimant is only treated as liable for—and is therefore only eligible for a loan in respect of—"the appropriate proportion of the payments for which s/he is responsible". "Appropriate proportion" is not defined and its meaning in individual cases may give rise to disputes.

Paragraph (4) provides that, if a UC claimant—or either joint UC claimant—has *any* earned income, they are not eligible for a loan in respect of owner-occupier payments. This replicates the rule in the Universal Credit Regulations, Sch.5, para.4.

Acceptance of loan payments offer

4. The offer of loan payments is accepted where the Secretary of State has received the loan agreement signed by, in the case of a single claimant, the claimant and his or her partner (if any), or, in the case of joint claimants, each member of the couple, and the documents referred to in regulation 5(2).

2.526

2.527

DEFINITIONS

"claimant"—reg.2(1).
"couple"—*ibid.*
"joint claimants"—*ibid.*
"loan agreement"—*ibid.*
"loan payments"—*ibid.*
"partner"—*ibid.*
"single claimant"—*ibid.*

GENERAL NOTE

2.528   Claimants do not have to accept the Secretary of State's offer. But if they do not do so, they will receive no help at all with owner-occupier payments because the legislation allowing such payments to be met by IS, IBJSA, SPC, IRESA or UC has been repealed.

To accept the Secretary of State's offer, the claimant—or both joint claimants—must sign the loan agreement and return it to the DWP with the documents set out in reg.5(2). The offer is not accepted until the Department has received the signed agreement ant those documents.

Conditions to meet before the loan payments can be made

2.529   **5.**—(1) The Secretary of State may make the loan payments if—
(a) the loan payments offer is accepted in accordance with regulation 4; and
(b) the conditions in paragraph (2) are met.
(2) The conditions are—
(a) in England and Wales—
   (i) where all of the legal owners are within the benefit unit, each legal owner has executed a charge by way of legal mortgage in favour of the Secretary of State in respect of the relevant accommodation;
   (ii) where one or more legal owners are not within the benefit unit, each legal owner within the benefit unit (if any) has executed an equitable charge in respect of their beneficial interest in the relevant accommodation;
(b) in Scotland, each legal owner within the benefit unit has executed a standard security in respect of his or her interest in the relevant accommodation;
(c) the Secretary of State has obtained the written consent referred to in paragraph (3); and
(d) the information condition in regulation 6 is met within the period of 6 months ending with the day on which the loan payments offer is accepted.
(3) The consent required by paragraph (2)(c) is consent given in writing to the creation of the charge or, in Scotland, the standard security by any person in the benefit unit in occupation of the relevant accommodation, who is not a legal owner.

DEFINITIONS

"benefit unit"—reg.2(1).
"charge by way of legal mortgage"—*ibid.*
"legal owner"—*ibid.*
"loan payments"—*ibid.*

"relevant accommodation"—*ibid.*
"standard security"—*ibid.*

GENERAL NOTE   2.530

Paragraph (1): The drafting of paragraph (1) seems over-cautious. It states that the Secretary of State may make loan payments if the offer is accepted in accordance with reg.4 and the conditions in paragraph (2) are met. However, under reg.4, the offer is only accepted when the Secretary of State receives "the documents referred to in regulation 5(2)", so—at most—all that all that reg.5(1)(b) achieves is to prevent loan payments from being made where the information condition in reg.6 has not been satisfied during the preceding six months: see para.(2)(d).

Paragraphs (2) and (3) require three things. First, all the legal owners of the "relevant accommodation" (*i.e.,* the accommodation which the claimant occupies, or is treated as occupying, as his or her home under Sch.3: see reg.2(1)) must give the Secretary of State security for the repayment of the loan payments (paras (2) (a) and (b)). In other words, they have to create a second mortgage in favour of the Secretary of State. Second, everyone occupying the relevant accommodation who is not a legal owner must consent to the giving of that security (paras (2)(c) and (3)). Third, the information condition in reg.6 must have been satisfied within the period of six months ending on the day on which the loan offer is accepted (para. (2)(d)).
The type of security that must be given depends upon whether the relevant accommodation is in England and Wales or in Scotland and, in the former case, on whether the legal ownership of the relevant accommodation is held entirely by people in the benefit unit or shared with someone outside that unit.
If the relevant accommodation is in England or Wales and the legal ownership is held entirely by those within the benefit unit each legal owner must execute a charge by way of legal mortgage (defined by reg.2(1) as having the same meaning as in s.132(1) of the Land Registration Act 2002) over it. Where the legal ownership of the relevant accommodation is jointly held with someone who is not in the benefit unit, each legal owner must execute an equitable charge over his or her beneficial interest in the property. For the difference between legal and beneficial ownership, see the commentary to reg.46 of the Income Support Regulations in Vol.II and, *e.g.,* *SSWP v LB Tower Hamlets and CT (IS & HB)* [2018] UKUT 25 (AAC) at paras 21-29.
If the relevant accommodation is in Scotland, then each legal owner within the benefit unit must execute a standard security in respect of her/his interest in the relevant accommodation. "Standard security" is defined by reg.2(1) as having "the meaning in Part 2 of the Conveyancing and Feudal Reform (Scotland) Act 1970".

Information condition

    6.—(1) The information condition is that the Secretary of State has pro-   2.531
vided relevant information about the loan payments to a single claimant
and his or her partner (if any) or each joint claimant.
    (2) For the purposes of this regulation, "relevant information" is informa-
tion about the loan payments which must include—
    (a) a summary of the terms and conditions included within the loan
        agreement;
    (b) where the circumstances in regulation 5(2)(a)(i) or (b) apply, an
        explanation that the Secretary of State will seek to obtain a charge
        or, in Scotland, a standard security in respect of the relevant accom-
        modation;
    (c) an explanation of the consent referred to in regulation 5(3); and

(d) information as to where a single claimant and his or her partner (if any) or each joint claimant can obtain further information and independent legal and financial advice regarding loan payments.

DEFINITIONS

"claimant"—reg.2(1).
"loan agreement"—*ibid.*
"loan payments"—*ibid.*
"partner"—*ibid.*
"relevant accommodation"—*ibid.*
"single claimant"—*ibid.*
"standard security"—*ibid.*

2.532   GENERAL NOTE

Taken together, reg.5(2)(d) and reg.6 require that the Secretary of State must have provided the claimant, and any partner, with the information specified in para. (2) at some point during the period of six months ending with the day on which the offer of loan payments is accepted. The regulations do not specify the consequences that are to follow if the information condition is not satisfied, or is not satisfied during that period.

Time of each loan payment

2.533   7. Each loan payment shall be made—
(a) in the case of a UC claimant, at monthly intervals in arrears; and
[¹(b) in the case of a legacy benefit claimant or SPC claimant, at 4 weekly intervals in arrears.]

AMENDMENT

1. Loans for Mortgage Interest and Social Fund Maternity Grant (Amendment) Regulations 2018 (SI 2018/307), reg.2(1) and (3) (April 6, 2018).

DEFINITIONS

"claimant"—reg.2(1).
"legacy benefit claimant"—*ibid.*
"qualifying benefit"—*ibid.*
"qualifying lender"—*ibid.*
"SPC claimant"—*ibid.*
"UC claimant"—*ibid.*

GENERAL NOTE

2.534   Loan payments are always made in arrears. For UC claimants, they are made at monthly intervals, presumably to coincide with the claimant's assessment period. For those on other benefits, payment is 4-weekly in arrears.

Period covered by loan payments

2.535   **8.—**(1) The period in respect of which the loan payments shall be made shall begin on the later of—
(a) 6th April 2018;
(b) in the case of a UC claimant or legacy benefit claimant, the day after the day on which the qualifying period ends;
[¹ (c) in the case of an SPC claimant, the first day of entitlement to state pension credit;]

(d) the transitional end day [¹;

(e) a date requested by the claimant.]

[¹ (2) If the day referred to in paragraph (1)(a) to (c) and (e) is not the first day of the claimant's benefit week, in the case of a legacy benefit claimant or SPC claimant, or assessment period, in the case of a UC claimant, the day referred to shall be the first day of the first benefit week or first assessment period that begins after that date.]

AMENDMENT

1. Loans for Mortgage Interest and Social Fund Maternity Grant (Amendment) Regulations 2018 (SI 2018/307), reg.2(1) and (4) (April 6, 2018).

DEFINITIONS

"claimant"—reg.2(1).
"legacy benefit claimant"—*ibid.*
"loan payments"—*ibid.*
"qualifying period"—*ibid.*
"SPC claimant"—*ibid.*
"transitional end day"—*ibid.* and regs 19(1), 19A(1) and (5) and 20(2).
"UC claimant"—reg,2(1).

GENERAL NOTE   2.536

Subject to para.(2), entitlement to loan payments begins on—and any entitlement to housing costs therefore ends the day before—the latest of the five days specified in para.(1). Para.(2) modifies that rule by providing that if the day identified by para. (1) is not the first day of an assessment period (for UC claimants) or of a benefit week (for claimants of IS, IBJSA or IRESA), entitlement to loan payments instead begins on the first day of the next assessment period or benefit week.

"Qualifying period"

The phrase "qualifying period" is defined in reg.2(1).   2.537

For UC claimants, the effect of that definition, taken with sub-para.(1) (b) is that there is no entitlement to a loan payment unless they have first been entitled to universal credit for nine consecutive assessment periods.

For claimants of IS, IBJSA, or IRESA the effect is that there is no entitlement to a loan payment unless they have been entitled to one of those benefits—or treated as so entitled by the provisions listed in head (1)(b)(ii) of the definition—for 39 consecutive weeks

Those provisions establish linking rules by which two or more periods of entitlement to one of those benefits are, in some circumstances treated as a single period of entitlement: see further Vol. II.

Where a claimant has moved from one of those benefits to another, see Sch.6, para.20(1)(c) to the ESA Regulations in Vol.I; and reg.32 of the Income Support (General) (Jobseeker's Allowance Consequential Amendments) Regulations 1996, and Sch.2, para.18(1)(c) to the JSA Regulations in Vol II.

See the commentary to reg.9(7) below for the circumstances in which claimants of IS, IBJSA and IRESA who were previously in receipt of loan payments may receive them again without serving a further qualifying period.

Transitional end day

2.538   The transitional end day applies where a claimant was entitled to housing costs before April 6, 2018 and benefits from the transitional provisions in regs 19, 19A and 20: see, further, the General Notes to those regulations.

Duration of loan payments

2.539   **9.**—(1) Subject to paragraph (2), loan payments shall continue to be made indefinitely at the intervals specified in regulation 7.

(2) If one of the circumstances in paragraph (3) occurs, the Secretary of State shall terminate the loan payments immediately but subject to paragraph (4).

(3) The circumstances are that—

(a) the claimant ceases to be entitled [¹, or treated as entitled to,] to a qualifying benefit;

(b) the claimant ceases to be, or to be treated as, liable to make owner-occupier payments under Schedule 2;

(c) the claimant ceases to be, or to be treated as, occupying the relevant accommodation under Schedule 3;

(d) the loan agreement is terminated in accordance with its terms;

(e) in the case of a UC claimant only, regulation 3(4) applies.

(4) The Secretary of State shall make the loan payments direct to the claimant for the period specified in paragraph (6) if—

(a) a claimant ceases to be entitled to a legacy benefit by reason that, in the case of a single claimant, the claimant or his or her partner (if any), or, in the case of joint claimants, either member of the couple, is engaged in remunerative work; and

(b) the conditions in paragraph (5) are met.

(5) The conditions are that, in the case of a single claimant, the claimant or his or her partner (if any), or, in the case of joint claimants, either member of the couple—

(a) is engaged in remunerative work which is expected to last for a period of no less than 5 weeks;

(b) is still liable or treated as liable to make owner-occupier payments under Schedule 2;

(c) has, for a continuous period of 26 weeks ending with the day on which he or she commences the work referred to in sub-paragraph (a), been entitled to a legacy benefit; and

(d) was, on the day before the day on which he or she commenced the work referred to in sub-paragraph (a), receiving loan payments under these Regulations.

(6) The period specified is the period of 4 weeks commencing with the day on which the relevant person is first engaged in remunerative work.

[¹(7) If a legacy benefit claimant ceases to be entitled to, or treated as entitled to, a legacy benefit ("the old entitlement") but becomes entitled, or treated as entitled, again to the benefit ("the new entitlement") within the period of 52 weeks beginning with the day on which the claimant ceased to be entitled, or treated as entitled, to the old entitlement, the loan payments may begin without a new qualifying period starting if the claimant wishes to receive loan payments on the basis of the new entitlement.]

AMENDMENT

1. Loans for Mortgage Interest and Social Fund Maternity Grant (Amendment) Regulations 2018 (SI 2018/307), reg.2(1) and (5) (April 6, 2018).

DEFINITIONS

"claimant"—reg.2(1).
"couple"—*ibid.*
"entitlement"—reg.2(2)(a).
"joint claimants"—reg.2(1).
"legacy benefit"—*ibid.*
"legacy benefit claimant"—*ibid.*
"loan agreement"—*ibid.*
"loan payments"—*ibid.*
"owner-occupier payments"—regs 2(1) and 3(2)(a).
"partner"—reg.2(1).
"qualifying benefit"—*ibid.*
"qualifying period"—*ibid.*
"relevant accommodation"—*ibid.*
"remunerative work"—reg.2(2)(e).
"single claimant"—reg.2(1).
"UC claimant"—*ibid.*

GENERAL NOTE

Paragraph (1). Once loan payments have started they continue indefinitely at monthly intervals for UC claimants, and four-weekly periods for other claimants, until one of the events in para.(2) occurs.   **2.540**

Paragraph (2). Loan payments come to an end if:

- the claimant ceases to be entitled, or treated as entitled, to a qualifying benefit (as defined in reg.2(1). However, where the benefit that has ended is IS, IBJSA or IRESA, and the reason that the benefit has come to an end is that the claimant or her/his partner has begun remunerative work, see paras (4)-(6);

- the claimant ceases to be liable, or to be treated as liable, to make owner occupier payments: see reg.3(2)(a) and (b) and Sch.1;

- the claimant ceases to occupy, or to be treated as occupying, the relevant accommodation: see reg.3(2)(c) and Sch.3;

- the loan agreement comes to an end; or

- for UC claimants, the claimant (or either joint claimant) begins to earn an income.

Paragraphs (4)-(6) create a four-week run-on for some claimants who are no longer eligible for loan payments because they have ceased to be entitled to IS, IBJSA or IRESA. The run-on applies if (1) the reason that entitlement to one of those benefits has ended is that the claimant or her/his partner (if any) have started remunerative work; (2) that work is expected to last for at least five weeks; (3) the claimant s still liable, or treated as liable to make owner-occupier payments; (4) on the day that the claimant or her/his partner commences remunerative work, the claimant has been entitled to one or more of those benefits for a continuous period of 26 weeks, and (5) on the previous day had been receiving loan payments.

Paragraph (7) is puzzling. What it appears to say is that where a claimant ceases to be entitled (or treated as entitled) to IS, IBJSA or IRESA but becomes entitled again within the following 52 weeks, it is not necessary for her/him to wait for a further qualifying period before loan payments can be made.

As the rule is about the circumstances in which the qualifying period does not apply, rather than about the circumstances in which loan payments come to an end, it might be thought to belong more naturally in reg.8 than reg.9.

More importantly, the rule has been drafted so narrowly that it seems unlikely that it will be of much practical benefit. To begin with, the reference to the claimant becoming "entitled, or treated as entitled, *again* to the benefit" (emphasis added) suggests that the old entitlement and the new entitlement must be to the same benefit. However, the roll-out of universal credit means that there are increasingly few districts in the country where it remains possible to make a fresh claim for IS, IBJSA or IRESA. Claimants who might otherwise have benefitted from this rule are likely to be required to claim universal credit, in which case, it will be necessary to serve a qualifying period of nine consecutive assessment periods.

Calculation of each loan payment

2.541   **10.**—Subject to any deduction under regulation 14 [¹ or 14A], each loan payment shall be the aggregate of the amounts resulting from regulations 11 and 12.

AMENDMENT

1. Loans for Mortgage Interest and Social Fund Maternity Grant (Amendment) Regulations 2018 (SI 2018/307), reg.2(1) and (6) (April 6, 2018).

GENERAL NOTE

2.542   Regulation 10 is self-explanatory. The amount of each loan payment is calculated by adding together the amount for interest on qualifying loans (calculated under reg.11) and the amount for alternative finance arrangements (calculated under reg.12) and then subtracting any non-dependant deduction that falls to be made under reg.14 and any insurance payment deduction under reg.14A.

Calculation in respect of qualifying loans

2.543   **11.**—(1) Subject to paragraphs (3) and (4), the amount to be included in each loan payment for owner-occupier payments which are payments of interest on qualifying loans is determined as follows.

Step 1

Determine the amount of capital for the time being owing in connection with each qualifying loan to which the owner-occupier payments relate.

Step 2

If there is more than one qualifying loan, add together the amounts determined in step 1.

Step 3

Determine the identified amount which is the lower of—
(a) the amount resulting from step 1 or 2; and
(b) the capital limit specified in paragraph (2)(a) or (b).
If both amounts in (a) and (b) are the same, that is the identified amount.

Step 4

In respect of a legacy benefit claimant or SPC claimant, apply the following formula to achieve a weekly sum—

$$\frac{A \times SR}{52} - I$$

In respect of a UC claimant, apply the following formula to achieve a monthly sum—

$$\frac{A \times SR}{12} - I$$

In either case—

"A" is the identified amount in step 3,

"SR" is the standard rate that applies at the end of the calculation (see regulation 13), and

"I" is the amount of any income, in the case of a legacy benefit or SPC claimant, or unearned income, in the case of a UC claimant, above the claimant's applicable amount.

The result is the amount to be included in each loan payment for owner-occupier payments which are payments of interest on qualifying loans.

(2) The capital limit is—

(a) £200,000—

    (i) in the case of a legacy benefit claimant or SPC claimant where the Modified Rules apply;

    (ii) in the case of a UC claimant;

(b) £100,000 in all other cases.

(3) In the application of paragraph (2) to a qualifying loan (or any part of a qualifying loan) which was taken out for the purpose of making necessary adaptations to the accommodation to meet the needs of a disabled person—

(a) the qualifying loan (or the part of the qualifying loan) is to be disregarded for the purposes of steps 2 and 3; and

(b) "A" in step 4 is to be read as the amount resulting from step 1 in respect of the qualifying loan (or the sum of those amounts if there is more than one qualifying loan taken out for the purpose of making such adaptations) plus the amount (if any) resulting from step 3 in relation to any other qualifying loan or loans.

(4) Subject to paragraph (5), any variation in the amount of capital for the time being owing in connection with a qualifying loan is not to be taken into account after the relevant date until such time as the Secretary of State recalculates the amount which shall occur—

(a) on the first anniversary of the relevant date; and

(b) in respect of any variation after the first anniversary, on the next anniversary which follows the date of the variation.

(5) In respect of an existing claimant, the Secretary of State shall recalculate the amount of capital owing in connection with a qualifying loan on the anniversary of the date on which the claimant's qualifying benefit first included an amount for owner-occupier payments.

DEFINITIONS

"applicable amount"—reg.2(1).
"claimant"—*ibid.*
"disabled person"—*ibid.*
"existing claimant"—*ibid.*
"income"—*ibid.*
"legacy benefit claimant"—*ibid.*
"Modified Rules"—*ibid.*
"owner-occupier payments"—regs 2(1) and 3(2)(a).
"qualifying benefit"—*ibid.*
"qualifying loan"—*ibid.*
"relevant date"—*ibid.*
"SPC claimant"—*ibid.*
"UC claimant"—*ibid.*
"unearned income"—*ibid.*

GENERAL NOTE

2.544   Regulation 11 provides for the calculation of loan payments in respect of interest of qualifying loans. The calculation of loan payments in respect of alternative finance payments is governed by reg.12.

Under para.(1), there are four steps to that calculation. However, in order to follow those steps, it is first necessary to identify the capital limit applicable to the claimant, by applying the rules in para.(2) and also the "standard interest rate" (see reg.13, below).

Capital Limit

2.545   The general rule is that the capital limit is £100,000 for those claiming IS, IBJSA, IRESA or SPC and £200,000 for those claiming UC: see para.(2)(a)(ii) and (b). There is one exception, and one modification, to that rule.

The exception is in para.(2)(a)(i). Claimants of IS, IBJSA, IRESA and SPC also have a capital limit of £200,000 where the "Modified Rules" apply. That phrase is defined by reg.2(1) as meaning the Social Security (Housing Costs Special Arrangements) (Amendment and Modification) Regulations 2008 (SI 2008/3195): see further Vol.II.

The modification is in paras (3)-(4) and applies where the whole, or part of, a qualifying loan was taken out in order to make "necessary" adaptations to the accommodation to meet the needs of a disabled person (*i.e.*, as defined in reg.2(1)). To avoid circumlocution, this General Note will refer to that purpose as "the specified purpose" even though reg.11 does not itself use that term.

The legislative intention appears to be that any part of a loan taken out for the specified purpose is excluded when the capital limit applies so that if, for example, a claimant on IBJSA with a capital limit of £100,000 has a loan of £250,000, of which £25,000 was taken out for the specified purpose, the loan payment is calculated on capital of £125,000, £100,000 for the part of the loan that was not taken out for the specified purpose plus the £25,000 that was taken out for that purpose.

However, there must be doubt as to whether the modification is effective. Para.(3) states that it has effect in the application of "*paragraph (2)*" to a qualifying loan taken out for the specified purpose. But the modifications in para.(3) relate to Steps 2, 3 and 4 of the calculation (see below), which do not form part of para.(2) but rather para.(1). Para. (2) is about the amount of the capital limit, which is the same irrespective of the amount of the loan (or loans) and the purposes for which those loans were taken out. Indeed, the whole point of the capital limit is that it is a cap on the actual amount of the claimant's loan or loans. It therefore appears that the reference to "paragraph (2)" in the opening words of para.(3) should instead be to "paragraph (1)".

Moreover, even if it is possible to read para.(3) as referring to para.(1) (perhaps by the application of the rule in *Inco Europe Ltd v First Choice Distribution (a firm)* [2000] UKHL 15), the drafting of the modification is unnecessarily complex, and it is arguable that it has effects that are far more favourable to claimants than was intended: see below.

The calculation

Where the calculation relates to a loan (or loans), no part of which was taken out for the specified purpose, it is relatively straightforward.   2.546

Step 1

The first step is to determine the amount of capital owing on each quali-   2.547 fying loan "to which the owner-occupier payments relate".

For claimants of IS, IBJSA, IRESA and SPC, "owner-occupier payments" are defined by reg.3(2)(a) and para.2(1)(a), (2) and (4) of Sch.1 by reference to the purposes for which the loans were taken out. To the extent that a loan was taken out for any purpose not specified in para.2(2) of Sch.1, the capital will not be capital "to which the owner-occupier payments relate" and therefore will not be taken into account in the calculation.

By the same reasoning, for claimants of UC, reg.3(2)(a)(ii) and para.5(1) (a) and (2), the owner-occupier payments will relate to the capital if, but only if, it is secured on the relevant accommodation: the purpose for which the loan was taken out is irrelevant.

Step 2

If there is more than one qualifying loan, then the amounts determined   2.548 separately in Step 1 are added together.

Step 3

The Step 1 or (if there is more than one qualifying loan) Step 2 figure   2.549 is then compared with the claimant's capital limit (see above) and if it is higher than that limit, then the amount of the loan payment is calculated using the capital limit, not the amount of capital the claimant has actually borrowed.

Step 4

Step 4 is the last step in the calculation. The standard interest rate (see   2.550 reg.13) is applied to the amount of capital identified in Step 3 and the product is then divided by either by 12 (to produce a monthly sum for UC claimants) or 52 (to produce a weekly sum for those on other qualifying benefits).

Then, finally, if UC claimants have *unearned* income—or those claiming other qualifying benefits have *any* income—in excess of their "applicable amount", the amount of the excess is deducted.

"Applicable amount" is defined in reg.2(1). For IS, IBJSA and IRESA it is the same as the applicable amount used in the calculation of those benefits. For SPC and universal credit, which do not use the concept of an "applicable amount" in the calculation of the award, the applicable amounts for the purpose of Step 4 are, respectively, the appropriate minimum guarantee (see s.2 SPCA 2002) and the maximum amount (see s.8(1) and (2) WRA 2012 and reg.23(1) of the UC Regulations).

Loans to adapt accommodation for disabled persons

2.551 How does that calculation differ, if the loan, or loans, or part of any loan is taken out for the specified purpose? As explained above, this depends upon the modifications made by para.(3) (and assumes that—contrary to what it actually says—para.(3) can be read as applying to para.(1), rather than para.(2)).

Step 1

2.552 At least at this stage, para.(3) does not modify Step 1.

Step 2

2.553 At Step 2, any part of the qualifying loan that was taken out to adapt the accommodation for the needs of a disabled person is disregarded: see para.(3)(a).

At this stage of the calculation the disregard of the capital disadvantages the claimant because it has the effect that capital borrowed to meet the needs of a disabled person does not count towards the total to which the standard rate of interest will be applied in Step 4.

As Step 2 only applies "[i]f there is more than one qualifying loan" and para.(3)(a) does not disregard the capital for the purposes of Step 1, the regulation creates the bizarre situation that—at this stage of the calculation—if a claimant has a single qualifying loan which includes amounts that were borrowed to adapt relevant accommodation to meet the needs of a disabled person, then no part of that capital is disregarded. However, if they have two or more such qualifying loans, all such capital is disregarded whichever loan it is part of.

Step 3

2.554 Where the loan includes capital that was borrowed for the specified purpose, it is difficult to work out what Step 3 requires. Para.(3)(a) says that such capital is to be disregarded for the purposes of that step. But from what amount or amounts is it to be disregarded?

Three amounts are mentioned in the unmodified Step 3, the capital limit, the Step 1 amount and the Step 2 amount.

It is not possible to disregard the amount of the loan taken out for the specified purpose from the capital limit because that figure is a notional amount. And, anyway, deducting the disregarded amount from that limit would reduce it and thereby work against the presumed policy intention that capital borrowed for this purpose should not be affected by the capital limit.

That leaves the Step 1 amount and the Step 2 amount. But capital borrowed to adapt accommodation for a disabled person has already been disregarded from the Step 2 amount. Should a second disregard now be made from that amount? And should such capital now be disregarded from the Step 1 amount as well? Given what is said below about the Step 4 calculation, the answers appear to be "no", and "the question is irrelevant".

Step 4

Where all or part of the qualifying loan (or loans) was taken out for the specified purpose, para.(3)(a) provides that the capital figure ("A" in the formula):

> "... is to be read as the amount resulting from step 1 in respect of the qualifying loan (or the sum of those amounts if there is more than one qualifying loan taken out for the purpose of making such adaptations) plus the amount (if any) resulting from step three in relation to any other qualifying loan or loans."

2.555

Finally, the drafting of the modification for loans taken out to adapt accommodation for the needs of a disabled person begins to make some sense. The aggregate of the full amounts of such loans (i.e., the aggregate of the amounts identified in Step 1) is taken into account. Then, in addition, loans, no part of which were taken out for that purpose are taken into account at the Step 3 figure (i.e., to the extent that, cumulatively, they do not exceed the capital limit). That is why no capital was disregarded at Step 1: for specified purpose loans, Step 4 takes the Step 1 figure into account in full without, in effect, going through the Step 3 process (which is why it is irrelevant whether specified purpose capital is disregarded from the Step 1 figure at the Step 3 stage). It is also why capital borrowed for the specified purpose is disregarded from the Step 2 figure: if it were not, it would be double-counted at Step 4.

Discussion

Even though the drafting becomes clear at the Step 4 stage, it is unnecessarily complex. Moreover, the wording does not achieve the result that appears to have been intended. An example may assist:

2.556

Estelle has been awarded IBJSA and is an owner-occupier. Her capital limit is £100,000. However she has a mortgage of £250,000, of which £25,000 was taken out to adapt her home for the needs of her daughter, Brittney, who is a disabled person.

What was (presumably) intended was that the loan payment should be calculated on £125,000 (i.e., the capital limit of £100,000 plus the £25,000 needed to carry out adaptations for Britney) and that is what would have been achieved if the £25,000 had been taken out as a separate loan.

However, Estelle has only one loan and what, because para.(3)(b) does not distinguish between loans and part loans, it appears to have the effect that the whole of that loan is taken into account at the Step 1 figure, namely £250,000.

Moreover, suppose that (before she claimed JSA) Estelle took out a further loan of £75,000 for purposes that are eligible under para.2(4) of Sch.1 but did not include the specified purpose. Para.(3)(b) now appears to have the effect that the second loan is taken into account at the Step 3 figure, which is £75,000 because it is less than Estelle's capital limit. If so, Estelle's loan payments should be calculated on a loan of £325,000.

Revaluation of capital

2.557   Even though Step 1 of the calculation says that what is to be determined is the amount of capital *for the time being owing* in connection with each qualifying loan, the Step 1 figure is not in fact revalued every month (for UC claimants) or every week (for other claimants). Instead, except where the claimant is an "existing claimant", the amount is re-calculated annually on the anniversary of the relevant date and on each subsequent such anniversary: see para.(4). For existing claimants, the recalculation is performed on the anniversary of the date on which owner-occupier payments were included in the claimant's qualifying benefit.

Calculation in respect of alternative finance payments

2.558   **12.**—(1) The amount to be included in each loan payment for owner-occupier payments which are alternative finance payments is determined as follows.

Step 1

Determine the purchase price of the accommodation to which the alternative finance payments relate.

Step 2

Determine the identified amount which is the lower of—
(a) the amount resulting from step 1; and
(b) the capital limit specified in paragraph (2)(a) or (b).
If both amounts are the same, that is the identified amount.

Step 3

In respect of an SPC claimant, apply the following formula to achieve a weekly sum—

$$\frac{A \times SR}{52} - I$$

In respect of a UC claimant, apply the following formula to achieve a monthly sum—

$$\frac{A \times SR}{12} - I$$

In either case—
"A" is the identified amount in step 2,
"SR" is the standard rate that applies at the date of the calculation (see regulation 13), and
"I" is the amount of any income, in the case of an SPC claimant, or unearned income, in the case of a UC claimant, above the claimant's applicable amount.
The result is the amount to be included in each loan payment for owner-occupier payments which are alternative finance payments.

(2) The capital limit is—

(a) £200,000 in the case of an SPC claimant where the Modified Rules apply or a UC claimant;

(b) £100,000 in all other cases.

(3) For the purposes of paragraph (1), "purchase price" means the price paid by a party to the alternative finance arrangements other than the claimant in order to acquire the interest in the accommodation to which those arrangements relate less—

(a) the amount of any initial payment made by the claimant in connection with the acquisition of that interest; and

(b) the amount of any subsequent payments made by the claimant or any partner to another party to the alternative finance arrangements before—

(i) the relevant date; or

(ii) in the case of an existing claimant, the date on which the claimant's qualifying benefit first included an amount for owner-occupier payments,

which reduce the amount owed by the claimant under the alternative finance arrangements.

(4) Subject to paragraph (5), any variation in the amount for the time being owing in connection with alternative finance arrangements is not to be taken into account after the relevant date until such time as the Secretary of State recalculates the amount which shall occur—

(a) on the first anniversary of the relevant date; and

(b) in respect of any variation after the first anniversary, on the next anniversary which follows the date of the variation.

(5) In respect of an existing claimant, the Secretary of State shall recalculate the amount for the time being owing [¹ in connection with alternative finance arrangements] on the anniversary of the date on which the claimant's qualifying benefit first included an amount for owner-occupier payments.

Amendment

1. Loans for Mortgage Interest and Social Fund Maternity Grant (Amendment) Regulations 2018 (SI 2018/307), reg.2(1) and (7) (April 6, 2018).

Definitions

"alternative finance payments"—reg.2(1).
"applicable amount"—*ibid.*
"claimant"—*ibid.*
"existing claimant"—*ibid.*
"income"—*ibid.*
"Modified Rules"—*ibid.*
"owner-occupier payments"—regs 2(1) and 3(2)(a).
"partner"—reg.2(1).
"qualifying benefit"—*ibid.*
"qualifying loan"—*ibid.*
"relevant date"—*ibid.*
"SPC claimant"—*ibid.*
"UC claimant"—*ibid.*
"unearned income"—*ibid.*

2.559 For the definition of "alternative finance payments" see Sch.1, para.5(3).

The calculation of loan payments made in respect of alternative finance payments is the same as that prescribed by reg.11 in respect of qualifying loans, except that:

- there is no modification where the alternative finance arrangements have been made in order to adapt the dwelling to meet the needs of a disabled person; and (more fundamentally)

- the Step 1 amount (*i.e.*, the capital element of the calculation) is the purchase price of the property (as set out in para.(3)), rather than the amount owing on a qualifying loan.

Standard rate to be applied under regulations 11 and 12

2.560 **13.**—(1) The standard rate is the average mortgage rate published by the Bank of England which has effect on the 5th April 2018.

(2) The standard rate is to be varied each time that paragraph (3) applies.

(3) This paragraph applies when, on any reference day, the Bank of England publishes an average mortgage rate which differs by 0.5 percentage points or more from the standard rate that applies on that reference day (whether it applies by virtue of paragraph (1) or by virtue of a previous application of this paragraph).

(4) The average mortgage rate published on that reference day then becomes the new standard rate in accordance with paragraph (5).

(5) Any variation in the standard rate by virtue of paragraphs (2) to (4) shall come into effect at the end of the period of 6 weeks beginning with the day referred to in paragraph (3).

(6) At least 7 days before a variation of the standard rate comes into effect under paragraph (5), the Secretary of State must arrange for notice to be published on a publicly accessible website of—

    (a) the new standard rate; and

    (b) the day on which the new standard rate comes into effect under paragraph (5).

(7) For the purposes of this Regulation—

"average mortgage rate" means the effective interest rate (non-seasonally adjusted) of United Kingdom resident banks and building societies for loans to households secured on dwellings, published by the Bank of England in respect of the most recent period specified for that rate at the time of publication; and

"reference day" means any day falling on or after 6th April 2018.

DEFINITIONS

"dwelling"—reg.2(1).

2.561 The interest rate applied in Step 4 of the calculations under regs 11 and 12 is not the contractual rate due under the qualifying loan (or the rate inherent in the alternative finance arrangements) but, rather, the standard rate as determined in accordance with para.(1) and as subsequently varied under paras (2)-(6).

At the time of going to press, the standard rate is 2.61% per annum.

It is difficult to identify any publicly available website on which the notice required by para.(6) has been published.

Non-dependant deductions

14.—(1) In the case of a legacy benefit claimant or SPC claimant, a deduction from each loan payment shall be made in respect of any non-dependant in accordance with paragraph (2).

(2) The amount to be deducted is calculated as follows.

Step 1

Identify the amount which is the sum of the loan payment calculated under regulation 10 and the amount of housing costs (if any) paid to a claimant under—
(a) paragraph 17 of Schedule 3 to the IS Regulations;
(b) paragraph 16 of Schedule 2 to the JSA Regulations;
(c) paragraph 18 of Schedule 6 to the ESA Regulations; or
(d) paragraph 13 of Schedule 2 to the SPC Regulations.

Step 2

Identify the total amount of the non-dependant deductions applicable to the claimant under—
(a) paragraph 18 of Schedule 3 to the IS Regulations;
(b) paragraph 17 of Schedule 2 to the JSA Regulations;
(c) paragraph 19 of Schedule 6 to the ESA Regulations; or
(d) paragraph 14 of Schedule 2 to the SPC Regulations.

Step 3

Identify the proportion of the non-dependant deductions applicable to the loan payment and housing costs (if any) in Step 1 by applying the formula—

$$A \times (B \div C)$$

where—
"A" is the total amount of the non-dependant deductions identified in Step 2,
"B" is the amount of the loan payment calculated under regulation 10, and
"C" is the amount identified in Step 1.

The result is the amount of the non-dependant deduction to be made from each loan payment in the case of a legacy benefit claimant or SPC claimant.

DEFINITIONS

"claimant"—reg.2(1).
"ESA Regulations"—*ibid*.
"IS Regulations"—*ibid*.
"JSA Regulations"—*ibid*.
"legacy benefit claimant"—*ibid*.
"non-dependant"—*ibid*.
"SPC claimant"—*ibid*.
"SPC Regulations"—*ibid*.

2.562

2.563   For claimants of IB, IBJSA, IRESA and SPC, some housing costs are still available as part their benefit: see the commentary to Sch.3 to the Income Support Regulations in Vol.II. Reg.14 is designed to ensure that such claimants do not have a non-dependant deduction made twice, once as part of their benefits and once under these regulations. This is achieved by adjusting the non-dependant deduction made when calculating the amount of a loan payment in accordance with the formula set out in Step 3.

Non-dependant deductions are not applied to loan payments where the claimant is on universal credit.

[¹ Insurance payment deduction

2.564   **14A.**—(1) In the case of a legacy benefit claimant or UC claimant, where the claimant or the claimant's partner is in receipt of a payment under a policy of insurance taken out to insure against the risk of being unable to maintain owner-occupier payments within the meaning of Schedule 1, a deduction from the loan payment calculated under regulation 10 shall be made equal to the amount received in respect of owner-occupier payments.

(2) Where the amount referred to in paragraph (1) is equal to or more than the loan payment, the amount of the loan payment shall be zero.]

AMENDMENT

1. Loans for Mortgage Interest and Social Fund Maternity Grant (Amendment) Regulations 2018 (SI 2018/307), reg.2(1) and (8) (April 6, 2018).

DEFINITIONS

"claimant"—reg.2(1).
"legacy benefit claimant"—*ibid*.
"loan payment"—*ibid*.
"owner-occupier payments"—*ibid*. and reg.3(2)(a) and Sch.1
"partner"—reg.2(1).
"UC claimant"—*ibid*.

GENERAL NOTE

2.565   This regulation is self-explanatory. No insurance payment deduction is made where the claimant's qualifying benefit is SPC.

Interest

2.566   **15.**—(1) The Secretary of State shall charge interest on the sum of the loan payments until the earlier of—

(a) the day on which the loan payments and accrued interest are repaid in full;

(b) the event referred to in regulation 16(1)(c) [¹;

(c) where the conditions in paragraph (1A) are met, the day on which the Secretary of State sends a completion statement to the claimant.]

[¹ (1A) The conditions are—

(a) the claimant requests a completion statement from the Secretary of State in order to repay all of the outstanding amount in accordance with regulation 16(8) and (9); and

(b) the outstanding amount is paid within 30 days beginning with the day on which the completion statement is sent by the Secretary of State to the claimant.

(1B) Where regulation 16(3) applies, the Secretary of State shall continue to charge interest on the outstanding amount until the day referred to in regulation 15(1).]

(2) Interest at the relevant rate shall accrue daily, with effect from the first day a loan payment is made to a qualifying lender or the claimant under regulation 17, and shall be added to the outstanding amount at the end of each month (or part month).

(3) The relevant rate is the interest rate for the relevant period.

(4) For the purposes of this regulation and regulation 16, the outstanding amount is the sum of the loan payments and interest which has been charged under paragraph (1).

[¹ (4A) For the purposes of this regulation, a "completion statement" means a written statement setting out the outstanding amount owed by the claimant to the Secretary of State.]

(5) The interest rate referred to in paragraph (3) is the weighted average interest rate on conventional gilts specified in the most recent report published before the start of the relevant period by the Office for Budget Responsibility under section 4(3) of the Budget Responsibility and National Audit Act 2011.

(6) The relevant period is the period starting on—

(a) 1st January and ending on 30th June in any year; or

(b) 1st July and ending on 31st December in any year.

AMENDMENT

1. Loans for Mortgage Interest and Social Fund Maternity Grant (Amendment) Regulations 2018 (SI 2018/307), reg.2(1) and (9) (April 6, 2018).

DEFINITIONS

"claimant"—reg.2(1).
"loan payments"—*ibid.*
"qualifying lender"—*ibid.*

GENERAL NOTE

2.567 In contrast with reg.13, this regulation is not about the rate of interest that is applied to calculate the amount of loan payments. Rather, it is the rate that the Secretary of State charges on the loan that she has made to the claimant (*i.e.*, by making the loan payments) and which must be repaid in accordance with reg.16.

The rate is currently 1.7% (and is therefore less than the standard rate). The derivation of that rate is complex. Section 4(3) of the Budget Responsibility and National Audit Act 2011 requires the Office for Budget Responsibility ("OBR") to prepare fiscal and economic forecasts "on at least two occasions for each financial year". This is usually done to coincide with the Budget and the Autumn Statement and the forecast, under the title, *Economic and Fiscal Outlook*, is published on the OBR's website (http://obr.uk/publications/). The relevant figure is in a table in that document. The best way to discover it is to download the document in PDF format and then search for "weighted average interest rate on conventional gilts" which is the criterion specified in para.(5). That rate is reviewed, twice yearly, with effect from January 1 and July 1: see para.(6).

Repayment

2.568 **16.**—(1) The outstanding amount shall become immediately due and payable, together with any further interest which accrues on that amount under regulation 15, where one of the following events occurs—

    (a) the relevant accommodation is sold;

    (b) legal or beneficial title in, or in Scotland, heritable or registered title to, the relevant accommodation is transferred, assigned or otherwise disposed of, unless paragraph (3) applies;

[¹ (c) in the case of—

      (i) a claimant who is the sole legal owner of the relevant accommodation or the legal owner of the accommodation with someone other than a partner, the claimant's death;

      (ii) a claimant with a partner who is the sole legal owner of the relevant accommodation or the legal owner of the accommodation with someone other than the claimant, the partner's death; or

      (iii) a claimant and partner who are both legal owners (whether or not with anyone else) of the relevant accommodation, the death of the last member of the couple.]

    (2) Subject to paragraphs (4) to (7), repayment shall occur—

    (a) in the event described in paragraph (1)(a) or (b), from the proceeds of sale, transfer, assignment or disposition;

    (b) in the event described in paragraph (1)(c), from the relevant person's estate.

    (3) This paragraph applies where legal or beneficial title is transferred to—

    (a) the claimant's partner, following the death of the claimant, where the partner is in occupation of the relevant accommodation; or

[¹(aa) the claimant, following the death of the claimant's partner, where the claimant is in occupation of the relevant accommodation; or]

    (b) the claimant, from a former spouse or civil partner, under a court order or an agreement for maintenance where the claimant is in occupation of the relevant accommodation.

    (4) Where, in England and Wales—

    (a) the Secretary of State has a charge by way of legal mortgage over the relevant accommodation; and

    (b) there is insufficient equity available in the relevant accommodation to discharge the outstanding amount,

repayment shall be limited to the amount of available equity in the relevant accommodation after any prior ranking charges by way of legal mortgage have been repaid, and, in the event described in paragraph (1)(c), this shall be taken to be the amount of equity at the date of death of the relevant person.

    (5) Where, in England and Wales—

    (a) the Secretary of State has an equitable charge over one legal owner's equitable interest in the relevant accommodation, repayment shall be limited to the amount of that legal owner's equitable interest in the relevant accommodation and, in the event described in paragraph (1)(c), this shall be taken to be the value of that equitable interest at the date of death of the relevant person;

    (b) the Secretary of State has an equitable charge over more than one legal owner's equitable interest in the relevant accommodation, repayment shall be limited to the sum of the equitable interests in the relevant accommodation of all legal owners within the benefit unit and, in the event described in paragraph (1)(c), this shall be taken to be the value of those equitable interests at the date of death of the relevant person.

(6) Where, in Scotland—

(a) the Secretary of State has a standard security over the whole or part of the relevant accommodation; and

(b) there is insufficient equity available in the whole or part of the relevant accommodation over which the standard security is held,

repayment shall be limited to the amount of available equity in the whole or part of the relevant accommodation over which the standard security is held after any prior ranking standard securities have been repaid, and, in the event described in paragraph (1)(c), this shall be taken to be the amount of equity at the date of death of the relevant person.

(7) In the event that the relevant accommodation is sold or legal or beneficial title in, or in Scotland, heritable or registered title to, the relevant accommodation is transferred, assigned or otherwise disposed of for less than market value, the disposal shall be treated as if it occurred at market value for the purposes of repayment.

(8) Subject to paragraph (9), a claimant shall be permitted to repay some or all of the outstanding amount before an event in paragraph (1) occurs if the amount of each repayment is equal to or more than £100.

(9) Where the outstanding amount is less than £100, a claimant shall be permitted to repay that sum in full in one repayment.

AMENDMENT

1. Loans for Mortgage Interest and Social Fund Maternity Grant (Amendment) Regulations 2018 (SI 2018/307), reg.2(1) and (10) (April 6, 2018).

DEFINITIONS

"benefit unit"—reg.2(1).
"charge by way of legal mortgage"—*ibid.*
"claimant"—*ibid.*
"legal owner"—*ibid.*
"partner"—*ibid.*
"relevant accommodation"—*ibid.*
"standard security"—*ibid.*

GENERAL NOTE

The loan from the Secretary of State is repayable   2.569

- when the relevant accommodation is sold: see para.(1)(a);

- when the title to the relevant accommodation changes hands (para.1(b)) unless para.(3) applies;

- when the claimant dies unless

  — the claimant's partner is either the sole legal owner of the relevant accommodation (or the joint legal owner with someone other than the claimant), in which case the loan is repayable when the partner dies; or

  — the claimant and partner are both legal owners of the relevant accommodation, in which case the loan is repayable on the death of the surviving member of the couple.

In *R (Vincent and others) v Secretary of State for Work and Pensions* [2020] EWHC 1976 (Admin), the High Court (Andrews J) rejected submissions that para.16(1)(a) unlawfully discriminated against the claimants under art.14 ECHR taken together with A1P1 and/or art.8, as severely disabled people with a partner in receipt of

Carer's Allowance and/or as dependent children of such persons. A challenge under the Public Sector Equality Duty was also dismissed.

Under para.(3) the loan is not repayable where the title is transferred (otherwise than by way of sale, in which case para.(1)(a) would apply) to the claimant or her/his partner on the death of the other member of the couple, where the person to whom title is transferred is in occupation of the relevant accommodation: see para.(3)(a) and (aa); or where the title is transferred to the claimant from a former spouse or civil partner either by court order or under a maintenance agreement and the claimant is occupying the relevant accommodation: see para.(3)(b).

The lack of any provision that deals with the reverse of the situation described in para.(3)(b) creates an apparent lacuna. What happens if the claimant deserts their spouse or civil partner and the accommodation is then transferred from the claimant to the civil partner? The answer seems to be that the loan, which is secured on the accommodation that has now been transferred to the former partner, becomes repayable under para.(1)(b). The practical answer may be that under para.(2)(a) repayment is to be made "from the proceeds of sale, transfer, assignment or disposition" and, depending upon the terms of the court order or maintenance agreement, there will often be no such proceeds.

Paragraphs (4)-(6) limit the amount repayable to the Secretary of State to the amount of the equity in the relevant accommodation after repayment of prior mortgages and charges.

Paragraph (7) prevents that rule from being abused by selling the relevant accommodation for less than its market value. In those circumstances the sale is treated as if it had been at market value for the purpose of repayment.

Paragraphs (8) and (9) allow the claimant to make voluntary repayments. Each repayment must be at least £100 unless the amount owing is less than £100 in which case the claimant may repay that amount in full in a single repayment.

Direct payments to qualifying lenders

2.570   **17.**—(1) Where the circumstances specified in paragraph (2) are met, the loan payments must be made by the Secretary of State direct to a claimant's lender.

(2) The circumstances referred to in paragraph (1) are that—

(a) money was lent to the claimant in respect of which owner-occupier payments in respect of the relevant accommodation are payable to a qualifying lender; and

(b) those owner-occupier payments are taken into account in calculating the amount of each loan payment under regulation 10.

(3) Where the circumstances in paragraph (2) are not met, the loan payments must be made to the claimant.

(4) Schedule 4 has effect in relation to payments made under paragraph (1).

DEFINITIONS

"claimant"—reg.2(1).
"loan payments"—*ibid.*
"owner-occupier payments"—regs 2(1) and 3(2)(a).
"qualifying lender"—*ibid.*
"relevant accommodation"—*ibid.*

GENERAL NOTE

2.571   In most cases, loan payments will be made to the lender rather than to the claimant. In fact, given the breadth of the circumstances specified in para.(2), loan payments will probably only ever be made to the claimant where the lender is not a "qualifying lender" as defined in reg.2(1) and s.19(7)-(9) WRWA 2016. Any financial institution or public authority is likely to come within that definition. All that remains seems to be private loans from one individual to another.

[¹ Consequential amendments

18.—(1) Subject to paragraph (2) and regulations 19, 19A and 20, the amendments in Schedule 5 have effect.

(2) The amendments made by Part 2 of Schedule 5 to the Social Security and Child Support (Decisions and Appeals) Regulations 1999 do not apply in relation to any decision or determination about an amount for owner-occupier payments under the substantive regulations as those regulations applied without the amendments made by Part 1 of Schedule 5.

(3) In this regulation, the "substantive regulations" means the ESA Regulations, IS Regulations, JSA Regulations, SPC Regulations and UC Regulations.]

2.572

AMENDMENT

1. Loans for Mortgage Interest and Social Fund Maternity Grant (Amendment) Regulations 2018 (SI 2018/307), reg.2(1) and (11) (April 6, 2018).

GENERAL NOTE

The consequential amendments made by Sch.5 have been taken in at the appropriate points in the text of the amended regulations. Those amendments are, however, subject to the transitional provisions made by regs 19, 19A and 20 below.

2.573

[¹ Transitional provision: loan offer made before 6th April 2018

19.—(1) Subject to regulation 20, in relation to an existing claimant in a case where the loan payments offer date occurs before 6th April 2018, the amendments made by Schedule 5 shall be treated as though they did not have effect until the earlier of the following days (where that day occurs after 6th April 2018) ("the transitional end day")—

(a) the day referred to in paragraph (2);
(b) the day after the day on which entitlement to a qualifying benefit ends.

(2) The day referred to is the later of—
(a) in the case of—
   (i) a legacy benefit claimant or SPC claimant, where 6th April 2018 is not the first day of the claimant's benefit week, the first day of the first benefit week that begins after 6th April 2018; or
   (ii) a UC claimant, where 6th April 2018 is not the first day of the claimant's assessment period, the first day of the first assessment period that begins after 6th April 2018;
(b) the relevant day in paragraph (3).

(3) The relevant day is the day after the day that is the earlier of—
(a) the day on which the Secretary of State receives notification from the claimant that the claimant does not wish to accept the offer of loan payments;
(b) the last day of the period of 4 weeks, beginning with the day after the day on which the Secretary of State has received both the loan agreement and the documents referred to in regulation 5(2), duly executed, where both the loan agreement and the documents are

2.574

received within the period of 6 weeks beginning with the loan payments offer date; or

(c) the last day of the period of 6 weeks, beginning with the loan payments offer date, where the Secretary of State has not received both the loan agreement and the documents referred to in regulation 5(2), duly executed, within that period.

(4) Where in the case of—

(a) a legacy benefit claimant or SPC claimant, the relevant day referred to in paragraph (3) is not the first day of the claimant's benefit week, then the relevant day shall be the first day of the first benefit week that begins after the relevant day; or

(b) a UC claimant, the relevant day referred to in paragraph (3) is not the first day of the claimant's assessment period, then the relevant day shall be the first day of the first assessment period that begins after the relevant day.]

Amendment

1. Loans for Mortgage Interest and Social Fund Maternity Grant (Amendment) Regulations 2018 (SI 2018/307), reg.2(1) and (12) (April 6, 2018).

Definitions

"assessment period"—reg.2(1) and reg.21 UC Regs 2013.
"benefit week"—reg.2(1).
"claimant"—*ibid.*
"entitlement"—reg.2(2)(a).
"existing claimant"—reg.2(1).
"legacy benefit claimant"—*ibid.*
"loan agreement"—*ibid.*
"loan payments"—*ibid.*
"loan payments offer date"—*ibid.*
"qualifying benefit"—*ibid.*
"SPC claimant"—*ibid.*
"transitional end day"—*ibid.* and para.(1).
"UC claimant"—reg.2(1).

General Note

2.575   Regs 19, 19A, 20 and 21 all establish transitional rules for "existing claimants" (*i.e.*, those entitled to a qualifying benefit including an amount for owner-occupier payments on April 5, 2018: see reg.2(1)). "Qualifying benefits" are IRESA, IS, IBJSA, SPC and universal credit. Reg.19 applies where the "loan payments offer date" (*i.e.*, the day on which the Secretary of State sent the loan agreement to the claimant under reg.3: see reg.2(1) (again)) was before April 6, 2018. In those circumstances:

- the consequential amendments made by Sch.5 do not come into effect until the "transitional end date": see also reg.8(1)(d); and

- section 11(1), (8), (9) and (11) of the Welfare Reform and Work Act 2016 (consequential amendments) are treated as though they are not in force in relation to the existing claimant: see reg.2(2) of SI 2018/438.

In the circumstances to which reg.19 applies, that date must be after April 6, 2018, and is either, the later of the days specified in para.(2), or (if earlier) the day after the day on which the claimant's entitlement to the qualifying benefit ends.

Ignoring, for the moment, the provisions about the "relevant day", the effect is that where April 6, 2018 is not the first day of the claimant's benefit week, or universal credit assessment period, the claimant continues to receive housing costs as part of his or her qualifying benefit until the first day of the benefit week or assessment period that begins after that date. This will mean that some universal credit claimants will get housing costs as part of their benefit for up to a month more than others purely because of the day of the month on which they first claimed universal credit.

For those claimants whose benefit weeks or assessment periods begin on April 6, 2018—and who are not affected by the rules in paras (3) and (4) about the relevant day—no transitional provision is required, and none has been made.

Paragraphs (3) and (4) deal with the position where the offer of loan payments was made before April 6, 2018 but is not accepted or rejected until after that date. In those circumstances, entitlement to payment of housing costs as part of a qualifying benefit ends and entitlement to a loan potentially begins on the "relevant day". Subject to the adjustment in para.(4), the rules are as follows:

- if the claimant does not execute and return the loan agreement and the other necessary documents so that the Secretary of State receives them by the last day of the period of six weeks beginning with the loan offer date, then the relevant day is the day after the last day of that six-week period;

- if the claimant does execute and return the loan agreement and the other necessary documents so that the Secretary of State receives them by the last day of that six-week period, the relevant day is the day after the last day of the period of four weeks beginning with the day on which the Secretary of State received those documents; and

- if the claimant notifies the Secretary of State that they do not wish to accept the offer of loan payments, the relevant day is the day after the Secretary of State receives that notification.

However, the need for the relevant day to be the first day of a benefit week or a universal credit assessment period means that the days identified by para.(3) are then adjusted by para.(4). If the relevant day is not the first day of a benefit week or assessment period, the first day of the following benefit week or assessment period becomes the new relevant day.

Reg.19 is subject to the rules about those who lack, or may lack, capacity in reg.20.

[¹ Transitional provision: loan offer made on or after 6th April 2018

19A.—(1) Subject to regulation 20 and paragraph (4), in relation to an existing claimant in a case where the loan payments offer date does not occur before 6th April 2018, the amendments made by Schedule 5 shall be treated as though they did not have effect until the earlier of the following days (where that day occurs after 6th April 2018) ("the transitional end day")— 2.576

(a) the relevant day in paragraph (2);

(b) the day after the day on which entitlement to a qualifying benefit ends;

(c) the day after the day on which the Secretary of State receives notification from the claimant that the claimant does not wish to receive loan payments.

(2) The relevant day is—

(a) 7th May 2018; or

(b) where the loan payments offer date occurs before 7th May 2018, the relevant day in regulation 19(3)(b) and (c) and (4).

(3) Where in the case of—

(a) a legacy benefit claimant or SPC claimant, the day referred to in paragraph (1)(c), or the relevant day as referred to in paragraph (2)(a), is not the first day of the claimant's benefit week, then that day or that relevant day is the first day of the first benefit week that begins after that day or that relevant day; or

(b) a UC claimant, the day referred to in paragraph (1)(c), or the relevant day as referred to in paragraph (2)(a), is not the first day of the claimant's assessment period, then that day or that relevant day is not the first day of the first assessment period that begins after that day or that relevant day.

(4) Paragraphs (1) to (3) do not apply in relation to an existing claimant where, as at the end of 5th April 2018—

(a) the Secretary of State, or a person authorised to exercise functions of the Secretary of State, has, before 19th March 2018 made a request to the claimant, whether orally or in writing, to provide information that is needed in order for the Secretary of State or that person to—

(i) take steps to ascertain whether the claimant wishes to receive an offer of loan payments or not; or

(ii) be able to send to the claimant the loan agreement and documents referred to in regulation 5(2); and

(b) the claimant has not provided that information to the Secretary of State or that person.

(5) Subject to regulation 20, in the case of an existing claimant referred to in paragraph (4), where 6th April 2018 is not the first day of the claimant's benefit week, in the case of a legacy benefit or SPC claimant, or assessment period, in the case of a UC claimant, the amendments made by Schedule 5 shall be treated as though they did not have effect until the first day of the first benefit week or first assessment period that begins after that date ("the transitional end day").

AMENDMENT

1. Loans for Mortgage Interest and Social Fund Maternity Grant (Amendment) Regulations 2018 (SI 2018/307), reg.2(1) and (12) (April 6, 2018).

DEFINITIONS

"assessment period"—reg.2(1) and reg.21 UC Regs 2013.
"benefit week"—reg.2(1).
"claimant"—*ibid.*
"existing claimant"—*ibid.*
"legacy benefit claimant"—*ibid.*
"loan agreement"—*ibid.*
"loan payments"—*ibid.*
"loan payments offer date"—*ibid.*
"qualifying benefit"—*ibid.*
"SPC claimant"—*ibid.*
"transitional end day"—*ibid.* and paras (1) and (5).
"UC claimant"—reg.2(1).

GENERAL NOTE

2.577   For transitional provision generally, see the General Note to reg.19. Reg.19A governs the position where the "loan payments offer date" was *after* April 6, 2018.

Paragraph (1): In those circumstances, the transitional end day is the earliest of the day after the day on which entitlement to a qualifying benefit ends; the day after the day on which the Secretary of State is notified that the claimant does not wish to receive loan payments; and the relevant day as identified in para.(2). Where the transitional end day is determined in accordance with the first two of those alternatives, and is not the first day of the claimant's benefit week (for claimants of IS. IBJSA, IRESA and SPC) or assessment period (for claimants of universal credit), then the date is adjusted to the first day of the claimant's following benefit week or assessment period.

Paragraph (2): Where the loan payments offer date is on or after April 6, 2018 but before May 7, 2018, the relevant day is determined in accordance with reg.19(3) (b) and (c) and (4): see the commentary to those provisions in the General Note to reg.19.

The effect of para.(2)(a) is that where the loan payments offer date is made on or after May 7, 2018, no transitional provision applies. So, entitlement to housing costs will end on May 7, 2018 (or the last day of the benefit week or assessment period that includes May 7, 2018: see para.(3)) and eligibility for loan payments will begin on the date specified in reg.8.

Paragraphs (4) and (5): In some circumstances, the reason why the loan payments offer date is on or after April 6, 2018 is that the Secretary of State—or an authorised person on his behalf: see reg.22—has asked the claimant for information that is needed to establish that they are eligible for loan payments or to complete the loan agreement or other documents and the claimant has not replied. Where that request was made before March 19, 2018, paras (1)-(3) do not apply. The lack of the transitional protection established by those rules means entitlement to housing costs will end on April 6, 2018, subject to the usual adjustments to ensure that the changes come into force on the first day of a benefit period or assessment period: see para.(5).

Reg.19A is subject to the rules about those who lack, or may lack, capacity in reg.20.

[¹ Transitional provision: persons who lack capacity or may lack capacity identified before 6th April 2018

20.—(1) Paragraph (2) applies in relation to an existing claimant where, before 6th April 2018—   2.578

   (a) the Secretary of State believes that the claimant is a person who lacks capacity to make some or all decisions about accepting an offer of loan payments; or

   (b) on the basis of information received by the Secretary of State, the Secretary of State suspects that the claimant is a person who may lack such capacity,

(a "relevant claimant").

(2) In relation to a relevant claimant, the amendments made by Schedule 5 shall be treated as though they were not in force until the day that is the earlier of ("the transitional end day")—

   (a) the relevant day in paragraph (3) or (8);

   (b) the day after the day on which entitlement to a qualifying benefit ends.

(3) Subject to paragraph (8), the relevant day is the later of—

   (a) 5th November 2018;

   (b) where, in a case where paragraph (1)(b) applies, the Secretary of State believes before 5th November 2018 that the claimant is a person who lacks capacity as referred to in paragraph (1)(a), the day after the last day of the period of 6 weeks beginning with the day on which the Secretary of State forms that belief;

   (c) where an application for a decision referred to in paragraph (7) is made before the later of 5th November 2018 and the relevant day under sub-paragraph (b), the day after the day specified in paragraph (4).

(4) The specified day is—

   (a) the last day of the period of 6 weeks beginning with the day on which a person referred to in paragraph (7) ("relevant person") makes a decision referred to in paragraph (7); or

   (b) the last day of the period of 6 weeks beginning with the day on which a relevant person receives notification that the application for such a decision is withdrawn.

(5) Where more than one application for a decision as referred to in paragraph (7) is made to a relevant person within the period referred to in paragraph (3)(c), then the periods in paragraph (4) do not start to run until the relevant person has made a decision with respect to the last of the applications to be dealt with, or the relevant person receives notification that all of the applications are withdrawn.

(6) Where an application for a decision as referred to in paragraph (7) is made to more than one relevant person within the period referred to in paragraph (3)(c), then, where the specified day under paragraph (4) would be different as between the applications made to the different relevant persons, the specified day is the later of the two days.

(7) The decisions referred to are—

   (a) in England and Wales—

      (i) a decision by the Court of Protection whether or not to appoint a deputy under section 16(2) of the Mental Capacity Act 2005 with power to act on the claimant's behalf in respect of accepting an offer of loan payments;

      (ii) a decision by the Court of Protection whether or not, by making an order under section 16(2) of the Mental Capacity Act 2005, to decide on behalf of the claimant to accept an offer of loan payments; or

     (iii) a decision by the Public Guardian whether or not to register a lasting power of attorney under the Mental Capacity Act 2005 where the power includes power to act on the claimant's behalf with respect to accepting an offer of loan payments; or

   (b) in Scotland—

      (i) a decision by the sheriff whether or not to make an order under section 58 of the Adults with Incapacity (Scotland) Act 2000 to appoint a guardian with power to act on the claimant's behalf with respect to accepting an offer of loan payments;

      (ii) a decision by the sheriff whether or not, by making an intervention order under section 53 of the Adults with Incapacity (Scotland) Act 2000, to decide on behalf of the claimant to accept an offer of loan payments; or

      (ii) a decision by the sheriff or the Court of Session whether or not to make an order under the Judicial Factors Act 1849 to appoint a judicial factor with power to act on the claimant's behalf with respect to accepting an offer of loan payments.

(8) Where, in a case where paragraph (1)(b) applies, the Secretary of State believes before 5th November 2018 that the claimant is not a person who lacks capacity as referred to in paragraph (1)(a), the relevant day is the day after the earlier of—

(a) the day specified in paragraph (9);
(b) the day on which the Secretary of State receives notification from the claimant that the claimant does not wish to receive loan payments.
(9) The specified day is—
(a) the last day of the period of 6 weeks beginning with the day on which the Secretary of State forms the belief in paragraph (8); or
(b) where the loan payments offer date occurs during the period in sub-paragraph (a), the day referred to in regulation 19(3)(b) and (c) and (4).
(10) Where in the case of—
(a) a legacy benefit claimant or SPC claimant, the relevant day referred to in paragraph (3) or (8) is not the first day of the claimant's benefit week, then the relevant day shall be the first day of the first benefit week that begins after the relevant day; or
(b) a UC claimant, the relevant day in paragraph (3) or (8) is not the first day of the claimant's assessment period, then the relevant day shall be the first day of the first assessment period that begins after the relevant day.]

Amendment

1. Loans for Mortgage Interest and Social Fund Maternity Grant (Amendment) Regulations 2018 (SI 2018/307), reg.2(1) and (12) (April 6, 2018). The fact that sub-para.7(b) has two heads lettered "(ii)" is a requirement of the amending instrument and is not an editorial error.

Definitions

"assessment period"—reg.2(1) and reg.21 UC Regs 2013.
"benefit week"—reg.2(1).
"claimant"—*ibid.*
"entitlement"—reg.2(2)(a).
"existing claimant"—reg.2(1).
"legacy benefit claimant"—*ibid.*
"loan agreement"—*ibid.*
"loan payments"—*ibid.*
"loan payments offer date"—*ibid.*
"person who lacks capacity"—*ibid.*
"qualifying benefit"—*ibid.*
"SPC claimant"—*ibid.*
"transitional end day"—*ibid.* and para.(2).
"UC claimant"—*ibid.*

General Note

Regs 19 and 19A are subject to reg.20, which applies where the Secretary of State believes the claimant lacks capacity to make some or all decisions about accepting an offer of loan payments or, on the basis of information he has received, suspects that to be the case. **2.579**

"Person who lacks capacity" is defined by reg.2(1) by reference to (in England and Wales) s.2 of the Mental Health Act 2005 or (in Scotland) as meaning a person who is incapable under s.1(2) of the Adults with Incapacity (Scotland) Act 2000. Under the former provision "a person lacks capacity in relation to a matter if at the material time he is unable to make a decision for himself in relation to the matter because of an impairment of, or a disturbance in the functioning of, the mind or brain". Under the latter, an "adult" is a person who aged 16 or more and "incapable" means incapable of acting, making decisions, communicating decisions, understanding decisions, or retaining the memory of decisions, by reason of mental disorder or of inability to communicate because of physical disability but not where the lack or deficiency in a faculty of communication can be made good by human or mechanical aid.

The capacity of the claimant is a matter of greater concern to the Secretary of State where what the claimant is being offered is a loan rather than a benefit payment. If the claimant lacks capacity to enter into the loan agreement or to execute the Secretary of State's charge or security over the property, the Secretary of State would be at risk that the agreement, and the charge or security, might be invalid.

The transitional provisions are complex but, in summary, have the effect that the new law does not come into force until any question about the claimant's capacity has been resolved.

Transition from legacy benefit to universal credit

2.580   **21.**—(1) Paragraph (3) applies where—

(a) an award of universal credit is made to a claimant who—

(i) was entitled to [¹, or was treated as entitled to,] a legacy benefit (a "relevant award") at any time during the period of one month ending with the day on which the claim for universal credit was made or treated as made (or would have been so entitled were it not for termination of that award by virtue of an order made under section 150(3) of the Welfare Reform Act 2012 or the effect of the Transitional Provisions Regulations); or

(ii) was at any time during the period of one month ending with the day on which the claim for universal credit was made or treated as made, the partner of a person ("P") who was at that time entitled to [¹, or was treated as entitled to,] a relevant award, where the award of universal credit is not a joint award to the claimant and P;

(b) on the relevant date—

(i) the relevant award included an amount in respect of housing costs under—

(aa) paragraphs 14 to 16 of Schedule 2 to the JSA Regulations;

(bb) paragraphs 16 to 18 of Schedule 6 to the ESA Regulations; or

(cc) paragraphs 15 to 17 of Schedule 3 to the IS Regulations; or

(ii) the claimant was entitled to loan payments under these Regulations; and

(c) the amendments made by Schedule 5 apply in relation to the award of universal credit.

(2) In this regulation, the "relevant date" means—

(a) where paragraph (1)(a)(i) applies and the claimant was not entitled to [¹, or was treated as entitled to,] the relevant award on the date on which the claim for universal credit was made or treated as made, the date on which the relevant award terminated;

(b) where paragraph (1)(a)(i) applies, the claimant is not a new claimant partner and he or she was entitled to [¹, or was treated as entitled to,] the relevant award on the date on which the claim for universal credit was made, that date;

(c) where paragraph (1)(a)(i) applies, the claimant is a new claimant partner and he or she was entitled to [¹, or was treated as entitled to,] the relevant award on the date on which the claim for universal credit was treated as made, that date;

(d) where paragraph (1)(a)(ii) applies, the date on which the claimant ceased to be the partner of P or, if earlier, the date on which the relevant award terminated.

(3) Where this paragraph applies, regulation 8(1)(b) does not apply.

(4) Paragraph (5) applies where paragraph (1)(a) applies and the amendments made by Schedule 5 apply in relation to the award of universal credit, but—

(a) the relevant award did not include an amount in respect of housing costs because the claimant's entitlement (or, as the case may be, P's entitlement) was nil by virtue of—
  (i) paragraph 7(1)(b) of Schedule 2 to the JSA Regulations;
  (ii) paragraph 9(1)(b) of Schedule 6 to the ESA Regulations; or
  (iii) paragraph 8(1)(b) of Schedule 3 to the IS Regulations; or

(b) the amendments made by Schedule 5 applied in relation to the relevant award but the claimant was not entitled to loan payments by virtue of regulation 8(1)(b).

(5) Where this paragraph applies—

(a) the definition of "qualifying period" in regulation 2(1) does not apply; and

(b) "qualifying period" means the period of 273 days starting with the first day on which the claimant (or, as the case may be, P) was entitled to the relevant award, taking into account any period which was treated as a period of continuing entitlement under—
  (i) paragraph 13 of Schedule 2 to the JSA Regulations;
  (ii) paragraph 15 of Schedule 6 to the ESA Regulations; or
  (iii) paragraph 14 of Schedule 3 to the IS Regulations,
  provided that, throughout that part of the qualifying period after the award of universal credit is made, receipt of universal credit is continuous and the claimant otherwise qualifies for loan payments under these Regulations.

(6) Paragraph (7) applies where—

(a) a claimant has an award of universal credit which becomes subject to the amendments made by Schedule 5; and

(b) regulation 29 of the Transitional Provisions Regulations applied in relation to the award.

(7) Where this paragraph applies—

(a) where paragraph (3) of regulation 29 of the Transitional Provisions Regulations applied in relation to the award, regulation 8(1)(b) does not apply; and

(b) where paragraph (5) of regulation 29 of the Transitional Provisions Regulations applied in relation to the award, paragraph (5) of this regulation applies in relation to the award.

AMENDMENT

1. Loans for Mortgage Interest and Social Fund Maternity Grant (Amendment) Regulations 2018 (SI 2018/307), reg. 2(1) and (13) (April 6, 2018).

DEFINITIONS

"claimant"—reg. 2(1).
"entitlement"—reg. 2(2)(a).

"ESA Regulations"—reg.2(1).
"IS Regulations"—*ibid*.
"JSA Regulations"—*ibid*.
"legacy benefit"—*ibid*.
"loan payments"—*ibid*.
"new claimant partner"—*ibid*.
"partner"—*ibid*.
"qualifying period"—reg.2(1) as modified by para.(5).
"relevant date"—para.(2).
"Transitional Provisions Regulations"—reg.2(1).

GENERAL NOTE

2.581   This regulation makes transitional provision where a claimant transfers to universal credit from IS, IBJSA or IRESA.

Delegation

2.582   **22.** A function of the Secretary of State under these Regulations may be exercised by a person authorised for that purpose by the Secretary of State.

GENERAL NOTE

2.583   This regulation is made under s.19(5) of the WRWA 2016 which provides that the regulations "may provide for the Secretary of State to make arrangements with another person for the exercise of functions under the regulations".

Regulation 3(2)(a)

SCHEDULE 1

MEANING OF OWNER-OCCUPIER PAYMENTS

PART 1

LEGACY BENEFIT CLAIMANTS AND SPC CLAIMANTS

Application of Part 1
2.584   1. This Part applies to legacy benefit claimants and SPC claimants.

Payments of interest on qualifying loans and alternative finance payments
2.585   2.—(1) "Owner-occupier payments" means—
(a) payments of interest on a loan which qualifies under sub-paragraph (2) or (4); and
(b) in respect of an SPC claimant only, alternative finance payments within the meaning of paragraph 5(3).
(2) A loan qualifies under this sub-paragraph where the loan was taken out to defray monies applied for any of the following purposes—
(a) acquiring an interest in the relevant accommodation; or
(b) paying off another loan which would have qualified under paragraph (a) had it not been paid off.
(3) For the purposes of sub-paragraph (2), references to a loan also include a reference to money borrowed under a hire purchase agreement, as defined in section 189 of the Consumer Credit Act 1974, for any purpose specified in paragraph (a) or (b) of sub-paragraph (2).
(4) A loan qualifies under this sub-paragraph if it was taken out, with or without security, for the purpose of—
(a) carrying out repairs and improvements to the relevant accommodation;
(b) paying any service charge imposed to meet the cost of repairs and improvements to the relevant accommodation;
(c) paying off another loan that would have qualified under paragraphs (a) and (b) had it not been paid off,

as long as the loan is used for that purpose within 6 months beginning with the date of receipt or as soon as reasonably practicable.

(5) In sub-paragraph (4), "repairs and improvements" means any of the following measures undertaken with a view to maintaining the fitness of the relevant accommodation, or any part of the building containing the relevant accommodation, for human habitation—

  (a) provision of a fixed bath, shower, wash basin, sink or lavatory, and necessary associated plumbing, including the provision of hot water not connected to a central heating system;
  (b) repairs to existing heating systems;
  (c) damp proof measures;
  (d) provision of ventilation and natural lighting;
  (e) provision of drainage facilities;
  (f) provision of facilities for preparing and cooking food;
  (g) provision of insulation;
  (h) provision of electric lighting and sockets;
  (i) provision of storage facilities for fuel or refuse;
  (j) repairs of unsafe structural defects;
  (k) adapting the accommodation for the special needs of a disabled person; or
  (l) provision of separate sleeping accommodation for persons of different sexes aged 10 or over but under the age of 20 who live with the claimant and for whom the claimant or the claimant's partner is responsible.

(6) Where a loan is applied only in part for the purposes specified in sub-paragraph (2) or (4), only that portion of the loan which is applied for that purpose shall qualify.

Loans incurred during relevant period

3.—(1) Subject to sub-paragraph (5), loans which, apart from this paragraph, qualify under paragraph 2(2) or (4) shall not so qualify where the loan was incurred during the relevant period.

2.586

(2) The "relevant period" for the purposes of this paragraph is any period during which the person to whom the loan was made—

  (a) is entitled to, or is treated as entitled to, a legacy benefit or state pension credit; or
  (b) is living as a member of a family one of whom is entitled to, or is treated as entitled to, a legacy benefit or state pension credit,

together with any period falling between two such periods of entitlement separated by not more than 26 weeks.

(3) For the purposes of sub-paragraph (2), a person shall be treated as entitled to either a legacy benefit or state pension credit during any period when the person, the person's partner, or, where that person is a member of a joint-claim couple, the other member of that couple was not so entitled because—

  (a) that person, the person's partner or, where that person is a member of a joint-claim couple, the other member of that couple, was participating in an employment programme specified in regulation 75(1)(a) of the JSA Regulations; and
  (b) in consequence of such participation that person, the person's partner, or, where that person is a member of a joint-claim couple, the other member of that couple, was a person engaged in remunerative work and had income equal to or in excess of the applicable amount.

(4) Where a loan which qualifies under paragraph 2(2) was incurred during the relevant period—

  (a) for paying off an earlier loan, and that earlier loan qualified under paragraph 2(2) and was incurred during the relevant period; or
  (b) to finance the purchase of a property where an earlier loan, which qualified under paragraph 2(2) or (4) and was incurred during the relevant period in respect of another property, is paid off (in whole or in part) with monies received from the sale of that property,

then the amount of the loan to which sub-paragraph (1) applies is the amount (if any) by which the new loan exceeds the earlier loan.

(5) Loans taken out during the relevant period shall qualify as loans under paragraph 2(2) or (4), where a claimant satisfies any of the conditions specified in sub-paragraphs (6), (8) and (9), but—

  (a) where the claimant satisfies the condition in sub-paragraph (6), [¹ the amount of each loan payment calculated under regulation 10] shall be subject to the additional limitation imposed by sub-paragraph (7); and
  (b) where the claimant satisfies the conditions in more than one of these sub-paragraphs,

only one sub-paragraph shall apply in the claimant's case, which shall be the one most favourable to the claimant.

(6) The first condition is that—

    (a) during the relevant period, the claimant or a member of the claimant's family acquires an interest ("the relevant interest") in the relevant accommodation; and

    (b) in the week preceding the week in which the relevant interest was acquired, the claimant or a member of the claimant's family was entitled to housing benefit.

(7) Where the condition in sub-paragraph (6) is satisfied, the amount of the loans which qualify shall initially not exceed the aggregate of—

    (a) the housing benefit entitlement referred to in sub-paragraph (6)(b); and

    (b) any amount included in the applicable amount of the claimant or a member of the claimant's family [¹ relating to housing costs] in that week,

    and shall be increased subsequently only to the extent that it is necessary to take account of any increase in the standard rate under regulation 13 arising after the date of acquisition.

(8) The second condition is that the loan was taken out, or an existing loan increased, to acquire alternative accommodation more suited to the needs of a disabled person than the relevant accommodation which was occupied before the acquisition by the claimant.

(9) The third condition is that—

    (a) the loan commitment increased in consequence of the disposal of the relevant accommodation and the acquisition of alternative accommodation; and

    (b) the change of accommodation was made solely by reason of the need to provide separate sleeping accommodation for persons of different sexes aged 10 or over but under the age of 20 who live with the claimant and for whom the claimant or the claimant's partner is responsible.

PART 2

UC CLAIMANTS

Application of Part 2

2.587   4. This Part applies to UC claimants.

Payments of interest on loans and alternative finance payments

2.588   5.—(1) "Owner-occupier payments" means—

    (a) payments of interest on a loan which qualifies under sub-paragraph (2);

    (b) alternative finance payments within the meaning of sub-paragraph (3).

(2) A loan qualifies under this sub-paragraph if it is secured on the relevant accommodation.

(3) "Alternative finance payments" means payments that are made under alternative finance arrangements which were entered into to enable a person to acquire an interest in the relevant accommodation.

(4) "Alternative finance arrangements" has the meaning given in Part 10A of the Income Tax Act 2007.

AMENDMENT

1. Loans for Mortgage Interest and Social Fund Maternity Grant (Amendment) Regulations 2018 (SI 2018/307), reg.2(1) and (14) (April 6, 2018).

DEFINITIONS

"alternative finance payments"—reg.2(1) and para. 5(3).
"alternative finance arrangements"—para.5(4).
"applicable amount"—reg.2(1).
"couple"—*ibid.*
"disabled person"—*ibid.*
"entitlement"—reg.2(2)(a).
"family"—reg.2(2)(b).
"income"—reg.2(1).
"joint-claim couple"—*ibid.*
"JSA Regulations"—*ibid.*
"legacy benefit"—*ibid.*

"legacy benefit claimant"—*ibid.*
"owner-occupier payments"—regs 2(1) and 3(2)(a) and paras 2(1) and 5(1).
"partner"—reg.2(1).
"qualifying loan"—*ibid.*
"relevant accommodation"—*ibid.*
"relevant period"—para.3(2).
"repairs and improvements"—para.2(5).
"remunerative work"—reg.2(2)(e).
"SPC claimant"—reg.2(1).
"UC claimant"—*ibid.*

GENERAL NOTE

The phrase, "owner-occupier payments" is defined by reg.2(1) as having "the meaning given in regulation 3(2)(a)" which, in turn, gives effect to this Schedule. **2.589**

The rules differ according to whether the claimant is on a "legacy benefit" or SPC, on the one hand, or on universal credit, on the other.

Paragraph 2: For the former group of claimants, owner-occupier payments are interest payments on:

- a loan to acquire an interest in the accommodation occupied, or treated as occupied as the claimant's home (see the definition of "relevant accommodation" in reg.2(1)) (or a loan to refinance such a loan): see para.2(2); or

- a loan to carry out repairs and improvements to the claimant's home, or to pay a service charge to meet the costs of such repairs or improvements (or a loan to refinance such a loan): see para.2(4).

For what counts as a repair or an improvement (para.2(5)), see the commentary to para.16 of Sch.3 to the IS Regulations in Vol.II.

Where a loan is only partly used to acquire an interest in the claimant's home or to carry out repairs and improvements, only that part qualifies for the purpose of para.2(1)(a) with the effect that a loan payment is only available to meet the interest on that part of the loan: see para.2(6).

For SPC claimants only, a payment in respect of "alternative finance arrangements" (see below) is also an owner occupier payment.

Paragraph 3 provides that, subject to the exceptions in sub-para.(5) loans that would otherwise qualify, do not qualify if they are taken out during the "relevant period" as defined in sub-para.(2). If a claimant refinances during the relevant period, then the amount that does not qualify is the amount by which the new loan exceeds the earlier loan: see sub-para.(4).

Paragraph 5: For UC claimants, the loan qualifies if it is secured on the relevant accommodation, irrespective of the purpose for which it was taken out: see sub-para.(1)(a). In addition, a payment in respect of "alternative finance arrangements" is also an owner occupier payment: see sub-para.(1)(b).

Alternative finance payments are defined by sub-para.(3) as payments that are made under "alternative finance arrangements" which were entered into to enable a person to acquire an interest in the relevant accommodation. Under sub-para.(4), "alternative finance arrangements" are defined by reference to Part 10A of the Income Tax Act 2007 and therefore "means ...(a) purchase and resale arrangements, (b) diminishing shared ownership arrangements, (c) deposit arrangements, (d) profit share agency arrangements, and (e) investment bond arrangements" (see section 564A(2) of that Act). All those types of arrangement are further defined by ss 564C–564G, and represent different types of what are known colloquially as an Islamic mortgage in which help from a financial institution to buy real property is structured in ways that do not involve the charging or payment of interest.

Regulation 3(2)(b)

SCHEDULE 2

CIRCUMSTANCES IN WHICH A CLAIMANT IS, OR IS TO BE TREATED AS, LIABLE TO MAKE OWNER-OCCUPIER PAYMENTS

PART 1

LEGACY BENEFIT CLAIMANTS AND SPC CLAIMANTS

Application of Part 1

2.590   1. This Part applies to legacy benefit claimants and SPC claimants.

Liable or treated as liable to make payments

2.591   2.—(1) A claimant is liable to make owner-occupier payments where—

(a) in the case of a single claimant, the claimant or the claimant's partner (if any), or, in the case of joint claimants, either member of the couple, has a liability to make the payments;

(2) A claimant is to be treated as liable to make owner-occupier payments where—

(a) all of the following conditions are met—

(i) the person who is liable to make the payments is not doing so;

(ii) the claimant has to make the payments in order to continue occupation of the relevant accommodation; and

(iii) it is reasonable in all the circumstances to treat the claimant as liable to make the payments; or

(b) all of the following conditions are met—

(i) the claimant in practice shares the responsibility for the owner-occupier payments with other members of the household, none of whom are close relatives of, in the case of a single claimant, the claimant or the claimant's partner (if any), or, in the case of joint claimants, either member of the couple;

(ii) one or more of those members is liable to meet those payments; and

(iii) it is reasonable in all the circumstances to treat that member as sharing responsibility.

(3) Where any one or more, but not all, members of the claimant's family are affected by a trade dispute, the owner-occupier payments shall be treated as wholly the responsibility of those members of the family not so affected.

(4) For the purposes of sub-paragraph (2), "trade dispute" has the meaning given in section 244 of the Trade Union and Labour Relations (Consolidation) Act 1992.

Treated as not liable to make payments

2.592   3. A claimant is to be treated as not liable to make owner-occupier payments where the liability to make the payments is owed to a person who is a member of the claimant's household.

PART 2

UC CLAIMANTS

Application of Part 2

2.593   4. This Part applies to UC claimants.

Liable or treated as liable to make payments

2.594   5.—(1) A claimant is liable to make owner-occupier payments where—

(a) in the case of a single claimant, the claimant or the claimant's partner (if any), or, in the case of joint claimants, either member of the couple, has a liability to make the payments;

(2) A claimant is to be treated as liable to make owner-occupier payments where—

(a) the person who is liable to make the payments is a child or qualifying young person for whom the claimant is responsible;

(b) all of the following conditions are met—

      (i) the person who is liable to make the payments is not doing so;

      (ii) the claimant has to make the payments in order to continue occupation of the relevant accommodation;

      (iii) the claimant's circumstances are such that it would be unreasonable to expect them to make other arrangements; and

      (iv) it is otherwise reasonable in all the circumstances to treat the claimant as liable to make the payments; or

  (c) the claimant—

      (i) has a liability to make the payments which is waived by the person ("P") to whom the liability is owed; and

      (ii) the waiver of that liability is by way of reasonable compensation for reasonable repair or re-decoration works carried out by the claimant to the relevant accommodation which P would otherwise have carried out or been required to carry out.

(3) [¹ Sub-paragraph (1)] does not apply to a person in a polygamous marriage who is a single claimant by virtue of regulation 3(4) of the UC Regulations.

Treated as not liable to make payments

6. A claimant is to be treated as not liable to make owner-occupier payments—   **2.595**

  (a) where the liability to make the payments is owed to a person who is a member of the claimant's household;

  (b) in respect of any amount which represents an increase in the sum that would otherwise be payable and is the result of—

      (i) outstanding arrears of any payment or charge in respect of the relevant accommodation;

      (ii) outstanding arrears of any payment or charge in respect of other accommodation previously occupied by the claimant; or

      (iii) any other unpaid liability to make a payment or charge; or

  (c) where the Secretary of State is satisfied that the liability to make the owner-occupier payments was contrived in order to secure the offer of loan payments or increase the amount of each loan payment.

AMENDMENT

1. Loans for Mortgage Interest and Social Fund Maternity Grant (Amendment) Regulations 2018 (SI 2018/307), reg.2(1) and (15) (April 6, 2018).

DEFINITIONS

"child"—reg.2(1).
"couple"—*ibid.*
"family"—reg.2(2)(b).
"joint claimants"—reg.2(1).
"legacy benefit claimant"—*ibid.*
"loan payments"—*ibid.*
"owner-occupier payments"—regs 2(1) and 3(2)(a).
"member of a household"—reg.2(2)(b).
"partner"—reg.2(1).
"polygamous marriage"—*ibid.*
"qualifying young person"—*ibid.*
"relevant accommodation"—*ibid.*
"single claimant"—*ibid.*
"SPC claimant"—*ibid.*
"trade dispute"—para.2(4).
"UC claimant"—*ibid.*
"UC Regulations"—*ibid.*

2.598   GENERAL NOTE

See the commentary to Sch.2 to the UC Regulations, which is to similar effect, except that   **2.596**
the grounds on which a claimant is treated as not liable to make owner-occupier payments are more restricted under this Schedule.

The fact that sub-para.2(1) has a single head (a) with no head (b) or (c) etc. is not an editorial error.

Regulation 3(2)(c)

SCHEDULE 3

CIRCUMSTANCES IN WHICH A CLAIMANT IS, OR IS TO BE, TREATED AS OCCUPYING ACCOMMODATION

PART 1

GENERAL

Interpretation

2.597

1.—(1) In this Schedule—

"Abbeyfield Home" means an establishment run by the Abbeyfield Society including all bodies corporate or incorporate which are affiliated to that Society;

"care home"—

(a) in England and Wales, has the meaning given in section 3 of the Care Standards Act 2000;

(b) in Scotland, means a care home service within the meaning of paragraph 2 of Schedule 12 to the Public Services Reform (Scotland) Act 2010,

and in either case includes an independent hospital;

"croft" means a croft within the meaning of section 3(1) of the Crofters (Scotland) Act 1993;

"full-time student" has the meaning given—

(a) in the case of income support, in regulation 61(1) of the IS Regulations;

(b) in the case of jobseeker's allowance, in regulation 1(3) of the JSA Regulations;

(c) in the case of employment and support allowance, in regulation 131 of the ESA Regulations;

(d) in the case of state pension credit, in regulation 1(2) of the SPC Regulations;

"independent hospital"—

(a) in England, means a hospital as defined in section 275 of the National Health Service Act 2006 that is not a health service hospital as defined by that section;

(b) in Wales, has the meaning given in section 2 of the Care Standards Act 2000;

(c) in Scotland means an independent healthcare service as defined in section 10F(1)(a) and (b) of the National Health Service (Scotland) Act 1978;

"medically approved" means certified by a medical practitioner;

"patient" means a person who is undergoing medical or other treatment as an inpatient in a hospital or similar institution;

"period of study" has the meaning given—

(a) in the case of income support and state pension credit, in regulation 2(1) of the IS Regulations;

(b) in the case of jobseeker's allowance, in regulation 1(3) of the JSA Regulations;

(c) in the case of employment and support allowance, in regulation 2 of the ESA Regulations;

"residential accommodation" means accommodation which is a care home, Abbeyfield Home or independent hospital;

"training course" means a course of training or instruction provided wholly or partly by or on behalf of or in pursuance of arrangements made with, or approved by or on behalf of, Skills Development Scotland, Scottish Enterprise, Highlands and Islands Enterprise, a government department or the Secretary of State.

(2) In this Schedule, a reference to a claimant being liable to make owner-occupier payments is to be read as a reference to a person being treated as liable to make owner-occupier payments under Schedule 2.

PART 2

Legacy benefit claimants and SPC claimants

Application of Part 2

2.598

2. This Part applies to legacy benefit claimants and SPC claimants.

Occupying accommodation: general rule

3.—(1) Subject to the following paragraphs of this Part, the accommodation which the claimant occupies as the claimant's home or, if the claimant is a member of a family, the claimant and the claimant's family occupy as their home, is the accommodation which is normally occupied as the home.

2.599

(2) In determining whether accommodation is the accommodation normally occupied as the home for the purposes of sub-paragraph (1), regard shall be had to any other dwelling occupied by the claimant or, if the claimant is a member of a family, by the claimant and the claimant's family, whether or not that other dwelling is in Great Britain.

Full-time study

4.—(1) Subject to sub-paragraph (2), where a claimant is a full-time student or on a training course and is liable to make owner-occupier payments in respect of either (but not both)—

2.600

(a) the accommodation which the claimant occupies for the purpose of attending the course of study or training course; or

(b) the accommodation which the claimant occupies when not attending the course of study or training course,

the claimant shall be treated as occupying as the claimant's home the accommodation in respect of which the claimant is liable to make the owner-occupier payments.

(2) A claimant who is a full-time student shall not be treated as occupying accommodation as the claimant's home for any week of absence from it outside the period of study, other than an absence occasioned by the need to enter hospital for treatment.

Living in other accommodation during essential repairs

5. Where the claimant—

2.601

(a) has been required to move into temporary accommodation by reason of essential repairs being carried out to the accommodation which the claimant occupies as the claimant's home ("the home accommodation"); and

(b) is liable to make owner-occupier payments in respect of either (but not both) the home accommodation or the temporary accommodation,

the claimant shall be treated as occupying as the claimant's home the accommodation in respect of which the claimant is liable to make those payments.

Living in other accommodation due to fear of violence, where a claimant's partner is a full-time student or where moving into new accommodation

6. Where a claimant is liable to make owner-occupier payments in respect of two dwellings, the claimant shall be treated as occupying both dwellings as the claimant's home—

2.602

(a) where—

(i) the claimant has left and remains absent from the accommodation which the claimant occupies as the claimant's home ("the home accommodation") through fear of violence in the home or of violence by a close relative or former partner; and

(ii) it is reasonable that owner-occupier payments should be met in respect of both the claimant's home accommodation and the claimant's present accommodation which the claimant occupies as the home;

(b) in the case of a couple or a member of a polygamous marriage, where—

(i) one partner is a full-time student or is on a training course and it is unavoidable that the members of the couple or polygamous marriage should occupy two separate dwellings; and

(ii) it is reasonable that owner-occupier payments should be met in respect of both dwellings; or

(c) where—

(i) the claimant has moved into new accommodation occupied as the claimant's home, except where paragraph 5 applies, for a period not exceeding four benefit weeks from the first day of the benefit week in which the move occurs; and

(ii) the claimant's liability to make owner-occupier payments in respect of both the new accommodation and the accommodation from which the move was made is unavoidable.

Moving in delayed for certain reasons

7.—(1) Where—

2.603

(a) a claimant was delayed in moving into accommodation ("the new accommodation") and was liable to make owner-occupier payments in respect of that accommodation before moving in; and

(b) the delay was reasonable and one of the conditions in sub-paragraphs (2) to (4) applies,

the claimant shall be treated as occupying the new accommodation as the claimant's home for the period of delay, not exceeding four weeks immediately prior to the date on which the claimant moved into the new accommodation.

(2) The first condition is that the delay occurred in order to adapt the accommodation to meet the needs of the claimant or a member of the claimant's family who is a disabled person.

(3) The second condition is that—

(a) the move was delayed pending local welfare provision to meet a need arising out of the move or in connection with setting up the claimant's home in the new accommodation; and

(b) in the case of a legacy benefit claimant only—

(i) a member of the claimant's family is aged 5 or under;

(ii) the claimant's applicable amount includes a pensioner premium or disability premium under Schedule 2 to the IS Regulations, Schedule 1 to the JSA Regulations or Schedule 4 to the ESA Regulations; or

(iii) a child tax credit is paid for a member of the claimant's family who is disabled or severely disabled for the purposes of section 9(6) of the Tax Credits Act 2002;

(4) The third condition is that the claimant became liable to make owner-occupier payments in respect of the accommodation while the claimant was a patient or was in a residential home.

Temporary absence to try new accommodation of up to 13 weeks

2.604   8.—(1) This sub-paragraph applies to a claimant who enters residential accommodation—

(a) for the purpose of ascertaining whether the accommodation suits the claimant's needs; and

(b) with the intention of returning to the accommodation which the claimant occupies as the claimant's home ("the home accommodation") in the event that the residential accommodation proves not to suit the claimant's needs,

and while in the residential accommodation, the home accommodation is not let or sub-let to another person.

(2) A claimant to whom sub-paragraph (1) applies shall be treated as occupying the home accommodation during the period of absence, not exceeding 13 weeks in which the claimant is resident in the residential accommodation, but only where the total absence from the home accommodation does not exceed 52 consecutive weeks.

Temporary absence of up to 13 weeks

2.605   9. A claimant, except where paragraph 10 applies, shall be treated as occupying accommodation as the claimant's home throughout any period of absence not exceeding 13 weeks, where—

(a) the claimant intends to return to occupy the accommodation as the claimant's home;

(b) the part of the accommodation occupied by the claimant has not been let or sub-let to another person; and

(c) the period of absence is unlikely to exceed 13 weeks.

Absences for certain reasons up to 52 weeks

2.606   10.—(1) Where sub-paragraph (2) applies, a claimant is to be treated as occupying accommodation as the claimant's home ("the home accommodation") during any period of absence from it not exceeding 52 weeks beginning with the first day of that absence.

(2) This paragraph applies where a claimant's absence from the home accommodation is temporary and—

(a) the claimant intends to return to occupy the home accommodation;

(b) the home accommodation has not been let or sub-let;

(c) the claimant is—

(i) detained in custody on remand pending trial or, as a condition of bail, required to reside—

(aa) in a dwelling, other than the home accommodation; or

(bb) in premises approved under section 13 of the Offender Management Act 2007;

(ii) detained pending sentence upon conviction;

(iii) resident in a hospital or similar institution as a patient;

(iv) undergoing or, the claimant's partner or child, or in the case of an SPC claimant, a person who has not attained the age of 20, is undergoing medical treatment, or medically approved convalescence, in accommodation other than residential accommodation;

   (v) undertaking a training course;

  (vi) undertaking medically approved care of another person;

 (vii) undertaking the care of a child or, in the case of an SPC claimant, a person under the age of 20 whose parent or guardian is temporarily absent from the dwelling occupied by that parent or guardian for the purpose of receiving medically approved care or medical treatment;

(viii) a person who is receiving medically approved care provided in accommodation other than a residential home;

  (ix) a full-time student to whom paragraph 4(1) or 6(b) does not apply;

   (x) a person, other than a person to whom paragraph 8(1) applies, who is receiving care provided in residential accommodation; or

  (xi) a person to whom paragraph 6(a) does not apply and who has left the home accommodation through fear of violence in that accommodation, or by a person who was formerly his or her partner or is a close relative; and

(d) the period of the claimant's absence is unlikely to exceed 52 weeks or, in exceptional circumstances, is unlikely substantially to exceed that period.

PART 3

UC CLAIMANTS

Application of Part 3

11. This Part applies to UC claimants.   **2.607**

Occupying accommodation: general rule

12.—(1) Subject to the following paragraphs of this Part, the accommodation which the   **2.608** claimant occupies as the claimant's home is the accommodation which the claimant normally occupies the home.

(2) Where the claimant occupies more than one dwelling, in determining whether accommodation is the accommodation normally occupied as the home for the purposes of sub-paragraph (1), regard is to be had to all the circumstances including (among other things) any persons with whom the claimant occupies each dwelling.

(3) Where accommodation which a claimant occupies as the claimant's home is situated on or pertains to a croft, croft land used for the purposes of the accommodation is to be treated as included in the accommodation.

Living in other accommodation due to essential repairs

13.—(1) Where a claimant—   **2.609**

(a) is required to move into accommodation ("the other accommodation") on account of essential repairs being carried out to the accommodation the claimant occupies as the claimant's home ("the home accommodation");

(b) intends to return to the home accommodation; and

(c) is liable to make owner-occupier payments in respect of either the other accommodation or the home accommodation (but not both),

the claimant is to be treated as occupying as the claimant's home the accommodation in respect of which the owner-occupier payments are made.

Moving homes: adaptations to new home for disabled person

14.—(1) Sub-paragraph (2) applies where—   **2.610**

(a) a claimant has moved into accommodation ("the new accommodation") and, immediately before the move, was liable to make owner-occupier payments in respect of the new accommodation; and

(b) there was a delay in moving in to adapt the new accommodation in order to meet the needs of a disabled person.

(2) The claimant is to be treated as occupying both the new accommodation and the accommodation from which the move was made ("the old accommodation") if—

(a) immediately before the move, the claimant was receiving loan payments or, in the case of an existing claimant, a qualifying benefit which includes an amount for owner-occupier payments, in respect of the old accommodation; and

(b) the delay in moving into the new accommodation was reasonable.

(3) A person is disabled under this Part if the person is—

(a) a claimant or any child or qualifying young person for whom the claimant is responsible; and

(b) in receipt of—
    (i) the care component of disability living allowance at the middle or highest rate;
    (ii) attendance allowance; or
    (iii) the daily living component of personal independence payment.

(4) No claimant may be treated as occupying both the old accommodation and the new accommodation under this paragraph for more than one month.

Living in other accommodation due to fear of violence

2.611   15.—(1) Sub-paragraph (2) applies where—
    (a) a claimant is occupying accommodation ("the other accommodation") other than the accommodation which the claimant occupies as the claimant's home ("the home accommodation");
    (b) it is unreasonable to expect the claimant to return to the home accommodation on account of the claimant's reasonable fear of violence in the home, or by a former partner, against the claimant or any child or qualifying young person for whom the claimant is responsible; and
    (c) the claimant intends to return to the home accommodation.

(2) The claimant is to be treated as occupying both the home accommodation and the other accommodation as the claimant's home if—
    (a) the claimant is liable to make payments in respect of both the other accommodation and the home accommodation; and
    (b) it is reasonable to make loan payments in respect of both the home accommodation and the other accommodation.

(3) Where the claimant is liable to make payments in respect of one accommodation only, the claimant is to be treated as occupying that accommodation as the claimant's home but only if it is reasonable to make loan payments in respect of that accommodation.

(4) No claimant may be treated as occupying both the home accommodation and the other accommodation under this paragraph for more than 12 months.

Moving in delayed by adaptations to accommodation to meet needs of disabled person

2.612   16.—(1) The claimant is to be treated as having occupied accommodation before the claimant moved into it where—
    (a) the claimant has since moved in and, immediately before the move, the claimant is liable to make payments in respect of that accommodation;
    (b) there was a delay in moving in that was necessary to enable the accommodation to be adapted to meet the needs of a disabled person; and
    (c) it was reasonable to delay moving in.

(2) No claimant may be treated as occupying accommodation under this paragraph for more than one month.

Moving into accommodation following a stay in hospital or care home

2.613   17.—(1) The claimant is to be treated as having occupied accommodation before he or she moved into it where—
    (a) the claimant has since moved in and, immediately before the move, the claimant was liable to make payments in respect of that accommodation; and
    (b) the liability to make the payments arose while the claimant was a patient or accommodated in a care home (or, in the case of joint claimants, where both individuals were patients or were accommodated in a care home).

(2) No claimant may be treated as occupying the accommodation under this paragraph for more than one month.

Temporary absence exceeding 6 months

2.614   18.—(1) Subject to sub-paragraph (2), a claimant is to be treated as no longer occupying accommodation from which the claimant is temporarily absent where the absence exceeds, or is expected to exceed, 6 months.

(2) Where a claimant who falls within [¹ paragraph 15] is temporarily absent from the relevant accommodation, the claimant is to be treated as no longer occupying that accommodation where the absence exceeds, or is expected to exceed, 12 months.

AMENDMENT

1. Loans for Mortgage Interest and Social Fund Maternity Grant (Amendment) Regulations 2018 (SI 2018/307), reg.2(1) and (16) (April 6, 2018).

DEFINITIONS

"applicable amount"—reg.2(1).
"benefit week"—*ibid.*
"care home"—para.1(1).
"child"—reg.2(1).
"close relative"—*ibid.*
"couple"—*ibid.*
"croft"—para.1(1).
"disabled person"—reg.2(1).
"dwelling"—*ibid.*
"ESA Regulations"—*ibid.*
"existing claimant"—*ibid.*
"family"—reg.2(2)(b).
"full-time student"—para.1(1).
"IS Regulations"—reg.2(1).
"joint claimants"—*ibid.*
"JSA Regulations"—*ibid.*
"legacy benefit claimant"—*ibid.*
"loan payments"—*ibid.*
"medically approved"—para.1(1).
"owner-occupier payments"—regs 2(1) and 3(2)(a).
"partner"—reg.2(1).
"patient"—para.1(1).
"period of study"—*ibid.*
"polygamous marriage"—reg.2(1).
"qualifying benefit"—*ibid.*
"qualifying young person"—*ibid.*
"relevant accommodation"—*ibid.*
"residential accommodation"—para.1(1).
"SPC claimant"—reg.2(1).
"SPC Regulations"—*ibid.*
"training course"—para.1(1).
"UC claimant"—reg.2(1).

2.617   GENERAL NOTE

See the commentary to Sch.3 to the UC Regulations (above), which is to similar   **2.615**
effect.

Regulation 17

SCHEDULE 4

Direct payments to qualifying lenders

Direct payments
1. Each loan payment made to a qualifying lender directly under regulation 17(1) shall be   **2.616**
the amount calculated under paragraph 2 [¹ ...] of this Schedule.

**[¹ Determining the amount to be paid to a qualifying lender: one or more qualifying
loans**
2.—(1) Where one qualifying loan or alternative finance arrangement has been provided   **2.617**
to a claimant by a qualifying lender, the amount that is to be paid direct to that lender is the
amount of each loan payment.
(2) Where more than one qualifying loan or alternative finance arrangement has been provided to a claimant by a qualifying lender, the amount that is to be paid direct to that lender
is the amount of each loan payment in respect of each of those loans or alternative finance
arrangements added together.]

Determining the amount to be paid to a qualifying lender: more than one qualifying loan

2.618   3. [¹ ...]

Qualifying lenders to apply direct payments to discharge of claimant's liability

2.619   4. Where a direct payment is made under regulation 17(1) to a qualifying lender, the lender must apply the amount of the payment determined under either paragraph 2 or 3 of this Schedule towards discharging the claimant's liability to make owner-occupier payments in respect of which the direct payment was made.

Application by qualifying lenders of any amount which exceeds liability

2.620   5.—(1) Where—

    (a) a direct payment is made to a qualifying lender under regulation 17(1); and

    (b) the amount paid exceeds the claimant's liability to make owner-occupier payments to the qualifying lender,

the qualifying lender must apply the amount of excess in accordance with sub-paragraph (2).

(2) Subject to sub-paragraph (3), the qualifying lender must apply the amount of excess as follows—

    (a) first, towards discharging the amount of any liability of the claimant for arrears of owner-occupier payments in respect of the qualifying loan or alternative finance arrangement in question;

    (b) if any amount of the excess is then remaining, towards discharging any liability of the claimant to repay—

      (i) the principal sum in respect of the qualifying loan or alternative finance arrangement; or

      (ii) any other sum payable by the claimant to that lender in respect of that qualifying loan or alternative finance arrangement.

(3) Where owner-occupier payments on two or more qualifying loans or alternative finance arrangements are payable to the same qualifying lender, the lender must apply the amount of the excess as follows—

    [¹ (a) first, towards discharging the amount of any liability of the claimant for arrears of owner-occupier payments in respect of the qualifying loan or alternative finance arrangement in respect of which the excess amount was paid;

    (b) if any amount of the excess is then remaining, towards discharging any liability of the claimant to repay—

      (i) in respect of the loan or alternative finance arrangement referred to in paragraph (a), the principal sum or any other sum payable by the claimant to that lender; or

      (ii) in respect of any other loan or alternative finance arrangement, any sum payable by the claimant to that lender where the liability to pay that sum is not already discharged.]

Fees payable by qualifying lenders

2.621   6.—(1) A fee is payable by a qualifying lender to the Secretary of State for the purpose of meeting the expenses of the Secretary of State in administering the making of direct payments to lenders.

(2) The fee is £0.39 in respect of each occasion on which a direct payment is made to the qualifying lender.

Election not to be regarded as a qualifying lender

2.622   7.—(1) A body or person who would otherwise be within the definition of "qualifying lender" in the Act—

    (a) may elect not to be regarded as such for the purposes of these Regulations by giving notice to the Secretary of State in writing; and

    (b) may revoke any such notice by giving a further notice in writing.

(2) In respect of any financial year, a notice under sub-paragraph (1) which is given not later than 1st February before the start of the financial year, takes effect on 1st April following the giving of the notice.

(3) Where a body or person becomes a qualifying lender in the course of a financial year—

    (a) any notice of an election by the body or person under sub-paragraph (1)(a) must be given within 6 weeks ("the initial period") beginning with the date on which the body or person becomes a qualifying lender; and

    (b) no direct payments may be made under regulation 17(1) to the body or person before the expiry of the initial period.

(4) Sub-paragraph (3)(b) does not apply in any case where—
  (a) the person or body gives the Secretary of State notice in writing that that provision should not apply; and
  (b) the notice is given before the start of the initial period or before that period expires.
(5) In relation to a notice under sub-paragraph (1)—
  (a) where the notice is given by an electronic communication, it must be given in accordance with Schedule 2 of the Universal Credit, Personal Independence Payment, Jobseeker's Allowance and Employment and Support Allowance (Claims and Payments) Regulations 2013;
  (b) where the notice is sent by post, it is to be treated as having been given on the day the notice was received.

Provision of information

8.—(1) A qualifying lender must, in respect of the claimant, provide the Secretary of State with information as to—

2.623

  (a) the owner-occupier payments payable by the claimant to the lender;
  (b) the amount of the qualifying loan or alternative finance arrangement in respect of which owner-occupier payments are payable;
  (c) the purpose for which the qualifying loan or alternative finance arrangement was made;
  (d) the amount outstanding on the qualifying loan or alternative finance arrangement;
  (e) the amount of arrears of owner-occupier payments due in respect of the qualifying loan or alternative finance payment;
  (f) any change in the owner-occupier payments payable by the claimant to the lender; and
  (g) the redemption of the qualifying loan or alternative finance arrangement, in the circumstances specified in paragraphs (2), (3) and (6).

(2) The information referred to in paragraph (1)(a) to (e) must be provided at the request of the Secretary of State where the claimant has made a claim for a qualifying benefit, provided that the Secretary of State may only make one request under this paragraph.

(3) The information referred to in paragraph (1)(d) and (f) must be provided where the Secretary of State makes a request for that information on or after the first day in respect of which loan payments are paid, or to be paid, to the qualifying lender on behalf of the claimant ("the first day"), provided that the Secretary of State may only make a request under this paragraph once in each period of 12 months referred to in paragraph (4).

(4) The period of 12 months is the period of 12 months beginning with the first day and each subsequent period of 12 months commencing on the anniversary of that day.

(5) A request may be made under paragraph (3) for the information referred to in paragraph (1)(d) even though that information has been requested in the same 12 month period (as referred to in paragraph (4)) under paragraph (2).

(6) The information referred to in sub-paragraph (1)(g) must be provided to the Secretary of State as soon as reasonably practicable once the qualifying lender has received notice that the qualifying loan or alternative finance arrangement is to be redeemed.

Recovery of sum wrongly paid

9.—(1) In the following circumstances, a qualifying lender must at the request of the Secretary of State repay any amount paid to the lender under regulation 17(1) which ought not to have been paid.

2.624

(2) The circumstances are that, in respect of a claimant—
  (a) the loan payments are terminated under regulation 9(2);
  (b) the qualifying loan or alternative finance arrangement in respect of which owner-occupier payments are made has been redeemed; or
  (c) both of the conditions in sub-paragraphs (3) and (4) are met.

(3) The first condition is that the amount of each loan payment determined under regulation 10 is reduced as a result of—
  (a) the standard rate determined under regulation 13 having been reduced; or
  (b) the amount outstanding on the qualifying loan or alternative finance arrangement having been reduced.

(4) The second condition is that no corresponding reduction was made to the amount calculated in respect of the qualifying lender under paragraph 2 or 3 of this Schedule.

(5) A qualifying lender is not required to make a repayment in the circumstances described in sub-paragraph (2)(a) unless the Secretary of State's request is made before the end of the period of two months starting with the date on which the loan payments are terminated.

AMENDMENT

1. Loans for Mortgage Interest and Social Fund Maternity Grant (Amendment) Regulations 2018 (SI 2018/307), reg.2(1) and (17) (April 6, 2018).

DEFINITIONS

"the Act"—reg.2(1)
"alternative finance payments"—reg.2(1).
"financial year"—*ibid.*
"loan payments"—*ibid.*
"owner-occupier payments"—regs 2(1) and 3(2)(a).
"qualifying benefit"—reg.2(1).
"qualifying lender"—*ibid.*
"qualifying loan"—*ibid.*

Regulation 18

SCHEDULE 5

CONSEQUENTIAL AMENDMENTS

2.625   *[Omitted]*

2.626   GENERAL NOTE

The consequential amendments made by Sch.5 have been incorporated at the appropriate places in the text of the amended regulations.

The Jobseeker's Allowance and Universal Credit (Higher-Level Sanctions) (Amendment) Regulations 2019

(SI 2019/1357)

Made by the Secretary of State for Work and Pensions under the powers conferred by sections 6J(5)(b) and (6), 19(4)(b) and (5), 35(1) and 36(4)(a) of the Jobseekers Act 1995 and sections 26(6)(b) and (7) and 42(1) and (3)(a) of the Welfare Reform Act 2012, the Social Security Advisory Committee having agreed that the proposals in respect of these Regulations should not be referred to it.

ARRANGEMENT OF REGULATIONS

1. Citation and commencement
2. Amendment of the Jobseeker's Allowance Regulations 1996
3. Amendment of the Universal Credit Regulations 2013
4. Amendment of the Jobseeker's Allowance Regulations 2013
5. Transitional provision

Citation and commencement

2.627   **1.** These Regulations may be cited as the Jobseeker's Allowance and Universal Credit (Higher-Level Sanctions) (Amendment) Regulations 2019 and come into force on 27th November 2019.

Amendment of the Jobseeker's Allowance Regulations 1996

2. (*Amendment incorporated into the text of the JSA Regulations 1996 in Part III of Vol. II of this series*)

2.628

Amendment of the Universal Credit Regulations 2013

3. (*Amendment incorporated into the text of the Universal Credit Regulations 2013*)

2.629

Amendment of the Jobseeker's Allowance Regulations 2013

4. (*Amendment incorporated into the text of the JSA Regulations 2013 in Part VI of Vol. II of this series*)

2.630

Transitional provision

5.—(1) Where, on the date that these Regulations come into force, the amount of an award of jobseeker's allowance is subject to a reduction under section 19 of the Jobseekers Act 1995 for a period of 156 weeks, the reduction is to be terminated where, since the date that the reduction took effect, the award has been reduced for a period of at least 26 weeks.

2.631

(2) Where, on the date that these Regulations come into force, the amount of an award of jobseeker's allowance is subject to a reduction under section 6J of the Jobseekers Act 1995 for a period of 1095 days, the reduction is to be terminated where, since the date that the reduction took effect, the award has been reduced for a period of at least 182 days.

(3) Where, on the date that these Regulations come into force, the amount of an award of universal credit is subject to a reduction under section 26 of the Welfare Reform Act 2012, or which is treated as a reduction under section 26 of that Act by virtue of regulation 32(3) of the Universal Credit (Transitional Provisions) Regulations 2014(**c**), for a period of 1095 days, the reduction is to be terminated where, since the date that the reduction took effect, the award has been reduced for a period of at least 182 days.

The Employment and Support Allowance and Universal Credit (Coronavirus Disease) Regulations 2020

(SI 2020/289)

Made by the Secretary of State for Work and Pensions under sections 10(3) and (6), 79(1), (4) and (6) and 84 of the Social Security Act 1998, sections 24(1) and 25(2), (3) and (5) of, and paragraphs 1(a) and 2 of Schedule 2 to, the Welfare Reform Act 2007 and sections 8(3)(a) and (4), 37(6), 40 and 42(1) to (3) of, and paragraph 4(1), (3)(a) and (4) of Schedule 1 to, the Welfare Reform Act 2012, it appearing inexpedient, by reason of urgency, to refer the proposals in respect of these Regulations to the Social Security Advisory Committee.

Citation, commencement and interpretation

1.—(1) These Regulations may be cited as the Employment and Support

2.632

Allowance and Universal Credit (Coronavirus Disease) Regulations 2020 and come into force on 13th March 2020.

(2) In these Regulations—

"the 2007 Act" means the Welfare Reform Act 2007;

"assessment period" has the meaning in regulation 21 of the Universal Credit Regulations 2013;

"Coronavirus disease" means COVID-19;

"employment and support allowance" means an employment and support allowance under Part 1 of the Welfare Reform Act 2007;

"existing award" means an award of universal credit or employment and support allowance that exists on the date on which these regulations come into force;

"isolation" in relation to a person, means the separation of that person from any other person in such a manner as to prevent infection or contamination with Coronavirus disease;

"qualifying young person" has the meaning in regulation 5 of the Universal Credit Regulations 2013;

"universal credit" means universal credit under Part 1 of the Welfare Reform Act 2012.

Waiting days

2.633

2.—(1) Paragraph 2 of Schedule 2 to the 2007 Act does not apply to a person to whom paragraph (2) applies.

(2) This paragraph applies to a person who is—

(a) infected or contaminated with Coronavirus disease;

(b) in isolation; or

(c) caring for a child or qualifying young person who is a member of the person's household and who falls within sub-paragraph (a) or (b),

where the Secretary of State is satisfied that paragraph 2 of Schedule 2 to the 2007 Act should not apply to the person.

[¹Treating a person as having limited capability for work

2.634

3.—*(1) This regulation applies to a person who makes a claim for universal credit or employment and support allowance or who has an existing award of universal credit or employment and support allowance.*

(2) Where this regulation applies the person is to be treated as having limited capability for work if the person is—

(a) infected or contaminated with Coronavirus disease;

(b) in isolation; or

(c) caring for a child or qualifying young person who is a member of the person's household and who falls within sub-paragraph (a) or (b),

where the Secretary of State is satisfied that the person should be treated as having limited capability for work.

(3) Regulations 26 and 35(6) to (9) of the Universal Credit, Personal Independence Payment, Jobseeker's Allowance and Employment and Support Allowance (Decisions and Appeals) Regulations 2013 apply to a determination that the person is to be treated as having limited capability for work in accordance with this regulation as if such a determination had been made under regulation 16 of the Employment and Support Allowance Regulations 2013 or Part 5 of the Universal Credit Regulations 2013.

(4) Regulation 6(2)(r) of the Social Security and Child Support (Decisions

and Appeals) Regulations 1999 applies to a determination that the person is to be treated as having limited capability for work in accordance with this regulation as if such a determination had been made under regulation 20 of the Employment and Support Allowance Regulations 2008.

AMENDMENT

1. Revoked in relation to universal credit by Social Security (Coronavirus) (Further Measures) Regulations 2020 (SI 2020/371) reg.10(3) (March 30, 2020).

2.635

[¹Suspension of the Minimum Income Floor

4. *Where a person ceases to be treated as having limited capability for work under regulation 3, the Secretary of State may determine that regulation 62 of the Universal Credit Regulations 2013 does not apply to the person for the assessment period in which they cease to be treated as having limited capability for work and the Secretary of State may further extend the period during which regulation 62 does not apply if the Secretary of State considers such an extension to be appropriate.*]

2.636

AMENDMENT

1. Revoked by Social Security (Coronavirus) (Further Measures) Regulations 2020 (SI 2020/371) reg.10(3) (March 30, 2020).

2.637

GENERAL NOTE

See the notes to reg.62 of the Universal Credit Regulations for the effect of this provision during its limited life.

2.638

Expiry

5.—(1) The Secretary of State must keep the operation of these Regulations under review.

(2) These Regulations cease to have effect at the end of the period of eight months beginning on the day on which they come into force.

2.639

The Social Security (Coronavirus) (Further Measures) Regulations 2020

(SI 2020/371)

Made by the Secretary of State for Work and Pensions under sections 70(8), 123(1)(d), 136(1), (3) and (5)(b), 137(1), 171D, 171G(2) and 175(1) and (3) to (5) of the Social Security Contributions and Benefits Act 1992, sections 6(4), 6E(5), 6F(1), 7(4), 35(1) and 36(2) and (4) of the Jobseekers Act 1995, sections 122(1) and (6) of the Housing Act 1996 and sections 9(2), 18(5), 22(2), 37(6), 40 and 42(1) to (3) and (5) of, and paragraph 4(4) of Schedule 1 and paragraphs 1(1) and 4(1), (2)(a), (c) and (d) and (3) of Schedule 6 to, the Welfare Reform Act 2012, it appearing inexpedient, by reason of urgency, to refer the proposals in respect of these Regulations to the Social Security Advisory Committee or to consult with representative bodies.

Citation, commencement and interpretation

2.640   **1.**—(1) These Regulations may be cited as the Social Security (Coronavirus) (Further Measures) Regulations 2020 and come into force on 30th March 2020.

(2) In these Regulations—

"coronavirus" means severe acute respiratory syndrome coronavirus 2 (SARS-CoV-2);

"coronavirus disease" means COVID-19 (the official designation of the disease which can be caused by coronavirus);

"isolation" in relation to a person, means the separation of that person from any other person in such a manner as to prevent infection or contamination with coronavirus disease;

"universal credit" means universal credit under Part 1 of the Welfare Reform Act 2012;

"Universal Credit Regulations" means the Universal Credit Regulations 2013.

Universal credit – minimum income floor

2.641   **2.**—(1) The Secretary of State may, where it appears expedient as a consequence of the outbreak of coronavirus disease, and in such cases or class of case, or for such period, as the Secretary of State determines—

(a) treat the amount of the individual threshold or the couple threshold in regulation 62 (minimum income floor) of the Universal Credit Regulations as if it were a lesser amount (including zero);

(b) where it falls to be determined whether a claimant is in gainful self-employment, delay that determination;

(c) where it has been determined that a claimant is in gainful self-employment, treat that claimant as not being in gainful self-employment;

(d) where a claimant is in a start-up period, extend that period for as long as the Secretary of State considers appropriate; or

(e) in relation to any claimant who would otherwise fall within section 22 of the Welfare Reform Act 2012 (all work-related requirements) as a result of this regulation, except that claimant from a work search requirement or a work availability requirement.

(2) In this regulation "start-up period" and "gainful self-employment" have the meanings given in regulations 63 and 64 respectively of the Universal Credit Regulations.

GENERAL NOTE

2.643   See the notes to reg.62 of the Universal Credit Regulations for discussion of the effect of this provision. Note that with effect from March 13, 2020 reg.4 of the Employment and Support Allowance and Universal Credit (Coronavirus Disease) Regulations 2020 (SI 2020/289) allowed the suspension of the minimum income floor provisions in certain limited circumstances. That regulation ceased to operate with effect from March 30, 2020 (reg.10(3) of the present Regulations), as also discussed in the notes to reg.62.

Universal credit – standard allowance modification

2.644   **3.** [*See the modifications to reg.36 of the Universal Credit Regulations.*]

Local housing allowance

4. [*See the amendments to the The Rent Officers (Universal Credit Functions)*   2.645
Order 2013.]

Housing benefit – disregards from income modification

5. [*Omitted as applying only to housing benefit*]   2.646

Universal credit and new style JSA – work-related requirements

6.—(1) As a consequence of the outbreak of coronavirus disease, where   2.647
a person has an award of new style JSA or an award of universal credit—
- (a) the Secretary of State must not impose a work search requirement on that person;
- (b) a work search requirement previously applying to such a person ceases to have effect from the date on which these Regulations come into force; and
- (c) "able and willing immediately to take up paid work" under a work availability requirement imposed on such a person means able and willing to take up paid work, or attend an interview, immediately once this regulation ceases to apply.

(2) This regulation applies for a period of 3 months beginning with the date that these Regulations come into force and the Secretary of State may extend that period for all cases or any class of case where it appears expedient as a consequence of the continuation of the outbreak of coronavirus disease.

(3) In this regulation, "new style JSA" means an allowance under the Jobseekers Act 1995 as amended by the amendments made by Part 1 of Schedule 14 to the Welfare Reform Act 2012 that remove references to an income-based allowance.

Old style JSA – availability for employment and actively seeking employment

7. [*Omitted as applying only to old style JSA—see Vol.II of this series*]   2.648

Jobseeker's Allowance – periods of sickness

8. [*Omitted as applying only to old style and new style JSA—see Vol.II of this*   2.649
series]

Carer's allowance

9. [*Omitted as applying only to carer's allowance – see Vol.I of this series*]   2.650

Expiry

10.—(1) The Secretary of State must keep the operation of these   2.651
Regulations under review.

(2) Regulations 2, 6, 7, 8 and 9 cease to have effect at the end of the period of eight months beginning on 13th March 2020.

(3) Regulation 3 (treating a person as having limited capability for work) and regulation 4 (suspension of the minimum income floor) of the Employment and Support Allowance and Universal Credit (Coronavirus Disease) Regulations 2020 no longer have effect in so far as they apply to universal credit.

PART IIIA

TRANSITIONAL PROVISIONS

The Universal Credit (Transitional Provisions) Regulations 2014

2014/1230 (AS AMENDED)

The Secretary of State for Work and Pensions makes the following Regulations in exercise of the powers conferred by section 42(2) and (3) of and paragraphs 1(1) and (2)(b), 3(1)(a) to (c), 4(1)(a), 5(1), (2)(c) and (d) and (3)(a) and 6 of Schedule 6 to the Welfare Reform Act 2012.

In accordance with section 172(1) of the Social Security Administration Act 1992 ("the 1992 Act"), the Secretary of State has referred proposals in respect of these Regulations to the Social Security Advisory Committee.

In accordance with section 176(1) of the 1992 Act and, in so far as these Regulations relate to housing benefit, the Secretary of State has consulted with organisations appearing to him to be representative of the authorities concerned in respect of proposals for these Regulations.

[In force: June 16, 2014]

ARRANGEMENT OF REGULATIONS

PART 1

PART 2

CHAPTER 1

CHAPTER 2

CHAPTER 3

GENERAL NOTE

3.2   The original Universal Credit (Transitional Provisions) Regulations 2013 (SI 2013/386) ("the 2013 Regulations") came into force on April 29, 2013 and provided for the introduction of universal credit to limited categories of claimant. A series of Commencement Orders has subsequently brought into force provisions relating to universal credit for claimants in specified postcodes, accompanied (in those areas) by repeals of the legislation relating to jobseeker's allowance and employment and support allowance for those claimants. The present Regulations ("the 2014 Transitional Regulations") made provision for the second phase of the introduction of universal credit, and represented a change from the structured plans for the roll out of universal credit set out in the 2013 Regulations. These Regulations accordingly provide for some of the more complex transitional situations that will arise when dealing with families and those on a wider range of existing benefits. The House of Lords' Secondary Legislation Scrutiny Committee expressed the following opinion on the draft 2014 Transitional Regulations (First Report, Session 2014/15, footnote omitted):

> "20. In line with an announcement made on 5 December 2013, the Department for Work and Pensions now expects the "majority" of existing benefit claimants to be transferred to Universal Credit by the end of 2017, that is, around 6.5 million people. DWP officials state that "decisions on the later stages of Universal Credit (UC) roll out will be informed by the development of the enhanced IT but some Employment Support Allowance claimants may be moved on to UC more slowly because they have already experienced the move from the old Incapacity Benefit and they would not immediately benefit from the improved work incentives of Universal Credit". The Committee was surprised to see this instrument accompanied by the original cost/benefit analysis from 2012, despite the well-publicised changes to the programme. DWP officials state that "the Impact Assessment published in December 2012 provides information based on the situation once Universal Credit (UC) is fully rolled out. Therefore, as there has not been any significant change since the Impact Assessment was published, we have not published an updated impact assessment for this instrument". However, the House may wish to note that the end date for completion of the transition to Universal Credit has been made more flexible and can be "managed" if problems arise in a particular area. Such changes will be made by Commencement Orders, which are not subject to parliamentary scrutiny. These Regulations also now include provision to allow the Secretary of State discretion temporarily to stop taking Universal Credit claims in certain geographic areas or for certain groups of claimants, so that any issues can be resolved. Where this provision is exercised, anyone prevented from claiming Universal Credit will be able to claim existing benefits or credits."

Note that most of these Regulations are also included in Vol.4 of this series, with extra commentary that focuses on the interaction between claims for tax credits and universal credit.

PART 1

Citation and commencement

1. (1) These Regulations may be cited as the Universal Credit (Transitional Provisions) Regulations 2014.

(2) These Regulations come into force on 16th June 2014.

Interpretation

2. (1) In these Regulations—

"the 2002 Act" means the Tax Credits Act 2002;

"the 2007 Act" means the Welfare Reform Act 2007;

"the Act" means the Welfare Reform Act 2012;

"assessment period" has the same meaning as in the Universal Credit Regulations;

3.3

3.4

[⁵"childcare costs element" has the meaning in the Universal Credit Regulations;]

"the Claims and Payments Regulations" means the Universal Credit, Personal Independence Payment, Jobseeker's Allowance and Employment and Support Allowance (Claims and Payments) Regulations 2013;

"contributory employment and support allowance" means a contributory allowance under Part 1 of the 2007 Act as that Part has effect apart from the amendments made by Schedule 3, and Part 1 of Schedule 14, to the Act that remove references to an income-related allowance; [¹ ...]

[⁵ "deadline day" has the meaning in regulation 44;]

[⁵ "earned income" has the meaning in Chapter 2 of Part 6 of the Universal Credit Regulations;]

"existing benefit" means income-based jobseeker's allowance, income-related employment and support allowance, income support, housing benefit and child tax credit and working tax credit under the 2002 Act, but see also [⁵paragraph (3) and] regulation 25(2);

[⁵ "final deadline" has the meaning in regulation 46;]

"First-tier Tribunal" has the same meaning as in the Social Security Act 1998;

[⁵ "HMRC" means Her Majesty's Revenue and Customs;]

"housing benefit" means housing benefit under section 130 of the Social Security Contributions and Benefits Act 1992;

"income-based jobseeker's allowance" has the same meaning as in the Jobseekers Act 1995;

"income-related employment and support allowance" means an income-related allowance under Part 1 of the 2007 Act;

"income support" means income support under section 124 of the Social Security Contributions and Benefits Act 1992;

[⁵ "indicative UC amount" has the meaning in regulation 54;]

"joint-claim jobseeker's allowance" means old style JSA, entitlement to which arises by virtue of section 1(2B) of the Jobseekers Act 1995;

[⁵ "migration day" has the meaning in regulation 49;]

[⁵ "migration notice" has the meaning in regulation 44;]

"new claimant partner" has the meaning given in regulation 7;

"new style ESA" means an allowance under Part 1 of the 2007 Act as amended by the amendments made by Schedule 3, and Part 1 of Schedule 14, to the Act that remove references to an income-related allowance;

"new style JSA" means an allowance under the Jobseekers Act 1995 as amended by the amendments made by Part 1 of Schedule 14 to the Act that remove references to an income-based allowance;

[⁵ "notified person" has the meaning in regulation 44;]

"old style ESA" means an employment and support allowance under Part 1 of the 2007 Act as that Part has effect apart from the amendments made by Schedule 3, and Part 1 of Schedule 14, to the Act that remove references to an income-related allowance;

"old style JSA" means a jobseeker's allowance under the Jobseekers Act 1995 as that Act has effect apart from the amendments made by Part 1 of Schedule 14 to the Act that remove references to an income-based allowance;

"partner" in relation to a person ("A") means a person who forms part of a couple with A;

[⁵ "qualifying claim" has the meaning in regulation 48;]

[² "qualifying young person" has the same meaning as in the Universal Credit Regulations, but see also regulation 28;]

[⁴ "severe disability premium" means the premium in relation to an employment and support allowance under paragraph 6 of Schedule 4 to the Employment and Support Allowance Regulations 2008 or, as the case may be, the corresponding premium in relation to income support, old style JSA or housing benefit;]

[¹ "specified accommodation" means accommodation to which one or more of sub-paragraphs (2) to (5) of paragraph 3A of Schedule 1 to the Universal Credit Regulations applies;]

[³ "temporary accommodation" means accommodation which falls within Case 1 or Case 2 under paragraph 3B of Schedule 1 to the Universal Credit Regulations;]

"tax credit" (including "child tax credit" and "working tax credit"), "tax credits" and "tax year" have the same meanings as in the 2002 Act;

"the Universal Credit Regulations" means the Universal Credit Regulations 2013;

[⁵ "total legacy amount" has the meaning in regulation 53;]

[⁵ "transitional capital disregard" has the meaning in regulation 51;]

[⁵ "transitional element" has the meaning in regulation 52;]

"Upper Tribunal" has the same meaning as in the Social Security Act 1998.

(2) For the purposes of these Regulations—

(a) the date on which a claim for universal credit is made is to be determined in accordance with the Claims and Payments Regulations;

(b) where a couple is treated, in accordance with regulation 9(8) of the Claims and Payments Regulations, as having made a claim for universal credit, references to the date on which the claim is treated as made are to the date of formation of the couple;

(c) where a regulation refers to entitlement to an existing benefit on the date on which a claim for universal credit is made or treated as made, such entitlement is to be taken into account notwithstanding the effect of regulations 5, 7 and 8 or termination of an award of the benefit before that date by virtue of an order made under section 150(3) of the Act.

[⁵(3) In these Regulations—

(a) references to an award of income-based jobseeker's allowance are to an award of old style JSA where the claimant is, or joint claimants are, entitled to the income-based allowance; and

(b) references to an award of income-related employment and support allowance are to an award of old style ESA where the claimant is entitled to the income-related allowance.

(4) In regulation 46 (termination of existing benefits if no claim before the deadline) and regulation 47 (notified persons who claim as a different benefit unit) "terminate" in relation to an award of income-based jobseeker's allowance or income-related employment and support allowance means treating that award as if the following provisions had come into force (including where a saving provision has ceased to apply) in relation to that award—

(a) section 33(1)(a) and (b) and (2) of the Act (abolition of benefits);

    (b) paragraphs 22 to 26 of Schedule 3 to the Act (abolition of benefits: consequential amendments) and section 33(3) of the Act in so far as it relates to those paragraphs; and

    (c) the repeals in Part 1 of Schedule 14 to the Act (abolition of benefits superseded by universal credit) that come into force if a claim is made for universal credit.]

AMENDMENTS

1. Universal Credit (Transitional Provisions) (Amendment) Regulations 2014 (SI 2014/1626) reg.3 (November 3, 2014).
2. Social Security (Restrictions on Amounts for Children and Qualifying Young Persons) Amendment Regulations 2017 (2017/376) reg.3(2) (April 6, 2017).
3. Universal Credit (Miscellaneous Amendments, Saving and Transitional Provision) Regulations 2018 (SI 2018/65) reg.6(3) (April 11, 2018).
4. Universal Credit (Transitional Provisions) (SDP Gateway) Amendment Regulations 2019 (SI 2019/10) reg.2(2) (January 16, 2019).
5. Universal Credit (Managed Migration Pilot and Miscellaneous Amendments) Regulations 2019 (SI 2019/1152) reg.3(2) (July 24, 2019).

DEFINITIONS

"the Act"–see reg.2(1).

GENERAL NOTE

Paragraph (1)

3.5   *"new claimant partner"*: where a single universal credit claimant becomes a member of a couple, and their award terminates, and the other member of the couple was not previously entitled to universal credit as a single person, but an award of universal credit is then made to the couple as joint claimants, then the other member of the couple is known as a "new claimant partner" (see also reg.7).

"new style ESA": in effect, this means (new variant) contribution-based ESA, shorn of its previous income-based element, and as defined in what were originally the Pathfinder areas as from April 29, 2013.

"new style JSA": similarly, this means (new variant) contribution-based JSA, again shorn of its income-related element, and as defined in those Pathfinder areas as from April 29, 2013.

Paragraph (2)(a)

3.6   The normal rule is that the date of a universal credit claim is the date the claim is received, whether electronically or by telephone or, if later, the first day for which the claim is made: see Claims and Payments Regulations 2013, reg.10.

Revocation and saving of the Universal Credit (Transitional Provisions) Regulations 2013

3.7   **3.**—(1) The Universal Credit (Transitional Provisions) Regulations 2013 ("the 2013 Regulations") are revoked, subject to the savings in paragraphs (2) to (4).

    (2) Chapters 2 and 3 of Part 2 (Pathfinder Group and treatment of invalid claims) of the 2013 Regulations continue to have effect in relation to a claim for universal credit—

(a) which was made before the date on which these Regulations come into force ("the commencement date"); and

(b) in respect of which no payment has been made to the claimant before the commencement date.

(3) Regulation 19 of the 2013 Regulations (advance payments of universal credit) continues to have effect in relation to an advance payment which was made in accordance with that regulation before the commencement date and regulation 17 of these Regulations does not apply to such a payment.

(4) Any other provision of the 2013 Regulations continues to have effect in so far as is necessary to give full effect to paragraphs (2) and (3).

DEFINITIONS

"the 2013 Regulations"–para.(1).
"the commencement date"–para.(2)(a).

GENERAL NOTE

This regulation provides for revocation of the Universal Credit (Transitional   **3.8** Provisions) Regulations 2013 (para.(1)), subject to certain savings (paras.(2)-(4)). These savings concern claimants who claimed universal credit before the date on which the 2014 Transitional Regulations came into force (June 16, 2014) and relate in particular to the treatment of invalid claims and recovery of advance payments of universal credit made under the 2013 Transitional Regulations. The intention is to ensure that the validity of a claim is judged in accordance with the provisions which were in force at the time the claim was made, and that advance payments made under the 2013 Transitional Regulations remain recoverable.

PART 2

CHAPTER 1

Secretary of State discretion to determine that claims for universal credit may not be made

4. (1) Where the Secretary of State considers it necessary, in order to—   **3.9**

(a) safeguard the efficient administration of universal credit; or

(b) ensure the effective testing of systems for the administration of universal credit,

to cease to accept claims in any area, or in any category of case (either in all areas or in a specified area), the Secretary of State may determine that claims for universal credit may not be made in that area, or in that category of case.

(2) A determination under paragraph (1) has effect until it ceases to have effect in accordance with a further determination made by the Secretary of State.

(3) More than one determination under paragraph (1) may have effect at the same time.

GENERAL NOTE

3.10   This regulation had no direct equivalent under the 2013 Transitional Regulations. It vests the Secretary of State with a discretion temporarily to exclude claims for universal credit in any area, or in any category of case, if he considers that this is necessary in order to safeguard the efficient administration of universal credit, or to ensure the effective testing of administrative systems. In the event that this provision is exercised, anyone prevented from claiming universal credit would be able to claim existing benefits or tax credits.

[¹ Restriction on claims for universal credit by persons entitled to a severe disability premium

3.10.1   **4A.**—[²(1)] No claim may be made for universal credit on or after 16th January 2019 by a single claimant who, or joint claimants either of whom—
[² (2) This regulation does not apply in relation to a claim for universal credit by a single claimant who is a notified person or by joint claimants both of whom are notified persons.]
> (a) is, or has been within the past month, entitled to an award of an existing benefit that includes a severe disability premium; and
> (b) in a case where the award ended during that month, has continued to satisfy the conditions for eligibility for a severe disability premium.]

AMENDMENTS

1. Universal Credit (Transitional Provisions) (SDP Gateway) Amendment Regulations 2019 (SI 2019/10) reg.2(3) (January 16, 2019).
2. Universal Credit (Managed Migration Pilot and Miscellaneous Amendments) Regulations 2019 (SI 2019/1152) reg.3(3) (July 24, 2019).

DEFINITION

"severe disability premium" – see reg.2(1).

GENERAL NOTE

3.10.2   There is a complex background to this provision inserted into the Regulations in January 2019. By way of context, universal credit, unlike the legacy means-tested benefits, does not include an equivalent component to severe disability premium (SDP). The Coalition Government maintained that universal credit would simplify means-tested support for disabled people, but disability organisations pointed out that the abolition of SDP could result in vulnerable claimants losing out financially. In response, the Government announced that transitional protection would be available to ensure that people moving onto universal credit did not lose out in cash terms at the point of transfer (i.e. if their universal credit entitlement was lower than their existing legacy benefits). However, it became apparent that transitional protection would only be available to claimants who were subject to "managed migration", i.e. having been required to transfer by the DWP. For claimants moving by "natural migration"—e.g. a change in their circumstances—there would be no such protection.
This differential treatment was challenged by way of judicial review in the High Court in R *(On the application of TP and AR) v Secretary of State for Work and Pensions* [2018] EWHC 1474 (Admin), in which two claimants previously in receipt of IR-ESA had to claim universal credit following a move to a full service area. In the absence of any equivalent to SDP they suffered a sudden and significant drop in their incomes. The judicial review claim was put on three grounds: (1) the absence of any additional payment in universal credit for those who previously qualified for

SDP amounted to unlawful discrimination contrary to art. 14 read with art. 1 of the First Protocol to the ECHR; (2) the Universal Credit (Transitional Provisions) Regulations 2014 involved unlawful discrimination (on the same basis) because of the absence of any element of transitional protection; and (3) the Secretary of State had breached the Equality Act 2010 by failing to have due regard to the impact of removing the premiums for disabled people when making the Universal Credit Regulations 2013 and the Transitional Provisions Regulations.

In June 2018 Lewis J. dismissed the challenges on the first and third grounds of judicial review, but allowed the application on the second ground, holding that the Transitional Provisions Regulations did not strike a fair balance between the interests of the individual and the community respectively in bringing about a phased transition to universal credit. The impact on the individuals was apparent—their cash payments were now significantly lower than the amounts they had previously received. The Judge found there appeared to have been no consideration given to the justification for requiring the individual to assume the entirety of the difference between their previous benefits and universal credit; this was all the more striking given Government statements over the years that such persons could need assistance and there was a need to define precisely the circumstances in which persons would not receive assistance. In this case, the operation of the implementation arrangements was "manifestly without reasonable foundation" and failed to strike a fair balance (at [88]). The differential treatment was based on status and had not been objectively justified. Accordingly, Lewis J. held that the universal credit implementing arrangements gave rise to unlawful discrimination contrary to art. 14 read with art. 1 of the First Protocol to the ECHR. The High Court granted a declaration that there was unlawful discrimination, leaving the Secretary of State to determine how to rectify the unlawful discrimination (at [114]). Thus, Lewis J concluded as follows:

"[113] The 2013 Regulations establishing universal credit do not involve discrimination contrary to Article 14 ECHR in so far as they do not include any element which corresponds to the additional disability premiums payable under the previous regime. Any differential treatment between different groups is objectively justifiable.

[114] The implementing arrangements do at present give rise to unlawful discrimination contrary to Article 14 ECHR read with Article 1 of the First Protocol to the ECHR. There is differential treatment between the group of persons who were in receipt of additional disability premiums (the SDP and EDP) and who transferred to universal credit on moving to a different local housing authority area and so receive less money by way of income related support than they previously received and the group of persons in receipt of SDP and EDP and who move house within the same local housing authority area but are not required to transfer to universal credit and continue to receive the basic allowance and SDP and EDP and suffer no loss of income. That differential treatment is based on status. That differential treatment has not been objectively justified at present. A declaration will be granted that there is unlawful discrimination. The defendant will then be able to determine how to rectify the unlawful discrimination."

In *R (on the application of AR & SXC) v SSWP* [2020] EWCA Civ 37, the Court of Appeal dismissed the Secretary of State's appeal against the judgment of Lewis J. The Department advanced four grounds of appeal. The first was that the judge had been wrong to conclude that there was any appearance of discriminatory treatment against TP and AR. The Court of Appeal rejected this ground for appeal on the basis that "there can be no realistic dispute that there is a difference of treatment between TP and AR on the one hand and, on the other hand, people in an analogous situation, who do not have to apply for universal credit" (at [87]). The second ground of appeal was that the High Court had erred in holding that the difference of treatment in these cases was on the ground of an 'other status' for the purpose of art. 14, namely a severely disabled person who moves to a different local authority area. The Court (Rose LJ dissenting) held that residence in a given local authority area could constitute a relevant status. The third ground of appeal was that Lewis J had been wrong to hold that the difference in treatment lacked an objective justification. This ground for appeal failed as, on the evidence that the DWP placed before Lewis J, there appeared to have been no consideration of the difference in treatment between the comparator groups. The final ground for appeal was that the High Court's declaration should have been limited to one that there had been a failure to 'consider' transitional payments, rather than that TP and AR had suffered unlawful discrimination by reason of the difference in payments. This ground was rejected as being based on a misunderstanding of Lewis J's reasoning. Moreover, the Court found that the DWP had failed in its duty of candour and co-operation by omitting to disclose to Lewis J that it had already made a policy decision both to stop moving more severely disabled people onto universal credit and to provide transitional payments for those who had already been transferred.

Following the High Court's decision in *R (on the application of TP and AR) v SSWP*, the DWP agreed to compensate the claimants in the case for the money they had lost as a result of moving onto universal credit, and to make ongoing payments of around £170 a month to reflect future loss which would be paid until changes to the regulations came into force.

The Government's immediate response, more broadly, was to issue a written statement explaining that "in order to support the transition for those individuals who live alone with substantial care needs and receive the Severe Disability Premium", the rules implementing universal credit would be changed. The Government announced that current claimants with an award including SDP who had a change of circumstances (normally meaning they would be subject to natural migration to universal credit) would not in fact move to the new benefit until they qualified for transitional protection—i.e. not until they were subject to "managed migration", i.e. as and when required to migrate by the DWP (written statement HCWS745, June 7, 2018, by the then Secretary of State, Esther McVey MP). The Secretary of State further stated that claimants who had already moved to universal credit and so lost their SDP would receive on-going compensation payments and an additional lump-sum payment to cover the period since they moved.

As a consequence there has been, in effect, a twin-track approach to further developments, namely first the relatively straightforward proposal to stop SDP claimants from transferring from legacy benefits to universal credit and, secondly, the more complex arrangements for providing transitional protection to those who have already transferred or will so transfer in due course.

As to the first track, the Universal Credit (Transitional Provisions) (SDP Gateway) Amendment Regulations 2019 (SI 2019/10), which came into force on January 16, inserted new reg.4A so as to prevent claimants of legacy benefits (IS, IR-ESA, IB-JSA or HB) with SDP from making a claim for universal credit. The exclusion also applies where an award of a legacy benefit has ended within the last month, so long as the claimant continued to satisfy the conditions for entitlement to the SDP. This exclusion is known as the "SDP gateway", although the "SDP roadblock" might be a more accurate description. DWP guidance to staff is available in Memo ADM 01/19 UC *Claimants entitled to Severe Disability Premium* (January 2019). As the Explanatory Memorandum to SI 2019/10 explains, "The regulations provide that these claimants will no longer naturally migrate to UC, but will remain on their existing benefits or be able to claim another existing benefit instead until such time as they are moved to Universal Credit as part of the Department's managed migration process." However, it should be noted that the SDP gateway has been prospectively repealed with effect from January 27, 2021 (see SI 2019/1152, reg.7), in response to the further High Court judgment in *R (on the application of TP, AR and SXC) v Secretary of State for Work and Pensions* [2019] EWHC 1116 (Admin). Swift J held there that the differential treatment between claimants with SDP who have already moved to universal credit and those who are prevented from doing so because of the SDP gateway was not justified (see further below).

As to the second track, it is fair to say that the DWP has had several attempts (to be precise, three goes as at the time of writing) at trying to develop a satisfactory solution for compensating those with financial losses.

First, transitional payment arrangements for claimants who had already moved to universal credit (and so had lost their SDP) were included in the draft Universal Credit (Managed Migration) Regulations laid before Parliament on November 5, 2018. An initial draft had been submitted to the SSAC, which undertook a public consultation on them over summer 2018. In the event, the DWP withdrew the draft regulations following wider concerns about its proposed approach to managed migration.

Secondly, the Department then included provisions on SDP transitional payments in the draft Universal Credit (Managed Migration Pilot and Miscellaneous Amendments) Regulations, laid before Parliament in January 2019. The regulations were subject to the affirmative procedure but no debate or vote took place in either House. In a case brought by the two claimants who had successfully challenged the DWP in the High Court in June 2018 (TP and AR), and a third claimant (SXC), the High Court (Swift J) ruled on May 3, 2019 that the Government's proposed scheme for SDP transitional payments was unlawful (*R (on the application of TP, AR and SXC) v Secretary of State for Work and Pensions* [2019] EWHC 1116 (Admin)). Under the proposed scheme set out in the second set of draft regulations, SDP recipients moving to universal credit on managed migration would receive top-ups of up to £180 a month, while those claimants who had already been subject to natural migration and lost their SDP would have received payments of £80 per months. Swift J. agreed that this difference in treatment could not be justified:

> "[59] …What needs to be justified extends to the difference in treatment between the SDP migrant group and the Regulation 4A group. The need for some form of explanation for the difference in treatment is all the more striking given the circumstances which, at the beginning of 2018, prompted the Secretary of State to consider the position of severely disabled benefits claimants. This was the point raised by the members of the House of Commons Select Committee on Work and Pensions on the effect that migration to Universal Credit was having on those who had previously been in receipt of SDP, and it was the point considered in the subsequent Departmental presentation (see above, at paragraphs 30 to 33).

> [60] No sufficient explanation for the difference in treatment has been provided. The Secretary of State's "bright line"/administrative efficiency submission explains the treatment of the SDP natural migrant group on its own terms, but does not explain why that group is treated differently to the Regulation 4A group. Both groups comprise severely disabled persons; all of whom meet the criteria for payment of SDP (or would continue to meet those criteria but for natural migration). The simple fact of natural migration is not a satisfactory ground of distinction because the trigger conditions for natural migration are not indicative of any material change in the needs of the Claimants (or the other members of the SDP natural migration group), as severely disabled persons. The same point is sufficient to dispose of the further suggestion in Miss Young's witness statement that the Secretary of State considered the SDP natural migrants as being in materially the same position as new welfare benefits claimants (i.e. severely disabled persons presenting themselves to the welfare benefits system for the first time, after the implementation of Universal Credit). There is no logical foundation for that view; if there were a logical foundation for it, it would negate the rationale for regulation 4A of the Transitional Provisions Regulations."

The High Court left it to the Government to decide what should happen next with regard to the regulations. The Court of Appeal subsequently dismissed the Secretary of State's appeal against Swift J's judgment (see *R (on the application of AR & SXC) v SSWP* [2020] EWCA Civ 37). A separate claim by SXC for compensation under the Human Rights Act 1988 was later dismissed by Swift J. (*SXC v Secretary of State for Work and Pensions* [2019] EWHC 2774 (Admin)). This takes us to the third attempt to deal with SDP transitional protection.

Thirdly, the final Universal Credit (Managed Migration Pilot and Miscellaneous Amendments) Regulations (SI 2019/1152) —which unlike the previous versions were subject to the negative procedure—were laid before Parliament on July 22, 2019 and (for present purposes) came into force two days later. They provide, among other things, for transitional payments for claimants who were in receipt of SDP who have already moved to universal credit, comprising ongoing monthly payments and an additional lump-sum covering the period since they moved.

CHAPTER 2

Exclusion of entitlement to certain benefits

3.11   **5.** (1) Except as provided in paragraph (2), a claimant is not entitled to—
   (a) income support;
   (b) housing benefit;
   (c) a tax credit; or
   (d) state pension credit under the State Pension Credit Act 2002,
in respect of any period when the claimant is entitled to universal credit.
   (2) Entitlement to universal credit does not preclude the claimant from entitlement—
   (a) to housing benefit in respect of [¹ specified accommodation] [², temporary accommodation or where regulation 8(2A) [³, 46(1) or 47(2)] applies]; or
   (b) during the first assessment period for universal credit, where the claimant is a new claimant partner, to—
      (i) income support, where an award to which the new claimant partner is entitled terminates, in accordance with regulation 7(4), after the first date of entitlement to universal credit;
      (ii) housing benefit, where regulation 7(5)(b) applies and an award of housing benefit to which the new claimant partner is entitled terminates after the first date of entitlement to universal credit; or
      (iii) a tax credit, where an award to which the new claimant partner is entitled terminates, in accordance with the 2002 Act, after the first date of entitlement to universal credit.

AMENDMENTS

1. Universal Credit (Transitional Provisions) (Amendment) Regulations 2014 (SI 2014/1626) reg.3 (November 3, 2014).
2. Universal Credit (Miscellaneous Amendments, Saving and Transitional Provision) Regulations 2018 (SI 2018/65) reg.6(4) (April 11, 2018).
3. Universal Credit (Managed Migration Pilot and Miscellaneous Amendments) Regulations 2019 (SI 2019/1152) reg.3(4) (July 24, 2019).

DEFINITIONS

"the 2002 Act"–see reg.2(1).
"assessment period"–*ibid.*
"housing benefit"–*ibid.*
"income support"–*ibid.*
"new claimant partner"–*ibid.*

"specified accommodation"–*ibid.*
"tax credit"–*ibid.*

GENERAL NOTE

This regulation broadly performs the same function as reg.15(1)-(2A) of the 2013   **3.12**
Transitional Regulations. The basic rule is that entitlement to universal credit and
entitlement to any of the benefits or tax credits in para.(1) are mutually exclusive.
Provision is made to similar effect in relation to "old style JSA" and "old style ESA"
by virtue of the various Commencement Orders made under s.150(3) of the Act,
which bring into force repeals of the legislation relating to those benefits. References
to "old style JSA" and "old style ESA" are to the versions of jobseeker's allowance and employment and support allowance which include an income-based, or
income-related, allowance (see reg.2 above).

[¹ Entitlement to universal credit and housing benefit: universal credit work allowance

5A. Where a claimant has an award of universal credit and, in any   **3.13**
assessment period, is also entitled to housing benefit for temporary accommodation and the award of universal credit does not include an amount
for housing costs, regulation 22(2) of the Universal Credit Regulations
(amount of the work allowance) is to apply in relation to that assessment
period as if the award did include an amount for housing costs.]

AMENDMENT

1. Universal Credit (Miscellaneous Amendments, Saving and Transitional
Provision) Regulations 2018 (SI 2018/65) reg.6(4) (April 11, 2018).

DEFINITIONS

"assessment period"–see reg.2(1).
"housing benefit"–*ibid.*
"temporary accommodation" –*ibid.*
"Universal Credit Regulations" –*ibid.*

GENERAL NOTE

The new reg.5A provides that where in a universal credit assessment period a   **3.14**
person is entitled to universal credit (without the housing costs element) and is also
entitled to housing benefit for temporary accommodation, then that person is to be
treated for the purposes of work allowances in universal credit as though they were
entitled to universal credit with the housing costs element.

Exclusion of claims for certain existing benefits

6. (1) Except as provided in paragraphs (5) to (9) a universal credit   **3.15**
claimant may not make a claim for income support, housing benefit or a
tax credit.
(2) For the purposes of this regulation, a person is a universal credit
claimant if—
   (a) the person is entitled to universal credit;
   (b) the person has made a claim for universal credit, a decision has not
       yet been made on that claim and the person has not been informed
       (in accordance with an order made under section 150(3) of the Act)
       that he or she is not entitled to claim universal credit;

[² (ba)(i) the conditions in regulation 6(1)(a), (b) and (c) or 6(2)(a), (b) and (c) of the Claims and Payments Regulations (claims not required for entitlement to universal credit in certain cases) are met in relation to the person;

    (ii) he or she may be entitled to an award of universal credit without making a claim if the conditions in regulation 6(1)(d) and (e) or, as the case may be, 6(2)(d) and (e) of those Regulations are also met; and

    (iii) either the Secretary of State has no information in relation to the person which may indicate a change of circumstances as referred to in regulation 6(1)(e) or, as the case may be, 6(2) (e) of those Regulations, or the Secretary of State has such information but no decision has been made that the person is entitled to universal credit;]

  (c) the person was previously entitled to a joint award of universal credit which terminated because the person ceased to be a member of a couple, he or she is not exempt (by virtue of regulation 9(6) of the Claims and Payments Regulations) from the condition of entitlement to universal credit that he or she makes a claim for it and the period of one month, starting with the date on which the person notified the Secretary of State that he or she had ceased to be a member of a couple, has not expired;

[² (ca) the person may be entitled to an award of universal credit in circumstances where, by virtue of regulation 9(6), (7) or (10) of the Claims and Payments Regulations (claims for universal credit by members of a couple), it is not a condition of entitlement that he or she makes a claim for it, but no decision has yet been made as to the person's entitlement;]

  (d) the person is treated, under the Claims and Payments Regulations, as having made a claim for universal credit, [² . . .] but no decision has yet been made as to the person's entitlement;

  (e) a decision has been made that the person is not entitled to universal credit and—

    (i) the Secretary of State is considering whether to revise that decision under section 9 of the Social Security Act 1998, whether on an application made for that purpose, or on the Secretary of State's own initiative; or

    (ii) the person has appealed against that decision to the First-tier Tribunal and that appeal or any subsequent appeal to the Upper Tribunal or to a court has not been finally determined.

(3) For the purposes of paragraph (1)—

(a) a universal credit claimant makes a claim for benefit mentioned in that paragraph if the claimant takes any action which results in a decision on a claim being required under the relevant Regulations; and

(b) except as provided in [² paragraphs (5) to (7B)], it is irrelevant that the effect of any provision of the relevant Regulations is that, for the purposes of those Regulations, the claim is made or treated as made at a time when the claimant was not a universal credit claimant.

(4) The relevant Regulations are—

(a) in relation to a claim for income support, the Social Security (Claims and Payments) Regulations 1987 ("the 1987 Regulations");

(b) in relation to a claim for housing benefit, the Housing Benefit Regulations 2006 ("the 2006 Regulations") or, as the case may be, the Housing Benefit (Persons who have attained the qualifying age for state pension credit) Regulations 2006 ("the 2006 (SPC) Regulations");

(c) in relation to a claim for a tax credit, the Tax Credits (Claims and Notifications) Regulations 2002.

(5) A universal credit claimant is not precluded from making a claim for income support if—

(a) first notification of the claimant's intention to make that claim was made, or deemed to be made, for the purposes of regulation 6(1A)(c) [² or 6(A)] of the 1987 Regulations, before the date on which the claim for universal credit was made or treated as made; and

(b) in accordance with the 1987 Regulations, the claimant's entitlement to income support in connection with the claim will (if the claimant is entitled to income support) pre-date—

(i) the date, or anticipated date, of the claimant's entitlement to universal credit in connection with the current award or claim; or

(ii) where the claimant is a new claimant partner and regulation 7(4) would apply to the award, the date on which it would terminate in accordance with that provision.

(6) A universal credit claimant is not precluded from making a claim for housing benefit if—

(a) first notification of the claimant's intention to make that claim was given (within the meaning of regulation 83(5)(d) of the 2006 Regulations or, as the case may be, regulation 64(6)(d) of the 2006 (SPC) Regulations before the date on which the claim for universal credit was made or treated as made; and

(b) in accordance with the 2006 Regulations or, as the case may be, the 2006 (SPC) Regulations, the claimant's entitlement to housing benefit in connection with the claim will (if the claimant is entitled to housing benefit) pre-date—

(i) the date, or anticipated date, of the claimant's entitlement to universal credit in connection with the current award or claim; or

(ii) where the claimant is a new claimant partner and regulation 7(5)(b) would apply to the award, the date on which it would terminate in accordance with the 2006 Regulations or, as the case may be, the 2006 (SPC) Regulations.

(7) A universal credit claimant is not precluded from correcting or completing a claim for housing benefit which was defective within the meaning of the 2006 Regulations or the 2006 (SPC) Regulations if—

(a) the defective claim was made before the date on which the claim for universal credit was made or treated as made; and

(b) in accordance with the 2006 Regulations or, as the case may be, the 2006 (SPC) Regulations, the claimant's entitlement to housing benefit in connection with the claim will (if the claimant is entitled to housing benefit) pre-date—

(i) the date, or anticipated date, of the claimant's entitlement to universal credit in connection with the current award or claim; or

(ii) where the claimant is a new claimant partner and regulation

567

7(5)(b) would apply to the award, the date on which it would terminate in accordance with the 2006 Regulations or, as the case may be, the 2006 (SPC) Regulations.

[² (7A) A claimant who is a universal credit claimant by virtue of sub-paragraph (ba) of paragraph (2) (and no other sub-paragraph) is not precluded from—

(a) making a claim for income support for a period starting on or after the relevant date if first notification of the claimant's intention to make that claim was made, or deemed to be made, for the purposes of regulation 6(1A)(c) or 6A of the 1987 Regulations, during the period starting with the relevant date and ending with 15th November 2015;

(b) making a claim for housing benefit for a period starting on or after the relevant date if first notification of the claimant's intention to make that claim was given (within the meaning of regulation 83(5) (d) of the 2006 Regulations or, as the case may be, regulation 64(6) (d) of the 2006 (SPC) Regulations, during the period starting with the relevant date and ending with 15th November 2015;

(c) correcting or completing a claim for housing benefit for a period starting on or after the relevant date, where that claim was defective within the meaning of the 2006 Regulations or the 2006 (SPC) Regulations and was made during the period starting with the relevant date and ending with 15th November 2015.

(7B) For the purposes of paragraph (7A), the "relevant date" is—

(a) where the conditions in regulation 6(1)(a), (b) and (c) of the Claims and Payments Regulations are met in relation to the claimant, the day after the claimant's last day of entitlement to universal credit;

(b) where the conditions in regulation 6(2)(a), (b) and (c) of the Claims and Payments Regulations are met in relation to the claimant, the first date on which the claimant would have been entitled to universal credit if the claimant had been so entitled.]

(8) A universal credit claimant is not precluded from making a claim for housing benefit in respect of [¹ specified accommodation] [³ or temporary accommodation].

(9) A universal credit claimant is not precluded from making a claim for a tax credit which the claimant is treated as having made by virtue of regulation 7(7) or 8(4)(a).

AMENDMENTS

1. Universal Credit (Transitional Provisions) (Amendment) Regulations 2014 (SI 2014/1626) reg.3 (November 3, 2014).

2. Universal Credit (Transitional Provisions) (Amendment) Regulations 2015 (SI 2015/1780) reg.2 (November 16, 2015).

3. Universal Credit (Miscellaneous Amendments, Saving and Transitional Provision) Regulations 2018 (SI 2018/65) reg.6(6)(a) (April 11, 2018).

DEFINITIONS

"the 1987 Regulations"–para.(4)(a).
"the 2006 Regulations"–para.(4)(b).
"the 2006 (SPC) Regulations"–*ibid.*
"the Act"–see reg.2(1).

"the Claims and Payments Regulations"–*ibid.*
"First-tier Tribunal"–*ibid.*
"housing benefit"–*ibid.*
"income support"–*ibid.*
"new claimant partner"–*ibid.*
"relevant date"–para.(7B).
"specified accommodation"–see reg.2(1).
"tax credit" –*ibid.*
"Upper Tribunal"–*ibid.*

GENERAL NOTE

This regulation broadly performs the same function as reg.15(3)-(5) of the 2013   **3.16**
Transitional Regulations, with various modifications. In summary, universal credit
claimants are excluded from claiming income support, housing benefit or tax
credits, except in certain cases where notice of intention to claim has previously
been given, or a defective claim has previously been made, and entitlement will run
from a date before the claimant became entitled to universal credit. Thus the new
regulation allows for further exceptions to the general rule that a universal credit
claimant may not also claim, or have entitlement to existing benefits. In particular, where the claimant has previously notified their intention to make a claim for
certain existing benefits (paras (5) and (6)), or has made a defective claim (para.
(7)), and entitlement to the existing benefit would pre-date the date of entitlement
to universal credit, the claim may now be completed, so that the claimant is not
disadvantaged by the move to universal credit. There is also provision for overlap of
awards of universal credit and certain existing benefits during the first assessment
period for universal credit, where this is necessary to protect the interests of a former
partner of the universal claimant. As with reg.5, similar provision is made in relation
to both "old style JSA" and "old style ESA" by Commencement Orders made under
s.150(3) of the Act.

The effect of the subsequent amendments made by the Universal Credit
(Transitional Provisions) (Amendment) Regulations 2015 (SI 2015/1780) is to add
certain claimants to the definition of a "Universal Credit claimant" contained in para.
(2) such that they too may not make a claim for income support, housing benefit or
tax credits. The further category of excluded claimants comprises those who:

- have been awarded universal credit and their earnings have reduced their
  universal credit award to nil; or

- have made a claim for universal credit, but are not entitled to an award
  because of the level of their earned income; and

- have entered a six month 're-award' period, during which universal credit
  may be awarded without a further claim if their earnings drop or there is
  another change of circumstances that would make universal credit payable.

Where claimants have been awarded or make a claim to universal credit and their
earnings have either reduced their award to nil (or they are not entitled to universal credit after making that claim after the work allowance and taper have been
applied), they enter a six month re-award period during which universal credit may
be awarded without a further claim (if either their earnings drop or there is another
change of circumstances that would make universal credit payable). Before the
2015 amendments, where claimants entered the six month re-award period and so
have no universal credit entitlement, they may claim existing benefits if so entitled.
However, if their earnings then drop (or their circumstances change so that universal credit becomes payable again), universal credit would also be re-awarded. The
parallel access both to existing benefits and universal credit created administrative
complexity and the risk of overpayments because of the difficulty in ensuring that
payments of existing benefits and universal credit are not made for the same or an
overlapping period.

These 2015 amendments do not apply to areas where universal credit is administered under relevant regulations as amended by the Universal Credit (Digital Service) Amendment Regulations 2014 (SI 2014/2887). In these areas the provision to re-award universal credit without a claim in these cases is revoked; and provisions in the relevant Commencement Orders bar claims for incomes support, housing benefit or tax credits by claimants who live in the relevant postcode districts.

Termination of awards of certain existing benefits: new claimant partners

3.17

7. (1) This regulation applies where—

(a) a person ("A") who was previously entitled to universal credit [² . . .] ceases to be so entitled on becoming a member of a couple;

(b) the other member of the couple ("the new claimant partner") was not entitled to universal credit [² . . .] immediately before formation of the couple;

(c) the couple is treated, in accordance with regulation 9(8) of the Claims and Payments Regulations, as having made a claim for universal credit; and

(d) the Secretary of State is satisfied that the claimants meet the basic conditions specified in section 4(1)(a) to (d) of the Act (other than any of those conditions which they are not required to meet by virtue of regulations under section 4(2) of the Act).

(2) Subject to paragraphs (4) and (5), where this regulation applies, all awards of income support or housing benefit to which the new claimant partner would (were it not for the effect of these Regulations) have been entitled during the relevant period are to terminate, by virtue of this regulation—

(a) on the day before the first date on which the joint claimants are entitled to universal credit in connection with the claim; or

(b) if the joint claimants are not entitled to universal credit, on the day before the first date on which they would have been so entitled, if all of the basic and financial conditions applicable to them had been met; or

(c) if the new claimant partner became entitled to an award after the date on which it would otherwise terminate under sub-paragraph (a) or (b), at the beginning of the first day of entitlement to that award.

(3) For the purposes of this regulation, "the relevant period" is the period starting with the first day of the assessment period (in relation to A's award of universal credit) during which A and the new claimant partner formed a couple and ending with the date of formation of the couple.

(4) Where the new claimant partner was entitled during the relevant period to income support, he or she was at that time a member of a couple and the award included an amount in respect of the new claimant partner and their partner at that time ("P"), the award of income support terminates, by virtue of this regulation, on the date on which the new claimant partner and P ceased to be a couple for the purposes of the Income Support (General) Regulations 1987, unless it terminates on that date in accordance with other legislative provision, or terminated on an earlier date.

(5) An award of housing benefit to which the new claimant partner is entitled does not terminate by virtue of this regulation where—

(a) the award is in respect of [¹ specified accommodation] [³ or temporary accommodation]; or

(b) the new claimant partner leaves the accommodation in respect of which housing benefit was paid, in order to live with A.

(6) Where an award terminates by virtue of this regulation, any legislative provision under which the award terminates on a later date does not apply.

(7) Where the new claimant partner was, immediately before forming a couple with A, treated by regulation 11 as being entitled to a tax credit, the new claimant partner is to be treated, for the purposes of the 2002 Act, as having made a claim for the tax credit in question for the current tax year.

AMENDMENTS

1. Universal Credit (Transitional Provisions) (Amendment) Regulations 2014 (SI 2014/1626) reg.3 (November 3, 2014).

2. Universal Credit (Digital Service) Amendment Regulations 2014 (SI 2014/2887) reg.3(3) (November 26, 2014).

3. Universal Credit (Miscellaneous Amendments, Saving and Transitional Provision) Regulations 2018 (SI 2018/65) reg.6(6)(b) (April 11, 2018).

DEFINITIONS

"the 2002 Act"–see reg.2(1).
"A"–para.7(1)(a).
"the Act"–see reg.2(1).
"assessment period"–*ibid.*
"the Claims and Payments Regulations"–*ibid.*
"housing benefit"–*ibid.*
"income support"–*ibid.*
"new claimant partner"–*ibid.*
"partner"–*ibid.*
"the relevant period"–para.(3).
"specified accommodation"–see reg.2(1).
"tax year"–*ibid.*

GENERAL NOTE

In broad terms this provision performs the same function as reg.16 of the 2013 **3.18** Transitional Regulations, with various modifications. As a general rule, all existing benefit or tax credit awards will terminate when an award of universal credit is made to a newly formed couple, one of whom was previously entitled to universal credit and the other to an existing benefit (or tax credit). The mechanics of this process are different for existing benefit and tax credits awards respectively.

Thus where the conditions in para.(1) are met, the new claimant partner's award of income support or housing benefit will terminate as provided for in para.(2). Para.(4) deals with the timing of the termination of an earlier award of income support where the new claimant partner was receiving that benefit together with their own previous partner ("P"). Para.(5) provides for special cases where an award of housing benefit does not end, despite the general rule.

The process is rather more complicated with tax credits – where the new partner is treated as having an ongoing tax credit award by virtue of reg.11, then they are treated as having made a new claim for the current year, whether or not they actually have made such a claim (para.(7)), and any award made under such a deemed claim likewise terminates on the day before the start of the joint award of universal credit.

Paragraph (1)

3.19   The amendments to para.(1)(a) and (b) (the omission of the words "as a single parent") are each subject to the saving provision as set out in reg.5 of the Universal Credit (Digital Service) Amendment Regulations 2014 (SI 2014/2887).

Paragraph (7)

3.20   See further reg.11.

Termination of awards of certain existing benefits: other claimants

3.21   **8.** (1) This regulation applies where—

(a) a claim for universal credit (other than a claim which is treated, in accordance with regulation 9(8) of the Claims and Payments Regulations, as having been made) is made; and

(b) the Secretary of State is satisfied that the claimant meets the basic conditions specified in section 4(1)(a) to (d) of the Act (other than any of those conditions which the claimant is not required to meet by virtue of regulations under section 4(2) of the Act).

(2) [²Where] this regulation applies, all awards of income support [² . . .] or a tax credit to which the claimant (or, in the case of joint claimants, either of them) is entitled on the date on which the claim is made are to terminate, by virtue of this regulation—

(a) on the day before the first date on which the claimant is entitled to universal credit in connection with the claim; or

(b) if the claimant is not entitled to universal credit, on the day before the first date on which he or she would have been so entitled, if all of the basic and financial conditions applicable to the claimant had been met.

[² (2A) Subject to paragraph (3), where this regulation applies, an award of housing benefit to which the claimant is entitled on the day mentioned in paragraph (2)(a) or (b) terminates on the last day of the period of two weeks beginning with the day after that day (whether or not the person is also entitled to an award of income support or a tax credit).]

(3) An award of housing benefit to which a claimant is entitled in respect of [¹ specified accommodation] [² or temporary accommodation] does not terminate by virtue of this regulation.

(4) Where this regulation applies and the claimant (or, in the case of joint claimants, either of them) is treated by regulation 11 as being entitled to a tax credit—

(a) the claimant (or, as the case may be, the relevant claimant) is to be treated, for the purposes of the 2002 Act and this regulation, as having made a claim for the tax credit in question for the current tax year; and

(b) if the claimant (or the relevant claimant) is entitled on the date on which the claim for universal credit was made to an award of a tax credit which is made in respect of a claim which is treated as having been made by virtue of sub-paragraph (a), that award is to terminate, by virtue of this regulation—

(i) on the day before the first date on which the claimant is entitled to universal credit; or

(ii) if the claimant is not entitled to universal credit, on the day before the first date on which he or she would have been so entitled, if all of the basic and financial conditions applicable to the claimant had been met.

(5) Where an award terminates by virtue of this regulation, any legislative provision under which the award terminates on a later date does not apply.

AMENDMENTS

1. Universal Credit (Transitional Provisions) (Amendment) Regulations 2014 (SI 2014/1626) reg.3 (November 3, 2014).
2. Universal Credit (Miscellaneous Amendments, Saving and Transitional Provision) Regulations 2018 (SI 2018/65) reg.6(7) (April 11, 2018).

DEFINITIONS

"the 2002 Act"–see reg.2(1).
"the Act"–*ibid.*
"the Claims and Payments Regulations"–*ibid.*
"housing benefit"–*ibid.*
"income support"–*ibid.*
"specified accommodation"–*ibid.*
"tax credit" –*ibid.*
"tax year"–*ibid.*

GENERAL NOTE

As a general rule, all existing benefit or tax credit awards will terminate when an award of universal credit is made to a claimant. This regulation essentially performs the same function as reg.7 but for claimants who do not have a new claimant partner.

In *AD (A child, by her litigation friend TD) & PR v SSWP* [2019] EWHC 462 (Admin) the High Court had held that the failure to provide transitional protection for claimants who transferred to universal credit following an incorrect legacy benefit decision was not unlawful.

However, the High Court's decision was reversed by the Court of Appeal in *R (TD & Ors) v SSWP* [2020] EWCA Civ 618.

TD was a single parent entitled to IS, CTC (with a disabled child element) and carer's allowance. Her total entitlement (excluding HB) was £1,005.45 per month. She also received DLA, on behalf of her daughter, of £333.23 per month. In March 2017, the DWP stopped her IS award and her Job Centre advised her to claim universal credit, which was awarded in April 2017. TD's universal credit award was £872.90 a month, which was £136.99 a month less than she had been entitled under the legacy benefits. TD was unable to return to legacy benefits due to the application of regs 8 and 13. In August 2018, the DWP increased her daughter's DLA, meaning she was entitled to the highest rate of the disabled child element of CTC (up to April 2017) and, thereafter, the highest rate of the disabled child element of universal credit. As a result, the household's combined entitlement was now at the same level under universal credit as it would have been had TD continued to receive her legacy benefits. However, TD continued to seek a declaration and damages for the distress caused to them resulting from the drop in income at the time of transfer. She argued that the declaration sought would also benefit others in the same position who remained on a lower entitlement under universal credit.

PR was in receipt of ESA with the SDP and support component, and was also entitled to PIP when, in March 2017, the DWP stopped her ESA. She challenged that decision and claimed universal credit in April 2017. PR's legacy benefits entitled her to receive £814.67 per month, while her universal credit award was £636.58 per month, £178.09 less. The ESA decision was reversed in August 2017 but, as with TD, the 2014 Regulations precluded her from receiving or claiming any legacy benefits after her claim for universal credit.

TD (and her daughter) and PR were given permission for the judicial review challenge on three grounds: (1) that the treatment amounted to unlawful discrimination

3.22

contrary to art.14 read with art.1 of the First Protocol to the ECHR (and in the case of TD and her daughter, it was said that their art.8 rights were also engaged); (2) that the decision of the Secretary of State to prevent those in the position of these claimants from returning to the legacy system, without providing for transitional protection, was irrational; and (3) that the SSWP had failed to comply with her Public Sector Equality Duty (PSED). In the High Court, May J. dismissed all three grounds.

However, the Court of Appeal accepted the Appellants' argument that, in their cases, the absence of transitional protection constituted discrimination contrary to art.14 of the ECHR. For art.14 purposes, the comparator group was, according to the Court of Appeal, "people who were entitled to legacy benefits and in whose cases no error was made by the Respondent". The High Court's analysis was flawed because, in considering whether the difference of treatment to which the Appellants had been subjected was justified, the judge failed to decide that matter for herself. Instead, the judge rejected the Appellants' case because she was persuaded that justification had been adequately considered by the Secretary of State. The Court of Appeal went on to decide that the difference of treatment was not justified and its effect was manifestly disproportionate for the Appellants, so that their rights under art.14 had been breached. The key consideration was identified in para.83 of the Court's judgment:

> "83...these Appellants were treated as they were despite their successful reviews, for reasons to do with administrative cost and complexity, which have nothing to do with the merits of their cases; and that the only reason in reality why they moved from legacy benefits to UC was as a result of errors of law by the state itself."

The Court of Appeal gave a declaration that the Appellants' art.14 rights had been breached but added "it will be a matter for the Secretary of State to decide how to respond to a declaration". Whether or not the response will be to introduce transitional protection for all claimants, rather than limiting it to those undergoing "managed migration", remains to be seen. The Court's decision was not based on a finding that the absence of transitional protection was, in general, discrimination contrary to art.14. However, nor did the Court rule that its absence was, in general, justified. As explained above, the Court decided the case by reference to the, hopefully, infrequent circumstance of a misadvised claimant. Whether, in the absence of such circumstances, the UK Government's policy of granting transitional protection to universal credit "managed migrants", but not "natural migrants", falls foul of art.14 remains to be determined.

[¹ Transitional housing payment

3.23   **8A.** Where an award of housing benefit terminates under regulation 8 [², 46 or 47]—

(a) the claimant is to be treated for the purposes of the Housing Benefit Regulations 2006 as entitled to universal credit during the period of two weeks mentioned in regulation 8(2A) [², 46(1) or 47(2)], even if no decision has been made on the claim; [²...]

(b) if a claim for universal credit is made because the claimant moves to new accommodation occupied as the claimant's home, then, notwithstanding anything in the Housing Benefit Regulations 2006, housing benefit is to be paid directly to the claimant during the period of two weeks mentioned in regulation 8(2A) [², 46(1) or 47(2)] [²; and

(c) if a claim for universal credit is made by a notified person then, notwithstanding anything in the Housing Benefit Regulations 2006, the weekly amount of housing benefit to which the person is entitled for that period of two weeks is the same as the weekly amount they were entitled to on the first day of that period.]

AMENDMENTS

1. Universal Credit (Miscellaneous Amendments, Saving and Transitional Provision) Regulations 2018 (SI 2018/65) reg.6(8) (April 11, 2018).
2. Universal Credit (Managed Migration Pilot and Miscellaneous Amendments) Regulations 2019 (SI 2019/1152) reg.3(5) (July 24, 2019).

DEFINITION

"housing benefit"–see reg.2(1).

GENERAL NOTE

The amendments to reg.8 effective from April 11, 2018 provide for a transitional housing payment for claimants who migrate to universal credit when they are in receipt of housing benefit. In addition, the new reg.8(2A) allows a housing benefit award to continue for a period of two weeks beyond the day on which the person becomes entitled to universal credit. The new reg.8A in turn provides that, pending the decision on the claim, the claimant is treated as entitled to universal credit for the purposes of the housing benefit award, and where the claimant makes a claim for universal credit because they have moved home, housing benefit will be paid directly to the claimant for the period of two weeks beginning with the day on which they become entitled to universal credit. The references to regs 46 and 47 provide for the amount of housing benefit to be frozen during the two-week run-on period in a case where the claimant is moved to universal credit.

3.24

Treatment of ongoing entitlement to certain benefits: benefit cap

9. (1) This regulation applies where a claimant who is a new claimant partner, or who has (in accordance with regulation 26 of the Universal Credit Regulations) been awarded universal credit in respect of a period preceding the date on which the claim for universal credit was made or treated as made—

3.25

(a) is entitled, in respect of the whole or part of the first assessment period for universal credit, to a welfare benefit (other than universal credit) mentioned in [¹section 96(10) of the Act (benefit cap)]; and
(b) is entitled to housing benefit at any time during the first assessment period for universal credit, or would be so entitled were it not for the effect of these Regulations.

(2) Where this regulation applies, regulation 79 of the Universal Credit Regulations applies, in relation to the claimant, as if the benefit in question was not included in the list of welfare benefits in [¹ section 96(10) of the Act].

AMENDMENT

1. Benefit Cap (Housing Benefit and Universal Credit) (Amendment) Regulations 2016 (SI 2016/909) reg.5(a) (November 7, 2016).

DEFINITIONS

"assessment period"–see reg.2(1).
"housing benefit"–*ibid.*
"new claimant partner"–*ibid.*
"the Universal Credit Regulations"–*ibid.*

GENERAL NOTE

This regulation provides for entitlement to some benefits (i.e. those listed in reg.79(4) of the Universal Credit Regulations 2013) to be disregarded for the pur-

3.26

poses of the benefit cap during the claimant's first assessment period for universal credit. This applies where a claimant is entitled to universal credit from a date before the date on which they made a claim, or were treated as making a claim, and they were also previously entitled to housing benefit (which may already have been subject to the benefit cap).

Treatment of overpayments

3.27   **10.** (1) This regulation applies where—

(a) an award of universal credit is made to a claimant who was previously entitled to an existing benefit other than a tax credit or a joint-claim jobseeker's allowance; and

(b) a payment of the existing benefit is made which includes payment ("the overpayment") in respect of a period—

(i) during which the claimant is not entitled to that benefit (including non-entitlement which arises from termination of an award by virtue of an order made under section 150(3) of the Act or regulation 7, 8, or 14); and

(ii) which falls within an assessment period for universal credit.

(2) Where this regulation applies, for the purposes of calculating the amount of an award of universal credit in respect of an assessment period—

(a) regulation 66 of the Universal Credit Regulations (what is included in unearned income?) applies as if the overpayment which was made in respect of that assessment period were added to the descriptions of unearned income in paragraph (1)(b) of that regulation; and

(b) regulation 73 of the Universal Credit Regulations (unearned income calculated monthly) does not apply to the overpayment.

(3) In so far as any overpayment is taken into account in calculating the amount of an award of universal credit in accordance with this regulation, that payment may not be recovered as an overpayment under—

(a) the Social Security (Payments on account, Overpayments and Recovery) Regulations 1988;

(b) the Housing Benefit Regulations 2006; or

(c) the Housing Benefit (Persons who have attained the qualifying age for state pension credit) Regulations 2006.

DEFINITIONS

"the Act"–see reg.2(1).
"assessment period"–*ibid.*
"existing benefit"–*ibid.*
"joint-claim jobseeker's allowance"–*ibid.*
"overpayment"–para.(1)(b).
"tax credit"–see reg.2(1).
"the Universal Credit Regulations"–*ibid.*

GENERAL NOTE

3.28   This regulation provides that overpayments of existing benefits (other than joint-claim jobseeker's allowance or tax credits) that may arise on transition to universal credit are to be off-set against entitlement to universal credit (para.(1)). Thus, overpayments of existing benefits which may arise on transition to universal credit can be offset as unearned income against the claimant's entitlement to universal credit (para.(2)) and may not then be recovered under other legislation (para.(3)). This is because it will be recovered as unearned income from the universal credit award rather than as an excess payment under existing overpayments legislation.

[¹ Arrears of benefit disregarded as capital

10A.—(1) This regulation applies in relation to the calculation of an award of universal credit (the "current award") where the claimant has received a payment of arrears of benefit [²or armed forces independence payment], or a payment made to compensate for arrears due to the non-payment of benefit [²or armed forces independence payment], of £5,000 or more, and the following conditions are met—

(a) the payment—
  (i) is received during the current award; or
  (ii) was received during an award of an existing benefit or state pension credit (the "earlier award") and the claimant became entitled to the current award within one month of the date of termination of the earlier award;
(b) in the case of a payment falling within sub-paragraph (a)(i), it would be disregarded from the calculation of the claimant's capital if the claimant were entitled to an existing benefit or state pension credit;
(c) in the case of a payment falling within sub-paragraph (a)(ii), it was disregarded from the calculation of the claimant's capital for the purposes of the earlier award; and
(d) the period of entitlement to benefit [²or armed forces independence payment] to which the payment relates commences before the first date on which, by virtue of section 33 of the Act (abolition of benefits), no claimant is entitled to an existing benefit.

(2) Where this regulation applies, notwithstanding anything in the Universal Credit Regulations, the payment is to be disregarded from the calculation of the claimant's capital for 12 months from the date of receipt of the payment, or until the termination of the current award (if later).]

[²(3) "Armed forces independence payment" means armed forces independence payment under the Armed Forces and Reserve Forces (Compensation Scheme) Order 2011.]

3.28.1

AMENDMENTS

1. Social Security (Treatment of Arrears of Benefit) Regulations 2018 (SI 2018/932) reg.8 (September 11, 2018).
2. Social Security (Capital Disregards) (Amendment) Regulations 2019 (SI 2019/1314) reg.9(2) (October 31, 2019).

DEFINITIONS

"armed forces independence payment" para.(3).
"current award" – see para.(1).
"earlier award" – see para.(1)(a)(ii).
"existing benefit" – see reg.2(1).

GENERAL NOTE

The UC Regs 2013 provide for arrears of a means-tested benefit, or a payment to compensate for arrears, to be disregarded for a period of 12 months from the date the payment is received (see Sch.10 para.18). As originally enacted, there was no provision for such a payment to be disregarded for a longer period if it had been paid out because of official error. This regulation provides for the longer disregard to apply until the termination of the universal credit award where a payment of arrears of £5,000 or more has been received during an earlier award of an income-related

3.28.2

benefit and the claimant becomes entitled to universal credit within one month of their earlier award terminating, or where it has been received during the universal credit award. Thus, the effect is that the arrears in question may be disregarded for the life of the benefit award rather than for the usual maximum of 52 weeks. This additional disregard only applies to a payment that relates to a period of entitlement to benefit which begins before migration of existing benefits to universal credit is completed.

[¹Arrears of maternity allowance disregarded as capital

3.28.3
10B.—(1) This regulation applies in relation to the calculation of an award of universal credit where—

    (a) the conditions set out in regulation 10A(1)(a) to (d) are met; and

    (b) the claimant has received a payment of arrears of maternity allowance, or a payment made to compensate for arrears due to the non-payment of maternity allowance, of under £5,000.

(2) Where this regulation applies, notwithstanding anything in the Universal Credit Regulations, the payment is to be disregarded from the calculation of the claimant's capital for 12 months from the date of receipt of the payment.

(3) "Maternity allowance" means a maternity allowance under section 35 of the Social Security Contributions and Benefits Act 1992 (state maternity allowance for employed or self-employed earner).]

AMENDMENT

1. Social Security (Capital Disregards) (Amendment) Regulations 2019 (SI 2019/1314) reg.9(3) (October 31, 2019).

DEFINITIONS

"maternity allowance" para.(3).
"Universal Credit Regulations" reg.2(1).

Ongoing awards of tax credits

3.29
11. (1) For the purposes of [²these Regulations]—

    (a) a person is to be treated as being entitled to working tax credit with effect from the start of the current tax year even though a decision has not been made under section 14 of the 2002 Act in respect of a claim for that tax credit for that tax year, if the person was entitled to working tax credit for the previous tax year and any of the cases specified in paragraph (2) applies; and

    (b) a person is to be treated as being entitled to child tax credit with effect from the start of the current tax year even though a decision has not been made under section 14 of the 2002 Act in respect of a claim for that tax credit for that tax year, if the person was entitled to child tax credit for the previous tax year and any of the cases specified in paragraph (2) applies[²;]

    [²and references to an award of a tax credit are to be read accordingly].

(2) The cases are—

    (a) a final notice has not been given to the person under section 17 of the 2002 Act in respect of the previous tax year;

    (b) a final notice has been given, which includes provision by virtue of subsection (2) or (4) of section 17, or a combination of those subsections and subsection (6) and—

(i) the date specified in the notice for the purposes of section 17(2) and (4) or, where different dates are specified, the later of them, has not yet passed and no claim for a tax credit for the current tax year has been made, or treated as made; or

(ii) a claim for a tax credit has been made, or treated as made, on or before the date mentioned in paragraph (i), but no decision has been made in relation to that claim under section 14(1) of the 2002 Act;

(c) a final notice has been given, no claim for a tax credit for the current year has been made, or treated as made, and no decision has been made under section 18(1) of the 2002 Act in respect of entitlement to a tax credit for the previous tax year; [¹. . .]

[¹(ca) a final notice has been given and the person made a declaration in response to a requirement included in that notice by virtue of section 17(2)(a), (4)(a) or (6)(a), or any combination of those provisions—

(i) by the date specified on the final notice;

(ii) if not in accordance with paragraph (i), within 30 days following the date on the notice to the person that payments of tax credit under section 24(4) of the 2002 Act have ceased due to the person's failure to make the declaration by the date specified in the final notice; or

(iii) if not in accordance with paragraph (i) or (ii), before 31 January in the tax year following the period to which the final notice relates and, in the opinion of Her Majesty's Revenue and Customs, the person had good reason for not making the declaration in accordance with paragraph (i) or (ii); or]

(d) a final notice has been given and—

(i) the person did not make a declaration in response to provision included in that notice by virtue of section 17(2)(a), (4)(a) or (6)(a), or any combination of those provisions, by the date specified in the notice;

(ii) the person was given due notice that payments of tax credit under section 24(4) of the 2002 Act had ceased due to his or her failure to make the declaration; and

(iii) the person's claim for universal credit is made during the period of 30 days starting with the date on the notice referred to in paragraph (ii) or, where the person is a new claimant partner, notification of formation of a couple with a person entitled to universal credit is given to the Secretary of State during that period.

AMENDMENTS

1. Universal Credit (Miscellaneous Amendments, Saving and Transitional Provision) Regulations 2018 (SI 2018/65) reg.6(9) (February 14, 2018).

2. Universal Credit (Managed Migration Pilot and Miscellaneous Amendments) Regulations 2019 (SI 2019/1152) reg.3(6) (July 24, 2019).

DEFINITIONS

"the 2002 Act"–see reg.2(1).
"new claimant partner"–*ibid.*
"tax credit" –*ibid.*
"tax year"–*ibid.*

GENERAL NOTE

3.30   This regulation provides for a claimant to be treated as entitled to an award of a tax credit in certain cases, for the purposes of regs.7 and 8.

Modification of tax credits legislation: overpayments and penalties

3.31   **12.** (1) This regulation applies where—

  (a) a claim for universal credit is made, or is treated as having been made;

  (b) the claimant is, or was at any time during the tax year in which the claim is made or treated as made, entitled to a tax credit; and

  (c) the Secretary of State is satisfied that the claimant meets the basic conditions specified in section 4(1)(a) to (d) of the Act (other than any of those conditions which the claimant is not required to meet by virtue of regulations under section 4(2) of the Act).

  (2) Where this regulation applies, the 2002 Act applies in relation to the claimant with the following modifications.

  (3) In section 28—

  (a) in subsection (1)—

    (i) after "tax year" in both places where it occurs, insert "or part tax year";

   [² (ii) in paragraph (b), for the words from "as if it were" to the end substitute "as an overpayment of universal credit"]

  (b) [²...]

  (c) omit subsection (5);

  (d) in subsection (6) omit "(apart from subsection (5))".

  [¹ (4) [²...]]

  (5) In section 48 after the definition of "overpayment" insert—

  ""part tax year" means a period of less than a year beginning with 6th April and ending with the date on which the award of a tax credit terminated,".

  (6) In Schedule 2, in paragraph 6(1)(a) and (c) and (2)(a), after "for the tax year" insert "or part tax year".

AMENDMENTS

  1. Universal Credit (Transitional Provisions) (Amendment) Regulations 2016 (SI 2016/232) reg.2 (April 1, 2016).

  2. Tax Credits (Exercise of Functions in relation to Northern Ireland and Notices for Recovery of Tax Credit Overpayments) Order 2017 (2017/781) art.7 (September 25, 2017).

DEFINITIONS

  "the 2002 Act"–see reg.2(1).
  "the Act"–*ibid.*
  "tax credit"–*ibid.*
  "tax year"–*ibid.*

GENERAL NOTE

3.32   This regulation provides that, where a claim for universal credit is made by a claimant who was previously entitled to a tax credit, the Tax Credits Act 2002 is to apply to that claimant with certain modifications. The effect is that that any overpayments of tax credits may be treated as overpayments of universal credit and appropriate time limits apply in relation to the imposition of penalties.

[¹ Modification of tax credits legislation: finalisation of tax credits

12A. (1) This regulation applies where— 3.33

(a) a claim for universal credit is made, or is treated as having been made;

(b) the claimant is, or was at any time during the tax year in which the claim is made or treated as made, entitled to a tax credit; and

(c) the Secretary of State is satisfied that the claimant meets the basic conditions specified in section 4(1)(a) to (d) of the Act (other than any of those conditions which the claimant is not required to meet by virtue of regulations under section 4(2) of the Act).

(2) Subject to paragraph (3), where this regulation applies, the amount of the tax credit to which the person is entitled is to be calculated in accordance with the 2002 Act and regulations made under that Act, as modified by the Schedule to these Regulations ("the modified legislation").

(3) Where, in the opinion of the Commissioners for Her Majesty's Revenue and Customs, it is not reasonably practicable to apply the modified legislation in relation to any case or category of cases, the 2002 Act and regulations made under that Act are to apply without modification in that case or category of cases.]

AMENDMENT

1. Universal Credit (Transitional Provisions) (Amendment) Regulations 2014 (SI 2014/1626) reg.4 (October 13, 2014).

DEFINITIONS

"the 2002 Act"–see reg.2(1).
"the 2002 Act"–*ibid.*
"the modified legislation"–para.(2).
"tax credit"–see reg.2(1).
"tax year"–*ibid.*

GENERAL NOTE

This amendment is designed to smooth the transition from receipt of tax credits 3.34 to an award of universal credit. It re-instates provision for in-year finalisation of tax credits for universal credit claimants (there was no equivalent to reg.17 of, and the Schedule to, the 2013 Transitional Regulations in the original version of the 2014 Transitional Regulations). By doing so, this provision allows tax credits awards to be finalised during the relevant tax year when a tax credit claimant makes the transition to universal credit (see paras.(1) and (2) and the Schedule), rather than after the end of the tax year. This is intended to reduce administrative complexity and confusion for the claimant by providing a clean break from tax credits, thus avoiding the claimant having to revert to providing HMRC with information about their circumstances and income after they have been receiving universal credit for some time. It also should thereby, in theory at least, ensure the claimant has a single interaction with HMRC so that HMRC only have to deal with their case once, as both the stopping of a tax credits award and the finalising of the award are dealt with upon transition to universal credit. Although the intention is that in-year finalisation of tax credits awards is the default approach in the majority of cases, provision has been made (see para.(3)) to allow HMRC to continue to finalise tax credits awards after the end of the tax year, if they think that it is not practicable to apply the modified legislation to a particular case or class of case, e.g. where it proved difficult to verify income that is particularly complex, such as those cases including particular combinations of self-employed and other income. Para.(3) might also be invoked as a contingency to guard against unforeseen operational or IT difficulties.

Appeals etc relating to certain existing benefits

3.35   **13.** (1) This regulation applies where, after an award of universal credit has been made to a claimant—

    (a) an appeal against a decision relating to the entitlement of the claimant to income support, housing benefit or a tax credit (a "relevant benefit") is finally determined;

    (b) a decision relating to the claimant's entitlement to income support is revised under section 9 of the Social Security Act 1998 ("the 1998 Act") or superseded under section 10 of that Act;

    (c) a decision relating to the claimant's entitlement to housing benefit is revised or superseded under Schedule 7 to the Child Support, Pensions and Social Security Act 2000; or

    (d) a decision relating to the claimant's entitlement to a tax credit is revised under section 19 or 20 of the 2002 Act, or regulations made under section 21 of that Act, or is varied or cancelled under section 21A of that Act.

(2) Where the claimant is a new claimant partner and, as a result of determination of the appeal or, as the case may be, revision or supersession of the decision the claimant would (were it not for the effect of these Regulations) be entitled to income support or housing benefit during the relevant period mentioned in regulation 7(3), awards of those benefits are to terminate in accordance with regulation 7.

(3) Where the claimant is not a new claimant partner and, as a result of determination of the appeal or, as the case may be, revision, supersession, variation or cancellation of the decision, the claimant would (were it not for the effect of these Regulations) be entitled to a relevant benefit on the date on which the claim for universal credit was made, awards of relevant benefits are to terminate in accordance with regulation 8.

(4) The Secretary of State is to consider whether it is appropriate to revise under section 9 of the 1998 Act the decision in relation to entitlement to universal credit or, if that decision has been superseded under section 10 of that Act, the decision as so superseded (in either case, "the UC decision").

(5) Where it appears to the Secretary of State to be appropriate to revise the UC decision, it is to be revised in such manner as appears to the Secretary of State to be necessary to take account of—

    (a) the decision of the First-tier Tribunal, Upper Tribunal or court, or, as the case may be, the decision relating to entitlement to a relevant benefit, as revised, superseded, varied or cancelled; and

    (b) any finding of fact by the First-tier Tribunal, Upper Tribunal or court.

DEFINITIONS

"the 1998 Act"–para.(1)(b).
"the 2002 Act"–see reg.2(1).
"First-tier Tribunal"–*ibid.*
"housing benefit"–*ibid.*
"income support"–*ibid.*
"new claimant partner"–*ibid.*
"relevant benefit"–para.(1)(a).
"tax credit"–see reg.2(1).
"the UC decision"–para.(4).
"Upper Tribunal"–see reg.2(1).

This regulation deals with appeals which are determined, and decisions about exist-   **3.36**
ing benefits which are revised or superseded, after the appellant has become entitled
to universal credit (see para.(1)). Entitlement to income support, housing benefit or a
tax credit arising from an appeal, revision or supersession will terminate in accordance
with regulation 7 or 8 (paras.(2) and (3)) and a decision made about entitlement to
universal credit may be revised to take account of any findings of fact by the relevant
appeal body (paras.(4) and (5)). The equivalent provision in the 2013 Transitional
Regulations (reg.18) applied only to new claimants partners; this provision applies to
all claimants and not just new claimant partners. See further the note to reg.8 above.

Appeals etc relating to universal credit

14.—(1) This regulation applies where—   **3.37**
  (a) a decision is made that a claimant is not entitled to universal credit
      ("the UC decision");
  (b) the claimant becomes entitled to income support, housing benefit or
      a tax credit (a "relevant benefit");
  (c) an appeal against the UC decision is finally determined, or the deci-
      sion is revised under section 9 of the Social Security Act 1998;
  (d) an award of universal credit is made to the claimant in consequence
      of entitlement arising from the appeal, or from the decision as
      revised; and
  (e) the claimant would (were it not for the effect of regulation 5 and this
      regulation) be entitled to both universal credit and a relevant benefit
      in respect of the same period.
  (2) Subject to paragraph (3), where this regulation applies—
  (a) all awards of a relevant benefit to which the claimant would (were it
      not for the effect of these Regulations) be entitled are to terminate,
      by virtue of this regulation, at the beginning of the first day of entitle-
      ment to that award; and
  (b) any legislative provision [² except regulation 8(2A)] under which an
      award would otherwise terminate on a later date does not apply.
  (3) An award of housing benefit to which a claimant is entitled in respect
of [¹ specified accommodation] [² or temporary accommodation] does not terminate by virtue of this regulation.

  1. Universal Credit (Transitional Provisions) (Amendment) Regulations 2014 (SI
2014/1626) reg.3 (November 3, 2014).
  2. Universal Credit (Miscellaneous Amendments, Saving and Transitional
Provision) Regulations 2018 (SI 2018/65) reg.6(10) (April 11, 2018).

  "housing benefit"–see reg.2(1).
  "income support"–*ibid.*
  "relevant benefit"–para.(1)(b).
  "specified accommodation"–see reg.2(1).
  "tax credit" –*ibid.*
  "the UC decision"–para.(1)(a).

This regulation concerns the situation where a claimant successfully appeals a   **3.38**
decision that they are not entitled to universal credit, or such a decision is revised,

but only after the claimant has become entitled to income support, housing benefit or a tax credit. In such a case, the award of the existing benefit terminates at the beginning of the first day of entitlement if there would otherwise be an overlap with the award of universal credit.

CHAPTER 3

Modification of Claims and Payments Regulations in relation to universal credit claimants

3.39   **15.** (1) Where a claim for universal credit is made by a person who was previously entitled to an existing benefit, regulation 26 of the Claims and Payments Regulations (time within which a claim for universal credit is to be made) applies in relation to that claim with the modification specified in paragraph (2).

(2) In paragraph (3) of regulation 26, after sub-paragraph (a) insert—

"(aa) the claimant was previously in receipt of an existing benefit (as defined in the Universal Credit (Transitional Provisions) Regulations 2014) and notification of expiry of entitlement to that benefit was not sent to the claimant before the date that the claimant's entitlement expired;".

DEFINITIONS

"the Claims and Payments Regulations"–see reg.2(1).
"existing benefit"–*ibid.*

GENERAL NOTE

3.40   Where a claim for universal credit is made by a claimant who was previously entitled to an existing benefit, this regulation modifies the application of reg.26(3) of the Claims and Payments Regulations 2013 in relation to the claimant. In practice it means that the time for claiming universal credit may be extended by up to one month, if the claimant was not given advance notice of termination of the award of existing benefit. The aim is to ensure that the same rule applies to claimants making the transition to universal credit from existing benefits as will apply in relation to universal credit and other benefits after the transitional period.

Persons unable to act

3.41   **16.** (1) Paragraph (2) applies where—

(a) a person ("P2") has been appointed, or treated as appointed, under regulation 33(1) of the Social Security (Claims and Payments) Regulations 1987 ("the 1987 Regulations") (persons unable to act) to exercise rights and to receive and deal with sums payable on behalf of a person who is unable to act ("P1"); or

(b) a person ("P2") has been appointed under regulation 18(3) of the Tax Credits (Claims and Notifications) Regulations 2002 ("the 2002 Regulations") (circumstances where one person may act for another in making a claim – other appointed persons) to act for a person who is unable to act ("P1") in making a claim for a tax credit.

(2) Where this paragraph applies and P1 is, or may be, entitled to universal credit, the Secretary of State may, if P2 agrees, treat the appointment of P2 as if it were made under regulation 57(1) of the Claims and Payments Regulations (persons unable to act) and P2 may carry out the functions set out in regulation 57(4) of those Regulations in relation to P1.

(3) Paragraph (4) applies where a person ("P2") was appointed, or treated as appointed, under regulation 57(1) of the Claims and Payments Regulations to carry out functions in relation to a person who is unable to act ("P1") and who was, or might have been, entitled to universal credit, but who has ceased to be so entitled, or was not in fact so entitled.

(4) Where this paragraph applies—

(a) the Secretary of State may, if P2 agrees, treat the appointment of P2 as if it were made under regulation 33(1) of the 1987 Regulations and P2 may exercise rights and receive and deal with sums payable in respect of existing benefits on behalf of P1; and

(b) the Board (within the meaning of the 2002 Regulations) may, if P2 agrees, treat the appointment of P2 as if it were made under regulation 18(3) of the 2002 Regulations and P2 may act for P1 in making a claim for a tax credit.

DEFINITIONS

"the 1987 Regulations"–para.(1)(a).
"the 2002 Regulations"–para.(1)(b).
"the Claims and Payments Regulations"–see reg.2(1).
"existing benefit"–*ibid.*
"tax credit"–*ibid.*

GENERAL NOTE

The effect of this regulation (which had no equivalent provision in the 2013 Transitional Regulations) is that a person who has been appointed to act on behalf of a claimant in relation to existing benefits and/or tax credits may be treated as having been appointed to act on their behalf in relation to universal credit and *vice versa*. This may be particularly relevant where claimants have mental health problems or where they suffer from other conditions that make communication with the Department very difficult or impossible. The aim of the provision is to make the process of transition between existing benefits and universal credit easier for claimants who are in this position.   3.42

[¹ Waiting days

16A. [²...]]   3.43

AMENDMENTS

1. Universal Credit (Waiting Days) (Amendment) Regulations 2015 (SI 2015/1362) reg.2(2) (August 3, 2015).
2. Universal Credit (Miscellaneous Amendments, Saving and Transitional Provision) Regulations 2018 (SI 2018/65) reg.6(11) (April 11, 2018).

Advance payments of universal credit

17. (1) This regulation applies where—   3.44

(a) the Secretary of State is deciding a claim for universal credit, other than a claim which is treated as having been made, in accordance with regulation 9(8) of the Claims and Payments Regulations;

(b) the claimant is, or was previously, entitled to an existing benefit ("the earlier award"); and

(c) if the earlier award terminated before the date on which the claim for universal credit was made, the claim for universal credit was made during the period of one month starting with the date of termination.

(2) Where this regulation applies—

(a) a single claimant may request an advance payment of universal credit;

(b) joint claimants may jointly request such a payment,

at any time during the first assessment period for universal credit.

(3) Where a request has been made in accordance with this regulation, the Secretary of State may make an advance payment to the claimant, or joint claimants, of such amount in respect of universal credit as the Secretary of State considers appropriate.

(4) After an advance payment has been made under this regulation, payments of any award of universal credit to the claimant or, in the case of joint claimants, to either or both of them, may be reduced until the amount of the advance payment is repaid.

DEFINITIONS

"assessment period"–see reg.2(1).
"the Claims and Payments Regulations"–*ibid.*
"the earlier award"–para.(1)(b).
"existing benefit"–see reg.2(1).

GENERAL NOTE

3.45   As a general rule universal credit is payable monthly in arrears (Claims and Payments Regulations 2013, reg.47(1)). Where a claim for universal credit is made by a claimant who was entitled to an existing benefit before they became entitled to universal credit, this regulation allows the claimant to apply for an advance payment of universal credit during their first assessment period (paras.(1) and (2)). The amount of any advance payment is at the discretion of the Secretary of State (para. (3)). Repayment is by reduction of subsequent payments (para.(4)).

This regulation differs from its predecessor in the 2013 Transitional Regulations (reg.19), in that new claimant partners are now no longer able to request such an advance. Instead, if the new couple require support they will have to apply for a universal credit (change of circumstances) advance. The justification for this change is that it is supposed to reduce complexity in the advance payment process.

Deductions from benefits

3.46   **18.** (1) This regulation applies where—

(a) an award of universal credit is made to a claimant who—

(i) was entitled to income-based jobseeker's allowance, income-related employment and support allowance or income support (a "relevant award") on the date on which the claim for universal credit was made or treated as made;

(ii) is a new claimant partner who was, immediately before forming a couple with a person entitled to universal credit, the partner of a person ("P") who was at that time entitled to a relevant award; or

(iii) is not a new claimant partner and was, immediately before making a claim for universal credit, the partner of a person ("P") who was at that time entitled to a relevant award, where the award of universal credit is not a joint award to the claimant and P; and

(b) on the relevant date, deductions in respect of fuel costs or water charges were being made under regulation 35 of the Social Security (Claims and Payments) Regulations 1987, in accordance with Schedule 9 to those Regulations.

(2) In this regulation, the "relevant date" means—

(a) where paragraph (1)(a)(i) applies and the claimant is not a new claimant partner, the date on which the claim for universal credit was made;

(b) where paragraph (1)(a)(i) applies and the claimant is a new claimant partner, the date on which the claim for universal credit was treated as made;

(c) where paragraph (1)(a)(ii) or (iii) applies, the date on which the claimant ceased to be the partner of P.

(3) Where this regulation applies, deductions in respect of fuel costs or, as the case may be, water charges, may be made from the award of universal credit in accordance with Schedule 6 to the Claims and Payments Regulations, without the need for any consent which would otherwise be required under paragraph 3(3) of that Schedule.

(4) For the purposes of this regulation, a deduction is to be taken into account even if the relevant award subsequently terminated by virtue of an order made under section 150(3) of the Act, regulation 7 or, as the case may be, regulation 8, before the date on which the deduction was first applied.

DEFINITIONS

"the Act"–see reg.2(1).
"the Claims and Payments Regulations"–*ibid.*
"income-based jobseeker's allowance"–*ibid.*
"income-related employment and support allowance"–*ibid.*
"income support"–*ibid.*
"new claimant partner"–*ibid.*
"partner"–*ibid.*
"relevant award"–para.(1)(a)(i).
"relevant date"–para.(2).

GENERAL NOTE

Where certain deductions were made from an award of an existing benefit (e.g. 3.47
for fuel costs or water charges), this regulation allows deductions in respect of the
same items to be made from an award of universal credit without the need for the
consents which might otherwise be required.

Transition from old style ESA

19. (1) This regulation applies where— 3.48

(a) an award of universal credit is made to a claimant who was entitled to old style ESA on the date on which the claim for universal credit was made or treated as made ("the relevant date"); and

[¹ (b) on or before the relevant date it had been determined that the claimant had limited capability for work or limited capability for work-related activity (within the meaning of Part 1 of the 2007 Act).]

(2) Where, on or before the relevant date, it had been determined that the claimant [¹ had limited capability for work (within the meaning of Part 1 of the 2007 Act)]—

(a) [¹ . . .]

(b) the claimant is to be treated as having limited capability for work for the purposes of [¹ . . .] section 21(1)(a) of the Act.

(3) [¹ . . .]

(4) Where, on or before the relevant date, it had been determined that

the claimant [¹ had limited capability for work-related activity (within the meaning of Part 1 of the 2007 Act) or was treated as having limited capability for work-related activity]—

    (a) regulation 27(3) of the Universal Credit Regulations does not apply; and

    (b) the claimant is to be treated as having limited capability for work and work-related activity for the purposes of regulation 27(1)(b) of those Regulations and section 19(2)(a) of the Act.

(5) Unless the assessment phase applied and had not ended at the relevant date, in relation to a claimant who is treated as having limited capability for work and work-related activity under paragraph (4)(4)(b)—

    (a) regulation 28 of the Universal Credit Regulations does not apply; and

    (b) the LCWRA element is (subject to the provisions of Part 4 of the Universal Credit Regulations) to be included in the award of universal credit with effect from the beginning of the first assessment period.

(6) For the purposes of this regulation, a determination that the claimant [¹ had limited capability for work or, as the case may be, limited capability for work-related activity (within the meaning of Part 1 of the 2007 Act)], is to be taken into account even if the award of old style ESA subsequently terminated (in so far as it was an award of income-related employment and support allowance) before the date on which that determination was made, by virtue of an order made under section 150(3) of the Act.

(7) Where a claimant is treated, by virtue of this regulation, as having limited capability for work or, as the case may be, limited capability for work and work-related activity, the Secretary of State may at any time make a fresh determination as to these matters, in accordance with the Universal Credit Regulations.

(8) In this regulation and in regulations 20 to 27—

[¹ "assessment phase" has the same meaning as in the 2007 Act;]

"incapacity benefit" and "severe disablement allowance" have the same meanings as in Schedule 4 to that Act;

[¹ "LCWRA element" has the same meaning as in the Universal Credit Regulations.]

(9) For the purposes of this regulation and regulation 20, references to cases in which the assessment phase applied are references to cases in which sections 2(2)(a)[¹ and 4(4)(a)] of the 2007 Act applied and references to cases in which the assessment phase did not apply are references to cases in which those sections did not apply.

[¹ (10) For the purposes of this regulation, references to a determination that the claimant had limited capability for work do not include a determination made under regulation 30 of the Employment and Support Allowance Regulations 2008 (conditions for treating a claimant as having limited capability for work until a determination about limited capability for work has been made).]

AMENDMENT

1. Employment and Support Allowance and Universal Credit (Miscellaneous Amendments and Transitional and Savings Provisions) Regulations 2017 (SI 2017/204) reg.5(2) (April 3, 2017).

DEFINITIONS

"the Act"–see reg.2(1).
"assessment period"–*ibid.*
"assessment phase"–para.(8).
"incapacity benefit"–*ibid.*
"income-based jobseeker's allowance"–see reg.2(1).
"LCW element"–para.(8).
"LCWRA element"–*ibid.*
"old style ESA"–see reg.2(1).
"the relevant date"–para.(1)(a).
"severe disablement allowance"–para.(8).
"support component"–*ibid.*
"the Universal Credit Regulations"–see reg.2(1).
"work-related activity component"–para.(8).

GENERAL NOTE

The purpose of this apparently complex provision is relatively simple. It provides   **3.49**
that a claimant may be treated as having limited capability for work, or limited capability for work and work-related activity, for the purposes of an award of universal
credit, if they were previously so assessed for the purpose of old style ESA. If the
claimant in question was in the process of assessment of their capability for work
in connection with an award of employment and support allowance at the time
the award terminated, the assessment period for universal credit will be adjusted
accordingly, under reg.20.

Transition from old style ESA before the end of the assessment phase

20. (1) This regulation applies where—   **3.50**
  (a) an award of universal credit is made to a claimant who was entitled
    to old style ESA on the date on which the claim for universal credit
    was made or treated as made ("the relevant date"); and
  (b) on the relevant date, the assessment phase in relation to the claimant
    applied and had lasted for less than 13 weeks.
  (2) Where this regulation applies—
  (a) regulation 28(2) of the Universal Credit Regulations (period for
    which the [¹ . . .] LCWRA element is not to be included) does not
    apply; and
  (b) for the purposes of regulation 28 of those Regulations, the relevant
    period is—
    (i) the period of 13 weeks starting with the first day of the assess-
      ment phase; or
    (ii) where regulation 5 of the Employment and Support Allowance
      Regulations 2008 (the assessment phase – previous claimants)
      applied to the claimant, the period which ends when the sum
      of the periods for which the claimant was previously entitled to
      old style ESA and the period for which the claimant is entitled
      to universal credit is 13 weeks.
  (3) Where, on the relevant date, the assessment phase in relation to
the claimant applied and had not ended and had lasted for more than 13
weeks—
  (a) regulation 28 of the Universal Credit Regulations does not apply;
  (b) [¹ . . .]
  (c) if it is subsequently determined in accordance with Part 5 of the

589

Universal Credit Regulations that the claimant has limited capability for work and work-related activity the LCWRA element is (subject to the provisions of Part 4 of those Regulations) to be included in the award of universal credit with effect from the beginning of the first assessment period.

(4) For the purposes of this regulation, the fact that an assessment phase applied in relation to a claimant on the relevant date is to be taken into account even if the award of old style ESA subsequently terminated (in so far as it was an award of income-related employment and support allowance) before that date by virtue of an order made under section 150(3) of the Act.

AMENDMENT

1. Employment and Support Allowance and Universal Credit (Miscellaneous Amendments and Transitional and Savings Provisions) Regulations 2017 (SI 2017/204) reg.5(3) (April 3, 2017).

DEFINITIONS

"the Act"–see reg.2(1).
"assessment period"–*ibid.*
"assessment phase"–see reg.19(8).
"income-based jobseeker's allowance"–*ibid.*
"LCW element"–see reg.19(8).
"LCWRA element"–*ibid.*
"old style ESA"–*ibid.*
"the relevant date"–para.(1)(a).
"the Universal Credit Regulations"–see reg.2(1).

GENERAL NOTE

3.51   This regulation provides that where a claimant was in the process of assessment of their capability for work in connection with an award of old style ESA at the time that award terminated, the assessment period for universal credit will be adjusted accordingly.

[¹ Transition from jobseeker's allowance following an extended period of sickness

3.52   **20A.**—(1) This regulation applies where—
  (a) the claimant's first day of entitlement to universal credit ("the relevant date"), immediately follows the claimant's last day of entitlement to a jobseeker's allowance; and
  (b) immediately before the relevant date, the claimant was treated as capable of work or as not having limited capability for work under regulation 55ZA of the Jobseeker's Allowance Regulations 1996 or regulation 46A of the Jobseeker's Allowance Regulations 2013 (extended period of sickness).
  (2) Where this regulation applies—
  (a) regulation 28(2) of the Universal Credit Regulations (period for which [¹ . . .] LCWRA element is not to be included) does not apply; and
  (b) for the purposes of regulation 28 of those Regulations, the relevant period is the period starting with the first day of the period for which

the claimant was treated as capable of work or as not having limited capability for work as specified in paragraph (1)(b).]

AMENDMENTS

1. Jobseeker's Allowance (Extended Period of Sickness) Amendment Regulations 2015 (SI 2015/339) reg.6 (March 30, 2015).
2. Employment and Support Allowance and Universal Credit (Miscellaneous Amendments and Transitional and Savings Provisions) Regulations 2017 (SI 2017/204) reg.5(4) (April 3, 2017).

DEFINITIONS

"the relevant date"–para.(1)(a).
"LCW element"–see reg.19(8).
"LCWRA element"–*ibid.*
"the Universal Credit Regulations"–see reg.2(1).

GENERAL NOTE

The Jobseeker's Allowance (Extended Period of Sickness) Amendment   3.53
Regulations 2015 (SI 2015/339) enabled jobseeker's allowance claimants suffering from a short (or third) period of sickness to choose to remain on that benefit while on what is termed as an "extended period of sickness" (EPS) for a continuous period of up to 13 weeks in a 12 month period. The same regulations also made provision to enable the employment and support allowance assessment phase (before any additional ESA components become payable) and the universal credit relevant period (before any additional universal credit elements become payable) to be reduced by the time a claimant spends on an EPS. This regulation is accordingly designed to ensure that the calculation of the universal credit relevant period includes the EPS where jobseeker's allowance claimants make a claim for universal credit and move immediately into the universal credit relevant period.

Other claimants with limited capability for work: credits only cases

21. (1) This regulation applies where—   3.54
(a) an award of universal credit is made to a claimant who was entitled to be credited with earnings equal to the lower earnings limit then in force under regulation 8B(2)(iv), (iva) or (v) of the Social Security (Credits) Regulations 1975 ("the 1975 Regulations") on the date on which the claim for universal credit was made or treated as made (the "relevant date"); and
(b) neither regulation 19 nor regulation 20 applies to that claimant (whether or not, in the case of joint claimants, either of those regulations apply to the other claimant).

(2) Where, on or before the relevant date, it had been determined that the claimant would have limited capability for work (within the meaning of Part 1 of the 2007 Act) if he or she was entitled to old style ESA—
(a) [¹ ...]
(b) the claimant is to be treated as having limited capability for work for the purposes of [¹ ...] section 21(1)(a) of the Act.
(3) [¹ ...]
(4) Where, on or before the relevant date, it had been determined that the claimant would have limited capability for work-related activity (within the meaning of Part 1 of the 2007 Act) if he or she was entitled to old style ESA—

(a) regulation 27(3) of the Universal Credit Regulations does not apply; and

(b) the claimant is to be treated as having limited capability for work and work-related activity for the purposes of regulation 27(1)(b) of those Regulations and section 19(2)(a) of the Act.

(5) Unless the notional assessment phase applied and had lasted for less than 13 weeks at the relevant date, in relation to a claimant who is treated as having limited capability for work and work-related activity under paragraph (4)—

(a) regulation 28 of the Universal Credit Regulations does not apply; and

(b) the LCWRA element is (subject to the provisions of Part 4 of the Universal Credit Regulations) to be included in the award of universal credit with effect from the beginning of the first assessment period.

(6) Where, on the relevant date, the notional assessment phase in relation to the claimant to whom the award was made applied and had lasted for less than 13 weeks—

(a) regulation 28(2) of the Universal Credit Regulations does not apply; and

(b) for the purposes of regulation 28 of those Regulations, the relevant period is the period of 13 weeks starting with the first day of the notional assessment phase.

(7) Where, on the relevant date, the notional assessment phase in relation to the claimant applied and had not ended and had lasted for more than 13 weeks—

(a) regulation 28 of the Universal Credit Regulations does not apply;

(b) [¹ . . .]

(c) if it is subsequently determined in accordance with Part 5 of those Regulations that the claimant has limited capability for work and work-related activity, the LCWRA element is (subject to the provisions of Part 4 of those Regulations) to be included in the award of universal credit with effect from the beginning of the first assessment period.

(8) Where a claimant is treated, by virtue of this regulation, as having limited capability for work or, as the case may be, limited capability for work and work-related activity, the Secretary of State may at any time make a fresh determination as to these matters, in accordance with the Universal Credit Regulations.

(9) For the purposes of this regulation—

(a) a determination that the claimant would have limited capability for work or, as the case may be, limited capability for work-related activity, if the claimant was entitled to old style ESA is to be taken into account even if the claimant subsequently ceased to be entitled as mentioned in paragraph (1)(a) before the date on which that determination was made because he or she became entitled to universal credit;

(b) the fact that a notional assessment phase applied in relation to a claimant on the relevant date is to be taken into account even if the claimant subsequently ceased to be entitled as mentioned in paragraph (1)(a) before that date because the claimant became entitled to universal credit.

(c) references to a determination that the claimant would have limited capability for work if the claimant was entitled to old style ESA do not include a determination made under regulation 30 of the Employment and Support Allowance Regulations 2008 (conditions for treating a claimant as having limited capability for work until a determination about limited capability for work has been made);

(d) references to cases in which the notional assessment phase applied are references to cases in which sections 2(2)(a) [¹ and 4(4)(a)] of the 2007 Act would have applied to the claimant if he or she had been entitled to old style ESA in addition to the entitlement mentioned in paragraph (1)(a), but do not include cases in which the claimant is entitled as mentioned in paragraph (1)(a) under regulation 8B(2) (iva) of the 1975 Regulations;

(e) subject to sub-paragraph (f), the "notional assessment phase" is the period of 13 weeks starting on the day on which the assessment phase would have started in relation to the claimant, if he or she had been entitled to old style ESA and sections 2(2)(a) [¹ and 4(4)(a)] of the 2007 Act had applied;

(f) the notional assessment phase has not ended if, at the end of the 13 week period referred to in sub-paragraph (e), no determination has been made as to whether a claimant would have limited capability for work (within the meaning of Part 1 of the 2007 Act) if the claimant was entitled to old style ESA.

AMENDMENT

1. Employment and Support Allowance and Universal Credit (Miscellaneous Amendments and Transitional and Savings Provisions) Regulations 2017 (SI 2017/204) reg.5(4) (April 3, 2017).

DEFINITIONS

"the 1975 Regulations"–para.(1)(a).
"the 2007 Act" –see reg.2(1).
"the Act"–*ibid.*
"assessment period"–*ibid.*
"assessment phase"–see reg.19(8).
"LCW element"–*ibid.*
"LCWRA element"–*ibid.*
"old style ESA"–*ibid.*
"the relevant date"–para.(1)(a).
"the Universal Credit Regulations"–see reg.2(1).

GENERAL NOTE

This regulation makes similar provision to reg.20 but for claimants who were not entitled to old style ESA, but who were entitled to credits of contributions and earnings on the grounds of limited capability for work. 3.55

Transition from income support payable on the grounds of incapacity for work or disability [¹ and other incapacity benefits]

22. (1) This regulation applies where an award of universal credit is made to a claimant [¹ (other than a claimant to whom regulation 23 or 24 applies)] who was entitled to income support on the grounds of incapacity 3.56

for work or disability on the date on which the claim for universal credit was made or treated as made [¹ or is entitled to incapacity benefit or severe disablement allowance].

(2) Where this regulation applies—

(a) if it is determined in accordance with Part 5 of the Universal Credit Regulations that the claimant has limited capability for work—

    (i) the claimant is to be treated as having had limited capability for work for the purposes of regulation 27(1)(a) of the Universal Credit Regulations (award to include LCW and LCWRA elements) from the beginning of the first assessment period;

    (ii) regulation 28 of those Regulations (period for which the LCW or LCWRA element is not to be included) does not apply; and

    (iii) the LCW element is (subject to the provisions of Part 4 of the Universal Credit Regulations) to be included in the award with effect from the beginning of the first assessment period;

(b) if it is determined in accordance with Part 5 of the Universal Credit Regulations that the claimant has limited capability for work and work-related activity—

    (i) the claimant is to be treated as having had limited capability for work and work-related activity for the purposes of regulation 27(1)(b) of the Universal Credit Regulations from the beginning of the first assessment period;

    (ii) regulation 28 of those Regulations does not apply; and

    (iii) the LCWRA element is (subject to the provisions of Part 4 of the Universal Credit Regulations) to be included in the award of universal credit with effect from the beginning of the first assessment period.

(3) In this regulation—

"income support on the grounds of incapacity for work or disability" means an award of income support which is an "existing award" within the meaning of Schedule 4 to the 2007 Act.

AMENDMENT

1. Universal Credit (Transitional Provisions) (Amendment) Regulations 2014 (SI 2014/1626) reg.5(1) (October 13, 2014).

DEFINITIONS

"the 2007 Act" –see reg.2(1).
"assessment period"–*ibid.*
"incapacity benefit"–see reg.19(8).
"income support"–*ibid.*
"income support on the grounds of incapacity for work or disability"–para.(3).
"LCW element"–see reg.19(8).
"LCWRA element"–*ibid.*
"severe disablement allowance"–*ibid.*
"the Universal Credit Regulations"–see reg.2(1).

GENERAL NOTE

3.57   The process of transition from existing incapacity benefits to universal credit is dealt with in regs.22 to 25. Transition from income support awarded on the grounds of incapacity for work or disability is dealt with in reg. 22 and transition from incapacity benefit or severe disablement allowance is dealt with in regs.23 to 25. In both cases, the limited capability for work (LCW) or limited capability for work and work-related activity (LCWRA) elements may be included in an award of universal credit with effect from the start of the first assessment period, if the claimant is subsequently assessed as having limited capability for work or, in the case of a claimant approaching pensionable age, is entitled to certain other benefits. Regulations 26 and 27 make similar provision to regs.22-25 but in respect of claimants who although they were not entitled to an incapacity benefit were entitled to credits of earnings on the grounds of incapacity for work.

The various amendments to regs 22-26 which came into effect on October 13, 2014 were designed to ensure that incapacity benefit or severe disablement allowance claimants can have the LCW or LCWRA elements applied to their universal credit award, from the start of the first assessment period where they joined or made a universal credit claim, as quickly as possible. This is sought to be achieved by ensuring they either:

- remain in the employment and support allowance conversion process and undergo a work capability assessment to determine whether their existing incapacity award qualifies for conversion to new style ESA, inclusive of either the WRA or support component and where it does, allow this decision to be used to apply the LCW or LCWRA element to their universal credit award; or

- enter the universal credit assessment process and undergo a universal credit work capability assessment to ascertain whether the LCW or LCWRA element should be applied to their award.

Before the October 2014 amendments, claimants who have not commenced ESA conversion had the choice of either entering the universal credit assessment process or waiting until they undergo conversion to ascertain whether the LCW or LCWRA element should be applied to their universal credit award. The amendments are intended to ensure that where the claimant has not entered the ESA conversion process they now have to enter the universal credit process, if they want to be assessed and have the LCW or LCWRA element backdated. The significance of this change is that if they do not enter the universal credit assessment process they would have to wait until they are scheduled for ESA conversion to see if their existing incapacity award qualified for conversion to new style ESA, before the LCW or LCWRA element could be applied to their universal credit award. This is supposed to avoid any delay in these claimants accessing the additional financial support they will be entitled to if it is decided that they have LCW or LCWRA.

The amending regulations also ensure that where incapacity benefit claimants are in receipt of National Insurance credits only, and are not entitled to the appropriate level or component of a prescribed benefit to allow them to qualify for the LCW or LCWRA element in universal credit, that they will be treated in the same way as those incapacity benefit or severe disablement allowance claimants and will not have to serve the universal credit relevant period but can have the LCW or LCWRA element applied to their universal credit award, with retrospective effect, back to the start of the first assessment period, if it is subsequently determined by a universal credit work capability assessment that they have either LCW or LCWRA.

Transition from other incapacity benefits [1: assessment under the 2010 Regulations]

23. (1) This regulation applies where—
   (a) an award of universal credit is made to a claimant who is entitled to incapacity benefit or severe disablement allowance [1 ("the relevant award")]; and
   [1(b) on or before the date on which the claim for universal credit is made

3.58

or treated as made, a notice has been issued to the claimant under regulation 4 of the Employment and Support Allowance (Transitional Provisions, Housing Benefit and Council Tax Benefit) (Existing Awards) (No.2) Regulations 2010 ("the 2010 Regulations") (notice commencing the conversion phase).]

[¹ (1A) Where this regulation applies, regulations 27(3) (award to include LCW and LCWRA elements) and 38 (determination of limited capability for work and work-related activity) of the Universal Credit Regulations do not apply and the question whether a claimant has limited capability for work, or for work and work-related activity, is to be determined, for the purposes of the Act and the Universal Credit Regulations, in accordance with this regulation.]

(2) [¹ Where it is determined in accordance with the 2010 Regulations that the relevant award qualifies for conversion into an award in accordance with regulation 7 of those Regulations (qualifying for conversion) and that award includes the work-related activity component]—

(a) [¹ ...];
(b) the claimant is to be treated as having had limited capability for work for the purposes of regulation 27(1)(a) of the Universal Credit Regulations from the beginning of the first assessment period;
(c) regulation 28(1) of those Regulations (period for which LCW or LCWRA element is not to be included) does not apply;
(d) the LCW element is (subject to the provisions of Part 4 of the Universal Credit Regulations) to be included in the award of universal credit with effect from the beginning of the first assessment period; and
(e) the claimant is to be treated as having limited capability for work for the purposes of section 21(1)(a) of the Act.

(3) [¹ Where it is determined in accordance with the 2010 Regulations that the relevant award qualifies for conversion into an award in accordance with regulation 7 of those Regulations and that award includes the support component]—

(a) [¹ ...];
(b) the claimant is to be treated as having had limited capability for work and work-related activity for the purposes of regulation 27(1)(b) of the Universal Credit Regulations from the beginning of the first assessment period;
(c) regulation 28(1) of those Regulations does not apply;
(d) the LCWRA element is (subject to the provisions of Part 4 of the Universal Credit Regulations) to be included in the award of universal credit with effect from the beginning of the first assessment period; and
(e) the claimant is to be treated as having limited capability for work and work-related activity for the purposes of section 19(2)(a) of the Act.

AMENDMENT

1. Universal Credit (Transitional Provisions) (Amendment) Regulations 2014 (SI 2014/1626) reg.5(2) (October 13, 2014).

DEFINITIONS

"the 2010 Regulations"–para.(1)(b).
"the Act"–see reg.2(1).

"assessment period"–*ibid.*
"incapacity benefit"–see reg.19(8).
"LCW element"–*ibid.*
"LCWRA element"–*ibid.*
"the relevant award"–para.(1)(a).
"severe disablement allowance"–see reg.19(8).
"support component"–*ibid.*
"the Universal Credit Regulations"–see reg.2(1).
"work-related activity component"–see reg.19(8).

GENERAL NOTE

See General Note to reg.22.   3.59

Transition from other incapacity benefits: claimants approaching pensionable age

24. (1) This paragraph applies where—   3.60

(a) an award of universal credit is made to a claimant who is entitled to incapacity benefit or severe disablement allowance;

(b) no notice has been issued to the claimant under regulation 4 (notice commencing the conversion phase) of the Employment and Support Allowance (Transitional Provisions, Housing Benefit and Council Tax Benefit) (Existing Awards) (No.2) Regulations 2010 ("the 2010 Regulations");

(c) the claimant will reach pensionable age (within the meaning of the 2010 Regulations) within the period of one year; and

(d) the claimant is also entitled to—

(i) personal independence payment, where neither the daily living component nor the mobility component is payable at the enhanced rate;

(ii) disability living allowance under section 71 of the Social Security Contributions and Benefits Act 1992 ("the 1992 Act"), where the care component is payable at the middle rate within the meaning of section 72(4) of that Act or the mobility component is payable at the lower rate within the meaning of section 73(11) of that Act (or both components are payable at those rates);

(iii) attendance allowance under section 64 of the 1992 Act, where the allowance is payable at the lower rate in accordance with section 65 of that Act;

(iv) an increase in the weekly rate of disablement pension under section 104 of the 1992 Act (increase where constant attendance needed), where the increase is of an amount which is equal to or less than the amount specified in paragraph 2(a) of Part V of Schedule 4 to that Act; or

(v) any payment based on the need for attendance which is paid as an addition to a war disablement pension (which means any retired pay or pension or allowance payable in respect of disablement under an instrument specified in section 639(2) of the Income Tax (Earnings and Pensions) Act 2003), where the amount of that payment is equal to or less than the amount specified in paragraph 2(a) of Part V of Schedule 4 to the 1992 Act.

(2) Where paragraph (1) applies and paragraph (3) does not apply—

(a) regulation 27(3) of the Universal Credit Regulations (award to include LCW and LCWRA elements) does not apply;

(b) the claimant is to be treated as having limited capability for work for the purposes of regulation 27(1)(a) of those Regulations from the beginning of the first assessment period;

(c) regulation 28(1) of the Universal Credit Regulations (period for which LCW or LCWRA element is not to be included) does not apply;

(d) the LCW element is (subject to the provisions of Part 4 of the Universal Credit Regulations) to be included in the award of universal credit with effect from the beginning of the first assessment period; and

(e) the claimant is to be treated as having limited capability for work for the purposes of section 21(1)(a) of the Act.

(3) This paragraph applies where—

(a) an award of universal credit is made to a claimant who is entitled to incapacity benefit or severe disablement allowance;

(b) no notice has been issued to the claimant under regulation 4 of the 2010 Regulations;

(c) the claimant will reach pensionable age (within the meaning of the 2010 Regulations) within the period of one year; and

(d) the claimant is also entitled to—

    (i) personal independence payment, where either the daily living component or the mobility component is (or both components are) payable at the enhanced rate;

    (ii) disability living allowance under section 71 of the 1992 Act, where the care component is payable at the highest rate within the meaning of section 72(4) of that Act or the mobility component is payable at the higher rate within the meaning of section 73(11) of that Act (or both components are payable at those rates);

    (iii) attendance allowance under section 64 of the 1992 Act, where the allowance is payable at the higher rate in accordance with section 65 of that Act;

    (iv) armed forces independence payment under the Armed Forces and Reserve Forces (Compensation Scheme) Order 2011;

    (v) an increase in the weekly rate of disablement pension under section 104 of the 1992 Act, where the increase is of an amount which is greater than the amount specified in paragraph 2(a) of Part V of Schedule 4 to that Act; or

    (vi) any payment based on the need for attendance which is paid as an addition to a war disablement pension (which means any retired pay or pension or allowance payable in respect of disablement under an instrument specified in section 639(2) of the Income Tax (Earnings and Pensions) Act 2003), where the amount of that payment is greater than the amount specified in paragraph 2(a) of Part V of Schedule 4 to the 1992 Act.

(4) Where paragraph (3) applies (whether or not paragraph (1) also applies)—

(a) regulation 27(3) of the Universal Credit Regulations does not apply;

(b) the claimant is to be treated as having limited capability for work and work-related activity for the purposes of regulation 27(1)(b) of those Regulations from the beginning of the first assessment period;

(c) regulation 28(1) of the Universal Credit Regulations does not apply;

(d) the LCWRA element is (subject to the provisions of Part 4 of the Universal Credit Regulations) to be included in the award of universal credit with effect from the beginning of the first assessment period; and

(e) the claimant is to be treated as having limited capability for work and work-related activity for the purposes of section 19(2)(a) of the Act.

DEFINITIONS

"the 1992 Act"–para.(1)(d)(ii).
"the 2010 Regulations"–para.(1)(b).
"the Act"–see reg.2(1).
"assessment period"–*ibid.*
"incapacity benefit"–see reg.19(8).
"LCW element"–*ibid.*
"LCWRA element"–*ibid.*
"severe disablement allowance"–*ibid.*
"the Universal Credit Regulations"–see reg.2(1).
"work-related activity component"–see reg.19(8).

GENERAL NOTE

See General Note to reg.22.   **3.61**

Transition from other incapacity benefits: supplementary

25. (1) Where an award of universal credit is made to a claimant who is **3.62** entitled to incapacity benefit or severe disablement allowance, regulation 66 of the Universal Credit Regulations (what is included in unearned income?) applies to the claimant as if incapacity benefit or, as the case may be, severe disablement allowance were added to the descriptions of unearned income in paragraph (1)(b) of that regulation.

(2) For the purposes of regulations [¹ 22,] 23 and 24 and this regulation only, incapacity benefit and severe disablement allowance are prescribed benefits under paragraph 1(2)(b) of Schedule 6 to the Act.

AMENDMENT

1. Universal Credit (Transitional Provisions) (Amendment) Regulations 2014 (SI 2014/1626) reg.5(3) (October 13, 2014).

DEFINITIONS

"the Act"–see reg.2(1).
"incapacity benefit"–see reg.19(8).
"severe disablement allowance"–*ibid.*
"the Universal Credit Regulations"–see reg.2(1).

GENERAL NOTE

See General Note to reg.22.   **3.63**

Other claimants with incapacity for work: credits only cases where claimant is approaching pensionable age

3.64

26. (1) This regulation applies where—

(a) an award of universal credit is made to a claimant who was entitled to be credited with earnings equal to the lower earnings limit then in force under regulation 8B(2)(a)(i), (ii) or (iii) of the Social Security (Credits) Regulations 1975 on the date on which the claim for universal credit was made or treated as made;

(b) the claimant will reach pensionable age within the meaning of the Employment and Support Allowance (Transitional Provisions, Housing Benefit and Council Tax Benefit) (Existing Awards) (No.2) Regulations 2010 within the period of one year; and

(c) [¹ none of regulations 22, 23 or 24 apply] to that claimant (whether or not, in the case of joint claimants, [¹ any] of those regulations apply to the other claimant).

(2) Where the claimant is entitled to a payment, allowance or increased rate of pension specified in regulation 24(1)(d) and is not entitled to a payment, allowance or increased rate of pension specified in regulation 24(3)(d)—

(a) regulation 27(3) of the Universal Credit Regulations (award to include LCW and LCWRA elements) does not apply;

(b) the claimant is to be treated as having limited capability for work for the purposes of regulation 27(1)(a) of those Regulations from the beginning of the first assessment period;

(c) regulation 28(1) of the Universal Credit Regulations (period for which the LCW or LCWRA element is not to be included) does not apply;

(d) the LCW element is (subject to the provisions of Part 4 of the Universal Credit Regulations) to be included in the award of universal credit with effect from the beginning of the first assessment period; and

(e) the claimant is to be treated as having limited capability for work for the purposes of section 21(1)(a) of the Act.

(3) Where the claimant is entitled to a payment, allowance or increased rate of pension specified in regulation 24(3)(d) (whether or not the claimant is also entitled to a payment, allowance or increased rate of pension specified in regulation 24(1)(d))—

(a) regulation 27(3) of the Universal Credit Regulations does not apply;

(b) the claimant is to be treated as having limited capability for work and work-related activity for the purposes of regulation 27(1)(b) of those Regulations from the beginning of the first assessment period;

(c) regulation 28(1) of the Universal Credit Regulations does not apply;

(d) the LCWRA element is (subject to the provisions of Part 4 of the Universal Credit Regulations) to be included in the award of universal credit with effect from the beginning of the first assessment period; and

(e) the claimant is to be treated as having limited capability for work and work-related activity for the purposes of section 19(2)(a) of the Act.

[¹ (4) Where the claimant is not entitled to a payment, allowance or increased rate of pension specified in either regulation 24(1)(d) or regulation 24(3)(d)—

(a) if it is determined in accordance with Part 5 of the Universal Credit Regulations that the claimant has limited capability for work—

    (i) the claimant is to be treated as having had limited capability for work for the purposes of regulation 27(1)(a) of the Universal Credit Regulations from the beginning of the first assessment period;

    (ii) regulation 28 of the Universal Credit Regulations does not apply; and

    (iii) the LCW element is (subject to the provisions of Part 4 of the Universal Credit Regulations) to be included in the award with effect from the beginning of the first assessment period; and

(b) if it is determined in accordance with Part 5 of the Universal Credit Regulations that the claimant has limited capability for work and work-related activity—

    (i) the claimant is to be treated as having had limited capability for work and work-related activity for the purposes of regulation 27(1)(b) of the Universal Credit Regulations from the beginning of the first assessment period;

    (ii) regulation 28 of the Universal Credit Regulations does not apply; and

    (iii) the LCWRA element is (subject to the provisions of Part 4 of the Universal Credit Regulations) to be included in the award of universal credit with effect from the beginning of the first assessment period.]

AMENDMENT

1. Universal Credit (Transitional Provisions) (Amendment) Regulations 2014 (SI 2014/1626) reg.5(4) (October 13, 2014).

DEFINITIONS

"the Act"–see reg.2(1).
"assessment period"–*ibid.*
"LCW element"–see reg.19(8).
"LCWRA element"–*ibid.*
"the Universal Credit Regulations"–see reg.2(1).
"the work-related activity component"–see reg.19(8).

GENERAL NOTE

Regulations 26 and 27 make similar provision to regs 22-25 but in respect of claimants who although they were not entitled to an incapacity benefit were entitled to credits of earnings under the Social Security (Credits) Regulations 1975 (SI 1975/556) on the grounds of incapacity for work.   3.65

Other claimants with incapacity for work: credits only cases

27. (1) This regulation applies where—   3.66

(a) an award of universal credit is made to a claimant who was entitled to be credited with earnings equal to the lower earnings limit then in force under regulation 8B(2)(a)(i), (ii) or (iii) of the Social Security (Credits) Regulations 1975 on the date on which the claim for universal credit was made or treated as made; and

(b) none of regulations 22, 23, 24 or 26 apply to that claimant (whether or not, in the case of joint claimants, any of those regulations apply to the other claimant).

(2) Where this regulation applies—

(a) if it is determined in accordance with Part 5 of the Universal Credit Regulations that the claimant has limited capability for work—

    (i) the claimant is to be treated as having had limited capability for work for the purposes of regulation 27(1)(a) of the Universal Credit Regulations (award to include LCW and LCWRA elements) from the beginning of the first assessment period;

    (ii) regulation 28 of the Universal Credit Regulations (period for which the LCW or LCWRA element is not to be included) does not apply; and

    (iii) the LCW element is (subject to the provisions of Part 4 of the Universal Credit Regulations) to be included in the award with effect from the beginning of the first assessment period;

(b) if it is determined in accordance with Part 5 of the Universal Credit Regulations that the claimant has limited capability for work and work-related activity—

    (i) the claimant is to be treated as having had limited capability for work and work-related activity for the purposes of regulation 27(1)(b) of the Universal Credit Regulations from the beginning of the first assessment period;

    (ii) regulation 28 of the Universal Credit Regulations does not apply; and

    (iii) the LCWRA element is (subject to the provisions of Part 4 of the Universal Credit Regulations) to be included in the award of universal credit with effect from the beginning of the first assessment period.

DEFINITIONS

"assessment period"–see reg.2(1).
"LCW element"–see reg.19(8).
"LCWRA element"–*ibid.*
"the Universal Credit Regulations"–see reg.2(1).

GENERAL NOTE

3.67   See General Notes to regs 22 and 26.

Meaning of "qualifying young person"

3.68   **28.** Where a person who would (apart from the provision made by this regulation) be a "qualifying young person" within the meaning of regulation 5 of the Universal Credit Regulations is entitled to an existing benefit—

(a) that person is not a qualifying young person for the purposes of the Universal Credit Regulations; and

(b) regulation 5(5) of those Regulations applies as if, after "a person who is receiving" there were inserted "an existing benefit (within the meaning of the Universal Credit (Transitional Provisions) Regulations 2014),".

Definitions

"existing benefit"–see reg.2(1).
"the Universal Credit Regulations"–*ibid.*

General Note

This regulation ensures that payments may not be made as part of an award of   **3.69**
universal credit in respect of a young person who is entitled to existing benefits in
their own right. Such persons cannot be claimed for by a parent or carer for the
purposes of the Universal Credit Regulations 2013.

Support for housing costs

29. (1) Paragraph (3) applies where—   **3.70**
(a) an award of universal credit is made to a claimant who—
  (i) was entitled to income-based jobseeker's allowance, income-
    related employment and support allowance or income support
    (a "relevant award") at any time during the period of one month
    ending with the day on which the claim for universal credit was
    made or treated as made (or would have been so entitled were it
    not for termination of that award by virtue of an order made under
    section 150(3) of the Act or the effect of these Regulations); or
  (ii) was at any time during the period of one month ending with the
    day on which the claim for universal credit was made or treated
    as made, the partner of a person ("P") who was at that time
    entitled to a relevant award, where the award of universal credit
    is not a joint award to the claimant and P; and
(b) on the relevant date, the relevant award included an amount in
  respect of housing costs under—
  (i) [² paragraph 16 of Schedule 2] to the Jobseeker's Allowance
    Regulations 1996 ("the 1996 Regulations");
  (ii) [² paragraph 18 of Schedule 6] to the Employment and Support
    Allowance Regulations 2008 ("the 2008 Regulations"); or, as
    the case may be,
  (iii) [² paragraph 17 of Schedule 3] to the Income Support (General)
    Regulations 1987 ("the 1987 Regulations").
(2) In this regulation, the "relevant date" means—
(a) where paragraph (1)(a)(i) applies and the claimant was not entitled
  to the relevant award on the date on which the claim for universal
  credit was made or treated as made, the date on which the relevant
  award terminated;
(b) where paragraph (1)(a)(i) applies, the claimant is not a new claimant
  partner and he or she was entitled to the relevant award on the date
  on which the claim for universal credit was made, that date;
(c) where paragraph (1)(a)(i) applies, the claimant is a new claimant
  partner and he or she was entitled to the relevant award on the date
  on which the claim for universal credit was treated as made, that date;
(d) where paragraph (1)(a)(ii) applies, the date on which the claimant
  ceased to be the partner of P or, if earlier, the date on which the relevant award terminated.
(3) Where this paragraph applies, paragraph 5 of Schedule 5 to the
Universal Credit Regulations (no housing costs element under this Schedule
for qualifying period) does not apply.

(4) Paragraph (5) applies where paragraph (1)(a) applies, but the relevant award did not include an amount in respect of housing costs because the claimant's entitlement (or, as the case may be, P's entitlement) was nil by virtue of—
  (a) paragraph 6(1)(c) or 7(1)(b) of Schedule 2 to the 1996 Regulations;
  (b) paragraph 8(1)(c) or 9(1)(b) of Schedule 6 to the 2008 Regulations; or, as the case may be,
  (c) paragraph 6(1)(c) or 8(1)(b) of Schedule 3(4) to the 1987 Regulations.
(5) Where this paragraph applies—
  (a) paragraph 5(2) of Schedule 5 to the Universal Credit Regulations does not apply; and
  (b) the "qualifying period" referred to in paragraph 5 of that Schedule is the period of [¹ 273] days starting with the first day on which the claimant (or, as the case may be, P) was entitled to the relevant award, taking into account any period which was treated as a period of continuing entitlement under—
    (i) paragraph 13 of Schedule 2 to the 1996 Regulations;
    (ii) paragraph 15 of Schedule 6 to the 2008 Regulations; or, as the case may be,
    (iii) paragraph 14 of Schedule 3 to the 1987 Regulations,
provided that, throughout that part of the qualifying period after the award of universal credit is made, receipt of universal credit is continuous and the claimant otherwise qualifies for the inclusion of an amount calculated under Schedule 5 to the Universal Credit Regulations in their award.
(6) For the purposes of—
  (a) paragraph (1)(b) of this regulation, inclusion of an amount in respect of housing costs in a relevant award is to be taken into account even if the relevant award subsequently terminated by virtue of an order made under section 150(3) of the Act, regulation 7 or, as the case may be, regulation 8, before the date on which that amount was included in the award;
  (b) paragraph (5)(b) of this regulation, entitlement to a relevant award is to be treated as having continued until the relevant date even if the award subsequently terminated by virtue of an order made under section 150(3) of the Act, regulation 7 or, as the case may be, regulation 8, before that date.

AMENDMENTS

1. Social Security (Housing Costs Amendments) Regulations 2015 (SI 2015/1647) reg.6 (April 1, 2016).
2. Loans for Mortgage Interest Regulations 2017 (2017/725) Sch.5 para.6 (April 6, 2018).

DEFINITIONS

"the 1987 Regulations"–para.(1)(b)(iii).
"the 1996 Regulations"–para.(1)(b)(i).
"the 2008 Regulations"–para.(1)(b)(ii).
"the Act" –see reg.2(1).
"income-based jobseeker's allowance"–*ibid.*
"income-related employment and support allowance"–*ibid.*

"income support"–*ibid.*
"new claimant partner"–*ibid.*
"partner"–*ibid.*
"qualifying period"–para.(5)(b).
"relevant award"–para.(1)(a)(i).
"relevant date"–para.(2).
"the Universal Credit Regulations"–see reg.2(1).

GENERAL NOTE

This is a hideously opaque regulation. Where a universal credit claimant or their   3.71
partner was previously entitled to old style JSA, old style ESA or income support,
this regulation allows for any support for housing costs which was included in that
award (paras.(1) and (2)), or time spent waiting to qualify for such support (paras.
(4)-(6)), to be carried over to the award of universal credit (para.(3)), providing
the claimant is entitled to the universal credit housing element. The amendment to
para.(5)(b) is subject to the saving provision in reg.8 of the Social Security (Housing
Costs Amendments) Regulations 2015 (SI 2015/1647).

Sanctions: transition from old style ESA

30. (1) This regulation applies where—   3.72
   (a) an award of universal credit is made to a claimant who was previ-
       ously entitled to old style ESA ("the ESA award"); and
   (b) on the relevant date, payments in respect of the ESA award were
       reduced under regulation 63 of the Employment and Support
       Allowance Regulations 2008 ("the 2008 Regulations").
(2) In this regulation, the "relevant date" means—
   (a) where the claimant was not entitled to old style ESA on the date on
       which the claim for universal credit was made or treated as made, the
       date on which the ESA award terminated;
   (b) where the claimant is not a new claimant partner and was entitled to
       old style ESA on the date on which the claim for universal credit was
       made, that date;
   (c) where the claimant is a new claimant partner and was entitled to old
       style ESA on the date on which the claim for universal credit was
       treated as made, that date.
(3) Where this regulation applies—
   (a) the failure which led to reduction of the ESA award ("the ESA
       failure") is to be treated, for the purposes of the Universal Credit
       Regulations, as a failure which is sanctionable under section 27 of
       the Act;
   (b) the award of universal credit is to be reduced in relation to the ESA
       failure, in accordance with the provisions of this regulation and
       Chapter 2 of Part 8 of the Universal Credit Regulations (sanctions),
       as modified by this regulation; and
   (c) the reduction is to be treated, for the purposes of the Universal
       Credit Regulations, as a reduction under section 27 of the Act.
(4) The reduction period for the purposes of the Universal Credit
Regulations is a period of the number of days which is equivalent to the
length of the fixed period applicable to the person under regulation 63(7)
of the 2008 Regulations in relation to the ESA failure, minus—
   (a) the number of days (if any) in that period in respect of which the
       amount of old style ESA was reduced; and
   (b) if the ESA award terminated before the first date of entitlement to

universal credit in connection with the current award, the number of days (if any) in the period after termination of that award, before the start of the universal credit award.

(5) Accordingly, regulation 101 of the Universal Credit Regulations (general principles for calculating reduction periods) applies in relation to the ESA failure as if, in paragraphs (1) and (3), for "in accordance with regulations 102 to 105", there were substituted "in accordance with regulation 30 of the Universal Credit (Transitional Provisions) Regulations 2014".

(6) For the purposes of this regulation, a determination that payments in respect of the ESA award are to be reduced under regulation 63 of the 2008 Regulations is to be taken into account even if the ESA award subsequently terminated (in so far as it was an award of income-related employment and support allowance) on a date before the date on which that determination was made, by virtue of an order made under section 150(3) of the Act.

DEFINITIONS

> "the 2008 Regulations"–para.(1)(b).
> "the Act"–see reg.2(1).
> "the ESA award"–para.(1)(a).
> "the ESA failure"–para.(3)(a).
> "income-related employment and support allowance"–*ibid.*
> "new claimant partner"–*ibid.*
> "old style ESA"–*ibid.*
> "relevant date"–para.(2).
> "the Universal Credit Regulations"–see reg.2(1).

GENERAL NOTE

3.73   Regulations 30 to 34 deal with the treatment of any sanctions which have been imposed on awards of old style JSA and old style ESA, prior to a claimant's transition to universal credit. The underlying principle is one of equivalence of treatment. Such pre-existing sanctions will continue to have effect by way of deductions from the award of universal credit and past sanctions will also be taken into account for the purposes of determining the level of sanction applicable to any future sanctionable failure. However, where there is a period of entitlement to an existing benefit between two periods of entitlement to universal credit, any sanctions arising prior to that intervening period will not be taken into account.

So, for example, where a new universal credit claimant was previously entitled to ESA, and subject to an ESA sanction for failure to take part in a work-focussed interview or to undertake a work-related activity, the ESA failure is treated as a sanctionable failure for the purposes of universal credit (paras.(1) and (3)). The reduction period is adjusted accordingly (para.(4)).

Escalation of sanctions: transition from old style ESA

3.74   **31.** (1) This regulation applies where an award of universal credit is made to a claimant who was at any time previously entitled to old style ESA.

(2) Where this regulation applies, for the purposes of determining the reduction period under regulation 104 of the Universal Credit Regulations (low-level sanction) in relation to a sanctionable failure by the claimant, other than a failure which is treated as sanctionable by virtue of regulation 30—

(a) a reduction of universal credit in accordance with regulation 30; and
(b) any reduction of old style ESA under the Employment and Support

Allowance Regulations 2008 ("the 2008 Regulations") which did
not result in a reduction under regulation 30,
is, subject to paragraph (3), to be treated as arising from a sanctionable
failure for which the reduction period which applies is the number of days
which is equivalent to the length of the fixed period which applied under
regulation 63 of the 2008 Regulations.

(3) In determining a reduction period under regulation 104 of the
Universal Credit Regulations in accordance with paragraph (2), no account
is to be taken of—

(a) a reduction of universal credit in accordance with regulation 30 if, at
any time after that reduction, the claimant was entitled to an existing
benefit;

(b) a reduction of old style ESA under the 2008 Regulations if, at any
time after that reduction, the claimant was entitled to universal
credit, new style ESA or new style JSA, and was subsequently entitled to an existing benefit.

DEFINITIONS

"the 2008 Regulations"–para.(2)(b).
"existing benefit" "–see reg.2(1).
"new style ESA"–*ibid.*
"new style JSA"–*ibid.*
"old style ESA"–*ibid.*
"the Universal Credit Regulations"–*ibid.*

GENERAL NOTE

This provision ensures that any previous ESA fixed period reductions are taken   3.75
into account when deciding the appropriate reduction period for the purposes of a
universal credit sanction.

Sanctions: transition from old style JSA

32. (1) This regulation applies where—   3.76

(a) an award of universal credit is made to a claimant who was previously entitled to old style JSA ("the JSA award");

(b) on the relevant date, payments in respect of the JSA award were
reduced under section 19 (as it applied either before or after substitution by the Act) or section 19A of the Jobseekers Act 1995 ("the
1995 Act"), or under regulation 69B of the Jobseeker's Allowance
Regulations 1996 ("the 1996 Regulations"); and

(c) if the JSA award was made to a joint-claim couple within the
meaning of the 1995 Act and the reduction related to—

(i) in the case of a reduction under section 19 as it applied before
substitution by the Act, circumstances relating to only one
member of the couple; or,

(ii) in the case of a reduction under section 19 as it applied after
substitution by the Act, a sanctionable failure by only one
member of the couple,

the award of universal credit was made to that person.

(2) In this regulation, the "relevant date" means—

(a) where the claimant was not entitled to old style JSA on the date on
which the claim for universal credit was made or treated as made, the
date on which the JSA award terminated;

(b) where the claimant is not a new claimant partner and was entitled to old style JSA on the date on which the claim for universal credit was made, that date;

(c) where the claimant is a new claimant partner and was entitled to old style JSA on the date on which the claim for universal credit was treated as made, that date.

(3) Where this regulation applies—

(a) the circumstances or failure which led to reduction of the JSA award (in either case, "the JSA failure") is to be treated, for the purposes of the Universal Credit Regulations, as—

    (i) a failure which is sanctionable under section 26 of the Act, where the reduction was under section 19 of the 1995 Act; or

    (ii) a failure which is sanctionable under section 27 of the Act, where the reduction was under section 19A of the 1995 Act or regulation 69B of the 1996 Regulations;

(b) the award of universal credit is to be reduced in relation to the JSA failure, in accordance with the provisions of this regulation and Chapter 2 of Part 8 of the Universal Credit Regulations (sanctions), as modified by this regulation; and

(c) the reduction is to be treated, for the purposes of the Universal Credit Regulations, as a reduction under section 26 or, as the case may be, section 27 of the Act.

(4) The reduction period for the purposes of the Universal Credit Regulations is a period of the number of days which is equivalent to the length of the period of reduction which is applicable to the person under regulation 69, 69A or 69B of the 1996 Regulations, minus—

(a) the number of days (if any) in that period in respect of which the amount of old style JSA was reduced; and

(b) if the award of old style JSA terminated before the first date of entitlement to universal credit in connection with the current award, the number of days (if any) in the period after termination of that award, before the start of the universal credit award.

(5) Accordingly, regulation 101 of the Universal Credit Regulations applies in relation to the JSA failure as if, in paragraphs (1) and (3), for "in accordance with regulations 102 to 105", there were substituted "in accordance with regulation 32 of the Universal Credit (Transitional Provisions) Regulations 2014".

(6) Where the JSA award was made to a joint-claim couple within the meaning of the 1995 Act and the JSA failure related to only one member of the couple, the daily reduction rate for the purposes of the Universal Credit Regulations is the amount calculated in accordance with regulation 70(3) of the 1996 Regulations in respect of the JSA award, divided by seven and rounded down to the nearest 10 pence, unless regulation 111(2) or (3) of the Universal Credit Regulations (daily reduction rate) applies.

(7) Where the daily reduction rate is to be determined in accordance with paragraph (6), regulation 111(1) of the Universal Credit Regulations applies in relation to the JSA failure as if, for the words from "an amount equal to" to the end there were substituted the words "an amount determined in accordance with regulation 32 of the Universal Credit (Transitional Provisions) Regulations 2014".

(8) For the purposes of this regulation, a determination that payments in respect of the JSA award are to be reduced under regulation 69, 69A or 69B

of the 1996 Regulations is to be taken into account even if the JSA award subsequently terminated (in so far as it was an award of income-based job-seeker's allowance) on a date before the date on which that determination was made, by virtue of an order made under section 150(3) of the Act.

DEFINITIONS

"the 1995 Act"–para.(1)(b).
"the 1996 Regulations"–para.(1)(b).
"the 2002 Act" –see reg.2(1).
"income-based jobseeker's allowance"–*ibid.*
"the JSA award"–para.(1)(a).
"the JSA failure"–para.(3)(a).
"new claimant partner" –see reg.2(1).
"new style ESA"–*ibid.*
"new style JSA"–*ibid.*
"old style JSA"–*ibid.*
"relevant date"–para.(2).
"the Universal Credit Regulations"–see reg.2(1).

GENERAL NOTE

This has similar effect for JSA as reg.30 does for ESA. It is designed to ensure that current JSA sanctions carry forward into the universal credit scheme.   3.77

Escalation of sanctions: transition from old style JSA

33. (1) This regulation applies where an award of universal credit is made   3.78
to a claimant who was at any time previously entitled to old style JSA.

(2) Where this regulation applies, for the purposes of determining the applicable reduction period under regulation 102 (higher-level sanction), 103 (medium-level sanction) or 104 (low-level sanction) of the Universal Credit Regulations in relation to a sanctionable failure by the person, other than a failure which is treated as sanctionable by virtue of regulation 32—

(a) a reduction of universal credit in accordance with regulation 32; and

(b) any reduction of old style JSA under section 19 or 19A of the Jobseekers Act 1995 ("the 1995 Act"), or under regulation 69B of the 1996 Regulations which did not result in a reduction under regulation 32,

is, subject to paragraph (3), to be treated as arising from a sanctionable failure for which the reduction period is the number of days which is equivalent to the length of the period which applied under regulation 69, 69A or 69B of the 1996 Regulations.

(3) In determining a reduction period under regulation 102, 103 or 104 of the Universal Credit Regulations in accordance with paragraph (2), no account is to be taken of—

(a) a reduction of universal credit in accordance with regulation 32 if, at any time after that reduction, the claimant was entitled to an existing benefit;

(b) a reduction of old style JSA under section 19 or 19A of the 1995 Act, or under regulation 69B of the 1996 Regulations if, at any time after that reduction, the claimant was entitled to universal credit, new style ESA or new style JSA, and was subsequently entitled to an existing benefit.

DEFINITIONS

"the 1995 Act"–para.(2)(b).
"the 1996 Regulations"–see reg.32(1)(b).
"existing benefit"–see reg.2(1).
"new style ESA"–*ibid.*
"new style JSA"–*ibid.*
"old style JSA"–*ibid.*
"the Universal Credit Regulations"–*ibid.*

GENERAL NOTE

3.79 This is the JSA equivalent of reg.31, which applies to ESA.

Sanctions: temporary return to certain existing benefits

3.80 **34.** If an award of universal credit terminates while there is an outstanding reduction period (within the meaning of regulation 107 of the Universal Credit Regulations) and the claimant becomes entitled to old style JSA, old style ESA or income support ("the relevant benefit") during that period—
 (a) regulation 107 of the Universal Credit Regulations (reduction period to continue where award terminates) ceases to apply; and
 (b) the reduction period is to terminate on the first date of entitlement to the relevant benefit.

DEFINITIONS

"income support"–see reg.2(1).
"old style ESA"–*ibid.*
"old style JSA"–*ibid.*
"relevant benefit"–see reg.34.
"the Universal Credit Regulations"–see reg.2(1).

GENERAL NOTE

3.81 This provision has the effect that where a claimant comes off universal credit and claims one of the former benefits (e.g. JSA, because he is no longer in a relevant area), then if he subsequently becomes entitled again to universal credit (e.g. by forming a couple with a universal credit claimant) then the universal credit sanction does not bite, even if it had on the face of it not expired. This is because the reduction period is deemed as having terminated on the first day of the award of the existing benefit such as JSA.

Loss of benefit penalties: transition from existing benefits other than tax credits

3.82 **35.** (1) Subject to paragraph (6), this regulation applies in the cases set out in paragraphs (2) to (4).
 (2) The first case is where—
 (a) an award of universal credit is made to a claimant who is an offender;
 (b) the claimant was entitled to old style JSA, old style ESA, income support or housing benefit ("the earlier award") at any time during the period of one month ending with the date on which the claim for universal credit was made or treated as made (or would have been so entitled were it not for termination of that award by virtue of an order made under section 150(3) of the Act or, as the case may be, the effect of these Regulations); and
 (c) payments in respect of the earlier award were, on the relevant date,

subject to a restriction under section 6B (loss of benefit in case of conviction, penalty or caution for benefit offence), 7 (repeated benefit fraud) or 8 (effect of offence on joint-claim jobseeker's allowance) of the 2001 Act.

(3) The second case is where—

(a) an award of universal credit is made to a claimant who is an offender;

(b) another person who was the offender's family member (but is no longer their family member) was entitled to old style JSA, old style ESA, income support or housing benefit ("the earlier award") at any time during the period of one month ending with the date on which the claim for universal credit was made or treated as made; and

(c) payments in respect of the earlier award were, on the relevant date, subject to a restriction under section 9 (effect of offence on benefits for members of offender's family) of the 2001 Act.

(4) The third case is where—

(a) an award of universal credit is made to a claimant who is an offender's family member;

(b) the offender, or the claimant, was entitled to old style JSA, old style ESA, income support or housing benefit ("the earlier award") at any time during the period of one month ending with the date on which the claim for universal credit was made or treated as made; and

(c) payments in respect of the earlier award were, on the relevant date, subject to a restriction under section 6B, 7, 8 or, as the case may be, 9 of the 2001 Act.

(5) Where this regulation applies—

(a) any subsequent payment of universal credit to the claimant in respect of an assessment period which falls wholly or partly within the remainder of the disqualification period applicable to the offender is to be reduced in accordance with regulation 36; and

(b) regulation 3ZB of the 2001 Regulations does not apply.

(6) This regulation does not apply if the earlier award was a joint-claim jobseeker's allowance and—

(a) payments in respect of the award were, on the relevant date, subject to a restriction under section 8(2) of the 2001 Act; or

(b) the award of universal credit is not made to joint claimants who were, on the relevant date, both entitled to the joint-claim jobseeker's allowance.

(7) In this regulation and in regulation 36—

"the 2001 Act" means the Social Security Fraud Act 2001;

"the 2001 Regulations" means the Social Security (Loss of Benefit) Regulations 2001;

"disqualification period" has the meaning given in the 2001 Act, interpreted in accordance with the 2001 Regulations;

"earlier award" is to be interpreted in accordance with paragraph (2)(b), (3)(b) or, as the case may be, (4)(b) and, for the purposes of regulation 36, where there is more than one earlier award, the term refers to the award to which the claimant became entitled most recently;

"offender" means an offender within the meaning of the 2001 Act;

"offender's family member" has the same meaning as in the 2001 Act;

"the relevant date" means—

(a) in relation to the first case—

(i) where the claimant was not entitled to the earlier award on the date on which the claim for universal credit was made or treated as made, the date on which the earlier award terminated;

    (ii) where the claimant is not a new claimant partner and was entitled to the earlier award on the date on which the claim for universal credit was made, that date;

    (iii) where the claimant is a new claimant partner and was entitled to the earlier award on the date on which the claim for universal credit was treated as made, that date;

(b) in relation to the second case, the date on which the person entitled to the earlier award ceased to be the offender's family member or, if the award terminated before that date, the date on which the earlier award terminated;

(c) in relation to the third case—

    (i) where the claimant was entitled to the earlier award but that entitlement terminated before the date on which the claim for universal credit was made or treated as made, the date on which the earlier award terminated;

    (ii) where the claimant is not a new claimant partner and was entitled to the earlier award on the date on which the claim for universal credit was made, that date;

    (iii) where the claimant is a new claimant partner and was entitled to the earlier award on the date on which the claim for universal credit was treated as made, that date;

    (iv) where the offender's family member was entitled to the earlier award, the date on which that person ceased to be the offender's family member or, if earlier, the date on which the earlier award terminated.

(8) For the purposes of this regulation, the fact that payments in respect of an earlier award were subject to a restriction is to be taken into account, even if the earlier award subsequently terminated before the date on which payments became subject to a restriction by virtue of an order made under section 150(3) of the Act (in so far as it was an award of income-based jobseeker's allowance or income-related employment and support allowance), regulation 7 or, as the case may be, regulation 8.

DEFINITIONS

"the 2001 Act"–para.(7).
"the 2001 Regulations"–*ibid.*
"the 2002 Act"–see reg.2(1).
"assessment period"–*ibid.*
"the disqualification period"–para.(7).
"earlier award"–*ibid.*
"housing benefit"–see reg.2(1).
"income support"–*ibid.*
"income-based jobseeker's allowance"–*ibid.*
"income-related employment and support allowance"–*ibid.*
"joint-claim jobseeker's allowance"–*ibid.*
"new claimant partner"–*ibid.*
"offender"—para.(7)
"offender's family member"—*ibid.*
"old style ESA"–see reg.2(1).
"old style JSA"–*ibid.*
"the relevant date"–para.(7).

GENERAL NOTE

This provision (taken with reg.36) has the effect that where a claimant moves to   **3.83**
universal credit within one month of the end of an award of an existing benefit and
is subject to a loss of benefit penalty, the penalty will in most cases continue on the
basis of the rate applicable to the existing benefit for the remainder of the disqualification period. The usual rules relating to calculation of penalties within universal
credit will not apply.

Loss of benefit penalties: reduction of universal credit

36. (1) Subject to paragraph (6) [¹ and to regulation 38], where regula-   **3.84**
tion 35 applies, the amount of a reduction of universal credit in respect of an
assessment period is to be calculated by multiplying the daily reduction rate
by the number of days in the assessment period, unless paragraph (2) applies.

(2) Where the disqualification period ends during an assessment period,
the amount of the reduction for that assessment period is (subject to paragraph (6)) to be calculated by multiplying the daily reduction rate by the
number of days in the assessment period which are within the disqualification period.

(3) Subject to paragraphs (4) and (5), the daily reduction rate where
regulation 35 applies is an amount which is equal to—

(a) the monetary amount by which payments in respect of the earlier
    award were reduced in accordance with section 6B or 7 of the 2001
    Act or, as the case may be, regulation 3, 3ZA or 17 of the 2001
    Regulations in respect of the last complete week before the relevant
    date (within the meaning of regulation 35);
(b) multiplied by 52;
(c) divided by 365; and
(d) rounded down to the nearest 10 pence.

(4) Where the monetary amount by which payments in respect of the
earlier award would have been reduced would, if the claimant had remained
entitled to the earlier award, have changed during the disqualification
period because of an order made under section 150 of the Social Security
Administration Act 1992 (annual up-rating of benefits)—

(a) the daily reduction rate is to be calculated in accordance with
    paragraph (3), but on the basis of the new amount by which pay-
    ments would have been reduced; and
(b) any adjustment to the reduction of universal credit is to take effect
    from the first day of the first assessment period to start after the date
    of the change.

(5) Where the earlier award was a joint-claim jobseeker's allowance, the
daily reduction rate is an amount which is equal to—

(a) the amount of the standard allowance applicable to the joint claim-
    ants under regulation 36 of the Universal Credit Regulations (table
    showing amounts of elements);
(b) multiplied by 12;
(c) divided by 365;
(d) reduced by 60%; and
(e) rounded down to the nearest 10 pence.

(6) The amount of the reduction under this regulation in respect of any
assessment period is not to exceed the amount of the standard allowance
which is applicable to the claimant in respect of that period.

AMENDMENTS

1. Universal Credit (Transitional Provisions) (Amendment) Regulations 2014 (SI 2014/1626) reg.6(1) (October 13, 2014).

DEFINITIONS

"the 2001 Act"–see reg.35(7).
"the 2001 Regulations"–*ibid.*
"assessment period"–see reg.2(1).
"the disqualification period"–see reg.35(7).
"earlier award"–*ibid.*
"joint-claim jobseeker's allowance"–see reg.2(1).
"the relevant date"–see reg.35(7).
"the Universal Credit Regulations"–see reg.2(1).

GENERAL NOTE

3.85   See General Note to reg.35. Note also that as compared with reg.35 of the 2013 Transitional Regulations provision for the transfer of loss of benefit penalties for fraudulent offences to a universal credit award has been amended in relation to the transfer of penalties from joint-claim JSA awards to an award of universal credit (para.(5)). In these cases the amount of the penalty applied to the universal credit award is reduced by 60%, if only one of the joint JSA claimants is subject to a penalty. This reflects the position in JSA where the member of the joint-claim couple who is not the benefit fraud offender can be paid JSA at the single person's rate.

[¹ Loss of benefit penalties: transition from working tax credit

3.86   **37.** (1) This regulation applies where an award of universal credit is made to a claimant who—

(a) was previously entitled to working tax credit; and
(b) is an offender, within the meaning of the 2002 Act.

(2) Where this regulation applies, the Social Security (Loss of Benefit) Regulations 2001 apply as if in regulation 3ZB of those Regulations—

(a) in paragraph (1) at the beginning there were inserted "Subject to regulation 38 of the Universal Credit (Transitional Provisions) Regulations 2014,";
(b) "disqualification period" includes a disqualification period within the meaning of the 2002 Act;
(c) "offender" includes an offender within the meaning of the 2002 Act; and
(d) "offender's family member" includes a person who is a member of the family (within the meaning of section 137(1) of the Social Security Contributions and Benefits Act 1992 of a person who is an offender within the meaning of the 2002 Act.]

AMENDMENTS

1.   Universal Credit (Transitional Provisions) (Amendment) Regulations 2014 (SI 2014/1626) reg.6(2) (October 13, 2014).

DEFINITIONS

"the 2002 Act"–see reg.2(1).
"working tax credit"–*ibid.*

This regulation provides that where a working tax credit (WTC) claimant has a **3.87** fraud penalty applied to their WTC award, the fraud penalty will be applied to the universal credit standard allowance, for the remaining period of that penalty. As a consequence, reg.38 below ensures that where a claimant has been in receipt of WTC and another existing benefit (e.g. housing benefit) and both awards have had a fraud penalty applied to them, the combination of these penalties will not exceed the universal credit standard allowance in any assessment period. This follows the approach taken with existing Department for Work and Pensions benefits where there is more than one fraud penalty applied to an existing benefit award upon the transition to universal credit.

[¹ Loss of benefit penalties: maximum total reduction

38. Where regulations 35 and 37 both apply to a claimant, the total amount **3.88** of a reduction of universal credit in respect of any assessment period under—
  (a) regulation 36; and
  (b) regulation 3ZB of the Social Security (Loss of Benefit) Regulations 2001,
must not exceed the amount of the standard allowance which is applicable to the claimant in respect of that period.]

Amendment

1. Universal Credit (Transitional Provisions) (Amendment) Regulations 2014 (SI 2014/1626) reg.6(2) (October 13, 2014).

Definitions

"assessment period"–see reg.2(1).

General Note

See General Note to reg.37. **3.89**

[¹ PART 3

ARRANGEMENTS REGARDING CHANGES TO THE CHILD ELEMENT FROM APRIL 2017

Restriction on claims for universal credit during the interim period

39.—[² ...]] **3.90**

Amendments

1. Social Security (Restrictions on Amounts for Children and Qualifying Young Persons) Amendment Regulations 2017 (2017/376) reg.3(3) (April 6, 2017).
2. Universal Credit (Restriction on Amounts for Children and Qualifying Young Persons) (Transitional Provisions) Amendment Regulations 2019 (SI 2019/27) reg.2 (February 1, 2019).

General Note

The repeal of this regulation is a consequence of the Government's decision to remove the retrospective application of the "two child rule" in universal credit. Under WRWA 2016, Government policy was to provide support in the CTC and universal credit regimes for a maximum of two children (with some exceptions). This rule applied to claims for children born on or after April 6, 2017 (the date that the legislation relating to the policy to provide support for a maximum of two children came into force). During an interim period following the introduction of the policy, new claims for families with three or more children were to be directed to tax credits and the child element in universal credit was to be paid for all children born before April 6, 2017. This interim period was due to come to an end on February 1, 2019. From that date, the policy was to apply to all new claims to universal credit regardless of the date of birth of the child. From that date, new claims for families with three or more children are no longer directed to tax credits and instead are made to universal credit. As a result of the Government announcement of January 11, 2019, families with three or more children will continue to receive an additional amount in universal credit for all children born before April 6, 2017.

[¹ Availability of the child element where maximum exceeded – transitionally protected children and qualifying young persons

3.91   **40.**—[² ...]]

AMENDMENTS

1. Social Security (Restrictions on Amounts for Children and Qualifying Young Persons) Amendment Regulations 2017 (2017/376) reg.3(3) (April 6, 2017).
2. Universal Credit (Restriction on Amounts for Children and Qualifying Young Persons) (Transitional Provisions) Amendment Regulations 2019 (SI 2019/27) reg.2 (February 1, 2019).

GENERAL NOTE

See General Note to reg.39.

[¹ Availability of the child element where maximum exceeded – continuation of exception from a previous award of child tax credit, income support or old style JSA

3.92   **41.**—(1) Where—
(a) the claimant ("C") is the step-parent of a child or qualifying young person ("A"); and
(b) within the 6 months immediately preceding the first day on which C became entitled to an award of universal credit, C had an award of child tax credit, income support or old style JSA in which an exception corresponding with an exception under paragraph 2, 3, 5 or 6 of Schedule 12 to the Universal Credit Regulations applied in respect of A,
paragraph 6 of that Schedule is to apply as if sub-paragraph (c) of that paragraph were satisfied, despite the fact that the previous award was not an award of universal credit.

(2) In this regulation, "step-parent" has the same meaning as in the Universal Credit Regulations.]

AMENDMENT

1. Social Security (Restrictions on Amounts for Children and Qualifying Young Persons) Amendment Regulations 2017 (2017/376) reg.3(3) (April 6, 2017).

[¹ Evidence for non-consensual conception where claimant previously had an award of child tax credit

3.93   **42.**—(1) This regulation applies for the purposes of paragraph 5 of Schedule 12(7) to the Universal Credit Regulations (exception for non-consensual conception).

(2) The Secretary of State may treat the condition in sub-paragraph (3)(a) of that paragraph 5 as met if the Secretary of State is satisfied that the claimant has previously provided the evidence referred to in that sub-paragraph to the Commissioners for her Majesty's Revenue and Customs for the purposes of the corresponding exception in relation to child tax credit.]

AMENDMENT

1. Social Security (Restrictions on Amounts for Children and Qualifying Young Persons) Amendment Regulations 2017 (2017/376) reg.3(3) (April 6, 2017).

[¹ Abolition of higher amount of the child element for first child or qualifying young person – saving where claimant responsible for a child or qualifying young person born before 6th April 2017

43. Section 14(5)(b) of the Welfare Reform and Work Act 2016(8) (which 3.94
amends the Universal Credit Regulations by omitting the amount of the child element payable for the first child or qualifying young person) does not apply where the claimant is responsible for a child or qualifying young person born before 6th April 2017.]

AMENDMENT

1. Social Security (Restrictions on Amounts for Children and Qualifying Young Persons) Amendment Regulations 2017 (2017/376) reg.3(3) (April 6, 2017).

[¹*Regulation 12A [²1]

[¹PART 4

MANAGED MIGRATION TO UNIVERSAL CREDIT

The Migration Process

Migration notice

44.—(1) The Secretary of State may, at any time, issue a notice ("a migra- 3.94.1
tion notice") to a person who is entitled to an award of an existing benefit—
   (a) informing the person that all awards of any existing benefits to which they are entitled are to terminate and that they will need to make a claim for universal credit; and
   (b) specifying a day ("the deadline day") by which a claim for universal credit must be made.

(2) The migration notice may contain such other information as the Secretary of State considers appropriate.

(3) The deadline day must not be within the period of three months beginning with the day on which the migration notice is issued.

(4) If the person who is entitled to an award of an existing benefit is, for the purposes of that award, a member of a couple or a member of a polygamous marriage, the Secretary of State must also issue the migration notice to the other member (or members).

(5) The Secretary of State may cancel a migration notice issued to any person—

(a) if it has been issued in error;

(b) if the Secretary of State has made a determination in accordance with regulation 4 (discretion to determine that claims for universal credit may not be made) that would affect a claim by that person; or

(c) in any other circumstances where the Secretary State considers it necessary to do so in the interests of the person, or any class of person, or to safeguard the efficient administration of universal credit.

(6) A "notified person" is a person to whom a migration notice has been issued.]

AMENDMENT

1. Universal Credit (Managed Migration Pilot and Miscellaneous Amendments) Regulations 2019 (SI 2019/1152) reg.3(7) (July 24, 2019).

DEFINITIONS

"deadline day" see para.(1)(b).
"existing benefit" see reg.2(1).
"migration notice" see para.(1).
"notified person" see para.(6).

GENERAL NOTE

3.94.2
Universal credit was first introduced on April 29, 2013. Initially claimants were required to satisfy the so-called "Pathfinder Group" and later the "gateway" conditions, in what were known as "live service" areas. As from November 26, 2014, it became possible to claim universal credit in "full service" or "digital service" areas without satisfying those criteria. Since December 12, 2018, all GB postcode districts and part-districts have been converted to digital service areas, in which universal credit must be claimed instead of one of the existing benefits (subject to certain exceptions where a legacy benefit may be claimed). Claimants of existing benefits who have had a change of circumstances have moved to universal credit by the process known as "natural migration". The next phase in the roll-out of universal credit is "managed migration", whereby claimants of existing benefits are invited to make a claim for universal credit under the new Pt 4 of these Regulations. In the first instance this is being introduced on a pilot basis. The full roll-out of "managed migration" is (currently) expected to take place between November 2020 and late 2023.

This regulation provides for the issue of a migration notice, which in effect formally kick-starts the process of managed migration (although, according to official guidance, "before a migration notice is issued, claimants are informed about the migration process to ensure that they are ready to claim UC": see *DMG Chapter M7: Managed migration pilot and Transitional protection* para.M7041). The migration notice informs a person that their existing benefits are to terminate and gives a deadline for claiming universal credit. Note that in the first instance at least this process is limited to a pilot, both geographically and numerically. The managed migration pilot, which is expected to last for up to 18 months, is initially confined to the Harrogate area and to a maximum of 10,000 awards of universal credit. However, the Harrogate pilot was temporarily suspended on March 30, 2020, owing to the coronavirus crisis.

Regulation 2 (Managed migration pilot: limit on number of cases migrated) of the Universal Credit (Managed Migration Pilot and Miscellaneous Amendments) Regulations 2019 (SI 2019/1152), in force with effect from July 24, 2019, provides as follows:

"2. When the number of awards of universal credit made to persons to whom a notice has been issued under regulation 44 (migration notice) of the Universal Credit (Transitional Provisions) Regulations 2014 reaches 10,000, the Secretary of State must not issue further notices under that regulation."

A person who receives a migration notice is a "notified person" (see para.(6)). A notice is only a migration notice if it contains two pieces of information (although other information may be included (para.(2)). First, the notice must inform "the person that all awards of any existing benefits to which they are entitled are to terminate and that they will need to make a claim for universal credit" (para.(1)(a))—thus transfer is not automatic, and a claim must be made. Second, the notice must also specify the day ("the deadline day") by which a claim for universal credit must be made (para.(1)(b)). Deadline day must not fall within 3 months of the date of issue of the migration notice (para.(3)) and may be extended (see reg.45). Where couples are concerned each member must be issued with a migration notice (para. (4)). Notices can be cancelled in the circumstances set out in para.(5)).

[¹Extension of the deadline day

45.—(1) The Secretary of State may determine that the deadline day should be changed to a later day either—   3.94.3

  (a) on the Secretary of State's own initiative; or

  (b) if a notified person requests such a change before the deadline day, where there is a good reason to do so.

(2) The Secretary of State must inform the notified person or persons of the new deadline day.]

AMENDMENT

1. Universal Credit (Managed Migration Pilot and Miscellaneous Amendments) Regulations 2019 (SI 2019/1152) reg.3(7) (July 24, 2019).

DEFINITIONS

"deadline day" see reg.44(1)(b).
"notified person" see reg.44(6).

GENERAL NOTE

This provides in very general terms for the circumstances in which the deadline   3.94.4
for making a universal credit claim following issue of a migration notice can be extended. The deadline may be extended by the Secretary of State on her own initiative or on receipt of a request from the notified person. All that is required (in either instance) is "a good reason to do so". There is no statutory definition of "good reason". The non-exhaustive list of examples in the official guidance refers to cases where the claimant has difficulty completing the universal credit claim because they have a physical or mental health condition, have learning difficulties, are in or about to go in to hospital as an in-patient, have significant caring responsibilities, are homeless or face a domestic emergency (*DMG Chapter M7: Managed migration pilot and Transitional protection* para M7080). Providing the criteria are met, there is no limit to the potential number of extensions that can be made (although cancellation under reg.44(5) may be more appropriate) but in any case the notified person must be advised of the new deadline (para.(2)). The official guidance also asserts that there is no right to a mandatory reconsideration or appeal about being issued with a migration notice, the deadline day or a refusal to extend a deadline or cancel the notice. This guidance is presumably based on the premise that such actions are not "made on a claim for, or on an award of, a relevant benefit" within s.12 SSA 1998 and, as they are not included within Sch.3 to that Act, do not carry a right of appeal.

It may, however, be possible to challenge such an action indirectly as a "building block" to an "outcome decision" (e.g. no valid migration notice served so decision to terminate existing award is incorrect). Such a challenge to extension notices may raise issues analogous to those in R(TC) 1/05. Failing that, in theory at least, judicial review must be available for a potential challenge.

[¹Termination of existing benefits if no claim before the deadline

3.94.5   **46.**—(1) Where a notified person has not made a claim for universal credit on or before the deadline day, all awards of any existing benefits to which the person is entitled terminate—

(a) in the case of housing benefit, on the last day of the period of two weeks beginning with the deadline day; and

(b) in the case of any other existing benefit, on the day before the deadline day.

(2) An award of housing benefit to which a claimant is entitled in respect of specified accommodation or temporary accommodation does not terminate by virtue of this regulation.

(3) Where paragraph (1) applies and the notified person makes a claim for universal credit—

(a) after the deadline day; and

(b) on or before the final deadline specified in paragraph (4),

then, notwithstanding anything in regulation 26 of the Claims and Payments Regulations (time within which a claim for universal credit is to be made) as modified by regulation 15 of these Regulations, the award is to commence on the deadline day.

(4) The final deadline is the day that would be the last day of the first assessment period in relation to an award commencing on the deadline day.

(5) This regulation is subject to regulation 47.]

AMENDMENT

1. Universal Credit (Managed Migration Pilot and Miscellaneous Amendments) Regulations 2019 (SI 2019/1152) reg.3(7) (July 24, 2019).

DEFINITIONS

"assessment period" see reg.2(1).
"deadline day" see reg.44(1)(b).
"existing benefit" see reg.2(1).
"final deadline" see para.(4).
"housing benefit" see reg.2(1).
"migration notice" see reg.44(1).
"notified person" see reg.44(6).
"specified accommodation" see reg.2(1).
"temporary accommodation *ibid.*

GENERAL NOTE

3.94.6   This provides for termination of all awards of any existing benefits where a notified person does not claim universal credit by the deadline day (para.(1)). However, the DWP has indicated that it has no intention to use these powers during the pilot phase – rather action will be taken to encourage the claimant to make a claim for universal credit.

In the case of an income-based JSA or income-related ESA, "terminate" means treating the award in the same way as if WRA 2012 s.33(1)(a) or (b) (abolition of those benefits) and associated provisions had come into force. This means that any contribution-based or contributory allowance to which a claimant is entitled becomes an award of new style JSA or new style ESA (as defined in reg.2 of the 2014 Regulations). Where the person claims universal credit by the final deadline (which is the last day of the first assessment period of an award commencing on the deadline day) the award is backdated to the deadline day (paras.(3) and (4)). See also reg.47 (para.(5)).

[¹Notified persons who claim as a different benefit unit

47.—(1) This regulation applies where—   3.94.7
  (a) notified persons who were a couple for the purposes of an award of an existing benefit when the migration notice was issued are single persons or members of a different couple for the purposes of a claim for universal credit; or
  (b) notified persons who were members of a polygamous marriage for the purposes of an award of an existing benefit when the migration notice was issued are a couple or single persons for the purposes of a claim for universal credit.

(2) If any of those notified persons makes a claim for universal credit on or before the deadline day then, notwithstanding anything in regulation 8 (termination of awards of certain existing benefits: other claimants), all awards of any existing benefits to which any of those persons is entitled terminate—
  (a) in the case of housing benefit, on the last day of the period of two weeks beginning with the earliest day on which any of those persons is entitled to universal credit in connection with a claim (or, in a case where the person is not entitled to universal credit, on the day they would have been entitled if all the basic and financial conditions had been met); or
  (b) in the case of any other existing benefit, on the day before the "earliest day" referred to in sub-paragraph (a).

(3) If, where paragraph (2) applies—
  (a) a notified person makes a claim for universal credit—
      (i) on or before the deadline day, or
      (ii) after the deadline day, but on or before the "final deadline" referred to in regulation 46(4); and
  (b) there would otherwise be a gap between the termination of existing benefits and the commencement of the award,
the award is to commence on the "earliest day" referred to in paragraph (2)(a).

(4) If none of those notified persons makes a claim for universal credit on or before the deadline day, all awards of any existing benefits to which any of them is entitled terminate in accordance with regulation 46(1), and regulation 46(3) applies in relation to any subsequent claim by any of those persons.

(5) An award of housing benefit to which a claimant is entitled in respect of specified accommodation or temporary accommodation does not terminate by virtue of this regulation.]

AMENDMENT

1. Universal Credit (Managed Migration Pilot and Miscellaneous Amendments) Regulations 2019 (SI 2019/1152) reg.3(7) (July 24, 2019).

"deadline day" see reg.44(1)(b).
"existing benefit" see reg.2(1).
"housing benefit" *ibid*.
"migration notice" see reg.44(1).
"notified person" see reg.44(6).
"specified accommodation" see reg.2(1).
"temporary accommodation *ibid*.

GENERAL NOTE

3.94.8 This provides for cases where notified persons have been treated as a couple (or members of a polygamous marriage) in relation to an existing benefit, but claim universal credit as different benefit units, for example as single persons, or as a different couple. If there is more than one possible date on which the existing benefits could terminate, they are to terminate on the earliest of those dates and a claim by the other notified person or persons is backdated to that date.

Transitional Protection

[¹Meaning of "qualifying claim"

3.94.9 **48.** A "qualifying claim" is a claim for universal credit by a single claimant who is a notified person or by joint claimants, both of whom are notified persons, where the claim is made on or before the final deadline (see regulation 46(4)).]

AMENDMENT

1. Universal Credit (Managed Migration Pilot and Miscellaneous Amendments) Regulations 2019 (SI 2019/1152) reg.3(7) (July 24, 2019).

DEFINITIONS

"final deadline" see reg.46(4).
"notified person" see reg.44(6).

GENERAL NOTE

3.94.10 The Secretary of State is required (see new regs 48 and 49) to determine whether transitional protection applies where the person makes a "qualifying claim" as defined by this provision. It follows these arrangements for transitional protection apply only to cases subject to *managed* migration, and not to cases affected by *natural* migration (e.g. owing to a change of circumstances). The two types of transitional protection are a "transitional capital disregard" (reg.51) and a "transitional element" (regs 52 to 55). The *transitional capital disregard* enables claimants entitled to tax credits and with capital above £16,000 to be entitled to universal credit for up to 12 months (technically 12 assessment periods). The *transitional element* is an additional amount of universal credit based on the difference between the total amount of existing benefits and the amount of universal credit entitlement. This is added to the award before income is deducted and erodes as other elements increase.

But see also reg.58, enabling the Secretary of State to specify a later commencement date for an award on a qualifying claim.

[¹Meaning of "migration day"

3.94.11 **49.** "Migration day", in relation to a qualifying claim, means the day before the first day on which the claimant is entitled to universal credit in connection with that claim.]

AMENDMENT

1. Universal Credit (Managed Migration Pilot and Miscellaneous Amendments) Regulations 2019 (SI 2019/1152) reg.3(7) (July 24, 2019).

DEFINITION

qualifying claim" see reg.48.

GENERAL NOTE

Migration day, being the day before the start of a universal credit award, is used as the marker to calculate any transitional protection due.

3.94.12

[¹Secretary of State to determine whether transitional protection applies

50.—(1) Before making a decision on a qualifying claim the Secretary of State must first determine whether—

3.94.13

(a) a transitional capital disregard is to apply; or

(b) a transitional element is to be included,

(or both) in the calculation of the award.

(2) But the Secretary of State is not to determine whether a transitional element is to be included in a case where regulation 47 (notified persons who claim as a different benefit unit) applies.]

AMENDMENT

1. Universal Credit (Managed Migration Pilot and Miscellaneous Amendments) Regulations 2019 (SI 2019/1152) reg.3(7) (July 24, 2019).

DEFINITIONS

"notified person" see reg.44(6).
"qualifying claim" see reg.48.
"transitional capital disregard" see reg.51.
"transitional element" see reg.52.

GENERAL NOTE

Subject to the special cases in para.(2), the Secretary of State is under a duty to determine whether transitional protection applies on a qualifying claim. This must be done "*before*" making a decision on a qualifying claim". The sequencing is important as otherwise the universal credit conditions of entitlement may not be satisfied or the amount of universal credit to which the claimant might be entitled might be less than any income taken into account. In addition, of course, transitional protection applies only to a qualifying claim (see reg.48), i.e. a claim made on or before the final deadline. Claimants who fail to claim under the managed migration rules will not be entitled to transitional protection even if they manage to make a successful claim at a later date. As the Explanatory Memorandum puts it:

3.94.14

"7.4 Provided that existing benefit claimants (and their partner, if they have one) make the UC claim by the deadline day specified in the notification, existing benefits will be paid up until the day before they made their UC claim and Transitional Protection will be considered. If they do not make a new UC claim by the deadline day, their existing benefits will end and will be paid up until the day before that day.

7.5 If claimants contact the Department after the deadline date but within one month of their existing benefits ending, their UC claim will automatically be backdated to the deadline date and Transitional Protection can be applied to the UC award. If a claimant does not contact the Department until after a month after the deadline date they were given, their claim will not be considered as a managed migration claim which means their claim will be assessed under the UC regulations5 without the consideration or award of Transitional Protection."

[¹The transitional capital disregard

3.94.15   **51.**—(1) A transitional capital disregard is to apply where, on the migration day, the claimant—

(a) is entitled to an award of a tax credit; and

(b) has capital exceeding £16,000.

(2) Where a transitional capital disregard applies, any capital exceeding £16,000 is to be disregarded for the purposes of—

(a) determining whether the financial condition in section 5(1)(a) or 5(2)(a) of the Act (capital limit) is met; and

(b) calculating the amount of an award of universal credit (including the indicative UC amount).

(3) Where a transitional capital disregard has been applied in the calculation of an award of universal credit but, in any assessment period, the claimant no longer has (or joint claimants no longer have) capital exceeding £16,000, the transitional capital disregard is not to apply in any subsequent assessment period.

(4) A transitional capital disregard is not to apply for more than 12 assessment periods.]

AMENDMENT

1. Universal Credit (Managed Migration Pilot and Miscellaneous Amendments) Regulations 2019 (SI 2019/1152) reg.3(7) (July 24, 2019).

DEFINITIONS

"assessment period" see reg.2(1).
"migration day" see reg.49.
"tax credit" see reg.2(1).

GENERAL NOTE

3.94.16   Tax credit entitlement is not subject to any capital limit whereas universal credit claimants must not have capital over £16,000. The transitional capital disregard allows capital over £16,000 in the hands of former tax credit claimants to be disregarded for 12 months where the relevant conditions are satisfied (the 12 months need not be consecutive). The transitional capital disregard ceases to apply in the circumstances set out in para.(3) or those in reg.56.

[¹The transitional element

3.94.17   **52.**—(1) A transitional element is to be included in the calculation of an award if the total amount of any awards of existing benefits determined in accordance with regulation 53 ("the total legacy amount") is greater than the amount of an award of universal credit determined in accordance with regulation 54 ("the indicative UC amount").

(2) Where a transitional element is to be included in the calculation of an award, the amount of that element is to be treated, for the purposes of section 8 of the Act (calculation of awards), as if it were an additional amount to be included in the maximum amount under section 8(2) before the deduction of income under section 8(3).]

AMENDMENT

1. Universal Credit (Managed Migration Pilot and Miscellaneous Amendments) Regulations 2019 (SI 2019/1152) reg.3(7) (July 24, 2019).

DEFINITIONS

"existing benefit" see reg.2(1).
"indicative UC amount" see reg.54.
"total legacy amount" see reg.53.

GENERAL NOTE

Transitional protection in the form of a "transitional element" applies (see para. (1)) if the "total legacy amount" (in effect the previous entitlement under existing benefits on the day before change-over—see reg.53) is more than the "indicative UC amount" (see reg.54). This method has been "designed to provide a balanced, like-for-like comparison of entitlement under the two regimes" (Explanatory Memorandum, para.7.15). Where transitional element applies, the difference is included in the universal credit award as a transitional element. It is treated as an additional amount to be included in the maximum amount of universal credit before the deduction of income (para.(2)). Rounding rules apply as under reg.61. The transitional element is no longer included in an award in the circumstances specified in reg.56. If the indicative UC amount is more than the total legacy amount, then obviously no such element is included.

3.94.18

[¹The transitional element – total legacy amount

53.—(1) The total legacy amount is the sum of the representative monthly rates of all awards of any existing benefits to which a claimant is, or joint claimants are, entitled on the migration day.

3.94.19

Tax credits

(2) To calculate the representative monthly rate of an award of working tax credit or child tax credit—
  (a) take the figure for the daily rate of the award on the migration day provided by HMRC and calculated on the basis of the information as to the claimant's circumstances held by HMRC on that day; and
  (b) convert to a monthly figure by multiplying by 365 and dividing by 12.

(3) For the purposes of paragraph (2)(a) "the daily rate" is—
  (a) in a case where section 13(1) of the 2002 Act applies (relevant income does not exceed the income threshold or the claimant is entitled to a prescribed social security benefit), the maximum rate of each element to which the claimant is entitled on the migration day divided by 365; and
  (b) in any other case, the rate that would be produced by applying regulations 6 to 9 of the Tax Credits (Income Thresholds and

Determination of Rates) Regulations 2002(**6**) as if the migration day were a relevant period of one day.

IS, JSA (IB) and ESA (IR)

(4) To calculate the representative monthly rate of an award of income support, income-based jobseeker's allowance or income-related employment and support allowance—
 (a) take the weekly rate on the migration day calculated in accordance with—
   (i) in the case of income support, Part 7 of the Social Security Contributions and Benefits Act 1992 and the Income Support (General) Regulations 1987,
   (ii) in the case of income-based jobseeker's allowance, Part 1 of the Jobseekers Act 1995 and the Jobseeker's Allowance Regulations 1996, or
   (iii) in the case of income-related employment and support allowance, Part 1 of the 2007 Act, the Employment and Support Allowance Regulations 2008 and the Employment and Support Allowance (Transitional Provisions, Housing Benefit and Council Tax Benefit) (Existing Awards) (No.2) Regulations 2010,
on the basis of the information held by the Secretary of State on that day; and
 (b) convert to a monthly figure by multiplying by 52 and dividing by 12.
(5) The amount of an award of income-related employment and support allowance or income-based jobseeker's allowance is to be calculated before any reduction for a sanction.
(6) Where—
 (a) a claimant who is entitled to income-based jobseeker's allowance is also entitled to contribution-based jobseeker's allowance; or
 (b) a claimant who is entitled to income-related employment and support allowance is also entitled to a contributory allowance,
then, notwithstanding section 4(8) to (11) of the Jobseekers Act 1995 and section 6(3) to (7) of the 2007 Act (excess over the contributory allowance to be treated as attributable to the income-based, or income-related, allowance) the weekly rate in paragraph (4) is to be calculated as the applicable amount less the claimant's income (if any).

Housing benefit

(7) To calculate the representative monthly rate of an award of housing benefit—
 (a) take the weekly rate on the migration day calculated in accordance with Part 7 of the Social Security Contributions and Benefits Act 1992 and the Housing Benefit Regulations 2006, on the basis of the information held by the Secretary of State on that day, and convert to a monthly figure by multiplying by 52 and dividing by 12; or
 (b) in a case where the claimant has rent free periods, calculate the annual rate by multiplying the weekly rate (as above) by the number of weeks in the year in respect of which the claimant is liable to pay rent, and convert to a monthly figure by dividing by 12.

(8) For the purposes of paragraph (7), if the migration day falls in a rent free period, the weekly rate of housing benefit is to be calculated by reference to the amount of rent for the last complete week that was not a rent free period.

(9) In paragraphs (7) and (8) "rent free period" has the meaning in regulation 81 of the Housing Benefit Regulations 2006.

(10) In a case where regulation 8(3) (continuation of housing benefit in respect of specified accommodation or temporary accommodation) applies, no amount is to be included in the total legacy amount in respect of housing benefit.

The benefit cap

(11) Where—

(a) the existing benefits do not include an award of housing benefit, or they include an award of housing benefit that has been reduced to the minimum amount by virtue of Part 8A of the Housing Benefit Regulations 2006 (the benefit cap);

(b) Part 7 of the Universal Credit Regulations (the benefit cap) applies in the calculation of the indicative UC amount; and

(c) the claimant's total entitlement to welfare benefits (as defined in section 96(10) of the Act) on the migration day is greater than the relevant amount,

the total legacy amount is reduced by the excess (minus the amount for childcare costs referred to regulation 54(2)(b) where applicable) over the relevant amount.

(12) For the purposes of paragraph (11)—

(a) the amount of each welfare benefit is the monthly equivalent calculated in the manner set out in regulation 73 (unearned income calculated monthly) of the Universal Credit Regulations; and

(b) the "relevant amount" is the amount referred to in regulation 80A of those Regulations which is applicable to the claimant.]

AMENDMENT

1. Universal Credit (Managed Migration Pilot and Miscellaneous Amendments) Regulations 2019 (SI 2019/1152) reg.3(7) (July 24, 2019).

DEFINITIONS

"contributory employment and support allowance" see reg.2(1).
"the daily rate" see para.(3).
"existing benefit" see reg.2(1).
"housing benefit" *ibid.*
"income support" *ibid.*
"income-based jobseeker's allowance" *ibid.*
"income-related employment and support allowance" *ibid.*
"migration day" see reg.49.
"HMRC" see reg.2(1).
"relevant amount" see para.(11).
"rent free period" see para.(9).
"tax credit" see reg.2(1).
"total legacy amount" see para.(1).

3.94.20   The total legacy amount is calculated by adding together the monthly rates of all awards of the existing benefits to which the claimant was entitled on migration day, i.e. the day before the universal credit award starts. That principle is established by para.(1). The remainder of the regulation deals with the necessary arithmetic with respect to tax credits (paras.(2) and (3)), income support, income-based JSA and income-related ESA (paras.(4)–(6)) and housing benefit (paras.(7)–(10)), subject to any benefit cap adjustment (paras.(11)–(12)).

[¹The transitional element - indicative UC amount

3.94.21   **54.**—(1) The indicative UC amount is the amount to which a claimant would be entitled if an award of universal credit were calculated in accordance with section 8 of the Act by reference to the claimant's circumstances on the migration day, applying the assumptions in paragraph (2).

(2) The assumptions are—

(a) if the claimant is entitled to an award of child tax credit, the claimant is responsible for any child or qualifying young person in respect of whom the individual element of child tax credit is payable;

(b) if the claimant is entitled to an award of working tax credit that includes the childcare element, the indicative UC amount includes the childcare costs element and, for the purposes of calculating the amount of that element, the amount of the childcare costs is equal to the relevant weekly childcare charges included in the calculation of the daily rate referred to in regulation 53(2), converted to a monthly amount by multiplying by 52 and dividing by 12;

(c) the amount of the claimant's earned income is—

(i) if the claimant is entitled to an award of a tax credit, the annual amount of any employment income or trading income, as defined by regulation 4 or 6 respectively of the Tax Credits (Definition and Calculation of Income) Regulations 2002, by reference to which the representative monthly rate of that tax credit is calculated for the purposes of regulation 53(2) converted to a net monthly amount by—

(aa) dividing by 12, and

(bb) deducting such amount for income tax and national insurance contributions as the Secretary of State considers appropriate,

(ii) if paragraph (i) does not apply and the claimant is entitled to an award of income support, income-based jobseeker's allowance or income-related employment and support allowance, the amount of earnings by reference to which the representative monthly rate of that benefit was calculated for the purposes of regulation 53(4) to (6) (including nil if none were taken into account) converted to a monthly amount by multiplying by 52 and dividing by 12, or

(iii) if paragraphs (i) and (ii) do not apply, but the claimant had an award of housing benefit, the amount of earnings by reference to which the representative monthly rate of that benefit was calculated for the purposes of regulation 53(7) to (10) (including nil if none were taken into account) converted to a monthly amount by multiplying by 52 and dividing by 12.

(3) If the claimant would not meet the financial condition in section 5(1)(b) of the Act (or, in the case of joint claimants, they would not meet the condition in section 5(2)(b) of the Act) the claimant is to be treated, for the purposes of calculating the indicative UC amount, as if they were entitled to an award of universal credit of a nil amount.

(4) If a transitional capital disregard is to apply, the claimant is to be treated as having met the financial condition in section 5(1)(a) or 5(2)(a) of the Act (capital limit).

(5) The indicative UC amount is to be calculated after any reduction under Part 7 of the Universal Credit Regulations (the benefit cap) but before any reduction under section 26 (higher-level sanctions) or 27 (other sanctions) of the Act.

(6) But there is to be no reduction for the benefit cap under that Part where the amount of the claimant's earned income (or, in the case of a couple their combined earned income) on the migration day, calculated in accordance with paragraph (2)(c), is equal to or exceeds the amount specified in paragraph (1)(a) of regulation 82 (exceptions – earnings) of the Universal Credit Regulations.

(7) The calculation of the indicative UC amount is to be based on the information that is used for the purposes of calculating the total legacy amount, supplemented as necessary by such further information or evidence as the Secretary of State requires.]

AMENDMENT

1. Universal Credit (Managed Migration Pilot and Miscellaneous Amendments) Regulations 2019 (SI 2019/1152) reg.3(7) (July 24, 2019).

DEFINITIONS

"childcare costs element" see reg.2(1).
"earned income" *ibid.*
"housing benefit" *ibid.*
"indicative UC amount" see reg.54.
"migration day" see reg.49.
"tax credit" see reg.2(1).
"total legacy amount" see reg.53.
"transitional capital disregard" see reg.51.

GENERAL NOTE

The total legacy amount (reg.53) is a relatively straightforward concept to grasp. It is what the claimant was in fact entitled to under the existing benefit regime. The indicative UC amount is a less readily understandable concept. According to para. (1) it represents the hypothetical amount of universal credit to which the claimant would have been entitled to on migration day (i.e. the day before the universal credit award commenced) but subject to the various assumptions in para.(2). In addition, if the claimant would not meet the income financial condition of entitlement, they are treated for these purposes as being entitled to a nil award (para.(3)). Claimants are also treated as satisfying the capital financial condition where the transitional capital disregard applies (para.(4)). The indicative UC amount is worked out *after* any reduction due to the benefit cap (but see para.(6)) and *before* any reduction for a sanction (para.(5)).

Note that for the purposes of any calculation under this regulation the amount of the standard allowance is to be the amount specified in reg.36 of the Universal Credit Regulations, as amended by the 2020 up-rating order, and not the enhanced

3.94.22

amounts specified in reg.3(1) of the Social Security (Coronavirus) (Further Measures) Regulations 2020 (SI 2020/371) .

[¹The transitional element – initial amount and adjustment where other elements increase

3.94.23

55.—(1) The initial amount of the transitional element is—

(a) if the indicative UC amount is greater than nil, the amount by which the total legacy amount exceeds the indicative UC amount; or

(b) if the indicative UC amount is nil, the total legacy amount plus any amount by which the income which fell to be deducted in accordance with section 8(3) of the Act exceeded the maximum amount.

(2) The amount of the transitional element to be included in the calculation of an award is—

(a) for the first assessment period, the initial amount;

(b) for the second assessment period, the initial amount reduced by the sum of any relevant increases in that assessment period;

(c) for the third and each subsequent assessment period, the amount that was included for the previous assessment period reduced by the sum of any relevant increases (as in sub-paragraph (b)).

(3) If the amount of the transitional element is reduced to nil in any assessment period, a transitional element is not to apply in the calculation of the award for any subsequent assessment period.

(4) A "relevant increase" is an increase in any of the amounts that are included in the maximum amount under sections 9 to 12 of the Act (including any of those amounts that is included for the first time), apart from the childcare costs element.]

AMENDMENT

1. Universal Credit (Managed Migration Pilot and Miscellaneous Amendments) Regulations 2019 (SI 2019/1152) reg.3(7) (July 24, 2019).

DEFINITIONS

"assessment period" see reg.2(1).
"childcare costs element" *ibid.*
"relevant increase" see para.(4).
"indicative UC amount" see reg.54.
"total legacy amount" see reg.53.
"transitional element" see reg.52.

GENERAL NOTE

3.94.24

The amount of the transitional element to be included in the calculation of a universal credit award is, for the first assessment period (para.(2)(a)), the initial amount as defined by para.(1). The amount for subsequent periods is governed by para.(2)(b) and (c) as appropriate. In these later periods the amount can be reduced by relevant increases, as defined by para.(4).

Note that for the purposes of any calculation under this regulation the amount of the standard allowance is to be the amount specified in reg.36 of the Universal Credit Regulations, as amended by the 2020 up-rating order, and not the enhanced amounts specified in reg.3(1) of the Social Security (Coronavirus) (Further Measures) Regulations 2020 (SI 2020/371) .

[¹Ending of transitional protection

Circumstances in which transitional protection ceases

56.—(1) A transitional capital disregard or a transitional element does not apply in any assessment period to which paragraph (2) or (4) applies, or in any subsequent assessment period. **3.94.25**

Cessation of employment or sustained drop in earnings

(2) This paragraph applies to an assessment period if the following condition is met—

    (a) in the case of a single claimant—

        (i) it is the assessment period after the third consecutive assessment period in which the claimant's earned income is less than the amount specified in regulation 99(6)(a) of the Universal Credit Regulations ("the single administrative threshold"), and

        (ii) in the first assessment period of the award, the claimant's earned income was equal to or more than that threshold; or

    (b) in the case of joint claimants—

        (i) it is the assessment period after the third consecutive assessment period in which their combined earned income is less than the amount specified in regulation 99(6)(b) of the Universal Credit Regulations ("the couple administrative threshold"), and

        (ii) in the first assessment period of the award, their combined earned income was equal to or more than that threshold.

(3) For the purposes of paragraph (2) a claimant is to be treated as having earned income that is equal to or more than the single administrative threshold (or, as the case may be, the couple administrative threshold) in any assessment period in respect of which regulation 62 (minimum income floor) of the Universal Credit Regulations applies to that claimant or would apply but for regulation 62(5) of those Regulations (minimum income floor not to apply in a start-up period).

Couple separating or forming

(4) This paragraph applies to an assessment period in which—

    (a) joint claimants cease to be a couple or become members of a different couple; or

    (b) a single claimant becomes a member of a couple, unless it is a case where the person may, by virtue of regulation 3(3) of the Universal Credit Regulations (claimant with an ineligible partner), claim as a single person.]

AMENDMENT

1. Universal Credit (Managed Migration Pilot and Miscellaneous Amendments) Regulations 2019 (SI 2019/1152) reg.3(7) (July 24, 2019).

DEFINITIONS

"assessment period" see reg.2(1).
"earned income" *ibid.*
"the couple administrative threshold" see para.(2)(b)(i).
"the single administrative threshold" see para.(2)(a)(i).
"transitional capital disregard" see reg.51.
"transitional element" see reg.52.

GENERAL NOTE

3.94.26   This provides for the circumstances in which transitional protection ceases. These are where there is a reduction in earnings over a three-month period or where an award ends (including where a couple separate or form—but note the exceptions turning on reg.3(3) of the Universal Credit Regulations). Exceptionally, transitional protection can be carried over to a subsequent award in certain circumstances under new reg.57.

[¹**Application of transitional protection to a subsequent award**

3.94.27   57.—(1) Where—

(a) a transitional capital disregard is applied, or a transitional element is included, in the calculation of an award, and that award terminates; or

(b) the Secretary State determines (in accordance with regulation 50) that a transitional capital disregard is to apply, or a transitional element is to be included in the calculation of an award, but the decision on the qualifying claim is that there is no entitlement to an award,

no transitional capital disregard is to apply and no transitional element is to be included in the calculation of any subsequent award unless paragraph (2) applies.

(2) This paragraph applies if—

(a) the reason for the previous award terminating or, as the case may be, there being no entitlement to an award, was that the claimant (or joint claimants) had earned income on account of which the financial condition in section 5(1)(b) or 5(2)(b) of the Act (income is such that the amount payable is at least 1p) was not met; and

(b) the claimant becomes entitled to an award within the period of three months beginning with—

(i) where paragraph (1)(a) applies, the last day of the month that would have been the final assessment period of the previous award (had it not terminated), or

(ii) where paragraph (1)(b) applies, the day that would have been the last day of the first assessment period had there been entitlement to an award.

(3) Where paragraph (2) applies in a case where a previous award has terminated, the new award is to be treated for the purposes of regulation 51 (transitional capital disregard), 55 (transitional element – initial amount and adjustment where other elements increase) and 56 (circumstances in which transitional protection ceases) as if it were a continuation of that award.]

AMENDMENT

1. Universal Credit (Managed Migration Pilot and Miscellaneous Amendments) Regulations 2019 (SI 2019/1152) reg.3(7) (July 24, 2019).

"assessment period" see reg.2(1).
"earned income" *ibid.*
"qualifying claim" see reg.48.
"transitional capital disregard" see reg.51.
"transitional element" see reg.52.

GENERAL NOTE

The basic rule is that where transitional protection on a universal credit claim has **3.94.28**
been lost (either because an award with transitional protection has ended or because
a qualifying claim with such protection has been disallowed) then it is lost forever
(para.(1)). However, there are exceptional cases in which transitional protection
once lost can be revived, as in the circumstances set out in para.(2).

[¹Miscellaneous

Qualifying claim – Secretary of State may set later commencement day

58. Where the Secretary of State decides a qualifying claim, and it is **3.94.29**
not a case where the award is to commence before the date of claim by
virtue of regulation 46(3) or 47(4) (claim made by the final deadline) or
regulation 26 of the Claims and Payments Regulations (time within which
a claim for universal credit is to be made) as modified by regulation 15 of
these Regulations, the Secretary of State may determine a day on which the
award of universal credit is to commence that is after, but no more than one
month after, the date of claim.]

AMENDMENT

1. Universal Credit (Managed Migration Pilot and Miscellaneous Amendments)
Regulations 2019 (SI 2019/1152) reg.3(7) (July 24, 2019).

DEFINITION

"qualifying claim" see reg.48.

GENERAL NOTE

This enables the Secretary State to set a date for commencement of the award **3.94.30**
of universal credit up to a month after the date of a qualifying claim (provided it
is not a case where the claim is to be backdated). According to the Explanatory
Memorandum, this provision "has been included to delay the start date of UC
claims if the number of claims that need to be assessed would put pressure on operational capacity to the point of threatening service delivery to claimants" (para.7.13).

[¹Minimum income floor not to apply for first 12 months

59. Where universal credit is awarded to a claimant who is a notified **3.94.31**
person, regulation 63 of the Universal Credit Regulations (start-up period)
is to apply as if paragraph (1)(a) (requirement that the claimant has begun
to carry on the trade, profession or vocation within the past 12 months)
were omitted.]

AMENDMENT

1. Universal Credit (Managed Migration Pilot and Miscellaneous Amendments) Regulations 2019 (SI 2019/1152) reg.3(7) (July 24, 2019).

DEFINITION

"notified person" see reg.44(6).

GENERAL NOTE

3.94.32   Where self-employed claimants are subject to managed migration to universal credit and are found to be "gainfully self-employed" they will enter the 12-month start-up period and will not have the minimum income floor (or MIF, under which certain self-employed claimants are to have an assumed level of earnings) applied to their award until this period has ended, regardless of how long they have been self-employed prior to being subject to managed migration. This applies irrespective of whether the gainful self-employment began before the universal credit claim is made or begins at a later date.

[¹Protection for full-time students until course completed

3.94.33   **60.** Where a notified person does not meet the basic condition in section 4(1)(d) of the Act (not receiving education) on the day on which all awards of any existing benefit are to terminate as a consequence of a claim for universal credit because the person is undertaking a full-time course (see regulation 12(2) and 13 of the Universal Credit Regulations), that condition is not to apply in relation to the notified person while they are continuing to undertake that course.]

AMENDMENT

1. Universal Credit (Managed Migration Pilot and Miscellaneous Amendments) Regulations 2019 (SI 2019/1152) reg.3(7) (July 24, 2019).

DEFINITIONS

"existing benefit" reg.2(1).
"notified person" see reg.44(6).

GENERAL NOTE

3.94.34   This provides for notified persons who are students, and entitled to existing benefits, to be exempt from the exclusion of full-time students from universal credit until they complete their course.

[¹Rounding

3.94.35   **61.** Regulation 6 of the Universal Credit Regulations (rounding) applies for the purposes of calculating any amount under this Part.]

AMENDMENT

1. Universal Credit (Managed Migration Pilot and Miscellaneous Amendments) Regulations 2019 (SI 2019/1152) reg.3(7) (July 24, 2019).

[¹Effect of revision, appeal etc. of an award of an existing benefit

3.94.36   **62.**—(1) Nothing in regulation 53 (total legacy amount) or 54 (indicative UC amount) requiring a calculation in relation to the transitional element to be made on the basis of information held on the migration day prevents the Secretary of State from revising or superseding a decision in relation to a claim for, or an award of, universal credit where—

(a) in the opinion of the Secretary of State, the information held on that day was inaccurate or incomplete in some material respect because of—

    (i) a misrepresentation by a claimant,

    (ii) a failure to report information that a claimant was required to report where that failure was advantageous to the claimant, or

    (iii) an official error; or

(b) a decision has been made on or after the migration day on—

    (i) an application made before migration day to revise or supersede a decision in relation to an award of an existing benefit (including the report of a change of circumstances), or

    (ii) an appeal in relation to such an application.

(2) In this regulation "official error" means an error that—

(a) was made by an officer of, or an employee of a body acting on behalf of, the Department for Work and Pensions, HMRC or a local authority that administers housing benefit; and

(b) was not caused, or materially contributed to, by any person outside that body or outside the Department, HMRC or local authority,

but excludes any error of law which is shown to have been such by a subsequent decision of the Upper Tribunal or of a court as defined in section 27(7) of the Social Security Act 1998.]

AMENDMENT

1. Universal Credit (Managed Migration Pilot and Miscellaneous Amendments) Regulations 2019 (SI 2019/1152) reg.3(7) (July 24, 2019).

DEFINITIONS

"HMRC" see reg.2(1).
"migration day" see reg.49.
"official error" see para.2.
"transitional element" see reg.52.
"Upper Tribunal" see reg.2(1).

GENERAL NOTE

This provision ensures that the requirement to apply the information held at the migration day when calculating transitional protection does not prevent the subsequent revision of the universal credit award in cases of misrepresentation or error or in order to give effect to an outstanding revision or appeal.   3.94.37

[¹Claimants previously entitled to a severe disability premium

63. Schedule 2 contains provision in respect of certain claimants who have been entitled to a benefit which included a severe disability premium.]   3.94.38

AMENDMENT

1. Universal Credit (Managed Migration Pilot and Miscellaneous Amendments) Regulations 2019 (SI 2019/1152) reg.3(7) (July 24, 2019).

DEFINITION

"severe disability premium" —see reg.2(1).

GENERAL NOTE

3.94.39   The new Schedule 2 in the 2014 Regulations provides for transitional payments in respect of certain claimants who were entitled to a severe disability premium (SDP) before claiming universal credit as a result of natural migration (e.g. a claim to universal credit prompted by a change in circumstances). Eligibility is governed by Sch.2, para.1; there is no need for individuals to make a claim, as the DWP has set up a specialist team to review universal credit claims and identify those claimants who may be eligible for a SDP transitional payment under Sch.2. The payments are based on a flat rate for each assessment period since the move to universal credit (see Sch.2, para.2). The flat rate is converted into a transitional element after a date determined by the Secretary of State; the effect is that a lump-sum payment is made to cover the period since the claimant moved to universal credit followed by an ongoing monthly payment thereafter (see Sch.2, para.3). Note that any such lump-sum payment can be disregarded as capital for 12 months or for the duration of the universal credit award, whichever is longer (see Sch.2, para.7). This provision is necessary as some of the backdated payments will be substantial (the average (in the sense of median) lump-sum payment is £2,280: see House of Commons Library, *Universal Credit and the Severe Disability Premium*, Briefing Paper 08494 November 5, 2019, p.7).

[¹Discretionary hardship payments

3.94.40   **64.** The Secretary of State may, in such circumstances and subject to such conditions as the Secretary of State considers appropriate, make payments to notified persons who appear to be in hardship as a result of the termination of an existing benefit in accordance with these Regulations or otherwise as a result of the provisions of this Part.]

AMENDMENT

1. Universal Credit (Managed Migration Pilot and Miscellaneous Amendments) Regulations 2019 (SI 2019/1152) reg.3(7) (July 24, 2019).

DEFINITIONS

"existing benefit" see reg.2(1).
"notified person" see reg.44(6).

SCHEDULE

MODIFICATION OF TAX CREDITS LEGISLATION (FINALISATION OF TAX CREDITS)

Modifications to the Tax Credits Act 2002

3.95   1. Paragraphs 2 to 10 prescribe modifications to the application of the 2002 Act where regulation 12A of these Regulations applies.
   2. In section 7 (income test)—
   (a)   in subsection (3), before "current year income" in each place where it occurs, insert "notional";
   (b)   in subsection (4)—
       (i)   for "current year" substitute "current part year";
       (ii) in paragraphs (a) and (b), before "tax year" insert "part";
   (c)   after subsection (4), insert—

"(4A) In this section "the notional current year income" means—

(a) in relation to persons by whom a joint claim for a tax credit is made, the aggregate income of the persons for the part tax year to which the claim relates, divided by the number of days in that part tax year, multiplied by the number of days in the tax year in which the part tax year is included and rounded down to the next whole number of pence; and

(b) in relation to a person by whom a single claim for a tax credit is made, the income of the person for that part tax year, divided by the number of days in that part tax year, multiplied by the number of days in the tax year in which the part tax year is included and rounded down to the next whole number of pence.".

3. In section 17 (final notice)—
  (a) in subsection (1)—
      (i) omit "the whole or"; and
      (ii) in sub-paragraph (a), before "tax year" insert "part";
  (b) in subsection (3), before "tax year" insert "part";
  (c) in subsections (4)(a) and (4)(b), for "current year" in both places where it occurs, substitute "current part year";
  (d) in subsection (5)(a) for "current year" in both places where it occurs, substitute "current part year";
  (e) omit subsection (8).
4. In section 18 (decisions after final notice)—
  (a) in subsection (1), before "tax year" insert "part";
  (b) omit subsections (6) to (9);
  (c) in subsection (10), for "subsection (1), (5), (6) or (9)" substitute "subsection (1) or (5)";
  (d) in subsection (11)—
      (i) after "subsection (5)" omit "or (9)";
      (ii) omit paragraph (a);
      (iii) in paragraph (b) omit "in any other case,";
      (iv) before "tax year" in each place where it occurs, insert "part".
5. In section 19 (power to enquire)—
  (a) in subsection (1)(a) and (b), before "tax year" insert "part";
  (b) in subsection (3), before "tax year" insert "part";
  (c) for subsection (5) substitute—

    "(5) "The relevant section 18 decision" means the decision under subsection (1) of section 18 in relation to the person or persons and the part tax year.";

  (d) for subsection (6) substitute—

    "(6) "The relevant section 17 date" means the date specified for the purposes of subsection (4) of section 17 in the notice given to a person or persons under that section in relation to the part tax year.";

  (e) in subsection (11), before "tax year" insert "part";
  (f) in subsection (12), before "tax year" in each place where it occurs, insert "part".
6. In section 20 (decisions on discovery)—
  (a) in subsection (1), before "tax year" insert "part";
  (b) in subsection (4)(a), before "tax year" insert "part";
  (c) in subsection (5)(b), before "tax year" insert "part";
  (d) in subsection (6)—
      (i) before "tax year" insert "part";
      (ii) in paragraph (a), for "section 18(1), (5), (6) or (9)" substitute "section 18(1) or (5)";
  (e) in subsection (7), before "tax year" in each place where it occurs, insert "part".
7. In section 21 (decisions subject to official error), for "18(1), (5), (6) or (9)" substitute "18(1) or (5)".
8. In section 23 (notice of decisions)—
  (a) in subsection (1), for "18(1), (5), (6) or (9)" substitute "18(1) or (5)";
  (b) in subsection (3)—
      (i) after "18(1)" omit "or (6)";
      (ii) for paragraph (b) substitute—

        "(b) the notice of the decision under subsection (1) of section 18,".

9. In section 30(1) (underpayments), before "tax year" in each place where it occurs, insert "part".

10. In section 38 (appeals)—

   (a)   in subsection (1)(b), before "tax year" insert "part";

   (b)   for subsection (2), substitute—

> "(2) "The relevant section 18 decision" means the decision under subsection (1) of section 18 in relation to the person or persons and the tax credit for the part tax year.".

Modifications to the Tax Credits (Definition and Calculation of Income) Regulations 2002

3.96   11. Paragraphs 12 to 23 prescribe modifications to the application of the Tax Credits (Definition and Calculation of Income) Regulations 2002 where regulation 12A of these Regulations applies.

12. In regulation 2(2) (interpretation), after the definition of "the Macfarlane Trusts" insert—

> ""part tax year" means a period of less than a year beginning with 6th April and ending with the date on which the award of a tax credit terminated;".

13. In regulation 3 (calculation of income of claimant)—

   (a)   in paragraph (1)—

      (i)   before "tax year" insert "part";

      (ii)   in Steps 1 and 2, after "of the claimant, or, in the case of a joint claim, of the claimants" insert "received in or relating to the part tax year";

      (iii) in the second and third sentences of Step 4, before "year" insert "part";

   (b)   in paragraph (6A), for the words from "ending on 31st March" to the end, substitute "ending on the last day of the month in which the claimant's award of a tax credit terminated";

   (c)   in paragraph (8)(b), before "year" insert "part".

14. In regulation 4 (employment income)—

   (a)   in paragraph (1)(a), before "tax year" insert "part";

   (b)   in paragraph (1)(b), (c), (d), (e), (g) and (k), before "year" insert "part";

   (c)   in paragraph (1)(f), after "ITEPA" insert "which is treated as received in the part tax year and in respect of which the charge arises in the part tax year";

   (d)   in paragraph (1)(h), after "week" insert "in the part tax year";

   (e)   in paragraph (1)(i), for "that year" substitute "the tax year" and after "ITEPA" insert "which is treated as received in the part tax year";

   (f)   in paragraph (1)(j), after "applies" insert "which is received in the part tax year";

   (g)   in paragraph (1)(l), for "that year" substitute "the tax year" and after "ITEPA" insert "in respect of which the charge arises in the part tax year";

   (h)   in paragraph (1)(m), after "paid" insert "in the part tax year";

   (i)   in paragraph (4), in the first sentence and in the title of Table 1, after "employment income" insert "received in the part tax year";

   (j)   in paragraph (5), after "calculating earnings" insert "received in the part tax year".

15. In regulation 5 (pension income)—

   (a)   in paragraph (1), after ""pension income" means" insert "any of the following received in or relating to the part tax year";

   (b)   in paragraph (2), in the first sentence and in the title of Table 2, after "pension income" insert "received in or relating to the part tax year";

   (c)   in paragraph (3), after "income tax purposes", insert "in relation to the part tax year".

16. In regulation 6 (trading income)—

   (a)   re-number the existing regulation as paragraph (1);

   (b)   in paragraph (1) (as so re-numbered)—

      (i)   in sub-paragraph (a), for "taxable profits for the tax year" substitute "actual or estimated taxable profits attributable to the part tax year";

      (ii)   in sub-paragraph (b), for "taxable profit for the" substitute "actual or estimated taxable profit attributable to the part tax";

   (c)   after paragraph (1) insert—

> "(2) Actual or estimated taxable profits attributable to the part tax year ("the relevant trading income") is to be calculated by reference to the basis period (determined by reference to the rules in Chapter 15 of Part 2 of ITTOIA) ending during the tax year in which the claimant made, or was treated as making, a claim for universal credit.

(3) The relevant trading income is to be calculated by—

(a) taking the figure for the actual or estimated taxable income earned in the basis period;

(b) dividing that figure by the number of days in the basis period to give the daily figure; and

(c) multiplying the daily figure by the number of days in the part tax year on which the trade, profession or vocation was carried on.".

17. In regulation 7 (social security income)—

(a) in paragraph (1), after "social security income" insert "received in the part tax year";

(b) in paragraph (3), in the opening words and in the title of Table 3, after "social security income" insert "received in the part tax year".

18. In regulation 8 (student income), after "in relation to a student" insert ", any of the following which is received in the part tax year".

19. In regulation 10 (investment income)—

(a) in paragraph (1), after "gross amount" insert "received in the part tax year";

(b) in paragraph (1)(e), before "year" insert "part tax";

(c) in paragraph (2), in the opening words and in the title of Table 4, after "investment income" insert "received in the part tax year".

20. In regulation 11(1) (property income)—

(a) omit "annual";

(b) after "taxable profits" insert "for the part tax year".

21. In regulation 12(1) (foreign income), before "year" insert "part tax".

22. In regulation 13 (notional income), after "means income" insert "received in the part tax year".

23. In regulation 18 (miscellaneous income), after "means income" insert "received in the part tax year".

Modifications to the Tax Credits (Income Thresholds and Determination of Rates) Regulations 2002

24. Paragraphs 25 to 27 prescribe modifications to the application of the Tax Credits (Income Thresholds and Determination of Rates) Regulations 2002 where regulation 12A of these Regulations applies.   **3.97**

25. In regulation 2 (interpretation)—

(a) after the definition of "the income threshold" insert—

""part tax year" means a period of less than a year beginning with 6th April and ending with the date on which the award of a tax credit terminated;";

(b) in the definition of "the relevant income" insert "as modified by the Universal Credit (Transitional Provisions) Regulations 2014" at the end.

26. In regulation 7(3) (determination of rate of working tax credit)—

(a) in Step 1, in the definition of "MR", after "maximum rate" insert "(determined in the manner prescribed at the date on which the award of the tax credit terminated)";

(b) in Step 3—

(i) in the definition of "I", before "tax year" insert "part";

(ii) in the definition of "N1", before "tax year" insert "part".

27. In regulation 8(3) (determination of rate of child tax credit)—

(a) in Step 1, in the definition of "MR", after "maximum rate" insert "(determined in the manner prescribed at the date on which the award of the tax credit terminated)";

(b) in Step 3—

(i) in the definition of "I", before "tax year" insert "part";

(ii) in the definition of "N1", before "tax year" insert "part".

Modifications to the Tax Credits (Claims and Notifications) Regulations 2002

28. Paragraphs 29 to 34 prescribe modifications to the application of the Tax Credits (Claims and Notifications) Regulations 2002 where regulation 12A of these Regulations applies.   **3.98**

29. In regulation 4 (interpretation), omit paragraph (b).

30. Omit regulation 11 (circumstances in which claims to be treated as made).

31. Omit regulation 12 (further circumstances in which claims to be treated as made).

32. In regulation 13 (circumstances in which claims made by one member of a couple to be treated as also made by the other)—

(a) in paragraph (1), after "prescribed by paragraph" omit "(2) or";

(b) omit paragraph (2).

33. In regulation 15(1)(c) (persons who die after making a claim)—

(a) omit "the whole or" and "after the end of that tax year but"; and

(b) for "section 18(1), (5), (6) or (9)" substitute "section 18(1) or (5)".

34. In regulation 33 (dates to be specified in notices)—
    (a) in paragraph (a), for the words from "not later than 31st July" to "if later", substitute "not less than 30 days after the date on which the notice is given";
    (b) omit paragraph (b) and the "and" which precedes it.

Modification to the Tax Credits (Payment by the Commissioners) Regulations 2002

3.99
    35. Paragraph 36 prescribes a modification to the application of the Tax Credits (Payment by the Commissioners) Regulations 2002 where regulation 12A of these Regulations applies.
    36. Omit regulation 7 (prescribed circumstances for certain purposes).

Modification to the Tax Credits (Residence) Regulations 2003

3.100
    37. Paragraph 38 prescribes a modification to the application of the Tax Credits (Residence) Regulations 2003 where regulation 12A of these Regulations applies.
    38. In regulation 3(5)(a) (circumstances in which a person is treated as not being in the United Kingdom)(26), omit "under regulation 11 or 12 of the Tax Credits (Claims and Notifications) Regulations 2002 or otherwise".]

AMENDMENTS

1. Universal Credit (Transitional Provisions) (Amendment) Regulations 2014 (SI 2014/1626) reg.4 (October 13, 2014).

2. Universal Credit (Managed Migration Pilot and Miscellaneous Amendments) Regulations 2019 (SI 2019/1152) reg.3(8) (July 24, 2019).

GENERAL NOTE

3.101
    See General Note to reg.12A.

[¹SCHEDULE 2   REGULATION 63

Claimants previously entitled to a severe disability premium: transitional payments

Determination by Secretary of State

3.101.1
    1. Where it comes to the attention of the Secretary of State that—
    (a) an award of universal credit has been made in respect of a claimant who, within the period of one month immediately preceding the first day on which the claimant became entitled to universal credit as a consequence of making a claim, was entitled to an award of income support, income-based jobseeker's allowance or income-related employment and support allowance that included a severe disability premium;
    (b) in a case where the award of income support, income-based jobseeker's allowance or income-related employment and support allowance ended during that month, the claimant continued to satisfy the conditions for eligibility for a severe disability premium for the remainder of that month;
    (c) the award of universal credit has not since terminated (whether by a claimant ceasing to meet the conditions of entitlement to universal credit or becoming, or ceasing to be, a member of a couple);
    (d) the claimant has not (or, in the case of joint claimants, neither of them has) ceased to be entitled to the care component, the daily living component, armed forces independence payment or attendance allowance (all of which have the same meaning as in paragraph 6 of Schedule 4 to the Employment and Support Allowance Regulations 2008); and
    (e) no person has become a carer for—
        (i) in the case of a single claimant, the claimant, or
        (ii) in the case of joint claimants—
            (aa) if a severe disability premium was payable at the higher rate, both of them, or
            (bb) if a severe disability premium was payable at the lower rate, the claimant who was the qualifying partner,
the Secretary of State must determine an additional amount of universal credit ("the transitional SDP amount") which is to be payable in respect of each assessment period that precedes

that determination and then for each subsequent assessment period that begins before the conversion day.

2. The transitional SDP amount, calculated by reference to the date of the determination, is—

(a) in the case of a single claimant—
   (i) £120, if the LCWRA element is included in the award, or
   (ii) £285, if the LCWRA element is not included in the award;

(b) in the case of joint claimants—
   (i) £405, if the higher SDP rate was payable and no person has since become a carer for either of them,
   (ii) £120, if paragraph (i) does not apply and the LCWRA element is included in the award in respect of either of them, or
   (iii) £285, if paragraph (i) does not apply and the LCWRA element is not included in the award in respect of either of them.

3. The Secretary of State must decide the manner in which the transitional SDP amount is to be paid, which may include payment of a lump sum covering all assessment periods preceding the determination under paragraph 1 and monthly payments thereafter.

4. If the LCWRA element is not included in the award at the time of the determination under paragraph 1, but is included in a later assessment period (and paragraph 2(b)(i) does not apply), the amount for that assessment period, and each subsequent assessment period beginning before the conversion day, is to be £120 (and the Secretary of State must make a further determination).

Conversion to a transitional element

5. In the first assessment period that begins on or after the conversion day, the calculation of the award is to include the amount of the transitional SDP payment as if it were the initial amount of a transitional element calculated under regulation 55(1).   **3.101.2**

6. In respect of each subsequent assessment period, the award is to be treated, for the purposes of regulation 55(2) (adjustment where other elements increase), regulation 56 (circumstances in which transitional protection ceases) and regulation 57 (application of transitional protection to a subsequent award), as if the transitional SDP payment had been converted into a transitional element.

Capital disregard

7. Any amount paid as a lump sum as a consequence of a determination under this Schedule is to be disregarded in the calculation of capital for 12 months from the date of that payment or, if longer, the remainder of the award.   **3.101.3**

Interpretation

8. In this Schedule—   **3.101.4**

"the conversion day" is a day determined by the Secretary of State having regard to the efficient administration of universal credit;

"LCWRA element" has the meaning in the Universal Credit Regulations;

"the lower SDP rate" and "the higher SDP rate" are the rates specified in sub-paragraph (i) and (ii) respectively of paragraph 11(2)(b) of Schedule 4 to the Employment and Support Allowance Regulations 2008 or, as the case may be, the corresponding rates of a severe disability premium in relation to income support or income-based jobseeker's allowance;

"the qualifying partner", in relation to a couple in respect of whom the lower SDP rate was payable, is the partner who had no carer or, as the case may be, had not been a patient for a period exceeding 28 days,

and references to a person being a carer for another person are to the person being entitled to, and in receipt of, a carer's allowance or having an award of universal credit which includes the carer element in respect of caring for that other person.]

AMENDMENTS

1. Universal Credit (Managed Migration Pilot and Miscellaneous Amendments) Regulations 2019 (SI 2019/1152) reg.3(8) (July 24, 2019).

GENERAL NOTE

See further the General Note to reg.63 above.   **3.101.5**

PART IIIB

COMMENCEMENT ORDERS

The Welfare Reform Act 2012 (Commencement No.9 and Transitional and Transitory Provisions and Commencement No.8 and Savings and Transitional Provisions (Amendment)) Order 2013

(SI 2013/983) (C. 41) (AS AMENDED)

The Secretary of State, in exercise of the powers conferred by section 150(3) and (4)(a), (b)(i) and (c) of the Welfare Reform Act 2012, makes the following Order:

ARRANGEMENT OF ARTICLES

23. Amendment of the Welfare Reform Act 2012 (Commencement No 8 and Savings and Transitional Provisions) Order 2013
24. Appeals relating to ESA and JSA

Schedule 1 Postcode districts
Schedule 2 Universal credit provisions coming into force in relation to certain claims and awards
Schedule 3 Commencement of repeals in Part 1 of Schedule 14 to the Act
Schedule 4 Modifications of the Transitional Provisions Regulations 2010
Schedule 5 The Gateway Conditions

GENERAL NOTE

3.103   This Commencement Order ("the Commencement No.9 Order") was the first to "roll out" the universal credit scheme. Originally it had to be read together with the Transitional Provisions Regulations 2013. This Order accordingly brought into force, albeit for limited purposes only, provisions of the WRA 2012 that related to both the introduction of universal credit and the abolition of income-related ESA and income-based JSA. This was achieved by reference to the specific categories of cases set out in arts. 3 and 4. However, these provisions applied only to four postcode districts in Manchester, Oldham and Stockport (or "the relevant districts"; see Sch.1) as from April 29, 2013 (also the date on which the Transitional Provisions Regulations 2013 came into force). The justification for the limited "roll out" was that it would "facilitate an evaluation of the Universal Credit business processes and information technology functionality in a live environment before it is rolled out nationally from October 2013" (*Explanatory Memorandum to the Transitional Provisions Regulations 2013*, Para.7.64).

In this Order and its following companions (see further below), an award of ESA under Part 1 of the Welfare Reform Act 2007, in a case where income-related ESA has been abolished (i.e. in a Pathfinder area), is referred to as a "new style ESA award". Likewise an award of JSA under the Jobseekers Act 1995, in a case where income-based JSA has been abolished, is referred to as a "new style JSA award". Conversely an award of ESA under Part 1 of the Welfare Reform Act 2007, in a case where income-related ESA has not been abolished, is referred to as an "old style ESA award". Similarly an award of JSA under the Jobseekers Act 1995, in a case where income-based JSA has not been abolished, is referred to as an "old style JSA award".

This Order was initially followed by the Commencement No.11 Order (certain postcodes in Wigan ("the No.2 relevant districts") and Oldham and Warrington ("the No.3 relevant districts") as from July 1, 2013), the Commencement No.13 Order (certain postcodes in Hammersmith, Manchester and Wigan ("the No.4 relevant districts") as from October 28, 2013) and the Commencement No.14 Order (certain postcodes in Rugby, Inverness and Perth ("the No.5 relevant districts") as from November 25, 2013). Further Commencement Orders duly followed.

In addition, of course, a claimant who lived in one of the four originally specified postcode districts had also to be a member of the Pathfinder Group, i.e. be a person who met the requirements of regulations 5 to 12 of the Transitional Provisions Regulations 2013. However, as noted above the No.9 Commencement Order (along with the No.11, 13, 14 and 16 Commencement Orders) was amended by the Welfare Reform Act 2012 (Commencement No.9, 11, 13, 14, 16 and 17 and Transitional and Transitory Provisions (Amendment)) Order 2014 (SI 2014/1661). In conjunction with these changes, the Transitional Provisions Regulations 2013 were revoked and replaced by the Universal Credit (Transitional Provisions) Regulations 2014 (SI 2014/1230). At the same time, the "Pathfinder Group" conditions, previously contained in regs.5 to 12 of the Transitional Provisions Regulations 2013 were omitted from the Transitional Regulations 2014. Instead, similar conditions (known as the "gateway conditions") appeared in Sch.5 to the Commencement No.9 Order as inserted by art.16 of (SI 2014/1661).

Citation

1. This Order may be cited as the Welfare Reform Act 2012 (Commencement No.9 and Transitional and Transitory Provisions and Commencement No.8 and Savings and Transitional Provisions (Amendment)) Order 2013.

3.104

Interpretation

2.—(1) In this Order—

3.105

"the Act" means the Welfare Reform Act 2012 (apart from in Schedule 4);

"the 1995 Act" means the Jobseekers Act 1995;

"the 2007 Act" means the Welfare Reform Act 2007;

"the amending provisions" means the provisions referred to in article 4(1)(a) to (c);

[¹] [⁴ "claimant"—

(a) in relation to an employment and support allowance, has the same meaning as in Part 1 of the Welfare Reform Act 2007, save as mentioned in article 5(1A);

(b) in relation to a jobseeker's allowance, has the same meaning as in the Jobseekers Act 1995 (as it applies apart from the amendments made by Part 1 of Schedule 14 to the Act that remove references to an income-based jobseeker's allowance), save as mentioned in article 5(1A);

(c) in relation to universal credit, has the same meaning as in Part 1 of the Act

"appointed day" means the day appointed for the coming into force of the amending provisions in accordance with article 4(3);]

"the Claims and Payments Regulations 1987" means the Social Security (Claims and Payments) Regulations 1987;

"the Claims and Payments Regulations 2013" means the Universal Credit, Personal Independence Payment, Jobseeker's Allowance and Employment and Support Allowance (Claims and Payments) Regulations 2013;

"contribution-based jobseeker's allowance" means a contribution-based allowance under the 1995 Act as it has effect apart from the amendments made by Part 1 of Schedule 14 to the Act that remove references to an income-based allowance;

"contributory employment and support allowance" means a contributory allowance under Part 1 of the 2007 Act as it has effect apart from the amendments made by Schedule 3, and Part 1 of Schedule 14, to the Act that remove references to an income-related allowance;

[¹ "conversion decision" has the meaning given by the 2010 Transitional Regulations;]

"the Decisions and Appeals Regulations 2013" means the Universal Credit, Personal Independence Payment, Jobseeker's Allowance and Employment and Support Allowance (Decisions and Appeals) Regulations 2013;

[⁵ "the Digital Service Regulations 2014" means the Universal Credit (Digital Service) Amendment Regulations 2014;]

[⁶ "disability living allowance" means an allowance under section 71 of the Social Security Contributions and Benefits Act 1992;]

"employment and support allowance" means an employment and support allowance under Part 1 of the 2007 Act;

"the ESA Regulations 2008" means the Employment and Support Allowance Regulations 2008;

"the ESA Regulations 2013" means the Employment and Support Allowance Regulations 2013;

[¹ [³ . . .]

"First-tier Tribunal" has the same meaning as in the Social Security Act 1998;

"gateway conditions" means the conditions specified in Schedule 5;

"housing benefit" means housing benefit under section 130 of the Social Security Contributions and Benefits Act 1992;]

"income-based jobseeker's allowance" means an income-based jobseeker's allowance under the 1995 Act;

"income-related employment and support allowance" means an income-related allowance under Part 1 of the 2007 Act;

[¹ "income support" means income support under section 124 of the Social Security Contributions and Benefits Act 1992;]

"jobseeker's allowance" means an allowance under the 1995 Act;

[¹ [² "joint claimants"], in relation to universal credit, has the same meaning as in Part 1 of the Act;]

"the JSA Regulations 1996" means the Jobseeker's Allowance Regulations 1996;

"the JSA Regulations 2013" means the Jobseeker's Allowance Regulations 2013;

[¹ "new style ESA" means an employment and support allowance under Part 1 of the 2007 Act as amended by the provisions of Schedule 3, and Part 1 of Schedule 14, to the Act that remove references to an income-related allowance and "new style ESA award" shall be construed accordingly;

"new style JSA" means a jobseeker's allowance under the 1995 Act as amended by the provisions of Part 1 of Schedule 14 to the Act that remove references to an income-based allowance and "new style JSA award" shall be construed accordingly;

"old style ESA" means an employment and support allowance under Part 1 of the 2007 Act as it has effect apart from the amendments made by Schedule 3, and Part 1 of Schedule 14, to the Act that remove references to an income-related allowance and "old style ESA award" shall be construed accordingly;

"old style JSA" means a jobseeker's allowance under the 1995 Act as it has effect apart from the amendments made by Part 1 of Schedule 14 to the Act that remove references to an income-based jobseeker's allowance and "old style JSA award" shall be construed accordingly;]

[⁶ "personal independence payment" means an allowance under Part 4 of the Act;]

"relevant districts" means the postcode districts specified in Schedule 1;

[¹ "single claimant", in relation to universal credit, has the same meaning as in Part 1 of the Act;

"state pension credit" means state pension credit under the State Pension Credit Act 2002;

"tax credit" (including "child tax credit" and "working tax credit") has the same meaning as in the Tax Credits Act 2002;]
[¹ . . .];
"the 2010 Transitional Regulations" means the Employment and Support Allowance (Transitional Provisions, Housing Benefit and Council Tax Benefit)(Existing Awards)(No.2) Regulations 2010.
[¹ "the 2014 Transitional Regulations" means the Universal Credit (Transitional Provisions) Regulations 2014;
"the Universal Credit Regulations" means the Universal Credit Regulations 2013;
"Upper Tribunal" has the same meaning as in the Social Security Act 1998.]
[¹ (2) For the purposes of this Order—
(a) the Claims and Payments Regulations 2013 apply for the purpose of deciding—
    (i) whether a claim for universal credit is made or is to be treated as made; and
    (ii) the date on which such a claim is made; and
(b) where a couple is treated, in accordance with regulation 9(8) of the Claims and Payments Regulations 2013, as making a claim for universal credit, references to the date on which the claim is treated as made are to the date of formation of the couple.]

AMENDMENTS

1. Welfare Reform Act 2012 (Commencement No.9, 11, 13, 14 and 16 and Transitional and Transitory Provisions (Amendment)) Order 2014 (SI 2014/1452) art.4 (June 16, 2014).
2. Welfare Reform Act 2012 (Commencement No.9, 11, 13 14, 16 and 17 and Transitional and Transitory Provisions (Amendment)) Order 2014 (SI 2014/1661) art. 4(1) (June 30, 2014).
3. Welfare Reform Act 2012 (Commencement No.9, 11, 13, 14, 16 and 17 and Transitional and Transitory Provisions (Amendment) (No.2)) Order 2014 (SI 2014/1923) art. 4(2) (July 28, 2014).
4. Welfare Reform Act 2012 (Commencement No.9, 11, 13 14, 16, 17 and 19 and Transitional and Transitory Provisions (Amendment)) Order 2014 (SI 2014/3067) art.6(2)(a) (November 24, 2014).
5. Welfare Reform Act 2012 (Commencement No.20 and Transitional and Transitory Provisions and Commencement No.9 and Transitional and Transitory Provisions (Amendment)) Order 2014 (SI 2014/3094) art.7(2)(a) (November 26, 2014).
6. Welfare Reform Act 2012 (Commencement No.9, 11, 13, 14, 16, 17 and 19 and Transitional and Transitory Provisions (Amendment)) Order 2015 (SI 2015/32) art.4(2) (January 26, 2015).

Day appointed for commencement of the universal credit provisions in Part 1 of the Act

3.—(1) 29th April 2013 is the day appointed for the coming into force of-   3.106
(a) sections 29 (delegation and contracting out), 37(1), (2), (8) and (9) (capability for work or work-related activity), 38 (information) and 39(1), (2), (3)(b) and (c) (couples) of the Act;
(b) the following paragraphs of Schedule 2 to the Act (universal credit:

amendments) and section 31 of the Act (supplementary and consequential amendments) in so far as it relates to those paragraphs, in so far as they are not already in force—

    (i) paragraphs 1, 2, 32 to 35, 37 to 42, 52 to 55 and 65;

    (ii) paragraphs 4, 8, 10 to 23, 25 and 27 to 31 and paragraph 3 in so far as it relates to those paragraphs; and

    (iii) paragraphs 44, 45, 47, 49, 50(2) and 50(1) in so far as it relates to 50(2), and paragraph 43 in so far as it relates to those paragraphs and sub-paragraphs; and

  (c) paragraph 1 of Schedule 5 to the Act (universal credit and other working-age benefits) and section 35 of the Act in so far as it relates to that paragraph.

(2) The day appointed for the coming into force of the provisions of the Act listed in Schedule 2, in so far as they are not already in force, in relation to the case of a claim referred to in paragraph (3)(a) to (d) and any award that is made in respect of such a claim, and in relation to the case of an award referred to in paragraph (3)(e) or (f), is the day appointed in accordance with paragraph (4).

[¹ (3) The claims and awards referred to are—

  (a) a claim for universal credit where, on the date on which the claim is made, the claimant resides in one of the relevant districts and meets the gateway conditions;

[²(b) a claim for universal credit where—

    (i) in the case of a single claimant, the claimant gives incorrect information regarding the claimant residing in a relevant district or meeting the gateway conditions and the claimant does not reside in such a district or does not meet the gateway conditions on the date on which the claim is made;

    (ii) in the case of joint claimants, either or both of the joint claimants gives or give incorrect information regarding his or her (or their) residing in such a district or meeting the gateway conditions and one or both of them does not or do not reside in such a district or does not or do not meet those conditions on the date on which the claim is made; and

    (iii) after a decision is made that the single claimant is, or the joint claimants are, entitled to universal credit and one or more payments have been made in respect of the single claimant or the joint claimants, the Secretary of State discovers that incorrect information has been given regarding residence or meeting the gateway conditions.]

  (c) a claim for universal credit that is treated as made by a couple in the circumstances referred to in regulation 9(8) of the Claims and Payments Regulations 2013 (claims for universal credit by members of a couple) where the claim complies with paragraph (7);

[²(d) a claim for universal credit by a former member of a couple who were joint claimants of universal credit, whether or not the claim is made jointly with another person, where the former member is not exempt from the requirement to make a claim by virtue of regulation 9(6) of the Claims and Payments Regulations 2013 (claims for universal credit by members of a couple), where the claim is made during the period of one month starting with the date on which notification is given to the Secretary of State that the former joint claimants have

ceased to be a couple, and where the claim complies with paragraph (8);]
(e) an award of universal credit that is made without a claim in the circumstances referred to in regulation 6(1) or (2) of the Claims and Payments Regulations 2013 (claims not required for entitlement to universal credit in some cases) where the circumstances referred to in paragraph (9) apply; and
(f) an award of universal credit that is made without a claim in the circumstances referred to in regulation 9(6), (7) or (10) of the Claims and Payments Regulations 2013 (claims for universal credit by members of a couple) where the circumstances referred to in paragraph (9) apply.]
(4) The day appointed in relation to the cases of the claims and awards referred to in paragraph (2) is—
(a) in the case of a claim referred to in paragraph (3)(a) to (d), the first day of the period in respect of which the claim is made or treated as made;
(b) in the case of an award referred to in paragraph (3)(e) or (f), the first day on which a person is entitled to universal credit under that award.
(5) [¹ ...];
(6) For the purposes of paragraph (4)(a), where the time for making a claim for universal credit is extended under regulation 26(2) of the Claims and Payments Regulations 2013, the reference to the first day of the period in respect of which the claim is made or treated as made is a reference to the first day of the period in respect of which the claim is, by reason of the operation of that provision, timeously made or treated as made.
[¹ (7) A claim that is treated as made by a couple in the circumstances referred to in regulation 9(8) of the Claims and Payments Regulations 2013 complies with this paragraph where, on the date on which the claim is treated as made, the member of the couple who did not previously have an award of universal credit [³ . . .] is not entitled to state pension credit.
(8) A claim by a former member of a couple that is made in the circumstances referred to in paragraph (3)(d) complies with this paragraph where, on the date on which the claim is made, [³ neither the former member nor his or her partner (if any) is entitled to state pension credit].
(9) The circumstances referred to are where the relevant person is not entitled to state pension credit and, save where an award of universal credit is made in the circumstances referred to in regulation 9(7) of the Claims and Payments Regulations 2013, his or her partner (if any) is not entitled to [³ state pension credit].
(10) For the purposes of paragraph (9), "relevant person" means—
(a) where an award of universal credit is made in the circumstances referred to in regulation 6(1) or (2) of the Claims and Payments Regulations 2013, the former claimant referred to in that regulation 6(1);
(b) where an award of universal credit is made in the circumstances referred to in paragraph (6) of regulation 9 of the Claims and Payments Regulations 2013, [³ as that paragraph has effect apart from the amendments made by the Digital Service Regulations 2014,] the member of the former couple referred to in that paragraph;

[³(ba) where an award of universal credit is made in the circumstances referred to in paragraph (6) of regulation 9 of the Claims and Payments Regulations 2013, as that paragraph has effect as amended by the Digital Service Regulations 2014, the former joint claimant of universal credit to whom a new award of universal credit is made as referred to in sub-paragraph (a) or (b) of that paragraph;]

(c) where an award of universal credit is made in the circumstances referred to in paragraph (7) of regulation 9 of the Claims and Payments Regulations 2013, each of the joint claimants referred to in that paragraph;

(d) where an award of universal credit is made in the circumstances referred to in paragraph (10) of regulation 9 of the Claims and Payments Regulations 2013, the surviving partner referred to in that paragraph.

[³ (10A) In paragraph (3)—

(a) in sub-paragraph (c), the reference to regulation 9(8) of the Claims and Payments Regulations 2013 is a reference to that provision both as it has effect as amended by the Digital Service Regulations 2014 and as it has effect apart from that amendment;

(b) in sub-paragraph (d), the reference to regulation 9(6) of the Claims and Payments Regulations 2013 is a reference to that provision as it has effect apart from the amendment made by the Digital Service Regulations 2014;

(c) in sub-paragraph (f), the reference to regulation 9(6) of the Claims and Payments Regulations 2013 is a reference to that provision both as it has effect as amended by the Digital Service Regulations 2014 and as it has effect apart from that amendment.]

(11) For the purposes of paragraphs (8) and (9), "partner" means a person who forms part of a couple with the person in question, where "couple" has the same meaning as it has in section 39 of the Act.]

AMENDMENTS

1. Welfare Reform Act 2012 (Commencement No.9, 11, 13, 14 and 16 and Transitional and Transitory Provisions (Amendment)) Order 2014 (SI 2014/1452) art.5 (June 16, 2014).

2. Welfare Reform Act 2012 (Commencement No.9, 11, 13, 14, 16 and 17 and Transitional and Transitory Provisions (Amendment) (No.2)) Order 2014 (SI 2014/1923) art. 4(3) (July 28, 2014).

3. Welfare Reform Act 2012 (Commencement No.20 and Transitional and Transitory Provisions and Commencement No.9 and Transitional and Transitory Provisions (Amendment)) Order 2014 (SI 2014/3094) art.7(2)(b) (November 26, 2014).

DEFINITIONS

"the Act"–art. 2(1).
"the Claims and Payments Regulations 2013"–*ibid.*
"relevant districts"–*ibid.*
"the Transitional Regulations"–*ibid.*

GENERAL NOTE

Paragraph (1)
This brings into force various provisions relating to universal credit (including some supplementary and consequential provisions set out in Sch.2 to the 2012 Act) on April 29, 2013.

3.107

Paragraph (2)
This tortuously worded provision has the effect of bringing into force those provisions relating to universal credit in Part 1 of the WRA 2012, as set out in Sch.2, where one of the different categories of case referred to in art.3(3) applies. These relate to claims for UC and any resulting award as well as to awards of universal credit without a claim.

3.108

Paragraph (3)
This specifies the various situations in which para.(2) has the effect of applying the new universal credit rules.

3.109

Sub-Paragraph (3)(a)
This covers the situation where a person makes a claim for universal credit in respect of a period that begins on or after April 29, 2013 where that individual both resides in a "relevant district" at the time that the claim is made and meets the gateway conditions.

3.110

Sub-Paragraph (3)(b)
Where a person claims universal credit and incorrectly states that they live in a relevant district, that person remains subject to the new regime.

3.111

Sub-Paragraph (3)(c)
This covers the case of a single person who becomes a member of a couple where the other member was already entitled to universal credit.

3.112

Sub-Paragraph (3)(d)
Where a couple separate, and the member of the couple who is not exempt from making a claim for universal credit makes a claim within a period of one month, the new rules apply.

3.113

Sub-Paragraph (3)(e)
A person may be awarded universal credit without making a claim as a result of changes in their income within six months of their income being such that they were not previously entitled to universal credit.

3.114

Sub-Paragraph (3)(f)
Again, a person may be awarded universal credit without making a claim where a couple cease to be a couple and an award is made to the member of the couple who is exempt from making a claim. Similarly, an award of universal credit may be made without a claim to a couple where the members of the couple were previously entitled to the new benefit as single claimants. In addition, the new regime applies where an award of universal credit is made without a claim to a member of a couple where the other member of the couple has died.

3.115

Paragraphs (4) – (11)
These make supplementary provision dealing with the effective date of universal credit claims and awards under the preceding rules.

3.116

[¹ [² [³ Incorrect information regarding residence in a relevant district or meeting the gateway conditions

3.117   **3A.**—(1) This article applies where a claim for universal credit is made and it is subsequently discovered that the single claimant or either or both of two joint claimants gave incorrect information regarding his or her (or their) residing in one of the relevant districts or meeting the gateway conditions and the conditions referred to in paragraph (2) are met.

(2) The conditions referred to are that, on the date on which the claim was made, the claimant—

(a) did not reside in one of the relevant districts (unless paragraph (3) applies); or

(b) did reside in one of the relevant districts but did not meet the gateway conditions.

(3) This paragraph applies where the claimant resided in an area apart from the relevant districts with respect to which the provisions of the Act referred to in Schedule 2 were in force in relation to a claim for universal credit and the conditions (if any) that applied to such a claim, for those provisions to come into force, were met.

(4) Where the discovery is made before the claim for universal credit has been decided—

(a) the claimant is to be informed that the claimant is not entitled to claim universal credit;

(b) if the claimant (or, in the case of joint claimants, either of them) makes a claim for old style ESA, old style JSA or income support ("the specified benefit") and the date on which that claim is made (as determined in accordance with the Claims and Payments Regulations 1987) is after the date on which the claim for universal credit was made, but no later than one month after the date on which the information required by sub-paragraph (a) was given—

(i) the claim for the specified benefit is to be treated as made on the date on which the claim for universal credit was made or the first date on which the claimant would have been entitled to the specified benefit if a claim had been made for it on that date, if later; and

(ii) any provision of the Claims and Payments Regulations 1987 under which the claim for the specified benefit is treated as made on a later date does not apply;

(c) if the claimant (or, in the case of joint claimants, either of them) makes a claim for housing benefit and the date of that claim (as determined in accordance with the Housing Benefit Regulations 2006 or, as the case may be, the Housing Benefit (Persons who have attained the qualifying age for state pension credit) Regulations 2006 (together referred to as "the Housing Benefit Regulations")) is after the date on which the claim for universal credit was made, but no later than one month after the date on which the information required by sub-paragraph (a) was given—

(i) the claim for housing benefit is to be treated as made on the date on which the claim for universal credit was made or the first date on which the claimant would have been entitled to housing benefit if a claim had been made for it on that date, if later; and

    (ii) any provision of the Housing Benefit Regulations under which the claim for housing benefit is treated as made on a later date does not apply;

(d) if the claimant (or, in the case of joint claimants, either of them) makes a claim for a tax credit and that claim is received by a relevant authority at an appropriate office (within the meaning of the Tax Credits (Claims and Notifications) Regulations 2002 ("the 2002 Regulations")) during the period of one month beginning with the date on which the information required by sub-paragraph (a) was given—

    (i) the claim for a tax credit is to be treated as having been received by a relevant authority at an appropriate office on the date on which the claim for universal credit was made or the first date on which the claimant would have been entitled to a tax credit if a claim had been so received on that date, if later; and

    (ii) any provision of the 2002 Regulations under which the claim is treated as having been made on a later date does not apply.

(5) Where the discovery is made after a decision has been made that the claimant is entitled to universal credit, but before any payment has been made—

(a) that decision is to cease to have effect immediately, by virtue of this article;

(b) the claimant is to be informed that they are not entitled to claim universal credit; and

(c) sub-paragraphs (b) to (d) of paragraph (4) apply.

(6) Where the discovery is made after a decision has been made that the claimant is entitled to universal credit and one or more payments have been made in respect of the claimant, the decision is to be treated as a decision under section 8 of the Social Security Act 1998.

(7) For the purposes of paragraph (4), a person makes a claim for old style ESA or old style JSA where he or she makes a claim for an employment and support allowance or a jobseeker's allowance and the claim is subject to Part 1 of the 2007 Act or the 1995 Act respectively as those provisions have effect apart from the amendments made by the amending provisions.]]]

AMENDMENTS

1. Welfare Reform Act 2012 (Commencement No.9, 11, 13, 14 and 16 and Transitional and Transitory Provisions (Amendment)) Order 2014 (SI 2014/1452) art.5 (June 16, 2014).

2. Welfare Reform Act 2012 (Commencement No.9, 11, 13 14, 16 and 17 and Transitional and Transitory Provisions (Amendment)) Order 2014 (SI 2014/1661) art. 4(3) (June 30, 2014).

3. Welfare Reform Act 2012 (Commencement No.9, 11, 13, 14, 16 and 17 and Transitional and Transitory Provisions (Amendment) (No.2)) Order 2014 (SI 2014/1923) art. 4(4) (July 28, 2014).

DEFINITIONS

"the 1995 Act"–see art. 2(1).
"the 2007 Act"–*ibid.*
"the 2002 Regulations"–para.(4)(d).
"the Act"–see art.2(1).
"the amending provisions"–*ibid.*

"the Claims and Payments Regulations 1987"–*ibid.*
"claimant"–*ibid.*
"employment and support allowance"–*ibid.*
"gateway conditions"–*ibid.*
"housing benefit"–*ibid.*
"the Housing Benefit Regulations"–para.(4)(c).
"income support"–see art.2(1).
"jobseeker's allowance"–*ibid.*
"joint claimants"–*ibid.*
"old style ESA"–*ibid.*
"old style JSA"–*ibid.*
"relevant districts"–*ibid.*
"single claimant"–*ibid.*
"the specified benefit"–para.(4)(b).
"tax credit"–see art.2(1).

GENERAL NOTE

3.118   This makes provision for the position where a person claims universal credit and provides incorrect information as to their place of residence or their compliance with the gateway conditions. This article is similar to reg.13 of the revoked 2013 Transitional Regulations.

Day appointed for the abolition of income-related employment and support allowance and income-based jobseeker's allowance

3.119   [¹4.—(1) The day appointed for the coming into force of—
(a) section 33(1)(a) and (b) and (2) of the Act (abolition of benefits);
(b) paragraphs 22 to 26 of Schedule 3 to the Act (abolition of benefits: consequential provisions) and section 33(3) of the Act in so far as it relates to those paragraphs; and
(c) the repeals in Part 1 of Schedule 14 to the Act (abolition of benefits superseded by universal credit) that are referred to in Schedule 3,
in relation to the case of a claim referred to in paragraph (2)(a) to (d) and (g) and any award that is made in respect of such a claim, and in relation to the case of an award referred to in paragraph (2)(e) and (f), is the day appointed in accordance with paragraph (3).
(2) The claims and awards referred to are—
(a) a claim for universal credit, an employment and support allowance or a jobseeker's allowance where, on the date on which the claim is made [² or treated as made], the claimant—
(i) resides in one of the relevant districts; and
(ii) meets the gateway conditions;
[² (b) a claim for universal credit where—
(i) in the case of a single claimant, the claimant gives incorrect information regarding the claimant residing in a relevant district or meeting the gateway conditions and does not reside in such a district or does not meet the gateway conditions on the date on which the claim is made;
(ii) in the case of joint claimants, either or both of the joint claimants gives or give incorrect information regarding his or her (or their) residing in such a district or meeting those conditions and one or both of them does not or do not reside in such a district or does not or do not meet those conditions on the date on which the claim is made; and

    (iii) after a decision is made that the single claimant is, or the joint claimants are, entitled to universal credit and one or more payments have been made in respect of the single claimant or the joint claimants, the Secretary of State discovers that incorrect information has been given regarding residence or meeting the gateway conditions;]

(c) a claim for universal credit that is treated as made by a couple in the circumstances referred to in regulation 9(8) of the Claims and Payments Regulations 2013 (claims for universal credit by members of a couple) where the claim complies with article 3(7) and [³ ...] ;

[²(d) a claim for universal credit by a former member of a couple who were joint claimants of universal credit, whether or not the claim is made jointly with another person, where the former member is not exempt from the requirement to make a claim by virtue of regulation 9(6) of the Claims and Payments Regulations 2013 (claims for universal credit by members of a couple), where the claim is made during the period of one month starting with the date on which notification is given to the Secretary of State that the former joint claimants have ceased to be a couple, and where the claim complies with article 3(8);]

(e) an award of universal credit that is made without a claim in the circumstances referred to in regulation 6(1) or (2) of the Claims and Payments Regulations 2013 (claims not required for entitlement to universal credit in some cases) where the circumstances referred to in article 3(9) apply;

(f) an award of universal credit that is made without a claim in the circumstances referred to in regulation 9(6), (7) or (10) the Claims and Payments Regulations 2013 (claims for universal credit by members of a couple) where the circumstances referred to in article 3(9) apply; and

(g) a claim for an employment and support allowance or a jobseeker's allowance [² other than one referred to in sub-paragraph (a) that is made or treated as made] —

    (i) during the relevant period by a single claimant of universal credit or, in the case of joint claimants of universal credit, by either of the joint claimants, where the single claimant has made or the joint claimants have made, or been treated as having made, a claim for universal credit within sub-paragraphs (a) to (d);

    (ii) during the relevant period by a single claimant of universal credit or, in the case of joint claimants of universal credit, by either of the joint claimants, where the single claimant has been awarded, or the joint claimants have been awarded, universal credit without a claim within sub-paragraph (e) or (f);

    (iii) by a person who is entitled to make a claim for universal credit in the circumstances referred to in sub-paragraph (d) but has not yet done so; or

    (iv) by a person who may be entitled to an award of universal credit in the circumstances referred to in sub-paragraph (e) or (f) but where no decision has yet been made as to the person's entitlement.

(3) Subject to paragraph (4), the day appointed in relation to the cases referred to in paragraph (2) is—

(a) in the case of a claim referred to in paragraph (2)(a) to (d) and (g), the first day of the period in respect of which the claim is made or (in the case of a claim for universal credit) treated as made;

(b) in the case of an award referred to in paragraph (2)(e) or (f), the first day on which a claimant is entitled to universal credit under that award.

(4) In relation to the case of a claim referred to in paragraph (2)(c) (claim for universal credit treated as made by a couple), where the member of the couple referred to in regulation 9(8)(b) of the Claims and Payments Regulations 2013 ("new claimant partner") was entitled during the prior period to an old style ESA award or an old style JSA award, the new claimant partner was at that time a member of a couple and the award included an amount in respect of the new claimant partner and his or her partner ("P"), the day appointed in relation to that case is the day after the day on which the new claimant partner and P ceased to be a couple for the purposes of the ESA Regulations 2008 or the JSA Regulations 1996 as the case may be.

(5) For the purposes of paragraph (4), the "prior period" means the period beginning with the first day of the period for which the claim for universal credit is treated as made and ending with the day before the day on which the claim for universal credit is treated as made.

(6) In paragraph (1), the reference to the case of a claim for universal credit referred to in paragraph (2)(a) to (d) (and any award made in respect of the claim), or of an award of universal credit referred to in paragraph (2)(e) and (f), includes a reference to—

(a) a case where a notice under regulation 4 of the 2010 Transitional Regulations (the notice commencing the conversion phase in relation to an award of incapacity benefit or severe disablement allowance) is issued to a single claimant or in the case of joint claimants, either of those claimants, during the designated period;

(b) where sub-paragraph (a) does not apply, a case where a conversion decision is made during that period in relation to an award of incapacity benefit or severe disablement allowance to which a single claimant or in the case of joint claimants, either of those claimants, is entitled; and

(c) where sub-paragraphs (a) and (b) do not apply, a case where the effective date of a conversion decision in relation to such an award occurs during that period (where "effective date" has the same meaning as in the 2010 Transitional Regulations),

and any award of an employment and support allowance that is made consequent on a conversion decision that relates to the notice referred to in sub-paragraph (a), the conversion decision referred to in sub-paragraph (b) or the conversion decision referred to in sub-paragraph (c), as the case may be.

(7) For the purposes of paragraph (6), the designated period means—

(a) in relation to a claim for universal credit referred to in paragraph (2)(a), (b)(i) [², (ii)] or (d), any period when a decision has not yet been made on the claim;

(b) in relation to a claim for universal credit that is treated as made as referred to in paragraph (2)(c), any period when no decision has yet been made as to the joint claimants' entitlement;

(c) any period, subsequent to the period referred to in sub-paragraph (a) or (b), when the single claimant or joint claimants is or are entitled to an award of universal credit in respect of the claim; and

(d) in relation to an award of universal credit referred to in paragraph (2) (e) or (f), any period when the single claimant or joint claimants to whom the award was made is or are entitled to that award.]

[³ (8) In paragraph (2)—

(a) in sub-paragraph (c), the reference to regulation 9(8) of the Claims and Payments Regulations 2013 is a reference to that provision both as it has effect as amended by the Digital Service Regulations 2014 and as it has effect apart from that amendment;

(b) in sub-paragraph (d), the reference to regulation 9(6) of the Claims and Payments Regulations 2013 is a reference to that provision as it has effect apart from the amendments made by the Digital Service Regulations 2014;

(c) in sub-paragraph (f), the reference to regulation 9(6) of the Claims and Payments Regulations 2013 is a reference to that provision both as it has effect as amended by the Digital Service Regulations 2014 and as it has effect apart from that amendment.]

[⁴ [⁵(9)] For the purposes of paragraph (1), the reference to the case of a claim for universal credit referred to in paragraph (2)(a) to (d) (and any award made in respect of the claim), or of an award of universal credit without a claim referred to in paragraph (2)(e) and (f), includes a reference to an old style ESA award or an old style JSA award that exists (or, as a result of an act as referred to in [⁵ paragraph (10)], is later found to have existed at that time) immediately before the day appointed (as referred to in paragraph (3) or (4)) in relation to that claim or award without a claim.

[⁵ (10)] For the purposes of [⁵ paragraph (9)], the acts referred to are–

(a) the revision of a decision that the claimant was not entitled to old style ESA or old style JSA; or

(b) an appeal to the First-tier Tribunal, the Upper Tribunal or a court against such a decision.]

AMENDMENTS

1. Welfare Reform Act 2012 (Commencement No.9, 11, 13, 14 and 16 and Transitional and Transitory Provisions (Amendment)) Order 2014 (SI 2014/1452) art.6 (June 16, 2014).

2. Welfare Reform Act 2012 (Commencement No.9, 11, 13, 14, 16 and 17 and Transitional and Transitory Provisions (Amendment) (No.2)) Order 2014 (SI 2014/1923) art. 4(5) (July 28, 2014).

3. Welfare Reform Act 2012 (Commencement No.20 and Transitional and Transitory Provisions and Commencement No.9 and Transitional and Transitory Provisions (Amendment)) Order 2014 (SI 2014/3094) art.7(2)(c) (November 26, 2014).

4. Welfare Reform Act 2012 (Commencement No.9, 11, 13, 14, 16, 17 and 19 and Transitional and Transitory Provisions (Amendment)) Order 2015 (SI 2015/32) art.4(3) (January 26, 2015).

5. Welfare Reform Act 2012 (Commencement No.22 and Transitional and Transitory Provisions) Order 2015 (SI 2015/101) art.7(2)(a) (February 11, 2015).

DEFINITIONS

"the Act"–art. 2(1).
"the Claims and Payments Regulations 2013"–*ibid.*
"employment and support allowance"–*ibid.*

"income-based jobseeker's allowance"–*ibid.*
"income-related employment and support allowance"–*ibid.*
"jobseeker's allowance"–*ibid.*
"relevant districts"–*ibid.*
"the Transitional Regulations"–*ibid.*
"the 2010 Transitional Regulations"–*ibid.*

GENERAL NOTE

Paragraph (1)

3.120   This brings into force provisions relating to the abolition of both income-related ESA and income-based JSA. This includes the repeal of various provisions relating to the abolished allowances as set out in Sch.3. However, these provisions are only brought into force where one of the various different categories of case set out in Paragraph (2) applies.

Paragraph (2)

3.121   This sets out the various categories of case affected by the amendments made by para.(1).

Paragraph (2)(a)

3.122   Where a person (i) resides in a relevant district (see Sch.1); (ii) meets the gateway conditions; and (iii) makes a claim for universal credit, ESA or JSA, then the amendments made by para.(1) above govern both the claim and any award made in respect of that claim.

Paragraph (2)(b)

3.123   This covers the situation here a person claims universal credit and incorrectly states that they live in a relevant district, or provides incorrect information as to their meeting the Pathfinder Group conditions. Such a claim remains within the universal credit regime despite the error.

Paragraph (2)(c)

3.124   This is analogous to art.3(3)(c).

Paragraph (2)(d)

3.125   This is analogous to art.3(3)(d).

Paragraph (2)(e)

3.126   This is analogous to art.3(3)(e).

Paragraph (2)(f)

3.127   This is analogous to art.3(3)(f).

Provisions that apply in connection with the abolition of income-related employment and support allowance and income-based jobseeker's allowance under article 4

3.128   [¹ 5.—(1) [². ..] [³ In determining, for the purposes of article 4(2)(a), whether a claim for an employment and support allowance or a jobseeker's allowance meets the gateway conditions, Schedule 5 is to be read as though—

(a) any reference in that Schedule to making a claim for universal credit included a reference to making a claim for an employment and support allowance or a jobseeker's allowance as the case may be; and

(b) the reference in paragraph 4 to a single claimant, or to joint claimants, of universal credit was a reference to a person who would be a single claimant of universal credit or to persons who would be joint claimants of universal credit, if the claimant of an employment and support allowance or a jobseeker's allowance had made a claim for universal credit.

(1A) For the purposes of article 4(2)(a), where a claim for an employment and support allowance or a jobseeker's allowance is made by a couple or a member of a couple, any reference in article 4(2)(a) or Schedule 5 (save in paragraph 4 of that Schedule) to "the claimant" is a reference to each member of the couple.

(1B) For the purposes of paragraph (1A), "couple" has the same meaning as it has in section 39 of the Act.]

(2) [⁴. ..]

(3) For the purposes of article 4(2)(g), "relevant period" means—

(a) in relation to a claim for universal credit within article 4(2)(a) to (d), any UC claim period, and any period subsequent to any UC claim period in respect of which the single claimant or the joint claimants is or are entitled to an award of universal credit in respect of the claim;

(b) in relation to an award of universal credit within article 4(2)(e) or (f), any period when the single claimant or the joint claimants to whom the award was made is or are entitled to the award.

(4) For the purposes of paragraph (3)(a), a "UC claim period" is a period when—

(a) a claim for universal credit within article 4(2)(a), (b)(i) [², (ii)] or (d) has been made but a decision has not yet been made on the claim;

(b) a claim for universal credit within article 4(2)(c) has been treated as made and no decision has yet been made as to the joint claimants' entitlement; or

(c) a decision has been made that a single claimant or joint claimants is or are not entitled to universal credit and—

(i) the Secretary of State is considering whether to revise that decision under section 9 of the Social Security Act 1998, whether on an application made for that purpose, or on the Secretary of State's own initiative; or

(ii) the single claimant or the joint claimants has or have appealed against that decision to the First-tier Tribunal and that appeal or any subsequent appeal to the Upper Tribunal or to a court has not been finally determined.

[⁵ (5) For the purposes of article 4(2)(a) and (g), the Claims and Payments Regulations 1987 apply, subject to paragraphs (6) and (7), for the purposes of deciding–

(a) whether a claim for an employment and support allowance or a jobseeker's allowance is made; and

(b) the date on which the claim is made or treated as made.

(6) Subject to paragraph (7),–

(a) a person makes a claim for an employment and support allowance or a jobseeker's allowance if he or she takes any action which results in a decision on a claim being required under the Claims and Payments Regulations 1987; and

(b) it is irrelevant that the effect of any provision of the Claims and Payments Regulations 1987 is that, for the purposes of those Regulations, the claim is made or treated as made at a date that is earlier than the date on which that action is taken.

(7) Where, by virtue of–

(a) regulation 6(1F)(b) or (c) of the Claims and Payments Regulations 1987, in the case of a claim for an employment and support allowance; or

(b) regulation 6(4ZA) to (4ZD) and (4A)(a)(i) and (b) of those Regulations, in the case of a claim for a jobseeker's allowance,

a claim for an employment and support allowance or a jobseeker's allowance is treated as made at a date that is earlier than the date on which the action referred to in paragraph (6)(a) is taken, the claim is treated as made on that earlier date.]

(8) For the purposes of article 4(3)(a)—

(a) in the case of a claim for universal credit, where the time for making a claim is extended under regulation 26(2) of the Claims and Payments Regulations 2013 (time within which a claim for universal credit is to be made), the reference to the first day of the period in respect of which the claim is made is a reference to the first day of the period in respect of which the claim is, by reason of the operation of that provision, timeously made;

(b) in the case of a claim for an employment and support allowance or a jobseeker's allowance, where the time for making a claim is extended under regulation 19 of, and Schedule 4 to, the Claims and Payments Regulations 1987, the reference to the first day of the period in respect of which the claim is made is a reference to the first day of the period in respect of which the claim is, by reason of the operation of those provisions, timeously made.]

AMENDMENTS

1. Welfare Reform Act 2012 (Commencement No.9, 11, 13, 14 and 16 and Transitional and Transitory Provisions (Amendment)) Order 2014 (SI 2014/1452) art.7 (June 16, 2014).

2. Welfare Reform Act 2012 (Commencement No.9, 11, 13, 14, 16 and 17 and Transitional and Transitory Provisions (Amendment) (No.2)) Order 2014 (SI 2014/1923) art. 4(6) (July 28, 2014).

3. Welfare Reform Act 2012 (Commencement No.9, 11, 13 14, 16, 17 and 19 and Transitional and Transitory Provisions (Amendment)) Order 2014 (SI 2014/3067) art.6(2)(b) (November 24, 2014).

4. Welfare Reform Act 2012 (Commencement No.20 and Transitional and Transitory Provisions and Commencement No.9 and Transitional and Transitory Provisions (Amendment)) Order 2014 (SI 2014/3094) art.7(2)(d) (November 26, 2014).

5. Welfare Reform Act 2012 (Commencement No.9, 11, 13, 14, 16, 17 and 19 and Transitional and Transitory Provisions (Amendment)) Order 2015 (SI 2015/32) art.4(4) (January 26, 2015).

DEFINITIONS

"the Claims and Payments Regulations 1987"–art. 2(1).
"the Claims and Payments Regulations 2013"–*ibid.*
"income-based jobseeker's allowance"–*ibid.*
"income-related employment and support allowance"–*ibid.*
"jobseeker's allowance"–*ibid.*
"the Transitional Regulations"–*ibid.*

GENERAL NOTE

3.129

These provisions supplement and further define the provisions of art.4.

[¹ Transitional provision where Secretary of State determines that claims for universal credit may not be made: effect on claims for employment and support allowance and jobseeker's allowance

5A.—(1) Where a person makes a claim for an employment and support allowance or a jobseeker's allowance at a time when they would not be able to make a claim for universal credit by virtue of a determination under regulation 4(1) of the 2014 Transitional Regulations (claims for universal credit may not be made in an area or category of case) [⁴, or by virtue of regulation [⁵ 4A of those Regulations (restriction on claims for universal credit by persons entitled to a severe disability premium) [⁶ ...] [⁷ or article 4(11) of the Welfare Reform Act 2012 (Commencement No. 32 and Savings and Transitional Provisions) Order 2019 (no claims for universal credit by frontier workers)] [² and where the amending provisions would otherwise have come into force in relation to the claim by virtue of article 4(2)(a) or any corresponding provision in any order made under section 150(3) of the Act other than this Order], then—

3.130

    (a) in relation to a claim for an employment and support allowance, Part 1 of the 2007 Act and the Welfare Reform Act 2009 are to apply as though the amending provisions and the provisions referred to in article 7(1)(c), (d) and (f) had not come into force in relation to the claim;

    (b) in relation to a claim for a jobseeker's allowance, the 1995 Act, the Social Security Administration Act 1992(2) and the Social Security Act 1998(3) are to apply as though the amending provisions and the provisions referred to in article 7(1)(a), (b) and (e) had not come into force in relation to the claim.]

[² (2) Paragraph (1) does not apply in relation to a claim for an employment and support allowance ("ESA") or a jobseeker's allowance ("JSA") where the claim is made or treated as made—

    (a) where the claimant of ESA or JSA has made or been treated as having made a claim for universal credit ("UC") within article 4(2)(a) to (d) (whether or not the claim for UC is made jointly with another person), or has been awarded UC without a claim within article 4(2)(e) or (f) (whether or not the award is made to the claimant of ESA or JSA and another person as joint claimants), during the "relevant period" in relation to that claim or award as referred to in article 5(3)(a) or (b);

    (b) where the claimant of ESA or JSA has made a claim for UC within any provision of an order made under section 150(3) of the Act, apart from this Order, that corresponds to article 4(2)(a) or (b) (whether or not the claim for UC is made by the claimant of ESA or JSA and another person as joint claimants), during the "relevant period" in relation to that claim as referred to in the provision of that order that corresponds to article 5(3)(a); or

    (c) at a time when the claimant of ESA or JSA may be entitled to an award of UC without a claim in the circumstances referred to in article 4(2)(e) or (f) (whether or not the award may be made to the claimant of ESA or JSA and another person as joint claimants) but where no decision has yet been made as to the claimant's entitlement.]

[³ (3) For the purposes of this article, paragraphs (5) to (7) of article 5 apply for the purpose of deciding—

    (a) whether a claim for ESA or JSA is made; and

    (b) the date on which the claim is made or treated as made.]

AMENDMENTS

1. Welfare Reform Act 2012 (Commencement No.9, 11, 13, 14 and 16 and Transitional and Transitory Provisions (Amendment)) Order 2014 (SI 2014/1452) art.8 (June 16, 2014).

2. Welfare Reform Act 2012 (Commencement No.19 and Transitional and Transitory Provisions and Commencement No.9 and Transitional and Transitory Provisions (Amendment)) Order 2014 (SI 2014/2321) art.7 (September 15, 2014).

3. Welfare Reform Act 2012 (Commencement No.23 and Transitional and Transitory Provisions) Order (2015/634) art.8(5) (March 18, 2015).

4. Welfare Reform Act 2012 (Commencement No.9 and 21 and Transitional and Transitory Provisions (Amendment)) Order 2017 (SI 2017/483) art.2(2) (April 6, 2017).

5. Universal Credit (Transitional Provisions) (SDP Gateway) Amendment Regulations 2019 (SI 2019/10) reg.3(1) (January 16, 2019).

6. Universal Credit (Restriction on Amounts for Children and Qualifying Young Persons) (Transitional Provisions) Amendment Regulations 2019 (SI 2019/27) reg.4(1) (February 1, 2019).

7. Welfare Reform Act 2012 (Commencement No. 32 and Savings and Transitional Provisions) Order 2019 SI 2019/167) art.5(2)(a) (February 1, 2019).

GENERAL NOTE

3.131   This provision has the effect that where a person claims ESA or JSA, and they would *not* be able to claim universal credit by virtue of a determination made by the Secretary of State that a claim for universal credit may not be made in a specified class of case or area (see reg.4(1) of the 2014 Transitional Regulations), then Part 1 of the Welfare Reform Act 2007, the Jobseekers Act 1995 and other relevant provisions apply in relation to the ESA or JSA claim as if the amending provisions had not come into force (see para.(1), subject to the exceptions in paras.(2)).

Transitional provision: where the abolition of income-related employment and support allowance and income-based jobseeker's allowance is treated as not applying

3.132   **6.**—(1) Paragraph (2) applies where—

    (a) a person has or had a new style ESA award or a new style JSA award ("the award") [¹ by virtue of the coming into force of the amending provisions under any secondary legislation];

    (b) in respect of all or part of the period to which the award relates, the person—

        (i) makes a claim, or is treated as making a claim, for universal credit; or

        (ii) makes an application to the Secretary of State for supersession of the decision to make the award, on the basis of a relevant change of circumstances that would relate to the grounds for entitlement to an income-related employment and support allowance or an income-based jobseeker's allowance if the amending provisions had not come into force [¹ ...];

    (c) if the amending provisions had not come into force under [¹ ...] and, in the case of a claim for universal credit, an application for supersession of the decision to make the award had been made, the person would be entitled to an income-related employment and support allowance or an income-based jobseeker's allowance, as the case may be, with respect to the period for which the claim for universal credit or application for supersession is made;

(d) where the person makes an application for supersession of the decision to make the award, the period in respect of which the application is made does not include any period in respect of which the person has been awarded universal credit; [¹ and]

[¹(e)(i) on the date on which the claim for universal credit is made, or the application for supersession is received, as the case may be, the claim does not, or, in the case of an application for supersession, a claim for universal credit by the person would not, fall within any case (including a case with respect to which an award of universal credit may be made without a claim) in relation to which the provisions of the Act referred to in Schedule 2 are in force ("the UC commencement case"); or

(ii) on that date, the claim for universal credit does, or, in the case of an application for supersession, a claim for universal credit by the person would, fall within the UC commencement case, but the claim does or would fall within a case (including a case that relates in whole or in part to residence in an area) that is the subject of a determination made by the Secretary of State under regulation 4(1) of the 2014 Transitional Regulations (determination that claims for universal credit may not be made) [²[³ or the claim is or would be one to which regulation 4A of those Regulations (restriction on claims for universal credit by persons entitled to a severe disability premium) or article 4(11) of the Welfare Reform Act 2012 (Commencement No. 32 and Savings and Transitional Provisions) Order 2019 (no claims for universal credit by frontier workers) applies]].]

(2) Where this paragraph applies, then, in relation to the award and with effect from the first day of the period in respect of which the claim is made or treated as made, or the application for supersession is made, the 1995 Act or Part 1 of the 2007 Act, as the case may be, is to apply as though the amending provisions had not come into force [¹ ...].

(3) For the purposes of paragraph (1) [¹ ...]—

(a) the Claims and Payments Regulations 2013 apply for the purpose of deciding—

(i) whether a claim for universal credit is made or is to be treated as made; and

(ii) the day on which the claim is made or is to be treated as made; [¹ ...]

(b) [¹ ...].

(4) For the purposes of paragraph (2), the reference to the period in respect of which the application for supersession is made is a reference to the period beginning with the day from which the superseding decision takes effect in accordance with section 10(5) of the Social Security Act 1998 and regulation 35 of, and Schedule 1 to, the Decisions and Appeals Regulations 2013 (effectives dates: Secretary of State decisions).

(5) For the purposes of paragraph (2), the reference to the first day of the period in respect of which the claim for universal credit is made or treated as made, in a case where the time for making a claim for universal credit is extended under regulation 26(2) of the Claims and Payments Regulations

2013, is a reference to the first day of the period in respect of which the claim is, by reason of the operation of that provision, timeously made or treated as made.

[[1] (6) For the purposes of this article, "secondary legislation" means an instrument made under an Act.]

AMENDMENTS

1. Welfare Reform Act 2012 (Commencement No.9, 11, 13, 14 and 16 and Transitional and Transitory Provisions (Amendment)) Order 2014 (SI 2014/1452) art.9 (June 16, 2014).
2. Welfare Reform Act 2012 (Commencement No.9 and 21 and Transitional and Transitory Provisions (Amendment)) Order 2017 (SI 2017/483) art.2(3) (April 6, 2017).
3. Welfare Reform Act 2012 (Commencement No. 32 and Savings and Transitional Provisions) Order 2019 SI 2019/167) art.5(2)(b) (February 1, 2019).

DEFINITIONS

"the 1995 Act"–art. 2(1).
"the 2007 Act"–*ibid.*
"the amending provisions"–*ibid.*
"the award"–para.1(a)
"the Claims and Payments Regulations 2013"–art.2(1).
"employment and support allowance"–*ibid.*
"the Decisions and Appeals Regulations 2013"–*ibid.*
"income-based jobseeker's allowance"–*ibid.*
"income-related employment and support allowance"–*ibid.*
"jobseeker's allowance"–*ibid.*
"new style ESA award"–*ibid.*
"new style JSA award"–*ibid.*
"relevant districts"–*ibid.*
"the Transitional Regulations"–*ibid.*

GENERAL NOTE

3.133   This makes transitional provision for cases where the conditions in para.(1) are met. These all concern cases where the claimant either moves out of a relevant district or is not in the Pathfinder Group. In these cases, the award is treated as though the provisions in art.4(1)(a)-(c) above had not come into force (para.(2); see further art.9(2)). In consequence the person concerned will be able to claim an existing benefit, i.e. income-related ESA or income-based JSA, once again. The six conditions set out in Para.(1) are (in summary) that (a) the claimant has a new style ESA award or new style JSA award; (b) they make a claim for universal credit or applies for supersession of the decision to make the award; (c) they would otherwise be entitled to income-related ESA or income-based JSA; (d) any award of universal credit has come to an end; (e), any claim for universal credit does not fall within the category of a "UC commencement case" or, if so, is the subject of a determination made by the Secretary of State under reg.4(1) of the 2014 Transitional Regulations. Paras.(3)-(5) make supplementary provision for paras.(1) and (2).

Day appointed for commencement of provisions relating to claimant responsibilities with respect to employment and support allowance and jobseeker's allowance, and transitional provisions

3.134   7.—(1) The day appointed for the coming into force of—

(a) section 44(2) of the Act and section 44(1) of the Act in so far as it relates to section 44(2) (claimant commitment for jobseeker's allowance);

(b) section 49(2) and (3) to (5) of the Act (and section 49(1) of the Act in so far as it relates to those provisions) (claimant responsibilities for jobseeker's allowance);

(c) section 54(2) of the Act (and section 54(1) of the Act in so far as it relates to that provision) (claimant commitment for employment and support allowance);

(d) section 57(2), (4), (5) and (9) of the Act (and section 57(1) of the Act in so far as it relates to those provisions) (claimant responsibilities for employment and support allowance);

(e) the repeals in Part 4 of Schedule 14 to the Act (jobseeker's allowance: responsibilities after introduction of universal credit); and

(f) the repeals in Part 5 of Schedule 14 to the Act (employment and support allowance: responsibilities after introduction of universal credit),

in so far as they are not already in force, is, in relation to a particular case, the day on which the amending provisions come into force, under any secondary legislation, in relation to that case.

[1 (2) Where, under any secondary legislation, in relation to a new style JSA award, the 1995 Act applies as though the amending provisions had not come into force, then, with effect from the day on which the 1995 Act so applies, the 1995 Act, the Social Security Administration Act 1992 and the Social Security Act 1998 are to apply in relation to the award as though the provisions referred to in paragraph (1)(a), (b) and (e) had not come into force.

(3) Where, under any secondary legislation, in relation to a new style ESA award, Part 1 of the 2007 Act applies as though the amending provisions had not come into force, then, with effect from the day on which Part 1 of the 2007 Act so applies, Part 1 of the 2007 Act and the Welfare Reform Act 2009 are to apply in relation to the award as though the provisions referred to in paragraph (1)(c), (d) and (f) had not come into force.]

(4) For the purposes of paragraphs (1) to (3), "secondary legislation" means an instrument made under an Act.

AMENDMENTS

1. Welfare Reform Act 2012 (Commencement No.11 and Transitional and Transitory Provisions and Commencement No.9 and Transitional and Transitory Provisions (Amendment)) Order 2013 (SI 2013/1511) art.6 (July 1, 2013).

DEFINITIONS

"the Act"–art. 2(1).
"the 1995 Act"–*ibid.*
"the 2007 Act"–*ibid.*
"the amending provisions"–*ibid.*
"employment and support allowance"–*ibid.*
"jobseeker's allowance"–*ibid.*
"new style ESA award"–*ibid.*
"new style JSA award"–*ibid.*
"secondary legislation"–para.(4).

GENERAL NOTE

This provides for the appointed day and transitional provisions for the measures in the WRA 2012 that relate to claimant responsibilities in relation to a new style ESA award or a new style JSA award.

3.135

Day appointed for commencement of provisions concerning consideration of revision before appeal

3.136　**8.** 29th April 2013 is the day appointed for the coming into force of paragraphs 1 to 11 and 15 to 18 of Schedule 11 to the Act (power to require consideration of revision before appeal) and section 102(6) of the Act in so far as it relates to those paragraphs, to the extent that those provisions are not already in force.

DEFINITIONS

"the Act"–art.2(1).

GENERAL NOTE

3.137　This simply brings into force those provisions of Sch.11 to the Act concerning consideration of revision before appeal.

Transitional provision: conversion of incapacity benefits

3.138　**9.**—(1) Subject to paragraph (2), where the amending provisions come into force under article 4(1) in relation to the case of a claim referred to in article 4(2)(a) to (d) [¹ or (g)] and any award made in respect of the claim, or the case of an award referred to in article 4(2)(e) or (f), the 2010 Transitional Regulations are to apply in relation to that case as if the modifications set out in Schedule 4 were made.

(2) Where article 6(2) applies in relation to a new style ESA award (such that the award continues as an old style ESA award), the 2010 Transitional Regulations are to apply in relation to the award, in its continuation as an old style ESA award, as if those modifications had not been made.

AMENDMENTS

1. Welfare Reform Act 2012 (Commencement No.9, 11, 13, 14 and 16 and Transitional and Transitory Provisions (Amendment)) Order 2014 (SI 2014/1452) art.10 (June 16, 2014).

DEFINITIONS

"the amending provisions"–art.2(1).
"new style ESA award"–*ibid*.
"old style ESA award"–*ibid*.
"the 2010 Transitional Regulations"–*ibid*.

GENERAL NOTE

3.139　The introduction of universal credit was always going to be complicated. That complexity has been made worse by the fact that many existing awards of ESA have not been assessed for conversion, sometimes described as "reassessment", to ESA, even though that process began on October 11, 2010. This regulation allows for transitional provisions whereby, in relation to cases with respect to which art.4 has come into force, the Transitional Provisions Regulations 2010 are to be read as if the amendments set out in Sch.4 were made. Those amendments substitute references to provisions that apply to new style ESA awards, including the ESA Regulations 2013.

[¹Transition from old style ESA]

10.—[¹ (1) This article applies where a person—   **3.140**

(a) makes, or is treated as making, a claim for an employment and support allowance and, under article 4, Part 1 of the 2007 Act, as amended by the provisions of Schedule 3, and Part 1 of Schedule 14, to the Act that remove references to an income-related allowance, applies in relation to the claim; or

(b) (i) has an old style ESA award immediately before the appointed day in relation to a case of a claim for universal credit referred to in article 4(2)(a) to (d) (and any award made in respect of the claim), or an award of universal credit referred to in article 4(2)(e) or (f); and

    (ii) the old style ESA award consists of or includes a contributory employment and support allowance (which allowance therefore continues as a new style ESA award),

and, in the case of sub-paragraph (a), the condition referred to in paragraph (1A) is satisfied.

(1A) The condition is that—

(a) the person previously made, or was treated as having made, a claim for an employment and support allowance and Part 1 of the 2007 Act, as it has effect apart from the provisions of Schedule 3, and Part 1 of Schedule 14, to the Act that remove references to an income-related allowance, applied in relation to the claim;

(b) a notice was issued to the person under regulation 4 of the 2010 Transitional Regulations and Part 1 of the 2007 Act, as that Part has effect apart from the provisions of Schedule 3, and Part 1 of Schedule 14, to the Act that remove references to an income-related allowance, applied in relation to the notice; or

(c) the person previously had a new style ESA award and article 6(2) applied in relation to the award (which award therefore continued as an old style ESA award).]

(2) Where this article applies, the ESA Regulations 2013 are to be read as if—

    (a)(i) in the definitions of "period of limited capability for work" in regulations 2 (interpretation) and 3 (further interpretation), the reference to a period throughout which a person has, or is treated as having, limited capability for work included a reference to a period throughout which the person in question had, or was treated as having, limited capability for work under the ESA Regulations 2008; and

    (ii) the reference, in the definition in regulation 2, to regulation 28 of the Claims and Payments Regulations 2013 (time within which a claim for employment and support allowance is to be made) included a reference to regulation 19 of, and Schedule 4 to, the Claims and Payments Regulations 1987 (prescribed times for claiming benefit);

(b) in regulation 6 (the assessment phase–previous claimants)—

    (i) any reference to an employment and support allowance included a reference to an old style ESA award; and

    (ii) in paragraph (2)(b)(v) and (c)(iii), the reference to regulation 26 (conditions for treating a claimant as having limited capability for work until a determination about limited capability for work has been made) included a reference to regulation 30 of the ESA Regulations 2008 (conditions for treating a claimant as having limited capability for work until a determination about limited capability for work has been made);

(c) in regulation 7 (circumstances where the condition that the assessment phase has ended before entitlement to the support component [³ . . .] arises does not apply)—

    (i) any reference to an employment and support allowance included a reference to an old style ESA award; and

    (ii) in paragraph (3)(b)(iv), (c)(iii), (c)(iv) and (d)(iii), the reference to regulation 26 included a reference to regulation 30 of the ESA Regulations 2008;

(d) in regulation 11 (condition relating to youth–previous claimants), any reference to an employment and support allowance included a reference to an old style ESA award;

(e) in regulation 15 (determination of limited capability for work)—

    (i) the reference in paragraph (7)(a) to a claimant having been determined to have limited capability for work included a reference to such a determination made under Part 5 of the ESA Regulations 2008; and

    (ii) the reference in paragraph (7)(b) to a person being treated as having limited capability for work included a reference to a person being so treated under regulation 20 (certain claimants to be treated as having limited capability for work), 25 (hospital patients), 26 (claimants receiving certain regular treatment) or 29 (exceptional circumstances) of the ESA Regulations 2008;

(f) in regulation 26 (conditions for treating a claimant as having limited capability for work until a determination about limited capability for work has been made)—

    (i) in paragraph (2)(b), the reference to regulation 18 (failure to provide information in relation to limited capability for work) and 19 (claimant may be called for a medical examination to determine whether the claimant has limited capability for work) included a reference to regulation 22 (failure to provide information in relation to limited capability for work) and 23 (claimant may be called for a medical examination to determine whether the claimant has limited capability for work) of the ESA Regulations 2008; and

    (ii) in paragraph (4)(c), the reference to regulation 18 included a reference to regulation 22 of the ESA Regulations 2008;

(g) in regulation 30(4) (determination of limited capability for work-related activity), the reference to a determination about whether a claimant has, or is to be treated as having or not having, limited capability for work-related activity included such a determination that was made under Part 6 of the ESA Regulations 2008; [¹ . . .]

[¹(ga) in regulation 39(6) (exempt work), the reference to an employment and support allowance included a reference to an old style ESA award;

(gb) in regulation 85(2)(a) (waiting days), where a claimant was entitled to an old style ESA award with effect from the first day of a period of limited capability for work by virtue of regulation 144(2)(a) of the ESA Regulations 2008 and, with effect from [² a day between the second and the seventh day of that period (including the second and the seventh day)], that award continued as a new style ESA award in the circumstances referred to in paragraph (1)(b) of this article, the reference to an employment and support allowance included a reference to the old style ESA award;]

(h) in regulation 87(1) (claimants appealing a decision), the reference to a determination that the claimant does not have limited capability for work under the ESA Regulations 2013 included a reference to such a determination under the ESA Regulations 2008.

(i) in regulation 89 (short absence), where—

    (i) a claimant had an old style ESA award in the circumstances referred to in paragraph (1)(b) of this article;

    (ii) a temporary absence from Great Britain commenced when regulation 152 of the ESA Regulations 2008 applied to the claimant; and

    (iii) the first 4 weeks of the temporary absence had not ended immediately before the first day of entitlement to the new style ESA award,

the initial words of regulation 89 included a reference to the claimant being entitled to the new style ESA award during the remainder of the first 4 weeks of the temporary absence that commenced when regulation 152 of the ESA Regulations 2008 applied to the claimant;

(j) in regulation 90 (absence to receive medical treatment), where—

    (i) a claimant had an old style ESA award in the circumstances referred to in paragraph (1)(b) of this article;

    (ii) a temporary absence from Great Britain commenced when regulation 153 of the ESA Regulations 2008 applied to the claimant; and

    (iii) the first 26 weeks of the temporary absence had not ended immediately before the first day of entitlement to the new style ESA award,

the initial words of paragraph (1) of regulation 90 included a reference to the claimant being entitled to the new style ESA award during the remainder of the first 26 weeks of the temporary absence that commenced when regulation 153 of the ESA Regulations 2008 applied to the claimant;

(k) in regulation 93 (disqualification for misconduct etc)—

    (i) in paragraph (3), for "Paragraph (2) does" there were substituted "Paragraphs (2) and (5) do"; and

    (ii) after paragraph (4) there were inserted—

"(5) Subject to paragraph (3), a claimant is to be disqualified for receiving an employment and support allowance for any period determined by the Secretary of State under regulation 157(2) of the Employment and Support Allowance Regulations 2008(3) less any days during that period on which those Regulations applied to the claimant.

(6) Where paragraph (5) applies to a claimant, paragraph (2) is not to apply to that claimant with respect to any matter referred to in paragraph (1) that formed the basis for the claimant's disqualification under regulation 157(2) of the Employment and Support Allowance Regulations 2008.";

(l) in regulation 95 (treating a claimant as not having limited capability for work), the existing words became paragraph (1) and—

 (i) at the beginning of paragraph (1), there were inserted "Subject to paragraph (2),"; and

 (ii) after paragraph (1), there were inserted—

"(2) A claimant is to be treated as not having limited capability for work if—

(a) under Part 1 of the Act as it has effect apart from the amendments made by Schedule 3, and Part 1 of Schedule 14, to the Welfare Reform Act 2012 that remove references to an income-related allowance ("the former law"), the claimant was disqualified for receiving a contributory employment and support allowance during a period of imprisonment or detention in legal custody;

(b) Part 1 of the Act as amended by the provisions of Schedule 3, and Part 1 of Schedule 14, to the Welfare Reform Act 2012 that remove references to an income-related allowance ("the current law") applied to the claimant with effect from a day that occurred during the period of imprisonment or detention in legal custody referred to in sub-paragraph (a) and during the period of six weeks with effect from the day on which the claimant was first disqualified as referred to in sub-paragraph (a); and

(c) the total of—

 (i) the period for which the claimant was disqualified for receiving a contributory employment and support allowance during the period of imprisonment or detention in legal custody when the former law applied to the claimant; and

 (ii) the period for which the claimant was disqualified for receiving an employment and support allowance during the period of imprisonment or detention in legal custody when the current law applied to the claimant,

amounts to more than six weeks."]

[¹ (3) Subject to paragraph (4), where this article applies, the 2007 Act is to be read as though—

(a) the reference to an employment and support allowance in section 1A(1) and (4) to (6);

(b) the first reference to an employment and support allowance in section 1A(3); and

(c) the first reference to an employment and support allowance in section 1B(4),

included a reference to a contributory employment and support allowance.

(4) Where this article applies and the 2010 Transitional Regulations apply to a person, paragraph (3)(c) becomes paragraph (3)(b) and, for paragraph (3)(a) and (b), there is substituted—

"(a) in section 1A as substituted by the 2010 Transitional Regulations—

 (i) the reference to an employment and support allowance in section 1A(1), (4) and (5); and

 (ii) the first reference to an employment and support allowance in section 1A(3); and".

(5) Where this article applies and a claimant—

(a) had an old style ESA award in the circumstances referred to in paragraph (1)(b); and

  (b) the old style ESA award had not been preceded by a new style ESA
      award in the circumstances referred to in paragraph (1A)(c),
the 2007 Act is to be read as if, in section 24(2), the beginning of the assessment phase (subject to section 24(3)) was the first day of the period for which the claimant was entitled to the old style ESA award.]

AMENDMENTS

  1. Welfare Reform Act 2012 (Commencement No.11 and Transitional and Transitory Provisions and Commencement No.9 and Transitional and Transitory Provisions (Amendment)) Order 2013 (SI 2013/1511) art.8 (July 1, 2013).
  2. Welfare Reform Act 2012 (Commencement No.9, 11, 13 14, 16, 17 and 19 and Transitional and Transitory Provisions (Amendment)) Order 2014 (SI 2014/3067) art.7(a) (November 24, 2014).
  3. Employment and Support Allowance and Universal Credit (Miscellaneous Amendments and Transitional and Savings Provisions) Regulations 2017 (SI 2017/204) reg.7 and Sch.1 para.9(2) (April 3, 2017).

DEFINITIONS

  "the amending provisions"–art. 2(1)
  "appointed day"–*ibid.*
  "the Claims and Payments Regulations 1987"–*ibid.*
  "the Claims and Payments Regulations 2013"–*ibid.*
  "contributory employment and support allowance"–*ibid.*
  "employment and support allowance"–*ibid.*
  "the ESA Regulations 2008"–*ibid.*
  "the ESA Regulations 2013"–*ibid.*
  "new style ESA award"–*ibid.*
  "old style ESA award"–*ibid.*

GENERAL NOTE

This makes transitional provisions for assessments of limited capability for work   **3.141**
or for work and work-related activity where a person has a new style ESA award and previously had an old style ESA award. Article 11 deals with the converse position.
  So, for example, under the new style ESA award the definition of a period of limited capability for work includes a period throughout which the claimant had, or was treated as having, limited capability for work for the purposes of old style ESA (para.(2)(a)). Similarly, where the old style and new style awards link, then days of entitlement to old styled ESA in the linked award are included in calculating the end of the assessment phase (para.(2)(b)). To the same end, any earlier period of limited capability for work under the old style ESA award is counted in working out whether the work related activity component or support component is payable from the first day of entitlement (para.(2)(c)). Likewise, the six months rule for the purposes of treating a claimant as having limited capability for work until a further determination is made includes having limited capability for work (or being treated as such) under an old style ESA award (subs.(2)(f)).

[¹ Transition from new style ESA]

  11.—[¹ (1) This article applies where a person—   **3.142**
  (a) makes, or is treated as making, a claim for an employment and support allowance and Part 1 of the 2007 Act, as it has effect apart from the provisions of Schedule 3, and Part 1 of Schedule 14, to the Act that remove references to an income-related allowance, applies in relation to the claim; or

(b) has a new style ESA award and article 6(2) applies in relation to the award (which award therefore continues as an old style ESA award),

and, in the case of sub-paragraph (a), the condition referred to in paragraph (1A) is satisfied.

(1A) The condition is that—

(a) the person previously made, or was treated as having made, a claim for an employment and support allowance and, under article 4, Part 1 of the 2007 Act, as amended by the provisions of Schedule 3, and Part 1 of Schedule 14, to the Act that remove references to an income-related allowance, applied in relation to the claim;

(b) a notice was issued to the person under regulation 4 of the 2010 Transitional Regulations and, under article 4, Part 1 of the 2007 Act, as amended by the provisions of Schedule 3, and Part 1 of Schedule 14, to the Act that remove references to an income-related allowance, applied in relation to the notice; or

(c) the person previously—

(i) had an old style ESA award immediately before the appointed day in relation to a case of a claim for universal credit referred to in article 4(2)(a) to (d) (and any award made in respect of the claim), or an award of universal credit referred to in article 4(2)(e) or (f); and

(ii) the old style ESA award consisted of or included a contributory employment and support allowance (which allowance therefore continued as a new style ESA award).]

(2) Where this article applies, the ESA Regulations 2008 are to be read as if—

(a)(i) in the definitions of "period of limited capability for work" in regulation 2(1) and (5) (interpretation), the reference to a period throughout which a person has, or is treated as having, limited capability for work included a reference to a period throughout which the person in question had, or was treated as having, limited capability for work under the ESA Regulations 2013; and

(ii) the reference, in the definition in regulation 2(1), to regulation 19 of the Claims and Payments Regulations 1987 (time for claiming benefit) included a reference to regulation 28 of the Claims and Payments Regulations 2013 (time within which a claim for an employment and support allowance is to be made);

(b) in regulation 5 (the assessment phase–previous claimants)—

(i) any reference to an employment and support allowance included a reference to a new style ESA award; and

(ii) in paragraph (2)(b)(v) and (c)(iii), the reference to regulation 30 (conditions for treating a claimant as having limited capability for work until a determination about limited capability for work has been made) included a reference to regulation 26 of the ESA Regulations 2013 (conditions for treating a claimant as having limited capability for work until a determination about limited capability for work has been made);

(c) in regulation 7 (circumstances where the condition that the assessment phase has ended before entitlement to the support component [5 . . .] arises does not apply)—

(i) any reference to an employment and support allowance included a reference to a new style ESA award; and

    (ii) in paragraph (1B)(b)(iv), (c)(iii), (c)(iv) and (d)(iii), the reference to regulation 30 included a reference to regulation 26 of the ESA Regulations 2013;

(d) in regulation 10 (condition relating to youth – previous claimants), any reference to an employment and support allowance included a reference to a new style ESA award;

(e) in regulation 19 (determination of limited capability for work)—

    (i) the reference in paragraph (7)(a) to a claimant having been determined to have limited capability for work included a reference to such a determination made under Part 4 of the ESA Regulations 2013; and

    (ii) the reference in paragraph (7)(b) to a person being treated as having limited capability for work included a reference to a person being so treated under regulation 16 (certain claimants to be treated as having limited capability for work), 21 (hospital patients), 22 (claimants receiving certain treatment) or 25 (exceptional circumstances) of the ESA Regulations 2013;

(f) in regulation 30 (conditions for treating a claimant as having limited capability for work until a determination about limited capability for work has been made)—

    (i) in the initial words of paragraph (2)(b), the reference to regulation 22 (failure to provide information in relation to limited capability for work) and 23 (claimant may be called for a medical examination to determine whether the claimant has limited capability for work) included a reference to regulation 18 (failure to provide information in relation to limited capability for work) and 19 (claimant may be called for a medical examination to determine whether the claimant has limited capability for work) of the ESA Regulations 2013; and

    (ii) in [² paragraph (4)(c)], the reference to regulation 22 included a reference to regulation 18 of the ESA Regulations 2013;

(g) in regulation 34(4) (determination of limited capability for work-related activity), the reference to a determination about whether a claimant has, or is to be treated as having or not having, limited capability for work-related activity included such a determination that was made under Part 5 of the ESA Regulations 2013; [¹ ...]

[¹(ga) in regulation 45(10) (exempt work), the reference to an employment and support allowance included a reference to a new style ESA award;

(gb) in regulation 144(2)(a) (waiting days), where the claimant was entitled to a new style ESA award with effect from the first day of a period of limited capability for work by virtue of regulation 85(2)(a) of the ESA Regulations 2013 and, with effect from [⁴ a day between the second and the seventh day of that period (including the second and the seventh day)], that award continued as an old style ESA award in the circumstances referred to in paragraph (1)(c) of this article, the reference to an employment and support allowance included a reference to the new style ESA award;]

(h) in regulation 147A(1) (claimants appealing a decision), the reference to a determination that the claimant does not have limited capability for work included a reference to such a determination under the ESA Regulations 2013.

(i) in regulation 152 (short absence), where—
  (i) a claimant had a new style ESA award in the circumstances referred to in paragraph (1)(b) of this article;
  (ii) a temporary absence from Great Britain commenced when regulation 89 of the ESA Regulations 2013 applied to the claimant; and
  (iii) the first 4 weeks of the temporary absence had not ended immediately before the first day of entitlement to the old style ESA award,
the initial words of regulation 152 included a reference to the claimant being entitled to the old style ESA award during the remainder of the first 4 weeks of the temporary absence that commenced when regulation 89 of the ESA Regulations 2013 applied to the claimant;
  (j) in regulation 153 (absence to receive medical treatment)—
  (i) a claimant had a new style ESA award in the circumstances referred to in paragraph (1)(b) of this article;
  (ii) a temporary absence from Great Britain commenced when regulation 90 of the ESA Regulations 2013 applied to the claimant; and
  (iii) the first 26 weeks of the temporary absence had not ended immediately before the first day of entitlement to the old style ESA award,
the initial words of paragraph (1) of regulation 153 included a reference to the claimant being entitled to the old style ESA award during the remainder of the first 26 weeks of the temporary absence that commenced when regulation 90 of the ESA Regulations 2013 applied to the claimant;
  (k) in regulation 157 (disqualification for misconduct etc)—
  (i) in paragraph (3), for "Paragraph (2) does" there were substituted "Paragraphs (2) and (4) do"; and
  (ii) after paragraph (3) there were inserted—
  "(4) Subject to paragraph (3), a claimant is to be disqualified for receiving an employment and support allowance for any period determined by the Secretary of State under regulation 93(2) of the Employment and Support Allowance Regulations 2013 less any days during that period on which those Regulations applied to the claimant.
  (5) Where paragraph (4) applies to a claimant, paragraph (2) is not to apply to that claimant with respect to any matter referred to in paragraph (1) that formed the basis for the claimant's disqualification under regulation 93(2) of the Employment and Support Allowance Regulations 2013."; [² ...]
  (l) in regulation 159 (treating a claimant as not having limited capability for work), the existing words became paragraph (1) and—
  (i) at the beginning of paragraph (1), there were inserted "Subject to paragraph (2),"; and
  (ii) after paragraph (1), there were inserted—
  "(2) A claimant is to be treated as not having limited capability for work if—
  (a) under Part 1 of the Act as amended by the provisions of Schedule 3, and Part 1 of Schedule 14, to the Welfare Reform Act 2012 that remove references to an income-related allowance ("the former law"), the claimant was disqualified for receiving an employment and support allowance during a period of imprisonment or detention in legal custody;

(b) Part 1 of the Act as it has effect apart from the amendments made by Schedule 3, and Part 1 of Schedule 14, to the Welfare Reform Act 2012 that remove references to an income-related allowance ("the current law") applied to the claimant with effect from a day that occurred during the period of imprisonment or detention in legal custody referred to in sub-paragraph (a) and during the period of six weeks with effect from the day on which the claimant was first disqualified as referred to in sub-paragraph (a); and

(c) the total of—

    (i) the period for which the claimant was disqualified for receiving an employment and support allowance during the period of imprisonment or detention in legal custody when the former law applied to the claimant; and

    (ii) the period for which the claimant was disqualified for receiving a contributory employment and support allowance during the period of imprisonment or detention in legal custody when the current law applied to the claimant,

amounts to more than six weeks."]; [³ and

(m) in Schedule 6 (housing costs), in paragraphs 8(1) and 9(1), each reference to an employment and support allowance included a reference to new style ESA.]

[¹ (3) Subject to paragraph (4), where this article applies, the 2007 Act is to be read as though—

(a) the reference to a contributory allowance in section (1A)(1) and (4) to (6);

(b) the first reference to a contributory allowance in section (1A)(3); and

(c) the first reference to a contributory allowance in section 1B,

included a reference to a new style ESA award.

(4) Where this article applies and the 2010 Transitional Regulations apply to a person, paragraph (3)(c) becomes paragraph (3)(b) and, for paragraph (3)(a) and (b), there is substituted—

"(a) in section 1A as substituted by the 2010 Transitional Regulations—

    (i) the reference to a contributory allowance in section 1A(1), (4) and (5); and

    (ii) the first reference to a contributory allowance in section 1A(3); and".

(5) Where this article applies and a claimant—

(a) had a new style ESA award in the circumstances referred to in paragraph (1)(b); and

(b) the new style ESA award had not been preceded by an old style ESA award in the circumstances referred to in paragraph (1A)(c),

section 24(2) of the 2007 Act is to be read as if the beginning of the assessment phase (subject to section 24(3)) was the first day of the period for which the claimant was entitled to the new style ESA award.]

AMENDMENTS

1. Welfare Reform Act 2012 (Commencement No.11 and Transitional and Transitory Provisions and Commencement No.9 and Transitional and Transitory Provisions (Amendment)) Order 2013 (SI 2013.1511) art.9 (July 1, 2013).

2. Welfare Reform Act 2012 (Commencement No.13 and Transitional and Transitory Provisions) Order 2013 (SI 2013/2657) art. 5(a) (October 29, 2013).

3. Welfare Reform Act 2012 (Commencement No.9, 11, 13, 14 and 16 and

Transitional and Transitory Provisions (Amendment)) Order 2014 (SI 2014/1452) art.11 (June 16, 2014).

4. Welfare Reform Act 2012 (Commencement No.9, 11, 13 14, 16, 17 and 19 and Transitional and Transitory Provisions (Amendment)) Order 2014 (SI 2014/3067) art.7(a) (November 24, 2014).

5. Employment and Support Allowance and Universal Credit (Miscellaneous Amendments and Transitional and Savings Provisions) Regulations 2017 (SI 2017/204) reg.7 and Sch.1 para.9(3) (April 3, 2017).

DEFINITIONS

"the Claims and Payments Regulations 1987"–art. 2(1)
"the Claims and Payments Regulations 2013"–*ibid.*
"employment and support allowance"–*ibid.*
"the ESA Regulations 2008"–*ibid.*
"the ESA Regulations 2013"–*ibid.*
"new style ESA award"–*ibid.*
"old style ESA award"–*ibid.*

GENERAL NOTE

3.143 This makes transitional provisions for assessments of limited capability for work or for work and work-related activity where a person has an old style ESA award and previously had a new style ESA award. Article 10 deals with the converse position. The modifications are to similar effect as in Art.10.

[¹Transition from old style JSA

3.144 **12.**—(1) This article applies where a person—
(a) makes, or is treated as making, a claim for a jobseeker's allowance and, under article 4, the 1995 Act, as amended by the provisions of Part 1 of Schedule 14 to the Act that remove references to an income-based jobseeker's allowance, applies in relation to the claim; or
(b) (i) has an old style JSA award (whether or not the award was made to the person as a member of a joint-claim couple) immediately before the appointed day in relation to a case of a claim for universal credit referred to in article 4(2)(a) to (d) (and any award made in respect of the claim), or an award of universal credit referred to in article 4(2)(e) or (f); and
(ii) the old style JSA award consists of or includes a contribution-based jobseeker's allowance (which allowance therefore continues as a new style JSA award),
and, in the case of sub-paragraph (a), the condition referred to in paragraph (2) is satisfied.
(2) The condition is that the person previously—
(a) made, or was treated as having made, a claim for a jobseeker's allowance (whether or not as a member of a joint-claim couple) and the 1995 Act, as it has effect apart from the provisions of Part 1 of Schedule 14 to the Act that remove references to an income-based jobseeker's allowance, applied in relation to the claim; or
(b) had a new style JSA award and article 6(2) applied in relation to the award (which award therefore continued as an old style JSA award).
(3) Where this article applies, the JSA Regulations 2013 are to be read as if—

(a) in regulation 15(3)(b) (victims of domestic violence), the reference to regulation 15 applying to the claimant included a reference to the claimant having been treated as being available for employment under regulation 14A(2) or (6) of the JSA Regulations 1996;

(b) in regulation 36(1) (waiting days), where a person was entitled to an old style JSA award with effect from the first day of a jobseeking period by virtue of regulation 46(1)(a) of the JSA Regulations 1996 and, with effect from [² a day between the second and the seventh day of that period (including the second and the seventh day)], that award continued as a new style JSA award in the circumstances referred to in paragraph (1)(b) of this article, the reference to a job-seeker's allowance included a reference to the old style JSA award;

(c) in regulation 37 (jobseeking period)—

    (i) the jobseeking period in relation to a claimant included any period that, under regulation 47 of the JSA Regulations 1996 (jobseeking period), forms part of the jobseeking period for the purposes of the 1995 Act; and

    (ii) in paragraph (3), the reference to a day that is to be treated as a day in respect of which the claimant was entitled to a jobseeker's allowance included a reference to any day that, under regulation 47(4) of the JSA Regulations 1996, is to be treated as a day in respect of which the claimant was entitled to a contribution-based jobseeker's allowance;

(d) in regulation 41 (persons temporarily absent from Great Britain), where a person had an old style JSA award in the circumstances referred to in paragraph (1)(b) of this article, the reference in paragraph (2)(b), (3)(a) and (c), (5)(a) and (6)(b) to entitlement to a jobseeker's allowance included a reference to the old style JSA award; and

(e) in regulation 46 (short periods of sickness), after paragraph (5) there were inserted—

"(6) Where—

(a) a person has been treated under regulation 55(1) of the Jobseeker's Allowance Regulations 1996 as capable of work or as not having limited capability for work for a certain period; and

(b) these Regulations apply to that person with effect from a day ("the relevant day") within that period,

the person is to be treated for the part of that period that begins with the relevant day as capable of work or as not having limited capability for work.

(7) Where paragraph (6) applies to a person and the conditions in paragraph (1)(a) to (c) are fulfilled in relation to that person on any day within the part of a period referred to in paragraph (6), the requirement of paragraph (1) to treat the person as capable of work or as not having limited capability for work is to be regarded as satisfied with respect to the fulfilment of those conditions on that day.

(8) For the purposes of paragraph (3), where paragraph (6) applies to a person, paragraph (3) is to apply to the person as though the preceding provisions of this regulation had applied to the person with respect to the person having been treated for a period, under regulation 55(1) of the Jobseeker's Allowance Regulations 1996 and paragraph (6), as capable of work or as not having limited capability for work.".

(4) Where this article applies, the 1995 Act is to be read as though, in

section 5 of the 1995 Act, the reference to a jobseeker's allowance in subsection (1) and the first reference to a jobseeker's allowance in subsection (2) included a reference to a contribution-based jobseeker's allowance.

(5) For the purposes of this article, "joint-claim couple" has the meaning given in section 1(4) of the 1995 Act.]

AMENDMENTS

1. Welfare Reform Act 2012 (Commencement No.11 and Transitional and Transitory Provisions and Commencement No.9 and Transitional and Transitory Provisions (Amendment)) Order 2013 (SI 2013/1511) art.10 (July 1, 2013).

2. Welfare Reform Act 2012 (Commencement No.9, 11, 13 14, 16, 17 and 19 and Transitional and Transitory Provisions (Amendment)) Order 2014 (SI 2014/3067) art.7(a) (November 24, 2014).

DEFINITIONS

"the amending provisions"–art. 2(1).
"the appointed day"–*ibid.*
"contribution-based jobseeker's allowance"–*ibid.*
"jobseeker's allowance"–*ibid.*
"joint-claim couple"—see para.(5).
"the JSA Regulations 1996"–art. 2(1).
"the JSA Regulations 2013"–*ibid.*
"new style JSA award"–*ibid.*
"old style JSA award"–*ibid.*

GENERAL NOTE

3.145   This makes transitional provisions for the continuity of jobseeking periods where a person has a new style JSA award and previously had an old style JSA award. Article 13 deals with the converse position.

[¹ Transition from new style JSA

3.146   **13.**—(1) This article applies where a person—
(a) makes, or is treated as making, a claim for a jobseeker's allowance (whether or not as a member of a joint-claim couple) and the 1995 Act, as it has effect apart from the provisions of Part 1 of Schedule 14 to the Act that remove references to an income-based jobseeker's allowance, applies in relation to the claim; or
(b) has a new style JSA award and article 6(2) applies in relation to the award such that it continues as an old style JSA award,
and, in the case of sub-paragraph (a), the condition referred to in paragraph (2) is satisfied.
(2) The condition is that the person previously—
(a) made, or was treated as having made, a claim for a jobseeker's allowance and, under article 4, the 1995 Act, as amended by the provisions of Part 1 of Schedule 14 to the Act that remove references to an income-based jobseeker's allowance, applied in relation to the claim; or
(b)(i) had an old style JSA award immediately before the appointed day in relation to a case of a claim for universal credit referred to in article 4(2)(a) to (d) (and any award made in respect of the claim), or an award of universal credit referred to in article 4(2) (e) or (f); and

(ii) the old style JSA award consisted of or included a contributory employment and support allowance (which allowance therefore continued as a new style JSA award).

(3) Where this article applies, the JSA Regulations 1996 are to be read as if—

[²(za) in regulation 11, the references in paragraph (2)(a) and (b) to a job-seeker's allowance included a reference to new style JSA;]

(a) in regulation 14A (victims of domestic violence), for the purposes of paragraph (3)(b) of that regulation, a person had been treated as available for employment on a day (under paragraph (2) of that regulation) where regulation 15 of the JSA Regulations 2013 applied to that person on that day;

[²(aa) in regulation 17A(7), in paragraph (a) of the definition of "benefit", the reference to a jobseeker's allowance included a reference to new style JSA;

(ab) in regulation 19(1)(r), the reference to a jobseeker's allowance included a reference to new style JSA;]

(b) in regulation 46 (waiting days)—

(i) where a person was entitled to a new style JSA award with effect from the first day of a jobseeking period by virtue of regulation 36(1) of the JSA Regulations 2013 and, with effect from [³ a day between the second and the seventh day of that period (including the second and the seventh day)], that award continued as an old style JSA award in the circumstances referred to in paragraph (1)(b) of this article, the reference to a jobseeker's allowance in paragraph (1)(a) included a reference to the new style JSA award; and

(ii) the second reference to a jobseeker's allowance in paragraph (1)(d) included a reference to a new style JSA award;

(c) in regulation 47 (jobseeking period)—

(i) the jobseeking period in relation to a claimant included any period that, under regulation 37 of the JSA Regulations 2013 (jobseeking period) forms part of the jobseeking period for the purposes of the 1995 Act; and

(ii) in paragraph (4), the reference to any day that is to be treated as a day in respect of which the claimant was entitled to a contribution-based jobseeker's allowance included a reference to a day that, under regulation 37(3) of the JSA Regulations 2013 (jobseeking period), is to be treated as a day in respect of which the claimant was entitled to a jobseeker's allowance;

(d) in regulation 50 (persons temporarily absent from Great Britain), where a person had a new style JSA award in the circumstances referred to in paragraph (1)(b) of this article, the reference in paragraph (2)(b), (3)(a) and (c), (5)(a) and (c), (6AA)(a) and (6D)(b) to entitlement to a jobseeker's allowance included a reference to the new style JSA award; [² . . .]

(e) in regulation 55 (short periods of sickness), after paragraph (5) there were inserted—

"(6) Where—

(a) a person has been treated under regulation 46(1) of the Jobseeker's Allowance Regulations 2013 as capable of work or as not having limited capability for work for a certain period; and

(b) these Regulations apply to that person with effect from a day ("the relevant day") within that period,

the person is to be treated for the part of that period that begins with the relevant day as capable of work or as not having limited capability for work.

(7) Where paragraph (6) applies to a person and the conditions in paragraph (1)(a) to (c) are fulfilled in relation to that person on any day within the part of a period referred to in paragraph (6), the requirement of paragraph (1) to treat the person as capable of work or as not having limited capability for work is to be regarded as satisfied with respect to the fulfilment of those conditions on that day.

(8) For the purposes of paragraph (3), where paragraph (6) applies to a person, paragraph (3) is to apply to the person as though the preceding provisions of this regulation had applied to the person with respect to the person having been treated for a period, under regulation 46(1) of the Jobseeker's Allowance Regulations 2013 and paragraph (6), as capable of work or as not having limited capability for work.".

[²(f) in paragraphs 6(1) and 7(1) of Schedule 2 (housing costs), each reference to a jobseeker's allowance included a reference to new style JSA; and

(g) in paragraph 13 of Schedule 2 (housing costs)—

    (i) in paragraph (a) of sub-paragraph (1) (apart from sub-paragraph (ii)(bb) of that paragraph), each of the references to a jobseeker's allowance included a reference to new style JSA;

    (ii) in sub-paragraph (1)(b), the reference to a jobseeker's allowance included a reference to new style JSA; and

    (iii) in sub-paragraph (1)(c)(iv) and (f)(iii), the reference to the making of a claim for a jobseeker's allowance included a reference to the making of a claim for a jobseeker's allowance where the 1995 Act, as it has effect as amended by the amending provisions, applied to the claim and the new style JSA award that resulted from the claim continued as an old style JSA award by virtue of article 6 of this Order.]

(4) Where this article applies, the 1995 Act is to be read as though, in section 5 of the 1995 Act, the reference to a contribution-based jobseeker's allowance in subsection (1) and the first reference to a contribution-based jobseeker's allowance in subsection (2) included a reference to a new style JSA award.

(5) For the purposes of this article, "joint-claim couple" has the meaning given in section 1(4) of the 1995 Act.]

AMENDMENTS

1. Welfare Reform Act 2012 (Commencement No.11 and Transitional and Transitory Provisions and Commencement No.9 and Transitional and Transitory Provisions (Amendment)) Order 2013 (SI 2013.1511) art.11 (July 1, 2013).

2. Welfare Reform Act 2012 (Commencement No.9, 11, 13, 14 and 16 and Transitional and Transitory Provisions (Amendment)) Order 2014 (SI 2014/1452) art.12 (June 16, 2014).

3. Welfare Reform Act 2012 (Commencement No.9, 11, 13 14, 16, 17 and 19 and Transitional and Transitory Provisions (Amendment)) Order 2014 (SI 2014/3067) art.7(a) (November 24, 2014).

DEFINITIONS

"contribution-based jobseeker's allowance"–art. 2(1).
"jobseeker's allowance"–*ibid.*
"joint-claim couple"—see para.(5).
"the JSA Regulations 1996"–art. 2(1).
"the JSA Regulations 2013"–*ibid.*
"new style JSA award"–*ibid.*
"old style JSA award"–*ibid.*

GENERAL NOTE

This makes transitional provisions for the continuity of jobseeking periods where   3.147
a person has an old style JSA award and previously had a new style JSA award.
Article 12 deals with the converse position.

Sanctions: transition from old style ESA in case of a new award

14.—(1) This article applies where—   3.148
  (a) a person is entitled to a new style ESA award and they were previously entitled to an old style ESA award that was not in existence immediately before the first day on which the person in question is entitled to the new style ESA award; and
  (b) immediately before the old style ESA award terminated, payments were reduced under regulation 63 of the ESA Regulations 2008 (reduction of employment and support allowance).
(2) Where this article applies—
  (a) the failure which led to reduction of the old style ESA award ("the relevant failure") is to be treated for the purposes of Part 8 of the ESA Regulations 2013, as a failure which is sanctionable under section 11J of the 2007 Act (sanctions);
  (b) the new style ESA award is to be reduced in relation to the relevant failure, in accordance with the provisions of this article and Part 8 of the ESA Regulations 2013 as modified by this article; and
  (c) the reduction referred to in sub-paragraph (b) is to be treated, for the purposes of the ESA Regulations 2013, as a reduction under section 11J of the 2007 Act.
(3) The reduction period for the purposes of the ESA Regulations 2013 is to be the number of days which is equivalent to the length of the fixed period applicable to the person under regulation 63 of the ESA Regulations 2008 in relation to the relevant failure, minus—
  (a) the number of days (if any) in that fixed period in respect of which the amount of the old style ESA award was reduced; and
  (b) the number of days (if any) in the period starting with the day after the day on which the old style ESA award terminated and ending with the day before the first day on which the person is entitled to the new style ESA award.
(4) Accordingly, regulation 51 of the ESA Regulations 2013 (general principles for calculating reduction periods) applies in relation to the relevant failure as if—
  (a) in paragraph (1), for the words "in accordance with regulations 52 and 53" there were substituted the words "in accordance with article 14 of the Welfare Reform Act 2012 (Commencement No.9 and Transitional and Transitory Provisions and Commencement

No.8 and Savings and Transitional Provisions (Amendment)) Order 2013"; and
(b) in paragraph (3), for the words "in accordance with regulation 52 or 53" there were substituted the words "in accordance with article 14 of the Welfare Reform Act 2012 (Commencement No.9 and Transitional and Transitory Provisions and Commencement No.8 and Savings and Transitional Provisions (Amendment)) Order 2013".

DEFINITIONS

"the 2007 Act"–art. 2(1).
"employment and support allowance"–*ibid.*
"the ESA Regulations 2008"–*ibid.*
"the ESA Regulations 2013"–*ibid.*
"new style ESA award"–*ibid.*
"old style ESA award"–*ibid.*

GENERAL NOTE

3.149   This makes transitional provision in relation to sanctions where a person has a new style ESA award and previously had an old style ESA award and was subject to sanctions.

Sanctions: transition from old style ESA in case of a continuing award

3.150   **15.**—(1) This article applies where—
(a) the amending provisions have come into force under article 4(1) in relation to the case of a claim for universal credit referred to in [¹ article 4(2)(a)] to (d) (and any award that is made in respect of the claim) or an award of universal credit referred to in article 4(2)(e) or (f);
(b) the person in question had an old style ESA award immediately before the appointed day which consisted of or included a contributory allowance (which allowance therefore continues as a new style ESA award); and
(c) immediately before the appointed day, payments under that award were reduced in accordance with regulation 63 of the ESA Regulations 2008 (reduction of employment and support allowance).
(2) Where this article applies—
(a) the failure which led to reduction of the old style ESA award ("the relevant failure") is to be treated for the purposes of Part 8 of the ESA Regulations 2013, as a failure which is sanctionable under section 11J of the 2007 Act (sanctions);
(b) on and after the appointed day, the award (in its continuation as a new style ESA award) is to be reduced in relation to the relevant failure, in accordance with the provisions of this article and Part 8 of the ESA Regulations 2013 as modified by this article; and
(c) the reduction referred to in sub-paragraph (b) is to be treated, for the purposes of the ESA Regulations 2013, as a reduction under section 11J of the 2007 Act.
(3) The reduction period for the purposes of the ESA Regulations 2013

is to be the number of days which is equivalent to the length of the fixed period applicable to the person under regulation 63 of the ESA Regulations 2008 in relation to the relevant failure, minus the number of days (if any) in that period in respect of which the amount of the old style ESA award was reduced.

(4) Accordingly, regulation 51 of the ESA Regulations 2013 (general principles for calculating reduction periods) applies in relation to the relevant failure as if—

(a) in paragraph (1), for the words "in accordance with regulations 52 and 53" there were substituted the words "in accordance with article 15 of the Welfare Reform Act 2012 (Commencement No.9 and Transitional and Transitory Provisions and Commencement No.8 and Savings and Transitional Provisions (Amendment)) Order 2013"; and

(b) in paragraph (3), for the words "in accordance with regulation 52 or 53" there were substituted the words "in accordance with article 15 of the Welfare Reform Act 2012 (Commencement No.9 and Transitional and Transitory Provisions and Commencement No.8 and Savings and Transitional Provisions (Amendment)) Order 2013".

AMENDMENT

1. Welfare Reform Act 2012 (Commencement No.9, 11, 13, 14 and 16 and Transitional and Transitory Provisions (Amendment)) Order 2014 (SI 2014/1452) art.13 (June 16, 2014).

DEFINITIONS

"the 2007 Act"–art. 2(1)
"the amending provisions"–*ibid.*
"the appointed day"–*ibid.*
"employment and support allowance"–*ibid.*
"the ESA Regulations 2008"–*ibid.*
"the ESA Regulations 2013"–*ibid.*
"new style ESA award"–*ibid.*

GENERAL NOTE

This makes transitional provision in relation to sanctions where a person has an award of universal credit and previously had an old style ESA award which was subject to sanctions.   3.151

Escalation of sanctions: transition from old style ESA

16.—(1) This article applies where a person is entitled to a new style ESA award and, at any time previously, the person was entitled to an old style ESA award.   3.152

(2) Where this article applies, for the purposes of determining the reduction period under regulation 52 of the ESA Regulations 2013 (low-level sanction) in relation to a sanctionable failure by the person to whom the new style award referred to in paragraph (1) was made, other than a failure which is treated as sanctionable under article 14 or 15—

(a) a reduction of a new style ESA award in accordance with article 14 or 15 as the case may be; and

(b) a reduction of an old style ESA award under the ESA Regulations 2008 which did not result in a reduction under article 14 or 15,

is, subject to paragraph (3), to be treated as arising from a sanctionable failure for which the reduction period which applies is the number of days which is equivalent to the length of the fixed period which applied under regulation 63 of the ESA Regulations 2008 (reduction of employment and support allowance).

(3) In determining a reduction period under regulation 52 of the ESA Regulations 2013 in accordance with paragraph (2), no account is to be taken of—

(a) a reduction of a new style ESA award in accordance with article 14 or 15, as the case may be, if, at any time after that reduction, the person was entitled to an old style ESA award, an old style JSA award or income support;

(b) a reduction of an old style ESA award under the ESA Regulations 2008 if, at any time after that reduction, the person was entitled to universal credit, a new style ESA award or a new style JSA award, and was subsequently entitled to an old style ESA award, an old style JSA award or income support.

Definitions

"employment and support allowance"–art. 2(1).
"the ESA Regulations 2008"–*ibid.*
"the ESA Regulations 2013"–*ibid.*
"new style JSA award"–*ibid.*
"old style ESA award"–*ibid.*
"old style JSA award"–*ibid.*

General Note

3.153   This ensures that any previous old style ESA fixed period reductions are taken into account when deciding the appropriate reduction period for the purposes of new style ESA award.

Sanctions: transition from old style JSA in case of a new award

3.154   17.—(1) This article applies where—

(a) a person is entitled to a new style JSA award and they were previously entitled to an old style JSA award that was not in existence immediately before the first day on which the person in question is entitled to the new style JSA award;

(b) immediately before that old style award terminated, payments were reduced under section 19 (as it applied both before and after substitution by the Act) (before substitution: circumstances in which a jobseeker's allowance is not payable; after substitution: higher-level sanctions) or 19A (other sanctions) of the 1995 Act, or under regulation 69B of the JSA Regulations 1996 (the period of a reduction under section 19B : Claimants ceasing to be available for employment etc.); and

(c) if the old style JSA award was made to a joint-claim couple within the meaning of the 1995 Act and the reduction related to—

(i) in the case of a reduction under section 19 as it applied before substitution by the Act, circumstances relating to only one member of the couple; or

(ii) in the case of a reduction under section 19 as it applied after substitution by the Act, a sanctionable failure by only one member of the couple,

the new style JSA award was made to that member of the couple.

(2) Where this article applies—

(a) the circumstances or failure which led to reduction of the old style JSA award (in either case "the relevant failure") is to be treated, for the purposes of the JSA Regulations 2013, as—

(i) a failure which is sanctionable under section 6J of the 1995 Act (higher-level sanctions), where the reduction was under section 19 of the 1995 Act; or

(ii) a failure which is sanctionable under section 6K of the 1995 Act (other sanctions), where the reduction was under section 19A of the 1995 Act or regulation 69B of the JSA Regulations 1996;

(b) the award of new style JSA is to be reduced in relation to the relevant failure, in accordance with the provisions of this article and Part 3 of the JSA Regulations 2013 (sanctions), as modified by this article; and

(c) the reduction is to be treated, for the purposes of the JSA Regulations 2013, as a reduction under section 6J or, as the case may be, section 6K of the 1995 Act.

(3) The reduction period for the purposes of the JSA Regulations 2013 is to be the number of days which is equivalent to the length of the period of reduction of a jobseeker's allowance which is applicable to the person under regulation 69, 69A or 69B of the JSA Regulations 1996, minus—

(a) the number of days (if any) in that period in respect of which the amount of a jobseeker's allowance was reduced; and

(b) the number of days (if any) in the period starting with the day after the day on which the old style JSA award terminated and ending with the day before the first day on which the person is entitled to a new style JSA award.

(4) Accordingly, regulation 18 of the JSA Regulations 2013 (general principles for calculating reduction periods) applies in relation to the relevant failure as if—

(a) in paragraph (1), for the words "in accordance with regulations 19, 20 and 21", there were substituted the words "in accordance with article 17 of the Welfare Reform Act 2012 (Commencement No.9 and Transitional and Transitory Provisions and Commencement No.8 and Savings and Transitional Provisions (Amendment)) Order 2013"; and

(b) in paragraph (3), for the words "in accordance with regulation 19, 20 or 21", there were substituted the words "in accordance with article 17 of the Welfare Reform Act 2012 (Commencement No.9 and Transitional and Transitory Provisions and Commencement No.8 and Savings and Transitional Provisions (Amendment)) Order 2013".

DEFINITIONS

"the Act"–art.2(1).
"the 1995 Act"–*ibid.*
"jobseeker's allowance"–*ibid.*
"the JSA Regulations 1996"–*ibid.*

"the JSA Regulations 2013"–*ibid.*
"new style JSA award"–*ibid.*
"old style JSA award"–*ibid.*

GENERAL NOTE

3.155   This makes transitional provision in relation to sanctions where a person has a new style JSA award and previously had an old style JSA award and was subject to sanctions.

Sanctions: transition from old style JSA in case of a continuing award

3.156   **18.**—(1) This article applies where—
   (a) the amending provisions have come into force under article 4(1) in relation to the case of a claim for universal credit referred to in [¹ article 4(2)(a)] to (d) (and any award that is made in respect of the claim) or an award of universal credit referred to in article 4(2)(e) or (f);
   (b) the person in question had an old style JSA award immediately before the appointed day which consisted of or included a contribution-based allowance (which allowance therefore continues as a new style JSA award);
   (c) immediately before the appointed day, payments under that award were reduced under section 19 (as it applied both before and after substitution by the Act) (before substitution: circumstances in which a jobseeker's allowance is not payable; after substitution: higher-level sanctions) or 19A (other sanctions) of the 1995 Act, or under regulation 69B of the JSA Regulations 1996) (the period of a reduction under section 19B : Claimants ceasing to be available for employment etc.); and
   (d) if the old style JSA award was made to a joint-claim couple within the meaning of the 1995 Act and the reduction related to—
       (i) in the case of a reduction under section 19 as it applied before substitution by the Act, circumstances relating to only one member of the couple; or
       (ii) in the case of a reduction under section 19 as it applied after substitution by the Act, a sanctionable failure by only one member of the couple,
   the new style JSA award was made to that member of the couple.
   (2) Where this article applies—
   (a) the circumstances or failure which led to reduction of the old style JSA award (in either case "the relevant failure") is to be treated, for the purposes of the JSA Regulations 2013, as—
       (i) a failure which is sanctionable under section 6J of the 1995 Act (higher-level sanctions), where the reduction was under section 19 of the 1995 Act; or
       (ii) a failure which is sanctionable under section 6K of the 1995 Act (other sanctions), where the reduction was under section 19A of the 1995 Act or regulation 69B of the JSA Regulations 1996;
   (b) the award (in its continuation as a new style JSA award) is to be reduced in relation to the relevant failure, in accordance with the provisions of this article and Part 3 of the JSA Regulations (sanctions), as modified by this article; and

(c) the reduction is to be treated, for the purposes of the JSA Regulations 2013, as a reduction under section 6J or, as the case may be, section 6K of the 1995 Act.

(3) The reduction period for the purposes of the JSA Regulations 2013 is to be the number of days which is equivalent to the length of the period of reduction of a jobseeker's allowance which is applicable to the person under regulation 69, 69A or 69B of the JSA Regulations 1996, minus the number of days (if any) in that period in respect of which the amount of a jobseeker's allowance was reduced.

(4) Accordingly, regulation 18 of the JSA Regulations 2013 (general principles for calculating reduction periods) applies in relation to the relevant failure as if—

(a) in paragraph (1), for the words "in accordance with regulations 19, 20 and 21", there were substituted the words "in accordance with article 18 of the Welfare Reform Act 2012 (Commencement No.9 and Transitional and Transitory Provisions and Commencement No.8 and Savings and Transitional Provisions (Amendment)) Order 2013"; and

(b) in paragraph (3), for the words "in accordance with regulation 19, 20 or 21", there were substituted the words "in accordance with article 18 of the Welfare Reform Act 2012 (Commencement No.9 and Transitional and Transitory Provisions and Commencement No.8 and Savings and Transitional Provisions (Amendment)) Order 2013".

AMENDMENT

1. Welfare Reform Act 2012 (Commencement No.9, 11, 13, 14 and 16 and Transitional and Transitory Provisions (Amendment)) Order 2014 (SI 2014/1452) art.13 (June 16, 2014).

DEFINITIONS

"the Act"–art. 2(1).
"the 1995 Act"–*ibid.*
"the amending provisions"–*ibid.*
"the appointed day"–*ibid.*
"jobseeker's allowance"–*ibid.*
"the JSA Regulations 1996"–*ibid.*
"the JSA Regulations 2013"–*ibid.*
"new style JSA award"–*ibid.*
"old style JSA award"–*ibid.*

GENERAL NOTE

This is the JSA equivalent to reg.15.   3.157

Escalation of sanctions: transition from old style JSA

19.—(1) This article applies where a person is entitled to a new style JSA   3.158
award and, at any time previously, the person was entitled to an old style JSA award.

(2) Where this article applies, for the purposes of determining the applicable reduction period under regulation 19 (higher-level sanction), 20 (medium-level sanction) or 21 (low-level sanction) of the JSA Regulations

2013 in relation to a sanctionable failure by the person other than a failure which is treated as sanctionable by virtue of article 17 or 18—

    (a) a reduction of a new style JSA award in accordance with article 17 or 18; and

    (b) a reduction of an old style JSA award under section 19 (as it applied both before and after substitution by the Act) or 19A of the 1995 Act, or under regulation 69B of the JSA Regulations 1996, which did not result in a reduction under article 17 or 18,

is, subject to paragraph (3), to be treated as arising from a sanctionable failure for which the reduction period is the number of days which is equivalent to the length of the period which applied under regulation 69, 69A or 69B of the JSA Regulations 1996.

(3) In determining a reduction period under regulation 19 (higher-level sanction), 20 (medium-level sanction) or 21 (low-level sanction) of the JSA Regulations 2013 in accordance with paragraph (2), no account is to be taken of—

    (a) a reduction of a new style JSA award in accordance with article 17 or 18 if, at any time after that reduction, the person was entitled to an old style JSA award, an old style ESA award or income support;

    (b) a reduction of an old style JSA award under section 19 (as it applied both before and after substitution by the Act) or 19A of the 1995 Act, or under regulation 69B of the JSA Regulations 1996, if, at any time after that reduction, the person was entitled to universal credit, a new style JSA award or a new style ESA award, and was subsequently entitled to an old style JSA award, an old style ESA award or income support.

DEFINITIONS

    "the Act"–art. 2(1).
    "the 1995 Act"–*ibid.*
    "the JSA Regulations 1996"–*ibid.*
    "the JSA Regulations 2013"–*ibid.*
    "new style JSA award"–*ibid.*
    "old style ESA award"–*ibid.*
    "old style JSA award"–*ibid.*

GENERAL NOTE

3.159   This is the JSA equivalent to reg.16.

Termination of sanctions under a new style ESA or JSA award

3.160   **20.**—(1) Paragraph (2) applies where—

    (a) a new style ESA award or new style JSA award terminates while there is an outstanding reduction period (within the meaning of regulation 55 of the ESA Regulations 2013 (reduction period to continue where award of employment and support allowance terminates) or regulation 23 of the JSA Regulations 2013 (reduction period to continue where award of jobseeker's allowance terminates)) and the claimant becomes entitled to an old style ESA award, an old style JSA award or income support during that period; or

    (b) article 6(2) applies to a new style ESA award or new style JSA award (such that it continues as an old style ESA award or an old style JSA award) and there is such an outstanding reduction period on the last day of the period of the new style ESA award or new style JSA award.

(2) Where this paragraph applies—

(a) regulation 55 of the ESA Regulations 2013 or regulation 23 of the JSA Regulations 2013, as the case may be, are to cease to apply; and

(b) the reduction period is to terminate on the first day of entitlement to an old style ESA award, old style JSA award or income support as the case may be.

DEFINITIONS

"employment and support allowance"–art.2(1).
"the ESA Regulations 2013"–*ibid.*
"jobseeker's allowance"–*ibid.*
"the JSA Regulations 2013"–*ibid.*
"new style ESA award"–*ibid.*
"new style JSA award"–*ibid.*
"old style JSA award"–*ibid.*

GENERAL NOTE

This provides that where a claimant has a new style ESA (or new style JSA)   **3.161**
award, is subject to sanctions and subsequently becomes entitled to an old style ESA (or old style JSA) award or income support, then the sanctions cease to have effect.

Transitory provisions: appeals

21.—(1) Paragraph (2) applies where—   **3.162**

(a) the amending provisions have come into force under article 4(1) in relation to the case of a claim referred to in article 4(2)(a) to (d) (and any award that is made in respect of the claim) or the case of an award referred to in article 4(2)(e) or (f);

(b) the person is sent notice of a decision relating to a new style ESA award or a new style JSA award; and

(c) the date of notification with respect to that decision is before 28th October 2013.

(2) Where this paragraph applies, the provisions mentioned in paragraph (3) apply for the purposes of any appeal in relation to that decision as if regulation 55 of the Decisions and Appeals Regulations 2013 (consequential amendments) did not apply in that person's case.

(3) The provisions referred to are the following provisions of the Social Security and Child Support (Decisions and Appeals) Regulations 1999—

(a) regulation 32 (late appeals);

(b) regulation 33 (notice of appeal); and

(c) regulation 34 (death of a party to an appeal).

(4) For the purposes of paragraph (1), "the date of notification" means the date on which the decision notice was posted to the person's last known address by the Secretary of State.

DEFINITIONS

"the amending provisions"–art.2(1).
"the Decisions and Appeals Regulations 2013"–*ibid.*
"new style JSA award"–*ibid.*

3.163 This makes limited transitory provision with respect to appeals where a person is sent a notice relating to a new style ESA award or a new style JSA award before October 29, 2013.

Transitional provision: references to contributory employment and support allowance and contribution-based jobseeker's allowance

3.164 22.—Where the amending provisions have come into force under article 4(1) in relation to the case of a claim referred to in article 4(2)(a) to (d) [¹ or (g)] (and any award that is made in respect of the claim) or the case of an award referred to in article 4(2)(e) or (f), then, in relation to such a case, any reference in the Social Security Administration Act 1992 or the Social Security Contributions and Benefits Act 1992 to—

> (a) a contributory employment and support allowance is to be read as if it included a reference to a new style ESA award; and
> (b) a contribution-based jobseeker's allowance is to be read as if it included a reference to a new style JSA award.

AMENDMENT

1. Welfare Reform Act 2012 (Commencement No.9, 11, 13, 14 and 16 and Transitional and Transitory Provisions (Amendment)) Order 2014 (SI 2014/1452) art.14 (June 16, 2014).

DEFINITIONS

"the amending provisions"–*ibid.*
"contribution-based jobseeker's allowance"–*ibid.*
"contributory employment and support allowance"–*ibid.*
"new style JSA award"–*ibid.*

GENERAL NOTE

3.165 This provision seeks to ensure that new style ESA and JSA awards are to be treated to all intents and purposes as awards of a contributory employment or support allowance or to a contribution-based jobseeker's allowance respectively. It does so by providing that, in relation to a case with respect to which art.4 has come into force, references in the SSAA 1992 and the SSCBA 1992 are to be construed as if they included a reference to a new style ESA award or to a new style JSA award respectively.

Amendment of the Welfare Reform Act 2012 (Commencement No 8 and Savings and Transitional Provisions) Order 2013

3.166 23.—(1) Article 5 of the Welfare Reform Act 2012 (Commencement No 8 and Savings and Transitional Provisions) Order 2013 (appointed day and saving for provisions relating to overpayments) is amended as follows.

(2) In paragraph (3)(a), at the beginning insert "subject to paragraph (3A),".

(3) After paragraph (3) insert—

"(3A) In so far as section 105(1) of the 2012 Act inserts section 71ZB(1)(b) and (c) of the 1992 Act, those paragraphs come into force on 29th April 2013 only in so far as they relate respectively to a new style JSA award and a new style ESA award.".

(4) In paragraph (6), for "those benefits have been claimed before 29th April 2013" substitute "they relate respectively to an old style JSA award and an old style ESA award".

(5) After paragraph (6) add—

"(7) In this article, "old style JSA award", "new style JSA award", "old style ESA award" and "new style ESA award" have the same meaning as in article 2(1) of the Welfare Reform Act 2012 (Commencement No.9 and Transitional and Transitory Provisions and Commencement No.8 and Savings and Transitional Provisions (Amendment)) Order 2013.".

DEFINITIONS

"the appointed day"–art. 2(1).
"new style JSA award"–*ibid.*
"old style ESA award"–*ibid.*
"old style JSA award"–*ibid.*

GENERAL NOTE

This amends art.5 of the Commencement No.8 Order as regards overpayments. **3.167** It is intended to make it clear that the new rules applying to overpayments of employment and support allowance and of jobseeker's allowance under the WRA 2012 apply only to overpayments of a new style ESA award and a new style JSA award respectively (para.(3)). The amendments also clarify that the old rules relating to overpayments of those benefits will continue to apply to overpayments of an old style ESA award and an old style JSA award respectively (para.(4)).

[¹ Appeals relating to ESA and JSA

24.—(1) This article applies where, after an award of universal credit has **3.168** been made to a claimant (where that award is made by virtue of the coming into force of the provisions of the Act referred to in Schedule 2, under any secondary legislation) —

(a) an appeal against a decision relating to the entitlement of the claimant to an old style ESA award or an old style JSA award is finally determined; or

(b) a decision relating to the claimant's entitlement to such an award is revised under section 9 of the Social Security Act 1998 ("the 1998 Act") or superseded under section 10 of that Act.

(2) Where this article applies, the Secretary of State is to consider whether it is appropriate to revise under section 9 of the 1998 Act the decision in relation to entitlement to universal credit or, if that decision has been superseded under section 10 of that Act, the decision as so superseded (in either case, "the UC decision").

(3) Where it appears to the Secretary of State to be appropriate to revise the UC decision, it is to be revised in such manner as appears to the Secretary of State to be necessary to take account of—

(a) the decision of the First-tier Tribunal, Upper Tribunal or court, or, as the case may be, the decision relating to entitlement to an old style ESA award or an old style JSA award, as revised or superseded; and

(b) any finding of fact by the First-tier Tribunal, Upper Tribunal or court.

(4) For the purposes of this article, "secondary legislation" means an instrument made under an Act.]

AMENDMENT

1. Welfare Reform Act 2012 (Commencement No.9, 11, 13, 14 and 16 and Transitional and Transitory Provisions (Amendment)) Order 2014 (SI 2014/1452) art.15 (June 16, 2014).

GENERAL NOTE

3.169   This makes provision relating to the possible revision of a decision to make a universal credit award in the situation where an appeal against a decision not to award old style ESA or old style JSA is made after a universal credit award has been made.

SCHEDULE 1

POSTCODE DISTRICTS

3.170   1. M43
2. OL6
3. OL7
4. SK16

Article 3(2)

SCHEDULE 2

UNIVERSAL CREDIT PROVISIONS COMING INTO FORCE IN RELATION TO CERTAIN CLAIMS AND AWARDS

3.171   1. Section 1 (universal credit).
2. Section 2(1) (claims).
3. Section 3 (entitlement).
4. Section 4(1) and (4) (basic conditions).
5. Section 5 (financial conditions).
6. Section 6 (restrictions on entitlement).
7. Section 7(1) and (4) (basis of awards).
8. Section 8 (calculation of awards).
9. Section 9(1) (standard allowance).
10. Section 10(1) (responsibility for children and young persons).
11. Section 11(1) and (2) (housing costs).
12. Section 12(1) and (2) (other particular needs or circumstances).
13. Section 13 (work-related requirements: introductory).
14. Section 14 (claimant commitment).
15. Section 15(1) and (4) (work-focused interview requirement).
16. Section 16 (work preparation requirement).
17. Section 17(1), (2), (3)(a) to (e), (4) and (5) (work search requirement).
18. Section 18 (work availability requirement).
19. Section 19(1), (2)(a) to (c), (5) and (6) (claimants subject to no work-related requirements).
20. Section 20 (claimants subject to work-focused interview requirement only).
21. Section 21 (claimants subject to work preparation requirement).
22. Section 22 (claimants subject to all work-related requirements).
23. Section 23 (connected requirements).
24. Section 24(2), (3) and (4) (imposition of requirements).
25. Section 26(1) to (5) (higher-level sanctions).
26. Section 27(1) to (3) and (6) to (8) (other sanctions).

SCHEDULE 3

COMMENCEMENT OF REPEALS IN PART 1 OF SCHEDULE 14 TO THE ACT

Article 9   **3.172**

Short title and chapter	Extent of repeal
Jobseekers Act 1995 (c.18)	Section 1(2A) to (2D) and (4). In section 2, in subsection (3C)(d), "contribution-based". Sections 3 to 3B. In section 4— (a) in subsection (1), "contribution-based"; (b) subsections (3), (3A) and (6) to (11A). Section 4A. In section 5— (a) in the heading and in subsection (1) "contribution-based"; (b) in subsection (2), "contribution-based" in the first two places; (c) in subsection (3), "contribution-based". Section 13. Sections 15 to 17. In section 17A(10), the definition of "claimant". Section 23. Sections 26. In section 35(1)— (a) in the definition of "claimant", the words from "except" to the end; (b) the definitions of "contribution-based jobseeker's allowance", "income-based jobseeker's allowance", "income-related employment and support allowance", "joint-claim couple", "joint-claim jobseeker's allowance" and "the nominated member". In section 38— (a) in subsections (3) and (4), "contribution-based"; (b) subsection (6). In Schedule 1— (a) in paragraph 6(1), "contribution-based"; (b) paragraphs 8 and 8A; (c) paragraphs 9 to 10; (d) in paragraph 11(1), "contribution-based"; (e) in paragraph 16(1) and (2)(d), "contribution-based"; (f) paragraph 18(b) and (c).
Welfare Reform and Pensions Act 1999 (c.30)	In Schedule 7, paragraphs 2(3) and (4), 4, 5(3) and (4), 6, 9 to 11, 15 and 16.
	In Schedule 8, paragraph 29(2).

Short title and chapter	Extent of repeal
State Pension Credit Act 2002 (c.16)	In Schedule 2, paragraphs 36 to 38.
Income Tax (Earnings and Payments) Act 2003 (c.1)	In Schedule 6, paragraphs 228 to 230.
Civil Partnership Act 2004 (c.33)	In Schedule 24, paragraphs 118 to 122.
Welfare Reform Act 2007 (c.5)	In section 1— (a) in subsection (2), in the opening words, "either"; (b) in subsection (2)(a), "Part 1 of" and "that Part of"; (c) subsection (2)(b) and the preceding "or"; (d) in subsection (3)(f), the words from "(and" to "allowance)"; (e) in subsection (3A), "Part 1 of"; (f) in subsection (6), the definition of "joint-claim jobseeker's allowance"; (g) subsections (6A) and (7). In subsection 1A— (a) in the heading "contributory"; (b) in subsections (1) (in both places), (3) and (4), "Part 1 of". Section 1B(2). In section 2, in the heading, "contributory". In section 3, in the heading, "contributory". Sections 4 to 6. Section 23. In section 24(1), the definitions of "contributory allowance" and "income-related allowance". In section 26(1)(a), "or 4(4)(c) or (5)(c)". Section 27(2)(a) and (4). In Schedule 1— (a) the heading to Part 1; (b) Part 2. In Schedule 2— (a) in the headings to paragraphs 6 and 7, "Contributory allowance:"; (b) paragraph 8; (c) paragraph 11(b) and (c); (d) paragraph 12, so far as not otherwise repealed.
Welfare Reform Act 2009 (c.24)	In Part 3 of Schedule 7, the entry relating to the Civil Partnership Act 2004.

SCHEDULE 4

MODIFICATIONS OF THE 2010 TRANSITIONAL REGULATIONS

3.173   1. The 2010 Transitional Regulations are to be read as if the amendments set out in this Schedule were made.

2. (1) Regulation 2 (interpretation) is amended as follows.

(2) In paragraph (1)—

(a) insert at the appropriate places in the alphabetical order of the definitions—

""the Claims and Payments Regulations" means the Universal Credit, Personal

Independence Payment, Jobseeker's Allowance and Employment and Support Allowance (Claims and Payments) Regulations 2013;";

""the Decisions and Appeals Regulations" means the Universal Credit, Personal Independence Payment, Jobseeker's Allowance and Employment and Support Allowance (Decisions and Appeals) Regulations 2013;";

""the ESA Regulations" means the Employment and Support Allowance Regulations 2013;";

(b) omit—

    (i) the definition of "income-related allowance";

    (ii) paragraphs (a) to (d) of the definition of "relevant deduction";

(c) in the definition of "benefit week", for "the 2008 Regulations" substitute "the ESA Regulations".

(3) In paragraph (3), omit "or awards".

3. In regulation 4 (the notice commencing the conversion phase), omit paragraph (6).

4. In regulation 5 (deciding whether an existing award qualifies for conversion)—

(a) in paragraph (1), omit "or awards";

(b) in paragraph (2)(a), for "or awards qualify" substitute "qualifies";

(c) in paragraph (2)(b), for "or awards do" substitute "does";

(d) in paragraph (6)(b), omit "or awards".

5. In regulation 6(2) (application of certain enactments for purpose of making conversion decisions)—

(a) for sub-paragraphs (b) and (c), substitute—

    "(b) the ESA Regulations;

    (c) regulation 38(2) and (3) of the Claims and Payments Regulations (evidence and information in connection with an award);";

(b) for sub-paragraph (e), substitute—

    "(e) the Decisions and Appeals Regulations."

6. In regulation 7 (qualifying for conversion)—

(a) in paragraph (1)—

    (i) omit "or awards";

    (ii) for "qualify" substitute "qualifies";

(b) in paragraphs (2)(b) and (3)(b), for "regulation 30 of the 2008 Regulations" substitute "regulation 26 of the ESA Regulations".

7. In regulation 8(1) (amount of an employment and support allowance on conversion), for "the 2008 Regulations" substitute "the ESA Regulations".

8. In regulation 9(1) (determining entitlement to a transitional addition)—

(a) for "or awards qualify" substitute "qualifies";

(b) omit "or 11(2) (transitional addition: income support)".

9. In regulation 10 (transitional addition: incapacity benefit or severe disablement allowance)—

(a) in paragraph (1), omit "(and for these purposes it is irrelevant whether the person is also entitled to any existing award of income support)";

(b) in paragraph (4)(a), for "paragraph (2) of regulation 67 of the 2008 Regulations (prescribed amounts for purpose of calculating a contributory allowance)" substitute "paragraph (1) of regulation 62 of the ESA Regulations (prescribed amounts)".

10. Omit regulation 11 (transitional addition: income support).

11. In regulation 12 (regulations 10 and 11: supplementary)—

(a) in the title, for "Regulations 10 and 11" substitute "Regulation 10";

(b) in paragraph (1), for "regulations 10 and 11" substitute "regulation 10";

(c) in paragraph (2), for "Amounts A and C are" substitute "Amount A is" and for "Amounts B and D are" substitute "Amount B is";

(d) for paragraph (3)(a), substitute—

    "(a) by virtue of an order made under section 150 of the Administration Act (annual up-rating of benefits), there is an increase in the weekly rate which, in accordance with regulation 10(3) (transitional addition: incapacity benefit or severe disablement allowance), is to be used to calculate Amount A; and";

(e) in paragraph (4)(a), for "paragraph (3)(a)(i) or (ii)" substitute "paragraph (3)(a)";

(f) in paragraphs (3) and (4), omit "or C" and "or applicable amount (as the case may be)".

12. In regulation 13(3) (the effective date of a conversion decision), omit "or awards".

13. In regulation 14 (conversion decision that existing award qualifies for conversion)—

(a) in paragraph (1)—

    (i) for "Subject to paragraph (2A), paragraphs (2) to (6)" substitute "Paragraphs (2) to (5)";

(ii) for "or awards qualify" substitute "qualifies";

(b) for paragraph (2), substitute—

"(2) On the effective date of the conversion decision P's existing award is by virtue of this paragraph converted into, and shall have effect on and after that date as, a single award of an employment and support allowance of such amount as is specified in the conversion decision.";

(c) omit paragraphs (2A), (2B) and (6);

(d) in paragraph (4), omit "or awards";

(e) for paragraph (7), substitute—

"(7) In this regulation paragraphs (2) to (5) are subject to regulation 17 (changes of circumstances before the effective date).".

14. In regulation 15 (conversion decision that existing award does not qualify for conversion)—

(a) in paragraph (1)—

(i) for "Subject to paragraphs (2A) and (4), paragraphs (2), (3) and (6)" substitute "Subject to paragraph (4), paragraphs (2) and (3)";

(ii) for "or awards do" substitute "does";

(b) for paragraph (2), substitute—

"(2) P's entitlement to an existing award of incapacity benefit or severe disablement allowance shall terminate by virtue of this paragraph immediately before the effective date of P's conversion decision.";

(c) omit paragraphs (2A), (2B) and (6);

(d) in paragraph (4)(a)—

(i) for "the 2008 Regulations" substitute "the ESA Regulations";

(ii) in paragraph (i), for "regulation 22(1) (failure to provide information or evidence requested in relation to limited capability for work)" substitute "regulation 18(1) (failure to provide information in relation to limited capability for work)";

(iii) in paragraph (ii), for "regulation 23(2) (failure to attend for a medical examination to determine whether the claimant has limited capability for work)" substitute "regulation 19(2) (claimant may be called for a medical examination to determine whether the claimant has limited capability for work)";

(e) in paragraph (5)—

(i) in sub-paragraph (c), omit "or awards";

(ii) in sub-paragraph (d), omit "or those existing awards";

(f) for paragraph (7), substitute—

"(7) In this regulation paragraphs (2) and (3) are subject to regulation 17 (changes of circumstances before the effective date).".

15. In regulation 16 (application of other enactments applying to employment and support allowance)—

(a) in paragraph (1A)(b), for "regulation 145(1) of the 2008 Regulations" substitute "regulation 86 of the ESA Regulations";

(b) in paragraph (2)(e)(ii), for "the 2008 Regulations" substitute "the ESA Regulations";

(c) in paragraph (2)(e)(iii), omit "(being regulations consequentially amended by regulations made under Part 1 of the 2007 Act)".

16. In regulation 17 (changes of circumstances before the effective date)—

(a) omit "or awards" in both places where it occurs;

(b) in paragraph (a)(ii)—

(i) omit "regulation 14(2B)(a) (termination of an existing award of incapacity benefit or severe disablement allowance where entitlement to award of income support continues),";

(ii) for "(termination of existing awards which do not qualify for conversion)" substitute "(termination of an existing award which does not qualify for conversion)";

(c) omit paragraph (c).

17. In regulation 18 (reducing the transitional addition: general rule), for paragraph (2) substitute—

"(2) For the purposes of paragraph (1), a relevant increase is an increase in any amount applicable to the person under regulation 62(1) or (2) of the ESA Regulations, which is not excluded by paragraph (3).".

18. In regulation 21 (termination of transitional addition)—

(a) in paragraph (1)(b)—

(i) for ", (3), (3A) and (4)" substitute ", (3) and (3A)"and (4)";

    (ii) omit "an employment and support allowance (entitlement to which arises from sections 1(2)(a) or 1(2)(b) of the 2007 Act), or to" and "or to an income-related allowance";

(b) omit paragraph (4);

(c) in paragraph (5)(a), for "regulation 145(1) of the 2008 Regulations (linking rules)" substitute "regulation 86 of the ESA Regulations (linking period)";

(d) in paragraph (5)(c)(ii), for "regulation 30 of the 2008 Regulations" substitute "regulation 26 of the ESA Regulations";

(e) in paragraph (5A)(c), for "regulation 145(1) of the 2008 Regulations (linking rules)" substitute "regulation 86 of the ESA Regulations (linking period)";

(f) omit paragraph (6);

(g) in paragraph (7)—

    (i) for ", 1A and 2" substitute "and 1A";

    (ii) omit "or additions, as the case may be," in both places where it occurs;

    (iii) for "an allowance which is referred to in paragraph (1)(b)" substitute "a contributory allowance".

19. In regulation 22 (disapplication of certain enactments following conversion decision), omit paragraphs (c) and (d).

20. In Schedule 1 (modification of enactments: making conversion decisions)—

(a) in paragraph 2(a), for the modified section 1(2) substitute—

"(2) Subject to the provisions of this Part, a notified person is entitled to an employment and support allowance if the person satisfies the basic conditions and is entitled to an existing award of incapacity benefit or severe disablement allowance.";

(b) for paragraph 6, substitute—

"6. Schedule 1 to the 2007 Act is to be read as if paragraphs 1 to 6 were omitted.";

(c) in the heading to Part 2, for "the 2008 Regulations" substitute "the ESA Regulations";

(d) in paragraph 10, for "Regulation 30" substitute "Regulation 26";

(e) omit paragraph 10A;

(f) in paragraph 11, for "Regulation 75" substitute "Regulation 68";

(g) in paragraph 12, for "Regulation 144" substitute "Regulation 85";

(h) in the sub-heading to Part 3, for "Social Security (Claims and Payments) Regulations 1987" substitute "The Claims and Payments Regulations";

(i) in paragraph 13—

    (i) for "Regulation 32 of the Social Security (Claims and Payments) Regulations 1987" substitute "Regulation 38 of the Claims and Payments Regulations";

    (ii) in sub-paragraph (a), for "paragraph (1)" substitute "paragraph (2)";

    (iii) in sub-paragraph (b), for "paragraph (1A)" substitute "paragraph (3)".

21. (1) Schedule 2 (modification of enactments: after the conversion phase) is amended as follows.

(2) In paragraph 2—

(a) in sub-paragraph (a), in the modified section 1(2)–

    (i) in paragraph (a), for "or awards into a single award of an employment and support allowance;" substitute "into an award of an employment and support allowance; and";

    (ii) omit paragraph (c) and for "; and" at the end of paragraph (b) substitute ",";

(b) in sub-paragraph (b) in the modified section 1(7)—

    [¹ (i) for the definition of "contributory allowance" substitute—

"employment and support allowance" means an employment and support allowance to which a person is entitled by virtue of the Employment and Support Allowance (Transitional Provisions, Housing Benefit and Council Tax Benefit) (Existing Awards)(No.2) Regulations 2010 which was based on an award of incapacity benefit or severe disablement allowance to which the person was entitled.] and for "; and" following that definition substitute "."];

    (ii) omit the definition of "income-related allowance".

[¹ (2A) In paragraph 2A—

(a) in paragraph (1), omit "contributory"; and

(b) in paragraph (2), in the substituted section 1A

    (i) in paragraphs (1) and (3) to (5), for " a contributory allowance" substitute "an employment and support allowance"; and

    (ii) in paragraph (3), omit "Part 1 of".]

(3) In paragraph 3(b), for "regulation 147A of the 2008 Regulations" substitute "regulation 87 of the ESA Regulations".

(4) Omit paragraphs 4 and 4A.

(5) In paragraph 6A—

  (a) in sub-paragraph (a), after paragraph (iv) insert "and";

  (b) in sub-paragraph (b), for "; and" substitute ".";

  (c) omit sub-paragraph (c).

(6) In the heading to Part 3, for "the 2008 Regulations" substitute "the ESA Regulations".

(7) In paragraph 8, for "regulation 147A of the 2008 Regulations" substitute "regulation 87 of the ESA Regulations".

(8) In paragraph 10, for "regulation 30" substitute "regulation 26".

"(9) For paragraph 11, substitute—

> **11.** Regulation 39 (exempt work) is to be read as if, in the definition of "work period" in paragraph (6), after "referred to in paragraph (1)(c)", in both places where it occurs, there were inserted ", or any work done in accordance with regulation 17(4)(a) of the Social Security (Incapacity for Work)(General) Regulations 1995.

(10) For paragraph 12, substitute—"

> "**12.** Regulation 62 (prescribed amounts) is to be read as if, in paragraph (1), for sub-paragraphs (a) and (b) there were substituted—

  (a)(i) where the claimant satisfies the conditions set out in section 2(2) or (3) of the Act, £71.70; or

    (ii) where the claimant does not satisfy the conditions set out in section 2(2) or (3) of the Act—

  (aa) where the claimant is aged not less than 25, £71.70; or

  (bb) where the claimant is aged less than 25, £56.80; and

  (b) the amount of any transitional addition to which the person is entitled under regulation 10 of the Employment and Support Allowance (Transitional Provisions, Housing Benefit and Council Tax Benefit) (Existing Awards) (No.2) Regulations 2010."

(9) Omit paragraph 13.

(10) In paragraph 14—

  (a) for "Regulation 75" substitute "Regulation 68";

  (b) for "paragraph 38" substitute "paragraph 11".

(11) In paragraph 15—

  (a) in the introductory words, for "Regulation 147A" substitute "regulation 87";

  (b) in the inserted regulation—

    (i) in the description of the number of the regulation, for "147A.—" substitute "87.—";

    (ii) in paragraph (2), for "regulation 19" substitute "regulation 15";

    (iii) in paragraph (4)(a), for "regulation 22 or 23" substitute "regulation 18 or 19";

    (iv) for "regulation 30", in all places where it occurs, substitute "regulation 26";

    (v) in paragraph (5)(c), for the words from ", struck out" to "(notice of appeal)", substitute "or struck out";

    (vi) in paragraph (5A), for "either—" and sub-paragraphs (a) and (b), substitute "receives the First-tier Tribunal's notification that the appeal is dismissed, withdrawn or struck out.".

(12) Omit paragraph 16.

(13) In the sub-heading before paragraph 17, for "Social Security (Claims and Payments) Regulations 1987" substitute "The Claims and Payments Regulations".

(14) In paragraph 17, for "The Social Security (Claims and Payments) Regulations 1987" substitute "The Claims and Payments Regulations".

(15) For paragraph 18 substitute—

> "**18.** Regulation 7 (claims not required for entitlement to an employment and support allowance in certain cases) is to read as if—

  (a) the existing provisions were renumbered as paragraph (1);

  (b) after paragraph (1) there were inserted—

(2) It is also not to be a condition of entitlement to an employment and support allowance that a claim be made for it where any of the following conditions are met—

  (a) the claimant—

    (i) has made and is pursuing an appeal against a conversion decision made by virtue of the Employment and Support Allowance (Transitional Provisions, Housing Benefit and Council Tax Benefit) (Existing Awards) (No.2) Regulations 2010 which embodies a determination that the beneficiary does not have limited capability for work; or

    (ii) was entitled to an employment and support allowance by virtue of the

Employment and Support Allowance (Transitional Provisions, Housing Benefit and Council Tax Benefit) (Existing Awards) (No.2) Regulations 2010 and has made and is pursuing an appeal against a later decision which embodies a determination that the claimant does not have limited capability for work; or
(b) the claimant is entitled to an existing award which is subject to conversion under the Employment and Support Allowance (Transitional Provisions, Housing Benefit and Council Tax Benefit) (Existing Awards) (No.2) Regulations 2010." "
(16) In paragraph 19, for "regulation 26C" substitute "regulation 51".
(17) In paragraph 20—
  (a) for "regulation 32(1B)" substitute "regulation 38(4)";
  (b) in sub-paragraph (a), for the words "sub-paragraph (a)" substitute "sub-paragraph (b)";
  (c) in sub-paragraph (b), for "(ab)" substitute "(bb)".
(18) Omit paragraph 21.
(19) In paragraph 22, for "Schedule 9B" substitute "Schedule 7".
(20) In paragraph 22A, in the inserted text omit paragraph (2B).
(21) In paragraph 23, in the inserted text omit paragraph (2B).
(22) In paragraph 24, in the inserted text omit paragraph (2B).
(23) In paragraph 25, in the inserted text omit paragraph (2B).
(24) In the sub-heading before paragraph 25A, for "Social Security and Child Support (Decisions and Appeals) Regulations 1999" substitute "Universal Credit, Personal Independence Payment, Jobseeker's Allowance and Employment and Support Allowance (Decisions and Appeals) Regulations 2013".
(25) In paragraph 25A—
  (a) in sub-paragraph (1), for "Regulation 3 of the Social Security and Child Support (Decisions and Appeals) Regulations 1999 (revision of decisions)" substitute "Regulation 5 of the Universal Credit, Personal Independence Payment, Jobseeker's Allowance and Employment and Support Allowance (Decisions and Appeals) Regulations 2013 (revision on any grounds)";
  (b) in sub-paragraph (1)(b), for "paragraph (9)(a)" substitute "paragraphs (2)(a) and (b)";
  (c) for sub-paragraph (1)(c), substitute—
    "(c) in paragraph (2)(a), for "in the case of an advance award under regulation 32, 33 or 34 of the Claims and Payment Regulations 2013" there were substituted, "in the case of an advance award under regulation 32, 33 or 34 of the Claims and Payment Regulations 2013 or a conversion decision within the meaning of regulation 5(2)(a) of the Employment and Support Allowance (Transitional Provisions, Housing Benefit and Council Tax Benefit) (Existing Awards) (No.2) Regulations 2010".";
  (d) for sub-paragraph (2), substitute—
    "(2) Regulation 23(1)(a) of those Regulations (change of circumstances) is to be read as if for "in the case of an advance award under regulation 32, 33 or 34 of the Claims and Payments Regulations 2013" there were substituted "in the case of an advance award under regulation 32, 33 or 34 of the Claims and Payments Regulations 2013 or a conversion decision within the meaning of regulation 5(2) (a) of the Employment and Support Allowance (Transitional Provisions, Housing Benefit and Council Tax Benefit) (Existing Awards) (No.2) Regulations 2010." "
(26) Omit paragraph 27.
22. In Schedule 3—
  (a) for "The Social Security (Claims and Payments) Regulations 1987" substitute "the Claims and Payments Regulations";
  (b) for " The Social Security and Child Support (Decisions and Appeals) Regulations 1999" substitute "the Decisions and Appeals Regulations".

AMENDMENT

1. Welfare Reform Act 2012 (Commencement No.11 and Transitional and Transitory Provisions and Commencement No.9 and Transitional and Transitory Provisions (Amendment)) Order 2013 (SI 2013/1511) art.7 (July 1, 2013).

[¹ SCHEDULE 5

THE GATEWAY CONDITIONS

Personal characteristics

3.174   1. The claimant must be—
(a) aged at least 18 years, but under 60 years and six months;
(b) [³ ...];
(c) a British citizen who—
   (i) has resided in the United Kingdom throughout the period of two years ending with the date on which the claim for universal credit is made; and
   (ii) has not, during that period, left the United Kingdom for a continuous period of four weeks or more.

Fitness to work

3.175   2. (1) The claimant must not—
(a) be pregnant; or
(b) have been pregnant, if the date of her confinement occurred during the period of 15 weeks ending with the date on which the claim for universal credit is made.
(2) In this paragraph, "confinement" has the same meaning as in regulation 8(4) of the Universal Credit Regulations.
(3) The claimant—
(a) must not have obtained from a doctor a statement given in accordance with the rules set out in Part 1 of Schedule 1 to the Social Security (Medical Evidence) Regulations 1976(1) ("a statement of fitness for work") in respect of the date on which the claim for universal credit is made, unless it has been determined, since the statement was given, that the claimant does not have limited capability for work within the meaning of the 2007 Act;
(b) must not have applied for a statement of fitness for work;
(c) must declare that the claimant does not consider himself or herself to be unfit for work; and
(d) must not have been the subject of a determination that the claimant has limited capability for work within the meaning of the 2007 Act, unless it has subsequently been determined that the claimant does not have limited capability for work within the meaning of that Act.

Existing benefits

3.176   3. (1) The claimant must not be entitled to—
[² (a) old style ESA;
(b) old style JSA;
(c) income support;]
(d) incapacity benefit or severe disablement allowance, as defined in Schedule 4 to the 2007 Act;
(e) disability living allowance [⁴ ...]; or
(f) personal independence payment [⁴ ...].
(2) [² ...]
(3) The claimant must not be awaiting—
[² (a) a decision on a claim for—
   (i) any benefit mentioned in sub-paragraph (1)(a) to (c);
   (ii) a tax credit; or
   (iii) housing benefit;]; or
(b) the outcome of an application—
   (i) to the Secretary of State to consider whether to revise, under section 9 of the Social Security Act 1998, a decision that the claimant is not entitled to old style JSA, old style ESA or income support; or
   (ii) to the relevant authority (within the meaning of the Child Support, Pensions and Social Security Act 2000) to consider whether to revise, under Schedule 7 to that Act, a decision that the claimant is not entitled to housing benefit.
(4) If the claimant has appealed against a decision that he or she is not entitled to a benefit mentioned in sub-paragraph (1)(a) to (c), the Secretary of State must be satisfied—

(a) that the appeal to the First-tier Tribunal, and any subsequent appeal to the Upper Tribunal or to a court, is not ongoing; and

(b) where an appeal has been finally determined, that there is no possibility of a further appeal by any party.

(5) [² ...]

(6) [² ...]

Income and capital

[³ 4. (1) If the claimant is a single claimant, the claimant must declare that, during the period of one month starting with the date on which the claim for universal credit is made, the claimant's earned income is expected not to exceed [⁴ £338].

(2) If the claim for universal credit is made by a couple as joint claimants, they must declare that, during the period of one month starting with the date on which the claim is made—

(a) in relation to each member of the couple, the earned income of that member is expected not to exceed [⁴ £338]; and

(b) the couple's total earned income is expected not to exceed [⁴ £541].

(3) If the claimant is a single claimant and is not a member of a couple, the claimant's capital must not exceed £6,000.

(4) If the claimant is a single claimant and is a member of a couple, the couple's total capital must not exceed £6,000.

(5) If the claim for universal credit is made by a couple as joint claimants, the couple's total capital must not exceed £6,000.

(6) For the purposes of this paragraph, "couple" has the same meaning as it has in section 39 of the Act and "earned income" and "capital" have the same meanings as they have in Part 6 of the Universal Credit Regulations.]

3.177

Housing

5. The claimant must not—

(a) be homeless (within the meaning of section 175 of the Housing Act 1996) and must currently reside at his or her usual address;

(b) reside in accommodation in which care, supervision, counselling, advice or other support services (other than services connected solely with the provision of adequate accommodation) are made available to the claimant by or on behalf of the person by whom the accommodation is provided, with a view to enabling the claimant to live there;

(c) reside in the same household as a person who is a member of the regular forces or the reserve forces (within the meaning of section 374 of the Armed Forces Act 2006) and who is absent from the household in connection with that role; or

(d) own, or partly own, the property in which he or she resides.

3.178

Caring responsibilities

6. [⁴ (1) There must not be a child or young person living with the claimant some or all of the time if the child or young person–

(a) has been certified as severely sight impaired or blind by a consultant ophthalmologist;

(b) is looked after by a local authority, within the meaning of section 22 of the Children Act 1989 or section 17(6) of the Children (Scotland) Act 1995, save where the child or young person is so looked after during any period referred to in regulation 4A(1)(a) of the Universal Credit Regulations; or

(c) is entitled to a disability living allowance or personal independence payment.]

(2) The claimant must not—

[⁴ (a) be an adopter (within the meaning of the Universal Credit Regulations) with whom a child has been placed during the period of 12 months ending immediately before the date on which the claim for universal credit is made or with whom a child is expected to be placed during the period of two months beginning with that date; or]

(b) be a foster parent;

(c) be liable to pay child support maintenance under the Child Support Act 1991; or

(d) have any responsibility for providing care to a person who has a physical or mental impairment, other than in the course of paid or voluntary employment.

(3) For the purposes of this paragraph—

(a) "child" has the same meaning as in Part 1 of the Act;

(b) "foster parent" means—

(i) in relation to England, a person who is approved as a foster parent under the Fostering Services (England) Regulations 2011;

3.179

   (ii) in relation to Wales, a person who is approved as a foster parent under the Fostering Services (Wales) Regulations 2003;

   (iii) in relation to Scotland, a person who is approved as a kinship carer or a foster carer under the Looked After Children (Scotland) Regulations 2009 [⁴;

  (c) "young person" means a person–

   (i) who is not a child but who is under the age of 20; and

   (ii) for whom the claimant would be responsible for the purposes of regulation 4 of the Universal Credit Regulations, if the person were a qualifying young person within the meaning of regulation 5 of those Regulations.]

Other requirements

3.180 7. The claimant—

[² (a) must not be carrying on a trade, profession or vocation in respect of which he or she receives self-employed earnings (within the meaning of regulation 57 of the Universal Credit Regulations) and must declare that he or she does not expect to carry on such a trade, profession or vocation during the period of one month starting with the date on which the claim for universal credit is made;]

  (b) must not be receiving education or undertaking a course of training of any kind and must declare that he or she does not intend to engage in education or training of any kind (other than where required to do so by the Secretary of State, or by agreement with the Secretary of State, in connection with an award of universal credit) during the period of one month starting with the date on which the claim for universal credit is made;

  (c) must not have—

   (i) a deputy appointed by the Court of Protection under Part 1 of the Mental Capacity Act 2005 ("the 2005 Act");

   (ii) a receiver appointed under Part 7 of the Mental Health Act 1983 and treated as a deputy by virtue of the 2005 Act; or

   (iii) any other person acting on the claimant's behalf in relation to the claim for universal credit;

  (d) must have a national insurance number;

[⁴ (e) must have an account with a bank, a building society, the Post Office, or a Credit Union (within the meaning of the Credit Unions Act 1979] [⁵ or, in the case of joint claimants(2), either member of the couple must have such an account] [²;

  (f) must not be—

   (i) a company director, within the meaning of the Companies Act 2006; or

   (ii) a member of a limited liability partnership, within the meaning of the Limited Liability Partnerships Act 2000.]

Declarations

3.181 8. [³ (1)] [² A] declaration which is required by paragraph 2(3)(c), 4(1) , [³ 4(2)] or 7(a) or (b) is to be made by such method as may be required by the Secretary of State in relation to the person by whom it is to be made.]

[³ (2) A declaration which is required by paragraph 4(2) in relation to a couple may be made on behalf of the couple by both members of the couple or by either of them.]

AMENDMENTS

1. Welfare Reform Act 2012 (Commencement No.9, 11, 13, 14 and 16 and Transitional and Transitory Provisions (Amendment)) Order 2014 (SI 2014/1452) art.16 (June 16, 2014).

2. Welfare Reform Act 2012 (Commencement No.9, 11, 13 14, 16 and 17 and Transitional and Transitory Provisions (Amendment)) Order 2014 (SI 2014/1661) art. 4(4) (June 30, 2014).

3. Welfare Reform Act 2012 (Commencement No.9, 11, 13, 14, 16 and 17 and Transitional and Transitory Provisions (Amendment) (No.2)) Order 2014 (SI 2014/1923) art. 4(7) (July 28, 2014).

4. Welfare Reform Act 2012 (Commencement No.9, 11, 13, 14, 16, 17 and 19 and Transitional and Transitory Provisions (Amendment)) Order 2015 (SI 2015/32) arts.4(5) and 5 (January 26, 2015).

5. Welfare Reform Act 2012 (Commencement No.24 and Transitional and Transitory Provisions and Commencement No.9 and Transitional and Transitory Provisions (Amendment)) Order 2015 (SI 2015/1537) art.5(2)(a) (July 21, 2015).

GENERAL NOTE

Paragraph 4

One of the gateway conditions is that a single claimant must declare that their **3.182** earned income for the next month "is not expected to exceed" a set figure (originally £330, now £338). The question on the original on-line claim form is subtly different, namely "Are you expecting take-home pay of £330 or more in the next month?" See AM v SSWP (UC) [2017] UKUT 131 for a discussion of the difficulties this may create. As Judge Rowland observed:

'25. The Secretary of State argues that, because those who are uncertain are not confident that they will receive take-home pay of £330 or more in the next month, the correct answer for them to give on the claim form is no. I accept that, as a matter of very strict logic, that is so and that therefore the advice given to the claimant on 20 July 2015 was, strictly speaking, correct insofar as it explained which answer on the claim form was appropriate. However, it seems to me to be unlikely that this claimant is the only one to have read the option no as requiring him to declare that he expected not to receive take-home pay of £330 or more in the next month even though he had no such clear expectation. People do not always distinguish between I am not expecting take-home pay of £330 or more in the next month and I am expecting not to receive take-home pay of £330 or more in the next month. Without some guidance, the claim form is apt to confuse and a cautious person may prefer to answer "yes" rather than "no" so as to avoid an apparent under-declaration that might be construed as deliberately misleading.'

Judge Rowland further held as a matter of law as follows (at para.23):

'23. Whether or not "highly likely" is the right phrase, I accept that in both paragraph 4(1) of Schedule 5 to the Commencement No.9 Order and in the question posed on the claim form, "expect" or "expecting" is used in the sense of the person concerned being reasonably confident about what will happen.'

The Welfare Reform Act 2012 (Commencement No.11 and Transitional and Transitory Provisions and Commencement No.9 and Transitional and Transitory Provisions (Amendment)) Order 2013

(SI 2013/1511) (C. 60) (AS AMENDED)

The Secretary of State, in exercise of the powers conferred by section 150(3) and (4)(a), (b)(i) and (c) of the Welfare Reform Act 2012, makes the following Order:

ARRANGEMENT OF ARTICLES

relation to claimant responsibilities with respect to employment and support allowance and jobseeker's allowance

7. Amendment of Schedule 4 to the No.9 Order
8. Amendment of the No.9 Order – transition from old style ESA to new style ESA
9. Transition from new style ESA to old style ESA
10. Transition from old style JSA to new style JSA
11. Transition from new style JSA to old style JSA

Schedule Part 1 The No.2 relevant districts
            Part 2 he No.3 relevant districts

GENERAL NOTE

3.184   Note that the text of this Commencement Order is not included in its entirety in this volume as it is now unlikely to give rise to live appeals. The full text can be found in the 2019/20 edn of this book at paras 3.183-3.212.

This Commencement Order ("the Commencement No.11 Order") extended the universal credit scheme to certain postcode districts in Wigan ("the No.2 relevant districts") and Manchester, Oldham and Warrington ("the No.3 relevant districts") as from July 1, 2013. The Order accordingly brought into force in those areas the provisions of the WRA 2012 that relate to both the introduction of universal credit and the abolition of income-related ESA and income-based JSA. This was achieved by reference to the specific categories of cases set out in arts.3 and 4. In addition, of course, the claimant had to fall within the Pathfinder Group, i.e. be a person who meets the requirements of regs.5 to 12 of the Transitional Provisions Regulations 2013 (or now meet the "gateway conditions" as set out in Sch.5 to the Commencement No.9 Order (as amended)).

An award of ESA under Part 1 of the Welfare Reform Act 2007, in a case where income-related ESA has been abolished, is referred to as a "new style ESA award". Likewise an award of a JSA under the Jobseekers Act 1995, in a case where income-based JSA has been abolished, is referred to as a "new style JSA award". Conversely an award of ESA under Part 1 of the Welfare Reform Act 2007, in a case where income-related ESA has not been abolished, is referred to as an "old style ESA award". Similarly an award of JSA under the Jobseekers Act 1995, in a case where income-based JSA has not been abolished, is referred to as an "old style JSA award".

This Order also amended certain transitional provisions in the Commencement No.9 Order.

The Welfare Reform Act 2012 (Commencement No.13 and Transitional and Transitory Provisions) Order 2013

(SI 2013/2657) (C.103) (AS AMENDED)

The Secretary of State, in exercise of the powers conferred by section 150(3) and (4)(a), (b)(i) and (c) of the Welfare Reform Act 2012, makes the following Order:

ARRANGEMENT OF ARTICLES

3.185   1. Citation

GENERAL NOTE

This Commencement Order ("the Commencement No.13 Order") extended   **3.186**
the universal credit scheme to certain postcode districts in West London (Hammersmith), Manchester and Wigan ("the No.4 relevant districts") as from October 28, 2013. In addition, of course, the claimant had initially to fall within the Pathfinder Group, i.e. be a person who met the requirements of regs.5 to 12 of the Transitional Provisions Regulations 2013, and subsequently the gateway conditions in Sch.5 to the Commencement No.9 Order.

Note that the text of this Commencement Order is not included in its entirety in this volume as it is now unlikely to give rise to live appeals. The full text can be found in the 2019/20 edn of this book at paras 3.213-3.235.

The Welfare Reform Act 2012 (Commencement No.14 and Transitional and Transitory Provisions) Order 2013

SI 2013/2846 (C.114) (AS AMENDED)

The Secretary of State, in exercise of the powers conferred by section 150(3) and (4)(a), (b)(i) and (c) of the Welfare Reform Act 2012, makes the following Order:

ARRANGEMENT OF ARTICLES

GENERAL NOTE

This Commencement Order ("the Commencement No.14 Order") extended the   **3.188**
universal credit scheme to certain postcode districts in Rugby, Inverness and Perth ("the No.5 relevant districts") as from November 25, 2013. In addition, of course, the claimant had to fall within the Pathfinder Group, i.e. be a person who met the requirements of regs.5 to 12 of the Transitional Provisions Regulations 2013, later the "gateway conditions" (see Sch.5 to the Commencement No.9 Order). Note that the text of this Commencement Order is not included in its entirety in this volume

as it is now unlikely to give rise to live appeals. The full text can be found in the 2019/20 edn of this book at paras 3.236-3.254.

The Welfare Reform Act 2012 (Commencement No.16 and Transitional and Transitory Provisions) Order 2014

SI 2014/209 (C. 7) (AS AMENDED)

The Secretary of State, in exercise of the powers conferred by section 150(3) and (4)(a), (b)(i) and (c) of the Welfare Reform Act 2012, makes the following Order:

ARRANGEMENT OF ARTICLES

3.189
1. Citation
2. Interpretation
3. Day appointed for commencement of the universal credit provisions in Part 1 of the Act
4. Day appointed for the abolition of income-related employment and support allowance and income-based jobseeker's allowance
5. Application of the No.9 Order
6. Day appointed for the coming into force of section 139 of the Act

Schedule: The No.6 and No.7 relevant districts

GENERAL NOTE

3.190   This Commencement Order ("the Commencement No.16 Order") extended the universal credit scheme to certain postcode districts in Bath and Harrogate ("the No.6 relevant districts") as from February 24, 2014 and to others in Shotton ("the No.7 relevant districts") as from April 7, 2014. In addition, of course, the claimant had to fall within the Pathfinder Group, i.e. be a person who met the requirements of regs.5 to 12 of the Transitional Provisions Regulations 2013, later the "gateway conditions" (see Sch.5 to the Commencement No.9 Order). Note that the text of this Commencement Order is not included in its entirety in this volume as it is now unlikely to give rise to live appeals. The full text can be found in the 2019/20 edn of this book at paras 3.255-3.267.

The Welfare Reform Act 2012 (Commencement No.9, 11, 13, 14 and 16 and Transitional and Transitory Provisions (Amendment)) Order 2014

(SI 2014/1452) (C.56)

The Secretary of State, in exercise of the powers conferred by section 150(3) and (4)(a), (b)(i) and (c) of the Welfare Reform Act 2012(1), makes the following Order:

ARRANGEMENT OF ARTICLES

PART 1

CITATION, INTERPRETATION AND APPLICATION

PART 2

AMENDMENT OF THE NO.9 ORDER

PART 3

AMENDMENT OF THE NO.11, 13, 14 AND 16 ORDERS

GENERAL NOTE

3.192   Note that the text of this Commencement Order is not included in its entirety in this volume as it is now unlikely to give rise to live appeals. However, the exception is that the myriad amendments made to the Commencement No.9 Order by Pt 2 of this Order are incorporated above in the text of the relevant Order. The full text of this Order can be found in the 2019/20 edn of this book at paras 3.268-3.274.

The Welfare Reform Act 2012 (Commencement No.17 and Transitional and Transitory Provisions) Order 2014Welfare Reform Act 2012 (Commencement No.17) Order 2014

SI 2014/1583 (C. 61) (AS AMENDED)

The Secretary of State, in exercise of the powers conferred by sections 150(3) and (4) (a), (b) (i) and (c) of the Welfare Reform Act 2012, makes the following Order:

ARRANGEMENT OF ARTICLES

GENERAL NOTE

3.194   This Commencement Order ("the Commencement No.17 Order") extended the universal credit scheme to certain postcode districts and as from various dates in areas known as the No.8, No.9, No.10, No.11, No.12 and No.13 relevant districts (see Schedule). All the scheduled postcode districts were in the North West. In addition, of course, the claimant had to fall within the Pathfinder Group, i.e. be a person who met the requirements of regs.5 to 12 of the Transitional Provisions Regulations 2013, later the "gateway conditions" (see Sch.5 to the Commencement No.9 Order).

For an example of an Upper Tribunal appeal involving a case subject to this Commencement Order, see *AM v SSWP (UC)* [2017] UKUT 131 (and especially paragraphs 12–14). Note that the text of this Commencement Order is not included in its entirety in this volume as it is now unlikely to give rise to live appeals. The full text can be found in the 2019/20 edn of this book at paras 3.275-3.287.

The Welfare Reform Act 2012 (Commencement No.9, 11, 13, 14, 16 and 17 and Transitional and Transitory Provisions (Amendment)) Order 2014

(SI 2014/1661) (C.69)

The Secretary of State, in exercise of the powers conferred by sections 150(3) and (4) (a), (b) (i) and (c) of the Welfare Reform Act 2012, makes the following Order:

ARRANGEMENT OF ARTICLES

GENERAL NOTE

Note that the text of this Commencement Order is not included in its entirety in this volume as it is now unlikely to give rise to live appeals. The text of this Order can be found in the 2019/20 edn of this book at paras 3.288-3.297.   **3.195**

The Welfare Reform Act 2012 (Commencement No.9, 11, 13, 14, 16 and 17 and Transitional and Transitory Provisions (Amendment) (No.2)) Order 2014

(SI 2014/1923) (C.88)

The Secretary of State, in exercise of the powers conferred by section 150(3) and (4) (a), (b) (i) and (c) of the Welfare Reform Act 2012, makes the following Order:

ARRANGEMENT OF ARTICLES

3.196

GENERAL NOTE

3.197   Note that the text of this Commencement Order is not included in its entirety in this volume as it is now unlikely to give rise to live appeals. The full text of this Order can be found in the 2019/20 edn of this book at paras 3.298-3.309. The main change made by this Order was the removal of the condition that a claimant had to be single in order for the universal credit provisions to come into force where a claim is made for universal credit (and for the amending provisions to come into force where a claim is made for universal credit, ESA or JSA). This meant that as from July 28, 2014, the universal credit provisions (and the amending provisions) came into force where a claim is made by members of a couple where they reside in an area covered by the relevant Commencement Orders and each member meets the remaining gateway conditions. These provisions were already in force for claims made by members of a couple who resided in certain areas by virtue of the Welfare Reform Act 2012 (Commencement No.9, 11, 13 14, 16 and 17 and Transitional and Transitory Provisions (Amendment)) Order 2014 (SI 2014/1661). To reflect the fact that the universal credit provisions (and the amending provisions) came into force where a claim is made by a couple who reside in one of the "relevant districts", art.4 makes consequential changes to articles 3, 4 and 5 of the Commencement No.9 Order and inserts a new article 3A into that Order.

The Welfare Reform Act 2012 (Commencement No.19 and Transitional and Transitory Provisions and Commencement No.9 and Transitional and Transitory Provisions (Amendment)) Order 2014

(SI 2014/2321) (C.99) (AS AMENDED)

The Secretary of State makes the following Order in exercise of the powers conferred by sections 150(3) and (4)(a), (b)(i) and (c) of the Welfare Reform Act 2012:

ARRANGEMENT OF ARTICLES

GENERAL NOTE

Note that the text of this Commencement Order is not included in its entirety **3.199** in this volume as it is now unlikely to give rise to live appeals. The full text of this Order can be found in the 2019/20 edn of this book at paras 3.310-3.332. This Commencement Order ("the Commencement No.19 Order") extended the UC scheme to certain postcode districts in a wide range of different areas in the North West of England (known as the No.14, No.15, No.16, No.17, No.18, No.19, No.20, No.21, No.22, No.23, No.24, No.25, No.26 or No.27 relevant districts – see Schedule). In addition, of course, the claimant must meet the gateway conditions in Sch.5 to the Commencement No.9 Order.

The Welfare Reform Act 2012 (Commencement No.9, 11, 13 14, 16, 17 and 19 and Transitional and Transitory Provisions (Amendment)) Order 2014

SI 2014/3067 (C.129)

The Secretary of State for Work and Pensions makes the following Order in exercise of the powers conferred by sections 150(3) and (4)(a), (b)(i) and (c) of the Welfare Reform Act 2012:

ARRANGEMENT OF ARTICLES

1. Citation   **3.200**
2. Interpretation
3. Amendment of the No.9, No.11, No.13, No.14, No.16, No.17 and No.19
   Orders: cases to which the amendments apply
4. Amendment of the No.11 Order: the gateway conditions
5. Amendment of the No.17 Order: the gateway conditions
6. Meaning of "claimant": amendment of the No.9, No.11, No.13, No.14, No.16,
   No.17 and No.19 Orders
7. Amendment of the No.9 Order: transitional provisions on waiting periods

GENERAL NOTE

The main effect of this Order was to amend the Commencement No.11 and the **3.201** Commencement No.17 Orders so as to modify the "gateway conditions" specified in Sch.5 to the Commencement No.9 Order by (in large part) removing the condition that a claimant must not have responsibility for children or young persons in a case where the claimant resides in certain postcode districts or part-districts in the North West of England (as covered by those Commencement No.11 and No.17 Orders). As a consequence the provisions listed in Sch.2 to the No.9 Order come into force where, on the date on which a claim for universal credit is made, the claimant resides in one of those postcode districts or part-districts and meets the modified gateway conditions. Note that the text of this Commencement Order is not included in its entirety in this volume as it is now unlikely to give rise to live appeals. The full text of this Order can be found in the 2019/20 edn of this book at paras 3.333-3.341.

The Welfare Reform Act 2012 (Commencement No.20 and Transitional and Transitory Provisions and Commencement No.9 and Transitional and Transitory Provisions (Amendment)) Order 2014

(SI 2014/3094) (C.133)

The Secretary of State for Work and Pensions makes the following Order in exercise of the powers conferred by sections 150(3) and (4)(a), (b)(i) and (c) of the Welfare Reform Act 2012:

ARRANGEMENT OF ARTICLES

GENERAL NOTE

3.203   Note that the text of this Commencement Order is not included in its entirety in this volume as it is now unlikely to give rise to live appeals. The full text of this Order can be found in the 2019/20 edn of this book at paras 3.342-3.350. This Commencement Order ("the Commencement No.20 Order") extended the universal credit scheme to the part postcode district in Sutton (SM5 2) known as "the No.28 relevant district". This applied for a limited test period only, namely November 26, 2014 until December 20, 2014. In this instance there was no further requirement that the claimant had to meet the gateway conditions (in Sch.5 to the Commencement No.9 Order). This was because this extension involved the testing of the enhanced digital (or full) service for universal credit for the full scope of universal credit households in a limited area (i.e. the part postcode SM5 2). See also the Universal Credit (Digital Service) Amendment Regulations 2014 (SI 2014/2887), introduced with effect from 26 November 2014, which were limited to any claimant who lived in the digital trial area and who was referred to as a 'Digital service claimant'. There is no Schedule to this Commencement Order as the relevant part postcode area is simply defined by reference to the definition of "the No.28 relevant district" in art.2(1). Provision for universal credit new claims in Sutton was subsequently resumed under the Commencement No.21 Order.

The Welfare Reform Act 2012 (Commencement No.9, 11, 13, 14, 16, 17 and 19 and Transitional and Transitory Provisions (Amendment)) Order 2015

(SI 2015/32) (C.3)

The Secretary of State for Work and Pensions makes the following Order in exercise of the powers conferred by section 150(3) and (4)(a) and (b)(i) of the Welfare Reform Act 2012:

ARRANGEMENT OF ARTICLES

3.204

GENERAL NOTE

This Commencement Order provided for the introduction of universal credit claims from claimants with children in all live service areas. This was implemented in two stages, with effect from January 26 and March 2, 2015. Thus Art.4 amended Sch.5 to the Commencement No.9 Order so that there is no longer a general condition that a claimant must not have responsibility for children or young persons. In its place is a condition that a claimant must not have responsibility for certain children and young persons (e.g. most children or young persons who are looked after by a local authority and children or young persons who are entitled to DLA or PIP). Article 3(1) in turn provides that those amendments to permit claims by those with responsibility for children came into effect on January 26, 2015 where a claimant resides in any of the areas covered by the Commencement No.9 Order. In addition, these changes also come into effect on the same date where a claimant resides in the areas covered by the Commencement No.11, No.13, No.14, No.16 and No.17 Orders (save for postcode districts and part-districts BL1 to BL4, BL5 1, BL5 3, BL6 4, BL6 9 and M26 3 in the No.9 relevant districts and the No.13 relevant districts (other than postcode part-district CH62 9). Article 3(2) meanwhile provides that the same changes came into effect on March 2, 2015 where a claimant resides in postcode districts and part-districts in the No.9 relevant districts listed above or in one of the No.13 relevant districts, covered by the Commencement No.17 Order, or in the areas covered by the Commencement No.19 Order. Note that the text of this Commencement Order is not included in its entirety in this volume as it is now unlikely to give rise to live appeals. The full text of this Order can be found in the 2019/20 edn of this book at paras 3.351-3.361.

3.205

The Welfare Reform Act 2012 (Commencement No.21 and Transitional and Transitory Provisions) Order 2015

(SI 2015/33) (C.4)

The Secretary of State for Work and Pensions makes the following Order in exercise of the powers conferred by section 150(3) and (4)(a), (b)(i) and (c) of the Welfare Reform Act 2012:

ARRANGEMENT OF REGULATIONS

3.206

1. Citation
2. Interpretation
3. Day appointed for the coming into force of the universal credit provisions
4. Day appointed for the abolition of income-related employment and support allowance and income-based jobseeker's allowance
5. Application of the No.9 Order
6. Transitional provision: claims for housing benefit, income support or a tax credit

GENERAL NOTE

3.207   This Order (the Commencement No.21 Order) provided for the resumption of universal credit new claims in Sutton as from January 28, 2015, following the pilot in place there from November 26 to December 19, 2014 (by virtue of the Commencement No.20 Order).

Citation

3.208   **1.** This Order may be cited as the Welfare Reform Act 2012 (Commencement No.21 and Transitional and Transitory Provisions) Order 2015.

Interpretation

3.209   **2.**—(1) In this Order–
"the Act" means the Welfare Reform Act 2012;
"the 1998 Act" means the Social Security Act 1998;
"the amending provisions" means the provisions referred to in article 4(1)(a) to (c) of the No.9 Order (day appointed for the abolition of income-related employment and support allowance and income-based jobseeker's allowance);
"claimant"–
(a) in relation to an employment and support allowance, has the same meaning as in Part 1 of the Welfare Reform Act 2007, save as mentioned in article 5(1A) of the No.9 Order as applied by article 4(7) of this Order;
(b) in relation to a jobseeker's allowance, has the same meaning as in the Jobseekers Act 1995 (as it applies apart from the amendments made by Part 1 of Schedule 14 to the Act that remove references to

an income-based jobseeker's allowance), save as mentioned in article 5(1A) of the No.9 Order as applied by article 4(7) of this Order;

(c) in relation to universal credit, has the same meaning as in Part 1 of the Act;

"the Claims and Payments Regulations 2013" means the Universal Credit, Personal Independence Payment, Jobseeker's Allowance and Employment and Support Allowance (Claims and Payments) Regulations 2013;

"employment and support allowance" means an employment and support

allowance under Part 1 of the Welfare Reform Act 2007;

"First-tier Tribunal" has the same meaning as in the 1998 Act;

"jobseeker's allowance" means a jobseeker's allowance under the Jobseekers Act 1995;

"joint claimants", in relation to universal credit, has the same meaning as in Part 1 of the Act;

"the No.9 Order" means the Welfare Reform Act 2012 (Commencement No.9 and Transitional and Transitory Provisions and Commencement No.8 and Savings and Transitional Provisions (Amendment)) Order 2013;

"the No.28 relevant district" means the postcode part-district SM5 2;

"single claimant", in relation to universal credit, has the same meaning as in Part 1 of the Act;

[¹...]

"Upper Tribunal" has the same meaning as in the 1998 Act.

(2) For the purposes of this Order, the Claims and Payments Regulations 2013 apply for the purpose of deciding–

(a) whether a claim for universal credit is made; and

(b) the date on which such a claim is made.

AMENDMENT

1. Welfare Reform Act 2012 (Commencement No.23 and Transitional and Transitory Provisions) Order 2015 (SI 2015/634) art.9(2) (June 10. 2015).

Day appointed for the coming into force of the universal credit provisions

3.—(1) The day appointed for the coming into force of the provisions   3.210
of the Act listed in Schedule 2 to the No.9 Order, in so far as they are not already in force, in relation to the case of a claim referred to in paragraph (2), and any award that is made in respect of the claim, is the day appointed in accordance with paragraph (3).

(2) The claims referred to are–

(a) a claim for universal credit that is made on or after 28th January 2015 in respect of a period that begins on or after 28th January 2015 where, on the date on which the claim is made, the claimant resides in the No.28 relevant district [¹...];

(b) a claim for universal credit that is made on or after 28th January 2015 in respect of a period that begins on or after 28th January 2015 where–

(i) in the case of a single claimant, the claimant gives incorrect information regarding the claimant residing in the No.28

relevant district [¹ . . .] and the claimant does not reside in that district [¹ . . .] on the date on which the claim is made;

(ii) in the case of joint claimants, either or both of the joint claim-ants gives or give incorrect information regarding his or her (or their) residing in that district [¹ . . .] and one or both of them does not or do not reside in that district [¹ . . .] on the date on which the claim is made,

and after a decision is made that the single claimant is, or the joint claim-ants are, entitled to universal credit and one or more payments have been made in respect of the single claimant or the joint claimants, the Secretary of State discovers that incorrect information has been given regarding such residence [¹ . . .].

(3) The day appointed in relation to the case of a claim referred to in paragraph (2), and any award that is made in respect of the claim, is the first day of the period in respect of which the claim is made.

(4) Article 3(6) of the No.9 Order applies for the purposes of paragraph (3) as it applies for the purposes of article 3(4)(a) of the No.9 Order.

(5) Article 3A of the No.9 Order applies in connection with a claim for universal credit where a single claimant, or, as the case may be, either or both of joint claimants, gives or give incorrect information regarding his or her (or their) residing in the No.28 relevant district [¹ . . .], as it applies in connection with the giving of incorrect information regarding a claimant residing in one of the relevant districts (as defined in the No.9 Order) [¹ . . .].

AMENDMENT

1. Welfare Reform Act 2012 (Commencement No.23 and Transitional and Transitory Provisions) Order 2015 (SI 2015/634) art.9(3) (June 10, 2015).

DEFINITIONS

"claimant"–see art.2(1).
"joint claimant"–*ibid.*
"single claimant"–*ibid.*
"No.9 Order"–*ibid.*
"No.28 relevant district"–*ibid.*
"specified condition"–*ibid.*

Day appointed for the abolition of income-related employment and support allowance and income-based jobseeker's allowance

3.211   4.—(1) The day appointed for the coming into force of the amending provisions, in relation to the case of a claim referred to in paragraph (2), and any award that is made in respect of the claim, is the day appointed in accordance with paragraph (3).

(2) The claims referred to are–

(a) a claim for universal credit that is made on or after 28th January 2015 in respect of a period that begins on or after 28th January 2015 where, on the date on which the claim is made, the claimant resides in the No.28 relevant district [² . . .];

(b) a claim for universal credit that is made on or after 28th January 2015 in respect of a period that begins on or after 28th January 2015 where–

(i) in the case of a single claimant, the claimant gives incorrect

information regarding the claimant residing in the No.28 relevant district [² . . .] and the claimant does not reside in that
district [² . . .] on the date on which the claim is made;

(ii) in the case of joint claimants, either or both of the joint claimants gives or give incorrect information regarding his or her (or
their) residing in that district [² . . .] and one or both of them
does not or do not reside in that district [² . . .] on the date on
which the claim is made,

and after a decision is made that the single claimant is, or the joint claimants are, entitled to universal credit and one or more payments have been
made in respect of the single claimant or the joint claimants, the Secretary
of State discovers that incorrect information has been given regarding such
residence [² . . .];

(c) a claim for an employment and support allowance or a jobseeker's allowance that is made or treated as made on or after 28th
January 2015 where, on the date on which the claim is made or
treated as made, the claimant resides in the No.28 relevant district
[² . . .];

(d) a claim for an employment and support allowance or a jobseeker's
allowance other than one referred to in sub-paragraph (c) that is
made or treated as made during the relevant period by a single claimant of universal credit or by either of two joint claimants of universal
credit who has or have made a claim for universal credit within sub-
paragraph (a) or (b).

(3) The day appointed in relation to the case of a claim referred to in
paragraph (2), and any award that is made in respect of the claim, is the first
day of the period in respect of which the claim is made.

(4) For the purposes of paragraph (2)(d), "relevant period" means, in
relation to a claim for universal credit within paragraph (2)(a) or (b), any
UC claim period, and any period subsequent to any UC claim period in
respect of which the claimant is entitled to an award of universal credit in
respect of the claim.

(5) For the purposes of paragraph (4), a "UC claim period" is a period
when–

(a) a claim for universal credit within sub-paragraph (a) of paragraph
(2), or within sub-paragraph (b)(i) or (ii) of that paragraph, has been
made but a decision has not yet been made on the claim; or

(b) a decision has been made that the claimant is not entitled to universal credit and–

(i) the Secretary of State is considering whether to revise that decision under section 9 of the 1998 Act, whether on an application
made for that purpose, or on the Secretary of State's own initiative; or

(ii) the claimant has appealed against that decision to the First-tier
Tribunal and that appeal or any subsequent appeal to the Upper
Tribunal or to a court has not been finally determined.

(6) [¹ Paragraphs (6), (7), (9) and (10)] of article 4 of the No.9 Order
apply in relation to a claim for universal credit referred to in paragraph (2)
(and any award that is made in respect of the claim) as they apply in relation to a claim for universal credit referred to in sub-paragraphs (a) and (b)
of article 4(2) of the No.9 Order (and any award that is made in respect of
the claim).

(7) Paragraphs (1A) and (1B) of article 5 of the No.9 Order apply for the purposes of paragraph (2)(c) as they apply for the purposes of article 4(2)(a) of the No.9 Order (but as if the references in paragraph (1A) to Schedule 5 to the No.9 Order were omitted).

(8) Paragraphs (5) to (7) of article 5 of the No.9 Order apply for the purposes of sub-paragraphs (c) and (d) of paragraph (2) as they apply for the purposes of subparagraphs (a) and (g) of article 4(2) of the No.9 Order.

(9) Article 5(8) of the No.9 Order applies for the purposes of paragraph (3) as it applies for the purposes of article 4(3)(a) of the No.9 Order.

AMENDMENTS

1. Welfare Reform Act 2012 (Commencement No.22 and Transitional and Transitory Provisions) Order 2015 (SI 2015/101), art.7(2)(b) (February 11, 2015).
2. Welfare Reform Act 2012 (Commencement No.23 and Transitional and Transitory Provisions) Order 2015 (SI 2015/634) art.9(4) (June 10, 2015).

DEFINITIONS

"the amending provisions"–see art.2(1).
"claimant"–*ibid.*
"employment and support allowance"–*ibid.*
"First-tier Tribunal"–*ibid.*
"jobseeker's allowance"–*ibid.*
"joint claimant"–*ibid.*
"No.9 Order"–*ibid.*
"No.28 relevant district"–*ibid.*
"relevant period"–para.(4).
"specified condition"–see art.2(1).
"UC claim period"–para.(5).
"Upper Tribunal"–see art.2(1).

Application of the No.9 Order

3.212   **5.** Articles 9 to 22 of the No.9 Order apply in connection with the coming into force of the amending provisions in relation to the case of a claim referred to in article 4(2), and any award made in respect of the claim, as they apply in connection with the coming into force of the amending provisions in relation to the case of a claim referred to in sub-paragraph (a), (b) or (g) of article 4(2) of the No.9 Order and any award made in respect of the claim.

DEFINITIONS

"the amending provisions"–see art.2(1).
"No.9 Order"–*ibid.*

Transitional provision: claims for housing benefit, income support or a tax credit

3.213   **6.**—(1) Except as provided by paragraphs [¹1(2) to (5) and (11)], a person may not make a claim for housing benefit, income support or a tax credit (in the latter case, whether or not as part of a Tax Credits Act couple) on any date where, if that person made a claim for universal credit on that date (in the capacity, whether as a single person or as part of a couple, in which he or she is permitted to claim universal credit under the Universal

Credit Regulations 2013), the provisions of the Act listed in Schedule 2 to the No.9 Order would come into force under article 3(1) and (2)(a) of this Order in relation to that claim for universal credit.

(2) Paragraph (1) does not apply to a claim for housing benefit in respect of specified accommodation [⁴ or temporary accommodation].

(3) Paragraph (1) does not apply to a claim for housing benefit [⁹ ...] where–

[⁵ [⁸ (a) in the case of a claim for housing benefit, the claim is made by a member of a State Pension Credit Act couple who has reached the qualifying age for state pension credit, where the other member has not reached that age, and entitlement begins, or in the case of claims made in advance of entitlement is to begin—

    (i) before 15th May 2019; or

    (ii) on or after 15th May 2019 where one of the savings in the sub-paragraphs of article 4(1) of the Welfare Reform Act 2012 (Commencement No. 31 and Savings and Transitional Provisions and Commencement No. 21 and 23 and Transitional and Transitory Provisions (Amendment)) Order 2019 applies to that person and the saving has not ceased to have effect under article 4(2) of that Order, and

entitlement to housing benefit is to be construed in accordance with article 2 of that Order;]]

(b) [⁹ ...]

(4) Paragraph (1) does not apply to a claim for a tax credit where a person or persons makes or make a claim for child tax credit or working tax credit and on the date on which he or she (or they) makes or make the claim he or she (or they) [⁹ has or have an award of working tax credit or child tax credit respectively]

(5) Paragraph (1) does not apply to a claim for a tax credit where a person [⁹ has or had, or persons have or had, an award of] child tax credit or working tax credit in respect of a tax year and that person or those persons makes or make (or is or are treated as making) a claim for that tax credit for the next tax year.

[⁹ (6) In paragraph (4), the reference to a person having an award of a tax credit includes where the person is "treated as being entitled to a tax credit" in the circumstances referred to in regulation 11(1) and (2)(a) to (ca) of the Universal Credit (Transitional Provisions) Regulations 2014 but as if, in regulation 11(1), for "For the purposes of regulations 7(7) and 8(4)" there were substituted "For the purposes of article 6(4) of the Welfare Reform Act 2012 (Commencement No. 21 and Transitional and Transitory Provisions) Order 2015".]

(7) Subject to paragraph (8), for the purposes of this article–

(a) a claim for housing benefit, income support or a tax credit is made by a person on the date on which he or she takes any action which results in a decision on a claim being required under the relevant Regulations; and

(b) it is irrelevant that the effect of any provision of the relevant Regulations is that, for the purpose of those Regulations, the claim is made or treated as made on a date that is earlier than the date on which that action is taken.

(8) Where under the provisions referred to in paragraph (9), a claim for housing benefit or income support is treated as made at a date that is earlier

than the date on which the action referred to in paragraph (7)(a) is taken, the claim is treated as made on that earlier date.

(9) The provisions referred to are–

(a) in the case of a claim for housing benefit, regulation 83(4E), (4F), (5)(d) or (8) of the Housing Benefit Regulations 2006 ("the 2006 Regulations") or, as the case may be, regulation 64(5F), (5G), (6)(d) or (9) of the Housing Benefit (Persons who have attained the qualifying age for state pension credit) Regulations 2006 ("the 2006 (SPC) Regulations")); or

(b) in the case of a claim for income support, [² regulation 6(1A)(b) or 6A] of the Social Security (Claims and Payments) Regulations 1987.

(10) For the purposes of this article–

(a) "couple" (apart from in the expressions "State Pension Credit Act couple" and "Tax Credit Act couple"), has the meaning given in section 39 of the Act;

(b) "housing benefit" means housing benefit under section 130 of the Social Security Contributions and Benefits Act 1992;

(c) "income support" means income support under section 124 of the Social Security Contributions and Benefits Act 1992;

(d) "qualifying age for state pension credit" means the qualifying age referred to in section 1(6) of the State Pension Credit Act 2002;

(e) the "relevant Regulations" means–

(i) in the case of a claim for housing benefit, the 2006 Regulations or, as the case may be, the 2006 (SPC) Regulations;

(ii) in the case of a claim for income support, the Social Security (Claims and Payments) Regulations 1987;

(iii) in the case of a claim for a tax credit, the Tax Credits (Claims and Notifications) Regulations 2002;

(f) "specified accommodation" means accommodation to which one or more of sub-paragraphs (2) to (5) of paragraph 3A of Schedule 1 to the Universal Credit Regulations 2013 applies;

(g) "state pension credit" means state pension credit under the State Pension Credit Act 2002;

(h) "State Pension Credit Act couple" means a couple as defined in section 17 of the State Pension Credit Act 2002;

(i) "tax credit" (including "child tax credit" and "working tax credit") and "tax year" have the same meanings as in the Tax Credits Act 2002;

(j) "Tax Credits Act couple" means a couple as defined in section 3(5A) of the Tax Credits Act 2002[⁴;

(k) "temporary accommodation" means accommodation which falls within Case 1 or Case 2 under paragraph 3B of Schedule 1 to the Universal Credit Regulations].

[¹ (11) Paragraph (1) does not apply to a claim for housing benefit, income support or a tax credit where, by virtue of a determination made under regulation 4 [³, or by virtue of regulation [⁶ 4A [⁷...]] [⁷...],] of the Universal Credit (Transitional Provisions) Regulations 2014, [⁹ or by virtue of article 4(11) of the Welfare Reform Act 2012 (Commencement No. 32 and Savings and Transitional Provisions) Order 2019] the person in question would be prevented from making a claim for universal credit as referred to in that paragraph.]

AMENDMENTS

1. Welfare Reform Act 2012 (Commencement No.23 and Transitional and Transitory Provisions) Order 2015 (SI 2015/634) art.9(5) (March 18, 2015).

2. Welfare Reform Act 2012 (Commencement No.23 and Transitional and Transitory Provisions) (Amendment) Order 2015 (SI 2015/740) art.2(b) (March 18, 2015).

3. Welfare Reform Act 2012 (Commencement No.9 and 21 and Transitional and Transitory Provisions (Amendment)) Order 2017 (SI 2017/483) art.3 (April 6, 2017).

4. Welfare Reform Act 2012 (Commencement No. 9, 21 and 23 (Amendment), Commencement No. 11, 13, 17, 19, 22, 23 and 24 (Modification), Transitional and Transitory Provisions) Order 2018 (2018/138) art.6(2) (April 11, 2018).

5. Welfare Reform Act 2012 (Commencement No. 31 and Savings and Transitional Provisions and Commencement No. 21 and 23 and Transitional and Transitory Provisions (Amendment)) Order 2019 (SI 2019/37) art.5(2) (January 15, 2019).

6. Universal Credit (Transitional Provisions) (SDP Gateway) Amendment Regulations 2019 (SI 2019/10) reg.3(2) (January 16, 2019).

7. Universal Credit (Restriction on Amounts for Children and Qualifying Young Persons) (Transitional Provisions) Amendment Regulations 2019 (SI 2019/27) reg.4(2) (February 1, 2019).

8. Welfare Reform Act 2012 (Commencement No. 31 and Savings and Transitional Provisions and Commencement No. 21 and 23 and Transitional and Transitory Provisions (Amendment)) Order 2019 (SI 2019/37) art.5 (January 15. 2019).

9. Welfare Reform Act 2012 (Commencement No. 32 and Savings and Transitional Provisions) Order 2019 (SI 2019/167) art 5(3) (February 1, 2019).

DEFINITIONS

"the 2006 Regulations"–para.(9)(a).
"the 2006 (SPC) Regulations"–*ibid.*
"child tax credit"–para.10(i).
"couple"–para.(10)(a).
"housing benefit"–para.(10)(b).
"income support"–para.(10)(c).
"qualifying age for state pension credit"–para.10(d).
"relevant Regulations"–para.10(e).
"specified accommodation"–para.10(f).
"state pension credit"–para.10(g).
"State Pension Credit Act couple"–para.10(h).
"tax credit"–para.(10)(i).
"Tax Credits Act couple"–para.10(j).
"working tax credit"–para.10(i).

The Welfare Reform Act 2012 (Commencement No.22 and Transitional and Transitory Provisions) Order 2015

(SI 2015/101) (C.6)

The Secretary of State for Work and Pensions makes the following Order, in exercise of the powers conferred by section 150(3) and (4) (a), (b) (i) and (c) of the Welfare Reform Act 2012:

ARRANGEMENT OF REGULATIONS

1. Citation
2. Interpretation

3.214

GENERAL NOTE

3.215   Note that the text of this Commencement Order is not included in its entirety in this volume as it is now unlikely to give rise to live appeals. The full text of this Order can be found in the 2019/20 edn of this book at paras 3.370-3.379. This Order made provision for the first phase of the national expansion of universal credit claims for single claimants for various dates (depending on the district concerned) between February 16 and July 20, 2015. It is important also to note that this Order has been subsequently modified for certain purposes by the Commencement No.26 and No.27 Orders, as well as by the Modification Order 2016.

The Welfare Reform Act 2012 (Commencement No.23 and Transitional and Transitory Provisions) Order 2015

(SI 2015/634) (C.32)

The Secretary of State for Work and Pensions makes the following Order in exercise of the powers conferred by section 150(3) and (4)(a), (b)(i) and (c) of the Welfare Reform Act 2012:

ARRANGEMENT OF ARTICLES

GENERAL NOTE

3.217   This Commencement Order ("the Commencement No.23 Order") provided for the expansion of universal credit to further postcode areas in the London Boroughs of Sutton, Croydon and Southwark in three phases. These a were the No.50, No.51 and No.52 relevant districts. Thus e.g. under art.3(1) and (2)(a), the universal credit provisions came into force in relation to a claim for universal credit, and any award that is made in respect of the claim, where the claim was made on or after March 18, 2015 with respect to a period that begins on or after that date and, on the date on which the claim was made, the claimant resides in one of the "No.50 relevant districts". The same provision was made for claims made on or after June 10, 2015 where the claimant resided in one of the "No.51 relevant districts" and for claims made on or after November 4, 2015 where the claimant resides in one of the "No.52 relevant districts".

Citation

1. This Order may be cited as the Welfare Reform Act 2012 (Commencement No.23 and Transitional and Transitory Provisions) Order 2015.

3.218

Interpretation

2.—(1) In this Order—

3.219

"the Act" means the Welfare Reform Act 2012;

"the amending provisions" means the provisions referred to in article 4(1)(a) to (c) of the No.9 Order (day appointed for the abolition of income-related employment and support allowance and income-based jobseeker's allowance);

"claimant"—

(a) in relation to an employment and support allowance, has the same meaning as in Part 1 of the Welfare Reform Act 2007, save as mentioned in article 5(1A) of the No.9 Order as applied by article 4(7) of this Order;

(b) in relation to a jobseeker's allowance, has the same meaning as in the Jobseekers Act 1995 (as it applies apart from the amendments made by Part 1 of Schedule 14 to the Act that remove references to an income-based jobseeker's allowance), save as mentioned in article 5(1A) of the No.9 Order as applied by article 4(7) of this Order;

(c) in relation to universal credit, has the same meaning as in Part 1 of the Act;

"the Claims and Payments Regulations 1987" means the Social Security (Claims and Payments) Regulations 1987;

"employment and support allowance" means an employment and support allowance under Part 1 of the Welfare Reform Act 2007;

"jobseeker's allowance" means a jobseeker's allowance under the Jobseekers Act 1995;

"joint claimants", in relation to universal credit, has the same meaning as in Part 1 of the Act;

"the No.9 Order" means the Welfare Reform Act 2012 (Commencement No.9 and Transitional and Transitory Provisions and Commencement No.8 and Savings and Transitional Provisions (Amendment)) Order 2013;

"the No.11 Order" means the Welfare Reform Act 2012 (Commencement No.11 and Transitional and Transitory Provisions and Commencement No.9 and Transitional and Transitory Provisions (Amendment)) Order 2013;

"the No.13 Order" means the Welfare Reform Act 2012 (Commencement No.13 and Transitional and Transitory Provisions) Order 2013;

"the No.14 Order" means the Welfare Reform Act 2012 (Commencement No.14 and Transitional and Transitory Provisions) Order 2013;

"the No.16 Order" means the Welfare Reform Act 2012 (Commencement No.16 and Transitional and Transitory Provisions) Order 2014;

"the No.17 Order" means the Welfare Reform Act 2012 (Commencement No.17 and Transitional and Transitory Provisions) Order 2014;

"the No.19 Order" means the Welfare Reform Act 2012 (Commencement No.19 and Transitional and Transitory Provisions and Commencement No.9 and Transitional and Transitory Provisions (Amendment)) Order 2014;

"the No.21 Order" means the Welfare Reform Act 2012 (Commencement No.21 and Transitional and Transitory Provisions) Order 2015;

"the No.22 Order" means the Welfare Reform Act 2012 (Commencement No.22 and Transitional and Transitory Provisions) Order 2015;

"the No.50 relevant districts" means the postcode part-districts SM6 7 and SM6 8;

"the No.51 relevant districts" means the postcode part-districts CR0 4 and SM6 9;

"the No.52 relevant districts" means the postcode part-districts CR0 2 and SE1 5;

"single claimant", in relation to universal credit, has the same meaning as in Part 1 of the Act.

(2) For the purposes of this Order, the Universal Credit, Personal Independence Payment, Jobseeker's Allowance and Employment and Support Allowance (Claims and Payments) Regulations 2013 apply for the purpose of deciding—

(a) whether a claim for universal credit is made; and

(b) the date on which such a claim is made.

(3) For the purposes of this Order, the Claims and Payments Regulations 1987 apply, subject to paragraphs (4) and (5), for the purposes of deciding—

(a) whether a claim for an employment and support allowance or a jobseeker's allowance is made; and

(b) the date on which the claim is made or treated as made.

(4) Subject to paragraph (5), for the purposes of this Order—

(a) a person makes a claim for an employment and support allowance or a jobseeker's allowance if he or she takes any action which results in a decision on a claim being required under the Claims and Payments Regulations 1987; and

(b) it is irrelevant that the effect of any provision of those Regulations is that, for the purposes of those Regulations, the claim is made or treated as made at a date that is earlier than the date on which that action is taken.

(5) Where, by virtue of—

(a) regulation 6(1F)(b) or (c) of the Claims and Payments Regulations 1987, in the case of a claim for an employment and support allowance; or

(b) regulation 6(4ZA) to (4ZD) and (4A)(a)(i) and (b) of those Regulations, in the case of a claim for a jobseeker's allowance,

a claim for an employment and support allowance or a jobseeker's allowance is treated as made at a date that is earlier than the date on which the action referred to in paragraph (4)(a) is taken, the claim is treated as made on that earlier date.

Day appointed for the coming into force of the universal credit provisions

3.—(1) The day appointed for the coming into force of the provisions   3.220
of the Act listed in Schedule 2 to the No.9 Order, in so far as they are not
already in force, in relation to the case of a claim referred to in paragraph
(2), and any award that is made in respect of the claim, is the day appointed
in accordance with paragraph (3).

(2) The claims referred to are—

(a) a claim for universal credit that is made on or after 18th March 2015
in respect of a period that begins on or after 18th March 2015 where,
on the date on which the claim is made, the claimant resides in one
of the No.50 relevant districts;

(b) a claim for universal credit that is made on or after 10th June 2015
in respect of a period that begins on or after 10th June 2015 where,
on the date on which the claim is made, the claimant resides in one
of the No.51 relevant districts;

(c) a claim for universal credit that is made on or after 4th November
2015 in respect of a period that begins on or after 4th November
2015 where, on the date on which the claim is made, the claimant
resides in one of the No.52 relevant districts;

(d) a claim for universal credit that is made on or after the date referred
to in any of subparagraphs (a) to (c), in respect of a period that
begins on or after that date where—

(i) in the case of a single claimant, the claimant gives incorrect
information regarding the claimant residing in a district as
referred to in the sub-paragraph in question and the claimant
does not reside in such a district on the date on which the claim
is made;

(ii) in the case of joint claimants, either or both of the joint claimants gives or give incorrect information regarding his or her (or
their) residing in such a district and one or both of them does
not or do not reside in such a district on the date on which the
claim is made, and after a decision is made that the single claimant is, or the joint claimants are, entitled to universal credit
and one or more payments have been made in respect of the
single claimant or the joint claimants, the Secretary of State
discovers that incorrect information has been given regarding
residence.

(3) The day appointed in relation to the case of a claim referred to in
paragraph (2), and any award that is made in respect of the claim, is the first
day of the period in respect of which the claim is made.

(4) Article 3(6) of the No.9 Order applies for the purposes of paragraph
(3) as it applies for the purposes of article 3(4)(a) of the No.9 Order.

(5) Article 3A of the No.9 Order applies in connection with a claim for
universal credit where a single claimant, or, as the case may be, either or
both of joint claimants, gives or give incorrect information regarding his or
her (or their) residing in one of the No.50, No.51 or No.52 relevant districts, as it applies in connection with the giving of incorrect information
regarding a claimant residing in one of the relevant districts (as defined in
the No.9 Order).

DEFINITIONS

    "the Act"–see art.2(1).
    "claimant"–*ibid.*
    "joint claimant"–*ibid.*
    "single claimant"–*ibid.*
    "No.9 Order"–*ibid.*
    "the No.50 relevant districts"–*ibid.*
    "the No.51 relevant districts"–*ibid.*
    "the No.52 relevant districts"–*ibid.*

GENERAL NOTE

3.221   See by analogy the commentary to art.3 of the Commencement No.22 Order.

Day appointed for the abolition of income-related employment and support allowance and income-based jobseeker's allowance

3.222   **4.**—(1) The day appointed for the coming into force of the amending provisions, in relation to the case of a claim referred to in paragraph (2), and any award that is made in respect of the claim, is the day appointed in accordance with paragraph (3).

    (2) The claims referred to are—

    (a) a claim for universal credit that is made on or after 18th March 2015 in respect of a period that begins on or after 18th March 2015 where, on the date on which the claim is made, the claimant resides in one of the No.50 relevant districts;

    (b) a claim for universal credit that is made on or after 10th June 2015 in respect of a period that begins on or after 10th June 2015 where, on the date on which the claim is made, the claimant resides in one of the No.51 relevant districts;

    (c) a claim for universal credit that is made on or after 4th November 2015 in respect of a period that begins on or after 4th November 2015 where, on the date on which the claim is made, the claimant resides in one of the No.52 relevant districts;

    (d) a claim for universal credit that is made on or after the date referred to in any of subparagraphs (a) to (c), in respect of a period that begins on or after that date where—

        (i) in the case of a single claimant, the claimant gives incorrect information regarding the claimant residing in a district as referred to in the sub-paragraph in question and the claimant does not reside in such a district on the date on which the claim is made;

        (ii) in the case of joint claimants, either or both of the joint claimants gives or give incorrect information regarding his or her (or their) residing in such a district and one or both of them does not or do not reside in such a district on the date on which the claim is made, and after a decision is made that the single claimant is, or the joint claimants are, entitled to universal credit and one or more payments have been made in respect of the single claimant or the joint claimants, the Secretary of State discovers that incorrect information has been given regarding residence;

    (e) a claim for an employment and support allowance or a jobseeker's allowance that is made or treated as made on or after 18th March 2015 where, on the date on which the claim is made or treated as made, the claimant resides in one of the No.50 relevant districts;

(f) a claim for an employment and support allowance or a jobseeker's allowance that is made or treated as made on or after 10th June 2015 where, on the date on which the claim is made or treated as made, the claimant resides in one of the No.51 relevant districts;

(g) a claim for an employment and support allowance or a jobseeker's allowance that is made or treated as made on or after 4th November 2015 where, on the date on which the claim is made or treated as made, the claimant resides in one of the No.52 relevant districts;

(h) a claim for an employment and support allowance or a jobseeker's allowance other than one referred to in sub-paragraphs (e) to (g) that is made or treated as made during the relevant period by a single claimant of universal credit or by either of two joint claimants of universal credit who has or have made a claim for universal credit within any of subparagraphs (a) to (d).

(3) The day appointed in relation to the case of a claim referred to in paragraph (2), and any award that is made in respect of the claim, is the first day of the period in respect of which the claim is made.

(4) For the purposes of paragraph (2)(h), "relevant period" means, in relation to a claim for universal credit within any of sub-paragraphs (a) to (d) of paragraph (2), any UC claim period, and any period subsequent to any UC claim period in respect of which the claimant is entitled to an award of universal credit in respect of the claim.

(5) For the purposes of paragraph (4), a "UC claim period" is a period when—

(a) a claim for universal credit within any of sub-paragraphs (a) to (c) of paragraph (2), or within sub-paragraph (d)(i) or (ii) of that paragraph, has been made but a decision has not yet been made on the claim; or

(b) a decision has been made that the claimant is not entitled to universal credit and—

    (i) the Secretary of State is considering whether to revise that decision under section 9 of the Social Security Act 1998, whether on an application made for that purpose, or on the Secretary of State's own initiative; or

    (ii) the claimant has appealed against that decision to the First-tier Tribunal and that appeal or any subsequent appeal to the Upper Tribunal or to a court has not been finally determined.

(6) Paragraphs (6), (7), (9) and (10) of article 4 of the No.9 Order apply in relation to a claim for universal credit referred to in paragraph (2) (and any award that is made in respect of the claim) as they apply in relation to a claim for universal credit referred to in sub-paragraphs (a) and (b) of article 4(2) of the No.9 Order (and any award that is made in respect of the claim).

(7) Paragraphs (1A) and (1B) of article 5 of the No.9 Order apply for the purposes of subparagraphs (e) to (g) of paragraph (2) as they apply for the purposes of article 4(2)(a) of the No.9 Order (but as if the references in paragraph (1A) to Schedule 5 to the No.9 Order were omitted).

(8) Article 5(8) of the No.9 Order applies for the purposes of paragraph (3) as it applies for the purposes of article 4(3)(a) of the No.9 Order.

"the amending provisions"–see art.2(1).
"claimant"–*ibid.*
"employment and support allowance"–*ibid.*
"jobseeker's allowance"–*ibid.*
"joint claimant"–*ibid.*
"No.9 Order"–*ibid.*
"the No.50 relevant districts"–*ibid.*
"the No.51 relevant districts"–*ibid.*
"the No.52 relevant districts"–*ibid.*
"relevant period"–para.(4).
"UC claim period"–para.(5).

Transitory provision – application of the "specified condition" for a period

3.223

5.—(1) Paragraphs (2) to (4) apply in relation to a case where a claim for universal credit, an employment and support allowance or a jobseeker's allowance is made on or after 18th March 2015 and before 10th June 2015.

(2) Where this paragraph applies, article 2(1) of this Order applies as if, after the definition of "single claimant" there were inserted—

";

"specified condition" means the condition that a claimant is a British citizen who—

(a) has resided in the United Kingdom throughout the period of two years ending with the date on which the claim for universal credit is made; and

(b) has not, during that period, left the United Kingdom for a continuous period of four weeks or more.".

(3) Where this paragraph applies, article 3 of this Order applies as if it were amended as follows—

(a) in sub-paragraph (a) of paragraph (2), after "relevant districts" insert "and meets the specified condition";

(b) in sub-paragraph (d)(i) of paragraph (2)—

(i) after "in question" insert "or meeting the specified condition"; and

(ii) after "in such a district" insert "or does not meet that condition";

(c) in sub-paragraph (d)(ii) of paragraph (2)—

(i) after "residing in such a district" insert "or meeting the specified condition"; and

(ii) after "reside in such a district" insert "or does not or do not meet that condition";

(d) in the closing words of sub-paragraph (d) of paragraph (2), after "regarding residence" insert "or meeting the specified condition as the case may be";

(e) in paragraph (5)—

(i) after "No.52 relevant districts" insert "or meeting the specified condition"; and

(ii) after "the No.9 Order)" insert "or meeting the gateway conditions (as defined in the No.9 Order)".

(4) Where this paragraph applies, article 4 of this Order applies as if it were amended as follows—

(a) in sub-paragraphs (a) and (e) of paragraph (2), after "relevant districts" insert "and meets the specified condition";
(b) in sub-paragraph (d)(i) of paragraph (2)—
  (i) after "in question" insert "or meeting the specified condition"; and
  (ii) after "in such a district" insert "or does not meet that condition";
(c) in sub-paragraph (d)(ii) of paragraph (2)—
  (i) after "residing in a such a district" insert "or meeting the specified condition"; and
  (ii) after "reside in such a district" insert "or does not or do not meet that condition";
(d) in the closing words of sub-paragraph (d) of paragraph (2), after "regarding residence" insert "or meeting the specified condition".

DEFINITIONS

"employment and support allowance"–see art.2(1).
"jobseeker's allowance"–*ibid.*

Application of the No.9 Order

6. Articles 9 to 22 of the No.9 Order apply in connection with the coming into force of the amending provisions in relation to the case of a claim referred to in article 4(2), and any award made in respect of the claim, as they apply in connection with the coming into force of the amending provisions in relation to the case of a claim referred to in sub-paragraph (a), (b) or (g) of article 4(2) of the No.9 Order and any award made in respect of the claim.   3.224

DEFINITIONS

"the amending provisions"–see art.2(1).
"No.9 Order"–*ibid.*

Transitional provision: claims for housing benefit, income support or a tax credit

7.—(1) Except as provided by paragraphs (2) to (6), a person may not make a claim for housing benefit, income support or a tax credit (in the latter case, whether or not as part of a Tax Credits Act couple) on any date where, if that person made a claim for universal credit on that date (in the capacity, whether as a single person or as part of a couple, in which he or she is permitted to claim universal credit under the Universal Credit Regulations 2013), the provisions of the Act listed in Schedule 2 to the No.9 Order would come into force under article 3(1) and [¹ (2)(a) to (c) of this Order in relation to that claim] for universal credit.   3.225

(2) Paragraph (1) does not apply to a claim for housing benefit, income support or a tax credit where, by virtue of a determination made under regulation 4 [², or by virtue of regulation [⁵ 4A [⁶...]] [⁶...],] of the Universal Credit (Transitional Provisions) Regulations 2014, [⁷ or by virtue of article 4(11) of the Welfare Reform Act 2012 (Commencement No. 32 and Savings and Transitional Provisions) Order 2019] the person in question would be prevented from making a claim for universal credit as referred to in that paragraph.

(3) Paragraph (1) does not apply to a claim for housing benefit in respect of specified accommodation [³ or temporary accommodation].

(4) Paragraph (1) does not apply to a claim for housing benefit [⁷...] where—

[⁴ [⁹ (a) in the case of a claim for housing benefit, the claim is made by a member of a State Pension Credit Act couple who has reached the qualifying age for state pension credit, where the other member has not reached that age, and entitlement begins, or in the case of claims made in advance of entitlement is to begin—

   (i) before 15th May 2019; or

   (ii) on or after 15th May 2019 where one of the savings in the sub-paragraphs of article 4(1) of the Welfare Reform Act 2012 (Commencement No. 31 and Savings and Transitional Provisions and Commencement No. 21 and 23 and Transitional and Transitory Provisions (Amendment)) Order 2019 applies to that person and the saving has not ceased to have effect under article 4(2) of that Order, and

entitlement to housing benefit is to be construed in accordance with article 2 of that Order;]]

   (b) [⁷...]

(5) Paragraph (1) does not apply to a claim for a tax credit where a person or persons makes or make a claim for child tax credit or working tax credit and on the date on which he or she (or they) makes or make the claim he or she (or they) [⁷ has or have an award of working tax credit or child tax credit respectively].

(6) Paragraph (1) does not apply to a claim for a tax credit where a person [⁷ has or had, or persons have or had, an award of] child tax credit or working tax credit in respect of a tax year and that person or those persons makes or make (or is or are treated as making) a claim for that tax credit for the next tax year.

[⁷ (7) In paragraph (5), the reference to a person having an award of a tax credit includes where the person is "treated as being entitled to a tax credit" in the circumstances referred to in regulation 11(1) and (2)(a) to (ca) of the Universal Credit (Transitional Provisions) Regulations 2014 but as if, in regulation 11(1), for "For the purposes of regulations 7(7) and 8(4)" there were substituted "For the purposes of article 7(5) of the Welfare Reform Act 2012 (Commencement No 23 and Transitional and Transitory Provisions) Order 2015".]

(8) Subject to paragraph (9), for the purposes of this article—

   (a) a claim for housing benefit, income support or a tax credit is made by a person on the date on which he or she takes any action which results in a decision on a claim being required under the relevant Regulations; and

   (b) it is irrelevant that the effect of any provision of the relevant Regulations is that, for the purpose of those Regulations, the claim is made or treated as made on a date that is earlier than the date on which that action is taken.

(9) Where under the provisions referred to in paragraph (10), a claim for housing benefit or income support is treated as made at a date that is earlier than the date on which the action referred to in paragraph (8)(a) is taken, the claim is treated as made on that earlier date.

(10) The provisions referred to are—

(a) in the case of a claim for housing benefit, regulation 83(4E), (4F), (5)(d) or (8) of the 2006 Regulations or, as the case may be, regulation 64(5F), (5G), (6)(d) or (9) of the the 2006 (SPC) Regulations; or

(b) in the case of a claim for income support, [¹ regulation 6(1A)(b) or 6A] of the Claims and Payments Regulations 1987.

(11) For the purposes of this article—

(a) "couple" (apart from in the expressions "State Pension Credit Act couple" and "Tax Credit Act couple"), has the meaning given in section 39 of the Act;

(b) "housing benefit" means housing benefit under section 130 of the Social Security Contributions and Benefits Act 1992;

(c) "income support" means income support under section 124 of the Social Security Contributions and Benefits Act 1992;

(d) "qualifying age for state pension credit" means the qualifying age referred to in section 1(6) of the State Pension Credit Act 2002;

(e) "the 2006 Regulations" means the Housing Benefit Regulations 2006;

(f) "the 2006 (SPC) Regulations" means the Housing Benefit (Persons who have attained the qualifying age for state pension credit) Regulations 2006;

(g) "the relevant Regulations" means—

(i) in the case of a claim for housing benefit, the 2006 Regulations or, as the case may be, the 2006 (SPC) Regulations;

(ii) in the case of a claim for income support, the Claims and Payments Regulations 1987;

(iii) in the case of a claim for a tax credit, the Tax Credits (Claims and Notifications) Regulations 2002;

(h) "specified accommodation" means accommodation to which one or more of subparagraphs (2) to (5) of paragraph 3A of Schedule 1 to the Universal Credit Regulations 2013 applies;

(i) "State Pension Credit Act couple" means a couple as defined in section 17 of the State Pension Credit Act 2002;

(j) "tax credit" (including "child tax credit" and "working tax credit") and "tax year" have the same meanings as in the Tax Credits Act 2002;

(k) "Tax Credits Act couple" means a couple as defined in section 3(5A) of the Tax Credits Act 2002 [³;

(l) "temporary accommodation" means accommodation which falls within Case 1 or Case 2 under paragraph 3B of Schedule 1 to the Universal Credit Regulations].

AMENDMENTS

1. Welfare Reform Act 2012 (Commencement No.23 and Transitional and Transitory Provisions) (Amendment) Order 2015 (SI 2015/740), art.2(a) (March 17, 2015).

2. Social Security (Restrictions on Amounts for Children and Qualifying Young Persons) Amendment Regulations 2017 (2017/376) reg.4 (April 6, 2017).

3. Welfare Reform Act 2012 (Commencement No. 9, 21 and 23 (Amendment), Commencement No. 11, 13, 17, 19, 22, 23 and 24 (Modification), Transitional and Transitory Provisions) Order 2018 (2018/138) art.6(3) (April 11, 2018).

4. Welfare Reform Act 2012 (Commencement No. 31 and Savings and Transitional Provisions and Commencement No. 21 and 23 and Transitional and Transitory Provisions (Amendment)) Order 2019 (SI 2019/37) art.5(2) (January 15, 2019).

5. Universal Credit (Transitional Provisions) (SDP Gateway) Amendment Regulations 2019 (SI 2019/10) reg.3(3) (January 16, 2019).

6. Universal Credit (Restriction on Amounts for Children and Qualifying Young Persons) (Transitional Provisions) Amendment Regulations 2019 (SI 2019/27) reg.4(3) (February 1, 2019).

7. Welfare Reform Act 2012 (Commencement No. 32 and Savings and Transitional Provisions) Order 2019 (SI 2019/167) art 5(4) (February 1, 2019).

8. Welfare Reform Act 2012 (Commencement No. 31 and Savings and Transitional Provisions and Commencement No. 21 and 23 and Transitional and Transitory Provisions (Amendment)) Order 2019 (SI 2019/37) art.5 (January 15, 2019).

DEFINITIONS

3.226

"the 2006 Regulations"–para.(11)(e).
"the 2006 (SPC) Regulations"–para.(11)(f).
"child tax credit"–para.11(j).
"couple"–para.(11)(a).
"housing benefit"–para.(11)(b).
"income support"–para.(11)(c).
"qualifying age for state pension credit"–para.11(d).
"relevant Regulations"–para.11(g).
"specified accommodation"–para.11(h).
"State Pension Credit Act couple"–para.11(i).
"tax credit"–para.(11)(j).
"Tax Credits Act couple"–para.11(k).
"working tax credit"–para.11(j).

Amendment of the Welfare Reform Act 2012 (Commencement No.9 and Transitional and Transitory Provisions and Commencement No.8 and Savings and Transitional Provisions (Amendment)) Order 2013

3.227

8.—(1) Paragraphs (2) and (3) apply in relation to a case where a claim for universal credit is made on or after 18th March 2015.

(2) Where this paragraph applies, in article 3A(3) of the No.9 Order, at the end insert "(and a determination had not been made under regulation 4 of the Universal Credit (Transitional Provisions) Regulations 2014, preventing a claim for universal credit being made with respect to the area in question or the category of case in question)".

(3) Where this paragraph applies, any reference in the No.11 Order, the No.13 Order, the No.14 Order, the No.16 Order, the No.17 Order, the No.19 Order, the No.21 Order or the No.22 Order to article 3A of the No.9 Order is a reference to that article as amended by paragraph (2).

(4) Paragraph (5) applies in relation to a case where a claim for an employment and support allowance or a jobseeker's allowance is made on or after 18th March 2015.

(5) Where this paragraph applies, for paragraph (3) of article 5A of the No.9 Order substitute—

"(3) For the purposes of this article, paragraphs (5) to (7) of article 5 apply for the purpose of determining—

(a) whether a claim for ESA or JSA is made; and

(b) the date on which the claim is made or treated as made.".

Amendment of the Welfare Reform Act 2012 (Commencement No.21 and Transitional and Transitory Provisions) Order 2015

9.—(1) Paragraphs (2) to (4) apply in relation to a case where a claim for universal credit, an employment and support allowance or a jobseeker's allowance is made on or after 10th June 2015.

3.228

(2) Where this paragraph applies, in article 2(1) of the No.21 Order, omit the definition of "specified condition".

(3) Where this paragraph applies, article 3 of the No.21 Order is amended as follows—

(a) in paragraph (2)(a), omit "and meets the specified condition";

(b) in sub-paragraph (b) of paragraph (2)—

    (i) in paragraph (i), omit "or meeting the specified condition" and "or does not meet the specified condition";

    (ii) in paragraph (ii), omit "or meeting the specified condition" and "or does not or do not meet the specified condition"; and

    (iii) in the closing words, omit "or meeting the specified condition as the case may be"; and

(c) in paragraph (5), omit "or meeting the specified condition" and "or meeting the gateway conditions (as defined in the No.9 Order)".

(4) Where this paragraph applies, article 4 of the No.21 Order is amended as follows—

(a) in sub-paragraphs (a) and (c) of paragraph (2), omit "and meets the specified condition"; and

(b) in sub-paragraph (b) of paragraph (2)—

    (i) in paragraph (i), omit "or meeting the specified condition" and "or does not meet the specified condition";

    (ii) in paragraph (ii), omit "or meeting the specified condition" and "or does not or do not meet the specified condition"; and

    (iii) in the closing words, omit "or meeting the specified condition as the case may be".

(5) With effect from 18th March 2015, article 6 of the No.21 Order is amended as follows—

(a) in paragraph (1), for "(2) to (5)" substitute "(2) to (5) and (11)";

(b) in paragraph (9)(b), for "regulation 6(1A)(b)" substitute "regulations 6(1A)(b) and 6A"; and

(c) after paragraph (10) insert—

"(11) Paragraph (1) does not apply to a claim for housing benefit, income support or a taxcredit where, by virtue of a determination made under regulation 4 of the Universal Credit (Transitional Provisions) Regulations 2014, the person in question would be prevented from making a claim for universal credit as referred to in that paragraph.".

Modification of the Universal Credit (Digital Service) Amendment Regulations 2014

10. With effect from 18th March 2015, the Universal Credit (Digital Service) Amendment Regulations 2014 have effect as if, in regulation 5(3)(a) of those Regulations (savings), for "the postcode part-district SM5 2" there were substituted "one of the postcode part-districts CR0 2 and CR0 4, SM5 2, SM6 7 to SM6 9 and SE1 5".

3.229

Modification of the Universal Credit (Surpluses and Self-employed Losses) (Digital Service) Amendment Regulations 2015

3.230   **11.** With effect from 18th March 2015, the Universal Credit (Surpluses and Self-employed Losses) (Digital Service) Amendment Regulations 2015 have effect as if, in regulation 4(3)(a) of those Regulations (savings), for "the postcode part-district SM5 2" there were substituted "one of the postcode part-districts CR0 2 and CR0 4, SM5 2, SM6 7 to SM6 9 and SE1 5."

The Welfare Reform Act 2012 (Commencement No.23 and Transitional and Transitory Provisions) (Amendment) Order 2015

(2015/740) (C.39)

The Secretary of State for Work and Pensions makes the following Order in exercise of the powers conferred by section 150(3) and (4)(a), (b)(i) and (c) of the Welfare Reform Act 2012:

ARRANGEMENT OF ARTICLES

12.   Citation
13.   Amendment of the Welfare Reform Act 2012 (Commencement No.23 and Transitional and Transitory Provisions) Order 2015

GENERAL NOTE

3.231   Note that the text of this Commencement Order is not included in this volume as it is now unlikely to give rise to live appeals. The full text of this Order can be found in the 2019/20 edn of this book at paras 3.394-3.396.

The Welfare Reform Act 2012 (Commencement No.24 and Transitional and Transitory Provisions and Commencement No.9 and Transitional and Transitory Provisions (Amendment)) Order 2015

(SI 2015/1537) (C.87)

The Secretary of State makes the following Order, in exercise of the powers conferred by section 150(3) and (4)(a), (b)(i) and (c) of the Welfare Reform Act 2012:

ARRANGEMENT OF ARTICLES

3.232   1.   Citation
2.   Interpretation
3.   Day appointed for the coming into force of the universal credit provisions
4.   Day appointed for the abolition of income-related employment and support allowance and income-based jobseeker's allowance
5.   Amendment of the No.9 Order and cases to which the amendment applies
6.   Application of the No.9 Order
7.   Modification of the Universal Credit (Digital Service) Amendment Regulations 2014

8. Revocation of modification of the Universal Credit (Digital Service) Amendment Regulations 2014
9. Modification of the Universal Credit (Surpluses and Self-Employed Losses) (Digital Service) Amendment Regulations 2015

GENERAL NOTE

Note that the text of this Commencement Order is not included in its entirety in this volume as it is now unlikely to give rise to live appeals. The full text of this Order can be found in the 2019/20 edn of this book at paras 3.397-3.408. The broad effect of this Commencement Order ("the Commencement No.24 Order") was to complete the national expansion of universal credit claims for single claimants in a series of stages from September 21, 2015 through to April 25, 2016.   3.233

Article 2 of the Order defines the gateway conditions, which are the requirements to be met to make a claim for universal credit. These are set out in Sch.5 to the Commencement No.9 Order (as amended). Article 5 of this Order amends para.7(e) of Sch.5 to allow the gateway condition requiring a universal credit claimant to have a particular type of account to be met in the case of a claim by a couple if either member of the couple has such an account.

It should be noted that para.(a) of the definition of the gateway conditions in Art.2 of this Order causes them to have effect apart from the amendments to Sch.5 made by art.4(5)(b) of the Welfare Reform Act 2012 (Commencement No.9, 11, 13, 14, 16, 17 and 19 and Transitional and Transitory Provisions (Amendment)) Order 2015 (S.I. 2015/32). That Order removed the condition that a claimant must not (at least for the great majority of cases) have responsibility for children or young persons. That particular gateway condition is reapplied for claims made with respect to the areas to which this Order applies. The gateway conditions are further modified by para.(b) of the definition and para.(3) to require that a claimant must be single, with consequent changes to alter or omit provisions relevant only to couples including the amendment by art.5 noted above ("the modified gateway conditions").

Article 3 then brought into force provisions relating to universal credit in Part 1 of the Act as set out in Sch.2 to the Commencement No.9 Order, in relation to a number of different types of cases and at different dates.

The Welfare Reform Act 2012 (Commencement No.25 and Transitional and Transitory Provisions) Order 2015

(2015/1930) (C.118)

The Secretary of State for Work and Pensions makes the following Order in exercise of the powers conferred by section 150(3) and (4)(a), (b)(i) and (c) of the Welfare Reform Act 2012:

ARRANGEMENT OF ARTICLES

1. Citation   3.234
2. Interpretation
3. Day appointed for the coming into force of the universal credit provisions
4. Day appointed for the abolition of income-related employment and support allowance and income-based jobseeker's allowance
5. Application of the No.9 Order

GENERAL NOTE

Note that the text of this Commencement Order is not included in its entirety in this volume as it is now unlikely to give rise to live appeals. The full text of this Order can be found in the 2019/20 edn of this book at paras 3.409-3.418. This Commencement Order provided for the expansion of universal credit to further designated postcodes in the London Borough of Sutton as from December 2, 2015 (see the definition of "the designated postcodes" in art.2(1)).

The Welfare Reform Act 2012 (Commencement No.26 and Transitional and Transitory Provisions and Commencement No.22, 23 and 24 and Transitional and Transitory Provisions (Modification)) Order 2016

(2016/33) (C.3)

3.235   *The Secretary of State for Work and Pensions makes the following Order in exercise of the powers conferred by section 150(3) and (4)(a), (b)(i) and (c) of the Welfare Reform Act 2012:*

ARRANGEMENT OF ARTICLES

GENERAL NOTE

3.236   Note that the text of this Commencement Order is not included in its entirety in this volume as it is now unlikely to give rise to live appeals. The full text of this Order can be found in the 2019/20 edn of this book at paras 3.419-3.435. The effect of this Commencement Order was to provide for the introduction of the universal credit digital or full service in postcodes administered by Sutton, London Bridge, Hounslow and Croydon jobcentres with effect from January 27, 2016 and February 24, 2016.

The Welfare Reform Act 2012 (Commencement No.27 and Transitional and Transitory Provisions and Commencement No.22, 23 and 24 and Transitional and Transitory Provisions (Modification)) Order 2016

(SI 2016/407) (C.20)

The Secretary of State for Work and Pensions makes the following Order in exercise of the powers conferred by section 150(3) and (4)(a), (b)(i) and (c) of the Welfare Reform Act 2012:

ARRANGEMENT OF ARTICLES

GENERAL NOTE

Note that the text of this Commencement Order is not included in its entirety   **3.238** in this volume as it is now unlikely to give rise to live appeals. The full text of this Order can be found in the 2019/20 edn of this book at paras 3.436-3.448. This Commencement Order provided for the further expansion of the universal credit digital or full service in various designated postcode areas with effect from March 23, 2016 (Croydon, London Bridge and Musselburgh) and April 27, 2016 (Purley, Thornton Heath and Great Yarmouth).

The Welfare Reform Act 2012 (Commencement No.13, 14, 16, 19, 22, 23 and 24 and Transitional and Transitory Provisions (Modification)) Order 2016

(SI 2016/596) (C.41)

The Secretary of State for Work and Pensions makes the following Order in   **3.239** *exercise of the powers conferred by section 150(3) and (4)(a), (b)(i) and (c) of the Welfare Reform Act 2012:*

ARRANGEMENT OF ARTICLES

GENERAL NOTE

3.240   Note that the text of this Commencement Order is not included in its entirety in this volume as it is now unlikely to give rise to live appeals. The full text of this Order can be found in the 2019/20 edn of this book at paras 3.449-3.462. This Order, amending and modifying a range of earlier Commencement Orders, provides for the expansion of the full or digital universal credit service in a number of designated postcode areas with effect from May 25, June 29 and July 27, 2016.

The Welfare Reform Act 2012 (Commencement No.19, 22, 23 and 24 and Transitional and Transitory Provisions (Modification)) Order 2016

(SI 2016/963) (C.86)

The Secretary of State for Work and Pensions makes the following Order in exercise of the powers conferred by section 150(3) and (4)(a), (b)(i) and (c) of the Welfare Reform Act 2012:

ARRANGEMENT OF ARTICLES

SCHEDULE   POSTCODE DISTRICTS AND PART-DISTRICTS

GENERAL NOTE

Note that the text of this Commencement Order is not included in its entirety in this volume as it is now unlikely to give rise to live appeals. The full text of this Order can be found in the 2019/20 edn of this book at paras 3.463-3.522. This Commencement Order provided for the expansion of the full Universal Credit service (or 'Digital Service' in the legislation) to postcodes administered by a total of 20 jobcentres on a weekly basis between October 5, and December 14, 2016 (along with a number of minor variations to the existing roll-out).   **3.242**

The Welfare Reform Act 2012 (Commencement No.11, 13, 16, 22, 23 and 24 and Transitional and Transitory Provisions (Modification)) Order 2017

(SI 2017/57) (C.5)

The Secretary of State for Work and Pensions makes the following Order in exercise of the powers conferred by section 150(3) and (4)(a), (b)(i) and (c) of the Welfare Reform Act 2012:

ARRANGEMENT OF ARTICLES

GENERAL NOTE

Note that the text of this Commencement Order is not included in its entirety in this volume as it is now unlikely to give rise to live appeals. The full text of this Order can be found in the 2019/20 edn of this book at paras 3.523-3.575. This Commencement Order provided for the expansion of the full Universal Credit service (or 'Digital Service' in legislation) to postcodes administered by a total of 15 jobcentres on a weekly basis between February 1 and April 26, 2017.

The Welfare Reform Act 2012 (Commencement No.9 and 21 and Transitional and Transitory Provisions (Amendment)) Order 2017

(SI 2017/483) (C.44)

The Secretary of State for Work and Pensions makes the following Order in exercise of the powers conferred by section 150(3) and (4)(a), (b)(i) and (c) of the Welfare Reform Act 2012:

ARRANGEMENT OF ARTICLES

1.Citation   **3.244**
2.Amendment of the Welfare Reform Act 2012 (Commencement No.9 and Transitional and Transitory Provisions and Commencement No.8 and Savings and Transitional Provisions (Amendment)) Order 2013
3.Amendment of the Welfare Reform Act 2012 (Commencement No.21 and Transitional and Transitory Provisions) Order 2015

GENERAL NOTE

Note that the text of this Commencement Order is not included in this volume as   **3.245**
it is now unlikely to give rise to live appeals. The full text of this Order can be found in the 2019/20 edition of this book at paras 3.576-3.579.

The Welfare Reform Act 2012 (Commencement No. 19, 22, 23 and 24 and Transitional and Transitory Provisions (Modification)) Order 2017

(SI 2017/584) (C. 53)

Made 24th April 2017

The Secretary of State for Work and Pensions makes the following Order in exercise of the powers conferred by section 150(3) and (4)(a), (b)(i) and (c) of the Welfare Reform Act 2012:

ARRANGEMENT OF ARTICLES

1. Citation   **3.246**
2. Interpretation
3. Modification of the No. 22 and 24 Orders: removal of the gateway conditions from 3rd May 2017
4. Modification of the No. 22 and 24 Orders: removal of the gateway conditions from 10th May 2017
5. Modification of the No. 19 Order: removal of the gateway conditions from 17th May 2017
6. Modification of the No. 22 and 24 Orders: removal of the gateway conditions from 24th May 2017

GENERAL NOTE

Note that the text of this Commencement Order is not included in its entirety in this volume as it is now unlikely to give rise to live appeals. The full text of this Order can be found in the 2019/20 edition of this book at paras 3.580-3.620. This Commencement Order provided for the expansion of the full Universal Credit service (or 'Digital Service' in legislation) to postcodes administered by a total of 13 jobcentres on a weekly basis between May 3 and June 28, 2017.

The Welfare Reform Act 2012 (Commencement No. 29 and Commencement No. 17, 19, 22, 23 and 24 and Transitional and Transitory Provisions (Modification)) Order 2017

2017 No. 664 (C. 56)

Made 19th May 2017

The Secretary of State for Work and Pensions makes the following Order in exercise of the powers conferred by section 150(3) and (4)(a), (b)(i) and (c) of the Welfare Reform Act 2012:

ARRANGEMENT OF ARTICLES

GENERAL NOTE

This Commencement Order provided for the expansion of the full Universal Credit service (or 'Digital Service' in legislation) to postcodes administered by a total of 30 jobcentres on a weekly basis between July 5 and 19, 2017, although in some postcodes on a phased basis until September 2017. Note that the text of this Commencement Order is not included in its entirety in this volume as it is now unlikely to give rise to live appeals. The full text of this Order can be found in the 2019/20 edition of this book at paras 3.621-3.682.

The Welfare Reform Act 2012 (Commencement No. 17, 19, 22, 23 and 24 and Transitional and Transitory Provisions (Modification)) Order 2017

2017 No. 952 (C. 86)

Made 28th September 2017

The Secretary of State for Work and Pensions makes the following Order in exercise of the powers conferred by section 150(3) and (4)(a), (b)(i) and (c) of the Welfare Reform Act 2012:

ARRANGEMENT OF ARTICLES

3.248

GENERAL NOTE

This Commencement Order provided for the expansion of the full Universal Credit service (or 'Digital Service' in legislation) to further postcodes between October 4, 2017 and January 24, 2018. Note that the text of this Commencement Order is not included in its entirety in this volume as it is now unlikely to give rise to live appeals. The full text of this Order can be found in the 2019/20 edn of this book at paras 3.683-3.689.

The Welfare Reform Act 2012 (Commencement No. 9, 21 and 23 (Amendment), Commencement No. 11, 13, 17, 19, 22, 23 and 24 (Modification), Transitional and Transitory Provisions) Order 2018

2018 No. 138 (C. 13)

Made 2nd February 2018

The Secretary of State for Work and Pensions makes the following Order in exercise of the powers conferred by section 150(3) and (4)(a), (b)(i) and (c) of the Welfare Reform Act 2012:

ARRANGEMENT OF ARTICLES

3.249

1 Citation
2 Interpretation
3 Amendment of the No. 9 Order: removal of the gateway conditions
4 Modification of the No. 11 Order, the No. 13 Order, the No. 17 Order, the No. 19 Order, the No. 22 Order and the No. 24 Order: removal of the gateway conditions
5 Modifications of the No. 11 Order, the No. 13 Order, the No. 17 Order, the No. 19 Order, the No. 22 Order and the No. 24 Order in consequence of removal of the gateway conditions
6 Amendment of the No. 21 Order and the No. 23 Order: claims for housing benefit in respect of temporary accommodation
7 Modification of the No. 23 Order: claims for housing benefit, income support or a tax credit
Sch. Postcode districts and part-districts where gateway conditions removed

GENERAL NOTE

This Commencement Order provided for the expansion of the full Universal Credit service (or 'Digital Service' in legislation) to further postcodes between February 7 and April 25, 2018. It also provided for universal credit claimants living in temporary accommodation to claim housing benefit instead of the universal credit housing element from April 11, 2018. Note that the text of this Commencement Order is not included in its entirety in this volume as it is now unlikely to give rise to live appeals. The full text of this Order can be found in the 2019/20 edn of this book at paras 3.690-3.698.

SI 2018/532 (C.43)

The Welfare Reform Act 2012 (Commencement No. 17, 19, 22, 23 and 24 and Transitional and Transitory Provisions (Modification)) Order 2018

SI 2018/532 (C.43)

Made 26th April 2018

The Secretary of State for Work and Pensions makes the following Order in exercise of the powers conferred by section 150(3) and (4)(a), (b)(i) and (c) of the Welfare Reform Act 2012:

3.250

ARRANGEMENT OF ARTICLES

GENERAL NOTE

This Order modified a series of prior Commencement Orders (as listed in art.2(1)), which in turn brought into force provisions of the WRA 2012 relating to universal credit and the abolition of IR-ESA and IB-JSA. Articles 3 and 4 of each of those prior Commencement Orders brought into force provisions in Part 1 of the WRA 2012 Act, as set out in Sch. 2 to the No. 9 Commencement Order, and provisions of the 2012 Act relating to the abolition of the two legacy benefits. Article 3 of this Order modified the provisions of the prior Commencement Orders as set out in the first column of the table in the Schedule. The effect was that the restrictions on claiming universal credit (i.e. the gateway conditions specified in Sch. 5 to the No. 9 Commencement Order) no longer applied. The modified provisions were specified by reference to the postcode districts and part-districts listed in the corresponding entry in the second column of the table. The modifications applied by reference to residence in those areas where claims were made for universal credit, ESA or JSA on or after the dates in the corresponding entry in the third column of the table. Article 4 of this Order made consequential modifications to several similar provisions in each of the prior Commencement Orders to remove references to meeting the gateway conditions. One consequence of the gateway conditions no longer applying was that claims by couples became possible for the first time in certain of the specified postcodes, namely those for which the universal credit provisions were commenced under the No. 22 Commencement Order and the No. 24 Commencement Order for single UC claimants only. Article 5 modified art. 7 of the No.23 Commencement Order such that, where the gateway conditions no longer applied to claims for universal credit (by virtue of art. 3 of this Order), a person could not (save in specified cases) make a claim for housing benefit, income

3.251

747

support or a tax credit on a date on which, if that person made a claim for universal credit on that date, the universal credit provisions would come into force under the provisions in question.

Citation

3.252   1. This Order may be cited as the Welfare Reform Act 2012 (Commencement No. 17, 19, 22, 23 and 24 and Transitional and Transitory Provisions (Modification)) Order 2018.

Interpretation

3.253   **2.**—(1) In this Order—
"claimant"—
   (a) in relation to an employment and support allowance, has the same meaning as in Part 1 of the Welfare Reform Act 2007;
   (b) in relation to a jobseeker's allowance, has the same meaning as in the Jobseekers Act 1995 (as it applies apart from the amendments made by Part 1 of Schedule 14 to the Welfare Reform Act 2012 that remove references to an income-based jobseeker's allowance);
   (c) in relation to universal credit, has the same meaning as in Part 1 of the Welfare Reform Act 2012;
   "the Claims and Payments Regulations 1987" means the Social Security (Claims and Payments) Regulations 1987;
   "employment and support allowance" means an employment and support allowance under Part 1 of the Welfare Reform Act 2007;
   "jobseeker's allowance" means a jobseeker's allowance under the Jobseekers Act 1995;
   "the No. 17 Order" means the Welfare Reform Act 2012 (Commencement No. 17 and Transitional and Transitory Provisions) Order 2014;
   "the No. 19 Order" means the Welfare Reform Act 2012 (Commencement No. 19 and Transitional and Transitory Provisions and Commencement No. 9 and Transitional and Transitory Provisions (Amendment)) Order 2014;
   "the No. 22 Order" means the Welfare Reform Act 2012 (Commencement No. 22 and Transitional and Transitory Provisions) Order 2015;
   "the No. 23 Order" means the Welfare Reform Act 2012 (Commencement No. 23 and Transitional and Transitory Provisions) Order 2015;
   "the No. 24 Order" means the Welfare Reform Act 2012 (Commencement No. 24 and Transitional and Transitory Provisions and Commencement No. 9 and Transitional and Transitory Provisions (Amendment)) Order 2015.
   (2) For the purposes of this Order, the Universal Credit, Personal Independence Payment, Jobseeker's Allowance and Employment and Support Allowance (Claims and Payments) Regulations 2013 apply for the purpose of deciding—
   (a) whether a claim for universal credit is made; and
   (b) the date on which the claim is made.
   (3) For the purposes of this Order, the Claims and Payments Regulations 1987 apply, subject to paragraphs (4) and (5), for the purposes of deciding—
   (a) whether a claim for an employment and support allowance or a jobseeker's allowance is made; and

(b) the date on which the claim is made or treated as made.

(4) Subject to paragraph (5), for the purposes of this Order—

(a) a person makes a claim for an employment and support allowance or a jobseeker's allowance if that person takes any action which results in a decision on a claim being required under the Claims and Payments Regulations 1987; and

(b) it is irrelevant that the effect of any provision of those Regulations is that, for the purposes of those Regulations, the claim is made or treated as made at a date that is earlier than the date on which that action is taken.

(5) Where, by virtue of—

(a) regulation 6(1F)(b) or (c) of the Claims and Payments Regulations 1987, in the case of a claim for an employment and support allowance; or

(b) regulation 6(4ZA) to (4ZD) and (4A)(a)(i) and (b) of those Regulations, in the case of a claim for a jobseeker's allowance,

a claim for an employment and support allowance or a jobseeker's allowance is treated as made at a date that is earlier than the date on which the action referred to in paragraph (4)(a) is taken, the claim is treated as made on that earlier date.

Modification of the No. 17 Order, the No. 19 Order, the No. 22 Order and the No. 24 Order: removal of the gateway conditions

3.—The provisions specified in the first column of the table in the Schedule have effect as though the reference in those provisions to meeting the gateway conditions were omitted, in respect of a claim for universal credit that is made, or a claim for an employment and support allowance or a jobseeker's allowance that is made or treated as made, by reference to the claimant's residence in any postcode district or part-district specified in the corresponding entry in the second column, on or after the date specified in the corresponding entry in the third column.

3.254

Modifications of the No. 17 Order, the No. 19 Order, the No. 22 Order and the No. 24 Order in consequence of removal of the gateway conditions

4.—(1) This article applies in respect of claims in relation to which provisions of the No. 17 Order, the No. 19 Order, the No. 22 Order and the No. 24 Order are modified by article 3.

3.255

(2) Where this article applies, the following modifications also have effect—

(a) those made to the No. 17 Order by article 10(2) of the Welfare Reform Act 2012 (Commencement No. 29 and Commencement No. 17, 19, 22, 23 and 24 and Transitional and Transitory Provisions (Modification)) Order 2017; and

(b) those made to the No. 19 Order, the No. 22 Order and the No. 24 Order by articles 13(2), 14(2) and 15(2) respectively of the Welfare Reform Act 2012 (Commencement No. 19, 22, 23 and 24 and Transitional and Transitory Provisions (Modification)) Order 2016.

Modification of the No. 23 Order: claims for housing benefit, income support or a tax credit

3.256

5.—(1) This article applies to claims in relation to which the provisions referred to in paragraph (2)(a) to (d) are modified by article 3.

(2) Where this article applies, article 7 of the No. 23 Order (prevention of claims for housing benefit, income support or a tax credit) applies as though the reference in paragraph (1) of that article to article 3(1) and (2)(a) to (c) of that Order included a reference to—

(a) paragraph (1) and sub-paragraphs (g), (i) and (k) of paragraph (2) of article 3 of the No. 17 Order;

(b) paragraph (1) and sub-paragraphs (a), (b), (d), (f), (h), (j), (k), (m) and (n) of paragraph (2) of article 3 of the No. 19 Order;

(c) paragraph (1) and sub-paragraphs (a), (c), (e) to (j), (l) to (n), (p) to (r) and (t) of paragraph (2) of article 3 of the No. 22 Order; and

(d) paragraph (1) and sub-paragraphs (a) to (d), (f) to (u), (w) to (y), (bb) and (cc) of paragraph (2) of article 3 of the No. 24 Order.

Article 3

SCHEDULE

3.257

POSTCODE DISTRICTS AND PART-DISTRICTS
WHERE GATEWAY CONDITIONS REMOVED

Provisions modified	Postcode			Date
Articles 3(2)(t) and 4(2)(mm) and (nn) of the No. 22 Order	LL22 7.	LL22 9.		2nd May 2018
Articles 3(2)(c) and 4(2)(e) and (f) of the No. 24 Order	CV23 1.			2nd May 2018
Articles 3(2)(f) and 4(2)(k) and (l) of the No. 24 Order	B45 9.			2nd May 2018
Articles 3(2)(j) and 4(2)(s) and (t) of the No. 24 Order	NE6 4. NE26 1 to NE26 3. NE30.	NE12. NE28.	NE25 8. NE29.	2nd May 2018
Articles 3(2)(k) and 4(2)(u) and (v) of the No. 24 Order	LN7.			2nd May 2018
Articles 3(2)(t) and 4(2)(mm) and (nn) of the No. 24 Order	NE13 6.	NE25 9.	NE27.	2nd May 2018
Articles 3(2)(cc) and 4(2)(eee) and (fff) of the No. 24 Order	IV2 8.	MK43 1 and MK43 2.		2nd May 2018

Articles 3(2)(f) and 4(2)(k) and (l) of the No. 22 Order	SY8 2.	SY8 3.		9th May 2018
Articles 3(2)(h) and 4(2)(o) and (p) of the No. 22 Order	SY1. SY4 1 to SY4 3. SY6. SY11. SY14 7. TF12.	SY2. SY4 5. SY10 1. SY12. TF9 1. WV16.	SY3. SY5 6 to SY5 8. SY10 8. SY13. TF9 3.	9th May 2018
Articles 3(2)(n) and 4(2)(aa) and (bb) of the No. 22 Order	SY4 4. TF11 9.	TF9 2. TF13 6.	TF9 4.	9th May 2018
Articles 3(2)(t) and 4(2)(mm) and (nn) of the No. 22 Order	LL14 5.			9th May 2018
Articles 3(2)(a) and 4(2)(a) and (b) of the No. 24 Order	WV15 5			9th May 2018
Articles 3(2)(b) and 4(2)(c) and (d) of the No. 24 Order	IP14.			9th May 2018
Articles 3(2)(c) and 4(2)(e) and (f) of the No. 24 Order	HG14 7. NG24. NN10.	NG22 0. NG25.	NG23 6. NN9 6.	9th May 2018
Articles 3(2)(f) and 4(2)(k) and (l) of the No. 24 Order	SY5 0. SY10 7.	SY5 9. SY10 9.	SY9.	9th May 2018
Articles 3(2)(h) and 4(2)(o) and (p) of the No. 24 Order	IP20, IP23.	IP21. NR15 2.	IP22.	9th May 2018
Articles 3(2)(i) and 4(2)(q) and (r) of the No. 24 Order	IP6 8.			9th May 2018
Articles 3(2)(k) and 4(2)(u) and (v) of the No. 24 Order	NG23 7.			9th May 2018
Articles 3(2)(l) and 4(2)(w) and (x) of the No. 24 Order	TF11 8.	WV15 6.		9th May 2018
Articles 3(2)(r) and 4(2)(ii) and (jj) of the No. 24 Order	WV5 7.			9th May 2018
Articles 3(2)(s) and 4(2)(kk) and (ll) of the No. 24 Order	NG23 5.			9th May 2018

Articles 3(2)(i) and 4(2)(i) of the No. 17 Order	L10 0. L10 8. L33 0 to L33 2. L35 1 to L35 3. L36 0 to L36 4.	L10 2 and L10 3. L28 3 to L28 7. L33 5 to L33 9. L35 5. L36 6 to L36 9.	L10 6. L32. L34. L35 7.	16th May 2018
Articles 3(2)(a) and 4(2)(a) of the No. 19 Order	L33 3 and L33 4. OL10. OL12 9. OL16.	M24 0 to M24 2. OL11. OL15 0.	M24 5 and M24 6. OL12 6. OL15 8.	16th May 2018
Articles 3(2)(b) and 4(2)(b) of the No. 19 Order	L10 1. L14. L36 5.	L10 4 and L10 5. L28 0 and L28 1. M24 4.	L10 7. L28 8.	16th May 2018
Articles 3(2)(d) and 4(2)(d) of the No. 19 Order	OL12 0.	OL12 7.		16th May 2018
Articles 3(2)(c) and 4(2)(e) and (f) of the No. 22 Order	EN5 1 and EN5 2. HA8 4. N2 8. N20. NW9 0 and NW9 1.	EN5 5. HA8 9. N3. NW4 NW9 5 to NW9 8	HA8 0. N2 2. N12. NW7. NW11.	16th May 2018
Articles 3(2)(i) and 4(2)(q) and (r) of the No. 22 Order	DG1. DG4 DG7. DG9. DG12.	DG2. DG5. DG8 0 and DG8 1. DG10. DG13.	DG3. DG6. DG8 7 to DG8 9. DG11. DG14.	16th May 2018
Articles 3(2)(l) and 4(2)(w) and (x) of the No. 22 Order	E10 7.	E10 9.	E17.	16th May 2018
Articles 3(2)(t) and 4(2)(mm) and (nn) of the No. 22 Order	EN4 8 and EN4 9. N18 9.	N9 0 and N9 1.	N18 2.	16th May 2018
Articles 3(2)(a) and 4(2)(a) and (b) of the No. 24 Order	DG16 5. L10 9.	EN4 0. N18 3.	EN5 3 and EN5 4. OL15 9.	16th May 2018
Articles 3(2)(c) and 4(2)(e) and (f) of the No. 24 Order	HA8 5 to HA8 8.	ML12 6.	NW9 9.	16th May 2018
Articles 3(2)(d) and 4(2)(g) and (h) of the No. 24 Order	DG8 6.			16th May 2018
Articles 3(2)(i) and 4(2)(q) and (r) of the No. 24 Order	EH27. EH47. EH52. EH55.	EH28. EH48. EH53. FK1 2.	EH29. EH49 6. EH54. ML7 5.	16th May 2018
Articles 3(2)(w) and 4(2)(ss) and (tt) of the No. 24 Order	N2 0.	N2 9.		16th May 2018

Articles 3(2)(cc) and 4(2)(eee) and (fff) of the No. 24 Order	NW9 4.			16th May 2018
Articles 3(2)(l) and 4(2)(w) and (x) of the No. 22 Order	PL22. PL25.	PL23. PL26.	PL24.	23rd May 2018
Articles 3(2)(p) and 4(2)(ee) and (ff) of the No. 22 Order	PL27. PL30. PL33. TR3 6. TR6.	PL28. PL31. TR1. TR4.	PL29. PL32. TR2. TR5.	23rd May 2018
Articles 3(2)(t) and 4(2)(mm) and (nn) of the No. 22 Order	TR7.	TR8.	TR9.	23rd May 2018
Articles 3(2)(b) and 4(2)(c) and (d) of the No. 24 Order	GU47 0. RG10 8. RG41. SL1 7.	GU47 9. RG12. RG42. SL5 8.	RG10 0. RG40. RG45. SL6 1 to SL6 9.	23rd May 2018
Articles 3(2)(i) and 4(2)(q) and (r) of the No. 24 Order	SL8.			23rd May 2018
Articles 3(2)(u) and 4(2)(oo) and (pp) of the No. 24 Order	SL5 0.	SL5 7.	SL5 9.	23rd May 2018
Articles 3(2)(y) and 4(2)(ww) and (xx) of the No. 24 Order	RG21. RG24. RG27.	RG22. RG25. RG28 9.	RG23. RG26. RG29.	23rd May 2018
Articles 3(2)(l) and 4(2)(w) and (x) of the No. 22 Order	DA11 0.	DA11 7.	DA12.	30th May 2018
Articles 3(2)(d) and 4(2)(g) and (h) of the No. 24 Order	DA13 0. ME3. ME7.	ME1. ME4. ME8.	ME2. ME5.	30th May 2018
Articles 3(2)(h) and 4(2)(o) and (p) of the No. 24 Order	LS25 6. YO11. YO14.	YO8 3 to YO8 5. YO12. YO21.	YO8 8 and YO8 9. YO13. YO22.	30th May 2018
Articles 3(2)(o) and 4(2)(cc) and (dd) of the No. 24 Order	DN14 0.			30th May 2018
Articles 3(2)(p) and 4(2)(ee) and (ff) of the No. 24 Order	CT18. CT21. DA13 9. TN29.	CT19. DA10. TN25 5 to TN25 7. TN26 2.	CT20. DA11 8 and DA11 9. TN28.	30th May 2018

Articles 3(2)(t) and 4(2)(mm) and (nn) of the No. 24 Order	NE31. NE34. SR6 7.	NE32. NE35.	NE33. NE36.	30th May 2018
Articles 3(2)(a) and 4(2)(a) and (b) of the No. 22 Order	BS20.	BS49.		6th June 2018
Articles 3(2)(j) and 4(2)(s) and (t) of the No. 22 Order	LL24. LL27. LL30. LL34.	LL25. LL28. LL31.	LL26. LL29. LL32.	6th June 2018
Articles 3(2)(l) and 4(2)(w) and (x) of the No. 22 Order	TR14.	TR15.	TR16.	6th June 2018
Articles 3(2)(p) and 4(2)(ee) and (ff) of the No. 22 Order	TR17. TR20.	TR18. TR26.	TR19. TR27.	6th June 2018
Articles 3(2)(r) and 4(2)(ii) and (jj) of the No. 22 Order	CF31. CF34.	CF32 7 to CF32 9. CF36.	CF33.	6th June 2018
Articles 3(2)(t) and 4(2)(mm) and (nn) of the No. 22 Order	LL2 8. TR11.	TR3 7. TR12.	TR10. TR13.	6th June 2018
Articles 3(2)(a) and 4(2)(a) and (b) of the No. 24 Order	BN5. RH10 4 to RH10 9. RH12 5. RH15. RH18. RH20 2 to RH20 4. TN7.	BN6. RH11. RH13. RH16. RH19 1 RH20 9	RH10 1. RH12 1 and RH12 2. RH14 9. RH17. RH19 4. TB6.	6th June 2018
Articles 3(2)(d) and 4(2)(g) and (h) of the No. 24 Order	RH20 1.	TN3 9.		6th June 2018
Articles 3(2)(f) and 4(2)(k) and (l) of the No. 24 Order	L33.			6th June 2018
Articles 3(2)(g) and 4(2)(m) and (n) of the No. 24 Order	BS1. BS4. BS9 1. BS40 6 to BS40 9.	BS2. BS6 5. BS13. BS41.	BS3. BS8. BS14.	6th June 2018
Articles 3(2)(l) and 4(2)(w) and (x) of the No. 24 Order	PO30. PO38. PO41. SO40 9.	PO31. PO39. SO40 4. SO45.	PO32. PO40. SO40 7.	6th June 2018
Articles 3(2)(m) and 4(2)(y) and (z) of the No. 24 Order	BN45.			6th June 2018

Articles 3(2)(s) and 4(2)(kk) and (ll) of the No. 24 Order	RH6 6. RH12 3 and RH142 4.	RH7 9. RH14 0.	RH10 3. RH19 2 and RH19 3.	6th June 2018
Articles 3(2)(t) and 4(2)(mm) and (nn) of the No. 24 Order	CF32 0.			6th June 2018
Articles 3(2)(x) and 4(2)(uu) and (vv) of the No. 24 Order	CF35.			6th June 2018
Articles 3(2)(cc) and 4(2)(eee) and (fff) of the No. 24 Order	RH12 0.			6th June 2018
Articles 3(2)(f) and 4(2)(k) and (l) of the No. 22 Order	HR1. HR6. SY8 1.	HR2. HR9 5 and HR9 6.	HR4. SY7 0.	13th June 2018
Articles 3(2)(g) and 4(2)(m) and (n) of the No. 22 Order	IP25. PE37.	NR19,	NR20 4.	13th June 2018
Articles 3(2)(i) and 4(2)(q) and (r) of the No. 22 Order	EH38. EH45. TD3. TD6. TD9 1, TD11.	EH43. TD1. TD4. TD7. TD9 7 to TD9 9. TD13.	EH44. TD2. TD5. TD8. TD10. TD14.	13th June 2018
Articles 3(2)(j) and 4(2)(s) and (t) of the No. 22 Order	HR9 7.			13th June 2018
Articles 3(2)(a) and 4(2)(a) and (b) of the No. 24 Order	TD9 0.			13th June 2018
Articles 3(2)(f) and 4(2)(k) and (l) of the No. 24 Order	DE5 DE56 4. HR3. HR8 1.	DE55 1. DE56 9. HR5. SY7 8.	DE56 0 and DE56 1. DE75. HR7. SY8 4.	13th June 2018
Articles 3(2)(g) and 4(2)(m) and (n) of the No. 24 Order	LN12 2. LN13 9. PE23.	LN12 9. NG16 2 to NG16 5. PE24.	LN13 3. PE22 8. PE25.	13th June 2018
Articles 3(2)(h) and 4(2)(o) and (p) of the No. 24 Order	NR20 3.			13th June 2018
Articles 3(2)(j) and 4(2)(s) and (t) of the No. 24 Order	DE55 2 to DE55 7. S42 5 and S42 6.	DE56 2. S45.	NG16 6.	13th June 2018

755

Articles 3(2)(l) and 4(2)(w) and (x) of the No. 24 Order	NR20 5.			13th June 2018
Articles 3(2)(p) and 4(2)(ee) and (ff) of the No. 24 Order	LE1. LE4. LE7. LE9 6. LE18.	LE2. LE5. LE8 4 to LE8 6. LE9 9. LE19.	LE3. LE6. LE9 1 to LE9 3. LE17 4 and LE17 5. LE87.	13th June 2018
Articles 3(2)(q) and 4(2)(gg) and (hh) of the No. 24 Order	ST1. ST4 1 to ST4 3. ST9. ST12.	ST2. ST6 1 to ST6 4. ST10. ST13.	ST3. ST6 6 to ST6 9. ST11.	13th June 2018
Articles 3(2)(w) and 4(2)(ss) and (tt) of the No. 24 Order	PE32 2.			13th June 2018
Articles 3(2)(bb) and 4(2)(ccc) and (ddd) of the No. 24 Order	KY13 0. PH2. PH5. PH8. PH11. PH14. PH17.	KY14. PH3. PH6. PH9. PH12. PH15. PH18.	PH1. PH4. PH7. PH10. PH13. PH16.	13th June 2018
Articles 3(2)(g) and 4(2)(m) and (n) of the No. 22 Order	TN23. TN26 1. TN30.	TN24. TN26 3.	TN25 4. TN27 0.	20th June 2018
Articles 3(2)(a) and 4(2)(a) and (b) of the No. 24 Order	DH1. DH6 1. DL5 4 and DL5 5. DL17.	DH2. DH6 4 and DH6 5. DL5 7.	DH3 2 to DH3 4. DH7. DL16.	20th June 2018
Articles 3(2)(d) and 4(2)(g) and (h) of the No. 24 Order	TN27 8.			20th June 2018
Articles 3(2)(g) and 4(2)(m) and (n) of the No. 24 Order	KT1. KT3 5. KT9 2. TW1. TW10. TW12 3.	KT2. KT5. SW13 TW2. TW11.	KT3 3. KT6 7. SW14. TW9. TW12 1.	20th June 2018
Articles 3(2)(h) and 4(2)(o) and (p) of the No. 24 Order	EC1A. EC1R 3. EC1V 7 and EC1V 8. N1 8. N19 3 and N19 4. SW1E. SW1V. SW1Y. W1C. W1G. W1K. W1U. W9 2. WC2N.	EC1M 4 to EC1M 7. EC1V 0. EC1Y. N5 1. NW8 8 and NW8 9. SW1H. SW1W. W1A. W1D. W1H. W1S. W1W. WC2E. WC2R.	EC1R 0 and EC1R 1. EC1V 2 and EC1V 4. N1 1 and N1 2. N7 6 to N7 8. SW1 A. SW1P. SW1X. W1B. W1F. W1J. W1T 3. W2. WC2H 7.	20th June 2018

Articles 3(2)(j) and 4(2)(s) and (t) of the No. 24 Order	DL1. DL4 2.	DL2 2 and DL2 3. DL5 6.	DL3. DL12 8.	20th June 2018
Articles 3(2)(k) and 4(2)(u) and (v) of the No. 24 Order	BD1. BD3 9. BD5. BD8. BD12. BD15. BD18. BD20 9.	BD2. BD4 6 and BD4 7. BD6. BD9. BD13. BD16. BD20 0. BD21.	BD3 0. BD4 9. BD7. BD10 8 and BD10 9. BD14. BD17. BD20 5 and BD20 6. BD22.	20th June 2018
Articles 3(2)(l) and 4(2)(w) and (x) of the No. 24 Order	DL2 1.	TS21 2.		20th June 2018
Articles 3(2)(o) and 4(2)(cc) and (dd) of the No. 24 Order	KT3 4. SW19 1 to SW19 5.	KT3 6. SW19 7 to SW19 9.	KT4 8.	20th June 2018
Articles 3(2)(q) and 4(2)(gg) and (hh) of the No. 24 Order	BD3 8.	BD4 0.	BD10 0.	20th June 2018
Articles 3(2)(s) and 4(2)(kk) and (ll) of the No. 24 Order	IG1. IG4. IG7 4. KT4 7. RM3. RM7. RM13.	IG2. IG5. IG8 0 and IG8 1. RM1. RM5. RM11. RM14 1 and RM14 2.	IG3. IG6. IG8 7 and IG8 8. RM2. RM6 4. RM12. RM14 9.	20th June 2018
Articles 3(2)(u) and 4(2)(oo) and (pp) of the No. 24 Order	KT6 4 to KT6 6.	KT9 1.	TW12 2.	20th June 2018
Articles 3(2)(w) and 4(2)(ss) and (tt) of the No. 24 Order	EC1M 3. N1C. N6. N19 5. NW8 6 and NW8 7. W9 1. WC1E. WC1R. WC2A. Wc2H 8 and WC2H 9.	EC1 N. N1 0. N7 0. NW1 1 to NW1 6. W1T1 and W1T 2. WC1A. WC1H. WC1V. WC2B.	EC1R 4 and EC1R 5. N1 9. N7 9. NW8 0. W1T4 to W1T 7. WC1B. WC1N. WC1X. WC2H 0.	20th June 2018
Articles 3(2)(y) and 4(2)(ww) and (xx) of the No. 24 Order	EC1V 1. N4.	EC1V 9. N5 2.	N1 3.	20th June 2018
Articles 3(2)(m) and 4(2)(y) and (z) of the No. 22 Order	AB41 8. AB44. AB53 4 to AB53 6.	AB42. AB45 1.	AB43. AB45 3.	27th June 2018

Articles 3(2)(a) and 4(2)(a) and (b) of the No. 24 Order	CF46. CF48 3 and CF48 4. NP7 8 and NP7 9. NP16.	CF47. NP7 0 and NP7 1. NP12 4. NP25.	CF48 1. NP7 5 and NP7 6. NP15. NP26.	27th June 2018
Articles 3(2)(f) and 4(2)(k) and (l) of the No. 24 Order	NP7 7.	NP8.		27th June 2018
Articles 3(2)(i) and 4(2)(q) and (r) of the No. 24 Order	AB37. AB54. IV30. IV36.	AB38. AB55. IV31.	AB45 2. AB56. IV32.	27th June 2018
Articles 3(2)(x) and 4(2)(uu) and (vv) of the No. 24 Order	CF48 2.			27th June 2018
Articles 3(2)(e) and 4(2)(i) and (j) of the No. 22 Order	CO1. CO4 0. CO5 7 and CO5 8.	CO2. CO4 3.	CO3. CO4 5.	4th July 2018
Articles 3(2)(g) and 4(2)(m) and (n) of the No. 22 Order	CO4 9.	CO11 2.	CO12.	4th July 2018
Articles 3(2)(a) and 4(2)(a) and (b) of the No. 24 Order	CO7 7. SO21 1 and SO21 2. SP9.	CO7 9. SO22. SP10.	SO20. SO23. SP11 7 to SP11 9.	4th July 2018
Articles 3(2)(b) and 4(2)(c) and (d) of the No. 24 Order	CO5 0. CO11 1.	CO6 3 and CO6 4.	CO7 6.	4th July 2018
Articles 3(2)(c) and 4(2)(e) and (f) of the No. 24 Order	CO5 9. HA2 HA7.	CO6 1. HA3.	HA1. HA5 5.	4th July 2018
Articles 3(2)(d) and 4(2)(g) and (h) of the No. 24 Order	BN11. BN14. BN17. BN44. PO10 8. PO20.	BN12. BN15. BN18. GU28. PO18. PO21.	BN13. BN16. BN43. GU29. PO19. PO22.	4th July 2018
Articles 3(2)(g) and 4(2)(m) and (n) of the No. 24 Order	HA5 1 to HA5 3.	HA6 1.		4th July 2018
Articles 3(2)(h) and 4(2)(o) and (p) of the No. 24 Order	EX10. EX13. EX16. EX24. EX33. EX36. EX39.	EX11. EX14. EX19. EX31. EX34. EX37.	EX12. EX15. EX22 7. EX32. EX35. EX38.	4th July 2018

Articles 3(2)(j) and 4(2)(s) and (t) of the No. 24 Order	HA5 4.	HA6 2 and HA6 3.		4th July 2018
Articles 3(2)(m) and 4(2)(y) and (z) of the No. 24 Order	BN42.			4th July 2018
Articles 3(2)(p) and 4(2)(ee) and (ff) of the No. 24 Order	CT1. CT3 4. CT6.	CT2. CT4.	CT3 1 and CT3 2. CT5.	4th July 2018
Articles 3(2)(r) and 4(2)(ii) and (jj) of the No. 24 Order	SE4. SE8 3 and SE8 4. SE23.	SE6 4. SE13. SE26.	SE6 9. SE19 2 and SE19 3. SO24 0.	4th July 2018
Articles 3(2)(y) and 4(2)(ww) and (xx) of the No. 24 Order	RG28 7. SP11 0.	SO21 3. SP11 6.	SO24 9.	4th July 2018
Articles 3(2)(cc) and 4(2)(eee) and (fff) of the No. 24 Order	CO4 6.			4th July 2018
Articles 3(2)(n) and 4(2)(aa) and (bb) of the No. 22 Order	LE11.	LE12 7 and LE12 8.		11th July 2018
Articles 3(2)(b) and 4(2)(c) and (d) of the No. 24 Order	LE12 9.			11th July 2018
Articles 3(2)(g) and 4(2)(m) and (n) of the No. 24 Order	PE11.	PE12 2.	PE12 6 to PE12 9.	11th July 2018
Articles 3(2)(j) and 4(2)(s) and (t) of the No. 24 Order	S21 1 to S21 3.	S43 3.	S44.	11th July 2018
Articles 3(2)(l) and 4(2)(w) and (x) of the No. 24 Order	CV1. CV4. CV7 7. S26. S61 3 and S61 4. S66. TS17 0. TS18. TS21 1. TS23.	CV2. CV5. CV8 3. S60. S62. TS15. TS17 5 and TS17 6. TS19. TS21 3.	CV3. CV6. S25. S61 1. S65. TS16. TS17 8. TS20. TS22.	11th July 2018
Articles 3(2)(m) and 4(2)(y) and (z) of the No. 24 Order	PE6 0.			11th July 2018

Articles 3(2)(o) and 4(2)(cc) and (dd) of the No. 24 Order	DN14 4 to DN14 9. HU13 3. HU17. S61 2. YO16.	HU10. HU14 HU18. YO8 6. YO25.	HU13 0. HU15. S21 4 and S21 5. YO15. YO43.	11th July 2018
Articles 3(2)(p) and 4(2)(ee) and (ff) of the No. 24 Order	DE1. DE6 9. DE23. SE72 2.	DE3. DE21. DE24. DE73 6 and DE73 7.	DE6 1 to DE6 4. DE22. DE65.	11th July 2018
Articles 3(2)(r) and 4(2)(ii) and (jj) of the No. 24 Order	TS17 7.	TS17 9.		11th July 2018
Articles 3(2)(s) and 4(2)(kk) and (ll) of the No. 24 Order	DE74.	LE12 5.		11th July 2018
Articles 3(2)(u) and 4(2)(oo) and (pp) of the No. 24 Order	HU4 7.	HU13 9.		11th July 2018
Articles 3(2)(w) and 4(2)(ss) and (tt) of the No. 24 Order	PE12 0.			11th July 2018
Articles 3(2)(g) and 4(2)(g) of the No. 17 Order	PR0. PR4 4 and PR4 5. PR25 1 to PR25 3.	PR1. PR5 4 and PR5 5. PR25 9.	PR2. PR11. PR26 6.	18th July 2018
Articles 3(2)(i) and 4(2)(i) of the No. 17 Order	L35 0. WA9. WA11 8 and WA11 9.	L35 4. WA10. WA12.	L35 8 and L35 9. WA11 0.	18th July 2018
Articles 3(2)(k) and 4(2)(k) of the No. 17 Order	CW12 1 and CW12 2. SK9.	CW12 4. WA16.	CW12 9.	18th July 2018
Articles 3(2)(a) and 4(2)(a) of the No. 19 Order	WA11 7.			18th July 2018
Articles 3(2)(f) and 4(2)(f) of the No. 19 Order	SK10.	SK11 6 to SK11 9.		18th July 2018
Articles 3(2)(h) and 4(2)(h) of the No. 19 Order	PR4 0.			18th July 2018
Articles 3(2)(j) and 4(2)(j) of the No. 19 Order	L35 6.			18th July 2018
Articles 3(2)(k) and 4(2)(k) of the No. 19 Order	PR5 0. PR6. PR26 7 to PR26 9.	PR5 6. PR7.	PR5 8. PR25 4 and PR25 5.	18th July 2018

Articles 3(2)(m) and 4(2)(m) of the No. 19 Order	PR3.			18th July 2018
Articles 3(2)(n) and 4(2)(aa) and (bb) of the No. 22 Order	SK11 0.			18th July 2018
Articles 3(2)(q) and 4(2)(gg) and (hh) of the No. 22 Order	B74 2 and B74 3. WS2. WS5 3.	WS1 1 to WS1 3. WS3 1 to WS3 3. WS9 0 and WS9 1.	WS1 9. WS4. WS9 8.	18th July 2018
Articles 3(2)(a) and 4(2)(a) and (b) of the No. 24 Order	CW12 3.			18th July 2018
Articles 3(2)(f) and 4(2)(k) and (l) of the No. 24 Order	NP13. NP23.	NP22 3 and NP22 4.	NP22 9.	18th July 2018
Articles 3(2)(g) and 4(2)(m) and (n) of the No. 24 Order	BS5 7 and BS5 8 BS7 8.	BS6 6 and BS6 7.	BS6 9.	18th July 2018
Articles 3(2)(i) and 4(2)(q) and (r) of the No. 24 Order	B43 7.			18th July 2018
Articles 3(2)(j) and 4(2)(s) and (t) of the No. 24 Order	WS1 4.			18th July 2018
Articles 3(2)(l) and 4(2)(w) and (x) of the No. 24 Order	BS5 0. BS16 3.	BS5 6. WS3 5.	BS5 9.	18th July 2018
Articles 3(2)(n) and 4(2)(aa) and (bb) of the No. 24 Order	BS7 9.	BS16 1 and BS16 2.		18th July 2018
Articles 3(2)(r) and 4(2)(ii) and (jj) of the No. 24 Order	WS10 8.			18th July 2018
Articles 3(2)(g) and 4(2)(g) of the No. 17 Order	BL0 9. BL9 0. M25 1. M26 1 and M26 2.	BL8 1 to BL8 3. BL9 5. M25 3. M26 4.	BL8 9. BL9 8 and BL9 9. M25 9. M45.	25th July 2018
Articles 3(2)(a) and 4(2)(a) of the No. 19 Order	BL9 7.			25th July 2018
Articles 3(2)(b) and 4(2)(b) of the No. 19 Order	M7 4. M22 0 to M22 2. M23.	M8. M22 5. M25 0.	M9. M22 8 and M22 9. M25 2.	25th July 2018

Articles 3(2)(d) and 4(2)(d) of the No. 19 Order	BL9 6.			25th July 2018
Articles 3(2)(j) and 4(2)(j) of the No. 19 Order	M22 4.			25th July 2018
Articles 3(2)(k) and 4(2)(k) of the No. 19 Order	BL8 4.			25th July 2018
Articles 3(2)(n) and 4(2)(n) of the No. 19 Order	CA1. CA4. CA7 0. CA8 0 and CA8 1. CA11.	CA2. CA5. CA7 5. CA8 9. CA16.	CA3. CA6. CA& 7 to CA7 9. CA10 1 to CA10 3. CA17.	25th July 2018
Articles 3(2)(g) and 4(2)(m) and (n) of the No. 22 Order	CO7 0. CO13. CO16.	CO7 5. CO14.	CO7 8. CO15.	25th July 2018
Articles 3(2)(l) and 4(2)(w) and (x) of the No. 22 Order	E4 6. E11 4. SS8.	E4 8 and E4 9. E11 9.	E10 5 and E10 6. SS7.	25th July 2018
Articles 3(2)(g) and 4(2)(m) and (n) of the No. 24 Order	DH4. NE37 9. SR2. SR5 2 to SR5 5.	DH5. NE38. SR3. SR5 9.	NE37 1 and NE37 2. SR1. SR4.	25th July 2018
Articles 3(2)(o) and 4(2)(cc) and (dd) of the No. 24 Order	BR1 1 to BR1 3. BR3 3 to BR3 6. BR5. SE20.	BR1 9. BR3 9. BR6. TN16 3.	BR2. BR4. BR7.	25th July 2018
Articles 3(2)(p) and 4(2)(ee) and (ff) of the No. 24 Order	BR8. DA2. DA9.	DA1 1 and DA1 2. DA3. TN14 7.	DA1 9. DA4. TN15 6 and TN15 7	25th July 2018
Articles 3(2)(q) and 4(2)(gg) and (hh) of the No. 24 Order	E4 7. SS6.		SS4. SS5.	25th July 2018
Articles 3(2)(r) and 4(2)(ii) and (jj) of the No. 24 Order	BR1 4 and BR1 5. DA1 5.	BR3 1. SE6 1 to SE6 3.	DA1 3.	25th July 2018
Articles 3(2)(s) and 4(2)(kk) and (ll) of the No. 24 Order	E6 1. E6 9. E12. E16. IG8 9.	E6 3. E7. E13. E18.	E6 5 to E6 7. E11 1 to E11 3. E15. E20 1 and E20 2.	25th July 2018
Articles 3(2)(t) and 4(2)(mm) and (nn) of the No. 24 Order	CA8 2. SR5 1.	CA9 3. SR6 0.	NE37 3. SR6 8 and SR6 9.	

Articles 3(2)(y) and 4(2)(ww) and (xx) of the No. 24 Order	E20 3.	25th July 2018

The Welfare Reform Act 2012 (Commencement No. 17, 19, 22, 23 and 24 and Transitional and Transitory Provisions (Modification) (No. 2)) Order 2018

SI 2018/881 (C.68)

Made 19th July 2018

The Secretary of State for Work and Pensions makes the following Order in exercise of the powers conferred by section 150(3) and (4)(a), (b)(i) and (c) of the Welfare Reform Act 2012:

3.258

ARRANGEMENT OF ARTICLES

1. Citation
2. Interpretation
3. Modification of the No. 17 Order, the No. 19 Order, the No. 22 Order and the No. 24 Order: removal of the gateway conditions
4. Modifications of the No. 17 Order, the No. 19 Order, the No. 22 Order and the No. 24 Order in consequence of removal of the gateway conditions
5. Modification of the No. 23 Order: claims for housing benefit, income support or a tax credit
SCH POSTCODE DISTRICTS AND PART-DISTRICTS WHERE GATEWAY CONDITIONS REMOVED

GENERAL NOTE

This Commencement Order follows the same format and has the same effect as the Welfare Reform Act 2012 (Commencement No. 17, 19, 22, 23 and 24 and Transitional and Transitory Provisions (Modification)) Order 2018 (SI 2018/532) except for different postcode districts and part districts.

3.259

Citation

1. This Order may be cited as the Welfare Reform Act 2012 (Commencement No. 17, 19, 22, 23 and 24 and Transitional and Transitory Provisions (Modification) (No. 2)) Order 2018.

3.260

Interpretation

2.—(1) In this Order—
"claimant"—
(a) in relation to an employment and support allowance, has the same meaning as in Part 1 of the Welfare Reform Act 2007;
(b) in relation to a jobseeker's allowance, has the same meaning as in the Jobseekers Act 1995 (as it applies apart from the amendments

3.261

made by Part 1 of Schedule 14 to the Welfare Reform Act 2012 that remove references to an income-based jobseeker's allowance);

(c) in relation to universal credit, has the same meaning as in Part 1 of the Welfare Reform Act 2012;

"the Claims and Payments Regulations 1987" means the Social Security (Claims and Payments) Regulations 1987;

"employment and support allowance" means an employment and support allowance under Part 1 of the Welfare Reform Act 2007;

"jobseeker's allowance" means a jobseeker's allowance under the Jobseekers Act 1995;

"the No. 17 Order" means the Welfare Reform Act 2012 (Commencement No. 17 and Transitional and Transitory Provisions) Order 2014;

"the No. 19 Order" means the Welfare Reform Act 2012 (Commencement No. 19 and Transitional and Transitory Provisions and Commencement No. 9 and Transitional and Transitory Provisions (Amendment)) Order 2014;

"the No. 22 Order" means the Welfare Reform Act 2012 (Commencement No. 22 and Transitional and Transitory Provisions) Order 2015;

"the No. 23 Order" means the Welfare Reform Act 2012 (Commencement No. 23 and Transitional and Transitory Provisions) Order 2015;

"the No. 24 Order" means the Welfare Reform Act 2012 (Commencement No. 24 and Transitional and Transitory Provisions and Commencement No. 9 and Transitional and Transitory Provisions (Amendment)) Order 2015.

(2) For the purposes of this Order, the Universal Credit, Personal Independence Payment, Jobseeker's Allowance and Employment and Support Allowance (Claims and Payments) Regulations 2013 apply for the purpose of deciding—

(a) whether a claim for universal credit is made; and

(b) the date on which the claim is made.

(3) For the purposes of this Order, the Claims and Payments Regulations 1987 apply, subject to paragraphs (4) and (5), for the purposes of deciding—

(a) whether a claim for an employment and support allowance or a jobseeker's allowance is made; and

(b) the date on which the claim is made or treated as made.

(4) Subject to paragraph (5), for the purposes of this Order—

(a) a person makes a claim for an employment and support allowance or a jobseeker's allowance if that person takes any action which results in a decision on a claim being required under the Claims and Payments Regulations 1987; and

(b) it is irrelevant that the effect of any provision of those Regulations is that, for the purposes of those Regulations, the claim is made or treated as made at a date that is earlier than the date on which that action is taken.

(5) Where, by virtue of—

(a) regulation 6(1F)(b) or (c) of the Claims and Payments Regulations 1987, in the case of a claim for an employment and support allowance; or

(b) regulation 6(4ZA) to (4ZD) and (4A)(a)(i) and (b) of those Regulations, in the case of a claim for a jobseeker's allowance,

a claim for an employment and support allowance or a jobseeker's allowance is treated as made at a date that is earlier than the date on which the action referred to in paragraph (4)(a) is taken, the claim is treated as made on that earlier date.

Modification of the No. 17 Order, the No. 19 Order, the No. 22 Order and the No. 24 Order: removal of the gateway conditions

3. The provisions specified in the first column of the table in the Schedule have effect as though the reference in those provisions to meeting the gateway conditions were omitted, in respect of a claim for universal credit that is made, or a claim for an employment and support allowance or a jobseeker's allowance that is made or treated as made, by reference to the claimant's residence in any postcode district or part-district specified in the corresponding entry in the second column, on or after the date specified in the corresponding entry in the third column. 3.262

Modifications of the No. 17 Order, the No. 19 Order, the No. 22 Order and the No. 24 Order in consequence of removal of the gateway conditions

4.—(1) This article applies in respect of claims in relation to which provisions of the No. 17 Order, the No. 19 Order, the No. 22 Order and the No. 24 Order are modified by article 3. 3.263

(2) Where this article applies, the following modifications also have effect—

(a) those made to the No. 17 Order by article 10(2) of the Welfare Reform Act 2012 (Commencement No. 29 and Commencement No. 17, 19, 22, 23 and 24 and Transitional and Transitory Provisions (Modification)) Order 2017; and

(b) those made to the No. 19 Order, the No. 22 Order and the No. 24 Order by articles 13(2), 14(2) and 15(2) respectively of the Welfare Reform Act 2012 (Commencement No. 19, 22, 23 and 24 and Transitional and Transitory Provisions (Modification)) Order 2016.

Modification of the No. 23 Order: claims for housing benefit, income support or a tax credit

5.—(1) This article applies to claims in relation to which the provisions referred to in paragraph (2)(a) to (d) are modified by article 3. 3.264

(2) Where this article applies, article 7 of the No. 23 Order (prevention of claims for housing benefit, income support or a tax credit) applies as though the reference in paragraph (1) of that article to article 3(1) and (2)(a) to (c) of that Order included a reference to—

(a) paragraph (1) and sub-paragraphs (c) and (i) of paragraph (2) of article 3 of the No. 17 Order;

(b) paragraph (1) and sub-paragraphs (b) to (h) and (j) to (n) of paragraph (2) of article 3 of the No. 19 Order;

(c) paragraph (1) and sub-paragraphs (a), (c) to (e), (g) to (k), (m) to (q), and (t) of paragraph (2) of article 3 of the No. 22 Order; and

(d) paragraph (1) and sub-paragraphs (a) to (d), (f) to (y), (aa) and (cc) of paragraph (2) of article 3 of the No. 24 Order.

SCHEDULE

3.265   POSTCODE DISTRICTS AND PART-DISTRICTS
                    WHERE GATEWAY CONDITIONS REMOVED

Provisions modified	Postcodes			Date
Articles 3(2)(i) and 4(2)(q) and (r) of the No. 22 Order	SW11 2 SW15 9	SW15 2 SW17 6 and SW17 7	SW15 4 SW18 1 to SW18 3	5th September 2018
Articles 3(2)(j) and 4(2)(s) and (t) of the No. 22 Order	CF81 NP11 3 and NP11 4 NP24	CF83 2 to CF83 4 NP11 6 and NP11 7	CF83 8 and CF83 9 NP12 0 to NP12 3	5th September 2018
Articles 3(2)(a) and 4(2)(a) and (b) of the No. 24 Order	CF82			5th September 2018
Articles 3(2)(f) and 4(2)(k) and (l) of the No. 24 Order	NP11 5	NP22 5		5th September 2018
Articles 3(2)(g) and 4(2)(m) and (n) of the No. 24 Order	SW15 1	SW15 3	SW15 5 and SW15 6	5th September 2018
Articles 3(2)(h) and 4(2)(o) and (p) of the No. 24 Order	EX7 SA63 SA66 SA69 SA72 TQ7 TQ10 TQ12 5 and TQ12 6	SA61 SA64 SA67 SA70 SA73 TQ8 TQ11 TQ13	SA62 SA65 SA68 SA71 TQ6 TQ9 TQ12 1 to TQ12 3 TQ14	5th September 2018
Articles 3(2)(i) and 4(2)(q) and (r) of the No. 24 Order	HP9 HP12 HP15 SL2 3 and SL2 4 SL9 7 to SL9 9	HP10 HP13 HP16 SL7	HP11 HP14 SL0 SL9 1	5th September 2018
Articles 3(2)(j) and 4(2)(s) and (t) of the No. 24 Order	SL9 0			5th September 2018
Articles 3(2)(l) and 4(2)(w) and (x) of the No. 24 Order	BS9 2 to BS9 4	BS10 5	BS11	5th September 2018

Articles 3(2)(n) and 4(2)(aa) and (bb) of the No. 24 Order	BS7 0 BS34	BS10 6 and BS10 7 BS35	BS32	5th September 2018
Articles 3(2)(o) and 4(2)(cc) and (dd) of the No. 24 Order	SW17 0	SW18 4 and SW18 5	SW19 6	5th September 2018
Articles 3(2)(p) and 4(2)(ee) and (ff) of the No. 24 Order	TQ1 TQ4	TQ2 TQ5	TQ3 TQ12 4	5th September 2018
Articles 3(2)(x) and 4(2)(uu) and (vv) of the No. 24 Order	CF83 1			5th September 2018
Articles 3(2)(g) and 4(2)(m) and (n) of the No. 22 Order	IP24 PE21	IP27 0 PE22 9	PE20 1 and PE 20 2	12th September 2018
Articles 3(2)(n) and 4(2)(aa) and (bb) of the No. 22 Order	SK13 SK23	SK17 6 and SK17 7	SK22	12th September 2018
Articles 3(2)(a) and 4(2)(a) and (b) of the No. 24 Order	NR16 2			12th September 2018
Articles 3(2)(c) and 4(2)(e) and (f) of the No. 24 Order	NG15 9 NG19 6 NG21	NG18 NG19 9 NG22 8 and NG22 9	NG19 0 NG20 0 NG70	12th September 2018
Articles 3(2)(f) and 4(2)(k) and (l) of the No. 24 Order	B60 B78 1 HR8 2 WR13	B61 CV9 HR8 9 WR14	B76 0 CV13 6 WR8 0	12th September 2018
Articles 3(2)(g) and 4(2)(m) and (n) of the No. 24 Order	LN11 PE22 0	LN12 1 PE22 7	LN13 0	12th September 2018
Articles 3(2)(j) and 4(2)(s) and (t) of the No. 24 Order	DE4 SK17 0	DE45 SK17 8 and SK17 9	NG19 7	12th September 2018
Articles 3(2)(k) and 4(2)(u) and (v) of the No. 24 Order	DN10 4 PE20 3	DN21	LN8 6	12th September 2018

Articles 3(2)(u) and 4(2)(oo) and (pp) of the No. 24 Order	CB6 3	CB7		12th September 2018
Articles 3(2)(w) and 4(2)(ss) and (tt) of the No. 24 Order	CB6 1 and CB6 2 PE14	IP26 PE15	PE13 PE16	12th September 2018
Articles 3(2)(o) and 4(2)(cc) and (dd) of the No. 22 Order	G51 1 to G51 3	G51 9	G52 1	19th September 2018
Articles 3(2)(q) and 4(2)(gg) and (hh) of the No. 22 Order	G51 4 PA1 PA2 9 PA5 PA8 PA12	G52 2 to G52 4 PA2 PA3 PA6 PA9	G52 9 PA2 6 and PA2 7 PA4 PA7 PA10	19th September 2018
Articles 3(2)(s) and 4(2)(kk) and (ll) of the No. 24 Order	PA2 8			19th September 2018
Articles 3(2)(v) and 4(2)(qq) and (rr) of the No. 24 Order	G83 7 PA21 PA24 PA27 PA30 PA33 PA36 PA41 PA44 PA47 PA60 PA63 PA66 PA69 PA72 PA75 PA78	G84 PA22 PA25 PA28 PA31 PA34 PA37 PA42 PA45 PA48 PA61 PA64 PA67 PA70 PA73 PA76	PA20 PA23 PA26 PA29 PA32 PA35 PA38 PA43 PA46 PA49 PA62 PA65 PA68 PA71 PA74 PA77	19th September 2018
Articles 3(2)(i) and 4(2)(i) of the No. 17 Order	M27 0 M28	M27 5 M30	M27 8 and M27 9 M38	26th September 2018
Articles 3(2)(g) and 4(2)(g) of the No. 19 Order	L16 L18 3 and L18 4 L24 0 to L24 3 L26	L17 0 L18 6 to L18 9 L24 6 to L249 L27	L17 5 and L17 6 L19 L25	26th September 2018
Articles 3(2)(j) and 4(2)(j) of the No. 19 Order	L24 4 and L24 5			26th September 2018
Articles 3(2)(l) and 4(2)(l) of the No. 19 Order	M1 M5 M27 4	M2 M6 M27 6	M3 M7 1 to M7 3 M50	26th September 2018

Articles 3(2)(m) and 4(2)(m) of the No. 19 Order	LA5 0 LA8 LA11 9 M44	LA6 1 and LA6 2 LA9 LA22	LA7 LA11 6 LA23	26th September 2018
Articles 3(2)(k) and 4(2)(u) and (v) of the No. 22 Order	HS1 HS4 HS7 KW15 LA10 5 ZE3	HS2 HS5 HS8 KW16 ZE1	HS3 HS6 HS9 KW17 ZE2	26th September 2018
Articles 3(2)(n) and 4(2)(aa) and (bb) of the No. 22 Order	BN7 BN10	BN8 5 and BN8 6 BN25	BN9 TN22	26th September 2018
Articles 3(2)(o) and 4(2)(cc) and (dd) of the No. 22 Order	G5 G43 G53 6	G41 G44 5 G53 9	G42 G44 9	26th September 2018
Articles 3(2)(p) and 4(2)(ee) and (ff) of the No. 22 Order	TR21 TR24	TR22 TR25	TR23	26th September 2018
Articles 3(2)(a) and 4(2)(a) and (b) of the No. 24 Order	BN8 4			26th September 2018
Articles 3(2)(c) and 4(2)(e) and (f) of the No. 24 Order	G44 4			26th September 2018
Articles 3(2)(h) and 4(2)(o) and (p) of the No. 24 Order	EX1 EX4 EX8 EX18	EX2 EX5 EX9 EX20	EX3 EX6 EX17 EX21	26th September 2018
Articles 3(2)(i) and 4(2)(q) and (r) of the No. 24 Order	HP5 HP8 HP19 HP22 MK18	HP6 HP17 HP20 HP27	HP7 HP18 HP21 MK17 0	26th September 2018
Articles 3(2)(l) and 4(2)(w) and (x) of the No. 24 Order	BH21 6 BH25 SO42	BH23 8 BH31 SP6	BH24 SO41	26th September 2018
Articles 3(2)(s) and 4(2)(kk) and (ll) of the No. 24 Order	G44 3 G76 0 G78	G46 G76 6 to G76 8	G53 7 G77	26th September 2018
Articles 3(2)(y) and 4(2)(ww) and (xx) of the No. 24 Order	PO1 PO4 PO7	PO2 PO5 PO8	PO3 PO6	26th September 2018

Articles 3(2)(o) and 4(2)(cc) and (dd) of the No. 24 Order	SE7 SE9 9 SE12 2	SE9 1 SE10 0 and SE10 1 SE18	SE9 5 and SE9 6 SE10 9	3rd October 2018
Articles 3(2)(q) and 4(2)(gg) and (hh) of the No. 24 Order	CM21 0 and CM21 1 EN11 SG3 SG5 9 SG9 SG12	CM22 7 SG1 SG4 SG6 SG10 SG13	CM23 SG2 SG5 1 and SG5 2 SG8 1 SG11 SG14	3rd October 2018
Articles 3(2)(r) and 4(2)(ii) and (jj) of the No. 24 Order	SE3 SE12 0 TS1 TS4 TS8	SE9 2 to SE9 4 SE12 8 and SE12 9 TS2 TS5	SE10 8 SE28 TS3 TS7 8	3rd October 2018
Articles 3(2)(u) and 4(2)(oo) and (pp) of the No. 24 Order	SG7	SG8 5	SG8 8 and SG8 9	3rd October 2018
Articles 3(2)(y) and 4(2)(ww) and (xx) of the No. 24 Order	E2 E9	E5 N1 4 to N1 7	E8 N16	3rd October 2018
Articles 3(2)(f) and 4(2)(k) and (l) of the No. 24 Order	LD1 LD4 LD7 LL36 SY15 SY18 SY21	LD2 LD5 LD8 SA9 SY16 SY19 SY22	LD3 LD6 LL35 SY10 0 SY17 SY20 9	10th October 2018
Articles 3(2)(h) and 4(2)(o) and (p) of the No. 24 Order	SY20 8			10th October 2018
Articles 3(2)(k) and 4(2)(u) and (v) of the No. 24 Order	LS29 0	LS29 7 to LS29 9		10th October 2018
Articles 3(2)(q) and 4(2)(gg) and (hh) of the No. 24 Order	BD3 7 LS1 LS4 LS7 LS10 LS13 LS16 LS18 LS21 LS24 8 and LS24 9 LS26 0 LS29 6	BD4 8 LS2 LS5 LS8 LS11 LS14 LS17 1 LS19 LS22 LS25 3 LS27 WF3 2	BD11 1 LS3 LS6 LS9 LS12 LS15 LS17 5 to LS17 9 LS20 LS23 LS25 5 LS28	10th October 2018

Articles 3(2)(t) and 4(2)(mm) and (nn) of the No. 24 Order	CF61 CF64	CF62 CF71	CF63	10th October 2018
Articles 3(2)(aa) and 4(2)(aaa) and (bbb) of the No. 24 Order	LS26 8	WF3 1		10th October 2018
Articles 3(2)(g) and 4(2)(m) and (n) of the No. 22 Order	IP11 IP13 6 IP16	IP12 IP13 9 IP17	IP13 0 IP15	17th October 2018
Articles 3(2)(n) and 4(2)(aa) and (bb) of the No. 22 Order	NN14 2 NN16 0	NN14 6 NN16 8 and NN16 9	NN15	17th October 2018
Articles 3(2)(q) and 4(2)(gg) and (hh) of the No. 22 Order	WS3 4 WS9 9	WS7 4	WS8 6	17th October 2018
Articles 3(2)(b) and 4(2)(c) and (d) of the No. 24 Order	IP13 7 and IP13 8 NR26	NR11 8 NR27	NR25	17th October 2018
Articles 3(2)(c) and 4(2)(e) and (f) of the No. 24 Order	B94 CV23 8 CV33 CV47 NN16 6	CV8 1 and CV8 2 CV31 CV34 NN14 1 WR1	CV23 0 CV32 CV35 8 NN14 3 and NN14 4 WR4 9	17th October 2018
Articles 3(2)(d) and 4(2)(g) and (h) of the No. 24 Order	WR3 WR7	WR4 0 WR9 0	WR5 1 WR9 8 and WR9 9	17th October 2018
Articles 3(2)(f) and 4(2)(k) and (l) of the No. 24 Order	WR2 WR9 7	WR5 2 and WR5 3	WR6	17th October 2018
Articles 3(2)(g) and 4(2)(m) and (n) of the No. 24 Order	NG16 1			17th October 2018
Articles 3(2)(l) and 4(2)(w) and (x) of the No. 24 Order	CV35 7 NR3 NR6 NR9 NR12 7 and NR12 8 NR15 1 NR18	NR1 NR4 NR7 NR10 NR13 4 to NR13 6 NR16 1 WS8 7	NR2 NR5 NR8 NR11 7 NR14 NR17	17th October 2018
Articles 3(2)(r) and 4(2)(ii) and (jj) of the No. 24 Order	WV12	WV13		17th October 2018

Articles 3(2)(s) and 4(2)(kk) and (ll) of the No. 24 Order	LE12 6 NG3 NG6 NG11 NG14 5	NG1 NG4 NG7 NG12 NG15 5 to NG15 8	NG2 NG5 1 and NG5 2 NG8 NG13 8 and NG13 9	17th October 2018
Articles 3(2)(u) and 4(2)(oo) and (pp) of the No. 24 Order	CB1 CB4 CB22 CB25 9 PE27 PE28 4 and PE28 5 SG8 0	CB2 CB5 CB23 PE19 PE28 0 PE28 9 SG8 6 and SG8 7	CB3 CB21 5 and CB21 6 CB24 PE26 1 PE28 2 PE29	17th October 2018
Articles 3(2)(w) and 4(2)(ss) and (tt) of the No. 24 Order	PE26 2	PE28 3		17th October 2018
Articles 3(2)(g) and 4(2)(m) and (n) of the No. 24 Order	HA4 UB7 UB10	UB3 UB8 UB11	UB4 UB9 4 and UB9 5	24th October 2018
Articles 3(2)(j) and 4(2)(s) and (t) of the No. 24 Order	UB9 6			24th October 2018
Articles 3(2)(l) and 4(2)(w) and (x) of the No. 24 Order	PO33 PO36	PO34 PO37	PO35	24th October 2018
Articles 3(2)(n) and 4(2)(aa) and (bb) of the No. 24 Order	BS15 BS30 GL9	BS16 4 to BS16 7 BS36 GL12 8	BS16 9 BS37 GL13	24th October 2018
Articles 3(2)(r) and 4(2)(ii) and (jj) of the No. 24 Order	DA1 4 DA7 DA15 DA18 GU14 GU34 9 GU52	DA5 DA8 DA16 GU11 GU30 GU35 SE2	DA6 DA14 DA17 GU12 4 GU34 1 to GU34 3 GU51	24th October 2018
Articles 3(2)(s) and 4(2)(kk) and (ll) of the No. 24 Order	CR3 6 and CR3 7 GU3 1 and GU3 2 GU6 GU9 GU26 KT18 KT21 KT23 RH2 RH5 RH7 6 SM7 1 and SM7 2	GU1 GU4 8 GU7 GU10 GU27 KT19 KT22 2 KT24 RH3 RH6 0 RH8 SM7 9	GU2 GU5 GU8 GU12 6 KT17 KT20 KT22 7 to KT22 9 RH1 RH4 RH6 7 to RH6 9 RH9	24th October 2018

Articles 3(2)(t) and 4(2)(mm) and (nn) of the No. 24 Order	LU1	LU2	LU5 5 and LU5 6	24th October 2018
Articles 3(2)(u) and 4(2)(oo) and (pp) of the No. 24 Order	GU3 3 GU21 GU24	GU4 7 GU22 KT14 6	GU12 5 GU23	24th October 2018
Articles 3(2)(w) and 4(2)(ss) and (tt) of the No. 24 Order	N8 N17	N10 N22	N15 3 to N15 5	24th October 2018
Articles 3(2)(y) and 4(2)(ww) and (xx) of the No. 24 Order	GU34 4 and GU34 5 N15 6			24th October 2018
Articles 3(2)(o) and 4(2)(cc) and (dd) of the No. 22 Order	G1 2 G4 G13 G21 G33 6	G2 G11 G14 G22	G3 G12 G20 G23	31st October 2018
Articles 3(2)(i) and 4(2)(q) and (r) of the No. 24 Order	AB10 AB13 AB16 AB23 AB31 AB34 AB39 AB51	AB11 AB14 AB21 AB24 AB32 AB35 AB41 6 and AB41 7 AB52	AB12 AB15 AB22 AB25 AB33 AB36 AB41 9 AB53 8	31st October 2018
Articles 3(2)(m) and 4(2)(y) and (z) of the No. 24 Order	G61	G62	G64 1 to G64 3	31st October 2018
Articles 3(2)(c) and 4(2)(c) of the No. 17 Order	BL1 BL4 BL6 4	BL2 BL5 1 BL6 9	BL3 BL5 3 M26 3	7th November 2018
Articles 3(2)(b) and 4(2)(b) of the No. 19 Order	L15	L18 0 to L18 2	L18 5	7th November 2018
Articles 3(2)(c) and 4(2)(c) of the No. 19 Order	L1 L6 0 and L6 1 L7 L17 7 to L17 9	L2 L6 3 and L6 4 L8	L3 L6 6 to L6 9 L17 1 to L17 4	7th November 2018
Articles 3(2)(e) and 4(2)(e) of the No. 19 Order	BL5 2			7th November 2018
Articles 3(2)(k) and 4(2)(k) of the No. 19 Order	BL6 5 to BL6 7	BL7		7th November 2018

Articles 3(2)(o) and 4(2)(cc) and (dd) of the No. 24 Order	S1 S4 S6 3 S9 S12 S32 S35 8 and S35 9	S2 S5 0 S7 S10 S14 S33	S3 S5 5 to S5 7 S8 S11 S17 S35 0 to S35 4	7th November 2018
Articles 3(2)(t) and 4(2)(mm) and (nn) of the No. 24 Order	NE20 NE61 NE65 7 and NE65 8 NE67 NE70 TD15	NE23 NE63 NE66 5 NE68 NE71	NE25 0 NE64 NE66 9 NE69 TD12	7th November 2018
Articles 3(2)(x) and 4(2)(uu) and (vv) of the No. 24 Order	CF37 CF40 CF43 CF72	CF38 CF41 CF44	CF39 CF42 CF45	7th November 2018
Articles 3(2)(n) and 4(2)(aa) and (bb) of the No. 22 Order	TF1 TF4 TF7	TF2 TF5 TF8	TF3 TF6 TF10 7	14th November 2018
Articles 3(2)(q) and 4(2)(gg) and (hh) of the No. 22 Order	NG5 0	NG5 7		14th November 2018
Articles 3(2)(a) and 4(2)(a) and (b) of the No. 24 Order	SY7 9			14th November 2018
Articles 3(2)(d) and 4(2)(g) and (h) of the No. 24 Order	DY10 1 and DY10 2 DY12 1 DY14 0 WR12	DY10 4 DY12 3 WR10	DY11 6 and DY11 7 DY13 8 and DY13 9 WR11	14th November 2018
Articles 3(2)(f) and 4(2)(k) and (l) of the No. 24 Order	DY12 2 WR8 9	DY13 0 WR15	DY14 8 and DY14 9	14th November 2018
Articles 3(2)(g) and 4(2)(m) and (n) of the No. 24 Order	NG9 1	NG9 3 to NG9 9		14th November 2018
Articles 3(2)(i) and 4(2)(q) and (r) of the No. 24 Order	B21 8 B66 B69 DY4	B43 5 and B43 6 B67 B70 WS5 4	B65 9 B68 B71 WS10 0	14th November 2018
Articles 3(2)(j) and 4(2)(s) and (t) of the No. 24 Order	MK16 8 NN2 NN5 NN12 OX17	MK19 NN3 NN7 1 to NN7 3 NN13 6 and NN13 7 WS10 7	NN1 NN4 NN7 9 NN13 9 WS10 9	14th November 2018

Articles 3(2)(k) and 4(2)(u) and (v) of the No. 24 Order	LN4 3 and LN4 4	LN10 6	NG32 3	14th November 2018
Articles 3(2)(l) and 4(2)(w) and (x) of the No. 24 Order	DY10 3	DY11 5	TF10 8 and TF10 9	14th November 2018
Articles 3(2)(s) and 4(2)(kk) and (ll) of the No. 24 Order	NG5 3 to NG5 6 NG4 6	NG5 8 and NG5 9	NG9 2	14th November 2018
Articles 3(2)(w) and 4(2)(ss) and (tt) of the No. 24 Order	PE30 PE33 PE36	PE31 6 and PE31 7 PE34 PE38	PE32 1 PE35	14th November 2018
Articles 3(2)(d) and 4(2)(d) of the No. 19 Order	BB4 BB9 4 and BB9 5 BB18 9 OL13	BB8 BB9 7 to BB9 9 BL0 O	BB9 0 BB18 5 OL12 8	21st November 2018
Articles 3(2)(j) and 4(2)(j) of the No. 19 Order	SK1 SK4 SK7	SK2 SK5 SK8	SK3 SK6 SK12	21st November 2018
Articles 3(2)(k) and 4(2)(k) of the No. 19 Order	BB9 6			21st November 2018
Articles 3(2)(n) and 4(2)(n) of the No. 19 Order	BB7			21st November 2018
Articles 3(2)(a) and 4(2)(a) and (b) of the No. 22 Order	BB18 6			21st November 2018
Articles 3(2)(c) and 4(2)(e) and (f) of the No. 22 Order	NW2 1 NW6 9	NW2 4 to NW2 7 NW10 2 and NW10 3	NW6 6 and NW6 7 NW10 8 and NW10 9	21st November 2018
Articles 3(2)(e) and 4(2)(i) and (j) of the No. 22 Order	ME14 ME17 1	ME15 ME17 3 and ME17 4	ME16 8 ME18 6	21st November 2018
Articles 3(2)(g) and 4(2)(m) and (n) of the No. 22 Order	ME17 2			21st November 2018
Articles 3(2)(h) and 4(2)(o) and (p) of the No. 22 Order	DE13 0 ST14 7	DE13 8 ST14 9	DE14	21st November 2018

Articles 3(2)(q) and 4(2)(gg) and (hh) of the No. 22 Order	NG15 0	NG17 0 to NG17 3	NG17 5 to NG17 9	21st November 2018
Articles 3(2)(t) and 4(2)(mm) and (nn) of the No. 22 Order	NW10 4	NW10 7		21st November 2018
Articles 3(2)(a) and 4(2)(a) and (b) of the No. 24 Order	TN12 9			21st November 2018
Articles 3(2)(b) and 4(2)(c) and (d) of the No. 24 Order	NN8 2 to NN8 6	NN8 9		21st November 2018
Articles 3(2)(c) and 4(2)(e) and (f) of the No. 24 Order	NG17 4 NN29	NN8 1	NN9 5	21st November 2018
Articles 3(2)(d) and 4(2)(g) and (h) of the No. 24 Order	ME6 ME18 5 TN1 TN3 8 TN10 TN13 TN15 8 and TN15 9 TN27 9	ME16 0 ME19 TN2 TN4 TN11 TN14 5 and TN14 6 TN17	ME16 9 ME20 TN 3 0 TN9 TN12 5 to TN12 8 TN15 0 TN18	21st November 2018
Articles 3(2)(f) and 4(2)(k) and (l) of the No. 24 Order	DE11 DE13 9 ST15 ST17 9 ST21	DE12 6 DE15 ST16 ST18 0	DE12 8 ST14 8 ST17 4 ST20	21st November 2018
Articles 3(2)(h) and 4(2)(o) and (p) of the No. 24 Order	NW10 5	W10 4		21st November 2018
Articles 3(2)(j) and 4(2)(s) and (t) of the No. 24 Order	DE6 5 NN6 0	NG19 8 ST14 5	NG20 8 and NG20 9	21st November 2018
Articles 3(2)(l) and 4(2)(w) and (x) of the No. 24 Order	ST17 0 WS6 WS15 1 and Ws15 2	ST18 9 WS11 WS15 4	ST19 WS12 WS15 9	21st November 2018
Articles 3(2)(o) and 4(2)(cc) and (dd) of the No. 24 Order	TN16 1			21st November 2018

Articles 3(2)(p) and 4(2)(ee) and (ff) of the No. 24 Order	DE73 5	DE73 8		21st November 2018
Articles 3(2)(r) and 4(2)(ii) and (jj) of the No. 24 Order	WV11 9			21st November 2018
Articles 3(2)(s) and 4(2)(kk) and (ll) of the No. 24 Order	TN8	TN16 2		21st November 2018
Articles 3(2)(t) and 4(2)(mm) and (nn) of the No. 24 Order	LU3 LU6 SG15 SG18	LU4 LU7 SG16 SG19 1	LU5 4 SG5 3 and SG5 4 SG17	21st November 2018
Articles 3(2)(u) and 4(2)(oo) and (pp) of the No. 24 Order	SG19 2 and SG19 3			21st November 2018
Articles 3(2)(w) and 4(2)(ss) and (tt) of the No. 24 Order	NW2 2 and NW2 3 W9 3	NW61 and NW6 2	NW6 5	21st November 2018
Articles 3(2)(d) and 4(2)(gg) and (hh) of the No. 22 Order	EH1 EH4 EH7 EH10 4 to EH10 6 EH12 EH15 G60 G82 1 to G82 4 G83 3	EH2 EH5 EH8 EH10 9 EH13 EH16 5 and EH16 6 G81 1 to G81 4 G82 9	EH3 EH6 EH9 EH11 EH14 EH17 7 G81 6 G83 0	28th November 2018
Articles 3(2)(i) and 4(2)(q) and (r) of the No. 22 Order	EH10 7	EH16 4	EH17 8	28th November 2018
Articles 3(2)(m) and 4(2)(y) and (z) of the No. 22 Order	G83 9			28th November 2018
Articles 3(2)(i) and 4(2)(q) and (r) of the No. 24 Order	EH30			28th November 2018
Articles 3(2)(m) and 4(2)(y) and (z) of the No. 24 Order	G81 5			28th November 2018

Articles 3(2)(r) and 4(2)(ii) and (jj) of the No. 24 Order	GU31	GU32	GU33	28th November 2018
Articles 3(2)(u) and 4(2)(oo) and (pp) of the No. 24 Order	GU15 GU18 GU25 KT7 KT11 KT14 7 KT16 TW16 TW19	GU16 GU19 GU46 KT8 KT12 KT14 9 KT22 0 TW17 TW20	GU17 GU20 GU47 7 and GU47 8 KT10 KT13 KT15 TW15 TW18	28th November 2018
Articles 3(2)(v) and 4(2)(qq) and (rr) of the No. 24 Order	G63 0	G82 5	G83 8	28th November 2018
Articles 3(2)(w) and 4(2)(ss) and (tt) of the No. 24 Order	TS6 TS9 6 TS12	TS7 0 TS10 TS13	TS7 9 TS11 TS14	28th November 2018
Articles 3(2)(y) and 4(2)(ww) and (xx) of the No. 24 Order	PO9 PO12 PO15 SO31 0 and SO31 1 SO32 3	PO10 7 PO13 PO16 SO31 6 and SO31 7	PO11 PO14 PO17 SO31 9	28th November 2018
Articles 3(2)(aa) and 4(2)(aaa) and (bbb) of the No. 24 Order	LS25 1 and LS25 2 LS26 9 WF3 3 and WF3 4 WF6 WF9	LS25 4 WF1 WF4 WF7 WF10	LS25 7 WF2 WF5 WF8 WF11	28th November 2018
Articles 3(2)(c) and 4(2)(c) of the No. 19 Order	L4 0 to L4 4 L62	L4 7 L6 5	L5	5th December 2018
Articles 3(2)(f) and 4(2)(f) of the No. 19 Order	L4 6	L4 8 and L4 9	L11	5th December 2018
Articles 3(2)(g) and 4(2)(g) of the No. 19 Order	L12	L13		5th December 2018
Articles 3(2)(h) and 4(2)(h) of the No. 19 Order	FY5	FY6	FY7	5th December 2018
Articles 3(2)(m) and 4(2)(m) of the No. 19 Order	FY1 FY4 LA12 LA15 LA18 LA21	FY2 FY8 LA13 LA16 LA19 PR4 1 to PR4 3	FY3 LA11 7 LA14 LA17 LA20	5th December 2018

Articles 3(2)(c) and 4(2)(e) and (f) of the No. 22 Order	HA0 2 to HA0 4	HA9	NW10 0 and NW10 1	5th December 2018
Articles 3(2)(o) and 4(2)(cc) and (dd) of the No. 22 Order	G1 1 G15 G33 1 to G33 5 G40 G69 6 to G69 8	G1 3 to G1 5 G31 G33 9 G45	G1 9 G32 G34 G69 1	5th December 2018
Articles 3(2)(t) and 4(2)(mm) and (nn) of the No. 22 Order	HA0 1			5th December 2018
Articles 3(2)(a) and 4(2)(a) and (b) of the No. 24 Order	HP1 LL58 LL62 LL65 LL68 LL71 LL74 LL77 7 and L77 8 WD7	HP2 LL60 LL63 LL66 LL69 LL72 LL75 LL78	HP3 9 LL61 LL64 LL67 LL70 LL73 LL76 WD6	5th December 2018
Articles 3(2)(b) and 4(2)(c) and (d) of the No. 24 Order	CM0 CM1 9 CM9 4 and CM9 5	CM1 to CM1 3 CM2 CM9 8	CM1 6 and CM1 7 CM3 5 to CM3 8 CM11 1	5th December 2018
Articles 3(2)(c) and 4(2)(e) and (f) of the No. 24 Order	CM1 4 CM9 6	CM3 1	CM3 3 and CM3 4	5th December 2018
Articles 3(2)(f) and 4(2)(k) and (l) of the No. 24 Order	LL59	LL77 9		5th December 2018
Articles 3(2)(h) and 4(2)(o) and (p) of the No. 24 Order	SA35 SA38 SA43 SA45 SA48 SY25	SA36 SA41 SA44 6 SA46 SY23	SA37 SA42 SA44 9 SA47 SY24	5th December 2018
Articles 3(2)(i) and 4(2)(q) and (r) of the No. 24 Order	HP4 2 and HP4 3 MK2 MK5 MK8 MK11 MK14 MK16 6	HP23 MK3 MK6 MK9 MK12 MK15 MK16 9	MK1 MK4 MK7 MK10 MK13 MK16 0 MK46	5th December 2018
Articles 3(2)(j) and 4(2)(s) and (t) of the No. 24 Order	HP3 0	HP3 8		5th December 2018

Articles 3(2)(q) and 4(2)(gg) and (hh) of the No. 24 Order	CM5 EN9 3	CM16 IG10	EN9 1	5th December 2018
Articles 3(2)(s) and 4(2)(kk) and (ll) of the No. 24 Order	IG7 5 and IG7 6	IG9	RM4	5th December 2018
Articles 3(2)(t) and 4(2)(mm) and (nn) of the No. 24 Order	HP4 1	MK17 8 and MK17 9		5th December 2018
Articles 3(2)(w) and 4(2)(ss) and (tt) of the No. 24 Order	NW1 0 NW5	NW1 7 to NW1 9 NW6 3 and NW6 4	NW3	5th December 2018
Articles 3(2)(g) and 4(2)(m) and (n) of the No. 22 Order	CB8 1	IP28 6 and IP28 7		12th December 2018
Articles 3(2)(h) and 4(2)(o) and (p) of the No. 22 Order	CW2 5 ST5 5 to ST5 9	CW3 9 ST7 1	ST5 2 and ST5 3 ST7 8	12th December 2018
Articles 3(2)(n) and 4(2)(aa) and (bb) of the No. 22 Order	ST7 3	ST8 6	ST8 9	12th December 2018
Articles 3(2)(b) and 4(2)(c) and (d) of the No. 24 Order	NR12 0 NR21 7 and NR21 8	NR12 9 NR24	NR21 0 NR28	12th December 2018
Articles 3(2)(f) and 4(2)(k) and (l) of the No. 24 Order	LL23 LL39 LL42 LL45 LL48 LL52 LL55 SA14 SA17 SA20 SA33	LL37 LL40 LL43 LL46 LL49 LL53 LL56 SA15 SA18 SA31 ST5 4	LL38 LL41 LL44 LL47 LL51 LL54 LL57 SA16 SA19 SA32	12th December 2018
Articles 3(2)(h) and 4(2)(o) and (p) of the No. 24 Order	SA34 SA44 4 and SA44 5	SA39	SA40	12th December 2018
Articles 3(2)(l) and 4(2)(w) and (x) of the No. 24 Order	NR11 6			12th December 2018

Articles 3(2)(o) and 4(2)(cc) and (dd) of the No. 24 Order	S5 8 and S5 9 S6 9 S36 1 to S36 4	S6 1 and S6 2 S13	S6 4 to S6 6 S20	12th December 2018
Articles 3(2)(q) and 4(2)(gg) and (hh) of the No. 24 Order	ST4 4 to ST4 9 ST7 4	ST5 0 and ST5 1 ST8 7	ST6 5	12th December 2018
Articles 3(2)(t) and 4(2)(mm) and (nn) of the No. 24 Order	CA8 7 NE24 NE43 NE46 NE49 NE65 9	NE19 NE26 4 NE44 NE47 NE62 NE66 1 to NE66 4	NE22 NE42 5 and NE42 6 NE45 NE48 NE65 0	12th December 2018
Articles 3(2)(u) and 4(2)(oo) and (pp) of the No. 24 Order	CB8 0 HU1 HU4 6 HU6 HU9 HU16 IP28 8	CB8 7 to CB8 9 HU2 HU4 9 HU7 HU11 HU19	CB25 0 HU3 HU5 HU8 HU12 HU20	12th December 2018
Articles 3(2)(w) and 4(2)(ss) and (tt) of the No. 24 Order	IP27 9 NR23	NR21 9 PE31 8	NR22	12th December 2018
Articles 3(2)(cc) and 4(2)(eee) and (fff) of the No. 24 Order	All further postcode districts and part-districts in England and Wales, and Scotland			12th December 2018

The Welfare Reform Act 2012 (Commencement No. 31 and Savings and Transitional Provisions and Commencement No. 21 and 23 and Transitional and Transitory Provisions (Amendment)) Order 2019

SI 2019/37

Made 14th January 2019

The Secretary of State for Work and Pensions makes the following Order in exercise of the powers conferred by section 150(3) and (4)(a), (b)(i) and (c) of the Welfare Reform Act 2012   **3.266**

ARRANGEMENT OF ARTICLES

1. Citation
2. Interpretation

GENERAL NOTE

3.267   Articles 1 and 2 of this Commencement Order are introductory and arts. 3 and 4 are concerned with state pension credit and do not directly affect this volume. Article 5 amends art.6(3)(a) of the No.21 and art.7(4)(a) of the No.23 Commencement Orders relating to the introduction of universal credit to supplement the provisions of those Orders that prevent claims to housing benefit by a member of a mixed-age couple of state pension credit qualifying age. Claims are prevented in the same cases as that member is excluded from entitlement to state pension credit, allowing for the savings cases in art.4(1) whilst they continue under art.4(2). Articles 6 and 7 make transitional provision in housing benefit cases and for parties to a polygamous marriage.

The High Court has ruled that the exclusion of mixed-age couples from pension credit is neither discriminatory nor in breach of the public sector equality duty (PSED): see *R (on the application of Prichard) v SSWP* [2020] EWHC 1495 (Admin), where the claimant was due to reach state pension age on July 6, 2020, but his wife would not do so for a further 6 years. As a result of the changes outlined above, the couple would have to continue to claim working-age benefits until 2026 and would be £65,000 worse off than they would have been had the changes not been made. Both the claimant and his wife had serious illnesses and were in receipt of disability benefits. The couple would be classed as a 'no-conditionality mixed-age couple' as the claimant was over pension age and his wife received carer's allowance (and so she would not be subject to any work-related requirements). On the application for judicial review, Laing J held that the Secretary of State had had appropriate regard to the relevant equality needs under the PSED (see further Equality Act 2010, s.149). She further held that the policy in question, in its application to no-conditionality mixed-age couples, was not manifestly without reasonable foundation. It followed that "the differential treatment of which the claimant complains is not a breach of article 14 (whether read with article 8 or with A1P1), and, therefore, that the 2019 Order, which provides for the commencement of paragraph 64 of the 2012 Act (and by that route, of section 4(1A) of the SPCA) is not incompatible with the claimant's Convention rights" (at [136]).

Citation

3.268   **1.** This Order may be cited as the Welfare Reform Act 2012 (Commencement No. 31 and Savings and Transitional Provisions and Commencement No. 21 and 23 and Transitional and Transitory Provisions (Amendment)) Order 2019.

Interpretation

3.269   **2.**—(1) In this Order—
[¹"the 1992 Act" means the Social Security Contributions and Benefits Act 1992;]
"the 2002 Act" means the State Pension Credit Act 2002;
"the 2012 Act" means the Welfare Reform Act 2012;

"the appointed day" means the day referred to in article 3;
[¹...];
"the Housing Benefit SPC Regulations" means the Housing Benefit (Persons who have attained the qualifying age for state pension credit) Regulations 2006;
"the No. 21 Order" means the Welfare Reform Act 2012 (Commencement No. 21 and Transitional and Transitory Provisions) Order 2015;
"the No. 23 Order" means the Welfare Reform Act 2012 (Commencement No. 23 and Transitional and Transitory Provisions) Order 2015;
"polygamous marriage" has the same meaning as in regulation 3(5) of the Universal Credit Regulations 2013;
"the qualifying age for state pension credit" has the same meaning as in the 2002 Act;
"secondary legislation" has the same meaning as in Part 1 of the 2012 Act;
"state pension credit" has the same meaning as in the 2002 Act(**9**).
[¹(1A) In this Order, "couple" has the same meaning as in the 2002 Act, save—
  (a) in reference to entitlement to housing benefit, where it has the same meaning as in Part VII of the 1992 Act; and
  (b) in article 7(3)(a), where it has the meaning given by article 7(2)(b)(ii).]
(2) In this Order—
  (a) "mixed-age couple" means a couple, one member of which has attained the qualifying age for state pension credit and the other of which has not; and
  (b) the definition in sub-paragraph (a) includes a polygamous marriage where at least one party to the marriage has attained the qualifying age for state pension credit and at least one has not.
(3) Save as stated to the contrary in article 6(2) [¹and article 8(2)(b)], all references in this Order to claims or entitlement to housing benefit are to claims or entitlement under the Housing Benefit SPC Regulations only.
(4) In this Order—
  (a) a person is entitled to state pension credit or housing benefit on any day where the person has made a claim for that benefit and the conditions of entitlement are met in relation to that person, regardless of whether, respectively, entitlement begins on a later day under—
    (i) regulation 16A (date of entitlement under an award of state pension credit for the purpose of payability and effective date of change of rate)(**10**) of the Social Security (Claims and Payments) Regulations 1987; or
    (ii) regulation 57 (date on which entitlement is to commence) of the Housing Benefit SPC Regulations; and
  (b) [¹save in article 7(3)(a),] a reference to claiming or entitlement to state pension credit or housing benefit as part of a [¹mixed-age] couple is a reference to [¹a person claiming or] being so entitled, on the basis that [¹the person] is a member of a couple or [¹...] a polygamous marriage.

AMENDMENT

1. Welfare Reform Act 2012 (Commencement No. 31 and Savings and Transitional Provisions (Amendment)) Order 2019 (SI 2019/935) art.2(2) (May 14, 2019).

Appointed day

3.270   **3.** 15th May 2019 is the appointed day for the coming into force of paragraph 64 (universal credit amendments: insertion of section 4(1A) into the 2002 Act) of Schedule 2 to the 2012 Act, and section 31 of the 2012 Act in so far as it relates to that paragraph.

Savings

3.271   **4.**—(1) Subject to paragraph (2), the 2002 Act shall have effect as though section 4(1A) (exclusion of mixed-age couples from state pension credit) had not come into force in relation to a member of a mixed-age couple who, on the day before the appointed day and as part of that couple, is entitled to—

    (a)   state pension credit;

    (b)   housing benefit; or

    (c)   state pension credit and housing benefit.

(2) The savings in the sub-paragraphs of paragraph (1) shall cease to have effect in relation to the member of the mixed-age couple referred to on any day after the appointed day when that person is not entitled to either state pension credit or housing benefit as part of the same mixed-age couple.

Transitional provision: termination of awards of housing benefit

3.272   **6.**—(1) The awards of housing benefit referred to in paragraph (2) are to terminate on the day referred to in paragraph (3), subject to paragraph (4).

(2) The awards are those where entitlement under the Housing Benefit SPC Regulations as part of a mixed-age couple begins on or after the appointed day and where the awards are made—

    (a)   at any time, under the Housing Benefit Regulations 2006 or the Housing Benefit SPC Regulations, to a person who, after the award, becomes a member of a mixed-age couple;

    (b)   at any time, under the Housing Benefit Regulations 2006, to a person who is a member of a mixed-age couple, where the award subsequently ceases to be subject to those Regulations and becomes subject to the Housing Benefit SPC Regulations; or

    (c)   on or before the day of making of this Order, to a person who claimed in advance of attaining the qualifying age for state pension credit.

(3) The termination takes effect—

    (a)   in the case of an award referred to in paragraph (2)(a) or (b), on the later of the appointed day and the day entitlement under the Housing Benefit SPC Regulations as part of a mixed-age couple takes effect on the award, as a change of circumstances, in accordance with the Housing Benefit and Council Tax Benefit (Decisions and Appeals) Regulations 2001; or

    (b)   in the case of an award referred to in paragraph (2)(c), on the day after the day of making of this Order.

(4) Paragraph (1) does not apply to awards in respect of specified accommodation or temporary accommodation, as defined respectively in sub-paragraphs (h) and (l) of article 7(11) of the No. 23 Order.

Transitional provision: [¹application of the rules in universal credit for treatment of couples and] polygamous marriages

7.—(1) Paragraph (3) applies where a [¹member of a mixed-age couple]—   3.273

(a) is excluded from entitlement to state pension credit under section 4(1A) of the 2002 Act;

(b) is prevented from claiming housing benefit under article 6 of the No. 21 Order or article 7 of the No. 23 Order; or

(c) has an award of housing benefit terminated under article 6.

[¹(2) For the purposes of paragraph (3) -

(a) all secondary legislation relevant to assessment of entitlement to state pension credit or housing benefit applies so that claims and awards may be made in respect of the party specified in paragraph (3)(a) or (b) as a part of a couple or as a single person respectively; and

(b) the following rules in regulation 3 of the Universal Credit Regulations 2013 apply—

   (i) the rule in paragraph (3) (treatment of certain couples), which establishes that a member of a couple may make a claim as a single person;

   (ii) the rule in paragraph (4) (treatment of polygamous marriages), which establishes that two of the parties to a polygamous marriage are to be treated as a couple and the remaining party (or parties) as a single person (or single persons);

   (iii) the rule in paragraph (6) (absence from the household), which establishes that members of a couple may cease to be treated as a couple.]

(3) Where this paragraph applies and the qualifying age for state pension credit has been attained by—

(a) both the parties to be treated as a couple by virtue of paragraph [¹(2)(b)(ii)], one of them may claim or remain entitled to state pension credit as part of that couple and one of them may claim or remain entitled to housing benefit as part of that couple;

(b) a party to be treated as a single person by virtue of paragraph [¹(2)(b)(i) to (iii)], that party may claim or remain entitled to state pension credit or housing benefit as a single person.

AMENDMENT

1. Welfare Reform Act 2012 (Commencement No. 31 and Savings and Transitional Provisions (Amendment)) Order 2019 (SI 2019/935) art.2(3) (May 14, 2019).

[¹Transitional provision: where restrictions on claims for universal credit are in place

8.—(1) This article applies to a member of a mixed-age couple who,   3.273.1
further to articles 3 to 7, is excluded from entitlement to state pension credit or housing benefit, and is also prevented from claiming universal credit by virtue of—

(a) regulation 4 of the Universal Credit (Transitional Provisions) Regulations 2014 (claims for universal credit may not be made in an area or category of case);

(b) regulation 4A of those Regulations (restriction on claims for universal credit by persons entitled to a severe disability premium); or

(c) article 4(11) of the Welfare Reform Act 2012 (Commencement No.

32 and Savings and Transitional Provisions) Order 2019 (no claims for universal credit by frontier workers).

(2) Where this article applies, the member of the mixed-age couple who has attained the qualifying age for state pension credit is, for the purposes of an award of benefit referred to in the following sub-paragraphs to that member, to be treated as—

    (a) meeting the basic condition of entitlement (upper age limit) for—

        (i) income support, in section 124(1)(aa) of the 1992 Act;

        (ii) a jobseeker's allowance, in section 1(2)(h) of the 1995 Act; or

        (iii) an employment and support allowance, in section 1(3)(c) of the 2007 Act; and

    (b) not having attained that age for housing benefit, for the purposes of regulation 5 of the Housing Benefit Regulations 2006 and regulation 5 of the Housing Benefit SPC Regulations, so that the Housing Benefit Regulations 2006 apply to the assessment of the award.

(3) This article continues to apply until the award of benefit referred to in paragraph (2)(a) or (b) terminates, regardless of whether paragraph (1)(a), (b) or (c) continues to apply throughout the award.

(4) Where a member of a mixed-age couple who has attained the qualifying age for state pension credit is entitled to income support by virtue of paragraph (2)(a)(i), references to a claimant's partner in paragraphs 9 and 9A (conditions for pensioner premium) and in paragraph 10 (condition for higher pensioner premium) of Schedule 2 to the Income Support (General) Regulations 1987 have effect as though they were references to the claimant.

(5) In this article—

"the 1995 Act" means the Jobseekers Act 1995;

"the 2007 Act" means the Welfare Reform Act 2007;

"employment and support allowance" means an employment and support allowance under Part 1 of the 2007 Act as it has effect apart from the amendments made by Schedule 3, and Part 1 of Schedule 14, to the 2012 Act that remove references to an income-related employment and support allowance;

"income support" has the same meaning as in Part VII of the 1992 Act;

"jobseeker's allowance" means a jobseeker's allowance under the 1995 Act as it has effect apart from the amendments made by Part 1 of Schedule 14 to the 2012 Act that remove references to an income-based jobseeker's allowance.]

AMENDMENT

1. Welfare Reform Act 2012 (Commencement No. 31 and Savings and Transitional Provisions (Amendment)) Order 2019 (SI 2019/935) art.2(4) (May 14, 2019).

The Welfare Reform Act 2012 (Commencement No. 32 and Savings and Transitional Provisions) Order 2019

SI 2019/167

Made 31st January 2019

3.274   *The Secretary of State for Work and Pensions makes the following Order in exercise of the powers conferred by section 150(3) and (4)(a), (b)(i) and (c) of the Welfare Reform Act 2012:*

ARRANGEMENT OF ARTICLES

GENERAL NOTE   3.275

This is no ordinary Commencement Order. Article 2 in effect repeals (as from February 1, 2019) Part 1 of the Tax Credits Act 2002 by commencing s.33(1) (f) of the WRA 2012, which abolishes child tax credit and working tax credit. However, these repeals are subject to the important savings provisions set out in Art.3. Meanwhile, Art.4 commences the provisions of Part 1 of the WRA 2012 that relate to universal credit and the abolition of both IR-ESA and IB-JSA for specified categories of cases. Art.5 simply makes consequential amendments to the No.9, 21 and 23 Commencement Orders, and are incorporated into those provisions in the text above.

Citation and Interpretation

1.—(1) This Order may be cited as the Welfare Reform Act 2012   3.276
(Commencement No. 32 and Savings and Transitional Provisions) Order 2019.

(2) In this Order—

"the Act" means the Welfare Reform Act 2012;

"the 2002 Act" means the Tax Credits Act 2002;

"the 2015 Order (N.I.)" means the Welfare Reform (Northern Ireland) Order 2015;

"the No. 8 Order (N.I.)" means the Welfare Reform (Northern Ireland) Order 2015 (Commencement No. 8 and Transitional and Transitory Provisions) Order 2017;

"the No. 9 Order" means the Welfare Reform Act 2012 (Commencement No. 9 and Transitional and Transitory Provisions and Commencement No. 8 and Savings and Transitional Provisions (Amendment)) Order 2013;

"the No. 21 Order" means the Welfare Reform Act 2012 (Commencement No. 21 and Transitional and Transitory Provisions) Order 2015;

"the No. 23 Order" means the Welfare Reform Act 2012 (Commencement No. 23 and Transitional and Transitory Provisions) Order 2015;

"the Claims and Payments Regulations 1987" means the Social Security (Claims and Payments) Regulations 1987;

"couple" means a couple as defined in section 3(5A) of the 2002 Act;

"employment and support allowance" means an employment and support allowance under Part 1 of the Welfare Reform Act 2007;

"jobseeker's allowance" means a jobseeker's allowance under the Jobseekers Act 1995;

"joint-claim couple" has the same meanings as in the Jobseeker's Act 1995;

"Her Majesty's forces" has the same meaning as in the Armed Forces Act 2006;

"mixed-age couple" means a couple, one member of which has attained the qualifying age and the other of which has not;

"polygamous unit" means a polygamous unit within the meaning of the Tax Credits (Polygamous Marriages) Regulations 2003;

"qualifying age" means the qualifying age for state pension credit as defined in section 1(6) of the State Pension Credit Act 2002;

"single claimant" means a person who makes a single claim for a tax credit as referred to in section 3(3)(b) of the 2002 Act;

"tax credit" (including "child tax credit" and "working tax credit") have the same meanings as in the 2002 Act and "tax year" has the same meaning as in Part 1 of that Act;

"UC age condition" means the condition in section 4(1)(b) of the Act for Great Britain or Article 9(1)(b) of the 2015 Order (N.I.) for Northern Ireland, subject to any exceptions in any instrument made under the Act or 2015 Order (N.I.);

"UC couple" means a couple as defined in section 39 of the Act for Great Britain or Article 45 of the 2015 Order (N.I.) for Northern Ireland (in article 4, as defined in that section 39);

"UC joint claimants" means joint claimants as defined in section 40 of the Act for Great Britain or Article 46 of the 2015 Order (N.I.) for Northern Ireland (in article 4, as defined in that section 40);

"UC provisions" means the provisions listed in Schedule 2 to the No. 9 Order;

"UC single claimant" means a single claimant as defined in section 40 of the Act for Great Britain or Article 46 of the 2015 Order (N.I.) for Northern Ireland (in article 4, as defined in that section 40);

"UC transitional provisions" means the orders made under section 150(3) of the Act or Article 2(2) of the 2015 Order (N.I.) that commence the UC provisions, or the provisions listed in Schedule 1 to the No. 8 Order (N.I.), respectively, and the regulations made under Schedule 6 to the Act or Schedule 6 to the 2015 Order (N.I.).

(3) In this Order—

(a) "frontier worker" means a person, other than a person referred to in sub-paragraph (b), who is in Great Britain for the purposes of section 4(1)(c) of the Act but who does not reside in Great Britain or Northern Ireland;

(b) the person referred to is a crown servant or member of Her Majesty's forces posted overseas (where "crown servant" and "posted overseas" have the same meanings as in regulation 10 of the Universal Credit Regulations 2013).

Commencement of provisions on abolition of tax credits

3.277   **2.** The day appointed for the coming into force of section 33(1)(f) of the Act (abolition of tax credits) and the repeal of Part 1 of the 2002 Act (but not Schedule 1 or 3), by Part 1 of Schedule 14 to the Act, is 1st February 2019.

GENERAL NOTE

3.278   Article 2, which extends to both Great Britain and Northern Ireland, commences s.33(1)(f) of the WRA 2012 , which abolishes child tax credit and working tax credit, and the repeal of Part 1 of the Tax Credits Act 2002 (but not Sch. 1 or 3), by Part 1 of Sch. 14 to the Act, on February 1, 2019, subject to the savings referred to below. In particular, art. 3 contains a saving for existing awards of a tax credit – e.g. one that has effect for a period that includes January 31, 2019. In these cases, s.33(1)(f) is treated as if it had not come into force.

Savings

3.—(1) Section 33(1)(f) of the Act, and the repeal of Part 1 of the 2002   3.279
Act (but not Schedule 1 or 3) by Part 1 of Schedule 14 to the Act, shall
be treated as though they had not come into force, in relation to a case as
referred to in paragraph (2), (3), (4), (5) or (9).

(2) The case referred to is the case of an award of a tax credit that has
effect for a period that includes 31st January 2019.

(3) The case referred to is the case of an award of a tax credit where the
period for which it has effect begins on or after 1st February 2019 and
where the claim for the award is made by—

(a) a single claimant who is, or a couple both members of which are,
aged under the qualifying age on the day that the claim is made;

(b) a mixed-age couple which is also a UC couple on that day; or

(c) a polygamous unit which on that day consists wholly of persons who,
ignoring any restrictions on claiming universal credit in the UC transitional provisions, could claim universal credit, and meet the UC
age condition, as—

(i) UC joint claimants and one or more UC single claimants; or

(ii) a number of UC single claimants.

(4) The case referred to is the case of an award of a tax credit where the
period for which it has effect begins on or after 1st February 2019 and
where the claim for the award is made by—

(a) a mixed-age couple apart from one referred to in paragraph (3)(b); or

(b) a polygamous unit apart from one referred to in paragraph (3)(c),

where, on the day on which the claim is made, a member of the couple,
or a member or members of the polygamous unit, would be able to claim
universal credit were it not for restrictions on claiming universal credit in
the UC transitional provisions.

(5) The case referred to is a case, not falling within paragraph (3) or (4),
of—

(a) an award of child tax credit where the period for which it has effect
begins on or after 1st February 2019 and where, on the day on which
the claimant or claimants of the award makes or make the claim for
it, he or she (or they) has or have an award of working tax credit;

(b) an award of working tax credit where the period for which it has effect
begins on or after 1st February 2019 and where, on the day on which
the claimant or claimants of the award makes or make the claim for it,
he or she (or they) has or have an award of child tax credit;

(c) an award of child tax credit or working tax credit where the period
for which it has effect begins on or after 1st February 2019 and
where the claimant or claimants who makes or make the claim for
the award had an award of the same type of tax credit for the previous tax year to the tax year for which the award is made.

(6) For the purposes of paragraph (5)(a) and (b)—

(a) a person is to be treated as having an award of working tax credit
with effect from the start of a tax year ("current tax year") even
though a decision has not been made under section 14 of the 2002
Act in respect of a claim for that tax credit for that tax year, if the
person had an award of working tax credit for the previous tax year
and any of the cases specified in paragraph (7) applies; and

(b) a person is to be treated as having an award of child tax credit with effect from the start of a tax year ("current tax year") even though a decision has not been made under section 14 of the 2002 Act in respect of a claim for that tax credit for that tax year, if the person had an award of child tax credit for the previous tax year and any of the cases specified in paragraph (7) applies.

(7) The cases are—

(a) a final notice has not been given to the person under section 17 of the 2002 Act in respect of that previous tax year;

(b) a final notice has been given, which includes provision by virtue of subsections (2) and (4) of section 17, or a combination of those subsections and subsection (6) of that section and—

    (i) the date specified in the notice for the purposes of section 17(2) and (4) or, where different dates are specified, the later of them, has not yet passed and no claim for a tax credit for the current tax year has been made, or treated as made; or

    (ii) a claim for a tax credit has been made, or treated as made, on or before the date mentioned in paragraph (i), but no decision has been made in relation to that claim under section 14(1) of the 2002 Act;

(c) a final notice has been given, no claim for a tax credit for the current tax year has been made, or treated as made, and no decision has been made under section 18(1) of the 2002 Act in respect of entitlement to a tax credit for the previous tax year;

(d) a final notice has been given and the person made a declaration in response to a requirement included in that notice by virtue of section 17(2)(a), (4)(a) or (6)(a), or any combination of those provisions—

    (i) by the date specified on the final notice;

    (ii) if not in accordance with paragraph (i), within 30 days following the date on the notice to the person that payments of a tax credit under section 24(4) of the 2002 Act have ceased due to the person's failure to make the declaration by the date specified in the final notice; or

    (iii) if not in accordance with paragraph (i) or (ii), before 31st January in the tax year following the period to which the final notice relates and, in the opinion of Her Majesty's Revenue and Customs, the person had good reason for not making the declaration in accordance with paragraph (i) or (ii).

(8) In this article, a reference to the date on which a claim for a tax credit is made is a reference to the date on which such a claim is made or treated as made as provided for in the Tax Credits (Claims and Notifications) Regulations 2002.

(9) The case referred to is the case of an award of a tax credit that had effect for a period that ended on or before 30th January 2019.

GENERAL NOTE

3.280   Article 2 above brings into force on February 1, 2019 s.33(1)(f) of the WRA 2012 which provides for the abolition of both child tax credit and working tax credit. Article 2 is subject to the savings provisions in art.3, which specifies five cases to which s.33(1)(f) does not apply. In these cases, s.33(1)(f) is treated as if it had not come into force.

Case 1 – article 3(2)

Case 1 applies to an award of a tax credit that has effect for a period that includes January 31, 2019. Since most tax credits awards are made for the entire tax year, the effect is that the majority of tax credits recipients for tax year 2018/19 will be unaffected by the commencement of s.33(1)(f).

Case 2 – article 3(3)

Case 2 applies to an award of a tax credit for a period beginning on or after February 1, 2019 where:

   (a) the claim for the tax credit was made by a single claimant, couple or polygamous unit; and

   (b) the single claimant, both members of the couple or all members of the polygamous unit could claim universal credit and meet the relevant age condition (in s.4 of the Welfare Reform Act 2012).

Case 3 – article 3(4)

Case 3 applies to an award of child tax credit or working tax credit that has effect for a period beginning on or after February 1, 2019 where:

   (a) the claim is made by a couple or a polygamous unit where only one member of the couple, or only some members of the polygamous unit, could claim universal credit and meet the age condition, and

   (b) where the member or members who could claim universal credit, and meet the age condition, cannot claim universal credit by virtue of restrictions in a transitional provisions order made under section 150(3) of the 2012 Act or regulations made under Sch.6 to that Act.

Cases 2 and 3 – persons who could claim Universal Credit

Cases 2 and 3 refer to a person who could claim universal credit. The Universal Credit (Transitional Provisions) Regulations 2014 (SI 2014/1230) set out the categories of person who are capable of claiming universal credit. The general rule is that a person who is able to make a claim for universal credit is unable to claim a tax credit (art.7 of the No.23 Commencement Order. Cases 2 and 3 operate as exemptions to this general rule.

Case 4 – article 3(5)

Case 4 applies to an award, not falling with Case 2 or Case 3, for a period beginning on or after February 1, 2019, of:

   (a) child tax credit where, on the date of claim, the person/s have an award of working tax credit; and

   (b) working tax credit where, on the date of claim, the person/s have an award of child tax credit;

   (c) either tax credit where the claimant/s had an award of the same type of tax credit for the previous tax year.

For these purposes, a person is treated as having an award of tax credit even if a decision on a claim for tax credit under s.14 of the Tax Credits Act 2002 is awaited, in the cases described in art.3(7).

Case 5 – article 3(9)

Case 5 applies to an award of a tax credit that had effect for a period that ended on or before January 30, 2019.

Appointed day – coming into force of universal credit provisions and abolition of income-related employment and support allowance and income-based jobseeker's allowance: persons resident outside Great Britain

4.—(1) The day appointed for the coming into force of the UC provisions, in so far as they are not already in force, in relation to the case of a   **3.281**

claim referred to in paragraph (2), and any award that is made in respect of the claim, is the day appointed in accordance with paragraph (3).

(2) The claim referred to is a claim for universal credit that is made on or after 1st February 2019 in respect of a period that begins on or after 1st February 2019 where, on the date that the claim is made, the claimant (in the case of UC joint claimants, either claimant) resides outside Great Britain.

(3) The day appointed in relation to the case of a claim referred to in paragraph (2), and any award that is made in respect of the claim, is the first day of the period in respect of which the claim is made.

(4) Article 3(6) of the No. 9 Order applies for the purposes of paragraph (3) as it applies for the purposes of article 3(4)(a) of the No. 9 Order.

(5) The day appointed for the coming into force of the provisions referred to in article 4(1)(a) to (c) of the No. 9 Order, in so far as they are not already in force, in relation to the case of a claim referred to in paragraph (6), and any award that is made in respect of the claim, is the day appointed in accordance with paragraph (7).

(6) The claims referred to are—

(a) a claim for universal credit that is made on or after 1st February 2019 in respect of a period that begins on or after 1st February 2019 where, on the date that the claim is made, the claimant (in the case of UC joint claimants, either claimant) resides outside Great Britain;

(b) a claim for an employment and support allowance or a jobseeker's allowance that is made on or after 1st February 2019 in respect of a period that begins on or after 1st February 2019 where, on the date that the claim is made, the claimant (in the case of a claim for a jobseeker's allowance by a joint-claim couple, or a claim for either allowance by a person who would form part of a UC couple for the purposes of universal credit, either member of the couple) resides outside Great Britain;

(c) a claim for an employment and support allowance or a jobseeker's allowance other than one referred to in sub-paragraph (b) that is made or treated as made during the relevant period by a UC single claimant or by either of two UC joint claimants who has or have made a claim for universal credit under sub-paragraph (a).

(7) The day appointed in relation to the case of a claim referred to in paragraph (6), and any award that is made in respect of the claim, is the first day of the period in respect of which the claim is made.

(8) Paragraphs (6), (7), (9) and (10) of article 4 of the No. 9 Order apply in relation to a claim for universal credit referred to in paragraph (6)(a) (and any award that is made in respect of the claim) as they apply to a claim for universal credit referred to in sub-paragraph (a) or (b) of article 4(2) of the No. 9 Order (and any award that is made in respect of the claim).

(9) Article 5(8) of the No. 9 Order applies for the purposes of paragraph (7) as it applies for the purposes of article 4(3)(a) of the No. 9 Order.

(10) Article 7 of the No. 23 Order applies as though the reference in paragraph (1) of that article to article 3(1) and (2)(a) to (c) of that Order included a reference to paragraphs (1) and (2).

(11) No claim may be made for universal credit on or after 1st February 2019 by a UC single claimant who is, or UC joint claimants each of whom is, a frontier worker.

(12) Articles 9 to 22 of the No. 9 Order apply in connection with the

coming into force of the provisions referred to in article 4(1)(a) to (c) of the No. 9 Order, in relation to the case of a claim referred to in paragraph (6), and any award made in respect of the claim, as they apply in connection with the coming into force of those provisions in relation to the case of a claim referred to in sub-paragraph (a) or (g) of article 4(2) of the No. 9 Order and any award that is made in respect of the claim.

(13) In this article—

(a) "claimant"—

    (i) in relation to an employment and support allowance, has the same meaning as in Part 1 of the Welfare Reform Act 2007;

    (ii) in relation to a jobseeker's allowance, has the same meaning as in the Jobseeker's Act 1995 (as it applies apart from the amendments made by Part 1 of Schedule 14 to the Act that remove references to an income-based jobseeker's allowance), save as mentioned in paragraph (6)(b);

    (iii) in relation to universal credit, has the same meaning as in Part 1 of the Act, save as mentioned in paragraph (2) and (6)(a);

(b) "relevant period" means, in relation to a claim for universal credit within paragraph (6)(a), any UC claim period, and any period subsequent to any UC claim period in respect of which the claimant is entitled to an award of universal credit in respect of the claim;

(c) "UC claim period" means a period when—

    (i) a claim for universal credit within paragraph (6)(a) has been made but a decision has not yet been made on the claim; or

    (ii) a decision has been made that the claimant is not entitled to universal credit and—

        (aa) the Secretary of State is considering whether to revise that decision under section 9 of the Social Security Act 1998, whether on an application made for that purpose or on the Secretary of State's own initiative; or

        (bb) the claimant has appealed against that decision to the First-tier Tribunal and that appeal, or any subsequent appeal to the Upper Tribunal or a court, has not yet been finally determined;

(d) the Universal Credit, Personal Independence Payment, Jobseeker's Allowance and Employment and Support Allowance (Claims and Payments) Regulations 2013 apply for the purpose of deciding—

    (i) whether a claim for universal credit is made;

    (ii) the date on which such a claim is made;

(e) the Claims and Payments Regulations 1987 apply, subject to sub-paragraphs (f) and (g), for the purpose of deciding—

    (i) whether a claim for an employment and support allowance or a jobseeker's allowance is made; and

    (ii) the date on which the claim is made or treated as made;

(f) subject to sub-paragraph (g)—

    (i) a person makes a claim for an employment and support allowance or a jobseeker's allowance if he or she takes any action which results in a decision on a claim being required under the Claims and Payments Regulations 1987; and

    (ii) it is irrelevant that the effect of any provision of those Regulations is that, for the purposes of those Regulations, the claim is made or treated as made at a date that is earlier than the date on which that action is taken;

(g) where, by virtue of—

(i) regulation 6(1F)(b) or (c) of the Claims and Payments Regulations 1987, in the case of a claim for an employment and support allowance; or

(ii) regulation 6(4ZA) to (4ZD) and (4A)(a)(i) and (b) of those Regulations, in the case of a claim for a jobseeker's allowance,

a claim for an employment and support allowance or a jobseeker's allowance is treated as made at a date that is earlier than the date on which the action referred to in sub-paragraph (f)(i) is taken, the claim is treated as made on that earlier date.

GENERAL NOTE

3.282   Article 4, which extends to Great Britain only, commences the provisions in Part 1 of the WRA 2012 that relate to universal credit and the abolition of IR-ESA and IB-JSA for the cases set out in this article.

Article 4(1) and (2) bring into force the provisions relating to universal credit (listed in Schedule 2 to the No.9 Commencement Order 2013 in relation to a claim for universal credit that is made on or after February 1, 2019 with respect to a period that begins on or after that date, where the claimant (in the case of joint claimants, either of them) resides outside Great Britain. This includes a Crown servant or a member of Her Majesty's forces posted overseas. Article 4(5) and (6) bring into force the provisions of the Act relating to the abolition of the two legacy benefits in relation to a claim for universal credit, ESA or JSA that is made on or after February 1, 2019 with respect to a period that begins on or after that date, where the claimant (in the case of joint claimants, either of them) resides outside Great Britain. Article 4(10) applies provisions in art.7 of the No. 23 Commencement Order to the commencement of the universal credit provisions such that a claim may not be made for housing benefit, income support or a tax credit where under this Order a claim may be made for universal credit, subject to the exceptions stated. Article 4(11) provides that a claim for universal credit may not be made by a single claimant or joint claimants where the claimant or each of the joint claimants is a "frontier worker" (see art.1(3)(a)).

Amendment of the No. 9, No. 21 and No. 23 Orders

3.283   **5.**—

GENERAL NOTE

3.284   The amendments made by art.5 to the No. 9, No. 21 and No. 23 Orders with effect from February 1, 2019 have been incorporated in the text of those Orders (above).

The Welfare Reform Act 2012 (Commencement No. 33) Order 2019

SI 2019/1135 (C. 34)

Made: 17th July 2019

The Secretary of State for Work and Pensions makes the following Order in exercise of the powers conferred by section 150(3) of the Welfare Reform Act 2012:

Citation

1. This Order may be cited as the Welfare Reform Act 2012 (Commencement No. 33) Order 2019.

3.285

Appointed day

2. The appointed day for the coming into force of section 36 of, and Schedule 6 to, the Welfare Reform Act 2012 in so far as they are not already in force, is the day after this Order is made.

3.286

GENERAL NOTE

This Order brings into force, on the day after it is made, the remaining regulation-making powers in Sch.6 to the Welfare Reform Act 2012. The Schedule enables the Secretary of State to make provision by regulations for the purpose of, or in connection with, replacing existing benefits (see s.33 of that Act, which specifies the "existing benefits" that are to be replaced) with universal credit.

3.287

PART IIIC

SAVINGS PROVISIONS

The Universal Credit (Digital Service) Amendment Regulations 2014

(2014/2887)

The Secretary of State for Work and Pensions, in exercise of the powers conferred by section 1(1) of the Social Security Administration Act 1992(1) and sections 4(3), 7(3), 8(3), 9(2), 10(3), 11(4), 12(1) and (3), 19(2)(d), 32(1) and (4), 42(2) and (3) of, and paragraph 3(2) of Schedule 1 to, the Welfare Reform Act 2012(2), makes the following Regulations:

In accordance with section 173(1)(b) of the Social Security Administration Act 1992, the Social Security Advisory Committee has agreed that the proposals for these Regulations need not be referred to it.

[In force November, 26 2014]

Citation and commencement

1. These Regulations may be cited as the Universal Credit (Digital Service) Amendment Regulations 2014 and, subject to regulation 5 (saving), come into force on 26th November 2014.

3.288

Universal credit - childcare costs

2. *[Omitted: see the amendments to regs. 33, 34 and 34A of the Universal Credit Regulations 2013, above.]*

3.289

Universal Credit - assessment periods

3. *[Omitted: see the amendments to regs 15, 21 and 22A of the Universal Credit Regulations 2013; regs 6, 9 and 26 of the Universal Credit, Personal Independence Payment, Jobseeker's Allowance and Employment and Support Allowance (Claims and Payments) Regulations 2013 above and reg. 7 of the Universal Credit (Transitional Provisions) Regulations 2013 below.]*

3.290

Universal Credit – calculation of unearned income

4. *[Omitted: see the amendment to reg. 73 of the Universal Credit Regulations 2013, above.]*

3.291

Saving

[⁴ **5.**—(1) The amendments made by these Regulations do not apply to an award of universal credit unless it is—

3.292

    (a) an award to which a person has become entitled by reference to residence in a digital service area (whether or not the person is still living in that area);

    (b) an award to which a person who is living in a digital service area is entitled (whether or not the person was living in that area at the time that person became entitled);

    (c) an award, not falling within sub-paragraph (a) or (b), to which a person who has lived in a digital service area at any time after it became a digital service area is entitled but only if that award has been administered on the digital service computer system;

(d) an award not falling within sub-paragraphs (a) to (c)—
    (i) which is made to members of a couple jointly as a consequence of a previous award having ended when the couple formed, or
    (ii) which is made to a single claimant as a consequence of a previous award having ended when the claimant ceased to be a member of a couple,

where that previous award was administered on the digital service computer system.

(2) Where the date on which these Regulations first apply to an existing award of universal credit by virtue of paragraph (1)(b) is not the first day of an assessment period, they are not to have effect in relation to that award until the first day of the next assessment period.

(3) In this regulation—

"a digital service area" means—
(a) postcode districts SM5 2, SM6 7 and SM6 8; and
(b) an area in respect of which no restrictions have been imposed in order for the universal credit provisions to come into force on a claim for universal credit (apart from with respect to residence and the date on which, or period in respect of which, universal credit is claimed) by an order under section 150 of the Welfare Reform Act 2012 or an area (apart from that referred to in (a)) in respect of which such restrictions have been, but are no longer, imposed;

"the digital service computer system" is the computer system operated by the Secretary of State in digital service areas;

"universal credit provisions" means the provisions listed in Schedule 2 to the Welfare Reform Act 2012 (Commencement No.9 and Transitional and Transitory Provisions and Commencement No.8 and Savings and Transitional Provisions (Amendment)) Order 2013.]

AMENDMENT

1. Welfare Reform Act 2012 (Commencement No.22 and Transitional and Transitory Provisions) Order 2015 (SI 2015/101) art 6 (February 16, 2015).
2. Welfare Reform Act 2012 (Commencement No.23 and Transitional and Transitory Provisions) Order 2015 (SI 2015/634) art.10 (March 18, 2015).
3. Welfare Reform Act 2012 (Commencement No.24 and Transitional and Transitory Provisions and Commencement No.9 and Transitional and Transitory Provisions (Amendment)) Order 2015 (SI 2015/1537) arts 7 and 8 (September 21, 2015).
4. Universal Credit and Miscellaneous Amendments Regulations 2015 (SI 2015/1754) reg.20 (November 4, 2015).

The Shared Parental Leave and Statutory Shared Parental Pay (Consequential Amendments to Subordinate Legislation) Order 2014

(2014/3255)

In force in accordance with art.1(2) and (3)
The Secretary of State makes the following Order in exercise of the powers

conferred by section 135(3) and 136(1) and (2) of the Children and Families Act 2014.

Citation and commencement

1.-(1) This Order may be cited as the Shared Parental Leave and Statutory Shared Parental Pay (Consequential Amendments to Subordinate Legislation) Order 2014.

(2) The provisions of this Order specified in article 37 come into force on 31st December 2014.

(3) The remaining provisions of this Order come into force on 5th April 2015

Amendment of Miscellaneous Regulations

2.-34. *[Omitted—Where relevant the amendments have been noted in the text of the Universal Credit Regulations (above) and in Vols I-IV]*

Transitional provisions

35.-(1) The amendments made by this Order in those articles which come into force on 5th April 2015 in accordance with 1(3) (amendments relating to references to ordinary and additional paternity leave and to ordinary and additional statutory paternity pay) do not have effect in relation to—
(a) ordinary statutory paternity pay which is paid;
(b) additional statutory paternity pay which is paid;
(c) a period in respect of which additional statutory paternity pay is payable which begins, or continues;
(d) ordinary paternity leave which is taken; or
(e) additional paternity leave which is taken;
on or after 5th April 2015.

(2) In this article—
"additional paternity leave" means leave under section 80AA or 80BB of the Employment Rights Act 1996;
"additional statutory paternity pay" means pay under section 171ZEA or 171ZEB of the Social Security Contributions and Benefits Act 1992;
"ordinary paternity leave" means leave under section 80A or 80B of the Employment Rights Act 1996;
"ordinary statutory paternity pay" means pay under section 171ZA or 171ZB of the Social Security Contributions and Benefits Act 1992.

36. *[Omitted as relating solely to Northern Ireland]*
Provisions coming into force on 31st December 2014
37. The provisions specified in article 1(2) are—
(a) this article;
(b) article 1;
(c)-(y) *[Omitted]*
(z) article 28(1), (2)(c), (3)(c) and (4)(c) and (d);
(aa)-(hh) *[Omitted]*
(gg) article 35;
(hh) *[Omitted]*.

3.293

3.294

3.295

3.296

3.297

The Social Security (Housing Costs Amendments) Regulations 2015

(SI 2015/1647)

Made by the Secretary of State for Work and Pensions under ss.123(1)(a), 135(1), 137(1) and 175(1), (3) and (4) of the Social Security Contributions and Benefits Act 1992, ss.4(5), 35(1) and 36(2) and (4) of the Jobseekers Act 1995, ss.4(2)(a), 24(1) and 25(2), (3) and (5) of the Welfare Reform Act 2007 and ss.11(4) and (5)(b), 40, 42(1), (2) and (3) of, and para.1 of Sch.6 to, the Welfare Reform Act 2012.

[In force April 1, 2016]

Citation and commencement

3.298   **1.** These Regulations may be cited as the Social Security (Housing Costs Amendments) Regulations 2015 and come into force on 1st April 2016.

Amendment of the Income Support (General) Regulations 1987, the Jobseeker's Allowance Regulations 1996 and the Employment and Support Allowance Regulations 2008

3.299   **2-4.** *[Omitted]*

Amendment of the Universal Credit Regulations 2013

3.300   **5.** *[Omitted – see the amendments to para.5(2)(a) and (b) of Sch. 5 to the Universal Credit Regulations 2013 in Pt. III]*

Amendment of the Universal Credit (Transitional Provisions) Regulations 2014

3.301   **6.** *[Omitted – see the amendment to reg. 29 of the Universal Credit (Transitional Provisions) Regulations 2014 in Pt. IV]*

Revocation

3.302   **7.** *[Omitted as not relevant to universal credit]*

Saving provision

3.303   **8.**—(1) This regulation applies to a person ("P") where, for the purpose of determining whether P's entitlement to a relevant benefit includes an amount for housing costs, the Secretary of State determines that P is entitled or required to be treated as entitled to one or more relevant benefits for a continuous period which includes 31st March 2016.

(2) Where this regulation applies to P, the provisions of—

(a) Schedule 6 to the Employment and Support Allowance Regulations 2008;

(b) Schedule 3 to the Income Support (General) Regulations 1987; and

(c) Schedule 2 to the Jobseeker's Allowance Regulations 1996,

as modified by the Social Security (Housing Costs Special Arrangements)

(Amendment and Modification) Regulations 2008 are to have effect in relation to P as if the amendments made by regulations 2 to 4 of these Regulations and the revocation made by regulation 7(1) had not been made.

(3) Where this regulation applies to P, the provisions of Schedule 5 to the Universal Credit Regulations 2013 are to have effect in relation to P as if the amendments made by regulations 5 and 6 of these Regulations had not been made.

(4) In this regulation, "relevant benefit" means—

(a) an employment and support allowance under Part 1 of the Welfare Reform Act 2007;

(b) income support under the Income Support (General) Regulations 1987;

(c) a jobseeker's allowance under the Jobseeker's Allowance Regulations 1996; and

(d) universal credit under Part 1 of the Welfare Reform Act 2012.

The Employment and Support Allowance and Universal Credit (Miscellaneous Amendments and Transitional and Savings Provisions) Regulations 2017

(SI 2017/204)

In Force April 3, 2017

REGULATIONS REPRODUCED

3.304

The Secretary of State for Work and Pensions makes the following Regulations in exercise of the powers conferred by sections 12(1), 17(4), 18(3), 19(2)(d), 25(a) and 42(3)(a) of the Welfare Reform Act 2012 and sections 15(4) and (5) and 34(1) of the Welfare Reform and Work Act 2016.

In accordance with section 173(5)(b) of the Social Security Administration Act 1992, this instrument contains only regulations made by virtue of, or consequential upon, sections 15, 16, 17 and 34 of the Welfare Reform and Work Act 2016 and is made before the end of the period of 6 months beginning with the coming into force of those sections.

In accordance with section 176(1) of the Social Security Administration Act 1992 the Secretary of State has consulted with organisations appearing to him to be representative of the authorities concerned.

GENERAL NOTE

3.305   Parts 1-3 of, and Sch.1 to, these Regulations, taken together and ss.15-17 of the Welfare Reform and Work Act 2016, abolish the LCW element of universal credit (and the work-related activity component of ESA) with effect from April 3, 2017 and make a number of consequential amendments. However, for universal credit, the abolition is subject to the transitional and savings provisions in Sch.2, Pt.2, to which effect is given by reg.2. Part 1 of the Schedule contains equivalent provisions for ESA and is reproduced in Vol.II.

Under Pt.2 of Sch.2, claimants who are found to have—or are treated as having—limited capability for work, but not limited capability for work-related activity, continue to be entitled to the LCW component in the following circumstances:

- There was an award of universal credit immediately before April 3, 2017 and that award included the LCW element, or would have done so if that element were not excluded by the three-month waiting period in reg.28(1) of the Universal Credit Regulations (para.9).

- There was an award of universal credit immediately before April 3, 2017 and that award included the LCWRA element, and it is subsequently decided that the claimant only has limited capability for work (para.10). This only applies where the claimant has had both limited capability for work and limited capability for work-related activity throughout the period from April 3, 2017 to the date on which it is determined that they only have limited capability for work.

- There was a claim for universal credit before April 3, 2017 and—also before that date—the claimant provided medical evidence of having limited capability for work. In those circumstances, the claimant will be entitled to the LCW element even if the determination that they have limited capability for work is not made until after April 3, 2017 and even if that determination is made on revision by the Secretary of State or on appeal by the First-tier Tribunal or Upper Tribunal (para.11).

- Article 24 of the Welfare Reform Act 2012 (Commencement No 9 and Transitional and Transitory Provisions and Commencement No 8 and Savings and Transitional Provisions (Amendment)) Order 2013 (see Part IVB below) provides that, where an award of universal credit is made and subsequently a decision is made to revise or supersede and earlier decision about old style ESA (or old style JSA) (or there is a final decision on an appeal against such a decision) the Secretary of State must consider whether to revise (or, in some circumstances, supersede) the universal credit decision. Where the claim for old style ESA was made, or treated as made, before April 3, 2013 and a decision is made to revise the universal credit decision after that date, then, if the revising decision includes a determination that the claimant has limited capability for work, the LCW element is to be included in the universal credit award (para.12).

- The claimant was entitled to employment and support allowance immediately before April 3, 2017 and remains so entitled until the date on which a subsequent claim for universal credit is made or treated as made (para.13).

- The claimant does not fall within the previous paragraph but was entitled to incapacity credits immediately before April 3, 2017 and remains so entitled until the date on which a subsequent claim for universal credit is made or treated as made (para.14).

- The claimant is entitled to income support on the grounds of incapacity for work or disability, or incapacity benefit or severe disablement allowance immediately before April 3, 2017 and regs 22-24, 26 or 27 of the Universal Credit (Transitional Provisions) Regulations 2014 applies to him or her from then until the date on which a subsequent claim for universal credit is made or treated as made (para.15).

The LCW element continues to be payable under Sch,2, Pt.2 for as long as continues to be entitled to universal credit and to have limited capability for work (para.8(1)(b)). Continuity of entitlement is not broken (i) where the award of universal credit but a further award begins immediately because the claimant ceased to be a member of a couple or became a member of a couple (para.8(2) (a)); or (ii) the award ends because the claimant's income (or the joint claimants' combined income) was too high but a further award is made within six months (para.8(2)(b)).

Citation and commencement

1. These Regulations may be cited as the Employment and Support Allowance and Universal Credit (Miscellaneous Amendments and Transitional and Savings Provisions) Regulations 2017 and come into force on 3rd April 2017.

3.306

PART 4

CONSEQUENTIAL, TRANSITIONAL AND SAVINGS PROVISIONS

Consequential, transitional and savings provisions

7.—(1) [Omitted]

(2) Schedule 2 contains transitional and savings provisions.

3.307

Regulation 7(2)

SCHEDULE 2

TRANSITIONAL AND SAVINGS PROVISIONS

PART 2

UNIVERSAL CREDIT: TRANSITIONAL AND SAVINGS PROVISIONS

Transitional and savings provisions: General

8.—(1) The amendments made by regulations 4 and 5 and paragraphs 13, 16 and 17 of Schedule 1 do not apply—

(a) where a claimant has an award of universal credit in any of the circumstances in the following paragraphs; and

(b) for so long as the claimant continues to be entitled to universal credit and to have limited capability for work.

(2) For the purposes of sub-paragraph (1)(b), the reference to continuous entitlement to universal credit includes where an award has terminated and a further award is made and—

(a) immediately before the further award commences, the previous award has terminated because the claimant ceased to be a member of a couple or became a member of a couple; or

(b) within the six months beginning with the date that the further award commences, the previous award has terminated because the financial condition in section 5(1)(b) or, if it was a joint claim, section 5(2)(b), of the Welfare Reform Act 2012 was not met.

(3) In this Part—

3.308

"employment and support allowance" means an employment and support allowance under Part 1 of the Welfare Reform Act 2007;

"LCW element" and "LCWRA element" have the meanings in regulation 27 of the Universal Credit Regulations 2013 as it has effect apart from the amendments made by regulation 4(4) (which remove references to the LCW element);

"limited capability for work" has the meaning given in section 37(1) of the Welfare Reform Act 2012.

(4) The Universal Credit, Personal Independence Payment, Jobseeker's Allowance and Employment and Support Allowance (Claims and Payments) Regulations 2013 apply for the purpose of deciding the date on which a claim for universal credit is made or is to be treated as made.

Claimants entitled to the LCW element before 3rd April 2017

3.309   9. The first circumstance is where immediately before 3rd April 2017 the award included the LCW element, or would have but for regulation 28(1) of the Universal Credit Regulations 2013, as it has effect apart from the amendments made by regulation 4(5)(a) (which removes the reference to the LCW element).

Claimants entitled to the LCWRA element before 3rd April 2017

3.310   10. The second circumstance is where—
  (a) immediately before 3rd April 2017 the award included the LCWRA element;
  (b) on or after 3rd April 2017 a determination that the claimant has limited capability for work is made; and
  (c) the claimant had limited capability for work and work-related activity throughout the period beginning immediately before 3rd April 2017 and ending with the date on which the determination that the claimant has limited capability for work is made.

Claimants who are providing evidence of having limited capability for work before 3rd April 2017

3.311   11. The third circumstance is where—
  (a) before 3rd April 2017—
    (i) it falls to be determined whether the claimant has limited capability for work; and
    (ii) the claimant has provided evidence of having limited capability for work in accordance with the Social Security (Medical Evidence) Regulations 1976; and
  (b) on or after 3rd April 2017 a determination that the claimant has limited capability for work is made on the basis of an assessment under Part 5 of the Universal Credit Regulations 2013, on revision under section 9 of the Social Security Act 1998 or on appeal.

Claimants who appeal or seek revision of a decision relating to employment and support allowance

3.312   12. The fourth circumstance is where—
  (a) the claimant appeals or seeks revision under section 9 of the Social Security Act 1998 of a decision relating to the entitlement of the claimant to an employment and support allowance, where the claim for employment and support allowance was made or treated as made before 3rd April 2017; and
  (b) on or after 3rd April 2017, in accordance with article 24 of the Welfare Reform Act 2012 (Commencement No 9 and Transitional and Transitory Provisions and Commencement No 8 and Savings and Transitional Provisions (Amendment)) Order 2013, the Secretary of State considers it appropriate to revise under section 9 of the Social Security Act 1998 an award of universal credit so as to include the LCW element.

Claimants entitled to employment and support allowance before 3rd April 2017

3.313   13. The fifth circumstance is where immediately before 3rd April 2017 the claimant was entitled to employment and support allowance and remains so entitled throughout the period beginning with 3rd April 2017 and ending with the date on which the claim for universal credit is made or treated as made.

Claimants entitled to be credited with earnings under the Social Security (Credits) Regulations 1975 before 3rd April 2017

3.314   14. The sixth circumstance is where—
  (a) immediately before 3rd April 2017—
    (i) the claimant entitled to the award was entitled to be credited with earnings

equal to the lower earnings limit then in force in respect of a week to which regulation 8B(2)(a)(iv), (iva) or (v) of the Social Security (Credits) Regulations 1975 applies; and

    (ii) paragraph 13 does not apply to that claimant; and

  (b) the claimant is so entitled in respect of each week that falls in the period beginning with 3rd April 2017 and ending with the date on which the claim for universal credit is made or treated as made.

Claimants entitled to income support or other incapacity benefits before 3rd April 2017

15. The seventh circumstance is where regulation 22, 23, 24, 26 or 27 of the Universal Credit (Transitional Provisions) Regulations 2014 applies to the claimant throughout the period beginning immediately before 3rd April 2017 and ending with the date on which the claim for universal credit is made or treated as made.

3.315

The Universal Credit (Housing Costs Element for claimants aged 18 to 21) (Amendment) Regulations 2017

(SI 2017/252)

Made by the Secretary of State under sections 11(5)(a) and 42(2) and (3) of the Welfare Reform Act 2012.

3.316

[In force April 1, 2017]

GENERAL NOTE

See the commentary to paras 4A-4C of Sch.4 to the Universal Credit Regulations at paras 2.386 – 2.388 of Vol.V of the 2018/19 edition.

3.317

These Regulations introduced the exclusions from entitlement to the housing costs element of universal credit contained in paras 4A-4C with effect from April 1, 2017. They were reproduced here because regs 3 and 4 contained transitional protection from those exclusion for, respectively, claimants not living in a digital service area and claimants who had been entitled to housing benefit or had an award of universal credit that included the housing costs element: see further paras 3.731-3.732 of Vol.V of the 2018/19 edition.

The Regulations were revoked with effect from December 31, 2018 by SI 2018/1129, which also revoked paras 4A-4C.

PART IV

UNIVERSAL CREDIT: CLAIMS &
PAYMENTS AND DECISIONS & APPEALS

The Universal Credit, Personal Independence Payment, Jobseeker's Allowance and Employment and Support Allowance (Claims and Payments) Regulations 2013

(SI 2013/380)

The Secretary of State, in exercise of the powers conferred upon him by the provisions set out in Schedule 1 to these Regulations, makes the following Regulations.

In accordance with section 172(1) of the Social Security Administration Act 1992, the Secretary of State has referred the proposals for these Regulations to the Social Security Advisory Committee.

The Secretary of State has consulted with organisations representing qualifying lenders likely to be affected by the fee specified in paragraph 9(2) of Schedule 5 to the Regulations (direct payment to lender of deductions in respect of interest on secured loans).

In accordance with section 176(2)(b) of the Social Security Administration Act 1992 and in so far as these Regulations relate to housing benefit, the Secretary of State has obtained the agreement of organisations appearing to him to be representative of the authorities concerned that proposals in respect of these Regulations should not be referred to them.

ARRANGEMENT OF REGULATIONS

PART I

GENERAL

PART II

CLAIMS

Part III

Evidence, information and notification of changes of circumstances

Part IV

Payments

Part V

Third parties

Part VI

Mobility component of personal independence payment

GENERAL NOTE

4.2   These Regulations are included in Vol.III. However, they are also reproduced in full below (except for Sch.3 which made consequential amendments to other legislation). The provisions which relate to universal credit are annotated in this volume. Readers are referred to Vol.III for commentary on the provisions which relate to personal independence payment or are of general application. These Regulations are in force from April 8, 2013 in relation to personal independence payment and April 29, 2013 in relation to universal credit, new-style ESA and new-style JSA.

PART I

GENERAL

Citation and commencement

4.3   **1.**—(1) These Regulations may be cited as the Universal Credit, Personal Independence Payment, Jobseeker's Allowance and Employment and Support Allowance (Claims and Payments) Regulations 2013.

(2) For the purpose of personal independence payment these Regulations come into force on 8th April 2013.

(3) For the purposes of universal credit, jobseeker's allowance and employment and support allowance these Regulations come into force on 29th April 2013.

Interpretation

4.4   **2.** In these Regulations—
"the 1991 Act" means the Child Support Act 1991;
"the 2012 Act" means the Welfare Reform Act 2012;
"the Administration Act" means the Social Security Administration Act 1992;
"the Contributions and Benefits Act" means the Social Security Contributions and Benefits Act 1992;
"the Jobseeker's Allowance Regulations" means the Jobseeker's Allowance Regulations 2013;
"the Personal Independence Payment Regulations" means the Social Security (Personal Independence Payment) Regulations 2013;
"the Universal Credit Regulations" means the Universal Credit Regulations 2013;
"appropriate office" means—
(a) an office of the Department for Work and Pensions or any other place designated by the Secretary of State in relation to any case or class of case as a place to, or at which, any claim, notice, document, evidence or other information may be sent, delivered or received for the purposes of these Regulations and includes a postal address specified by the Secretary of State for that purpose; or
(b) in the case of a person who is authorised or required by these Regulations to use an electronic communication for any purpose, an

address to which such communications may be sent in accordance with Schedule 2;

"assessment period" has the meaning given by regulation 21 of the Universal Credit Regulations;

"attendance allowance" means an allowance payable by virtue of section 64 of the Contributions and Benefits Act;

"benefit", except in regulation 60 and Schedules 5 and 6, means universal credit, personal independence payment, a jobseeker's allowance or an employment and support allowance;

"child" has the meaning given by section 40 of the 2012 Act;

"claimant" in relation to—

(a) universal credit, has the meaning given by section 40 of the 2012 Act;

(b) personal independence payment, means any person who is a claimant for the purposes of regulations made under Part 4 (personal independence payment) of that Act;

(c) a jobseeker's allowance, has the meaning given by section 35(1) of the Jobseekers Act 1995; and

(d) an employment and support allowance, has the meaning given by section 24(1) of the Welfare Reform 2007 Act;

"couple" has the meaning given by section 39 of the 2012 Act;

"disability living allowance" means an allowance payable by virtue of section 71 of the Contributions and Benefits Act;

"earned income" has the meaning given by regulation 52 of the Universal Credit Regulations;

"electronic communication" has the meaning given by section 15(1) of the Electronic Communications Act 2000;

"employment and support allowance" means an allowance under Part 1 of the Welfare Reform Act 2007 as amended by the provisions of Schedule 3, and Part 1 of Schedule 14, to the 2012 Act that remove references to an income-related allowance;

"jobseeker's allowance" means an allowance under the Jobseekers Act 1995 as amended by the provisions of Part 1 of Schedule 14 to the 2012 Act that remove references to an income-based allowance;

"limited capability for work" has the meaning given by section 1(4) of the Welfare Reform Act 2007;

"local authority" has the meaning given by section 191 of the Administration Act;

"maternity allowance" means an allowance payable by virtue of section 35 of the Contributions and Benefits Act;

"official computer system" means a computer system maintained by or on behalf of the Secretary of State to—

(a) send or receive any claim or information; or

(b) process or store any claim or information;

"partner" means one of a couple;

"personal independence payment" means the allowance under Part 4 of the 2012 Act;

"qualifying young person" has the meaning given by regulation 5 of the Universal Credit Regulations;

"regular and substantial caring responsibilities for a severely disabled person" has the meaning given by regulation 30 of the Universal Credit Regulations;

"universal credit" means the benefit under Part 1 of the 2012 Act;
"writing" includes writing produced by means of electronic communications used in accordance with Schedule 2.

Use of electronic communications

4.5   **3.** Schedule 2 makes provision as to the use of electronic communications.

DEFINITION

"electronic communication"—see reg.2.

Consequential amendments

4.6   **4.** Schedule 3 makes amendments to other regulations which are consequential upon these Regulations.

Disapplication of section 1(1A) of the Administration Act

4.7   **5.** Section 1(1A) of the Administration Act (requirements in respect of a national insurance number) is not to apply to a child or a qualifying young person in respect of whom universal credit is claimed.

DEFINITIONS

"the Administration Act"—see reg.2.
"universal credit"—*ibid.*

PART II

CLAIMS

Claims not required for entitlement to universal credit in certain cases

4.8   **6.** [¹ . . .]

AMENDMENT

1. Universal Credit (Digital Service) Amendment Regulations 2014 (SI 2014/2887) reg.3(2)(a) (November 26, 2014). The amendment is subject to the saving provision in reg.5 of SI 2014/2887 (see Pt IV).

GENERAL NOTE

4.9   SSAA 1992 s.1(1) provides that except in such cases as may be prescribed, no person shall be entitled to any benefit unless, in addition to satisfying any other conditions of entitlement, he or she "makes a claim for it in the manner, and within the time, prescribed in relation to that benefit by regulations" under SSAA Pt 1.

From April 29, 2014, reg.6 set out the exceptions to that general rule, in which a former entitlement to universal credit could revive without a claim being made, if not more than six months had elapsed since the previous entitlement ended. As a result of the saving provision in reg.5 of SI 2014/2887, those exceptions continue in "Live Service" cases and readers are referred to pp.432-3 of the 2013/14 edition for the text of the revoked regulation.

However, in "Full Service" or "Digital Service" cases (see *Universal Credit—An Introduction* (above)) reg.6 has been revoked from November 26, 2014. and the only such exceptions relate to people who cease to be—or become—members of a couple and are to be found in reg.9(6) and (7). Claimants who are subject to the Full Service rules, who were formerly entitled to universal credit and become so entitled again must now make a new claim. However, more favourable rules apply if the claim is made within six months of the old entitlement ending and (if applicable) within seven days of any claimant ceasing paid work: see UC Regulations regs 21(3C) and 22A.

Claims not required for entitlement to an employment and support allowance in certain cases

[¹ **7.**—(1) It is not to be a condition of entitlement to an employment and support allowance that a claim be made for it where—   4.10
  (a) the claimant has made and is pursuing an appeal against a relevant decision of the Secretary of State, and
  (b) the appeal relates to a decision to terminate or not to award an employment and support allowance for which a claim was made.
(2)   In this regulation—
"appellate authority" means the First-tier Tribunal, the Upper Tribunal, the Court of Appeal, the Court of Session, or the Supreme Court; and
"relevant decision" means—
  (a) a decision that embodies the first determination by the Secretary of State that the claimant does not have limited capability for work; or
  (b) a decision that embodies the first determination by the Secretary of State that the claimant does not have limited capability for work since a previous determination by the Secretary of State or appellate authority that the claimant does have limited capability for work.]

AMENDMENT

1. Employment and Support Allowance (Repeat Assessments and Pending Appeal Awards) (Amendment) Regulations 2015 (SI 2015/437) reg.6 (March 30, 2015).

DEFINITIONS

  "claimant"—see reg.2.
  "employment and support allowance"—*ibid.*

Making a claim for universal credit

8.—(1) Except as provided in paragraph (2), a claim for universal credit   4.11
must be made by means of an electronic communication in accordance with the provisions set out in Schedule 2 and completed in accordance with any instructions given by the Secretary of State for that purpose.
  (2) A claim for universal credit may be made by telephone call to the telephone number specified by the Secretary of State if the claim falls within a class of case for which the Secretary of State accepts telephone claims or where, in any other case, the Secretary of State is willing to do so.
  (3) A claim for universal credit made by means of an electronic communication in accordance with the provisions set out in Schedule 2 is defective if it is not completed in accordance with any instructions of the Secretary of State.

(4) A claim made by telephone in accordance with paragraph (2) is properly completed if the Secretary of State is provided during that call with all the information required to determine the claim and the claim is defective if not so completed.

(5) If a claim for universal credit is defective the Secretary of State must inform the claimant of the defect and of the relevant provisions of regulation 10 relating to the date of claim.

(6) The Secretary of State must treat the claim as properly made in the first instance if—

    (a) in the case of a claim made by telephone, the person corrects the defect; or

    (b) in the case of a claim made by means of an electronic communication, a claim completed in accordance with any instructions of the Secretary of State is received at an appropriate office,

within one month, or such longer period as the Secretary of State considers reasonable, from the date on which the claimant is first informed of the defect.

DEFINITIONS

    "appropriate office"—see reg.2.
    "claimant"—*ibid.*
    "electronic communication"—*ibid.*
    "universal credit"—*ibid.*

GENERAL NOTE

4.12   Regulation 8 and Sch.2 prescribe the manner in which a claim for universal credit must be made. The general rule (in accordance with the aspiration that universal credit is to be "digital by default") is that the claim must be made by "an electronic communication" in accordance with Sch.2. In brief, the claim must be made by completing and submitting an online claim form (para.(1)). However, a claim may instead be made by telephone if the Secretary of State is prepared to accept it in that form (para.(2)). For a detailed description of the online claim process see *GDC v SSWP (UC)* [2020] UKUT 108 (AAC), which holds that the claim is made when it has been submitted in accordance with all the requirements of Sch.2 below. In practice this is when the claimant, having entered all the data required by the online form, and confirmed the truth of that information, clicks on the "Submit claim" button, which automatically has the effect of delivering the claim to the Secretary of State. A claimant does not make a "defective claim" for the purposes of paras (3) and (5)-(6) by completing some of the information required by the form and saving the form online for future completion and submission.

Claims for universal credit by members of a couple

4.13   **9.**—(1) Where a person is a member of a couple and may make a claim as a single person by virtue of regulation 3(3) (couples) of the Universal Credit Regulations, but instead makes a claim for universal credit jointly, that claim is to be treated as a claim made by that person as a single person.

(2) Where a claim for universal credit is made jointly by a member ("M1") of a polygamous marriage with another member of the polygamous marriage ("M2"), that claim is to be treated as a claim made by M1 as a single person where—

    (a) M1 is not a party to an earlier marriage in the polygamous marriage, and

(b) any party to an earlier marriage is living in the same household as M1 and M2.

(3) In paragraph (2) "polygamous marriage" means a marriage during which a party to it is married to more than one person and which took place under the laws of a country which permits polygamy.

(4) The Secretary of State may treat a claim made by members of a couple as single persons as a claim made jointly by the couple where it is determined by the Secretary of State that they are a couple.

(5) Where the Secretary of State considers that one member of a couple is unable to make a joint claim with the other member of that couple, the other member of the couple may make a claim jointly for both of them.

[² (6) Where an award of universal credit to joint claimants is terminated because they cease to be a couple an award may be made, without a claim, to either or each one of them—

(a) as a single person; or

(b) if either of them has formed a new couple with a person who is already entitled to universal credit, jointly with that person.]

(7) Where awards of universal credit to two single claimants are terminated because they form a couple who are joint claimants, it is not to be a condition of entitlement to universal credit that the couple make a claim for it and universal credit may be awarded to them jointly.

(8) A couple who are joint claimants are to be treated as making a claim for universal credit where—

[² (a) one of them ceased to be entitled to an award of universal credit (whether as a single person or as a member of a different couple) on the formation of that couple;]

(b) the other member of the couple did not have an award of universal credit as a single person before formation of the couple

[¹ and the claim is to be treated as made on the day after the member of the couple mentioned in sub-paragraph (a) ceased to be entitled to universal credit.]

(9) In relation to an award which may be made by virtue of paragraph (6) or (7) without a claim being required, a claimant and every person by whom or on whose behalf, sums by way of universal credit are receivable must supply in such manner and at such times as the Secretary of State may determine such information or evidence as the Secretary of State may require in connection with the formation or dissolution of a couple.

(10) Where an award of universal credit to joint claimants is terminated because one of them has died it is not to be a condition of entitlement to universal credit that the surviving partner makes a claim for it.

DEFINITIONS

"couple"—see reg.2 and WRA 2012 s.39.
"universal credit"—see reg.2.

AMENDMENT

1. Social Security (Miscellaneous Amendments) (No.2) Regulations 2013 (SI 2013/1508) reg.6(1) and (2) (July 29, 2013).

2. Universal Credit (Digital Service) Amendment Regulations 2014 (SI 2014/2887) reg.3(2)(b) (November 26, 2014). The amendment is subject to the saving provision in reg.5 of SI 2014/2887 (see Pt IV).

GENERAL NOTE

4.14   See the commentary to reg.3 of the Universal Credit Regulations. The effect of the saving provision in reg.5 of SI 2014/2887 is that the amendments with effect from November 26, 2014 only apply in "Full Service" (aka "Digital Service" cases), see *Universal Credit—An Introduction* above. For the text of the regulation before those amendments, which continues to apply in "Live Service" cases, see pp.435-6 of the 2013/14 edition.

Date of claim for universal credit

4.15   **10.**—(1) Where a claim for universal credit is made, the date on which the claim is made is—

   (a) subject to sub-paragraph (b), in the case of a claim made by means of an electronic communication in accordance with regulation 8(1), the date on which the claim is received at an appropriate office;

   (b) in the case of a claim made by means of an electronic communication in accordance with regulation 8(1), where the claimant receives assistance at home or at an appropriate office from the Secretary of State, or a person providing services to the Secretary of State, which is provided for the purpose of enabling that person to make a claim, the date of first notification of a need for such assistance;

   (c) subject to sub-paragraph (d), in the case of a claim made by telephone in accordance with regulation 8(2), the date on which that claim is properly completed in accordance with regulation 8(4); or

   (d) where the Secretary of State is unable to accept a claim made by telephone in accordance with regulation 8(2) on the date of first notification of intention to make the claim, the date of first notification, provided a claim properly completed in accordance with regulation 8(4) is made within one month of that date,

or the first day in respect of which the claim is made if later than the above.

(2) In the case of a claim which is defective by virtue of regulation 8, the date of claim is to be the first date on which the defective claim is received or made but is treated as properly made in the first instance in accordance with regulation 8(6).

DEFINITIONS

   "appropriate office"—see reg.2.
   "claimant"—*ibid.*
   "electronic communication"—*ibid.*
   "universal credit"—*ibid.*

GENERAL NOTE

4.16   Regulation 10 identifies the date on which a claim for universal credit is made. Online claims are made when received by the DWP (para.(1)(a)), unless the person received assistance to complete the form from an officer of the Department (or a contractor providing services to the Secretary of State) in which case the date of claim is the date on which the Secretary of State was told that assistance was needed (para.(1)(b)). A telephone claim is made on the day reg.8(4) is satisfied (i.e., when the Secretary of State is provided with all the information required to determine the claim) (para.(1)(c)). But if the Department cannot accept a telephone claim on the same day as the claimant first notifies it that it would like to make one, then the claim is made on that day as long as a properly completed telephone claim is made within a month of that day (para.(1)(d)).

Paragraph (2) applies where a defective claim is treated as properly made in the first instance under reg.8(6). Such a claim is made on the first date the defective claim was received.

Making a claim for personal independence payment

11.—(1) A claim for personal independence payment must be made—

    4.17

(a) in writing on a form authorised by the Secretary of State for that purpose and completed in accordance with the instructions on the form;

(b) by telephone call to the telephone number specified by the Secretary of State; or

(c) by receipt by the claimant of a telephone call from the Secretary of State made for the purpose of enabling a claim for personal independence payment to be made,

unless in any case or class of case the Secretary of State decides only to accept a claim made in one of the ways specified in paragraph (a), (b) or (c).

(2) In the case of a claim made in writing the claim must be sent to or received at the appropriate office.

(3) A claim for personal independence payment made in writing is defective if it is not completed in accordance with any instructions of the Secretary of State.

(4) A claim made by telephone in accordance with paragraph (1) is properly completed if the Secretary of State is provided during that call with all the information required to determine the claim and the claim is defective if not so completed.

(5) If a claim for personal independence payment is defective the Secretary of State must inform the claimant of the defect and of the relevant provisions of regulation 12 relating to the date of claim.

(6) The Secretary of State must treat the claim as properly made in the first instance if a claim completed in accordance with any instructions of the Secretary of State is received within one month, or such longer period as the Secretary of State may consider reasonable, from the date on which the claimant is first informed of the defect.

(7) Paragraph (8) applies where—

(a) a person ("P1") makes a claim for personal independence payment on behalf of another person ("P2") whom P1 asserts to be a person unable for the time being to act; and

(b) the Secretary of State makes a decision not to appoint P1 under regulation 57.

(8) The Secretary of State must treat the claim made by P1 as properly made by P2 in the first instance if a further claim made by P2 is received within one month, or such longer period as the Secretary of State may consider reasonable, from the date the Secretary of State notified the decision not to appoint P1 under regulation 57.

DEFINITIONS

    "claimant"—see reg.2.
    "personal independence payment"—*ibid.*
    "writing"—*ibid.*

Date of claim for personal independence payment

4.18   **12.**—(1) Subject to paragraph (4), where a claim for personal independence payment is made in accordance with regulation 11 the date on which the claim is made is—

(a) in the case of a claim in writing made by means of an electronic communication in accordance with the provisions set out in Schedule 2, the date on which the claim is received at the appropriate office;

(b) in the case of a claim made by telephone, the date on which a claim made by telephone is properly completed; or

(c) where a person first notifies an intention to make a claim and provided that a claim made in writing produced other than by means of an electronic communication is properly completed and received at the appropriate office designated by the Secretary of State in that claimant's case within one month or such longer period as the Secretary of State considers reasonable of the date of first notification, the date of first notification,

or the first day in respect of which the claim is made if later than the above.

(2) In the case of a claim which is defective by virtue of regulation 11(3) or (4)—

(a) subject to sub-paragraph (b) and paragraph (4), the date of claim is to be the first date on which the defective claim is received or made but is treated as properly made in the first instance in accordance with regulation 11(6);

(b) the date of claim is to be the date of first notification of an intention to make a claim where a claim made by a person to whom paragraph (1)(c) applies is defective but is treated as properly made in the first instance in accordance with regulation 11(6).

(3) In the case of a claim which is treated as properly made by the claimant in accordance with regulation 11(8), the date on which the claim is made is the date on which it was received in the first instance.

(4) Where a further claim made by a person ("P2") in the circumstances set out in regulation 11(8) is defective and that further claim is treated as properly made in the first instance in accordance with regulation 11(6), the date of claim is to be the date on which the claim made by the person ("P1") whom the Secretary of State decided not to appoint under regulation 57 was received in the first instance.

(5) In a case where the Secretary of State decides not to award personal independence payment following a claim for it being made on behalf of another expressly on the ground of terminal illness (which has the meaning given by section 82(4) of the 2012 Act), the date of claim is to be—

(a) the date that claim was made if a further claim, made in accordance with regulation 11, is received within one month, or such longer period as the Secretary of State may consider reasonable, from the date the Secretary of State notified the decision not to award personal independence payment on the ground of terminal illness; or

(b) the date that claim was made where the further claim is defective but is treated as properly made in the first instance in accordance with regulation 11(6).

DEFINITIONS

"appropriate office"—see reg.2.
"claimant"—*ibid.*
"electronic communication"—*ibid.*
"personal independence payment"—*ibid.*
"writing"—*ibid.*

Making a claim for an employment and support allowance by telephone

13.—(1) Except where the Secretary of State directs in any case or class   **4.19**
of case that a claim must be made in writing, a claim for an employment
and support allowance may be made by telephone call to the telephone
number specified by the Secretary of State.

(2) Where the Secretary of State, in any particular case, directs that the
person making the claim approves a written statement of the person's circumstances provided for the purpose by the Secretary of State, a telephone
claim is not a valid claim unless the person complies with the direction.

(3) A claim made by telephone in accordance with paragraph (1) is properly completed if the Secretary of State is provided during that call with all
the information required to determine the claim and the claim is defective
if not so completed.

(4) Where a telephone claim is defective, the Secretary of State must
advise the person making it of the defect and of the effect on the date of
claim of the provisions of regulation 14.

(5) If the person corrects the defect so that the claim then satisfies the
requirements of paragraph (3) and does so within one month, or such
longer period as the Secretary of State considers reasonable, of the date the
Secretary of State first drew attention to the defect, the Secretary of State
must treat the claim as if it had been properly made in the first instance.

DEFINITION

"employment and support allowance"—see reg.2.

Date of claim for an employment and support allowance where claim made by telephone

14. In the case of a telephone claim, the date on which the claim is made   **4.20**
is to be the first date on which—
(a) a claim made by telephone is properly completed;
(b) a person first notifies the Secretary of State of an intention to make
a claim, provided that a claim made by telephone is properly completed within one month or such longer period as the Secretary of
State considers reasonable of first notification; or
(c) a defective claim is received but is treated as properly made in the
first instance in accordance with regulation 13(5),
or the first day in respect of which the claim is made if later than the
above.

Making a claim for an employment and support allowance in writing

4.21   **15.**—(1) A claim for an employment and support allowance may be made to the Secretary of State in writing on a form authorised by the Secretary of State for that purpose and must be completed in accordance with the instructions on the form.

(2) A written claim for an employment and support allowance, which is made on the form approved for the time being, is properly completed if completed in accordance with the instructions on the form and defective if not so completed.

(3) If a written claim is defective when first received, the Secretary of State must advise the person making it of the defect and of the effect on the date of claim of the provisions of regulation 16.

(4) If the person corrects the defect so that the claim then satisfies the requirements of paragraph (2) and does so within one month, or such longer period as the Secretary of State considers reasonable, of the date the Secretary of State first drew attention to the defect, the Secretary of State must treat the claim as if it had been properly made in the first instance.

DEFINITIONS

"employment and support allowance"—see reg.2.
"writing"—*ibid.*

Date of claim for an employment and support allowance where claim made in writing

4.22   **16.** In the case of a written claim for an employment and support allowance, the date on which the claim is made is to be the first date on which—

(a) a properly completed claim is received in an appropriate office;

(b) a person first notifies an intention to make a claim, provided that a properly completed claim form is received in an appropriate office within one month, or such longer period as the Secretary of State considers reasonable, of first notification; or

(c) a defective claim is received but is treated as properly made in the first instance in accordance with regulation 15(4),

or the first day in respect of which the claim is made if later than the above.

DEFINITIONS

"appropriate office"—see reg.2.
"employment and support allowance"—*ibid.*

Claims for an employment and support allowance where no entitlement to statutory sick pay

4.23   **17.**—(1) Paragraph (2) applies to a claim for an employment and support allowance for a period of limited capability for work in relation to which the claimant gave the claimant's employer a notice of incapacity under regulation 7 of the Statutory Sick Pay (General) Regulations 1982 and for which the claimant has been informed in writing by the employer that there is no entitlement to statutory sick pay.

(2) A claim to which this paragraph applies is to be treated as made on the date accepted by the claimant's employer as the first day of incapacity,

provided that the claimant makes the claim within the period of 3 months beginning with the day on which the claimant is informed in writing by the employer that the claimant was not entitled to statutory sick pay.

DEFINITIONS

"claimant"—see reg.2.
"employment and support allowance"—*ibid.*
"limited capability for work"—*ibid.*
"writing"—*ibid.*

Special provisions where it is certified that a woman is expected to be confined or where she has been confined

18. Where, in a certificate issued or having effect as issued under the Social Security (Medical Evidence) Regulations 1976, it has been certified that it is to be expected that a woman will be confined and she makes a claim for maternity allowance in expectation of that confinement, any such claim may, unless the Secretary of State otherwise directs, be treated as a claim for an employment and support allowance, made in respect of any days in the period beginning with either—
  (a) the beginning of the sixth week before the expected week of confinement; or
  (b) the actual date of confinement,
whichever is the earlier, and ending in either case on the 14th day after the actual date of confinement.

(2) Where, in a certificate issued under the Social Security (Medical Evidence) Regulations 1976 it has been certified that a woman has been confined and she claims maternity allowance within three months of the date of her confinement, her claim may be treated in the alternative or in addition as a claim for an employment and support allowance for the period beginning with the date of her confinement and ending 14 days after that date.

4.24

DEFINITIONS

"employment and support allowance"—see reg.2.
"maternity allowance"—*ibid.*

Making a claim for a jobseeker's allowance: attendance at an appropriate office

19. A person wishing to make a claim for a jobseeker's allowance, unless the Secretary of State otherwise directs, is required to attend for the purpose of making a claim for that allowance, in person at an appropriate office or such other place, and at such time, as the Secretary of State may specify in that person's case.

4.25

DEFINITIONS

"appropriate office"—see reg.2.
"jobseeker's allowance"—*ibid.*

Date of claim where a person claiming a jobseeker's allowance is required to attend at an appropriate office

20.—(1) Subject to regulation 29(6), where a person is required to attend in accordance with regulation 19, if the person subsequently attends for the

4.26

purpose of making a claim for a jobseeker's allowance at the place and time specified by the Secretary of State and, if so requested, provides a properly completed claim form at or before the time when the person is required to attend, the claim is to be treated as made on whichever is the later of the date of first notification of intention to make that claim or the first day in respect of which the claim is made.

(2) Where a person who is required to attend in accordance with regulation 19 without good cause fails to attend at either the place or time specified in that person's case, or does not, if so requested, provide a properly completed claim form at or before the time when the person is required to attend, the claim is to be treated as made on the first day on which the person does attend at the specified place or time or does provide a properly completed claim form, or if later the first day in respect of which the claim is made.

(3) The Secretary of State may direct that the time for providing a properly completed claim form may be extended to a date no later than the date one month after the date of first notification of intention to make that claim.

DEFINITION

"jobseeker's allowance"—see reg.2.

Making a claim for a jobseeker's allowance in writing

4.27   **21.**—(1) Except where a person is required to attend in accordance with regulation 19, a claim for a jobseeker's allowance may be made in writing on a form authorised by the Secretary of State for that purpose and may be delivered or sent to the Secretary of State at an appropriate office.

(2) A claim made in accordance with paragraph (1) must be completed in accordance with the instructions on the form.

(3) A written claim for a jobseeker's allowance made under this regulation or regulation 20, which is made on the form approved for the time being, is properly completed if completed in accordance with the instructions on the form and defective if not so completed.

(4) If a written claim made under this regulation is defective when first received, the Secretary of State must advise the person making it of the defect and of the effect on the date of claim of the provisions of regulation 22.

(5) If that person corrects the defect so that the claim then satisfies the requirements of paragraph (3) and does so within one month, or such longer period as the Secretary of State considers reasonable, from the date the Secretary of State first drew attention to the defect, the claim must be treated as having been properly made in the first instance.

DEFINITIONS

"appropriate office"—see reg.2.
"jobseeker's allowance"—*ibid.*
"writing"—*ibid.*

Date of claim for a jobseeker's allowance where claim made in writing

4.28   **22.** Subject to regulation 29(6), in the case of a written claim for a jobseeker's allowance made under regulation 21, the date on which the claim is made or treated as made is to be the first date on which—

(a) a properly completed claim is received in an appropriate office;
(b) a person first notifies an intention to make a claim, provided that a properly completed claim form is received in an appropriate office within one month or such longer period as the Secretary of State considers reasonable of first notification; or
(c) a defective claim is received but is treated as properly made in the first instance in accordance with regulation 21(5),

or the first day in respect of which the claim is made if later than the above.

DEFINITIONS

"appropriate office"—see reg.2.
"jobseeker's allowance"—*ibid.*

Making a claim for a jobseeker's allowance by telephone

23.—(1) Except where a person is required to attend in accordance with regulation 19, or where the Secretary of State in any case directs that the claim must be made in writing in accordance with regulation 21, a claim for a jobseeker's allowance may be made by telephone call to the telephone number specified by the Secretary of State where such a claim falls within a class of case for which the Secretary of State accepts telephone claims or in any other case where the Secretary of State is willing to do so.

4.29

(2) A claim made by telephone in accordance with paragraph (1) is properly completed if the Secretary of State is provided during that call with all the information required to determine the claim and the claim is defective if not so completed.

(3) Where a telephone claim is defective, the Secretary of State must advise the person making it of the defect and of the effect on the date of claim of the provisions of regulation 24.

(4) If the person corrects the defect so that the claim then satisfies the requirements of paragraph (2) and does so within one month, or such longer period as the Secretary of State considers reasonable, of the date the Secretary of State first drew attention to the defect, the Secretary of State must treat the claim as if it had been properly made in the first instance.

DEFINITIONS

"jobseeker's allowance"—see reg.2.
"writing"—*ibid.*

Date of claim for a jobseeker's allowance where claim made by telephone

24. Subject to regulation 29(6), in the case of a telephone claim made under regulation 23, the date on which the claim is made or treated as made is to be the first date on which—

4.30

(a) a claim made by telephone is properly completed;
(b) a person first notifies an intention to make a claim, provided that a claim made by telephone is properly completed within one month or such longer period as the Secretary of State considers reasonable of first notification; or

(c) a defective claim is received but is treated as properly made in the first instance in accordance with regulation 23(4),

or the first day in respect of which the claim is made if later than the above.

Interchange with claims for other benefits

4.31   **25.**—(1) The Secretary of State may treat a claim for an employment and support allowance by a woman in addition or in the alternative as a claim for maternity allowance.

(2) The Secretary of State may treat a claim for a maternity allowance in addition or in the alternative as a claim for an employment and support allowance.

(3) Where it appears that a person who has made a claim for personal independence payment is not entitled to it but may be entitled to disability living allowance or attendance allowance, the Secretary of State may treat any such claim alternatively, or in addition, as a claim for either disability living allowance or attendance allowance as the case may be.

(4) Where it appears that a person who has made a claim for disability living allowance or attendance allowance is not entitled to it but may be entitled to personal independence payment, the Secretary of State may treat any such claim alternatively, or in addition, as a claim for personal independence payment.

(5) In determining whether the Secretary of State should treat a claim as made alternatively or in addition to another claim ("the original claim") under this regulation the Secretary of State must treat the alternative or additional claim, whenever made, as having been made at the same time as the original claim.

DEFINITIONS

    "attendance allowance"—see reg.2.
    "disability living allowance"—*ibid.*
    "employment and support allowance"—*ibid.*
    "maternity allowance"—*ibid.*
    "personal independence payment"—*ibid.*

Time within which a claim for universal credit is to be made

4.32   **26.**—(1) Subject to the following provisions of this regulation, a claim for universal credit must be made on the first day of the period in respect of which the claim is made.

(2) Where the claim for universal credit is not made within the time specified in paragraph (1), the Secretary of State is to extend the time for claiming it, subject to a maximum extension of one month, to the date on which the claim is made, if—

(a) any one or more of the circumstances specified in paragraph (3) applies or has applied to the claimant; and

(b) as a result of that circumstance or those circumstances the claimant could not reasonably have been expected to make the claim earlier.

(3) The circumstances referred to in paragraph (2) are—

(a) the claimant was previously in receipt of a jobseeker's allowance or an employment and support allowance and notification of expiry of entitlement to that benefit was not sent to the claimant before the date that the claimant's entitlement expired;

(b) the claimant has a disability;

(c) the claimant has supplied the Secretary of State with medical evidence that satisfies the Secretary of State that the claimant had an illness that prevented the claimant from making a claim;

(d) the claimant was unable to make a claim in writing by means of an electronic communication used in accordance with Schedule 2 because the official computer system was inoperative;

[¹ . . .]

(f) where—

    (i) the Secretary of State decides not to award universal credit to members of a couple jointly because one of the couple does not meet the basic condition in section 4(1)(e) of the 2012 Act;

    (ii) they cease to be a couple; and

    (iii) the person who did meet the basic condition in section 4(1)(e) makes a further claim as a single person;

(g) where—

    (i) an award of universal credit to joint claimants has been terminated because one of the couple does not meet the basic condition in section 4(1)(e) of the 2012 Act;

    (ii) they cease to be a couple; and

    (iii) the person who did meet the basic condition in section 4(1)(e) makes a further claim as a single person.

(4) In the case of a claim for universal credit made by each of joint claimants, the prescribed time for claiming is not to be extended under paragraph (2) unless both claimants satisfy that paragraph.

[¹ (5) In the case of a claim for universal credit referred to in regulation 21(3C) of the Universal Credit Regulations (assessment period applied from a previous award within the last 6 months) the claim for universal credit must be made before the end of the assessment period in respect of which it is made]

AMENDMENT

1. Universal Credit (Digital Service) Amendment Regulations 2014 (SI 2014/2887) reg.3(2)(c) (November 26, 2014). The amendment is subject to the saving provision in reg.5 of SI 2014/2887 (see Pt IV). The absence of a full-stop at the end of para.(5) is a consequence of the amending instrument and is not an editorial error.

MODIFICATION

With effect from June 16, 2014, para.(3) is modified by reg.15 of the Universal Credit (Transitional Provisions) Regulations 2014 (SI 2014/1230). The modification applies where a claim for universal credit is made by a person who was previously entitled to an "existing benefit" (namely JSA(IB), ESA(IR), IS, HB and CTC, WTC and, in some circumstances, incapacity benefit and severe disablement allowance: see regs 2(1) and 25(2) of SI 2014/1230). The modified text includes the following sub-para.(aa) after sub-para.(a):

""(aa) the claimant was previously in receipt of an existing benefit (as defined in the Universal Credit (Transitional Provisions) Regulations 2014) and notification of expiry of entitlement to that benefit was not sent to the claimant before the date that the claimant's entitlement expired;"

"the 2012 Act"—see reg.2.
"benefit"—*ibid.*
"claimant"—*ibid.*
"couple"—see reg.2 and WRA 2012, s.39.
"jobseeker's allowance"—see reg.2.
"universal credit"—*ibid.*

GENERAL NOTE

4.33   The effect of the saving provision in reg.5 of SI 2014/2887 is that the amended text of reg.26 only applies in "Full Service" (aka "Digital Service" cases), see *Universal Credit—An Introduction* above. For the text of the unamended regulation, which continues to apply in "Live Service" cases, see pp.445-6 of the 2013/14 edition.

A claim for universal credit must normally be made on the first day for which the claimant wishes to receive it (para.(1)). However, under para.(2), the Secretary of State must extend that time limit by up to one month (but no more) if at least one circumstances in para.(3) applies, or has applied, to the claimant; and, as a result of that circumstance or those circumstances, the claimant could not reasonably have been expected to make the claim earlier. In the case of joint claimants, both must satisfy para.(2) before the time limit can be extended (para.(4)).

For a discussion of the circumstances in which a computer can be said to have been "inoperative" (para.(3)(d)), see *AM v SSWP (UC)* [2017] UKUT 131 (AAC).

Time within which a claim for personal independence payment is to be made

4.34   **27.** A claim for personal independence payment must be made on the first day of the period in respect of which the claim is made.

DEFINITION

"personal independence payment"—see reg.2.

Time within which a claim for an employment and support allowance is to be made

4.35   **28.** A claim for an employment and support allowance must be made on the first day of the period in respect of which the claim is made or within the period of three months immediately following that day.

DEFINITION

"employment and support allowance"—see reg.2.

Time within which a claim for a jobseeker's allowance is to be made

4.36   **29.**—(1) Subject to paragraphs (2) and (4), a claim for a jobseeker's allowance must be made on the first day of the period in respect of which the claim is made.

(2) In a case where the claim is not made within the time specified in paragraph (1), the Secretary of State is to extend the time for claiming a jobseeker's allowance, subject to a maximum extension of three months, to the date on which the claim is made, where—

(a) any one or more of the circumstances specified in paragraph (3) applies or has applied to the claimant; and

   (b) as a result of that circumstance or those circumstances the claimant could not reasonably have been expected to make the claim earlier.

(3) The circumstances referred to in paragraph (2) are—

   (a) the claimant has difficulty communicating because—

       (i) the claimant has learning, language or literacy difficulties; or

      (ii) the claimant is deaf or blind,

and it was not reasonably practicable for the claimant to obtain assistance from another person to make the claim;

   (b) the claimant was caring for a person who is ill or disabled and it was not reasonably practicable for the claimant to obtain assistance from another person to make the claim;

   (c) the claimant was given information by an officer of the Department for Work and Pensions which led the claimant to believe that a claim for a jobseeker's allowance would not succeed;

   (d) the claimant was given written advice by a solicitor or other professional adviser, a medical practitioner, a local authority or a person working in a Citizens Advice Bureau or a similar advice agency, which led the claimant to believe that a claim for a jobseeker's allowance would not succeed;

   (e) the claimant was required to deal with a domestic emergency affecting the claimant and it was not reasonably practicable for the claimant to obtain assistance from another person to make the claim; or

   (f) the claimant was prevented by adverse weather conditions from attending an appropriate office.

(4) In a case where the claim is not made within the time specified in paragraph (1), the prescribed time for claiming a jobseeker's allowance is to be extended, subject to a maximum extension of one month, to the date on which the claim is made, where—

   (a) any one or more of the circumstances specified in paragraph (5) applies or has applied to the claimant; and

   (b) as a result of that circumstance or those circumstances the claimant could not reasonably have been expected to make the claim earlier.

(5) The circumstances referred to in paragraph (4) are—

   (a) the appropriate office where the claimant would be expected to make a claim was closed and alternative arrangements were not available;

   (b) the claimant was unable to attend the appropriate office due to difficulties with the claimant's normal mode of transport and there was no reasonable alternative available;

   (c) there were adverse postal conditions;

   (d) the claimant was previously in receipt of an employment and support allowance and notification of expiry of entitlement to that benefit was not sent to the claimant before the date that the entitlement expired;

   (e) the claimant had ceased to be a member of a couple within the period of one month before the claim was made;

   (f) during the period of one month before the claim was made a close relative of the claimant had died and for this purpose "close relative" means partner, parent, son, daughter, brother or sister;

   (g) the claimant was unable to make telephone contact with the appropriate office where the claimant would be expected to notify an intention of making a claim because the telephone lines to that office were busy or inoperative;

(h) the claimant was unable to make contact by means of an electronic communication used in accordance with Schedule 2 where the claimant would be expected to notify an intention of making a claim because the official computer system was inoperative.

(6) In a case where the time for claiming a jobseeker's allowance is extended under paragraph (2) or (4), the claim is to be treated as made on the first day of the period in respect of which the claim is, by reason of the operation of those paragraphs, timeously made.

DEFINITIONS

"appropriate office"—see reg.2.
"claimant"—*ibid.*
"electronic communication"—*ibid.*
"jobseeker's allowance"—*ibid.*
"official computer system"—*ibid.*
"partner"—*ibid.*

Amendment of claim

4.37   **30.**—(1) A person who has made a claim for benefit may amend it at any time before a determination has been made on the claim by notice in writing received at an appropriate office, by telephone call to a telephone number specified by the Secretary of State or in such other manner as the Secretary of State may decide or accept.

(2) Any claim amended in accordance with paragraph (1) may be treated as if it had been so amended in the first instance.

DEFINITIONS

"benefit"—see reg.2.
"writing"—*ibid.*

Withdrawal of claim

4.38   **31.**—(1) A person who has made a claim for benefit may withdraw it at any time before a determination has been made on it by notice in writing received at an appropriate office, by telephone call to a telephone number specified by the Secretary of State or in such other manner as the Secretary of State may decide or accept.

(2) Any notice of withdrawal given in accordance with paragraph (1) has effect when it is received.

DEFINITION

"appropriate office"—see reg.2.

Advance claim for and award of universal credit

4.39   **32.**—(1) This regulation applies where—
(a) although a person does not satisfy the conditions of entitlement to universal credit on the date on which a claim is made, the Secretary of State is of the opinion that unless there is a change of circumstances that person will satisfy those conditions for a period beginning on a day not more than one month after the date on which the claim is made; and
(b) the case falls within a class for which Secretary of State accepts

advance claims or is a case where Secretary of State is otherwise willing to do so.

(2) The Secretary of State is to treat the claim as if made on the first day of that period.

(3) The Secretary of State may award universal credit accordingly, subject to the requirement that the person satisfies the conditions for entitlement on the first day of that period.

DEFINITION

"universal credit"—see reg.2.

GENERAL NOTE

Regulation 32 permits claims for universal credit to be made up to one month in advance.   4.40

Advance claim for and award of personal independence payment

33.—(1) Where, although a person does not satisfy the requirements for entitlement to personal independence payment on the date on which the claim is made, the Secretary of State is of the opinion that unless there is a change of circumstances the person will satisfy those requirements for a period beginning on a day ("the relevant day") not more than 3 months after the date on which the decision on the claim is made, the Secretary of State may award personal independence payment from the relevant day subject to the condition that the person satisfies the requirements for entitlement on the relevant day.   4.41

(2) A person who has an award of personal independence payment may make a further claim for personal independence payment during the period of 6 months immediately before the existing award expires.

(3) Where a person makes a claim in accordance with paragraph (2) the Secretary of State may—

(a) treat the claim as if made on the first day after the expiry of the existing award; and

(b) award personal independence payment accordingly, subject to the condition that the person satisfies the requirements for entitlement on that first day after the expiry of the existing award.

DEFINITION

"personal independence payment"—see reg.2.

Advance claim for and award of an employment and support allowance or a jobseeker's allowance

34. Where, although a person does not satisfy the requirements of entitlement to an employment and support allowance or a jobseeker's allowance on the date on which a claim is made, the Secretary of State is of the opinion that unless there is a change of circumstances that claimant will satisfy those requirements for a period beginning on a day ("the relevant day") not more than three months after the date on which the claim is made, then the Secretary of State may—   4.42

(a) treat the claim as if made for a period beginning with the relevant day; and

(b) award an employment and support allowance or a jobseeker's allowance accordingly, subject to the condition that the person satisfies the requirements for entitlement when those benefits become payable under an award.

DEFINITIONS

"employment and support allowance"—see reg.2.
"jobseeker's allowance"—*ibid.*

Attendance in person

4.43   **35.** Except in a case where regulation 9 of the Personal Independence Payment Regulations applies, every person who makes a claim for benefit, other than a jobseeker's allowance, or any person entitled to benefit, other than a jobseeker's allowance, and any other person by whom, or on whose behalf, payments by way of such a benefit are receivable, must attend at such place and on such days and at such times as the Secretary of State may direct, for the purpose of supplying any information or evidence under regulations 37, 38, 39 and 41, if reasonably so required by the Secretary of State.

DEFINITIONS

"benefit"—see reg.2.
"jobseeker's allowance"—*ibid.*

Duration of awards

4.44   **36.**—(1) A claim for universal credit is to be treated as made for an indefinite period and any award of universal credit on that claim is to be made for an indefinite period.

(2) The provisions of Schedule 4 are to have effect in relation to claims for a jobseeker's allowance made during periods connected with public holidays.

GENERAL NOTE

4.45   Under para.(1), claims for universal credit are treated as made for an indefinite period and any award made is also for an indefinite period. However, this does not prevent the Secretary of State from revising the decision making the award, or from superseding that decision so as to change the award or bring it to an end if there is a subsequent change of circumstances. For revision and supersession of decisions about universal credit see ss.9 and 10 SSA 1998 and regs. 5–37 of the Decisions and Appeals Regulations 2013.

PART III

EVIDENCE, INFORMATION AND NOTIFICATION OF CHANGES OF CIRCUMSTANCES

DEFINITION

"universal credit"—see reg.2.

Evidence and information in connection with a claim

37.—(1) Subject to regulation 8 of the Personal Independence Payment Regulations, paragraphs (2) and (3) apply to a person who makes a claim for benefit, other than a jobseeker's allowance, or on whose behalf a claim is made.

(2) The Secretary of State may require the person to supply information or evidence in connection with the claim, or any question arising out of it, as the Secretary of State considers appropriate.

(3) The person must supply the Secretary of State with the information or evidence in such manner as the Secretary of State determines within one month of first being required to do so or such longer period as the Secretary of State considers reasonable.

(4) Where joint claimants have made a claim for universal credit, information relating to that claim may be supplied by the Secretary of State to either or both members of the couple for any purpose connected with the claim.

(5) Where a person is a member of a couple and may make a claim as a single person by virtue of regulation 3(3) (couples) of the Universal Credit Regulations and entitlement to or the amount of any universal credit is or may be affected by the circumstances of their partner, the Secretary of State may require the partner to do any of the following, within one month of being required to do so or such longer period as the Secretary of State may consider reasonable—

  (a) to confirm the information given about the partner's circumstances;

  (b) to supply information or evidence in connection with the claim, or any question arising out of it, as the Secretary of State may require.

(6) The Secretary of State may require a landlord or a rent officer to supply information or evidence in connection with a claim for universal credit that may include in the calculation of an award an amount in respect of housing costs, and any information or evidence so requested must be supplied within one month of the request or such longer period as the Secretary of State considers reasonable.

(7) Every person providing relevant childcare as defined in regulation 35 of the Universal Credit Regulations, in a case where the calculation of a claimant's award of universal credit may include an amount in respect of childcare costs under regulation 31 of those Regulations, must supply such information or evidence in connection with the claim made by the claimant, or any question arising out of it, as may be required by the Secretary of State, and must do so within one month of being required to do so or such longer period as the Secretary of State may consider reasonable.

(8) In this regulation any reference to a person or joint claimants making a claim for a benefit, other than a jobseeker's allowance, is to be interpreted as including a person or joint claimants in a case where it is not a condition of entitlement to benefit that a claim be made for it.

(9) In this regulation any reference to a claim for a benefit, other than a jobseeker's allowance, is to be interpreted as including a potential award of benefit in a case where it is not a condition of entitlement to benefit that a claim be made for it.

DEFINITIONS

"the Personal Independence Payment Regulations"—see reg.2.
"the Universal Credit Regulations"—*ibid.*

"benefit"—*ibid.*
"claimant"—*ibid.*
"couple"—see reg.2 and WRA 2012 s.39.
"jobseeker's allowance"—see reg.2.
"partner"—*ibid.*
"personal independence payment"—*ibid.*
"universal credit"—see reg.2.

Evidence and information in connection with an award

4.47   **38.**—(1) This regulation, apart from paragraph (7), applies to any person entitled to benefit, other than a jobseeker's allowance, and any other person by whom, or on whose behalf, payments by way of such a benefit are receivable.

(2) Subject to regulation 8 of the Personal Independence Payment Regulations, a person to whom this regulation applies must supply in such manner as the Secretary of State may determine and within the period applicable under regulation 45(4)(a) of the Universal Credit, Personal Independence Payment, Jobseeker's Allowance and Employment and Support Allowance (Decisions and Appeals) Regulations 2013 such information or evidence as the Secretary of State may require for determining whether a decision on the award of benefit should be revised under section 9 of the Social Security Act 1998 or superseded under section 10 of that Act.

(3) A person to whom this regulation applies must supply in such manner and at such times as the Secretary of State may determine such information or evidence as the Secretary of State may require in connection with payment of the benefit awarded.

(4) A person to whom this regulation applies must notify the Secretary of State of any change of circumstances which the person might reasonably be expected to know might affect—

(a) the continuance of entitlement to benefit;

(b) the amount of benefit awarded; or

(c) the payment of benefit,

as soon as reasonably practicable after the change occurs.

(5) A notification of any change of circumstances under paragraph (4) must be given—

(a) in writing or by telephone (unless the Secretary of State determines in any case that notice must be given in a particular way or to accept notice given otherwise than in writing or by telephone); or

(b) in writing if in any class of case the Secretary of State requires written notice (unless the Secretary of State determines in any case to accept notice given otherwise than in writing),

and must be sent or delivered to, or received at, the appropriate office.

(6) Where universal credit has been awarded to joint claimants, information relating to that award may be supplied by the Secretary of State to either or both members of the couple for any purpose connected with that award.

(7) Every person providing relevant childcare as defined in regulation 35 of the Universal Credit Regulations, in a case where the claimant's award of universal credit includes an amount in respect of childcare costs under regulation 31 of those Regulations, must supply such information or evidence in connection with the award, or any question arising out of it, as

the Secretary of State may require, and must do so within one month of being required to do so or such longer period as the Secretary of State may consider reasonable.

(8) Where the calculation of an award of universal credit includes, by virtue of regulation 29 of the Universal Credit Regulations, an amount in respect of the fact that a claimant has regular and substantial caring responsibilities for a severely disabled person, the Secretary of State may require a person to whom this regulation applies to furnish a declaration signed by such severely disabled person confirming the particulars respecting the severely disabled person which have been given by that person.

DEFINITIONS

"the Universal Credit Regulations"—see reg.2.
"benefit"—*ibid.*
"claimant"—*ibid.*
"jobseeker's allowance"—*ibid.*
"personal independence payment"—*ibid.*
"regular and substantial caring responsibilities for a severely disabled person"—*ibid.*
"universal credit"—*ibid.*
"writing"—*ibid.*

Alternative means of notifying changes of circumstances

39. In such cases and subject to such conditions as the Secretary of State may specify, the duty in regulation 38(4) to notify a change of circumstances may be discharged by notifying the Secretary of State as soon as reasonably practicable—

4.48

(a) where the change of circumstances is a birth or death, through a local authority, or a county council in England, by personal attendance at an office specified by that authority or county council, provided the Secretary of State has agreed with that authority or county council for it to facilitate such notification; or

(b) where the change of circumstances is a death, by telephone to a telephone number specified for that purpose by the Secretary of State.

DEFINITION

"local authority"—see reg.2.

Information to be provided to rent officers

40.—(1) The Secretary of State must provide to the rent officer such information as the rent officer may reasonably require to carry out functions under section 122 of the Housing Act 1996.

4.49

(2) The information referred to in paragraph (1) may include information required to make a determination under the Rent Officers Order and may include—

(a) the name and address of a universal credit claimant in respect of whom the Secretary of State has applied for a determination;

(b) the amount of any rent (within the meaning of paragraph 2 of Schedule 1 to the Universal Credit Regulations) (meaning of payments in respect of accommodation);

    (c) the amount of any service charge payments (within the meaning of paragraph 2 of Schedule 1 to the Universal Credit Regulations);

    (d) the number of bedrooms in the accommodation in respect of which a determination is made;

    (e) the name and address of a claimant's landlord.

(3) A landlord must provide to the rent officer such information or evidence as the rent officer may reasonably require to make a determination in accordance with the Rent Officers Order and which the rent officer is not able to obtain from the Secretary of State.

(4) The evidence referred to in paragraph (3) may include evidence as to whether a property is let at an Affordable Rent within the meaning in Schedule 2 to the Rent Officers Order.

(5) In this regulation and regulation 37 "landlord" means any person to whom a claimant or partner is liable to make payments in respect of the occupation of the claimant's accommodation.

(6) In this regulation "the Rent Officers Order" means the Rent Officer (Universal Credit Functions) Order 2013.

DEFINITIONS

    "the Universal Credit Regulations"—see reg.2.
    "claimant"—*ibid.*
    "universal credit"—*ibid.*

Evidence and information required from pension fund holders

4.50   **41.**—(1) Where a claimant or the claimant's partner is aged not less than 60 and is a member of, or a person deriving entitlement to a pension under a personal pension scheme or an occupational pension scheme, such a person must, where the Secretary of State so requires, furnish the following information—

    (a) the name and address of the pension fund holder;

    (b) such other information including any reference or policy number as is needed to enable the personal pension scheme or occupational pension scheme to be identified.

(2) Where the pension fund holder receives from the Secretary of State a request for details concerning the personal pension scheme or occupational pension scheme relating to a person to whom paragraph (1) refers, the pension fund holder must provide the Secretary of State with any information to which the following paragraph refers.

(3) The information to which this paragraph refers is—

    (a) where the purchase of an annuity under a personal pension scheme or occupational pension scheme has been deferred, the amount of any income which is being withdrawn from the personal pension scheme or occupational pension scheme;

    (b) in the case of—

        (i) a personal pension scheme or occupational pension scheme where income withdrawal is available, the [1 rate of the annuity which may have been purchased with the funds held under the scheme]; or

        (ii) a personal pension scheme or occupational pension scheme where income withdrawal is not available, the [1 rate of the annuity which might have been purchased with the fund] if the fund were held under a personal pension scheme or occupational pension scheme where income withdrawal was available,

calculated by or on behalf of the pension fund holder by means of tables prepared from time to time by the Government Actuary which are appropriate for this purpose.

(4) In this regulation any reference to a claimant is to be interpreted as including a person in a case where it is not a condition of entitlement to benefit that a claim be made for it.

(5) This regulation does not apply to a person claiming personal independence payment.

(6) In this regulation—

(a) "pension fund holder" means with respect to a personal pension scheme or an occupational pension scheme, the trustees, managers or scheme administrators of the scheme concerned;

(b) "personal pension scheme" means—

(i) a personal pension scheme as defined by section 1 of the Pension Schemes Act 1993;

(ii) an annuity contract or trust scheme approved under section 620 or 621 of the Income and Corporation Taxes Act 1988 or a substituted contract within the meaning of section 622(3) of that Act which is treated as having become a registered pension scheme by virtue of paragraph 1(1)(f) of Schedule 36 to the Finance Act 2004;

(iii) a personal pension scheme approved under Chapter 4 of Part 14 of the Income and Corporation Taxes Act 1988 which is treated as having become a registered pension scheme by virtue of paragraph 1(1)(g) of Schedule 36 to the Finance Act 2004;

(c) "occupational pension" means any pension or other periodical payment under an occupational pension scheme but does not include any discretionary payment out of a fund established for relieving hardship in particular cases.

AMENDMENT

1. Social Security (Miscellaneous Amendments No. 4) Regulations 2017 (SI 2017/1015) reg.15 (November 16, 2017).

DEFINITIONS

"claimant"—see reg.2.
"partner"—*ibid.*

Notification for purposes of sections 111A and 112 of the Administration Act

42. Regulations 43 to 44 below prescribe the person to whom, and manner in which, a change of circumstances must be notified for the purposes of sections 111A(1A) to (1G) and 112(1A) to (1F) of the Administration Act (offences relating to failure to notify a change of circumstances).

4.51

DEFINITION

"the Administration Act"—see reg.2.

Notification of changes of circumstances affecting a jobseeker's allowance or an employment and support allowance for purposes of sections 111A and 112 of the Administration Act

4.52

43.—(1) Subject to paragraphs (2) and (3), where the benefit affected by the change of circumstances is a jobseeker's allowance or an employment and support allowance, notice must be given to the Secretary of State at the appropriate office—

    (a) in writing or by telephone (unless the Secretary of State determines in any case that notice must be in writing or may be given otherwise than in writing or by telephone); or

    (b) in writing if in any class of case the Secretary of State requires written notice (unless the Secretary of State determines in any case to accept notice given otherwise than in writing).

(2) Where the notice in writing referred to in paragraph (1) is given or sent by an electronic communication that notice must be given or sent in accordance with the provisions set out in Schedule 2 to these Regulations (electronic communications).

(3) In such cases and subject to such conditions as the Secretary of State may specify, the duty in regulation 38(4) of these Regulations or regulation 31(4) of the Jobseeker's Allowance Regulations to notify a change of circumstances may be discharged by notifying the Secretary of State as soon as reasonably practicable—

    (a) where the change of circumstances is a birth or death, through a local authority, or a county council in England, by personal attendance at an office specified by that authority or county council, provided the Secretary of State has agreed with that authority or county council for it to facilitate such notification; or

    (b) where the change of circumstances is a death, by telephone to a telephone number specified for that purpose by the Secretary of State.

DEFINITIONS

> "the Jobseeker's Allowance Regulations"—see reg.2.
> "appropriate office"—*ibid.*
> "benefit"—*ibid.*
> "electronic communication"—*ibid.*
> "employment and support allowance"—*ibid.*
> "jobseeker's allowance"—*ibid.*
> "writing"—*ibid.*

Notification of changes of circumstances affecting personal independence payment or universal credit for purposes of sections 111A and 112 of the Administration Act

4.53

44.—(1) Subject to paragraphs (2) and (3), where the benefit affected by the change of circumstances is personal independence payment or universal credit, notice must be given to the Secretary of State ("S") at the appropriate office—

    (a) in writing or by telephone (unless S determines in any case that notice must be in writing or may be given otherwise than in writing or by telephone); or

    (b) in writing if in any class of case S requires written notice (unless

S determines in any case to accept notice given otherwise than in writing).

(2) Where the notice in writing referred to in paragraph (1) is given or sent by an electronic communication that notice must be given or sent in accordance with the provisions set out in Schedule 2 to these Regulations (electronic communications).

(3) In such cases and subject to such conditions as the Secretary of State may specify, the duty in regulation 38(4) to notify a change of circumstances may be discharged by notifying the Secretary of State as soon as reasonably practicable—

(a) where the change of circumstances is a birth or death, through a local authority, or a county council in England, by personal attendance at an office specified by that authority or county council, provided the Secretary of State has agreed with that authority or county council for it to facilitate such notification; or

(b) where the change of circumstances is a death, by telephone to a telephone number specified for that purpose by the Secretary of State.

DEFINITIONS

"the Administration Act"—see reg.2.
"electronic communication"—*ibid.*
"local authority"—*ibid.*
"personal independence payment"—*ibid.*
"universal credit"—*ibid.*
"writing"—*ibid.*

GENERAL NOTE

SSAA ss.111A(1A) to (1F) and 112(1A) to (1D) create various offences where   4.54
a person "fails to give a prompt notification of [a change of circumstances] in the prescribed manner to the prescribed person". The main difference between the two sections is that offences under s.111A require proof of dishonesty whereas those under s.112 do not. Regulation 44 provides that the "prescribed person" to whom notice must be given is the Secretary of State and that the "prescribed manner" of giving notice is as set out in paras (1)–(3). The general rule (para.(1)) is that notice may be given by telephone or in writing unless the Secretary of State requires notice to be given in writing. That is subject to the special rules about reporting births and deaths in para.(3). Written notices that are "given or sent by an electronic communication" (i.e., by email and, when the technology permits, online) must satisfy the rules in Sch.2 (para.(2)).

PART IV

PAYMENTS

Time of payment: general provision

45. Subject to the other provisions of this Part, benefit is to be paid in   4.55
accordance with an award as soon as is reasonably practicable after the award has been made.

DEFINITION

"benefit"—see reg.2.

Direct credit transfer

4.56   **46.**—(1) The Secretary of State may arrange for benefit to be paid by way of direct credit transfer into a bank or other account—

     (a) in the name of the person entitled to benefit, the person's partner, a person appointed under regulation 57(1) or a person referred to in regulation 57(2);

     (b) in the joint names of the person entitled to benefit and the person's partner;

     (c) in the joint names of the person entitled to benefit and a person appointed under regulation 57(1) or a person referred to in regulation 57(2); or

     (d) in the name of such persons as are mentioned in regulation 57(2).

    (2) A Jobseeker's Allowance or an Employment and Support Allowance are to be paid in accordance with paragraph (1) within seven days of the last day of each successive period of entitlement.

DEFINITIONS

    "benefit"—see reg.2.
    "partner"—*ibid.*

Payment of universal credit

4.57   **47.**—(1) Universal credit is payable monthly in arrears in respect of each assessment period unless in any case or class of case the Secretary of State arranges otherwise.

    (2) Where universal credit is to be paid in accordance with regulation 46, it is to be paid within seven days of the last day of the assessment period but if it is not possible to pay universal credit within that period of seven days, it is to be paid as soon as reasonably practicable thereafter.

    (3) In respect of an award of universal credit which is the subject of an arrangement for payment under regulation 46, the Secretary of State may make a particular payment by credit transfer otherwise than is provided by paragraph (2), if it appears to the Secretary of State appropriate to do so for the purpose of—

     (a) paying any arrears of benefit; or

     (b) making a payment in respect of a terminal period of an award or for any similar purpose.

    (4) Where the Secretary of State has arranged for universal credit to be paid in accordance with regulation 46, joint claimants may nominate a bank or other account into which that benefit is to be paid.

    (5) Where joint claimants of universal credit have not nominated a bank or other account into which that benefit is to be paid, the Secretary of State may nominate a bank or other account.

    (6) The Secretary of State may, in any case where the Secretary of State considers it is in the interests of—

     (a) the claimants;

     (b) a child or a qualifying young person for whom one or both of the claimants are responsible; or

     (c) a severely disabled person, where the calculation of an award of universal credit includes, by virtue of regulation 29 of the Universal Credit Regulations, an amount in respect of the fact that a claimant has regular and substantial caring responsibilities for that severely disabled person,

arrange that universal credit payable in respect of joint claimants be paid wholly to only one member of the couple or be split between the couple in such proportion as the Secretary of State considers appropriate.

(7) Where a superseding decision takes effect in accordance with paragraph 26 of Schedule 1 to the Universal Credit, Personal Independence Payment, Jobseeker's Allowance and Employment and Support Allowance (Decisions and Appeals) Regulations 2013, the amount payable in respect of that last assessment period is to be calculated as follows—

$$N \times \left(\frac{A \times 12}{365} \right)$$

where N is the number of days in the period and A is the amount calculated in relation to that period as if it were an assessment period of one month.

DEFINITIONS

"assessment period"—see reg.2 and Universal Credit Regs reg.21.
"benefit"—see reg.2.
"child"—see reg.2 and WRA 2012 s.40.
"couple"—see reg.2 and WRA 2012 s.39.
"employment and support allowance"—see reg.2.
"jobseeker's allowance"—*ibid.*
"qualifying young person"—*ibid.*
"regular and substantial caring responsibilities for a severely disabled person"—*ibid.*
"universal credit"—*ibid.*

GENERAL NOTE

Regulation 47 contains important rules about the payment of universal credit.   **4.58**

Paragraph (1)

Universal credit is normally paid monthly in arrears after the end of the relevant assessment period. This is in contrast to the rules for income support, income-based JSA and income-related ESA. The change in policy is linked to the provisions under which earned income for each assessment period is taken to be the amount reported to HMRC by the claimant's (or claimants') employers. Monthly payment in arrears after the end of the assessment period is intended to ensure that no payment is made until after changes in circumstances relating to earned income have been reported and that overpayments will be reduced.

Paragraphs (2) to (5)

These apply where universal credit is paid by direct transfer under reg.46 which will be the usual method of payment. They are largely administrative. However, the rule in para.(2) that payment by direct transfer must be paid within seven days of the last day of the assessment period or as soon as reasonably practicable thereafter will be important to claimants.

Paragraph (6)

Allows the Secretary of State pay universal credit to one of two joint claimants or to split that payment between them in the circumstances specified. See also reg.58(1).

Paragraph (7)

Changes of circumstance relating to universal credit normally take effect from the first day of the assessment period in which they occur. However, Sch.1, para.26 of the Decisions and Appeals Regulations 2013 provides that where a claimant reaches the qualifying age for state pension credit during an assessment period and has made an advance claim for SPC, the change in circumstances takes effect when it occurs. In those circumstances, it is necessary to make a payment which covers less than a full assessment period and para.(7) specifies how that payment is to be calculated. The rule is the same as that which applies under reg.21(6) of the Universal Credit Regulations where a payment has to be made covering less than a full assessment period because the time limit for claiming has been extended and entitlement therefore begins before the date of claim.

Payment of personal independence payment

4.59   **48.**—(1) Subject to the following provisions of this regulation and regulation 50, personal independence payment is to be paid at intervals of four weeks in arrears.

(2) In the case of any person to whom section 82 of the 2012 Act (terminal illness) applies, the Secretary of State may arrange that personal independence payment is to be paid at intervals of one week in advance.

(3) Where the amount of personal independence payment payable is less than £5.00 a week the Secretary of State may arrange that it is to be paid in arrears at such intervals as may be specified not exceeding 12 months.

DEFINITION

"personal independence payment"—see reg.2.

Days for payment of personal independence payment

4.60   **49.**—(1) Subject to the following provisions of this regulation, a personal independence payment is payable on the day of the week on which the Secretary of State makes a decision to award that benefit, except that where that decision is made on a Saturday or a Sunday the benefit is to be paid on such day of the week as the Secretary of State may direct in any case.

(2) The Secretary of State may, in any case or class of case, arrange that personal independence payment or any part of it be paid on any day of the week.

(3) Where personal independence payment is in payment to any person and the day on which it is payable is changed, it is to be paid at a daily rate of 1/7th of the weekly rate in respect of any of the days for which payment would have been made but for that change.

(4) Where there is a change in the amount of any personal independence payment payable, or where entitlement to personal independence payment ends, and these events do not occur on the day of the week referred to in paragraph (1) or (2), personal independence payment is to be paid at a daily rate of 1/7th of the weekly rate.

DEFINITIONS

"benefit"—see reg.2.
"personal independence payment"—*ibid.*

Payment of personal independence payment at a daily rate between periods in hospital or other accommodation

50.—(1) Personal independence payment is to be paid in respect of any person, for any day falling within a period to which paragraph (2) applies, at the daily rate (which is to be equal to 1/7th of the weekly rate) and personal independence payment payable in pursuance of this regulation is to be paid weekly or as the Secretary of State may direct in any case.

(2) This paragraph applies to any period which is not a period of residence—

  (a) but which commences immediately following such a period; and

  (b) on the first day of which it is expected that, before the expiry of the term of 28 days beginning with that day, the person will commence another period of residence.

(3) Where paragraph (2) applies, the period referred to in that paragraph is to end—

  (a) at the expiry of the term of 28 days beginning with the first day of the period referred to in that paragraph; or

  (b) if earlier, on the day before the day which is the first day of a period of residence.

(4) In this regulation a "period of residence" means a period of residence where—

  (a) the person is a resident of a care home, as defined in section 85(3) of the 2012 Act, and no amount of personal independence payment which is attributable to the daily living component is payable in respect of the person by virtue of regulation 28(1) of the Personal Independence Payment Regulations; or

  (b) the person is undergoing medical or other treatment as an in-patient at a hospital or similar institution and no amount of personal independence payment which is attributable to the daily living component or the mobility component is payable in respect of the person by virtue of regulation 29 of the Personal Independence Payment Regulations,

and such period is to be deemed to begin on the day after the day on which the person enters the care home, hospital or similar institution and to end on the day before the day on which the person leaves the care home, hospital or similar institution.

DEFINITIONS

  "the 2012 Act"—see reg.2.
  "the Personal Independence Payment Regulations"—*ibid.*
  "personal independence payment"—*ibid.*

Payment of an employment and support allowance

51.—(1) Subject to paragraphs (3) to (8), an employment and support allowance paid in accordance with regulation 46 is to be paid fortnightly in arrears on the day of the week determined in accordance with paragraph (2).

(2) The day specified for the purposes of paragraph (1) is the day in column (2) which corresponds to the series of numbers in column (1) which includes the last two digits of the claimant's national insurance number—

4.61

4.62

(1)	(2)
00 to 19	Monday
20 to 39	Tuesday
40 to 59	Wednesday
60 to 79	Thursday
80 to 99	Friday

(3) The Secretary of State may, in any case or class of case, arrange that the claimant be paid otherwise than fortnightly.

(4) In respect of an award of an employment and support allowance which is the subject of an arrangement for payment under regulation 46, the Secretary of State may make a particular payment by credit transfer otherwise than as provided by paragraph (1), if it appears to the Secretary of State appropriate to do so for the purpose of—

(a) paying any arrears of benefit; or

(b) making a payment in respect of a terminal period of an award or for any similar purpose.

(5) The Secretary of State may, in any case or class of case, arrange that an employment and support allowance be paid on any day of the week and where it is in payment to any person and the day on which it is payable is changed, it is to be paid at a daily rate of 1/7th of the weekly rate in respect of any of the days for which payment would have been made but for that change.

(6) Where the weekly amount of an employment and support allowance is less than £1.00 it may be paid in arrears at intervals of not more than 13 weeks.

(7) Where the weekly amount of an employment and support allowance is less than 10 pence that allowance is not payable.

(8) Where an employment and support allowance is normally payable in arrears and the day on which that benefit is payable by reason of paragraph (2) is affected by office closure, it may for that benefit week be paid wholly in advance or partly in advance and partly in arrears and on such day as the Secretary of State may direct.

(9) Where under paragraph (8) an employment and support allowance is paid either in advance or partly in advance and partly in arrears it is for any other purposes to be treated as if it were paid in arrears.

(10) For the purposes of paragraph (8), "benefit week" means a period of seven days beginning or ending with such day as the Secretary of State may direct.

(11) For the purposes of paragraph (8), "office closure" means a period during which an appropriate office is closed in connection with a public holiday.

(12) For the purposes of paragraph (11), "public holiday" means—

(a) in England and Wales, Christmas Day, Good Friday or a bank holiday under the Banking and Financial Dealings Act 1971;

(b) in Scotland, a bank holiday under the Banking and Financial Dealings Act 1971 or a local holiday.

"appropriate office"—see reg.2.
"benefit"—*ibid.*
"claimant"—*ibid.*
"employment and support allowance"—*ibid.*

Payment of a jobseeker's allowance

52.—(1) Subject to paragraphs (2) to (4), a jobseeker's allowance paid in accordance with regulation 46 is to be paid fortnightly in arrears unless in any case or class of case the Secretary of State arranges otherwise.

4.63

(2) In respect of an award of a jobseeker's allowance which is the subject of an arrangement for payment under regulation 46, the Secretary of State may make a particular payment by credit transfer otherwise than as provided by paragraph (1), if it appears to the Secretary of State appropriate to do so for the purpose of—

(a) paying any arrears of benefit; or

(b) making a payment in respect of a terminal period of an award or for any similar purpose.

(3) Where the amount of a jobseeker's allowance is less than £1.00 a week the Secretary of State may direct that it is to be paid at such intervals, not exceeding 13 weeks, as may be specified in the direction.

(4) Where a jobseeker's allowance is normally payable in arrears and the day on which that benefit is normally payable is affected by office closure, it may for that benefit week be paid wholly in advance or partly in advance and partly in arrears and on such day as the Secretary of State may direct.

(5) Where under paragraph (4) a jobseeker's allowance is paid either in advance or partly in advance and partly in arrears it is for any other purposes to be treated as if it were paid in arrears.

(6) For the purposes of paragraph (4), "benefit week" means a period of seven days ending with a day determined in accordance with the definition of that term in regulation 2(2) (general interpretation) of the Jobseeker's Allowance Regulations.

(7) For the purposes of paragraph (4), "office closure" means a period during which an appropriate office is closed in connection with a public holiday.

(8) For the purposes of paragraph (7), "public holiday" means—

(a) in England and Wales, Christmas Day, Good Friday or a bank holiday under the Banking and Financial Dealings Act 1971;

(b) in Scotland, a bank holiday under the Banking and Financial Dealings Act 1971 or a local holiday.

"benefit"—see reg.2.
"jobseeker's allowance"—*ibid.*

Fractional amounts of benefit

53. Where the amount of any benefit payable would, but for this regulation, include a fraction of a penny, that fraction is to be disregarded if it is less than half a penny and is otherwise to be treated as a penny.

4.64

"benefit"—see reg.2.

Payment to persons under age 18

4.65   54. Where a benefit is paid to a person under the age of 18, a direct credit transfer under regulation 46 into any such person's account, or the receipt by the person of a payment made by some other means, is sufficient discharge for the Secretary of State.

Extinguishment of right to payment if payment is not obtained within the prescribed period

4.66   55.—(1) The right to payment of any sum by way of benefit is to be extinguished where payment of that sum is not obtained within the period of 12 months from the date on which the right is treated as having arisen.

(2) For the purposes of this regulation, the right to payment of any sum by way of benefit is to be treated as having arisen—

(a) where notice is given or sent that the sum contained in the notice is ready for collection, on the date of the notice or, if more than one such notice is given or sent, the date of the first such notice;

(b) in relation to any such sum which the Secretary of State has arranged to be paid by means of direct credit transfer in accordance with regulation 46 into a bank or other account, on the due date for payment of the sum or in the case of universal credit on the date of payment of the sum; or

(c) in relation to any such sum to which neither sub-paragraph (a) or (b) applies, on such date as the Secretary of State determines.

(3) The giving or sending of a notice under paragraph (2)(a) is effective for the purposes of that paragraph, even where the sum contained in that notice is more or less than the sum which the person concerned has the right to receive.

(4) Where a question arises whether the right to payment of any sum by way of benefit has been extinguished by the operation of this regulation and the Secretary of State is satisfied that—

(a) the Secretary of State first received written notice requesting payment of that sum after the expiration of 12 months from the date on which the right is treated as having arisen;

(b) from a day within that period of 12 months and continuing until the day the written notice was given, there was good cause for not giving the notice; and

(c) no payment has been made under the provisions of regulation 46 (direct credit transfer),

the period of 12 months is extended to the date on which the Secretary of State decides that question, and this regulation is to apply accordingly as though the right to payment had arisen on that date.

(5) This regulation applies to a person appointed under regulation 57(1) to act on behalf of a claimant or a person referred to in regulation 57(2) as it applies to a claimant.

"benefit"—see reg.2.
"claimant"—*ibid.*

Payments on death

56.—(1) On the death of a person who has made a claim for benefit, the $\qquad$ 4.67
Secretary of State may appoint such person as the Secretary of State thinks
fit to proceed with the claim and any related issue of revision, supersession
or appeal under the Social Security Act 1998.

(2) Subject to paragraphs (6) and (7), any sum payable by way of benefit
which is payable under an award on a claim proceeded with under paragraph (1) may be paid or distributed by the Secretary of State to or amongst
persons over the age of 16 claiming as personal representatives, legatees,
next of kin or creditors of the deceased and the provisions of regulation 55
(extinguishment of right to payment if payment is not obtained within the
prescribed period) are to apply to any such payment or distribution.

(3) Subject to paragraphs (2), (6) and (7), any sum payable by way of
benefit to the deceased, payment of which the deceased had not obtained
at the date of the deceased's death, may, unless the right to payment was
already extinguished at that date, be paid or distributed to or amongst any
persons mentioned in paragraph (2), and regulation 55 is to apply to any
such payment or distribution, except that, for the purpose of that regulation, the period of 12 months is to be calculated from the date on which the
right to payment of any sum is treated as having arisen in relation to any
such person and not from the date on which that right is treated as having
arisen in relation to the deceased.

(4) A direct credit transfer under regulation 46 into an account in the
name of any person mentioned in paragraph (2), or the receipt by such a
person of a payment made by some other means, is sufficient discharge for
the Secretary of State for any sum so paid.

(5) Where the Secretary of State is satisfied that any sum payable by way
of benefit under paragraph (2) or (3), or part of it, is needed for the well-
being of any person under the age of 16, the Secretary of State may obtain
sufficient discharge for it by paying the sum or part of it to a person over
that age who satisfies the Secretary of State that that person will apply the
sum so paid for the well-being of the person under the age of 16.

(6) Paragraphs (2) and (3) are not to apply in any case unless written
application for the payment of any sum is made to the Secretary of State
within 12 months from the date of the deceased's death or within such
longer period as the Secretary of State may allow in any case.

(7) The Secretary of State may dispense with strict proof of the title of
any person claiming in accordance with the provisions of this regulation.

(8) In paragraph (2) "next of kin" means—
 (a) in England and Wales, the persons who would take beneficially on an
 intestacy;
 (b) in Scotland, the persons entitled to the moveable estate of the
 deceased on intestacy.

DEFINITION

"benefit"—see reg. 2.

PART V

THIRD PARTIES

Persons unable to act

4.68   57.—(1) Where a person ("P1") is, or may be, entitled to benefit (whether or not a claim for benefit has been made by P1 or on P1's behalf) but P1 is unable for the time being to act, the Secretary of State may, if all the conditions in paragraph (2) and the additional conditions in paragraph (3) are met, appoint a person ("P2") to carry out the functions set out in paragraph (4).

(2) The conditions are that—

(a) no deputy has been appointed by the Court of Protection under Part 1 of the Mental Capacity Act 2005;

(b) no receiver has been appointed under Part 7 of the Mental Health Act 1983 who is treated as a deputy by virtue of the Mental Capacity Act 2005 with power to claim or receive benefit on P1's behalf;

(c) no attorney with a general power, or a power to claim or receive benefit, has been appointed by P1 under the Powers of Attorney Act 1971, the Enduring Powers of Attorney Act 1985, the Mental Capacity Act 2005 or otherwise; and

(d) in Scotland, P1's estate is not being administered by a judicial factor or any guardian acting or appointed under the Adults with Incapacity (Scotland) Act 2000 who has power to claim or receive benefit on P1's behalf.

(3) The additional conditions are that—

(a) P2 has made a written application to the Secretary of State to be appointed; and

(b) if P2 is a natural person, P2 is over the age of 18.

(4) The functions are exercising on behalf of P1 any right to which P1 may be entitled and receiving and dealing on behalf of P1 with any sums payable to P1.

(5) Anything required by these Regulations to be done by or in relation to P1 may be done by or in relation to P2 or any person mentioned in paragraph (2).

(6) Where a person has been appointed under regulation 82(3) of the Housing Benefit Regulations 2006 by a relevant authority within the meaning of those Regulations to act on behalf of another in relation to a benefit claim or award, the Secretary of State may, if the person so appointed agrees, treat that person as if the Secretary of State had appointed that person under paragraph (1).

(7) A direct credit transfer under regulation 46 into the account of P2 or any person mentioned in paragraph (2), or the receipt by such a person of a payment made by some other means, is sufficient discharge for the Secretary of State for any sum paid.

(8) An appointment under paragraph (1) or (6) comes to an end if—

(a) the Secretary of State at any time revokes it;

(b) P2 resigns P2's office having given one month's notice in writing to the Secretary of State of an intention to do so; or

(c) the Secretary of State is notified that any condition in paragraph (2) is no longer met.

DEFINITION

"benefit"—see reg.2.

Payment to another person on the claimant's behalf

58.—(1) The Secretary of State may direct that universal credit be paid wholly or in part to another person on the claimant's behalf if this appears to the Secretary of State necessary to protect the interests of— 4.69

(a) the claimant;

(b) their partner;

(c) a child or qualifying young person for whom the claimant or their partner or both are responsible; or

(d) a severely disabled person, where the calculation of the award of universal credit includes, by virtue of regulation 29 of the Universal Credit Regulations, an amount in respect of the fact that the claimant has regular and substantial caring responsibilities for that severely disabled person.

(2) The Secretary of State may direct that personal independence payment be paid wholly to another person on the claimant's behalf if this appears to the Secretary of State necessary to protect the interests of the claimant.

DEFINITIONS

"the Universal Credit Regulations"—see reg.2.
"claimant"—*ibid.*
"partner"—*ibid.*
"regular and substantial caring responsibilities for a severely disabled person"—*ibid.*
"universal credit"—*ibid.*

GENERAL NOTE

Paragraph (1)
Universal credit may be paid to third parties in the specified circumstances. 4.70

Direct payment to lender of deductions in respect of interest on secured loans

59. [¹ ...] 4.71

AMENDMENT

1. Loans for Mortgage Interest Regulations 2017 (SI 2017/725) reg.18 and Sch.5 para.8(a) (April 6, 2018).

GENERAL NOTE

Where, prior to April 6, 2018, an award of universal credit included the housing costs element based on mortgage interest payments, that part of the award was normally paid directly to the lender under the provisions of reg.59 and Sch.5. From that date, UC housing costs for mortgage interest have been replaced with loans (see SI 2017/725 above) and both reg.59 and Sch.5 have therefore been revoked. 4.72

Deductions which may be made from benefit and paid to third parties

4.73   **60.** [¹ ...] Deductions may be made from benefit and direct payments may be made to third parties on behalf of a claimant in accordance with the provisions of Schedule 6 and Schedule 7.

AMENDMENT

1. Loans for Mortgage Interest Regulations 2017 (SI 2017/725) reg.18 and Sch.5, para.8(b) (April 6, 2018).

DEFINITIONS

"benefit"—see reg.2.
"claimant"—*ibid.*

GENERAL NOTE

4.74   Regulation 60 gives effect to Schs 6 and 7. Under Sch.6, the Secretary of State may make deductions from certain benefits (including universal credit) and pay them to third parties where the claimant is in arrears of mortgage payments, rent or service charge, charges for fuel, water charges, or the payments due under certain loans. It also allows deductions to be made in respect of payments in lieu of child support due under s.43 Child Support Act 1991 and reg.28 Child Support (Maintenance Assessments and Special Cases) Regulations 1992, and to recover integration loans made to refugees.

Under Sch.7, deductions from universal credit may be made to enforce payment of child support maintenance due under the Child Support Act 1991. Deductions under that schedule are then paid to the person with care of the qualifying child.

PART VI

MOBILITY COMPONENT OF PERSONAL INDEPENDENCE PAYMENT

Cases where mobility component of personal independence payment not payable

4.75   **61.**—(1) Subject to the following provisions of this regulation, personal independence payment by virtue of entitlement to the mobility component is not payable to any person who would otherwise be entitled to it during any period in respect of which that person has received, or is receiving, any payment—

    (a) by way of grant under section 5 of, and paragraph 10 of Schedule 1 to, the National Health Service Act 2006, section 5 of, and paragraph 10 of Schedule 1 to, the National Health Service (Wales) Act 2006 or section 46 of the National Health Service (Scotland) Act 1978 towards the costs of running a private car;

    (b) of mobility supplement under—

        (i) the Naval, Military and Air Forces etc., (Disablement and Death) Service Pensions Order 2006;

        (ii) the Personal Injuries (Civilians) Scheme 1983; or

        (iii) the Order referred to in paragraph (i) by virtue of the War Pensions (Naval Auxiliary Personnel) Scheme 1964, the

Pensions (Polish Forces) Scheme 1964, the War Pensions (Mercantile Marine) Scheme 1964 or an Order of Her Majesty in relation to the Home Guard dated 21st or 22nd December 1964 or in relation to the Ulster Defence Regiment dated 4th January 1971; or

(c) out of public funds which the Secretary of State is satisfied is analogous to a payment under sub-paragraph (a) or (b).

(2) Paragraph (3) applies where a person in respect of whom personal independence payment is claimed for any period has received any such payment as is referred to in paragraph (1) for a period which, in whole or in part, covers the period for which personal independence payment is claimed.

(3) Such payment referred to in paragraph (1) is to be treated as an aggregate of equal weekly amounts in respect of each week in the period for which it is made and, where in respect of any such week a person is treated as having a weekly amount so calculated which is less than the weekly rate of mobility component of personal independence payment to which, apart from paragraph (1), they would be entitled, any personal independence payment to which that person may be entitled for that week is to be payable at a weekly rate reduced by the weekly amount so calculated.

Payment of personal independence payment on behalf of a claimant (Motability)

62.—(1) This regulation applies where— 4.76

(a) personal independence payment is payable in respect of a claimant by virtue of entitlement to the mobility component at the enhanced rate; and

(b) under arrangements made or negotiated by Motability, an agreement has been entered into by or on behalf of the claimant for the hire or hire-purchase of a vehicle.

(2) Where this regulation applies, the Secretary of State may arrange that any personal independence payment by virtue of entitlement to the mobility component at the enhanced rate be paid in whole or in part on behalf of the claimant in settlement of liability for payments due under the agreement mentioned in paragraph (1).

(3) Subject to regulations 63 and 64, in the case of the hire of a vehicle, an arrangement made by the Secretary of State under paragraph (2) terminates—

(a) where the vehicle is returned to the owner at or before the expiration of the term of hire or any agreed extension of the term of hire, on expiry of the period of the term or extended term;

(b) where the vehicle is retained by or on behalf of the claimant with the owner's consent after the expiration of the term of hire or any agreed extension of the term of hire, on expiry of the period of the term or extended term; or

(c) where the vehicle is retained by or on behalf of the claimant otherwise than with the owner's consent after the expiration of the term of hire or any agreed extension of the term of hire, or its earlier termination, on expiry of whichever is the longer of the following periods—

> > (i) the period ending with the return of the vehicle to the owner; or
> > (ii) the period of the term of hire or any agreed extension of the term of hire.

(4) Subject to regulations 63 and 64 in the case of a hire-purchase agreement, an arrangement made by the Secretary of State under paragraph (2) terminates—

> (a) on the purchase of the vehicle; or
> (b) where the vehicle is returned to, or is repossessed by, the owner under the terms of the agreement before the completion of the purchase, at the end of the original period of the agreement.

(5) In this regulation "Motability" means the company, set up under that name as a charity and originally incorporated under the Companies Act 1985 and subsequently incorporated by Royal Charter.

Power for the Secretary of State to terminate an arrangement (Motability)
63. The Secretary of State may terminate an arrangement under regulation 62(2) on such date as the Secretary of State decides—

> (a) if requested to do so by the owner of the vehicle to which the arrangement relates; or
> (b) if it appears to the Secretary of State that the arrangement is causing undue hardship to the claimant and that it should be terminated earlier than provided for by regulation 62(3) or (4).

Restriction on duration of arrangements by the Secretary of State (Motability) 64. The Secretary of State must terminate an arrangement under regulation 62(2) where the Secretary of State is satisfied that—

> (a) the vehicle to which the arrangement relates has been returned to the owner; and
> (b) the expenses of the owner arising out of the hire or hire-purchase agreement have been recovered following the return of the vehicle.

DEFINITIONS

> "claimant"—see reg.2.
> "personal independence payment"—*ibid.*

[¹ **Recovery of expenses**

4.77

62A.—(1) Paragraph 2 applies where—

> (a) an agreement referred to in regulation 62(1)(b) has been entered into; and
> (b) a relevant provider is receiving payments of personal independence payment in settlement of liability for payments due under that agreement.

(2) The Secretary of State may require the relevant provider to make payments to meet the reasonable expenses of the Secretary of State in administering the making of the payments of personal independence payment to the relevant provider.

(3) The method by which the expenses under paragraph (2) are to be met is for the Secretary of State to issue an invoice to the relevant provider setting out the expenses that have been incurred and for the relevant provider to pay the sum stated to the Secretary of State.

(4) The first invoice issued by the Secretary of State may recover expenses incurred between 21st July 2016 and the date of the invoice.

(5) Subsequently the Secretary of State may issue invoices no more frequently than annually and only in respect of expenses incurred since the period covered by the previous invoice.

(6) The expenses that the Secretary of State may take into account for the purposes of paragraph (2) include—

(a) the salaries and other costs relating to the employment of staff wholly engaged in the administering of the payments of personal independence payment and where staff have other responsibilities, an apportioned amount of those costs; and

(b) overheads, including rent and other shared costs, relating to those staff.

(7) In determining what expenses were reasonably incurred in administering the making of payments of personal independence payment to a relevant provider, the Secretary of State must have regard to any agreement between the Secretary of State and the relevant provider concerning the level of service to be provided by the Secretary of State in the making of such payments to that relevant provider.]

AMENDMENT

1. Social Security (Expenses of Paying Sums in Relation to Vehicle Hire) Regulations 2016 (SI 2016/674) regs 4 and 5 9 (July 21, 2016).

Preamble

SCHEDULE 1

POWERS EXERCISED IN MAKING THESE REGULATIONS

1. The following provisions of the Administration Act— 4.78

(a) section 1(1), (1C);

(b) section 5(1)(a), (b), (c), (d), (g), (i), (j), (k), (l), (m), (p), (q), (1A), (2A), (2B), (2C), (3B);

(c) section 7A(2)(b);

(d) section 15A(2);

(e) section 111A(1A)(d), (1B)(d), (1D)(c), (1E)(c);

(f) section 112(1A)(d), (1B)(d), (1C)(c), (1D)(c);

(g) section 189(1) and (5) to (6);

(h) section 191.

2. Paragraph 7A of Schedule 2 to the Abolition of Domestic Rates etc. (Scotland) Act 1987.

3. Paragraph 6 of Schedule 4 to the Local Government Finance Act 1988.

4. Section 24(2)(b), (c) and (d) and section 30 of the Criminal Justice Act 1991.

5. Section 43(2) of the 1991 Act.

6. Paragraphs 1 and 6(2)(b) of Schedule 4 and paragraph 6 of Schedule 8 to, the Local Government Finance Act 1992.

7. Sections 32 and 92 of, and paragraph 3(1)(a), (b), (2)(a), (b) and (c) of Schedule 1 to the 2012 Act.

DEFINITIONS

"the Administration Act"—see reg.2.
"electronic communication"—*ibid.*

SCHEDULE 2

ELECTRONIC COMMUNICATIONS

PART I

USE OF ELECTRONIC COMMUNICATIONS

Use of electronic communications by the Secretary of State

4.79   1. The Secretary of State may use an electronic communication in connection with claims for, and awards of, any benefit.

Conditions for the use of electronic communications by other persons

2.—(1) A person other than the Secretary of State may use an electronic communication in connection with the matters referred to in paragraph 1 if the conditions specified in sub-paragraphs (2) to (5) are satisfied.

(2) The first condition is that the person is for the time being permitted to use an electronic communication for the purpose in question by an authorisation given by means of a direction of the Secretary of State.

(3) The second condition is that the person uses an approved method of—

     (a)   authenticating the identity of the sender of the communication where required to do so;

     (b)   electronic communication;

     (c)   authenticating any claim or information delivered by means of an electronic communication; and

     (d)   subject to sub-paragraph (6), submitting any claim or information to the Secretary of State.

(4) The third condition is that any claim or information sent by means of an electronic communication is in an approved form.

(5) The fourth condition is that the person maintains such records as may be specified in a direction given by the Secretary of State.

(6) Where the person uses any method other than the method approved by the Secretary of State of submitting any claim or information, it is to be treated as not having been submitted.

(7) In this paragraph "approved" means approved by means of a direction given by the Secretary of State for the purposes of this Schedule.

Use of intermediaries

3. The Secretary of State may use intermediaries in connection with—

     (a)   the delivery of any claim or information by means of an electronic communication; and

     (b)   the authentication or security of anything transmitted by such means,

and may require other persons to use intermediaries in connection with those matters.

PART II

EVIDENTIAL PROVISIONS

Effect of delivering information by electronic communications

4.80   4.—(1) Any claim or information which is delivered by means of an electronic communication is to be treated as having been delivered in the manner or form required by any provision of these Regulations on the day on which the conditions imposed—

     (a)   by this Schedule; and

     (b)   by or under an applicable enactment (except to the extent that the condition thereby imposed is incompatible with this Schedule), are satisfied.

(2) The Secretary of State may, by a direction, determine that any claim or information is to be treated as delivered on a different day (whether earlier or later) from the day specified in sub-paragraph (1).

(3) Any claim or information is not to be taken to have been delivered to an official computer system by means of an electronic communication unless it is accepted by the system to which it is delivered.

Proof of delivery

5.—(1) The use of an approved method of electronic communication is to be presumed,   **4.81**
unless the contrary is proved, to have resulted in delivery—

    (a) in the case of any claim or information falling to be delivered to the Secretary of State,
if the delivery of that claim or information is recorded on an official computer system;
or

    (b) in the case of any information that falls to be delivered by the Secretary of State, if the
despatch of that information is recorded on an official computer system.

(2) The use of an approved method of electronic communication is to be presumed, unless
the contrary is proved, not to have resulted in delivery—

    (a) in the case of any claim or information falling to be delivered to the Secretary of State,
if the delivery of that claim or information is not recorded on an official computer
system; or

    (b) in the case of information that falls to be delivered by the Secretary of State, if the
despatch of that information is not recorded on an official computer system.

(3) The time and date of receipt of any claim or information sent by an approved method of
electronic communication is to be presumed, unless the contrary is proved, to be that recorded
on an official computer system.

Proof of identity

6.—(1) The identity of—   **4.82**

    (a) the sender of any claim or information delivered by means of an electronic communi-
cation to an official computer system; or

    (b) the recipient of any claim or information delivered by means of an electronic com-
munication from an official computer system,

is to be presumed, unless the contrary is proved, to be the person whose name is recorded
as such on that official computer system.

(2) Any claim or information delivered by an approved method of electronic communication
on behalf of another person ("P") is to be deemed to have been delivered by P unless P proves
that it was delivered without P's knowledge or connivance.

Proof of content

7. The content of any claim or information sent by means of an electronic communication
is to be presumed, unless the contrary is proved, to be that recorded on an official computer
system.

DEFINITIONS

    "electronic communication"—see reg.2.
    "official computer system"—*ibid.*

Regulation 36(2)

SCHEDULE 4

SPECIAL PROVISIONS RELATING TO CLAIMS FOR A JOBSEEKER'S ALLOWANCE
DURING PERIODS CONNECTED WITH PUBLIC HOLIDAYS

1. In this Schedule and regulation 36(2)—   **4.83**

    (a) "public holiday" means—

        (i) in England and Wales, Christmas Day, Good Friday or a bank holiday under the
Banking and Financial Dealings Act 1971,

        (ii) in Scotland, a bank holiday under the Banking and Financial Dealings Act 1971
or a local holiday;

    (b) "Christmas and New Year holidays" means—

        (i) in England and Wales, the period beginning at the start of Christmas Day and
terminating at the end of New Year's Day, or if New Year's Day is a Sunday at
the end of 2nd January,

        (ii) in Scotland, the period beginning at the start of Christmas Day and terminating
at the end of 2nd January, or where New Year's Day is a Saturday or a Sunday
terminating at the end of 3rd January;

    (c) "Easter Holidays" means the period beginning at the start of Good Friday and terminating at the end of Easter Monday;

    (d) "office closure" means a period during which an appropriate office is closed in connection with a public holiday.

  2. Where a claim for a jobseeker's allowance is made during any period set out in paragraph 3, the Secretary of State may treat that claim as a claim for a period, to be specified in a decision of the Secretary of State, not exceeding—

    (a) 35 days after the date of the claim where the claim is made during the period specified in sub-paragraph (a) of paragraph 3; or

    (b) 21 days after the date of claim where the claim is made during the period specified in either sub-paragraph (b) or (c) of paragraph 3.

  3. For the purposes of paragraph 2 the periods are—

    (a) in the case of Christmas and New Year holidays, a period beginning with the start of the 35th day before the first day of office closure and terminating at the end of the last day of office closure;

    (b) in the case of Easter Holidays, a period beginning with the start of the 16th day before the first day of office closure and terminating at the end of the last day of office closure;

    (c) in the case of any other public holiday, a period beginning with the start of the 14th day before the first day of office closure and terminating at the end of the last day of office closure.

DEFINITIONS

  "appropriate office"—see reg.2.
  "jobseeker's allowance"—*ibid.*

Regulation 59

SCHEDULE 5

DIRECT PAYMENT TO LENDER OF DEDUCTIONS IN RESPECT OF INTEREST ON SECURED LOANS

4.84   *[Revoked by the Loans for Mortgage Interest Regulations 2017 (SI 2017/725) reg. 18 and Sch. 5, para. 8(c) with effect from April 6, 2018]*

Regulation 60

SCHEDULE 6

DEDUCTIONS FROM BENEFIT AND DIRECT PAYMENT TO THIRD PARTIES

Interpretation

4.85   **1.**[²(1)] In this Schedule—

  "assessment period" has the meaning given by regulation 21 (assessment periods) of the Universal Credit Regulations;

  "the work allowance" means, in relation to any claimant, the amount applicable to that claimant under regulation 22(2) (deduction of income and work allowance) of the Universal Credit Regulations;

  "child element" means, in relation to any claimant, any amount included in the claimant's award of universal credit under regulation 24 (the child element) of the Universal Credit Regulations;

  "the Community Charges Regulations" means the Community Charges (Deductions from Income Support) (No. 2) Regulations 1990;

  "the Community Charges (Scotland) Regulations" means the Community Charges (Deductions from Income Support) (Scotland) Regulations 1989;

  "the Council Tax Regulations" means the Council Tax (Deductions from Income Support) Regulations 1993;

  "the Fines Regulations" means the Fines (Deductions from Income Support) Regulations 1992;

"standard allowance" means, in relation to any claimant, any amount included in the claimant's award of universal credit under section 9(1) of the 2012 Act;
"water charges" means—
- (a) as respects England and Wales, any water and sewerage charges under Chapter 1 of Part 5 of the Water Industry Act 1991;
- (b) as respects Scotland, any such charges established by Scottish Water under a charges scheme made under section 29A of the Water Industry (Scotland) Act 2002;

[² ...]
[² (2) For the purposes of this Schedule, where the relevant percentage of the standard allowance results in a fraction of a penny, that fraction is to be disregarded if it is less than half a penny and otherwise it is to be treated as a penny.]

General
2.—(1) The Secretary of State may deduct an amount from a claimant's award of universal credit and pay that amount to a third party in accordance with the following provisions of this Schedule to discharge (in whole or part) a liability of the claimant to that third party.   **4.86**

(2) A payment made to a third party in accordance with this Schedule may be made at such intervals as the Secretary of State may direct.

Limitations applicable to deductions made under this Schedule
3.—(1) The Secretary of State may not deduct an amount from a claimant's award of universal credit under this Schedule and pay that amount to a third party if, in relation to any assessment period, that would—   **4.87**
- (a) reduce the amount payable to the claimant to less than one penny; or
- (b) result in more than three deductions being made, in relation to that assessment period, under one or more of the provisions mentioned in sub-paragraph (2).

(2) The provisions are—
- (a) paragraph 6 (housing costs) of this Schedule;
- (b) paragraph 7 (rent and service charges included in rent) of this Schedule;
- (c) paragraph 8 (fuel costs) of this Schedule;
- (d) paragraph 9 (water charges) of this Schedule;
- (e) paragraph 10 (payments in place of payments of child support maintenance) of this Schedule;
- (f) paragraph 11 (eligible loans) of this Schedule;
- (g) paragraph 12 (integration loans) of this Schedule;
- (h) regulation 3 (deductions from income support etc.) of the Community Charges Regulations;
- (i) regulation 3 (deductions from income support etc.) of the Community Charges (Scotland) Regulations;
- (j) regulation 5 (deduction from debtor's income support etc.) of the Council Tax Regulations; and
- (k) regulation 4 (deductions from offender's income support etc.) of the Fines Regulations.

(3) The aggregate amount deducted from a claimant's award of universal credit in relation to any assessment period and paid to a third party under paragraphs 8 (fuel costs) and 9 (water charges) of this Schedule must not, without the claimant's consent, exceed a sum equal to [² 25%] of the aggregate of the standard allowance and any child element.

Maximum amount
4.—(1) Except as provided for in sub-paragraph (4), the Secretary of State may not deduct an amount from a claimant's award of universal credit under a provision mentioned in paragraph 5(2) of this Schedule if, in relation to any assessment period, that would result in the Secretary of State deducting an amount in excess of [² 40%] of the standard allowance ("the maximum amount") from the claimant's award under one or more relevant provisions.   **4.88**

(2) The relevant provisions are—
- (a) those mentioned in paragraph 5(2) of this Schedule;
- (b) section 26 (higher-level sanctions) of the 2012 Act;
- (c) section 27 (other sanctions) of the 2012 Act;
- (d) section 71ZG (recovery of payments on account) of the Administration Act;
- (e) section 6B of the Social Security Fraud Act 2001 ("the 2001 Act");
- (f) section 7 of the 2001 Act; and
- (g) section 9 of the 2001 Act.

(3) For the purposes of determining whether the maximum amount would be exceeded, no account is to be taken of any liability for continuing need mentioned in—
- (a) paragraph 8(4)(b) (fuel costs) of this Schedule; or

(b) paragraph 9(6)(b) or (7)(b)(water charges) of this Schedule.

(4) Subject to paragraph 3 of this Schedule, the Secretary of State may deduct an amount from the claimant's award under paragraph 6 (housing costs), [⁵ . . .] paragraph 8 (fuel costs) [⁵ , or the minimum amount which may be deducted under paragraph 7 (rent and service charges included in rent)] of this Schedule and pay that amount to a third party where the deduction appears to the Secretary of State to be in the claimant's best interests, even though the deduction would result in the maximum amount being exceeded.

Priority as between certain debts

4.89 **5.**—(1) This paragraph applies to a claimant ("C") where, in relation to any assessment period—

- (a) a deduction could otherwise be made from C's award under more than one of the provisions mentioned in sub-paragraph (2); and
- (b) the amount of universal credit payable to C in relation to that assessment period is insufficient to enable the Secretary of State to meet all of the liabilities for which in C's case deductions may be made under those provisions or the deduction, were it to be made, would mean that the maximum amount referred to in paragraph 4(1) would be exceeded.

(2) The provisions are—

- (a) paragraph 6 (housing costs) of this Schedule;
- (b) paragraph 7 (rent and service charges included in rent) of this Schedule [⁵ where the amount of the deduction equals 10% of the standard allowance];
- (c) paragraph 8 (fuel costs) of this Schedule;
- (d) regulation 3 (deductions from income support etc.) of the Community Charges Regulations, regulation 3 (deductions from income support etc.) of the Community Charges (Scotland) Regulations or (because no such payments are being made in C's case) regulation 5 (deduction from debtor's income support etc.) of the Council Tax Regulations;
- (e) regulation 4 (deductions from offender's income support etc.) of the Fines Regulations where the amount of the deduction equals 5% of the standard allowance;
- (f) paragraph 9 (water charges) of this Schedule;
- (g) paragraph 10 (payments in place of child support maintenance) of this Schedule;
- (h) Schedule 7 (deductions from benefit in respect of child support maintenance and payment to persons with care) to these Regulations;
- (i) section 78(2) (recovery of social fund awards) of the Administration Act;
- (j) section 71ZH(1)(a) or (b) (recovery of hardship payments etc.) of the [⁶ Administration Act];
- (k) section 115A (penalty as alternative to prosecution) of the Administration Act where an overpayment is recoverable from a person by, or due from a person to, the Secretary of State or an authority under or by virtue of section 71 (overpayments – general), section 75 (overpayments of housing benefit) or section 71ZB (recovery of overpayments of certain benefits) of that Act;
- (l) section 71 (overpayments – general), section 71ZC (deduction from benefit) or section 75(4) (overpayments of housing benefit) of the Administration Act or an over-payment of working tax credit or child tax credit, where in each case, the overpayment (or part of it) is the result of fraud;
- (m) section 115C(4) (incorrect statements etc.) and section 115D(4) (failure to disclose information) of the Administration Act;
- (n) section 71 (overpayments – general), section 71ZC (deduction from benefit) or section 75(4) (overpayments of housing benefit) of the Administration Act or an over-payment of working tax credit or child tax credit, where in each case, the overpayment (or part of it) is not the result of fraud;
- (o) paragraph 12 (integration loans) of this Schedule;
- (p) paragraph 11 (eligible loans) of this Schedule;
- [⁵ (pa) paragraph 7 (rent and service charges included in rent) where the amount of deduction exceeds the minimum amount that may be deducted under that para-graph;]
- (q) regulation 4 (deductions from offender's income support etc.) of the Fines Regulations where the amount of the deduction exceeds the minimum amount that may be deducted in accordance with those Regulations.

(3) Where this paragraph applies to a claimant, the Secretary of State must make a deduc-tion under any of the provisions mentioned sub-paragraph (2) in accordance with sub-para-graphs (4) and (5).

(4) The Secretary of State must give priority to any such deductions in the order in which they are listed in sub-paragraph (2), with housing costs having the priority.

(5) Where two or more provisions mentioned in any single paragraph of sub-paragraph (2) apply to the claimant, unless the Secretary of State directs otherwise, those deductions have equal priority with each other and the amount of such deductions are to be apportioned accordingly.

(6) For the purposes of sub-paragraph (2)(l) and (n), an overpayment is the result of fraud if, in relation to that overpayment or that part of it, the claimant—

   (a) has been found guilty of an offence whether under statute or otherwise;

   (b) made an admission after caution of deception or fraud for the purpose of obtaining benefit under the Administration Act, or in the case of a tax credit, under the Tax Credits Act 2002; or

   (c) agreed to pay a penalty under section 115A of the Administration Act (penalty as an alternative to prosecution) and the agreement has not been withdrawn.

Housing costs

6.—(1) This paragraph applies where the following condition is met.   **4.90**

(2) The condition is that in any assessment period the claimant is in debt for any item of housing costs which is included in the claimant's award of universal credit under Schedule 5 (housing costs element for owner-occupiers) to the Universal Credit Regulations.

(3) Where this paragraph applies, but subject to sub-paragraph (4), the Secretary of State may, in such cases and circumstances as the Secretary of State may determine, in relation to that assessment period deduct an amount from the claimant's award equal to 5% of the standard allowance in respect of any debt mentioned in sub-paragraph (2) and pay that amount or those amounts to the person to whom any such debt is owed.

(4) Before the Secretary of State may commence (or re-commence) making deductions in respect of any such debt, the claimant's earned income (or in the case of joint claimants their combined earned income) in relation to the previous assessment period must not exceed the work allowance.

(5) [⁷. . .]

(6) [⁷. . .]

Rent and service charges included in rent

7.—(1) This paragraph applies where all of the following conditions are met.   **4.91**

(2) The first condition is that in any assessment period the claimant—

   (a) has an award of universal credit which includes an amount under Schedule 4 (housing costs element for renters) to the Universal Credit Regulations; or

   (b) occupies exempt accommodation and has an award of housing benefit under section 130 (housing benefit) of the Contributions and Benefits Act.

(3) The second condition is that the claimant is in debt for any—

   (a) rent payments;

   (b) service charges which are paid with or as part of the claimant's rent.

(4) The third condition is that the claimant occupies the accommodation to which the debt relates.

(5) Where this paragraph applies, but subject to sub-paragraphs (6) and (7), the Secretary of State may, in such cases and circumstances as the Secretary of State may determine, deduct in relation to that assessment period an amount from the claimant's award [⁵ which is no less than 10% and no more than 20%] of the standard allowance and pay that amount to the person to whom the debt is owed.

(6) Before the Secretary of State may commence (or re-commence) making deductions in respect of such a debt, the claimant's earned income (or in the case of joint claimants their combined earned income) in relation to the previous assessment period must not exceed the work allowance.

(7) The Secretary of State must stop making such deductions if, in relation to the three assessment periods immediately preceding the date on which the next deduction could otherwise be made, the claimant's earned income (or in the case of joint claimants their combined earned income) equals or exceeds the work allowance.

(8) In this paragraph—

"exempt accommodation" has the meaning given by paragraph 1 of Schedule 1 (interpretation) to the Universal Credit Regulations;

"rent payments" includes any elements included in the claimant's rent which would not fall to be treated as rent under the Housing Benefit Regulations 2006 or as rent payments under the Universal Credit Regulations;

"service charges" includes any items in a charge for services in respect of the accommodation occupied by the claimant which would not fall to be treated as service charges under the Universal Credit Regulations.

Fuel costs

4.92   8.—(1) This paragraph applies where the following condition is met.

(2) The condition is that in any assessment period the claimant is in debt for any [¹ fuel item].

(3) Where this paragraph applies, but subject to sub-paragraphs (5) and (6), the Secretary of State may, in such cases and circumstances as the Secretary of State may determine, deduct in relation to that assessment period the following amounts from the claimant's award and pay them to the person to whom the payment is due.

(4) The amount which may be deducted in respect of any fuel item is—

(a)   an amount equal to 5% of the standard allowance; and

(b)   an additional amount which the Secretary of State estimates is equal to the average monthly cost necessary to meet the claimant's continuing need for [¹ the fuel in respect of which the debt arose, plus such monthly amount as is required to meet any payments required to be made under a green deal plan within the meaning of section 1 of the Energy Act 2011 ("the 2011 Act")], except where current consumption is paid for by other means such as a pre-payment meter.

(5) Before the Secretary of State may commence (or re-commence) making deductions in respect of such a debt, the claimant's earned income (or in the case of joint claimants their combined earned income) in relation to the previous assessment period must not exceed the work allowance.

(6) The Secretary of State must stop making such deductions if, in relation to the three assessment periods immediately preceding the date on which the next deduction could otherwise be made, the claimant's earned income (or in the case of joint claimants their combined earned income) equals or exceeds the work allowance.

(7) As between liabilities for items of gas or electricity, the Secretary of State must give priority to whichever liability the Secretary of State considers it would, having regard to the circumstances and to any requests of the claimant, be appropriate to discharge.

[¹(8) In this paragraph, "fuel item" means—

(a)   any charge for mains gas, including for the reconnection of mains gas;

(b)   any charge for mains electricity and including any charge for the disconnection and reconnection of mains electricity and including any payments required to be made under a green deal plan within the meaning of section 1 of the 2011 Act.]

Water charges

4.93   9.—(1) This paragraph applies where the following condition is met.

(2) The condition is that in any assessment period the claimant is in debt for water charges, including any charges for reconnection ("the original debt").

(3) Where this paragraph applies, but subject to sub-paragraphs (4) and (5), the Secretary of State may, in such cases and circumstances as the Secretary of State may determine, deduct an amount from the claimant's award in accordance with sub-paragraphs (6) to (8) and pay it to a water undertaker to whom the payment is due or to the person or body authorised to collect water charges for that undertaker.

(4) Before the Secretary of State may commence (or re-commence) making deductions in respect of such a debt, the claimant's earned income (or in the case of joint claimants their combined earned income) in relation to the previous assessment period must not exceed the work allowance.

(5) The Secretary of State must stop making such deductions if, in relation to the three assessment periods immediately preceding the date on which the next deduction could otherwise be made, the claimant's earned income (or in the case of joint claimants their combined earned income) equals or exceeds the work allowance.

(6) Where water charges are determined by means of a water meter, the amount to be deducted under this paragraph in relation to any assessment period is to be—

(a)   an amount equal to 5% of the standard allowance towards discharging the original debt; and

(b)   an additional amount which the Secretary of State estimates to be the average monthly cost necessary to meet the claimant's continuing need for water consumption.

(7) Where water charges are determined otherwise than by means of a water meter, the amount to be deducted in relation to any assessment period under this paragraph is to be—

(a)   the amount referred to in sub-paragraph (6)(a); and

(b) an additional amount equal to the cost necessary to meet the continuing need for water consumption in that assessment period.

(8) Where the claimant is in debt to two water undertakers—

(a) only one amount under sub-paragraph (6)(a) or (7)(a) may be deducted;

(b) a deduction in respect of an original debt for sewerage may only be made after the whole debt in respect of an original debt for water has been paid; and

(c) deductions in respect of continuing charges for both water and for sewerage may be made at the same time.

(9) In this paragraph "water undertaker" means—

(a) in relation to any area in England and Wales, a company holding an appointment as a water undertaker or a sewerage undertaker under the Water Industry Act 1991; or

(b) in relation to any area in Scotland, Scottish Water.

Payments in place of payments of child support maintenance
10. [⁸ . . .]   **4.94**

Eligible loans
11.—(1) This paragraph applieswhere [⁴ in any assessment period the claimant is in arrears   **4.95**
in respect of a loan entered into (whether solely or jointly) with an eligible lender in respect
of an eligible loan].

(2) [⁴ . . .]

(3) [⁴ . . .]

(4) Where the claimant has an award of universal credit, the Secretary of State may, in such cases and circumstances as the Secretary of State may determine, deduct in relation to the assessment period referred to in sub-paragraph (2) an amount from the claimant's award equal to 5% of the standard allowance and pay that amount to the eligible lender towards discharging the amount owing under the loan agreement.

(5) In a case where the claimant has an award of universal credit but the amount payable to the claimant in relation to that assessment period is insufficient to enable such a deduction to be made, the Secretary of State may instead deduct a weekly amount equal to 5% of the personal allowance for a single claimant aged not less than 25 from any employment and support allowance or jobseeker's allowance awarded to the claimant and pay that amount to the eligible lender.

(6) In a case where the claimant does not have an award of universal credit, but has an award of an employment and support allowance or a jobseeker's allowance, the Secretary of State may deduct a weekly amount equal to 5% of the personal allowance for a single claimant aged not less than 25 from any such award and pay that amount to the eligible lender.

(7) The Secretary of State must not make deductions from a claimant's employment and support allowance or a jobseeker's allowance under this paragraph if that would reduce the amount payable to the claimant to less than 10 pence.

(8) In this paragraph—
"eligible benefit" means—

(a) an employment and support allowance;

(b) a jobseeker's allowance;

(c) universal credit;

"eligible lender" means—

(a) a body registered under section 1 (societies which may be registered) of the Industrial and Provident Societies Act 1965;

(b) a credit union within the meaning of section 1 (registration under the Industrial and Provident Societies Act 1965) of the Credit Unions Act 1979;

(c) a charitable institution within the meaning of section 58(1) (interpretation of Part 2) of the Charities Act 1992;

(d) a body entered on the Scottish Charity Register under section 3 (Scottish Charities Register) of the Charities and Trustee Investment (Scotland) Act 2005;

(e) a community interest company within the meaning of Part 2 of the Companies (Audit, Investigations and Community Enterprise) Act 2004,

which, except for a credit union, [³ has permission under the Financial Services and Markets Act 2000 to enter into a contract of the kind mentioned in paragraph 23 or paragraph 23B of Schedule 2 to that Act (credit agreements and contracts for hire of goods)] and which the Secretary of State considers is an appropriate body to which payments on behalf of the claimant may be made in respect of loans made by that body;

"eligible loan" means a loan made by a lender who is, at the time the loan agreement is made, an eligible lender, to a claimant except a loan which—

(a) is secured by a charge or pledge;

(b) is for the purpose of business or self-employment; or

(c) was made by means of a credit card;

"loan agreement" means an agreement between the eligible lender and the claimant in respect of an eligible loan;

"5% of the personal allowance" means 5% of the personal allowance applicable in the claimant's case, rounded up (in any case where that calculation produces a result which is not a multiple of five pence) to the next higher multiple of five pence.

[³ (9) The definition of "eligible lender" must be read with—

(a) section 22 of the Financial Services and Markets Act 2000,

(b) any relevant order under that section, and

(c) Schedule 2 to that Act.]

Integration loans

4.96

12.—(1) This paragraph applies where [⁴ the claimant has an integration loan which is recoverable by deductions].

(2) The first condition is that the claimant has an integration loan which is recoverable by deductions.

(3) The second condition is that, as at the date on which the Secretary of State receives an application for deductions to be made under this paragraph, no deductions are being made from the claimant's universal credit in respect of an amount recoverable under—

(a) section 71 (overpayments – general) or 71ZB (recovery of overpayments of certain benefits) of the Administration Act; or

(b) section 78 (recovery of social fund awards) of that Act.

(4) Where this paragraph applies, the amount payable by deductions in any assessment period is to be equal to 5% of the standard allowance.

(5) In this paragraph, "integration loan which is recoverable by deductions" means an integration loan which is made under the Integration Loans for Refugees and Others Regulations 2007 and which is recoverable from the claimant by deductions from the claimant's award of universal credit under regulation 9 of those Regulations.

AMENDMENTS

1. Social Security (Miscellaneous Amendments) Regulations 2013 (SI 2013/443) reg.10 (April 29, 2013).

2. Social Security (Miscellaneous Amendments) (No. 2) Regulations 2013 (SI 2013/1508) reg.6(1) and (3) (July 29, 2013).

3. Financial Services and Markets Act 2000 (Regulated Activities) (Amendment) (No.2) Order 2013 (SI 2013/1881) art.28 and Sch. para.45 (April 1, 2014).

4. Universal Credit and Miscellaneous Amendments Regulations 2014 (SI 2014/597) reg.5 (April 28, 2014).

5. Universal Credit and Miscellaneous Amendments (No.2) Regulations 2014 (SI 2014/2888) reg.6 (Assessment periods beginning on or after November 26, 2014).

6. Universal Credit and Miscellaneous Amendments Regulations 2015 (SI 2015/1754) reg.9 (Assessment periods beginning on or after November 4, 2015).

7. Loans for Mortgage Interest Regulations 2017 (SI 2017/725) reg.18 and Sch.5, para.8(d) (April 6, 2018).

8. Child Support (Miscellaneous Amendments) Regulations 2019 (SI 2019/1084) regs 6 and 7 (July 4, 2019).

DEFINITIONS

"the 1991 Act"—see reg.2.

"the 2012 Act"—*ibid.*

"the Administration Act"—*ibid.*

"assessment period"—see reg.2 and Universal Credit Regs., reg.21.

"benefit"—see reg.2.

"child" —see reg.2 and WRA 2012 s.40.

"claimant"—see reg.2.
"earned income"—see reg.2 and Universal Credit Regs., reg.52.
"employment and support allowance"—see reg.2.
"jobseeker's allowance"—*ibid.*
"universal credit"—*ibid.*
"the Universal Credit Regulations"— *ibid.*

Regulation 60

Schedule 7

Deductions from Benefit in Respect of Child Support Maintenance and
Payment to Persons with Care

Interpretation
1. In this Schedule—   **4.97**
"beneficiary" means a person who has been awarded a specified benefit;
"maintenance", except in [¹ paragraph 3(1)], means child support maintenance which
a non-resident parent is liable to pay under the 1991 Act at a flat rate (or would be so
liable but for a variation having been agreed to) where that rate applies (or would have
applied) because the non-resident parent falls within [¹ paragraph 4(1)(a), (b)], (c) or (2)
of Schedule 1 to the 1991 Act, and includes such maintenance payable at a transitional rate
in accordance with regulations made under section 29(3)(a) of the Child Support, Pensions
and Social Security Act 2000;
"person with care" has the same meaning as in section 3 (meaning of certain terms used in
this Act) of the 1991 Act;
"specified benefit" means—
   (a) an employment and support allowance;
   (b) a jobseeker's allowance;
   (c) universal credit.

Deductions
2.—(1) Subject to the following provisions of this paragraph and to paragraph 5 (flat rate   **4.98**
maintenance), the Secretary of State may deduct from any specified benefit awarded to a beneficiary, an amount equal to the amount of maintenance which is payable by the beneficiary
and pay the amount deducted to or among the person or persons with care in discharge (in
whole or in part) of the liability to pay maintenance.
(2) A deduction may only be made from one specified benefit in respect of the same period.
(3) No amount may be deducted under this Schedule from any employment and support
allowance or any jobseeker's allowance awarded to the claimant if that would reduce the
amount of the benefit payable to the claimant to less than 10 pence.
(4) No amount may be deducted from any universal credit awarded to the claimant under
this Schedule if that would reduce the amount payable to the claimant to less than one penny.

Arrears
3.—(1) [¹ . . .] the Secretary of State may deduct the sum of [¹ £8.40] per week from any   **4.99**
employment and support allowance [¹ , jobseeker's allowance or universal credit] which the
beneficiary has been awarded and [¹ . . .] pay the amount deducted to or among the person or
persons with care in discharge (in whole or in part) of the beneficiary's liability to pay arrears
of maintenance.
[¹ (1A) No deduction may be made under sub-paragraph (1) if the beneficiary is liable to
pay maintenance.]
(2) [¹ . . .]
(3) In sub-paragraph (1) "maintenance" means child support maintenance as defined by
section 3(6) of the 1991 Act whether before or after the amendment of the definition of such
maintenance by section 1(2)(a) of the Child Support, Pensions and Social Security Act 2000,
and includes maintenance payable at a transitional rate in accordance with regulations made
under section 29(3)(a) of that Act.

Apportionment
4. Where maintenance is payable to more than one person with care, the amount deducted   **4.100**
must be apportioned between the persons with care in accordance with paragraphs 6, 7 and 8
of Schedule 1 (maintenance assessments) to the 1991 Act.

Flat rate maintenance

4.101　　5.—(1) This paragraph applies where the beneficiary and that person's partner are each liable to pay maintenance at a flat rate in accordance with paragraph 4(2) of Schedule 1 to the 1991 Act and either of them has been awarded universal credit (whether as a single claimant or as joint claimants).

(2) Where this paragraph applies, an amount not exceeding an amount equal to the flat rate of maintenance may be deducted from such an award in respect of the total liability of both partners to pay maintenance, in the proportions described in regulation 4(3) of the Child Support (Maintenance Calculations and Special Cases) Regulations 2001 or regulation 44(3) of the Child Support Maintenance Calculation Regulations 2012 and must be paid in discharge (in whole or in part) of the respective liabilities to pay maintenance.

Notice

4.102　　6. Where the Secretary of State commences making deductions under this Schedule, the Secretary of State must notify the beneficiary in writing of the amount and frequency of the deduction and the benefit from which the deduction is made and must give further such notice when there is a change to any of the particulars specified in the notice.

AMENDMENT

1. Child Support (Miscellaneous Amendments) Regulations 2019 (SI 2019/1084) regs 6 and 8 (July 4, 2019).

DEFINITIONS

"the 1991 Act"—see reg.2.
"beneficiary"—see para.(1).
"benefit"—see reg.2.
"child"—see reg.2 and WRA 2012 s.40.
"claimant"—see reg.2.
"employment and support allowance"—*ibid.*
"jobseeker's allowance"—*ibid.*
"maintenance"—see para.(1).
"person with care"—*ibid.*
"specified benefit"—*ibid.*
"universal credit"—see reg.2.

The Universal Credit, Personal Independence Payment, Jobseeker's Allowance and Employment and Support Allowance (Decisions and Appeals) Regulations 2013

(SI 2013/381)

4.103　　*The Secretary of State makes the following Regulations in exercise of the powers conferred by sections: 5(1A), 159D(1) and (6), 189(1), (4) to (6) and section 191 of the Social Security Administration Act 1992; 9(1), (4) and (6), 10(3) and (6), 10A, 11(1), 12(2), (3), (3A), (3B), (6) and (7)(b), 16(1), 17, 18(1), 21(1) to (3), 22 and 23, 25(3)(b) and (5)(c), 26(6)(c), 28(1), 31(2), 79(1) and (4) to (7) and 84 of, and paragraph 9 of Schedule 2, paragraphs 1, 4 and 9 of Schedule 3 and Schedule 5 to, the Social Security Act 1998.*

A draft of this instrument was laid before and approved by a resolution of each House of Parliament in accordance with section 80(1) of the Social Security Act 1998.

The Social Security Advisory Committee has agreed that the proposals in respect of these Regulations should not be referred to it.

ARRANGEMENT OF REGULATIONS

PART I

GENERAL

PART II

REVISION

CHAPTER 1

REVISION ON ANY GROUNDS

CHAPTER 2

REVISION ON SPECIFIC GROUNDS

CHAPTER 3

PROCEDURE AND EFFECTIVE DATE

PART III

SUPERSESSIONS

CHAPTER 1

GROUNDS FOR SUPERSESSION

CHAPTER 2

SUPERSEDING DECISIONS: LIMITATIONS AND PROCEDURE

CHAPTER 3

EFFECTIVE DATES FOR SUPERSESSIONS

PART IV

OTHER MATTERS RELATING TO DECISION- MAKING

PART V

SUSPENSION

PART VI

TERMINATION

PART VII

APPEALS

GENERAL NOTE

An annotated version of these Regulations is included in Vol. III. They are repeated   **4.104**
in this volume so as to provide a complete text of the law governing universal credit.
Readers are referred to Vol. III for commentary on the individual provisions. These
Regulations are in force from April 8, 2013 in relation to personal independence
payment and April 29, 2013 in relation to universal credit, new-style employment
and support allowance and new-style jobseeker's allowance.

PART I

GENERAL

Citation, commencement and application

4.105   **1.**—(1) These Regulations may be cited as the Universal Credit, Personal Independence Payment, Jobseeker's Allowance and Employment and Support Allowance (Decisions and Appeals) Regulations 2013.

(2) They come into force—

(a) in so far as they relate to personal independence payment and for the purposes of this regulation, on 8th April 2013;

(b) for all remaining purposes, on 29th April 2013.

(3) These Regulations apply in relation to—

(a) an employment and support allowance payable under Part 1 of the 2007 Act as amended by Schedule 3 and Part 1 of Schedule 14 to the 2012 Act (to remove references to an income-related allowance);

(b) a jobseeker's allowance payable under the Jobseekers Act as amended by Part 1 of Schedule 14 to the 2012 Act (to remove references to an income-based allowance);

(c) personal independence payment; and

(d) universal credit.

Interpretation

4.106   **2.** In these Regulations—

"the 1998 Act" means the Social Security Act 1998;

"the 2007 Act" means the Welfare Reform Act 2007;

"the 2012 Act" means the Welfare Reform Act 2012;

"the Administration Act" means the Social Security Administration Act 1992;

"appeal", except where the context otherwise requires, means an appeal to the First-tier Tribunal established under the Tribunals, Courts and Enforcement Act 2007;

"appropriate office" means—

(a) in the case of a contributions decision which falls within Part 2 (contributions decisions) of Schedule 3 (decisions against which an appeal lies) to the 1998 Act, any National Insurance Contributions office of HMRC or any office of the Department for Work and Pensions; or

(b) in any other case, the office of the Department for Work and Pensions, or other place, the address of which is specified on the notification of the original decision referred to in regulation 5(1) (revision on any grounds);

"assessment period" is to be construed in accordance with regulation 21 (assessment periods) of the Universal Credit Regulations;

"benefit" means a benefit or an allowance in relation to which these Regulations apply;

"benefit week" has the same meaning as in—

(a) regulation 2 (interpretation) of the Employment and Support Allowance Regulations 2013 in the case of an employment and support allowance;

(b) regulation 2 (general interpretation) of the Jobseeker's Allowance Regulations 2013, in the case of a jobseeker's allowance;

"child" means a person under the age of 16;

"claimant" means—

(a) any person who has claimed—
  (i) an employment and support allowance;
  (ii) a jobseeker's allowance;
  (iii) personal independence payment;

(b) in the case of universal credit, any person who is a claimant for the purposes of section 40 (interpretation) of the 2012 Act; and

(c) any other person from whom an amount of benefit is alleged to be recoverable;

"the Claims and Payments Regulations 2013" means the Universal Credit, Personal Independence Payment, Jobseeker's Allowance and Employment and Support Allowance (Claims and Payments) Regulations 2013;

"the Contributions and Benefits Act" means the Social Security Contributions and Benefits Act 1992;

"the date of notification", in relation to a decision of the Secretary of State, means the date on which the notification of the decision is treated as having been given or sent in accordance with—

(a) regulation 3 (service of documents); or

(b) where the notification is given or sent using an electronic communication, Schedule 2 (electronic communications) to the Claims and Payments Regulations 2013;

"designated authority" means—

(a) the Secretary of State; or

(b) a person providing services to the Secretary of State;

"electronic communication" has the same meaning as in section 15(1) of the Electronic Communications Act 2000;

"employment and support allowance" means an employment and support allowance in relation to which these Regulations apply;

"the Fraud Act" means the Social Security Fraud Act 2001;

"fraud penalty", in relation to any claimant of an employment and support allowance, a jobseeker's allowance or universal credit, means any period during which the provisions of section 6B, 7 or 9 of the Fraud Act apply to the award;

"family" means the claimant's partner and any—

(a) child; or

(b) qualifying young person, within the meaning of regulation 5 (meaning of "qualifying young person") of the Universal Credit Regulations,

who is a member of the same household as the claimant and for whom the either the claimant or their partner is, or both of them are, responsible;

"HMRC" means Her Majesty's Revenue and Customs;

"the Jobseekers Act" means the Jobseekers Act 1995;

"jobseeker's allowance" means a jobseeker's allowance in relation to which these Regulations apply;

"limited capability for work" has the same meaning as in—

(a) section 1(4) of the 2007 Act in relation to an employment and support allowance;

(b) section 37(1) of the 2012 Act in relation to universal credit;

"limited capability for work determination" means—

(a) where the determination relates to an employment and support allowance, a determination whether a person has limited capability for work following a limited capability for work assessment in accordance with regulation 15(1) (determination of limited capability for work) of the Employment and Support Allowance Regulations 2013, or a determination that a person is to be treated as having limited capability for work in accordance with regulation 16 (certain claimants to be treated as having limited capability for work) or 25 (exceptional circumstances) of those Regulations;

(b) where the determination relates to universal credit, a determination whether a person has limited capability for work following a limited capability for work assessment referred to in regulation 39(2) (limited capability for work) of the Universal Credit Regulations, or a determination that a person is to be treated as having limited capability for work in accordance with regulation 39(6) of those Regulations;

"official error" means an error made by—

(a) an officer of the Department for Work and Pensions or HMRC acting as such which was not caused or materially contributed to by any person outside the Department or HMRC;

(b) a person employed by, and acting on behalf of, a designated authority which was not caused or materially contributed to by any person outside that authority,

but excludes any error of law which is shown to have been such by a subsequent decision of the Upper Tribunal, or of the court as defined in section 27(7) of the 1998 Act;

"partner" means one of a couple within the meaning of section 39 (couples) of the 2012 Act;

"personal independence payment" means an allowance payable under Part 4 (personal independence payment) of the 2012 Act;

"relevant benefit" has the same meaning as in Chapter 2 (social security decisions and appeals) of Part 1 (decisions and appeals) of the 1998 Act;

"the Rent Officers Order 2013" means the Rent Officers (Universal Credit Functions) Order 2013;

"terminally ill", in relation to a claimant, means that the claimant is suffering from a progressive disease and that death in consequence of that disease can reasonably be expected within 6 months;

"the Tribunal Procedure Rules" means the Tribunal Procedure (First-tier Tribunal) (Social Entitlement Chamber) Rules 2008;

"the Universal Credit Regulations" means the Universal Credit Regulations 2013;

"universal credit" means the benefit payable under Part 1 (universal credit) of the 2012 Act;

"writing" includes writing produced by means of electronic communications used in accordance with regulation 4 (electronic communications).

Service of documents

4.107   **3.**—(1) Where, under any provision of these Regulations, any notice or other document is given or sent by post to the Secretary of State, it is to be treated as having been given or sent on the day on which it is received by the Secretary of State.

(2) Where, under any provision of these Regulations, the Secretary of State sends a notice or other document by post to a person's last known address, it is to be treated as having been given or sent on the day on which it was posted.

Electronic communications

4. Schedule 2 (electronic communications) to the Claims and Payments Regulations 2013 applies to the delivery of electronic communications to or by the Secretary of State for the purposes of these Regulations in the same manner as it applies to the delivery of electronic communications for the purposes of the Claims and Payments Regulations 2013.

4.108

DEFINITIONS

"the Claims and Payments Regulations 2013"—see reg.2.
"electronic communication"—*ibid.*

PART II

REVISION

CHAPTER 1

REVISION ON ANY GROUNDS

Revision on any grounds

5.—(1) Any decision of the Secretary of State under section 8 or 10 of the 1998 Act ("the original decision") may be revised by the Secretary of State if—

4.109

 (a) the Secretary of State commences action leading to the revision within one month of the date of notification of the original decision; or

 (b) an application for a revision is received by the Secretary of State at an appropriate office within—

  (i) one month of the date of notification of the original decision (but subject to regulation 38(4)(correction of accidental errors));

  (ii) 14 days of the expiry of that period if a written statement of the reasons for the decision is requested under regulation 7 (consideration of revision before appeal) or regulation 51 (notice of a decision against which an appeal lies) and that statement is provided within the period specified in paragraph (i);

  (iii) 14 days of the date on which that statement was provided if the statement was requested within the period specified in paragraph (i) but was provided after the expiry of that period; or

  (iv) such longer period as may be allowed under regulation 6 (late application for a revision).

(2) Paragraph (1) does not apply—

 (a) in respect of a relevant change of circumstances which occurred since the decision had effect or, in the case of an advance award under reg-

873

ulation 32, 33 or 34 of the Claims and Payments Regulations 2013, since the decision was made;

(b) where the Secretary of State has evidence or information which indicates that a relevant change of circumstances will occur;

(c) in respect of a decision which relates to an employment and support allowance or personal independence payment where the claimant is terminally ill, unless the application for a revision contains an express statement that the claimant is terminally ill.

DEFINITIONS

"appeal"—see reg.2.
"claimant"—*ibid.*
"the date of notification"—*ibid.*
"personal independence payment"—*ibid.*
"terminally ill"—*ibid.*

Late application for a revision

4.110   **6.**—(1) The Secretary of State may extend the time limit specified in regulation 5(1) (revision on any grounds) for making an application for a revision if all of the following conditions are met.

(2) The first condition is that the person wishing to apply for the revision has applied to the Secretary of State at an appropriate office for an extension of time.

(3) The second condition is that the application—

(a) explains why the extension is sought;

(b) contains sufficient details of the decision to which the application relates to enable it to be identified; and

(c) is made within [¹ 12] months of the latest date by which the application for revision should have been received by the Secretary of State in accordance with regulation 5(1)(b)(i) to (iii).

(4) The third condition is that the Secretary of State is satisfied that it is reasonable to grant the extension.

(5) The fourth condition is that the Secretary of State is satisfied that due to special circumstances it was not practicable for the application for revision to be made within the time limit specified in regulation 5(1)(b)(i) to (iii) (revision on any grounds).

(6) In determining whether it is reasonable to grant an extension of time, the Secretary of State must have regard to the principle that the greater the amount of time that has elapsed between the end of the time limit specified in regulation 5(1)(b)(i) to (iii) (revision on any grounds) and the date of the application, the more compelling should be the special circumstances on which the application is based.

(7) An application under this regulation which has been refused may not be renewed.

AMENDMENT

1. Social Security (Miscellaneous Amendments No. 4) Regulations 2017 (SI 2017/1015) reg.16 (November 16, 2017).

DEFINITION

"appropriate office"—see reg.2.

Consideration of revision before appeal

7.—(1) This regulation applies in a case where—

(a) the Secretary of State gives a person written notice of a decision under section 8 or 10 of the 1998 Act (whether as originally made or as revised under section 9 of that Act); and

(b) that notice includes a statement to the effect that there is a right of appeal in relation to the decision only if the Secretary of State has considered an application for a revision of the decision.

(2) In a case to which this regulation applies, a person has a right of appeal under section 12(2) of the 1998 Act in relation to the decision only if the Secretary of State has considered on an application whether to revise the decision under section 9 of that Act.

(3) The notice referred to in paragraph (1) must inform the person—

(a) of the time limit under regulation 5(1) (revision on any grounds) for making an application for a revision; and

(b) that, where the notice does not include a statement of the reasons for the decision ("written reasons"), the person may, within one month of the date of notification of the decision, request that the Secretary of State provide written reasons.

(4) Where written reasons are requested under paragraph (3)(b), the Secretary of State must provide that statement within 14 days of receipt of the request or as soon as practicable afterwards.

(5) Where, as the result of paragraph (2), there is no right of appeal against a decision, the Secretary of State may treat any purported appeal as an application for a revision under section 9 of the 1998 Act.

4.111

DEFINITIONS

"the 1998 Act"—see reg.2.
"appeal"—*ibid.*

CHAPTER 2

REVISION ON SPECIFIC GROUNDS

Introduction

8. A decision of the Secretary of State under section 8 or 10 of the 1998 Act may be revised at any time by the Secretary of State in any of the cases and circumstances set out in this Chapter.

4.112

Official error, mistake etc.

9. A decision may be revised where the decision—

(a) arose from official error; or

(b) was made in ignorance of, or was based on a mistake as to, some material fact and as a result is more advantageous to a claimant than it would otherwise have been.

4.113

DEFINITION

"official error"—see reg.2.

Decisions against which no appeal lies

4.114   **10.** A decision may be revised where the decision is one which is—

    (a) specified in Schedule 2 (decisions against which no appeal lies) to the 1998 Act; or

    (b) prescribed by regulation 50(2) (decisions which may or may not be appealed).

DEFINITIONS

> "the 1998 Act"—see reg.2.
> "appeal"—*ibid.*

Decisions where there is an appeal

4.115   **11.**—(1) A decision may be revised where there is an appeal against the decision within the time prescribed by the Tribunal Procedure Rules but the appeal has not been decided.

    (2) Where—

    (a) the Secretary of State makes a decision under section 8 or 10 of the 1998 Act or such a decision is revised under section 9(1) of the 1998 Act ("decision A");

    (b) the claimant appeals against decision A;

    (c) after the appeal has been made, but before it results in a decision by the First-tier Tribunal, the Secretary of State makes another decision ("decision B") which—

      (i) supersedes decision A; or

      (ii) decides a further claim by the claimant;

    (d) after the making of decision B, the First-tier Tribunal makes a decision on the appeal ("decision C"); and

    (e) the Secretary of State would have made decision B differently if, at the time, the Secretary of State had been aware of decision C,

the Secretary of State may revise decision B.

DEFINITIONS

> "the 1998 Act"—see reg.2.
> "appeal"—*ibid.*
> "claimant"—*ibid.*

Award of another benefit

4.116   **12.** Where—

    (a) the Secretary of State makes a decision to award a benefit to a claimant ("the original award"); and

    (b) an award of another relevant benefit or of an increase in the rate of another relevant benefit is made to the claimant or, in the case of universal credit, to a member of their family, for a period which includes the date on which the original award took effect,

the Secretary of State may revise the original award.

DEFINITIONS

> "benefit"—see reg.2.
> "claimant"—*ibid.*
> "relevant benefit"—*ibid.*
> "universal credit"—*ibid.*

Advance awards etc.

13. A decision pursuant to regulation 32, 33 or 34 of the Claims and Payments Regulations 2013 to make an advance award of benefit may be revised if the conditions for entitlement are found not to have been satisfied at the start of the period for which the claim is treated as having been made.

4.117

DEFINITION

"the Claims and Payments Regulations 2013"—see reg.2.

Sanctions cases etc.

14.—(1) The following decisions may be revised—
  (a) a decision that the amount of an employment and support allowance is to be reduced by virtue of section 11J(1) (sanctions) of the 2007 Act;
  (b) a decision that the amount of a jobseeker's allowance is to be reduced by virtue of section 6J (higher-level sanctions) or 6K(1) (other sanctions) of the Jobseekers Act;
  (c) a decision that the amount of universal credit is to be reduced by virtue of section 26(1) (higher-level sanctions) or 27(1) (other sanctions) of the 2012 Act.
  (d) A decision under section 6B, 7 or 9 ("the loss of benefit provisions") of the Fraud Act that benefit ceases to be payable or falls to be reduced as a result of the person—
  (e) being convicted of an offence; or
  (f) agreeing to pay a penalty as an alternative to prosecution,
may be revised where that conviction is quashed or set aside by a court or where the person withdraws the agreement to pay the penalty.

4.118

DEFINITIONS

"the 2007 Act"—see reg.2.
"benefit"—*ibid.*
"employment and support allowance"—*ibid.*
"the Fraud Act"—*ibid.*
"the Jobseekers Act"—*ibid.*
"jobseeker's allowance"—*ibid.*

Other decisions relating to an employment and support allowance

15.—(1) A decision awarding an employment and support allowance may be revised in any of the following circumstances.
  (2) The first circumstance is where—
  (a) the decision was made on the basis that the claimant had made and was pursuing an appeal against a decision of the Secretary of State that the claimant did not have limited capability for work ("the original decision"); and
  (b) the appeal in relation to the original decision is successful.
  (3) The second circumstance is where—
  (a) the decision incorporates a determination that the conditions in regulation 26(2) (conditions for treating claimant as having limited capability for work until a determination about limited capability for work has been made) of the Employment and Support Allowance Regulations 2013 are satisfied;
  (b) those conditions were not satisfied when the claim was made; and

4.119

(c) a decision falls to be made concerning entitlement to that award in respect of a period before the date on which the award took effect.

(4) The third circumstance is where the claimant's current period of limited capability for work is treated as a continuation of another such period under regulation 86 (linking period) of the Employment and Support Allowance Regulations 2013.

[¹ (4A) The fourth circumstance is where the decision—

(a) immediately follows the last day of a period for which the claimant was treated as capable of work or as not having limited capability for work under regulation 55ZA of the Jobseeker's Allowance Regulations or regulation 46A of the Jobseeker's Allowance Regulations 2013 (extended period of sickness) and that period lasted 13 weeks; and

(b) is not a decision which embodies a determination that the person is treated as having limited capability for work under regulation 26 of the Employment and Support Allowance Regulations 2013 (conditions for treating a claimant as having limited capability for work until a determination about limited capability for work has been made).]

(5) A decision terminating a person's entitlement to an employment and support allowance may be revised where—

(a) that entitlement was terminated because of section 1A (duration of contributory allowance) of the 2007 Act; and

(b) it is subsequently determined, in relation to the period of entitlement before that decision, that the person had or is treated as having had limited capability for work-related activity.

Amendment

1. Jobseeker's Allowance (Extended Period of Sickness) Amendment Regulations 2015 (SI 2015/339) reg.8(1) and (2) (March 30, 2015).

Definitions

"appeal"—see reg.2.
"claimant"—*ibid.*
"employment and support allowance"—*ibid.*
"limited capability for work"—*ibid.*

Other decisions relating to a jobseeker's allowance

4.120
16.—(1) A decision awarding a jobseeker's allowance may be revised in any of the following circumstances.

(2) The first circumstance is where—

(a) the Secretary of State makes a conversion decision (within the meaning of regulation 5(2)(b) of the Employment and Support Allowance (Transitional Provisions, Housing Benefit and Council Tax Benefit) (Existing Awards) (No.2) Regulations 2010 (deciding whether an existing award qualifies for conversion)) in respect of a person;

(b) the person appeals against that decision;

(c) before or after the appeal is made, there is a decision to award a jobseeker's allowance as the result of a claim being made by that person; and

(d) the appeal in relation to the conversion decision referred to in subparagraph (a) is successful.

(3) The second circumstance is where—

(a) a person's entitlement to an employment and support allowance is terminated because of a decision which embodies a determination that the person does not have limited capability for work;

(b) the person appeals against that decision;

(c) before or after the appeal is made, there is a decision to award a job-seeker's allowance as the result of a claim being made by that person; and

(d) the appeal in relation to the termination decision referred to in sub-paragraph (a) is successful.

DEFINITIONS

"appeal"—see reg.2.
"benefit"—*ibid.*
"employment and support allowance"—*ibid.*
"jobseeker's allowance"—*ibid.*

Contributions cases

17.—(1) A decision ("the original decision") may be revised where—   4.121

(a) on or after the date of the original decision—

    (i) a late paid contribution is treated under regulation 5 (treatment of late paid contributions where no consent, connivance or negligence by the primary contributor) of the Social Security (Crediting and Treatment of Contributions and National Insurance Numbers) Regulations 2001 ("the Crediting Regulations") as paid on a date which falls on or before the date on which the original decision was made;

    (ii) a direction is given under regulation 6 (treatment of contributions paid late through ignorance or error) of those Regulations that a late paid contribution is to be treated as paid on a date which falls on or before the date on which the original decision was made; or

    (iii) an unpaid contribution is treated under regulation 60 (treatment of unpaid contributions where no consent, connivance or negligence by the primary contributor) of the Social Security (Contributions) Regulations 2001 as paid on a date which falls on or before the date on which the original decision was made; and

(b) either an award of benefit would have been made or the amount of benefit awarded would have been different.

(2) A decision may be revised where, by virtue of regulation 6C (treatment of Class 3 contributions paid under section 13A of the Act) of the Crediting Regulations, a contribution is treated as paid on a date which falls on or before the date on which the decision was made.

[¹ (3) A decision in relation to a claim for a jobseeker's allowance or an employment and support allowance may be revised at any time where—

(a) on or after the date of the decision a contribution is treated as paid as set out in regulation 7A of the Social Security (Crediting and Treatment of Contributions, and National Insurance Numbers) Regulations 2001 (treatment of Class 2 contributions paid on or before the due date); and

(b) by virtue of the contribution being so treated, the person satisfies the contribution conditions of entitlement specified in paragraph (6) in relation to that benefit.

(4) A decision to award a jobseeker's allowance or an employment and support allowance may be revised at any time where on or after the date of the decision—

(a) any of the circumstances in paragraph (5) occur; and

(b) by virtue of the circumstance occurring, the person ceases to satisfy the contribution conditions of entitlement specified in paragraph (6) in relation to that benefit.

(5) The circumstances are—

(a) a Class 2 contribution is repaid to a person in consequence of an amendment or correction of the person's relevant profits under section 9ZA or 9ZB of the Taxes Management Act 1970 (amendment or correction of return by taxpayer or officer of the Board);

(b) a Class 2 contribution is returned to a person under regulation 52 of the Social Security (Contributions) Regulations 2001 (contributions paid in error); or

(c) a Class 1 or a Class 2 contribution paid by a person to Her Majesty's Revenue and Customs under section 223 of the Finance Act 2014 (accelerated payment in respect of notice given while tax enquiry is in progress) is repaid to the person.

(6) The contribution conditions of entitlement are—

(a) in relation to a jobseeker's allowance, the conditions set out in section 2(1)(a) and (b) of the Jobseekers Act (the contribution-based conditions); or

(b) in relation to an employment and support allowance, the first and second conditions set out in paragraphs 1(1) and 2(1) of Schedule 1 to the 2007 Act (conditions relating to national insurance).

(7) In this regulation "relevant profits" has the meaning given in section 11(3) of the Contributions and Benefits Act]

AMENDMENT

1. Social Security (Credits, and Crediting and Treatment of Contributions) (Consequential and Miscellaneous Amendments (SI 2016/1145) reg.6 (January 1, 2017).

DEFINITION

"benefit"—see reg.2.

Other decisions relating to personal independence payment

4.122   **18.**—(1) Where the Secretary of State makes a decision awarding personal independence payment which takes effect immediately after the expiry of an existing award under regulation 33(3) (advance claim for and award of personal independence payment) of the Claims and Payments Regulations 2013, that decision may be revised if the requirements for entitlement are found not to have been met on the date on which the decision takes effect.

(2) A decision that personal independence payment is not payable to a person for any period may be revised where—

(a) the Secretary of State determines that the person meets the condition in section 85(2) of the 2012 Act (care home residents where the costs of qualifying services are borne out of local or public funds) on incomplete evidence in accordance with regulation 39(5); and

(b) after that determination is made, any of the costs of the qualifying

services are recovered from the person for whom they are provided.

(3) A decision of the Secretary of State made in consequence of a
negative determination may be revised at any time if it contains an error to
which the claimant did not materially contribute.

DEFINITIONS

"the 2012 Act"—see reg.2.
"personal independence payment"—*ibid.*

Other decisions relating to universal credit

19.—(1) Where the Secretary of State has reduced the amount of an
award of universal credit as a consequence of regulation 81 (reduction of
universal credit) of the Universal Credit Regulations, that decision may be
revised.

4.123

(2) A decision in relation to universal credit which adopts a determination made under the Rent Officers Order 2013 may be revised at any
time in consequence of a rent officer's redetermination made under that
Order which resulted in an increase in the amount which represents rent
for the purposes of calculating the housing costs element in universal
credit.

DEFINITIONS

"the Universal Credit Regulations"—see reg.2.
"universal credit"—*ibid.*

CHAPTER 3

PROCEDURE AND EFFECTIVE DATE

Procedure for making an application for a revision

20.—(1) The Secretary of State may treat an application for a supersession under section 10 of the 1998 Act as an application for a revision under
section 9 of that Act.

4.124

(2) The following paragraph applies where the Secretary of State, in
order to consider all the issues raised by the application, requires further
evidence or information from a person who has applied for a revision ("the
applicant").

(3) The Secretary of State must notify the applicant that—

(a) the further evidence or information specified in the notification is
required;

(b) if the applicant provides the relevant evidence or information within
one month of the date of notification or such longer period as the
Secretary of State may allow, the decision may be revised taking such
evidence or information into account; and

(c) if the applicant does not provide such evidence or information within
that period, the decision may be revised using such evidence or information as was submitted with the application for revision.

DEFINITION

"the date of notification"—see reg.2.

Effective date of a revision

4.125   **21.** Where, on a revision under section 9 of the 1998 Act, the Secretary of State decides that the date from which the decision under section 8 or 10 of that Act ("the original decision") took effect was wrong, the revision takes effect from the date from which the original decision would have taken effect had the error not been made.

DEFINITION

"the 1998 Act"—see reg.2.

PART III

SUPERSESSIONS

CHAPTER 1

GROUNDS FOR SUPERSESSION

Introduction

4.126   **22.** Subject to regulation 32 (decisions which may not be superseded), the Secretary of State may make a decision under section 10 ("a superseding decision") of the 1998 Act in any of the cases and circumstances set out in this Chapter.

Changes of circumstances

4.127   **23.**—(1) The Secretary of State may supersede a decision in respect of which—

   (a) there has been a relevant change of circumstances since the decision to be superseded had effect or, in the case of an advance award under regulation 32, 33 or 34 of the Claims and Payments Regulations 2013, since it was made; or

   (b) it is expected that a relevant change of circumstances will occur.

(2) The fact that a person has become terminally ill is not a relevant change of circumstances for the purposes of paragraph (1) unless an application for supersession is made which contains an express statement that the person is terminally ill.

DEFINITIONS

"the Claims and Payments Regulations 2013"—see reg.2.
"terminally ill"—*ibid.*

Error of law, ignorance, mistake etc.

4.128   **24.** A decision of the Secretary of State, other than one to which regulation 25 (decisions against which no appeal lies) refers, may be superseded where—

   (a) the decision was wrong in law, or was made in ignorance of, or was based on a mistake as to, some material fact; and

   (b) an application for a supersession was received, or a decision was taken by the Secretary of State to act on the Secretary of State's own initiative, more than one month after the date of notification of the decision to be superseded or after the expiry of such longer period as may have been allowed under regulation 6 (late application for a revision).

Decisions against which no appeal lies

25. A decision specified in Schedule 2 (decisions against which no appeal **4.129**
lies) to the 1998 Act or prescribed in regulation 50(2) (decisions which may
or may not be appealed) may be superseded.

DEFINITIONS

"the 1998 Act"—see reg.2.
"appeal"—*ibid.*

Medical evidence and limited capability for work etc.

26.—(1) An employment and support allowance decision, a personal **4.130**
independence payment decision or universal credit decision may be superseded where, since the decision was made, the Secretary of State has—
  (a) received medical evidence from a healthcare professional or other
      person approved by the Secretary of State; or
[¹ (b) made a determination that the claimant is to be treated as having—
        (i) limited capability for work in accordance with regulation
            16, 21, 22 or 29 of the Employment and Support Allowance
            Regulations 2013; or
       (ii) limited capability for work or for work and work-related activity
            in accordance with Part 5 (capability for work or work-related
            activity) of the Universal Credit Regulations.]
  (2) The decision awarding personal independence payment may be
superseded where there has been a negative determination.
  (3) In this regulation—
"an employment and support allowance decision", "personal independ-
    ence payment decision" and "universal credit decision" each has the
    meaning given in Schedule 1 (effective dates for superseding decisions
    made on the ground of a change of circumstances);
"healthcare professional" means—
  (a) a registered medical practitioner;
  (b) a registered nurse; or
  (c) an occupational therapist or physiotherapist registered with a
      regulatory body established by an Order in Council under section 60
      (regulation of health professions, social workers, other care workers
      etc.) of the Health Act 1999.

AMENDMENT

1. Universal Credit and Miscellaneous Amendments Regulations 2014 (SI
2014/597) reg.6 (April 28, 2014).

DEFINITIONS

"claimant"—see reg.2.
"employment and support allowance"—*ibid.*
"limited capability for work"—*ibid.*
"personal independence payment"—*ibid.*
"universal credit"—*ibid.*

GENERAL NOTE

With effect from March 13, 2020, reg.3(1) and (2) of the Employment and
Support Allowance and Universal Credit (Coronavirus Disease) Regulations 2020
(SI 2020/289) applied to those who claimed, or had an existing award of, universal

credit and were—or were caring for a child or qualifying young person who was a member their household and who was—either infected or contaminated with Coronavirus disease or were in isolation. The regulation provided that such people were to be treated as having limited capability for work where the Secretary of State was satisfied that they should be so treated.

By reg.3(3) of SI 2020/289, reg.26 (i.e., reg.26(1)(b)(ii)) applied to such a determination as if it had been made under Pt.5 of the Universal Credit Regulations. The determination therefore amounted to a ground for the supersession of the existing award of universal credit. For the effective date of the superseding decision see reg.35(9) below.

For most purposes, the provisions of SI 2020/289 are to expire at the end of November 12, 2020: see reg.5(2). As it applied to universal credit, however, reg.3 of SI 2020/289 ceased to have effect on March 30, 2020: see regs 1(1) and 10(3) of the Social Security (Coronavirus) (Further Measures) Regulations 2020 (SI 2020/371).

Sanctions cases

4.131

27.—(1) A decision as to the amount of an award of benefit may be superseded where the amount of that award is to be reduced by virtue of—

(a) section 11J(1) (sanctions) of the 2007 Act;

(b) section 6J(1) (higher-level sanctions) or 6K(1) (other sanctions) of the Jobseekers Act; or

(c) section 26(1) (higher-level sanctions) or 27(1) (other sanctions) of the 2012 Act.

(2) A decision reducing an award of benefit by virtue of any of those provisions may be superseded where the reduction falls to be suspended or terminated.

DEFINITIONS

"the 2007 Act"—see reg.2.
"benefit"—*ibid.*

Loss of benefit cases

4.132

28. A decision that a benefit is payable to a claimant may be superseded where that benefit ceases to be payable or falls to be reduced by virtue of section 6B, 7 or 9 of the Fraud Act (loss of benefit provisions).

DEFINITION

"benefit"—see reg.2.

Contributions cases

4.133

29. The Secretary of State may supersede a decision ("the original decision") where, on or after the date on which the decision is made, a late or an unpaid contribution is treated as paid under—

(a) regulation 5 of the Social Security (Crediting and Treatment of Contributions and National Insurance Numbers) Regulations 2001 (treatment of late paid contributions where no consent, connivance or negligence by the primary contributor) on a date which falls on or before the date on which the original decision was made;

(b) regulation 6 of those Regulations (treatment of contributions paid late through ignorance or error) on a date which falls on or before the date on which the original decision was made; or

(c) regulation 60 of the Social Security (Contributions) Regulations

2001 (treatment of unpaid contributions where no consent, connivance or negligence by the primary contributor) on a date which falls
on or before the date on which the original decision was made.

Housing costs: universal credit

30.—(1) A decision in relation to universal credit which adopts a determination made under the Rent Officers Order 2013 may be superseded
where, in consequence of a rent officer's redetermination made in under
that Order, the amount which represents rent for the purposes of calculating the housing costs element in universal credit is reduced.

4.134

DEFINITIONS

"the Rent Officers Order 2013"—see reg.2.
"universal credit"—*ibid.*

Tribunal decisions

31. The Secretary of State may supersede a decision of the First-tier
Tribunal or Upper Tribunal which—

4.135

(a) was made in ignorance of, or was based upon a mistake as to, some
material fact; or
(b) in a case where section 26(5) (appeals involving issues that arise in
other cases) of the 1998 Act applies, was made in accordance with
section 26(4)(b)of that Act.

CHAPTER 2

SUPERSEDING DECISIONS: LIMITATIONS AND PROCEDURE

Decisions which may not be superseded

32. A decision which may be revised under section 9 of the 1998 Act may
not be superseded under Chapter 1 of this Part unless—

4.136

(a) circumstances arise in which the Secretary of State may revise the
decision under Part 2; and
(b) further circumstances arise in relation to that decision which—
   (i) are not set out in that Part; but
   (ii) are set out in Chapter 1 of this Part or are ones where a superseding decision may be made in accordance with regulation 33(3).

DEFINITION

"the 1998 Act"—see reg.2.

Procedure for making an application for a supersession

33.—(1) The Secretary of State may treat an application for a revision
under section 9 of the 1998 Act, or a notification of a change of circumstances, as an application for a supersession under section 10 of that Act.

4.137

(2) The following paragraph applies where the Secretary of State, in
order to consider all the issues raised by the application, requires further
evidence or information from a person who has applied for a supersession
("the applicant").

(3) The Secretary of State must notify the applicant that—

(a) the further evidence or information specified in the notification is required;

(b) if the applicant provides the relevant evidence or information within one month of the date of notification or such longer period as the Secretary of State may allow, the decision may be superseded taking such information or evidence into account; and

(c) if the applicant does not provide such evidence or information within that period, the decision to be superseded may be superseded taking into account only such evidence or information as was submitted with the application for a supersession.

[¹ (4) In relation to an applicant who is supplying information or evidence of a change of circumstances which is advantageous to the applicant in relation to an award of universal credit, paragraph (3)(b) has effect as if for "one month" there were substituted "14 days."]

AMENDMENT

1. Universal Credit (Miscellaneous Amendments, Saving and Transitional Provision) Regulations 2018 (SI 2018/65) reg.5(1) and (2) (April 11, 2018).

DEFINITION

"the date of notification"—see reg.2.

CHAPTER 3

EFFECTIVE DATES FOR SUPERSESSIONS

Introduction

4.138   **34.** This Chapter and Schedule 1 (effective dates for superseding decisions made on the ground of a change of circumstances) contains exceptions to the provisions of section 10(5) of the 1998 Act as to the date from which a decision under section 10 of that Act which supersedes an earlier decision takes effect.

DEFINITION

"the 1998 Act"—see reg.2.

Effective dates: Secretary of State decisions

4.139   **35.**—(1) Schedule 1 (effective dates for superseding decisions made on the ground of a change of circumstances) makes provision for the date from which a superseding decision takes effect where there has been, or it is anticipated that there will be, a relevant change of circumstances since the earlier decision took effect.

(2) This paragraph applies where the Secretary of State supersedes a decision—

(a) on the ground that the decision was wrong in law, or was made in ignorance of, or was based on a mistake as to, some material fact, in accordance with regulation 24 (error of law, ignorance, mistake etc.); or

(b) under regulation 25 (decisions against which no appeal lies).

(3) In a case where paragraph (2) applies and the superseding decision relates to a jobseeker's allowance or an employment and support allowance, the superseding decision takes effect from the first day of the benefit week in which the superseding decision, or where applicable, the application for supersession, was made.

(4) In a case where paragraph (2) applies and the superseding decision relates to universal credit, the superseding decision takes effect from the first day of the assessment period in which the superseding decision, or where applicable, the application for supersession, was made.

(5) A superseding decision made in consequence of a decision which is a relevant determination for the purposes of section 27 of the 1998 Act (restrictions on entitlement to benefit in certain cases of error) takes effect from the date of the relevant determination.

(6) In the case of an employment and support allowance, a superseding decision made in accordance with regulation 26(1) (medical evidence and limited capability for work etc.), following an application by the claimant, that embodies a determination that the claimant has limited capability for work-related activity, takes effect from the date of the application.

(7) In the case of an employment and support allowance, a superseding decision made on the Secretary of State's own initiative in accordance with regulation 26(1) that embodies a determination that the claimant has—

(a) limited capability for work; or

(b) limited capability for work-related activity; or

(c) limited capability for work and limited capability for work-related activity,

takes effect [¹ the day after the last day of the relevant period as defined in regulation 5(4) of the Employment and Support Allowance Regulations 2013] where the determination is the first such determination.

(8) In the case of an employment and support allowance where regulation 6 of the Employment and Support Allowance Regulations 2013 (assessment phase – previous claimants) applies, a superseding decision made in accordance with regulation 26(1) of these Regulations that embodies a determination that the claimant has—

(a) limited capability for work; or

(b) limited capability for work-related activity; or

(c) limited capability for work and limited capability for work-related activity,

takes effect from the beginning of the 14th week of the claimant's continuous period of limited capability for work.

(9) In the case of universal credit, a superseding decision made in accordance with regulation 26(1) that embodies a determination that the claimant has limited capability for work or limited capability for work and work-related activity takes effect—

(a) in a case to which regulation 28(1) (period for which the LCW or LCWRA element is not to be included) of the Universal Credit Regulations applies, from the beginning of the assessment period specified in that paragraph; or

(b) in any other case, from the beginning of the assessment period in which the decision (if made on the Secretary of State's own initiative) or the application for a supersession was made.

(10) A superseding decision to which regulation 27(1) (sanctions cases:

reduction in an award) applies takes effect from the beginning of the period specified in—

    (a) regulation 54 of the Employment and Support Allowance Regulations 2013, where the decision relates to the start of a reduction in the amount of an employment and support allowance;

    (b) regulation 56 of the Employment and Support Allowance Regulations 2013, where the decision relates to ending the suspension of a such a reduction where a fraud penalty ceases to apply;

    (c) regulation 22 of the Jobseeker's Allowance Regulations 2013, where the decision relates to the start of a reduction in the amount of a jobseeker's allowance;

    (d) regulation 24 of the Jobseeker's Allowance Regulations 2013, where the decision relates to ending the suspension of such a reduction where a fraud penalty ceases to apply;

    (e) regulation 106 of the Universal Credit Regulations, where the decision relates to the start of a reduction in the amount of universal credit;

    (f) regulation 108 of the Universal Credit Regulations, where the decision relates to ending the suspension of such a reduction where a fraud penalty ceases to apply.

(11) A superseding decision to which regulation 27(2) (sanctions cases: suspension and termination of a reduction) applies takes effect from the beginning of the period specified in—

    (a) regulation 56 of the Employment and Support Allowance Regulations 2013, where the decision relates to the start of a suspension where a fraud penalty applies;

    (b) regulation 57 of the Employment and Support Allowance Regulations 2013, where the decision relates to the termination of a reduction in the amount of an employment and support allowance;

    (c) regulation 24 of the Jobseeker's Allowance Regulations 2013, where the decision relates to the start of a suspension where a fraud penalty applies;

    (d) regulation 25 of the Jobseeker's Allowance Regulations 2013, where the decision relates to the termination of a reduction in the amount of a jobseeker's allowance;

    (e) regulation 108 of the Universal Credit Regulations, where the decision relates to the start of a suspension where a fraud penalty applies;

    (f) regulation 109 of the Universal Credit Regulations, where the decision relates to the termination of a reduction in the amount of an award of universal credit.

(12) A superseding decision to which regulation 28 (loss of benefit provisions) applies takes effect from the date prescribed for the purposes of section 6B or 7 of the Fraud Act.

(13) Where a decision is superseded in accordance with regulation 29 (contributions cases), the superseding decision takes effect from the date referred to in regulation 29(a), (b) or (c) on which the late or unpaid contribution is treated as paid.

(14) A superseding decision made in consequence of a redetermination in accordance with regulation 30 (housing costs: universal credit) takes effect on the first day of the first assessment period following the day on which that redetermination is received by Secretary of State.

AMENDMENT

1. Jobseeker's Allowance (Extended Period of Sickness) Amendment Regulations 2015 (SI 2015/339) reg.8(1) and (3) (March 30, 2015).

DEFINITIONS

"assessment period"—see reg.2 and Universal Credit Regs reg.21.
"benefit"—see reg.2.
"claimant"—*ibid.*
"employment and support allowance"—*ibid.*
"the Fraud Act"—*ibid.*
"fraud penalty"—*ibid.*
"jobseeker's allowance"—*ibid.*
"limited capability for work"—*ibid.*
"the Universal Credit Regulations"—*ibid.*
"universal credit"—*ibid.*

GENERAL NOTE

From March 13 to 29, 2020, the Secretary of State had power to determine that universal credit claimants who were—or were caring for a child or qualifying young person who was a member their household and who was—either infected or contaminated with Coronavirus disease or were in isolation were to be treated as having limited capability for work: see the General Note to reg.26 above and reg.3(1) and (2) of SI 2020/289. Regulation 26(1)(b)(ii) had the effect that such determination amounted to a ground for the supersession of an existing award of universal credit. By reg.3(3) of SI 2020/289, the effective date of such a superseding decision is governed by para.(9) of reg.36.

For most purposes, the provisions of SI 2020/289 are to expire on November 13, 2020: see reg.5(2). As it applied to universal credit, however, reg.3 of SI 2020/289 ceased to have effect on March 30, 2020: see regs 1(1) and 10(3) of the Social Security (Coronavirus) (Further Measures) Regulations 2020 (SI 2020/371).

Effective dates for superseding decisions where changes notified late

36.—(1) For the purposes of regulation 35(1) (effective dates: Secretary of State decisions) and paragraphs 6, 14 and 21 of Schedule 1 (effective dates for superseding decisions made on the ground of a change of circumstances), the Secretary of State may extend the time allowed for a person ("the applicant") to give notice of a change of circumstances in so far as it affects the effective date of the change if all of the following conditions are met.

(2) The first condition is that an application is made to the Secretary of State at an appropriate office for an extension of time.

(3) The second condition is that the application—

(a) contains particulars of the change of circumstances and the reasons for the failure to give notice of the change of circumstances on an earlier date; and

(b) is made—

    (i) within 13 months of the date on which the change occurred; or

    (ii) in the case of personal independence payment where a notification is given under paragraph 15 of Part 2 of Schedule 1 (effective dates for superseding decisions made on the ground of a change of circumstances), within 13 months of the date on

4.140

which the claimant first satisfied the conditions of entitlement to the particular rate of personal independence payment.

(4) The third condition is that the Secretary of State is satisfied that it is reasonable to grant the extension.

(5) The fourth condition is that the change of circumstances notified by the applicant is relevant to the decision which is to be superseded.

(6) The fifth condition is that the Secretary of State is satisfied that, due to special circumstances, it was not practicable for the applicant to give notice of the change of circumstances within the relevant notification period.

(7) In determining whether it is reasonable to grant an extension of time—

    (a) the Secretary of State must have regard to the principle that the greater the amount of time that has elapsed between the end of the relevant notification period and the date of the application, the more compelling should be the special circumstances on which the application is based;

    (b) no account must be taken of the fact that the applicant or any person acting for them was unaware of, or misunderstood, the law applicable to the case (including ignorance or misunderstanding of the time limits imposed by these Regulations); and

    (c) no account must be taken of the fact that the Upper Tribunal or a court has taken a different view of the law from that previously understood and applied.

(8) An application under this regulation which has been refused may not be renewed.

(9) In this regulation, "the relevant notification period" means—

    (a) in the case of universal credit, the assessment period in which the change of circumstances occurs; or

    (b) in any other case, a period of one month, beginning with the date on which the change of circumstances occurred.

DEFINITION

"personal independence payment"—see reg.2.

Effective dates: tribunal cases

4.141   **37.**—(1) This paragraph applies where—

    (a) the Secretary of State supersedes a decision of the First-tier Tribunal or the Upper Tribunal on the ground that it is made in ignorance of, or based on a mistake as to, a material fact in accordance with regulation 31(a) (tribunal decisions), and

    (b) as a result of that ignorance or mistake, the decision to be superseded was more advantageous to the claimant than it would otherwise have been.

(2) In a case where paragraph (1) applies where the decision relates to—

    (a) a jobseeker's allowance;

    (b) personal independence payment,

the superseding decision takes effect from the date on which the decision of the First-tier Tribunal or the Upper Tribunal took, or was to take, effect.

(3) In a case where paragraph (1) applies and the decision relates to an employment and support allowance or universal credit where—

(a) the material fact does not relate to a limited capability for work determination embodied in or necessary to the decision; or

(b) the material fact does relate to such a determination and the Secretary of State is satisfied that at the time the decision was made the claimant knew or could reasonably be expected to know of it and that it was relevant,

the superseding decision takes effect from the first day of the benefit week or (as the case may be) the assessment period in which in the Tribunal's decision took or was to take effect.

(4) Where the Secretary of State supersedes a decision of the First-tier Tribunal or the Upper Tribunal in accordance with regulation 31(b) (tribunal decisions), the decision takes effect—

(a) if the decision relates to personal independence payment, from the date on which the decision of the First-tier Tribunal or the Upper Tribunal would have taken effect had it been decided in accordance with the determination of the Upper Tribunal or the court in the appeal referred to in section 26(1)(b) of the 1998 Act;

(b) if the decision relates to a jobseeker's allowance or an employment and support allowance, from the first day of the benefit week in which the Tribunal's decision would have taken effect had it been so decided;

(c) if the decision relates to universal credit, from the first day of the assessment period in which the Tribunal's decision would have taken effect had it been so decided.

(5) Paragraph (6) applies where—

(a) the Upper Tribunal, or the court as defined in section 27(7) (restrictions on entitlement to benefit in certain cases of error) of the 1998 Act, determines an appeal as mentioned in subsection (1)(a) of that section ("the relevant determination");

(b) the Secretary of State makes a decision of the kind specified in subsection (1)(b) of that section;

(c) there is an appeal against the relevant determination;

(d) after the Secretary of State's decision, payment is suspended in accordance with regulation 44 (suspension in prescribed cases); and

(e) on appeal a court, within the meaning of section 27, reverses the relevant determination in whole or part.

(6) A consequential decision by the Secretary of State under section 10 of the 1998 Act which supersedes an earlier decision of the Secretary of State under paragraph (5)(b) takes effect from the date on which the earlier decision took effect.

Definitions

"the 1998 Act"—see reg.2.
"appeal"—*ibid.*
"assessment period"—see reg.2 and Universal Credit Regs reg.21.
"benefit"—see reg.2.
"benefit week"—*ibid.*
"claimant"—*ibid.*
"employment and support allowance"—*ibid.*
"jobseeker's allowance"—*ibid.*
"personal independence payment"—*ibid.*
"universal credit"—*ibid.*

PART IV

OTHER MATTERS RELATING TO DECISION-MAKING

Correction of accidental errors

4.142   **38.**—(1) An accidental error in a decision of the Secretary of State, or in any record of such a decision, may be corrected by the Secretary of State at any time.

(2) Such a correction is to be treated as part of that decision or of that record.

(3) The Secretary of State must give written notice of the correction as soon as practicable to the person to whom the decision was given.

(4) In calculating the time within which an application may be made under regulation 5 (revision on any grounds) for a decision to be revised, no account is to be taken of any day falling before the day on which notice of the correction was given.

Determinations on incomplete evidence

4.143   **39.**—(1) The following provisions of this regulation apply for the purposes of a decision under section 8 or 10 of the 1998 Act.

(2) Where—

(a) a determination falls to be made by the Secretary of State concerning the matter mentioned in paragraph (3); and

(b) it appears to the Secretary of State that the Secretary of State is not in possession of all of the evidence or information which is relevant for the purposes of the determination,

the Secretary of State must make the determination on the assumption that the relevant evidence or information which is not in the Secretary of State's possession is adverse to the claimant.

(3) The matter is whether, for the purposes of regulation 45 (relevant education) of the Jobseeker's Allowance Regulations 2013 a person is by virtue of that regulation to be treated as receiving relevant education.

(4) Where—

(a) a determination falls to be made by the Secretary of State as to what costs are to be included in claimant's award of universal credit under section 11 (housing costs) of the 2012 Act; and

(b) it appears to the Secretary of State that the Secretary of State is not in possession of all of the evidence or information which is relevant for the purposes of the determination,

the Secretary of State may make the determination on the assumption that the costs to be included in the claimant's award under that section are those that the Secretary of State is able to determine using such evidence or information as is in the Secretary of State's possession.

(5) Where, in the case of personal independence payment—

(a) a determination falls to be made by the Secretary of State as to whether a person meets the condition in section 85(2) (care home residents where the costs of qualifying services are borne out of local or public funds) of the 2012 Act; and

(b) it appears to the Secretary of State that, having made reasonable enquiries, the Secretary of State is not in possession of all of the evidence or information which is or could be relevant for the purposes of the determination,

the Secretary of State may make the determination using such information or evidence as is in the Secretary of State's possession.

DEFINITIONS

"the 2012 Act"—see reg.2.
"claimant"—*ibid.*

Determinations as to limited capability for work

40.—(1) Where, in relation to an award of an employment and support allowance, the Secretary of State makes a determination (including a determination made following a change of circumstances) whether a person—

(a) has or does not have limited capability for work; or

(b) is to be treated as having or not having limited capability for work,

which is embodied in or necessary to a decision under Chapter 2 of Part 1 of the 1998 Act (decisions and appeals) or on which such a decision is based, that determination is to be conclusive for the purposes of any further decision relating to such an allowance.

(2) Paragraph (1) applies to determinations made in relation to universal credit as it applies in the case of an employment and support allowance.

(3) Where, in relation to any purpose for which Part 1 (employment and support allowance) of the 2007 Act or Part 1 (universal credit) of the 2012 Act applies, a determination falls to be made as to whether a person—

(a) is, or is to be treated as, having or not having limited capability for work; or

(b) is terminally ill,

that issue is to be determined by the Secretary of State, notwithstanding the fact that any other matter falls to be determined by another authority.

4.144

DEFINITIONS

"the 1998 Act"—see reg.2.
"employment and support allowance"—*ibid.*
"limited capability for work"—*ibid.*
"universal credit"—*ibid.*

Effect of alterations affecting universal credit

41.—(1) Subject to paragraph (3), an alteration in the amount of a person's employed earnings (within the meaning of regulation 55(1) of the Universal Credit Regulations) made in accordance with Chapter 2 of Part 6 (earned income) of the Universal Credit Regulations in consequence of information provided to the Secretary of State by HMRC is prescribed for the purposes of section 159D(1)(b)(vi) (effect of alterations affecting universal credit) of the Administration Act.

(2) For the purposes of this regulation, "alteration" means an increase or decrease in such earnings.

(3) Where the person disputes the figure used in accordance with regulation 55 (employed earnings) of the Universal Credit Regulations to calculate employed earnings in relation to any assessment period, the Secretary of State must—

(a) inform the person that they may request that the Secretary of State

4.145

gives a decision in relation to the amount of universal credit payable in relation to that assessment period; and

(b) where such a decision is requested, give it within 14 days of receiving the request or as soon as practicable afterwards.

(4) Paragraph (3) does not affect the validity of anything done under section 159D(2) or (3) of the Administration Act in relation to the person's award.

(5) A decision made in accordance with paragraph (3) takes effect on the date on which the alteration under section 159(D)(2) or (3) came into force in relation to the person.

DEFINITIONS

"the Administration Act"—see reg.2.
"assessment period"—see reg.2 and Universal Credit Regs reg.21.
"the Universal Credit Regulations"—see reg.2.
"universal credit"—*ibid.*

GENERAL NOTE

4.145.1   See further the commentary to reg.61 of the Universal Credit Regulations, dealing with the interaction of this regulation, s.159D of the SSAA 1992 and para.6(b)(v) of Sch.2 to the SSA 1998 on rights of appeal where there is an alteration to the amount of earned income to be taken into account.

Issues for HMRC

4.146   **42.**—(1) Where, on consideration of any claim or other matter, it appears to the Secretary of State that an issue arises which, by virtue of section 8 of the Transfer Act, falls to be decided by an officer of HMRC, the Secretary of State must refer that issue to HMRC.

(2) Where—

(a) the Secretary of State has decided any claim or other matter on an assumption of facts—

(i) which appeared to the Secretary of State not to be in dispute, but

(ii) concerning which, had an issue arisen, that issue would have fallen, by virtue of section 8 of the Transfer Act, to be decided by HMRC;

(b) an application for a revision or supersession is made, or an appeal is brought, in relation to that claim or other matter; and

(c) it appears to the Secretary of State on receipt of that application or appeal that such an issue arises,

the Secretary of State must refer that issue to HMRC.

(3) Pending the final decision of any issue which has been referred to HMRC in accordance with paragraph (1) or (2), the Secretary of State may—

(a) determine any other issue arising on consideration of the claim, application or other matter,

(b) seek a preliminary opinion from HMRC on the issue referred and decide the claim, application or other matter in accordance with that opinion; or

(c) defer making any decision on the claim, application or other matter.

(4) On receipt by the Secretary of State of the final decision of an issue which has been referred to HMRC under paragraph (1) or (2), the Secretary of State must—

(a) in a case where the Secretary of State made a decision under paragraph (3)(b), decide whether to revise the decision under section 9 of the 1998 Act or to supersede it under section 10 of that Act;

(b) in a case to which paragraph (3)(a) or (c) applies, decide the claim, application or other matter in accordance with the final decision of the issue so referred.

(5) In this regulation—

(a) "final decision" means the decision of HMRC under section 8 (decisions by officers of Board) of the Transfer Act or the determination of any appeal in relation to that decision; and

(b) "the Transfer Act" means the Social Security Contributions (Transfer of Functions, etc.) Act 1999.

DEFINITIONS

"appeal"—see reg.2.
"HMRC"—*ibid.*

Appeals raising issues for HMRC

43.—(1) This regulation applies where—

4.147

(a) a person has appealed to the First-tier Tribunal and it appears to the First-tier Tribunal that an issue arises which, by virtue of section 8 of the Transfer Act, falls to be decided by HMRC; and

(b) the tribunal has required the Secretary of State to refer that issue to HMRC.

(2) Pending the final decision of any issue which has been referred to HMRC in accordance with paragraph (1), the Secretary of State may revise the decision under appeal under section 9 of the 1998 Act, or make a further decision under section 10 of that Act superseding that decision, in accordance with the Secretary of State's determination of any issue other than one which has been so referred.

(3) On receipt by the Secretary of State of the final decision of an issue which has been referred to HMRC in accordance with paragraph (1), the Secretary of State must consider whether the decision under appeal ought to be revised or superseded under the 1998 Act, and—

(a) if so, revise it or make a further decision which supersedes it; or

(b) if not, invite the First-tier Tribunal to determine to appeal.

(4) In this regulation, "final decision" and "Transfer Act" have the same meaning as in regulation 42 (issues for HMRC).

DEFINITIONS

"the 1998 Act"—see reg.2.
"appeal"—*ibid.*
"HMRC"—*ibid.*

PART V

SUSPENSION

Suspension in prescribed cases

44.—(1) The Secretary of State may suspend, in whole or part, payment of any benefit to a person ("P") in the circumstances described in paragraph (2).

4.148

(2) The circumstances are where—

(a) it appears to the Secretary of State that—

  (i) an issue arises whether the conditions for entitlement to the benefit are or were fulfilled;
  (ii) an issue arises whether a decision relating to an award of the benefit should be revised under section 9 or superseded under section 10 of the 1998 Act,
  (iii) an issue arises whether any amount of benefit paid to P is recoverable under or by virtue of section 71ZB, 71ZG or 71ZH of the Administration Act,
  (iv) the last address notified to the Secretary of State of P is not the address at which P resides,
 (b) an appeal is pending in P's case against a decision of the First-tier Tribunal, the Upper Tribunal or a court; or
 (c) an appeal is pending against a decision given by the Upper Tribunal or a court in a different case and it appears to the Secretary of State that, if the appeal were to be decided in a particular way, an issue would arise as to whether the award of any benefit to P (whether the same benefit or not) ought to be revised or superseded.

(3) For the purposes of section 21(2)(c) (suspension in prescribed circumstances) of the 1998 Act, where an appeal against the decision has not been brought or an application for permission to appeal against the decision has not been made but the time for doing so has not yet expired, an appeal is pending in the circumstances described in paragraph (4).

(4) The circumstances are where a decision of the First-tier Tribunal, the Upper Tribunal or a court has been made and the Secretary of State—
 (a) is awaiting receipt of that decision; or
 (b) in the case of a decision of the First-tier Tribunal, is considering whether to apply for a statement of reasons for the decision or has applied for such a statement and is awaiting receipt; or
 (c) has received that decision or, if it is a decision of the First-tier Tribunal has received the statement of reasons for it, and is considering whether to apply for permission to appeal, or where permission to appeal has been granted, is considering whether to appeal.

(5) Where payment of any benefit is suspended as the result of paragraph (2)(b) or (c), the Secretary of State must, as soon as reasonably practicable, give written notice to P of any proposal to—
 (a) request a statement of the reasons for a tribunal decision;
 (b) apply for permission to appeal; or
 (c) make an appeal.

DEFINITIONS

 "the 1998 Act"—see reg.2.
 "appeal"—*ibid.*
 "benefit"—*ibid.*

Provision of information or evidence

4.149   **45.**—(1) This regulation applies where the Secretary of State requires information or evidence from a person mentioned in paragraph (2) ("P") in order to determine whether a decision awarding a benefit should be revised under section 9 of the 1998 Act or superseded under section 10 of that Act.
 (2) The persons are—
 (a) a person in respect of whom payment of any benefit has been sus-

pended in the circumstances set out in regulation 44(2)(a) (suspension in prescribed cases);

(b) a person who has made an application for a decision of the Secretary of State to be revised or superseded;

(c) a person from whom the Secretary of State requires information or evidence under regulation 38(2) (evidence and information in connection with an award) of the Claims and Payments Regulations 2013;

(d) a person from whom the Secretary of State requires documents, certificates or other evidence under regulation 31(3) (evidence and information) of the Jobseeker's Allowance Regulations 2013;

(e) a person whose entitlement to an employment and support allowance or universal credit is conditional on their having, or being treated as having, limited capability for work.

(3) The Secretary of State must notify P of the requirements of this regulation.

(4) P must either—

(a) supply the information or evidence within—

    (i) a period of 14 days beginning with the date on which the notification under paragraph (3) was given or sent to P or such longer period as the Secretary of State allows in that notification, or

    (ii) such longer period as P satisfies the Secretary of State is necessary in order to comply with the requirements, or

(b) satisfy the Secretary of State within the period applicable under sub-paragraph (a)(i) that either—

    (i) the information or evidence does not exist, or

    (ii) it is not possible for P to obtain it.

(5) In relation to a person to whom paragraph (2)(d) refers, paragraph (4)(a)(i) has effect as if for "14 days" there were substituted "7 days".

(6) The Secretary of State may suspend the payment of a benefit, in whole or part, to any person to whom paragraph (2)(b), (c), (d) or (e) applies who fails to satisfy the requirements of paragraph (4).

(7) In this regulation, "evidence" includes evidence which a person is required to provide in accordance with regulation 2 (evidence of incapacity for work, limited capability for work and confinement) of the Social Security (Medical Evidence) Regulations 1976.

DEFINITIONS

"benefit"—see reg.2.
"jobseeker's allowance"—*ibid.*
"limited capability for work"—*ibid.*

Making of payments which have been suspended

46. The Secretary of State must pay a benefit which has been suspended where— **4.150**

(a) in a case where regulation 44(2)(a) (suspension in prescribed cases) applies, the Secretary of State is satisfied that the benefit is properly payable and that there are no outstanding issues to be resolved;

(b) in a case to which regulation 45(6) (provision of information or evidence) applies, the Secretary of State is satisfied that the benefit is properly payable and that the requirements of regulation 45(4) have been satisfied;

    (c) in a case to which regulation 44(2)(b) (suspension in prescribed cases) applies, the Secretary of State—

        (i) does not, in the case of a decision of the First-tier Tribunal, apply for a statement of the reasons for that decision within the period specified under the Tribunal Procedure Rules;

        (ii) does not, in the case of a decision of the First-tier Tribunal, the Upper Tribunal or a court, make an application for permission to appeal or (where permission to appeal is granted) make the appeal within the time prescribed for the making of such application or appeal;

        (iii) withdraws an application for permission to appeal or withdraws the appeal; or

        (iv) is refused permission to appeal, in circumstances where it is not open to the Secretary of State to renew the application for permission or to make a further application for permission to appeal;

    (d) in a case to which regulation 44(2)(c) (suspension in prescribed cases) applies, the Secretary of State, in relation to the decision of the Upper Tribunal or a court in a different case—

        (i) does not make an application for permission to appeal or (where permission to appeal is granted) make the appeal within the time prescribed for the making of such application or appeal;

        (ii) withdraws an application for permission to appeal or withdraws the appeal;

        (iii) is refused permission to appeal, in circumstances where it is not open to the Secretary of State to renew the application for permission or to make a further application for permission to appeal.

DEFINITIONS

"appeal"—see reg.2.
"benefit"—*ibid.*
"the Tribunal Procedure Rules"—*ibid.*

PART VI

TERMINATION

Termination for failure to furnish information or evidence

4.151   **47.**—(1) This regulation applies where payment of a benefit to a person ("P") has been suspended in full under—

    (a) regulation 44 (suspension in prescribed cases) and P subsequently fails to comply with a requirement for information or evidence under regulation 45 (provision of information or evidence) and more than one month has elapsed since the requirement was made; or

    (b) regulation 45(6) and more than one month has elapsed since the first payment was suspended.

(2) In a case to which this regulation applies, except where entitlement ceases on an earlier date other than under this regulation, the Secretary of State must decide that P ceases to be entitled to that benefit with effect from the date on which the payment of the benefit was suspended.

DEFINITION

"benefit"—see reg.2.

Termination in the case of entitlement to alternative benefits

48.—(1) This paragraph applies where an award of a jobseeker's allowance ("the existing benefit") exists in favour of a person and, if that award did not exist and a claim was made by that person for an employment and support allowance ("the alternative benefit"), an award of the alternative benefit would be made on that claim.

(2) This paragraph applies where an award of an employment and support allowance ("the existing benefit") exists in favour of a person and, if that award did not exist and a claim was made by that person for a jobseeker's allowance ("the alternative benefit"), an award of the alternative benefit would be made on that claim.

(3) In a case where paragraph (1) or (2) applies, if a claim for the alternative benefit is made, the Secretary of State may bring to an end the award of the existing benefit if satisfied that an award of the alternative benefit will be made.

(4) Where the Secretary of State brings an award of the existing benefit to an end under paragraph (3), the Secretary of State must end the award on the day immediately preceding the first day on which an award of the alternative benefit takes effect.

(5) Where an award of a jobseeker's allowance is made in accordance with this regulation, paragraph 4 of Schedule 1 to the Jobseekers Act (waiting days) does not apply.

(6) Where an award of an employment and support allowance is made in accordance with this regulation, paragraph 2 (waiting days) of Schedule 2 (supplementary provisions) to the 2007 Act does not apply.

4.152

DEFINITIONS

"the 2007 Act"—see reg.2.
"benefit"—*ibid.*
"employment and support allowance"—*ibid.*
"the Jobseekers Act"—*ibid.*
"jobseeker's allowance"—*ibid.*

PART VII

APPEALS

Other persons with a right of appeal

49. In addition to the claimant, but subject to regulation 7 (consideration of revision before appeal), the following persons have the right of appeal under section 12(2) of the 1998 Act—

(a) any person appointed by the Secretary of State under regulation 56 (payments on death) of the Claims and Payments Regulations 2013 to proceed with the claim of a person who claimed benefit and subsequently died;

(b) any person appointed by the Secretary of State under regulation

4.153

57 (persons unable to act) of those Regulations to act on behalf of another;

(c) any person claiming personal independence payment on behalf of another under section 82(5) of the 2012 Act (terminal illness); and

(d) in the case of a decision under section 71ZB, 71ZG or 71ZH of the Administration Act to recover any amount paid by way of benefit, any person from whom such an amount is recoverable, but only if their rights, duties or obligations are affected by that decision.

DEFINITIONS

"the 1998 Act"—see reg.2.
"the 2012 Act"—*ibid.*
"the Administration Act"—*ibid.*
"appeal"—*ibid.*
"benefit"—*ibid.*
"the Claims and Payments Regulations 2013"—*ibid.*
"personal independence payment"—*ibid.*

Decisions which may or may not be appealed

4.154   **50.**—(1) An appeal lies against a decision set out in Schedule 2 (decisions against which an appeal lies).

(2) No appeal lies against a decision set out in Schedule 3 (decisions against which no appeal lies).

(3) In paragraph (2) and Schedule 3, "decision" includes a determination embodied in or necessary to a decision.

DEFINITION

"appeal"—see reg.2.

Notice of a decision against which an appeal lies

4.155   **51.**—(1) This regulation applies in the case of a person ("P") who has a right of appeal under the 1998 Act or these Regulations.

(2) The Secretary of State must—

(a) give P written notice of the decision and of the right to appeal against that decision; and

(b) inform P that, where that notice does not include a statement of the reasons for the decision, P may, within one month of the date of notification of that decision, request that the Secretary of State provide a written statement of the reasons for that decision.

(3) If the Secretary of State is requested under paragraph (2)(b) to provide a written statement of reasons, the Secretary of State must provide such a statement within 14 days of the request or as soon as practicable afterwards.

DEFINITION

"appeal"—see reg.2.

Appeals against decisions which have been revised

4.156   **52.**—(1) An appeal against a decision of the Secretary of State does not lapse where—

(a) the decision is revised under section 9 of the 1998 Act before the appeal is decided; and

(b) the decision of the Secretary of State as revised is not more advantageous to the appellant than the decision before it was revised.

(2) In a case to which paragraph (1) applies, the appeal must be treated as though it had been brought against the decision as revised.

(3) The Secretary of State must inform the appellant that they may, within one month of the date of notification of the decision as revised, make further representations as to the appeal.

(4) After the end of that period, or within that period if the appellant consents in writing, the appeal to the First-tier Tribunal must proceed, except where—

(a) the Secretary of State further revises the decision in light of further representations from the appellant; and

(b) that decision is more advantageous to the appellant than the decision before it was revised.

(5) Decisions which are more advantageous for the purpose of this regulation include those where—

(a) the amount of any benefit payable to the appellant is greater, or any benefit is awarded for a longer period, as a result of the decision;

(b) the decision would have resulted in the amount of benefit in payment being greater but for the operation of any provision of the Administration Act or the Contributions and Benefits Act restricting or suspending the payment of, or disqualifying a claimant from receiving, some or all of the benefit;

(c) as a result of the decision, a denial or disqualification for the receipt of any benefit is lifted, wholly or in part;

(d) the decision reverses a decision to pay benefit to a third party instead of to the appellant;

(e) in consequence of the decision, benefit paid is not recoverable under section 71ZB, 71ZG or 71ZH of the Administration Act or regulations made under any of those sections, or the amount so recoverable is reduced; or

(f) a financial gain accrued or will accrue to the appellant in consequence of the decision.

DEFINITIONS

"the 1998 Act"—see reg.2.
"the Administration Act"—*ibid.*
"appeal"—*ibid.*
"benefit"—*ibid.*
"claimant"—*ibid.*
"the date of notification"—*ibid.*
"writing"—*ibid.*

Decisions involving issues that arise on appeal in other cases

53.—(1) For the purposes of section 25(3)(b) of the 1998 Act (prescribed cases and circumstances in which a decision may be made on a prescribed basis)—

(a) a prescribed case is a case in which the claimant would be entitled to the benefit to which the decision relates, even if the other appeal

4.157

referred to in section 25(1)(b) of the 1998 Act were decided in a way which is the most unfavourable to the claimant; and

(b) the prescribed basis on which the Secretary of State may make the decision is as if—

    (i) the other appeal referred to in section 25(1)(b) of the 1998 Act had already been decided; and

    (ii) that appeal had been decided in a way which is the most unfavourable to the claimant.

(2) For the purposes of section 25(5)(c) of the 1998 Act (appeal treated as pending against a decision in a different case, even though an appeal against the decision has not been brought or an application for permission to appeal against the decision has not been made but the time for doing so has not yet expired), the prescribed circumstances are that the Secretary of State—

(a) certifies in writing that the Secretary of State is considering appealing against that decision; and

(b) considers that, if such an appeal were to be decided in a particular way—

    (i) there would be no entitlement to benefit in that case; or

    (ii) the appeal would affect the decision in that case in some other way.

DEFINITIONS

    "the 1998 Act"—see reg.2.
    "appeal"—*ibid.*
    "benefit"—*ibid.*
    "claimant"—*ibid.*

Appeals involving issues that arise in other cases

4.158   **54.** For the purposes of section 26(6)(c) of the 1998 Act (appeal is treated as pending against a decision in a different case, even though an appeal against the decision has not been brought or an application for permission to appeal has not been made but the time for doing so has not yet expired) the prescribed circumstances are that the Secretary of State—

(a) certifies in writing that the Secretary of State is considering appealing against that decision; and

(b) considers that, if such an appeal were already decided, it would affect the determination of the appeal referred to in section 26(1)(a) of the 1998 Act.

DEFINITIONS

    "the 1998 Act"—see reg.2.
    "appeal"—*ibid.*
    "writing"—*ibid.*

Consequential amendments

4.159   **55.** [Omitted]

SCHEDULE 1

EFFECTIVE DATES FOR SUPERSEDING DECISIONS MADE ON THE
GROUND OF A CHANGE OF CIRCUMSTANCES

PART I

EMPLOYMENT AND SUPPORT ALLOWANCE AND JOBSEEKER'S ALLOWANCE

1. Subject to the following provisions of this Part and to Part 4, in the case of an employment **4.160** and support allowance or a jobseeker's allowance, a superseding decision made on the ground of a change of circumstances takes effect from the first day of the benefit week in which the relevant change of circumstances occurs or is expected to occur.

2. Paragraph 1 does not apply where—
(a) the superseding decision is not advantageous to the claimant; and
(b) there has been an employment and support allowance decision where the Secretary of State is satisfied that, in relation to a limited capability for work determination, the claimant—
  (i) failed to notify an appropriate office of a change of circumstances which the claimant was required by regulations under the Administration Act to notify; and
  (ii) could not reasonably have been expected to know that the change of circumstances should have been notified.

3. Where a relevant change of circumstances results, or is expected to result, in a reduced award and the Secretary of State is of the opinion that it is impracticable for a superseding decision to take effect from the day set out in paragraph 1, that superseding decision takes effect—
(a) where the relevant change has occurred, from the first day of the benefit week following that in which that superseding decision is made; or
(b) where the relevant change is expected to occur, from the first day of the benefit week following that in which that change of circumstances is expected to occur.

4. Where entitlement ends, or is expected to end, as the result of a change of circumstances, the superseding decision takes effect from the day on which the relevant change of circumstances occurs or is expected to occur.

5. In the case of an employment and support allowance where a person who is subject to—
(a) section 45A or 47 of the Mental Health Act 1983 (power of higher courts to direct hospital admission; removal to hospital of persons serving sentences of imprisonment etc.);
(b) section 59A (hospital direction) of the Criminal Procedure (Scotland) Act 1995; or
(c) section 136 (transfer of prisoners for treatment for mental disorder) of the Mental Health (Care and Treatment) (Scotland) Act 2003,
ceases, or is expected to cease, to be detained in a hospital (as defined in the Act, or the Act of the Scottish Parliament, to which the person is subject) for a period of less than a week, a superseding decision related to that person's departure from, or return to, hospital takes effect from the day on which that change of circumstances occurs or is expected to occur.

6. Where the superseding decision is advantageous to the claimant and the change of circumstances was notified to an appropriate office more than one month after the change occurred or after the expiry of such longer period as may be allowed under regulation 36 (effective dates for superseding decisions where changes notified late), the superseding decision takes effect from the beginning of the benefit week in which the notification was given.

7. In the case of an employment and support allowance decision where the Secretary of State is satisfied that, in relation to a limited capability for work determination, the claimant—
(a) failed to notify an appropriate office of a change of circumstances which the claimant was required by regulations under the Administration Act to notify; and
(b) could reasonably have been expected to know that the change of circumstances should have been notified,
the superseding decision takes effect in accordance with paragraph 8.

8. The superseding decision takes effect—
(a) from the date on which the claimant ought to have notified the change of circumstances; or
(b) if more than one change has taken place between the date from which the decision to

be superseded took effect and the date of the superseding decision, from the date on which the first change ought to have been notified.

9. In the case of a claimant who makes an application for a supersession which contains an express statement that they are terminally ill, the superseding decision takes effect from the date on which the claimant became terminally ill.

10. Where the superseding decision is advantageous to the claimant and is made on the Secretary of State's own initiative, the decision takes effect from the beginning of the benefit week in which the Secretary of State commenced action with a view to supersession.

11. In this Part—

"employment and support allowance decision" means a decision to award an employment and support allowance embodied in or necessary to which is a determination that the claimant has, or is to be treated as having, limited capability for work;

"week" means a period of 7 days, beginning with midnight between Saturday and Sunday.

PART II

PERSONAL INDEPENDENCE PAYMENT

4.161 12. Subject to the following provisions of this Part and to Part 4, in the case of personal independence payment, a superseding decision made on the ground of a change of circumstances takes effect on the date on which the relevant change of circumstances occurs or is expected to occur.

13. Paragraph 12 does not apply where—

(a) the superseding decision is not advantageous to the claimant; and

(b) there has been a personal independence payment decision where the Secretary of State is satisfied that, in relation to such a decision, the claimant—

(i) failed to notify an appropriate office of a change of circumstances which the claimant was required by regulations under the Administration Act to notify; and

(ii) could not reasonably have been expected to know that the change of circumstances should have been notified.

14. Except in a case where paragraph 15 or 31 applies, where the superseding decision is advantageous to the claimant and the change of circumstances was notified to an appropriate office more than one month after the change occurred or after the expiry of such longer period as may be allowed under regulation 36 (effective dates for superseding decisions where changes notified late), the superseding decision takes effect from the date of notification of the change.

15. Where—

(a) the change is relevant to entitlement to a particular rate of personal independence payment; and

(b) the claimant notifies an appropriate office of the change no later than one month after the date on which they first satisfied the conditions of entitlement to that rate or within such longer period as may be allowed by regulation 36 (effective dates for superseding decisions where changes notified late),

the superseding decision takes effect from the date on which the claimant first satisfied those conditions.

16. Where the Secretary of State is satisfied that, in relation to a personal independence payment decision, the claimant—

(a) failed to notify an appropriate office of a change of circumstances which the claimant was required by regulations under the Administration Act to notify; and

(b) could reasonably have been expected to know that the change of circumstances should have been notified,

the superseding decision takes effect in accordance with paragraph 17.

17. The superseding decision takes effect—

(a) from the date on which the claimant ought to have notified the change of circumstances; or

(b) if more than one change has taken place between the date from which the decision to be superseded took effect and the date of the superseding decision, from the date on which the first change ought to have been notified.

18. Where the superseding decision is advantageous to the claimant and is made on the Secretary of State's own initiative, the decision takes effect from the date on which the Secretary of State commenced action with a view to supersession.

19. In paragraphs 13 and 16, "personal independence payment decision" means a decision to award personal independence payment, embodied in or necessary to which is a determi-

nation whether the claimant satisfies any of the requirements in section 78(1) and (2) (daily living component) or section 79(1) and (2) (mobility component) of the 2012 Act.

PART III

UNIVERSAL CREDIT

20. Subject to the following paragraphs and to Part 4, in the case of universal credit, a superseding decision made on the ground of a change of circumstances takes effect from the first day of the assessment period in which that change occurred or is expected to occur.

4.162

21. Except in a case to which paragraph 22 or 31 applies, where the superseding decision is advantageous to the claimant and the change of circumstances was notified to an appropriate office after the end of the assessment period in which the change occurred or after the expiry of such longer period as may be allowed under regulation 36 (effective dates for superseding decisions where changes notified late), the superseding decision takes effect from the first day of the assessment period in which the notification was given.

22. In the case of a person to whom regulation 61 (information for calculating earned income) of the Universal Credit Regulations applies, where—

    (a) the relevant change of circumstances is that the person's employed earnings are reduced; and

    (b) the person provides such information for the purposes of calculating those earnings at such times as the Secretary of State may require,

the superseding decision takes effect from the first day of the assessment period in which that change occurred.

23. In the case of a universal credit decision where the Secretary of State is satisfied that, in relation to a limited capability for work determination, the claimant—

    (a) failed to notify an appropriate office of a change of circumstances which the claimant was required by regulations under the Administration Act to notify; and

    (b) could reasonably have been expected to know that the change of circumstances should have been notified,

the superseding decision takes effect in accordance with paragraph 24.

24. The superseding decision takes effect—

    (a) from the first day of the assessment period in which the claimant ought to have notified the change of circumstances; or

    (b) if more than one change has taken place between the date from which the decision to be superseded took effect and the date of the superseding decision, from the first day of the assessment period in which the first change ought to have been notified.

25. Where—

    (a) the superseding decision is not advantageous to the claimant; and

    (b) there has been a universal credit decision where the Secretary of State is satisfied that, in relation to a limited capability for work determination, the claimant—

      (i) failed to notify an appropriate office of a change of circumstances which the claimant was required by regulations under the Administration Act to notify; and

      (ii) could not reasonably have been expected to know that the change of circumstances should have been notified,

the superseding decision takes effect on the first day of the assessment period in which the Secretary of State makes that decision.

26. Where, in any assessment period, a claimant—

    (a) reaches the qualifying age for state pension credit under the State Pension Credit Act 2002; and

    (b) has made an advance claim for an award of state pension credit,

a superseding decision made in consequence of the person reaching that age takes effect on the date on which that change of circumstances occurs or is expected to occur.

27. A superseding decision of the Secretary of State to make or to cease making a hardship payment takes effect in accordance with regulation 117 (period of hardship payments) of the Universal Credit Regulations.

28. In the case of a claimant who makes an application for a supersession which contains an express statement that they are terminally ill, the superseding decision takes effect from the first day of the assessment period in which the claimant became terminally ill.

29. Where the superseding decision is advantageous to a claimant and is made on the Secretary of State's own initiative, it takes effect from the first day of the assessment period in which the Secretary of State commenced action with a view to supersession.

30. In this Part, "a universal credit decision" means a decision to award universal credit embodied in or necessary to which is a determination that the claimant has or is to be treated as having limited capability for work.

PART IV

COMMON PROVISIONS

4.163

31.—(1) This paragraph applies in relation to an award of personal independence payment or universal credit where the change of circumstances is that the claimant or, in the case of universal credit, a member of their family, becomes entitled to another relevant benefit, ceases so to be entitled or the rate of another such benefit alters.

(2) Where this paragraph applies, the superseding decision takes effect from—

    (a) where the superseding decision concerns universal credit, the first day of the assessment period in which—

        (i) the entitlement to the other benefit arises;

        (ii) the entitlement to the other benefit ends; or

        (iii) entitlement to a different rate of the other benefit arises;

    (b) where the superseding decision concerns personal independence payment, the date on which—

    (i) the entitlement to the other benefit arises;

    (ii) the entitlement to the other benefit ends; or

    (iii) entitlement to a different rate of the other benefit arises.

(3) For the purpose of sub-paragraph (1), where the superseding decision relates to personal independence payment, "relevant benefit" includes any payment made under any of the provisions mentioned in regulation 61(1) (cases where mobility component of personal independence payment not payable) of the Claims and Payments Regulations 2013.

4.164

[¹ **32.** Where the change of circumstances is that there has been a change in the legislation, the superseding decision takes effect—

    (a) in relation to an award of universal credit that exists on the date on which the change in legislation comes into force—

        (i) if there is an assessment period for the award that begins on the date on which that change in legislation has effect, from that date; or

        (ii) in any other case, from the first day of the next assessment period for the award beginning after the date on which that change had effect;

    (b) in any other case, from the date on which that change in the legislation had effect.]

4.165

[¹ **33.** Where the change of circumstances is the expected coming into force of a change in the legislation, the superseding decision takes effect—

    (a) in relation to an award of universal credit that exists on the date on which the change in legislation comes into force—

        (i) if there is an assessment period for the award that begins on the date on which that change in legislation has effect, from that date; or

        (ii) in any other case, from the first day of the next assessment period for the award beginning after the date on which that change has effect;

    (b) in any other case, from the date on which that change in the legislation has effect.]

AMENDMENTS

1. Universal Credit (Miscellaneous Amendments, Saving and Transitional Provision) Regulations 2018 (SI 2018/65) reg.5(1) and (3) (February 14, 2018).

DEFINITIONS

    "the Administration Act"—see reg.2.

    "appropriate office"—*ibid.*

    "assessment period"—see reg.2 and Universal Credit Regulations, reg.21.

    "benefit week"—see reg.2.

    "benefit"—*ibid.*

    "claimant"—*ibid.*

    "employment and support allowance"—*ibid.*

    "family"—*ibid.*

"jobseeker's allowance"—*ibid.*
"limited capability for work determination"—*ibid.*
"limited capability for work"—*ibid.*
"personal independence payment"—*ibid.*
"relevant benefit"—*ibid.*
"terminally ill"—*ibid.*
"universal credit"—*ibid.*

Regulation 50(1)

SCHEDULE 2

DECISIONS AGAINST WHICH AN APPEAL LIES

1. A decision as to whether a person is entitled to a benefit for which no claim is required by virtue of regulation 6, 7 or 9(6) and (7) of the Claims and Payments Regulations 2013.　　**4.166**

DEFINITIONS

"appeal"—see reg. 2.
"the Claims and Payments Regulations 2013"—*ibid.*

Regulation 50(2)

SCHEDULE 3

DECISIONS AGAINST WHICH NO APPEAL LIES

Claims and Payments
1. A decision under any of the following provisions of the Claims and Payments Regulations 2013—　　**4.167**
- (a) regulation 18 (special provisions where it is certified that a woman is expected to be confined or where she has been confined);
- (b) regulation 25 (interchange with claims for other benefits);
- (c) regulation 37 (evidence and information in connection with a claim);
- (d) regulation 46 (direct credit transfer);
- (e) regulation 47 (payment of universal credit);
- (f) regulation 48 (payment of personal independence payment);
- (g) regulation 49 (days for payment of personal independence payment);
- (h) regulation 50(1) (payment of personal independence payment at a daily rate between periods in hospital or other accommodation);
- (i) regulation 51 (payment of an employment and support allowance);
- (j) regulation 52 (payment of a jobseeker's allowance);
- (k) regulation 55, except a decision under paragraph (4) (extinguishment of right to payment if payment is not obtained within the prescribed period);
- (l) regulation 56 (payments on death);
- (m) regulation 57 (persons unable to act);
- (n) regulation 58 (payment to another person on the claimant's behalf);
- (o) [¹. . .]
- (p) Part 6 (mobility component of personal independence payment).

Other Jobseeker's Allowance Decisions
2. A decision made in accordance with regulation 39(2) (jobseeker's allowance determinations on incomplete evidence) of these Regulations.　　**4.168**

Other Decisions relating to Universal Credit
3. A decision in default of a nomination under regulation 21(4) (assessment periods) of the Universal Credit Regulations.　　**4.169**
4. A decision in default of an election under regulation 29 (award to include the carer element) of the Universal Credit Regulations.
5. A decision as to the amount of universal credit to which a person is entitled, where it appears to the Secretary of State that the amount is determined by reference to the claimant's entitlement to an increased amount of universal credit in the circumstances referred to

in section 160C(2) (implementation of increases in universal credit due to attainment of a particular age) of the Administration Act.

6. So much of a decision as adopts a decision of a rent officer under an order made by virtue of section 122 of the Housing Act 1996 (decisions of rent officers for the purposes of universal credit).

Suspension

4.170   **7.** A decision of the Secretary of State relating to suspending payment of benefit, or to the payment of a benefit which has been suspended, under Part 5 (suspension) of these Regulations.

Decisions Depending on Other Cases

4.171   **8.** A decision of the Secretary of State in accordance with section 25 or 26 of the 1998 Act (decisions and appeals depending on other cases).

Expenses

4.172   **9.** A decision of the Secretary of State whether to pay travelling expenses under section 180 of the Administration Act.

Deductions

4.173   **10.** A decision of the Secretary of State under the Fines (Deductions from Income Support) Regulations 1992, other than a decision whether benefit is sufficient for a deduction to be made.

11. Any decision of the Secretary of State under the Community Charges (Deductions from Income Support) (No. 2) Regulations 1990, the Community Charges (Deductions from Income Support) (Scotland) Regulations 1989 or the Council Tax (Deductions from Income Support) Regulations 1993, except a decision—

    (a) whether there is an outstanding sum due of the amount sought to be deducted;
    (b) whether benefit is sufficient for the deduction to be made; or
    (c) on the priority of the deductions.

Loss of Benefit

4.174   **12.**—(1) In the circumstances referred to in sub-paragraph (2), a decision of the Secretary of State that a sanctionable benefit as defined in section 6A(1) of the Fraud Act is not payable (or is to be reduced) pursuant to section 6B, 7 or 9 of that Act as a result of—

    (a) a conviction for one or more benefit offences in one set of proceedings;
    (b) an agreement to pay a penalty as an alternative to prosecution;
    (c) a caution in respect of one or more benefit offences; or
    (d) a conviction for one or more benefit offences in each of two sets of proceedings, the later offence or offences being committed within the period of 5 years after the date of any of the convictions for a benefit offence in the earlier proceedings.

(2) The circumstances are that the only ground of appeal is that any of the convictions was erroneous, or that the offender (as defined in section 6B(1) of the Fraud Act) did not commit the benefit offence in respect of which there has been an agreement to pay a penalty or a caution has been accepted.

Payments on Account, Overpayments and Recovery

4.175   **13.** In the case of personal independence payment, a decision of the Secretary of State under the Social Security (Payments on account, Overpayments and Recovery) Regulations 1988, except a decision of the Secretary of State under the following provisions of those Regulations—

    (a) regulation 5, as to the offsetting of a prior payment against a subsequent award;
    (b) regulation 11(1), as to whether a payment in excess of entitlement has been credited to a bank or other account;
    (c) regulation 13, as to the sums to be deducted in calculating recoverable amounts.

14. A decision of the Secretary of State under the Social Security (Payments on Account of Benefit) Regulations 2013, except a decision under regulation 10 (bringing payments on account of benefit into account) of those Regulations.

15. A decision of the Secretary of State under the Social Security (Overpayments and Recovery) Regulations 2013, except a decision of the Secretary of State under the following provisions of those Regulations—

    (a) regulation 4(3), as to the person from whom an overpayment of a housing payment is recoverable;
    (b) regulation 7, as to the treatment of capital to be reduced;
    (c) regulation 8, as to the sums to be deducted in calculating recoverable amounts;
    (d) regulation 9 (sums to be deducted: change of dwelling).

Reciprocal Agreements

16. A decision of the Secretary of State made in accordance with an Order made under section 179 (reciprocal agreements with countries outside the United Kingdom) of the Administration Act.

4.176

European Community Regulations

17. An authorisation given by the Secretary of State in accordance with Article 22(1) or 55(1) of Council Regulation (EEC) No 1408/71 [² , as amended from time to time,] on the application of social security schemes to employed persons, to self-employed persons and to members of their families moving within the European Union.

4.177

Up-rating

18. A decision of the Secretary of State relating to the up-rating of benefits under Part 10 (review and alteration of benefits) of the Administration Act.

4.178

AMENDMENTS

1. Loans for Mortgage Interest Regulations 2017 (SI 2017/725) reg.18 and Sch.5 para.12 (April 6, 2018).

2. Social Security (Updating of EU References) (Amendment) Regulations 2018 (SI 2018/1084 reg.4 and Sch. para.12 (November 15, 2018).

DEFINITIONS

"the Administration Act"—see reg.2.
"assessment period"—see reg.2 and Universal Credit Regs., reg.21.
"benefit"—see reg.2.
"claimant"—*ibid.*
"the Fraud Act"—*ibid.*
"jobseeker's allowance"—*ibid.*
"personal independence payment"—*ibid.*
"universal credit"—*ibid.*
"the Universal Credit Regulations"—*ibid.*

PART V

IMMIGRATION STATUS AND THE RIGHT TO RESIDE

The Social Security (Immigration and Asylum) Consequential Amendments Regulations 2000

(SI 2000/636) (AS AMENDED)

Made by the Secretary of State under ss.115(3), (4) and (7), 123(5) and (6), 166(3) and 167 of the Immigration and Asylum Act 1999, ss.64(1), 68(4), 70(4), 71(6), 123(1)(a), (d) and (e), 135(1), 136(3) and (4), 137(1) and (2) (i) and 175(1), (3) and (4) of the Social Security Contributions and Benefits Act 1992, ss.5(1)(a) and (b), 189(1) and (4) and 191 of the Social Security Administration Act 1992, ss.12(1) and (2), 35(1) and 36(2) and (4) of the Jobseekers Act 1995

[In force April 3, 2000]

GENERAL NOTE

The United Kingdom's withdrawal from the European Union

The United Kingdom left the European Union on January 31, 2020 at 11.00 pm. However, these Regulations continue to apply in an unamended form—including references to EU law and the EEA—during the "implementation period". At the time of going to press, it is anticipated that the implementation period will end on December 31, 2020 at 11.00 pm. See further under the heading, *The United Kingdom's withdrawal from the European Union*, in the General Note to the Immigration (European Economic Area) Regulations 2016 below.

The law during the implementation period

These regulations are made under s.115 of the Immigration and Asylum Act   **5.1**
1999 (see Part II above), which excludes "persons subject to immigration control" from entitlement to most non-contributory benefits (including universal credit). Regulation 2 and the Schedule provide for exceptions to that exclusion. The combined effect of those provisions is as follows.

"Person subject to immigration control" is defined by s.115(9). Note first of all that a British citizen can never be a person subject to immigration control for social security purposes—*R(PC)2/07*. Neither can a person who is a national of a European Economic Area ("EEA") state (i.e. of the 27 EU countries—Austria, Belgium, Bulgaria, Croatia, Cyprus, the Czech Republic, Denmark, Estonia, Finland, France, Germany, Greece, Hungary, Ireland, Italy, Latvia, Lithuania, Luxembourg, Malta, the Netherlands, Poland, Portugal, Romania, Slovakia, Slovenia, Spain, and Sweden—or of Iceland, Liechtenstein or Norway).

Nationals of other countries are subject to immigration control if they are within one of the following four categories:

(a) A person who requires leave to enter or remain in the UK but does not have it

This category (s.115(9)(a)) covers illegal entrants, overstayers, people who are   **5.2**
subject to a deportation order, those allowed temporary admission to the UK and, subject to *R(SB) 11/88* (below), anyone whose immigration status has yet to be determined.

The practice of the Home Office is to grant temporary admission to asylum seekers (except those who are detained) pending investigation of their claims (see *CIS/3108/97*). Section 115 therefore has the effect of excluding all asylum seekers from benefit with effect from April 3, 2000. Asylum seekers who are destitute will instead receive support from a Home Office agency, the National Asylum Support Service, under ss.95–100 of the Immigration and Asylum Act.

For social security purposes, whether or not a person requires leave to enter or remain in the UK is a matter for the decision-maker (or, on appeal, for the First-tier Tribunal or Upper Tribunal) to determine and any decision by the Home Office is not binding (*R(SB) 11/88* but see *R(SB) 2/85* and *R(SB) 25/85* as to the terms on which leave is granted).

Nationals of the Isle of Man and the Channel Islands have freedom of travel within the UK and do not require leave to enter or remain (Immigration Act 1971 s.1(3)). Certain commonwealth citizens cannot be deported (Immigration Act 1971 s.7(1)).

Finally, note the Displaced Persons (Temporary Protection) Regulations 2005 (SI 2005/1379) (below), which, for benefit purposes, treat some displaced persons as if they have been granted exceptional leave to remain (i.e. with the result that those persons are not persons subject to immigration control under s.115(9)(a)).

(b) A person who has leave to enter or remain but subject to a condition that he does not have recourse to public funds

5.3   Limited leave to enter or remain subject to there being no recourse to public funds is given under s.33(1) of the Immigration Act 1971. From April 6, 2016, "public funds" are defined by rule 6 of the Immigration Rules as attendance allowance, severe disablement allowance, carer's allowance, disability living allowance, income support, (the former) council tax benefit and housing benefit, a social fund payment, child benefit, income-based JSA, income-related ESA, state pension credit, child tax credit, working tax credit, universal credit, personal independence payment, council tax reduction, certain publicly funded housing, and payments from local welfare funds under s.1 of the Localism Act 2011, the Welfare Funds (Scotland) Act 2015, or regulations made under art.135 of the Welfare Reform (Northern Ireland) Order 2015. Note however the clarifications of that definition in rules 6A–6C, as follows:

> "6A. For the purpose of these Rules, a person (P) is not to be regarded as having (or potentially having) recourse to public funds merely because P is (or will be) reliant in whole or in part on public funds provided to P's sponsor unless, as a result of P's presence in the United Kingdom, the sponsor is (or would be) entitled to increased or additional public funds (save where such entitlement to increased or additional public funds is by virtue of P and the sponsor's joint entitlement to benefits under the regulations referred to in paragraph 6B).

> 6B. Subject to paragraph 6C, a person (P) shall not be regarded as having recourse to public funds if P is entitled to benefits specified under section 115 of the Immigration and Asylum Act 1999 by virtue of regulations made under subsections (3) and (4) of that section or section 42 of the Tax Credits Act 2002. For an example of this principle, see *OD v SSWP (JSA)* [2015] UKUT 0438 (AAC).

> 6C. A person (P) making an application from outside the United Kingdom will be regarded as having recourse to public funds where P relies upon the future entitlement to any public funds that would be payable to P or to P's sponsor as a result of P's presence in the United Kingdom, (including those benefits to which P or the sponsor would be entitled as a result of P's presence in the United Kingdom under the regulations referred to in to paragraph 6B)."

The circumstances in which a "no recourse to public funds" condition will be imposed are set out in Appendix FM to the Immigration Rules. In *R. (on the application of W (A Child)) v Secretary of State for the Home Department* [2020] EWHC 1299 (Admin), the Divisional Court (Bean LJ and Chamberlain J) summarised the provisions of that Appendix as follows:

> "16. As a result [*i.e.*, of the events set out earlier in the judgment], the criteria for deciding whether to impose or lift the NRPF condition were included in the Immigration Rules. That was done by way of amendment to Appendix FM to the

Immigration Rules. Appendix FM provides a number of bases on which a person may be granted LTR with a view to eventual settlement by virtue of a connection with a family member who is a British citizen, settled in the UK or a refugee or person entitled to humanitarian protection. There are separate provisions governing applications for entry clearance or LTR as a partner (D-ECP and D-LTRP), a child (D-ECC and DLTRC) and a parent (D-ECPT and D-LTRPT) of such a person. The rules for those applying as partners and parents stipulate that entry clearance or LTR, if granted, will be subject to a condition of NRPF "unless the decision-maker considers, with reference to paragraph GEN 1.11A, that the applicant should not be subject to such a condition". The rules for those applying as children provide that the child will be subject to the same condition as the parent.

17.   Paragraph GEN 1.11A provides as follows:

"Where entry clearance or leave to remain as a partner, child or parent is granted under paragraph D-ECP.1.2., D-LTRP.1.2., D-ECC.1.1., DLTRC.1.1., D-ECPT.1.2. or D-LTRPT.1.2., it will normally be granted subject to a condition of no recourse to public funds, unless the applicant has provided the decision-maker with:
(a)   satisfactory evidence that the applicant is destitute as defined in section 95 of the Immigration and Asylum Act 1999; or
(b)   satisfactory evidence that there are particularly compelling reasons relating to the welfare of a child of a parent in receipt of a very low income."

In *Re W*, the Divisional Court held (at [73]) that:

"The NRPF regime ... [does] not adequately recognise, reflect or give effect to the Secretary of State's obligation not to impose, or to lift, the condition of NRPF in cases where the applicant is not yet, but will imminently suffer inhuman or degrading treatment [*i.e.*, by becoming destitute] without recourse to public funds. In its current form the NRPF regime is apt to mislead caseworkers in this critical respect and gives rise to a real risk of unlawful decisions in a significant number of cases. To that extent it is unlawful."

It is suggested, however, that it is not open to a tribunal to decide on an appeal against a decision refusing a social security benefit on the basis that the claimant is a person subject to immigration control, that a no recourse to public funds condition that has in fact been imposed, should not have been: see *R(SB) 2/85* and *R(SB) 25/85* below. Such an argument must be pursued by an appeal against the immigration decision or by judicial review.

For this category (s.115(9)(b)) and the following two (s.115(9)(c) and (d)) to apply, it is necessary that the person should actually require leave to enter or remain in the UK. So, for example, if the Home Office mistakenly grants conditional leave to a person who is in fact a British citizen and does not require leave at all, the mistake does not cause that person to become subject to immigration control for social security purposes (see *R(SB) 11/88*). However, where leave is required, the decision of the Home Office as to the terms on which leave is granted is conclusive (see *R(SB) 2/85* and *R(SB) 25/85*). A proper statement of the terms of leave should be obtained from the Home Office (*CSSB/137/82*).

Until October 28, 2013 there was one exception to the exclusion from benefit in s.115(9)(b). That exception was established by reg.2(1) and para.1 of Pt I of the Schedule and applied to those who had previously supported themselves without recourse to public funds but found themselves temporarily without money because remittances from abroad had been disrupted. In such circumstances, income support, income-based JSA, income-related ESA and social fund payments could be paid as long as there was a reasonable expectation that the supply of funds would be resumed. However, that exception was abolished with effect from October 29, 2013, by reg.9(1) and (3) of the Social Security (Miscellaneous Amendments) (No.3)

Regulations 2013 (SI 2013/2536). For details of the law as it stood before that date, see pp.375, 800–801 and 809–810 of Vol.II of the 2013/14 edition.

(c) A person who has leave to enter or remain which was given as a result of a maintenance undertaking

5.4   "Maintenance undertaking" is defined by s.115(10) as "a written undertaking given by another person in pursuance of the immigration rules to be responsible for [the claimant's] maintenance and accommodation". Under r.35 of the Immigration Rules such undertakings may be demanded from "a sponsor of a person seeking leave to enter or variation of leave to enter or remain in the United Kingdom" but are normally only required from the sponsors of elderly or other dependent relatives.

Rule 6 defines "sponsor" as meaning:

> "the person in relation to whom an applicant is seeking leave to enter or remain as their spouse, fiancé, civil partner, proposed civil partner, unmarried partner, same-sex partner or dependent relative, as the case may be, under paragraphs 277 to 295O or 317 to 319 or the person in relation to whom an applicant is seeking entry clearance or leave as their partner or dependent relative under Appendix FM."

A promise of support given by someone who is not a "sponsor" as so defined cannot amount to a "maintenance undertaking" for the purposes of s.115(10) or para.3 of the Schedule: see *Leeds City Council v EO (HB)* [2019] UKUT 96 (AAC).

The purpose of the undertaking is to reinforce a condition that the person seeking leave to enter or remain should not have recourse to public funds by

- demonstrating that the sponsor has sufficient resources to maintain and accommodate the relative without the latter claiming public funds; and

- making the sponsor legally "liable to maintain" the relative. This has the effect that, if the Secretary of State does for any reason have to pay income support to the relative (and, in most cases, the mere existence of an undertaking will mean that the relative has no such entitlement), the sponsor may, in certain circumstances, be subject to a criminal penalty and the Secretary of State may recoup the benefit paid by making a complaint in a magistrates' court (see, respectively ss.105 and 106 of the SSAA 1992 in Vol.III).

The requirement in the definition that the undertaking has been given "in pursuance of the immigration rules" cannot mean "in pursuance of a requirement in the immigration rules" because the decision whether to ask for an undertaking is a discretionary one. Rather, it means "under" or "further to" the immigration rules, see *CIS/1697/2004*, paras 41 and 42. In that case, the Deputy Commissioner held that it was sufficient that the sponsor was making a promise in furtherance of the claimant's application for indefinite leave to remain.

It is not necessary that the undertaking should be given on one of the official Home Office forms (either Form RON 112 or the Form SET(F) that replaced it)—see *R. (Begum) v Social Security Commissioner* [2003] EWHC 3380 (Admin), QBD (Sir Christopher Bellamy), November 6, 2003 confirming *CIS/2474/1999*, *CIS/2816/2002* and, on this point, *CIS/47/2002*. Those forms "are expressly in the language of undertaking and emphasise the significance of such undertakings" (see Rix LJ at [36] of *Ahmed v Secretary of State for Work & Pensions* [2005] EWCA Civ 535, CA (May, Rix and Jacob LJJ), April 19, 2005 (reported as *R(IS) 8/05*). But if an official form is not used, consideration may need to be given to whether the document signed by the sponsor amounts to an "undertaking" at all. In *Ahmed* the Court of Appeal held (upholding the Commissioner in *CIS/426/2003* and disagreeing, on this point, with the Commissioner in *CIS/47/2002* in which the disputed document was in similar terms) that the issue is one of substance rather than form and that the legal test is whether or not the document contains a promise or agreement about what the sponsor will do in the future rather than a statement about his or her present abilities and intentions:

> "**47.** . . . It seems to me that an undertaking has to be something in the nature of a promise or agreement and the language that 'I am able and willing to maintain and accommodate' is language which has reference, essentially, to current ability and intention and does not amount to a promise for the future. The essence of an undertaking is a promise as to the future, as typically found in the language 'I will.'

> **48.** I accept that the use of any particular language is not a condition precedent. The absence of an express reference to 'I undertake', such as is found in the Home Office's forms, or to 'I promise' or 'I agree', will not necessarily be critical if it is still clear that the substance of what is said is a promise for the future." (per Rix LJ)

So, the declaration in the *Ahmed* case that the sponsor was "able and willing to maintain and accommodate the applicant without recourse to public funds and in suitable accommodation" was not an undertaking because it only related to present facts and intentions. For a further example (in which the opposite conclusion was reached on the facts) see *CIS/1697/2004*. That decision also holds that neither a commissioner, nor (by necessary implication) a tribunal, has any power to grant rectification of a defective maintenance undertaking .

5.5

In *CIS 3508/2001* it was held that leave to enter or remain was given "as a result of" a maintenance undertaking if the existence of that undertaking was a factor in the decision to grant leave. It does not have to be the only, or even a major, factor. It is sufficient that it was of some relevance. It seems that that will almost always be the case if the immigration decision-maker acts within the Immigration Rules. In *Shah v Secretary of State for Work and Pensions* [2002] EWCA Civ 285 (reported as *R(IS) 2/02*), the Court of Appeal held that a maintenance undertaking should be regarded as a continuing obligation and therefore applied even if the claimant had left the UK (thereby causing his or her indefinite leave to remain to lapse) and had been made a fresh grant of indefinite leave to remain as a returning resident on his or her return. *Shah* was decided under the pre-April 2000 law, but it is suggested that the same principles also apply to s.115(9)(c).

Under the principles set out by the House of Lords in *Kerr v Department for Social Development* [2004] UKHL 23; *R1/04 (SF)*, it is for the Secretary of State to show that the maintenance undertaking was a factor in the decision to grant leave: see *R(PC) 1/09*. In that case, where the decision to grant leave was made outside the Immigration Rules, the causal connection could not be inferred and had not been established: see also *SSWP v SS (SPC)* [2010] UKUT 483 (AAC) and *SJ v SSWP* [2015] UKUT 505 (AAC).

People who are granted leave to enter or remain as a result of a maintenance undertaking are not entitled to income support income-based JSA until they have been resident in the UK for a period of at least five years from the date of entry or the date on which the undertaking was given, whichever is later. The only exceptions are where the sponsored immigrant becomes a British citizen during the five-year period (see *R(PC) 2/07*) and where the person (or all the people if there was more than one) who gave the maintenance undertaking has died before the end of the five-year period. See para.3 of Pt I of the Schedule. The five years' residence need not be continuous: it can be made up of shorter periods (see paras 74–75 of the Commissioner's decision in *R(IS) 2/02*). In *CPC/1035/2005* the Commissioner considered the position of a Pakistani national who had been given leave to enter the UK under a maintenance undertaking. Since entering the UK in October 1996, she had returned to Pakistan for periods of 17 months, nearly 14 months and 21 months in order to look after her parents. In July 2004, over 7½ years after she first entered, she claimed—and, in August 2004, was refused—SPC. The Commissioner upheld that refusal. Although it was not necessary for the claimant to be physically present in the UK in order to be resident here, "whether a person is or is not resident in a particular place during a period of physical absence depends on a calculus consisting of the duration and circumstances of the absence". Some absences affect residence simply on account of their length. Each period of absence had to be considered individually but none of the periods listed above, not even the shortest, was compatible with the claimant remaining resident in the UK. It followed that as the claimant had not been resident in the UK for nearly 58 months (4 years and 10 months) of the period between October 1996 and August 2004, she had not been resident for a total of five years since the date of her entry and was therefore still excluded from benefit.

Sponsored immigrants are not excluded from social fund payments (see para.4 of Pt II of the Schedule) but in practice are unlikely to be eligible for anything other than a crisis loan or a winter fuel payment. This is because, as persons subject to immigration control, they are excluded from the qualifying benefits for maternity and funeral expenses payments, community care grants, budgeting loans and cold weather payments. Sponsored immigrants are also not excluded from entitlement to attendance allowance, severe disablement allowance, (the former) health in pregnancy grants, carer's allowance or disability living allowance.

(d) A person who has leave to enter or remain only because he is appealing against certain immigration decisions

5.6   Section 115(9)(d) provides that a person who "has leave to enter or remain in the United Kingdom only as a result of paragraph 17 of Schedule 4 [*i.e.*, Sch.4 to the Immigration and Asylum Act 1999 itself]" is a person subject to immigration control. Para.17 of Sch. was repealed by Sch.9, para.1 to the Nationality, Immigration and Asylum Act 2002 with effect from 1 April 2003. However, s.17(2) of the Interpretation Act 1978 has the effect that the reference to para.17 of Schedule 4 in s.115(9)(d) must be read as a reference to that provision as re-enacted in section 3C(1) and (2)(b) and (c) of the Immigration Act 1971: see *EE v City of Cardiff (HB)* [2018] UKUT 418 (AAC).

Under s.82 of the 2002 Act (the successor to s.61 of the 1999 Act referred to in to para.17 of Sch.4 to that Act), a person with limited leave to enter or remain in the UK has a right of appeal against a decision to vary, or to refuse to vary, his leave. Section 3C of the Immigration Act 1971 provides that while such an appeal is pending, the leave to which the appeal relates and any conditions subject to which it was granted continue to have effect. The effect of s.115(9)(d) is therefore now that those whose leave has automatically been extended by s.3C are persons subject to immigration control.

The former section 3D of the Immigration Act (which was in force from 31 August 2006 to 30 November 2016) is also potentially relevant. It applied where a person's leave to enter or remain in the United Kingdom is "varied with the result that he has no leave to enter or remain in the United Kingdom, or ... is revoked" and had the effect that the former leave to enter or remain was extended during any period when the person was appealing against it. The reference in s.115(9)(d) to of paragraph 17 of Schedule 4 is not to be treated as a reference to section 3D—see *EE* (above) at paras 37-40—so anyone within s.3D was not a person who "requires leave to enter or remain in the United Kingdom but does not have it" within s.115(9)(a): see *GO v HMRC (CHB)* [2018] UKUT 328 (AAC).

The ECSMA Agreement and the European Social Charter

5.7   Nationals of those countries which are not members of the EEA but which have ratified the European Convention on Social and Medical Assistance ("the ECSMA Agreement") or the European Social Charter (both of which are treaties concluded under the auspices of the Council of Europe (ETS Nos 14 and 35 respectively) are not excluded from income support, income-based jobseeker's allowance, income-related ESA, universal credit, housing benefit, social fund payments or (before April 1, 2013) council tax benefit: see *OD v SSWP (JSA)* [2015] UKUT 438 (AAC). This affects nationals of Turkey (ECSMA Agreement and Social Charter), Switzerland (Social Charter) and the Republic of Northern Macedonia (Social Charter). Turkey ratified the Social Charter on November 24, 1999 and the ECSMA Agreement on December 2, 1996. Switzerland ratified the Social Charter on May 6, 1976 and Northern Macedonia ratified it on March 31, 2005. Records of which States have ratified a Council of Europe treaty are maintained by the Council's Treaty Office and are available from its website at *http://www.conventions.coe.int/*.

Note, finally, that there are two European Social Charters. For the purposes of these regulations it is the original Charter (which was opened for signature in Turin on October 18, 1961) that is relevant, not the Revised Social Charter (ETS 163) (which was opened for signature in Strasbourg on May 3, 1996).

The meaning of "lawfully present" was considered by the House of Lords in *Szoma v Secretary of State for Work and Pensions* [2005] UKHL 64 (reported as *R(IS)* 2/06). That appeal was a challenge to the decision of the Court of Appeal in *Kaya v Haringey LBC* [2001] EWCA Civ 677, in which it had been held, following the decision of the House of Lords in *In re Muisi* (reported *sub nom. R. v Home Secretary Ex p. Bugdaycay* [1987] A.C. 514), that a person granted temporary admission to the UK could not be "lawfully present" because he or she was deemed by s.11 of the Immigration Act 1971 not to be present in the UK at all. In *Szoma*, their Lordships overruled *Kaya* and held that lawful presence did not require

". . . more by way of positive legal authorisation for someone's presence in the UK than that they are at large here pursuant to the express written authority of an immigration officer provided for by statute."

Note that an ECSMA national who is not excluded from benefit by virtue of para.4 of Pt I of the Schedule, may nevertheless be excluded by virtue of the habitual residence and right to reside tests—see *Yesiloz v Camden LBC and SSWP* [2009] EWCA Civ 415 *(R(H) 7/09)*.

Spouses and family members of EEA nationals

A person who is not an EEA national but who is a family member of such a national is not excluded from social fund payments (and certain non-contributory, non-means-tested benefits covered by Vol.I) (para.1 of Pt II of the Schedule. In *CDLA/708/2007*, the Deputy Commissioner held that para.1 only applied where the EEA national is "exercising his or her rights or freedoms under the EEA Agreement (whether or not he or she also has equivalent rights under EC law) and where the family member is a person who has rights under the EEA Agreement as a family member. However, in *JFP v DSD (DLA)* [2012] NI Com 267, the Chief Commissioner of Northern Ireland declined to follow *CDLA/708/2007*. In his view, there was no reason not to give para.1 of Pt II of the Schedule its natural meaning so that s.115 does not exclude any family member of any EEA national from entitlement to attendance allowance, disability living allowance, carer's allowance, child benefit, a social fund payment or any of the other benefits set out in the heading to that Part of the Schedule. In *MS v SSWP (DLA)* [2016] UKUT 42 (AAC) a judge of the Upper Tribunal in Great Britain considered the reasoning in both decisions and preferred that in *CDLA/708/2007*. The judge's views on this point were *obiter* because he had already decided that the claimant did not satisfy the conditions of entitlement to DLA. However, the practical effect of *MS v SSWP* is to create a conflict of precedent between Great Britain and Northern Ireland. The strict position has always been that the FTT in Great Britain was bound to follow *CDLA/708/2007* and appeal tribunals in Northern Ireland were bound by the decision of the Chief Commissioner. However, most tribunals in Great Britain would in practice have regarded themselves as free to follow *JFP v DSD* because, although it was given in another jurisdiction, it was of considerable persuasive authority, had considered *CDLA/708/2007* in detail, and disapproved it. That line of argument is no longer open following *MS v SSWP*.

As regards entitlement to social fund payments, see the note on sponsored immigrants (above) as to the practical restrictions on eligibility.

5.8

EEA reciprocal agreements

5.9   Under art.310 (formerly art.238) of the Treaty establishing the European Community (as amended by the Treaty of Amsterdam), the EC "may conclude with one or more States or international organisations agreements establishing an association involving reciprocal rights and obligations, common action and special procedure". Paragraphs 2 and 3 of Pt II of the Schedule apply when such a reciprocal agreement provides for equal treatment in the field of social security of workers who are nationals of the signatory State and their families. In those circumstances, nationals of the non-EC State who are lawfully working in the UK and members of their families who are living with them are not excluded by s.115 from entitlement to social fund payments, attendance allowance, SDA, health in pregnancy grants, carer's allowance, DLA and child benefit. For an example of how an association agreement affected entitlement to family credit under the pre-April 3, 2000 law see *R(FC) 1/01* which also decides that where such an Agreement does not provide for equal treatment in the field of social security but a Decision of an Association Council constituted under the Agreement and required by the Agreement to adopt social security measures does so provide, the Decision of the Association Council must be regarded as made under the Agreement so that (in terms of the current law) paras 2 and 3 of Pt II of the Schedule would apply.

From time to time, tribunals can be called on to decide legal issues arising under the terms of the individual Association Agreements and the Decisions of the Association Councils established by those Agreements. Useful guidance for those who need to apply the Agreement between the EC and Turkey may be found in two decisions of Commissioner Mesher, *CJSA/4705/1999* and *CIS/5707/1999*. In the latter appeal, the Commissioner holds that income support is not within the material scope of Decision 3/80 of the Association Council under that Agreement (and therefore that IS claimants may not benefit from its terms). In the former appeal, it was held that JSA was within the material scope of the Decision but, following the decision of the ECJ in *Sürül v Bundesanstalt für Arbeit* (C–262/96) [1999] E.C.R. I-2685, a person may only rely on the Decision if authorised to reside in the Member State concerned and lawfully resident there. In *CJSA/4705/1999*, the claimant was an overstayer and therefore not authorised to reside in the United Kingdom. He could not therefore benefit from Decision 3/80.

The habitual residence test and the right to reside

5.10   Note that, even if claimants are not excluded from benefit as a person subject to immigration control, entitlement to universal credit, IS, IBJSA, IRESA, HB and SPC is also dependent upon their being (or treated as being) habitually resident. For EEA and Swiss nationals, this includes a requirement that they should have a "right to reside" in the Common Travel Area. See the notes to the Immigration (European Economic Area) Regulations 2016 (below).

Citation, commencement and interpretation

5.11   **1.**—(1) These Regulations may be cited as the Social Security (Immigration and Asylum) Consequential Amendments Regulations 2000.

(2) These Regulations shall come into force on 3rd April 2000.

(3) In these Regulations—

"the Act" means the Immigration and Asylum Act 1999;

"the Attendance Allowance Regulations" means the Social Security (Attendance Allowance) Regulations 1991;

"the Claims and Payments Regulations" means the Social Security (Claims and Payments) Regulations 1987;

"the Contributions and Benefits Act" means the Social Security Contributions and Benefits Act 1992;

[¹ . . .];

"the Disability Living Allowance Regulations" means the Social Security (Disability Living Allowance) Regulations 1991;

[² "the Employment and Support Allowance Regulations" means the Employment and Support Allowance Regulations 2008;]

[¹ . . .];

"the Income Support Regulations" means the Income Support (General) Regulations 1987;

"the Invalid Care Allowance Regulations" means the Social Security (Invalid Care Allowance) Regulations 1976;

"the Jobseeker's Allowance Regulations" means the Jobseeker's Allowance Regulations 1996;

[³ "personal independence payment" means personal independence payment under Part 4 of the Welfare Reform Act 2012;]

"the Persons from Abroad Regulations" means the Social Security (Persons from Abroad) Miscellaneous Amendments Regulations 1996;

"the Severe Disablement Allowance Regulations" means the Social Security (Severe Disablement Allowance) Regulations 1984.

[² "income-related employment and support allowance" means an income-related allowance under Part 1 of the Welfare Reform Act 2007 (employment and support allowance) [⁴ ;

"universal credit" means universal credit under Part 1 of the Welfare Reform Act 2012].]

(4) In these Regulations, unless the context otherwise requires, a reference—

(a) to a numbered regulation or Schedule is to the regulation in, or the Schedule to, these Regulations bearing that number;

(b) in a regulation or Schedule to a numbered paragraph is to the paragraph in that regulation or Schedule bearing that number.

AMENDMENTS

1. Housing Benefit and Council Tax Benefit (Consequential Provisions) Regulations 2006 (SI 2006/217) reg.3 and Sch.1 (March 6, 2006).

2. Employment and Support Allowance (Consequential Provisions) (No.2) Regulations 2008 (SI 2008/1554) reg.69(1) and (2) (October 27, 2008).

3. Personal Independence Payment (Supplementary Provisions and Consequential Amendments) Regulations 2013 (SI 2013/388) reg.8 and Sch. para.23(1) and (2) (April 8, 2013).

4. Universal Credit (Consequential, Supplementary, Incidental and Miscellaneous Provisions) Regulations 2013 (SI 2013/630) reg.31(1) and (2) (April 29, 2013).

GENERAL NOTE

With effect from April 7, 2003 the definition of "the Claims and Payments Regulations" was revoked in so far as it related to child benefit and guardian's allowance (reg.43 of and Pt I of Sch.3 to the Child Benefit and Guardian's Allowance (Administration) Regulations 2003). The definition remains in force for the purposes of other benefits.   5.12

Persons not excluded from specified benefits under section 115 of the Immigration and Asylum Act 1999

5.13
    2.—(1) For the purposes of entitlement to income-based jobseeker's allowance, income support, a social fund payment, housing benefit [⁶ ...] under the Contributions and Benefits Act, [³ income-related employment and support allowance,] [² or state pension credit under the State Pension Credit Act 2002,] as the case may be, a person falling within a category or description of persons specified in Part I of the Schedule is a person to whom section 115 of the Act does not apply.

[⁸ (1A) For the purposes of entitlement to universal credit, a person falling within a category or description of persons specified in paragraphs 2, 3 and 4 of Part I of the Schedule is a person to whom section 115 of the Act does not apply.]

(2) For the purposes of entitlement to attendance allowance, severe disablement allowance, [¹ carer's allowance], disability living allowance, a social fund payment [⁴ , health in pregnancy grant] or child benefit under the Contributions and Benefits Act [⁷ or personal independence payment], as the case may be, a person falling within a category or description of persons specified in Part II of the Schedule is a person to whom section 115 of the Act does not apply.

(3) For the purposes of entitlement to child benefit, attendance allowance or disability living allowance under the Contributions and Benefits Act [⁷ or personal independence payment], as the case may be, a person in respect of whom there is an Order in Council made under section 179 of the Social Security Administration Act 1992 giving effect to a reciprocal agreement in respect of one of those benefits, as the case may be, is a person to whom section 115 of the Act does not apply.

(4) For the purposes of entitlement to—

    (a) income support, a social fund payment, housing benefit [⁶ ...] under the Contributions and Benefits Act, [³ or income-related employment and support allowance,] as the case may be, a person who is entitled to or is receiving benefit by virtue of paragraph (1) or (2) of regulation 12 of the Persons from Abroad Regulations is a person to whom section 115 of the Act does not apply;

    (b) attendance allowance, disability living allowance, [¹carer's allowance, severe disablement allowance, a social fund payment or child benefit under the Contributions and Benefits Act, as the case may be, a person who is entitled to or is receiving benefit byvirtue of paragraph (10) of regulation 12 is a person to whom section 115 of the Act does not apply.

[²(c) state pension credit under the State Pension Credit Act 2002, a person to whom sub-paragraph (a) would have applied but for the fact that they have attained the qualifying age for the purposes of state pension credit, is a person to whom section 115 of the Act does not apply.]

[⁵ (5) For the purposes of entitlement to [⁸ universal credit,] income support, [⁸ an income-based jobseeker's allowance under the Jobseekers Act 1995], an [⁸ income-related] employment and support allowance or a social fund payment under the Contributions and Benefits Act, as the case may be, a person who is an asylum seeker within the meaning of paragraph (4) of regulation 12 who has not ceased to be an asylum seeker by virtue of paragraph (5) of that regulation is a person to whom section 115 of the Act does not apply.]

(6) For the purposes of entitlement to housing benefit [⁶ . . .] or a social fund payment under the Contributions and Benefits Act, as the case may be, a person to whom regulation 12(6) applies is a person to whom section 115 of the Act does not apply.

[² (7) For the purposes of entitlement to state pension credit under the State Pension Credit Act 2002, a person to whom paragraph (5) would have applied but for the fact that they have attained the qualifying age for the purposes of state pension credit, is a person to whom section 115 of the Act does not apply.

(8) [⁹ . . .]]

AMENDMENTS

1. Social Security Amendment (Carer's Allowance) Regulations 2002 (SI 2002/2497) reg.3 and Sch.2 (April 1, 2003).
2. State Pension Credit (Transitional and Miscellaneous Provisions) Amendment Regulations 2003 (SI 2003/2274) reg.6 (October 6, 2003).
3. Employment and Support Allowance (Consequential Provisions) (No.2) Regulations 2008 (SI 2008/1554) reg.69(1) and (3) (October 27, 2008).
4. Health in Pregnancy Grant (Entitlement and Amount) Regulations 2008 (SI 2008/3108) reg.8(2) (January 1, 2009).
5. Social Security (Miscellaneous Amendments) (No.5) Regulations 2009 (SI 2009/3228) reg.3(5) (January 25, 2010).
6. Council Tax Benefit Abolition (Consequential Provision) Regulations 2013 (SI 2013/458) reg.3 and Sch.1 (April 1, 2013).
7. Personal Independence Payment (Supplementary Provisions and Consequential Amendments) Regulations 2013 (SI 2013/388) reg.8 and Sch. para.23(1) and (3) (April 8, 2013).
8. Universal Credit (Consequential, Supplementary, Incidental and Miscellaneous Provisions) Regulations 2013 (SI 2013/630) reg.31(1) and (3) (April 29, 2013).
9. Social Security (Miscellaneous Amendments) (No.3) Regulations 2013 (SI 2013/2536) reg.9(2) (October 29, 2013).

Transitional arrangements and savings

12.—(1) and (2) [² . . .]   5.14
(3) [³ . . .]
(4) An asylum seeker within the meaning of this paragraph is a person who—
  (a) submits on his arrival (other than on his re-entry) in the United Kingdom from a country outside the Common Travel Area a claim for asylum on or before 2nd April 2000 to the Secretary of State that it would be contrary to the United Kingdom's obligations under the Convent for him to be removed or required to leave, the United Kingdom and that claim is recorded by the Secretary of State as having been made before that date; or
  (b) on or before 2nd April 2000 becomes, while present in Great Britain, an asylum seeker when—
    (i) the Secretary of State makes a declaration to the effect that the country of which he is a national is subject to such a fundamental change of circumstances that he would not normally order the return of a person to that country; and

    (ii) he submits, within a period of three months from the date that declaration was made, a claim for asylum to the Secretary of State under the Convention relating to the Status of Refugees, and

    (iii) his claim for asylum under that Convention is recorded by the Secretary of State has having been made; and

  (c) in the case of a claim for jobseeker's allowance, holds a work permit or has written authorisation from the Secretary of state permitting him to work in the United Kingdom.

(5) A person ceases to be an asylum seeker for the purposes of this paragraph when his claim for asylum is recorded by the Secretary of State as having been decided (other than on appeal) or abandoned

(6)–(8) [*Omitted as applying only to housing benefit and council tax benefit.*]

(9) In paragraphs (4) and (7) "the Common Travel Area" means the United Kingdom, the Channel Islands, the Isle of Man and the Republic of Ireland collectively and "the Convention" means the Convention relating to the Status of Refugees done at Geneva on 28th July 1951 as extended by Article 2(1) of the Protocol relating to the Status of Refugees done at New York on 31st January 1967.

(10) Where, before the coming into force of these Regulations, a person has claimed benefit to which he is entitled or is receiving benefit by virtue of regulation 12(3) of the Persons from Abroad Regulations or regulation 14B(g) of the Child Benefit (General) Regulations 1976, as the case may be, those provisions shall continue to have effect, for the purposes of entitlement to attendance allowance, disability living allowance, [¹ carer's allowance], severe disablement allowance or child benefit, as the case may be, until such time as—

  (a) his claim for asylum (if any) is recorded by the Secretary of State as having been decided or abandoned; or

  (b) his entitlement to that benefit is revised or superseded under section 9 or 10 of the Social Security Act 1998, if earlier,

as if regulations 8, 9, 10 and 11 and paragraph (2) or paragraph (3), as the case may be, of regulation 13, had not been made.

(11) In the Persons from Abroad Regulations—

  (a) in paragraph (1) of regulation 12, after the words "shall continue to have effect" there shall be inserted the words "both as regards him as regards persons who are members of his family at the coming into force of these Regulations)"; and

  (b) notwithstanding the amendments and revocations in regulations 3, 6 and 7, regulations 12(1) and (2) of the Persons from Abroad Regulations shall continue to have effect as they had effect before those amendments and revocations came into force.

AMENDMENTS

1. Social Security Amendment (Carer's Allowance) Regulations 2002 (SI 2002/2497) reg.3 and Sch.2 (April 1, 2003).

2. Asylum and Immigration (Treatment of Claimants, etc.) Act 2004 (c.19) s.12(3) (June 14, 2007).

3. Social Security (Miscellaneous Amendments) (No.5) Regulations 2009 (SI 2009/3228) reg.2(1)(c) (January 25, 2010).

GENERAL NOTE

Paragraphs (1) and (2) made transitional provision for asylum seekers who claimed   **5.15**
asylum before April 3, 2000, by preserving the effect of s.11(2) of the Asylum and
Immigration Act 1996 (which was repealed by the Immigration and Asylum Act
1999 with effect from that date). They were revoked on June 14, 2007. However, by
art.2(3) of the Asylum and Immigration (Treatment of Claimants, etc.) Act 2004
(Commencement No.7 and Transitional Provisions) Order 2007 (SI 2007/1602),
the revocation of reg.21ZB "shall not apply to a person who is recorded as a refugee
on or before June 14, 2007". For those purposes a person is recorded as a refugee on
the day on which the Home Secretary notifies him that he has been recognised as a
refugee and granted asylum in the UK (see art.2(4)). For cases in which the claim for
asylum was made before April 3, 2000 and the decision granting refugee status was
notified on or before June 14, 2007, see pp.698–699 of the 2007 edition.

Until January 25, 2010, para.(3) allowed pre-April 3, 2000 asylum seekers to claim
income support (and, from October 27, 2008, employment and support allowance:
see reg.69(1) and (4) of SI 2008/1554) at the reduced "urgent cases" rate. Paragraph
(3) was revoked on January 25, 2010. From that date, if there are still any pre-April
3, 2000 asylum seekers (as defined in para.(4)) who have not ceased to be an asylum
seekers under para.(5), they can claim income support, jobseeker's allowance, employment and support allowance and social fund payments at the full rate under reg.2(5).
For income support, such claimants will fall within the amended prescribed category
"Persons from abroad" in para.21 of Sch.1B to the Income Support Regulations.

SCHEDULE   **Regulation 2**

PERSONS NOT EXCLUDED FROM CERTAIN BENEFITS UNDER SECTION 115
OF THE IMMIGRATION AND ASYLUM ACT 1999

PART I

Persons not excluded under section 115 of the Immigration and Asylum Act from entitlement   **5.16**
to [⁵ universal credit,] income-based jobseeker's allowance, income support, [3 income-related
employment and support allowance,] a social fund payment, housing benefit or council tax benefit.

1.[⁷ . . .]

2. A person who has been given leave to enter or remain in, the United Kingdom by the
Secretary of State upon an undertaking by another person or persons pursuant to the immigration rules within the meaning of the Immigration Act 1971, to be responsible for his maintenance and accommodation and who has not been resident in the United Kingdom for a period
of at least five years beginning on the date of entry or the date on which the undertaking was
given in respect of him, whichever date is the later and the person or persons who gave the
undertaking to provide for his maintenance and accommodation has, or as the case may be,
have died

3. A person who—
  (a) has been given leave to enter or remain in, the United Kingdom by the Secretary of
      State upon an undertaking by another person or persons pursuant to the immigra-
      tion rules within the meaning of the Immigration Act 1971, to be responsible for his
      maintenance and accommodation; and
  (b) has been resident in the United Kingdom for a period of at least five years beginning
      on the date of entry or the date on which the undertaking was given in respect of him,
      whichever date is the later.

4. A person who is a national of a state which has ratified the European Convention on
Social and Medical Assistance (done in Paris on 11th December 1953) or a state which has
ratified the Council of Europe Social Charter (signed in Turin on 18th October 1961) and who
is lawfully present in the United Kingdom.

Part II

5.17   *Persons not excluded under section 115 of the Immigration and Asylum Act from entitlement to attendance allowance, severe disablement allowance, [1carer's allowance], disability living allowance, [4 personal independence payment,] a social fund payment [2 , Health in Pregnancy Grant] or child benefit.*

1. A member of a family of a national of a State contracting party to the Agreement on the European Economic Area signed at Oporto on 2nd May 1992 as adjusted by the Protocol signed at Brussels on 17th March 1993 [6 as modified or supplemented from time to time].

2. A person who is lawfully working in Great Britain and is a national of a State with which the Community has concluded an agreement under Article 310 of the Treaty of Amsterdam amending the Treaty on European Union, the Treaties establishing the European Communities and certain related Acts providing, in the field of social security, for the equal treatment of workers who are nationals of the signatory State and their families.

3. A person who is a member of a family of, and living with, a person specified in paragraph 2.

4. A person who has been given leave to enter, or remain in, the United Kingdom by the Secretary of State upon an undertaking by another person or persons pursuant to the immigration rules within the meaning of the Immigration Act 1971, to be responsible for his maintenance and accommodation.

Amendments

1. Social Security Amendment (Carer's Allowance) Regulations 2002 (SI 2002/2497) reg.3 and Sch.2 (April 1, 2003).

2. Health in Pregnancy Grant (Entitlement and Amount) Regulations 2008 (SI 2008/3108) reg.8(3) (January 1, 2009).

3. Employment and Support Allowance (Consequential Provisions) (No.2) Regulations 2008 (SI 2008/1554) reg.69(1) and (5) (October 27, 2008).

4. Personal Independence Payment (Supplementary Provisions and Consequential Amendments) Regulations 2013 (SI 2013/388) reg.8 and Sch. para.23(1) and (4) (April 8, 2013).

5. Universal Credit (Consequential, Supplementary, Incidental and Miscellaneous Provisions) Regulations 2013 (SI 2013/630) reg.31(1) and (4) (April 29, 2013).

6. Social Security (Croatia) Amendment Regulations 2013 (SI 2013/1474) reg.8 (July 1, 2013).

7. Social Security (Miscellaneous Amendments) (No.3) Regulations 2013 (SI 2013/2536) reg.9(3) (October 29,2013).

The Accession (Immigration and Worker Registration) Regulations 2004

(SI 2004/1219) (as amended)

Made by the Home Secretary, under section 2(2) of the European Communities Act 1972 and section 2 of the European Union (Accessions) Act 2003

[In force May 1, 2004]

General Note

5.18   See the commentary to the Immigration (European Economic Area) Regulations 2016: see below

With two exceptions, these Regulations were revoked by reg.2 of the Accession (Immigration and Worker Registration) (Revocation, Savings and Consequential

926

Provisions) Regulations 2011 (SI 2011/544) with effect from May 1, 2011. For the text of the Regulations prior to revocation, see pp.792–798 of Vol.II of the 2011/12 edition.

The exceptions are that:

- reg.8 remains in force (as amended) until April 30, 2012 (see reg.3(1)–(3) of SI 2011/544); and

- the whole of the regulations continue to have effect to the extent necessary for the purposes of reg.7A of the Immigration (European Economic Area) Regulations 2006 which is introduced by reg.5 of and Sch.2 to SI 2011/544.

Registration card and registration certificate

8.—(1) An application for a registration certificate authorising an acces-   5.19
sion State worker requiring registration to work for an employer may only be made by an applicant who is working for that employer at the date of the application.

(2) The application shall be in writing and shall be made to the Secretary of State.

(3) The application shall state—

(a) the name, address, and date of birth of the applicant;

(b) the name and address of the head or main office of the employer;

(c) the date on which the applicant began working for that employer;

(d) where the applicant has been issued with a registration card, the reference number of that card.

(4) Unless the applicant has been issued with a registration card under paragraph (5), the application shall be accompanied by—

(a) a registration fee of [¹[²£90]];

(b) two passport size photographs of the applicant;

(c) the applicant's national identity card or passport issued by the applicant's State;

(d) a letter from the employer concerned confirming that the applicant began working for the employer on the date specified in the application.

(5) In the case of an application by an applicant who has not been issued with a registration card under this paragraph, the Secretary of State shall, where he is satisfied that the application is made in accordance with this regulation and that the applicant—

[³ (a) was an accession State worker requiring registration at the date on which the applicant began working for that employer; and]

(b) began working for the employer on the date specified in the application,
send the applicant a registration card and a registration certificate authorising the worker to work for the employer specified in the application, and shall return the applicant's national identity card or passport.

(6) In the case of any other application, the Secretary of State shall, if he is satisfied as mentioned in paragraph (5), send the applicant a registration certificate authorising the worker to work for the employer specified in the application.

(7) A registration card issued under paragraph (5) shall contain—

(a) the name, nationality and date of birth of the applicant;

(b) a photograph of the applicant;

(c) a reference number.

(8) A registration certificate issued under paragraph (5) or (6) shall contain—

    (a) the name of the applicant;

    (b) the reference number of the applicant's registration card;

    (c) the name and address of the head or main office of the employer, as specified in the application;

    (d) the date on which the applicant began working for the employer, as specified in the application; and

    (e) the date on which the certificate is issued.

(9) Where the Secretary of State receives an application made in accordance with this regulation and he is not satisfied as mentioned in paragraph (5), he shall—

    (a) send the applicant a notice of refusal; and

    (b) return any documents and fee that accompanied the application to the applicant.

(10) Where the Secretary of State sends a registration certificate or notice of refusal to an applicant under this regulation he shall, at the same time, send a copy of the certificate or notice to the employer concerned at the address specified in the application for that employer.

(11) Certificates and notices, and copies of these documents, sent under this regulation shall be sent by post.

AMENDMENTS

1. Accession (Immigration and Worker Registration) (Amendment) Regulations 2005 (SI 2005/2400) reg.2 (October 1, 2005).

2. Accession (Immigration and Worker Registration) (Amendment) Regulations 2007 (SI 2007/928) regs 2 and 3 (April 2, 2007).

3. Accession (Immigration and Worker Registration) (Revocation, Savings and Consequential Provisions) Regulations 2011 (SI 2011/1544) reg.3 (May 1, 2011).

The Displaced Persons (Temporary Protection) Regulations 2005

(SI 2005/1379)

Made by the Secretary of State under s.2(2) of the European Communities Act 1972

[In force June 15, 2005]

GENERAL NOTE

The United Kingdom's withdrawal from the European Union

The United Kingdom left the European Union on January 31, 2020 at 11.00 pm. However, these Regulations continue to apply in an unamended form—including references to EU law and the EEA—during the "implementation period". At the time of going to press, it is anticipated that the implementation period will end on December 31, 2020 at 11.00 pm. See further under the heading, *The United Kingdom's withdrawal from the European Union*, in the General Note to the Immigration (European Economic Area) Regulations 2016 below.

The law during the implementation period

5.20   These Regulations form part of the implementation of Council Directive 2001/55 on minimum standards for giving temporary protection in the event of a mass influx of displaced persons. Essentially, those granted temporary protection as displaced persons are treated for benefit purposes as if they had been granted exceptional leave to remain. They are therefore not "persons subject to immigration control" within s.115 of the Immigration and Asylum Act 1999. In addition, they do not have to satisfy the right to reside test for universal credit, income support, income-based JSA, income-related ESA, and SPC (see reg.9(4)(e)(iii) of the Universal Credit Regulations, reg.21AA(4)(h)(iii) of the Income Support Regulations, reg.85A(4)(h) (iii) of the Jobseeker's Allowance Regulations, reg.70(4)(h)(iii) of the Employment and Support Allowance Regulations, reg.2(4)(h)(iii) of the State Pension Credit Regulations).

Interpretation

2.—(1) In these Regulations—   5.21

(a)–(g) *[Omitted]*

(h) "temporary protection" means limited leave to enter or remain granted pursuant to Part 11A of the Immigration Rules; and

(i) "Temporary Protection Directive" means Council Directive 2001/55/ EC of 20 July 2001 on minimum standards for giving temporary protection in the event of a mass influx of displaced persons and on measures promoting a balance of efforts between member States in receiving such persons and bearing the consequences thereof.

Means of subsistence

3.—(1) Any person granted temporary protection as a result of a deci-   5.22
sion of the Council of the European Union made pursuant to Article 5 of the Temporary Protection Directive shall be deemed for the purposes of the provision of means of subsistence to have been granted leave to enter or remain in the United Kingdom exceptionally, outside the Immigration Rules.

(2) Subject to paragraph (3), paragraph (1) shall cease to apply on the date when the period of mass influx of displaced persons to which the grant of temporary protection relates ends in accordance with Chapter II of the Temporary Protection Directive.

(3) Paragraph (1) shall continue to apply for a period not exceeding 28 days from the date referred to in paragraph (2) for as long as the conditions in paragraph (4) are satisfied and the person is in the United Kingdom.

(4) Those conditions are—

(a) the person's grant of temporary protection has expired; and

(b) the person is taking all reasonable steps to leave the United Kingdom or place himself in a position in which he is able to leave the United Kingdom, which may include co-operating with a voluntary return programme.

4.—"Means of subsistence" in regulation 3 means any means of subsist-   5.23
ence governed by—

(a) Part VII of the Social Security Contributions and Benefits Act 1992;

(b) Part VII of the Social Security Contributions and Benefits (Northern Ireland) Act 1992;

(c) sections 1 and 3 of Part I of the Jobseekers Act 1995;

(d) articles 3 and 5 of Part II of the Jobseekers (Northern Ireland) Order 1995;

(e) the State Pension Credit Act 2002; or

(f) the State Pension Credit Act (Northern Ireland) 2002.

The Immigration (European Economic Area) Regulations 2006

(SI 2006/1003)

REGULATIONS REPRODUCED

PART 1
INTERPRETATION ETC

5.24   7A.   Application of the Accession Regulations
       7B.   Application of the EU2 Regulations

GENERAL NOTE

These Regulations were revoked by reg.45 of, and Pt.1 of Sch.1 to, the Immigration (European Economic Area) Regulations 2016 (SI 2016/1052). That revocation is subject to the savings and modifications in Sch.1 Pt.2 para.2, which provides that—subject to the modifications noted below—regs 7A and 7B continue to have effect in relation to any EEA national to whom they applied immediately before February 1, 2017.

[¹ Application of the Accession Regulations

5.25   **7A.**—(1) This regulation applies to an EEA national who was an accession State worker requiring registration on 30th April 2011 ("an accession worker").

(2) In this regulation—

"accession State worker requiring registration" has the same meaning as in regulation 1(2)(d) of the Accession Regulations;

"legally working" has the same meaning as in regulation 2(7) of the Accession Regulations.

(3) In regulation 5(7)(c), where the worker is an accession worker, periods of involuntary unemployment duly recorded by the relevant employment office shall be treated only as periods of activity as a worker—

(a) during any period in which regulation 5(4) of the Accession Regulations applied to that person; or

(b) when the unemployment began on or after 1st May 2011.

(4) Regulation 6(2) applies to an accession worker where he—

(a) was a person to whom regulation 5(4) of the Accession Regulations applied on 30th April 2011; or

(b) became unable to work, became unemployed or ceased to work, as the case maybe, on or after 1st May 2011.

(5) For the purposes of regulation 15, an accession worker shall be treated as having resided in accordance with these Regulations during any period before 1st May 2011 in which the accession worker—

(a) was legally working in the United Kingdom; or

(b) was a person to whom regulation 5(4) of the Accession Regulations applied.

(6) Subject to paragraph (7), a registration certificate issued to an accession worker under regulation 8 of the Accession Regulations shall, from 1st May 2011, be treated as if it was a registration certificate issued under these Regulations where the accession worker was legally working in the United Kingdom for the employer specified in that certificate on—

(a) 30th April 2011; or

(b) the date on which the certificate is issued where it is issued after 30th April 2011.

(7) Paragraph (6) does not apply—

(a) if the Secretary of State issues a registration certificate in accordance with regulation 16 to an accession worker on or after 1st May 2011; and

(b) from the date of registration stated on that certificate.]

AMENDMENT

1. Accession (Immigration and Worker Registration) (Revocation, Savings and Consequential Provisions) Regulations 2011 (SI 2011/544) reg.5 and Sch.2 para.4 (May 1, 2011).

MODIFICATIONS

Regulation 7A is modified by reg.45 of, and Sch.1 Pt.2 para.2(a) to, the **5.26** Immigration (European Economic Area) Regulations 2016 (SI 2016/1052) ("the 2016 Regulations"). As modified, the regulation is to be read as though:

• the references in para.(3) to treating periods of involuntary unemployment duly recorded by the relevant employment office as periods of work for the purposes of reg.5(7)(c) of the 2006 Regulations were to treating such periods of involuntary unemployment as periods of work for the purposes of reg.6(2) of the 2016 Regulations; and

• the references to reg.6(2) (persons who continue to be treated as a worker) in para.(4), and reg.15 (right of permanent residence) in para.(5), were references to those provisions in the 2016 Regulations.

DEFINITIONS

"EEA national"—see reg.2(1).
"registration certificate"—*ibid.*

[¹ Application of the EU2 Regulations

7B.—(1) This regulation applies to an EEA national who was an acces-   **5.27** sion State national subject to worker authorisation before 1st January 2014.

(2) In this regulation—

"accession State national subject to worker authorisation" has the same meaning as in regulation 2 of the EU2 Regulations;

"the EU2 Regulations" means the Accession (Immigration and Worker Authorisation) Regulations 2006.

(3) Regulation 2(12) of the EU2 Regulations (accession State national subject to worker authorisation: legally working) has effect for the purposes of this regulation as it does for regulation 2(3) and (4) of the EU2 Regulations.

(4) In regulation 5(7)(c), where the worker is an accession State national subject to worker authorisation, periods of involuntary unemployment duly recorded by the relevant employment office must only be treated as periods of activity as a worker when the unemployment began on or after 1st January 2014.

(5) Regulation 6(2) applies to an accession State national subject to worker authorisation where the accession State national subject to worker authorisation became unable to work, became unemployed or ceased to work, as the case may be, on or after 1st January 2014.

(6) For the purposes of regulation 15, an accession State national subject to worker authorisation must be treated as having resided in accordance with these Regulations during any period before 1st January 2014 in which the accession State national subject to worker authorisation was legally working in the United Kingdom.

(7) An accession worker card issued to an accession State national subject to worker authorisation under regulation 11 of the EU2 Regulations before 1st January 2014 must be treated as if it were a registration certificate issued under these Regulations so long as it has not expired.]

AMENDMENT

1. Immigration (European Economic Area) (Amendment) (No.2) Regulations 2013 (SI 2013/3032) reg.4 and Sch.1 para.4 (January 1, 2014).

MODIFICATIONS

Regulation 7B is modified by reg.45 of, and Sch.1 Pt.2 para.2(a) to, the Immigration (European Economic Area) Regulations 2016 (SI 2016/1052) ("the 2016 Regulations"). As modified the regulation is to be read as though:

- the references in para.(4) to treating periods of involuntary unemployment duly recorded by the relevant employment office as periods of work for the purposes of reg.5(7)(c) of the 2006 Regulations were to treating such periods of involuntary unemployment as periods of work for the purposes of reg.6(2) of the 2016 Regulations; and

- the references to reg.6(2) (persons who continue to be treated as a worker) in para.(5), and reg.15 (right of permanent residence) in para.(6), were references to those provisions in the 2016 Regulations.

The Accession of Croatia (Immigration and Worker Authorisation) Regulations 2013

(SI 2013/1460)

IN FORCE JULY 1, 2013

ARRANGEMENT OF REGULATIONS

PART 1

INTERPRETATION ETC.

PART 2

APPLICATION OF THE EEA REGULATIONS AND OTHER INSTRUMENTS

PART 3

ACCESSION STATE WORKER AUTHORISATION AND ASSOCIATED DOCUMENTATION

PART 4

PENALTIES AND OFFENCES

SCHEDULE

CONSEQUENTIAL AMENDMENTS

GENERAL NOTE

The United Kingdom's withdrawal from the European Union

The United Kingdom left the European Union on January 31, 2020 at 11.00 pm. However, these Regulations continue to apply in an unamended form—including references to EU law and the EEA—during the "implementation period". At the time of going to press, it is anticipated that the implementation period will end on December 31, 2020 at 11.00 pm. See further under the heading, *The United Kingdom's withdrawal from the European Union,* in the General Note to the Immigration (European Economic Area) Regulations 2016 below.   **5.28.1**

The law during the implementation period

Croatia acceded to the EU on July 1, 2013 under the Treaty concerning the accession of the Republic of Croatia to the European Union, signed at Brussels on December 9, 2011, to which effect is given in UK domestic law by ss.1 and 3 of the European Union (Croatian Accession and Irish Protocol) Act 2013. Section 4 of that Act empowers the Secretary of State to make provision for "the entitlement of a Croatian national to enter or reside in the United Kingdom as a worker, and . . . any matter ancillary to that entitlement". That power has been exercised to make these Regulations, which provide that during a transitional period of five years, a Croatian national who is an "accession State national subject to worker authorisation" (i.e. any Croatian national who does not fall within the exceptions listed in reg.2(2)–(20)) does not have a right of residence of the UK as a "jobseeker" and only has a right to reside as a worker during a period in which s/he "holds an accession worker authorisation document and is working in accordance with the conditions set out in that document".   **5.29**

The structure of the scheme is similar to that which applied to nationals of Bulgaria and Romania before January 1, 2014 under the Accession (Immigration and Worker Authorisation) Regulations 2006 (see above). It requires that the employment of accession state national subject to worker authorisation should be authorised in advance in order to be lawful. It therefore differs from the scheme of registration that applied to nationals of the A8 states between May 1, 2004 and April 30, 2011.

The final day of the accession period for Croatian nationals was June 30, 2018. However, the regulations (which were last amended in 2015) continue in force.

See further the commentary to the Immigration (European Economic Area) Regulations 2016 below.

The Secretary of State makes the following Regulations in exercise of the powers conferred by section 4 of the European Union (Croatian Accession and Irish Protocol) Act 2013.

In accordance with section 5(1) of that Act, a draft of this instrument was laid before Parliament and approved by resolution of each House of Parliament.

PART 1

INTERPRETATION ETC

Citation, commencement, interpretation and consequential amendments

5.30   **1.**—(1) These Regulations may be cited as the Accession of Croatia (Immigration and Worker Authorisation) Regulations 2013 and come into force on 1st July 2013.

(2) In these Regulations—

"the 1971 Act" means the Immigration Act 1971;

"the 2006 Act" means the Immigration, Asylum and Nationality Act 2006;

"accession period" means the period beginning with 1st July 2013 and ending with 30th June 2018;

"accession State national subject to worker authorisation" has the meaning given in regulation 2;

"accession worker authorisation document" has the meaning given in regulation 8(2);

"authorised category of employment" means—

(a) employment for which the applicant has been issued by a sponsor with a valid certificate of sponsorship under Tier 2 or Tier 5 of the Points-Based System; or

(b) employment as—

    (i) a representative of an overseas business;

    (ii) a postgraduate doctor or dentist; or

    (iii) a domestic worker in a private household;

"certificate of sponsorship" has the meaning given in paragraph 6 of the immigration rules, except that the reference to an application or potential application for entry clearance or leave to enter or remain as a Tier 2 migrant or a Tier 5 migrant is to be read as including a reference to an application or potential application for a worker authorisation registration certificate;

"certificate of sponsorship checking service" has the meaning given in paragraph 6 of the immigration rules, except that the reference to an application or potential application for entry clearance or leave to enter or remain as a Tier 2 migrant or a Tier 5 migrant is to be read as including a reference to an application or potential application for a worker authorisation registration certificate;

"civil partner" does not include a party to a civil partnership of convenience;

"EEA registration certificate" means a certificate issued in accordance with regulation 16 of the EEA Regulations;

"the EEA Regulations" means the Immigration (European Economic Area) Regulations 2006;

"EEA State" excludes the United Kingdom and includes Switzerland;

"employer" means, in relation to a worker, the person who directly pays the wage or salary of that worker, and "employ", "employment" and "employs" shall be construed accordingly;

"the EU2 Regulations" means the Accession (Immigration and Worker Authorisation) Regulations 2006;

"extended family member" has the meaning given in regulation 8 of the EEA Regulations;

"family member" has the meaning given in regulation 7 of the EEA Regulations;

"highly skilled person" has the meaning given in regulation 3;

"immigration rules" means the rules laid down as mentioned in section 3(2) of the 1971 Act applying (except for in the definition of "relevant requirements") [2 —

(a) for the purposes of regulation 3(1)(a) (highly skilled person: Tier 1 (Exceptional Talent) migrant), on 6th November 2014; and

(b) for all other purposes, on 1st July 2013];

"Points-Based System" means the system established under Part 6A of the immigration rules;

"relevant requirements" means, in relation to an authorised category of employment, the requirements which, subject to any necessary modifications, a person in that category of employment was obliged to meet under the immigration rules in force on 9th December 2011 in order to obtain entry clearance or leave to enter or remain in the United Kingdom and which are set out in the relevant statement;

[1 "relevant statement" means the statement entitled "the Statement of relevant requirements" dated [2 March 2015] and published by the Secretary of State;]

"right to reside" shall be interpreted in accordance with the EEA Regulations and "entitled to reside" and "right of residence" shall be construed accordingly;

"sponsor" means the holder of a sponsor licence;

"sponsor licence" has the meaning given in paragraph 6 of the immigration rules;

"spouse" does not include a party to a marriage of convenience;

"student" has the meaning given in regulation 4(1)(d) of the EEA Regulations;

[2 "Student Union Sabbatical Officer" and "national National Union of Students (NUS) position" have the same meaning as in paragraph 245ZW of the immigration rules;]

"Tier 2" and "Tier 5" shall be construed in accordance in paragraph 6 of the immigration rules, except that the reference to the grant of leave is to be read as including a reference to the issuing of a worker authorisation registration certificate;

"unmarried or same sex partner" means a person who is in a durable relationship with another person;

"work" and "working" shall be construed in accordance with the meaning of "worker"; and

"worker authorisation registration certificate" means a certificate issued in accordance with regulation 10 of these Regulations.

(3) The Schedule (consequential amendments) shall have effect.

AMENDMENTS

1. Accession of Croatia (Immigration and Worker Authorisation) (Amendment) Regulations 2014 (SI 530/2014) reg.2(1) and (2) (April 6, 2014).

2. Immigration (European Economic Area) (Amendment) Regulations 2015 (SI 2015/694) reg.5 and Sch.2 para.1 (April 6, 2015).

"Accession State national subject to worker authorisation"

5.31   **2.**—(1) Subject to the following paragraphs of this regulation, other than where these Regulations expressly refer to an accession State national subject to worker authorisation within the meaning of regulation 2 of the EU2 Regulations, in these Regulations "accession State national subject to worker authorisation" means a Croatian national.

(2) A Croatian national is not an accession State national subject to worker authorisation if, on 30th June 2013, he had leave to enter or remain in the United Kingdom under the 1971 Act that was not subject to any condition restricting his employment [[1] (other than a condition restricting his employment as a doctor in training or as a dentist in training or as a professional sportsperson (including as a sports coach))], or he is given such leave after that date.

(3) A Croatian national is not an accession State national subject to worker authorisation if he was legally working in the United Kingdom on 30th June 2013 and had been legally working in the United Kingdom without interruption throughout the preceding period of 12 months ending on that date.

(4) A Croatian national who legally works in the United Kingdom without interruption for a period of 12 months falling partly or wholly after 30th June 2013 ceases to be an accession State national subject to worker authorisation at the end of that period of 12 months.

(5) For the purposes of paragraphs (3) and (4) of this regulation—

(a) a person working in the United Kingdom during a period falling before 1st July 2013 was legally working in the United Kingdom during that period if—

  (i) he had leave to enter or remain in the United Kingdom under the 1971 Act for that period, that leave allowed him to work in the United Kingdom, and he was working in accordance with any condition of that leave restricting his employment;

  (ii) he was exempt from the provisions of the 1971 Act by virtue of section 8(2) or (3) of that Act (persons exempted by order or membership of diplomatic mission); or

  (iii) he was entitled to reside in the United Kingdom for that period under the EEA Regulations without the requirement for such leave;

    (b) a person working in the United Kingdom on or after 1st July 2013 is legally working in the United Kingdom during any period in which he—

        (i) falls within any of paragraphs (6) to (16) or (18); or

        (ii) holds an accession worker authorisation document and is working in accordance with the conditions set out in that document; and

    (c) a person shall be treated as having worked in the United Kingdom without interruption for a period of 12 months if—

        (i) he was legally working in the United Kingdom at the beginning and end of that period; and

        (ii) during that period of 12 months, if his work in the United Kingdom was interrupted, any intervening periods of interruption did not exceed 30 days in total.

(6) Other than during any period in which he is also an accession State national subject to worker authorisation within the meaning of regulation 2 of the EU2 Regulations, a Croatian national is not an accession State national subject to worker authorisation during any period in which he is also a national of—

    (a) the United Kingdom; or

    (b) an EEA State, other than Croatia.

(7) A Croatian national is not an accession State national subject to worker authorisation during any period in which he is also an accession State national subject to worker authorisation within the meaning of regulation 2 of the EU2 Regulations and is working in accordance with those Regulations.

(8) A Croatian national is not an accession State national subject to worker authorisation during any period in which he is the spouse, civil partner, unmarried or same sex partner, or child under 18 of a person who has leave to enter or remain in the United Kingdom under the 1971 Act and that leave allows him to work in the United Kingdom.

(9) A Croatian national is not an accession State national subject to worker authorisation during any period in which he is the spouse, civil partner, unmarried or same sex partner of—

    (a) a national of the United Kingdom; or

    (b) a person that is settled in the United Kingdom in accordance with the meaning given in section 33(2A) (interpretation – meaning of "settled") of the 1971 Act.

(10) A Croatian national is not an accession State national subject to worker authorisation during any period in which he is a member of a mission or other person mentioned in section 8(3) (member of a diplomatic mission, the family member of such a person, or a person otherwise entitled to diplomatic immunity) of the 1971 Act, other than a person who, under section 8(3A) (conditions of membership of a mission) of that Act, does not count as a member of a mission for the purposes of section 8(3).

(11) A Croatian national is not an accession State national subject to worker authorisation during any period in which he is a person who is exempt from all or any of the provisions of the 1971 Act by virtue of an order made under section 8(2) (exemption for persons specified by order) of that Act.

(12) A Croatian national is not an accession State national subject to worker authorisation during any period in which he has a permanent right of residence under regulation 15 of the EEA Regulations.

(13) Subject to paragraph (14), a Croatian national is not an accession State national subject to worker authorisation during any period in which he is a family member (X) of an EEA national (Y) who has a right to reside in the United Kingdom.

(14) Where Y is an accession State national subject to worker authorisation under these Regulations or an accession State national subject to worker authorisation within the meaning of regulation 2 of the EU2 Regulations, paragraph (13) only applies where X is the—

    (a) spouse or civil partner of Y;

    (b) unmarried or same sex partner of Y; or

    (c) a direct descendant of Y, Y's spouse or Y's civil partner who is—

        (i) under 21; or

        (ii) dependant of Y, Y's spouse or Y's civil partner.

(15) A Croatian national is not an accession State national subject to worker authorisation during any period in which he is a highly skilled person and holds an EEA registration certificate issued in accordance with regulation 7 that includes a statement that he has unconditional access to the United Kingdom labour market.

(16) A Croatian national is not an accession State national subject to worker authorisation during any period in which he is in the United Kingdom as a student and either—

    (a) holds an EEA registration certificate that includes a statement that he is a student who may work in the United Kingdom whilst a student in accordance with the condition set out in paragraph (17) and complies with that condition; or

    (b) has leave to enter or remain under the 1971 Act as a student and is working in accordance with any conditions attached to that leav

(17) The condition referred to in paragraph (16)(a) is that the student shall not work for more than 20 hours a week unless—

    (a) he is following a course of vocational training and is working as part of that training; [² . . .]

    (b) he is working during his vacation [; or

    (c) he works for no more than 2 years as a Student Union Sabbatical Officer, provided the appointment to the post is by election and the post is—

        (i) either at the institution at which the Croatian national is enrolled as a student; or

        (ii) a national National Union of Students (NUS) position].

(18) A Croatian national who ceases to be a student at the end of his course of study is not an accession State national subject to worker authorisation during the period of four months beginning with the date on which his course ends provided he holds an EEA registration certificate that was issued to him before the end of the course that includes a statement that he may work during that period.

(19) A Croatian national is not an accession State national subject to worker authorisation during any period in which he is a posted worker.

(20) In paragraph (19), "posted worker" means a worker who is posted to the United Kingdom, within the meaning of Article 1(3) of the Council Directive 96/71/EC of the European Parliament and of the Council of 16 December 1996 concerning the posting of workers in the framework of the provision of services, by an undertaking established in an EEA State.

AMENDMENTS

1. Accession of Croatia (Immigration and Worker Authorisation) (Amendment) Regulations 2014 (SI 530/2014) reg.2(1) and (3) (April 6, 2014).

2. Immigration (European Economic Area) (Amendment) Regulations 2015 (SI 2015/694) reg.5 and Sch.2 para.2 (April 6, 2015).

"Highly skilled person"

3.—(1) In these Regulations "highly skilled person" means a person who—   **5.32**

(a) meets the requirements specified by the Secretary of State for the purpose of paragraph 245BB(c) (requirements for entry clearance as a Tier 1 (Exceptional Talent) migrant) of the immigration rules; or

(b) has been awarded one of the following qualifications and applies for an EEA registration certificate within 12 months of being awarded the qualification—

(i) a recognised bachelor, masters or doctoral degree;

(ii) a postgraduate certificate in education or professional graduate diploma of education; or

(iii) a higher national diploma awarded by a Scottish higher education institution.

(2) For the purposes of paragraph (1)(b), the qualification must have been awarded by a higher education institution which, on the date of the award, is a UK recognised body or an institution that is not a UK recognised body but which provides full courses that lead to the award of a degree by a UK recognised body.

(3) For the purposes of paragraph (1)(b)(iii), to qualify as a higher national diploma from a Scottish institution, a qualification must be at level 8 on the Scottish credit and qualifications framework.

(4) In this regulation, a "UK recognised body" means an institution that has been granted degree awarding powers by a Royal Charter, an Act of Parliament or the Privy Council.

PART 2

APPLICATION OF THE EEA REGULATIONS AND OTHER INSTRUMENTS

Derogation from provisions of European Union law relating to workers

4.—Pursuant to Annex V of the treaty concerning the accession of the Republic of Croatia to the European Union, signed at Brussels on 9 December 2011, Regulations 5 and 7 to 10 derogate during the accession period from Article 45 of the Treaty on the Functioning of the European Union, Articles 1 to 6 of Regulation (EEC) No. 1612/68 of the Council of 15 October 1968 on freedom of movement for workers within the Community and Directive 2004/38/EC of the European Parliament and of the Council of 29 April 2004 on the right of citizens of the Union and their family members to move and reside freely within the territory of the member States, amending Regulation (EEC) No. 1612/68, and repealing Directives 64/221/EEC, 68/360/EEC, 72/194/EEC, 73/148/EEC, 75/34/EEC, 75/35/EEC, 90/364/EEC, 90/365/EEC and 93/96/EEC.   **5.33**

Right of residence of an accession State national subject to worker authorisation

5.34

[¹ 5.—During the accession period, an accession State national subject to worker authorisation who is seeking employment in the United Kingdom shall not be treated as a jobseeker and shall be treated as a worker only in so far as it gives him a right to reside and only during a period in which he holds an accession worker authorisation document and is working in accordance with the conditions set out in that document.]

AMENDMENT

1. Accession of Croatia (Immigration and Worker Authorisation) (Amendment) Regulations 2014 (SI 530/2014) reg.2(1) and (4) (April 6, 2014).

Transitional provisions to take account of the application of the EEA Regulations to Croatian nationals and their family members on 1st July 2013

5.35

6.—(1) Where, before 1st July 2013, any direction has been given for the removal of a Croatian national or the family member of such a national under paragraphs 8 to 10A of Schedule 2 (removal of persons refused leave to enter and illegal entrants) to the 1971 Act, section 10 (removal of certain persons unlawfully in the United Kingdom) of the 1999 Act or section 47 (removal: persons with statutorily extended leave) of the 2006 Act, that direction shall cease to have effect on that date.

(2) Where before 1st July 2013 the Secretary of State has made a deportation order against a Croatian national or the family member of such a national under section 5(1) (deportation orders) of the 1971 Act—

  (a) that order shall, on and after 1st July 2013, be treated as if it were a decision under regulation 19(3)(b) of the EEA Regulations; and

  (b) any appeal against that order, or against the refusal of the Secretary of State to revoke the deportation order, made before 1st July 2013 under section 63 (deportation orders) of the 1999 Act, or under section 82(2)(j) or (k) (right of appeal: general) of the 2002 Act shall, on or after that date, be treated as if it had been made under regulation 26 of the EEA Regulations.

(3) In this regulation—

  (a) "the 1999 Act" means the Immigration and Asylum Act 1999;

  (b) "the 2002 Act" means the Nationality, Immigration and Asylum Act 2002; and

  (c) any reference to the family member of a Croatian national is, in addition to the definition set out in regulation 1(2), a reference to a person who on 1st July 2013 acquires a right to reside in the United Kingdom under the EEA Regulations as the family member of a Croatian national.

Issuing EEA registration certificates and residence cards

5.36

7.—(1) During the accession period, regulation 6 of the EEA Regulations has effect as if, in paragraph (1), after "EEA national", there were inserted

", except an accession State national subject to worker authorisation within the meaning of regulation 2 of the Croatian Regulations," and after paragraph (1), there were inserted—

"(1A) In these Regulations, a "qualified person" also means a person who is an accession State national subject to worker authorisation within the meaning of regulation 2 of the Croatian Regulations and in the United Kingdom as—

(a) a self-employed person;

(b) a self-sufficient person;

(c) a student; or

(d) a highly skilled person who is seeking employment or is employed in the United Kingdom.

[¹ (1B) In regulation 14(2), regulation 16(3) and (5) and regulation 17(1) and (4) a "qualified person" includes an accession State national subject to worker authorisation within the meaning of regulation 2 of the Croatian Regulations where that accession State national subject to worker authorisation has a right to reside.]

(1C) In these Regulations—

(a) "the Croatian Regulations" means the Accession of Croatia (Immigration and Worker Authorisation) Regulations 2013; and

(b) "highly skilled worker" has the meaning given in regulation 1 of the Croatian Regulations."

(2) Subject to paragraph (6), an EEA registration certificate issued to a Croatian national during the accession period shall include a statement that the holder of the certificate has unconditional access to the United Kingdom labour market, unless that person is not an accession State national subject to worker authorisation solely by virtue of falling within paragraph (16) or (18) of regulation 2.

(3) A Croatian national who holds an EEA registration certificate that does not include a statement that he has unconditional access to the United ingdom labour market may, during the accession period, submit the certificate to the Secretary of State for the inclusion of such a statement.

(4) The Secretary of State must re-issue a EEA certificate submitted to her under paragraph (3) with the inclusion of a statement that the holder has unconditional access to the United Kingdom labour market if she is satisfied that the holder—

(a) is a qualified person within the meaning of paragraph (1A) of regulation 6 of the EEA Regulations as applied by paragraph (1); or

(b) has ceased to be an accession State national subject to worker authorisation other than solely by virtue of falling within paragraph (16) or (18) of regulation 2.

(5) An EEA registration certificate issued to a Croatian national who is a student during the accession period shall include a statement that the holder of the certificate is a student who may work in the United Kingdom whilst a student in accordance with the condition set out in paragraph (17) of regulation 2 and who, on ceasing to be a student, may work during the period referred to in paragraph (18) of regulation 2, unless it includes a statement under paragraph (2) or (4) that the holder has unconditional access to the United Kingdom labour market.

(6) Where under paragraph (5) of regulation 16 of the EEA Regulations an EEA registration certificate is issued to a Croatian national extended family member [¹ , with the exception of an extended family member who is an unmarried partner (including a same sex partner),] of an accession

State national subject to worker authorisation, the certificate must include a statement that the certificate does not confer a permission to work.

[¹ (7) Where under paragraph (1) or (4) of regulation 17 of the EEA Regulations a residence card is issued to a family member or an extended family member of an accession State national subject to worker authorisation—

(a) paragraph (6) of regulation 17 of the EEA Regulations shall not apply;

(b) the duration of that card shall be twelve months from the date of issue; and

(c) that card shall be entitled "Accession Residence Card".]

AMENDMENT

1. Accession of Croatia (Immigration and Worker Authorisation) (Amendment) Regulations 2014 (SI 530/2014) reg.2(1) and (5) (April 6, 2014).

PART 3

ACCESSION STATE WORKER AUTHORISATION AND ASSOCIATED DOCUMENTATION

Requirement for an accession State national subject to worker authorisation to be authorised to work

5.37 **8.**—(1) An accession State national subject to worker authorisation shall only be authorised to work in the United Kingdom during the accession period if he holds an accession worker authorisation document and is working in accordance with the conditions set out in that document.

(2) For the purpose of these Regulations, an accession worker authorisation document means—

(a) a passport or other travel document endorsed before 1st July 2013 to show that the holder has leave to enter or remain in the United Kingdom under the 1971 Act, subject to a condition restricting his employment in the United Kingdom to a particular employer or category of employment; or

(b) a worker authorisation registration certificate endorsed with a condition restricting the holder's employment to a particular employer and authorised category of employment.

(3) In the case of a document mentioned in paragraph (2)(a), the document ceases to be a valid accession worker authorisation document at the point at which—

(a) the period of leave to enter or remain expires; or

(b) the document holder ceases working for the employer, or in the employment, specified in the document for a period of time that exceeds 30 days in total.

(4) In the case of a document mentioned in paragraph (2)(b), the document ceases to be a valid accession worker authorisation document at the point at which—

(a) the document expires;

(b) the document holder ceases working for the employer, or in the authorised category of employment, specified in the document for a period of time that exceeds 30 days in total; or

(c) the document is revoked.

(5) For the purposes of this regulation, and regulations 9 and 11, the ref-

erence to a travel document other than a passport is a reference to a document which relates to a Croatian national and which can serve the same purpose as a passport.

Application for a worker authorisation registration certificate as an accession worker authorisation document

9.—(1) An application for a worker authorisation registration certificate may be made by an accession State national subject to worker authorisation who wishes to work for an employer in the United Kingdom if the employment concerned falls within an authorised category of employment.

(2) The application shall be in writing and shall be made to the Secretary of State.

(3) The application shall state—

(a) the name, address in the United Kingdom or in Croatia, and date of birth, of the applicant;

(b) the name and address of the employer for whom the applicant wishes to work; and

(c) the authorised category of employment covered by the application.

(4) The application shall be accompanied by—

(a) proof of the applicant's identity in the form of—
    (i) a national identity card;
    (ii) a passport; or
    (iii) other travel document as defined by regulation 8(5);

(b) two passport size photographs of the applicant;

(c) where the relevant requirements require the applicant to hold a certificate of sponsorship, the certificate of sponsorship reference number;

(d) where sub-paragraph (c) does not apply, a letter from the employer specified in the application confirming that the applicant has an offer of employment with the employer; and

(e) a fee of £55.

(5) In this regulation "address" means, in relation to an employer which is a body corporate or partnership, the head or main office of that employer.

Issuing and revoking a worker authorisation registration certificate

10.—(1) Subject to paragraph (3), the Secretary of State shall issue a worker authorisation registration certificate pursuant to an application made in accordance with the provisions of regulation 9 if the Secretary of State is satisfied that the applicant is an accession State national subject to worker authorisation who meets the relevant requirements.

(2) A worker authorisation registration certificate shall include—

(a) a condition restricting the employment of the document holder to the employer and the authorised category of employment specified in the application;

(b) a statement that the document holder has a right of residence in the United Kingdom as a worker whilst working in accordance with any conditions specified in the certificate;

(c) where the authorised category of employment specified in the application is one for which a certificate of sponsorship is required, a statement that the holder of the document has a right to engage in supplementary employment; and

5.38

5.39

(d) where the period of authorised employment is less than 12 months, a statement specifying the date on which the worker authorisation registration certificate expires.

(3) The Secretary of State may—

(a) refuse to issue, revoke or refuse to renew a worker authorisation registration certificate if the refusal or revocation is justified on grounds of public policy, public security or public health,

(b) refuse the application where the Secretary of State is not satisfied that regulation 9 or this regulation has been complied with or satisfied, or

(c) revoke a worker authorisation registration certificate where—

   (i) the document holder ceases working for the employer, or in the employment, specified in the document for a period of time that exceeds 30 days in total,

   (ii) deception was used in order to obtain the document, or

   (iii) the document was obtained on the basis of sponsorship by a sponsor whose licence has been withdrawn,

and where the Secretary of State has refused to issue, revoked or refused to renew a worker authorisation registration certificate, she shall issue a notice setting out the reasons.

(4) A worker authorisation registration certificate or notice of refusal or revocation issued under this regulation shall be sent to the applicant by post together with the identity card or passport that accompanied the application.

(5) Subject to paragraph (6), in this regulation, "supplementary employment" means—

(a) employment in a job which appears on the shortage occupation list in Appendix K of the immigration rules; or

(b) employment in the same profession and at the same professional level as the employment for which the applicant has been issued with a certificate of sponsorship.

(6) "Supplementary employment" is subject to the condition that—

   (i) the applicant remains working for the sponsor in the employment that the certificate of sponsorship checking service records that the applicant has been sponsored to do; and

   (ii) the supplementary employment does not exceed 20 hours per week and takes place outside of the hours when the applicant is contracted to work for the sponsor in the employment the applicant is being sponsored to do.

(7) The Secretary of State shall ensure that the relevant statement is available to the public through her website and the library of the Home Office.

PART 4

PENALTIES AND OFFENCES

Unauthorised employment of accession State national - penalty for employer

5.40   **11.**—(1) It is contrary to this regulation to employ an accession State national subject to worker authorisation during the accession period if that person is not the holder of a valid accession worker authorisation document or, where that person holds such a document, the person would be in breach of a condition of that document in undertaking the employment.

(2) The Secretary of State may give an employer who acts contrary to this regulation a notice requiring him to pay a penalty of a specified amount not exceeding £5,000.

(3) The Secretary of State may give a penalty notice without having established whether the employer is excused under paragraph (5).

(4) A penalty notice must—

(a) state why the Secretary of State thinks the employer is liable to the penalty;

(b) state the amount of the penalty;

(c) specify a date, at least 28 days after the date specified in the notice as the date on which it is given, before which the penalty must be paid;

(d) specify how the penalty must be paid;

(e) provide a reference number;

(f) explain how the employer may object to the penalty; and

(g) explain how the Secretary of State may enforce the penalty.

(5) Subject to paragraph (7), an employer is excused from paying a penalty under this regulation if—

(a) before the commencement of the employment, the employee or prospective employee produces to the employer any of the following documents—

   (i) an accession worker authorisation document that authorises the employee or prospective employee to take the employment in question;

   (ii) an EEA registration certificate which includes a statement that the holder has unconditional access to the United Kingdom labour market; or

   (iii) one of the following documents confirming that the document holder is not an accession State national subject to worker authorisation by virtue of regulation 2(6)—

      (aa) a passport;

      (bb) a national identity card; or

      (cc) other travel document as defined by regulation 8(5); and

(b) the employer complies with the requirements set out in paragraph (6) of this regulation.

(6) The requirements are that—

(a) the employer takes all reasonable steps to check the validity of the document;

(b) the employer has satisfied himself that the photograph on the document is of the employee or prospective employee;

(c) the employer has satisfied himself that the date of birth on the document is consistent with the appearance of the employee or prospective employee;

(d) the employer takes all other reasonable steps to check that the employee or prospective employee is the rightful holder of the document; and

(e) the employer securely retains a dated copy of the whole of the document in a format which cannot be subsequently altered for a period of not less than two years after the employment has come to an end.

(7) An employer is not excused from paying a penalty if the employer

knew, at any time during the period of the employment, that the employment was contrary to this regulation.

(8) Nothing in these regulations permits an employer to retain documents produced by an employee or prospective employee for the purposes of paragraph (5) for any period longer than is necessary for the purposes of ensuring compliance with paragraph (6).

(9) The Secretary of State may issue a code of practice specifying factors to be considered by her in determining the amount of a penalty imposed under paragraph (2) of this regulation.

(10) The Secretary of State shall lay a code issued under paragraph (9) before Parliament and publish it.

(11) The Secretary of State may from time to time review the code and may revoke, or revise and re-issue it, following a review; and a reference in this section to the code includes a reference to the code as revised.

Unauthorised employment of accession State national – penalty for employer – objection

5.41   **12.** *[Omitted.]*

Unauthorised employment of accession State national – penalty for employer – appeal

5.42   **13.** *[Omitted.]*

Unauthorised employment of accession State national – penalty for employer – enforcement

5.43   **14.** *[Omitted.]*

Unauthorised employment of accession State national – employer offence

5.44   **15.**—(1) A person commits an offence if he employs another ("the employee") knowing that the employee is an accession State national subject to worker authorisation and that—

(a) the employee is not the holder of a valid accession worker authorisation document; or

(b) the employee is prohibited from undertaking the employment because of a condition in his accession worker authorisation document.

(2) A person guilty of an offence under this section shall be liable on summary conviction—

(a) to imprisonment for a term not exceeding 51 weeks in England and Wales or 6 months in Scotland or Northern Ireland;

(b) to a fine not exceeding level 5 on the standard scale; or

(c) to both.

(3) An offence under this regulation shall be treated as—

(a) a relevant offence for the purpose of sections 28B (search and arrest by warrant) and 28D (entry and search of premises) of the 1971 Act; and

(b) an offence under Part 3 of that Act (criminal proceedings) for the purposes of sections 28E (entry and search of premises following arrest), 28G (searching arrested persons) and 28H (searching persons in police custody).

(4) In relation to an offence committed before the commencement of section 281(5) (alteration of penalties for other summary offences) of the Criminal Justice Act 2003, the reference to 51 weeks in paragraph (2)(a) shall be read as a reference to 6 months.

(5) For the purposes of paragraph (1), a body (whether corporate or not) shall be treated as knowing a fact about an employee if a person who has responsibility within the body for an aspect of the employment knows the fact.

Unauthorised working by accession State national – employee offence and penalty

16.—(1) Subject to paragraph (2), an accession State national subject to worker authorisation who works in the United Kingdom during the accession period shall be guilty of an offence if he does not hold a valid accession worker authorisation document.

5.45

(2) A person guilty of an offence under this regulation shall be liable on summary conviction—

(a) to imprisonment for a term not exceeding more than three months;

(b) to a fine not exceeding level 5 on the standard scale; or

(c) to both.

(3) A constable or immigration officer who has reason to believe that a person has committed an offence under this regulation may give that person a notice offering him the opportunity of discharging any liability to conviction for that offence by payment of a penalty of £1000 in accordance with the notice.

(4) Where a person is given a notice under paragraph (3) in respect of an offence under this regulation—

(a) no proceedings may be instituted for that offence before the expiration of the period of 21 days beginning with the day after the date of the notice; and

(b) he may not be convicted of that offence if, before the expiration of that period, he pays the penalty in accordance with the notice.

(5) A notice under paragraph (3) must give such particulars of the circumstances alleged to constitute the offence as are necessary for giving reasonable information of the offence.

(6) A notice under paragraph (3) must also state—

(a) the period during which, by virtue of paragraph (4), proceedings will not be instituted for the offence;

(b) the amount of the penalty; and

(c) that the penalty is payable to the Secretary of State at the address specified in the notice.

(7) Without prejudice to payment by any other method, payment of a penalty in pursuance of a notice under paragraph (3) may be made by pre-paying and posting a letter by registered post or the recorded delivery service containing the amount of the penalty (in cash or otherwise) to the Secretary of State at the address specified in the notice.

(8) Where a letter is sent in accordance with paragraph (7) payment is to be regarded as having been made at the time at which that letter would be delivered in the ordinary course of registered post or the recorded delivery service.

(9) A constable or immigration officer may withdraw a penalty notice given under paragraph (3) if the constable or immigration officer decides that—

(a) the notice was issued in error;

(b) the notice contains material errors; or

(c) he has reasonable grounds to believe that the employee has committed an offence under regulation 17.

(10) A penalty notice may be withdrawn—

(a) whether or not the period specified in paragraph (4)(a) has expired;

(b) under paragraph (9)(a) and (b), whether or not the penalty has been paid; and

(c) under paragraph (9)(c), only where the penalty has not yet been paid.

(11) Where a penalty notice has been withdrawn under paragraph (9)—

(a) notice of the withdrawal must be given to the recipient; and

(b) any amount paid by way of penalty in pursuance of that notice must be repaid to the person who paid it.

(12) Subject to paragraph (13), proceedings shall not be continued or instituted against an employee for an offence under paragraph (1) in connection with which a withdrawal notice was issued.

(13) Proceedings may be continued or instituted for an offence in connection with which a withdrawal notice was issued if—

(a) where the withdrawal notice was withdrawn pursuant to paragraph (9)(b)—

(i) a further penalty notice in respect of the offence was issued at the same time as the penalty notice was withdrawn; and

(ii) the penalty has not been paid pursuant to that further penalty notice in accordance with paragraph (4)(a); or

(b) the withdrawal notice was withdrawn pursuant to paragraph (9)(c).

Deception—employee offence

5.46   **17.** *[Omitted.]*

Offences under regulations 16 and 17—search, entry and arrest

5.47   **18.** *[Omitted.]*

The Immigration (European Economic Area) Regulations 2016

(SI 2016/1052)

REGULATIONS REPRODUCED

The Secretary of State, being a Minister designated for the purposes of section 2(2) of the European Communities Act 1972 in relation to measures relating to rights of entry into, and residence in, the United Kingdom, in exercise of the powers conferred by that section and those conferred by section 109 of the Nationality, Immigration and Asylum Act 2002, makes the following Regulations.
[In force November 25, 2016 (reg. 44 and Sch. 5) and February 1, 2017]

PART 1

PRELIMINARY

PART 2

EEA RIGHTS

PART 3

RESIDENCE DOCUMENTATION

PART 4

REFUSAL OF ADMISSION AND REMOVAL ETC

PART 5

Procedure in Relation to EEA Decisions

29-34. *Omitted*

PART 6

Appeals under these Regulations

35-42. *Omitted*

PART 7

General

43.   Effect on other legislation
44.   *Revoked*
45.   Revocations, savings, transitory and transitional provisions and consequential modifications
46.   Revocation of regulation 44 and Schedule 5

Schedules

1.   *Omitted*
2.   *Omitted*
3.   Effect on other legislation
4.   Revocations and savings
5.   *Revoked*
6.   Transitional provisions
7.   Consequential modifications

General Note

5.48.1   *The United Kingdom's withdrawal from the European Union*
        The United Kingdom left the European Union on January 31, 2020 at 11.00 pm. Section 1 of the European Union (Withdrawal) Act 2018 ("the Withdrawal Act") repealed the European Communities Act 1972 at that date and time: see the definition of "exit day" in s.20(1) of the Withdrawal Act as supplemented by s.20(2)–(5) and reg.2 of the European Union (Withdrawal) Act 2018 (Exit Day) (Amendment) (No. 3) Regulations 2019 (SI 2019/1423).
        However, s.1A and 1B of the Withdrawal Act (inserted by ss.1 and 2 of the European Union (Withdrawal Agreement) Act 2020 ("the Withdrawal Agreement Act")) which came into force at the same date and time (see the European Union (Withdrawal Agreement) Act 2020 (Commencement No.1) Regulations 2020 (SI 2020/75) provided that, despite the repeal of the 1972 Act:

- it continues to have effect in domestic UK law during the "implementation period" "as it [had] effect in domestic law … immediately before exit day": see s.1A(1), and (2) of the Withdrawal Agreement Act; and

- EU-derived domestic legislation also continues to have effect in domestic UK law during the implementation period "as it [had] effect in domestic law … immediately before exit day": see s.1B(1) and (2) of the Withdrawal Agreement Act.

The "implementation period" is defined by s.1A(6) of the Withdrawal Act as meaning "the transition or implementation period provided for by Part 4 of the withdrawal agreement and beginning with exit day and ending on IP completion day". "IP completion day" is, in turn, defined by s.1A(6) and by s.39(1) of the Withdrawal Agreement Act as "31 December 2020 at 11.00 p.m". By s.39(4), a Minister of the Crown has power to amend that definition so as "to ensure that the day and time specified in the definition are the day and time that the transition or implementation period provided for by Part 4 of the withdrawal agreement is to end". However, the UK government has expressed a firm intention that the implementation period will not in fact be extended beyond December 31, 2020.

"EU-derived domestic legislation" is defined by s.1B(7) as meaning:

"… any enactment so far as—

(a) made under section 2(2) of, or paragraph 1A of Schedule 2 to, the European Communities Act 1972,

(b) passed or made, or operating, for a purpose mentioned in section 2(2)(a) or (b) of that Act,

(c) relating to—

(i) anything which falls within paragraph (a) or (b), or

(ii) any rights, powers, liabilities, obligations, restrictions, remedies or procedures which are recognised and available in domestic law by virtue of section 2(1) of the European Communities Act 1972, or

(d) relating otherwise to the EU or the EEA,

but does not include any enactment contained in the European Communities Act 1972 or any enactment contained in this Act or the European Union (Withdrawal Agreement) Act 2020 or in regulations made under this Act or the Act of 2020."

The definition is therefore amply broad to cover the domestic immigration law of the UK that is relevant to the social security right to reside test.

Moreover, by s.41(4) of, and Sch.5 para.1(1) and (2) to, the Withdrawal Agreement Act:

"Subordinate legislation with commencement by reference to exit day

1 (1) Any provision in subordinate legislation made before exit day under—

(a) any provision of the European Union (Withdrawal) Act 2018 (or any provision made under any such provision), or

(b) any other enactment, which provides, by reference to exit day (however expressed), for all or part of that or any other subordinate legislation to come into force immediately before exit day, on exit day or at any time after exit day is to be read instead as providing for the subordinate legislation or (as the case may be) the part to come into force immediately before IP completion day, on IP completion day or (as the case may be) at the time concerned after IP completion day.

(2)   Sub-paragraph (1) does not apply so far as it is expressly disapplied by the subordinate legislation that provides as mentioned in that sub-paragraph."

Paragraph 1(1) has the effect that a number of Regulations that would affect the right to reside test, and which on their face, came into effect on exit day, did not in fact do so and will not come into effect until December 31, 2020 at 11.00 pm. Those Regulations include:

The Social Security (Amendment) (EU Exit) Regulations 2019	SI 2019/128
The Immigration (European Economic Area Nationals) (EU Exit) Regulations 2019	SI 2019/468
The Immigration (European Economic Area Nationals) (EU Exit) Order 2019 (in part)	SI 2019/686
The European Union (Withdrawal) Act 2018 (Consequential Modifications and Repeals and Revocations) (EU Exit) Regulations 2019 (in part)	SI 2019/628
The Tax Credits and Child Trust Funds (Amendment) (EU Exit) Regulations 2019	SI 2019/713
The Immigration, Nationality and Asylum (EU Exit) Regulations 2019	SI 2019/745
The Immigration (Amendment) (EU Exit) Regulations 2019	SI 2019/1383
The Freedom of Establishment and Free Movement of Services (EU Exit) Regulations 2019	SI 2019/1401
The Social Security, Child Benefit and Child Tax Credit (Amendment) (EU Exit) Regulations 2019	SI 2019/1431

It appears probable that, after the implementation period has expired, the right to reside test will be replaced by a rule that (no doubt subject to exceptions) those who are not British citizens will be entitled to means-tested benefits if they have indefinite leave to remain in the UK or settled status (as to which, see the General Note to reg.9 of the Universal Credit Regulations).

In the meantime, however, the law relating to the right to reside test continues to be as set out in the regulations and commentary below.

The law during the implementation period

5.49   These Regulations ("the 2016 Regulations") implement Directive 2004/38/EC "on the right of citizens of the Union and their family members to move and reside freely within the territory of the Member States" ("the Citizenship Directive"): see Vol.III. They therefore govern whether EEA nationals and their family members have a right to reside for the purposes of universal credit IS, HB, income-based JSA, SPC, child benefit, CTC and income-related ESA.

In the commentary to these Regulations, references to numbered articles (*e.g.*, "art.7") are to the Citizenship Directive unless the contrary is stated.

Introduction and historical background

5.50   Claimants who are "persons from abroad" as defined in reg.21AA of the IS Regulations, reg.85A of the JSA Regulations and reg.70 of the ESA Regulations are not entitled to IS, JSA or ESA. This is because they are treated as a special case with an applicable amount of nil (see para.17 of Sch.7 to the IS Regulations, para.14 of Sch.5 to the JSA Regulations and para.11 of Sch.5 to the ESA Regulations). For child benefit, SPC, and universal credit, the same result is achieved by treating such claimants as "not in Great Britain" (see reg.23(2) of the Child Benefit (General) Regulations 2006, reg.2 of the SPC Regulations and reg.9 of the Universal Credit

Regulations) and, therefore, as failing to satisfy the conditions of entitlement in, respectively, s.146(2) of SSCBA 1992, s.1(2)(a) of SPCA 2002 and s.4(1)(c) of WRA 2012. Similarly, CTC claimants with no right to reside are treated as "not in the United Kingdom" (reg.3(5) of the Tax Credits (Residence) Regulations 2003) and, therefore, as having no entitlement to claim under s.3 TCA 2002.

From the introduction of the IS and HB Schemes in April 1988 until the Immigration and Asylum Act 1999 came into force on April 3, 2000, the exclusion of "persons from abroad" from benefit was the principal mechanism for denying income-related benefits to those claimants who were considered to have insufficiently close links with Great Britain. The approach was extended to community charge benefit when that benefit was introduced on April 1, 1990 and then to CTB, JSA and ESA when they were introduced on April 1, 1993, October 7, 1996 and October 27, 2008 respectively.

Originally, the definition of "person from abroad" was in reg.21(3) of the IS Regulations. It was a wide definition and encompassed those who did not have leave to enter or remain in the UK or whose leave had been granted on a sponsorship undertaking or was conditional upon not having recourse to public funds (see pp.164–167 of the 1999 edition of Mesher & Wood, *Income-related Benefits: the Legislation* for further details).

That definition was widened on August 1, 1994 by the introduction of the "habitual residence test". That test was aimed principally at EEA nationals (although it affects many others) but EC law prohibiting discrimination against the citizens of other Member States meant that, to be valid, it had to apply to British citizens as well. One of the results of the change was therefore that, for the first time, a British citizen could be excluded from income-related benefits as a "person from abroad".

In the early days of the test there were a number of challenges to its validity both on the grounds that it was *ultra vires* s.124(1) of the Contributions and Benefits Act and as being unlawful under EC law. However, these challenges were all unsuccessful (see pp.290–291 of the 1999 edition of Mesher and Wood, *Income-related Benefits: the Legislation*).

Subsequently, in *Couronne v Crawley BC and Secretary of State for Work and Pensions* [2007] EWCA Civ 1086, the Court of Appeal held that the test did not discriminate unlawfully against British Citizens from the Chagos Islands in comparison with British Citizens of Irish ethnic or national origin either under the Race Relations Act 1976 or art.14 and art.8 and or art.1 First Protocol ECHR. In that case, the appellants had been unlawfully prevented by the British government from returning to their homeland but the Court held that it was not irrational for the habitual residence test to be applied to them.

With effect from April 3, 2000, the definition of "person from abroad" was narrowed to such an extent that only the habitual residence test remained. Most claimants who had previously fallen within other heads of the definition were re-categorised as "persons subject to immigration control" and excluded from income-related benefits by s.115 of the Immigration and Asylum Act 1999. **5.51**

On May 1, 2004, 10 additional countries joined the EU and the habitual residence test was supplemented by the introduction (as reg.21(3G) of the IS Regulations, reg.85(4B) of the JSA Regulations and reg.2(2) of the SPC Regulations) of the "right to reside" test. The test was also applied to child benefit and child tax credit by amendments to reg.23 of the Child Benefit Regulations and reg.3 of the Tax Credits (Residence) Regulations 2003.

In addition, the Accession (Immigration and Worker Registration) Regulations 2004 (SI 2004/1219) ("the A8 Regulations") established a registration scheme which imposed greater restrictions on the rights of "A8 Nationals" (see below) to reside in the UK as workers or jobseekers than applied to the nationals of other member States.

From that point on, EEA nationals who did not have a legal right to reside—very broadly, those who had never been, or (in certain circumstances) were no longer, economically active and were not the family members of people who were, or had been, economically active—ceased to be regarded as habitually resident unless they had the benefit of transitional protection, and stood no chance of becoming habitually resident in the future, irrespective of their intentions and the length of time for which they had actually lived in the UK.

On April 30, 2006, the Citizenship Directive came into force and repealed the previous Directives upon which EC immigration law had been based. The Citizenship Directive was implemented in UK domestic law by the Immigration (European Economic Area) Regulations 2006 ("the 2006 Regulations").

On the same day, the right to reside test was revised to reflect the new EU Law and the definition of "person from abroad" was moved from reg.21 to reg.21AA of the IS Regulations, and from reg.85 to reg.85A of the JSA Regulations.

5.52 On January 1, 2007, Bulgaria and Romania joined the EU and the Accession (Immigration and Worker Authorisation) Regulations 2006 (SI 2006/3317) ("the A2 Regulations") (see below) established an authorisation scheme which restricted the rights of "A2 nationals" (see below) to reside in the UK as workers or jobseekers. With effect from the same day, the right to reside test was further amended.

On May 1, 2009 (although, at the time, the law purported to end the A8 Scheme on May 1, 2011: see the discussion of *Secretary of State for Work and Pensions v Gubeladze* [2019] UKSC 31 below), the A8 States became full members of the EU and their nationals ceased to be subject to additional restrictions on their right to reside in the UK (i.e., over and above those that apply to the nationals of other EU states) from that date. Whether previous periods of residence were lawful under the former A8 Scheme remains relevant to whether an A8 national has acquired a permanent right of residence (see reg.7A of the 2006 Regulations).

On July 1, 2013, Croatia joined the EU and the Accession of Croatia (Immigration and Worker Authorisation) Regulations 2013 (SI 2013 No. 1460) (see below) established a further authorisation scheme which restricted the rights of Croatian nationals to reside in the UK as workers or jobseekers (see below), along similar lines to the A2 scheme.

On January 1, 2014, Bulgaria and Romania became full members of the EU and their nationals ceased to be subject to additional restrictions on their right to reside in the UK (i.e., over and above those that apply to the nationals of other EU states) from that date. Whether previous periods of residence were lawful under the former A8 Scheme remains relevant to whether an A8 national has acquired a permanent right of residence (see reg.7B of the 2006 Regulations).

Also on January 1, 2014, the habitual residence test for jobseeker's allowance was amended to include an additional requirement that the claimant should have been living in the Common Travel Area for the past three months.

On February 1, 2017, the 2006 Regulations (other than regs 7A and 7B) were consolidated and revoked by the 2016 Regulations. There is a table of equivalences in Sch.7 to the Regulations.

On July 1, 2018, Croatian nationals became full members of the EU and their nationals ceased to be subject to additional restrictions on their right to reside in the UK (i.e., over and above those that apply to the nationals of other EU states) from that date. Whether previous periods of residence were lawful between July 1, 2013 and June 30, 2018 remains relevant to whether a Croatian national has acquired a permanent right of residence.

On January 31, 2020 at 11.00 pm, the United Kingdom left the EU. However, the EU and domestic law relating to the right to reside test was preserved during the implementation period: see under the heading, *The United Kingdom's withdrawal from the European Union*, above.

Overview

5.53 Given that background, the framework of the law is now as follows:

(1) under s.115(1) and (3) of the Immigration and Asylum Act 1999, a "person subject to immigration control" is not entitled to a wide range of benefits including income support, income-based jobseeker's allowance, income-

related ESA, state pension credit, universal credit and social fund payments. However, EEA nationals and their family members cannot fall within the definition of "person subject to immigration control" in s.115(9), EEA nationals because they are expressly excluded and family members because they do not require leave to enter or remain in the UK: see s.7 of the Immigration Act 1988;

(2) this general rule is subject to the limited exceptions that are set out in the Social Security (Immigration and Asylum) Consequential Amendments Regulations 2000 (SI 2000/636—see below);

(3) even if a claimant is not a "person subject to immigration control", he may nevertheless be a "person from abroad" if he is not habitually resident in the Common Travel Area ("CTA") (i.e. the UK, Channel Islands, Isle of Man and Republic of Ireland). This includes British and Irish nationals;

(4) claimants who are nationals of EEA countries (other than the UK and the Republic of Ireland), or of Switzerland, only satisfy the habitual residence test if they have a "right to reside" in the CTA—see reg.21AA(2).

For a more detailed discussion of points (1) and (2) above, see the notes to SI 2000/636.

Subject to what is said about the burden of proof in *Kerr v Department for Social Development* [2004] UKHL 23 (*R 1/04 (SF)*), it is for the Secretary of State to prove that a claimant is not habitually resident, rather than for the claimant to show that he is, although it is preferable to resolve any doubts by enquiring further into the facts rather than relying on the burden of proof—see *R(IS) 6/96*.

EEA nationals

Although, conceptually, the "right to reside" test applies to all claimants, the legal framework explained above means that, as a matter of practice, it will only affect nationals of the EEA states and their family members (including, in exceptional cases, the parents of British children: see reg.16(5)). This is because non-EEA nationals will either have a right of abode in the UK, in which case, they will obviously also have a right to reside here; or they will have some type of leave to remain here, in which case, they will have a right to reside here for the duration of that leave—and any extension of it (although they will not necessarily be entitled to income-related benefits); or they will be illegal entrants or overstayers, in which case they are already excluded from benefit as persons subject to immigration control so that the additional requirement that they have should have the right to reside before being entitled to benefit has no practical effect.

5.54

By contrast, under s.7 of the Immigration Act 1988, EEA nationals do not usually require leave to enter or remain in the UK and, in principle, "must be admitted to the United Kingdom if [they produce], on arrival, a valid national identity card or passport issued by an EEA state" (see reg.11). It is therefore possible for EEA nationals to be admitted to the UK who have no legal right to reside here: whether or not they have such a right depends on EU Law.

The EEA now consists of the 27 EU countries (namely Austria, Belgium, Bulgaria, Croatia, Cyprus, the Czech Republic, Denmark, Estonia, Finland, France, Germany, Greece, Hungary, Ireland, Italy, Latvia, Lithuania, Luxembourg, Malta, the Netherlands, Poland, Portugal, Romania, Slovakia, Slovenia, Spain and Sweden) together with Norway, Liechtenstein and Iceland.

During the implementation period, nationals of Norway, Liechtenstein and Iceland continue to have the same rights of residence in the UK as EU nationals: see the definition of "EEA national" in reg.2 below.

The rights of A8 nationals (i.e., nationals of the Czech Republic, Estonia, Hungary, Latvia, Lithuania, Poland, Slovakia and Slovenia, which joined the EU on May 1, 2004), of A2 nationals (i.e., nationals of Bulgaria and Romania), and of Croatian nationals, to reside in the UK as workers or work seekers were once more restricted than for nationals of most other Member States. The A8 restrictions applied from May 1, 2004 until April 30, 2009—but see the discussion of *Secretary of State for Work and Pensions v Gubeladze* [2019] UKSC 31—and the A2 restrictions applied from January 1, 2007 to December 31, 2013. The Croatian restrictions applied from July 1, 2013 to June 30, 2018. The former restrictions remain relevant to the question whether the residence of an A8, A2 or Croatian national during those periods counts towards the acquisition of a permanent right of residence.

The rights of Croatian, A8 and A2 nationals are considered in more detail below.

British nationals

5.55 British nationals have a right of abode in the UK (see s.2(1)(a) of the Immigration Act 1971 and *R(PC)2/07*) and therefore automatically have a right to reside in the CTA.

In some circumstances—for example, the treatment of family members—EU Law is more favourable to the nationals of other Member States than domestic UK law is to British nationals. In such circumstances, British nationals cannot rely upon their status as EU citizens to obtain the more favourable treatment unless the unfavourable treatment is the consequence of having exercised an EU right, such as the rights to freedom of movement or establishment.

For similar reasons, British nationals who have not exercised any EU right are subject to the habitual residence test as it applies to non-EEA nationals (see below) because they cannot take advantage of the exemptions in para.(4)(a)–(e). For the position of British nationals who are also nationals of another EEA State see the discussion of the *McCarthy* case below.

For the rights of non-British nationals who are parents of British children, see reg.16(5).

Irish and Island nationals

5.56 Ireland, the Channel Islands and the Isle of Man are part of the CTA and their nationals automatically have a right to reside in the UK. However, the Channel Islands and the Isle of Man are not part of the EU or the EEA (see *SSWP v JG (RP)* [2013] UKUT 300 (AAC) at para.34) and their nationals are subject to the habitual residence test as it applies to non-EEA nationals (see the commentary to reg.21AA of the IS Regulations). The exemptions in para.(4)(a)–(e) cannot apply to them. There are reciprocal agreements between the UK and the Isle of Man (SI 2016/187) and Jersey and Guernsey (SI 1994/2802).

As Ireland is a member of the EU, Irish nationals in the UK may well be exercising EU rights and therefore have a right to reside under EU law in addition to their rights under domestic UK law. Therefore, even though Irish nationals have a right to reside, it may be to their advantage to establish that they fall within one of the EU categories in para.(4)(a)–(e) in order to obtain exemption from the habitual residence test. Those Irish nationals who are unable to establish such an exemption will be subject to the habitual residence test as it applies to non-EEA nationals.

The special treatment accorded by the UK to Irish nationals, but not accorded to citizens of other member States, which might otherwise be thought to be contrary to the various prohibitions in EU law against discrimination on the ground of nationality, is lawful because the provision for Irish citizens is protected by art.2 of the Protocol on the Common Travel Area (Protocol 20 annexed to the TFEU and TEU). That article states that the United Kingdom and Ireland "may continue to make arrangements between themselves relating to the movement of persons between their territories" and provides that nothing in articles 26 and 77 of the Treaty on the Functioning of the European Union or in any other provision of that Treaty or of the Treaty on European Union or in any other measure adopted under them shall affect any such arrangements: see *Patmalniece v SSWP* [2011] UKSC 11 at paras 54–61.

Complications sometimes arise because, before January 1, 2005, the domestic law of the Republic of Ireland entitled anyone born on the island of Ireland (i.e. including Northern Ireland) to Irish citizenship, irrespective of the nationality of their parents or the existence of any other connection with the Republic. In particular, non-EEA nationals have sometimes arranged for a child to be born in Northern Ireland (or in the Republic) so as to obtain a right to reside in the UK by virtue of that child's Irish citizenship. It is clear from the decision of the ECJ in *Zhu and Chen v Home Secretary* (Case C–200/02) that this stratagem will sometimes work as far as immigration law is concerned. But its success depends upon the parents and child being self-sufficient and having health insurance (see *W(China) v Home Secretary* [2006] EWCA Civ 1494) and it will therefore be of limited efficacy in establishing a right to reside for the purpose of entitlement to income-related benefits.

Gibraltar

The status of Gibraltar was explained by Upper Tribunal Judge White in *SSWP v JG (RP)* (above) at paras 29-32.   5.57

> "29.   Gibraltar was ceded in perpetuity by Spain to Great Britain under the Treaty of Utrecht 1713. It is a British Crown Colony. It is not part of the United Kingdom. This separate status is recognized under national law, international law and European Union law.
> 30.   In Case C-145/04 *Spain v United Kingdom* [2006] ECR I-7917, the Court of Justice described the status of Gibraltar as follows:
>
> > '19.   In Community law, Gibraltar is a European territory for whose external relations a Member State is responsible within the meaning of Article 299(4) EC and to which the provisions of the EC Treaty apply. The Act concerning the conditions of accession of the Kingdom of Denmark, Ireland and the United Kingdom of Great Britain and Northern Ireland and the adjustments to the Treaties (OJ 1972 L 73, p. 14) provides, however, that certain parts of the Treaty are not to apply to Gibraltar.'
>
> 31.   European Union law on citizenship of the Union and the free movement of persons applies to Gibraltar.
> 32.   The Family Allowances, National Insurance and Industrial Injuries (Gibraltar) Order 1974 (SI 1974 No 555) ("the Gibraltar Order") provides:
>
> > '1.   Any reference in the following paragraphs to a territory shall be construed as a reference to the territory of the United Kingdom or Gibraltar or both as the case may be and any reference to a child shall be construed as a reference to any person for whom family allowances are payable under the legislation in question.
> >
> > 2(a).   Any person shall have the same rights and liabilities in relation to social security other than family allowances, as he would have had if the United Kingdom and Gibraltar had been separate Member States of the European Economic Community.
> >
> > For the purpose of giving effect to paragraph (a) above the same procedures shall so far as is practicable be adopted in relation to the person and benefit concerned as would have been applicable had the United Kingdom and Gibraltar been such separate Member States.'"

Nationals of Norway, Iceland and Liechtenstein:

Nationals of the three EEA states that are not EU members enjoy the same   5.58
rights as EU citizens by virtue of the EEA Treaty (also known as the "Oporto Agreement"): see *Ullusow v Secretary of State for Work and Pensions* [2007] EWCA Civ 657 (July 5, 2007, CA, Sir Andrew Morritt C., Lloyd and Moses L.JJ.) overturning *CPC/2920/2005* in which a tribunal of Commissioners held that, on a true interpretation of the Oporto Agreement, Directive 90/364 only conferred a right

to reside on those (non-EU) EEA nationals who are seeking to exercise a right of establishment (i.e. to set up a business in the UK).

The 2016 Regulations do not distinguish between EEA nationals who are EU citizens and those who are not. The exemptions in reg.21AA(4) of the IS Regulations, reg.85A(4) of the JSA Regulations, and reg.2(4) of the SPC Regulations apply to nationals of Iceland, Liechtenstein and Norway, and to their family members (see reg.7), as if they were EU nationals (see reg.10(e) of SI 1026/2006).

Swiss nationals

5.59   Switzerland is not a member of either the EU or the EEA. However, since June 1, 2002, Swiss nationals have had rights of residence in Britain that are similar to those enjoyed by EEA nationals. Those rights are conferred by the Luxembourg Agreement (*Agreement between the European Community and its Member States, of the one part, and the Swiss Confederation, of the other, on the Free Movement of Persons*, Luxembourg, June 21, 1999, Cm.5639).

Before April 30, 2006, that agreement was implemented as a matter of domestic law by the Immigration (Swiss Free Movement of Persons) (No.3) Regulations 2002 (SI 2002/1241). From that date, SI 2002/1241 was revoked and reg.2(1) of the 2006 Regulations deemed Switzerland to be an EEA state, even though it is not actually one. That approach is continued in the 2016 Regulations. In addition, the exemptions in reg.21AA(4) of the IS Regulations, reg.85A(4) of the JSA Regulations, and reg.2(4) of the SPC Regulations apply to Swiss nationals, and to their family members (see reg.7), as if they were EU nationals (see reg.10(e) of SI 2006/1026).

The effect is that Swiss nationals have the full range of rights conferred on EEA nationals by the 2016 Regulations. Switzerland is also a party to the European Social Charter (see immediately below), but that Charter does not confer any additional right to reside on Swiss nationals.

Turkish nationals and nationals of the Republic of Northern Macedonia

5.60   Although not EEA States, Turkey has ratified the European Convention on Social and Medical Assistance ("the ECSMA Agreement") and the European Social Charter, and the Republic of Northern Macedonia has ratified the Social Charter. In some circumstances, this will have the effect that Turkish and Northern Macedonian nationals are not excluded from benefit as "persons subject to immigration control" (see the commentary to SI 2000/636). However, the right to reside and habitual residence tests remain applicable (*CH/2321/2007*) and neither the ECSMA Agreement nor the Social Charter confers any direct right of residence or right to benefit: see *Yesiloz v Camden LBC and SSWP* [2009] EWCA Civ 415 (R(H) 7/09. This is because, as the Commissioner pointed out at para.6 of *CIS/1773/2007*, the ECSMA Agreement "requires the Contracting Powers to enact legislation conferring rights to benefit but it does not confer those rights itself. In the United Kingdom, it is for Parliament to give effect to ECSMA through domestic legislation" (see also para.24 of *CJSA/4705/999, CIS/259/2008* and paras 27–40 of the decision of the Court of Appeal in *Abdirahman v Secretary of State for Work and Pensions* [2007] EWCA Civ 657). Therefore, it is not possible for an ECSMA national who is not also an EEA national to assert in the domestic courts of the UK that legislation breaches the UK's international obligations under ECSMA: s/he can only rely on the rights conferred by domestic law. The same is true of the Social Charter (see para.39 of *Abdirahman*).

The Citizenship Directive

5.61   The phrase "right to reside" is not defined in social security legislation and whether or not a claimant has such a right therefore falls to be determined by the ordinary rules of immigration law and, in particular, EU Law.

That Law changed with effect from April 30, 2006 when the Citizenship Directive came into force and it is therefore necessary to ascertain the period with which one is dealing in order to know which law to apply. Readers are referred to pp.298-306 of Vol.II of the 2006 edition, and to the Updating Material for those pages in the Supplement to that edition, for a full discussion of the law as it stood before April 30, 2006.

The purpose of the Citizenship Directive is to extend the rights of EU citizens. Therefore, arguments suggesting that the rights it confers are less extensive than those conferred by the former law need to be treated with caution. As the ECJ held in Case C-127/08 *Metock v Minister for Justice, Equality and Law Reform* at para.59:

> "As is apparent from recital 3 in the preamble to Directive 2004/38, it aims in particular to 'strengthen the right of free movement and residence of all Union citizens', so that Union citizens cannot derive less rights from that directive than from the instruments of secondary legislation which it amends or repeals."

The only exception to this principle in UK law occurred in the decision of the Court of Appeal in *State for Work and Pensions v Elmi* [2011] EWCA Civ 1403 (see below). However the principle appears to have been ignored rather than disapplied in that case.

The changes in EU Law from April 30, 2006 were reflected by amendments to domestic social security law and, in particular, the introduction of reg.21AA and of reg.85A of the JSA Regulations, and the substitution of a new reg.2 in the SPC Regulations.

The most important conceptual change in the domestic law is that, whereas, before April 30, 2006, any right of residence was sufficient to satisfy the right to reside test, it is now necessary to ask whether the particular right of residence enjoyed by the claimant counts for the purpose of the particular benefit that s/he has claimed (see para.(3) of each of those Regulations). For example, the initial right of residence (see below) does not count for the purposes of any income-related benefit and the extended right of residence enjoyed by jobseekers only counts for the purposes of JSA.

The personal scope of the Citizenship Directive

By art.3(1) of the Citizenship Directive, it applies to "all Union citizens who   5.62
move to or reside in a Member State other than that of which they are a national, and to their family members . . . who accompany or join them". For the definition of "family members", see reg.7.

The rights under the Citizenship Directive are extended to the nationals of the other EEA States and to Switzerland by, respectively, the Oporto Agreement and the Luxembourg Agreement (see above). The commentary to these Regulations will therefore follow the Regulations themselves by describing the beneficiaries of the Directive as "EEA nationals" and their family members.

It follows the words "who move to or reside in a Member State other than that of which they are a national" in art.3(1) that, whatever rights they may have under the EU *Treaties*, EU citizens do not have rights *under the Citizenship Directive* against the Member States of which they are nationals unless they have exercised their rights to freedom of movement to live in another EU state.

The leading case on this point is *McCarthy v Secretary of State for the Home Department* (Case C-434/09). Mrs McCarthy was a dual British/Irish citizen who was born in, and had always lived in, the UK. She was in receipt of social security benefits. She married a Jamaican citizen who did not have leave to remain in the UK. She then obtained an Irish passport and she and her husband applied for a residence permit and a residence document as, respectively, an EU citizen and the family member of an EU citizen. Those applications were refused, on the basis that Mrs McCarthy was not a qualifying person (see below). On appeal, the Supreme Court referred the following question to the ECJ for a preliminary ruling:

"1. Is a person of dual Irish and United Kingdom nationality who has resided in the United Kingdom for her entire life a 'beneficiary' within the meaning of Article 3 of [the Citizenship Directive]?"

The ECJ reformulated that question and answered as follows:

"— Article 3(1) of [the Citizenship Directive] must be interpreted as meaning that that directive is not applicable to a Union citizen who has never exercised his right of free movement, who has always resided in a Member State of which he is a national and who is also a national of another Member State."

Note, however, that the Citizenship Directive is not the only source of rights of residence. Such rights can arise directly under arts 20, 21 and 45 of TFEU, under EU Regulations (particularly, Regulation 492/2011, formerly Regulation 1612/68), and under the domestic law of the UK. Such rights do not necessarily depend upon the exercise by the EU citizen of his or her free movement rights. In particular:

- an EU citizen who has never exercised his/her rights of free movement, who has always resided in a Member State of which s/he is a national may, exceptionally, derive rights against such a Member State under art.21 TFEU where the application of measures by that Member State would have the effect of depriving him or her of "the genuine enjoyment of the substance of the rights conferred by virtue of his [or her] status as a Union citizen or of impeding the exercise of his [or her] right of free movement and residence within the territory of the Member States: see the discussion of *Zambrano* below.

- until October 15, 2012, a British citizen who is a dual national of another EU State, was able to derive rights from his or her other nationality under domestic UK law (i.e. the 2006 Regulations) where those Regulations were more favourable to him or her than EU law would be (see the decisions of the Upper Tribunal in *SSWP v AA* [2009] UKUT 249 (AAC) and HG v SSWP (SPC) [2011] UKUT 382 (AAC). However, from October 16, 2012, the 2006 Regulations were amended by SI 2012/1547 to reflect the Citizenship Directive as interpreted in *McCarthy*. The changes, which effectively reverse the decisions of the Upper Tribunal referred to above, are subject to transitional protection set out in para.9 of Sch.6.

The position of British nationals who are also nationals of another EEA State (and of their family members) has recently changed as a result of the decision of the Grand Chamber of the CJEU in *Lounes Secretary of State for the Home Department (Case C-165/16)*.

The Court was considering circumstances in which Ms O, a Spanish national, had exercised her rights to freedom of movement to live and work in the UK and become a naturalised British citizen, while retaining her Spanish nationality. She subsequently married Mr Lounes who was an Algerian national and, under domestic immigration law, an illegal overstayer. Mr Lounes then applied for the issue of a residence card as a family member of an EEA national (i.e., under reg.18). That application was refused and he was served with notice of a decision to remove him from the UK as an overstayer.

Under the 2016 Regulations, an EEA national who becomes a naturalised British citizen ceases to be an "EEA National" as defined in see reg.2(1). Therefore third country national family members cannot derive a right of residence as his/her family member.

The Grand Chamber ruled that the UK was correct to say that Ms O (and Mr Lounes) ceased to be beneficiaries of the Directive when she became British. However, Mr Lounes derived a right of residence directly from Art 21(1) TFEU "on conditions which must not be stricter than those provided for by [the]Directive".

The Court's formal ruling was in the following terms:

"[The Citizenship Directive] must be interpreted as meaning that, in a situation in which a citizen of the European Union (i) has exercised his freedom of movement by moving to and residing in a Member State other than that of which he is a national, under Article 7(1) or Article 16(1) of that directive, (ii) has then acquired the nationality of that Member State, while also retaining his nationality of origin, and (iii) several years later, has married a third-country national with whom he continues to reside in that Member State, that third-country national does not have a derived right of residence in the Member State in question on the basis of [the Citizenship Directive].

The third-country national is however eligible for a derived right of residence under Article 21(1) TFEU, on conditions which must not be stricter than those provided for by [the Citizenship Directive] for the grant of such a right to a third-country national who is a family member of a Union citizen who has exercised his right of freedom of movement by settling in a Member State other than the Member State of which he is a national."

The Lounes principle is not confined to cases in which the family member is a third-country national. It also applies where s/he is an EEA national: see ODS v SSWP (UC) [2019] UKUT 192 (AAC) and AS v SSWP (UC) [2018] UKUT 260 (AAC) at paras 31-36.

The *Lounes* principle does not, however, apply where the EU National worked in the UK and became a naturalised British citizen before the EU before Member State of which she is a national acceded to the EU: see the decision of the Immigration Appeals Chamber of the Upper Tribunal in *Kovacevic (British citizen – Art 21 TFEU) Croatia* [2018] UKUT 273 (IAC). Ms Kovacevic is a national of Croatia who lawfully entered the UK in 1995 and naturalised as a British citizen in 2007 (i.e., before Croatia acceded to the EU on 1 July 2013). Since arriving in the UK, she had resided and worked lawfully under UK domestic law and she retained her Croatian nationality following naturalisation. In June 2014, (i.e., after Croatia acceded to the EU) she married an Algerian national. The Upper Tribunal distinguished *Lounes*. Although she was a dual British/Croatian national, Ms Kovacevic had neither lived nor worked in the UK in the exercise of her Treaty rights. Her rights were therefore analogous to those of the Mrs McCarthy in *McCarthy v Secretary of State for the Home Department* C-434/09 and no right arose under art.21.

"Residence" and "lawful presence"

Lawful presence is not the same as a right of residence. A claimant who is lawfully present in the UK (i.e. who has been admitted under the right of entry in reg.11 of the 2016 Regulations, is in fact present in the UK, and would have an immediate right of re-entry if ever removed) does not *ipso facto* have a right to reside (see *Abdirahman* and *Ulluslow*). 5.63

Whether a claimant is lawfully present in the UK is, however, relevant for other social security purposes (see, in particular, the commentary on the ECSMA Agreement and the European Social Charter in the General Note to SI 2000/636).

Meaning of "right to reside"

"Right to reside" is defined by reg.2(1) as meaning "a right to reside in the United Kingdom under these Regulations (or where so specified, a right to reside under a particular regulation)". 5.64

However, these Regulations implement the Citizenship Directive and may sometimes do so imperfectly, in which case a right to reside for social security purposes will arise by virtue of the Directive and will take precedence over domestic UK immigration law. Conversely, there are a number of occasions when these Regulations confer rights that have no equivalent in the Directive. These Regulations must therefore be understood in the context of the relevant EU law.

The starting point must be that under art.20 of the Treaty on the Functioning of the European Union ("TFEU") (formerly art.17 of the EC Treaty ("TEC")) "[e]very person holding the nationality of a Member State shall be a citizen of the Union" and that, under art.21 (ex-art.18 TEC).

"1. Every citizen of the Union shall have the right to move and reside freely within the territory of the Member States, subject to the limitations and conditions laid down in this Treaty and by the measures adopted to give it effect. . .."

It is also of potential relevance that, under art.18 (Ex-art.12 TEC):

"Within the scope of application of this Treaty, and without prejudice to any special provisions contained therein, any discrimination on grounds of nationality shall be prohibited"

and that, under art.45 (Ex-art.39 TEC):

"1. Freedom of movement for workers shall be secured within the Community.
2. Such freedom of movement shall entail the abolition of any discrimination based on nationality between workers of the Member States as regards employment, remuneration and other conditions of work and employment.
3. It shall entail the right, subject to limitations justified on grounds of public policy, public security or public health:. . .

    (c)   to stay in a Member State for the purpose of employment in accordance with the provisions governing the employment of nationals of that State laid down by law, regulation or administrative action;
    (d)   to remain in the territory of a Member State after having been employed in that State, subject to conditions which shall be embodied in implementing regulations to be drawn up by the Commission."

The "limitations and conditions" authorised by art.20(1) are contained in the Citizenship Directive, see art.1(a) and (c). In that context, the drafting of the Citizenship Directive can often seem confusing because it appears to *grant* rights subject to limitations and conditions, rather than to *limit* rights that have already been conferred by the Treaty. However, except in relation to the right of permanent residence (which does not derive directly from the Treaty), the Directive has to be read on the basis that Treaty rights only apply to the extent set out. The circumstances in which it is possible to go behind the Directive and derive a right of residence directly from the Treaty are now extremely narrow: see below).

Compatibility of the right to reside test with EU law

5.65   In the past, it has been controversial whether the right to reside test, both as it affects A8 and A2 nationals, and as it affects some economically-inactive nationals of all Member States, is fully in accordance with EU law. However, that controversy has been put to rest by the decisions of the Court of Appeal of England and Wales in *Abdirahman* (above) and *Kaczmarek v SSWP* [2008] EWCA Civ 1310; (also reported as R(IS) 5/09), of the House of Lords in *Zalewska v Department for Social Development* [2008] UKHL 67, (also reported as R 1/09(IS)), and by the decisions of the Supreme Court in *Patmalniece v SSWP* [2011] UKSC 11 and *Mirga v Secretary of State for Work and Pensions* [2016] UKSC 1.

Abdirahman was the appeal against the decisions of the tribunal of Commissioners in *CIS/3573/2005* and *CH/2484/2005*. The challenge was to the right to reside test as a whole. Mrs Abdirahman was a Swedish national who, at the time under consideration had not been economically active in the UK and did not have a right to reside under the Citizenship Directive or the 2006 Regulations. She argued that she had a right to reside as a citizen of the European Union under art.21 TFEU (ex-art.18 TEC) and that the right to reside test discriminated against her on the grounds of nationality contrary to art.18 TFEU (ex-art.12 TEC). Both those arguments were rejected. Her art.21 (ex-art.18) right was "subject to the limitations and conditions laid down in [the] Treaty and by the measures adopted to give it effect" and on the authority of the *Trojani* case (above) and of a number of previous Court of Appeal decisions, including *W (China) v Secretary of State for the Home Department* (below), that article did not confer a right of residence in circumstances where the limitations imposed by the relevant Directive (in that case Directive 90/364) were not satisfied. Although the right to reside test was discriminatory, that discrimination was not "within the scope of application of the Treaty" because art.12 did not extend to cases in which there was no right to reside under either the Treaty or the relevant domestic law. Moreover, even if art.12 were engaged, the discrimination was in any event justified by the need to prevent benefit tourism and as an aspect of immigration control.

In *Kaczmarek*, the claimant had been economically active for a period of three years in the past but was no longer so. She relied on a passage from the judgment in *Trojani* (para.43) in submitting that "a citizen of the Union who is not economically active may rely on art.12 EC [now art.18 TFEU] where he has been lawfully resident in the host Member State for a certain time or possesses a residence permit" (emphasis added). However, the Court decided that "the reference to 'a certain time' is a reference to specific qualifying periods which give rise to an express right of residence".

Zalewska was about the validity of one aspect of the former registration scheme for A8 nationals (and, by implication, the equivalent provisions of the former authorisation scheme for A2 nationals and the current authorisation scheme for Croatian nationals). Specifically, it concerned the position of an A8 national who worked lawfully in the UK but became involuntarily unemployed or temporarily incapable of work before completing 12 months' lawful work. Any other EEA national would be regarded in those circumstances as a "person retaining the status of worker" with an entitlement to benefit. However, the effect of the former A8 Regulations was that an A8 national in that position was treated as a "workseeker" with no such entitlement. By the time the appeal reached the House of Lords, the issue was whether that treatment amounted to the unlawful denial of a social advantage that was available to UK nationals (i.e. contrary to art.7(2) of the former Regulation 1612/68). This, in turn depended on whether the exclusion from benefit was a proportionate exercise of the authority given by the relevant derogation in the Treaty of Accession. Although that derogation did not mention art.7 of Regulation 1612/68, it was not necessary to do so because, if the A8 scheme was proportionate, an A8 national who did not comply with it was not a worker for the purposes of art.7 and was therefore not entitled to its protection. Their Lordships decided by a majority (Lords Hope, Carswell and Brown, Baroness Hale and Lord Neuberger dissenting) that the A8 scheme was compatible with the EU law principle of proportionality. See also in this context the decision of the Court of Appeal in England and Wales in *R. (D) v Secretary of State for Work and Pensions* [2004] EWCA Civ 1468 (October 11, 2004, CA, Mummery and Kay L.JJ.) and *CIS/3232/2006*.

Patmalniece was concerned with the application of the "Equality of Treatment" provisions of art.3 of the former Regulation 1408/71 to the claimant's claim for SPC. In that case, the claimant was within the personal scope of the Regulation and SPC was within the material scope. It therefore could not be said, as had been held in *Abdirahman*, that the subject matter of the appeal was not within the scope of the anti-discrimination provision in question. Relying on the decision of the ECJ in *Bressol v Gouvernement de la Communauté Française*, Case C-73/08, the Supreme Court held unanimously that the right to reside test was indirectly rather than directly discriminatory. Regulation 2 of the SPC Regulations was said to impose:

> "a composite test, one element of which [i.e., the right to reside test] could be satisfied by a person who was not a national of the host Member State only if he met certain additional conditions but which every national of the host member state would automatically satisfy"

and that the effect of the conditions in that regulation (i.e. both the right to reside test and the habitual residence test) had to be looked at cumulatively. It was not directly discriminatory on grounds of nationality but, as it put nationals of other member States at a particular disadvantage, it was indirectly discriminatory and needed to be justified. By a majority (Lord Walker dissenting), it found that discrimination to be justified by:

> "the principle that those who are entitled to claim social assistance in the host Member State should have achieved a genuine economic tie with it or a sufficient degree of social integration as a pre-condition for entitlement to it"

and that justification was not undermined by the more favourable treatment accorded by the UK to Irish nationals because of art.2 of Protocol 20 to the TFEU and TEU (the Protocol on the Common Travel Area, see above).

The decision in *Patmalniece* applies to child benefit and child tax credit as it does to other social security benefits. In *AS v HMRC (CB)* [2013] NICom 15, the Chief Commissioner of Northern Ireland distinguished *Patmalniece* and held that the right to reside test in reg.27(3) of the Child Benefit (General) Regulations 2006 (i.e. of the Northern Ireland regulations which is equivalent to reg.23(4) of the GB regulations) is unlawfully discriminatory on the grounds of nationality contrary to art.3 of Regulation 1408/71. However, the Court of Appeal in Northern Ireland allowed HMRC's appeal (*HM Revenue & Customs v Spiridonova* [2014] NICA 63) and confirmed the validity of the test.

That leaves the question of whether it is possible to derive a right of residence directly from art.21(1) TFEU (ex-art.18(1) TEC) in circumstances where no such right is expressly conferred by the Citizenship Directive or the Regulations. In *Kaczmarek*, the Court followed the approach adopted by the Commissioner in that case (*CIS/2538/2006*), namely that there is no direct right of residence under art.21 unless the denial of such a right would offend the general principles of community law and, in particular, the principle of proportionality. In such cases, there may be a freestanding right of residence under art.21(1). However, the Citizenship Directive provides the benchmark for proportionality (even in cases arising before that Directive came into force) and art.21(1) cannot be interpreted so as to confer rights that go beyond the Citizenship Directive except where it can be shown that there is a lacuna in the Directive.

For examples of post-Kaczmarek decisions on proportionality see *SSWP v DWP* [2009] UKUT 17 (AAC), *SSWP v IM-M* [2009] UKUT 71 (AAC), *SSWP v CA* [2009] UKUT 169 (AAC), *RM v SSWP (IS)* [2010] UKUT 238 (AAC), *SSWP v PS-B (IS)* [2016] UKUT 511 (AAC), *SSWP v AC (UC)* [2017] UKUT 130 (AAC) and *JK v SSWP (SPC)* [2017] UKUT 179 (AAC). Cases in which a right to reside is conferred on the basis that it is disproportionate to apply the normal rules will be exceptional. For examples, see *R(IS)* 4/09 and *JK* (above). *AC* holds that "the circumstances in which a lacuna may be avoided must relate to a potential gap in the EU legislation" rather than under domestic law. However, this is difficult to reconcile with *JK*.

More recently, the issue of proportionality has been considered again by the Supreme Court in *Mirga v Secretary of State for Work and Pensions* [2016] UKSC 1. The claimant was a Polish national who had come to the UK in 1998 at the age of 10 with her parents and siblings. The family went back to Poland in 2002 but returned to the UK in June 2004. After completing her education, the claimant started work in April 2005. Her first period of work of seven months was registered under the former worker registration scheme for A8 nationals but the two subsequent short periods were not. She left home in June 2006, having fallen out with her father because she was pregnant (her mother had died in October 2004). Her claim for income support made in August 2006 was refused on the ground that she did not have a right to reside. The Court of Appeal ([2012] EWCA Civ 1952) rejected the argument that in these circumstances the refusal of income support was disproportionate and therefore offensive to EU law. The Court relied, firstly, on *Zalewska* and, secondly, on the distinction drawn in para. 5 of *Kaczmarek* between lawful presence and right to reside. The protection of the claimant's fundamental rights did not require that she be accorded a right of residence. She was lawfully present, and if the Home Office decided to remove her, would have a right of appeal against that decision and be able to raise any argument based on fundamental rights arising out of EU law or Art. 8 ECHR at that point. On further appeal, the Supreme Court upheld the decision of the Court of Appeal. On the issue of proportionality, the Court decided, following the judgments of the CJEU in *Dano v Jobcenter Leipzig* (C-333/13) and *Jobcenter Berlin Neukölln v Alimanovic* (Case C-67/14), that the provisions of Directive 2004/38/EC "guarantees a significant level of legal certainty and transparency in the context of the award of social assistance by way of basic provision while complying with the principle of proportionality" so that an examination of proportionality in the context of an individual case was not necessary, except (possibly) in exceptional cases, of which Ms Mirga's case was not one.

For examples of cases decided by the Upper Tribunal after the decision of the Supreme Court in *Mirga*, see *MM v SWP (ESA)* [2017] UKUT 437 (AAC) and *LO v SSWP (IS)* [2017] UKUT 440 (AAC) both of which demonstrate how very exceptional a claimant's circumstances would have to be to fall into the (possible) category of exceptional cases in which an individual consideration of those circumstances might be required by the principle of proportionality. For guidance on how to approach issues of proportionality following *Kaczmarek* and *Mirga*, see *JS v SSWP (IS)* [2019] UKUT 135 (AAC).

The UK case law which holds that there is no general right for EEA nationals who are not economically active to reside in a member state of which they are not a national is reinforced by the Grand Chamber of the ECJ in *Dano v Jobcenter Leipzig* (C-333/13). The court ruled that: "Article 24(1) of Directive 2004/38/EC …, read in conjunction with Article 7(1)(b) thereof, and Article 4 of Regulation No 883/2004, … must be interpreted as not precluding legislation of a Member State under which nationals of other Member States are excluded from entitlement to certain 'special non-contributory cash benefits' within the meaning of Article 70(2) of Regulation No 883/2004, although those benefits are granted to nationals of the host Member State who are in the same situation, in so far as those nationals of other Member States do not have a right of residence under Directive 2004/38 in the host Member State." The Court's decision received considerable publicity in the UK but does not actually change the law as it was previously understood: economically inactive EEA nationals who are without sufficient resources do not have a right to reside and so are not entitled to social assistance.

PART 1

PRELIMINARY

Citation and commencement

1.—(1) These Regulations may be cited as the Immigration (European Economic Area) Regulations 2016.   5.66

(2) These Regulations come into force—

(a) for the purposes of this regulation, regulation 44 and Schedule 5 (transitory provisions), on 25th November 2016;

(b) for all other purposes, on 1st February 2017.

General interpretation

2.—(1) In these Regulations—   5.67

"the 1971 Act" means the Immigration Act 1971;

"the 1999 Act" means the Immigration and Asylum Act 1999;

"the 2002 Act" means the Nationality, Immigration and Asylum Act 2002;

"the 2006 Regulations" means the Immigration (European Economic Area) Regulations 2006;

[¹ "the 2016 Act" means the Immigration Act 2016;]

"civil partner" does not include—

(a) a party to a civil partnership of convenience; or

(b) the civil partner ("C") of a person ("P") where a spouse, civil partner or durable partner of C or P is already present in the United Kingdom;

"civil partnership of convenience" includes a civil partnership entered into for the purpose of using these Regulations, or any other right conferred by the EU Treaties, as a means to circumvent—

(a) immigration rules applying to non-EEA nationals (such as any applicable requirement under the 1971 Act to have leave to enter or remain in the United Kingdom); or

(b) any other criteria that the party to the civil partnership of convenience would otherwise have to meet in order to enjoy a right to reside under these Regulations or the EU Treaties;

"Common Travel Area" has the meaning given in section 1(3) of the 1971 Act;

"decision maker" means the Secretary of State, an immigration officer or an entry clearance officer (as the case may be);

"deportation order" means an order made under regulation 32(3);

"derivative residence card" means a card issued to a person under regulation 20;

"derivative right to reside" means a right to reside under regulation 16;

"document certifying permanent residence" means a document issued under regulation 19(1);

"durable partner" does not include—

(a) a party to a durable partnership of convenience; or

(b) the durable partner ("D") of a person ("P") where a spouse, civil partner or durable partner of D or P is already present in the United Kingdom and where that marriage, civil partnership or durable partnership is subsisting;

"durable partnership of convenience" includes a durable partnership entered into for the purpose of using these Regulations, or any other right conferred by the EU Treaties, as a means to circumvent—

(a) immigration rules applying to non-EEA nationals (such as any applicable requirement under the 1971 Act to have leave to enter or remain in the United Kingdom); or

(b) any other criteria that the party to the durable partnership of convenience would otherwise have to meet in order to enjoy a right to reside under these Regulations or the EU Treaties;

"EEA decision" means a decision under these Regulations that concerns—

(a) a person's entitlement to be admitted to the United Kingdom;

(b) a person's entitlement to be issued with or have renewed, or not to have revoked, [⁴ an EEA family permit,] a registration certificate, residence card, derivative residence card, document certifying permanent residence or permanent residence card (but does not include [⁴ a decision to reject an application for the above documentation as invalid]);

(c) a person's removal from the United Kingdom; or

(d) the cancellation, under regulation 25, of a person's right to reside in the United Kingdom,

but does not include [³ ...] a decision to [⁴ refuse] an application under regulation 26(4) (misuse of a right to reside: material change of circumstances), or any decisions under regulation 33 (human rights considerations and interim orders to suspend removal) or 41 (temporary admission to submit case in person);

"EEA family permit" means a document issued under regulation 12;

[² "EEA national" means—

(a) a national of an EEA State who is not also a British citizen; or

(b) a national of an EEA State who is also a British citizen and who prior to acquiring British citizenship exercised a right to reside as such a national, in accordance with regulation 14 or 15,

save that a person does not fall within paragraph (b) if the EEA State of which they are a national became a member State after that person acquired British citizenship.]

"EEA State" means—

(a) a member State, other than the United Kingdom; or

(b) Liechtenstein, Iceland, Norway or Switzerland;

"entry clearance" has the meaning given in section 33(1) of the 1971 Act;

"entry clearance officer" means a person responsible for the grant or refusal of entry clearance;

"exclusion order" means an order made under regulation 23(5);

"indefinite leave", "immigration laws" and "immigration rules" have the meanings given in section 33(1) of the 1971 Act;

"marriage of convenience" includes a marriage entered into for the purpose of using these Regulations, or any other right conferred by the EU Treaties, as a means to circumvent—

(a) immigration rules applying to non-EEA nationals (such as any applicable requirement under the 1971 Act to have leave to enter or remain in the United Kingdom); or

(b) any other criteria that the party to the marriage of convenience would otherwise have to meet in order to enjoy a right to reside under these Regulations or the EU Treaties;

"military service" means service in the armed forces of an EEA State;

"permanent residence card" means a document issued under regulation 19(2);

"qualifying EEA State residence card" means a valid document called a "Residence card of a family member of a Union Citizen" issued under Article 10 of Council Directive 2004/38/EC (as applied, where relevant, by the EEA agreement) by any EEA State (except Switzerland) to a non-EEA family member of an EEA national as proof of the holder's right of residence in that State;

"registration certificate" means a certificate issued under regulation 17;

"relevant EEA national" in relation to an extended family member has the meaning given in regulation 8(6);

"residence card" means a card issued under regulation 18;

"right to reside" means a right to reside in the United Kingdom under these Regulations (or where so specified, a right to reside under a particular regulation);

"spouse" does not include—

(a) a party to a marriage of convenience; or

(b) the spouse ("S") of a person ("P") where a spouse, civil partner or durable partner of S or P is already present in the United Kingdom.

(2) Section 11 of the 1971 Act (construction of references to entry) applies for the purpose of determining whether a person has entered the United Kingdom for the purpose of these Regulations as it applies for the purpose of determining whether a person has entered the United Kingdom for the purpose of that Act.

AMENDMENT

1. Immigration Act 2016 (Consequential Amendments) (Immigration Bail) Regulations 2017 (SI 2017/1242) reg.2 and Sch. para.8(1) and (2) (January 15, 2018).

2. Immigration (European Economic Area) (Amendment) Regulations 2018 (SI 2018/801) reg.2 and Sch., para.1 (July 24, 2018).

3. Immigration (European Economic Area Nationals) (EU Exit) Regulations 2019 (SI 2019/468) reg.3(2) (March 28, 2019).

4. Immigration (European Economic Area) (Amendment) Regulations 2019 (SI 2019/1155) reg.2(1) and (2) (August 15, 2019).

DEFINITIONS

"extended family member"—see reg.8.
"family member"—see reg.7.

GENERAL NOTE

5.68   *Paragraph (1)*: Most of these definitions are either self-explanatory or are discussed in the commentary to the regulations where the defined terms are used. The following merit comment here.

"*Common Travel Area*" is defined by reference to Immigration Act 1971 s.1(3) which states:

"(3) Arrival in and departure from the United Kingdom on a local journey from or to any of the Islands (that is to say, the Channel Islands and Isle of Man) or the Republic of Ireland shall not be subject to control under this Act, nor shall a person require leave to enter the United Kingdom on so arriving, except in so far as any of those places is for any purpose excluded from this subsection under the powers conferred by this Act; and in this Act the United Kingdom and those places, or such of them as are not so excluded, are collectively referred to as 'the common travel area'."

See also Immigration Act 1971 s.11(2) and (4) (quoted in the commentary to para.(2) below) and *Irish and Island Nationals* in the General Note to these Regulations, above.

"*entry clearance*" is defined by Immigration Act 1971 s.33(1) as meaning "a visa, entry certificate or other document which, in accordance with the immigration rules, is to be taken as evidence or the requisite evidence of a person's eligibility, though not a British citizen, for entry into the United Kingdom (but does not include a work permit)".

"*indefinite leave*" is defined by Immigration Act 1971 s.33(1) as meaning "leave under this Act to enter or remain in the United Kingdom . . . which is not . . . limited as to duration".

"*immigration laws*" is defined by Immigration Act 1971 s.33(1) as meaning "this Act and any law for purposes similar to this Act which is for the time being or has (before or after the passing of this Act) been in force in any part of the United Kingdom and Islands".

"immigration rules" is defined by Immigration Act 1971 s.33(1) as meaning the rules laid down under s.3(2) of that act. Section 3(2) is in the following terms:

"(2) The Secretary of State shall from time to time (and as soon as may be) lay before Parliament statements of the rules, or of any changes in the rules, laid down by him as to the practice to be followed in the administration of this Act for regulating the entry into and stay in the United Kingdom of persons required by this Act to have leave to enter, including any rules as to the period for which leave is to be given and the conditions to be attached in different circumstances; and section 1(4) above shall not be taken to require uniform provision to be made by the rules as regards admission of persons for a purpose or in a capacity specified in section 1(4) (and in particular, for this as well as other purposes of this Act, account may be taken of citizenship or nationality).

If a statement laid before either House of Parliament under this subsection is disapproved by a resolution of that House passed within the period of forty days beginning with the date of laying (and exclusive of any period during which Parliament is dissolved or prorogued or during which both Houses are adjourned for more than four days), then the Secretary of State shall as soon as may be make such changes or further changes in the rules as appear to him to be required in the circumstances, so that the statement of those changes be laid before Parliament at latest by the end of the period of forty days beginning with the date of the resolution (but exclusive as aforesaid)."

The text of the current immigration rules can be found online at *https://www.gov. uk/guidance/immigration-rules* and an archive of previous versions of the rules is at *https://www.gov.uk/government/collections/archive-immigration-rules.*

"indefinite leave" is defined by Immigration Act 1971 s.33(1) as meaning "leave under this Act to enter or remain in the United Kingdom . . . which is not . . . limited as to duration".

Paragraph 2 requires that the question whether a person has entered the United Kingdom for the purpose of the 2016 Regulations should be determined in accordance with Immigration Act 1971 s.11. That section is in the following terms:

"Construction of references to entry, and other phrases relating to travel.

11.—(1) A person arriving in the United Kingdom by ship or aircraft shall for purposes of this Act be deemed not to enter the United Kingdom unless and until he disembarks, and on disembarkation at a port shall further be deemed not to enter the United Kingdom so long as he remains in such area (if any) at the port as may be approved for this purpose by an immigration officer; and a person who has not otherwise entered the United Kingdom shall be deemed not to do so as long as he is detained, or temporarily admitted or released while liable to detention, under the powers conferred by Schedule 2 to this Act or section 62 of the Nationality, Immigration and Asylum Act 2002 or by section 68 of the Nationality, Immigration and Asylum Act 2002.

(2) In this Act "disembark" means disembark from a ship or aircraft, and "embark" means embark in a ship or aircraft; and, except in subsection (1) above,

   (a) references to disembarking in the United Kingdom do not apply to disembarking after a local journey from a place in the United Kingdom or elsewhere in the common travel area; and

   (b) references to embarking in the United Kingdom do not apply to embarking for a local journey to a place in the United Kingdom or elsewhere in the common travel area.

(3) Except in so far as the context otherwise requires, references in this Act to arriving in the United Kingdom by ship shall extend to arrival by any floating structure, and "disembark" shall be construed accordingly; but the provisions of this Act specially relating to members of the crew of a ship shall not by virtue of this provision apply in relation to any floating structure not being a ship.

(4) For purposes of this Act "common travel area" has the meaning given by section 1(3), and a journey is, in relation to the common travel area, a local journey if but only if it begins and ends in the common travel area and is not made by a ship or aircraft which—

5.69

(a) in the case of a journey to a place in the United Kingdom, began its voyage from, or has during its voyage called at, a place not in the common travel area; or

(b) in the case of a journey from a place in the United Kingdom, is due to end its voyage in, or call in the course of its voyage at, a place not in the common travel area.

(5) A person who enters the United Kingdom lawfully by virtue of section 8(1) above, and seeks to remain beyond the time limited by section 8(1), shall be treated for purposes of this Act as seeking to enter the United Kingdom."

Continuity of residence

5.70   **3.**—(1) This regulation applies for the purpose of calculating periods of continuous residence in the United Kingdom under these Regulations.

(2) Continuity of residence is not affected by—

(a) periods of absence from the United Kingdom which do not exceed six months in total in any year;

(b) periods of absence from the United Kingdom on compulsory military service; or

(c) one absence from the United Kingdom not exceeding twelve months for an important reason such as pregnancy and childbirth, serious illness, study or vocational training or an overseas posting.

(3) Continuity of residence is broken when—

(a) a person serves a sentence of imprisonment;

(b) a deportation or exclusion order is made in relation to a person; or

(c) a person is removed from the United Kingdom under these Regulations.

(4) Paragraph (3)(a) applies, in principle, to an EEA national who has resided in the United Kingdom for at least ten years, but it does not apply where the Secretary of State considers that—

(a) prior to serving a sentence of imprisonment, the EEA national had forged integrating links with the United Kingdom;

(b) the effect of the sentence of imprisonment was not such as to break those integrating links; and

(c) taking into account an overall assessment of the EEA national's situation, it would not be appropriate to apply paragraph (3)(a) to the assessment of that EEA national's continuity of residence.

DEFINITION

"EEA national"—see reg.2(1).
"exclusion order"—*ibid.*
"military service"—*ibid.*

GENERAL NOTE

5.71   Continuity of residence is relevant to the acquisition of a permanent right of residence under art.16(1) and (2) and reg.15(1)(a) and (b). Regulation 3 implements art.16(3)

Paragraph (2): Continuity of residence is not affected by absence on military service, absences for any reason that do not in total exceed six months in any year or by a single absence of no more than 12 months "for an important reason such as pregnancy and childbirth, serious illness, study or vocational training or an overseas posting".

As is clear from the quoted words, that list is not exhaustive. In *Babajanov v Secretary of State for the Home Department (Continuity of residence – Immigration (EEA) Regulations 2006)* [2013] UKUT 513 (IAC), the Upper Tribunal held that when deciding whether absence for a non-listed reason falls within art.16(3), the purpose of the absence needs to be considered and should involve compelling events and/or an activity linked to the exercise of Treaty rights in the UK.

Absences within art.16(3)/reg.3(2) do not break continuity of residence, but do they count towards the five-year period required by art.16(1) and reg.15(1)(a) and (b)? In *CIS/2258/2008* at para.17 the Commissioner held that they did not. However, in *Idezuna (EEA—permanent residence) Nigeria* [2011] UKUT 474 (IAC) the Immigration Appeals Chamber of the Upper Tribunal held—without expressly addressing the point or being referred to *CIS/2258/2008*—that the appellant had acquired a permanent right of residence through a period of five years' continuous residence beginning on April 23, 2004 and ending on April 23, 2009 even though there was evidence that he had been absent from the UK for two periods including one from October 29, 2006 to December 17, 2006. Previous editions have suggested that the reasoned decision of the Commissioner in *CIS/2258/2008* should be followed in preference to *Idezuna*. However, the weight of authority now favours the opposite conclusion. In *Babajanov* (above), a two-judge panel of the Immigration Appeals Chamber of the Upper Tribunal held that the right of permanent residence is capable of being established whilst a national of a Member State or a family member of that national is outside the host country. If that is correct, it follows that periods of absence within art.16(3)/reg.3(2) do count towards the five-year period.

Under reg.15(1)(a) and (b), a permanent right of residence is conferred on EEA nationals and their family members who have "resided in the United Kingdom in accordance with these Regulations for a continuous period of five years". In *Secretary of State for the Home Department v Ojo* [2015] EWCA Civ 1301, the Court of Appeal held that "[t]he acquisition of a permanent right of residence depends on continuous residence in a qualifying status". It is therefore not possible for a claimant who has resided in the UK continuously, but whose residence has not been continuously legal—in the sense of being in accordance with the Regulations— to aggregate separate periods of legal residence to achieve a total of five years. The decision of the Upper Tribunal in *OB v SSWP (ESA)* [2017] UKUT 255 (AAC) and, to the extent that it followed *OB*, in *AP v SSWP (IS)* [2018] UKUT 307 (AAC), were per incuriam and wrongly decided: see *Cardiff CC v HM (HB)* [2019] UKUT 271 (AAC).

Imprisonment – paras (3) and (4): Any period during which an EEA national is serving a sentence of imprisonment in this country is not to be included when calculating whether he has resided in the United Kingdom for a continuous period and breaks continuity of residence so that a the person must reside lawfully for five years after his or her release from prison before acquiring a permanent right of residence: *Onuekwere v Secretary of State for the Home Department* (Case C-378/12); *Secretary of State for the Home Department v MG* (Case C-400/12), *HR (Portugal) v Secretary of State for the Home Office* [2009] EWCA Civ 371; *Carvalho v Secretary of State for the Home Department [2010] EWCA Civ* 1406; *Jarusevicius (EEA Reg 21—effect of imprisonment)* [2012] UKUT 120 (IAC) and *SO (imprisonment breaks continuity of residence) Nigeria* [2011] UKUT 164 (IAC). For the purposes of para.(3)(a), a "sentence of imprisonment" includes a sentence of detention in a Young Offenders' Institution: see *Secretary of State for the Home Department v Viscu* [2019] EWCA Civ 1052.

However, an EEA national does not cease to be a qualified person as a result of being detained in a hospital pursuant to an order of the court under the Mental Health Act 1983, having not been convicted of any criminal offence: *JO (qualified person – hospital order – effect) Slovakia* [2012] UKUT 237(IAC).

"Worker", "self-employed person", "self-sufficient person" and "student"

4.—(1) In these Regulations—   5.72
   (a) "worker" means a worker within the meaning of Article 45 of the
       Treaty on the Functioning of the European Union;

(b) "self-employed person" means a person who is established in the United Kingdom in order to pursue activity as a self-employed person in accordance with Article 49 of the Treaty on the Functioning of the European Union;

(c) "self-sufficient person" means a person who has—

    (i) sufficient resources not to become a burden on the social assistance system of the United Kingdom during the person's period of residence; and

(ii) comprehensive sickness insurance cover in the United Kingdom;

(d) "student" means a person who—

    (i) is enrolled, for the principal purpose of following a course of study (including vocational training), at a public or private establishment which is—

    (aa) financed from public funds; or

    (bb) otherwise recognised by the Secretary of State as an establishment which has been accredited for the purpose of providing such courses or training within the law or administrative practice of the part of the United Kingdom in which the establishment is located;

    (ii) has comprehensive sickness insurance cover in the United Kingdom; and

    (iii) has assured the Secretary of State, by means of a declaration, or by such equivalent means as the person may choose, that the person has sufficient resources not to become a burden on the social assistance system of the United Kingdom during the person's intended period of residence.

(2) For the purposes of paragraphs (3) and (4) below, "relevant family member" means a family member of a self-sufficient person or student who is residing in the United Kingdom and whose right to reside is dependent upon being the family member of that student or self-sufficient person.

(3) In sub-paragraphs (1)(c) and (d)—

(a) the requirement for the self-sufficient person or student to have sufficient resources not to become a burden on the social assistance system of the United Kingdom during the intended period of residence is only satisfied if the resources available to the student or self-sufficient person and any of their relevant family members are sufficient to avoid the self-sufficient person or student and all their relevant family members from becoming such a burden; and

(b) the requirement for the student or self-sufficient person to have comprehensive sickness insurance cover in the United Kingdom is only satisfied if such cover extends to cover both the student or self-sufficient person and all their relevant family members.

(4) In paragraph (1)(c) and (d) and paragraph (3), the resources of the student or self-sufficient person and, where applicable, any of their relevant family members, are to be regarded as sufficient if—

(a) they exceed the maximum level of resources which a British citizen (including the resources of the British citizen's family members) may possess if the British citizen is to become eligible for social assistance under the United Kingdom benefit system; or

(b) paragraph (a) does not apply but, taking into account the personal circumstances of the person concerned and, where applicable, all their relevant family members, it appears to the decision maker that the resources of the person or persons concerned should be regarded as sufficient.

(5) For the purposes of regulation 16(2) (criteria for having a derivative right to reside), references in this regulation to "family members" includes a "primary carer" as defined in regulation 16(8).

DEFINITIONS

"decision maker"—see reg.2(1).
"derivative right to reside"—see regs 2(1) and 16.
"family member"—see reg.7.
"primary carer"—see reg.16(8).
"right to reside"—see reg.2(1).

GENERAL NOTE

Workers, self-employed persons, self-sufficient persons and students are all "qualified persons" as defined in reg.6 and have an extended right of residence by virtue of art.7(1) and reg.14 that counts for the purposes of entitlement to all income-related benefits. They are also exempt from the habitual residence test under reg.21AA(4)(za) of the IS Regs, reg.85(4)(za) of the JSA Regulations, reg.2(4)(za) of the SPC Regulations, reg.70(4)(za) of the ESA Regulations 2008 and reg.9(4)(a) of the Universal Credit Regulations. 5.73

Worker

Paragraph (1)(a) defines "worker" as meaning a worker within the meaning of art.45 TFEU (ex-39 TEC), which is reproduced in Vol.III. That definition is not as helpful as it appears, because neither that Treaty nor the measures that have implemented it (including the Citizenship Directive) include a definition of the term "worker" and case law makes it clear that it means different things in different contexts and sometimes even in different parts of the same Regulation (see Case C–85/96 *Martinez Sala v Freistaat Bayern*; Case C–138/02 *Collins v Secretary of State for Work and Pensions* [2005] Q.B. 145 (reported as *R(JSA) 3/06* and *CJSA/1475/2006*). However, the reference to art.45 TFEU in the definition does make it clear that the word is to be interpreted in accordance with EU law and hence in accordance with the established case law of the ECJ. A number of principles can be derived from those cases: 5.74

- The term "worker" has a Community meaning and may not be defined by reference to the national laws of Member States (Case C–75/63 *Hoekstra (née Unger) v Bestuur der Bedrijfsvereniging voor Detailhandel en Ambachten* [1964] E.C.R. 177).

- As a concept that defines the field of application of one of the fundamental freedoms guaranteed by the Treaty, it may not be interpreted restrictively (Case C–53/81 *Levin v Staatssecretaris van Justitie* [1982] E.C.R. 1035).

- The term applies to those who are employees rather than self-employed. For these purposes "the essential characteristic of an employment relationship is that for a certain period a person performs services for and under the direction of another person in return for which he receives remuneration" (Case C–357/89 *Raulin v Minister Van Onderwijs en Wetenschappen* [1992] E.C.R. I-1027 at para.10). However, the existence of a legally-binding employment relationship is not conclusive of whether the employee is a worker (Case C–344/87 *Bettray v Staatssecretaris Van Justitie* [1989] E.C.R. 1621). A person who has been a worker, but is no longer employed, may retain worker status under art.7(3) and reg.6(2): see the commentary to reg.6, below.

- The requirement that a "worker" should receive remuneration means that voluntary activity is not "work" for these purposes (*CIS/868/2008* and

CIS/1837/2006). Similarly, a person who receives carer's allowance for caring for a severely disabled person is not providing services for remuneration and so is not a worker for the purposes of art.7(1)(a) of the Citizenship Directive: see *JR v SSWP (IS) and JR v Leeds CC and another (HB)* [2014] UKUT 154 (AAC).

- The concept extends to part-time workers but only to the extent that the work undertaken is "effective and genuine. . . to the exclusion of activities on such a small scale as to be regarded as purely marginal and ancillary" (*Levin*, at para.17).

- As long as the work undertaken, is "effective and genuine" in this sense, it is irrelevant whether it "yields an income lower than that which, in the [host] state, is considered as the minimum required for subsistence, whether that person supplements the income from his activity as an employed person with other income so as to arrive at that minimum or is satisfied with means of support lower than the said minimum" (*Levin*, at para.18). Moreover, "where a national of a Member State pursues within the territory of another Member State by way of employment activities which may in themselves be regarded as effective and genuine work, the fact that he claims financial assistance payable out of the public funds of the latter Member State in order to supplement the income he receives from those activities does not exclude him from the provisions of community law relating to freedom of movement for workers" (Case C–139/85 *Kempf v Staatssecretaris Van Justitie* [1986] E.C.R. 1741 (formal ruling of the Court)).

- The motives which may have prompted the worker to seek employment in another Member State are irrelevant provided s/he pursues, or wishes to pursue, an effective and genuine activity (*Levin*, at para.23).

- In assessing whether a person is a worker, account should be taken of all the occupational activities s/he has undertaken in the host State (although activities pursued in other Member States do not count) (*Raulin*). In principle, there seems to be no reason why this should not include work done during a claimant's previous stay in the UK (even if on this occasion the person has not yet obtained employment) although this will depend on the length of time which has passed since the previous stay, the circumstances in which that employment came to an end, and the extent to which it can be said that the work now sought is connected to the work previously undertaken—see also the discussion of *Collins*, below.

Whether work undertaken by a particular claimant is, on the facts, "effective and genuine" within the case law of the ECJ is a matter for the national courts (i.e. the First-tier Tribunal and, on appeal, the Upper Tribunal) (*Levin*, at para.13).

Traditionally, the "effective and genuine" test was thought to present a low threshold. It excluded cases of abuse (i.e. relationships not really entered into for the purpose of pursuing economic activity but for the sole purpose of obtaining some other advantage: see the Advocate General in *Raulin* at para.9) and cases in which the work undertaken was not really economic activity at all (such as the rehabilitative work in *Bettray*) or "if it is done pursuant to some other relationship between the parties which is not an employment relationship, as where a lodger performs some small task for his landlord as part of the terms of his tenancy" (see the decision of the Court of Appeal in *Barry v London Borough of Southwark* [2008] EWCA Civ 1440 at para.20). Although the duration of the work is a relevant factor (*Raulin*), work undertaken for very short periods and for a very few hours a week has been held to qualify. For example, in *R(IS) 12/98* an au pair who had worked for five weeks (being paid £35 for a 13-hour week, plus free board and lodging) was held to be a worker.

However, there was a difference of opinion between Commissioners over whether, for work to be effective and genuine, the claimant's hours of work and earnings (or, in the case of a jobseeker (see the commentary to reg.6, below), the prospective hours of work and earnings) had to be such that s/he was not eligible to claim social assistance: see pp.312–313 of Vol.II of the 2010/11 edition. The current position is that, whilst the level of the claimant's hours and earnings are a relevant factor, the decision cannot be taken on a formulaic basis, and the correct approach is to consider what is proportionate, taking into account all relevant matters: see *SS v Slough Borough Council* [2011] UKUT 128 (AAC) at para.25.

The issue of sufficiency of earnings has also been considered by the ECJ in Cases C-22/08 and C-23/08 *Vatsouras and Koupatantze v Arbeitsgemeinschaft (ARGE) Nürnberg 900* and Case C-14/09 *Hava Genc v Land Berlin*. In the former case, the Court stated:

"27. Neither the origin of the funds from which the remuneration is paid nor the limited amount of that remuneration can have any consequence in regard to whether or not the person is a 'worker' for the purposes of Community law (see Case 344/87 *Bettray* [1989] ECR 1621, paragraph 15, and Case C-10/05 *Mattern and Cikotic* [2006] ECR I-3145, paragraph 22).

28. The fact that the income from employment is lower than the minimum required for subsistence does not prevent the person in such employment from being regarded as a 'worker' within the meaning of Article 39 EC (see Case 53/81 *Levin* [1982] ECR 1035, paragraphs 15 and 16, and Case C-317/93 *Nolte* [1995] ECI-4625, paragraph 19), even if the person in question seeks to supplement that remuneration by other means of subsistence such as financial assistance drawn from the public funds of the State in which he resides (see Case 139/85 *Kempf* [1986] ECR 1741, paragraph 14)."

In the latter, it reiterated that:

"20. Neither the origin of the funds from which the remuneration is paid nor the limited amount of that remuneration, nor indeed the fact that the person in question seeks to supplement that remuneration by other means of subsistence such as financial assistance drawn from the public funds of the State in which he resides, can have any consequence in regard to whether or not the person is a 'worker' for the purposes of European Union law (see, to that effect, Case 139/85 *Kempf* [1986] ECR 1741, paragraph 14; Case 344/87 *Bettray* [1989] ECR 1621, paragraph 15; and Case C-10/05 *Mattern and Cikotic* [2006] ECR I-3145, paragraph 22)."

In *CSIS/467/2007*, the Commissioner held that the claimant's physical incapacity to do the work she had undertaken and the fact that she had been dismissed from it after a short period were relevant to the issue of whether the work was effective and genuine.

Even though s/he will not be a "worker", person who is engaged in work that is not effective and genuine may still be a jobseeker if s/he satisfies the conditions in art.7(3) and reg.6. As the duration of work is a factor that is relevant to whether the work is effective and genuine, it is possible that work which would not have been regarded as effective and genuine at the outset will become so through repetition. In other words, a jobseeker can become a worker through the passage of time while s/he continues in a job. Guidance on this issue was given by the Upper Tribunal in *NE v SSWP* [2009] UKUT 38 (AAC). The claimant had worked for 15 hours in December 2004 and (possibly) for three weeks for an agency in January 2005 before claiming IS in July 2005. Judge Rowland stated:

"9. The issue in a case like the present may be said to be whether the claimant has genuinely and effectively (to borrow that phrase from its usual context) become a worker rather than a workseeker. I do not accept [counsel for the claimant]'s submission that agency work is by its nature ancillary and insufficient to confer on a claimant the status of worker. Although agency work is often temporary and for short periods, it is not necessarily so. However, I do accept that a distinction is to be drawn between temporary employment for a short period and indefinite employment that has been curtailed prematurely. Where work is undertaken for what is expected from the outset to be for a very short period and is known to be temporary, the person concerned is obliged to keep looking for work and often he or she cannot realistically be said to have become established in work and to have ceased to be a workseeker. It does not follow that all agency workers always remain workseekers. Where short periods of temporary work are not separated by longer periods of no work, it will often be appropriate to regard the person concerned as having become a worker rather than a workseeker. There will be cases where work that is temporarily is nonetheless for a prolonged period or where there is a high likelihood of further work being obtained and, in particular, many agency workers will be able to show that the agency has regularly found them work albeit for short periods and they have, for practical purposes, become established members of the national workforce. On the other hand, where a person has worked only intermittently for very short periods, as in *CIS/1793/2007*, the claimant is more likely to have remained a workseeker because the work performed has been marginal. The case-law shows that whether work is marginal is a matter of judgement on the facts of each case. In *Ninni-Orasche v Bundesminister für Wissenschaft, Verkehr und Kunst* (Case C-413/01) [2003] E.C.R. I-13187, the Court did not rule out the possibility that work under a fixed-term contract for two and a half months might be marginal and ancillary."

The duration of work was also an issue in *Barry*, in which a citizen of the Netherlands was held to be a worker on the basis of having done two weeks' work as a steward at the All England Tennis Championships at Wimbledon for which he was paid £789.86 net. See, however, the comments of Judge Rowland at para.8 of *NE v SSWP*.

An employee undertaking genuine and effective work is a worker for the purposes of the Citizenship Directive even if employed under a contract that is performed illegally (e.g., because the employer does not account to HMRC for the PAYE and national insurance contributions due on the employee's wages): see *JA v SSWP (ESA)* [2012] UKUT 122 (AAC) (CE/2190/2011) at paras 15–20. Similarly, undeclared work by a person claiming benefit can still be genuine and effective, see *Barry* at paras 28, 31 and 45 and *NE v SSWP* at para.4.

A person may acquire worker status by virtue of work done as a victim of illegal people trafficking: see *EP v SSWP (JSA)* [2016] UKUT 445 (AAC).

Minimum earnings threshold

5.75   Although there has been no change in the law governing whether work is effective and genuine, there was a change in the administrative practice followed by the DWP when deciding that issue with effect from March 1, 2014. The change was set out in DMG Memo 1/14 which establishes a "Minimum Earnings Threshold". The DWP will accept that claimants who have had average gross earnings of at least the primary earnings threshold for national insurance contributions (£157 pw in 2017/18, £162 in 2018/19 and £166 in 2019/20) for the three months before the claim are (or were) in effective and genuine work, without making further enquiries. The circumstances of claimants who do not meet that threshold, or have not done so for a continuous period of three months before the claim, will be investigated in more detail.

Contrary to the way in which the change was misrepresented in the press, the law does not require that a claimant must earn at least £155 pw before s/he can be accepted as being in effective and genuine work: see *RF v London Borough of Lambeth* [2019] UKUT 52 (AAC).

Self-employed person

5.76   Paragraph 1(b) defines "self-employed person" as meaning a person who is established in the United Kingdom in order to pursue activity as a self-employed person in accordance with art.49 TFEU (ex-43 TEC), which is reproduced in Vol.III. That definition is narrower than the equivalent definition in the 2000 Regulations, which included the words "or who seeks to do so" at the end. It follows that to have an extended right of residence as a self-employed person it is not sufficient to arrive in the UK with the wish to establish oneself. It is necessary to have taken active steps to pursue self-employment. This accords with the previous law; see *R(IS)* 6/00, para.31 (a case on the former Directive 73/148). Exactly what steps will suffice to give rise to the extended right of residence will depend upon the particular circumstances of individual cases.

RM v SSWP (IS) [2014] UKUT 401 (AAC), [2015] AACR 11 contains guidance on the concept of self-employment in EU law.

It is not necessary to register as self-employed with HMRC in order to have a right to reside as a self-employed person (see *SSWP v IM-M* [2009] UKUT 71 (AAC)). However, registration with HMRC is evidence of self-employed status.

The Upper Tribunal has decided that, as is the case for work as an employee, activity as a self-employed person must be "effective and genuine", rather than "marginal or ancillary" in order to give rise to a right of residence (see *Bristol City Council v FV (HB)* [2011] UKUT 494 (AAC) (CH/2859/2011), in which Judge Rowland upheld a decision of the First-tier tribunal that the activities of a Big Issue seller were effective and genuine and amounted to self-employment). The authority cited for that proposition, namely *Jany v Staatssecretarie van Justitie* (Case C-268/99) at para.33 is equivocal, as are the authorities from which *Jany* is itself derived: see *Deliège v Ligue Francophone de Judo and others* (Joined Cases C-56/91 and C-191/97) at paras 52–55 and *Steymann v Staatssecretaris van Justitie* (Case 196/87) at paras 14–15. Nevertheless, it is suggested that *Bristol City Council* is correctly decided on the point. For a case in which self-employed work was held by the Upper Tribunal not to be effective and genuine, see *SSWP v HH (SPC)* [2015] UKUT 583 (AAC).

Fostering is not self-employment (see *SSWP v SY (IS)* [2012] UKUT 233 (AAC) at paras 10–11). Similarly, a person who receives carer's allowance for caring for a severely disabled person is not providing services for remuneration and so is not a self-employed person for the purposes of art.7(1)(a) of the Citizenship Directive: see *JR v SSWP (IS) and JR v Leeds CC and another (HB)* [2014] UKUT 154 (AAC).

For the circumstances in which a person who has ceased self-employment retains the status of a "self-employed person" see the commentary to reg.6, below.

Self-sufficient persons

The status of "self-sufficient person" is governed by paras (1)(c), (3) and (4). **5.77**
The general rule (in para.(1)(c)) is that, to count as self-sufficient, a person must have "sufficient resources not to become a burden on the social assistance system of the United Kingdom during the person's period of residence" (para.(1)(c)(i)) and "comprehensive sickness insurance cover in the United Kingdom" (para.(1)(c)(ii)). That definition follows art.7(1)(b) of the Citizenship Directive.

Social assistance

The decision of the ECJ in *Pensionsversicherungsanstalt v Brey* Case C-140/12 **5.78**
holds (at para.61) that "social assistance":

"must be interpreted as covering all assistance introduced by the public authorities, whether at national, regional or local level, that can be claimed by an individual who does not have resources sufficient to meet his own basic needs and the needs of his family and who, by reason of that fact, may become a burden on the public finances of the host Member State during his period of residence which could have consequences for the overall level of assistance which may be granted by that State".

Further, the fact that a benefit is a special non-contributory cash benefit for the purposes of Regulation (EC) 883/2004 does not prevent its being social assistance for the purposes of art.7(1)(b) of the Citizenship Directive (*ibid.* at para.58). In

Brey, an Austrian benefit called the *Ausgleichzulage* (compensatory supplement), which appears to be similar to state pension credit, was held (at para.62) to be social assistance. Housing benefit and the former council tax benefit are also social assistance *SG v Tameside Metropolitan Borough Council (HB)* [2010] UKUT 243 (AAC) at para.50. However, tax credits may not be (see *R (A, B and C) v Secretary of State for the Home Department* [2013] EWHC 1272 at para.46, although the observations were made when granting permission to apply for judicial review and are therefore not binding).

Burden
5.79 "Burden" in para.(1)(c)(i) and art.7(1)(b) means "unreasonable burden": see Recitals (10) and (16) to the Citizenship Directive and *Brey*, above, paras 53-54, 57 and generally. The Court in Brey places particular emphasis (at para.72) on whether "the difficulties which a beneficiary of the right of residence encounters are temporary" as a relevant factor in assessing whether the grant of a social security benefit could place a burden on the host Member State's social assistance system as a whole.

Sufficient resources
5.80 The person's resources are "sufficient" if (taking into account the resources of any relevant family member) they exceed the maximum level of resources which a British citizen and his family members may possess if he is to become eligible for social assistance under the United Kingdom benefit system; or, if that is not the case, it appears those resources should be regarded as sufficient "taking into account the personal situation of the person concerned and, where applicable, any family members": see para.(4), which follows art.8(4).

If a person "has" sufficient resources then, with one exception, the origin of those resources is irrelevant. So, for example, where accommodation is made available to a claimant by a third party, the claimant "is in principle entitled to have that taken into account towards determining the sufficiency of their resources" (*SG v Tameside MBC* (HB) [2010] UKUT 243 (AAC). at paras 51-52, following the decision of the ECJ in Case C-408/03 *Commission v Kingdom of Belgium*). This includes the earnings of a spouse or partner who is a third-country national: see *Singh and others v Minister for Justice and Equality* (Case C-218/14).

The exception is that a person who has earnings, but who is nevertheless not a worker, cannot rely upon those earnings to establish self-sufficiency (*VP v SSWP (JSA)* [2014] UKUT 32 (AAC) at para.92, agreeing with the Chief Commissioner for Northern Ireland in *AS v HMRC (CB)* [2013] NICom 15 at para.110 and with the former Asylum and Immigration Tribunal in *MA & Others (EU national; self-sufficiency; lawful employment) Bangladesh* [2006] UKAIT 90 at para.44).

5.81 It will often seem self-evident that a person who has been driven by circumstances to claim an income-related benefit, no longer satisfies that definition of a "self-sufficient person". However, the decision in *Brey* means that that consequence does not follow automatically. There may be cases in which a person can assert that, although they are without resources at present, they should still be regarded as self-sufficient because their claim for benefit does not represent an unreasonable burden on the social assistance system of the United Kingdom. The reasoning underlying that conclusion is stated at paras 63-78 of *Brey*:

> "63. . . . . the fact that a national of another Member State who is not economically active may be eligible, in light of his low pension, to receive [a social assistance] benefit could be an indication that that national does not have sufficient resources to avoid becoming an unreasonable burden on the social assistance system of the host Member State for the purposes of Article 7(1)(b) of [the Citizenship] Directive . . . .
>
> 64. However, the competent national authorities cannot draw such conclusions without first carrying out an overall assessment of the specific burden which granting that benefit would place on the national social assistance system as a

whole, by reference to the personal circumstances characterising the individual situation of the person concerned.

65. First, it should be pointed out that there is nothing in [the Citizenship] Directive . . . to preclude nationals of other Member States from receiving social security benefits in the host Member State . . . .

66. On the contrary, several provisions of that directive specifically state that those nationals may receive such benefits. Thus, as the Commission has rightly pointed out, the very wording of Article 24(2) of that directive shows that it is only during the first three months of residence that, by way of derogation from the principle of equal treatment set out in Article 24(1), the host Member State is not to be under an obligation to confer entitlement to social assistance on Union citizens who do not or no longer have worker status. In addition, Article 14(3) of that directive provides that an expulsion measure is not to be the automatic consequence of recourse to the social assistance system of the host Member State by a Union citizen or a member of his family.

67. Second, it should be noted that the first sentence of Article 8(4) of [the Citizenship] Directive . . . expressly states that Member States may not lay down a fixed amount which they will regard as 'sufficient resources', but must take into account the personal situation of the person concerned. Moreover, under the second sentence of Article 8(4), the amount ultimately regarded as indicating sufficient resources may not be higher than the threshold below which nationals of the host Member State become eligible for social assistance, or, where that criterion is not applicable, higher than the minimum social security pension paid by the host Member State.

68. It follows that, although Member States may indicate a certain sum as a reference amount, they may not impose a minimum income level below which it will be presumed that the person concerned does not have sufficient resources, irrespective of a specific examination of the situation of each person concerned . . . .

69. Furthermore, it is clear from recital 16 in the preamble to [the Citizenship] Directive 2004/38 that, in order to determine whether a person receiving social assistance has become an unreasonable burden on its social assistance system, the host Member State should, before adopting an expulsion measure, examine whether the person concerned is experiencing temporary difficulties and take into account the duration of residence of the person concerned, his personal circumstances, and the amount of aid which has been granted to him.

70. Lastly, it should be borne in mind that, since the right to freedom of movement is – as a fundamental principle of EU law – the general rule, the conditions laid down in Article 7(1)(b) of [the Citizenship] Directive . . . must be construed narrowly . . . and in compliance with the limits imposed by EU law and the principle of proportionality . . . .

71. In addition, the margin for manoeuvre which the Member States are recognised as having must not be used by them in a manner which would compromise attainment of the objective of [the Citizenship] Directive . . ., which is, inter alia, to facilitate and strengthen the exercise of Union citizens' primary right to move and reside freely within the territory of the Member States, and the practical effectiveness of that directive . . . .

72. By making the right of residence for a period of longer than three months conditional upon the person concerned not becoming an 'unreasonable' burden on the social assistance 'system' of the host Member State, Article 7(1)(b) of [the Citizenship] Directive . . ., interpreted in the light of recital 10 to that directive, means that the competent national authorities have the power to assess, taking into account a range of factors in the light of the principle of proportionality, whether the grant of a social security benefit could place a burden on that Member State's social assistance system as a whole. [The Citizenship] Directive . . . thus recognises a certain degree of financial solidarity between nationals of a host Member State and nationals of other Member States, particularly if the difficulties which a beneficiary of the right of residence encounters are temporary . . . .

. . .

75. It can be seen from paragraphs 64 to 72 above that the mere fact that a national of a Member State receives social assistance is not sufficient to show that he constitutes an unreasonable burden on the social assistance system of the host Member State.

76. As regards the legislation at issue in the main proceedings, it is clear from the explanation provided by the Austrian Government at the hearing that, although the amount of the compensatory supplement depends on the financial situation of the person concerned as measured against the reference amount fixed for granting that supplement, the mere fact that a national of another Member State who is not economically active has applied for that benefit is sufficient to preclude that national from receiving it, regardless of the duration of residence, the amount of the benefit and the period for which it is available, that is to say, regardless of the burden which that benefit places on the host Member State's social assistance system as a whole.

77. Such a mechanism, whereby nationals of other Member States who are not economically active are automatically barred by the host Member State from receiving a particular social security benefit, even for the period following the first three months of residence referred to in Article 24(2) of the Citizenship Directive . . ., does not enable the competent authorities of the host Member State. . . to carry out – in accordance with the requirements under, inter alia, Articles 7(1)(b) and 8(4) of that directive and the principle of proportionality – an overall assessment of the specific burden which granting that benefit would place on the social assistance system as a whole by reference to the personal circumstances characterising the individual situation of the person concerned.

78. In particular, in a case such as that before the referring court, it is important that the competent authorities of the host Member State are able, when examining the application of a Union citizen who is not economically active and is in Mr Brey's position, to take into account, inter alia, the following: the amount and the regularity of the income which he receives; the fact that those factors have led those authorities to issue him with a certificate of residence; and the period during which the benefit applied for is likely to be granted to him. In addition, in order to ascertain more precisely the extent of the burden which that grant would place on the national social assistance system, it may be relevant, as the Commission argued at the hearing, to determine the proportion of the beneficiaries of that benefit who are Union citizens in receipt of a retirement pension in another Member State."

5.82 *Brey* was considered by the Upper Tribunal in *VP v SSWP (JSA)* [2014] UKUT 32 (AAC). For the reasons given are paras 71-79 of his decision, Judge Ward held that "*Brey* is concerned with what follows where a right of residence has arisen in the first place": it does not operate to confer a right of residence on a claimant who has not previously had such a right.

Judge Ward also expressed the view (at para.84) that the requirement for a person to have sufficient resources not to become a burden on the social assistance system of the United Kingdom "during his period of residence" meant that:

"a person wishing to assert self-sufficiency at the beginning of a five year period (with a view to subsequent permanent residence) would have to point to "resources" to see them through five years. . . . [i]t may often be the case . . . that consideration is only given to the topic at the end of the five year period when a right of permanent residence is asserted (whether as part of a benefit claim or otherwise). . . . In my view the question, whenever asked, remains: was the person at the beginning of year 1 – and in principle at any other times in the period – able to show sufficient resources to meet the test? I do not accept that a person who could not meet the test on that basis could simply lie low for five years and through a combination of luck and an unusually frugal lifestyle avoid being any kind of burden to the social assistance system and then argue that they have retrospectively shown that they had throughout had the resources to be self-sufficient."

In *Gusa v Minister for Social Protection, Attorney General, Ireland* (Case C-442/16), Advocate General Wathelet recomended that the Court should rule that art.16(1) of the Citizenship Directive confers a right of permanent residence on a Member State national who has resided in the territory of the host Member State for an uninterrupted period of five years without relying on the social assistance system of that host Member State. However, the Court did not follow that recommendation.

The requirement for (in para.64 of *Brey*) for "an overall assessment of the specific burden which granting that benefit would place on the national social assistance system as a whole, by reference to the personal circumstances characterising the individual situation of the person concerned" may seem to conflict with the subsequent decisions of the CJEU in *Dano v Jobcenter Leipzig* (C-333/13), *Jobcenter Berlin Neukölln v Alimanovic* (Case C-67/14) and *Vestische Arbeit Jobcenter Kreis Recklinghausen v Garcia-Nieto and others* (C-299/14) and with the decision of the Supreme Court in *Mirga v Secretary of State for Work and Pensions* [2016] UKSC 1 (see below). However, those decisions were dealing with a different issue. None of the claimants in *Dano, Alimanovic, Garcia-Nieto* or *Mirga* was claiming to be self-sufficient. They all accepted—or were the subject of final findings of fact—that they did not fall within any head of art.7. Rather they argued that the principle of equal treatment required that they should receive social assistance in a Member State of which they were not a national on the same basis as those who were nationals of that State, which in turn raised the question of the scope of the derogation in art.24(2). Such derogations have to be applied proportionately but the CJEU and Supreme Court held that the Citizenship Directive itself ensured proportionality, so that there was no need for an individual assessment in such cases. That is very different from saying that an individual assessment is not required when a claimant is saying that he has a right of residence under art.7(1)(b) in circumstances where art.8(4) provides that:

"Member States may not lay down a fixed amount which they regard as "sufficient resources", *but must take into account the personal situation of the person concerned*" (emphasis added).

In other words, by requiring an individual assessment of the "unreasonable burden" question in the context of a claim to be self-sufficient, Brey does no more than give effect to what the Citizenship Directive says.

Comprehensive sickness insurance

SG v Tameside MBC (HB) also considered the requirement for "comprehensive sickness insurance". In that appeal, the claimant, a Polish national who had been living in Sweden for many years and was receiving Swedish invalidity benefit in the UK under the provisions of the former Regulation (EEC) No. 1408/71. The Upper Tribunal accepted a concession from the Secretary of State that the claimant could rely on the UK's right to the reimbursement of healthcare costs under arts 27–34 of that Regulation and art.95 of Regulation (EEC) No. 574/72 as meeting the requirement for comprehensive sickness insurance. However, in *SSWP v HH (SPC)* [2015] UKUT 583 (AAC), it was emphasised that, under art.28a of Regulation 1408/71 the Member State competent in respect of pensions was only responsible for the costs of healthcare "to the extent that the pensioner and members of his family would have been entitled to such benefits under the legislation [of that Member State] if they resided in the territory of [that] Member State". Whether a claimant and her/his family members would have been so entitled was a question of foreign law that had to be proved by evidence: see paras 5-6 of *HH*.

The rights of reimbursement referred to in *SG v Tameside MBC (HB)* are now to be found in arts 35 and 41 of Regulation (EC) 883/2004 and arts 62-86 of Regulation (EC) 987/2009.

5.83

In *SSWP v GS(PC)* [2016] UKUT 394 (AAC), [2017] AACR 7, the Upper Tribunal considered the position of an Italian National who held an EHIC card issued by Italy which entitled him to medical benefits in kind (*i.e.,* in this case, NHS treatment) "during a stay in the territory of another Member State": see art.19 of Regulation (EC) 883/2004 (equivalent to art.22(1)(a) of the former Regulation (EEC) 1408/71) and art.25 of Regulation (EC) 987/2009 (equivalent to art.21 of Regulation (EEC) 574/72). In some circumstances, the UK would have been entitled to seek reimbursement from Italy for the costs of any such treatment. But whether those circumstances exist in any given case raises complicated issues of law and fact, particularly as to whether the UK has become the competent state—in which case no reimbursement would be possible—and at what point a "stay" (defined by art.1(k) of Regulation (EC) 883/2004 as meaning "temporary residence") becomes "residence" (defined by art.1(j) as meaning "habitual residence"): see the decision of the CJEU in *I v Health Service Executive* C-255/13. In *GS*, Judge Ward held that the claimant had become habitually resident in the UK and that the UK therefore would have had no right to seek reimbursement of NHS costs from Italy merely because he held an EHIC card. However, Judge Ward added (at para.40):

> "40. It does not however follow from what I have said that there are no circumstances in which reliance could be placed on an EHIC as amounting to CSIC. The conditions governing the scope of the coverage must be considered and applied to the circumstances of the case. While, as C-255/13–with its exceptional facts–demonstrates, very lengthy periods would not necessarily always be precluded from constituting a "stay", it will be for temporary–and so, in practice though not as a matter of law, probably shorter–periods that such reliance is most likely to be possible."

In the absence of a right to reimbursement from another Member State, the ability to obtain free medical treatment under the National Health Service does not amount to comprehensive sickness insurance (see *Ahmad v Secretary of State for the Home Department* [2014] EWCA Civ 988; *FK (Kenya) v Secretary of State for the Home Department* [2010] EWCA Civ 1302; *W (China) and X (China) v Secretary of State for the Home Department* [2006] EWCA Civ 1494 and *VP v SSWP (JSA)* [2014] UKUT 32 (AAC) at paras 98-105).

It follows from the decision in *Ahmad* that the observations made by Judge Rowland in *SSWP v SW (IS)* [2011] UKUT 508 (AAC) at [20] and by the Chief Commissioner of Northern Ireland in *AS v HMRC (CB)* at para.128 (xi) and (xii) do not correctly state the law.

Students

5.84   Under the definition in para.(1)(d), the students who have a right of residence are those who are "enrolled, for the principal purpose of following a course of study (including vocational training), at a public or private establishment which is . . . financed from public funds; or . . . otherwise recognised by the Secretary of State as an establishment which has been accredited for the purpose of providing such courses or training within the law or administrative practice of the part of the United Kingdom in which the establishment is located".

It is necessary for students to make a declaration to the Secretary of State (or satisfy him in some other manner) that they have sufficient resources to avoid them (and any family members) becoming a burden on the social assistance system of the United Kingdom" (see reg.4(1)(d)). For the level of resources that is sufficient, and the approach to be taken where a student claims an income-related benefit, see the note on "self-sufficient persons" (above).

It is also necessary for students to have comprehensive sickness insurance cover in the United Kingdom (see the discussion under *Comprehensive sickness insurance,* above). From April 6, 2015 such insurance must cover family members as well as the student (see the amendment to reg.4(2) and (3) of the 2006 Regulations by reg.4 of SI 2015/694 and para.(3)(b)).

In *CIS/419/2007*, the Commissioner held that a Polish single parent intercalating student who was not looking for work does not have a right of residence under the former Directive 93/96/EEC.

Paragraph (5): see the commentary to reg.16, below. 5.85

"Worker or self-employed person who has ceased activity"

5.—(1) In these Regulations, "worker or self-employed person who has 5.86
ceased activity" means an EEA national who satisfies a condition in paragraph (2), (3), (4) or (5).

(2) The condition in this paragraph is that the person—

(a) terminates activity as a worker or self-employed person and—

    (i) had reached the age of entitlement to a state pension on termi-
nating that activity; or

    (ii) in the case of a worker, ceases working to take early retirement;

(b) pursued activity as a worker or self-employed person in the United
Kingdom for at least 12 months prior to the termination; and

(c) resided in the United Kingdom continuously for more than three
years prior to the termination.

(3) The condition in this paragraph is that the person terminates activity
in the United Kingdom as a worker or self-employed person as a result of
permanent incapacity to work; and—

(a) had resided in the United Kingdom continuously for more than two
years [¹ immediately] prior to the termination; or

(b) the incapacity is the result of an accident at work or an occupational
disease that entitles the person to a pension payable in full or in part
by an institution in the United Kingdom.

(4) The condition in this paragraph is that the person—

(a) is active as a worker or self-employed person in an EEA State but
retains a place of residence in the United Kingdom and returns, as a
rule, to that place at least once a week; and

(b) [¹ immediately] prior to becoming so active in the EEA State, had
been continuously resident and continuously active as a worker or
self-employed person in the United Kingdom for at least three years.

(5) A person who satisfied the condition in paragraph (4)(a) but not the
condition in paragraph (4)(b) must, for the purposes of paragraphs (2) and
(3), be treated as being active and resident in the United Kingdom during
any period during which that person is working or self-employed in the
EEA State.

(6) The conditions in paragraphs (2) and (3) as to length of residence and
activity as a worker or self-employed person do not apply in relation to a
person whose spouse or civil partner is a British citizen.

(7) Subject to regulation 6(2), periods of—

(a) inactivity for reasons not of the person's own making;

(b) inactivity due to illness or accident; and

(c) in the case of a worker, involuntary unemployment duly recorded by
the relevant employment office,

must be treated as periods of activity as a worker or self-employed person,
as the case may be.

AMENDMENT

1. Immigration (European Economic Area) (Amendment) Regulations 2019 (SI
2019/1155) reg.2(1) and (3) (August 15, 2019).

DEFINITION

> "civil partner"—see reg.2(1).
> "EEA national"—*ibid.*
> "EEA State"—*ibid.*
> Self-employed person—see reg.4(1)(b).
> "spouse"—*ibid.*
> "worker"—see reg.4(1)(a).

GENERAL NOTE

5.87   Workers and self-employed persons who have ceased activity have a permanent right of residence under reg.15(1)(c) and art.17, even if they have lived in the UK for less than five years. This regulation implements the conditions established by art.17 for the exercise of that right.

There are three routes to the status of a worker or self-employed person who has ceased activity. They are set out in paras (2) to (4).

Paragraph (2) implements art.17(1)(a). It applies to people who have resided continuously in the UK for more than three years and worked in the UK as a worker or a self-employed person for at least 12 months and who then "terminate activity as a worker or self-employed person"—or, in plain English, retire. To qualify under this paragraph, the former worker or self-employed person must have reached state pension age before terminating activity or, if s/he was a worker, have ceased working to take early retirement. In *AT v Pensionsversicherungsanstalt* (Case C-32/19) the CJEU rejected an interpretation of art.17, under which the requirements of a year's work and three years' residence only applied to those taking early retirement and not those ceasing work after reaching retirement age. It follows that para.(2) correctly implements art.17(a) of the Directive.

Ceasing paid employment to take early retirement requires a definitive step by the worker or self-employed person to leave the labour market and one which involves a positive decision by the worker or self-employed person to take early retirement. It is not simply a status that may be identified retrospectively by the application of hindsight. How such a positive decision is shown will be a matter for the evidence in the individual case. It may, most obviously, be shown by the person accessing some early retirement allowance or pension from an employer or private/occupational pension provider: see *JP v SSWP (ESA)* [2018] UKUT 161 (AAC) at para.39.

Paragraph (3) implements art.17(1)(b). It applies to people terminating activity as a worker or self-employed person as a result of permanent incapacity for work. The former worker or self-employed person must also either have resided continuously in the UK for more than two years before terminating activity or have become permanently incapable of work as a result of an accident at work or an occupational disease that entitles him or her to "a pension payable in full or in part by an institution in the United Kingdom". It is suggested that industrial injuries disablement benefit would amount to such a pension as would employment and support allowance. However, public service pensions payable following early retirement on medical grounds may also count as—depending on the meaning of "institution"—a private occupational pension payable in those circumstances.

Paragraph (4) implements art.17(1)(c). It applies to cross-border workers.

Legal or actual residence?

5.88   The word "reside" in Article 17(1)(a) of the Citizens Directive and reg.5 means "actually reside" and not "legally reside": see the decision of the Supreme Court in Secretary of State for Work and Pensions v Gubeladze [2019] UKSC 31 (at paras 76-92) overruling the decision of the Court of Appeal ([2017] EWCA Civ 1751) and upholding the decision of Upper Tribunal Judge Ward in TG v SSWP (PC) [2015] UKUT 50 (AAC). The earlier decision of Upper Tribunal Judge Jacobs in ID v SSWP (IS) [2011] UKUT 401 (AAC), which is to the contrary effect, is no longer good law.

"Qualified person"

6.—(1) In these Regulations—   5.89
"jobseeker" means an EEA national who satisfies conditions A, B and, where relevant, C;
"qualified person" means a person who is an EEA national and in the United Kingdom as—
(a) a jobseeker;
(b) a worker;
(c) a self-employed person;
(d) a self-sufficient person; or
(e) a student;
"relevant period" means—
(a) in the case of a person retaining worker status under paragraph (2)
    (b) [¹ or self-employed person status under paragraph (4)(b)], a continuous period of six months;
(b) in the case of a jobseeker, 91 days, minus the cumulative total of any days during which the person concerned previously enjoyed a right to reside as a jobseeker, not including any days prior to a continuous absence from the United Kingdom of at least 12 months.
(2) A person who is no longer working must continue to be treated as a worker provided that the person—
(a) is temporarily unable to work as the result of an illness or accident;
(b) is in duly recorded involuntary unemployment after having been employed in the United Kingdom for at least one year, provided the person—
    (i) has registered as a jobseeker with the relevant employment office; and
    (ii) satisfies conditions A and B;
(c) is in duly recorded involuntary unemployment after having been employed in the United Kingdom for less than one year, provided the person—
    (i) has registered as a jobseeker with the relevant employment office; and
    (ii) satisfies conditions A and B;
(d) is involuntarily unemployed and has embarked on vocational training; or
(e) has voluntarily ceased working and has embarked on vocational training that is related to the person's previous employment.
(3) A person to whom paragraph (2)(c) applies may only retain worker status for a maximum of six months.
[¹ (4) A person who is no longer in self-employment must continue to be treated as a self-employed person provided that the person—
(a) is temporarily unable to engage in activities as a self-employed person as the result of an illness or accident;
(b) is in duly recorded involuntary unemployment after having worked as a self-employed person in the United Kingdom for at least one year provided the person—

    (i) has registered as a jobseeker with the relevant employment office; and

    (ii) satisfies conditions D and E;

(c) is in duly recorded involuntary unemployment after having worked as a self-employed person in the United Kingdom for less than one year, provided the person—

    (i) has registered as a jobseeker with the relevant employment office; and

    (ii) satisfies conditions D and E;

(d) is involuntarily no longer in self-employment and has embarked on vocational training; or

(e) has voluntarily ceased self-employment and has embarked on vocational training that is related to the person's previous occupation.

(4A) A person to whom paragraph (4)(c) applies may only retain self-employed person status for a maximum of six months.

(4B) Condition D is that the person—

(a) entered the United Kingdom as a self-employed person or in order to seek employment as a self-employed person; or

(b) is present in the United Kingdom seeking employment or self-employment, immediately after enjoying a right to reside under sub-paragraphs (c) to (e) of the definition of qualified person in paragraph (1) (disregarding any period during which self-employed status was retained pursuant to paragraph (4)(b) or (c)).

(4C) Condition E is that the person provides evidence of seeking employment or self-employment and having a genuine chance of being engaged.]

(5) Condition A is that the person—

(a) entered the United Kingdom in order to seek employment; or

(b) is present in the United Kingdom seeking employment, immediately after enjoying a right to reside under [¹ sub-paragraphs (b), (d) or (e)] of the definition of qualified person in paragraph (1) (disregarding any period during which worker status was retained pursuant to paragraph (2)(b) or (c)).

(6) Condition B is that the person provides evidence of seeking employment and having a genuine chance of being engaged.

(7) A person may not retain the status of—

(a) a worker under paragraph (2)(b); [¹ ...]

(b) a jobseeker; [¹ or

(c) a self-employed person under paragraph (4)(b)]

for longer than the relevant period without providing compelling evidence of continuing to seek employment and having a genuine chance of being engaged.

(8) Condition C applies where the person concerned has, previously, enjoyed a right to reside under this regulation as a result of satisfying Conditions A and B [¹ or, as the case may be, conditions D and E]—

(a) in the case of a person to whom paragraph (2)(b) or (c) [¹ or (4)(b) or (c)] applied, for at least six months; or

(b) in the case of a jobseeker, for at least 91 days in total,

unless the person concerned has, since enjoying the above right to reside, been continuously absent from the United Kingdom for at least 12 months.

(9) Condition C is that the person has had a period of absence from the United Kingdom.

(10) Where condition C applies—

(a) paragraph (7) does not apply; and

(b) condition B [¹ or, as the case may be, condition E] has effect as if "compelling" were inserted before "evidence".

AMENDMENT

1. Immigration (European Economic Area) (Amendment) Regulations 2018 (SI 2018/801) reg.2 and Sch., para.2 (July 24, 2018).

DEFINITION

"EEA national"—see reg.2(1).
"right to reside"—*ibid.*
"Self-employed person"—see reg.4(1)(b).
"self-sufficient person"—see reg.4(1)(c).
"student"—see reg.4(1)(d).
"worker"—see reg.4(1)(a).

GENERAL NOTE

Regulation 6 specifies the categories of EEA National who are "qualified persons", namely jobseekers, workers, self-employed persons, self-sufficient persons and students. Qualified persons have an extended right of residence under reg.14 and residence as a qualified person counts towards the continuous period of five years' residence required by reg.15(1)(a) for the acquisition of a permanent right of residence. They are also exempt from the habitual residence test (see reg.21AA(4) of the IS Regulations, reg.85A(4) of the JSA Regulations 1996, and reg.2(4) of the SPC Regulations and reg.9(4) of the Universal Credit Regulations).

5.90

British nationals are not "EEA nationals" for the purposes of the 2016 Regulations even if they are dual nationals of another Member State (see the definition of that phrase in reg.2(1)). From October 16, 2012, they can only be "qualified persons" if they benefit from the transitional provisions in para.9 of Sch.6.

For commentary on who counts as a worker, self-employed person, self-sufficient person or a student, see the General Note to reg.4.

Persons who retain the status of worker and "jobseekers"

Under para.(2) it is possible for people who were, but are not now, workers to retain that status. EEA nationals who have not previously worked in the UK—or who have ceased to be members of the UK labour market since they last worked here—but are looking for work potentially have a right to reside as "jobseekers".

5.91

The use of "jobseeker" in this context is unfortunate. In domestic UK social security law, "jobseeker" is used colloquially to describe anyone who claims JSA or, possibly, jobseeking credits. But such a person may be a worker (because part-time work may be genuine and effective but the claimant may be looking for full-time employment), a person who has retained worker status, or a "jobseeker" in the sense described above. The rights of residence that attach to each of those categories are different and it is therefore important not to assume that a person is a "jobseeker" merely because they are claiming JSA.

In particular, it can be difficult to distinguish those who are retaining worker status on the basis of involuntary employment and those who are "mere" jobseekers. However, the rights of the two groups are markedly different because Member States are not obliged to pay social assistance to nationals of other member states whose only right of residence is as a jobseeker, and in that respect, are not obliged to treat jobseekers equally with their own nationals (see *Jobcenter Berlin Neukölln v Alimanovic* (Case C-67/14)). In practice this means that:

- A right to reside as a jobseeker (or the family member of a jobseeker) only counts for the purposes of JSA. This is because the UK seems to accept that JSA is not social assistance but a benefit designed to facilitate access to the labour market and, therefore, the UK has to treat EEA nationals equally in relation to it. In contrast, those who retain worker status *also* have a right to reside for the purposes of ESA, IS, SPC, housing benefit and, increasingly importantly, universal credit. Jobseekers do not. (Note, in this context, that the Housing Benefit (Habitual Residence) Amendment Regulations 2014 (SI 2014/539), which removed entitlement to housing benefit from jobseekers with effect from April 1, 2014 is neither *ultra vires*—see the decision of the three-judge panel of the UT in *IC v Glasgow City Council and SSWP (HB)* [2016] UKUT 321 (AAC), [2017] AACR 1—nor contrary to the ECHR: see the decision of the Court of Appeal in Northern Ireland in *Stach v Department for Communities and Department for Work and Pensions* [2020] NICA 4.)

- If a person who retains worker status becomes ill, s/he may continue to retain worker status on the basis that s/he is temporarily incapable of work. This means s/he can receive ESA. If a jobseeker becomes too ill to work, s/he ceases to be entitled to JSA and cannot receive ESA because s/he does not have a right to reside that counts for ESA purposes.

- To qualify for JSA, jobseekers have to show that they are actually habitually resident in the UK. This means that jobseekers are also subject to the three-months' test (see the commentary to reg.21AA of the IS Regulations). Those who retain worker status do not have to be actually habitually resident (although they often will be) because they are exempt from the HRT (see reg.85A(4)(za) of the JSA Regulations 1996) and do not need to have lived in the UK for the past three months.

Given the importance of the distinction and the potential for confusion, previous editions of this work have fought a rearguard action to retain the use of the word "workseeker", which, before the Citizenship Directive, was the word used to describe those who are now called "jobseekers". More than ten years later, the time has come to admit defeat and this edition now uses "jobseeker" except when quoting directly from cases in which the judge has used "workseeker". However, a surrender over nomenclature does not mean that the distinction between jobseekers who claim JSA and workers (including those retaining that status) who claim JSA is any less important.

Retaining worker status

5.92 The rules about retaining worker status relate to people who do not have subsisting contracts of employment. Those who are still employed, even though, temporarily, they are not actually working, *e.g.*, because of illness or pregnancy or because they have been laid off, continue to be "workers" and therefore do not need to rely on the rules (see *CS v SSWP* [2009] UKUT 16 (AAC) and *CIS/185/2008* at para.8).

Although the Citizenship Directive and the 2016 Regulations contain detailed rules about the circumstances in which worker status is retained, the underlying principle by which those rules should be interpreted is whether the former worker continues to be in the labour market. As was explained by the Commissioner in *CIS/3789/2006* (at para.8):

"... It may seem harsh, but the status of a "worker" is accorded only to those actually engaged in economic activity in the labour market or as self-employed persons at the material time. Accepting that this description can extend to those temporarily unable to be at their work because of illness or accident, or an involuntary spell of unemployment, it is still not apt to include a person who has withdrawn from employment voluntarily and has been and remains economically inactive, neither in work nor seeking it: albeit for entirely proper and understandable practical reasons such as having had to take a break from the world of work because of the breakdown of a relationship and the continuing family responsibilities of having a young child under school age to look after and another one on the way"

See also the observations of the Court of Appeal to similar effect at paras 21 and 22 of *SSWP v Dias*.

Former workers who retain that status are treated as workers by these Regulations and are therefore qualified persons with an extended right of residence under reg.14. They are also exempt from the habitual residence test (see reg.21AA(4)(c), reg.85A(4) of the JSA Regulations, reg.2(4)(c) of the SPC Regulations, reg.70(4)(c) of the ESA Regulations 2008 and reg.9(4)(a) of the Universal Credit Regulations).

Whether worker status has been retained can involve a detailed analysis of the facts of the case. Tribunals need to investigate the issues and make proper findings of fact (see *SSWP v IR* [2009] UKUT 11 (AAC)).

In domestic UK law, the question is governed by reg.6(2), and (5) –(7), which implements art.7(3).

Temporarily unable to work

As used in reg.6(2)(a), inability to work is a concept of EU law and must be interpreted the same way throughout the EU *(CIS/4304/2007)*. It therefore does not depend upon the domestic legislation governing incapacity benefits in the individual member States. The Commissioner stated (at para.35): 5.93

"The context provides some guidance. It ensures continuity of worker status for someone who would otherwise be employed or looking for work. That employment or search for employment provides the touchstone against which the claimant's disabilities must be judged. The question is: can she fairly be described as unable to do the work she was doing or the sort of work that she was seeking?"

The meaning of "temporarily" was considered by the Commissioner in *CIS/3890/2005*. The tribunal had taken the view that a temporary incapacity was one "which had a certainty of recovery". The Commissioner stated:

"5. . . . The tribunal was entitled to take the view that the condition from which the claimant was suffering was a permanent one. However, it does not follow that incapacity was not temporary, if the claimant was to be regarded as incapable of work at all. The fact that the claimant had returned to work was sufficient to show that the condition was not one that would permanently incapacitate the claimant in respect of all work. (Although the return to work was after the date of the Secretary of State's decision, it was evidence that could be taken into account in considering what could have been anticipated at the date of that decision.) However, it is reasonable to consider a person to be incapable of work for a period after he or she has become incapable of following previous employment, even if there is other work that he or she might undertake. Moreover, the British system in respect of incapacity benefit deems a person to be incapable of work for benefit purposes if a personal capability assessment is satisfied and also pending such an assessment. Such a person may not actually be incapable of work and may be looking for a job. If such a person is not to be treated as incapable of work for the purposes of the 2000 Regulations, there would arise the question whether that person should be treated as a workseeker instead. However, there are practical difficulties in treating a person who is entitled to benefit on the basis of incapacity as a workseeker, not the least of which is arranging for registration as being available for work. There is therefore much to be said for what appears to be implied in the Secretary of State's submission, which is that a person should be treated as incapable of work if entitled to benefits on that basis.
6. It seems to me that the tribunal erred in assuming that because the claimant may have had a permanent disability, she was necessarily permanently incapable of work or, alternatively, in failing to consider whether she was a workseeker if she was not incapable of work. I therefore set aside the tribunal's decision and I accept the Secretary of State's suggestion that I should find that the claimant was temporarily incapable of work. . .".

In *Secretary of State for the Home Department v FB* [2010] UKUT 447 (IAC), a two-judge panel of the Upper Tribunal held that a "temporary" incapacity is one that is not "permanent". See also the decisions of the Court of Appeal in *De Brito v Secretary of State for the Home Department* [2012] EWCA Civ 709 (at para.33), *Konodyba v Royal Borough of Kensington & Chelsea* [2012] EWCA Civ 982 (at paras 18-23) and in *Samin v City of Westminster* [2012] EWCA Civ 1468 where the relevant law was summarised as follows (para.31):

> "Temporary is to be contrasted with permanent. The question is one of fact in every case; plainly the circumstances which will fall to be examined will vary infinitely. It will generally be helpful to ask whether there is or is not a realistic prospect of a return to work. It will generally not be helpful to ask if the interruption is indefinite; an indefinite absence from work may well not be temporary, but it might be, for example if an injured man is awaiting surgery which can be expected to restore him to fitness to work, but the date when it will be available is uncertain".

The meaning of "temporarily unable to work" was further considered by the Upper Tribunal (Judge Jacobs) in *HK v SSWP* [2017] UKUT 421 (AAC). After quoting from para.35 in his previous decision, CIS/4304/2007 he added:

> "4. ... In other words, the claimant's ability to work has to be decided as a purely factual matter without regard to the particular tests applied by domestic legislation, in this case the employment and support allowance legislation. This is subject to two qualifications.
> 5. First, there is a difference between the test that has to be applied and the evidence that is relevant to the test. Accordingly, the way that the employment and support allowance legislation would apply to the claimant may be relevant as evidence of inability to work.
> 6. Second, there is a difference between the basis of the right to reside and the entitlement to benefit. If the claimant wishes to claim for a period before the date when he submitted his claim, his entitlement during that period will be determined by the domestic legislation."

The temporary incapacity for work must be the result of an illness or accident suffered by the EEA national and not, for example, the illness of a dependent child—*CIS/3182/2005.*

Pregnancy

5.94   The position of pregnant women requires particular mention here.

Some pregnant women who are EEA nationals will be entitled to benefits that are not subject to the right to reside test or because they satisfy that test:

- A woman who has worked may have an entitlement to statutory maternity pay, maternity allowance or, in some very limited circumstances, incapacity benefit (none of which depends on her having a right to reside).

- A woman who still has a contract of employment but takes time off to give birth will still be a "worker" (in the same way as a person who takes leave for other reasons) and will therefore not need to show that she has "retained" that status (see *CIS/185/2008* at para.8 and *CIS/4237/2007* in which an A8 national was held to be legally working while on maternity leave).

However, for other women a problem arises because of the conditions of entitlement for IS, JSA and ESA under domestic law.

Under para.14 of Sch.1B to the IS Regulations, a woman falls within a prescribed category if she is "incapable of work by reason of pregnancy" and also during the period from eleven weeks before the expected week of confinement until seven weeks after the end of the pregnancy. Women in this category may claim IS but, subject to what is said below, may also claim JSA if they can satisfy the labour market conditions. Regulations 20(d) and (f) of the ESA Regulations (see Vol.I) treat pregnant women as having limited capability for work either if working would endanger their health or the health of the unborn child or (in the case of women with no entitlement to statutory maternity pay or maternity allowance) from the sixth week before the expected week of confinement and the fourteenth day after the actual date of confinement. A woman who is treated as having limited capability for work may not claim JSA and, if she is to be entitled to an income-related benefit at all, must claim either IS or ESA.

But many pregnant women who are EEA nationals will be unable to make such a claim. Those who have never worked in the UK (or have worked but since withdrawn from the labour-market) will, at most, have a right to reside as a jobseeker (in the narrow sense described below) and that right does not count for the purposes of IS or ESA. Women who have worked in the UK but who give up their jobs because of their pregnancies, or those who—when they became pregnant—were involuntarily unemployed (see below) and claiming JSA as a person who had retained worker status, need to rely on art.7 of the Citizenship Directive or reg.6(2)(a). In the past, they could not always do so. In an individual case a pregnant woman might be suffering from an illness by reason of her pregnancy (see *CIS/731/2007*) but pregnancy *per se* is not an "illness or accident" (*CIS/4010/2006* and the judgment of the ECJ in *Saint Prix* (below) at paras 29–30). The question therefore arises whether a woman who gives up employment (or the search for employment in cases where she was previously retaining worker status on the basis of involuntary unemployment) can retain (or continue to retain) worker status simply by virtue of being pregnant.

The answer to that question is yes. In *Saint Prix v Secretary of State for Work and Pensions* (Case C-507/12) [2014] AACR 18, the claimant was a French national who had worked until she was nearly six months pregnant but then gave up because the demands of her job had become too strenuous for her. She spent about a week looking for less strenuous work and then, at the beginning of the eleventh week before her expected date of confinement, she claimed income support. She returned to work three months after the premature birth of her child.

The Secretary of State refused her income support claim on the ground that she had no longer retained worker status. An appeal tribunal upheld her appeal against that decision. However, the Upper Tribunal (*JS v SSWP (IS)* [2010] UKUT 131 (AAC)) upheld the Secretary of State's appeal as did the Court of Appeal (*JS v Secretary of State for Work and Pensions* [2011] EWCA Civ 806, [2012] AACR 7). The claimant then appealed to the Supreme Court, which referred the following questions to the CJEU (see *Saint Prix v Secretary of State for Work and Pensions* [2012] UKSC 49):

"1. Is the right of residence conferred upon a 'worker' in Article 7 of the Citizenship Directive to be interpreted as applying only to those (i) in an existing employment relationship, (ii) (at least in some circumstances) seeking work, or (iii) covered by the extensions in article 7(3), or is the Article to be interpreted as not precluding the recognition of further persons who remain 'workers' for this purpose?

2. (i) If the latter, does it extend to a woman who reasonably gives up work, or seeking work, because of the physical constraints of the late stages of pregnancy (and the aftermath of childbirth)?

(ii) If so, is she entitled to the benefit of the national law's definition of when it is reasonable for her to do so?"

The CJEU answered those questions by ruling that:

"Article 45 TFEU must be interpreted as meaning that a woman who gives up work, or seeking work, because of the physical constraints of the late stages of pregnancy and the aftermath of childbirth retains the status of 'worker', within the meaning of that article, provided she returns to work or finds another job within a reasonable period after the birth of her child."

The Court's reasoning is set out at paras 38–46 of its judgment:

"38. . . . it cannot be argued, contrary to what the United Kingdom Government contends, that Article 7(3) of [the Citizenship] Directive lists exhaustively the circumstances in which a migrant worker who is no longer in an employment relationship may nevertheless continue to benefit from that status.

39. In the present case, ... Ms Saint Prix was employed in the territory of the United Kingdom before giving up work, less than three months before the birth of her child, because of the physical constraints of the late stages of pregnancy and the immediate aftermath of childbirth. She returned to work three months after the birth of her child, without having left the territory of that Member State during the period of interruption of her professional activity.

40. The fact that such constraints require a woman to give up work during the period needed for recovery does not, in principle, deprive her of the status of 'worker' within the meaning Article 45 TFEU.

41. The fact that she was not actually available on the employment market of the host Member State for a few months does not mean that she has ceased to belong to that market during that period, provided she returns to work or finds another job within a reasonable period after confinement ....

42. In order to determine whether the period that has elapsed between childbirth and starting work again may be regarded as reasonable, the national court concerned should take account of all the specific circumstances of the case in the main proceedings and the applicable national rules on the duration of maternity leave, in accordance with Article 8 of Council Directive 92/85/EEC of 19 October 1992 on the introduction of measures to encourage improvements in the safety and health at work of pregnant workers and workers who have recently given birth or are breastfeeding ...

43. The approach adopted in paragraph 41 of the present judgment is consistent with the objective pursued by Article 45 TFEU of enabling a worker to move freely within the territory of the other Member States and to stay there for the purpose of employment ....

44. As the Commission contends, a Union citizen would be deterred from exercising her right to freedom of movement if, in the event that she was pregnant in the host State and gave up work as a result, if only for a short period, she risked losing her status as a worker in that State.

45. Furthermore, it must be pointed out that EU law guarantees special protection for women in connection with maternity. In that regard, it should be noted that Article 16(3) of [the Citizenship] Directive provides, for the purpose of calculating the continuous period of five years of residence in the host Member State allowing Union citizens to acquire the right of permanent residence in that territory, that the continuity of that residence is not affected, inter alia, by an absence of a maximum of 12 consecutive months for important reasons such as pregnancy and childbirth.

46. If, by virtue of that protection, an absence for an important event such as pregnancy or childbirth does not affect the continuity of the five years of residence in the host Member State required for the granting of that right of residence, the physical constraints of the late stages of pregnancy and the immediate aftermath of childbirth, which require a woman to give up work temporarily, cannot, a fortiori, result in that woman losing her status as a worker."

Tribunals must therefore assess whether the woman has claimed IS or ESA because she gave up work, or seeking work, because of the physical constraints of the late stages of pregnancy and the aftermath of childbirth and, if so, whether—taking into account paras 40–42 of the judgment—she remains in the labour market. In *SSWP v SFF, ADR v SSWP, CS v LB Barnet & SSWP* [2015] UKUT 502, the Upper Tribunal considered a number of legal and practical issues arising from that assessment namely:

(a) What is the nature of the *Saint Prix* right: in particular, is it a right to be assessed prospectively or retrospectively?
(b) To whom is the *Saint Prix* right available?
(c) When does a *Saint Prix* right start?

(d) How long does the "reasonable period" last?

(e) Does a woman have to return to work (or find another job) or will a return to seeking work suffice?

(f) Can a *Saint Prix* right contribute to the period of time necessary to acquire the right of permanent residence under art.16 of Directive 2004/38?

Judge Ward answered those questions as follows:

(a) The *Saint Prix* right is to be assessed prospectively. The proviso in para.41 of the CJEU's judgment—namely that in order to retain worker status a formerly-pregnant woman should "[return] to work or find another job within a reasonable period after confinement"—did not create "a condition precedent to the [*Saint Prix*] right coming into existence, which would have the consequence that the existence of the right could only be assessed retrospectively, but . . . a condition subsequent for terminating it where it is not met . . .". The issue was "primarily one of the woman's intention, but subject to the special protection conferred by the CJEU's judgment". Approaching it in that way "means that a woman is protected by her worker status until such time, not exceeding the end of the "reasonable period" contemplated by para.47 of *Saint-Prix*, as she by her words or actions shows an intention not to be part of the employment market": see para.22 of *SFF*. This approach avoids the potential problem with s.12(8)(b) of the Social Security Act 1998, *i.e.,* that any return to work will often occur after the date of the decision under appeal.

(b) As is implicit in the CJEU's decision itself—and as was not in dispute in before the Upper Tribunal—the *Saint Prix* right is available to women who have exercised the right of freedom of movement for workers and have been employed in a Member State other than that of their residence and to those who by meeting the conditions of Article 7(3) retain worker status while looking for work. It has yet to be decided whether a "jobseeker" in the EU sense—*i.e.,* a woman who has never previously worked in the UK or who, having worked in the UK, has left the labour market but is now seeking work—can avail herself of the right. That is because none of the claimants in *SFF* fell within that category.

(c) Judge Ward ruled that "the 11th week before the expected date of childbirth which appears as the earliest permitted commencement of a maternity pay period and for payment of maternity allowance and, more importantly, as the start of the period when a claimant for income support fulfils, without more, the requirement to fall within a "prescribed category" of person . . . provides a convenient yardstick by which to assess whether the test is fulfilled but one that is capable of being displaced in particular cases".

(d) Contrary to the guidance issued by the Secretary of State in DMG Memo 25/14—which had advised decision makers that the maximum reasonable period was the 26 weeks during which a woman is entitled to ordinary maternity leave—Judge Ward ruled that the reasonable period is to be determined taking account of the 52-week period covered by the rights to ordinary and additional maternity leave and of the circumstances of the particular case: see para.35. He added:

"As a matter of practice rather than of law, it seems likely that it will be an unusual case in which the period is other than the 52 week period".

(e) A return to seeking work will suffice. Judge Ward accepted (at para.39) a submission from the Secretary of State, that:

"if a woman with rights under Article 7(3)(b) or (c) had to find a job within the reasonable period after childbirth rather than merely returning to qualifying work seeking, then she would have to do more as the result of leaving the labour market temporarily because of pregnancy and the aftermath of childbirth than if she had remained as a person with retained worker status under Article 7(3)(b) or (c)."

The same was true of a woman who was in employment at the beginning of the reasonable period but whose job had come to an end during that period (para.40). The reference in the CJEU's judgment to a condition that a woman "returns to work or finds another job" could be explained by the fact that that is what had happened on the facts of *Saint Prix* (para.41).

(f) The *Saint Prix* right does count towards the continuous period of legal residence necessary to acquire the right of permanent residence. The Secretary of State did not dispute that in *SFF* and therefore the reason why it is so is not explained. It is because a woman exercising the *Saint Prix* right retains worker status while she does so. Therefore, that period counts towards the qualifying residence period for the permanent right of residence in the same way as any other period of residence as a retained-status worker.

Note that receipt of maternity allowance does not lead to a woman automatically abandoning her worker status: see *Secretary of State for Work and Pensions v MM (IS)* [2015] UKUT 128 (AAC) at para.57.

Where a pregnant woman was formerly *self*-employed – and where self-employment does not continue while she is on maternity leave: see *HMRC v GP (final decision)* below – it remains to be decided whether *Saint Prix* can apply. In *HMRC v HD (CHB) (Second interim decision)* [2018] UKUT 148 (AAC), Judge Ward decided to refer the following question (or one substantially in the same form) to the CJEU:

"In circumstances where an EU citizen who is a national of one Member State (i) is present in another Member State (the host Member State), (ii) has been active as a self-employed person within the meaning of Article 49 TFEU in the host Member State, (iii) was paid a maternity allowance from May 2014 (a point at which she considered herself less able to work on account of pregnancy), (iv) has been found to have ceased to be in genuine and effective self-employed activity from July 2014, (v) gave birth in August 2014, and (vi) did not return to genuine and effective self-employed activity in the period following the birth and prior to claiming jobseekers' allowance as a jobseeker in February 2015:

Must Article 49 TFEU be interpreted as meaning that such a person, who ceases self-employed activity in circumstances where there are physical constraints in the late stages of pregnancy and the aftermath of childbirth, retains the status of being self-employed, within the meaning of that Article, provided she returns to economic activity or seeking work within a reasonable period after the birth of her child?"

Where a pregnant woman is wrongly advised to claim IS or ESA rather than JSA, see the discussion below.

Saint-Prix is a case which should be treated as being unique to the special circumstances with which it was concerned, *i.e.*, pregnancy. It is not an authority that provides any basis for drawing analogies with its circumstances: see *JS v SSWP (IS)* [2019] UKUT 135 (AAC) at para.33. In that case, the claimant—a Polish national—was told by social services that he had to give up work to look after his children or they would be take into care. However, he did not retain worker status by analogy with *Saint Prix*.

Involuntary unemployment

5.95 The provisions on involuntary unemployment in reg.6 of the 2016 Regulations purport to implement art.7(3)(b)–(d) of the Citizenship Directive. Until December 31, 2013, the equivalent provisions of the 2006 Regulations were more generous to claimants than art.7(3) strictly required. The provisions were substantially amended with effect from January 1, 2014, July 1, 2014 and November 10, 2014 and there must now be a question as to whether they are more restrictive than art.7(3) permits.

For the position until December 31, 2013, see pp.321-325 of Vol.II of the 2013-2014 edition. The position from January 1, 2014 to June 30, 2014 is set out at p.329 of Vol.II of the 2014–2015 edition. From July 1, 2014, the domestic law of the UK is as follows.

Under para.(2)(b) and (c), as drafted, EEA nationals who have ceased to be workers retain worker status if they are in duly recorded involuntary unemployment provided they have registered as a jobseeker with the relevant employment office and satisfy two conditions, namely Condition A and Condition B.

Condition A is that they either entered the United Kingdom in order to seek employment or are present in the United Kingdom seeking employment, immediately after enjoying a right to reside as a worker, a self-employed person, a self-sufficient person, or as a student: see para.(5). When applying the "immediately after" test, "any period during which worker status was retained" is disregarded.

Condition B is that they "can provide evidence that [they are] seeking employment and [have] a genuine chance of being engaged": see reg.6(6).

Under para.(2)(c) and (3), EEA nationals who have been employed in the UK for less than a year, cannot retain worker status for longer than six months.

Under reg.6(2)(b) and (7), EEA nationals who have been employed in the UK for at least a year may retain the status of worker for longer than six months but only if they can provide "compelling evidence" that they are continuing to seek employment and have a genuine chance of being engaged.

However, in *KH v Bury MBC and SSWP* [2020] UKUT 50 (AAC), the Upper Tribunal (Judge Wright) held that, for those who had worked in the UK for at least a year—i.e., those within reg.6(2)(b)—the requirement to provide evidence of "having a genuine chance of being engaged" was contrary to EU law and that the FTT had erred by applying reg.6(2)(b)(ii) (as it relates to Condition B) and (7) to such a claimant. The judge accepted the submission made by CPAG on behalf of the appellant as follows:

> "38. The crux of the appellant's argument, which I accept, is that EU law draws a distinction between mere workseekers (i.e. what are termed 'jobseekers' under regulation 6(1)(a) of the 2006 EEA Regs), primarily those who have never worked in the Member State in which they are seeking work, and those who have worked in the Member State in question (here the UK) and have become 'workers' by so doing and who then retain that worker status by remaining in the labour market and looking for work.
> 39. For the latter group ... their status as persons who have worked in the Member State is recognised by the differing periods for which that status may be retained depending on the length of time they previously worked in the Member State. A person who has worked for less than a year retains the status of worker for no less than six months under Article 7(3)(c) of the Directive, provided he or she is involuntarily unemployed and has registered as a jobseeker with the relevant employment office. The person who has worked for more than one year has no temporal limitation on the period when his or her worker status may be maintained under Article 7(3)(b), provided he or she is involuntarily unemployed and has registered as a jobseeker with the relevant employment office. The retention for this second category of person is indefinite. But beyond this, those who have been employed for more than a year are entitled under EU law to retain worker status for as long as they remain involuntarily employed in the labour market and registered as a jobseeker at the employment office. It is no part of meeting those requirements, however, that such a person must show they have a genuine chance of being engaged in employment. By contrast, the test of a genuine chance of being engaged in employment is an appropriate means of identifying whether mere workseekers continue to have a connection with the Member State's employment or labour markets."

By implication, the decision in *KH* also applies to those who have worked in the UK for less than a year during the six month period specified in reg.6(3). However, for the reasons given in the passage quoted above, it does not apply to those who are jobseekers (in the narrow meaning of "mere workseekers").

The Secretary of State was given permission to appeal to the Court of Appeal against the decision in *KH,* but it is understood that the appeal will not be pursued.

EEA nationals who cease to retain worker status under the six months rule but remain in the UK and continue to seek work will become "jobseekers" (see below) if they continue to satisfy Condition A (as they inevitably will), Condition B and (where relevant) an additional condition ("Condition C").

The meaning of "voluntary" (and hence "involuntary") unemployment was considered by the Commissioner in *CIS/3315/2005*. Following *R(IS) 12/98*, he held that the term:

> ". . . must be regarded as focussing on the question whether the claimant is still in the labour market rather than on the circumstances in which he or she ceased to be employed, although the latter may be relevant as evidence as to whether the clamant is still genuinely in the labour market".

It was therefore unnecessary for the claimant to argue that she was forced to give up her job by her circumstances and therefore did not give it up voluntarily and, depending on those circumstances—for example, if she were unable to work or be available for work because of child care responsibilities—such an argument would be detrimental to her case.

An EU citizen who retains worker status by virtue of reg.6(2)(b) will not lose that worker status merely because his or her JSA is disallowed on the grounds of "not actively seeking work: see *SSWP v WN (rule 17)* [2018] UKUT 268 (AAC).

"Duly recorded" and "registered as a jobseeker"

5.96   The Commissioner in *CIS/3315/2005* also considered the requirement (in the 2000 Regulations) that such unemployment should be "duly recorded by the relevant employment office" and accepted a concession from the Secretary of State that the requirement was met by an income support claimant who declared that s/he was seeking work at the first opportunity (in this case in answer to a question on the "Right To Reside Stencil"). The Commissioner left open the question of whether an income support claimant who was in fact looking for work but, for some reason, answered "no" to that question would nevertheless meet the requirement.

The position from April 30, 2006 was less clear but has now been clarified. From that date, it was no longer sufficient for claimants to be in "duly recorded involuntary unemployment": they also had to have "registered as a jobseeker with the relevant employment office" (arts 7(3)(b) and (c) of the Citizenship Directive and reg.6(2)(b) of the 2006 Regulations). In *CIS/3799/2007* (paras 17 and 18) and *CIS/184/2008*, the Secretary of State did not repeat the concession that had been made in *CIS/3315/2005*. The Commissioner held that, in order to satisfy the additional requirement of registration as a jobseeker with the relevant employment office, a claimant must claim JSA rather than IS. However, in *SSWP v FE* [2009] UKUT 287 (AAC) a Three-Judge Panel decided (by a majority, Walker J., CP, and Judge Ward, Judge Howell QC dissenting) that claiming JSA or registering for NI credits were not the only means of "registering as a jobseeker". Summarising its conclusions, the majority stated:

> "29. We conclude that the Secretary of State has not shown that the UK has defined specific mechanisms as being the only ways in which an individual can, for the purposes of Article 7(3)(c) "register as a jobseeker with the relevant employment office". That being so, the tribunal was entitled to hold that the Secretary of State's factual concessions meant that the claimant succeeded in her appeal. In summary:
>
> a. What the Directive contemplates is that a claimant has done what is needed in order to have his or her name recorded as looking for work by the relevant employment office
> b. Whether or not this has been done is a question of fact
> c. There is no rule of law that such registration can be effected only by way of registering for jobseeker's allowance or national insurance credits, less still only by successfully claiming one or other of those benefits

   d. Nor was there at the material time an administrative practice to that effect (even assuming—without deciding—that to be a lawful way of implementing the Directive)

   e. Successfully claiming jobseeker's allowance or national insurance credits will no doubt provide sufficient evidence to satisfy Article 7(3)(c); but

   f. Those who are able to show not merely that they were seeking work, but that they had done what is needed in order to have their name recorded as looking for work by the relevant employment office—will meet the registration requirement of Article 7(3)(c).

   g. It being conceded that the claimant had stated on the Habitual Residence Test documents that she was seeking work and that the extent of the work being sought was sufficient, it follows that she met the relevant test."

Therefore, the claimant who (as the Secretary of State conceded, the relevant documents having been lost) had ticked the "Yes" box on the HRT2 form in response to the question "Are you looking for work in the UK?" and was actually seeking work retained her former worker status. The decision of the majority of the Upper Tribunal in *SSWP v FE* was subsequently upheld by the Court of Appeal in *Secretary of State for Work and Pensions v Elmi* [2011] EWCA Civ 1403, [2012] AACR 22.

This issue highlights the unfortunate consequences that can flow from the use of the word "jobseeker" to denote what the French text of the Citizenship Directive describes as a *demandeur d'emploi* and what EU law previously described as a "workseeker": see above. If the English text had required those who wished to retain worker status to register "as a workseeker" with the relevant employment office, no one would have thought that requirement necessarily involved making a claim for JSA.

The decision in *FE* means that former workers who retain worker status may be entitled to claim IS. However, they would be much better advised to claim JSA. The risk with claiming IS is that the efforts of IS claimants' to find work are not actively monitored by the Department. It will therefore be up to them to prove that they satisfy Conditions A and B (above) and (where relevant) Condition C (below). If they are unable to do so, they will be classed as jobseekers, and therefore not entitled to IS.

Participation in a work-focused interview by an IS claimant does not amount to or involve registration for work: see *SSWP v ZW* [2009] UKUT 25 (AAC). The decision was doubted by Maurice Kay LJ in *Elmi* (at para.20) but has not been overruled and remains binding, at least on the First-tier Tribunal.

Two further issues arise. The first is whether, in order to satisfy the requirement of registration, the claim for JSA (or IS) must be made immediately after the cessation of employment. The second concerns the position of the, mostly female, claimants who are wrongly advised by the DWP to claim IS or ESA rather than JSA.

The first issue was considered by the Commissioner in *CIS/1934/2006* (at para.8) and *CIS/0519/2007* and by the Upper Tribunal in *SSWP v IR (IS)* [2009] UKUT 11 (AAC), *SSWP v MK (IS)* [2013] UKUT 163 (AAC) and *VP v SSWP (JSA)* [2014] UKUT 32 (AAC) (AAC), [2014] AACR 25. In *IR*, the judge stated (at para.15):

"There is still a question of the speed with which the claim must be made. A gap between becoming involuntarily unemployed and claiming jobseeker's allowance is not necessarily fatal. Whether it is significant or not will depend on the length of the gap and the reasons for it. Put into the legal terms of EC analysis, the question is whether the gap shows that the claimant has withdrawn from the labour market. A claimant may take a few days to think about the future or to rest after a stressful period leading to redundancy. That may be consistent with remaining in the labour market. In contrast, a claimant who decides to spend six months backpacking in the Australian outback before looking for work has clearly left the labour market for the time being. The tribunal must investigate this issue at the rehearing."

However, *IR* was a decision on the pre-Directive law under which it was only necessary for claimants to establish that they were in duly-recorded involuntary unemployment. The Upper Tribunal has decided that, because the Citizenship Directive introduced an additional requirement that a claimant should be "registered as a jobseeker with the relevant unemployment office", the appropriate test is now whether there has been "undue delay" in so registering (*VP* at paras 51-57, following *MK* at para.69).

The law as stated in *VP* and *MK* is problematic. The concept of "undue delay" is not found in the Citizenship Directive or the 2016 Regulations. Further, the basis for the conclusion that *IR* does not apply after the Citizenship Directive came into force appears to be the decision of the Court of Appeal in *Elmi*. In that case, the majority of the Upper Tribunal had concluded that words requiring registration "as a jobseeker with the relevant employment office" did not add anything to the pre-April 2006 law. A clear majority of the Court (Moses LJ at para.26 and Baron J. at para.29) held that that conclusion was incorrect and that registration as a jobseeker was an additional requirement. However, the majority decision of the Upper Tribunal was based on the authority of the ECJ in *Metock* that "Union citizens cannot derive less rights from that directive than from the instruments of secondary legislation which it amends or repeals" (see above). It is implicit in the Court of Appeal decision that the majority of the Upper Tribunal was wrong to follow *Metock*. However, no explanation is given why that is the case: *Metock* is not even mentioned either in the Court of Appeal decision or in the minority decision of the Upper Tribunal with which, on this point, the Court of Appeal agreed.

What amounts to undue delay will depend heavily on the facts of individual cases. However, in *SSWP v MM (IS)* [2015] UKUT 128 (AAC) the Upper Tribunal held that a delay of five weeks did not amount to undue delay where the claimant did not claim JSA while she waited to see if she would get more work from her agency and made a claim promptly as soon as it became apparent that there was no further work. And in *FT v (1) LB of Islington and (2) SSWP (HB)* [2015] UKUT 121 (AAC)) the Secretary of State and the local authority accepted that the same was true of a delay of six weeks. The claimant had previously obtained jobs quickly, had savings to tide her over and had provided specific details of her steps to find work during the period between the end of her previous employment and her registration as a jobseeker.

As to the second issue, EEA nationals who are looking for work in the UK would always have been well-advised to claim JSA rather than IS. But people are not always well-advised. In particular, lone parents, and women in the late stages of pregnancy (see above), are often advised to claim IS or ESA rather than JSA. As pointed out in *SSWP v CA* [2009] UKUT 169 (AAC), it will usually be incorrect for Jobcentre staff to advise lone parents and pregnant women to claim income support rather than jobseeker's allowance, even if they are CTA nationals. As the judge explained:

> "18. In cases where the claimant is a British or Irish citizen, or has leave to remain in the UK, there may be circumstances in which it is correct for Jobcentre staff to advise a lone parent who is receiving jobseeker's allowance to cease her jobsearch and claim income support instead.
>
> 19.   However, such cases are likely to be few and far between because:
>
> (a) even if the lone parent would be entitled to income support, ceasing to sign on may affect her eventual entitlement to retirement pension by making her ineligible for unemployment credits under regulation 8A of the Social Security (Credits) Regulations 1975 and forcing her instead to rely upon the less advantageous rules for home responsibilities protection; and
>
> (b) in any event, it is government policy that lone parents should be encouraged and assisted to seek work.
>
> 20. In cases where the right to reside is an issue, such advice will almost always be incorrect. The structure of the right to reside test means that a lone parent who is an EEA national (other than a citizen of the United Kingdom or Ireland) will only be entitled to income support if they have acquired a permanent right of

residence or are the separated (but not divorced) spouse of another EEA national who has right to reside in the UK."

If the EEA national has never been on JSA and is wrongly advised to claim IS, the only remedy is to seek compensation either under the Department's *Financial Redress for Maladministration* scheme (details of which can be found on its website) or, less easily, through the courts as damages for negligent misstatement. However, where the claimant was already on JSA and has been wrongly advised to cease claiming that benefit and claim IS instead, s/he should appeal against the decision to terminate the JSA claim (which will often not have been notified expressly) as well as the refusal of IS (see para.5 of *CIS/571/2007* and paras 29–32 of *CIS/4144/2007*). Note that an extension of time may be necessary. The claimant should argue that s/he did not give informed consent to the withdrawal of the JSA award. In addition, the power to supersede a decision awarding benefit is just that, a power not a duty. Claimants should argue that for the Secretary of State to exercise that power so as to disadvantage a claimant for having relied on the advice of his own staff would be an abuse of power contrary to the principle in *CIS/6249/1999* (see para.32 of *CIS/4144/2007*).

Vocational Training

In *SSWP v EM* [2009] UKUT 146 (AAC), Judge Rowland held (at para.10) that what is now reg.6(2)(d) of the 2016 Regulations gives effect to art.7(3)(d) of Directive, which in turn codifies the effects of *Lair* and *Raulin*. It applies: **5.97**

"... only where a person has to retrain in order to find work reasonably equivalent to his or her former employment. Like regulation 6(2)(b), it does not look back at the circumstances in which the person has become unemployed, although that may be part of the background; it is concerned with the situation where a person cannot reasonably be expected to be in the labour market because there is no appropriate market. That is not the case here. Jobs in education have obvious attractions for parents with young children, but the claimant in the present case could have looked for work equivalent to her former employment."

The claimant, who had worked in a chicken-processing factory and had left to train as a teaching assistant, was therefore not "involuntarily unemployed" within what is now reg.6(2)(d) and could not rely upon what is now reg.6(2)(e) because her training was not "related to [her] previous employment".

"Jobseekers"

The right to reside granted by regs 6(1)(a) and 14 to "a jobseeker" is not conferred by the Citizenship Directive but is derived directly from art.45 TFEU (ex. art.39 TEC) (see Case C–292/89 *R. v Immigration Appeal tribunal Ex p. Antonissen* [1991] E.C.R. I-745). **5.98**

Since July 1, 2014, "jobseeker" has been defined for the purposes of the 2016 Regulations (and the 2006 Regulations) by para.(1) as "a person who satisfies conditions A, B and, where relevant, C". Condition A is described above in the discussion of retention of worker status.

Condition B is that is that the person provides evidence of seeking employment and having a genuine chance of being engaged. Following the decision of the Upper Tribunal in *KH v Bury MBC and SSWP* [2020] UKUT 50 (AAC), the Condition only applies to jobseekers (in the narrow EU sense of that word). In *KH*, Judge Wright held that the requirement to provide evidence of "having a genuine chance of being engaged" in order to retain worker status was contrary to EU law and that the FTT had erred by applying reg.6(2)(b)(ii) (as it relates to Condition B) and (7) to such a claimant. It therefore follows that no question arises as to what evidence retained status workers must provide to establish a genuine chance of being engaged.

Condition B does, however, apply to jobseekers. The "genuine chance of being engaged" test is a derived from para.21 of the decision of the ECJ in *R v Immigration*

Appeal Tribunal ex p. Antonissen (Case C-292/89) which first established that a limited right of residence to seek work in another Member State was part of the principle of free movement of workers.

The Secretary of State can assess whether there is a genuine chance of being engaged using the evidence supplied by the claimant to demonstrate that the domestic law "labour market" conditions of entitlement to JSA are satisfied. However, it may be necessary for HMRC to apply the test without such detailed evidence in order to determine entitlement to child benefit: see, further, *DD v HMRC and SSWP (CB)* [2020] UKUT 66 (AAC).

Further, by para.(7) a person cannot remain a jobseeker for more than the "relevant period" of "91 days, minus the cumulative total of any days during which the person concerned previously enjoyed a right to reside as a jobseeker, not including any days prior to a continuous absence from the United Kingdom of at least 12 months" (see para.(1)) without providing "compelling" evidence of continuing to seek employment and having a genuine chance of being engaged.

The way in which the requirements to have a genuine chance of being engaged and to provide compelling evidence of that chance were applied in practice by the DWP was considered by the Upper Tribunal (Judge Ward) in *SSWP v MB (JSA)* (and linked cases) [2016] UKUT 372 (AAC), [2017] AACR 6, in which the claimants were all jobseekers. The DWP had implemented the requirement for "compelling evidence" administratively by the establishment of a "genuine prospects of work" test ("GPoW"). That test treated "genuine prospects of work" as synonymous with "a genuine chance of being engaged" and as effectively requiring either a definite job offer of genuine and effective work or that there had been a change of circumstances which made it likely that the claimant will receive a job offer imminently.

However, following *MB*, this does not reflect the law. To begin with, the legal test in reg.6 requires a jobseeker to show that s/he has "a genuine chance of being engaged" rather than that s/he has genuine prospects of work. Judge Ward confirmed that the rights of jobseekers under EU law are derived from what is now art.45 TFEU as interpreted by the decision of the ECJ in *Antonissen*. There is no requirement in *Antonissen* that a genuine chance of being engaged must be established by evidence that is more "compelling" than would usually be required. Moreover, as Lord Hoffmann stated in *Re B (Children)* [2008] UKHL 35 at para.13:

> "13.   [T]here is only one civil standard of proof and that is proof that the fact in issue more probably occurred than not."

Applying that principle, Judge Ward stated:

> "54.   The test under *Antonissen* remains whether a person has "genuine chances of being engaged" and that is a matter which falls to be decided on the civil standard of proof. In assessing whether a person has genuine chances of being engaged, the (flexible) principle that "regard should be had, to whatever extent appropriate, to inherent probabilities" (*Re B*) is available to a tribunal. However, that is a matter of "common sense, not law" per Lord Hoffmann. ...
>
> 56.   If regulation 6(7) of the 2006 Regulations does not go beyond the process which *Re B* permits and requiring *Antonissen* to be fully applied in accordance with its terms, then in my judgment it is unexceptionable. It does not detract from the Community interpretation of who is a "worker" and does not interpret the term, as regards jobseekers, any more restrictively than the Court of Justice already has. It may be said that on that view the requirement for "compelling evidence" does not add anything, save for making express to decision-makers and tribunals what was the case anyway, but that is not necessarily an inappropriate purpose for legislation.
>
> 57.   What in my view the amendment cannot do and does not do is anything more than that. In particular, it cannot raise the bar for what constitutes a genuine chance (or chances) of being engaged higher than it falls to be set in accordance with *Antonissen*, which I have sought to interpret in this decision. ... Insistence on

'compelling' evidence may, if care is not taken, all too easily result in raising the bar above the level I have found to be required, namely chances that are founded on something objective and offer real prospects of success in obtaining genuine and effective work within a reasonable period."

Judge Ward also made the following points about the way in which whether or not a jobseeker has a genuine chance of being engaged should be assessed.

- "Genuine" is an everyday word. In the context of a chance, it "implies both the need for the chance to be founded on something objective (i.e., it is genuine as opposed to illusory or speculative) but also something about the likelihood that the chance will come to fruition". "What is contemplated are chances that, as well as being founded on something objective, offer real prospects of success in obtaining work".

- There has to be a genuine chance of being engaged in work that is "genuine and effective" (i.e., in the *Levin* sense).

- A "genuine chance of being engaged" is not something that can only be satisfied if the person can point to a particular job.

- A "chance" is something which by its nature necessitates a degree of looking forward. Qualifications that the person has obtained, or is in the process of obtaining, in the UK may be relevant.

- There is no absolute time limit on a right under *Antonissen*. A Member State may wish to conduct more frequent reviews after a certain time but that must be distinguished from only granting the right for a set period of time. There is nothing to stop a Member State conducting a review after 6 months but nor is there anything in EU law which permits any kind of step change in what has to be proved at that (or any other) point.

- However, a tribunal will need to take a period of 6 months (or indeed longer) unsuccessful jobseeking into account, along with other factors, in assessing whether a person did have "genuine chances" as at the date that needs to be looked at.

In *OS v SSWP (JSA)* [2017] UKUT 107 (AAC), Judge Ward confirmed that where a claimant obtains employment after the date of the Secretary of State's decision refusing jobseeker's allowance, that circumstance can be taken into account as evidence that she had a genuine chance of being engaged as at the date of that decision. Section 12(8)(b) of the Social Security Act 1998, which prevents the First-tier Tribunal from considering circumstances not obtaining at the date of the decision under appeal, "does not preclude inferences being drawn from events which occurred after the decision date about circumstances obtaining when, or before, the decision was made: see, inter alia, R(DLA) 2/01 and 3/01".

The relationship between the inaccurately-named "genuine prospects of work" test and participation in the New Enterprise Allowance ("NEA") scheme was considered by the Upper Tribunal in *EG v SSWP (JSA)* [2018] UKUT 285 (AAC). Judge Poole QC accepted a concession by the Secretary of State that the First-tier Tribunal had erred in law by failing 'to consider the implications of the claimant's participation in the NEA scheme in relation to whether he had a genuine prospect of work and retained jobseeker's status" but rejected the claimant's submission that, while participating in the scheme he did not have to show that he had a genuine chance of being engaged.

As far as any right to reside the claimant may have had as a jobseeker is concerned, the decision cannot be faulted. However, it is strongly arguable that the First-tier Tribunal erred more fundamentally by failing to consider whether his participation in the NEA scheme had given rise to a separate right of residence as a self-employed person. The NEA scheme is established under Jobseekers Act 1995, s.17A and the Jobseeker's Allowance (Schemes for Assisting Persons to Obtain Employment)

Regulations 2013. And, as its name suggests, it is designed to help people into self-employment. Regulation 3(5) of those Regulations states that it is "designed to assist a claimant into self-employed earner's employment comprising guidance and support provided by a business mentor, access to a loan to help with start-up costs (subject to status) and a weekly allowance for a period of 26 weeks once the claimant starts trading." It is implicit in the definition that a claimant may have begun to trade as a self-employed person but still be participating in the NEA scheme: it cannot be assumed that, just because a claimant is claiming jobseeker's allowance and participating in a scheme under s.17A, he can only have a right of residence as a jobseeker. The point is a potentially important one for claimants. Claimants who are self-employed persons have a right of residence that counts for the purposes of all working-age means-tested benefits, not just JSA, and so can claim HB if they live in rented accommodation and can claim ESA if they become ill.

Condition C is that "the person has had a period of absence from the United Kingdom" (see para.(9)).

By para.(8), Condition C applies:

"where the person concerned has, previously, enjoyed a right to reside under [regulation 6] as a result of satisfying conditions A and B—

    (a) in the case of a person to whom paragraph (2)(b) or (ba) applied, for at least 6 months; or

    (b) in the case of a jobseeker for at least 91 days in total.

unless the person concerned has, since enjoying the above right to reside, been continuously absent from the United Kingdom for at least 12 months."

The length of the period of absence is not specified. In particular, para.(8) does not say that the period of absence must be at least 12 months. It only says that Condition C does not apply at all where there has been a continuous absence for 12 months or more.

A period of absence of more than three months may have the effect that the claimant will not be entitled to JSA immediately on return to the UK: see the commentary to reg.21AA of the IS Regulations.

The decision in SSWP v RR (IS)

5.99   Previous editions drew attention to the fact that unnecessarily broad language in the decision of a Three-Judge Panel in *SSWP v RR (IS)* [2013] UKUT 21 (AAC) seemed to have blurred the distinction between "workers" and "jobseekers" by suggesting that anyone who could bring themselves within art.39 TEC (which would include *Antonissen* jobseekers) are thereby workers for the purposes of art.7(1)(a) of the Citizenship Directive: for more details, see pp.344-345 of Vol.II of the 2015/16 edition. However, *RO v SSWP (JSA)* [2015] UKUT 533 (AAC), confirms that *RR* is not authority for that proposition. *RR* remains authority that a national of another EEA state who comes to the UK in order to take up an offer of employment but has not yet been able to take it up for medical reasons and has therefore never worked in the UK, she has a right to reside under art.39(3)(a) and (b) TEC (now art.45 TFEU) as the holder of a job offer—at least while the job offer was being kept open for her—and so was a worker for the purposes of art.7(1)(a) of the Citizenship Directive.

Pre-accession work

5.100   In *CIS/1833/2006*, the Commissioner held, applying the decision of the ECJ in Case C-171/91 *Tsiotras v Landeshauptstadt Stuttgart*, that work undertaken by a Maltese national in the UK before Malta acceded to the EU on May 1, 2004 did not count for the purposes of the predecessor to reg.6(2). However, that position decision cannot stand in the light of the subsequent decision of the Grand Chamber of the CJEU in *Ziolkowski and Szeja* (see below).

Retaining self-employed status

A person who has ceased self-employment because they are temporarily incapable   **5.101**
of work retains the status of a "self-employed person" in the same way as a worker
(see above and art.7(3)(a) of the Citizenship Directive).

In the past, however, the view was taken that a formerly self-employed person did
not retain self-employed status during periods of involuntary unemployment: see in
SSWP v RK [2009] UKUT 209 (AAC) and *R. (Tilianu) v Secretary of State for Work
and Pensions* [2010] EWCA Civ 1397.

That view is no longer tenable. In *Gusa v Minister for Social Protection, Ireland,
Attorney General* (Case C-442/16), the CJEU ruled that:

> "Article 7(3)(b) of [the Citizenship Directive] must be interpreted as meaning
> that a national of a Member State retains the status of self-employed person
> for the purposes of Article 7(1)(a) of that directive where, after having lawfully
> resided in and worked as a self-employed person in another Member State for
> approximately four years, that national has ceased that activity, because of a duly
> recorded absence of work owing to reasons beyond his control, and has registered
> as a jobseeker with the relevant employment office of the latter Member State."

That ruling reflects the facts of the individual case. Paragraph 45 of the judgment
makes it clear that it applies whenever anyone has been self-employed for over a year.
And the decision of Judge Ward in *SB v SSWP* (UC) [2019] UKUT 219 (AAC),
following the decision of the CJEU in *Tarola v Minister of Social Protection* (Case
C-483/17), holds that the *Gusa* principle also applies where the claimant has been
self-employed for less than a year (although, in those circumstances, self-employed
status is retained for "no less than six months" (i.e., in the same way as worker status
is retained by an EEA national who has been employed for less than a year).

Such a person retains self-employed status and is not a jobseeker (*i.e.*, in the EU
sense). S/he can therefore claim social assistance (i.e., IS. HB, IRESA, SPC and,
importantly, UC).

The decisions in *RK* and *Tilianu* cannot be reconciled with the decision in *Gusa*
and are therefore no longer good law.

On July 24, 2018, reg.6 was amended by SI 2018/801, reg.2 and Sch., para.2,
to bring domestic UK law into line with EU law as set out in *Gusa*. New paras (4)
(b)-(e) and (4A)-(4C) have the effect that a formerly self-employed person retains
self-employed status in the same circumstances that a formerly employed person
retains worker status, the only difference being that Conditions D and E (equivalent
to Conditions A and B for former workers) can be satisfied by seeking self-employment as well as employment.

However, the issue whether a formerly self-employed person has to retain self-
employed status only arises if that person has actually ceased to be self-employed.
That is a question of fact in each case: see the decisions of the Upper Tribunal in
RJ v SSWP (JSA) [2011] UKUT 477 (AAC), [2012] AACR 12; SSWP v AL (JSA)
[2010] UKUT 451 (AAC) and *SSWP v JS* [2010] UKUT 240 (AAC). In the last
of those cases, Judge Jacobs stated (at para.5):

> "5.   I do not accept that a claimant who is for the moment doing no work is
> necessarily no longer self-employed. There will commonly be periods in a per-
> son's self-employment when no work is done. Weekends and holiday periods
> are obvious examples. There may also be periods when there is no work to do.
> The concept of self-employment encompasses periods of both feast and famine.
> During the latter, the person may be engaged in a variety of tasks that are prop-
> erly seen as part of continuing self-employment: administrative work, such as
> maintaining the accounts; in marketing to generate more work; or developing the
> business in new directions. Self-employment is not confined to periods of actual
> work. It includes natural periods of rest and the vicissitudes of business life. This
> does not mean that self-employment survives regardless of how little work arrives.
> It does mean that the issue can only be decided in the context of the facts at any
> particular time. The amount of work is one factor. Whether the claimant is taking

any other steps in the course of self-employment is also relevant. The claimant's motives and intentions must also be taken into account, although they will not necessarily be decisive."

Similarly, in *HMRC v GP (final decision)* [2017] UKUT 11 (AAC) (one of two cases with that neutral citation: see *HD* below), Judge Ward accepted that a pregnant woman could retain self-employed status while on maternity leave. Whether or not that status is retained is a question of fact (paras 10 and 23–34). For the position where a pregnant woman does not continue to be self-employed see the discussion of *HMRC v HD (interim decision)* [2017] UKUT 11 (AAC) (above).

"Family member"

5.102   **7.**—(1) In these Regulations, "family member" means, in relation to a person ("A")—

(a) A's spouse or civil partner;

(b) A's direct descendants, or the direct descendants of A's spouse or civil partner who are either—

    (i) aged under 21; or

    (ii) dependants of A, or of A's spouse or civil partner;

(c) dependent direct relatives in A's ascending line, or in that of A's spouse or civil partner.

(2) Where A is a student residing in the United Kingdom otherwise than under regulation 13 (initial right of residence), a person is not a family member of A under paragraph (1)(b) or (c) unless—

(a) in the case of paragraph (1)(b), the person is the dependent child of A or of A's spouse or civil partner; or

(b) A also falls within one of the other categories of qualified person mentioned in regulation 6(1).

(3) A person ("B") who is an extended family member and has been issued with an EEA family permit, a registration certificate or a residence card must be treated as a family member of A, provided—

(a) B continues to satisfy the conditions in regulation [² 8(1A),] 8(2), (3), (4) or (5); and

(b) the EEA family permit, registration certificate or residence card remains in force.

(4) A must be an EEA national unless regulation 9 applies (family members [¹ and extended family members] of British citizens).

AMENDMENT

1. Immigration (European Economic Area Nationals) (EU Exit) Regulations 2019 (SI 2019/468) reg.3(3) (March 28, 2019).

2. Immigration (European Economic Area) (Amendment) Regulations 2019 (SI 2019/1155) reg.2(1) and (4) (August 15, 2019).

DEFINITION

    "civil partner"—see reg.2(1).
    "EEA family permit"—see regs 2(1) and 12.
    "EEA national"—see reg.2(1).
    "qualified person"—see reg.6(1).
    "registration certificate"—see regs 2(1) and 17.
    "residence card"—see regs 2(1) and 18.
    "spouse"—see reg.2(1).
    "student"—see reg.4(1)(d).

GENERAL NOTE

The "family members" of a qualified person and of a person with a permanent   **5.103**
right of residence have an extended right of residence in the UK: see reg.14(2). In
addition residence as such a family member counts towards the continuous period
of five years' residence required by reg.15(1)(a) and (b) for the acquisition of a
permanent right of residence. In *CIS/1685/2007*, the Commissioner held that, in an
appropriate case, a tribunal must consider whether the claimant has a right of residence as a family member of a qualified person as well as considering his/her rights
as a qualified person. See also *CIS/2431/2006*.

Family members who are EEA nationals can become qualified persons in their
own right by, for example, looking for or accepting work.

Family members

Regulation 7 reflects the definition of the phrase "family member" in art.2(2).   **5.104**
Under art.3(1), the family members of an EEA national are "beneficiaries" of (*i.e.*,
are within the personal scope of) the Citizenship Directive, even if they are not
themselves EEA Nationals.

Paragraph (1) provides that, except where the qualified person only has a right
of residence as a student, the phrase means the qualified person's spouse or civil
partner, the "direct descendants" (i.e. children, grandchildren, etc.) of the qualified
person (or of the spouse or civil partner) who are either their dependants or are under
the age of 21, and "dependent direct relatives in the ascending line", i.e. parents and
grandparents, etc. of the qualified person (or of the spouse or civil partner).

A child who has been placed in the permanent legal guardianship of a citizen of
the Union under the Algerian *kafala* system (and—by implication—any other type
of guardianship that does not create the legal relationship of parent and child), is not
a "direct descendant of the guardian and therefore cannot derive a right of residence
as a "family member" of the guardian. However:

> "... it is for the competent national authorities to facilitate the entry and residence
> of such a child as one of the other family members of a citizen of the Union pur-
> suant to Article 3(2)(a) of [the Citizenship Directive], read in the light of Article 7
> and Article 24(2) of the Charter of Fundamental Rights of the European Union,
> by carrying out a balanced and reasonable assessment of all the current and rel-
> evant circumstances of the case which takes account of the various interests in
> play and, in particular, of the best interests of the child concerned. In the event
> that it is established, following that assessment, that the child and its guardian,
> who is a citizen of the Union, are called to lead a genuine family life and that that
> child is dependent on its guardian, the requirements relating to the fundamental
> right to respect for family life, combined with the obligation to take account of
> the best interests of the child, demand, in principle, that that child be granted a
> right of entry and residence in order to enable it to live with its guardian in his or
> her host Member State."

see the decision of the Grand Chamber of the CJEU in *SM v Entry Clearance Officer*
(Case C-129/18).

Paragraph (2) provides that, where the qualified person's sole right of residence
is as a student, only the qualified person's spouse or civil partner and their dependent children count as "family members" after the initial period of three months has
expired.

"Spouse" does not include a party to a UK same sex marriage under the Marriage
(Same Sex Couples) Act 2013: see the Marriage (Same Sex Couples) Act 2013
(Consequential and Contrary provisions and Scotland) Order 2014 (SI 2014/560),
art.3 and Sch.2, Pt 2. (The phrase "EU instruments" used in that Schedule is
defined in Sch.1 to the European Communities Act 1972 (as amended) as "any
instrument issued by an EU institution".) However, a party to a same sex marriage

might nevertheless be a "family member" within art.2(2)(b) of the Citizenship Directive, (*i.e.*, the provision that treats civil partners as family members).

Moreover, it has recently become clear that that in certain circumstances, a third-country national same-sex spouse of an EEA national will have a right of residence under art.21 TFEU: see *Coman, Hamilton & Anor. v Inspectoratul General pentru Imigrări & Ors* (Case C-673/16). Mr Coman is a dual national of Romania and the USA. He met Mr Hamilton, a US citizen in New York and lived with him there. He then moved to Brussels to work as a parliamentary assistant at the European Parliament. The couple were married in Brussels. In due course, Mr Coman wished to return to Romania. However. Romania neither permits same-sex marriage, nor recognises same-sex marriages contracted elsewhere. It therefore did not accept that Mr Hamilton was Mr Coman's family member and refused him a right of residence. However, the Grand Chamber of the CJEU ruled as follows:

"1. In a situation in which a Union citizen has made use of his freedom of movement by moving to and taking up genuine residence, in accordance with the conditions laid down in Article 7(1) of [the Citizenship] Directive ..., in a Member State other than that of which he is a national, and, whilst there, has created and strengthened a family life with a third-country national of the same sex to whom he is joined by a marriage lawfully concluded in the host Member State, Article 21(1) TFEU must be interpreted as precluding the competent authorities of the Member State of which the Union citizen is a national from refusing to grant that third-country national a right of residence in the territory of that Member State on the ground that the law of that Member State does not recognise marriage between persons of the same sex.

2. Article 21(1) TFEU is to be interpreted as meaning that, in circumstances such as those of the main proceedings, a third-country national of the same sex as a Union citizen whose marriage to that citizen was concluded in a Member State in accordance with the law of that state has the right to reside in the territory of the Member State of which the Union citizen is a national for more than three months. That derived right of residence cannot be made subject to stricter conditions than those laid down in Article 7 of [the Citizenship] Directive ...."

"Spouse" and "civil partner" are defined by reg.2(1) as not including a party to a marriage of convenience or a civil partnership of convenience. Those definitions also exclude parties to polygamous and quasi-polygamous relationships: where either party to a marriage or civil partnership has a spouse, civil partner, or "durable partner" (see regs 2(1) and 8) already present in the UK, other spouses, civil partners and durable partners do not count as family members.

The spouse of a qualified person retains that status until finally divorced (Case C–267/83 *Diatta v Land Berlin* [1985] E.C.R. 567). By the same reasoning, the civil partner of a qualified person should retain that status until the partnership is finally dissolved. For the circumstances in which the former spouse or civil partner of a qualified person can retain a right of residence in the UK following divorce or dissolution of the partnership, see the General Note to reg.10.

Paragraph (3). Some people who do not satisfy the criteria, may nevertheless fall within the definition of "extended family member": see reg.8. Such people are treated as family members as long as reg.8 continues to apply to them and they have been issued with an EEA family permit, registration certificate or residence card that remains in force. See further, the General Note to reg.8.

Paragraph (4) provides that, with one exception, reg.7 only applies to the family members of EEA nationals. As the definition of EEA National in reg.2(1) excludes British citizens, the effect is that the family members of British citizens have no rights under the 2016 Regulations, require leave to enter and remain, and are subject to the more restrictive provisions in Pt 8 of the Immigration Rules. The exception is that, in the circumstances set out in reg.9, the family members of a British citizen are treated as if they were the family members of an EEA national. See further the General Note to reg.9.

Dependency

The requirement that certain family members should be "dependent" on the EEA national or his/her spouse has been considered by the Court of Appeal in *Jeleniewicz v SSWP* [2008] EWCA Civ 1163 reported as R(1S)3/09 and by the Commissioner in *CIS/2100/2007* and *CPC/1433/2008*.

5.105

In *Jeleniewicz*, the Court upheld a finding by the Commissioner (in *CIS/1545/2007*) that (under the law as it stood before April 30, 2006) where a student had contact with his daughter twice a week and made irregular payments towards her maintenance averaging £10 per week, the daughter did not have a right to reside as his dependent child (and the daughter's mother did not have a right to reside as the daughter's primary carer). It was not enough that there should be some emotional dependency. There must be material support which, though not necessarily financial, must provide for or contribute towards, the basic necessities of life.

In *CIS/2100/2007*, the Commissioner reviewed the ECJ case law (Case C–316/85 *Centre Public D'Aide Sociale de Courcelles v Lebon* [1987] E.C.R. 2811, Case C–200/02 *Chen v Secretary of State for the Home Department* [2005] Q.B. 325 and Case C–1/05 *Jia v Migrationsverket* [2007] Q.B. 545) and concluded as follows:

"44. In summary, the case law is authority for these propositions:

• A person is only dependent who actually receives support from another.

• There need be no right to that support and it is irrelevant that there are alternative sources of support available.

• That support must be material, although not necessarily financial, and must provide for, or contribute towards, the basic necessities of life."

"Material support" does not include emotional or social support or linguistic support (i.e., translation) : see *SSWP v MF (SPC)* [2018] UKUT 179 (AAC).

In *Pedro v SSWP* [2009] EWCA Civ 1358, the Court of Appeal (Mummery, Sullivan and Goldring L.JJ.) (an appeal from the decision of the Deputy Commissioner in *CPC/1433/2008*) considered whether, to be dependent, the family member had to prove that they needed the support of the EEA national or their spouse in the country of origin rather than in the host Member State. In *Jia*, the Grand Chamber of the ECJ held that dependence in the country of origin was required for the purposes of the former Directive 73/148 on the freedom of establishment and provision of services. However, the Court—in reliance on *Metock* (see above)—confined the application of *Jia* to cases arising under the pre-April 30, 2006 law. Therefore it was only necessary for Mrs Pedro to prove that she was dependent on her son in the United Kingdom in order to be a "dependent direct relative in the ascending line" for the purposes of art.2(2)(d) of the Citizenship Directive. Giving the judgment of the Court, Goldring L.J. stated:

"67. Article 2(2) [i.e., of the Citizenship Directive] does not specify when the dependency has to have arisen. Neither does it require that the relative must be dependent in the country of origin. Article 3(2)(a), on the other hand, requires actual dependency at a particular time and place. That difference, as I have said, is reflected by Article 8(5)(d) as compared with 8(5)(e). It cannot be an accident of drafting. It contemplates, as it seems to me, that where in an Article 2(2)(d) case reliance is placed on dependency, it can be proved by a document from the host state without input from the state of origin. Taking Article 2(2)(d) together with Article 8(5)(d) suggests that dependency in the state of origin need not be proved for family members. It is sufficient if, as is alleged here, the dependency arises in the host state."

The authority of *Pedro* may be somewhat compromised because it does not refer to the decision of the Court of Appeal (Sullivan, Ward and Etherton L.JJ.) in *SM (India) v Entry Clearance Officer* [2009] EWCA Civ 1426 which was given approximately two weeks earlier. In *SM (India)*, the Court applied *Jia* to a post-April 30, 2006 case: the appeal was stated to be against the refusal to issue the appellants with "EEA family permits under Regulation 12 of the Immigration (European Economic Area) Regulations 2006". The decision in *SM (India)* was given after the hearing in *Pedro* but before judgment in that case was handed down. However, it cannot be that the Court in *SM (India)* was unaware of the issue in *Pedro* because Sullivan L.J. was a member of both panels. The decisions can be reconciled on the basis that *SM (India)* was about entry clearance and therefore inevitably involved people who had yet to come to the UK. In such circumstances, the only type of dependence that could arise was dependence in the country of origin, so that the possibility or reliance on dependence in the UK did not arise. The aspect of *Jia* that was in issue in *SM (India)* was whether dependence had to arise as a matter of necessity or whether it could be a matter of choice. Therefore the Court in *SM (India)* was not dealing with the issue that had to be considered in *Pedro* and which led the Court in that case to confine the operation of *Jia* to circumstances arising before April 30, 2006.

Dependency is a question of fact. If one person is in fact dependent on another, the reasons why that is so are irrelevant. *Entry Clearance Officer, Manila v Lim (EEA – dependency)* [2013] UKUT 437 (IAC) concerned a Malaysian citizen, aged 60, who owned a three-bedroom house in Malaysia (valued at £80,000) and had savings of approximately £55,000 in an Employers Provident Fund based on her past employment, which she was entitled to withdraw. However, she wished to leave her savings and her house to her children and grandchildren and so relied on remittances from her daughter, who was married to a Finnish national working in the UK. Judge Storey confirms that, subject to there being no abuse of rights, the jurisprudence of the Court of Justice allows for dependency of choice and that there was no discernible reason why this should not include dependency of choice in the form of choosing not to live off savings. Similarly in *Reyes v Migrationsverket* (Case C-423/12) the ECJ confirmed that there was no need to determine the reasons for the dependence. Ms Reyes was a Philippines citizen born in 1987 who moved to Sweden in March 2011 to join her mother who was married to a Norwegian. Her mother had moved to Germany to work when she was three years old and had regularly sent money to support her family in the Philippines. The Court ruled that Ms Reyes did not have to show that she had tried to find work or subsistence support in the Philippines in order to establish her dependency, nor did the fact that Ms Reyes was well placed to obtain employment and intended to start work affect the interpretation of dependency. The ECJ did refer to the fact that following *Jia* it was necessary for Ms Reyes to have been dependent in the country from which she had come (*cf. Pedro* above). However, on the facts, Ms Reyes was dependent in the Philippines so the point cannot have been essential to the Court's reasoning.

Note that, even in those categories of family member where dependence on the qualified person forms part of the definition, it is not necessary for the family member to live in the same household as the qualified person in order to have a right of residence. This is important because family breakdown will often be the reason the family member claims an income-related benefit.

"Extended family member"

5.106   **8.**—(1) In these Regulations "extended family member" means a person who is not a family member of an EEA national under regulation 7(1)(a), (b) or (c) and who satisfies a condition in paragraph [[1] (1A),] (2), (3), (4) or (5).

[¹ (1A) The condition in this paragraph is that the person—
  (a) is under the age of 18;
  (b) is subject to a non-adoptive legal guardianship order in favour of an EEA national that is recognised under the national law of the state in which it was contracted;
  (c) has lived with the EEA national since their placement under the guardianship order;
  (d) has created family life with the EEA national; and
  (e) has a personal relationship with the EEA national that involves dependency on the EEA national and the assumption of parental responsibility, including legal and financial responsibilities, for that person by the EEA national.]

(2) The condition in this paragraph is that the person is—
  (a) a relative of an EEA national; and
  (b) residing in a country other than the United Kingdom and is dependent upon the EEA national or is a member of the EEA national's household; and either—
    (i) is accompanying the EEA national to the United Kingdom or wants to join the EEA national in the United Kingdom; or
    (ii) has joined the EEA national in the United Kingdom and continues to be dependent upon the EEA national, or to be a member of the EEA national's household.

(3) The condition in this paragraph is that the person is a relative of an EEA national and on serious health grounds, strictly requires the personal care of the EEA national [¹ or the spouse or civil partner of the EEA national].

(4) The condition in this paragraph is that the person is a relative of an EEA national and would meet the requirements in the immigration rules (other than those relating to entry clearance) for indefinite leave to enter or remain in the United Kingdom as a dependent relative of the EEA national.

(5) The condition in this paragraph is that the person is the partner (other than a civil partner) of, and in a durable relationship with, an EEA national [¹ or the child (under the age of 18) of that partner] and is able to prove this to the decision maker.

(6) In these Regulations, "relevant EEA national" means, in relation to an extended family member—
  (a) referred to in paragraph (2), (3) or (4), the EEA national to whom the extended family member is related;
  (b) referred to in paragraph (5), the EEA national who is the durable partner of the extended family member.

(7) In [¹ paragraphs (2), (3) and (4)], "relative of an EEA national" includes a relative of the spouse or civil partner of an EEA national [¹ ...].

[¹ (8) Where an extensive examination of the personal circumstances of the applicant is required under these Regulations, it must include examination of the following—
  (a) the best interests of the applicant, particularly where the applicant is a child;
  (b) the character and conduct of the applicant; and
  (c) whether an EEA national would be deterred from exercising their free movement rights if the application was refused.]

AMENDMENT

1. Immigration (European Economic Area) (Amendment) Regulations 2019 (SI 2019/1155) reg.2(1) and (5) (August 15, 2019).

DEFINITION

"civil partner"—see reg.2(1).
"decision maker"—*ibid.*
"durable partner"—*ibid.*
"EEA family permit"—see regs 2(1) and 12.
"EEA national"—see reg.2(1).
"entry clearance"—*ibid.*
"family member"—see reg.7.
"immigration rules"—see reg.2(1).
"registration certificate"—see regs 2(1) and 17.
"relevant EEA national"—see General Note.
"residence card"—see regs 2(1) and 18.
"spouse"—*ibid.*

GENERAL NOTE

5.107   Under art.3(2), a host Member State is required, in accordance with its national legislation, to facilitate entry and residence for "any other family members, irrespective of their nationality, not falling under the definition in [art.2(2): see the General Note to reg.7 above] who, in the country from which they have come, are dependants or members of the household of the Union citizen having the primary right of residence, or where serious health grounds strictly require the personal care of the family member by the Union citizen" and for "the partner with whom the Union citizen has a durable relationship, duly attested". Regulation 8, taken together with reg.7(3), implements the UK's obligations under art.3(2) by treating "extended family members" as if they were family members as long as they have a valid EEA family permit (see reg.12(4) and (5)), registration certificate (see reg.17(5) and (6)) or residence card (see reg.18.(4) and (5)).

The requirement for an extended family member to have been issued with one of those documents in order to have a right of residence, reflects the fact that the obligation imposed by art.3(2) on Member States is not to allow extended family members rights of free movement but only to facilitate entry and residence in accordance with national law. It follows that, for extended family members, the issue of an EEA family permit, registration certificate or residence card is constitutive of the right to reside. The right only exists if the host state grants it. The issue of a family permit, registration certificate or residence card is the mechanism by which the UK grants the right (see *CIS/612/2008*). This is in contrast to the usual situation in which the issue of a residence document under the Citizenship Directive is merely evidence of a right that has arisen independently: see the General Note to Pt 3. Note, however, that although the issue of an EEA family permit, registration certificate or residence card is a necessary condition of the right to reside, it is not sufficient. Under reg.7(3), a tribunal considering a right to reside appeal involving an extended family member must be satisfied both that a relevant residence document has been issued and that the conditions in paras (2)–(5) (see below) continue to be satisfied.

The UK is not obliged to issue an EEA family permit, registration certificate or residence card to every extended family member. However, art.3(2) also requires that "[the] host Member State shall undertake an extensive examination of the personal circumstances and shall justify any denial of entry or residence to these people". In *Secretary of State for the Home Department v Rahman* (Case C-83/11) the Grand Chamber of the CJEU ruled that:

"1. On a proper construction of Article 3(2) of [the Citizenship Directive]:

- the Member States are not required to grant every application for entry or residence submitted by family members of a Union citizen who do not fall under the definition in Article 2(2) of that directive, even if they show, in accordance with Article 10(2) thereof, that they are dependants of that citizen;
- it is, however, incumbent upon the Member States to ensure that their legislation contains criteria which enable those persons to obtain a decision on their application for entry and residence that is founded on an extensive examination of their personal circumstances and, in the event of refusal, is justified by reasons;
- the Member States have a wide discretion when selecting those criteria, but the criteria must be consistent with the normal meaning of the term 'facilitate' and of the words relating to dependence used in Article 3(2) and must not deprive that provision of its effectiveness; and
- every applicant is entitled to a judicial review of whether the national legislation and its application satisfy those conditions."

Extended family members who are EEA nationals can become qualified persons in their own right by, for example, looking for or accepting work.

Extended family member

Paragraph (1). "Extended family member" is defined by para.(1) as a person who is not a family member of an EEA national (*i.e.*, as defined in reg.7) and satisfies at least one of the five conditions in paras (1A) to (5).   **5.108**

Paragraph (1A) sets out the first condition. It applies to a person who is under 18, is "subject to a non-adoptive legal guardianship order in favour of an EEA national that is recognised under the national law of the state in which it was contracted" and who meets the other specified criteria.

Paragraph (2) sets out the second condition. The drafting is not as clear as it might be, because of the problem with the opening words of para.(2)(b) identified below. Overall, it is important to remember that the 2016 Regulations are primarily about immigration. It follows that para.(2) is mainly concerned with circumstances in which the putative extended family member is outside the UK and wishes to enter in order to accompany or join the EEA national.

However, for social security purposes, the issue whether someone is an extended family member can only arise once they have arrived in the UK. In such a case, the position is governed by para.(2)(a) and (b)(ii). To qualify as an extended family member, the person must be "a relative of the EEA national" who has formerly resided in a country other than the UK and was either dependent on the EEA national, or a member of the EEA national's household in that country, and has joined the EEA national in the UK and continues to be dependent on him/her or to be a member of his/her household. "Relative" is not defined and therefore bears its normal meaning.

Although the opening words of para.(2)(b) are in the present tense (*"residing* in a country other than the United Kingdom") they must also include *former* residence in such a country. This is required by the express words of art.3(2) ("the country from which they have come") and also because any other interpretation would make para.(2)(b)(ii) meaningless by requiring the putative extended family member to have joined the EEA national in the UK and to be still residing in a country other than the UK at the same time.

The words "and continues to be dependent" in what is now para.(2)(b)(ii) require the non-EEA national to establish that there has not been a break in his or her dependency on the EEA national: see *Chowdhury (Extended family members: dependency)* [2020] UKUT 188 (IAC). The same is presumably also the case where the non-EEA national is a member of the EEA national's household. If so, there would seem to be no reason why the non-EEA national should not move from dependency to household membership (or vice versa) without breaking continuity.

VN (EEA rights – dependency) Macedonia [2010] UKUT 380 (IAC) confirms (without expressly addressing the point made above) that the decision in *Pedro* (see the General Note to reg.7 above) does not apply to extended family members with the effect that, to establish a right of residence, extended family members are required to show both dependence in the country from which they have come and dependence in the UK.

In *Soares v Secretary of State for the Home Department* [2013] EWCA Civ 575 the Court of Appeal held that the predecessor to para.(2)(aa) and (b)(ii) require dependence on, or household membership of, the EEA national him/herself. Dependence on, or household membership of, the EEA national's spouse or civil partner does not count for this purpose. However, para.(7) provides that the phrase "relative of an EEA national" includes a relative of the spouse or civil partner of an EEA national where, before February 1, 2017, a person has been issued with an EEA family permit, a registration certificate or a residence card on the basis of being an extended family member and, since the most recent issue of such a document been continuously resident in the UK. This is a puzzling provision and has no equivalent in the 2006 Regulations. Given the decision in *Soares*, there should not be anyone who has been granted a UK residence document on the basis of being an extended family member of the spouse or civil partner of an EEA national. Presumably, the purpose is to protect the *status quo* in cases where such a mistake has been made.

It is not necessary for the putative extended family member to establish the prior and present connection with the EEA national in the same capacity. So, for example, a relative who was a member of the EEA national's household (but not a dependant) before coming to the UK and is now dependant on the EEA national (but not a household member) within the UK satisfies the definition (see *Dauhoo (EEA Regulations—reg.8(2))* [2012] UKUT 79 (IAC)). However, it is necessary that the situation of dependence (or household membership) must have existed "in the country from which the family member concerned comes" and must have done so "at the very least at the time when [the extended family member] applies to join the Union citizen on whom he is dependent": see the paras 32–35 of the decision of the CJEU in *Secretary of State for the Home Department v Rahman & Others* (Case C-83/11). See also *CIS/612/2008* and *AP and FP (Citizens Directive Article 3(2); discretion; dependence) India* [2007] UKAIT 48.

Paragraph (3) sets out the third condition. It is that the putative extended family member "is a relative of an EEA national and on serious health grounds, strictly requires the personal care of the EEA national". Again, subject to para.(7), the putative extended family member must be related to the EEA national and not the EEA national's spouse or civil partner: see the discussion of *Soares* above.

Paragraph (4) sets out the fourth condition, namely that the putative extended family member "is a relative of an EEA national and would meet the requirements in the immigration rules (other than those relating to entry clearance) for indefinite leave to enter or remain in the United Kingdom as a dependent relative of the EEA national". This condition has no express equivalent in art.3(2) but is implicit in the obligation to facilitate entry and residence in accordance with national law and in the principle of equal treatment in art.24. The UK could hardly be said to be "facilitating" the entry or residence of an extended family member, or treating the EEA national equally, if it were not to allow a right of residence on the same, very strict, terms that apply to the family members of British citizens.

Paragraph (5) sets out the final condition. The putative extended family member qualifies if he or she is "the partner (other than a civil partner) of, and in a durable relationship with, an EEA national, and is able to prove this to the decision maker." The wording is broad enough to cover irregular, but durable, relationships between both heterosexual and same sex partners.

"Durability" was considered by the Commissioner in *CIS/612/2008*. It was stated that:

"36. 'Durable' has an element of ambiguity. It may mean that it has lasted or that it is capable of lasting. Too much should not be made of this. If the focus is on the past, the length of time for which the partnership has survived will not be the only factor that is relevant. The circumstances will be as important as the duration of the relationship. Survival in times of wealth, health and good fortune is less an indication of durability than survival in terms of poverty, poor health and misfortune. And if the focus in on the present and future, the fact that it has lasted may, depending on the circumstances, be very good evidence that it is and will remain durable.

37. 'Durable' governs the relationship, not the partnership. However, the relationship has to be with the partner. It may, and usually will, have existed before the couple became partners and evidence of the relationship at that time is relevant to its durability.

38. Subject to these points, the durability of a relationship is an issue of fact."

"Durable partner" is defined by reg.2(1) as not including "a party to a durable partnership of convenience" or to those in a quasi-polygamous durable partnership. "Durable partnership of convenience" is further defined as including:

"a durable partnership entered into for the purpose of using these Regulations, or any other right conferred by the EU Treaties, as a means to circumvent—

(a) immigration rules applying to non-EEA nationals (such as any applicable requirement under the 1971 Act to have leave to enter or remain in the United Kingdom); or

(b) any other criteria that the party to the durable partnership of convenience would otherwise have to meet in order to enjoy a right to reside under these Regulations or the EU Treaties".

However, it is difficult to see how any partnership that fell within that definition could satisfy the criteria for assessing durability in *CIS/612/2008*.

Paragraph (6). The phrase "relevant EEA national" is not used in reg.8, other than to define that phrase as it appears in other regulations. It means the EEA national to whom the extended family member is related, or of whom s/he is the durable partner.

Family members [² and extended family members] of British citizens

9.—(1) If the conditions in paragraph (2) are satisfied, these Regulations apply to a person who is the family member ("F") of a British citizen ("BC") as though the BC were an EEA national.   5.109

[² (1A) These Regulations apply to a person who is the extended family member ("EFM") of a BC as though the BC were an EEA national if—

(a) the conditions in paragraph (2) are satisfied; and

(b) the EFM was lawfully resident in the EEA State referred to in paragraph (2)(a)(i).]

(2) The conditions are that—

(a) BC—

(i) is residing in an EEA State as a worker, self-employed person, self-sufficient person or a student, or so resided immediately before returning to the United Kingdom; or

(ii) has acquired the right of permanent residence in an EEA State;

(b) F [² or EFM] and BC resided together in the EEA State; [¹ ...]

(c) F [² or EFM] and BC's residence in the EEA State was genuine

[¹ [³ (d) either—

(i) F was a family member of BC during all or part of their joint residence in the EEA State;

    (ii) F was an EFM of BC during all or part of their joint residence in the EEA State, during which time F was lawfully resident in the EEA State; or

    (iii) EFM was an EFM of BC during all or part of their joint residence in the EEA State, during which time EFM was lawfully resident in the EEA State;]

  (e) genuine family life was created or strengthened during [² F or EFM and BC's] joint residence in the EEA State] [³ and]

[³ (f) the conditions in sub-paragraphs (a), (b) and (c) have been met concurrently.]

(3) Factors relevant to whether residence in the EEA State is or was genuine include—

  (a) whether the centre of BC's life transferred to the EEA State;

  (b) the length of F [² or EFM] and BC's joint residence in the EEA State;

  (c) the nature and quality of the F [² or EFM] and BC's accommodation in the EEA State, and whether it is or was BC's principal residence;

  (d) the degree of F [² or EFM] and BC's integration in the EEA State;

  (e) whether F's [² or EFM's] first lawful residence in the EU with BC was in the EEA State.

(4) This regulation does not apply—

  (a) where the purpose of the residence in the EEA State was as a means for circumventing any immigration laws applying to non-EEA nationals to which F [² or EFM] would otherwise be subject (such as any applicable requirement under the 1971 Act to have leave to enter or remain in the United Kingdom); [² ...]

  (b) [² ...]

(5) Where these Regulations apply to F [² or EFM], BC is to be treated as holding a valid passport issued by an EEA State for the purposes of the application of these Regulations to F [² or EFM].

(6) In paragraph (2)(a)(ii), BC is only to be treated as having acquired the right of permanent residence in the EEA State if such residence would have led to the acquisition of that right under regulation 15, had it taken place in the United Kingdom.

(7) For the purposes of determining whether, when treating the BC as an EEA national under these Regulations in accordance with paragraph (1), BC would be a qualified person—

    (a) any requirement to have comprehensive sickness insurance cover in the United Kingdom still applies, save that it does not require the cover to extend to BC;

  (b) in assessing whether BC can continue to be treated as a worker under regulation 6(2)(b) or (c), BC is not required to satisfy condition A;

  (c) in assessing whether BC can be treated as a jobseeker as defined in regulation 6(1), BC is not required to satisfy conditions A and, where it would otherwise be relevant, condition C.

AMENDMENT

1. Immigration (European Economic Area) (Amendment) Regulations 2018 (SI 2018/801) reg.2 and Sch., para.3 (July 24, 2018).

2. Immigration (European Economic Area Nationals) (EU Exit) Regulations 2019 (SI 2019/468) reg.3(4) and (5) (March 28, 2019).

3. Immigration (European Economic Area) (Amendment) Regulations 2019 (SI 2019/1155) reg.2(1) and (6) (August 15, 2019).

DEFINITION

"the 1971 Act"—see reg.2(1).
"EEA national"—*ibid.*
"EEA State"—*ibid.*
"extended family member"—see reg.8.
"family member"—see reg.7.
"immigration laws"—*ibid.*
"jobseeker"—see reg.6(1).
"qualified person"—*ibid.*
"Self-employed person"—see reg.4(1)(b).
"self-sufficient person"—see reg.4(1)(c).
"student"—see reg.4(1)(d).
"worker"—see reg.4(1)(a).

GENERAL NOTE

The Citizenship Directive does not confer an automatic right of residence on **5.110** the third-country national family members of EEA nationals in the Member State of nationality. However, where the EEA national has resided with a third country national family member in a member state of which the EEA national is not a national, while exercising rights under art.7, the Member State of nationality must grant the third-country national family member a derived right of residence on the EEA national's return: see *R v Immigration Appeal Tribunal and Surinder Singh, ex p. Secretary of State for the Home Department* (Case C-370/90); *Minister voor Vreemdelingenzaken en Integratie v Eind* (Case C-291/05) and *O and B v Minister voor Immigratie, Integratie en Asiel* (Case C-456/12). That principle is implemented in UK domestic law by reg.9.

Regulation 9 in (more or less) its present form was inserted in the 2006 Regulations by reg.44 and Sch.5 with effect from November 25, 2016 because the UK government considered that, as it was previously worded, the regulation was open to abuse and was being used to circumvent the family reunification provisions of domestic UK immigration law (which are less generous than the rules for the family members or EEA nationals exercising their rights of free movement here). Adopting the approach of the CJEU in the *O and B* case, there is now a requirement (in para.(2)(c)) that the residence of the British citizen and the family member in the other EEA state should have been "genuine" and para.(3) lists a number of factors that must be taken into account when deciding whether that is the case. In addition, an anti-abuse provision in para.(4)(a) disapplies the regulation where "the purpose of the residence in the EEA State was as a means for circumventing any immigration laws applying to non-EEA nationals to which F would otherwise be subject (such as any applicable requirement under the 1971 Act to have leave to enter or remain in the United Kingdom)": see, *e.g., Kaur v Secretary of State for the Home Department* [2020] EWCA Civ 98.

Before March 28, 2019, para,(4)(b) also disapplied the Regulation where the third-country national was only a "family member" by virtue of the rules treating "extended family members" as family members. However, that restriction became unsustainable following the decision in following the decision of in the CJEU in *Banger v Secretary of State for the Home Department* (Case C-89/17). In *Banger (Unmarried Partner of British National)* [2017] UKUT 125 (IAC), the Immigration Appeals Chamber of the Upper Tribunal referred the following questions:

"(1) Do the principles contained in the decision in Immigration Appeal Tribunal and Surinder Singh, ex parte Secretary of State for the Home Department (Case C-370/90) [1992] operate so as to require a Member State to issue or, alternatively, facilitate the provision of a residence authorisation to the non-Union unmarried partner of a EU citizen who, having exercised his Treaty right of freedom of movement to work in a second Member State, returns with such partner to the Member State of his nationality?

(2) Alternatively, is there a requirement to issue or alternatively, facilitate the provision of such residence authorisation by virtue of European Parliament and Council Directive 2004/38/EC on the right of citizens of the Union and their family members to move and reside freely within the territory of the Member States ("the Directive")?

(3) Where a decision to refuse a residence authorisation is not founded on an extensive examination of the personal circumstances of the Applicant and is not justified by adequate or sufficient reasons is such decision unlawful as being in breach of Article 3(2) of the Citizens Directive?

(4) Is a rule of national law which precludes an appeal to a court or tribunal against a decision of the executive refusing to issue a residence card to a person claiming to be an extended family member compatible with the Directive?

The CJEU answered those questions as follows:

1. Article 21(1) TFEU must be interpreted as requiring the Member State of which a Union citizen is a national to facilitate the provision of a residence authorisation to the unregistered partner, a third-country national with whom that Union citizen has a durable relationship that is duly attested, where the Union citizen, having exercised his right of freedom of movement to work in a second Member State, in accordance with the conditions laid down in [the Citizenship] Directive ..., returns with his partner to the Member State of which he is a national in order to reside there.

2. Article 21(1) TFEU must be interpreted as meaning that a decision to refuse a residence authorisation to the third-country national and unregistered partner of a Union citizen, where that Union citizen, having exercised his right of freedom of movement to work in a second Member State, in accordance with the conditions laid down in [the Citizenship] Directive ..., returns with his partner to the Member State of which he is a national in order to reside there, must be founded on an extensive examination of the applicant's personal circumstances and be justified by reasons.

3. Article 3(2) of [the Citizenship] Directive ... must be interpreted as meaning that the third-country nationals envisaged in that provision must have available to them a redress procedure in order to challenge a decision to refuse a residence authorisation taken against them, following which the national court must be able to ascertain whether the refusal decision is based on a sufficiently solid factual basis and whether the procedural safeguards were complied with. Those safeguards include the obligation for the competent national authorities to undertake an extensive examination of the applicant's personal circumstances and to justify any denial of entry or residence.

With effect from March 28, 2019, reg.3(4) and (5) of SI 2019/468 amended reg.9 so as to bring domestic UK law into line with EU law as set out in *Banger*. The new para.(1A) gives extended family members of British citizens the same rights as British citizens, provided only that the extended family member was lawfully resident in the state in which the British citizen was residing in accordance with his or her rights under art.7 of the Citizenship Directive: see para.(1A)(b).

The right of facilitation recognised by the CJEU in *Banger* is not subject to the limitations on the right recognised in the *O and B* case. So, it is not necessary for a *Banger* durable partner to have made an application to the immigration authorities of the Member State in which the relationship was formed or strengthened under art.3(2) of the Directive or, to have obtained an immigration decision from those authorities based on that provision: see the decision of the Court of Appeal (Underhill, Sharp and Sales LJJ) in *Secretary of State for the Home Department v Christy* [2018] EWCA Civ 2378.

In *GA v SSWP (SPC)* [2018] UKUT 172 (AAC), the claimant was an Italian national. On the assumed facts, he had met and married a British citizen while she was living and working in Italy in 1968. They moved to the UK in 1969 and the claimant had worked in the UK from 1970 to 2000, when he left the UK. In the meantime, the couple had separated but did not divorce. The claimant returned to the UK in 2013 and the couple were finally divorced in March 2015. Judge Markus QC held that in those circumstances, the Surinder Singh principle did not apply because, at the time the British Citizen was working in Italy, and at the time of her return to the UK with her husband, the UK was not a member of the (then) EEC and so was not exercising her Treaty rights to freedom of movement on either occasion.

In *HK v SSWP (PC) [2020] UKUT 73* (AAC), the issue was whether the words "these Regulations apply to a person who is the family member ("F") of a British citizen ("BC") as though the BC were an EEA national" had the effect that BC had to be the equivalent of a qualified person or a person with a right of permanent residence in order for F to acquire a right to reside. Judge Ward summarised the facts as follows:

> "2. The background is that the appellant (Mr K) is an Austrian national. His wife, Mrs K, is a British citizen. It is common ground that in 1979, before the couple had met, Mrs K went to Germany to work and did so for many years, eventually accruing a right of permanent residence there under [the Directive]. It was while living and working in Germany that she met and married Mr K. In November 2014, by which time Mrs K was not in good health, they moved to live in Scotland, initially living on savings and the pension from Mr K's job in Germany and staying with a relative. In around April 2018, ... the couple applied for social housing, housing benefit and council tax reduction and Mr K applied for state pension credit. Under section 1(2) of the State Pension Credit Act 2002 and Regulations 2(1) and 2(2) of the State Pension Credit Regulations 2002/1792, it is a condition of entitlement that a claimant has a qualifying right to reside. On 30 July 2018 the Secretary of State decided that Mr K did not have such a right and so his claim was refused."

The reason for the refusal was that, if regulation 9(1) is read literally and the 2016 Regulations applied to her "as though [she] were an EEA national", then she would not have had a right to reside herself and Mr K could therefore have no better right as her family member. Mrs K was above state pension credit age, ill, and would not have fallen within any of the categories of "qualified person" in reg. 6. Neither would she have a right of permanent residence in the UK under reg. 15 because she had not lived in the UK as a qualified person for a continuous period of five years. As a matter of immigration law, she did not need those rights because she had a right of abode as a British citizen. Nevertheless, if the 2016 Regulations were applied to her "as though [she] were an EEA national", then she did not have them.

Relying in particular on the decision of the CJEU in *Minister voor Vremdelingenzaken en Integratie v RNG Eind* (C-456/12), Judge Ward held at [44] that "reg 9(1) is to be interpreted as not requiring, as part of how "these Regulations apply", "BC" to fulfil the condition of being a "qualified person" under reg. 6". The reasoning behind that conclusion is summarised at [31]:

> "31. The requirement is to apply the Directive "by analogy", a somewhat ill-defined process. We know, however, that, whatever this means, it does not extend to the ability to impose a requirement to be economically active upon return (*Eind*), even though either that, or being a student or self-sufficient, would be a requirement if one was starting *ab initio* in another Member State. Nor can it be the case that the conditions imposed could derogate from the effectiveness of allowing a person who has acquired a right of permanent residence elsewhere to return with the family member concerned (*O and B* at [45]), as would occur if a condition were to be imposed requiring the citizen to re-qualify for permanent residence by a further 5 years as a qualified person before reliance could be

placed on the second limb of reg 14(2) . . . . This view is consistent with the idea, seen in both *Eind* and *O and B*, that what earned the Union citizen's ability to confer a derived right upon his family member was his initial exercise of freedom of movement rights to go to another Member State to an extent which passes the *O and B* tests of strengthening family life there.

Finally Judge Ward observed (at [44]):

"While the issue has been raised in these proceedings only tangentially, I cannot see that the condition in reg 14(2) could be applied so as to require the returning British citizen to have a right of permanent residence (as if under the Directive) either".

[¹ Dual national: national of an EEA State who acquires British citizenship

5.111 **9A.**—(1) In this regulation "DN" means a person within paragraph (b) of the definition of "EEA national" in regulation 2(1).

(2) DN who comes within the definition of "qualified person" in regulation 6(1) is only a qualified person for the purpose of these Regulations if DN—

(a) came within the definition of "qualified person" at the time of acquisition of British citizenship; and

(b) has not at any time subsequent to the acquisition of British citizenship lost the status of qualified person.

(3) Regulation 15 only applies to DN, or to the family member of DN who is not an EEA national, if DN satisfies the condition in paragraph (4).

(4) The condition in this paragraph is that at the time of acquisition of British citizenship DN either—

(a) was a qualified person; or

(b) had acquired a right of permanent residence in accordance with these Regulations.]

AMENDMENT

1. Immigration (European Economic Area) (Amendment) Regulations 2018 (SI 2018/801) reg.2 and Sch., para.4 (July 24, 2018).

DEFINITIONS

"EEA national"—see reg.2(1).
"qualified person"—see reg.6.
"right of permanent residence"—see reg.15.

GENERAL NOTE

Regulation 9A was inserted with effect from July 24, 2018 by SI 2018/801 in order to bring domestic law into line with EU law as set out by the CJEU in *Toufik Lounes v Secretary of State for the Home Department* (Case C-165/16): see, further, the discussion under the heading, *The personal scope of the Citizenship* Directive, in the introductory General Note to these Regulations.

Paragraph (1) defines "DN" (obviously short for "dual national") as meaning a person within para.(b) of the definition of "EEA National" in reg.2(1), namely "a national of an EEA State who is also a British citizen and who prior to acquiring British citizenship exercised a right to reside as such a national, in accordance with regulation 14 or 15".

Paragraph (2) provides that such a dual national is only a "qualified person" within reg.6 if s/he was a qualified person when s/he acquired British citizenship and has not lost that status at any time since. The consequence, which is not spelled out in the regulation, is that where the dual national satisfies those requirements, his or her family members and extended family members have the same rights as the family members and extended family members of any qualified person.

Paragraphs (3) and (4) provide that neither the dual national, nor his or her non-EEA family members, are treated as having a permanent right of residence under reg.15 unless the dual national was either a qualified person, or had acquired a permanent right of residence, when s/he acquired British citizenship. This does not affect the dual national who, *ex hypothesi*, is a British citizen (see note to para.(1) above). However, it may restrict the circumstances in which family members and extended family members may derive a permanent right of residence from the dual national.

"Family member who has retained the right of residence"

10.—(1) In these Regulations, "family member who has retained the 5.112 right of residence" means, subject to paragraphs (8) and (9), a person who satisfies a condition in paragraph (2), (3), (4) or (5).

(2) The condition in this paragraph is that the person—

(a) was a family member of a qualified person or of an EEA national with a right of permanent residence when the qualified person or the EEA national with the right of permanent residence died;

(b) resided in the United Kingdom in accordance with these Regulations for at least the year immediately before the death of the qualified person or the EEA national with a right of permanent residence; and

(c) satisfies the condition in paragraph (6).

(3) The condition in this paragraph is that the person—

(a) is the direct descendant of—

(i) a qualified person or an EEA national with a right of permanent residence who has died;

(ii) a person who ceased to be a qualified person on ceasing to reside in the United Kingdom;

(iii) the spouse or civil partner of the qualified person or EEA national described in sub-paragraph (i) immediately preceding that qualified person or EEA national's death; or

(iv) the spouse or civil partner of the person described in sub-paragraph (ii); and

(b) was attending an educational course in the United Kingdom immediately before the qualified person or the EEA national with a right of permanent residence died, or ceased to be a qualified person, and continues to attend such a course.

(4) The condition in this paragraph is that the person is the parent with actual custody of a child who satisfies the condition in paragraph (3).

(5) The condition in this paragraph is that the person ("A")—

(a) ceased to be a family member of a qualified person or an EEA national with a right of permanent residence on the termination of the marriage or civil partnership of A;

(b) was residing in the United Kingdom in accordance with these Regulations at the date of the [¹ initiation of proceedings for the termination];

(c) satisfies the condition in paragraph (6); and

(d) either—

(i) prior to the initiation of the proceedings for the termination of the marriage or the civil partnership, the marriage or civil partnership had lasted for at least three years and the parties to the marriage or civil partnership had resided in the United Kingdom for at least one year during its duration;

(ii) the former spouse or civil partner of the qualified person or the EEA national with a right of permanent residence has custody of a child of that qualified person or EEA national;

(iii) the former spouse or civil partner of the qualified person or the EEA national with a right of permanent residence has the right of access to a child of that qualified person or EEA national, where the child is under the age of 18 and where a court has ordered that such access must take place in the United Kingdom; or

(iv) the continued right of residence in the United Kingdom of A is warranted by particularly difficult circumstances, such as where A or another family member has been a victim of domestic violence whilst the marriage or civil partnership was subsisting.

(6) The condition in this paragraph is that the person—

(a) is not an EEA national but would, if the person were an EEA national, be a worker, a self-employed person or a self-sufficient person under regulation 6; or

(b) is the family member of a person who falls within paragraph (a).

(7) In this regulation, "educational course" means a course within the scope of Article 10 of Council Regulation (EU) No. 492/2011.

(8) A person ("P") does not satisfy a condition in paragraph (2), (3), (4) or (5) if, at the first time P would otherwise have satisfied the relevant condition, P had a right of permanent residence under regulation 15.

(9) A family member who has retained the right of residence ceases to enjoy that status on acquiring a right of permanent residence under regulation 15.

AMENDMENT

1. Immigration (European Economic Area) (Amendment) Regulations 2019 (SI 2019/1155) reg.2(1) and (7) (August 15, 2019).

DEFINITION

"civil partner"—see reg.2(1).
"EEA national"—*ibid*.
"family member"—see reg.7.
"qualified person"—see reg.6(1).
"self-employed person"—see reg.4(1)(b).
"self-sufficient person"—see reg.4(1)(c).
"spouse"—see reg.2(1).
"worker"—see reg.4(1)(a).

GENERAL NOTE

5.113   Regulation 10 implements arts 12 and 13. A family member who has retained the right of residence has an extended right of residence in the UK for as long as s/he retains that status (see reg.14(3)). In addition residence as a family member who has retained the right of residence counts towards the continuous period of five years' residence required by reg.15(1)(a) and (b) for the acquisition of a permanent right of residence. Note that a family member who has already acquired a right of permanent residence (i.e., by residing with the EEA national for a continuous period of five years) does not need to rely on—and is not subject to the restrictions in—reg.10: see *MS v SSWP* (ESA) [2020] UKUT 235 (AAC) (and also para.(9)).

Family member who has retained the right of residence

Paragraph (1)."Family member who has retained the right of residence" is defined **5.114** by para.(1). The phrase means a person—other than a person with a right of permanent residence (see para.(8))—who satisfies at least one of four conditions.

Paragraph (2) sets out the first condition. It applies to those who were family members of a qualified person, or of an EEA national with a permanent right residence, when that person died and who had resided in the UK in accordance with the 2016 Regulations for at least a year immediately before the death. This only applies where the person seeking to retain the right of residence either:

- is not an EEA national, but would qualify as a worker, a self-employed person or a self-sufficient person if s/he were;

- or is a family member of such a person,

(see para.(6)). In other words, to retain the right of residence by satisfying para. (2), the former family member must be economically active or the family member of someone else who is. The first option excludes EEA nationals because an EEA national who would qualify as a worker, a self-employed person or a self-sufficient person would be a qualified person with an extended right of residence in any event and would not need to have such a right under reg.10.

Paragraph (3) sets out the second condition. It applies to the direct descendants of a qualified person, or of an EEA national with a permanent right residence, who has died or ceased to be a qualifying person on ceasing to reside in the UK (or of the spouse or civil partner of such a qualified person) who were attending an educational course (within the scope of art.10 of regulation 492/2011 (formerly art.12 of Regulation 1612/68): see para.(7)) in the UK immediately before the qualified person died or ceased to live in the UK and who continue to attend such a course.

Paragraph (4) sets out the third condition. It applies to parents who have "actual custody" of a child who satisfies the conditions in para.(3).

Paragraph (5) sets out the fourth condition. It applies to former spouses or civil partners of a qualified person, or of an EEA national with a permanent right residence (a "former spouse or partner"), who were residing in the UK on the date when the marriage or civil partnership came to an end, where either:

- the marriage or civil partnership had lasted for at least three years before the commencement of the legal proceedings to terminate it and the parties had both resided in the UK for at least one year during its duration. The decision of the CJEU in *Singh and others v Minister for Justice and Equality* (Case C-218/14) holds that art.13(2) of the Citizenship Directive (which is implemented by para.(5)) only applies where the qualified person or EEA national with a permanent right of residence was still resident in the host member State at the time when the divorce proceedings (or proceedings to terminate the civil partnership) were commenced; or

- the former spouse or partner has custody of a child of the qualified person, or of the EEA national with a permanent right residence, or a right of access to such a child that, by court order, can only take place in the UK; or

- there are "particularly difficult circumstances" that warrant the former spouse or partner continuing to have a right of residence in the UK. The example that is given is where the former spouse or partner or another family member has "been a victim of domestic violence while the marriage or civil partnership was subsisting"

As with para.(2), para.(5) only applies where the person seeking to retain the right of residence is not an EEA national, but would qualify as a worker, a self-employed person or a self-sufficient person if s/he were, or is a family member of such a person (see para.(6) and the commentary to para.(2) above).

Residence in the UK before February 1, 2017 counts as residence in accordance with the 2016 Regulations if it was in accordance with the 2000 Regulations or the 2006 Regulations (see Sch.6, para.8).

For the date on which a marriage or civil partnership ends, see the commentary to reg.7 above.

PART 2

EEA RIGHTS

Right of admission to the United Kingdom

5.115   **11.**—(1) An EEA national must be admitted to the United Kingdom on arrival if the EEA national produces a valid national identity card or passport issued by an EEA State.

(2) A person who is not an EEA national must be admitted to the United Kingdom if that person is—

   (a) a family member of an EEA national and produces on arrival a valid passport and qualifying EEA State residence card, provided the conditions in regulation 23(4) (family member of EEA national must accompany or join EEA national with right to reside) are met; or

   (b) a family member of an EEA national, a family member who has retained the right of residence, a person who meets the criteria in paragraph (5) or a person with a right of permanent residence under regulation 15 and produces on arrival—

     (i) a valid passport; and

     (ii) a valid EEA family permit, residence card, derivative residence card or permanent residence card.

(3) An immigration officer must not place a stamp in the passport of a person admitted to the United Kingdom under this regulation who is not an EEA national if the person produces a residence card, a derivative residence card, a permanent residence card or a qualifying EEA State residence card.

(4) Before an immigration officer refuses admission to the United Kingdom to a person under this regulation because the person does not produce on arrival a document mentioned in paragraph (1) or (2), the immigration officer must provide every reasonable opportunity for the document to be obtained by, or brought to, the person or allow the person to prove by other means that the person is—

   (a) an EEA national;

   (b) a family member of an EEA national with a right to accompany that EEA national or join that EEA national in the United Kingdom;

   (c) a person who meets the criteria in paragraph (5); or

   (d) a family member who has retained the right of residence or a person with a right of permanent residence under regulation 15.

(5) The criteria in this paragraph are that a person ("P")—

   (a) previously resided in the United Kingdom under regulation 16(3) and would be entitled to reside in the United Kingdom under that regulation were P in the country;

   (b) is accompanying an EEA national to, or joining an EEA national in, the United Kingdom and P would be entitled to reside in the United Kingdom under regulation 16(2) were P and the EEA national both in the United Kingdom;

(c) is accompanying a person ("the relevant person") to, or joining the relevant person in, the United Kingdom and—
   (i) the relevant person is residing, or has resided, in the United Kingdom under regulation 16(3); and
   (ii) P would be entitled to reside in the United Kingdom under regulation 16(4) were P and the relevant person both in the United Kingdom;
(d) is accompanying a person who meets the criteria in sub-paragraph (b) or (c) ("the relevant person") to the United Kingdom and—
   (i) P and the relevant person are both—
      (aa) seeking admission to the United Kingdom in reliance on this paragraph for the first time; or
      (bb) returning to the United Kingdom having previously resided there pursuant to the same provisions of regulation 16 in reliance on which they now base their claim to admission; and
   (ii) P would be entitled to reside in the United Kingdom under regulation 16(6) were P and the relevant person there; or
(e) is accompanying a British citizen to, or joining a British citizen in, the United Kingdom and P would be entitled to reside in the United Kingdom under regulation 16(5) were P and the British citizen both in the United Kingdom.
(6) Paragraph (7) applies where—
(a) a person ("P") seeks admission to the United Kingdom in reliance on paragraph (5)(b), (c) or (e); and
(b) if P were in the United Kingdom, P would have a derived right to reside under regulation 16(8)(b)(ii).
(7) Where this paragraph applies a person ("P") must only be regarded as meeting the criteria in paragraph (5)(b), (c) or (e) where P—
(a) is accompanying the person with whom P would on admission to the United Kingdom jointly share care responsibility for the purpose of regulation 16(8)(b)(ii); or
(b) has previously resided in the United Kingdom pursuant to regulation 16(2), (4) or (5) as a joint primary carer and seeks admission to the United Kingdom in order to reside there again on the same basis.
(8) But this regulation is subject to regulations 23(1), (2), (3) and (4) and 31.
[¹ (9) A person is not entitled to be admitted by virtue of this regulation where that person is subject to a decision under regulation 23(6)(b) (removal decision).]

AMENDMENT

1. Immigration (European Economic Area) (Amendment) Regulations 2018 (SI 2018/801) reg.2 and Sch., para.5 (July 24, 2018).

DEFINITION

"derivative residence card"—see regs 2(1) and 20.
"EEA family permit"—see regs 2(1) and 12.
"EEA national"—see reg.2(1).
"EEA State"—*ibid*.
"family member"—see reg.7.
"family member who has retained the right of residence"—see reg.10.

"permanent residence card"—see regs 2(1) and 19(2).
"qualifying EEA State residence card"—see reg.2(1).
"residence card"—see regs 2(1) and 18.
"right to reside"—see reg.2(1).

GENERAL NOTE

5.116   Regulation 11 is about rights of entry, rather than rights of residence and therefore does not require detailed commentary in a publication about social security. It is, however, worth noting that it is the right of EEA nationals and their family members to enter the UK without leave under Immigration Act 1988 s.7 and reg.11 that means they are not excluded from entitlement to benefits as "persons subject to immigration control" under Immigration and Asylum Act 1999, s.115.

Issue of EEA family permit

5.117   **12.**—(1) An entry clearance officer must issue an EEA family permit to a person who applies for one if the person is a family member of an EEA national and—
   (a) the EEA national—
      (i) is residing in the United Kingdom in accordance with these Regulations; or
      (ii) will be travelling to the United Kingdom within six months of the date of the application and will be an EEA national residing in the United Kingdom in accordance with these Regulations on arrival in the United Kingdom; and
   (b) the family member will be accompanying the EEA national to the United Kingdom or joining the EEA national there.
(2) An entry clearance officer must issue an EEA family permit to a person who applies and provides evidence demonstrating that, at the time at which the person first intends to use the EEA family permit, the person—
   (a) would be entitled to be admitted to the United Kingdom because that person would meet the criteria in regulation 11(5); and
   (b) will (save in the case of a person who would be entitled to be admitted to the United Kingdom because that person would meet the criteria for admission in regulation 11(5)(a)) be accompanying to, or joining in, the United Kingdom any person from whom the right to be admitted to the United Kingdom under the criteria in regulation 11(5) is derived.
(3) An entry clearance officer must issue an EEA family permit to—
   (a) a family member who has retained the right of residence; or
   (b) a person who is not an EEA national but who has acquired the right of permanent residence under regulation 15.
(4) An entry clearance officer may issue an EEA family permit to an extended family member of an EEA national (the relevant EEA national) who applies for one if—
   (a) the relevant EEA national satisfies the condition in paragraph (1)(a);
   (b) the extended family member wants to accompany the relevant EEA national to the United Kingdom or to join that EEA national there; and
   (c) in all the circumstances, it appears to the entry clearance officer appropriate to issue the EEA family permit.
(5) Where an entry clearance officer receives an application under paragraph (4) an extensive examination of the personal circumstances of the

applicant must be undertaken by the Secretary of State and if the application is refused, the entry clearance officer must give reasons justifying the refusal unless this is contrary to the interests of national security.

[¹ (5A) An EEA family permit issued under this regulation may be issued in electronic form.]

(6) An EEA family permit issued under this regulation must be issued free of charge and as soon as possible.

(7) But an EEA family permit must not be issued under this regulation if the applicant or the EEA national concerned is not entitled to be admitted to the United Kingdom as a result of regulation 23(1), (2) or (3) or falls to be excluded in accordance with regulation 23(5).

(8) An EEA family permit must not be issued under this regulation to a person ("A") who is the spouse, civil partner or durable partner of a person ("B") where a spouse, civil partner or durable partner of A or B holds a valid EEA family permit.

AMENDMENT

1. Immigration (European Economic Area) (Amendment) Regulations 2018 (SI 2018/801) reg.2 and Sch., para.6 (July 24, 2018).

DEFINITION

"civil partner"—see reg.2(1).
"durable partner"—*ibid.*
"EEA family permit"—see General Note to Pt.3.
"EEA national"—see reg.2(1).
"entry clearance officer"—*ibid.*
"extended family member"—see reg.8.
"family member"—see reg.7.
"family member who has retained the right of residence"—see reg.10.
"relevant EEA national"—see regs 2(1) and 8(6).
"spouse"—see reg.2(1).

GENERAL NOTE

See the General Note to Pt 3.   5.118

Initial right of residence

13.—(1) An EEA national is entitled to reside in the United Kingdom for   5.119
a period not exceeding three months beginning on the date of admission to the United Kingdom provided the EEA national holds a valid national identity card or passport issued by an EEA State.

(2) A person who is not an EEA national but is a family member who has retained the right of residence or the family member of an EEA national residing in the United Kingdom under paragraph (1) is entitled to reside in the United Kingdom provided that person holds a valid passport.

(3) An EEA national or the family member of an EEA national who is an unreasonable burden on the social assistance system of the United Kingdom does not have a right to reside under this regulation.

(4) A person who otherwise satisfies the criteria in this regulation is not entitled to a right to reside under this regulation where the Secretary of State or an immigration officer has made a decision under regulation 23(6)(b) (decision to remove on grounds of public policy, public security or public health), 24(1) (refusal to issue residence documentation etc),

25(1) (cancellation of a right of residence), 26(3) (misuse of right to reside) or 31(1) (revocation of admission) [¹ or an order under regulation 23(5) (exclusion order) or 32(3) (deportation order), unless that decision or order, as the case may be, is set aside, revoked or otherwise no longer has effect].

AMENDMENT

1. Immigration (European Economic Area) (Amendment) Regulations 2018 (SI 2018/801) reg.2 and Sch., para.7 (July 24, 2018).

DEFINITION

"EEA national"—see reg.2(1).
"EEA State"—*ibid.*
"family member"—see reg.7.
"family member who has retained the right of residence"—see reg.10.
"right to reside"—see reg.2(1).

GENERAL NOTE

5.120   Regulation 13 implements art .6. It permits EEA nationals, and their non-EEA national family members, to reside in the UK for up to three months for any reason. That right is subject to reg.13(3)(b) (implementing art.14) and therefore ceases if either the EEA national or the family member "becomes an unreasonable burden on the social assistance system of the United Kingdom".

Rights of residence under the Citizenship Directive normally carry with them the right to equal treatment under art.24. However, the right to equal treatment that accompanies the initial right of residence is subject to a derogation in art.24(2) which states that "the host Member State shall not be obliged to confer entitlement to social assistance during the first three months of residence". In *Vestische Arbeit Jobcenter Kreis Recklinghausen v Garcia-Nieto* and others (C-299/14), the CJEU confirmed that neither art.24, nor the principle of equality of treatment in art.4 of Regulation (EC) No 883/2004, prevented Member States from excluding those whose only right of residence arose under art.6 of the Citizenship Directive from entitlement to special non-contributory cash benefits (see art.70(2) of Regulation No 883/2004) which also constitute "social assistance" within the meaning of Article 24(2). In such circumstances, (following *Alimanovic* (C-67/14) and distinguishing *Brey* (C-140/12): see further below) it was unnecessary to carry out an individual assessment of the circumstances of the person concerned.

In accordance with those derogations, reg.21AA(3)(a) and (c) of the IS Regulations, reg.85A(3) of the JSA Regulations, reg.70(a) and (c) of the ESA Regulations, reg.2(3)(a) and (c) of the SPC Regulations, and reg.9(3)(a) of the Universal Credit Regulations provide that the initial right of residence does not qualify a claimant to any of those benefits.

However, under domestic law, though not EU law, residence pursuant to reg.13 is "in accordance with these regulations" within reg.15(1)(a) and therefore counts towards the period of five years' continuous residence required by that regulation for the acquisition of a permanent right of residence: see *GE v SSWP (ESA)* [2017] UKUT 145 (AAC), [2017] AACR 34.

Extended right of residence

5.121   **14.**—(1) A qualified person is entitled to reside in the United Kingdom for as long as that person remains a qualified person.

(2) A person ("P") who is a family member of a qualified person residing in the United Kingdom under paragraph (1) or of an EEA national with a

right of permanent residence under regulation 15 is entitled to remain in the United Kingdom for so long as P remains the family member of that person or EEA national.

(3) A family member who has retained the right of residence is entitled to reside in the United Kingdom for so long as that person remains a family member who has retained the right of residence.

(4) A person who otherwise satisfies the criteria in this regulation is not entitled to a right to reside in the United Kingdom under this regulation where the Secretary of State or an immigration officer has made a decision under regulation 23(6)(b), 24(1), 25(1), 26(3) or 31(1), [¹ or an order under regulation 23(5) (exclusion order) or 32(3) (deportation order), unless that decision or order, as the case may be, is set aside, revoked or otherwise no longer has effect].

AMENDMENT

1. Immigration (European Economic Area) (Amendment) Regulations 2018 (SI 2018/801) reg.2 and Sch., para.8 (July 24, 2018).

DEFINITION

"EEA national"—see reg.2(1).
"family member"—see reg.7.
"family member who has retained the right of residence"—see reg.10.
"qualified person"—see reg.6(1).
"right to reside"—see reg.2(1).

GENERAL NOTE

Regulation 14 implements art.7. It establishes an extended right of residence for three categories of people:

5.122

- qualified persons (para.(1));

- family members of qualified persons or of EEA nationals with a permanent right of residence (para.2); and

- family members who have retained the right of residence (para.(3)).

Those categories are discussed in detail in the General Notes to regs 4, 6, 7 and 10 above.

Where an extended right of residence exists, it does so in addition to any initial or permanent right of residence that may exist during the same period.

The extended right of residence conferred on a "family member who has retained the right of residence" by para.(3) is not a right that is excluded by reg.21AA(3)(b) (ii) of the IS Regulations (or, by parity of reasoning, by the equivalent provisions of the JSA Regulations, the SPC Regulations, the ESA Regulations and the UC Regulations): see the decision of the Inner House of the Court of Session in *Slezak v Secretary of State for Work and Pensions* [2017] CSIH 4, [2017] AACR 21.

Right of permanent residence

15.—(1) The following persons acquire the right to reside in the United Kingdom permanently—

5.123

(a) an EEA national who has resided in the United Kingdom in accordance with these Regulations for a continuous period of five years;

(b) a family member of an EEA national who is not an EEA national but who has resided in the United Kingdom with the EEA national in accordance with these Regulations for a continuous period of five years;

    (c) a worker or self-employed person who has ceased activity;

    (d) the family member of a worker or self-employed person who has ceased activity, provided—

        (i) the person was the family member of the worker or self-employed person at the point the worker or self-employed person ceased activity; and

       (ii) at that point, the family member enjoyed a right to reside on the basis of being the family member of that worker or self-employed person;

    (e) a person who was the family member of a worker or self-employed person where—

        (i) the worker or self-employed person has died;

       (ii) the family member resided with the worker or self-employed person immediately before the death; and

      (iii) the worker or self-employed person had resided continuously in the United Kingdom for at least two years immediately before dying or the death was the result of an accident at work or an occupational disease;

    (f) a person who—

        (i) has resided in the United Kingdom in accordance with these Regulations for a continuous period of five years; and

       (ii) was, at the end of the period, a family member who has retained the right of residence.

(2) Residence in the United Kingdom as a result of a derivative right to reside does not constitute residence for the purpose of this regulation.

(3) The right of permanent residence under this regulation is lost through absence from the United Kingdom for a period exceeding two years.

(4) A person who satisfies the criteria in this regulation is not entitled to a right to permanent residence in the United Kingdom where the Secretary of State or an immigration officer has made a decision under regulation 23(6)(b), 24(1), 25(1), 26(3) or 31(1), [¹ or an order under regulation 23(5) (exclusion order) or 32(3) (deportation order), unless that decision or order, as the case may be, is set aside, revoked or otherwise no longer has effect].

AMENDMENT

    1. Immigration (European Economic Area) (Amendment) Regulations 2018 (SI 2018/801) reg.2 and Sch., para.9 (July 24, 2018).

DEFINITIONS

    "derivative right to reside"—see regs 2(1) and 16.
    "EEA national"—see reg.2(1).
    "family member"—see reg.7.
    "family member who has retained the right of residence"—see reg.10.
    "right to reside"—see reg.2(1).
    "self-employed person"—see reg.4(1)(b).
    "worker"—see reg.4(1)(a).
    "worker or self-employed person who has ceased activity"—see reg.5.

GENERAL NOTE

5.124   Regulation 15 implements arts 16 and 17 of the Citizenship Directive. It establishes a permanent right of residence for five categories of people:

- EEA nationals who have "resided in the UK in accordance with these Regulations for a continuous period of five years";

- family members of an EEA national who have resided in the UK with the EEA national "in accordance with these Regulations for a continuous period of five years". This category only applies where the family member is not an EEA national him or herself: otherwise there would be a permanent right of residence because of the previous category;

- a "worker or self-employed person who has ceased activity" and the family members of such a person;

- (in certain circumstances) family members of workers or self-employed persons who have died;

- (in certain circumstances) people who were formerly "family members who ha[d] retained the right of residence".

Those whose right of residence arises under paras (1)(c)–(e) (i.e., those who fall within the third and fourth of the five categories set out above) are exempt from the habitual residence test (and therefore also from the right to reside test) under reg.21AA(4)(zb) of the IS Regulations, reg.85A(4)(zb) of the JSA Regulations 1996, and reg.2(4)(zb) of the SPC Regulations and reg.9(4)(zb) of the Universal Credit Regulations. Those whose right arises under paras (1)(a), (b) and (f) (*i.e.,* on the basis of five years' continuous residence) are not automatically exempt but will almost inevitably have been living in the UK for considerably longer than would be required to become actually habitually resident.

Paragraphs (1)(a) and (b) – Continuous residence
Residence "in accordance with" these Regulations includes certain types of residence before February 1, 2017 including residence under the 2006 Regulations, the 2000 Regulations, and before October 2, 2000, in accordance the Immigration (European Economic Area) Order 1994 (see below). **5.125**
For continuity of residence, see the commentary to reg.3.

Legal residence—Ziolkowski and Szeja:
The question of what type or types of residence can form the basis of a permanent right to reside under art.16 of the Citizenship Directive was once an area of considerable legal uncertainty (see pp.334–340 of Vol.II of 2011–12 edition). The problem arose because although reg.15 requires that the period of five years' continuous residence should have been "in accordance with" what are now the 2016 Regulations, art.16 merely provides that the EEA national should have "resided legally" for that period. As it is possible for EEA national to reside legally in the UK without such residence being in accordance with the 2016 Regulations, it was unclear whether reg.15 correctly implemented art.16 and, if not, what other types of lawful residence would give rise to the permanent right. **5.126**
However, the law has been clarified—at least in relation to this point—by the decision of the Grand Chamber of the ECJ in *Tomasz Ziolkowski v Land Berlin* and *Barbara Szeja, Maria-Magdalena Szeja, Marlon Szeja v Land Berlin* (Joined Cases C-424/10 and C-425/10). In the light of that decision, it now appears that reg.15 not only fully implements art.16 but—at least as regards the rights of jobseekers—is more generous to certain EEA nationals than art.16 strictly requires.
In *Ziolkowski and Szeja*, the appellants in the proceedings before the *Bundesverwaltungsgericht* (the German Federal Administrative Court) were Polish nationals who had lived in Germany since 1989 and 1988 respectively. At that time, Poland had not acceded to the EU and both were granted residence permits on humanitarian grounds under German domestic law. Although Mr Ziolkowski (at least) had worked in Germany in the past, by the time Poland acceded to the EU on May 1, 2004, neither was in employment or had sufficient resources to support

him or herself economically so as not to be a burden on the German social assistance system. In 2005, both applied to the State of Berlin to extend their residence permits under German domestic law or to issue a residence permit under EU law. Those applications were refused on the basis that the applicants were unable to support themselves financially and did not have a right of residence under EU law. Mr Ziolkowski and Mrs Szeja appealed and it was ultimately argued on their behalf that they had resided legally in Germany under German domestic law (i.e., by virtue of the residence permits) for a continuous period in excess of five years before Poland acceded to the EU and that—following the principle in *Lassal* (see below)— each acquired a right of permanent residence under art.16 when the Citizenship Directive came into force on April 30, 2006. The *Bundesverwaltungsgericht* took the view that residence which was lawful under national law alone did not amount to legal residence for the purposes of art.16. It nevertheless referred the following questions to the ECJ:

> "1. Is the first sentence of Article 16(1) of Directive 2004/38 to be interpreted as conferring on Union citizens who have resided legally for more than five years in the territory of a Member State on the basis of national law alone, but who did not during that period fulfil the conditions laid down in Article 7(1) of Directive 2004/38, a right of permanent residence in that Member State?
>
> 2. Are periods of residence by Union citizens in the host Member State which took place before the accession of their Member State of origin to the European Union also to be counted towards the period of lawful residence under Article 16(1) of Directive 2004/38?"

The ECJ answered those questions as follows:

> "1. Article 16(1) of [the Citizenship] Directive ... must be interpreted as meaning that a Union citizen who has been resident for more than five years in the territory of the host Member State on the sole basis of the national law of that Member State cannot be regarded as having acquired the right of permanent residence under that provision if, during that period of residence, he did not satisfy the conditions laid down in Article 7(1) of the directive.
>
> 2. Periods of residence completed by a national of a non-Member State in the territory of Member State before the accession of the non-Member State to the European Union must, in the absence of specific provisions in the Act of Accession, be taken into account for the purpose of the acquisition of the right of permanent residence under Article 16(1) of Directive 2004/38, provided those periods were completed in compliance with the conditions laid down in Article 7(1) of the directive."

It follows that *Lekpo-Bozua v Hackney LBC* [2010] EWCA Civ 909 and *Okafor v Secretary of State for the Home Department* [2011] EWCA Civ 499 are correctly decided. It also follows that previously binding UK authority to the effect that pre-accession residence cannot count towards the five-year period (including *GN (EEA Regulations: Five years' residence) Hungary* [2007] UKAIT 73 and *CPC/3764/2007* at para.18) should no longer be followed.

The Court's reasoning on the first question is set out at paras 31–51 of its judgment as follows:

- Article 16 made no express reference to the law of the Member States for the purpose of determining how the phrase "resided legally" was to be interpreted, that phrase must be regarded "as designating an autonomous concept of EU law which must be interpreted in a uniform manner throughout the Member States" (paras 31–33).

- As the Citizenship Directive contained no definition of that phrase, its meaning must be determined by considering, among other things, the context in which it occurs and the purposes of the rules of which it forms part. The aim of the Directive was to facilitate and strengthen the exercise of each EU citizen's right to move and reside freely within the territory of the Member States by providing a single legislative act codifying and revising the instruments of EU law which preceded the Citizenship Directive. But the subject matter of the Citizenship Directive, as was apparent from art.1(a) and (b), concerned the conditions governing the exercise of that right and the right of permanent residence (paras 34–37).

- The Citizenship Directive introduced a gradual system as regards the right of residence in a host Member State (para.38).

- First, for periods of residence of up to three months, art.6 limits the conditions and formalities of the right of residence to the requirement to hold a valid identity card or passport and the requirement, under art.14(1), for the EU citizen and any family members not to become an unreasonable burden on the social assistance system of the host Member State (para.39).

- Then, for periods of residence of longer than three months, the right is subject to the conditions set out in art.7(1) and, under art.14(2), is retained only if the EU citizen and any family members satisfy those conditions. Recital 10 in the preamble to the Citizenship Directive in particular showed that those conditions are intended, inter alia, to prevent nationals of other Member States becoming an unreasonable burden on the social assistance system of the host Member State. (para.40).

- Finally, EU citizens acquire the right of permanent residence after residing legally for a continuous period of five years in the host Member State and that right is not subject to the conditions referred to above. Recital 17 in the preamble states that such a right should be laid down for all EU citizens and their family members who have resided in the host Member State 'in compliance with the conditions laid down in this Directive' during a continuous period of five years without becoming subject to an expulsion measure. The *travaux préparatoires* showed that the relevant part of recital 17 was included "in order to clarify the content of the term "legal residence"" for the purpose of art.16(1) (paras 41–42).

- Further the Citizenship Directive stated explicitly that, to acquire a permanent right of residence, family members of an EU citizen who retain a right of residence following the death of the EU citizen; or his or her departure from the host State; or following divorce, annulment of marriage or the termination of a registered partnership must satisfy the conditions in art.7(1) (see arts 12, 13 and 18) (paras 43–44).

- It follows that "resided legally" in art.16(1) of the Citizenship Directive should be construed as meaning residence which complies with the conditions laid down in the Citizenship Directive, in particular those set out in art.7(1). Consequently, a period of residence which complies with the law of a Member State but does not satisfy the conditions in art.7(1) cannot be regarded as a "legal" period of residence within the meaning of art.16(1) (paras 45–47).

- Article 37 of the Citizenship Directive does not affect that analysis. It simply provides that the Directive does not preclude the laws of the Member States from introducing provisions that are more favourable than those established by the Directive. That does not mean that such provisions must be incorporated into the system introduced by the Citizenship Directive. It is for each Member State to decide not only whether it will introduce more favourable provision but also the conditions to which the more favourable rules are subject and, in particular, the legal consequences of a right of residence granted on the basis of national law alone (paras 47–50).

On the second question (i.e. that concerning pre-accession residence), the Court reasoned that, on the Accession of a new Member State, the principle is that EU law applies to that State in full from the outset unless there are express derogations which establish transitional provisions. Nationals of any Member State may rely on EU law as regards the present effects of circumstances which existed previously including circumstances which arose before the accession of a Member State to the EU (e.g., *Saldanha and MTS* (Case C-122/96) [1997] E.C.R. I-5325, at para.14; *Österreichischer Gewerkschaftsbund* (Case C-195/98) [2000] E.C.R. I-10497, at para.55; and *Duchon* (Case C-290/00) [2002] ECR I-3567 at para.44)). As there are no transitional provisions that are relevant to the question, art.16(1) can be applied to the present and future effects of situations arising before the accession of the Member State of which the EU citizen is a national to the EU. Although periods of residence completed in the territory of the host Member State by a national of another State before the accession of the latter State to the EU do not fall within the scope of EU law but solely within the domestic law of the host Member State, provided the person concerned can demonstrate that such periods were completed in compliance with the conditions laid down in art.7(1) of Directive, taking such periods into account from the date of accession of the Member State of nationality to the EU does not give retroactive effect to art.16, but simply gives present effect to situations which arose before the date of transposition of that Directive.

Residence from April 30, 2006:

5.127   Following *Ziolkowski and Szeja*, the position as regards residence for periods from April 30, 2006 (when the Citizenship Directive came into force) may be summarised as follows.

Such residence is "legal" for the purposes of art.16(1)—and therefore counts towards the acquisition of a right of permanent residence—only if the person whose residence is under consideration satisfies the conditions in art.7(1) of the Citizenship Directive (i.e. if that person is a worker (or has retained that status), self-employed (or has retained that status), self-sufficient, a student or a family member of someone who falls into those categories).

Therefore residence that is lawful solely by virtue of rights enjoyed:

- as a jobseeker (i.e. under art.45 TFEU (ex-art.39 TEC): see *R. v IAT Ex p. Antonissen*, Case C-292/89); or

- as the child of a migrant worker or former migrant worker who has established him or herself in education (i.e. under art.10 of Regulation 492/2011 (formerly art.12 of Regulation 1612/68) or as the primary carer of such a child (i.e. under the principles established in *Ibrahim* and *Teixeira*). See further *Okafor* at para.31; or

- under arts 20 and 21 TFEU (including the rights enjoyed by some parents of British children under the principle established in *Zambrano*: see below); or

- (to the extent that the resident does not satisfy the conditions in art.7(1)) under the domestic law of the UK.

is **not** "legal" for the purposes of art.16(1) and does not count towards the acquisition of a right of permanent residence.

In *Ziolkowski and Szeja* none of the applicants had any of the rights of residence listed immediately above. Thus the question of whether residence pursuant to such rights is "legal" for the purposes of art.16 was not strictly before the Court. However, it was subsequently confirmed by the ECJ at paras 32–48 of *Alarape and Tijani v Secretary of State for the Home Department* (Case C–529/11) that:

"Periods of residence in a host Member State which are completed by family members of a Union citizen who are not nationals of a Member State solely on the basis of Article 12 of Regulation No 1612/68, as amended by Directive 2004/38, where the conditions laid down for entitlement to a right of residence under that directive are not satisfied, may not be taken into consideration for the purposes of acquisition by those family members of a right of permanent residence under that directive."

However, although residence as a jobseeker does not count towards the acquisition of a permanent right of residence under EU law, it counts towards the acquisition of such a right under the more favourable provisions of para.(1): see below. The more favourable provisions of reg.15 apply only to residence as a jobseeker and not to residence in any of the other capacities listed above.

Residence before April 30, 2006

As is apparent from the Court's answer to the second question in *Ziolkowski and Szeja*, it is also possible for certain types of residence during periods before the Citizenship Directive came into force on April 30, 2006 to count towards the acquisition of the right of permanent residence after that date.

5.128

Where the member State of nationality was a member of the EU at the time when the claimant was resident in the UK, the decision of the ECJ in *Secretary of State for Work and Pensions v Lassal* (Case C-162/09) holds that pre-Directive residence will count towards the five-year period, if it is "in accordance with earlier European Union law instruments". In *Alarape and Tijani v Secretary of State for the Home Department*, the ECJ confirmed that that phrase only refers to the instruments that were repealed by, and consolidated in, the Citizenship Directive and does not include instruments, such as art.12 of Regulation 1612/68 (now art.10 of Regulation 492/2011), which are unaffected by the Citizenship Directive.

Where the member State of nationality was not a member of the EU at the time when the claimant was resident in the UK, *Ziolkowski and Szeja* holds that—in the absence of specific provisions in the Act of Accession—pre-Directive residence counts towards the five-year period if it was "in compliance with the conditions laid down in Article 7(1) of the [Directive]". Previously binding UK authority to the effect that pre-accession residence cannot count towards the five year period (including *R(IS) 3/08* and *CPC/3764/2007*) should no longer be followed.

This aspect of the decision in *Ziolkowski and Szeja* raises two further issues:

- First, there is the obvious conceptual problem about how residence can have been "in compliance with" the conditions in art.7(1) at a time when that provision was not in force and the resident's state of nationality was not even a member of the EU. The answer to that problem can be found in the Court's insistence that it was not applying art.16 retrospectively but rather giving present and future effect to circumstances which had arisen in the past. Articles 7(1) and 16(1) exist now. Although the Citizenship Directive as a whole may only affect those who are "beneficiaries" as defined by art.3(1), none of the, relatively well-established, criteria for establishing whether the conditions in art.7(1) are satisfied require that the person to whom they are applied should be an EU citizen at the relevant time. If, for example, it is possible to conclude that a Polish national was a self-employed person in May 2004, there is no reason why one cannot also conclude that she was a self-employed person during the previous month, or year, or years and therefore say that, during that period, she satisfied the condition that is now laid down in art.7(1)(a). Analysed in that way, the difficulties are likely to be evidential rather than conceptual.

- However that analysis leads to the second issue, namely that the narrow criteria for establishing whether the conditions in art.7(1) are satisfied do not require that the residence or work under consideration must also have been legal under the domestic law of the host state at the time. Suppose that the same Polish national referred to in the previous bullet point entered the UK illegally in March 2001 and worked here illegally on a self-employed basis for a continuous period ending on or before April 2006. Presumably she did not acquire a permanent right of residence as soon as the Citizenship Directive came into force on April 30, 2006, but nothing in *Ziolkowski and Szeja* actually says otherwise. The contrary outcome could, perhaps, be achieved by holding that a person in that position was not resident at all but only present, so that even if her activities would otherwise bring her within art.7(1), there would still be no "residence" for the purposes of art.16. Some support for that approach can be found in *R(IS) 3/08* which holds that temporary admission as an asylum seeker does not amount to a right of residence and *SSWP v LS (IS)* [2012] UKUT 207 (AAC).

The 2006 Regulations were amended with effect from July 16, 2012 to codify what was said in *Ziolkowski and Szeja* about pre-accession residence. Under para.6(3)(a) of Sch.4 to those Regulations, the codified right became conditional on the person concerned having had leave to enter or remain in the UK at the relevant time. That provision has now been consolidated as para.8(3)(b) of Sch.6. The codification refers to residence "in accordance with these Regulations" (para.8(3)(c) of Sch.6) and will therefore include jobseekers in addition to people who come within art.7 of the Citizenship Directive.

Loss of the *Lassal* right

5.129   Once the inchoate permanent right of residence conferred by *Lassal* has accrued, it can potentially be lost by:

- a period of absence from the UK (see *Lassal* at paras 56–58); or

- a period of residence in the UK that was not legal (i.e. in the sense that it was not "in accordance with earlier European Union law instruments") (see *Secretary of State for the Home Department v Dias* (Case C-325/09) at paras 62–66); between the date on which the five years' continuous residence was completed and April 30, 2006.

Although there is no ECJ authority on the point, it seems probable that the inchoate right of permanent residence based on pre-Directive, pre-accession, residence that was recognised in *Ziolkowski and Szeja*, will be lost in the same circumstances as the *Lassal* right.

That conclusion in *Lassal* that the inchoate right can be lost through absence from the UK is unexceptionable. As the Court rightly points out, any other interpretation would have required Member States "to grant the right of permanent residence... even in cases of prolonged absences which [called] into question the link between the person concerned and the host Member State".

However, the rule was extended by analogy in *Dias* to cover situations in which a concluded period of five years' lawful residence before April 30, 2006 is followed by a period of residence for which there is no legal basis. The Court ruled that:

> "periods of residence of less than two consecutive years, completed on the basis solely of a residence permit validly issued pursuant to Directive 68/360, without the conditions governing entitlement to a right of residence having been satisfied, which occurred before 30 April 2006 and after a continuous period of five years' legal residence completed prior to that date, are not such as to affect the acquisition of the right of permanent residence under Article 16(1) of Directive 2004/38."

The ECJ's justification for that ruling was that:

> "64. ....it should be noted, as the Advocate General has stated in points 106 and 107 of her Opinion, that the integration objective which lies behind the acquisition of the right of permanent residence laid down in Article 16(1) of Directive 2004/38 is based not only on territorial and time factors but also on qualitative elements, relating to the level of integration in the host Member State.

65. As the situations are comparable, it follows that the rule laid down in Article 16(4) of Directive 2004/38 must also be applied by analogy to periods in the host Member State completed on the basis solely of a residence permit validly issued under Directive 68/360, without the conditions governing entitlement to a right of residence of any kind having been satisfied, which occurred before 30 April 2006 and after a continuous period of five years' legal residence completed prior to that date."

The analogy drawn by the ECJ is false or, at any rate, is not inevitably true. Leaving a country for a period of two consecutive years obviously reduces one's level of integration in that country. The same cannot be said of Mrs Dias' decision to remain in the country but to spend time looking after her child instead of working, even if that decision meant that she left the labour market for a period. On the contrary, the process of raising a child in the UK probably increases one's level of integration in British society. One could go further. It is arguable that even claiming UK social security benefits involves being integrated in Britain: the process necessitates interacting with institutions of the state and involves doing something that almost every UK citizen will do at some time during his or her life. Finally, as it stands the analogy proves too much. It is being asserted that two years of economic inactivity is to be equated with two years' absence from the host State, but if that were the case before April 30, 2006 it is equally the case after that date. If, therefore, the analogy were correct, the implication would be that those who acquired a permanent right of residence after April 30, 2006 should be deprived of that right after two years of economic inactivity in the same way as they would be after two years' absence.

The passages from the Advocate General's opinion in *Dias* (to which the Court refers) explain the analogy on a slightly different basis:

"106. First, the integration objective which lies behind Article 16 of the directive is based not only on territorial and time factors but also on qualitative elements. It therefore seems to me quite possible that unlawful conduct of a Union citizen may diminish his integration in the host State from a qualitative point of view. In so far as a Union citizen, following a period of legal residence in the host Member State, remains without a right of residence based on European Union law or national law in the host Member State, and the national authorities do not grant leave to remain, that can clearly in my view be taken into account from the perspective of integration.

107. Second, the principle of equal treatment also supports that point of view. A Union citizen who complies with the law, who did not remain unlawfully contrary to the wishes of the host Member State in that State, would not be entitled to a right of permanent residence on 30 April 2006 following absence for more than two years, pursuant to Article 16(4) of Directive 2004/38. It does not seem justified to reward a Union citizen who does not comply with the law."

At least in the UK, the premise on which those passages are based is incorrect. An EEA national who stays in the UK after a positive right of residence comes to an end is not acting unlawfully. S/he commits no criminal offence; remains lawfully present here; is not, without more, subject to removal; and, if removed, would have an immediate right of re-entry. Even if it is the case that "unlawful conduct" can diminish the level of integration, no unlawful conduct occurs in these circumstances. For that reason, treating a period of lawful presence after the acquisition of an inchoate right of residence as neutral, rather than as potentially preventing the right from crystallising, would not involve "rewarding" a Union citizen who does not comply with the law.

The 2006 Regulations were amended with effect from July 16, 2012 by (SI 2012/1547) to reflect the Citizenship Directive as interpreted in *Dias*. The amended Regulations provide for the automatic loss of the *Lassal* right after two years' residence that is not in accordance with the Regulations. The 2016 Regulations have consolidated that rule at para.8(4)(b) of Sch.6.

The position of jobseekers and their family members under UK domestic law

5.130   As noted above, jobseekers do not satisfy the conditions in art.7(1) of the Citizenship Directive and therefore, under EU law as declared in *Ziolkowski and Szeja*, residence as a jobseeker—though lawful by virtue of art.45 TFEU—does not count towards the acquisition of the permanent right of residence under art.16(1). The same is true of residence as the family member of a jobseeker.

However, domestic UK law is more favourable to jobseekers and their family members. Since April 30, 2006, first reg.6 of the 2006 Regulations and now reg.6 of these Regulations have included jobseekers in the definition of as "qualified persons". They therefore have an extended right of residence under reg.14. The consequence is that residence as a jobseeker, or as the family member of a jobseeker, is "in accordance with these regulations" for the purposes of reg.15(1) so that if it lasts for a continuous period of five years—or, more probably, forms part of a continuous period of five years throughout which the claimant was a qualified person for a number of different reasons (or a family member of such a person)—the claimant will acquire a permanent right of residence by virtue of that regulation: see *GE v SSWP (ESA)* [2017] UKUT 145 (AAC), [2017] AACR 34.

The definition of "jobseeker" in reg.6 does not contain any requirement to register as a jobseeker. Therefore it is suggested that periods during which a claimant can show that s/he was seeking employment and had a genuine chance of being engaged will count towards the five-year period even if s/he was not claiming JSA or jobseeking credits.

Regulation 5 of the 2000 Regulations, did not expressly include "jobseekers" in the definition of "qualified person". However, "workers" were so included and "worker" was defined as meaning "a worker within the meaning of Article 39 of the EC Treaty". "Worker" in art.39 TEC (now art.45 TFEU) has a wider meaning than it has in art.7 of the Citizenship Directive. It is therefore arguable that a jobseeker who would have been treated as "worker" under art.39 was a qualified person with a right of residence under reg.14(1) of those Regulations and that family members of such a jobseeker had a right of residence under reg.14(2). As already noted, the types of residence before April 30, 2006 specified in para.8 of Sch.6 count towards the five-year period in reg.15.

A8 and A2 nationals

5.131   The A8 Regulations have largely been revoked. The text immediately before revocation is set out at pp.792–798 of Vol.II of the 2011/2012 edition and detailed commentary is to be found at paras 2.274–2.276 of Vol.II of the 2016/17 edition. However, the Regulations remain relevant to the acquisition of a permanent right of residence under paras (1)(a) and (b) because residence that was not within the A8 Regulations is not "in accordance with" the 2016 Regulations: see reg.7A of the 2006 Regulations and Sch.6, para.(8). The same is true of the A2 Regulations (above): see reg.7B of the 2006 Regulations. However, as the A2 Scheme required prior authorisation for work done by Bulgarian and Romanian nationals, it now raises fewer practical problems than the A8 Regulations, which only required that work employment should be registered with the Home Office once it had commenced; a requirement that was often overlooked.

Until recently, the main issues arising under the A8 Regulations concerned their legality and duration.

As to legality, in *RP v SSWP* [2016] UKUT 422 (AAC), the Upper Tribunal (Judge Ward) referred the following questions to the CJEU:

"Did Annex XII of the Treaty of Accession permit Member States to exclude Polish nationals from the benefits of Article 7(2) of the Workers Regulation and Article 7(3) of the Citizenship Directive where the worker, though he had belatedly complied with the national requirement that his employment be registered, had not yet worked for an uninterrupted registered twelve month period?

If the answer to the first question is "no," may a Polish national worker in the circumstances in question 1 rely on Article 7(3) of the Citizenship Directive which concerns retention of worker status?"

The CJEU answered question 1 as follows (see *Rafal Prefeta v Secretary of State for Work and Pensions* (Case C-618/165)):

"Chapter 2 of Annex XII to the Act concerning the conditions of accession of the [A8 States, Cyprus, and Malta] and the adjustments to the Treaties on which the European Union is founded, must be interpreted as permitting, during the transitional period provided for by that act, the United Kingdom . . . to exclude a Polish national, such as Mr Rafal Prefeta, from the benefits of Article 7(3) of [the Citizenship Directive], when that person has not satisfied the requirement imposed by national law of having completed an uninterrupted 12-month period of registered work in the United Kingdom."

The A8 Regulations were therefore in accordance with EU law.

As to duration, in *Secretary of State for Work and Pensions v Gubeladze* [2019] UKSC 31 at paras 1-75, the Supreme Court upheld the decisions of the Court of Appeal ([2017] EWCA Civ 1751) and Upper Tribunal Judge Ward in *TG v SSWP (PC)* [2015] UKUT 50 (AAC) that the two-year extension of the A8 accession period from May 1, 2009 to April 30, 2011 by the Accession (Immigration and Worker Registration) (Amendment) Regulations 2009 (SI 2009/892) was not compatible with EU law because it was not a proportionate exercise of the UK's powers under the Treaty of Accession. It follows that, from May 1, 2009, the rights of A8 nationals to reside in the UK as workers or jobseekers were the same as for other EU citizens (other than A2 nationals) and were no longer subject to restriction. The decision is of potential benefit to A8 nationals who need to rely on residence during that period to establish a permanent right of residence: see, e.g., *AM v SSWP (ESA)* [2019] UKUT 215 (AAC).

Finally, in *SSWP v NZ (ESA) (Third interim decision)* [2017] UKUT 0360 (AAC), the Upper Tribunal (Judge Ward) decided that neither the Accession (Immigration and Worker Registration) Regulations 2004 nor any other provision effected a valid derogation from art.17 of the Directive. As a person who would—but for the impact of the worker registration scheme—otherwise on any view have been a worker, the claimant's inability to point to 12 months of registered work did not preclude her from relying on art.17 if she could satisfy its remaining conditions.

Paragraphs (1) (c) and (d)– worker or self-employed person who has ceased activity and their family members
See the commentary to regs 5 and 7.   5.132
The family members of a worker or self-employed person who has ceased activity only acquire a permanent right of residence to the extent that they were family members of the worker or self-employed person at the time s/he ceased activity and had a right of residence in that capacity at that time. These rules prevent family members who join the worker or self-employed person in the UK after s/he has retired—and, it would seem, those who become family members by marriage or birth after that date—from acquiring a permanent right of residence immediately. However, such a person would have an extended right of residence under reg.14(2) and would acquire a permanent right of residence under reg.15(1)(b) after five years' continuous residence in the UK pursuant to that right.

Paragraph (1) (e) – Family members of workers or self-employed persons who have died:
A family member (see reg.7) of a worker or self-employed person who has died   5.133
has a permanent right of residence where the family member resided with the deceased person immediately before his or her death, and either:

- the deceased person had resided continuously in the UK for at least two years immediately before his death; or

- the death was the result of an accident at work or an occupational disease.

Paragraph (1) (f) – Family members who have retained the right of residence

5.134   A person who has lived in the UK in accordance with the 2016 Regulations for a continuous period of five years acquires a permanent right of residence if, at the end of that period, s/he is a family member who has retained the right of residence.

In practice, this category only affects non-EEA nationals: an EEA national who had lived in the UK in accordance with the 2016 Regulations for a continuous period of five years would acquire a permanent right of residence under para.(1) (a), irrespective of whether s/he was a family member who has retained the right of residence at the end of that period.

For the definition of "family member who has retained the right of residence" see reg.10. One consequence of that definition is that the permanent right of residence conferred by para.(1)(f) replaces rather than supplements, the extended right of residence granted by reg.14(3). Under reg.10(8), the acquisition of the permanent right of residence brings an end to the person's former status as a family member who has retained the right of residence; by ceasing to hold that status, the person loses his or her former rights under reg.14(3).

Paragraph (2) – Derivative right to reside

5.135   Residence under a derivative right to reside (see reg.16) does not count as residence for the purpose of para.(1).

Paragraph (3) – Loss of the permanent right of residence

5.136   Paragraph (3) implements art.16(4). The right of permanent residence is lost if the EEA national is absent from the UK for more than two years.

Derivative right to reside

5.137   **16.**—(1) A person has a derivative right to reside during any period in which the person—

(a) is not an exempt person; and

(b) satisfies each of the criteria in one or more of paragraphs (2) to (6).

(2) The criteria in this paragraph are that—

(a) the person is the primary carer of an EEA national; and

(b) the EEA national—

(i) is under the age of 18;

(ii) resides in the United Kingdom as a self-sufficient person; and

(iii) would be unable to remain in the United Kingdom if the person left the United Kingdom for an indefinite period.

(3) The criteria in this paragraph are that—

(a) any of the person's parents ("PP") is an EEA national who resides or has resided in the United Kingdom;

(b) both the person and PP reside or have resided in the United Kingdom at the same time, and during such a period of residence, PP has been a worker in the United Kingdom; and

(c) the person is in education in the United Kingdom.

(4) The criteria in this paragraph are that—

(a) the person is the primary carer of a person satisfying the criteria in paragraph (3) ("PPP"); and

(b) PPP would be unable to continue to be educated in the United Kingdom if the person left the United Kingdom for an indefinite period.

(5) The criteria in this paragraph are that—

(a) the person is the primary carer of a British citizen ("BC");

(b) BC is residing in the United Kingdom; and

(c) BC would be unable to reside in the United Kingdom or in another

EEA State if the person left the United Kingdom for an indefinite period.

(6) The criteria in this paragraph are that—

(a) the person is under the age of 18;

(b) the person does not have leave to enter, or remain in, the United Kingdom under the 1971 Act [² but see paragraph (7A)];

(c) the person's primary carer is entitled to a derivative right to reside in the United Kingdom under paragraph (2), (4) or (5); and

(d) the primary carer would be prevented from residing in the United Kingdom if the person left the United Kingdom for an indefinite period.

(7) In this regulation—

(a) "education" excludes nursery education but does not exclude education received before the compulsory school age where that education is equivalent to the education received at or after the compulsory school age;

(b) "worker" does not include a jobseeker or a person treated as a worker under regulation 6(2);

(c) an "exempt person" is a person—

  (i) who has a right to reside under another provision of these Regulations;

  (ii) who has the right of abode under section 2 of the 1971 Act;

  (iii) to whom section 8 of the 1971 Act, or an order made under subsection (2) of that section, applies; or

  (iv) who has indefinite leave to enter or remain in the United Kingdom [² but see paragraph (7A)].

[² (7A) Leave to enter, or remain in, the United Kingdom under the 1971 Act which has been granted by virtue of Appendix EU to the immigration rules is not to be treated as leave for the purposes of paragraph (6)(b) or (7)(c)(iv).]

(8) A person is the "primary carer" of another person ("AP") if—

(a) the person is a direct relative or a legal guardian of AP; and

(b) either—

  (i) the person has primary responsibility for AP's care; or

  (ii) shares equally the responsibility for AP's care with one other person [¹ ...].

(9) In paragraph (2)(b)(iii), (4)(b) or (5)(c), if the role of primary carer is shared with another person in accordance with paragraph (8)(b)(ii), the words "the person" are to be read as "both primary carers".

(10) Paragraph (9) does not apply if the person with whom care responsibility is shared acquired a derivative right to reside in the United Kingdom as a result of this regulation prior to the other person's assumption of equal care responsibility.

(11) A person is not be regarded as having responsibility for another person's care for the purpose of paragraph (8) on the sole basis of a financial contribution towards that person's care.

(12) A person does not have a derivative right to reside where the Secretary of State or an immigration officer has made a decision under regulation 23(6)(b), 24(1), 25(1), 26(3) or 31(1), unless that decision is set aside or otherwise no longer has effect.

AMENDMENT

1. Immigration (European Economic Area) (Amendment) Regulations 2018 (SI 2018/801) reg.2 and Sch., para.10 (July 24, 2018).

2 Immigration (European Economic Area Nationals) (EU Exit) Regulations 2019 (SI 2019/468) reg.3(6) (March 28, 2019).

DEFINITION

"the 1971 Act"—see reg.2(1).
"derivative right to reside"—see reg.2(1) and the General Note.
"EEA national"—see reg.2(1).
"EEA State"—*ibid.*
"jobseeker"—see reg.6(1).
"right to reside"—see reg.2(1).
"self-sufficient person"—see reg.4(1)(c).
"worker"—see reg.4(1)(a).

GENERAL NOTE

5.138   Regulation 16 codifies a number of different decisions of the CJEU by conferring a "derivative right of residence" for various categories of people whose rights do not arise directly under the Citizenship Directive but have been held to arise from the TFEU or from other provisions of EU law, notably art.10 of Regulation (EU) 492/2011. Under para.(1), a person has a derivative right of residence during any period in which s/he is not an exempt person and satisfies all criteria in one or more of paras (2)–(7).

Residence pursuant to a derivative right to reside does not count as residence within reg.15 and therefore does not lead to a permanent right of residence.

5.139   *Paragraphs (1)(a) and (7) – Exempt persons*
"Exempt person" is defined by para.(7) as a person who has a right to reside under another provision of these Regulations, or is a British citizen or a Commonwealth citizen with the right of abode, or is entitled to enter or remain in the UK under s.8 Immigration Act 1971 (Exceptions for seamen, aircrews and other special cases), or has indefinite leave to remain. The effect of that definition, taken with para.(1)(a) is that a derivative right to reside is a right of last resort. People with most other rights of residence do not qualify for a derivative right to reside. For a practical example, see *SSWP v MH (IS)* [2016] UKUT 526 (AAC).

Primary carers of self-sufficient children
5.140   Paragraph (2) applies to a person who is the primary carer (as defined in para.(8)) of an EEA national aged under 18, who is living in the UK as a self-sufficient person and would be unable to remain in the United Kingdom if that person left the UK for an indefinite period. It therefore consolidates the decision of the ECJ in *Zhu and Chen v Home Secretary* (Case C–200/02).

In *Bajratari v Secretary of State for the Home Department* [2017] NICA 74, the question arose whether a child's resources could be "sufficient" where they were derived from work undertaken unlawfully (i.e., without the necessary work permit) by a third-country national parent. The Court of Appeal in Northern Ireland referred the following questions to the CJEU:

"[i]   Can income from employment that is unlawful under national law establish, in whole or in part, the availability of sufficient resources under Article 7(1) (b) of the Citizens Directive?

[ii] If 'yes', can Article 7(1) (b) be satisfied where the employment is deemed precarious solely by reason of its unlawful character?"

The reference has been registered at the CJEU as Case C-93/18 and Advocate General Szpunar has issued an opinion recommending that the Court should answer those questions as follows:

"Article 7(1)(b) of [the Citizenship Directive] must be interpreted as meaning that a young child who is a Union citizen has sufficient resources not to become a burden on the social assistance system of the host Member State during his period of residence where, in circumstances such as those of the case in the main proceedings, those resources are provided from income derived from the activity unlawfully carried on in that Member State, without a residence or work permit, by the child's father, a national of a third country."

At the time of going to press, no date had been fixed for the delivery of the Court's judgment.

Regulation 4(5) provides that "[for] the purposes of regulation 16(2) (criteria for having a derivative right to reside), references in this regulation to "family members" includes a "primary carer" as defined in regulation 16(8). What this means is that the comprehensive sickness insurance that the EEA national must have in order to be a self-sufficient person must cover his or her primary carers as well.

Children of migrant workers in education

Paragraph (3) applies to a person who is the child of a migrant worker or former migrant worker and who is in education (as defined in reg.7(a)) in the UK. It therefore codifies the decision of the ECJ in *Baumbast and R v Secretary of State for the Home Department* (Case C-413/99). It is not necessary for the child to be self-sufficient or to have comprehensive sickness insurance.   **5.141**

However, it is necessary for the child to satisfy all the requirements of the paragraph. In *JS v SSWP (ESA)* [2016] UKUT 314 (AAC), the Upper Tribunal (Judge Wright) held (in relation to the equivalent, though differently worded, provisions of reg.15A of the 2006 Regulations) that those requirements are not met where it is one of the child's grandparents, rather than a parent, who was the EEA national who had been a worker in the UK. That was so even though, under the definition in para.(8), a grandparent can be the child's "primary carer" for the purposes of paras (4)-(6).

Similarly, it is not sufficient for the EEA national who has been a worker in the UK to be a person who is not the child's biological parent and is not in a legally recognised relationship with the parent: see *IP v SSWP* [2015] UKUT 691 (AAC) and *OFNATS v Ahmed* (Case C-45/12). It is also necessary for there to have been a period when the child lived in the UK and the parent was a worker here: see *Bolton MBC v HY (HB)* [2018] UKUT 103 (AAC).

The right codified in para.(3) does not extend to the children of EEA nationals who have been self-employed in the UK but have not been workers: see the decisions of the CJEU in *Secretary of State for Work and Pensions v Czop* (Case C-147/11) and of the Court of Appeal in *Hrabkova v Secretary of State for Work and Pensions* [2017] EWCA Civ 794. Ms Hrabkova has been refused permission to appeal to the Supreme Court (ref: UKSC 2018/0018).

Primary carers of children of migrant workers in education

Paragraph (4) codifies the right of residence established for the primary carers of the children of migrant workers who are in education in the UK that was established by the ECJ in *Ibrahim v London Borough of Harrow* (Case C-310/08) and *Teixeira v London Borough of Lambeth* (Case C-480/08). Again the primary carer does not need to be self-sufficient or to have comprehensive sickness insurance. However, under the definition of "primary carer" in para.(8), the carer does have to be a "direct relative" of the child. In *MS v SSWP (IS)* [2016] UKUT 348 (AAC), the Upper Tribunal (Judge Jacobs) held that this did not include the child's elder brother, even though he had been appointed her legal guardian. Guardianship creates rights and responsibilities but it does not create a parental relationship. The position would probably be different if the putative primary carer were the child's adoptive parent.   **5.142**

The right does not extend to the primary carers of children who have not established themselves in education even where the child has a right of residence as the family member of an EEA national who is a worker: see *AM v SSWP and City and County of Swansea Council* [2019] UKUT 361 (AAC).

Carers of British citizens

5.143   Paragraph (5) codifies the right of residence for some people who care for British citizens derived from art.21 TFEU by the Grand Chamber of the CJEU in *Zambrano v Office national de l'emploi (ONEm)* (Case C-34/09). In *DM v SSWP (PIP)* [2019] UKUT 26 (AAC), Upper Tribunal Judge Ward accepted a concession from the Secretary of State that "Regulation 16(5) of the Immigration (European Economic Area) Regulations 2016 (and regulation 15A(4A) of the 2006 Regulations) applies to carers of adult British citizens as well as children, and this reflects the relevant EU case law": see also the decision of the High Court (Lane J.) in *R (Hamid Saeed) v Secretary of State for the Home Department* [2018] EWHC 1707 (Admin).

Under reg.9(3) of the Universal Credit Regulations, reg.21AA(3) of the IS Regulations, reg.85A(3) of the JSA Regulations 1996, and reg.2(4) of the SPC Regulations, the *Zambrano* right of residence has not counted for the purposes of any social security benefit since November 8, 2012. That position was confirmed by the decision of the Supreme Court in *R (HC) v Secretary of State for Work and Pensions and others* [2017] UKSC 73.

Other children of primary carers

5.144   Where the primary carer with a derivative right of residence under paras (2), (4) or (5) is also the primary carer of another child (who is not an exempt person) and who does not have leave to enter or remain in the UK, the other child will have a derivative right of residence under para.(6) if the primary carer would not be able to remain in the UK if the other child left the UK for an indefinite period.

PART 3

RESIDENCE DOCUMENTATION

GENERAL NOTE

5.145   It is unnecessary for a publication about social security law to go into detail about the various documents issued to those with rights under these Regulations. Those documents are:

- a registration certificate

  Registration certificates are issued by the Secretary of State under reg.17 to qualified persons, to EEA nationals who are family members of a qualified person or an EEA national with the right of permanent residence, and to family members who have retained the right of residence. They may also be issued to extended family members who are EEA nationals.

- a residence card

  Residence cards are issued by the Secretary of State under reg.18 to the family members of a qualified person or an EEA national with the right of permanent residence, but who are not themselves EEA nationals. They may also be issued to extended family members who are not EEA nationals.

- a document certifying permanent residence

  Documents certifying permanent residence are issued by the Secretary of State under reg.19 to EEA nationals with a right of permanent residence.

- a permanent residence card

  Permanent residence cards are issued by the Secretary of State under reg.19 to those with a right of permanent residence who are not EEA nationals.

- a derivative residence card

Derivative residence cards are issued by the Secretary of State under reg.20 to those (whether EEA nationals or not) who have a derivative right to reside under reg.16.

- an EEA family permit

  EEA family permits are issued by entry clearance officers under reg.12 to family members of EEA national who are outside the UK and wish to accompany the EEA national to the UK or to join him or her here, to family members who have retained the right of residence, and to people who are not EEA nationals but have a right of permanent residence under reg.16. They may also be issued to extended family members.

The main value of these documents in social security cases is as evidence that the Home Office has accepted the claimant has a right to reside. However, it must be born in mind that—except in the case of extended family members: see reg.8—regs 17–20 all provide that the documents to which they refer are:

"(a) proof of the holder's right to reside on the date of issue;
(b) no longer valid if the holder ceases to have a right to reside under these Regulations; [and]
(c) invalid if the holder never had a right to reside under these Regulations."

This follows the ruling of the CJEU in *Dias v Secretary of State for Work and Pensions* (Case C-325/09), [2012] AACR 36. The Court held, confirming the provisional view expressed by the Court of Appeal (*Secretary of State for Work and Pensions v Dias* [2009] EWCA Civ 807), that the mere possession of a (former) residence permit did not make the claimant's residence "legal" for the purposes of art.16(1) of the Citizenship Directive. The ECJ's formal answer to the question referred by the Court of Appeal was that:

"periods of residence completed before 30 April 2006 on the basis solely of a residence permit validly issued pursuant to Directive 68/360, without the conditions governing entitlement to any right of residence having been satisfied, cannot be regarded as having been completed legally for the purposes of the acquisition of the right of permanent residence under Article 16(1) of Directive 2004/38"

and its reasoning is summarised succinctly at para.54 of its judgment:

". . . the declaratory character of residence permits means that those permits merely certify that a right already exists. Consequently, just as such a declaratory character means that a citizen's residence may not be regarded as illegal, within the meaning of European Union law, solely on the ground that he does not hold a residence permit, it precludes a Union citizen's residence from being regarded as legal, within the meaning of European Union law, solely on the ground that such a permit was validly issued to him."

A registration certificate does not have retrospective effect (*CIS/4237/2007*, para.9).

Issue of registration certificate

17.—(1) The Secretary of State must issue a registration certificate to a qualified person immediately on application and production of—   **5.146**
(a) a valid national identity card or passport issued by an EEA State; and
(b) proof that the applicant is a qualified person.
(2) In the case of a worker, confirmation of the worker's engagement from the worker's employer or a certificate of employment is sufficient proof for the purposes of paragraph (1)(b).
(3) The Secretary of State must issue a registration certificate to an EEA

national who is the family member of a qualified person or of an EEA national with a right of permanent residence under regulation 15 immediately on application and production of—

(a) a valid national identity card or passport issued by an EEA State; and

(b) proof that the applicant is such a family member.

(4) The Secretary of State must issue a registration certificate to an EEA national who is a family member who has retained the right of residence on application and production of—

(a) a valid national identity card or passport; and

(b) proof that the applicant is a family member who has retained the right of residence.

(5) The Secretary of State may issue a registration certificate to an extended family member not falling within regulation 7(3) who is an EEA national on application if—

(a) the application is accompanied or joined by a valid national identity card or passport;

(b) the relevant EEA national is a qualified person or an EEA national with a right of permanent residence under regulation 15; and

(c) in all the circumstances it appears to the Secretary of State appropriate to issue the registration certificate.

(6) Where the Secretary of State receives an application under paragraph (5) an extensive examination of the personal circumstances of the applicant must be undertaken by the Secretary of State and if the application is refused, the Secretary of State must give reasons justifying the refusal unless this is contrary to the interests of national security.

(7) A registration certificate issued under this regulation must state the name and address of the person registering and the date of registration.

(8) A registration certificate is—

(a) proof of the holder's right to reside on the date of issue;

(b) no longer valid if the holder ceases to have a right to reside under these Regulations;

(c) invalid if the holder never had a right to reside under these Regulations.

(9) This regulation is subject to regulations 24 (refusal to issue or renew and revocation of residence documentation) and 25 (cancellation of a right of residence).

MODIFICATION

Where regs 7A and 7B of the Immigration (European Economic Area) Regulations 2006 continue to have effect by virtue of reg.45 of, and Sch.1 Pt.2 para.2(1) to, the 2016 Regulations (see below), para.(9) has effect as though the words "regulations 7A and 7B of the 2006 Regulations and regulation 24 of these Regulations" were substituted for the words "regulation 24": see Sch.1 Pt.2 para.2(2)(b).

DEFINITIONS

"EEA national"—see reg.2(1).

"EEA State"—*ibid.*

"extended family member"—see reg.8.

"family member"—see reg.7.

"family member who has retained the right of residence"—see reg.10.

"qualified person"—see reg.6(1).

"registration certificate"—see reg.2(1) and the General Note to Pt 3.

"relevant EEA national"—see regs 2(1) and 8(6).

"right to reside"—see reg.2(1).
"worker"—see reg.4(1)(a).

Issue of residence card

18.—(1) The Secretary of State must issue a residence card to a person 5.147
who is not an EEA national and is the family member of a qualified person
or of an EEA national with a right of permanent residence under regulation
15 on application and production of—

(a) a valid passport; and

(b) proof that the applicant is such a family member.

(2) The Secretary of State must issue a residence card to a person who is
not an EEA national but who is a family member who has retained the right
of residence on application and production of—

(a) a valid passport; and

(b) proof that the applicant is a family member who has retained the
right of residence.

(3) On receipt of an application under paragraph (1) or (2) and the
documents that are required to accompany the application the Secretary
of State must immediately issue the applicant with a certificate of application for the residence card and the residence card must be issued no later
than six months after the date on which the application and documents are
received.

(4) The Secretary of State may issue a residence card to an extended
family member not falling within regulation 7(3) who is not an EEA
national on application if—

(a) the application is accompanied or joined by a valid passport;

(b) the relevant EEA national is a qualified person or an EEA national
with a right of permanent residence under regulation 15; and

(c) in all the circumstances it appears to the Secretary of State appropriate to issue the residence card.

(5) Where the Secretary of State receives an application under paragraph
(4) an extensive examination of the personal circumstances of the applicant must be undertaken by the Secretary of State and if the application is
refused, the Secretary of State must give reasons justifying the refusal unless
this is contrary to the interests of national security.

(6) A residence card issued under this regulation is valid for—

(a) five years from the date of issue; or

(b) in the case of a residence card issued to the family member or
extended family member of a qualified person, the envisaged period
of residence in the United Kingdom of the qualified person,

whichever is the shorter.

(7) A residence card—

(a) must be called "Residence card of a family member of [¹ a Union
Citizen]";

(b) is proof of the holder's right to reside on the date of issue;

(c) is no longer valid if the holder ceases to have a right to reside under
these Regulations;

(d) is invalid if the holder never had a right to reside under these
Regulations.

(8) This regulation is subject to regulations 24 and 25.

AMENDMENT

1. Immigration (European Economic Area) (Amendment) Regulations 2017 (SI 2017/1) reg.2 and Sch.1, para.1 (January 31, 2017).

DEFINITIONS

"EEA national"—see reg.2(1).
"extended family member"—see reg.8.
"family member"—see reg.7.
"family member who has retained the right of residence"—see reg.10.
"qualified person"—see reg.6(1).
"relevant EEA national"—see regs 2(1) and 8(6).
"residence card"— see reg.2(1) and the General Note to Pt 3.
"right to reside"— see reg.2(1).

Issue of a document certifying permanent residence and a permanent residence card

5.148   **19.**—(1) The Secretary of State must, as soon as possible, issue an EEA national with a right of permanent residence under regulation 15 with a document certifying permanent residence on application and the production of—

(a) a valid national identity card or passport issued by an EEA State; and
(b) proof that the EEA national has a right of permanent residence.

(2)   The Secretary of State must issue a person who is not an EEA national who has a right of permanent residence under regulation 15 with a permanent residence card no later than six months after an application is received and the production of—

(a) a valid passport; and
(b) proof that the person has a right of permanent residence.

(3) Subject to paragraph (4) a permanent residence card is valid for ten years from the date of issue and must be renewed on application.

(4) A document certifying permanent residence and a permanent residence card is—

(a) proof that the holder had a right to reside under regulation 15 on the date of issue;
(b) no longer valid if the holder ceases to have a right of permanent residence under regulation 15;
(c) invalid if the holder never had a right of permanent residence under regulation 15.

(5) This regulation is subject to regulations 24 and 25.

DEFINITIONS

"document certifying permanent residence"— see reg.2(1) and the General Note to Pt 3.
"EEA national"—see reg.2(1).
"EEA State"—*ibid.*
"permanent residence card"— see reg.2(1) and the General Note to Pt 3.
"right to reside"— see reg.2(1).

Issue of a derivative residence card

5.149   **20.**—(1) The Secretary of State must issue a person with a derivative residence card on application and on production of—

(a) a valid national identity card issued by an EEA State or a valid passport; and

(b) proof that the applicant has a derivative right to reside under regulation 16.

(2) On receipt of an application under paragraph (1) the Secretary of
State must issue the applicant with a certificate of application as soon as
possible.

(3) A derivative residence card issued under paragraph (1) is valid until—

(a) the date five years from the date of issue; or

(b) any earlier date specified by the Secretary of State when issuing the
derivative residence card.

(4) A derivative residence card issued under paragraph (1) must be
issued as soon as practicable.

(5) A derivative residence card is—

(a) proof of the holder's derivative right to reside on the day of issue;

(b) no longer valid if the holder ceases to have a derivative right to reside
under regulation 16;

(c) invalid if the holder never had a derivative right to reside under regulation 16.

(6) This regulation is subject to regulations 24 and 25.

DEFINITIONS

"derivative residence card"— see reg.2(1) and the General Note to Pt 3.
"derivative right to reside"—see regs 2(1) and 16.
"EEA State"—see reg.2(1).
"right to reside"—*ibid.*

Procedure for applications for documentation under this Part and regulation 12

21.—(1) An application for documentation under this Part, or for an EEA
family permit under regulation 12, must be made—

    5.150

(a) online, submitted electronically using the relevant pages of www.gov.
uk; or

(b) by post or in person, using the relevant application form specified by
the Secretary of State on www.gov.uk.

(2)   All applications must—

(a) be accompanied [2 ...] by the evidence or proof required by this Part
or regulation 12, as the case may be, as well as that required by paragraph [1(5)], within the time specified by the Secretary of State on
www.gov.uk; and

(b) be complete.

(3) An application for a residence card or a derivative residence card
must be submitted while the applicant is in the United Kingdom.

(4) When an application is submitted otherwise than in accordance with
the requirements in this regulation, it is invalid [3 and must be rejected].

[2 (4A) An application for documentation under this Part, or for an EEA
family permit under regulation 12, is invalid where the person making the
application is subject to a removal decision made under regulation 23(6)
(b), a deportation order made under regulation 32(3) or an exclusion order
made under regulation 23(5).]

(5) Where an application for documentation under this Part is made by
a person who is not an EEA national on the basis that the person is or was

the family member of an EEA national or an extended family member of
an EEA national, the application must be accompanied [² ...] by a valid
national identity card or passport in the name of that EEA national.

(6) Where—

(a) there are circumstances beyond the control of an applicant for documentation under this Part; and

(b) as a result, the applicant is unable to comply with the requirements
to submit an application online or using the application form specified by the Secretary of State,

the Secretary of State may accept an application submitted by post or in
person which does not use the relevant application form specified by the
Secretary of State.

AMENDMENT

1. Immigration (European Economic Area) (Amendment) Regulations 2017 (SI
2017/1) reg.2 and Sch.1, para.2 (January 31, 2017).

2. Immigration (European Economic Area) (Amendment) Regulations 2018 (SI
2018/801) reg.2 and Sch., para.11 (July 24, 2018).

3. Immigration (European Economic Area) (Amendment) Regulations 2019 (SI
2019/1155) reg.2(1) and (8) (August 15, 2019).

DEFINITION

"derivative residence card"—see regs 2(1) and 20.
"EEA family permit"—see regs 2(1) and 12.
"EEA national"—see reg.2(1).
"extended family member"—see reg.8.
"family member"—see reg.7.
"residence card"—see regs 2(1) and 18.

Verification of a right of residence

5.151   22.—(1) This regulation applies where the Secretary of State—

(a) has reasonable doubt as to whether a person ("A") has a right to
reside or a derivative right to reside; or

(b) wants to verify the eligibility of a person ("A") to apply for an EEA
family permit or documentation issued under Part 3.

(2) Where this regulation applies, the Secretary of State may invite A to—

(a) provide evidence to support the existence of a right to reside or a
derivative right to reside (as the case may be), or to support an application for an EEA family permit or documentation under this Part;
or

(b) attend an interview with the Secretary of State.

(3) If A purports to have a right to reside on the basis of a relationship
with another person ("B"), (including, where B is a British citizen, through
having lived with B in another EEA State), the Secretary of State may invite
B to—

(a) provide information about their relationship or residence in another
EEA State; or

(b) attend an interview with the Secretary of State.

(4) If without good reason A or B (as the case may be)—

(a) fails to provide the information requested;

(b) on at least two occasions, fails to attend an interview if so invited;

the Secretary of State may draw any factual inferences about A's entitlement to a right to reside as appear appropriate in the circumstances.

(5) The Secretary of State may decide following the drawing of an inference under paragraph (4) that A does not have or ceases to have a right to reside.

(6) But the Secretary of State must not decide that A does not have or ceases to have a right to reside on the sole basis that A failed to comply with this regulation.

(7) This regulation may not be invoked systematically.

DEFINITION

"derivative right to reside"—see regs 2(1) and 16.
"EEA family permit"—see regs 2(1) and 12.
"EEA State"—see reg.2(1).
"right to reside"—*ibid.*

PART 4

REFUSAL OF ADMISSION AND REMOVAL ETC   5.152

PART 5

PROCEDURE IN RELATION TO EEA DECISIONS   5.153

PART 6

APPEALS UNDER THESE REGULATIONS   5.154

PART 7

GENERAL

Effect on other legislation

43. Schedule 3 (effect on other legislation) has effect.   5.155

Substitution of regulation 9 of the 2006 Regulations

44.   [¹ . . .]   5.156

AMENDMENT

1. Regulation 46(a) (January 31, 2017).

GENERAL NOTE

Unlike the other provisions of these Regulations, reg.55 and Sch.5 came into   5.157
force on November 25, 2016 (see reg.1(2)(a)). They inserted a new reg.9 into the
2006 Regulations (see pp.175–6 of the Supplement to the 2016/17 edition). The
inserted regulation was in the same terms as reg.9 of these Regulations. Accordingly,
when the main provisions in these Regulations came into force on February 1, 2017
(thereby revoking the 2006 Regulations), reg.46 below revoked reg.44 and Sch.5.

Revocations, savings, transitory and transitional provisions and consequential modifications

5.158   45. Schedule 4 (revocations and savings), Schedule 6 (transitional provisions) and Schedule 7 (consequential modifications) have effect.

GENERAL NOTE

The combined effect of reg.45 and Sch.6, and the former reg.44 and Sch.5 is that:

- All decisions made on or after 1 February 2017 are to be treated as having been made under the 2016 Regs, whatever the date of the application;

- Regulation 9 of the 2016 Regs applied to all decisions made on or after 25 November 2016 whatever the date of the application;

- In all other respects the 2006 Regulations apply if the application was made before 25 November 2016 *and* the decision was made before 1 February 2017:

see the decision of the Immigration and Asylum Chamber of the Upper Tribunal in *Oksuzoglu (EEA appeal – "new matter")* [2018] UKUT 385 (IAC).

Revocation of regulation 44 and Schedule 5

5.159   46. The following are revoked—
(a) regulation 44;
(b) Schedule 5.

GENERAL NOTE

5.160   See the General Note to reg.44, above.

Regulation 27

SCHEDULE 1

CONSIDERATIONS OF PUBLIC POLICY, PUBLIC SECURITY AND THE FUNDAMENTAL INTERESTS OF SOCIETY ETC.

5.161   *Omitted*

Regulation 36

SCHEDULE 2

APPEALS TO THE FIRST-TIER TRIBUNAL

5.162   *Omitted*

SCHEDULE 3

EFFECT ON OTHER LEGISLATION

Leave under the 1971 Act

5.163   1. Where a person has leave to enter or remain under the 1971 Act which is subject to conditions and that person also has a right to reside under these

Regulations, those conditions do not have effect for as long as the person has that right to reside.

Person not subject to restriction on the period for which they may remain

2.—(1) For the purposes of the 1971 Act and British Nationality Act 1981, a person who has a right of permanent residence under regulation 15 must be regarded as a person who is in the United Kingdom without being subject under the immigration laws to any restriction on the period for which the person may remain.

(2) But a qualified person, the family member of a qualified person, a person with a derivative right to reside and a family member who has retained the right of residence must not, by virtue of that status, be so regarded for those purposes.

5.164

Carriers' liability under the 1999 Act

3. *Omitted*

5.165

Definitions

"the 1971 Act"—see reg.2(1).
"the 1999 Act"—*ibid.*
"derivative right to reside"—see regs 2(1) and 16.
"family member"—see reg.7.
"family member who has retained the right of residence"—see reg.10.
"immigration laws"—see reg.2(1).
"qualified person"—see reg.6(1).
"right to reside"—see reg.2(1).

Regulation 45

SCHEDULE 4

Revocations and savings

PART 1

Table of Revocations

1. *Omitted*

5.166

PART 2

Savings and modifications

Accession member States: savings and modifications

2.—(1) Regulations 7A and 7B of the 2006 Regulations (arrangements for accession member States) continue to have effect in relation to any EEA national to whom they applied immediately before 1st February 2017.

(2) Where regulations 7A and 7B continue to have effect—
(a) they do so with the following modifications—
(i) in paragraph (3) of regulation 7A and paragraph (4) of regulation 7B, as though the references to treating periods of involun-

5.167

tary unemployment duly recorded by the relevant employment office as periods of work for the purposes of regulation 5(7)(c) of the 2006 Regulations were to treating such periods of involuntary unemployment as periods of work for the purposes of regulation 6(2) of these Regulations; and

    (ii) as though the references to regulations 6(2) (persons who continue to be treated as a worker) and 15 (right of permanent residence) were references to those provisions in these Regulations; and

  (b) these Regulations have effect save that regulation 17 (issue of registration certificate) has effect as though, in paragraph (9), for "regulation 24" there were substituted "regulations 7A and 7B of the 2006 Regulations and regulation 24 of these Regulations".

[¹ Appeals

5.168   **3.**—(1) Notwithstanding the revocation of the 2006 Regulations by paragraph 1(1), those Regulations continue to apply—

  (a) in respect of an appeal under those Regulations against an EEA decision which is pending (within the meaning of regulation 25(2) of the 2006 Regulations) on 31st January 2017;

  (b) in a case where a person has, on 31st January 2017, a right under those Regulations to appeal against an EEA decision.

(2) For the purposes of this paragraph, "EEA decision" has the meaning given in regulation 2 of the 2006 Regulations and the definition of "EEA decision" in regulation 2 of these Regulations does not apply.]

AMENDMENT

1. Immigration (European Economic Area) (Amendment) Regulations 2017 (SI 2017/1) reg.2 and Sch.1, para.4 (January 31, 2017).

DEFINITIONS

    "the 2006 Regulations"—see reg.2(1).
    "EEA decision"—see General Note.
    "EEA national"—see reg.2(1).
    "registration certificate"—see regs 2(1) and 17.

GENERAL NOTE

5.169   In para.3, "EEA decision" is defined by reg.2 of the 2006 Regulations as follows:

"'EEA decision' means a decision under these Regulations that concerns—

  (a) a person's entitlement to be admitted to the United Kingdom;

  (b) a person's entitlement to be issued with or have renewed, or not to have revoked, a registration certificate, residence card, derivative residence card, document certifying permanent residence or permanent residence card;

  (c) a person's removal from the United Kingdom; or

  (d) the cancellation, pursuant to regulation 20A, of a person's right to reside in the United Kingdom;"

rather than by reg.2 (see sub-para.(2)). The difference is that the 2006 definition does not include the words, "(but does not include a decision that an application for the above documentation is invalid)" in head (b) or the full-out exclusory words:

"but does not include a decision to refuse to issue a document under regulation 12(4) (issue of an EEA family permit to an extended family member), 17(5) (issue of a registration certificate to an extended family member) or 18(4) (issue of a residence card to an extended family member), a decision to reject an application under regulation 26(4) (misuse of a right to reside: material change of circumstances), or any decisions under regulation 33 (human rights considerations and interim orders to suspend removal) or 41 (temporary admission to submit case in person);"

at the end.

Regulation 44

SCHEDULE 5

TRANSITORY PROVISIONS

[Revoked by reg.46(b) with effect from January 31, 2017]

GENERAL NOTE

See the commentary to reg.44, above.   5.170

Regulation 45

SCHEDULE 6

TRANSITIONAL PROVISIONS

Interpretation

1.—(1) In this Schedule, "permission to be temporarily admitted in order   5.171
to make submissions in person" means—
  (a) in relation to the 2006 Regulations, permission to be temporarily admitted under regulation 29AA(2) of the 2006 Regulations;
  (b) in relation to these Regulations, permission to be temporarily admitted under regulation 41(2).

(2) References to documents applied for or issued under the 2006 Regulations are to those documents as defined in regulation 2(1) of the 2006 Regulations.

Existing documents

2.—(1) An EEA family permit issued under regulation 12 of the 2006   5.172
Regulations before 1st February 2017 is to be treated as an EEA family permit issued under regulation 12 of these Regulations.

(2) Any document issued or treated as though issued under Part 3 of the 2006 Regulations is to be treated as though issued under Part 3 of these Regulations.

(3) Nothing in this paragraph extends the validity of any document issued under the 2006 Regulations beyond that document's original period of validity.

Verification of a right of residence

3. Where, before 1st February 2017, the Secretary of State had invited a   5.173
person to provide evidence or information or to attend an interview under regulation 20B of the 2006 Regulations (verification of a right of residence), the Secretary of State's invitation is to be treated as though made under regulation 22 of these Regulations.

Outstanding applications

5.174   **4.**—(1) An application for—

(a) an EEA family permit;

(b) a registration certificate;

(c) a residence card;

(d) a document certifying permanent residence;

(e) a permanent residence card;

(f) a derivative residence card; or

(g) permission to be temporarily admitted in order to make submissions in person;

made but not determined before 1st February 2017 is to be treated as having been made under these Regulations.

(2) But regulation 21 and the words in parentheses in paragraph (b) of the definition of an EEA decision in regulation 2(1) are of no application to such an application made before 1st February 2017

Removal decisions, deportation orders and exclusion orders under the 2006 Regulations

5.175   **5.**—(1) A decision to remove a person under regulation 19(3)(a), (b) or (c) of the 2006 Regulations must, upon the coming into force of Part 4 of these Regulations in its entirety, be treated as a decision to remove that person under regulation 23(6) (a), (b) or (c) of these Regulations, as the case may be.

(2) A deportation order made under regulation 24(3) of the 2006 Regulations must be treated as a deportation order made under regulation 32(3) of these Regulations.

(3) Until the coming into force of Part 4 in its entirety, a deportation order to which sub-paragraph (2) applies has effect until revoked by the Secretary of State.

(4) An exclusion order made under regulation 19(1B) of the 2006 Regulations must, upon the coming into force of Part 4 in its entirety, be treated as though having been made under regulation 23(5) of these Regulations.

(5) A person removed under regulation 19(3)(a) of the 2006 Regulations before 1st February 2017 is to be taken into account for the purposes of regulation 26(2).

(6) Where sub-paragraph (5) applies to a person, regulation 26 has effect as though the references to "12" were to "36".

Certification under regulations 24AA and 29AA of the 2006 Regulations

5.176   **6.**—(1) Where the Secretary of State certified under regulation 24AA of the 2006 Regulations (human rights considerations and interim orders to suspend removal) that a person's removal from the United Kingdom would not be unlawful under section 6 of the Human Rights Act 1998 (public authority not to act contrary to the Human Rights Convention), the removal of that person is to be treated as though certified under regulation 33 of these Regulations.

(2) Where sub-paragraph (1) applies, certification treated as though given under regulation 33 does not amount to certification under that regulation

for the purposes of paragraph 2(1)(b) of Schedule 2 to these Regulations (appeals to the First-tier Tribunal).

(3) Where the Secretary of State granted a person permission to be temporarily admitted to the United Kingdom to make submissions in person under regulation 29AA of the 2006 Regulations, that permission is to be treated as though given under regulation 41 of these Regulations.

(4) A person temporarily admitted to the United Kingdom in order to make submissions in person under regulation 29AA(6) of the 2006 Regulations is to be treated as though having been temporarily admitted under regulation 41(6) of these Regulations.

Appeals to the Commission

7. *Omitted*   5.177

Periods of residence prior to the coming into force of these Regulations

8.—(1) Any period of time during which an EEA national ("P") resided   5.178
in the United Kingdom in accordance with the conditions listed in sub-paragraphs (2) or (3) is to be taken into account for the purpose of calculating periods of residence in the United Kingdom in accordance with these Regulations.

(2) The condition in this paragraph is that P resided in, or was treated as though having resided in, the United Kingdom in accordance with—
  (a) the Immigration (European Economic Area) Regulations 2000; or
  (b) the 2006 Regulations.

(3) The condition in this paragraph is that P resided in the United Kingdom in circumstances where—
  (a) P was a national of a State which at that time was not an EEA State;
  (b) P had leave to enter or remain in the United Kingdom under the 1971 Act for the duration of P's residence; and
  (c) P would have been residing in the United Kingdom in accordance with these Regulations, had P's State of origin been an EEA State at that time, and had these Regulations been in force.

(4) Any period during which P resided in the United Kingdom in circumstances which met the conditions in sub-paragraph (2) or (3) is not to be taken into account for the purposes of sub-paragraph (1) where that residence was followed by a period of at least two continuous years during which—
  (a) P was absent from the United Kingdom; or
  (b) P's residence in the United Kingdom—
      (i) did not meet the conditions in sub-paragraph (2) or (3); or
      (ii) was not otherwise in accordance with these Regulations.

[¹ Preservation of transitional provisions in relation to family members of dual nationals

9.—(1) Where—   5.179
  (a) the right of a family member ("F") to be admitted to, or reside in, the United Kingdom pursuant to these Regulations depends on a person ("P") being an EEA national;
  (b) P would be an EEA national if P was not also a British citizen; and
  (c) any of the criteria in sub-paragraphs (2), (3) and (4) is met;

P will, notwithstanding the effect of the definition of an EEA national in regulation 2, be regarded as an EEA national for the purpose of these Regulations.

(2) The criterion in this sub-paragraph is met where F was on 16th July 2012 a person with the right of permanent residence in the United Kingdom under the 2006 Regulations.

(3) Subject to sub-paragraph (5), the criterion in this sub-paragraph is met where F—

(a) was on 16th July 2012 a person with a right of residence in the United Kingdom under the 2006 Regulations; and

(b) on 16th October 2012—

   (i) held a valid registration certificate or residence card issued under the 2006 Regulations;

   (ii) had made an application under the 2006 Regulations for a registration certificate or residence card which had not been determined; or

   (iii) had made an application under the 2006 Regulations for a registration certificate or residence card which had been refused and in respect of which an appeal under regulation 26 of the 2006 Regulations could be brought while the appellant was in the United Kingdom (excluding the possibility of an appeal out of time with permission) or was pending (within the meaning of section 104 of the Nationality, Immigration and Asylum Act 2002(5), as it applied on 16th July 2012).

(4) Subject to sub-paragraph (6), the criterion in this sub-paragraph is met where F—

(a) had, prior to 16th July 2012, applied for an EEA family permit pursuant to regulation 12 of the 2006 Regulations; or

(b) had applied for and been refused an EEA family permit and where, on 16th July 2012, an appeal under regulation 26 of the 2006 Regulations against that decision could be brought (excluding the possibility of an appeal out of time with permission) or was pending (within the meaning of section 104 of the Nationality, Immigration and Asylum Act 2002 Act, as it applied on 16th July 2012).

(5) The criterion in sub-paragraph (3) is not met in a case to which sub-paragraph (3)(b)(ii) or (iii) applies where no registration certificate or residence card was, in fact, issued pursuant to that application.

(6) The criterion in sub-paragraph (4) is not met where—

(a) F was issued with an EEA family permit pursuant to an application made prior to 16th July 2012 but F had not been admitted to the United Kingdom within six months of the date on which it was issued; or

(b) no EEA family permit was, in fact, issued pursuant to that application.

(7) Where met, the criteria in sub-paragraphs (2), (3) and (4) remain satisfied until the occurrence of the earliest of the following events—

(a) the date on which F ceases to be the family member of P; or

(b) the date on which F's right of permanent residence is lost.

(8) P will only continue to be regarded as an EEA national for the purpose of considering the position of F under these Regulations.]

AMENDMENT

1. Immigration (European Economic Area) (Amendment) Regulations 2017 (SI 2017/1) reg.2 and Sch.1, para.5 (January 31, 2017).

DEFINITIONS

"the 1971 Act"—see reg.2(1).
"the 2006 Regulations"—*ibid.*
"derivative residence card"—see regs 2(1) and 20.
"deportation order"—see reg.2(1).
"document certifying permanent residence"—see regs 2(1) and 19(1).
"EEA decision"—see reg. 2(1).
"EEA family permit"—see regs 2(1) and 12.
"EEA national"—see reg.2(1).
"EEA State"—*ibid.*
"exclusion order"—*ibid.*
"family member"—see reg.7.
"permanent residence card"—see regs 2(1) and 19(2).
"registration certificate"—see regs 2(1) and (17).
"residence card"—see regs 2(1) and 18.

Regulation 45

SCHEDULE 7

CONSEQUENTIAL MODIFICATIONS

1.—(1) Unless the context otherwise requires—

(a) any reference in any enactment to the 2006 Regulations, or a provision of the 2006 Regulations, has effect as though referring to these Regulations, or the corresponding provision of these Regulations, as the case may be;

(b) but—

    (i) any reference to a provision of the 2006 Regulations in column 1 of the table has effect as though it were a reference to the corresponding provision of these Regulations listed in column 2; and

    (ii) any reference to a provision of the 2006 Regulations with no corresponding provision in these Regulations ceases to have effect.

(2) Unless otherwise specified in the table, sub-divisions of the provisions of the 2006 Regulations listed in column 1 correspond to the equivalent sub-division in the corresponding provision of these Regulations.

(3) This paragraph is of no application where the reference to the 2006 Regulations had the effect of amending the 2006 Regulations. Additionally this paragraph has no application to amendments to the 2006 Regulations made under Schedule 5 of these Regulations.

5.180

TABLE OF EQUIVALENCES

	(1)	(2)	(3)
5.181	*Provision in the 2006 Regulations*	*Corresponding provision in these Regulations*	*Description of provision*
	1	1(1) to (2)	Citation and commencement
	2(3)	2(2)	General interpretation
	3(3)	3(3)(c)	Continuity of residence
	4(2)	4(2) and (3)	"Worker", "self-employed person", "self-sufficient person" and "student"
	4(4)	4(2) and (4)	
	6(2)(ba)	6(2)(c)	"Qualified person"
	6(2)(c)	6(2)(d)	
	6(2)(d)	6(2)(e)	
	6(2A)	6(3)	
	6(3)	6(4)	
	6(4) and 6(8)	Relevant definitions in 6(1)	
	6(9)	6(8)	
	6(10)	6(9)	
	6(11)	6(10)	
	8(2)	8(2) and (7)	Extended family member
	8(3)	8(3) and (7)	
	9(1)	9(1) and (7)	Family members of British citizens
	9(3)(a) to (c)	9(3)(a) to (e)	
	9(4)	9(5)	
	11(4)(ba)	11(4)(c)	Right of admission to the United Kingdom
	11(4)(c)	11(4)(d)	
	12(1A)	12(2)	Issue of EEA family permit
	12(1B)	12(3)(a)	
	12(2)	12(4)	
	12(3)	12(5)	
	12(4)	12(6)	
	12(5)	12(7)	
	12(6)	12(8)	
	14(5)	14(4)	Extended right of residence
	15(1A)	15(2)	Right of permanent residence
	15(2)	15(3)	
	15(3)	15(4)	

(1)	(2)	(3)
Provision in the 2006 Regulations	*Corresponding provision in these Regulations*	*Description of provision*
15A	16	Derivative right to reside
15A(1)	16(1)	
15A(2)	16(2)	
15A(3)	16(3)	
15A(4)	16(4)	
15A(4A)	16(5)	
15A(5)	16(6)	
15A(6)	16(7)	
15A(7)	16(8)	
15A(7A)	16(9)	
15A(7B)	16(10)	
15A(8)	16(11)	
15A(9)	16(12)	
16	17	Issue of registration certificate
16(8)	17(9)	
17	18	Issue of residence card
17(6A)	18(7)	
18	19	Issue of a document certifying permanent residence and a permanent residence card
18(5)	19(4)(b)	
18(6)	19(5)	
18A	20	Issue of a derivative residence card
18A(5)	20(6)	
19	23	Exclusion and removal from the United Kingdom
19(1A)	23(2)	
19(1AB)	23(3)	
19(1B)	23(5)	
19(2)	23(4)	
19(3)	23(6)	
19(4)	23(7)(a)	
19(5)	23(7)(b)	
20	24	Refusal to issue or renew and revocation of residence documentation
20(1A)	24(2)	
20(2)	24(3)	
20(3)	24(4)	
20(4)	24(5)	
20(5)	24(6)	
20(6)	24(7)	
20A	25	Cancellation of a right of residence

(1)	(2)	(3)
Provision in the 2006 Regulations	*Corresponding provision in these Regulations*	*Description of provision*
20B	22	Verification of a right of residence
20B(8)	Relevant definition in 2(1)	
21	27	Decisions taken on public policy, public security and public health grounds
21(5)	27(5) and (8) and Schedule 1	
21A	28	Application of Part 4 to persons with a derivative right to reside
21A(1)	28(2)	
21A(2)	28(1)	
21A(3)(c)	28(2)(a)	
21A(3)(d)	28(2)(b)	
21A(3)(f)	28(2)(c)	
21A(3)(g)	28(2)(d)	
21B	26	Misuse of a right to reside
21B(1)	26(1) and (2)	
21B(2)	26(3)	
21B(3)	26(4)	
21B(4)	26(5)	
21B(5)	26(6)	
21B(6)	Relevant definition in 2(1)	
22	29	Person claiming right of admission
23	30	Person refused admission
23A	31	Revocation of admission
24	32	Person subject to removal
24A	34	Revocation of deportation and exclusion orders
24A(1)	34(1) and (2)	
24A(2)	34(3)	
24A(3)	34(4)	
24A(4)	34(5)	
24A(5)	34(6)	
24AA	33	Human rights considerations and interim orders to suspend removal
25	35	Interpretation of Part 6

(1)	(2)	(3)
Provision in the 2006 Regulations	*Corresponding provision in these Regulations*	*Description of provision*
26	36	Appeal rights
26(2A)	36(3)	
26(3)	36(4)	
26(3A)	36(5)	
26(4)	36(8)	
26(5)	36(7)	
26(6)	36(9)	
26(7)	36(10)	
26(8)	36(11)	
27	37	Out of country appeals
27(1)(zaa)	37(1)(b)	
27(1)(aa)	37(1)(c)	
27(1)(b)	37(1)(d)	
27(1)(c)	37(1)(e)	
27(1)(ca)	37(1)(f)	
27(1)(d)	37(1)(g)	
28	38	Appeals to the Commission
28(8)	38(8) and (9)	
28A	39	National security: EEA Decisions
29	40	Effect of appeals to the First-tier Tribunal or Upper Tribunal
29(4A)	40(5)	
29(5)	40(6)	
29A	42	Alternative evidence of identity and nationality
29AA	41	Temporary admission in order to submit case in person
30	43	Effect on other legislation
31	45 and 46	Revocations etc.
Schedule 1	Schedule 2	Appeals to the First-tier Tribunal
Schedule 1, paragraph 1	Schedule 2, paragraph 2	
Schedule 1, paragraph 2	Schedule 2, paragraph 3	
Schedule 2	Schedule 3	Effect on other legislation
Schedule 2, paragraph 1(2)	Schedule 3, paragraph 1	
Schedule 2, paragraph 3	Schedule 3, paragraph 3	
Schedule 2, paragraph 4	Schedule 2, paragraph 2	

Definition

"the 2006 Regulations"—see reg.2(1).

SCHEDULE

Consequential Amendments

[Omitted.]

2019 No. 468

The Immigration (European Economic Area Nationals) (EU Exit) Regulations 2019

IN FORCE MARCH 28, 2019

Made by the Secretary of State for the Home Department under section 2(2) of the European Communities Act 1972, section 9(2) and (6) of the Immigration Act 1971 and section 109 of the Nationality, Immigration and Asylum Act 2002,

General Note

5.181   The amendments made by these Regulations to reg.9(2) of the Immigration (European Economic Area) Regulations 2016, are noted in the text of that regulation (above). Reg.4 is a transitional provision. Where a decision is made on or after March 29, 2019—the regulation refers to " any decision made *after* the day on which regulation 3 comes into force" and that day is March 28, 2019—reg.4 treats the amended reg.9(2) of the 2016 Regulations as having being in force at all relevant times.

Part 1

Introductory

Introductory Citation and commencement

5.182   1.—(1) These Regulations may be cited as the Immigration (European Economic Area Nationals) (EU Exit) Regulations 2019.

(2) This regulation, regulation 3 (amendment of the Immigration (European Economic Area) Regulations 2016) and regulation 4 (transitional provision) come into force on the twenty-first day after the day on which these Regulations are laid before Parliament.

(3) Otherwise, these Regulations come into force on exit day.

PART 2

LEAVE TO ENTER THROUGH REPUBLIC OF IRELAND

Amendment of the Immigration (Control of Entry through Republic of Ireland) Order 1972

2. *[Omitted]* 5.183

PART 3

AMENDMENTS TO THE IMMIGRATION (EUROPEAN ECONOMIC AREA) REGULATIONS 2016

Amendments to the Immigration (European Economic Area) Regulations 2016

3. *[Where appropriate, these amendments have been incorporated in the text of* 5.184 *the amended regulations in SI 2016/1052 above]*

Transitional provision

4. In any decision made after the day on which regulation 3 comes into 5.185 force as to whether a person satisfies the conditions in regulation 9(2) of the Immigration (European Economic Area) Regulations 2016 (family members and extended family members), the amendments made by regulation 3(4) and (5) are to be treated as if they had been in force at all times relevant to such a decision.

INDEX

(All references are to paragraph number)